ELEMENTS
OF LITERATURE
3

ELEMENTS OF LITERATURE

3 Revised Edition

Fiction ROBERT SCHOLES
Brown University

Poetry NANCY R. COMLEY
University of Oklahoma

Drama CARL H. KLAUS
University of Iowa

New York • Oxford
OXFORD UNIVERSITY PRESS
1982

Library of Congress Cataloging in Publication Data

Main entry under title:

Elements of literature 3.

  This work, plus two sections on essay and film,
is published as: Elements of literature 5.
  Includes index.
  1. Literature—Collections. I. Scholes,
Robert E. II. Comley, Nancy. III. Klaus, Carl H.
IV. Title: Elements of literature three.
PN6014.E42   808.8   81-18895
ISBN 0-19-503071-0 (pbk.)   AACR2

Acknowledgments

Sherwood Anderson. "I'm a Fool" from *The Portable Sherwood Anderson*, edited by Horace Gregory. Copyright 1922, copyright renewed 1950 by Eleanor Copenhaver Anderson. Reprinted by permission of Viking Penguin, Inc.

Aristophanes. "Lysistrata," trans. Charles T. Murphy, from *Greek Literature in Translation*, edited by Whitney J. Oates and Charles T. Murphy. Copyright © 1944 by Longman, Inc. Reprinted by permission of Longman, Inc., New York.

W. H. Auden. From *W. H. Auden: Collected Poems*, edited by Edward Mendelson. "Who's Who" and "On This Island" copyright 1937, renewed 1965 by W. H. Auden. "Lullaby," "The Unknown Citizen," "Musée des Beaux Arts," "In Memory of W. B. Yeats," and "As I Walked Out One Evening" copyright 1940, renewed 1968 by W. H. Auden. Reprinted by permission of Random House, Inc.

James Baldwin. "Sonny's Blues" from *Going to Meet the Man*, originally appeared in *Partisan Review*. Copyright © 1948, 1951, 1957, 1958, 1960, 1965 by James Baldwin. Reprinted by permission of The Dial Press.

Amiri Baraka (LeRoi Jones). "The Turncoat" from *Preface to a Twenty-Volume Suicide Note*, copyright 1961 by LeRoi Jones. "An Agony. As Now" from *The Dead Lecturer* copyright 1964 by LeRoi Jones. "Legacy" and "Ka'Ba" from *Black Magic Poetry* copyright 1969 by LeRoi Jones. Reprinted by permission of The Sterling Lord Agency.

John Barth. "Lost in the Funhouse" from *Lost in the Funhouse*. Copyright © 1967 by The Atlantic Monthly Company. Reprinted by permission of Doubleday & Company, Inc.

Samuel Beckett. *Krapp's Last Tape*. Copyright © 1957 by Samuel Beckett. Copyright © 1958, 1959, 1960 by Grove Press, Inc. Reprinted by permission of Grove Press, Inc.

William Blake. From *The Poetry and Prose of William Blake*, edited by David V. Erdman, commentary by Harold Bloom. "The Clod and the Pebble," "The Chimney-Sweeper," "The Sick Rose," "The Tyger," "London," and "Auguries of Innocence." Copyright © 1965 by David V. Erdman and Harold Bloom. Reprinted by permission of Doubleday & Company, Inc.

Giovanni Boccaccio. "Federigo and Giovanna," an excerpt from *The Decameron*, trans. Richard Aldington. Copyright 1930 by Garden City Publishing Company, Inc. Reprinted by permission of Doubleday & Company, Inc.

Jorge Luis Borges. From *Labyrinths*. "The Lottery in Babylon," trans. John M. Fein, and "Theme of the Traitor and the Hero," trans. James E. Irby. Copyright © 1962, 1964 by New Directions Publishing Corporation.

Elizabeth Bowen. "The Demon Lover" copyright 1946, renewed 1974 by Elizabeth Bowen. Reprinted from *Collected Stories of Elizabeth Bowen*, by Elizabeth Bowen, by permission of Alfred A. Knopf, Inc.

Kay Boyle. "Winter Night" published in *The New Yorker*, January 19, 1946, to the F-R Publishing Corporation. Reprinted by permission of Doubleday & Company, Inc.

Bertolt Brecht. "The Threepenny Opera" from *Collected Plays, Volume 2*, trans. Ralph Manheim and John Willett. Copyright © 1976, 1977 by Stefan S. Brecht. Reprinted by permission of Random House, Inc.

Gwendolyn Brooks. From *The World of Gwendolyn Brooks*. "The Mother" and "Kitchenette Building" copyright 1944 by Gwendolyn Brooks Blakely. "The Rites for Cousin Vit" copyright 1949 by Gwendolyn Brooks Blakely. "We Real Cool: The Pool Players. Seven at the Golden Shovel" copyright © 1959 by Gwendolyn Brooks. "The Lovers of the Poor" copyright © 1960 by Gwendolyn Brooks. Reprinted by permission of Harper & Row, Publishers, Inc.

Angela Carter. "The Snow Child" from *The Bloody Chamber and Other Adult Tales*, by Angela Carter. Copyright © 1979 by Angela Carter. Reprinted by permission of Harper & Row, Publishers, Inc.

John Cheever. "The Swimmer" from *The Stories of John Cheever*. Copyright © 1964 by John Cheever. Reprinted by permission of Aldred A. Knopf, Inc.

Anton Chekhov. "Heartache" from *The Portable Chekhov*, edited by Avrahm Yarmolinsky. Copyright 1947, © renewed 1975 by Avrahm Yarmolinsky. Reprinted by permission of Viking Penguin Inc.

Robert Coover. "The Hat Act" from *Pricksongs & Descants* by Robert Coover. Copyright © 1969 by Robert Coover. Reprinted by permission of the publisher, E.P. Dutton.

Julio Cortazar. "Blow-Up" from *End of the Game and Other Stories*, translated by Paul Blackburn. Copyright © 1967, 1963 by Random House, Inc. Reprinted by permission of Pantheon Books, a Division of Random House, Inc.

E. E. Cummings. "Buffalo Bill's" and "Spring is like a perhaps hand" reprinted from *Tulips & Chimneys*. Copyright 1923, 1925 and renewed 1951, 1953 by E. E. Cummings. Copyright © 1973, 1976 by Nancy T. Andrews. Copyright © 1973, 1976 by George James Firmage. "next to of course god america i" reprinted from *IS 5*, poems by E. E. Cummings. Copyright 1926 by Horace Liveright. Copyright renewed 1953 by E. E. Cummings. "Somewhere i have never travelled, gladly beyond" reprinted from *Viva* by E. E. Cummings, edited by George James Firmage. Copyright 1931, 1959 by E. E. Cummings. Copyright © 1979, 1973 by Nancy T. Andrews. Copyright © 1979, 1973 by George James Firmage. "r-p-o-p-h-e-s-s-a-g-r" reprinted from *No Thanks* by E. E. Cummings, edited by George James Firmage. Copyright © 1935 by E. E. Cummings. Copyright © 1968 by Marion Morehouse Cummings. Copyright © 1973, 1978 by Nancy T. Andrews. Copyright © 1973, 1978 by George James Firmage. All reprinted by permission of Liveright Publishing Corporation. "my father moved through dooms of love" copyright 1940 by E. E. Cummings, renewed 1968 by Marion Morehouse Cummings. "pity this busy monster" copyright 1944 by E. E. Cummings, renewed 1972 by Nancy T. Andrews. Both reprinted from *Complete Poems 1913-1962* by E. E. Cummings by permission of Harcourt Brace Jovanovich, Inc.

Emily Dickinson. From *The Poems of Emily Dickinson*, edited by Thomas H. Johnson (Cambridge, Mass.: The Belknap Press of Harvard University Press). "Success Is Counted Sweetest," "I Never Hear the Word," "I'm 'Wife' — I've Finished That," "What Is — 'Paradise'," "I Heard a Fly Buzz," "The Heart Asks Pleasure — First," "Because I Could Not Stop for Death," and "A Narrow Fellow in the Grass." Reprinted by permission of the publishers and the Trustees of Amherst College. Copyright 1951, © 1955, 1979 by the President and Fellows of Harvard College.

T. S. Eliot. "Macavity: The Mystery Cat" from *Old Possum's Book of Practical Cats*. Copyright 1939 by T. S. Eliot, renewed 1967 by Esme Valerie Eliot. "The Love Song of J. Alfred Prufrock," "Morning at the Window," "The Hollow Men," and "Journey of the Magi" from *Collected Poems 1909-1962*. Copyright 1936 by Harcourt Brace Jovanovich, Inc., copyright © 1963, 1964 by T. S. Eliot. All reprinted by permission of the publisher.

Ralph Ellison. "Battle Royal" from Chapter 7 of *Invisible Man*. Copyright 1947 by Ralph Ellison. Reprinted by permission of Random House, Inc.

Everyman, edited by Kate Franks. Reprinted by permission of Kate Franks.

William Faulkner. "A Rose for Emily" from *Collected Stories of William Faulkner*. Copyright 1930, renewed 1958 by William Faulkner. Reprinted by permission of Random House, Inc.

F. Scott Fitzgerald. "Babylon Revisited" from *Taps at Reveille*. Copyright 1931 by The Curtis Publishing Company, copyright renewed. Copyright 1935 by Charles Scribner's Sons, copyright renewed. Reprinted with the permission of Charles Scribner's Sons.

Robert Frost. From *The Poetry of Robert Frost*, edited by Edward Connery Lathem. "Mending Wall," "After Apple-Picking," "Stopping by Woods on a Snowy Evening," "Two Tramps in Mud Time," "Design," "Provide, Provide," and "The Silken Tent." Copyright 1923, 1930, 1939, © 1969 by Holt, Rinehart and Winston. Copyright 1936, 1942, 1951, © 1958 by Robert Frost. Copyright © 1964, 1967, 1970 by Lesley Frost Ballantine. Reprinted by permission of Holt, Rinehart and Winston, Publishers.

Ernest Hemingway. "Hills Like White Elephants" in *Men Without Women*. Copyright 1927 by Charles Scribner's Sons, copyright renewed. Reprinted with the permission of Charles Scribner's Sons.

Herodotus. From *The Histories*, trans. Aubrey de Sélincourt. Copyright © 1954 by the Estate of Aubrey de Sélincourt. Copyright © 1972 by A. R. Burn. Reprinted by permission of Penguin Books Ltd.

Gerard Manley Hopkins. "God's Grandeur," "The Windhover," "Pied Beauty," "Spring and Fall . . .," and "Thou Art Indeed Just, O Lord" from *The Poems of Gerard Manley Hopkins*, Fourth Edition, edited by W. H. Gardner and N. H. MacKenzie, Oxford University Press, 1967.

A. E. Housman. "Loveliest of trees . . .," "To an Athlete Dying Young," "When I was One-and-Twenty," "Is my team ploughing," and "Terence, this is stupid stuff" from "A Shropshire Lad" (Authorized Edition) from *The Collected Poems of A. E. Housman*. Copyright 1939, 1940, © 1965 by Holt, Rinehart and Winston. Copyright © 1967, 1968 by Robert E. Symons. "Eight O'Clock" from *The Collected Poems of A. E. Housman*. Copyright 1922 by Holt, Rinehart and Winston. Copyright 1950 by Barclays Bank Ltd. All reprinted by permission of Holt, Rinehart and Winston, Publishers.

Langston Hughes. "On the Road" from *Laughing To Keep from Crying*. Copyright © 1934 by Langston Hughes, renewed 1962. "Mother and Child" from *Black Drama Anthology*. Copyright © 1961 by Langston Hughes. Both reprinted by permission of Harold Ober Associates Incorporated.

Henrik Ibsen. "A Doll's House" from *Ghosts and Three Other Plays* by Henrik Ibsen, translated by Michael Meyer. Copyright © 1966 by Michael Meyer. Reprinted by permission of Harold Ober Associates Incorporated.

James Joyce. "The Boarding House" and "Clay" from *Dubliners*. Originally published by B. W. Heubsch, Inc. in 1916. Copyright © 1967 by the Estate of James Joyce. Reprinted by permission of Viking Penguin, Inc.

Franz Kafka. "On Parables" and "An Imperial Message" from *The Complete Stories*. Copyright © 1946, 1947, 1948, 1949, 1954, 1958, 1971 by Schocken Books, Inc. Reprinted by permission of Schocken Books, Inc.

D. H. Lawrence. "The Rocking-Horse Winner" from *The Complete Short Stories of D. H. Lawrence*, Volume III. Copyright 1934 by Frieda Lawrence, © renewed 1962 by Angelo Ravagli and C. M. Weekley, Executors of the Estate of Frieda Lawrence Ravagli. "The Christening" from *The Complete Short Stories of D. H. Lawrence*, Volume I. Copyright 1922 by Thomas Seltzer, Inc., renewal copyright 1950 by Frieda Lawrence. "Piano" (2 versions) from *The Complete Poems of D. H. Lawrence*, edited by Vivian de Sola Pinto and F. Warren Roberts. Copyright © 1964, 1971 by Angelo Ravagli and C. M. Weekley, Executors of the Estate of Frieda Lawrence Ravagli. All reprinted by permission of Viking Penguin, Inc.

Ursula K. Le Guin. "The Ones Who Walk Away from Omelas" from *The Wind's Twelve Quarters*. Copyright © 1973, 1975 by Ursula K. Le Guin. Reprinted by permission of the author and her agent, Virginia Kidd.

John Lennon and Paul McCartney. "Eleanor Rigby" copyright © 1966 by Northern Songs Ltd. All rights for the U.S.A., Canada, Mexico, and the Philippines controlled by Maclen Music, Inc., c/o ATV Music Corp. Used by permission. All rights reserved.

Doris Lessing. "Sunrise on the Veld" from *African Stories*. Copyright © 1951, 1953, 1954, 1957, 1958, 1962, 1963, 1964, 1965 by Doris Lessing. Reprinted by permission of Simon & Schuster, a Division of Gulf & Western Corporation.

Philip Levine. "Hold Me" from *1933* copyright © 1974 by Philip Levine; "No One Remembers" from *The Names of the Lost* copyright © 1976 by Philip Levine. "Let Me Begin Again" from *7 Years from Somewhere* copyright © 1979 by Philip Levine. Reprinted with the permission of Atheneum Publishers. "From Fran" from *On the Edge* and this version of "Ricky" (first published in *The Iowa Review*) reprinted by permission of the author.

Livy. From *The Early History of Rome*, trans. Aubrey de Sélincourt. Copyright © 1960 by the Estate of Aubrey de Sélincourt. Reprinted by permission of Penguin Books Ltd.

Adrienne Rich. From *Poems, Selected and New, 1950–1974*. "Amnesia," "The Afterwake," "Novella," "Night-Pieces: For a Child," "5:30 A.M.," "Moving in Winter," and "Rape." Copyright © 1975, 1973, 1971, 1969, 1966 by W.W. Norton & Company, Inc. Copyright © 1967, 1963, 1962, 1961, 1960, 1959, 1958, 1957, 1956, 1955, 1954, 1953, 1952, 1951 by Adrienne Rich. All reprinted by permission of W.W. Norton & Company, Inc.

Edwin Arlington Robinson. From *Collected Poems*. "Eros Turannos" copyright 1916 by Edwin Arlington Robinson, renewed 1944 by Ruth Nivison. "Mr. Flood's Party" copyright 1921 by Edwin Arlington Robinson, renewed 1949 by Ruth Nivison. Reprinted with permission of Macmillan Publishing Co., Inc. "Richard Cory" and "The Pity of the Leaves" from *The Children of the Night*, reprinted with the permission of Charles Scribner's Sons.

Theodore Roethke. From *The Collected Poems of Theodore Roethke*. "Old Florist" copyright 1946 by Harper & Brothers. "My Papa's Waltz" copyright 1942 by Hearst Magazines, Inc. "The Premonition" copyright 1941 by Theodore Roethke. "Dolor" copyright 1943 by Modern Poetry Association, Inc. "Elegy for Jane" copyright 1950 by Theodore Roethke. "The Waking" copyright 1953 by Theodore Roethke. "I Knew a Woman" copyright 1954 by Theodore Roethke. "The Manifestation" copyright © 1959 by Beatrice Roethke, Administratrix for the Estate of Theodore Roethke. Reprinted by permission of Doubleday & Company, Inc.

Bernard Shaw. *Major Barbara*. Copyright 1907, 1913, 1930, 1941, George Bernard Shaw. Copyright © 1957, The Public Trustee as Executor of the Estate of George Bernard Shaw. Copyright © 1971, The Trustees of the British Museum, The Governors and Guardians of The National Gallery of Ireland and Royal Academy of Dramatic Art. Reprinted by permission of Dodd, Mead & Company, Inc. and The Society of Authors for the Estate of George Bernard Shaw.

Gary Snyder. "Looking at Pictures To Be Put Away" from *Back Country*. Copyright © 1968 by Gary Snyder. Reprinted by permission of New Directions. "Mid-August at Sourdough Mountain Lookout," "Riprap," "An Autumn Morning in Shokoku-ju," and "It Was When" are all reprinted by permission of the author.

Sophocles. *The Oedipus Rex of Sophocles*, trans. Dudley Fitts and Robert Fitzgerald. Copyright 1949 by Harcourt Brace Jovanovich, Inc., renewed 1977 by Cornelia Fitts and Robert Fitzgerald. Reprinted by permission of the publisher.

Caution: All rights, including professional, amateur, motion picture, recitation, lecturing, public reading, radio broadcasting, and television are strictly reserved. Inquiries on all rights should be addressed to Harcourt Brace Jovanovich, Inc., 757 Third Avenue, New York, NY 10017.

Wallace Stevens. From *The Collected Poems of Wallace Stevens*. "Of Mere Being" copyright © 1957 by Elsie Stevens and Holly Stevens. "Of Modern Poetry" copyright 1942 by Wallace Stevens, renewed 1970 by Holly Stevens. "Sunday Morning" copyright 1923, renewed 1951 by Wallace Stevens. "Anecdote of the Jar," "Thirteen Ways of Looking at a Blackbird," "The Snow Man," and "A High-Toned Old Christian Woman." All reprinted by permission of Alfred A. Knopf, Inc.

August Strindberg. "The Stronger," from *Six Plays*, trans. Elizabeth Sprigge. Reprinted by permission of the Estate of Elizabeth Sprigge and A.P. Watt Ltd.

Tacitus. From *The Annals of Imperial Rome*, trans. Michael Grant. Copyright © 1956, 1959, 1971 by Michael Grant Publications Ltd. Reprinted by permission of Penguin Books Ltd.

Dylan Thomas. From *The Poems of Dylan Thomas*. "The Force That Through the Green Fuse Drives the Flower," "This Bread I Break," "A Refusal To Mourn the Death, by Fire, of a Child," "Do Not Go Gentle into That Good Night," and "Fern Hill." Copyright 1939 by New Directions Publishing Corporation. Copyright 1952 by Dylan Thomas; Copyright 1945, © 1967 by The Trustees for the copyrights of Dylan Thomas. Reprinted by permission of New Directions.

James Thurber. "The Moth and the Star" copyright © 1940 by James Thurber, copyright © 1968 by Helen Thurber. From *Fables for Our Time*, published by Harper & Row. "Courtship Through the Ages" copyright © 1942 James Thurber, copyright © 1970 Helen W. Thurber and Rosemary T. Sauers. From *My World—and Welcome To It*, published by Harcourt Brace Jovanovich. All reprinted by permission of Mrs. James Thurber.

Mark Twain. "In the Animals' Court" from *The Works of Mark Twain: What Is Man?* Reprinted by permission of the publisher, the University of Iowa Press.

Kurt Vonnegut, Jr. "Harrison Bergeron" from *Welcome to the Monkey House*, originally published in *Fantasy and Science Fiction*. Copyright © 1961 by Kurt Vonnegut, Jr. Reprinted by permission of Delacorte Press/Seymour Lawrence.

Rosmarie Waldrop. "Deflecting Forces" and "Stroke" from *The Aggressive Ways of the Casual Stranger*. "76 (as drowsiness mists lines)," "77 (the body's angle at a)," "78 (the cigarette still burning)," "79 (it's not enough to think to see)," and "80 (the signs)" from *The Road Is Everywhere or Stop This Body*. Reprinted by permission of the author.

H. G. Wells. "The Country of the Blind" from *The Country of the Blind*. Reprinted by permission of the Executors of the Estate of H. G. Wells.

Eudora Welty. "Why I Live at the P.O." from *A Curtain of Green and Other Stories*. Copyright 1941, 1969 by Eudora Welty. Reprinted by permission of Harcourt Brace Jovanovich, Inc.

E. B. White. "Spring" from *One Man's Meat* by E. B. White. Copyright 1941 by E. B. White. Reprinted by permission of Harper & Row, Publishers, Inc.

Tennessee Williams. "Cat on a Hot Tin Roof" from *Theatre of Tennessee Williams, Volume III*. Copyright © 1954, 1955, 1971, 1975 by Tennessee Williams. Reprinted by the permission of New Directions.

William Carlos Williams. "Landscape with the Fall of Icarus" from *Pictures from Brueghel and Other Poems*. Copyright 1960 by William Carlos Williams. "Spring and All," "Flowers by the Sea," "The Yachts," "The Widow's Lament in Springtime," "Nantucket," "This Is Just To Say," "The Last Words of My English Grandmother," and "The Red Wheelbarrow" from *Collected Earlier Poems*. Copyright 1938 by New Directions Publishing Corporation. All reprinted by permission of New Directions.

William Butler Yeats. From *Collected Poems*. "The Song of Wandering Aengus" copyright 1906 by Macmillan Publishing Co., Inc., renewed 1934 by William Butler Yeats. "Leda and the Swan" and "Sailing to Byzantium" copyright 1928 by Macmillan Publishing Co., Inc., renewed 1956 by Georgie Yeats. "For Anne Gregory" and "After Long Silence" copyright 1933 by Macmillan Publishing Co., renewed 1961 by Bertha Georgie Yeats. "The Circus Animals' Desertion" copyright 1940 by Georgie Yeats, renewed by Bertha Georgie Yeats, Michael Butler Yeats and Anne Yeats. "The Wild Swans at Coole" and "The Fisherman" copyright 1928 by Macmillan Publishing Co., Inc., renewed 1947 by Bertha Georgie Yeats. "The Lake Isle of Innisfree." Reprinted by permission of Macmillan Publishing Co., Inc.

Preface

In making this anthology we have tried to do two things: get as many outstanding works of fiction, poetry, and drama as we can between the covers of a single book; and give as much help as we can to people who want to learn how to understand and enjoy works of literature. To these ends we have gathered together here a collection of fifty-two stories, two hundred twenty poems, and twelve plays by major writers from the classical period to the contemporary period. And for each of these forms of literature we have prepared separate explanatory discussions, each approximately thirty pages in length. Beyond these guides to understanding we have provided biographical headnotes for each author in the collection and a glossary of critical terms after the text of the book. Thus we have no further explanations to offer in this preface. But we do have a number of people to thank for helping us to put this book together.

For their good advice about the table of contents and the critical apparatus, we are grateful to Professors Stephen V. Armstrong (University of Alabama), Ronald L. Ballard (Hagerstown Junior College), David E. Boudreaux (Nicholls State University), Luana F. Clayton (Jackson State University), Robert Cox (University of the Pacific), Robert R. Craven (New Hampshire College), Joan B. Crawford (Garrett Community College), Robert W. Crone (Garrett Community College), William R. Epperson (Oral Roberts University), Diane Turner Everson (Frederick Community College), Miriam Gilbert (University of Iowa), Eric Gould (University of Denver), Paula Johnson (New York University), William Rea Keast (University of Texas), Robert T. Knighton (University of the Pacific), Frank McHugh (Eastern Michigan University), John Means (Hagerstown Junior College), Marguerite H. Norris (Nicholls State University), Evelyn D. Pace (Virginia Wesleyan College), Bobby L. Smith (Kent State University), Idelle Sullens (Monterey Peninsula College), Donald P. Veith (California State University–Chico), Fred White (Goucher College), and Christopher Zinn (New York University). For his fine theatrical drawings, we are grateful to Professor A. G. Smith (University of Windsor). And for their expert work in bringing this book into print, we are indebted to all the good people at Oxford University Press, especially Natalie Tutt, Permissions Editor, Ellen B. Fuchs, Managing Editor, and John Wright, our Sponsoring Editor.

R.S.
C.H.K.
N.C.

Contents

1. FICTION

Realism: *Introduction,* **183**

2. POETRY

3. DRAMA

ELEMENTS
OF LITERATURE
3

1
FICTION

The Elements of Fiction

FICTION, FACT, AND TRUTH

A fiction is a made-up story. This definition covers a lot of territory. It includes the homemade lies we tell to protect ourselves from annoying scrutiny, and the casual jokes we hear and re-tell as polite (or impolite) conversation, as well as great visionary works of literature like Milton's *Paradise Lost* or the Bible itself. Yes, we are saying that the Bible is fiction; but before you either bristle with smug piety or nod with complacent skepticism, read a few words more. The Bible is fiction because it is a made-up story. This does not mean that it necessarily lacks truth. Nor does it mean that the Bible may not contain fact. The relation between fact and fiction is by no means as simple as one might think; and, since it is very important to an understanding of fiction, it must be considered with some care.

Fact and fiction are old acquaintances. They are both derivatives of Latin words. Fact comes from *facere*—to make or do. Fiction comes from *fingere*—to make or shape. Plain enough words, one would think—not necessarily loaded with overtones of approval or disapproval. But their fortunes in the world of words have not been equal. Fact has prospered. In our ordinary conversation, "fact" is associated with those pillars of verbal society, "reality" and "truth." "Fiction," on the other hand, is known to consort with such suspicious characters as "unreality" and "falsehood." Still, if we look into the matter, we can see that the relation of "fact" and "fiction" with "the real" and "the true" is not exactly what appears on the surface. Fact still means for us quite literally "a thing done." And fiction has never lost its meaning of "a thing made." But in what sense do things done or things made partake of truth or reality? A thing done has no real existence once it has been done. It may have consequences, and there may be many records that point to its former existence (think of the Civil War, for

3

example); but once it is done its existence is finished. A thing made, on the other hand, exists until it decays or is destroyed. Once it is finished, its existence begins (think of a Civil War story like Stephen Crane's *Red Badge of Courage*, for example). Fact, finally, has no real existence, while fiction may last for centuries.

We can see this rather strange relation between fact and fiction more clearly if we consider one place where the two come together: the place we call history. The word "history" itself hides a double meaning. It comes from a Greek word that originally meant inquiry or investigation. But it soon acquired the two meanings that interest us here: on the one hand, history can mean "things that have happened"; on the other, it can refer to "a recorded version of things that are supposed to have happened." That is, history can mean both the events of the past and the story of these events: fact—or fiction. The very word "story" lurks in the word "history," and is derived from it. What begins as investigation must end as story. Fact, in order to survive, must become fiction. Seen in this way, fiction is not the opposite of fact, but its complement. It gives a more lasting shape to the vanishing deeds of men.

But this is, in fact, only one aspect of fiction. We *do* think of it also as something quite different from historical records or mere data. We think of it not just as made but as made-up, a non-natural, unreal product of the human imagination. It is helpful to see fiction in both the ways outlined here. It can be very factual, maintaining the closest possible correspondence between its story and things that have actually happened in the world. Or it can be very fanciful, defying our sense of life's ordinary possibilities.

Taking these two extremes as the opposite ends of a whole spectrum of fictional possibilities, between the infra-red of pure history and the ultra-violet of pure imagination, we can distinguish many shades of coloration. But all are fragments of the white radiance of truth, which is present in both history books and fairy tales, but only partly present in each—fragmented by the prism of fiction, without which we should not be able to see it at all. For truth is like ordinary light, present everywhere but invisible, and we must break it to behold it. To fracture truth in a purposeful and pleasing way—that is the job of the writer of fiction, with whatever shades from the spectrum he or she chooses to work.

FICTION: EXPERIENCE AND ANALYSIS

Though fiction itself has a real existence—a book has weight and occupies space—our experience of fiction is unreal. When we are reading a story we are not "doing" anything. We have stopped the ordinary course of our existence, severed our connections with friends and family, in order to withdraw temporarily into a private and unreal world. Our experience of fiction is more like dreaming than like our normal waking activity. It makes us physically inert yet exercises our imagination. In terms of our performing any action in it, this special world is absolutely unreal, whether we are reading a history book or a science fiction story. We can do nothing to affect either the Battle of Waterloo or the War of the Worlds. And yet, in a way, we participate. We are engaged and involved in the events we are reading about, even though powerless to alter them. We *experience* the events of a story, but without the consequences—emerging from John Hersey's *Hiroshima*, for example, without a scratch on our bodies. Emotionally, however, and intellectually, we are different. We have experienced something.

All discussion of literature, all classes and instruction in literary matters, can have only one valid end: to prepare us for our part in the literary experience. Just as the dull routine exercises and repetitious practice for an athletic event or a dramatic performance are devoted to the end of physical and mental readiness for the actual game or play, exercises in literature are preparations for the act of reading. The successful athlete must do much "instinctively," moving faster than thought to make the most of his time. The painstaking analysis of "game movies" by football coach and players, the searching criticism of each player's reactions to every situation, the drill to counteract past errors—all these wait upon the test of the game itself. Then ability, experience, and training will reveal their quality. It is similar with reading. Classroom, teacher, the artificially assembled anthology—all these must give place to that final confrontation between individual reader and story. Except that this is not a struggle like an athletic contest, but something more intimate and more rewarding. Ideally, it is a kind of consummation—an embrace.

Everything that follows in this section is intended to help readers toward an enriched experience of fiction. Such special terminology as is presented is presented not because critical terminology is an important object of study. Its acquisition is not an end in itself. We learn terminology in order to analyze more accurately. We learn the process of analysis in order to read better.

THE SPECTRUM OF FICTION

The fictional spectrum mentioned earlier can be of use in the analysis of fiction, so long as we remember that it is just a metaphor, a handy linguistic tool to be discarded when it becomes more of a hindrance to understanding than a help. In terms of this metaphor, you will remember, it was possible to think of fiction as resembling the spectrum of color to be found in ordinary light, but in the fictional spectrum the ends were not infra-red and ultra-violet but history and fantasy.

Now only a recording angel, taking note of all the deeds of men without distorting or omitting anything, could be called a "pure" historian. And only a kind of deity, creating a world out of his own imagination, could be called a "pure" fantasist. Both ends of the spectrum are invisible to mortal eyes. All history recorded by men becomes fictional. All human fantasy involves some resemblance—however far-fetched—to life. For the student of fiction, then, the *combination* of historical and imaginative materials becomes crucial. This is so because our understanding of fiction depends on our grasping the way in which any particular work is related to life.

Life itself is neither tragic nor comic, neither sentimental nor ironic. It is a sequence of sensations, action, thoughts, and events that we try to tame with language. Every time we say a word about our existence we are engaged in this taming process. An art like fiction is a highly developed method of domestication, in which life is not merely subdued but is asked to perform tricks as well. The tricks, if well done, please us in a very complicated way. In the first place they *please* because their order and intelligibility are a welcome relief from the confusions and pressures of daily existence. In the second place this artificial order may be mastered by us and used to help *make sense of our own experience*. Having read Hemingway or Lawrence, we will begin to recognize certain situations in our existence as having a family resemblance to situations we have encountered in the pages of Lawrence or Hemingway.

Literature offers us an "escape" from life, but also provides us with new equipment for our inevitable return. It offers us an "imitation" of life. It helps us understand life, and life helps us understand fiction. We recognize aspects of ourselves and our situations in the more ordered perspectives of fiction, and we also see ideal and debased extremes of existence—both possible and impossible—that are interesting in themselves and interestingly different from our own experience. Fiction interests us because of the complicated ways in which it is at once like and unlike life—which is what we mean when we call it an "imitation." Our experience of fiction, then, involves both pleasure and understanding. We may think of understanding either as a result of the pleasurable experience of fiction or as a necessary preliminary to that pleasure. But no matter how we view the complicated relation between pleasure and understanding, we must recognize that the two are inseparable in the reading of fiction.

Now it happens that education has more to do with understanding than with pleasure. This is regrettable, perhaps, but unavoidable. In our study of fiction, then, we must concentrate on understanding, and hope that pleasure will follow because of the connection between the two. Understanding a work of fiction begins with recognizing what kind of fiction it is. This is where the notion of a spectrum becomes useful. We can adjust to the special qualities of any given work more readily if we begin it with a clear and flexible view of fictional possibilities.

Any attempt to give every shade of fiction a place would be cumbersome and misleading. What we want is a rough scale only, with the primary possibilities noted and located in relation to one another. Between the extremes of history and fantasy on such a scale we might locate two major points of reference something like this:

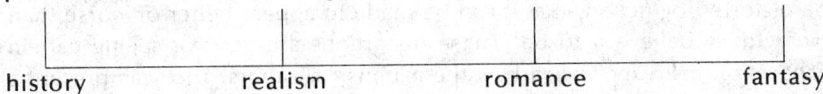

history	realism	romance	fantasy

"Realism" and "romance" are names of the two principal ways that fiction can be related to life. Realism is a matter of perception. The realist presents his impressions of the world of experience. A part of his vocabulary and other technical instruments he shares with the social scientists—especially the psychologists and sociologists. The realistic writer seeks always to give the reader a sense of the way things are, but he feels that a made-up structure of character and event can do better justice to the way things are than any attempt to copy reality directly. The realist's truth is a bit more general and typical than the reporter's fact. It may also be more vivid and memorable.

Romance is a matter of vision. The romancer presents not so much his impressions of the world as his ideas about it. The ordinary world is seen at a greater distance, and its shape and color are deliberately altered by the lenses and filters of philosophy and fantasy. In the world of romance, ideas are allowed to play less encumbered by data. Yet, though "what is" often gives way in romance to "what ought to be" or "might be," *ought* and *might* always imply what *is* by their distortion of it.

Realism and romance are not absolutely different: they share some qualities between them. Realism itself is more romantic than history or journalism. (It is not reality, after all, but real*ism*.) And romance is more realistic than fantasy. Many important works of fiction are rich and complicated blends of romance and realism. In fact, it is possible to say that the greatest works are those that successfully blend the realist's perception and the romancer's vision, giving us fictional worlds remarkably close to our sense of the actual, but skillfully shaped so as to make us intensely aware of the meaningful potential of existence.

FICTIONAL MODES AND PATTERNS

The usefulness of the concept of a fictional spectrum will depend upon our ability to adapt it to various works of fiction. Such adaptation will inevitably require a certain amount of complication. The additional concepts of fictional modes and patterns will be a step in that direction. The spectrum assumed that romance diverges from realism in one way only, along that line which leads from history to fantasy. But it is possible to see this divergence in a more complete way by observing that there are actually two quite different modes of what we have been calling romance.

We may begin by noting that there are two obvious ways that reality can be distorted by fiction, that it can be made to appear better or worse than we actually believe it to be. These distortions are ways of seeing certain aspects of reality more clearly at the expense of others. They can present a "true" picture of either the heroic or the debased side of human existence. A fictional work that presents a world better than the real world is in the mode of romance. A work that presents a fictional world worse than the real world is in the mode of anti-romance, or satire. Because they represent certain potentialities that we recognize as present in our world, both these distorted views depend on our sense of the actual to achieve their effects.

The world of romance emphasizes beauty and order. The world of satire emphasizes ugliness and disorder. The relations between individual characters and these distorted worlds constitute a crucial element of fiction, for these relations determine certain patterns or master plots that affect the shaping of the particular plot of every story. One of these master patterns deals with the kind of character who begins out of harmony with his world and is gradually educated or initiated into a harmonious situation in it. This pattern may operate in either the ordered world of romance or the chaotic world of satire, but the same pattern will have a quite different effect on us when we observe it working out in such different situations. Education that adapts the inept or foolish character for a role in the orderly world presents a comic rise that we observe with approval and pleasure. An initiation into a world of ugliness and disorder, however, amounts to corruption, an ironic rise to what Milton called a "bad eminence"; and we react with disapproval and disgust. (For some reason we find both reactions pleasurable.)

Another master pattern reverses this process of accommodation and presents us with change of another sort: the character who begins in harmony with his world but is finally rejected or destroyed by it. Again, depending on our view of the world presented, we react differently. The heroic figure who falls from his position in the orderly world through some flaw in his character is *tragic*. The lowly creature whose doom is the result of his unfortunate virtue or delicacy is *pathetic*. His fall is, ironically, a kind of rise. (It is traditionally assumed, for complicated reasons, that tragedy is superior to pathos. That assumption is not made here. These patterns are presented as descriptions only, not evaluations.)

The *comic* rise and the *tragic* fall are straightforward because the values of the orderly world represent human virtue raised to a heroic power. The *satiric* rise and *pathetic* fall are ironic because of the inverted values of the debased world. Satire and pathos debase the world in order to criticize it. Tragedy and comedy elevate it to make it acceptable. The two romantic patterns promote resignation. The two satiric patterns promote opposition.

One other pair of fictional patterns may be added to the two already considered. When characters begin and end in a harmonious relation to their respective worlds, the fictional pattern is one not of change but of movement. The characters will have adventures or encounters but will not make any fundamental change in themselves or their relation to the world around them. In this kind of story the hero himself will not be as important as the things he meets. In the romantic world the adventures of the hero will take the form of a quest or voyage that ends with his triumphant return and/or his marriage to the heroine. This pattern moves us to admiration of the wonderful, offering us more of an escape from the actual than a criticism of it. In the satiric world the adventures of a born anti-hero or rogue will parody the quest pattern, often reflecting the chaos of the debased world by becoming endless themselves. Stories of this kind are likely to end when the rogue heads for new territory or another tour of the familiar chaos. This picaresque pattern moves us to recognition and acceptance of the chaotic.

Thus, we have distinguished three pairs of fictional patterns, or six kinds in all: the comic and the satiric rise; the tragic and the pathetic fall; the heroic (romantic) and the anti-heroic (picaresque) quest. But we have done this only with regard to the fantasy worlds of romance and satire, leaving open the question of what happens as these patterns are introduced into a more realistic fictional universe. What happens is, naturally, very complicated indeed. These neat, schematic distinctions fade; the various patterns combine and interact; and values themselves are called into question: rise and fall, success and failure—all become problematic. And this problematic quality is one of the great sources of interest in realistic fiction. Realism uses the familiar patterns of education, expulsion, and quest, but often in such a way as to call into question the great issues of whether the education is beneficial, the expulsion or death justified, the quest worthwhile. Our recognition of the traces of traditional patterns in realistic fiction will be of use, then, mainly in helping us to see what questions are being raised.

Viewed historically, realism developed later than romance and satire; thus it will be useful for us to see realistic fiction as combining the elements of its predecessors in various ways. It would be a mistake, however, to think of realism as superseding the earlier forms just because it uses some of their elements in a new way. In fact, the development of realism has led to a kind of counterflow of realistic elements into the older forms of fiction, reinvigorating them with its problematical qualities. The reader of contemporary fiction in particular will require the flexibility of response that can be attained by careful attention to the workings of traditional patterns in modern fiction. But our discernment of these patterns in any work of fiction will depend on our grasp of the specific elements of that work. We must be alert to the way that *its* characters, *its* plot, and *its* point of view adapt the traditional elements we have been considering.

PLOT

Fiction is movement. A story is a story because it tells about a process of change. A person's situation changes. Or the person is changed in some way. Or our understanding of the person changes. These are the essential movements of fiction. Learning to read stories involves learning to "see" these movements, to follow them, and to interpret them. In the classroom we often—perhaps too often—put our emphasis on interpretation. But you cannot interpret what you cannot see. Thus, before getting into more complicated questions of interpretation, we want to give the plainest and most direct advice possible about how to perceive and follow fictional plotting. This advice includes things to be done while reading and things to be done after a first reading. A good story may be experienced pleasurably many times, and often a second or third reading will be more satisfying in every respect than the first time through.

1. *Look at beginnings and endings.* Movement in fiction is always movement *from* and *to*. A grasp of the start and the finish should lead to a sense of the direction taken to get *from* start *to* finish.

2. *Isolate the central characters.* The things that happen in fiction happen *to* somebody. A few major characters or even a single central character may be the real focus of our concern. Explore the situation of the major characters (or central character) at the beginning and at the end of the story. The nature of the changes revealed by this exploration should begin to suggest what the story is all about.

3. *Note the stages in all important changes.* If a character has moved from one situation to another, or one state of mind to another, the steps leading to the completed change should be illuminating. Through them the reader can get to "how" and "why." But, as always, "what" comes first.

4. *Note the things working against the movement of the story.* Usually, the interest of a story may be seen as the product of two forces: the things that work to move it toward its end, and those that work against that movement, delaying its completion. If the story moves toward a marriage, for example, consider what things delay the happy occasion. When we see the obstacles clearly, we should have a better sense of the direction of the plot itself.

5. *In a long story or novel, consider the various lines of action.* A complex fiction is likely to involve a number of actions, each with its own central character. The actions may or may not interact. The central character in one line of action may be insignificant in another. By isolating the various lines of action and separating them from one another in our

thoughts, we should gain a better sense of those things that connect them. Often these connections will lead us to thematic relations that cast a direct light on the meaning of the whole fiction.

6. *Note carefully characters or events that seem to make no contribution to plot or movement.* This negative advice is a way of moving from the plot to the meaning of a story. Often elements that are not important in the plot have a special thematic importance.

CHARACTER

The greatest mistake we can make in dealing with characters in fiction is to insist on their "reality." No character in a book is a real person. Not even if he is in a history book and is called Ulysses S. Grant. Characters in fiction are *like* real people. They are also unlike them. In realistic fiction, which includes most novels and short stories, writers have tried to emphasize the lifelikeness of their characters. This means that such writers have tried to surround these characters with details drawn from contemporary life. And they have tried to restrict the events of their narrative to things likely to happen in ordinary life. As a result, the writers of realistic fiction have had to abandon certain kinds of plots that are too fanciful for characters supposed to typify ordinary life. Such writers have tried to draw the reader away from his interest in the movement of fiction and to lead him toward an interest in character for its own sake.

Using the newly developed ideas we have learned to call psychology and sociology, the realistic writers have offered us instruction in human nature. The motivation of characters, the workings of conscience and consciousness, have been made the focal point of most novels and short stories. Perhaps the most extreme movement in this direction has been the development of the stream of consciousness technique, through which fiction writers offer us a version of mental process at the level where impressions of things seen and heard converge with confused thoughts and longings arising from the subconscious mind. In reading this kind of fiction we must check the validity of its characterization against our own sense of the way people behave. The best realists always offer us a shock of recognition through which we share their perception of human behavior.

It may be useful for us to think of character as a function of two impulses: the impulse to individualize and the impulse to typify. Great and memorable characters are the result of a powerful combination of these two impulses. We remember the special, individualizing quirks—habitual patterns of speech, action, or appearance—and we remember the way the character represents something larger than himself. These individualizing touches are part of the storyteller's art. They amuse us or engage our sympathy for the character. The typifying touches are part of a story's meaning. In realistic fiction a character is likely to be representative of a social class, a race, a profession; or he may be a recognizable psychological type, analyzable in terms of this or that "complex" or "syndrome." Or he may be a mixture of social and psychological qualities. In allegorical fiction the characters are more likely to represent philosophical positions. In a story of adventure we will encounter types belonging to the traditional pattern of romantic quest: hero, heroine, villain, monster.

The important thing for a reader to remember about characterization is that there are many varieties—and many combinations of the varieties. An adventure story may have an important realistic or allegorical dimension that will be observable in its characterizations. Characters in realistic novels may also be meaningful as illustrations of philosophical ideas or attitudes. As readers we must be alert and ready to respond to different kinds of characterization on their own terms. A story by Jorge Luis Borges and a story by James Joyce are not likely to yield equally to the same kind of reading. It is the reader's business to adapt himself to whatever fictional world he enters. It is the writer's business to make such adaptation worthwhile.

MEANING

More often than not, when we talk about a story after our experience of it, we talk about its meaning. In the classroom, "What is the theme of this work?" is a favorite question. This interpretive aspect of literary analysis is the most difficult, we should say, for the reason that in order to attempt it we must not only look carefully at the work itself but also look away from the work toward the world of ideas and experiences. Discovering themes or meanings in a work involves us in making connections between the work and the world outside it. These connections *are* the meaning. The great problem for the interpreter, then, becomes that of the validity of the thematic materials he discovers. Are these ideas *really* there? we want to know. Are they being "read out" of the story or "read into" it? Is any given set of connections between story and world necessarily implied by the story itself or are they arbitrarily imposed by an overly clever interpreter?

A story is always particular, always an instance. How do we properly move from any given instance to a general notion? When is it legitimate to conclude from the presence of a husband and wife in a story (for example) that the story is "about" marriage—that it makes a statement or raises a question about this aspect of human relations? It is impossible to provide a single method that will always work. In fact, as T. S. Eliot once observed, "There is no method except to be very intelligent." But there are certain procedures that will frequently prove helpful, even for the very intelligent.

If we isolate everything that is not just narration, description, or dialogue, some clues are likely to appear in a story. The title of a work is often a striking instance of this kind of material. Sometimes it will point our thinking about the work in a particular direction, or it will emphasize for us the importance of a particular element in the work. Like the title, passages in the writing that are themselves commentary or interpretation are of especial importance for thematic discussion.

Often, however, interpretive passages will not be presented directly by a narrator, with all his authority behind them. They will be spoken instead by a character, and this means that we must assess the reliability of the character before we decide to accept his interpretation as valid. Sometimes the narrator will be characterized to the extent that we must question even *his* reliability. In similar ways narration and description may also be colored by thematic materials. A character or a scene may be presented by the author so as to lead us toward a certain way of thinking about the materials presented. A school called "Dotheboys Hall" or a teacher named "Gradgrind" is presented to us with a name that carries some not too subtle advice as to how we are to understand the presentation.

In less obvious cases, where the author refrains from direct commentary, we must look for subtler clues. Patterns of repetition, ironic juxtaposition, the tone of the narration—devices like these must lead us to the connections between the particular world of the book and the generalized world of ideas. And the more delicate and subtle the story is, the more delicate our interpretation must be. Thus, taking care that our interpretation is rooted in the work itself is only one aspect of the problem.

The other aspect involves the outside knowledge that the interpreter brings to the work. If the story is realistic it will be understood best by those readers whose experience has equipped them with information about the aspect of reality toward which the story points. This does not mean that one must have lived the life of a black American to understand "Battle Royal" or "Sonny's Blues." But these stories do depend on the reader's having some understanding of injustice and prejudice, and some sense of the way impersonal social forces can act destructively upon individuals and even whole groups of human beings.

Often a realistic story may point to an aspect of life we have encountered but never understood, and the fiction may help us clarify and order that experience. D. H. Lawrence's story "The Christening" can teach us something about personal relations, especially the way that a strong father can dominate and inhibit the lives of his children, causing them to hate him. But Lawrence requires us to bring some experience of family life to that story, for without that it must remain virtually meaningless for the reader. Fantasy and adventure are the principal ingredients of the child's literary diet, for the reason that the child lacks the experience that would make realism meaningful to him, and he lacks the learning necessary for the interpretation of complex allegorical fiction.

Often, however, allegorical fiction takes the form of fantasy or adventure, so that it can be read by the child "at one level" and by the adult on two.

Jonathan Swift's *Gulliver's Travels* has been read in that way for over two centuries. D. H. Lawrence's "The Rocking-Horse Winner" is an exciting story about a boy with a kind of magical power, but it is also a criticism of an excessively materialistic society. Kurt Vonnegut's "Harrison Bergeron" may seem to be just a strangely imagined vision of the future, and yet it asks to be read as an allegory that raises questions about the ability of a country like the United States to deliver on its promises to equalize human life while promoting human freedom. We call such modern allegories "fabulation," and we recognize their ancient ancestors in the simple fable and the homely parable. These two early forms of fiction will be discussed in the next part of this section, and a number of examples of modern fabulation will be found in the anthology of short stories that concludes our study of fiction.

Fiction generates its meanings in innumerable ways, but always in terms of some movement from the particular characters and events of the story to general ideas or human situations suggested by them. The reader comes to an understanding of a fictional work by locating the relevant generalities outside the work and fitting them to the specific instances within the work. The process of understanding can be crudely represented as a sequence something like this:

1. The reader determines whether the work points mainly toward experience itself (i.e., is "realistic"), or toward ideas about experience (i.e., is "allegorical"), or is self-contained.

2. Using the clues in the work, the reader sifts his or her store of general notions drawn from experience or systematic thought to find those appropriate to the specific materials of the story.

3. He or she checks back against the story to test the relevance of the general notions summoned up.

4. He or she seeks for the way the story refines, qualifies, questions, or reinforces those notions.

Something like the process described—performed not a single time but in rapid oscillation into the work and back out—should leave the reader with an understanding of the story and with an enriched store of general notions that he has been led to develop in order to understand. In addition to acquiring new notions, the reader may have refined his attitudes toward his old notions and toward experience itself. Fiction is justified not as a means of conveying ideas but as a means of generating attitudes toward ideas. The meaning of fiction must finally be seen in terms of emotions directed toward impressions of experience or toward ideas about life.

POINT OF VIEW: PERSPECTIVE AND LANGUAGE

Point of view is a technical term for the way a story is told. A stage play normally has no particular point of view: no one stands between the audience and the action. But if we *read* a play, the stage directions—the words of someone who is not a character—provide the beginnings of a special point of view. A story told all in dialogue would be similarly without a point of view. But as soon as a descriptive phrase is added—such as "he said *cruelly*" or "she *whined viciously*"—we begin to have a special viewpoint. A voice outside the action is reaching us, shaping our attitude toward the events being presented. In our experience of fiction, the attitude we develop toward the events presented, and our understanding of those events, will usually be controlled by the author through his or her technical management of point of view.

For convenience we may divide the subject of fictional viewpoint into two related parts—one dealing with the nature of the storyteller in any given fiction, the other dealing with his language. Obviously the two are not really separate. Certain kinds of narration require certain kinds of language—Huck Finn must talk like Huck Finn—but we may consider them apart for analytical purposes.

The nature of the storyteller is itself far from a simple matter. It involves such things as the extent to which he is himself a character whose personality affects our understanding of his statements, and the extent to which his view of events is limited in time and space or in his ability to see into the minds of various characters. The complications and refinements in fictional point of view can be classified at considerable length. But for the reader the classifications themselves are less important than his awareness of many possibilities. The reader's problem comes down to knowing how to take the things presented to him. This means paying special attention to any limitations in the narrator's viewpoint. If the viewpoint in the story is "partial"—in the sense of incomplete or in the sense of biased—the reader must be ready to compensate in appropriate ways.

The language of narration presents a similar problem for the reader—that is, a problem of adjustment and compensation. Of all the dimensions of language that can be considered, two are especially important for the reader of fiction. Both these dimensions may be seen as ways in which wit—or artistic intelligence—operates through language. One has to do with *tone*, or the way unstated attitudes are conveyed through language. The other has to do with *metaphor*, or the way language can convey the richest and most delicate kinds of understanding by bringing together different images and ideas. Consider first this small passage from Virginia Woolf's novel *Mrs. Dalloway*:

> But Sir William Bradshaw stopped at the door to look at a picture. He looked in the corner for the engraver's name. His wife looked too. Sir William Bradshaw was so interested in art.

What is the tone of this? Sarcastic, we should say. The paragraph asks us to be critical of the Bradshaws, but it does not do so directly. It uses the indirection of verbal irony in which the real meaning is different from the apparent sense of the words. The last sentence might be read aloud with a drawn-out emphasis on the word "soooo." How do we know this? How do we supply the appropriate tone of voice for words that we see on the page but do not hear prounounced? We pay attention to the clues given. In *Mrs. Dalloway* the Bradshaws appear in a similar light several times; so that by this, their last appearance, we have been prepared to regard them unsympathetically. But just on the strength of these four sentences we should be able to catch the tone.

The banal "Dick and Jane" sentence patterns reinforce the banality of an approach to art by way of the artist's name. Sir William looks not at the picture itself but at the signature. The implication of this action is that (a) he cannot tell who the artist is by considering the work alone, and (b) he attaches too much importance to the name. His interest in art is fraudulent. Thus, the statement that he is "so" interested in art conflicts with both the actions narrated and the tone of the narration. We resolve the conflict by reading the sentence as *ironic,* meaning the opposite of what it seems to say, and acquiring thereby a sarcastic tone. The way his wife's behavior mechanically mimics his own adds another satiric dimension to the little scene.

As an earlier passage in the novel has revealed, she has no life of her own but has been reduced by him to the status of an object:

> Fifteen years ago she had gone under. It was nothing you could put your finger on; there had been no scene, no snap; only the slow sinking, water-logged, of her will into his.

Thus, the short sentence—"His wife looked too"—picks up the earlier statement about the "submersion" of her will in his, and reminds us of it with satiric brevity. Catching the tone of a passage in a matter of paying attention to clues in sentence pattern and choice of words, and also of keeping in mind the whole context of the story we are reading. The more we read a particular author, the better we become at catching her tone—at perceiving the emotional shades that color the sense of her words.

The second passage quoted from *Mrs. Dalloway* (which comes first in the book) is also a good introductory example of a writer's use of metaphor. The expression "gone under" has been used often enough to refer to defeat or failure—so often, in fact, that it is quite possible to use it without any sense that it is metaphorical. But actually the notion of drowning—going under water to the point of death—is present in the expression. A writer who, like

Virginia Woolf, is sensitive to metaphor, can pick up the submerged (!) implications of such an expression and use them to strengthen her meaning: "the slow sinking, water-logged, of her will into his." The metaphor—which implicitly compares her to a floating object and him to the engulfing waters—conveys a sense of how slowly and inexorably this process has taken place, and it generates in us an appropriate feeling of horror at a human being's lingering destruction.

Similar metaphors can be used in different ways. In another part of the same novel, Virginia Woolf employs the metaphor of drowning in a related but distinct context. When Peter Walsh, who wanted to marry Clarissa Dalloway in his youth, returns from India to tell her that he is in love with a young woman whom he intends to marry, Mrs. Dalloway reacts in this way:

> "In love!" she said. That he at his age should be sucked under in his little bow-tie by that monster! And there's no flesh on his neck; his hands are red; and he's six months older than I am! her eye flashed back to her; but in her heart she felt, all the same, he is in love. He has that, she felt; he is in love.

Love is seen here as a monstrous whirlpool that sucks people under. It is dangerous and destructive: one loses one's identity when sucked in by that monster. But it is also heroic to be involved in such dangerous matters. While her "eye" tells Mrs. Dalloway that Peter is unheroic and even ridiculous, with his little bow tie and skinny neck, her "heart" accepts the heroism of this venture. It is absurd to "be sucked under" in a "little bow-tie," but it is also intensely real: "He has that, she felt; he is in love." By comparing these two metaphors of drowning we can see more accurately certain dimensions of Virginia Woolf's view of marriage: it involves a submergence or submission, but a violent conquest by an emotional whirlpool is superior to a "slow sinking, water-logged," of one will into another. We need not go outside the novel to understand this discrimination, but when we learn or remember that in a state of depression Ms. Woolf took her own life by drowning, we get a hint of why this metaphor has such intensity in her hands.

These uses of the metaphor of drowning are actually just brief examples of the way metaphorical possibilities can be exploited in the language of fiction. We present now a fuller example of metaphorical development, for the student to explore. Marcel Proust's multi-volume novel, The Remembrance of Things Past, is constructed upon the recovery of the past in the memory of the central character and narrator, Marcel. The process of recollection is described in a famous passage in which, on being given a piece of cake (a madeleine) dipped in tea, Marcel suddenly finds that the taste of this morsel has brought to mind much that he had forgotten. In the part of this passage quoted here, Marcel first discusses the persistence of

sensations of taste and smell, and then considers the manner in which
recollection can emerge from these sensations. The passage should be read
with an eye to the metaphors (including similes) operative in it:

> But when from a long-distant past nothing subsists, after the people are
> dead, after the things are broken and scattered, still, alone, more fragile,
> but with more vitality, more unsubstantial, more persistent, more faithful,
> the smell and taste of things remain poised a long time, like souls, ready to
> remind us, waiting and hoping for their moment, amid the ruins of all the
> rest; and bear unfaltering, in the tiny and almost impalpable drop of their
> essence, the vast structure of recollection.
>
> And once I had recognised the taste of the crumb of madeleine soaked in
> her decoction of lime-flowers which my aunt used to give me (although I
> did not yet know and must long postpone the discovery of why this
> memory made me so happy) immediately the old grey house upon the
> street, where her room was, rose up like the scenery of a theatre, to attach
> itself to the little pavilion, opening on to the garden, which had been built
> out behind it for my parents (the isolated panel which until that moment
> had been all that I could see); and with the house the town, from morning
> to night and in all weathers, the Square where I was sent before luncheon,
> the streets along which I used to run errands, the country roads we took
> when it was fine. And just as the Japanese amuse themselves by filling a
> porcelain bowl with water and steeping in it little crumbs of paper which
> until then are without character or form, but, the moment they become
> wet, stretch themselves and bend, take on colour and distinctive shape,
> become flowers or houses or people, permanent and recognisable, so in
> that moment all the flowers in our garden and in M. Swann's park, and the
> water-lilies on the Vivonne and the good folk of the village and their little
> dwellings and the parish church and the whole of Combray and of its
> surroundings, taking their proper shapes and growing solid, sprang into
> being, town and gardens alike, from my cup of tea.

While it is not our intention to encroach too much on what should be
matter for the student's consideration and discussion, we should point out
two of the principal metaphors in the passage and offer a suggestion or two
about them. The first is the comparison of the smell and taste of things to
"souls" in whose "essence" a shape or structure is housed. Proust is here
using an ancient Greek notion of the soul as an essence that gives its shape
to the body it inhabits. The second, the final metaphor of the passage, takes
the form of an extended analogy: "*just as* the Japanese . . . *so* in that
moment. . . ." In examining Proust's use of this particular metaphor, the
student might begin by considering the ways in which the metaphor is
appropriate to the situation—that is, to both the eating of a cake dipped in
tea and the ensuing recovery of the past. Beyond that, he might consider
how the Japanese paper metaphor is related to the soul metaphor, and how
both of these are related to the theatrical simile ("like the scenery") that
links them.

Finally, this consideration of metaphor should lead back to an awareness
of tone. Though this passage is a translation from the original French, it

captures the tone of the original with high fidelity. How would you describe this tone? How should the passage sound if read aloud? What is the function of the repeated use of "and" in the last sentence (which is the last sentence in a whole section of the book)? How is the tone related to the metaphoric structure and the meaning of the passage? In sum, how do these two most important dimensions of the art of language—tone and metaphor—operate in this passage to control the response of a sensitive and careful reader?

In getting at this question the student might try to paraphrase the passage without its metaphors and tonal qualities. Considering such a paraphrase, he might then ask to what extent the meaning *is* paraphrasable, and to what extent the meaning requires the images and rhythms of the passage itself.

DESIGN: JUXTAPOSITION AND REPETITION IN THE STRUCTURE OF FICTION

When we look at a painting up close, we can see its details clearly and the texture of its brush strokes, but we cannot really see it as a whole. When we back away, we lose our perception of these minute qualities but gain, with this new perspective, a sense of its design. Similarly, as we read a story, we are involved in its details. And in a story we are involved especially because we experience it as a flow of words in time, bringing us impressions and ideas, moving us emotionally and stirring us intellectually. It is natural to back away from a painting and see it as a whole. But it is less natural and more difficult to get a similar perspective on a book. We can never "see" it all at once. Yet design is an important part of the writer's art, and a sense of design is essential to a full reading experience.

Design in fiction takes many forms, but these may be seen as mainly of two kinds. One has to do with juxtaposition: with what is put next to what in the arrangement of the story. The other has to do with repetition: with images, ideas, or situations that are repeated—often with interesting variations—in the course of the narrative. Juxtaposition is more important in some kinds of fiction than it is in others. If a single action is presented in a simple, chronological arrangement, the order of events is not likely to assume any special significance. But if the action is rearranged in time so that we encounter events out of their chronological sequence—through flashbacks or some other device—the order should be given some attention. We must look for reasons behind this manipulation of chronology by the author. Why has he chosen to place this particular scene from the "past" next to this particular scene in the "present"? Similarly, if we are following two actions in one story, now one and now the other, we should look for reasons why an incident from one sequence should be placed next to a particular incident in the other.

Often we will find interesting parallels: similar situations that amount to a kind of repetition with variation. If character A gets into a situation and takes one kind of action, while character B, in a similar situation, takes a different action, we should be able to compare the two and contrast their distincitve behavior, thus learning more about both. This kind of comparison can also lead us quite properly to generalizations about the meaning of a work.

Significant kinds of repetition occur also in sections of a story that are not placed next to one another. This kind of repetition is an important element of design, and serves to tie separate parts of a story together, enriching and strengthening the whole structure. Structure in fiction is a very complicated notion, because it involves so many factors. We can think of structure in one sense as the elements that shape our experience as we move through the story. In this sense structure is close to plot. We can also think of structure as the elements that enable us to see a meaningful pattern in the whole work. In this sense structure is close to design. For if plot has to do with the dynamics or movement of fiction, design has to do with the statics of fiction—the way we see a whole story after we have stopped moving through it. When we become aware of design in reading, so that one part of a story reminds us of parts we have read earlier, we are actually involved in a movement counter to our progress through from beginning to end. Plot wants to move us along; design wants to delay our movement, to make us pause and "see." The counteraction of these two forces is one of the things which enrich our experience of fiction.

Design is often a matter of the repetition of images or metaphors. In considering the metaphors of drowning in *Mrs. Dalloway*, we have already begun an examination of the way metaphoric design can tie together quite different characters and situations. Now we present a striking example of a rather different use of repetition in the design of a story. This is a case in which two episodes in the life of the same character—separated both by pages of our reading and by weeks in the life of the character—are brought together into powerful contrast by means of repetition with variation.

At the end of the second chapter of James Joyce's novel *A Portrait of the Artist as a Young Man*, the young man of the title, Stephen Dedalus, has been led by the urgings of physical desire into the arms of a prostitute. This is the last paragraph of that chapter:

> With a sudden movement she bowed his head and joined her lips to his and he read the meaning of her movements in her frank uplifted eyes. It was too much for him. He closed his eyes, surrendering himself to her, body and mind, conscious of nothing in the world but the dark pressure of her softly parting lips. They pressed upon his brain as upon his lips as though they were the vehicle of vague speech; and between them he felt an unknown and timid pressure, darker than the swoon of sin, softer than sound or odour.

By the end of the third chapter, Joyce has taken Stephen Dedalus through a period of disgust, remorse, and repentance. In the last paragraphs of the chapter we find Stephen receiving Holy Communion:

He knelt before the altar with his classmates, holding the altar cloth with them over a living rail of hands. His hands were trembling, and his soul trembled as he heard the priest pass with the ciborium from communicant to communicant.

—*Corpus Domini nostri.*

Could it be? He knelt there sinless and timid: and he would hold upon his tongue the host and God would enter his purified body.

—*In vitam eternam. Amen.*

Another life! A life of grace and virtue and happiness! It was true.

—*Corpus Domini nostri.*

The ciborium had come to him.

In the last sentence of the second chapter, Stephen felt the woman's tongue, pressing through her kiss—"an unknown and timid pressure." In the last lines of the third chapter, his tongue receives the body of Our Lord. Could the contrast be made more striking, or more rich in emotional and intellectual implications? Design here is powerfully carrying out Joyce's intention, which is to make us see Stephen poised between sinful and holy extremes, both of which attract him powerfully but neither of which can hold him finally—as the later chapters demonstrate. The focus on tongues in these two episodes is the crucial repeated element that makes the contrast Joyce wishes. And in the context of the whole story, it reminds us that tongues are not only for kissing or receiving the sacrament. They are also instruments of expression. Stephen ultimately must strive to express himself as an artist of languages, using his gift of tongues. In these two episodes, Stephen has been passive, the receiver. Later he will learn to speak out.

What we have been considering is the way that an object—in this case the tongue—can by its use in a fictional design acquire a metaphorical value that points in the direction of meaning. When this happens, the object becomes a symbol. The process of symbolism will be examined further in the commentary on "Clay" below.

Early Forms of Fiction

KINDS OF STORY

Long before the modern novel and short story developed, human beings were telling one another stories, acting them and singing them, too. When systems of writing were developed, stories began to be recorded for future times. In this brief section we present some illustrative examples of the ancestors of modern fiction, since modern works of fiction usually offer us a combination of elements that were more distinctly separated in these earlier forms. In order to isolate these elements for inspection, we include, first, three different kinds of story: the myth, the fable (or parable), and the tale; followed by examples of three different types of characterization.

In the study of fiction it is never really possible to separate plot from character. After all, a character *is* what he or she does; and a story must be about *someone*. In the most primitive forms of fiction—myth and legend—it is impossible to say whether the character or the plot is the center of interest, since the character is known specifically for the action that defines his or her mythic or legendary status. In more sophisticated forms, as we shall see later on, character can be presented in terms of description, analysis, and a few illustrative actions, without anything like a complete story being required.

Myth

Myths are expressions in narrative form of the deepest human concerns. The myths of primitive peoples are closely associated with their religious beliefs and tribal values. The Orpheus myth presented here is based on ancient celebrations of the fertility/sterility cycle that follows the annual march of the seasons. But the myth has already been given a personal touch; it is also the story of any husband mourning the loss of a beloved wife, a story of death and bereavement.

The following two versions of the Orpheus myth are, first, the plainest possible telling (by C. S. Lewis) of the events that compose the myth; and, second, a modern translation of the sophisticated Roman poet Ovid's elaboration of the mythic story. Taken together, the two versions allow us to see how different the "same story" may appear when it is told differently. Some people prefer the plain version; others, the fancy one. Ask yourself which one you prefer. Can you locate any specific parts of Ovid's version that seem to you especially effective or, on the other hand, too elaborate for your taste? Do you find anything lacking in the plain version?

C. S. LEWIS
1898–1963
Orpheus

There was a man who sang and played the harp so well that even beasts and trees crowded to hear him. And when his wife died he went down alive into the land of the dead and made music before the King of the Dead till even he had compassion and gave him back his wife, on condition that he led her up out of that land without once looking back to see her until they came out into the light. But when they were nearly out, one moment too soon, the man looked back, and she vanished from him forever.

OVID
43 B.C.–?A.D.17
Orpheus

From there Hymen, clad in his saffron robes, was summoned by Orpheus, and made his way across the vast reaches of the sky to the shores of the Cicones. But Orpheus' invitation to the god to attend his marriage was of no avail, for though he was certainly present, he did not bring good luck. His expression was gloomy, and he did not sing his accustomed refrain. Even the torch he carried sputtered and smoked, bringing tears to the eyes, and no amount of tossing could make it burn. The outcome was even worse than the omens foretold: for while the new bride was wandering in the meadows, with her band of naiads, a serpent bit her ankle, and she sank lifeless to the ground. The Thracian poet mourned her loss; when he had wept for her to the full in the upper world, he made so bold as to descend through the gate of Taenarus to the Styx, to try to rouse the sympathy of the shades as well. There he passed among the thin ghosts, the wraiths of the dead, till he reached Persephone and her lord, who holds sway over these dismal regions, the king of the shades. Then, accompanying his words with the music of his lyre, he said:

"Deities of this lower world, to which all we of mortal birth descend, if I have your permission to dispense with rambling insincerities and speak the simple truth, I did not come here to see the dim haunts of Tartarus, nor yet to chain Medusa's monstrous dog, with its three heads and snaky ruff. I came because of my wife, cut off before she reached her prime when she trod on a serpent and it poured its poison into her veins. I wished to be strong enough to endure my grief, and I will not deny that I tried to do so; but Love was too much for me. He is a god well-known in the world above; whether he may be so here too, I do not know, but I imagine that he is familiar to you also and, if there is any truth in the story of that rape of long ago, then you yourselves were brought together by Love. I beg you, by these awful regions, by this boundless chaos, and by the silence of your vast realms, weave again Eurydice's destiny, brought too swiftly to a close. We mortals and all that is ours are fated to fall to you, and after a little time, sooner or later, we hasten to this one abode. We are all on our way here, this is our final home, and yours the most lasting sway over the human race. My wife, like the rest, when she has completed her proper span of years will, in the fullness of time, come within your power. I ask as a gift from you only the enjoyment of her: but if the fates refuse her a reprieve, I have made up my mind that I do not wish to return either. You may exult in my death as well as hers!"

As he sang these words to the music of his lyre, the bloodless ghosts were in tears: Tantalus made no effort to reach the waters that ever shrank away, Ixion's wheel stood still in wonder, the vultures ceased to gnaw Tityus' liver, the daughters of Danaus rested from their pitchers, and Sisyphus sat idle on his rock. Then for the first time, they say, the cheeks of the Furies were wet with tears, for they were overcome by his singing. The king and queen of the underworld could not bear to refuse his pleas. They called Eurydice. She was among the ghosts who had but newly come, and walked slowly because of her injury. Thracian Orpheus received her, but on condition that he must not look back until he had emerged from the valleys of Avernus, or else the gift he had been given would be taken from him.

Up the sloping path, through the mute silence they made their way, up the steep dark track, wrapped in impenetrable gloom, till they had almost reached the surface of the earth. Here, anxious in case his wife's strength be failing and eager to see her, the lover looked behind him, and straightway Eurydice slipped back into the depths. Orpheus stretched out his arms, straining to clasp her and be clasped; but the hapless man touched nothing but yielding air. Eurydice, dying now a second time, uttered no complaint against her husband. What was there to complain of, but that she had been loved? With a last farewell which scarcely reached his ears, she fell back again into the same place from which she had come.

At his wife's second death, Orpheus was completely stunned. He was like that timid fellow who, when he saw three-headed Cerberus led along, chained by the middle one of his three necks, was turned to stone in every limb, and lost his fear only when he lost his original nature too: or like Olenus and hapless Lethaea, once fond lovers, now stones set on well-watered Ida, all because Lethaea was too confident in her beauty, while Olenus sought to take her guilt upon his own shoulders, and wished to be considered the culprit. In vain did the poet long to cross the Styx a second time, and prayed that he might do so. The ferryman thrust him aside. For seven days, unkempt and neglected, he sat on the river bank, without tasting food: grief, anxiety and tears were his nourishment. Then he retired to lofty Rhodope and windswept Haemus, complaining of the cruelty of the gods of Erebus.

Fable and Parable

The fable and parable are ancient forms of fiction that share two important elements. They are very short, and they are allegorical in nature. That is, they tell, very briefly, a story about one thing while really directing attention to something else. Thus, there are always "two levels" to the fable and parable—a *literal* level and a *figurative* level.

In the fables of Aesop (a Greek of very ancient times) the literal level always involves animals, and the figurative level always points toward some aspect of human social behavior. Aesop invariably concludes his fable with a moral generalization that brings home the figurative point made by the fable. Jesus, on the other hand, usually bases his parables on some ordinary human action. He tells an anecdote about human behavior which is intended to illustrate a moral or spiritual truth at the figurative level. As Jesus explains in the Parable of the Sower, a parable has a hidden meaning that can function as a kind of test. Those who are enlightened will understand. Those who are not, will fail to comprehend. If and when they finally see the light, they will join the enlightened.

These little allegorical fictions are related to such truly primitive forms as the riddle. In ancient rituals, initiation often involved the answering of riddles as a qualification test for admission to the inner circle. The parable works in somewhat the same way. The fable, on the other hand, is a more socialized form: it is related to the primitive proverb—and, indeed, many a "moral" attached to the end of a fable also circulates on its own as a maxim or proverb.

You could, for instance, invent a story to go before such familiar sayings as "Look before you leap" or "He who hesitates is lost." You could also retell the stories of Aesop and Jesus so as to make different points from those made in the originals. You might even suggest alternatives to the morals or spiritual values regularly attached to the fables and parables presented here. Kurt Vonnegut (whose modern fable "Harrison Bergeron" you may read later in this volume) has rather impudently suggested, for instance, that the whole life story of Jesus may be read as a fable leading to a moral like this one: You shouldn't hassle a kid whose family has connections. Could you rewrite or reinterpret the fables or parables presented here, or invent others of your own?

FABLES OF AESOP
c. 620–c. 560 B.C.
The Wolf and the Mastiff

A Wolf, who was almost skin and bone—so well did the dogs of the neighborhood keep guard—met, one moonshiny night, a sleek Mastiff, who was, moreover, as strong as he was fat. Bidding the Dog good-night very humbly, he praised his good looks. "It would be easy for you," replied the Mastiff, "to get as fat as I am if you liked." "What shall I have to do?" asked the Wolf. "Almost nothing," answered the Dog. They trotted off together, but, as they went along, the Wolf noticed a bare spot on the Dog's neck. "What is that mark?" said he. "Oh, the merest trifle," answered the Dog; "the collar which I wear when I am tied up is the cause of it." "Tied up!" exclaimed the Wolf, with a sudden stop; "tied up? Can you not always then run where you please?" "Well, not quite always," said the Mastiff; "but what can that matter?" "It matters much to me, " rejoined the Wolf, and, leaping away, he ran once more to his native forest.

Moral: Better starve free, than be a fat slave.

The Dog in the Manger

A Dog was lying in a Manger full of hay. An Ox, being hungry, came near and was going to eat of the hay. The Dog, getting up and snarling at him, would not let him touch it. "Surly creature," said the Ox, "you cannot eat the hay yourself, and yet you will let no one else have any."

Moral: People often grudge others what they cannot enjoy themselves.

The Fox and the Grapes

A famished Fox saw some clusters of ripe black grapes hanging from a trellised vine. She resorted to all her tricks to get at them, but wearied herself in vain, for she could not reach them. At last she turned away, beguiling herself of her disappointment and saying: "The Grapes are sour, and not ripe as I thought."

Moral: It is easy to despise what we cannot have.

PARABLES OF JESUS
1–34 A.D.
The Sower and the Seed

And when much people were gathered together, and were come to him out of every city, he spake by a parable: A sower went out to sow his seed: and as he sowed, some fell by the way side; and it was trodden down, and the fowls of the air devoured it. And some fell upon a rock; and as soon as it was sprung up, it withered away, because it lacked moisture. And some fell among thorns; and the thorns sprang up with it, and choked it. And other fell on good ground, and sprang up, and bare fruit an hundredfold. And when he had said these things, he cried, He that hath ears to hear, let him hear. And his disciples asked him, saying, What might this parable be? And he said, Unto you it is given to know the mysteries of the kingdom of God: but to others in parables; that seeing they might not see, and hearing they might not understand. Now the parable is this: The seed is the word of God. Those by the way side are they that hear; then cometh the devil, and taketh away the word out of their hearts, lest they should believe and be saved. They on the rock are they, which, when they hear, receive the word with joy; and these have no root, which for a while believe, and in time of temptation fall away. And that which fell among thorns are they, which, when they have heard, go forth, and are choked with cares and riches and pleasures of this life, and bring no fruit to perfection. But that on the good ground are they, which in an honest and good heart, having heard the word, keep it, and bring forth fruit with patience.

These excerpts are from the King James version of the Gospel according to Luke, chapters 8, 10, and 15.

The Good Samaritan

And, behold, a certain lawyer stood up, and tempted him, saying, Master, what shall I do to inherit eternal life? He said unto him, What is written in the law? how readest thou? And he answering said, Thou shalt love the Lord thy God with all thy heart, and with all thy soul, and with all thy strength, and with all thy mind; and thy neighbour as thyself. And he said unto him, Thou hast answered right: this do, and thou shalt live. But he, willing to justify himself, said unto Jesus, And who is my neighbour? And Jesus answering said, A certain man went down from Jerusalem to Jericho, and fell among thieves, which stripped him of his raiment, and wounded him, and departed, leaving him half dead. And by chance there came down a certain priest that way: and when he saw him, he passed by on the other side. And likewise a Levite, when he was at the place, came and looked on him, and passed by on the other side. But a certain Samaritan, as he journeyed, came where he was: and when he saw him, he had compassion on him, and went to him, and bound up his wounds, pouring in oil and wine, and set him on his own beast, and brought him to an inn, and took care of him. And on the morrow when he departed, he took out two pence, and gave them to the host, and said unto him, Take care of him; and whatsoever thou spendest more, when I come again, I will repay thee. Which now of these three, thinkest thou, was neighbour unto him that fell among the thieves? And he said, He that shewed mercy on him. Then said Jesus unto him, Go, and do thou likewise.

Three Parables on Lost and Found

Then drew near unto him all the publicans and sinners for to hear him. And the Pharisees and scribes murmured, saying, This man receiveth sinners, and eateth with them.

And he spake this parable unto them, saying, What man of you, having an hundred sheep, if he lose one of them, doth not leave the ninety and nine in the wilderness, and go after that which is lost, until he find it? And when he hath found it, he layeth it on his shoulders, rejoicing. And when he cometh home, he calleth together his friends and neighbours, saying unto them, Rejoice with me; for I have found my sheep which was lost. I say unto you, that likewise joy shall be in heaven over one sinner that repenteth, more than over ninety and nine just persons, which need no repentance.

Either what woman having ten pieces of silver, if she lose one piece, doth not light a candle, and sweep the house, and seek diligently till she find it? And when she hath found it, she calleth her friends and her neighbours together, saying, Rejoice with me; for I have found the piece which I had lost. Likewise, I say unto you, there is joy in the presence of the angels of God over one sinner that repenteth.

And he said, A certain man had two sons: and the younger of them said to his father, Father, give me the portion of goods that falleth to me. And he divided unto them his living. And not many days after the younger son gathered all together, and took his journey into a far country, and there wasted his substance with riotous living. And when he had spent all, there arose a mighty famine in that land; and he began to be in want. And he went and joined himself to a citizen of that country; and he sent him into his fields to feed swine. And he would fain have filled his belly with the husks that the swine did eat: and no man gave unto him. And when he came to himself, he said, How many hired servants of my father's have bread enough and to spare, and I perish with hunger! I will arise and go to my father, and will say unto him, Father, I have sinned against heaven, and before thee, and am no more worthy to be called thy son: make me as one of thy hired servants. And he arose, and came to his father. But when he was yet a great way off, his father saw him, and had compassion, and ran, and fell on his neck, and kissed him. And the son said unto him, Father, I have sinned against heaven, and in thy sight, and am no more worthy to be called thy son. But the father said to his servants, Bring forth the best robe, and put it on him; and put a ring on his hand, and shoes on his feet: and bring hither the fatted calf, and kill it; and let us eat, and be merry: for this my son was dead, and is alive again; he was lost, and is found. And they began to be merry. Now his elder son was in the field: and as he came and drew nigh to the house, he heard musick and dancing. And he called one of the servants, and asked what these things meant. And he said unto him, Thy brother is come; and thy father hath killed the fatted calf, because he hath received him safe and sound. And he was angry, and would not go in: therefore came his father out, and intreated him. And he answering said to his father, Lo, these many years do I serve thee, neither transgressed I at any time thy commandment: and yet thou never gavest me a kid, that I might make merry with my friends: but as soon as this thy son was come, which hath devoured thy living with harlots, thou hast killed for him the fatted calf. And he said unto him, Son, thou art ever with me, and all that I have is thine. It was meet that we should make merry, and be glad: for this thy brother was dead, and is alive again; and was lost, and is found.

The Tale

The tale is a complete story that exists for its own sake, because it is "a good story." Even though it may make a point or illustrate an argument, and thus be reduced to a kind of fable or parable, there is always something about its own form that justifies it for us whether it has a moral or not. The tale, of all the ancient forms of story, is also the most deeply rooted in everyday life. The tale turns on points of human behavior, and thus tends to focus on the things that move people most immediately: love, money, and social position.

Of all the early forms of short fiction, the tale is the one most concerned to produce an emotional reaction in an audience. The simplest tales call for either laughter or tears from their audience. More complicated fictions call for both—or something in between that partakes of both. The greatest tales seem always to have an ironic dimension. They exploit the difference between what humans hope for and what they get, or between what they say and what they do, producing either the pathetic irony of frustrated dreams or the ironic comedy of satire and ridicule.

More modern fictions have been frequently based upon the difference between what a character thinks to be true about the world and what is actually the case. Such an ironic gap between appearance and reality may lead to the realistic story of education. The ancient tales seldom if ever took this form. Most of them were in fact simple stories of hopes and wishes fulfilled, like many fairy tales. But the two tales included for examination here are not so simple. Although both have "happy endings," neither is a simple story of wish fulfillment.

The tale began as an oral form, and both examples here preserve some oral quality. The first, taken from the *Satyricon* of the first-century (A.D.) Roman courtier Petronius, is presented as a story that proves a point, but it is also considered a real anecdote, of "something that happened in our own time." In the hands of Petronius the tale reveals its connection to the ancient form of the joke, as well as to the fable and parable. The second, taken from the *Decameron* of Giovanni Boccaccio (a Florentine of the fourteenth century), is also presented as a story told aloud to an audience. And it, too, is said to be a real story about real people. In Boccaccio's case, this "reality" is insisted upon even more, through the device of naming a real person, known to the audience, who is alleged to be the authority for the tale's authenticity.

The hundred stories of the *Decameron* are presented as being told to one another by a group of ladies and gentlemen, to while away the time they must spend in the country avoiding a siege of plague in the city of Florence. The stories were called *novelli*, or novels, by Boccaccio, since they were supposed to be "new" or "novel" stories set in contemporary places, rather than traditional tales retold. Many of them, however, were far from new, but Boccaccio modernized them as best he could, and the very best, like the tale included here, he must have shaped himself.

The word "novel" became the word for short story in all the Romance languages, as opposed to the word "romance," which meant long story. When the English took over these words, they made a different distinction, designating both "novel" and "romance" as terms for long fictions in prose, but thinking of the novel as being closer to ordinary life—more realistic— and romance as extraordinary or fantastic. But the *novello* of Boccaccio is the ancestor not of the modern novel but of the modern short story. It is just a step from "Federigo and Giovanna" to certain stories of Maupassant —but it took humanity almost five centuries to manage that little step.

PETRONIUS
First century A.D.
The Widow of Ephesus

Meanwhile Eumolpus, our spokesman in the hour of danger and the author of our present reconciliation, anxious that our gaiety should not be broken, began, in a sudden movement of silence, to gibe at the fickleness of women, the wonderful ease with which they became infatuated, their readiness to abandon their children for their lovers, and so forth. In fact, he declared, no woman was so chaste or faithful that she couldn't be seduced; sooner or later she would fall head over heels in love with some passing stranger. Nor, he added, was he thinking so much of the old tragedies and the classics of love betrayed as of something that had happened in our own time; in fact, if we were willing to hear, he would be delighted to tell the story. All eyes and ears were promptly turned to our narrator, and he began:

Once upon a time there was a certain married woman in the city of Ephesus whose fidelity to her husband was so famous that the women from all the neighboring towns and villages used to troop into Ephesus merely to stare at this prodigy. It happened, however, that her husband one day died. Finding the normal custom of following the cortege with hair unbound and beating her breast in public quite inadequate to express her grief, the lady insisted on following the corpse right into the tomb, an underground vault of the Greek type, and there set herself to guard the body, weeping and wailing night and day. Although in her extremes of grief she was clearly courting death from starvation, her parents were utterly unable to persuade her to leave, and even the magistrates, after one last supreme attempt, were rebuffed and driven away. In short, all Ephesus had gone into mourning for this extraordinary woman, all the more since the lady was now passing her fifth consecutive day without once tasting food. Beside the failing woman sat her devoted maid, sharing her mistress' grief and relighting the lamp whenever it flickered out. The whole city could speak, in fact, of nothing else: here at last, all classes alike agreed, was the one true example of conjugal fidelity and love.

In the meantime, however, the governor of the province gave orders that several thieves should be crucified in a spot close by the vault where the lady was mourning her dead husband's corpse. So, on the following night, the soldier who had been assigned to keep watch on the crosses so that nobody could remove the thieves' bodies for burial suddenly noticed a light blazing among the tombs and heard the sounds of groaning. And prompted by a natural human curiosity to know who or what was making those sounds, he descended into the vault.

But at the sight of a strikingly beautiful woman, he stopped short in terror, thinking he must be seeing some ghostly apparition out of hell. Then, observing the corpse and seeing the tears on the lady's face and the scratches her fingernails had gashed in her cheeks, he realized what it was: a widow, in inconsolable grief. Promptly fetching his little supper back down to the tomb, he implored the lady not to persist in her sorrow or break her heart with useless mourning. All men alike, he reminded her, have the same end; the same resting place awaits us all. He used, in short, all those platitudes we use to comfort the suffering and bring them back to life. His consolations, being unwelcome, only exasperated the widow more; more violently than ever she beat her breast, and tearing out her hair by the roots, scattered it over the dead man's body. Undismayed, the soldier repeated his arguments and pressed her to take some food, until the little maid, quite overcome by the smell of the wine, succumbed and stretched out her hand to her tempter. Then, restored by the food and wine, she began herself to assail her mistress' obstinate refusal.

"How will it help you," she asked the lady, "if you faint from hunger? Why should you bury yourself alive, and go down to death before the Fates have called you? What does Vergil say?—

> Do you suppose the shades and ashes of the dead are by such sorrow touched?

No, begin your life afresh. Shake off these woman's scruples; enjoy the light while you can. Look at that corpse of your poor husband:

doesn't it tell you more eloquently than any words that you should live?"

None of us, of course, really dislikes being told that we must eat, that life is to be lived. And the lady was no exception. Weakened by her long days of fasting, her resistance crumbled at last, and she ate the food the soldier offered her as hungrily as the little maid had eaten earlier.

Well, you know what temptations are normally aroused in a man on a full stomach. So the soldier, mustering all those blandishments by means of which he had persuaded the lady to live, now laid determined siege to her virtue. And chaste though she was, the lady found him singularly attractive and his arguments persuasive. As for the maid, she did all she could to help the soldier's cause, repeating like a refrain the appropriate line of Vergil:

If love is pleasing, lady, yield yourself to love.

To make the matter short, the lady's body soon gave up the struggle; she yielded and our happy warrior enjoyed a total triumph on both counts. That very night their marriage was consummated, and they slept together the second and the third night too, carefully shutting the door of the tomb so that any passing friend or stranger would have thought the lady of famous chastity had at last expired over her dead husband's body.

As you can perhaps imagine, our soldier was a very happy man, utterly delighted with his lady's ample beauty and that special charm that a secret love confers. Every night, as soon as the sun had set, he bought what few provisions his slender pay permitted and smuggled them down to the tomb. One night, however, the parents of one of the crucified thieves, noticing that the watch was being badly kept, took advantage of our hero's absence to remove their son's body and bury it. The next morning, of course, the soldier was horror-struck to discover one of the bodies missing from its cross, and ran to tell his mistress of the horrible punishment which awaited him for neglecting his duty. In the circumstances, he told her, he would not wait to be tried and sentenced, but would punish himself then and there with his own sword. All he asked of her was that she make room for another corpse and allow the same gloomy tomb to enclose husband and lover together.

Our lady's heart, however, was no less tender than pure. "God forbid," she cried, "that I should have to see at one and the same time the dead bodies of the only two men I have ever loved. No, better far, I say, to hang the dead than kill the living." With these words, she gave orders that her husband's body should be taken from its bier and strung up on the empty cross. The soldier followed this good advice, and the next morning the whole city wondered by what miracle the dead man had climbed up on the cross.

GIOVANNI BOCCACCIO
1313–1375
Federigo and Giovanna

It is now my turn to speak, dearest ladies, and I shall gladly do so with a tale similar in part to the one before, not only that you may know the power of your beauty over the gentle heart, but because you may learn yourselves to be givers of rewards when fitting, without allowing Fortune always to dispense them, since Fortune most often bestows them, not discreetly but lavishly.

You must know then that Coppo di Borghese Domenichi, who was and perhaps still is one of our fellow citizens, a man of great and revered authority in our days both from his manners and his virtues (far more than from nobility of blood), a most excellent person worthy of eternal fame, and in the fullness of his years delighted often to speak of past matters with his neighbors and other men. And this he could do better and more orderly and with a better memory and more ornate speech than anyone else.

Among other excellent things, he was wont to say that in the past there was in Florence a young man named Federigo, the son of Messer Filippo Alberighi, renowned above all other young gentlemen of Tuscany for his prowess in arms and his courtesy. Now, as most often happens to gentlemen, he fell in love with a lady named Monna Giovanna, in her time held to be one of the gayest and most beautiful women ever known in Florence. To win her love, he went to jousts and tourneys, made and gave feasts, and spent his money without stint. But she, no less chaste than beautiful, cared nothing for the things he did for her nor for him who did them.

Now as Federigo was spending far beyond his means and getting nothing in, as easily happens, his wealth failed and he remained poor with nothing but a little farm, on whose produce he lived very penuriously, and one falcon which was among the best in the world. More in love than ever, but thinking he would never be able to live in the town any more as he desired, he went to Campi where his farm was. There he spent his time hawking, asked nothing of anybody, and patiently endured his poverty.

Now while Federigo was in this extremity it happened one day that Monna Giovanna's husband fell ill, and seeing death come upon him, made his will. He was a very rich man and left his estate to a son who was already growing up. And then, since he had greatly loved Monna Giovanna, he made her his heir in case his son should die without legitimate children; and so died.

Monna Giovanna was now a widow, and as is customary with our women, she went with her son to spend the year in a country house she had near Federigo's farm. Now the boy happened to strike up a friendship with Federigo, and delighted in dogs and hawks. He often saw Federigo's falcon fly, and took such great delight in it that he very much wanted to have it, but did not dare ask for it, since he saw how much Federigo prized it.

While matters were in this state, the boy fell ill. His mother was very much grieved, as he was her only child and she loved him extremely. She spent the day beside him, trying to help him, and often asked him if there was anything he wanted, begging him to say so, for if it were possible to have it, she would try to get it for him. After she had many times made this offer, the boy said:

"Mother, if you can get me Federigo's falcon, I think I should soon be better."

The lady paused a little at this, and began to think what she should do. She knew that Federigo had loved her for a long time, and yet had never had one glance from her, and she said to herself:

"How can I send or go and ask for this falcon, which is, from what I hear, the best that ever flew, and moreover his support in life? How can I be so thoughtless as to take this away from a gentleman who has no other pleasure left in life?"

Although she knew she was certain to have the bird for the asking, she remained in embarrassed thought, not knowing what to say, and did not answer her son. But at length love for her child got the upper hand and she determined that to please him in whatever way it might be, she would not send, but go herself for it and bring it back to him. So she replied:

"Be comforted, my child, and try to get better somehow. I promise you that tomorrow morning I will go for it, and bring it to you."

The child was so delighted that he became a little better that same day. And on the morrow the lady took another woman to accompany her, and as if walking for exercise went to Federigo's cottage, and asked for him. Since it was not the weather for it, he had not been hawking for some days, and was in his garden employed in certain work there. When he heard that Monna Giovanna was asking for him at the door, he was greatly astonished, and ran there happily. When she saw him coming, she got up to greet him with womanly charm, and when Federigo had courteously saluted her, she said:

"How do you do, Federigo? I have come here to make amends for the damage you have suffered through me by loving me more than was needed. And in token of this, I intend to dine today familiarly with you and my companion here."

"Madonna," replied Federigo humbly, "I do not remember ever to have suffered any damage through you, but received so much good that if I was ever worth anything it was owing to your worth and the love I bore it. Your generous visit to me is so precious to me that I could spend again all that I have spent; but you have come to a poor host."

So saying, he modestly took her into his house, and from there to his garden. Since there was nobody else to remain in her company, he said:

"Madonna, since there is nobody else, this good woman, the wife of this workman, will keep you company, while I go to set the table."

Now, although his poverty was extreme, he had never before realised what necessity he had fallen into by his foolish extravagance in spending his wealth. But he repented of it that morning when he could find nothing with which to do honour to the lady, for love of whom he had entertained vast numbers of men in the past. In his anguish he cursed himself and his fortune and ran up and down like a man out of his senses, unable to find money or anything to pawn. The hour was late and his desire to honour the lady extreme, yet he would not apply to anyone else, even to his own workman; when suddenly his eye fell upon his falcon, perched on a bar in the sitting room. Having no one to whom he could appeal, he took the bird, and finding it plump, decided it would be food worthy such a lady. So, without further thought, he wrung its neck, made his little maid servant quickly pluck and prepare it, and put it on a spit to roast. He spread the table with the whitest napery, of which he had some left, and returned to the lady in the garden with a cheerful face, saying that the meal he had been able to prepare for her was ready.

The lady and her companion arose and went to table, and there together with Federigo, who served it with the greatest devotion, they ate the good falcon, not knowing what it was. They left the table and spent some time in cheerful conversation, and the lady, thinking the time had now come to say what she had come for, spoke fairly to Federigo as follows:

"Federigo, when you remember your former life and my chastity, which no doubt you considered harshness and cruelty, I have no doubt that you will be surprised at my presumption when you hear what I have come here for chiefly. But if you had children, through whom you could know the power of parental love, I am certain that you would to some extent excuse me.

"But, as you have no child, I have one, and I cannot escape the common laws of mothers. Compelled by their power, I have come to ask you—against my will, and against all good manners and duty—for a gift, which I know is something especially dear to you, and reasonably so, because I know your straitened fortune has left you no other pleasure, no other recreation, no other consolation. This gift is your falcon, which has so fascinated my child that if I do not take it to him, I am afraid his present illness will grow so much worse that I may lose him. Therefore I beg you, not by the love you bear me (which holds you to nothing), but by your own nobleness, which has shown itself so much greater in all courteous usage than is wont in other men, that you will be pleased to give it me, so that through this gift I may be able to say that I have saved my child's life, and thus be ever under an obligation to you."

When Federigo heard the lady's request and knew that he could not serve her, because he had given her the bird to eat, he began to weep in her presence, for he could not speak a word. The lady at first thought that his grief came from having to part with his good falcon, rather than from anything else, and she was almost on the point of retraction. But she remained firm and waited for Federigo's reply after his lamentation. And he said:

"Madonna, ever since it has pleased God that I should set my love upon you, I have felt that Fortune has been contrary to me in many things, and have grieved for it. But they are all light in comparison with what she has done to me now, and I shall never be at peace with her again when I reflect that you came to my poor house, which you never deigned to visit when it was rich, and asked me for a little gift, and Fortune has so acted that I cannot give it to you. Why this cannot be, I will briefly tell you.

"When I heard that you in your graciousness desired to dine with me and I thought of your excellence and your worthiness, I thought it right and fitting to honor you with the best food I could obtain; so, remembering the falcon you asked me for and its value, I thought it a meal worthy of you, and today you had it roasted on the dish and set forth as best I could. But now I see that you wanted the bird in another form, it is such a grief to me that I cannot serve you that I think I shall never be at peace again."

And after saying this, he showed her the feathers and the feet and the beak of the bird in proof. When the lady heard and saw all this, she first blamed him for having killed such a falcon to make a meal for a woman; and then she inwardly commended his greatness of soul which no poverty could or would be able to abate. But, having lost all hope of obtaining the falcon, and thus perhaps the health of her son, she departed sadly and returned to the child. Now, either from disappointment at not having the falcon or because his sickness must inevitably have led to it, the child died not many days later, to the mother's extreme grief.

Although she spent some time in tears and bitterness, yet, since she had been left very rich and was still young, her brothers often urged her to marry again. She did not want to do so, but as they kept on pressing her, she remembered the worthiness of Federigo and his last act of generosity, in killing such a falcon to do her honor.

"I will gladly submit to marriage when you please," she said to her brothers, "but if you want me to take a husband, I will take no man but Federigo degli Alberighi."

At this her brothers laughed at her, saying:

"Why, what are you talking about, you fool? Why do you want a man who hasn't a penny in the world?"

But she replied:

"Brothers, I know it is as you say, but I would rather have a man who needs money than money which needs a man."

Seeing her determination, the brother, who knew Federigo's good qualities, did as she wanted, and gave her with all her wealth to him, in spite of his poverty. Federigo, finding that he had such a woman, whom he loved so much, with all her wealth to boot, as his wife, was more prudent with his money in the future, and ended his days happily with her.

TYPES OF CHARACTER

One of the major lines of development in the history of fiction may be traced in the examples presented here. As humans have developed their knowledge of the social and psychological forces conditioning human behavior, they have learned to write about people with greater insight into the motives behind their actions. Of course, the more we have discovered about the extent to which human actions are indeed conditioned by forces beyond our control, the less heroic our fictional characters have become.

If we think of Orpheus, that mythic hero whose story was presented earlier, as the most ancient kind of characterization, we can trace a steady movement in types of character from ancient times to the modern era. First, the mythic figures, who can deal even with the gods face to face; then heroes, whose brave deeds affect the fate of kingdoms; then social types, such as one might encounter on the street or at home; and, finally, individuals who are unique. This is not a simple progression through time: the Germanic and Scandinavian peoples (including the Anglo-Saxons) were still writing a heroic kind of fiction a thousand years after sophisticated Greeks had developed characterizations of different social types. But the general tendency is clear: a movement from heroic figures, defined by their valorous deeds, toward social and psychological portraiture.

When English and French writers of the seventeenth century rediscovered ways of writing about social types and historic individuals, the features of characterization that we recognize in the realistic modern novel and short story were finally achieved, and a recognizably modern fiction could begin its development. As we shall see later on, this development culminated in the fictional achievements of the nineteenth and twentieth centuries.

Legendary Hero

The Legendary Hero is to be found in the writings of certain historians who emphasize battlefield heroics in their histories. These writers are poised between the world of myth and the world of science, between fantastic invention and sober recording. Their heroes in a sense are actual historical personages, in that people bearing those names may well have lived and even been present at the events described. But the deeds recounted are so colored by myth and epic poetry that no modern historian dares to accept them uncritically.

The first historian represented here is the Greek Herodotus (fifth century B.C.), called the "father of history" because he was the first to call his writing *Histories* (or, more literally, *Inquiries*) and to attempt a kind of historical research—not easy in a world with few written records of the past. He has also been called, by later historians, the "father of lies." Our second historian is the Roman, Livy (first century B.C.) who, like Herodotus, loved a good story whether it was entirely accurate or not.

The tendency to make legendary heroes out of more ordinary or more complicated human beings did not die with the fall of Rome. It was one of the most powerful forces operating in European literature during the Middle Ages, and it is still powerful wherever folk literature flourishes. Historians and folklore scholars have shown how strongly the popular image of General Custer was colored by the same heroic pattern you will find in the stories of Leonidas and Horatius. The more recent bumper sticker "Custer Died for Your Sins" suggests—with tongue in cheek—that we should see Custer in a rather different mythic pattern. But whenever a modern folk singer tries to cash in on an actual event, the result is likely to be a song about a figure cast in the old heroic mold, made into a "legend in his own time."

HERODOTUS
Fifth Century B.C.
Leonidas

The Greeks at Thermopylae had their first warning of the death that was coming with the dawn from the seer Megistias, who read their doom in the victims of sacrifice; deserters, too, came in during the

night with news of the Persian flank movement, and lastly, just as
day was breaking, the look-out men came running from the hills. In
council of war their opinions were divided, some urging that they
must not abandon their post, others the opposite. The result was that
the army split: some dispersed, contingents returning to their
various cities, while others made ready to stand by Leonidas. It is
said that Leonidas himself dismissed them, to spare their lives, but
thought it unbecoming for the Spartans under his command to desert
the post which they had originally come to guard. I myself am
inclined to think that he dismissed them when he realized that they
had no heart for the fight and were unwilling to take their share of
the danger; at the same time honor forbade that he himself should
go. And indeed by remaining at his post he left a great name behind
him, and Sparta did not lose her prosperity, as might otherwise have
happened; for right at the outset of the war the Spartans had been
told by the Delphic oracle that either their city must be laid waste by
the foreigner or a Spartan king be killed. The prophecy was in
hexameter verse and ran as follows:

Hear your fate, O dwellers in Sparta of the wide spaces;
Either your famed, great town must be sacked by Perseus' sons,
Or, if that be not, the whole land of Lacedaemon
Shall mourn the death of a king of the house of Heracles,
For not the strength of lions or of bulls shall hold him,
Strength against strength; for he has the power of Zeus,
And will not be checked till one of these two he has consumed.

I believe it was the thought of this oracle, combined with his wish
to lay up for the Spartans a treasure of fame in which no other city
should share, that made Leonidas dismiss those troops; I do not
think that they deserted, or went off without orders, because of a
difference of opinion. Moreover, I am strongly supported in this view
by the case of the seer Megistias, who was with the army—an
Acarnanian, said to be of the clan of Melampus—who foretold the
coming doom from his inspection of the sacrificial victims. He quite
plainly received orders from Leonidas to quit Thermopylae, to save
him from sharing the army's fate. He refused to go, but he sent his
only son, who was serving with the forces.

Thus it was that the confederate troops, by Leonidas' orders,
abandoned their posts and left the pass, all except the Thespians and
the Thebans who remained with the Spartans. The Thebans were
detained by Leonidas as hostages very much against their will; but
the Thespians of their own accord refused to desert Leonidas and his

men, and stayed, and died with them. They were under the command of Demophilus the son of Diadromes.

In the morning Xerxes poured a libation to the rising sun, and then waited till it was well up before he began to move forward. This was according to Ephilates' instructions, for the way down from the ridge is much shorter and more direct than the long and circuitous ascent. As the Persian army advanced to the assault, the Greeks under Leonidas, knowing that they were going to their deaths, went out into the wider part of the pass much further than they had done before; in the previous days' fighting they had been holding the wall and making sorties from behind it into the narrow neck, but now they fought outside the narrows. Many of the invaders fell; behind them the company commanders plied their whips indiscriminately, driving the men on. Many fell into the sea and were drowned, and still more were trampled to death by their friends. No one could count the number of the dead. The Greeks, who knew that the enemy were on their way round by the mountain track and that death was inevitable, put forth all their strength and fought with fury and desperation. By this time most of their spears were broken, and they were killing Persians with their swords.

In the course of that fight Leonidas fell, having fought most gallantly, and many distinguished Spartans with him—their names I have learned, as those of men who deserve to be remembered; indeed, I have learned the names of all the three hundred. Amongst the Persian dead, too, were many men of high distinction, including two brothers of Xerxes, Habrocomes and Hyperanthes, sons of Darius by Artanes' daughter Phratagune. Artanes, the son of Hystaspes and grandson of Arsames, was Darius' brother; as Phratagune was his only child, his giving her to Darius was equivalent to giving him his entire estate.

There was a bitter struggle over the body of Leonidas; four times the Greeks drove the enemy off, and at last by their valour rescued it. So it went on, until the troops with Ephialtes were close at hand; and then, when the Greeks knew that they had come, the character of the fighting changed. They withdrew again into the narrow neck of the pass, behind the wall, and took up a position in a single compact body—all except the Thebans—on the little hill at the entrance to the pass, where the stone lion in memory of Leonidas stands today. Here they resisted to the last, with their swords, if they had them, and, if not, with their hands and teeth, until the Persians, coming on from the front over the ruins of the wall and closing in from behind, finally overwhelmed them with missile weapons.

Of all the Spartans and Thespians who fought so valiantly the most signal proof of courage was given by the Spartan Dieneces. It is said that before the battle he was told by a native of Trachis that, when the Persians shot their arrows, there were so many of them that they hid the sun. Dieneces, however, quite unmoved by the thought of the strength of the Persian army, merely remarked: "This is pleasant news that the stranger from Trachis brings us: if the Persians hide the sun, we shall have our battle in the shade." He is said to have left on record other sayings, too, of a similar kind, by which he will be remembered. After Dieneces the greatest distinction was won by two Spartan brothers, Alpheus and Maron, the sons of Orsiphantus; and of the Thespians the man to gain the highest glory was a certain Dithyrambus, the son of Harmatides.

The dead were buried where they fell, and with them the men who had been killed before those dismissed by Leonidas left the pass. Over them is this inscription, in honor of the whole force:

Four thousand here from Pelops' land
Against three million once did stand.

The Spartans have a special epitaph; it runs:

Go tell the Spartans, you who read:
We took their orders, and are dead.

For the seer Megistias there is the following:

Here lies Megistias, who died
When the Mede passed Spercheius' tide.
A prophet; yet he scorned to save
Himself, but shared the Spartans' grave.

The columns with the epitaphs inscribed on them were erected in honor of the dead by the Amphictyons—though the epitaph upon the seer Megistias was the work of Simonides, the son of Leoprepes, who put it there for friendship's sake.

LIVY

59 B.C.—A.D. 17

Horatius

On the approach of the Etruscan army, the Romans abandoned their farmsteads and moved into the city. Garrisons were posted. In some sections the city walls seemed sufficient protection, in others the barrier of the Tiber. The most vulnerable point was the wooden bridge, and the Etruscans would have crossed it and forced an entrance into the city, had it not been for the courage of one man, Horatius Cocles—that great soldier whom the fortune of Rome gave to be her shield on that day of peril. Horatius was on guard at the bridge when the Janiculum was captured by a sudden attack. The enemy forces came pouring down the hill, while the Roman troops, throwing away their weapons, were behaving more like an undisciplined rabble than a fighting force. Horatius acted promptly: as his routed comrades approached the bridge, he stopped as many as he could catch and compelled them to listen to him. "By God," he cried, "can't you see that if you desert your post escape is hopeless? If you leave the bridge open in your rear, there will soon be more of them in the Palatine and the Capitol than on the Janiculum." Urging them with all the power at his command to destroy the bridge by fire or steel or any means they could muster, he offered to hold up the Etruscan advance, so far as was possible, alone. Proudly he took his stand at the outer end of the bridge; conspicuous amongst the rout of fugitives, sword and shield ready for action, he prepared himself for close combat, one man against an army. The advancing enemy paused in sheer astonishment at such reckless courage. Two other men, Spurius Lartius and Titus Herminius, both aristocrats with a fine military record, were ashamed to leave Horatius alone, and with their support he won through the first few minutes of desperate danger. Soon, however, he forced them to save themselves and leave him; for little was now left of the bridge, and the demolition squads were calling them back before it was too late. Once more Horatius stood alone; with defiance in his eyes he confronted the Etruscan chivalry, challenging one after another to single combat, and mocking them all as tyrants' slaves who, careless of their own liberty, were coming to destroy the liberty of others. For a while they hung back, each waiting for his neighbor to make the first move, until shame at the unequal battle drove them to action, and with a fierce cry they hurled their spears at the solitary figure which barred their way. Horatius caught the missiles on his shield and, resolute as ever, straddled the bridge and held his ground. The Etruscans moved forward, and would have thrust him aside by the sheer weight of numbers, but their advance was suddenly checked by the crash of the falling bridge and the simultaneous shout of triumph from the Roman soldiers who had done their work in time. The Etruscans could only stare in bewilderment as Horatius, with a prayer to Father Tiber to bless him and his sword, plunged fully armed into the water and swam, through the missiles which fell thick about him, safely to the other side where his friends were waiting to receive him. It was a noble piece of work—legendary, maybe, but destined to be celebrated in story through the years to come.

For such courage the country showed its gratitude. A statue of Horatius was placed in the Comitium, and he was granted as much land as he could drive a plough round in a day. In addition to public honours many individuals marked their admiration of his exploit in the very hard times which were to follow, by going short themselves in order to contribute something, whatever they could afford, to his support.

The Social Type

The word "characters" was used by the Greek writer Theophrastus (fourth century B.C.) to describe his collection of sketches of typical Athenian social types. The sketches that have come down to us are comic and satirical, apparently designed for recitation at parties and other social functions. They are fictional in two senses. First, they are slightly exaggerated portraits, and, second, they represent a "type" of behavior rather than the actions of any individual person. The exaggeration, in fact, comes from the putting together of so many similar traits as the sketch of a single character. Yet each trait represents a kind of actual behavior. The types represented by Theophrastus are not social types in the sense of being defined by class or trade; they are behavioral types who violate the standards of good manners in some particular way.

In seventeenth-century England there was a great revival of "Character"-making. The inspiration for this came from the rediscovery of the work of Theophrastus himself, but the nature of the English Characters changed the form somewhat. In the two samples presented here (modernized a bit but quite faithful to the originals), you will find the work of Thomas Overbury and some friends of his, which sees each Character as linked to a particular profession or trade. One question to ask in considering these is how the Overburian Character differs from the Theophrastian. Another is how authentically historical these Characters may be. Are these types confined to ancient Athens and the England of three centuries ago? Or do they represent human functions sufficiently universal to be recognized today? Would it be possible to produce contemporary imitations of Theophrastus or Overbury? Overbury's own definition of a Character offers some clues as to how to proceed:

> . . . it is a picture (real or personal) quaintly drawn in various colors, all of them heightened by one shadowing.
> It is a quick and soft touch of many strings, all shutting up in one musical close. It is wit's descant [variation] on any plain song.

THEOPHRASTUS
Fourth century B.C.
The Rough

Roughness is coarse conduct, whether in word or act. The rough takes an oath lightly and is insensible to insult and ready to give it. In character he is a sort of town bully, obscene in manner, ready for anything and everything. He is willing, sober and without a mask, to dance the vulgar cordax[1] in comic chorus. At a show he goes around from man to man and collects the pennies, quarrelling with the spectators who present a pass and therefore insist on seeing the performance free.

He is the sort of man to keep a hostelry,[2] or brothel, or to farm the taxes. There is no business he considers beneath him, but he is ready to follow the trade of crier, cook, or gambler. He does not support his mother, is caught at theft and spends more time in jail than in his home. He is the type of man who collects a crowd of bystanders and harangues them in a loud brawling voice; while he is talking, some are going and others coming, without listening to him; to one part of the moving crowd he tells the beginning of his story, to another part a sketch of it, and to another part a mere fragment. He regards a holiday as the fittest time for the full exhibition of his roughness.

He is a great figure in the courts as plaintiff or defendant. Sometimes he excuses himself on oath from trial but later he appears with a bundle of papers in the breast of his cloak, and a file of documents in his hands. He enjoys the role of generalissimo in a band of rowdy loafers; he lends his followers money and on every quarter collects a penny interest per day. He visits the bakeshops, the markets for fresh and pickled fish, collects his tribute from them, and stuffs it in his cheek.

1. Lewd dance
2. Innkeepers were in ill-repute in antiquity.

The Gross Man

Grossness is such neglect of one's person as gives offense to others. The gross man is one who goes about with an eczema, or white eruption, or diseased nails, and says that these are congenital ailments; for his father had them, and his grandfather, too, and it would be hard to foist an outsider upon their family. He's very apt to have sores on his shins and bruises on his toes, and to neglect these things so that they grow worse.

His armpits are hairy like an animal's for a long distance down his sides; his teeth are black and decayed. As he eats, he blows his nose with his fingers. As he talks, he drools, and has no sooner drunk wine than up it comes. After bathing he uses rancid oil to anoint himself; and when he goes to the marketplace, he wears a thick tunic and a thin outer garment disfigured with spots of dirt.

When his mother goes to consult the soothsayer, he utters words of evil omen; and when people pray and offer sacrifices to the gods he lets the goblet fall, laughing as though he had done something amusing. When there's playing on the flute, he alone of the company claps his hands, singing an accompaniment and upbraiding the musician for stopping so soon.

Often he tries to spit across the table,—only to miss the mark and hit the butler.

THOMAS OVERBURY
1581–1613
A Mere Scholar

A mere scholar is an intelligible ass, or a silly fellow in black that speaks sentences more familiarly than sense. The antiquity of his University is his creed, and the excellency of his College (though but for a match of football) is an article of his faith. He speaks Latin better than his mother tongue, and is a stranger in no part of the world but in his own country. He does usually tell great stories of himself to small purpose, for they are commonly ridiculous, be they true or false. His ambition is that he either is, or shall be, a graduate, but if he ever gets a fellowship, he has then no fellow. In spite of all logic he dare swear and maintain it, that a cuckold and a townsman are *termini convertibles*,[1] though his mother's husband be an Alderman. He was never begotten (as it seems) without much wrangling, for his whole life is spent in *Pro & Contra*.[2] His tongue goes always before his wit, like a gentleman-usher, but somewhat faster. That he is a complete gallant in all points, from head to toe, witness his horsemanship and the wearing of his weapons. He is commonly long-winded, able to speak more with ease than any man can hear with patience.

University jests are his universal discourse, and his news the demeanor of the Proctors. His phrase, the apparel of his mind, is made up of diverse shreds like a cushion, and when it goes plainest

1. I.e., that a deceived husband and a man who lives in town are identical concepts.
2. Disputation

has a rash outside and rough linings. The current of his speech is closed with an "*ergo*," and whatever be the question, the truth is on his side. 'Tis a wrong to his reputation to be ignorant of anything, and yet he knows not that he knows nothing. He gives directions for husbandry from Virgil's *Georgics;* for cattle, from his *Bucolics;* for warlike strategems, from his *Aeneid* or Caesar's *Commentaries.* He orders all things by the book, is skillful in all trades, and thrives in none. He is led more by his ears than his understanding, taking the sound of words for their true sense. His ill luck is not so much in being a fool, as in being put to such pains to express it to the world; for what in others is natural, in him (with much ado) is artificial. His poverty is his happiness, for it makes some men believe that he is none of fortune's favorites. That learning which he has, was in his youth put in backwards like an enema, and 'tis now like ware mislaid in a peddler's pack: he has it, but knows not where it is. In a word, he is the index of a man, and the title page of a scholar, or a Puritan in morality; much in profession, nothing in practice.

A Jailer

Is a creature mistaken in the making, for he should be a tiger. But the shape being thought too terrible, it is covered, and he wears the mask of a man, yet retains the qualities of his former fierceness, currishness, and ravenousness. Of that red earth of which he was fashioned, this piece was the basest. Of the rubbish which was left and thrown aside came a jailer. Or if God had something else to do than to regard such trash, his descent, then, is more ancient but more ignoble, for he comes of the race of those angels that fell with Lucifer from heaven, whither he never (or hardly ever) returns. Of all his bunches of keys not one has the power to open that door. For a jailer's soul stands not upon those two pillars that support heaven (justice and mercy), it rather sits upon those two footstools of hell, wrong and cruelty. He is a judge's slave, a prisoner is his. In this they differ: he is a voluntary one, the other compelled. He is the hangman of the law with a lame hand, and if the law gave him all his limbs perfect, he would strike those on whom he is glad to fawn. In fighting against a debtor he is a creditor's second, but observes not the laws of the dueller's code, for his play is foul and he takes base advantages. His conscience and his shackles hang up together and are made very nearly of the same metal, saving that the one is harder than the other and has one property greater than iron, for it never melts. He distills money out of the poor's tears, and grows fat by their curses. No man coming to the practical part of hell can discharge it better, because here he does nothing but study the theory of it. His house is a picture of hell, and the original of the Letters Patent of his office stand exemplified there. A chamber of lousy beds is better worth to him than the best acre of corn-land in England. Two things are hard to him (nay, almost impossible), *viz:* to save all his prisoners that none ever escape, and to be saved himself. His ears are stopped to the cries of others, and God's to his. And good reason, for lay the life of a man in one scale, and his fees in another—he will lose the first to find the second. He must look for no mercy (if he desires justice to be done to him) for he shows none; and I think he cares less, because he knows heaven has no need of jailers. The doors there want no porters, for they stand ever open. If it were possible for all creatures in the world to sleep every night, he only and a Tyrant cannot. That blessing is taken from them, and this curse comes instead: to be ever in fear, and ever hated. What estate can be worse?

The Historical Personage

As we have seen, the earliest historians were interested especially in presenting heroic figures taken from a legendary past. Even in ancient times, however, certain writers made a serious effort to describe the events of their own times and to record the lives of important people for posterity. Little more than a century after Livy wrote, Tacitus, his fellow Roman, produced a brilliant study of Imperial Rome, which, though it is heightened with the colors of rhetoric, is also valuable as documentation of Rome in the time of Nero. We have excerpted from the *Annals* of Tacitus two passages dealing with the life and death of Seneca, a famous playwright and philosopher, who had been Nero's tutor and became his victim. Even in a modern translation we can appreciate how Tacitus used language to create dramatic scenes and to color events and situations with his own harshly ironical view of life.

The other two portraits of individuals presented here are modern English translations from the eighteenth-century French *Memoirs* of Louis de Rouvroy, Duc de Saint-Simon. Less formal than Tacitus, and less dramatic, Saint-Simon offers posterity intimate sketches of life at the court of Louis XIV. The portraits or sketches of Saint-Simon were written roughly a century after the Characters of the Englishman Thomas Overbury. It will be instructive to compare the work of Overbury and Saint-Simon, to see what distinguishes the memoir-sketch of an actual historical personage from the invented character-type produced by Overbury and his friends. Certainly, in both cases, we find a fierce delight in capturing the unpleasant detail, but the methods are interestingly different. And, taken together, they show very clearly where the realistic characterizations of modern fiction have their roots.

TACITUS

55(?)–117(?) A.D.

Seneca

Burrus' death undermined Seneca's influence. Decent standards carried less weight when one of their two advocates was gone. Now Nero listened to more disreputable advisers. These attacked Seneca, first for his wealth, which was enormous and excessive for any subject, they said, and was still increasing; secondly, for the grandeur of his mansions and beauty of his gardens, which outdid even the emperor's; and thirdly, for his alleged bids for popularity. They also charged Seneca with allowing no one to be called eloquent but himself. "He is always writing poetry," they suggested, "now that Nero has become fond of it. He openly disparages the emperor's amusements, underestimates him as a charioteer, and makes fun of his singing. How long must merit at Rome be conferred by Seneca's certificate alone? Surely Nero is a boy no longer! He is a grown man and ought to discharge his tutor. His ancestors will teach him all he needs." Seneca knew of these attacks. People who still had some decency told him of them. Nero increasingly avoided his company.

Seneca, however, requested an audience, and when it was granted, this is what he said. "It is nearly fourteen years, Caesar, since I became associated with your rising fortunes, eight since you became emperor. During that time you have showered on me such distinctions and riches that, if only I could retire to enjoy them unpretentiously, my prosperity would be complete.

"May I quote illustrious precedents drawn from your rank, not mine? Your great-great-grandfather Augustus allowed Marcus Agrippa to withdraw to Mytilene, and allowed Gaius Maecenas the equivalent of retirement at Rome itself. The one his partner in wars, the other the bearer of many anxious burdens at Rome, they were greatly rewarded, for great services. I have had no claim on your generosity, except my learning. Though acquired outside the glare of public life, it has brought me the wonderful recompense and distinction of having assisted in your early education.

"But you have also bestowed on me measureless favours, and boundless wealth. Accordingly, I often ask myself: 'Is it I, son of a provincial non-senator, who am accounted a national leader? Is it my unknown name which has come to glitter among ancient and glorious pedigrees? Where is my old self, that was content with so little? Laying out these fine gardens? Grandly inspecting these estates? Wallowing in my vast revenues?' I can only find one excuse. It was not for me to obstruct your munificence.

"But we have both filled the measure—you, of what an emperor

49

can give his friend, and I, of what a friend may receive from his emperor. Anything more will breed envy. Your greatness is far above all such mortal things. But I am not; so I crave your help. If, in the field or on a journey, I were tired, I should want a stick. In life's journey, I need just such a support.

"For I am old and cannot do the lightest work. I am no longer equal to the burden of my wealth. Order your agents to take over my property and incorporate it in yours. I do not suggest plunging myself into poverty, but giving up the things that are too brilliant and dazzle me. The time now spent on gardens and mansions shall be devoted to the mind. You have abundant strength. For years the supreme power has been familiar to you. We older friends may ask for our rest. This, too, will add to your glory—that you have raised to the heights men content with lower positions."

The substance of Nero's reply was this. "My first debt to you is that I can reply impromptu to your premeditated speech. For you taught me to improvise as well as to make prepared orations. True, my great-great-grandfather Augustus permitted Agrippa and Maecenas to rest after their labors. But he did so when he was old enough to assure them, by his prestige, of everything—of whatever kind—that he had given them. Besides, he certainly deprived neither of the rewards which they had earned from him in the wars and crises of Augustus' youthful years. If my life had been warlike, you too would have fought for me. But you gave what our situation demanded: wisdom, advice, philosophy, to support me as boy and youth. Your gifts to me will endure as long as life itself! My gifts to you, gardens and mansions and revenues, are liable to circumstances.

"They may seem extensive. But many people far less deserving than you have had more. I omit, from shame, to mention ex-slaves who flaunt greater wealth. I am even ashamed that you, my dearest friend, are not the richest of all men. You are still vigorous and fit for State affairs and their rewards. My reign is only beginning. Or do you think you have reached your limit? If so you must rank yourself below Lucius Vitellius, thrice consul, and my generosity below that of Claudius, and my gifts as inferior to the lifelong savings of Lucius Volusius Saturninus (II).

"If youth's slippery paths lead me astray, be at hand to call me back! You equipped my manhood; devote even greater care to guiding it! If you return my gifts and desert your emperor, it is not your unpretentiousness, your retirement, that will be on everyone's lips, but *my* meanness, your dread of *my* brutality. However much your self-denial were praised, no philosopher could becomingly gain credit from an action damaging to his friend's reputation."

Then he clasped and kissed Seneca. Nature and experience had fitted Nero to conceal hatred behind treacherous embraces. Seneca expressed his gratitude (all conversations with autocrats end like that). But he abandoned the customs of his former ascendancy. Terminating his large receptions, he dismissed his entourage, and rarely visited Rome. Ill-health or philosophical studies kept him at home, he said. . . .

Seneca's death followed. It delighted the emperor. Nero had no proof of Seneca's complicity but was glad to use steel against him when poison had failed. The only evidence was a statement of Antonius Natalis that he had been sent to visit the ailing Seneca and complain because Seneca had refused to receive Piso. Natalis had conveyed the message that friends ought to have friendly meetings; and Seneca had answered that frequent meetings and conversations would benefit neither, but that his own welfare depended on Piso's.

A colonel of the Guard, Gavius Silvanus, was ordered to convey this report to Seneca and ask whether he admitted that those were the words of Natalis and himself. Fortuitously or intentionally, Seneca had returned that day from Campania and halted at a villa four miles from Rome. Towards evening the officer arrived. Surrounding the villa with pickets, he delivered the emperor's message to Seneca as he dined with his wife Pompeia Paulina and two friends. Seneca replied as follows: "Natalis was sent to me to protest, on Piso's behalf, because I would not let him visit me. I answered excusing myself on grounds of health and love of quiet. I could have had no reason to value any private person's welfare above my own. Nor am I a flatterer. Nero knows this exceptionally well. He has had more frankness than servility from Seneca!"

The officer reported this to Nero in the presence of Poppaea and Tigellinus, intimate counsellors of the emperor's brutalities. Nero asked if Seneca was preparing for suicide. Gavius Silvanus replied that he had noticed no signs of fear or sadness in his words or features. So Silvanus was ordered to go back and notify him of the death-sentence. According to one source,[1] he did not return by the way he had come but made a detour to visit the commander of the Guard, Faenius Rufus; he showed Faenius the emperor's orders asking if he should obey them; and Faenius, with that ineluctable weakness which they all revealed, told him to obey. For Silvanus was himself one of the conspirators—and now he was adding to the crimes which he had conspired to avenge. But he shirked communicating or witnessing the atrocity. Instead he sent in one of his staff-officers to tell Seneca he must die.

Unperturbed, Seneca asked for his will. But the officer refused.

1. Fabius Rusticus

Then Seneca turned to his friends. "Being forbidden," he said, "to show gratitude for your services, I leave you my one remaining possession, and my best: the pattern of my life. If you remember it, your devoted friendship will be rewarded by a name for virtuous accomplishments." As he talked—and sometimes in sterner and more imperative terms—he checked their tears and sought to revive their courage. Where had their philosophy gone, he asked, and that resolution against impending misfortunes which they had devised over so many years? "Surely nobody was unaware that Nero was cruel!" he added. "After murdering his mother and brother, it only remained for him to kill his teacher and tutor."

These words were evidently intended for public hearing. Then Seneca embraced his wife and, with a tenderness very different from his philosophical imperturbability, entreated her to moderate and set a term to her grief, and take just consolation, in her bereavement, from contemplating his well-spent life. Nevertheless, she insisted on dying with him, and demanded the executioner's stroke. Seneca did not oppose her brave decision. Indeed, loving her wholeheartedly, he was reluctant to leave her for ill-treatment. "Solace in life was what I commended to you," he said. "But you prefer death and glory. I will not grudge your setting so fine an example. We can die with equal fortitude. But yours will be the nobler end."

Then, each with one incision of the blade, he and his wife cut their arms. But Seneca's aged body, lean from austere living, released the blood too slowly. So he also severed the veins in his ankles and behind his knees. Exhausted by severe pain, he was afraid of weakening his wife's endurance by betraying his agony—or of losing his own self-possession at the sight of her sufferings. So he asked her to go into another bedroom. But even in his last moments his eloquence remained. Summoning secretaries, he dictated a dissertation. (It has been published in his own words, so I shall refrain from paraphrasing it.)

Nero did not dislike Paulina personally. In order, therefore, to avoid increasing his ill-repute for cruelty, he ordered her suicide to be averted. So, on instructions from the soldiers, slaves and ex-slaves bandaged her arms and stopped the bleeding. She may have been unconscious. But discreditable versions are always popular, and some took a different view—that as long as she feared there was no appeasing Nero, she coveted the distinction of dying with her husband, but when better prospects appeared life's attractions got the better of her. She lived on for a few years, honorably loyal to her husband's memory, with pallid features and limbs which showed how much vital blood she had lost.

Meanwhile Seneca's death was slow and lingering. Poison, such as was formerly used to execute State criminals at Athens, had long been prepared; and Seneca now entreated his well-tried doctor, who was also an old friend,[1] to supply it. But when it came, Seneca drank it without effect. For his limbs were already cold and numbed against the poison's action. Finally he was placed in a bath of warm water. He sprinkled a little of it on the attendant slaves, commenting that this was his libation to Jupiter. Then he was carried into a vapor-bath, where he suffocated. His cremation was without ceremony, in accordance with his own instructions about his death—written at the height of his wealth and power.

1. Annaeus Statius

DUC DE SAINT-SIMON
1675–1755

Two Portraits

Princesse d'Harcourt

The Princesse d'Harcourt was a sort of personage whom it is good to make known, in order better to lay bare a Court which did not scruple to receive such as she. She had once been beautiful and gay; but though not old, all her grace and beauty had vanished. The rose had become an ugly thorn. At the time I speak of she was a tall, fat creature, mightily brisk in her movements, with a complexion like milk-porridge; great, ugly, thick lips, and hair like tow, always sticking out and hanging down in disorder, like all the rest of her fittings out. Dirty, slatternly, always intriguing, pretending, enterprising, quarrelling—always low as the grass or high as the rainbow, according to the person with whom she had to deal: she was a blonde Fury, nay more, a harpy: she had all the effrontery of one, and the deceit and violence; all the avarice and the audacity; moreover, all the gluttony, and all the promptitude to relieve herself from the effects thereof; so that she drove out of their wits those at whose house she dined; was often a victim of her confidence; and was many a time sent to the devil by the servants of M. du Maine and *M. le Grand.* She, however, was never in the least embarrassed, tucked up her petticoats and went her way; then returned, saying she had been unwell. People were accustomed to it.

Whenever money was to be made by scheming and bribery, she was there to make it. At play she always cheated, and if found out stormed and raged; but pocketed what she had won. People looked upon her as they would have looked upon a fishfag, and did not like to commit themselves by quarrelling with her.

Sometimes the Duchesse de Bourgogne used to send about twenty Swiss guards, with drums, into her chamber, who roused her from her first sleep by their horrid din. Another time—and these scenes were always at Marly—they waited until very late for her to go to bed and sleep. She lodged not far from the post of the Captain of the Guards, who was at that time the Maréchal de Lorges. It had snowed very hard, and had frozen. Madame la Duchesse de Bourgogne and her suite gathered snow from the terrace which is on a level with their lodgings; and, in order to be better supplied, waked up to assist them, the Maréchal's people, who did not let them want for ammunition. Then, with a false key, and lights, they gently slipped into the chamber of the Princesse d'Harcourt; and, suddenly drawing the curtains of her bed, pelted her amain with snowballs. The filthy creature, waking up with a start, bruised and stifled in snow, with which even her ears were filled, with disheveled hair, yelling at the top of her voice, and wriggling like an eel, without knowing where to hide, formed a spectacle that diverted people more than half an hour: so that at last the nymph swam in her bed, from which the water flowed everywhere, slushing all the chamber. It was enough to make one die of laughter.

She was very violent with her servants, beat them, and changed them every day. Upon one occasion, she took into her service a strong and robust chambermaid, to whom, from the first day of her arrival, she gave many slaps and boxes on the ear. The chambermaid said nothing, but after submitting to this treatment for five or six days, conferred with the other servants; and one morning, while in her mistress's room, locked the door without being perceived, said something to bring down punishment upon her, and at the first box on the ear she received, flew upon the Princesse d'Harcourt, gave her no end of thumps and slaps, knocked her down, kicked her, mauled her from her head to her feet, and when she was tired of this exercise, left her on the ground, all torn and disheveled, howling like a devil.

Madame de Montespan

On Wednesday, the 27th of May, 1707, at three o'clock in the morning, Madame de Montespan, aged sixty, died very suddenly at the waters of Bourbon. Her death made much stir, although she had long retired from the Court and from the world, and preserved no trace of the commanding influence she had so long possessed. I need not go back beyond my own experience, and to the time of her reign as mistress of the King. I will simply say, because the anecdote is little known, that her conduct was more the fault of her husband than her own. She warned him as soon as she suspected the King to be in love with her; and told him when there was no longer any doubt upon her mind. She assured him that a great entertainment that the King gave was in her honor. She pressed him, she entreated him in the most eloquent manner, to take her away to his estates of Guyenne, and leave her there until the King had forgotten her or chosen another mistress. It was all to no purpose; and Montespan was not long before repentance seized him; for his torment was that he loved her all his life, and died still in love with her—although he would never consent to see her again after the first scandal.

At last God touched her. Her sin had never been accompanied by forgetfulness; she used often to leave the King to go and pray in her cabinet; nothing could ever make her evade any fast-day or meagre day; her austerity in fasting continued amidst all her dissipation. She gave alms, was esteemed by good people, never gave way to doubt or impiety; but she was imperious, haughty and overbearing, full of mockery, and of all the qualities by which beauty with the power it bestows is naturally accompanied. Being resolved at last to take advantage of an opportunity which had been given her against her will, she put herself in the hands of Père de la Tour, that famous General of the Oratory. From that moment to the time of her death her conversion continued steadily, and her penitence augmented.

Little by little she gave almost all she had to the poor. She worked for them several hours a day, making stout shirts and such things for them. Her table, that she had loved to excess, became the most frugal; her fasts multiplied; she would interrupt her meals in order to go and pray. Her mortifications were continued; her chemises and her sheets were of rough linen, of the hardest and thickest kind, but hidden under others of ordinary kind. She unceasingly wore bracelets, garters, and a girdle, all armed with iron points, which oftentimes inflicted wounds upon her; and her tongue, formerly so dangerous, had also its peculiar penance imposed on it.

She received the last sacrament with an ardent piety. The fear of death which all her life had so continually troubled her, disappeared suddenly, and disturbed her no more. She died, without regret, occupied only with thoughts of eternity, and with a sweetness and tranquility that accompanied all her actions.

Madame de Montespan was bitterly regretted by all the poor of the province, amongst whom she spread an infinity of alms, as well as amongst others of different degree.

Three Stories and Commentaries

INTRODUCTION

These three stories are intended to illustrate something of the range and variety of modern short fiction. The commentaries illustrate ways in which the procedures outlined at the beginning of this section may be employed in the reading of specific texts. They may also be thought of as developments or refinements of those procedures. In preparing them we have sought not to put the stories mechanically through every analytical process mentioned earlier, but rather to fit the relevant and useful procedures to the appropriate aspects of each story.

In the anthology section ahead, students and teachers will find an even greater range of fiction for discussion and study. The examples of analysis offered here should suggest approaches that may apply to other stories but should not be allowed to limit the analytical procedures applied to the stories to come. Every discussion of a story must be adapted to that particular story. There is no single analytical method that works for everything. In considering these examples of critical analysis, it might be especially appropriate to ask why each discussion takes the form it does, emphasizing the aspects of the story it does, and whether it leaves out anything important about the story it treats.

GUY DE MAUPASSANT
1850–1893
Moonlight

His warlike name well suited the Abbé Marignan.[1] He was a tall thin priest, full of zeal, his soul always exalted but just. All his beliefs were fixed; they never wavered. He sincerely believed that he understood his God, entered into His plans, His wishes, His intentions.

As he strode down the aisle of his little country church, sometimes a question would take shape in his mind: "Now why has God done that?" He would seek the answer stubbornly, putting himself in

---

1. The Battle of Marignan (1515) was a great and bloody victory for Francis I and France.

Translated by R.S., with valuable advice and criticism from Peter Clothier and the students in his University of Iowa Translation Workshop.

God's place, and he nearly always found it. He was not one of those who murmur with an air of pious humility, "O Lord, your designs are impenetrable!" He would say to himself: "I am the servant of God, I should know His purposes, and if I don't know them I should divine them."

Everything in nature seemed to him created with an absolute and admirable logic. The "why" and the "because" always balanced out. Dawns existed to make waking up a pleasure, days to ripen the crops, rain to water them, evening to prepare for slumber, and the night was dark for sleeping.

The four seasons were perfectly fitted to all the needs of agriculture; and it would never have occurred to the priest to suspect that nature has no intentions at all, and that, on the contrary, every living thing has bowed to the hard necessities of times, climates, and matter itself.

But he hated women, he hated them unconsciously and despised them by instinct. He often repeated the words of Christ: "Woman, what have I to do with thee?" and he added, "You'd think that not even God himself was happy with that particular piece of work." Woman for him was precisely that child twelve times unclean of whom the poet speaks. She was the temptress who had ensnared the first man and who still continued her damnable work—a weak creature, dangerous, curiously disturbing. And even more than her devilish body he hated her loving soul.

He had often felt the yearning affection of women, and, even though he knew himself invulnerable, he was exasperated by this need to love which always trembled in them.

God, in his opinion, had made woman only to tempt man and test him. Thus man should approach her with great care, ever fearful of traps. She was, in fact, even shaped like a trap, with her arms extended and her lips parted for a man.

He was indulgent only of nuns, made inoffensive by their vows; and he treated even them severely, because he felt stirring in the depths of their fettered hearts—those hearts so humbled—that eternal yearning which still sought him out, even though he was a priest.

He felt it in their gaze—more steeped in piety than that of monks—in their religious ecstasy tainted with sex, in their transports of love for Christ, which infuriated him because it was woman's love, fleshly love. He felt it—this wicked yearning—even in their docility, in the sweetness of their voices in talking to him, in their lowered eyes, and in their submissive tears when he rebuffed them rudely.

And he shook out his soutane on leaving the gates of a convent and strode quickly away as though fleeing from danger.

He had a niece who lived with her mother in a little house nearby. He was determined to make her a Sister of Charity.

She was pretty, light-headed, and impish. When the Abbé preached, she laughed; and when he got angry at her she kissed him eagerly, clasping him to her heart while he tried instinctively to escape this embrace which nevertheless gave him a taste of sweet happiness, waking deep within him those paternal impulses which slumber in every man.

Often he spoke to her of God—of his God—while walking beside her along country lanes. She scarcely listened but looked at the sky, the grass, the flowers, with a lively joy which showed in her eyes. Sometimes she leaped to catch some flying thing and brought it back to him, crying: "Look, uncle, how pretty it is. I want to pet it." And this impulse to "pet bugs" or nuzzle lilac blossoms disturbed, annoyed, sickened the priest, who discerned in it that ineradicable yearning which always springs up in the female heart.

Then, it happened that one day the sacristan's wife, who kept house for the Abbé Marignan, cautiously told him that his niece had a lover. The news shocked him terribly and he stopped, choking, with his face full of soap, for he was busy shaving.

When he recovered so that he could think and speak, he shouted: "It is not true, you are lying, Mélanie!"

But the good woman put her hand on her heart: "May the Good Lord strike me dead if I'm lying, M. le Curé. She goes out there every night, I tell you, as soon as your sister's in bed. They meet down by the river. You've only to go and watch there between ten and midnight."

He stopped scraping his chin and started walking up and down violently, as he always did in his hours of solemn meditation. When he tried to finish shaving he cut himself three times between the nose and the ear.

All day he was silenced, swollen with indignation and rage. To his fury as a priest, confronted by love, the invincible, was added the exasperation of a strict father, of a guardian, of a confessor fooled, cheated, tricked by a child. He shared that self-centered feeling of suffocation experienced by parents whose daughter tells them she has—without them and despite them—chosen a husband.

After dinner he tried to read a bit, but he could not get into it. He got more and more exasperated. When ten o'clock struck he took down his walking stick, a formidable oaken cudgel he always used when making his evening rounds to visit the sick. And he smiled as he looked at this big club, whirling it about fiercely in his great countryman's fist. Then, suddenly, he raised it and, gritting his teeth, brought it down on a chair, knocking its splintered back to the floor.

He opened the door to go out, but stopped on the sill, surprised by a splendor of moonlight such as he had rarely seen.

And, endowed as he was with an exalted spirit—such as those poetical dreamers the Fathers of the Church might have had—he was immediately distracted, moved by the glorious and serene beauty of the pale night.

In his little garden, all bathed in soft light, the ordered ranks of his fruit trees traced on the path the shadows of their slender limbs, lightly veiled with foliage, while the giant honeysuckle, clinging to the wall of the house, exhaled a delicious, sugary breath that floated through the calm clear air like a ghostly perfume.

He began to breathe deeply, drinking the air as a drunkard drinks wine, and he took a few slow, dreaming, wondering steps, almost forgetting his niece.

When he reached the open country, he stopped to contemplate the fields all flooded with tender light, bathed in the delicate and languid charm that calm nights have. Incessantly the frogs gave out their short metallic note, and distant nightingales, inspiring dream not thought, blended their unstrung tune—a rapid throbbing music made for kisses—with the enchantment of the moonlight.

The Abbé pressed on, losing heart, though he could not tell why. He felt feeble, suddenly drained; he wanted to sit down, to stay there, to contemplate, to admire God in His handiwork.

Below, following the undulations of the little river, a tall line of poplars wound like a snake. A fine mist, a white vapor which the moonbeams pierced and turned to glowing silver, hung around and above the banks wrapping the whole tortuous watercourse in a sort of delicate and transparent gauze.

The priest halted again, struck to the depths of his soul by an irresistible wave of yearning.

And a doubt, a vague disturbance, came over him. He sensed within himself another of those questions he sometimes posed.

Why had God done this? Since the night is intended for sleep, for unconsciousness, for repose, for oblivion, why make it more charming than the day, sweeter than dawn or evening? And why this slow and seductive moon, which is more poetic than the sun and seems intended by its very delicacy to illumine things too fragile and mysterious for daylight, why should it come to make the shadows so transparent?

Why should the loveliest of songbirds not go to sleep with the others but linger on to sing in the disturbing shade?

Why this half-veil thrown over the world? Why this thrill in the heart, this stirring of the soul, this languor of the flesh?

Why this display of delights that men never see, since they are asleep in their beds? For whom was it intended, this sublime spectacle, this flood of poetry poured from the sky over the earth?

And the Abbé found no answer.

But then, down below, on the edge of the fields, under the vault of trees drenched with glowing mist, two shadows appeared, walking side by side.

The man was taller and held the neck of his lover and sometimes kissed her forehead. Their sudden appearance brought the still countryside to life, and it enfolded the young lovers like a setting divinely made for them. They seemed, the pair, a single being, the being for whom this calm and silent night was intended, and they moved toward the priest like a living answer, the answer to his question, flung back by his Master.

He stood still, his heart pounding in confusion, and he felt as if he were looking at a biblical scene, like the love of Ruth and Boaz, like the accomplishment of the will of God as presented in one of the great scenes of holy scripture. In his head echoed verses of the Song of Songs: the passionate cries, the calls of the flesh, all the ardent poetry of this poem that seethes with passionate yearning.

And he said to himself: "Perhaps God has made such nights to veil the loves of men with ideal beauty."

He recoiled before the couple who kept walking arm in arm. It was certainly his niece. But he asked himself now if he was not on the verge of disobeying God. Must not God permit love since He lavished upon it such visible splendor?

And he fled, distraught, almost ashamed, as if he had entered a temple where he had no right to be.

A Commentary

This tale is essentially realistic. The events are ordinary, the geography recognizable; the characters can be assigned to a particular time, place, religion, and class. But the imposition of a pattern on this realistic material moves it in the direction of comic romance. It contains no detail presented for its own sake or as documentation of a way of life. Every piece of information given to us contributes to the comic pattern of the plot. We can see this if we consider the central character and what we know about him.

In this uncomplicated tale the Abbé Marignan is not only the central character, he is almost the only character. His niece and the housekeeper, Mélanie, exist only to the extent that they contribute to the Abbé's story.

And the Abbé's story, if we consider its beginning and end, is a story of education, of a change in attitude. The change involves a dramatic shift in the priest's view of women and love.

The story falls naturally into three sections of nearly equal length, of which the first is entirely devoted to the presentation of the Abbé's character. Even here a striking selectivity prevails. We learn about two facets of this character only: one is the nature of the priest's religious belief, presented in the first paragraph and elaborated in the next three; the other is the priest's attitude toward women and love, presented in the fourth paragraph and elaborated in the next five. These two attributes are absolutely vital to the story because his attitude toward love must be changed— this is what the story is "about"—and his religious belief is the lever by means of which the change is accomplished. All the information in the first four paragraphs prepares us for the priest's mental process as we follow it in the closing paragraphs of the story.

If we accept the justice of the priest's comic education, we accept with it a particular view of life. There is a touch of satire as well as comedy in this tale. The priest's view of the workings of the universe is being subjected to an ironic scrutiny that is implicit in the way the story is worked out, and is almost explicit in the point of view from which the story is told. Even the priest's name, Marignan, is touched with irony for those who recognize what it alludes to, since the victor of the Battle of Marignan, Francis I, was defeated and captured in his next campaign, as the Abbé is in *his* little struggle.

Exactly what is our perspective on the events of this little tale? We look into the mind of the Abbé but we do not see things from his point of view. The narrator has his own perspective which is revealed to us by the allusion to the Battle of Marignan and by other means. Consider the fourth paragraph:

> The four seasons were perfectly fitted to all the needs of agriculture; and it would never have occurred to the priest to suspect that nature has no intentions at all, and that, on the contrary, every living thing has bowed to the hard necessities of times, climates, and matter itself.

Up to the semicolon, we are receiving a report on the priest's view—actually a continuation of the preceding paragraph. But after the semicolon, we are being given another view of the world, one which "would never have occurred" to the Abbé himself. This other viewpoint—the narrator's—is in direct opposition to the priest's. Where the Abbé sees God's intentions everywhere, the narrator sees a nature without plan or purpose but still determining the quality of existence. There is a touch of naturalism in this view (a satiric hint of a chaotic, destructive world), which is counteracted by the purposeful pattern of the story itself.

The narrator's views are closest to the surface in this paragraph, but once we are alert to them we can see them operating more subtly elsewhere. In the very first paragraph, for instance, the last two sentences are so emphatic in their repetition that they acquire a somewhat mocking tone. In them we learn not only that the priest's views are "fixed," but also that they "never wavered." We learn that the Abbé entered not only into God's "plans," but also into "His wishes, His intentions." This underlining of the rigidity and presumption of the priest's beliefs prepares us for his comeuppance and at the same time makes us unconsciously begin to wish for it.

Some of the metaphors used by the narrator also enrich the meaning of the work. The last sentence employs a simile which is appropriate and ironic. The priest flees from this love scene "as if he had entered into a temple where he had no right to be." The word "entered" (pénétré), of course, echoes ironically the penetration of the priest into God's designs, and is an interesting example of such designed repetition, but this penetration in the last sentence of the story is part of a metaphoric structure—an analogy introduced by the expression "as if." The key word in the simile is "temple." The priest does not flee from a scene that outrages religion in order to take sanctuary in his church. In a comic reversal he flees from a scene which is itself religious, as he now understands it, and where he is the infidel profaning holy ground. This image of the temple, we should also note, has been prepared for by our first sight of the two lovers, under the "vault" of the trees.

Other metaphors operate with comparable subtlety. Consider the priest's first vision of this scene, as he pauses above it and looks at the winding river and the poplars lining its banks. The narrator, in describing the trees, says they "wound like a snake" (serpentait). He must have chosen this expression specifically to remind us of a similar idyllic love scene—the Garden of Eden—which also had its serpent. The suggestion is delicate and rich. The priest usually thinks of woman as "the temptress who had ensnared the first man," but in this scene nature itself and finally God seem to have conspired to surround this "sin" with beauty. And the Abbé enters a world in which he is as much an alien as the devil in paradise, though his intention is not to tempt but to prevent a fall.

Although this story is essentially a plot, it is not without design. The early sample of the Abbé's reasoning process is repeated at the end with its startling new conclusion that God "must permit love." And the temple simile in the last sentence reminds us of two related scenes: the Abbé striding so confidently down the aisle of his own church, and the Abbé leaving a convent of nuns with that same stride, after having shaken its contaminating dust of femininity off his soutane. He, who had been too pure to accept these nuns as his spiritual equals, is finally seen as profaning a temple of love. The design and the tone reinforce in various subtle ways the irony of the plot. The strength of this little story lies in the way all these elements cooperate to achieve its comic effect.

JAMES JOYCE
1882–1941
Clay

The matron had given her leave to go out as soon as the women's tea was over and Maria looked forward to her evening out. The kitchen was spick and span: the cook said you could see yourself in the big copper boilers. The fire was nice and bright and on one of the side-tables were four very big barmbracks. These barmbracks seemed uncut; but if you went closer you would see that they had been cut into long thick even slices and were ready to be handed round at tea. Maria had cut them herself.

Maria was a very, very small person indeed but she had a very long nose and a very long chin. She talked a little through her nose, always soothingly: *Yes, my dear,* and *No, my dear.* She was always sent for when the women quarrelled over their tubs and always succeeded in making peace. One day the matron had said to her:

—Maria, you are a veritable peace-maker!

And the sub-matron and two of the Board ladies had heard the compliment. And Ginger Mooney was always saying what she wouldn't do to the dummy who had charge of the irons if it wasn't for Maria. Everyone was so fond of Maria.

The women would have their tea at six o'clock and she would be able to get away before seven. From Ballsbridge to the Pillar, twenty minutes; from the Pillar to Drumcondra, twenty minutes; and twenty minutes to buy the things. She would be there before eight. She took out her purse with the silver clasps and read again the words *A Present from Belfast.* She was very fond of that purse because Joe had brought it to her five years before when he and Alphy had gone to Belfast on a Whit-Monday trip. In the purse were two half-crowns and some coppers. She would have five shillings clear after paying tram fare. What a nice evening they would have, all the children singing! Only she hoped that Joe wouldn't come in drunk. He was so different when he took any drink.

Often he had wanted her to go and live with them; but she would have felt herself in the way (though Joe's wife was ever so nice with her) and she had become accustomed to the life of the laundry. Joe was a good fellow. She had nursed him and Alphy too; and Joe used often say:

—Mamma is mamma but Maria is my proper mother.

After the break-up at home the boys had got her that position in the *Dublin by Lamplight* laundry, and she liked it. She used to have such a bad opinion of Protestants but now she thought they were very nice people, a little quiet and serious, but still very nice people to live with. Then she had her plants in the conservatory and she liked looking after them. She had lovely ferns and wax-plants and, whenever anyone came to visit her, she always gave the visitor one or two slips from her conservatory. There was one thing she didn't like and that was the tracts on the walls; but the matron was such a nice person to deal with, so genteel.

When the cook told her everything was ready she went into the women's room and began to pull the big bell. In a few minutes the women began to come in by twos and threes, wiping their steaming hands in their petticoats and pulling down the sleeves of their blouses over their red steaming arms. They settled down before their huge mugs which the cook and the dummy filled up with hot tea, already mixed with milk and sugar in huge tin cans. Maria superintended the distribution of the barmbrack and saw that every woman got her four slices. There was a great deal of laughing and joking during the meal. Lizzie Fleming said Maria was sure to get the ring and, though Fleming had said that for so many Hallow Eves, Maria had to laugh and say she didn't want any ring or man either; and when she laughed her grey-green eyes sparkled with disappointed shyness and the tip of her nose nearly met the tip of her chin. Then Ginger Mooney lifted up her mug of tea and proposed Maria's health while all the other women clattered with their mugs on the table, and said she was sorry she hadn't a sup of porter to drink it in. And Maria laughed again till the tip of her nose nearly met the tip of her chin and till her minute body nearly shook itself asunder because she knew that Mooney meant well though, of course, she had the notions of a common woman.

But wasn't Maria glad when the women had finished their tea and the cook and the dummy had begun to clear away the tea-things! She went into her little bedroom and, remembering that the next morning was a mass morning, changed the hand of the alarm from seven to six. Then she took off her working skirt and her house-boots and laid her best skirt out on the bed and her tiny dress-boots beside the foot of the bed. She changed her blouse too and, as she stood before the mirror, she thought of how she used to dress for mass on Sunday morning when she was a young girl; and she looked with quaint affection at the diminutive body which she had so often adorned. In spite of its years she found it a nice tidy little body.

When she got outside the streets were shining with rain and she was glad of her old brown raincloak. The tram was full and she had to sit on the little stool at the end of the car, facing all the people, with her toes barely touching the floor. She arranged in her mind all she was going to do and thought how much better it was to be independent and to have your own money in your pocket. She hoped they would have a nice evening. She was sure they would but she could not help thinking what a pity it was Alphy and Joe were not speaking. They were always falling out now but when they were boys together they used to be the best of friends: but such was life.

She got out of her tram at the Pillar and ferreted her way quickly among the crowds. She went into Downes's cake-shop but the shop was so full of people that it was a long time before she could get herself attended to. She bought a dozen of mixed penny cakes, and at last came out of the shop laden with a big bag. Then she thought what else would she buy: she wanted to buy something really nice. They would be sure to have plenty of apples and nuts. It was hard to know what to buy and all she could think of was cake. She decided to buy some plumcake but Downes's plumcake had not enough almond icing on top of it so she went over to a shop in Henry Street. Here she was a long time in suiting herself and the stylish young lady behind the counter, who was evidently a little annoyed by her, asked her was it wedding-cake she wanted to buy. That made Maria blush and smile at the young lady; but the young lady took it all very seriously and finally cut a thick slice of plumcake, parcelled it up and said:

—Two-and-four, please.

She thought she would have to stand in the Drumcondra tram because none of the young men seemed to notice her but an elderly gentleman made room for her. He was a stout gentleman and he wore a brown hard hat; he had a square red face and a greying moustache. Maria thought he was a colonel-looking gentleman and she reflected how much more polite he was than the young men who simply stared straight before them. The gentleman began to chat with her about Hallow Eve and the rainy weather. He supposed the bag was full of good things for the little ones and said it was only right that the youngsters should enjoy themselves while they were young. Maria agreed with him and favoured him with demure nods and hems. He was very nice with her, and when she was getting out at the Canal Bridge she thanked him and bowed, and he bowed to her and raised his hat and smiled agreeably; and while she was going up along the terrace, bending her tiny head under the rain, she thought how easy it was to know a gentleman even when he has a drop taken.

Everybody said: *O, here's Maria!* when she came to Joe's house. Joe was there, having come home from business, and all the children had their Sunday dresses on. There were two big girls in from next door and games were going on. Maria gave the bag of cakes to the eldest boy, Alphy, to divide and Mrs Donnelly said it was too good of her to bring such a big bag of cakes and made all the children say:

—Thanks, Maria.

But Maria said she had brought something special for papa and mamma, something they would be sure to like, and she began to look for her plumcake. She tried in Downes's bag and then in the pockets of her raincloak and then on the hallstand but nowhere could she find it. Then she asked all the children had any of them eaten it—by mistake, of course—but the children all said no and looked as if they did not like to eat cakes if they were to be accused of stealing. Everybody had a solution for the mystery and Mrs Donnelly said it was plain that Maria had left it behind her in the tram. Maria, remembering how confused the gentleman with the greyish moustache had made her, coloured with shame and vexation and disappointment. At the thought of the failure of her little surprise and of the two and fourpence she had thrown away for nothing she nearly cried outright.

But Joe said it didn't matter and made her sit down by the fire. He was very nice with her. He told her all that went on in his office, repeating for her a smart answer which he had made to the manager. Maria did not understand why Joe laughed so much over the answer he had made but she said that the manager must have been a very overbearing person to deal with. Joe said he wasn't so bad when you knew how to take him, that he was a decent sort so long as you didn't rub him the wrong way. Mrs Donnelly played the piano for the children and they danced and sang. Then the two next-door girls handed round the nuts. Nobody could find the nutcrackers and Joe was nearly getting cross over it and asked how did they expect Maria to crack nuts without a nutcracker. But Maria said she didn't like nuts and that they weren't to bother about her. Then Joe asked would she take a bottle of stout and Mrs Donnelly said there was port wine too in the house if she would prefer that. Maria said she would rather they didn't ask her to take anything: but Joe insisted.

So Maria let him have his way and they sat by the fire talking over old times and Maria thought she would put in a good word for Alphy. But Joe cried that God might strike him stone dead if ever he spoke a word to his brother again and Maria said she was sorry she had mentioned the matter. Mrs Donnelly told her husband it was a great shame for him to speak that way of his own flesh and blood but Joe said that Alphy was no brother of his and there was nearly being a row on the head of it. But Joe said he would not lose his temper on account of the night it was and asked his wife to open some more stout. The two next-door girls had arranged some Hallow Eve games and soon everything was merry again. Maria was delighted to see the children so merry and Joe and his wife in such good spirits. The next-door girls put some saucers on the table and then led the children up to the table, blindfold. One got the prayer-book and the other three got the water; and when one of the next-door girls got the ring Mrs Donnelly shook her finger at the blushing girl as much as to say: *O, I know all about it!* They insisted then on blindfolding Maria and leading her up to the table to see what she would get; and, while they were putting on the bandage, Maria laughed and laughed again till the top of her nose nearly met the tip of her chin.

They led her up to the table amid laughing and joking and she put her hand out in the air as she was told to do. She moved her hand about here and there in the air and descended on one of the saucers. She a felt a soft wet substance with her fingers and was surprised that nobody spoke or took off her bandage. There was a pause for a few seconds; and then a great deal of scuffling and whispering. Somebody said something about the garden, and at last Mrs Donnelly said something very cross to one of the next-door girls and told her to throw it out at once: that was no play. Maria understood that it was wrong that time and so she had to do it over again: and this time she got the prayer-book .

After that Mrs Donnely played Miss McCloud's Reel for the children and Joe made Maria take a glass of wine. Soon they were all quite merry again and Mrs Donnelly said Maria would enter a convent before the year was out because she had got the prayer-book. Maria had never seen Joe so nice to her as he was that night, so full of pleasant talk and reminiscences. She said they were all very good to her.

At last the children grew tired and sleepy and Joe asked Maria would she not sing some little song before she went, one of the old songs. Mrs Donnelly said *Do, please, Maria!* and so Maria had to get up and stand beside the piano. Mrs Donnelly bade the children be quiet and listen to Maria's song. Then she played the prelude and said *Now, Maria!* and Maria, blushing very much, began to sing in a tiny quavering voice. She sang *I Dreamt that I Dwelt*, and when she came to the second verse she sang again:

I dreamt that I dwelt in marble halls
  With vassals and serfs at my side
And of all who assembled within those walls
  That I was the hope and the pride.
I had riches too great to count, could boast
  Of a high ancestral name,
But I also dreamt, which pleased me most,
  That you loved me still the same.

But no one tried to show her her mistake; and when she had ended her song Joe was very much moved. He said that there was no time like the long ago and no music for him like poor old Balfe, whatever other people might say; and his eyes filled up so much with tears that he could not find what he was looking for and in the end he had to ask his wife to tell him where the corkscrew was.

A Commentary by R. S.

I can remember vividly my first encounter with "Clay," and this is partly why I have included it here. I was a freshman in college, and my roommate handed me the anthology they were using in his English class and asked me what I made of one story that baffled him. The story was "Clay," and I remember that it baffled me as well. It was not like the stories I knew and admired—by Poe, O. Henry, Maupassant. It seemed to me to have no plot and to be about nothing in particular. By one of those ironies that operate in life as well as in art, I have since devoted a good deal of my time to studying Joyce. So "Clay" is here both because I know it well and respect it and because I can remember so well what it was like not to understand it.

Like "Moonlight" it is realistic, dealing with ordinary people and situations. It is, in fact, much more concerned to document a kind of reality than to tell a crisp and comic tale. It is more realistic than "Moonlight" and more pathetic than comic in its effect. As the Abbé Marignan's story is amusing, Maria's is sad. And as his story is one of education, hers is one of revelation. He *learns* from his experience; she *is revealed* to us through her experience, but without any increase in awareness on her part. The Abbé's day, after all, is an extraordinary one in his life. Maria's is merely typical. Nothing of great importance happens in it. This is one reason why "Clay" can be so baffling. It is hard to "see" a story in it, since nothing of any consequence happens. Nevertheless, it is a story, and it will respond to a careful consideration of its elements.

To begin with the matter of plot, it is not easy to find one in "Clay," but one is there all the same. Part of it has to do with the Halloween game that Maria and the others play. The game is not explained but there are enough clues in the story for us to reconstruct its method. We first hear of the game while Maria is still at the laundry:

> There was a great deal of laughing and joking during the meal. Lizzie Fleming said Maria was sure to get the ring and, though Fleming had said that for so many Hallow Eves, Maria had to laugh and say she didn't want any ring or any man either; and when she laughed her grey-green eyes sparkled with disappointed shyness and the tip of her nose nearly met the tip of her chin.

Later, Maria plays the game at her brother's house, so that, taken together, the two scenes make the beginning and end of a line of action in the story. And, since the title points directly toward the second of these scenes, we are surely right to consider it important. In this scene we first learn more about the operation of the game, as the children and the next-door girls play it:

> The next-door girls put some saucers on the table and then led the children up to the table, blindfold. One got the prayer-book and the other three got the water; and when one of the next-door girls got the ring Mrs Donnelly shook her finger at the blushing girl as much as to say: *O, I know all about it!*

And later, after the game has gone "wrong" once and been played over, Maria is gently teased by Mrs Donnelly also:

> ... Mrs Donnelly said Maria would enter a convent before the year was out because she had got the prayer-book.

The game, as we can reconstruct it from the clues in these three passages, is a simple, fortunetelling affair. A blindfolded person chooses among three saucers and the choice indicates the future event. The ring indicates marriage, the prayerbook foretells entering the Church, and the water—we are not told, but I should guess a sea voyage. In reading this story we must continue to perform exactly this kind of reconstruction. Where Maupassant told us everything he wanted us to know in the most direct way possible, Joyce is *in*direct, making us do a good deal of interpretive labor ourselves. But having figured out the game, we must now arrive at an understanding of its significance in Maria's story.

At the beginning of this line of action, Maria was teased by Lizzie Fleming about being "sure to get the ring"—which would mean marriage. At the end she is teased about having got the prayerbook, which means a life of chaste seclusion from the world. But between these moments, Maria has actually made her real selection:

> They led her up to the table amid laughing and joking and she put out her hand out in the air as she was told to do. She moved her hand about here and there in the air and descended on one of the saucers. She felt a soft wet substance with her fingers and was surprised that nobody spoke or took off her bandage. There was a pause for a few seconds; and then a great deal of scuffling and whispering. Somebody said something about the garden, and at last Mrs Donnelly said something very cross to one of the next-door girls and told her to throw it out at once: that was no play. Maria understood that it was wrong that time and so she had to do it over again: and this time she got the prayer-book.

By calling his story "Clay," Joyce made sure that we would be able to understand this episode and its significance, even though Maria herself, from whose point of view we are perceiving things, never realizes what substance she has encountered. The next-door girls have played a trick on her by putting clay into one of the saucers. We know what the ring, prayerbook, and water signify in this game. But clay is not regularly a part of it. Its significance is a matter for our interpretation. Clearly, we will not be far wrong if we associate it with death, realizing that Maria is not likely to marry or enter a convent, but certainly is destined to die and become clay—as are we all. Clay is the substance out of which the first man was made. It conveys the essence of human frailty. Indeed, "that was no play." The clay intrudes on this Halloween scene like a ghostly presence, reminding us of the reality of death and decomposition. Thus, with some scrutiny, this strand of the action becomes both clear and meaningful. But at least one other must be accounted for. If we are to grasp the entire story we must understand such episodes as Maria admiring her body in the mirror, Maria responding to the "colonel-looking gentlemen," Maria losing her plum-cake, and Maria mistaking the verses of her song.

Since the mistake in singing is the very last thing in "Clay," we might well consider it for possible revelations. What mistake does Maria make? "When she came to the second verse she sang again: . . . . But no one tried to show her her mistake." She repeats the first verse, which is to say, she leaves out the second. What does she leave out? The omitted second verse goes this way:

> I dreamt that suitors sought my hand,
>   That knights on bended knee,
> And with vows no maiden heart could withstand,
>   They pledged their faith to me.
> And I dreamt that one of that noble band,
>   Came forth my heart to claim,
> But I also dreamt, which charmed me most,
>   That you loved me all the same.

Joyce could have told us what was in this verse that Maria omitted, but he chose simply to leave out what she left out and include the verse she repeated. He made sure we knew she had left something out, but he did not tell us its nature. As with the game, he insists that we do the work of interpretation, which in this case includes research into "I Dreamt that I Dwelt," so that we can supply the missing verse. He continually requires us to share the work of constructing this story in order to understand it. But what does the missing verse tell us? It tells us that Maria unconsciously rebelled at singing "suitors sought my hand"; that a subject such as "vows that no maiden heart could withstand" bothered her enough that she repressed it and "forgot" the second verse. Can we relate this to the other episodes in the story?

When Lizzie Fleming teased her and predicted she would "get the ring,"

Maria "had to laugh and say she didn't want any ring or man either." But she adorns her "nice tidy little body," and she gets so flustered by an inebriated "colonel-looking gentleman" that she misplaces her plumcake while talking to him. In its very different way from Maupassant's, Joyce's story is also about feminine *tendresse*, or "yearning." The missing verse fits into this pattern perfectly. Maria is a reluctant spinster, homely as a Halloween witch, with the tip of her nose nearly meeting the tip of her chin. She feels superior to the "common" women who work in the *Dublin by Lamplight* laundry (a title intended to suggest that the laundresses have been reclaimed from a distinctly "fallen" status), but she takes several drinks when Joe "makes" her. Her appetites are more like those of the "common" women than she would admit. All in all, she is a pathetic figure—a "peacemaker" whose "children" have quarreled so bitterly that she is powerless to reconcile them, and whose suspicions that the children ate her missing plumcake turn them temporarily against her and perhaps lead to the trick by the next-door girls. Clay certainly, common clay.

The title of this story points much more insistently toward its meaning than does the title of "Moonlight" (though the French title, "Clair de lune," is stronger than its English equivalent in suggesting a metaphoric "light" in the sense of mental illumination). Like the title of "Moonlight," the title of "Clay" points toward something that is present in the story, but this clay of Joyce's story is more richly and subtly meaningful than Maupassant's moonlight. The substance, clay, acquires metaphorical suggestions of mortality and common human weakness. The object in the story—that dish of clay in the Halloween game—becomes a symbol for these complicated qualities. And symbolism is the richest and most complicated of metaphorical processes.

Metaphorical possibilities range from the simple and straightforward simile to the symbol. The simile indicates precisely the nature of the comparison it makes with words like "as" and "so." But the symbol opens out from an object or image in the direction of an unspecified meaning. We should add that though the meaning of a symbol is extensive and not precisely limited, this meaning is always directed and controlled in some way. A symbol in a work of fiction, like the clay in this story, cannot be made to "mean" anything we happen to associate with the word "clay." Only those associations both suggested by the substance clay and actually related to Maria's fictional situation belong in our interpretation of the story. Meanings like "mortality" and "common weakness" are traditionally associated with clay in Western tradition, from the Bible on, and clay is used to symbolize similar things in other cultures as well. But we must demonstrate a connection between these traditional meanings and the story in order to establish their appropriateness. Plot, character, and symbol work together to shape our final understanding of the story.

We should note in passing that "Clay" is a special kind of short story in that it is actually part of a sequence of stories put together by its author for a purpose beyond that realizable in any single short piece. In this case, Joyce called his sequence *Dubliners* and meant it as a representation of life in his native city of Dublin. In its proper setting, the meaning of "Clay" chimes with the meaning of the other stories, as Maria's spinsterhood and common humanity are echoed by and contrasted with the situations and qualities of other Dubliners. But even though it gains in resonance when placed in *Dubliners*, "Clay" is sufficient to be of interest by itself.

Aside from its central symbol, Joyce is sparing of metaphor in "Clay." But he is very careful about his control of tone. The tone he establishes at the beginning never falters. How should it be described? "The kitchen was spick and span. . . . The fire was nice and bright." What kind of prose is this? Or consider the short fourth paragraph:

> And the sub-matron and two of the Board ladies had heard the compliment. And Ginger Mooney was always saying what she wouldn't do to the dummy who had charge of the irons if it wasn't for Maria. Everyone was so fond of Maria.

The syntactical pattern of "And . . . and . . . . And" is just one facet of the excessive simplicity of this prose. It is echoed by the quality of cliché that we find in phrases like "spick and span" or "nice and bright." Though Maria herself is not telling this story to us, the narrator is using language closely approaching her own. That is one reason why any striking use of metaphor has been ruled out. Complicated sentences, complex words, and brilliant turns of phrase are all inappropriate here. Joyce said once that he had written *Dubliners* in a style of "scrupulous meanness." That expression is exactly appropriate to the style of "Clay."

In the paragraph we are considering, this linguistic situation is actually somewhat like the one in the first paragraph quoted from *Mrs. Dalloway* in the section on point of view (see p. 114 above): simple, even banal language; and a "so" in the last sentence. Is the tone of the two paragraphs—or of the two "so's"—exactly the same? I think not. The excessive simplicity of Virginia Woolf's prose at this point is entirely devoted to mockery of Sir William Bradshaw. But Joyce's simplicity is in considerable part devoted to giving us Maria's own view of her situation. Her view is undoubtedly limited. Everyone is not *so* fond of her as she would like to think. But we are not really standing off from her and subjecting her to an ironic scrutiny. We are *with* her to some extent here, as well as detached from her. The paragraph in *Mrs. Dalloway* is almost pure satire. The paragraph in "Clay" is pathos mainly, with perhaps a slight admixture of satire.

All the way through the story, Joyce keeps very close not only to a style of language appropriate to Maria, but also to Maria's perspective. Only rarely, as when Maria responds to Lizzie's teasing, does he tell us directly something she could not perceive herself. And there, when he tells us her "eyes sparkled with disappointed shyness," he is giving us an important clue to the "disappointed" quality of her spinsterhood. Usually he avoids such direct transcendence of Maria's perspective and makes us do the work of inference ourselves. Even at the end, when he tells us something that Maria does not know—that she has left out a verse of the song—he does not tell us what is in the verse, for to do so would take us too far from her perspective. By holding us so close to the viewpoint of his central character, Joyce makes it necessary for us to infer a good deal in order to achieve a distance from her sufficient to focus on her with the clarity of detachment. In effect, he makes us see Maria with a double vision, engaged and detached, sympathetic and ironic. And not only Maria but the other characters as well must be seen in this way. Joe, at the close of the story, weeping so much he cannot find the corkscrew to open another bottle, could be seen as a caricature only—another drunken, sentimental, stage Irishman. But Joe's booze-induced sentimentality is also genuine warmth—a mixture of the genuine and the spurious which is, for better or worse, very common in life. Joyce leaves the evaluation to us.

The comic clarity of Maupassant does make, in a sense, a better story. The delicacy and complexity of Joyce make a more realistic one. Fortunately, we do not have to choose between one and the other. We can have both ways, and many more, whenever we want.

Design in "Clay" is mainly a matter of the organization of parts to bear on the revelation of Maria's common disappointments. The central symbol of the clay itself, which is established in the story's climactic episode, is the pivot around which everything else turns. The story appears to us to be almost a plotless, designless "slice of life," and we have to look carefully to note the care of its construction. Actually, design operates much more powerfully in *Dubliners* as a whole than in any single story. The arrangement of stories was very carefully worked out by Joyce to achieve certain juxtapositions, and the stories are designed so that each contains elements that repeat and echo their counterparts in the others. The larger any work is, the more important plot and design become as elements of coherence. A collection of stories, which has no plot, must depend extensively on design for its structural interconnections. But Joyce preferred design to plot, and his longest narratives, *Ulysses* and *Finnegans Wake*, are scantily plotted and elaborately designed.

You will encounter another story from *Dubliners* in the anthology section that follows. At that point, it should be interesting to see how the two stories work together, treating similar thematic materials with a similar technique—yet managing to be entirely unique.

JORGE LUIS BORGES
1899–
Theme of the Traitor and the Hero

> So the Platonic year
> Whirls out new right and wrong,
> Whirls in the old instead;
> All men are dancers and their tread
> Goes to the barbarous clangour of a gong.
>> W. B. Yeats: *The Tower*

Under the notable influence of Chesterton (contriver and embellisher of elegant mysteries) and the palace counselor Leibniz (inventor of the pre-established harmony), in my idle afternoons I have imagined this story plot which I shall perhaps write some-day and which already justifies me somehow. Details, rectifications, adjustments are lacking; there are zones of the story not yet revealed to me; today, January 3rd, 1944, I seem to see it as follows:

The action takes place in an oppressed and tenacious country: Poland, Ireland, the Venetian Republic, some South American or Balkan state . . . Or rather it has taken place, since, though the narrator is contemporary, his story occurred towards the middle or the beginning of the nineteenth century. Let us say (for narrative convenience) Ireland; let us say in 1824. The narrator's name is Ryan; he is the great-grandson of the young, the heroic, the beautiful, the assassinated Fergus Kilpatrick, whose grave was mysteriously violated, whose name illustrated the verses of Browning and Hugo, whose statue presides over a gray hill amid red marshes.

Kilpatrick was a conspirator, a secret and glorious captain of conspirators: like Moses, who from the land of Moab glimpsed but could not reach the promised land, Kilpatrick perished on the eve of the victorious revolt which he had premeditated and dreamt of. The first centenary of his death draws near; the circumstances of the crime are enigmatic; Ryan, engaged in writing a biography of the hero, discovers that the enigma exceeds the confines of a simple police investigation. Kilpatrick was murdered in a theater; the British police never found the killer; the historians maintain that this scarcely soils their good reputation, since it was probably the police themselves who had him killed. Other facets of the enigma disturb Ryan. They are of a cyclic nature: they seem to repeat or combine events of remote regions, or remote ages. For example, no one is unaware that the officers who examined the hero's body found a sealed letter in which he was warned of the risk of attending the theater that evening; likewise Julius Caesar, on his way to the place where his friends' daggers awaited him, received a note he never read, in which the treachery was declared along with the traitors' names. Caesar's wife, Calpurnia, saw in a dream the destruction of a tower decreed him by the Senate; false and anonymous rumors on the eve of Kilpatrick's death publicized throughout the country that the circular tower of Kilgarvan had burned, which could be taken as a presage, for he had been born in Kilgarvan. These parallelisms (and others) between the story of Caesar and the story of an Irish conspirator lead Ryan to suppose the existence of a secret form of time, a pattern of repeated lines. He thinks of the decimal history conceived by Condorcet, of the morphologies proposed by Hegel, Spengler and Vico, of Hesiod's men, who degenerate from gold to iron. He thinks of the transmigration of souls, a doctrine that lends horror to Celtic literature and that Caesar himself attributed to the British druids: he thinks that, before having been Fergus Kilpatrick, Fergus Kilpatrick was Julius Caesar. He is rescued from these circular labyrinths by a curious finding, a finding which then sinks him into other, more inextricable and heterogeneous labyrinths: certain words uttered by a beggar who spoke with Fergus Kilpatrick the day of his death were prefigured by Shakespeare in the tragedy *Macbeth*. That history should have copied history was already sufficiently astonishing; that history should copy literature was inconceivable. . . . Ryan finds that, in 1814, James Alexander Nolan, the oldest of the hero's companions, had translated the principal dramas of Shakespeare into Gaelic; among these was *Julius Caesar*. He also discovers in the archives the manuscript of an article by Nolan on the Swiss *Festspiele:* vast and errant theatrical representations which require thousands of actors and repeat historical episodes in the very cities and mountains where they took place. Another unpublished document reveals to him that, a few days before the end, Kilpatrick, presiding over the last meeting, had signed the order for the execution of a traitor whose name had been deleted from the records. This order does not accord with Kilpatrick's merciful nature. Ryan investigates the matter (this investigation is one of the gaps in my plot) and manages to decipher the enigma.

Kilpatrick was killed in a theater, but the entire city was a theater as well, and the actors were legion, and the drama crowned by his death extended over many days and many nights. This is what happened:

On the 2nd of August, 1824, the conspirators gathered. The country was ripe for revolt; something, however, always failed: there was a traitor in the group. Fergus Kilpatrick had charged James Nolan with the responsibility of discovering the traitor. Nolan carried out his assignment: he announced in the very midst of the meeting that the traitor was Kilpatrick himself. He demonstrated the truth of his accusations with irrefutable proof; the conspirators condemned their president to die. He signed his own sentence, but begged that his punishment not harm his country.

It was then that Nolan conceived his strange scheme. Ireland idolized Kilpatrick; the most tenuous suspicion of his infamy would have jeopardized the revolt; Nolan proposed a plan which made of the traitor's execution an instrument for the country's emancipation. He suggested that the condemned man die at the hands of an unknown assassin in deliberately dramatic circumstances which would remain engraved in the imagination of the people and would hasten the revolt. Kilpatrick swore he would take part in the scheme, which gave him the occasion to redeem himself and for which his death would provide the final flourish.

Nolan, urged on by time, was not able to invent all the circumstances of the multiple execution; he had to plagiarize another dramatist, the English enemy William Shakespeare. He repeated scenes from *Macbeth,* from *Julius Caesar.* The public and secret enactment comprised various days. The condemned man entered Dublin, discussed, acted, prayed, reproved, uttered words of pathos, and each of these gestures, to be reflected in his glory, had been pre-established by Nolan. Hundreds of actors collaborated with the protagonist; the role of some was complex; that of others momentary. The things they did and said endure in the history books, in the impassioned memory of Ireland. Kilpatrick, swept along by this minutely detailed destiny which both redeemed him and destroyed him, more than once enriched the text of his judge with improvised acts and words. Thus the populous drama unfolded in time, until on the 6th of August, 1824, in a theater box with funereal curtains prefiguring Lincoln's, a long-desired bullet entered the breast of the traitor and hero, who, amid two effusions of sudden blood, was scarcely able to articulate a few foreseen words.

In Nolan's work, the passages imitated from Shakespeare are the *least* dramatic; Ryan suspects that the author interpolated them so that in the future someone might hit upon the truth. He understands that he too forms part of Nolan's plot. . . . After a series of tenacious hesitations, he resolves to keep his discovery silent. He publishes a book dedicated to the hero's glory; this too, perhaps, was foreseen.

A Commentary

The first paragraph of Borges's story indicates unmistakably how far removed it is from the realism of Maupassant and Joyce. Instead of presenting us with a character situated in a world, it presents us with an idea for a "story plot which I shall perhaps write someday." This story does not pretend to be a slice of life. It does not even pretend to be a finished story: "Details, rectifications, adjustments are lacking; there are zones of the story not yet revealed to me." It is hard to see how fiction could insist more resolutely on its fictional character. Moreover, despite its shortness, the story consists of a number of separate plots or lines of action. The narrator himself, whom we might call *Borges* (italicized to distinguish him from the author, Borges), is telling us about Ryan, a man who is trying to write a biography. Ryan, himself a narrator, is trying to write the life of his ancestor Fergus Kilpatrick. In particular, Ryan is trying to account for the mysterious manner of Kilpatrick's death in a theater.

In the first sentence *Borges* tells us he has "imagined" this story under the influence of two other writers: Chesterton, author of the still popular "Father Brown" detective-mysteries, and Leibniz (or Leibnitz), a politician-mathematician-historian-philosopher who developed a theory in which the world is seen as an arrangement of harmoniously related substances. By notifying us that a mystery writer and a philosopher have inspired this tale, *Borges* suggests that we should be alert for clues and ideas. The story offers us a mystery about the death of Fergus Kilpatrick, complete with clues and solution; and the solution suggests a certain view of the world, a philosophical position.

Along with Ryan, the detective-biographer, we follow the clues about the murder of Fergus Kilpatrick. We discover not only that James Nolan was responsible for his death but that Nolan also stage-managed all the events surrounding that death: "Kilpatrick was killed in a theater, but the entire city was a theater as well." Nolan, who was an expert on the Swiss *Festspiele*, had arranged a gigantic play. But this one, with its cast of thousands, was not a reenactment of history in the form of fiction. It was fiction becoming history: "The things they did and said endure in the history books." The whole episode, which also prefigured the actual death of Lincoln, is referred to as Nolan's "work"—which it is, since he created it. *Borges*'s story closes with this paragraph:

> In Nolan's work, the passages imitated from Shakespeare are the *least* dramatic; Ryan suspects that the author interpolated them so that in the future someone might hit upon the truth. He understands that he too forms part of Nolan's plot . . . After a series of tenacious hesitations, he resolves to keep his discovery silent. He publishes a book dedicated to the hero's glory; this too, perhaps, was foreseen.

Ryan, the historian, has set out to discover historical truth about certain characters who lived in the past. He will then put them in a history book. What he discovers, however, is that he himself is perhaps a character in a fictional work designed by James Nolan; and his part is not that of truthful historian but of deceitful falsifier of history. He accepts the role as Kilpatrick accepted his, and plays the assigned part. But of course this part was really assigned by *Borges,* who tells us that he has made the whole thing up "in my idle afternoons." And behind this fictional *Borges* there stands another Borges who has made up this one, idle afternoons and all. And perhaps behind that one. . . .

We end, finally, as characters in someone's great design ourselves, as we sit reading Borges's pages, wondering whether the world is really organized according to a "pre-established harmony". The quotation from Yeats, which is set before the story as its epigraph, proposes a cyclical theory of history. It is taken from a poem, "Nineteen Hundred and Nineteen," written by the poet during the Irish "Troubles," which began with an uprising, like many others plotted in Ireland, but ended in success—only to be followed by civil war.

The poem, which Yeats included in his volume *The Tower,* is appropriate to the story in a very immediate way. But its main purpose is to add its voice to the cyclical theory of history that Borges is proposing in his story. The story is not a logical argument for this view. It merely asks "What if . . . ?" If history moves in cycles according to a pre-established harmony, then the sort of thing presented here might well occur. Questions like, "Does this sort of thing actually occur?" are left open to our thought. But Borges directs our thought along these lines. Instead of simply moving continually from old to new, history may—as Yeats suggests—whirl out the new and whirl in the old. It may move not in a line but in a circle or spiral. Borges's story can be seen as a variation on this theme in the philosophy of history.

Thus, in his tale Borges displays no special interest in the psychology of his characters or in the specific sociology of their environment. His Ireland is not Joyce's. Nor is it Yeats's. It is not even necessarily Ireland. It could be Poland or "some South American or Balkan state," as long as it is "op-pressed and tenacious." The crowded plot and elaborate design of this little story overwhelm the characters. Idea and pattern, and the idea *of* pattern, dominate our vision. Borges has moved far from realism in telling us the stories of Ryan, Kilpatrick, and Nolan. Their tragi-comic histories exist for us mainly as a way of encouraging a pleasurable speculation—what Poe called "ratiocination." Philosophy can be seen as a serious playing with ideas. Borges embraces this playfulness and makes philosophy into fiction.

The title of this fable also encourages us to take a detached and speculative view of its "theme." What are traitors and heroes, it asks? One answer proposed is that traitors and heroes are people whom the history books present as traitors and heroes. Kilpatrick, of course, could be seen as either or both: his death being the execution of a traitor and the martyrdom of a hero who redeems himself by playing a role. Which is the "real" Kilpatrick? And is James Alexander Nolan, the stage-manager and execu-tioner, a hero or traitor? And Ryan, who falsifies history for the sake of an ideal?

Whereas Joyce took a day in the life of an insignificant person and presented it with great care and seriousness, Borges takes the ideas of philosophers of history (like those he mentions: Condorcet, Hegel, Spengler, and Vico) and plays a fictional game with them. The possibilities of fiction are as various as man himself, and are continually renewed and refreshed by writers who offer us new perspectives on the universe. What every writer of fiction proposes to us is his own view of the world. He may look at it with a microscope or an inverted telescope. His lenses may be clear or colored. He may seek a photographic verisimilitude or offer us idealization or caricature. But every genuine writer of fiction offers us refined perception or expanded vision. It is because fiction enlarges and enhances our dealings with reality that we cherish it so highly.

In the stories in the anthology that follows, you will find two groups of tales that may be related to this one. This story is a modern kind of fable, similar to others collected under the heading "Fabulation." But it is also a "Metafiction," a story about the processes involved in creating fiction and in writing history. Thus, if this fable has a moral, it is a metafictional one, one that asks us to wonder whether there is really any difference between acting on the stage of history and performing in a theater. Borges suggests that in believing that we have separated the factual from the fictional in writing, we may have made a great mistake—or created yet another fiction.

A Collection of Modern Fiction

Fabulation, Realism, Metafiction

FABULATION: *INTRODUCTION*

Modern fabulation looks back to the ancient forms of fable and parable, but instead of leading us toward a clear moral or spiritual conclusion, modern fabling may simply raise a question or play with an idea. Thus, Kafka's parables bear upon the impossibility of reaching final interpretations: they grow out of the gap between literal and figurative levels of meaning, a gap crossed so easily in the fables of Aesop or the parables of Jesus. What all the works of fabulation here collected have in common is a concern for ideas and values rather than for the social surface of existence or the psychological depths of character—or even our notion of what is possible or impossible in this world. Some of these modern tales and fables approach realism in one way or another. There is a good deal of social detail in "The Rocking-Horse Winner," for instance, or in "The Magic Barrel." In fact, each one of them has its realistic dimensions. But in every case there is at least one break with what we recognize as normal or probable; there is some moving away from realism for the sake of ideas that may ordinarily be concealed by the surface of reality.

The justification for this kind of fabling lies precisely in the way that it can open up questions of value for us, and prompt us to consider the assumptions upon which we act. Where ancient fables tried to settle questions of behavior, modern fables try to unsettle, to disturb, patterns of thought and action that have become so habitual that they conceal important dimensions of existence. In studying or discussing such tales it is most important to ask what ideas and values are called into question by the tale in question. Often, the best way to do that is to locate the most *fabulous* elements in each work and ask why the author chose to break with ordinary probabilities or possibilities at this particular point. To take the simplest and most graphic illustration, why should Merwin decide to describe in painstaking detail the *un*-chopping of a tree? With this question in mind, it should be possible to examine the way any given feature of a fable relates to the larger concerns of the whole story.

NATHANIEL HAWTHORNE
1804–1864

Born in Salem, Massachusetts, at a time when the American revolution was still living history and the Puritan heritage of Salem was very much alive, Hawthorne absorbed its preoccupation with sin and its remembrance of witch-hunts. Four years at Bowdoin College in Maine, a job at the Boston Custom House, and a short stay at Brook Farm—an idealistic commune that ran into practical problems—broadened his horizons, but his best work came from brooding over the past more than from observation of the present. He called his short fiction "tales" and his longer works "romances," insisting that his imagination have a certain latitude in which to work. He knew what he was about. *The Scarlet Letter* (1850) has become a classic of world literature and many of his shorter tales have proved equally durable.

My Kinsman, Major Molineux

After the kings of Great Britain had assumed the right of appointing the colonial governors, the measures of the latter seldom met with the ready and generous approbation which had been paid to those of their predecessors, under the original charters. The people looked with most jealous scrutiny to the exercise of power which did not emanate from themselves, and they usually rewarded their rulers with slender gratitude for the compliances by which, in softening their instructions from beyond the sea, they had incurred the reprehension of those who gave them. The annals of Massachusetts Bay will inform us, that of six governors in the space of about forty years from the surrender of the old charter, under James II, two were imprisoned by a popular insurrection; a third, as Hutchinson inclines to believe, was driven from the province by the whizzing of a musket-ball; a fourth, in the opinion of the same historian, was hastened to his grave by continual bickerings with the House of

Representatives; and the remaining two, as well as their successors, till the Revolution, were favored with few and brief intervals of peaceful sway. The inferior members of the court party, in times of high political excitement, led scarcely a more desirable life. These remarks may serve as a preface to the following adventures, which chanced upon a summer night, not far from a hundred years ago.[1] The reader, in order to avoid a long and dry detail of colonial affairs, is requested to dispense with an account of the train of circumstances that had caused much temporary inflammation of the popular mind.

It was near nine o'clock of a moonlight evening, when a boat crossed the ferry with a single passenger, who had obtained his conveyance at that unusual hour by the promise of an extra fare. While he stood on the landing-place, searching in either pocket for the means of fulfilling his agreement, the ferryman lifted a lantern, by the aid of which, and the newly risen moon, he took a very accurate survey of the stranger's figure. He was a youth of barely eighteen years, evidently country-bred, and now, as it should seem, upon his first visit to town. He was clad in a coarse gray coat, well worn, but in excellent repair; his under garments were durably constructed of leather, and fitted tight to a pair of serviceable and well-shaped limbs; his stockings of blue yarn were the incontrovertible work of a mother or a sister; and on his head was a three-cornered hat, which in its better days had perhaps sheltered the graver brow of the lad's father. Under his left arm was a heavy cudgel formed of an oak sapling, and retaining a part of the hardened root; and his equipment was completed by a wallet, not so abundantly stocked as to incommode the vigorous shoulders on which it hung. Brown, curly hair, well-shaped features, and bright, cheerful eyes were nature's gifts, and worth all that art could have done for his adornment.

The youth, one of whose names was Robin, finally drew from his pocket the half of a little province bill of five shillings, which, in the depreciation in that currency, did but satisfy the ferryman's demand, with the surplus of a sexangular piece of parchment, valued at three pence. He then walked forward into the town, with as light a step as if his day's journey had not already exceeded thirty miles, and with as eager an eye as if he were entering London city, instead of the little metropolis of a New England colony. Before Robin had proceeded far, however, it occurred to him that he knew not whither to direct his steps; so he paused, and looked up and down the narrow street, scrutinizing the small and mean wooden buildings that were scattered on either side.

"This low hovel cannot be my kinsman's dwelling," thought he,

1. The time of this tale is the eve of the American revolution. The place is Boston.

"nor yonder old house, where the moonlight enters at the broken casement; and truly I see none hereabouts that might be worthy of him. It would have been wise to inquire my way of the ferryman, and doubtless he would have gone with me, and earned a shilling from the Major for his pains. But the next man I meet will do as well."

He resumed his walk, and was glad to perceive that the street now became wider, and the houses more respectable in their appearance. He soon discerned a figure moving on moderately in advance, and hastened his steps to overtake it. As Robin drew nigh, he saw that the passenger was a man in years, with a full periwig of gray hair, a wide-skirted coat of dark cloth, and silk stockings rolled above his knees. He carried a long and polished cane, which he struck down perpendicularly before him at every step; and at regular intervals he uttered two successive hems, of a peculiarly solemn and sepulchral intonation. Having made these observations, Robin laid hold of the skirt of the old man's coat, just when the light from the open door and windows of a barber's shop fell upon both their figures.

"Good evening to you, honored sir," said he, making a low bow, and still retaining his hold of the skirt. "I pray you tell me whereabouts is the dwelling of my kinsman, Major Molineux."

The youth's question was uttered very loudly; and one of the barbers, whose razor was descending on a well-soaped chin, and another who was dressing a Ramillies wig, left their occupations, and came to the door. The citizen, in the mean time, turned a long-favored countenance upon Robin, and answered him in a tone of excessive anger and annoyance. His two sepulchral hems, however, broke into the very centre of his rebuke, with most singular effect, like a thought of the cold grave obtruding among wrathful passions.

"Let go my garment, fellow! I tell you, I know not the man you speak of. What! I have authority, I have—hem, hem—authority; and if this be the respect you show for your betters, your feet shall be brought acquainted with the stocks[2] by daylight, tomorrow morning!"

Robin released the old man's skirt, and hastened away, pursued by an ill-mannered roar of laughter from the barber's shop. He was at first considerably surprised by the result of his question, but, being a shrewd youth, soon thought himself able to account for the mystery.

"This is some country representative," was his conclusion, "who has never seen the inside of my kinsman's door, and lacks the

2. The stocks were an outdoor engine of imprisonment.

breeding to answer a stranger civilly. The man is old, or verily—I might be tempted to turn back and smite him on the nose. Ah, Robin, Robin! even the barber's boys laugh at you for choosing such a guide! You will be wiser in time, friend Robin."

He now became entangled in a succession of crooked and narrow streets, which crossed each other, and meandered at no great distance from the water-side. The smell of tar was obvious to his nostrils, the masts of vessels pierced the moonlight above the tops of the buildings, and the numerous signs, which Robin paused to read, informed him that he was near the centre of business. But the streets were empty, the shops were closed, and lights were visible only in the second stories of a few dwelling-houses. At length, on the corner of a narrow lane, through which he was passing, he beheld the broad countenance of a British hero swinging before the door of an inn, whence proceeded the voices of many guests. The casement of one of the lower windows was thrown back, and a very thin curtain permitted Robin to distinguish a party at supper, round a well-furnished table. The fragrance of the good cheer steamed forth into the outer air, and the youth could not fail to recollect that the last remnant of his travelling stock of provision had yielded to his morning appetite, and that noon had found and left him dinnerless.

"Oh, that a parchment three-penny might give me a right to sit down at younder table!" said Robin, with a sigh. "But the Major will make me welcome to the best of his victuals; so I will even step boldly in, and inquire my way to his dwelling."

He entered the tavern, and was guided by the murmur of voices and the fumes of tobacco to the public-room. It was a long and low apartment, with oaken walls, grown dark in the continual smoke, and a floor which was thickly sanded, but of no immaculate purity. A number of persons—the larger part of whom appeared to be mariners, or in some way connected with the sea—occupied the wooden benches, or leather-bottomed chairs, conversing on various matters, and occasionally lending their attention to some topic of general interest. Three or four little groups were draining as many bowls of punch, which the West India trade had long since made a familiar drink in the colony. Others, who had the appearance of men who lived by regular and laborious handicraft, preferred the insulated bliss of an unshared potation, and became more taciturn under its influence. Nearly all, in short, evinced a predilection for the Good Creature in some of its various shapes, for this is a vice to which, as Fast Day sermons of a hundred years ago will testify, we have a long hereditary claim. The only guests to whom Robin's sympathies inclined him were two or three sheepish countrymen, who were using the inn somewhat after the fashion of a Turkish caravansary; they had gotten themselves into the darkest corner of the room, and heedless of the Nicotian atmosphere, were supping on the bread of their own ovens, and the bacon cured in their own chimney-smoke. But though Robin felt a sort of brotherhood with these strangers, his eyes were attracted from them to a person who stood near the door, holding whispered conversation with a group of ill-dressed associates. His features were separately striking almost to grotesqueness, and the whole face left a deep impression on the memory. The forehead bulged out into a double prominence, with a vale between; the nose came boldly forth in an irregular curve, and its bridge was of more than a finger's breadth; the eyebrows were deep and shaggy, and the eyes glowed beneath them like fire in a cave.

While Robin deliberated of whom to inquire respecting his kinsman's dwelling, he was accosted by the innkeeper, a little man in a stained white apron, who had come to pay his professional welcome to the stranger. Being in the second generation from a French Protestant, he seemed to have inherited the courtesy of his parent nation; but no variety of circumstances was ever known to change his voice from the one shrill note in which he now addressed Robin.

"From the country, I presume, sir?" said he, with a profound bow. "Beg leave to congratulate you on your arrival, and trust you intend a long stay with us. Fine town here, sir, beautiful buildings, and much that may interest a stranger. May I hope for the honor of your commands in respect to supper?"

"The man sees a family likeness! the rogue has guessed that I am related to the Major!" thought Robin, who had hitherto experienced little superfluous civility.

All eyes were now turned on the country lad, standing at the door, in his worn three-cornered hat, gray coat, leather breeches, and blue yarn stockings, leaning on an oaken cudgel, and bearing a wallet on his back.

Robin replied to the courteous innkeeper, with such an assumption of confidence as befitted the Major's relative. "My honest friend," he said, "I shall make it a point to patronize your house on some occasion, when"—here he could not help lowering his voice—"when I may have more than a parchment three-pence in my pocket. My present business," continued he, speaking with lofty confidence, "is merely to inquire my way to the dwelling of my kinsman, Major Molineux."

There was a sudden and general movement in the room, which Robin interpreted as expressing the eagerness of each individual to become his guide. But the innkeeper turned his eyes to a written paper on the wall, which he read, or seemed to read, with occasional recurrences to the young man's figure.

"What have we here?" said he, breaking his speech into little dry fragments. " 'Left the house of the subscriber, bounden servant, Hezekiah Mudge,—had on, when he went away, gray coat, leather breeches, master's third-best hat. One pound currency reward to whosoever shall lodge him in any jail of the providence.' Better trudge, boy; better trudge!"

Robin had begun to draw his hand towards the lighter end of the oak cudgel, but a strange hostility in every countenance induced him to relinquish his purpose of breaking the courteous innkeeper's head. As he turned to leave the room, he encountered a sneering glance from the bold-featured personage whom he had before noticed; and no sooner was he beyond the door, than he heard a general laugh, in which the innkeeper's voice might be distinguished, like the dropping of small stones into a kettle.

"Now, is it not strange," thought Robin, with his usual shrewdness,—"is it not strange that the confession of an empty pocket should outweigh the name of my kinsman, Major Molineux? Oh, if I had one of those grinning rascals in the woods, where I and my oak sapling grew up together, I would teach him that my arm is heavy though my purse be light!"

On turning the corner of the narrow lane, Robin found himself in a spacious street, with an unbroken line of lofty houses on each side, and a steepled building at the upper end, whence the ringing of a bell announced the hour of nine. The light of the moon, and the lamps from the numerous shop-windows, discovered people promenading on the pavement, and amongst them Robin had hoped to recognize his hitherto inscrutable relative. The result of his former inquiries made him unwilling to hazard another, in a scene of such publicity, and he determined to walk slowly and silently up the street, thrusting his face close to that of every elderly gentleman, in search of the Major's lineaments. In his progress, Robin encountered many gay and gallant figures. Embroidered garments of showy colors, enormous periwigs, gold-laced hats, and silver-hilted swords glided past him and dazzled his optics. Travelled youths, imitators of the European fine gentlemen of the period, trod jauntily along, half dancing to the fashionable tunes which they hummed, and making poor Robin ashamed of his quiet and natural gait. At length, after many pauses to examine the gorgeous display of goods in the shop-windows, and after suffering some rebukes for the impertinence of his scrutiny into people's faces, the Major's kinsman found himself near the steepled building, still unsuccessful in his search. As yet, however, he had seen only one side of the thronged street; so Robin crossed, and continued the same sort of inquisition down the opposite pavement, with stronger hopes than the philosopher seeking an honest man, but with no better fortune. He had arrived about midway towards the lower end, from which his course began, when he overheard the approach of some one who struck down a cane on the flag-stones at every step, uttering at regular intervals, two sepulchral hems.

"Mercy on us!" quoth Robin, recognizing the sound.

Turning a corner, which chanced to be close at his right hand, he hastened to pursue his researches in some other part of the town. His patience now was wearing low, and he seemed to feel more fatigue from his rambles since he crossed the ferry, than from his journey of several days on the other side. Hunger also pleaded loudly within him, and Robin began to balance the propriety of demanding, violently, and with lifted cudgel, the necessary guidance from the first solitary passenger whom he should meet. While a resolution to this effect was gaining strength, he entered a street of mean appearance, on either side of which a row of ill-built houses was straggling towards the harbor. The moonlight fell upon no passenger along the whole extent, but in the third domicile which Robin passed there was a half-opened door, and his keen glance detected a woman's garment within.

"My luck may be better here," said he to himself.

Accordingly, he approached the door, and beheld it shut closer as he did so; yet an open space remained, sufficing for the fair occupant to observe the stranger, without a corresponding display on her part. All that Robin could discern was a strip of scarlet petticoat, and the occasional sparkle of an eye, as if the moonbeams were trembling on some bright thing.

"Pretty mistress," for I may call her so with a good conscience, thought the shrewd youth, since I know nothing to the contrary,— "my sweet pretty mistress, will you be kind enough to tell me whereabouts I must seek the dwelling of my kinsman, Major Molineux?"

Robin's voice was plaintive and winning, and the female, seeing nothing to be shunned in the handsome country youth, thrust open the door, and came forth into the moonlight. She was a dainty little figure, with a white neck, round arms, and a slender waist, at the extremity of which her scarlet petticoat jutted out over a hoop, as if she were standing in a balloon. Moreover, her face was oval and pretty, her hair dark beneath the little cap, and her bright eyes possessed a sly freedom, which triumphed over those of Robin.

"Major Molineux dwells here," said this fair woman.

Now, her voice was the sweetest Robin had heard that night, yet he could not help doubting whether that sweet voice spoke Gospel truth. He looked up and down the mean street, and then surveyed the house before which they stood. It was a small, dark edifice of two stories, the second of which projected over the lower floor, and the front apartment had the aspect of a shop for pretty commodities.

"Now, truly, I am in luck," replied Robin, cunningly, "and so indeed is my kinsman, the Major, in having so pretty a house-keeper. But I prithee trouble him to step to the door; I will deliver him a message from his friends in the country, and then go back to my lodgings at the inn."

"Nay, the Major has been abed this hour or more," said the lady of the scarlet petticoat; "and it would be to little purpose to disturb him to-night, seeing his evening draught was of the strongest. But he is a kind-hearted man, and it would be as much as my life's worth to let a kinsman of his turn away from the door. You are the good old gentleman's very picture, and I could swear that was his rainy-weather hat. Also he has garments very much resembling those leather small-clothes. But come in, I pray, for I bid you hearty welcome in his name."

So saying, the fair and hospitable dame took our hero by the hand; and the touch was light, and the force was gentleness, and though Robin read in her eyes what he did not hear in her words, yet the slender-waisted woman in the scarlet petticoat proved stronger than the athletic country youth. She had drawn his half-willing footsteps nearly to the threshold, when the opening of a door in the neighborhood startled the Major's housekeeper, and, leaving the Major's kinsman, she vanished speedily into her own domicile. A heavy yawn preceded the appearance of a man, who, like the Moonshine of Pyramus and Thisbe, carried a lantern, need-lessly aiding his sister luminary in the heavens. As he walked sleepily up the street, he turned his broad, dull face on Robin, and displayed a long staff, spiked at the end.

"Home, vagabond, home!" said the watchman, in accents that seemed to fall asleep as soon as they were uttered. "Home, or we'll set you in the stocks by peep of day!"

"This is the second hint of the kind," thought Robin. "I wish they would end my difficulties, by setting me there to-night."

Nevertheless, the youth felt an instinctive antipathy towards the guardian of midnight order, which at first prevented him from ask-ing his usual question. But just when the man was about to vanish behind the corner, Robin resolved not to lose the opportunity, and shouted lustily after him,—

"I say, friend! will you guide me to the house of my kinsman, Major Molineux?"

The watchman made no reply, but turned the corner and was gone; yet Robin seemed to hear the sound of drowsy laughter steal-ing along the solitary street. At that moment, also, a pleasant titter saluted him from the open window above his head; he looked up, and caught the sparkle of a saucy eye; a round arm beckoned to him, and next he heard light footsteps descending the staircase within. But Robin, being of the household of a New England clergyman, was a good youth, as well as a shrewd one; so he resisted temptation, and fled away.

He now roamed desperately, and at random, through the town, almost ready to believe that a spell was on him, like that by which a wizard of his country had once kept three pursuers wandering, a whole winter night, within twenty paces of the cottage which they sought. The streets lay before him, strange and desolate, and the lights were extinguished in almost every house. Twice, however, little parties of men, among whom Robin distinguished individuals in outlandish attire, came hurrying along; but, though on both occasions, they paused to address him, such intercourse did not at all enlighten his perplexity. They did but utter a few words in some language of which Robin knew nothing, and perceiving his inability to answer, bestowed a curse upon him in plain English and hastened away. Finally, the lad determined to knock at the door of every mansion that might appear worthy to be occupied by his kinsman, trusting that perseverance would overcome the fatality that had hitherto thwarted him. Firm in this resolve, he was passing beneath the walls of a church, which formed the corner of two streets, when, as he turned into the shade of its steeple, he encountered a bulky stranger, muffled in a cloak. The man was proceeding with the speed of earnest business, but Robin planted himself full before him, holding the oak cudgel with both hands across his body as a bar to further passage.

"Halt, honest man, and answer me a question," said he, very resolutely. "Tell me, this instant, whereabouts is the dwelling of my kinsman, Major Molineux!"

"Keep your tongue between your teeth, fool, and let me pass!" said a deep, gruff voice, which Robin partly remembered. "Let me pass, or I'll strike you to the earth!"

"No, no, neighbor!" cried Robin, flourishing his cudgel, and then thrusting its larger end close to the man's muffled face. "No, no, I'm not the fool you take me for, nor do you pass till I have an answer to my question. Whereabouts is the dwelling of my kinsman, Major Molineux?"

The stranger, instead of attempting to force his passage, stepped back into the moonlight, unmuffled his face, and stared full into that of Robin.

"Watch here an hour, and Major Molineux will pass by," said he.

Robin gazed with dismay and astonishment on the unprecedented physiognomy of the speaker. The forehead with its double prominence, the broad hooked nose, the shaggy eyebrows, and fiery eyes were those which he had noticed at the inn, but the man's complexion had undergone a singular, or more properly, a twofold change. One side of the face blazed an intense red, while the other was black as midnight, the divison line being in the broad bridge of the nose; and a mouth which seemed to extend from ear to ear was black or red, in contrast to the color of the cheek.[3] The effect was as if two individual devils, a fiend of fire and a fiend of darkness had united themselves to form this infernal visage. The stranger grinned in Robin's face, muffled his party-colored features, and was out of sight in a moment.

"Strange things we travellers see!" ejaculated Robin.

He seated himself, however, upon the steps of the church-door, resolving to wait the appointed time for his kinsman. A few moments were consumed in philosophical speculations upon the species of man who had just left him; but having settled this point shrewdly, rationally, and satisfactorily, he was compelled to look elsewhere for his amusement. And first he threw his eyes along the street. It was of more respectable appearance than most of those into which he had wandered; and the moon, creating, like the imaginative power, a beautiful strangeness in familiar objects, gave something of romance to a scene that might not have possessed it in the light of day. The irregular and often quaint architecture of the houses, some of whose roofs were broken into numerous little peaks, while others ascended, steep and narrow, into a single point, and others again were square; the pure snow-white of some of their complexions, the aged darkness of others, and the thousand sparklings, reflected from bright substances in the walls of many; these matters engaged Robin's attention for a while, and then began to grow wearisome. Next he endeavored to define the forms of distant objects, starting away, with almost ghostly indistinctness, just as his eye appeared to grasp them; and finally he took a minute survey of an edifice which stood on the opposite side of the street, directly in front of the church-door, where he was stationed. It was a large, square mansion, distinguished from its neighbors by a balcony, which rested on tall pillars, and by an elaborate Gothic window, communicating therewith.

"Perhaps this is the very house I have been seeking," thought Robin.

Then he strove to speed away the time, by listening to a murmur which swept continually along the street, yet was scarcely audible, except to an unaccustomed ear like his; it was a low, dull, dreamy sound, compounded of many noises, each of which was at too great a distance to be separately heard. Robin marvelled at this snore of a sleeping town, and marvelled more whenever its continuity was broken by now and then a distant shout, apparently loud where it

3. The disguise of an Indian in war paint was much used by the early revolutionaires, as in the Boston tea party.

originated. But altogether it was a sleep-inspiring sound, and, to shake off its drowsy influence, Robin arose, and climbed a window-frame, that he might view the interior of the church. There the moonbeams came trembling in, and fell down upon the deserted pews, and extended along the quiet aisles. A fainter yet more awful radiance was hovering around the pulpit, and one solitary ray had dared to rest upon the open page of the great Bible. Had nature, in that deep hour, become a worshipper in the house which man had builded? Or was that heavenly light the visible sanctity of the place,—visible because no earthly and impure feet were within the walls? The scene made Robin's heart shiver with a sensation of loneliness stronger than he had ever felt in the remotest depths of his native woods; so he turned away and sat down again before the door. There were graves around the church, and now an uneasy thought obtruded into Robin's breast. What if the object of his search, which had been so often and so strangely thwarted, were all the time mouldering in his shroud? What if his kinsman should glide through yonder gate, and nod and smile to him in dimly passing by?

"Oh that any breathing thing were here with me!" said Robin.

Recalling his thoughts from this uncomfortable track, he sent them over forest, hill, and stream, and attempted to imagine how that evening of ambiguity and weariness had been spent by his father's household. He pictured them assembled at the door, beneath the tree, the great old tree, which had been spared for its huge twisted trunk and venerable shade, when a thousand leafy brethen fell. There, at the going down of the summer sun, it was his father's custom to perform domestic worship, that the neighbors might come and join with him like brothers of the family, and that the wayfaring man might pause to drink at that fountain, and keep his heart pure by freshening the memory of home. Robin distinguished the seat of every individual of the little audience; he saw the good man in the midst, holding the Scriptures in the golden light that fell from the western clouds; he beheld him close the book and all rise up to pray. He heard the old thanksgivings for daily mercies, the old supplications for their continuance, to which he had so often listened in weariness, but which were now among his dear remembrances. He perceived the slight inequality of his father's voice when he came to speak of the absent one; he noted how his mother turned her face to the broad and knotted trunk; how his elder brother scorned, because the beard was rough upon his upper lip to permit his features to be moved; how the younger sister drew down a low hanging branch before her eyes; and how the little one of all, whose sports had hitherto broken the decorum of the scene, understood the prayer for her playmate, and burst into clamorous grief.

Then he saw them go in at the door; and when Robin would have entered also, the latch tinkled into its place, and he was excluded from his home.

"Am I here, or there?" cried Robin, starting; for all at once, when his thoughts had become visible and audible in a dream, the long, wide, solitary street shone out before him.

He aroused himself, and endeavored to fix his attention steadily upon the large edifice which he had surveyed before. But still his mind kept vibrating between fancy and reality; by turns, the pillars of the balcony lengthened into the tall, bare stems of pines, dwindled down to human figures, settled again into their true shape and size, and then commenced a new succession of changes. For a single moment, when he deemed himself awake, he could have sworn that a visage—one which he seemed to remember, yet could not absolutely name as his kinsman's—was looking towards him from the Gothic window. A deeper sleep wrestled with and nearly overcame him, but fled at the sound of footsteps along the opposite pavement. Robin rubbed his eyes, discerned a man passing at the foot of the balcony, and addressed him in a loud, peevish, and lamentable cry.

"Hallo, friend! must I wait here all night for my kinsman, Major Molineux?"

The sleeping echoes awoke, and answered the voice; and the passenger, barely able to discern a figure sitting in the oblique shade of the steeple, traversed the street to obtain a nearer view. He was himself a gentleman in his prime, of open, intelligent, cheerful, and altogether prepossessing countenance. Perceiving a country youth, apparently homeless and without friends, he accosted him in a tone of real kindness, which had become strange to Robin's ears.

"Well, my good lad, why are you sitting here?" inquired he. "Can I be of service to you in any way?"

"I am afraid not, sir," replied Robin, despondingly; "yet I shall take it kindly, if you'll answer me a single question. I've been searching, half the night, for one Major Molineux; now, sir, is there really such a person in these parts, or am I dreaming?"

"Major Molineux! The name is not altogether strange to me," said the gentleman, smiling. "Have you any objection to telling me the nature of your business with him?"

Then Robin briefly related that his father was a clergyman, settled on a small salary, at a long distance beck in the country, and that he and Major Molineux were brothers' children. The Major, having inherited riches, and acquired civil and military rank, had visited his cousin, in great pomp, a year or two before; had manifested much interest in Robin and an elder brother, and, being childless himself, had thrown out hints respecting the future establishment of one of them in life. The elder brother was destined to succeed to the farm which his father cultivated in the interval of sacred duties; it was therefore determined that Robin should profit by his kinsman's generous intentions, especially as he seemed to be rather the favorite, and was thought to possess other necessary endowments.

"For I have the name of being a shrewd youth," observed Robin, in this part of his story.

"I doubt not you deserve it," replied his new friend, good-naturedly; "but pray proceed."

"Well, sir, being nearly eighteen years old, and well grown, as you see," continued Robin, drawing himself up to his full height, "I thought it high time to begin in the world. So my mother and sister put me in handsome trim, and my father gave me half the remnant of his last year's salary, and five days ago I started for this place, to pay the Major a visit. But, would you believe it, sir! I crossed the ferry a little after dark, and have yet found nobody that would show me the way to his dwelling; only, an hour or two since, I was told to wait here, and Major Molineux would pass by."

"Can you describe the man who told you this?" inquired the gentleman.

"Oh, he was a very ill-favored fellow, sir," replied Robin, "with two great bumps on his forehead, a hook nose, fiery eyes; and, what struck me as the strangest, his face was of two different colors. Do you happen to know such a man, sir?"

"Not intimately," answered the stranger, "but I chanced to meet him a little time previous to your stopping me. I believe you may trust his word, and that the Major will very shortly pass through this street. In the mean time, as I have a singular curiosity to witness your meeting, I will sit down here upon the steps and bear you company."

He seated himself accordingly, and soon engaged his companion in animated discourse. It was but of brief continuance, however, for a noise of shouting, which had long been remotely audible, drew so much nearer that Robin inquired its cause.

"What may be the meaning of this uproar?" asked he. "Truly, if your town be always as noisy, I shall find little sleep while I am an inhabitant."

"Why, indeed, friend Robin, there do appear to be three or four riotous fellows abroad to-night," replied the gentleman. "You must not expect all the stillness of your native woods here in our streets. But the watch will shortly be at the heels of these lads and"—

"Ay, and set them in the stocks by peep of day," interrupted Robin, recollecting his own encounter with the drowsy lantern-bearer. "But, dear sir, if I may trust my ears, an army of watchmen would never make head against such a multitude of rioters. There were at least a thousand voices went up to make that one shout."

"May not a man have several voices, Robin, as well as two complexions?" said his friend.

"Perhaps a man may; but Heaven forbid that a woman should!" responded the shrewd youth, thinking of the seductive tones of the Major's housekeeper.

The sounds of a trumpet in some neighboring street now became so evident and continual, that Robin's curiosity was strongly excited. In addition to the shouts, he heard frequent bursts from many instruments of discord, and a wild and confused laughter filled up the intervals. Robin rose from the steps, and looked wistfully towards a point whither people seemed to be hastening.

"Surely some prodigious merry-making is going on," exclaimed he. "I have laughed very little since I left home, sir, and should be sorry to lose an opportunity. Shall we step round the corner by that darkish house, and take our share of the fun?"

"Sit down again, sit down, good Robin," replied the gentleman, laying his hand on the skirt of the gray coat. "You forget that we must wait here for your kinsman; and there is reason to believe that he will pass by, in the course of a very few moments."

The near approach of the uproar had now disturbed the neighborhood; windows flew open on all sides; and many heads, in the attire of the pillow, and confused by sleep suddenly broken, were protruded to the gaze of whoever had leisure to observe them. Eager voices hailed each other from house to house, all demanding the explanation, which not a soul could give. Half-dressed men hurried towards the unknown commotion, stumbling as they went over the stone steps that thrust themselves into the narrow foot-walk. The shouts, the laughter, and the tuneless bray, the antipodes of music, came onwards with increasing din, till scattered individuals, and then denser bodies, began to appear round a corner at the distance of a hundred yards.

"Will you recognize your kinsman, if he passes in this crowd?" inquired the gentleman.

"Indeed, I can't warrant it, sir; but I'll take my stand here, and keep a bright lookout," answered Robin, descending to the outer edge of the pavement.

A mighty stream of people now emptied into the street, and came rolling slowly towards the church. A single horseman wheeled the corner in the midst of them, and close behind him came a band of fearful wind-instruments, sending forth a fresher discord now that no intervening buildings kept it from the ear. Then a redder light disturbed the moon-beams, and a dense multitude of torches shone along the street, concealing, by their glare, whatever object they illuminated. The single horseman, clad in a military dress, and bearing a drawn sword, rode onward as the leader, and, by his fierce and variegated countenance, appeared like war personified; the red of one cheek was an emblem of fire and sword; the blackness of the other betokened the mourning that attends them. In his train were wild figures in the Indian dress, and many fantastic shapes without a model, giving the whole march a visionary air, as if a dream had broken forth from some feverish brain, and were sweeping visibly through the midnight streets. A mass of people, inactive, except as applauding spectators, hemmed the procession in; and several women ran along the sidewalk, piercing the confusion of heavier sounds with their shrill voices of mirth or terror.

"The double-faced fellow has his eye upon me," muttered Robin, with an indefinite but an uncomfortable idea that he was himself to bear a part in the pageantry.

The leader turned himself in the saddle, and fixed his glance full upon the country youth, as the steed went slowly by. When Robin had freed his eyes from those fiery ones, the musicians were passing before him, and the torches were close at hand; but the unsteady brightness of the latter formed a veil which he could not penetrate. The rattling of wheels over the stones sometimes found its way to his ear, and confused traces of a human form appeared at intervals, and then melted into the vivid light. A moment more, and the leader thundered a command to halt: the trumpets vomited a horrid breath, and then held their peace; the shouts and laughter of the people died away, and there remained only a universal hum, allied to silence. Right before Robin's eyes was an uncovered cart. There the torches blazed the brightest, there the moon shone out like day, and there, in tar-and-feathery dignity,[4] sat his kinsman, Major Molineux!

He was an elderly man, of large and majestic person, and strong, square features, betokening a steady soul; but steady as it was, his enemies had found means to shake it. His face was pale as death, and far more ghastly; the broad forehead was contracted in his agony, so that his eyebrows formed one grizzled line; his eyes were red and wild, and the foam hung white upon his quivering lip. His whole frame was agitated by a quick and continual tremor, which his pride strove to quell, even in those circumstances of overwhelming humiliation. But perhaps the bitterest pang of all was when his eyes met those of Robin; for he evidently knew him on the instant, as the youth stood witnessing the foul disgrace of a head grown gray in honor. They stared at each other in silence, and Robin's knees shook, and his hair bristled, with a mixture of pity and terror.

---

4. In this rough punishment a man was stripped naked, covered with hot tar, and sprinkled with feathers. It was frequently visited upon those suspected of resisting the revolution.

Soon, however, a bewildering excitement began to seize upon his mind; the preceding adventures of the night, the unexpected appearance of the crowd, the torches, the confused din and the hush that followed, the spectre of his kinsman reviled by that great multitude,—all this, and more than all, a perception of tremendous ridicule in the whole scene, affected him with a sort of mental inebriety. At that moment a voice of sluggish merriment saluted Robin's ears; he turned instinctively, and just behind the corner of the church stood the lantern-bearer, rubbing his eyes, and drowsily enjoying the lad's amazement. Then he heard a peal of laughter like the ringing of silvery bells; a woman twitched his arm, a saucy eye met his, and he saw the lady of the scarlet petticoat. A sharp, dry cachinnation appealed to his memory, and, standing on tiptoe in the crowd, with his white apron over his head, he beheld the courteous little innkeeper. And lastly, there sailed over the heads of the multitude a great, broad laugh, broken in the midst by two sepulchral hems; thus, "haw, haw, haw,—hem, hem,—haw, haw, haw, haw!"

The sound proceeded from the balcony of the opposite edifice, and thither Robin turned his eyes. In front of the Gothic window stood the old citizen, wrapped in a wide gown, his gray periwig exchanged for a nightcap, which was thrust back from his forehead, and his silk stockings hanging about his legs. He supported himself on his polished cane in a fit of convulsive merriment, which manifested itself on his solemn old features like a funny inscription on a tombstone. Then Robin seemed to hear the voices of the barbers, of the guests of the inn, and of all who had made sport of him that night. The contagion was spreading among the multitude, when all at once, it seized upon Robin, and he sent forth a shout of laughter that echoed through the street,—every man shook his sides, every man emptied his lungs, but Robin's shout was the loudest there. The cloud-spirits peeped from their silvery islands, as the congregated mirth went roaring up the sky! The Man in the Moon heard the far bellow. "Oho," quoth he, "the old earth is frolicsome tonight!"

When there was a momentary calm in that tempestuous sea of sound, the leader gave the sign, the procession resumed its march. On they went, like fiends that throng in mockery around some dead potentate, mighty no more, but majestic still in his agony. On they went, in counterfeited pomp, in senseless uproar, in frenzied merriment, trampling all on an old man's heart. On swept the tumult, and left a silent street behind.

.   .   .   .

"Well, Robin, are you dreaming?" inquired the gentleman, laying his hand on the youth's shoulder.

Robin started, and withdrew his arm from the stone post to which he had instinctively clung, as the living stream rolled by him. His cheek was somewhat pale, and his eye not quite as lively as in the earlier part of the evening.

"Will you be kind enough to show me the way to the ferry?" said he, after a moment's pause.

"You have, then, adopted a new subject of inquiry?" observed his companion, with a smile.

"Why, yes, sir," replied Robin, rather dryly. "Thanks to you, and to my other friends, I have at last met my kinsman, and he will scarce desire to see my face again. I begin to grow weary of a town life, sir. Will you show me the way to the ferry?"

"No, my good friend Robin,—not to-night, at least," said the gentleman. "Some few days hence, if you wish it, I will speed you on your journey. Or, if you prefer to remain with us, perhaps, as you are a shrewd youth, you may rise in the world without the help of your kinsman, Major Molineux."

H. G. WELLS
1866–1946

Herbert George Wells was born in Bromley, Kent, England. His father was a semi-professional cricket player who kept various kinds of shops not too successfully, and his mother worked from time to time as a lady's maid. He had an irregular education, but made the most of the chance to read in the library of a great house where his mother worked. Later he failed as a draper's apprentice and was lucky enough to get some good instruction and win a scholarship to the Royal College of Science in London, where he studied under Thomas H. Huxley. But he did not develop as a scientist, turning gradually to journalism and fiction as a way of supporting himself. His "scientific romances" —The Time Machine (1895), The War of the Worlds (1898), etc.—made him immensely popular and he continued to write, trying his hand at realistic fiction, popular science, social criticism, and history in a perpetual effort to educate the English people and finally the whole world. It is ironic that his early stories and short novels are now his best known works, while his later more "serious" productions are largely ignored.

The Country of the Blind

Three hundred miles and more from Chimborazo, one hundred from the snows of Cotopaxi, in the wildest wastes of Ecuador's Andes, there lies that mysterious mountain valley, cut off from the world of men, the Country of the Blind. Long years ago that valley lay so far open to the world that men might come at last through frightful gorges and over an icy pass into its equable meadows; and thither indeed men came, a family or so of Peruvian half-breeds fleeing from the lust and tyranny of an evil Spanish ruler. Then came the stupendous outbreak of Mindobamba, when it was night in Quito for seventeen days, and the water was boiling at Yaguachi and all the fish floating dying even as far as Guayaquil; everywhere along the Pacific slopes there were landslips and swift thawings and sudden floods, and one whole side of the old Arauca crest slipped and came down in thunder, and cut off the Country of the Blind for ever from the exploring feet of men. But one of these early settlers had chanced to be on the hither side of the gorges when the world had so terribly shaken itself, and he perforce had to forget his wife and his child and all the friends and possessions he had left up there, and start life over again in the lower world. He started it again but ill, blindness overtook him, and he died of punishment in the mines; but the story he told begot a legend that lingers along the length of the Cordilleras of the Andes to this day.

He told of his reason for venturing back from that fastness, into which he had first been carried lashed to a llama, beside a vast bale of gear, when he was a child. The valley, he said, had in it all that the heart of man could desire—sweet water, pasture, an even climate, slopes of rich brown soil with tangles of a shrub that bore an excellent fruit, and on one side great hanging forests of pine that held the avalanches high. Far overhead, on three sides, vast cliffs of grey-green rock were capped by cliffs of ice; but the glacier stream came not to them but flowed away by the farther slopes, and only now and then huge ice masses fell on the valley side. In this valley it neither rained nor snowed, but the abundant springs gave a rich green pasture, that irrigation would spread over all the valley space. The settlers did well indeed there. Their beasts did well and multiplied, and but one thing marred their happiness. Yet it was enough to mar it greatly. A strange disease had come upon them, and had made all the children born to them there—and indeed, several older children also—blind. It was to seek some charm or antidote against this plague of blindness that he had with fatigue and danger and difficulty returned down the gorge. In those days, in such cases, men did not think of germs and infections but of sins; and it seemed to him that the reason of this affliction must lie in the

negligence of these priestless immigrants to set up a shrine so soon
as they entered the valley. He wanted a shrine—a handsome, cheap,
effectual shrine—to be erected in the valley; he wanted relics and
such-like potent things of faith, blessed objects and mysterious medals and prayers. In his wallet he had a bar of native silver for which
he would not account; he insisted there was none in the valley with
something of the insistence of an inexpert liar. They had all clubbed
their money and ornaments together, having little need for such
treasure up there, he said, to buy them holy help against their ill. I
figure this dim-eyed young mountaineer, sunburnt, gaunt, and anxious, hat-brim clutched feverishly, a man all unused to the ways of
the lower world, telling this story to some keen-eyed, attentive
priest before the great convulsion; I can picture him presently seeking to return with pious and infallible remedies against that trouble,
and the infinite dismay with which he must have faced the tumbled
vastness where the gorge had once come out. But the rest of his
story of mischances is lost to me, save that I know of his evil death
after several years. Poor stray from that remoteness! The stream that
had once made the gorge now bursts from the mouth of a rocky
cave, and the legend his poor, ill-told story set going developed into
the legend of a race of blind men somewhere 'over there' one may
still hear to-day.

And amidst the little population of that now isolated and forgotten valley the disease ran its course. The old became groping and
purblind, the young saw but dimly, and the children that were born
to them saw never at all. But life was very easy in that snow-rimmed
basin, lost to all the world, with neither thorns nor briars, with no
evil insects nor any beasts save the gentle breed of llamas they had
lugged and thrust and followed up the beds of the shrunken rivers
in the gorges up which they had come. The seeing had become
purblind so gradually that they scarcely noted their loss. They
guided the sightless youngsters hither and thither until they knew
the whole valley marvellously, and when at last sight died out
among them the race lived on. They had even time to adapt themselves to the blind control of fire, which they made carefully in
stoves of stone. They were a simple strain of people at the first,
unlettered, only slightly touched with the Spanish civilisation, but
with something of a tradition of the arts of old Peru and of its lost
philosophy. Generation followed generation. They forgot many
things; they devised many things. Their tradition of the greater
world they came from became mythical in colour and uncertain. In
all things save sight they were strong and able; and presently the
chance of birth and heredity sent one who had an original mind and
who could talk and persuade among them, and then afterwards

another. These two passed, leaving their effects, and the little community grew in numbers and in understanding, and met and settled social and economic problems that arose. Generation followed generation. There came a time when a child was born who was fifteen generations from that ancestor who went out of the valley with a bar of silver to seek God's aid, and who never returned. Thereabouts it chanced that a man came into this community from the outer world. And this is the story of that man.

He was a mountaineer from the country near Quito, a man who had been down to the sea and had seen the world, a reader of books in an original way, an acute and enterprising man, and he was taken on by a party of Englishmen who had come out to Ecuador to climb mountains, to replace one of their three Swiss guides who had fallen ill. He climbed here and he climbed there, and then came the attempt on Parascotopetl, the Matterhorn of the Andes, in which he was lost to the outer world. The story of the accident has been written a dozen times. Pointer's narrative is the best. He tells how the party worked their difficult and almost vertical way up to the very foot of the last and greatest precipice, and how they built a night shelter amidst the snow upon a little shelf of rock, and, with a touch of real dramatic power, how presently they found Núñez had gone from them. They shouted, and there was no reply; shouted and whistled, and for the rest of that night they slept no more.

As the morning broke they saw the traces of his fall. It seems impossible he could have uttered a sound. He had slipped eastward towards the unknown side of the mountain; far below he had struck a steep slope of snow, and ploughed his way down it in the midst of a snow avalanche. His track went straight to the edge of a frightful precipice, and beyond that everything was hidden. Far, far below, and hazy with distance, they could see trees rising out of a narrow, shut-in valley—the lost Country of the Blind. But they did not know it was the lost Country of the Blind, nor distinguish it in any way from any other narrow streak of upland valley. Unnerved by this disaster, they abandoned their attempt in the afternoon, and Pointer was called away to the war before he could make another attack. To this day Parascotopetl lifts an unconquered crest, and Pointer's shelter crumbles unvisited amidst the snows.

And the man who fell survived.

At the end of the slope he fell a thousand feet, and came down in the midst of a cloud of snow upon a snow slope even steeper than the one above. Down this he was whirled, stunned and insensible, but without a bone broken in his body; and then at last came to gentler slopes, and at last rolled out and lay still, buried amidst a softening heap of the white masses that had accompanied and saved him. He came to himself with a dim fancy that he was ill in bed; then realised his position with a mountaineer's intelligence, and worked himself loose, and after a rest or so, out until he saw the stars. He rested flat upon his chest for a space, wondering where he was and what had happened to him. He explored his limbs, and discovered that several of his buttons were gone and his coat turned over his head. His knife had gone from his pocket and his hat was lost, though he had tied it under his chin. He recalled that he had been looking for loose stones to raise his piece of the shelter wall. His ice-axe had disappeared.

He decided he must have fallen, and looked up to see, exaggerated by the ghastly light of the rising moon, the tremendous flight he had taken. For a while he lay, gazing blankly at that vast pale cliff towering above, rising moment by moment out of a subsiding tide of darkness. Its phantasmal mysterious beauty held him for a space, and then he was seized with a paroxysm of sobbing laughter. . . .

After a great interval of time he became aware that he was near the lower edge of the snow. Below, down what was now a moonlit and practicable slope, he saw the dark and broken appearance of rock-strewn turf. He struggled to his feet aching in every joint and limb, got down painfully from the heaped loose snow about him, went downward until he was on the turf, and there dropped rather than lay beside a boulder, drank deep from the flask in his inner pocket, and instantly fell asleep. . . .

He was awakened by the singing of birds in the trees far below.

He sat up and perceived he was on a little alp at the foot of a vast precipice, that was grooved by the gully down which he and his snow had come. Over against him another wall of rock reared itself against the sky. The gorge between these precipices ran east and west and was full of the morning sunlight, which lit to the westward the mass of fallen mountain that closed the descending gorge. Below him it seemed there was a precipice equally steep, but behind the snow in the gully he found a sort of chimney-cleft dripping with snow-water down which a desperate man might venture. He found it easier than it seemed, and came at last to another desolate alp, and then after a rock climb of no particular difficulty to a steep slope of trees. He took his bearings and turned his face up the gorge, for he saw it opened out above upon green meadows, among which he now glimpsed quite distinctly a cluster of stone huts of unfamiliar fashion. At times his progress was like clambering along the face of a wall, and after a time the rising sun ceased to strike along the gorge, the voices of the singing birds died away, and the air grew cold and dark about him. But the distant valley with its houses was all the brighter for that. He came presently to talus, and among the rocks he noted—for he was an observant man—an unfamiliar fern that seemed to clutch out of the crevices with intense green hands. He picked a frond or so and gnawed its stalk and found it helpful.

About midday he came at last out of the throat of the gorge into the plain and the sunlight. He was stiff and weary; he sat down in the shadow of a rock, filled up his flask with water from a spring and drank it down, and remained for a time resting before he went on to the houses.

They were very strange to his eyes, and indeed the whole aspect of that valley became, as he regarded it, queerer and more unfamiliar. The greater part of its surface was lush green meadow, starred with many beautiful flowers, irrigated with extraordinary care, and bearing evidence of systematic cropping piece by piece. High up and ringing the valley about was a wall, and what appeared to be a circumferential water-channel, from which the little trickles of water that fed the meadow plants came, and on the higher slopes above this flocks of llamas cropped the scanty herbage. Sheds, apparently shelters or feeding-places for the llamas, stood against the boundary wall here and there. The irrigation streams ran together into a main channel down the centre of the valley, and this was enclosed on either side by a wall breast high. This gave a singularly urban quality to this secluded place, a quality that was greatly enhanced by the fact that a number of paths paved with black and white stones, and each with a curious little kerb at the side, ran hither and thither in an orderly manner. The houses of the central village were quite unlike the casual and higgledy-piggledy agglomeration of the mountain villages he knew; they stood in a continuous row on either side of a central street of astonishing cleanness; here and there their parti-coloured façade was pierced by a door, and not a solitary window broke their even frontage. They were parti-coloured with extraordinary irregularity; smeared with a sort of plaster that was sometimes grey, sometimes drab, sometimes slate-coloured or dark brown; and it was the sight of this wild plastering that first brought the word "blind" into the thoughts of the explorer. "The good man who did that," he thought, "must have been as blind as a bat."

He descended a steep place, and so came to the wall and channel that ran about the valley, near where the latter spouted out its surplus contents into the deeps of the gorge in a thin and wavering thread of cascade. He could now see a number of men and women resting on piled heaps of grass, as if taking a siesta, in the remoter part of the meadow, and nearer the village a number of recumbent children, and then nearer at hand three men carrying pails on yokes along a little path that ran from the encircling wall towards the houses. These latter were clad in garments of llama cloth and boots and belts of leather, and they wore caps of cloth with back and ear flaps. They followed one another in single file, walking slowly and yawning as they walked, like men who have been up all night. There was something so reassuringly prosperous and respectable in their bearing that after a moment's hesitation Núñez stood forward as conspicuously as possible upon his rock, and gave vent to a mighty shout that echoed round the valley.

The three men stopped, and moved their heads as though they were looking about them. They turned their faces this way and that, and Núñez gesticulated with freedom. But they did not appear to see him for all his gestures, and after a time, directing themselves towards the mountains far away to the right, they shouted as if in answer. Núñez bawled again, and then once more, and as he gestured ineffectually the word "blind" came up to the top of his thoughts. "The fools must be blind," he said.

When at last, after much shouting and wrath, Núñez crossed the stream by a little bridge, came through a gate in the wall, and approached them, he was sure that they were blind. He was sure that this was the Country of the Blind of which the legends told. Conviction had sprung upon him, and a sense of great and rather enviable adventure. The three stood side by side, not looking at him, but with their ears directed towards him, judging him by his unfamiliar steps. They stood close together like men a little afraid, and he could see their eyelids closed and sunken, as though the very balls beneath had shrunk away. There was an expression near awe on their faces.

"A man," one said, in hardly recognisable Spanish—"a man it is—a man or a spirit—coming down from the rocks."

But Núñez advanced with the confident steps of a youth who enters upon life. All the old stories of the lost valley and the Country of the Blind had come back to his mind, and through his thoughts ran this old proverb, as if it were a refrain—

"In the Country of the Blind the One-eyed Man is King."

"In the Country of the Blind the One-eyed Man is King."

And very civilly he gave them greeting. He talked to them and used his eyes.

"Where does he come from, brother Pedro?" asked one.

"Down out of the rocks."

"Over the mountains I come," said Núñez, "out of the country beyond there—where men can see. From near Bogotá, where there are a hundred thousands of people, and where the city passes out of sight."

"Sight?" muttered Pedro. "Sight?"

"He comes," said the second blind man, "out of the rocks."

The cloth of their coats Núñez saw was curiously fashioned, each with a different sort of stitching.

They startled him by a simultaneous movement towards him, each with a hand outstretched. He stepped back from the advance of these spread fingers.

"Come hither," said the third blind man, following his motion and clutching him neatly.

And they held Núñez and felt him over, saying no word further until they had done so.

"Carefully," he cried, with a finger in his eye, and found they thought that organ, with its fluttering lids, a queer thing in him. They went over it again.

"A strange creature, Correa," said the one called Pedro. "Feel the coarseness of his hair. Like a llama's hair."

"Rough he is as the rocks that begot him," said Correa, investigating Núñez's unshaven chin with a soft and slightly moist hand. "Perhaps he will grow finer." Núñez struggled a little under their examination, but they gripped him firm.

"Carefully," he said again.

"He speaks," said the third man. "Certainly he is a man."

"Ugh!" said Pedro, at the roughness of his coat.

"And you have come into the world?" asked Pedro.

"*Out* of the world. Over mountains and glaciers; right over above there, halfway to the sun. Out of the great big world that goes down, twelve days' journey to the sea."

They scarcely seemed to heed him. "Our fathers have told us men may be made by the forces of Nature," said Correa. "It is the warmth of things and moisture, and rottenness—rottenness."

"Let us lead him to the elders," said Pedro.

"Shout first," said Correa, "lest the children be afraid. This is a marvellous occasion."

So they shouted, and Pedro went first and took Núñez by the hand to lead him to the houses.

He drew his hand away. "I can see," he said.

"See?" said Correa.

"Yes, see," said Núñez, turning towards him, and stumbled against Pedro's pail.

"His senses are still imperfect," said the third blind man. "He stumbles, and talks unmeaning words. Lead him by the hand."

"As you will, " said Núñez, and was led along, laughing.

It seemed they knew nothing of sight.

Well, all in good time he would teach them.

He heard people shouting, and saw a number of figures gathering together in the middle roadway of the village.

He found it taxed his nerve and patience more than he had anticipated, that first encounter with the population of the Country of the Blind. The place seemed larger as he drew near to it, and the smeared plasterings queerer, and a crowd of children and men and women (the women and girls, he was pleased to note, had some of them quite sweet faces, for all that their eyes were shut and sunken) came about him holding on to him, touching him with soft, sensitive hands, smelling at him, and listening at every word he spoke. Some of the maidens and children, however, kept aloof as if afraid, and indeed his voice seemed coarse and rude beside their softer notes. They mobbed him. His three guides kept close to him with an effect of proprietorship, and said again and again, "A wild man out of the rocks."

"Bogotá," he said. "Bogotá. Over the mountain crests."

"A wild man—using wild words," said Pedro. "Did you hear that—*Bogotá*? His mind is hardly formed yet. He has only the beginnings of speech."

A little boy nipped his hand. "Bogotá!" he said mockingly.

"Ay! A city to your village, I come from the great world—where men have eyes and see."

"His name's Bogotá," they said.

"He stumbled," said Correa, "stumbled twice as we came hither."

"Bring him to the elders."

And they thrust him suddenly through a doorway into a room as black as pitch, save at the end there faintly glowed a fire. The crowd closed in behind him and shut out all but the faintest glimmer of day, and before he could arrest himself he had fallen headlong over the feet of a seated man. His arm, out-flung, struck the face of someone else as he went down; he felt the soft impact of features and heard a cry of anger, and for a moment he struggled against a number of hands that clutched him. It was a one-sided fight. An inkling of the situation came to him, and he lay quiet.

"I fell down," he said; "I couldn't see in this pitchy darkness."

There was a pause as if the unseen persons about him tried to understand his words. Then the voice of Correa said: "He is but newly formed. He stumbles as he walks and mingles words that mean nothing with his speech."

Others also said things about him that he heard or understood imperfectly.

"May I sit up?" he asked, in a pause. "I will not struggle against you again."

They consulted and let him rise.

The voice of an older man began to question him, and Núñez found himself trying to explain the great world out of which he had fallen, and the sky and mountains and sight and such-like marvels,

to these elders who sat in darkness in the Country of the Blind. And
they would believe and understand nothing whatever he told them,
a thing quite outside his expectation. They would not even understand many of his words. For fourteen generations these people had
been blind and cut off from all the seeing world; the names for all
the things of sight had faded and changed; the story of the outer
world was faded and changed to a child's story; and they had ceased
to concern themselves with anything beyond the rocky slopes above
their circling wall. Blind men of genius had arisen among them and
questioned the shreds of belief and tradition they had brought with
them from their seeing days, and had dismissed all these things as
idle fancies, and replaced them with new and saner explanations.
Much of their imagination had shrivelled with their eyes, and they
had made for themselves new imaginations with their ever more
sensitive ears and finger-tips. Slowly Núñez realised this; that his
expectation of wonder and reverence at his origin and his gifts was
not to be borne out; and after his poor attempt to explain sight to
them had been set aside as the confused version of a new-made
being describing the marvels of his incoherent sensations, he subsided, a little dashed, into listening to their instruction. And the
eldest of the blind men explained to him life and philosophy and
religion, how that the world (meaning their valley) had been first an
empty hollow in the rocks, and then had come, first, inanimate
things without the gift of touch, and llamas and a few other creatures that had little sense, and then men, and at last angels, whom
one could hear singing and making fluttering sounds, but whom no
one could touch at all, which puzzled Núñez greatly until he
thought of the birds.

He went on to tell Núñez how this time had been divided into the
warm and the cold, which are the blind equivalents of day and
night, and how it was good to sleep in the warm and work during
the cold, so that now, but for his advent, the whole town of the
blind would have been asleep. He said Núñez must have been specially created to learn and serve the wisdom they had acquired, and
for that all his mental incoherency and stumbling behavior he must
have courage and do his best to learn, and at that all the people in
the doorway murmured encouragingly. He said the night—for the
blind call their day night—was now far gone, and it behooved
everyone to go back to sleep. He asked Núñez if he knew how to
sleep, and Núñez said he did, but that before sleep he wanted food.

They brought him food—llama's milk in a bowl, and rough salted
bread—and led him to a lonely place to eat out of their hearing, and
afterwards to slumber until the chill of the mountain evening roused
them to begin their day again. But Núñez slumbered not at all.

Instead, he sat up in the place where they had left him, resting his limbs and turning the unanticipated circumstances of his arrival over and over in his mind.

Every now and then he laughed, sometimes with amusement, and sometimes with indignation.

"Unformed mind!" he said. "Got no senses yet! They little know they've been insulting their heaven-sent king and master. I see I must bring them to reason. Let me think—let me think."

He was still thinking when the sun set.

Núñez had an eye for all beautiful things, and it seemed to him that the glow upon the snowfields and glaciers that rose about the valley on every side was the most beautiful thing he had ever seen. His eyes went from that inaccessible glory to the village and irrigated fields, fast sinking into the twilight, and suddenly a wave of emotion took him, and he thanked God from the bottom of his heart that the power of sight had been given him.

He heard a voice calling to him from out of the village.

"Ya ho there, Bogotá! Come hither!"

At that he stood up smiling. He would show these people once and for all what sight would do for a man. They would seek him, but not find him.

"You move not, Bogotá," said the voice.

He laughed noiselessly, and made two stealthy steps aside from the path.

"Trample not on the grass, Bogotá; that is not allowed."

Núñez had scarcely heard the sound he made himself. He stopped, amazed.

The owner of the voice came running up the piebald path towards him.

He stepped back into the pathway. "Here I am," he said.

"Why did you not come when I called you?" said the blind man. "Must you be led like a child? Cannot you hear the path as you walk?"

Núñez laughed. "I can see it," he said.

"There is no such word as *see*," said the blind man, after a pause. "Cease this folly, and follow the sound of my feet."

Núñez followed, a little annoyed.

"My time will come," he said.

"You'll learn," the blind man answered. "There is much to learn in the world."

"Has no one told you, 'In the Country of the Blind the One-eyed Man is King'?"

"What is blind?" asked the blind man carelessly over his shoulder.

Four days passed, and the fifth found the King of the Blind still incognito, as a clumsy and useless stranger among his subjects.

It was, he found, much more difficult to proclaim himself than he had supposed, and in the meantime, while he meditated his *coup d'état*, he did what he was told and learned the manners and customs of the Country of the Blind. He found working and going about at night a particularly irksome thing, and he decided that that should be the first thing he would change.

They led a simple, laborious life, these people, with all the elements of virtue and happiness, as these things can be understood by men. They toiled, but not oppressively; they had food and clothing sufficient for their needs; they had days and seasons of rest; they made much of music and singing, and there was love among them, and little children.

It was marvellous with what confidence and precision they went about their ordered world. Everything, you see, had been made to fit their needs; each of the radiating paths of the valley area had a constant angle to the others, and was distinguished by a special notch upon its kerbing; all obstacles and irregularities of path or meadow had long since been cleared away; all their methods and procedure arose naturally from their special needs. Their senses had become marvellously acute; they could hear and judge the slightest gesture of a man a dozen paces away—could hear the very beating of his heart. Intonation had long replaced expression with them, and touches gesture, and their work with hoe and spade and fork was as free and confident as garden work can be. Their sense of smell was extraordinarily fine; they could distinguish individual differences as readily as a dog can, and they went about the tending of the llamas, who lived among the rocks above and came to the wall for food and shelter, with ease and confidence. It was only when at last Núñez sought to assert himself that he found how easy and confident their movements could be.

He rebelled only after he had tried persuasion.

He tried at first on several occasions to tell them of sight. "Look you here, you people," he said. "There are things you do not understand in me."

Once or twice one or two of them attended to him; they sat with faces downcast and ears turned intelligently towards him, and he did his best tell them what it was to see. Among his hearers was a girl, with eyelids less red and sunken than the others, so that one could almost fancy she was hiding eyes, whom especially he hoped to persuade. He spoke of the beauties of sight, of watching the mountains, of the sky and the sunrise, and they heard him with amused incredulity that presently became condemnatory. They told him there were indeed no mountains at all, but that the end of the rocks where the llamas grazed was indeed the end of the world;

thence sprang a cavernous roof of the universe, from which the dew and the avalanches fell; and when he maintained stoutly the world had neither end nor roof such as they supposed, they said his thoughts were wicked. So far as he could describe sky and clouds and stars to them it seemed to them a hideous void, a terrible blankness in the place of the smooth roof to things in which they believed—it was an article of faith with them that the cavern roof was exquisitely smooth to the touch. He saw that in some manner he shocked them, and gave up that aspect of the matter altogether, and tried to show them the practical value of sight. One morning he saw Pedro in the path called Seventeen and coming towards the central houses, but still too far off for hearing or scent and he told them as much. "In a little while," he prophesied, "Pedro will be here." An old man remarked that Pedro had no business on Path Seventeen, and then, as if in confirmation, that individual as he drew near turned and went transversely into Path Ten, and so back with nimble paces towards the outer wall. They mocked Núñez when Pedro did not arrive, and afterwards, when he asked Pedro questions to clear his character, Pedro denied and outfaced him, and was afterwards hostile to him.

Then he induced them to let him go a long way up the sloping meadows towards the wall with one complacent individual, and to him he promised to describe all that happened among the houses. He noted certain goings and comings, but the things that really seemed to signify to these people happened inside of or behind the windowless houses—the only things they took note of to test him by—and of these he could see or tell nothing; and it was after the failure of this attempt, and the ridicule they could not repress, that he resorted to force. He thought of seizing a spade and suddenly smiting one or two of them to earth, and so in fair combat showing the advantage of eyes. He went so far with that resolution as to seize his spade, and then he discovered a new thing about himself, and that was that it was impossible for him to hit a blind man in cold blood.

He hesitated, and found them all aware that he snatched up the spade. They stood alert, with their heads on one side, and bent ears towards him for what he would do next.

"Put that spade down," said one, and he felt a sort of helpless horror. He came near obedience.

Then he thrust one backwards against a house wall, and fled past him and out of the village.

He went athwart one of their meadows, leaving a track of trampled grass behind his feet, and presently sat down by the side of one of their ways. He felt something of the buoyancy that comes to all men in the beginning of a fight, but more perplexity. He began to realise that you cannot even fight happily with creatures who stand upon a different mental basis to yourself. Far away he saw a number of men carrying spades and sticks come out of the street of houses, and advance in a spreading line along the several paths towards him. They advanced slowly, speaking frequently to one another, and ever and again the whole cordon would halt and sniff the air and listen.

The first time they did this Núñez laughed. But afterwards he did not laugh.

One struck his trail in the meadow grass, and came stooping and feeling his way along it.

For five minutes he watched the slow extension of the cordon, and then his vague disposition to do something forthwith became frantic. He stood up, went a pace or so towards the circumferential wall, turned, and went back a little way. There they all stood in a crescent, still and listening.

He also stood still, gripping his spade very tightly in both hands. Should he charge them?

The pulse in his ears ran into the rhythm of "In the Country of the Blind the One-eyed Man is King!"

Should he charge them?

He looked back at the high and unclimbable wall behind—unclimbable because of its smooth plastering, but withal pierced with many little doors, and at the approaching line of seekers. Behind these, others were now coming out of the street of houses.

Should he charge them?

"Bogotá!" called one. "Bogotá! where are you?"

He gripped his spade still tighter, and advanced down the meadows towards the place of habitations, and directly he moved they converged upon him. "I'll hit them if they touch me," he swore; "by Heaven, I will. I'll hit." He called aloud, "Look here, I'm going to do what I like in this valley. Do you hear? I'm going to do what I like and go where I like!"

They were moving in upon him quickly, groping, yet moving rapidly. It was like playing blind man's buff, with everyone blindfolded except one. "Get hold of him!" cried one. He found himself in the arc of a loose curve of pursuers. He felt suddenly he must be active and resolute.

"You don't understand," he cried in a voice that was meant to be great and resolute, and which broke. "You are blind, and I can see. Leave me alone!"

"Bogotá! Put down that spade, and come off the grass!"

The last order, grotesque in its urban familiarity, produced a gust of anger.

"I'll hurt you," he said, sobbing with emotion. "By Heaven, I'll hurt you. Leave me alone!"

He began to run, not knowing clearly where to run. He ran from the nearest blind man, because it was a horror to hit him. He stopped, and then made a dash to escape from their closing ranks. He made for where a gap was wide, and the men on either side, with a quick perception of the approach of his paces, rushed in on one another. He sprang forward, and then saw he must be caught, and *swish!* the spade had struck. He felt the soft thud of hand and arm, and the man was down with a yell of pain, and he was through.

Through! And then he was close to the street of houses again, and blind men, whirling spades and stakes, were running with a sort of reasoned swiftness hither and thither.

He heard steps behind him just in time, and found a tall man rushing forward and swiping at the sound of him. He lost his nerve, hurled his spade a yard wide at his antagonist, and whirled about and fled, fairly yelling as he dodged another.

He was panic-stricken. He ran furiously to and fro, dodging when there was no need to dodge, and in his anxiety to see on every side of him at once, stumbling. For a moment, he was down and they heard his fall. Far away in the circumferential wall a little doorway looked like heaven, and he set off in a wild rush for it. He did not even look round at his pursuers until it was gained, and he had stumbled across the bridge, clambered a little way among the rocks, to the surprise and dismay of a young llama, who went leaping out of sight, and lay down sobbing for breath.

And so his *coup d'état* came to an end.

He stayed outside the wall of the valley of the Blind for two nights and days without food or shelter, and meditated upon the unexpected. During these meditations he repeated very frequently and always with a profounder note of derision the exploded proverb: "In the Country of the Blind the One-Eyed Man is King." He thought chiefly of ways of fighting and conquering these people, and it grew clear that for him no practicable way was possible. He had no weapons, and now it would be hard to get one.

The canker of civilisation had got to him even in Bogotá, and he could not find it in himself to go down and assassinate a blind man. Of course, if he did that, he might then dictate terms on the threat of assassinating them all. But—sooner or later he must sleep! . . .

He tried also to find food among the pine trees, to be comfortable under pine boughs while the frost fell at night, and—with less confidence—to catch a llama by artifice in order to try to kill it—perhaps by hammering it with a stone—and so finally, perhaps, to eat some of it. But the llamas had a doubt of him and regarded him with distrustful brown eyes, and spat when he drew near. Fear came on him the second day and fits of shivering. Finally he crawled down to the wall of the Country of the Blind and tried to make terms. He crawled along by the stream shouting, until two blind men came out to the gate and talked to him.

"I was mad," he said. "But I was only newly made."

They said that was better.

He told them he was wiser now, and repented of all he had done.

Then he wept without intention, for he was very weak and ill now, and they took that as a favourable sign.

They asked him if he still thought he could "*see.*"

"No," he said. "That was folly. The word means nothing—less than nothing!"

They asked him what was overhead.

"About ten times ten the height of a man there is a roof above the world—of rock—and very, very smooth." . . . He burst again into hysterical tears. "Before you ask me any more, give me some food or I shall die."

He expected dire punishments, but these blind people were capable of toleration. They regarded his rebellion as but one more proof of his general idiocy and inferiority; and after they had whipped him they appointed him to do the simplest and heaviest work they had for anyone to do, and he, seeing no other way of living, did submissively what he was told.

He was ill for some days, and they nursed him kindly. That refined his submission. But they insisted on his lying in the dark, and that was a great misery. And blind philosophers came and talked to him of the wicked levity of his mind, and reproved him so impressively for his doubts about the lid of rock that covered their cosmic casserole that he almost doubted whether indeed he was not the victim of hallucination in not seeing it overhead.

So Núñez became a citizen of the Country of the Blind, and these people ceased to be a generalised people and became individualities and familiar to him, while the world beyond the mountains became more and more remote and unreal. There was Yacob, his master, a kindly man when not annoyed; there was Pedro, Yacob's nephew; and there was Medina-saroté, who was the youngest daughter of Yacob. She was little esteemed in the world of the Blind, because she had a clear-cut face, and lacked that satisfying, glossy smoothness that is the blind man's ideal of feminine beauty; but Núñez thought her beautiful at first, and presently the most beautiful thing in the whole creation. Her closed eyelids were not sunken and red after the common way of the valley, but lay as though they might open again at any moment; and she had long eyelashes, which were considered a grave disfigurement. And her voice was strong, and did not satisfy the acute hearing of the valley swains. So that she had no lover.

There came a time when Núñez thought that, could he win her, he would be resigned to live in the valley for all the rest of his days.

He watched her; he sought opportunities of doing her little services, and presently he found that she observed him. Once at a rest-day gathering they sat side by side in the dim starlight, and the music was sweet. His hand came upon hers and he dared to clasp it. Then very tenderly she returned his pressure. And one day, as they were at their meal in the darkness, he felt her hand very softly seeking him, and as it chanced the fire leaped then and he saw the tenderness of her face.

He sought to speak to her.

He went to her one day when she was sitting in the summer moonlight spinning. The light made her a thing of silver and mystery. He sat down at her feet and told her he loved her, and told her how beautiful she seemed to him. He had a lover's voice, he spoke with a tender reverence that came near to awe, and she had never before been touched by adoration. She made him no definite answer, but it was clear his words pleased her.

After that he talked to her whenever he could take an opportunity. The valley became the world for him, and the world beyond the mountains where men lived in sunlight seemed no more than a fairy tale he would some day pour into her ears. Very tentatively and timidly he spoke to her of sight.

Sight seemed to her the most poetical of fancies, and she listened to his descriptions of the stars and the mountains and her own sweet white-lit beauty as though it was a guilty indulgence. She did not believe, she could only half understand, but she was mysteriously delighted, and it seemed to him that she completely understood.

His love lost its awe and took courage. Presently he was for demanding her of Yacob and the elders in marriage, but she became fearful and delayed. And it was one of her elder sisters who first told Yacob that Medina-saroté and Núñez were in love.

There was from the first very great opposition to the marriage of Núñez and Medina-saroté; not so much because they valued her as because they held him as a being apart, an idiot, incompetent thing below the permissible level of a man. Her sisters opposed it bitterly as bringing discredit on them all; and old Yacob, though he had formed a sort of liking for his clumsy, obedient serf, shook his head and said the thing could not be. The young men were all angry at the idea of corrupting the race, and one went so far as to revile and strike Núñez. He struck back. Then for the first time he found an advantage in seeing, even by twilight, and after that fight was over no one was disposed to raise a hand against him. But they still found his marriage impossible.

Old Yacob had a tenderness for his last little daughter, and was grieved to have her weep upon his shoulder.

"You see, my dear, he's an idiot. He has delusions; he can't do anything right."

"I know," wept Medina-saroté. "But he's better than he was. He's getting better. And he's strong, dear father, and kind—stronger and kinder than any other man in the world. And he loves me—and, Father, I love him."

Old Yacob was greatly distressed to find her inconsolable, and, besides—what made it more distressing—he liked Núñez for many things. So he went and sat in the windowless council-chamber with the other elders and watched the trend of the talk, and said, at the proper time, "He's better than he was. Very likely; some day, we shall find him as sane as ourselves."

Then afterwards one of the elders, who thought deeply, had an idea. He was the great doctor among these people, their medicine-man, and he had a very philosophical and inventive mind, and the idea of curing Núñez of his peculiarities appealed to him. One day when Yacob was present he returned to the topic of Núñez.

"I have examined Bogotá," he said, "and the case is clearer to me. I think very probably he might be cured."

"That is what I have always hoped," said old Yacob.

"His brain is affected," said the blind doctor.

The elders murmured assent.

"Now *what* affects it?"

"Ah!" said old Yacob.

"*This,*" said the doctor, answering his own question. "Those queer things that are called the eyes, and which exist to make an agreeable soft depression in the face, are diseased, in the case of Bogotá, in such a way as to affect his brain. They are greatly distended, he has eyelashes, and his eyelids move, and consequently his brain is in a state of constant irritation and distraction."

"Yes?" said old Yacob. "Yes?"

"And I think I may say with reasonable certainty that, in order to cure him completely, all we need do is a simple and easy surgical operation—namely, to remove these irritant bodies."

"And then he will be sane?"

"Then he will be perfectly sane, and a quite admirable citizen."

"Thank Heaven for science!" said old Yacob, and went forth at once to tell Núñez of his happy hopes.

But Núñez's manner of receiving the good news struck him as being cold and disappointing.

"One might think," he said, "from the tone you take, that you did not care for my daughter."

It was Medina-saroté who persuaded Núñez to face the blind surgeons.

"*You* do not want me," he said, "to lose my gift of sight?"

She shook her head.

"My world is sight."

Her head drooped lower.

"There are the beautiful things, the beautiful little things—the flowers, the lichens among the rocks, the lightness and softness on a piece of fur, the far sky with its drifting down of clouds, the sunsets and the stars. And there is *you*. For you alone it is good to have sight, to see your sweet, serene face, your kindly lips, your dear, beautiful hands folded together. . . . It is these eyes of mine you won, these eyes that hold me to you, that these idiots seek. I must touch you, hear you, and never see you again. I must come under that roof of rock and stone and darkness, that horrible roof under which your imagination stoops. . . . No; you would not have me do that?"

A disagreeable doubt had arisen in him. He stopped, and left the thing a question.

"I wish," she said, "sometimes——" She paused.

"Yes?" said he, a little apprehensively.

"I wish sometimes—you would not talk like that."

"Like what?"

"I know it's pretty—it's your imagination. I love it, but *now*——"

He felt cold. "*Now?*" he said faintly.

She sat still.

"You mean—you think—I should be better, better perhaps——"

He was realising things very swiftly. He felt anger, indeed, anger at the dull course of fate, but also sympathy for her lack of understanding—sympathy near akin to pity.

"*Dear,*" he said, and he could see by her whiteness how intensely her spirit pressed against the things she could not say. He put his arms about her, he kissed her ear, and they sat for a time in silence.

"If I were to consent to this?" he said at last, in a voice that was very gentle.

She flung her arms about him, weeping wildly. "Oh, if you would," she sobbed, "if only you would!"

For a week before the operation that was to raise him from his servitude and inferiority to the level of a blind citizen Núñez knew nothing of sleep, and all through the warm sunlit hours, while the others slumbered happily, he sat brooding or wandered aimlessly, trying to bring his mind to bear on his dilemma. He had given his answer, he had given his consent, and still he was not sure. And at last work-time was over, the sun rose in splendour over the golden crests, and his last day of vision began for him. He had a few minutes with Medina-saroté before she went apart to sleep.

"To-morrow," he said, "I shall see no more."

"Dear heart!" she answered, and pressed his hands with all her strength.

"They will hurt you but little," she said; "and you are going through this pain—you are going through it, dear lover, for *me*. . . . Dear, if a woman's heart and life can do it, I will repay you. My dearest one, my dearest with the tender voice, I will repay."

He was drenched in pity for himself and her.

He held her in his arms, and pressed his lips to hers, and looked on her sweet face for the last time. "Good-bye!" he whispered at that dear sight, "good-bye!"

And then in silence he turned away from her.

She could hear his slow retreating footsteps, and something in the rhythm of them threw her into a passion of weeping.

He had fully meant to go to a lonely place where the meadows were beautiful with white narcissus, and there remain until the hour of his sacrifice should come, but as he went he lifted up his eyes and saw the morning, the morning like an angel in golden armour, marching down the steeps. . . .

It seemed to him that before this splendour he, and this blind world in the valley, and his love, and all, were no more than a pit of sin.

He did not turn aside as he had meant to do, but went on, and passed through the wall of the circumference and out upon the rocks, and his eyes were always upon the sunlit ice and snow.

He saw their infinite beauty, and his imagination soared over them to the things beyond he was now to resign for ever.

He thought of that great free world he was parted from, the world that was his own, and he had a vision of those further slopes, distance beyond distance, with Bogotá, a place of multitudinous stirring beauty, a glory by day, a luminous mystery by night, a place of palaces and fountains and statues and white houses, lying beautifully in the middle distance. He thought how for a day or so one might come down through passes, drawing ever nearer and nearer to its busy streets and ways. He thought of the river journey, day by day, from great Bogotá to the still vaster world beyond, through towns and villages, forest and desert places, the rushing river day by day, until its banks receded and the big steamers came splashing by, and one had reached the sea—the limitless sea, with its thousand islands, its thousands of islands, and its ships seen dimly far away in their incessant journeyings round and about that greater world. And there, unpent by mountains, one saw the sky— the sky, not such a disc as one saw it here, but an arch of immeasurable blue, a deep of deeps in which the circling stars were floating. . . .

His eyes scrutinised the great curtain of the mountains with a keener inquiry.

For example, if one went so, up that gully and to that chimney there, then one might come out high among those stunted pines that ran round in a sort of shelf and rose still higher and higher as it passed above the gorge. And then? That talus might be managed. Thence perhaps a climb might be found to take him up to the precipice that came below the snow; and if that chimney failed, then another farther to the east might serve his purpose better. And then? Then one would be out upon the amber-lit snow there, and halfway up to the crest of those beautiful desolations.

He glanced back at the village, then turned right round and regarded it steadfastly.

He thought of Medina-saroté, and she had become small and remote.

He turned again towards the mountain wall, down which the day had come to him.

Then very circumspectly he began to climb.

When sunset came he was no longer climbing, but he was far and high. He had been higher, but he was still very high. His clothes were torn, his limbs were blood-stained, he was bruised in many places, but he lay as if he were at his ease, and there was a smile on his face.

From where he rested the valley seemed as if it were in a pit and nearly a mile below. Already it was dim with haze and shadow, though the mountain summits around him were things of light and fire, and the little details of the rocks near at hand were drenched with subtle beauty—a vein of green mineral piercing the grey, the flash of crystal faces here and there, a minute, minutely beautiful orange lichen close beside his face. There were deep mysterious shadows in the gorge, blue deepening into purple, and purple into a luminous darkness, and overhead was the illimitable vastness of the sky. But he heeded these things no longer, but lay quite inactive there, smiling as if he were satisfied merely to have escaped from the valley of the Blind in which he had thought to be King.

The glow of the sunset passed, and the night came, and still he lay peacefully contented under the cold stars.

FRANZ KAFKA

1883–1924

He was born in Prague, Czechoslovakia, to Jewish parents, and went to German schools in Prague. His father, the son of a butcher, was a tall, strong patriarch, who built a large and successful wholesale clothing business in Prague. In 1901 Kafka began studying at the German University in Prague, obtaining his doctorate in jurisprudence there in 1906. Two years later he found a job with the Workers' Accident Insurance Company that allowed him some time to write. He was engaged twice and fathered a child whose existence was kept from him. He never married. In 1912 he began to write his most serious work. In 1917 he was diagnosed as tubercular, and his health declined steadily from then until his death in 1924. In 1919 two volumes of his stories were published: *A Country Doctor* and *In the Penal Colony*. On his death he left the manuscripts of three nearly finished novels and many diaries and stories, with instructions that they should all be destroyed. His wishes were not obeyed, and the novels *Amerika*, *The Castle*, and *The Trial*, along with many other works, were saved for publication, bringing him posthumous fame.

On Parables

Many complain that the words of the wise are always merely parables and of no use in daily life, which is the only life we have. When the sage says: "Go over," he does not mean that we should cross to some actual place, which we could do anyhow if the labor were worth it; he means some fabulous yonder, something unknown to us, something that he cannot designate more precisely either, and therefore cannot help us here in the very least. All these parables really set out to say merely that the incomprehensible is incomprehensible, and we know that already. But the cares we have to struggle with every day: that is a different matter.

Concerning this a man once said: Why such reluctance? If you only followed the parables you yourselves would become parables and with that rid of all your daily cares.

Another said: I bet that is also a parable.

The first said: You have won.

The second said: But unfortunately only in parable.

The first said: No, in reality: in parable you have lost.

Translated by Willa and Edwin Muir

An Imperial Message

The emperor, so a parable runs, has sent a message to you, the humble subject, the insignificant shadow cowering in the remotest distance before the imperial sun; the Emperor from his deathbed has sent a message to you alone. He has commanded the messenger to kneel down by the bed, and has whispered the message to him; so much store did he lay on it that he ordered the messenger to whisper it back into his ear again. Then by a nod of the head he has confirmed that it is right. Yes, before the assembled spectators of his death—all the obstructing walls have been broken down, and on the spacious and loftily mounting open staircases stand in a ring the great princes of the Empire—before all these he has delivered his message. The messenger immediately sets out on his journey; a powerful, an indefatigable man; now pushing with his right arm, now with his left, he cleaves a way for himself through the throng; if he encounters resistance he points to his breast, where the symbol of the sun glitters; the way is made easier for him than it would be for any other man. But the multitudes are so vast; their numbers have no end. If he could reach the open fields how fast he would fly, and soon doubtless you would hear the welcome hammering of his fists on your door. But instead how vainly does he wear out his strength; still he is only making his way through the chambers of the innermost palace; never will he get to the end of them; and if he succeeded in that nothing would be gained; he must next fight his way down the stair; and if he succeeded in that nothing would be gained; the courts would still have to be crossed; and after the courts the second outer palace; and once more stairs and courts; and once more another palace; and so on for thousands of years; and if at last he should burst through the outermost gate—but never, never can that happen—the imperial capital would lie before him, the center of the world, crammed to bursting with its own sediment. Nobody could fight his way through here even with a message from a dead man. But you sit at your window when evening falls and dream it to yourself.

Translated by Willa and Edwin Muir

D. H. LAWRENCE
1885–1930

David Herbert Lawrence was born at Eastwood, a coal-mining village in the English Midlands. His father was a miner, his mother a woman from the middle class who never accepted her husband's way of life. Lawrence was torn between them: close to his mother during her life, appreciating his father only after his death. The story of this family struggle is told in one of Lawrence's finest works, his novel *Sons and Lovers* (1913). In 1901 Lawrence nearly died of pneumonia. His health was delicate after this until his death of tuberculosis at the age of forty-five. In 1904 he took the King's Scholarship examination and came out first in all England and Wales. He seems to have been good at all academic subjects from mathematics to botany, painting, and writing. He began a career as a teacher, but trouble with his health and his early success as a writer took him away from teaching. In 1912 he ran off with the wife of a former professor of his at Nottingham University, and in 1914, when her divorce became final, he married her. From then on the Lawrences traveled, staying in England at times, but also living in Germany, Italy, Ceylon, Australia, the United States, and Mexico. After Lawrence died in southern France, his body was cremated and the ashes were brought to the United States and buried on a hill near Taos, New Mexico.

Lawrence's personality has drawn almost as much attention as his books. He spoke and wrote informally with the same vitality that animates all his literary work. And some of the informality of talk and personal correspondence can be found in his poetry and fiction. For a time censorship of his works and controversy over the supposed immorality of his views on sex obscured the seriousness and beauty of his work for many readers. But now his books are in print and his place in English letters is secure.

The Rocking-Horse Winner

There was a woman who was beautiful, who started with all the advantages, yet she had no luck. She married for love, and the love turned to dust. She had bonny children, yet she felt they had been thrust upon her, and she could not love them. They looked at her coldly, as if they were finding fault with her. And hurriedly she felt she must cover up some fault in herself. Yet what it was that she must cover up she never knew. Nevertheless, when her children were present, she always felt the centre of her heart go hard. This troubled her, and in her manner she was all the more gentle and anxious for her children, as if she loved them very much. Only she herself knew that at the centre of her heart was a hard little place that could not feel love, no, not for anybody. Everybody else said of her: "She is such a good mother. She adores her children." Only she herself, and her children themselves, knew it was not so. They read it in each other's eyes.

There were a boy and two little girls. They lived in a pleasant house, with a garden, and they had discreet servants, and felt themselves superior to anyone in the neighbourhood.

Although they lived in style, they felt always an anxiety in the house. There was never enough money. The mother had a small income, and the father had a small income, but not nearly enough for the social position which they had to keep up. The father went into town to some office. But though he had good prospects, these prospects never materialised. There was always the grinding sense of the shortage of money, though the style was always kept up.

At last the mother said: "I will see if *I* can't make something." But she did not know where to begin. She racked her brains, and tried this thing and the other, but could not find anything successful. The failure made deep lines come into her face. Her children were growing up, they would have to go to school. There must be more money, there must be more money. The father, who was always very handsome and expensive in his tastes, seemed as if he never *would* be able to do anything worth doing. And the mother, who had a great belief in herself, did not succeed any better, and her tastes were just as expensive.

And so the house came to be haunted by the unspoken phrase: *There must be more money! There must be more money!* The children could hear it all the time, though nobody said it aloud. They heard it at Christmas, when the expensive and splendid toys filled the nursery. Behind the shining modern rocking-horse, behind the smart doll's house, a voice would start whispering: "There *must* be more money! There *must* be more money!" And the children would stop playing, to listen for a moment. They would look into each other's eyes, to see if they had all heard. And each one saw in the eyes of the other two that they too had heard. "There *must* be more money! There *must* be more money!"

It came whispering from the springs of the still-swaying rocking-horse, and even the horse, bending his wooden, champing head, heard it. The big doll, sitting so pink and smirking in her new pram, could hear it quite plainly, and seemed to be smirking all the more self-consciously because of it. The foolish puppy, too, that took the place of the teddy-bear, he was looking so extraordinarily foolish for no other reason but that he heard the secret whisper all over the house: "There *must* be more money!"

Yet nobody ever said it aloud. The whisper was everywhere, and therefore no one spoke it. Just as no one ever says: "We are breathing!" in spite of the fact that breath is coming and going all the time.

"Mother," said the boy Paul one day, "why don't we keep a car of our own? Why do we always use uncle's, or else a taxi?"

"Because we're the poor members of the family," said the mother.

"But why *are* we, mother?"

"Well—I suppose," she said slowly and bitterly, "it's because your father has no luck."

The boy was silent for some time.

"Is luck money, mother?" he asked, rather timidly.

"No, Paul. Not quite. It's what causes you to have money."

"Oh!" said Paul vaguely. "I thought when Uncle Oscar said *filthy lucker*, it meant money."

"*Filthy lucre* does mean money," said the mother. "But it's lucre, not luck."

"Oh!" said the boy. "Then what *is* luck, mother?"

"It's what causes you to have money. If you're lucky you have money. That's why it's better to be born lucky than rich. If you're rich, you may lose your money. But if you're lucky, you will always get more money."

"Oh! Will you? And is father not lucky?"

"Very unlucky, I should say," she said bitterly.

The boy watched her with unsure eyes.

"Why?" he asked.

"I don't know. Nobody ever knows why one person is lucky and another unlucky."

"Don't they? Nobody at all? Does *nobody* know?"

"Perhaps God. But He never tells."

"He ought to, then. And aren't you lucky either, mother?"

"I can't be, if I married an unlucky husband."

"But by yourself, aren't you?"

"I used to think I was, before I married. Now I think I am very unlucky indeed."

"Why?"

"Well—never mind! Perhaps I'm not really," she said.

The child looked at her to see if she meant it. But he saw, by the lines of her mouth, that she was only trying to hide something from him.

"Well, anyhow," he said stoutly, "I'm a lucky person."

"Why?" said his mother, with a sudden laugh.

He stared at her. He didn't even know why he had said it.

"God told me," he asserted, brazening it out.

"I hope He did, dear!" she said, again with a laugh, but rather bitter.

"He did, mother!"

"Excellent!" said the mother, using one of her husband's exclamations.

The boy saw she did not believe him; or rather, that she paid no attention to his assertion. This angered him somewhere, and made him want to compel her attention.

He went off by himself, vaguely, in a childish way, seeking for the clue to "luck." Absorbed, taking no heed of other people, he went about with a sort of stealth, seeking inwardly for luck. He wanted luck, he wanted it, he wanted it. When the two girls were playing dolls in the nursery, he would sit on his big rocking-horse, charging madly into space, with a frenzy that made the little girls peer at him uneasily. Wildly the horse careered, the waving dark hair of the boy tossed, his eyes had a strange glare in them. The little girls dared not speak to him.

When he had ridden to the end of his mad little journey, he climbed down and stood in front of his rocking-horse, staring fixedly into its lowered face. Its red mouth was slightly open, its big eye was wide and glassy-bright.

"Now!" he would silently command the snorting steed. "Now, take me to where there is luck! Now take me!"

And he would slash the horse on the neck with the little whip he had asked Uncle Oscar for. He *knew* the horse could take him to where there was luck, if only he forced it. So he would mount again and start on his furious ride, hoping at last to get there. He knew he could get there.

"You'll break your horse, Paul!" said the nurse.

"He's always riding like that! I wish he'd leave off!" said his elder sister Joan.

But he only glared down on them in silence. Nurse gave him up. She could make nothing of him. Anyhow, he was growing beyond her.

One day his mother and his Uncle Oscar came in when he was on one of his furious rides. He did not speak to them.

"Hallo, you young jockey! Riding a winner?" said his uncle.

"Aren't you growing too big for a rocking-horse? You're not a very little boy any longer, you know," said his mother.

But Paul only gave a blue glare from his big, rather close-set eyes. He would speak to nobody when he was in full tilt. His mother watched him with an anxious expression on her face.

At last he suddenly stopped forcing his horse into the mechanical gallop and slid down.

"Well, I got there!" he announced fiercely, his blue eyes still flaring, and his sturdy long legs straddling apart.

"Where did you get to?" asked his mother.

"Where I wanted to go," he flared back at her.

"That's right, son!" said Uncle Oscar. "Don't you stop till you get there. What's the horse's name?"

"He doesn't have a name," said the boy.

"Gets on without all right?" asked the uncle.

"Well, he has different names. He was called Sansovino last week."

"Sansovino, eh? Won the Ascot. How did you know this name?"

"He always talks about horse-races with Bassett," said Joan.

The uncle was delighted to find that his small nephew was posted with all the racing news. Bassett, the young gardener, who had been

wounded in the left foot in the war and had got his present job through
Oscar Cresswell, whose batman he had been, was a perfect blade of
the "turf." He lived in the racing events, and the small boy lived with
him.

Oscar Cresswell got it all from Bassett.

"Master Paul comes and asks me, so I can't do more than tell him,
sir," said Bassett, his face terribly serious, as if he were speaking of
religious matters.

"And does he ever put anything on a horse he fancies?"

"Well—I don't want to give him away—he's a young sport, a fine
sport, sir. Would you mind asking him himself? He sort of takes a
pleasure in it, and perhaps he'd feel I was giving him away, sir, if you
don't mind."

Bassett was serious as a church.

The uncle went back to his nephew and took him off for a ride in the
car.

"Say, Paul, old man, do you ever put anything on a horse?" the
uncle asked.

The boy watched the handsome man closely.

"Why, do you think I oughtn't to?" he parried.

"Not a bit of it! I thought perhaps you might give me a tip for the
Lincoln."

The car sped on into the country, going down to Uncle Oscar's place
in Hampshire.

"Honour bright?" said the nephew.

"Honour bright, son!" said the uncle.

"Well, then, Daffodil."

"Daffodil! I doubt it, sonny. What about Mirza?"

"I only know the winner," said the boy. "That's Daffodil."

"Daffodil, eh?"

There was a pause. Daffodil was an obscure horse comparatively.

"Uncle!"

"Yes, son?"

"You won't let it go any further, will you? I promised Bassett."

"Bassett be damned, old man! What's he got to do with it?"

"We're partners. We've been partners from the first. Uncle, he lent
me my first five shillings, which I lost. I promised him, honour bright,
it was only between me and him; only you gave me that ten-shilling
note I started winning with, so I thought you were lucky. You won't let
it go any further, will you?"

The boy gazed at his uncle from those big, hot, blue eyes, set rather
close together. The uncle stirred and laughed uneasily.

"Right you are, son! I'll keep your tip private. Daffodil, eh? How
much are you putting on him?"

"All except twenty pounds," said the boy. "I keep that in reserve."

The uncle thought it a good joke.

"You keep twenty pounds in reserve, do you, you young romancer? What are you betting, then?"

"I'm betting three hundred," said the boy gravely. "But it's between you and me, Uncle Oscar! Honour bright?"

The uncle burst into a roar of laughter.

"It's between you and me all right, you young Nat Gould," he said, laughing. "But where's your three hundred?"

"Bassett keeps it for me. We're partners."

"You are, are you! And what is Bassett putting on Daffodil?"

"He won't go quite as high as I do, I expect. Perhaps he'll go a hundred and fifty."

"What, pennies?" laughed the uncle.

"Pounds," said the child, with a surprised look at his uncle. "Bassett keeps a bigger reserve than I do."

Between wonder and amusement Uncle Oscar was silent. He pursued the matter no further, but he determined to take his nephew with him to the Lincoln races.

"Now, son," he said, "I'm putting twenty on Mirza, and I'll put five on for you on any horse you fancy. What's your pick?"

"Daffodil, uncle."

"No, not the fiver on Daffodil!"

"I should if it was my own fiver," said the child.

"Good! Good! Right you are! A fiver for me and a fiver for you on Daffodil."

The child had never been to a race-meeting before, and his eyes were blue fire. He pursed his mouth tight and watched. A Frenchman just in front had put his money on Lancelot. Wild with excitement, he flayed his arms up and down, yelling *"Lancelot! Lancelot!"* in his French accent.

Daffodil came in first, Lancelot second, Mirza third. The child, flushed and with eyes blazing, was curiously serene. His uncle brought him four five-pound notes, four to one.

"What am I do with these?" he cried, waving them before the boy's eyes.

"I suppose we'll talk to Bassett," said the boy. "I expect I have fifteen hundred now; and twenty in reserve; and this twenty."

His uncle studied him for some moments.

"Look here, son!" he said. "You're not serious about Bassett and that fifteen hundred, are you?"

"Yes, I am. But it's between you and me, uncle. Honour bright?"

"Honour bright all right, son! But I must talk to Bassett."

"If you'd like to be a partner, uncle, with Bassett and me, we could all be partners. Only, you'd have to promise, honour bright, uncle, not to let it go beyond us three. Bassett and I are lucky, and you must be lucky, because it was your ten shillings I started winning with. . . ."

Uncle Oscar took both Bassett and Paul into Richmond Park for an afternoon, and there they talked.

"It's like this, you see, sir," Bassett said. "Master Paul would get me talking about racing events, spinning yarns, you know, sir. And he was always keen on knowing if I'd made or if I'd lost. It's about a year since, now, that I put five shillings on Blush of Dawn for him: and we lost. Then the luck turned, with that ten shillings he had from you: that we put on Singhalese. And since that time, it's been pretty steady, all things considering. What do you say, Master Paul?"

"We're all right when we're sure," said Paul. "It's when we're not quite sure that we go down."

"Oh, but we're careful then," said Bassett.

"But when are you *sure?*" smiled Uncle Oscar.

"It's Master Paul, sir," said Bassett in a secret, religious voice. "It's as if he had it from heaven. Like Daffodil, now, for the Lincoln. That was as sure as eggs."

"Did you put anything on Daffodil?" asked Oscar Cresswell.

"Yes, sir. I made my bit."

"And my nephew?"

Bassett was obstinately silent, looking at Paul.

"I made twelve hundred, didn't I, Bassett? I told uncle I was putting three hundred on Daffodil."

"That's right," said Bassett, nodding.

"But where's the money?" asked the uncle.

"I keep it safe locked up, sir. Master Paul he can have it any minute he likes to ask for it."

"What, fifteen hundred pounds?"

"And twenty! And *forty*, that is, with the twenty he made on the course."

"It's amazing!" said the uncle.

"If Master Paul offers you to be partners, sir, I would, if I were you: if you'll excuse me," said Bassett.

Oscar Cresswell thought about it.

"I'll see the money," he said.

They drove home again, and, sure enough, Bassett came round to the garden-house with fifteen hundred pounds in notes. The twenty pounds reserve was left with Joe Glee, in the Turf Commission deposit.

"You see, it's all right, uncle, when I'm *sure!* Then we go strong, for all we're worth. Don't we, Bassett?"

"We do that, Master Paul."

"And when are you sure?" said the uncle, laughing.

"Oh, well, sometimes I'm *absolutely* sure, like about Daffodil," said the boy; "and sometimes I have an idea; and sometimes I haven't even an idea, have I, Bassett? Then we're careful, because we mostly go down."

"You do, do you! And when you're sure, like about Daffodil, what makes you sure, sonny?"

"Oh, well, I don't know," said the boy uneasily. "I'm sure, you know, uncle; that's all."

"It's as if he had it from heaven, sir," Bassett reiterated.

"I should say so!" said the uncle.

But he became a partner. And when the Leger was coming on Paul was "sure" about Lively Spark, which was a quite inconsiderable horse. The boy insisted on putting a thousand on the horse, Bassett was for five hundred, and Oscar Cresswell two hundred. Lively Spark came in first, and the betting had been ten to one against him. Paul had made ten thousand.

"You see," he said, "I was absolutely sure of him."

Even Oscar Cresswell had cleared two thousand.

"Look here, son," he said, "this sort of thing makes me nervous."

"It needn't, uncle! Perhaps I shan't be sure again for a long time."

"But what are you going to do with your money?" asked the uncle.

"Of course," said the boy, "I started it for mother. She said she had no luck, because father is unlucky, so I thought if I was lucky, it might stop whispering."

"What might stop whispering?"

"Our house. I *hate* our house for whispering."

"What does it whisper?"

"Why—why"—the boy fidgeted—"why, I don't know. But it's always short of money, you know, uncle."

"I know it, son, I know it."

"You know people send mother writs, don't you, uncle?"

"I'm afraid I do," said the uncle.

"And then the house whispers, like people laughing at you behind your back. It's awful, that is! I thought if I was lucky——"

"You might stop it," added the uncle.

The boy watched him with big blue eyes, that had an uncanny cold fire in them, and he said never a word.

"Well, then!" said the uncle. "What are we doing?"

"I shouldn't like mother to know I was lucky," said the boy.

"Why not, son?"

"She'd stop me."

"I don't think she would."

"Oh!"—and the boy writhed in an odd way—"I *don't* want her to know, uncle."

"All right, son! We'll manage it without her knowing."

They managed it very easily. Paul, at the other's suggestion, handed over five thousand pounds to his uncle, who deposited it with the family lawyer, who was then to inform Paul's mother that a relative had put five thousand pounds into his hands, which sum was to be paid out a thousand pounds at a time, on the mother's birthday, for the next five years.

"So she'll have a birthday present of a thousand pounds for five successive years," said Uncle Oscar. "I hope it won't make it all the harder for her later."

Paul's mother had her birthday in November. The house had been "whispering" worse than ever lately, and, even in spite of his luck, Paul could not bear up against it. He was very anxious to see the effect of the birthday letter, telling his mother about the thousand pounds.

When there were no visitors, Paul now took his meals with his parents, as he was beyond the nursery control. His mother went into town nearly every day. She had discovered that she had an odd knack of sketching furs and dress materials, so she worked secretly in the studio of a friend who was the chief "artist" for the leading drapers. She drew the figures of ladies in furs and ladies in silk and sequins for the newspaper advertisements. This young woman artist earned several thousand pounds a year, but Paul's mother only made several hundreds, and she was again dissatisfied. She so wanted to be first in something, and she did not succeed, even in making sketches for drapery advertisements.

She was down to breakfast on the morning of her birthday. Paul watched her face as she read her letters. He knew the lawyer's letter. As his mother read it, her face hardened and became more expressionless. Then a cold, determined look came on her mouth. She hid the letter under the pile of others, and said not a word about it.

"Didn't you have anything nice in the post for your birthday, mother?" said Paul.

"Quite moderately nice," she said, her voice cold and absent.

She went away to town without saying more.

But in the afternoon Uncle Oscar appeared. He said Paul's mother had had a long interview with the lawyer, asking if the whole five thousand could not be advanced at once, as she was in debt.

"What do you think, uncle?" said the boy.

"I leave it to you, son."

"Oh, let her have it, then! We can get some more with the other," said the boy.

"A bird in the hand is worth two in the bush, laddie!" said Uncle Oscar.

"But I'm sure to *know* for the Grand National; or the Lincolnshire; or else the Derby. I'm sure to know for *one* of them," said Paul.

So Uncle Oscar signed the agreement, and Paul's mother touched the whole five thousand. Then something very curious happened. The voices in the house suddenly went mad, like a chorus of frogs on a spring evening. There were certain new furnishings, and Paul had a tutor. He was *really* going to Eton, his father's school, in the following autumn. There were flowers in the winter, and a blossoming of the luxury Paul's mother had been used to. And yet the voices in the house, behind the sprays of mimosa and almondblossom, and from under the piles of iridescent cushions, simply trilled and screamed in a sort of ecstasy: "There *must* be more money! Oh-h-h; there *must* be more money. Oh, now, now-w! Now-w-w—there *must* be more money!—more than ever! More than ever!"

It frightened Paul terribly. He studied away at his Latin and Greek with his tutor. But his intense hours were spent with Bassett. The Grand National had gone by: he had not "known," and had lost a hundred pounds. Summer was at hand. He was in agony for the Lincoln. But even for the Lincoln he didn't "know," and he lost fifty pounds. He became wild-eyed and strange, as if something were going to explode in him.

"Let it alone, son! Don't you bother about it!" urged Uncle Oscar. But it was as if the boy couldn't really hear what his uncle was saying.

"I've got to know for the Derby! I've got to know for the Derby!" the child reiterated, his big blue eyes blazing with a sort of madness.

His mother noticed how overwrought he was.

"You'd better go to the seaside. Wouldn't you like to go now to the seaside, instead of waiting? I think you'd better," she said, looking down at him anxiously, her heart curiously heavy because of him.

But the child lifted his uncanny blue eyes.

"I couldn't possibly go before the Derby, mother!" he said. "I couldn't possibly!"

"Why not?" she said, her voice becoming heavy when she was opposed. "Why not? You can still go from the seaside to see the Derby with your Uncle Oscar, if that's what you wish. No need for you to wait here. Besides, I think you care too much about these races. It's a bad sign. My family has been a gambling family, and you won't know till you grow up how much damage it has done. But it has done damage. I shall have to send Bassett away, and ask Uncle Oscar not to talk racing to you, unless you promise to be reasonable about it: go away to the seaside and forget it. You're all nerves!"

"I'll do what you like, mother, so long as you don't send me away till after the Derby," the boy said.

"Send you away from where? Just from this house?"

"Yes," he said, gazing at her.

"Why, you curious child, what makes you care about this house so much, suddenly? I never knew you loved it."

He gazed at her without speaking. He had a secret within a secret, something he had not divulged, even to Bassett or to his Uncle Oscar.

But his mother, after standing undecided and a little bit sullen for some moments, said:

"Very well, then! Don't go to the seaside till after the Derby, if you don't wish it. But promise me you won't let your nerves go to pieces. Promise you won't think so much about horse-racing and *events,* as you call them!"

"Oh no," said the boy casually. "I won't think much about them, mother. You needn't worry. I wouldn't worry, mother, if I were you."

"If you were me and I were you," said his mother, "I wonder what we *should* do!"

"But you know you needn't worry, mother, don't you?" the boy repeated.

"I should be awfully glad to know it," she said wearily.

"Oh, well, you *can,* you know. I mean, you *ought* to know you needn't worry," he insisted.

"Ought I? Then I'll see about it," she said.

Paul's secret of secrets was his wooden horse, that which had no name. Since he was emancipated from a nurse and a nursery-governess, he had had his rocking-horse removed to his own bedroom at the top of the house.

"Surely you're too big for a rocking-horse!" his mother had remonstrated.

"Well, you see, mother, till I can have a *real* horse, I like to have *some* sort of animal about," had been his quaint answer.

"Do you feel he keeps you company?" she laughed.

"Oh yes! He's very good, he always keeps me company, when I'm there," said Paul.

So the horse, rather shabby, stood in an arrested prance in the boy's bedroom.

The Derby was drawing near, and the boy grew more and more tense. He hardly heard what was spoken to him, he was very frail, and his eyes were really uncanny. His mother had sudden strange seizures of uneasiness about him. Sometimes, for half an hour, she would feel a sudden anxiety about him that was almost anguish. She wanted to rush to him at once, and know he was safe.

Two nights before the Derby, she was at a big party in town, when one of her rushes of anxiety about her boy, her first-born, gripped her heart till she could hardly speak. She fought with the feeling, might and main, for she believed in common sense. But it was too strong. She had to leave the dance and go downstairs to telephone to the country. The children's nursery-governess was terribly surprised and startled at being rung up in the night.

"Are the children all right, Miss Wilmot?"

"Oh yes, they are quite all right."

"Master Paul? Is he all right?"

"He went to bed as right as a trivet. Shall I run up and look at him?"

"No," said Paul's mother reluctantly. "No! Don't trouble. It's all right. Don't sit up. We shall be home fairly soon." She did not want her son's privacy intruded upon.

"Very good," said the governess.

It was about one o'clock when Paul's mother and father drove up to their house. All was still. Paul's mother went to her room and slipped off her white fur cloak. She had told her maid not to wait up for her. She heard her husband downstairs, mixing a whisky and soda.

And then, because of the strange anxiety at her heart, she stole upstairs to her son's room. Noiselessly she went along the upper corridor. Was there a faint noise? What was it?

She stood, with arrested muscles, outside his door, listening. There was a strange, heavy, and yet not loud noise. Her heart stood still. It was a soundless noise, yet rushing and powerful. Something huge, in violent, hushed motion. What was it? What in God's name was it? She ought to know. She felt that she knew the noise. She knew what it was.

Yet she could not place it. She couldn't say what it was. And on and on it went, like a madness.

Softly, frozen with anxiety and fear, she turned the doorhandle.

The room was dark. Yet in the space near the window, she heard and saw something plunging to and fro. She gazed in fear and amazement.

Then suddenly she switched on the light, and saw her son, in his green pyjamas, madly surging on the rocking-horse. The blaze of light suddenly lit him up, as he urged the wooden horse, and lit her up, as she stood, blonde, in her dress of pale green and crystal, in the doorway.

"Paul!" she cried. "Whatever are you doing?"

"It's Malabar!" he screamed in a powerful, strange voice. "It's Malabar!"

His eyes blazed at her for one strange and senseless second, as he ceased urging his wooden horse. Then he fell with a crash to the ground, and she, all her tormented motherhood flooding upon her, rushed to gather him up.

But he was unconscious, and unconscious he remained, with some brain-fever. He talked and tossed, and his mother sat stonily by his side.

"Malabar! It's Malabar! Bassett, Bassett, I *know*! It's Malabar!"

So the child cried, trying to get up and urge the rocking-horse that gave him his inspiration.

"What does he mean by Malabar?" asked the heart-frozen mother.

"I don't know," said the father stonily.

"What does he mean by Malabar?" she asked her brother Oscar.

"It's one of the horses running for the Derby," was the answer.

And, in spite of himself, Oscar Cresswell spoke to Bassett, and himself put a thousand on Malabar: at fourteen to one.

The third day of the illness was critical: they were waiting for a change. The boy, with his rather long, curly hair, was tossing ceaselessly on the pillow. He neither slept nor regained consciousness, and his eyes were like blue stones. His mother sat, feeling her heart had gone, turned actually into a stone.

In the evening, Oscar Cresswell did not come, but Bassett sent a message, saying could he come up for one moment, just one moment? Paul's mother was very angry at the intrusion, but on second thoughts she agreed. The boy was the same. Perhaps Bassett might bring him to consciousness.

The gardener, a shortish fellow with a little brown moustache and sharp little brown eyes, tiptoed into the room, touched his imaginary cap to Paul's mother, and stole to the bedside, staring with glittering, smallish eyes at the tossing, dying child.

"Master Paul!" he whispered. "Master Paul! Malabar came in first all right, a clean win. I did as you told me. You've made over seventy thousand pounds, you have; you've got over eighty thousand. Malabar came in all right, Master Paul."

"Malabar! Malabar! Did I say Malabar, mother? Did I say Malabar? Do you think I'm lucky, mother? I knew Malabar, didn't I? Over eighty thousand pounds! I call that lucky, don't you, mother? Over eighty thousand pounds! I knew, didn't I know I knew? Malabar came in all right. If I ride my horse till I'm sure, then I tell you, Bassett, you can go as high as you like. Did you go for all you were worth, Bassett?"

"I went a thousand on it, Master Paul."

"I never told you, mother, that if I can ride my horse, and *get there*, then I'm absolutely sure—oh, absolutely! Mother, did I ever tell you? I *am* lucky!"

"No, you never did," said his mother.

But the boy died in the night.

And even as he lay dead, his mother heard her brother's voice saying to her: "My God, Hester, you're eighty-odd thousand to the good, and a poor devil of a son to the bad. But, poor devil, poor devil, he's best gone out of a life where he rides his rocking-horse to find a winner."

ELIZABETH BOWEN
1899–1973

The only child of Henry and Isabel Bowen, of County Cork, Ireland, she was raised at the family mansion, Bowen's Court, in Ireland, until her father went insane, when she moved, with her mother, to East Kent, England. From childhood on she was handicapped by a pronounced stammer. She went to school at Downe House in Westerham (West Kent), where she was quite happy. She began writing fiction early, publishing her first collection of stories in 1923, the year in which she married. She traveled in Europe and America, building a reputation for sensitive, witty fiction with novels like *The House in Paris* (1938) and *The Death of the Heart* (1938) and stories, sometimes with a touch of the supernatural like those in *The Demon Lover* collection of 1945.

The Demon Lover

Towards the end of her day in London Mrs. Drover went round to her shut-up house to look for several things she wanted to take away. Some belonged to herself, some to her family, who were by now used to their country life. It was late August; it had been a steamy, showery day: at the moment the trees down the pavement glittered in an escape of humid yellow afternoon sun. Against the next batch of clouds, already piling up ink-dark, broken chimneys and parapets stood out. In her once familiar street, as in any unused channel, an unfamiliar queerness had silted up; a cat wove itself in and out of railings, but no human eye watched Mrs. Drover's return. Shifting some parcels under her arm, she slowly forced round her latchkey in an unwilling lock, then gave the door, which had warped, a push with her knee. Dead air came out to meet her as she went in.

The staircase window having been boarded up, no light came down into the hall. But one door, she could just see, stood ajar, so she went quickly through into the room and unshuttered the big window in there. Now the prosaic woman, looking about her, was more perplexed than she knew by everything that she saw, by traces of her long former habit of life—the yellow smoke-stain up the white marble mantelpiece, the ring left by a vase on the top of the escritoire; the bruise in the wallpaper where, on the door being thrown open widely, the china handle had always hit the wall. The piano, having gone away to be stored, had left what looked like claw-marks on its part of the parquet. Though not much dust had seeped in, each object wore a film of another kind; and, the only ventilation being the chimney, the whole drawing-room smelled of the cold hearth. Mrs. Drover put down her parcels on the escritoire and left the room to proceed upstairs; the things she wanted were in a bedroom chest.

She had been anxious to see how the house was—the part-time caretaker she shared with some neighbours was away this week on his holiday, known to be not yet back. At the best of times he did not look in often, and she was never sure that she trusted him. There were some cracks in the structure, left by the last bombing, on which she was anxious to keep an eye. Not that one could do anything—

A shaft of refracted daylight now lay across the hall. She stopped dead and stared at the hall table—on this lay a letter addressed to her.

She thought first—then the caretaker *must* be back. All the same, who, seeing the house shuttered, would have dropped a letter in at the box? It was not a circular, it was not a bill. And the post office redirected, to the address in the country, everything for her that came through the post. The caretaker (even if he *were* back) did not know she was due in London to-day—her call here had been planned to be a surprise—so his negligence in the manner of this letter, leaving it to wait in the dusk and the dust, annoyed her. Annoyed, she picked up the letter, which bore no stamp. But it cannot be important, or they would know . . . She took the letter rapidly upstairs with her, without a stop to look at the writing till she reached what had been her bedroom, where she let in light. The room looked over the garden and other gardens: the sun had gone in; as the clouds sharpened and lowered, the trees and rank lawns seemed already to smoke with dark. Her reluctance to look again at the letter came from the fact that she felt intruded upon—and by someone contemptuous of her ways. However, in the tenseness preceding the fall of rain she read it: it was a few lines.

> Dear Kathleen,
> You will not have forgotten that to-day is our anniversary, and the day we said. The years have gone by at once slowly and fast. In view of the fact that nothing has changed, I shall rely upon you to keep your promise. I was sorry to see you leave London, but was satisfied that you would be back in time. You may expect me, therefore, at the hour arranged.
>
> Until then . . .
>
> K.

Mrs. Drover looked for the date: it was to-day's. She dropped the letter on to the bed-springs, then picked it up to see the writing again—her lips, beneath the remains of lipstick, beginning to go white. She felt so much the change in her own face that she went to the mirror, polished a clear patch in it and looked at once urgently and stealthily in. She was confronted by a woman of forty-four, with eyes starting out under a hat-brim that had been rather carelessly pulled down. She had not put on any more powder since she left the shop where she ate her solitary tea. The pearls her husband had given her on their marriage hung loose round her now rather thinner throat, slipping into the V of the pink wool jumper her sister knitted last autumn as they sat round the fire. Mrs. Drover's most normal expression was one of controlled worry, but of assent. Since the birth of the third of her little boys, attended by a quite serious illness, she had had an intermittent muscular flicker to the left of her mouth, but in spite of this she could always sustain a manner that was at once energetic and calm.

Turning from her own face as precipitately as she had gone to meet it, she went to the chest where the things were, unlocked it, threw up the lid and knelt to search. But as rain began to come crashing down she could not keep from looking over her shoulder at the stripped bed on which the letter lay. Behind the blanket of rain the clock of the church that still stood struck six—with rapidly heightening apprehension, she counted each of the slow strokes. "The hour arranged . . . My God," she said, "*what* hour? How should I . . . ? After twenty-five years. . . ."

The young girl talking to the soldier in the garden had not ever completely seen his face. It was dark; they were saying good-bye under a tree. Now and then—for it felt, from not seeing him at this intense moment, as though she had never seen him at all—she verified his presence for these few moments longer by putting out a hand, which he each time pressed, without very much kindness, and painfully, on to one of the breast buttons of his uniform. That cut of the button on the palm of her hand was, principally, what she was to carry away. This was so near the end of a leave from France that she could only wish him already gone. It was August 1916. Being not kissed, being drawn away from and looked at intimidated Kathleen till she imagined spectral glitters in the place of his eyes. Turning away and looking back up the lawn she saw, through branches of trees, the drawing-room window alight: she caught a breath for the moment when she could go running back there into the safe arms of her mother and sister, and cry: "What shall I do, what shall I do? He has gone."

Hearing her catch her breath, her fiancé said, without feeling: "Cold?"

"You're going away such a long way."

"Not so far as you think."

"I don't understand?"

"You don't have to," he said. "You will. You know what we said."

"But that was—suppose you—I mean, suppose."

"I shall be with you," he said, "sooner or later. You won't forget that. You need do nothing but wait."

Only a little more than a minute later she was free to run up the silent lawn. Looking in through the window at her mother and sister, who did not for the moment perceive her, she already felt that unnatural promise drive down between her and the rest of all human kind. No other way of having given herself could have made her feel so apart, lost and foresworn. She could not have plighted a more sinister troth.

Kathleen behaved well when, some months later, her fiancé was reported missing, presumed killed. Her family not only supported her but were able to praise her courage without stint because they could not regret, as a husband for her, the man they knew almost nothing about. They hoped she would, in a year or two, console herself—and had it been only a question of consolation things might have gone much straighter ahead. But her trouble, behind just a little grief, was a complete dislocation from everything. She did not reject other lovers, for these failed to appear: for years she failed to attract men—and with the approach of her thirties she became natural enough to share her family's anxiousness on this score. She began to put herself out, to wonder; and at thirty-two she was very greatly relieved to find herself being courted by William Drover. She married him, and the two of them settled down in this quiet, arboreal part of Kensington: in this house the years piled up, her children were born and they all lived till they were driven out by the bombs of the next war. Her movements as Mrs. Drover were circumscribed, and she dismissed any idea that they were still watched.

As things were—dead or living the letter-writer sent her only a threat. Unable, for some minutes, to go on kneeling with her back exposed to the empty room, Mrs. Drover rose from the chest to sit on an upright chair whose back was firmly against the wall. The desuetude of her former bedroom, her married London home's whole air of being a cracked cup from which memory, with its reassuring power, had either evaporated or leaked away, made a crisis—and at just this crisis the letter-writer had, knowledgeably, struck. The hollowness of the house this evening cancelled years on years of voices, habits and steps. Through the shut windows she only heard rain fall on the roofs around. To rally herself, she said she was in a mood—and, for two or three seconds shutting her eyes, told herself that she had imagined the letter. But she opened them—there it lay on the bed.

On the supernatural side of the letter's entrance she was not permitting her mind to dwell. Who, in London, knew she meant to call at the house to-day? Evidently, however, this had been known. The caretaker, *had* he come back, had had no cause to expect her: he would have taken the letter in his pocket, to forward it, at his own time, through the post. There was no other sign that the caretaker had been in—but, if not? Letters dropped in at doors of deserted houses do not fly or walk to tables in halls. They do not sit on the dust of empty tables with the air of certainty that they will be found. There is needed some human hand—but nobody but the caretaker had a key. Under circumstances she did not care to consider, a house can be entered without a key. It was possible that she was not alone now. She might be being waited for, downstairs. Waited for—until when? Until "the hour arranged." At least that was not six o'clock: six has struck.

She rose from the chair and went over and locked the door.

The thing was, to get out. To fly? No, not that: she had to catch her train. As a woman whose utter dependability was the keystone of her family life she was not willing to return to the country, to her husband, her little boys and her sister, without the objects she had come up to fetch. Resuming work at the chest she set about making up a number of parcels in a rapid, fumbling-decisive way. These, with her shopping parcels, would be too much to carry; these meant a taxi—at the thought of the taxi her heart went up and her normal breathing resumed. I will ring up the taxi now; the taxi cannot come too soon: I shall hear the taxi out there running its engine, till I walk calmly down to it through the hall. I'll ring up—But no: the telephone is cut off . . . She tugged at a knot she had tied wrong.

The idea of flight . . . He was never kind to me, not really. I don't remember him kind at all. Mother said he never considered me. He was set on me, that was what it was—not love. Not love, not meaning a person well. What did he do, to make me promise like that? I can't remember— But she found that she could.

She remembered with such dreadful acuteness that the twenty-five years since then dissolved like smoke and she instinctively looked for the weal left by the button on the palm of her hand. She remembered not only all that he said and did but the complete suspension of *her* existence during that August week. I was not myself—they all told me so at the time. She remembered—but with one white burning blank as where acid has dropped on a photograph: *under no conditions* could she remember his face.

So, wherever he may be waiting, I shall not know him. You have no time to run from a face you do not expect.

The thing was to get to the taxi before any clock struck what could be the hour. She would slip down the street and round the side of the square to where the square gave on the main road. She would return in the taxi, safe, to her own door, and bring the solid driver into the house with her to pick up the parcels from room to room. The idea of the taxi driver made her decisive, bold: she unlocked her door, went to the top of the staircase and listened down.

She heard nothing—but while she was hearing nothing the *passé* air of the staircase was disturbed by a draught that travelled up to her face. It emanated from the basement: down there a door or window was being opened by someone who chose this moment to leave the house.

The rain had stopped; the pavements steamily shone as Mrs. Drover let herself out by inches from her own front door into the empty street. The unoccupied houses opposite continued to meet her look with their damaged stare. Making towards the thoroughfare and the taxi, she tried not to keep looking behind. Indeed, the silence was so intense—one of those creeks of London silence exaggerated this summer by the damage of war—that no tread could have gained on hers unheard. Where her street debouched on the square where people went on living she grew conscious of and checked her unnatural pace. Across the open end of the square two buses impassively passed each other; women, a perambulator, cyclists, a man wheeling a barrow signalized, once again, the ordinary flow of life. At the square's most populous corner should be—and was—the short taxi rank. This evening, only one taxi—but this, although it presented its blank rump, appeared already to be alertly waiting for her. Indeed, without looking round the driver started his engine as she panted up from behind and put her hand on the door. As she did so, the clock struck seven. The taxi faced the main road: to make the trip back to her house it would have to turn—she had settled back on the seat and the taxi *had* turned before she, surprised by its knowing movement, recollected that she had not "said where." She leaned forward to scratch at the glass panel that divided the driver's head from her own.

The driver braked to what was almost a stop, turned round and slid the glass panel back: the jolt of this flung Mrs. Drover forward till her face was almost into the glass. Through the aperture driver and passenger, not six inches between them, remained for an eternity eye to eye. Mrs. Drover's mouth hung open for some seconds before she could issue her first scream. After that she continued to scream freely and to beat with her gloved hands on the glass all round at the taxi, accelerating without mercy, made off with her into the hinterland of deserted streets.

JORGE LUIS BORGES

1899–

Borges (pronounced Bor'hace) was born in the heart of Buenos Aires, Argentina, where his father was a lawyer and a teacher of psychology. Borges's grandmother was English and this language was much used in the family, so that most of his early reading was in English. He began writing in Spanish and English when he was six, and had a translation of an Oscar Wilde story published in a Buenos Aires newspaper when he was nine, after which he began to go to school. When he was fifteen his family moved to Switzerland, where he studied at the college founded by John Calvin. Here all his classes were in French and the most important subject was Latin. On his own, he studied German and Italian. He was always destined to be a writer, it seems, and his love of languages was a part of his equipment. After a stay in Spain, where he wrote political poems and essays which he destroyed before leaving, he returned to Buenos Aires in 1921. He has been called a leader of the "ultraist" movement in Hispanic literature, but he says now that ultraism was obsessed with modernity and gadgets. He regrets his brief flirtation with it. Back in Buenos Aires he began to write the plainer poems and the philosophical fables that have made him famous. He has since lived a quiet life as a librarian (except for a time when dictator Perón made him a chicken inspector) and teacher of Old English literature, with his eyesight failing and his reputation growing.

The Lottery in Babylon

Like all men in Babylon, I have been proconsul; like all, a slave. I have also known omnipotence, opprobrium, imprisonment. Look: the index finger on my right hand is missing. Look: through the rip in my cape you can see a vermilion tatoo on my stomach. It is the second symbol, Beth. This letter, on nights when the moon is full, gives me power over men whose mark is Gimmel, but it subordinates me to the men of Aleph, who on moonless nights owe obedience to those marked with Gimmel. In the half light of dawn, in a cellar, I have cut the jugular vein of sacred bulls before a black stone. During a lunar year I have been declared invisible. I shouted and they did not answer me; I stole bread and they did not behead me. I have known what the Greeks do not know, incertitude. In a bronze chamber, before the silent handkerchief of the strangler, hope has been faithful to me, as has panic in the river of pleasure. Heraclides Ponticus tells with amazement that Pythagoras remembered having been Pyrrhus and before that Euphorbus and before that some other mortal. In order to

Translated by John M. Fein.

remember similar vicissitudes I do not need to have recourse to death or even to deception.

I owe this almost atrocious variety to an institution which other republics do not know or which operates in them in an imperfect and secret manner: the lottery. I have not looked into its history; I know that the wise men cannot agree. I know of its powerful purposes what a man who is not versed in astrology can know about the moon. I come from a dizzy land where the lottery is the basis of reality. Until today I have thought as little about it as I have about the conduct of indecipherable divinities or about my heart. Now, far from Babylon and its beloved customs, I think with a certain amount of amazement about the lottery and about the blasphemous conjectures which veiled men murmur in the twilight.

My father used to say that formerly—a matter of centuries, of years?—the lottery in Babylon was a game of plebeian character. He recounted (I don't know whether rightly) that barbers sold, in exchange for copper coins, squares of bone or of parchment adorned with symbols. In broad daylight a drawing took place. Those who won received silver coins without any other test of luck. The system was elementary, as you can see.

Naturally these "lotteries" failed. Their moral virtue was nil. They were not directed at all of man's faculties, but only at hope. In the face of public indifference, the merchants who founded these venal lotteries began to lose money. Someone tried a reform: The interpolation of a few unfavorable tickets in the list of favorable numbers. By means of this reform, the buyers of numbered squares ran the double risk of winning a sum and of paying a fine that could be considerable. This slight danger (for every thirty favorable numbers there was one unlucky one) awoke, as is natural, the interest of the public. The Babylonians threw themselves into the game. Those who did not acquire chances were considered pusillanimous, cowardly. In time, that justified disdain was doubled. Those who did not play were scorned, but also the losers who paid the fine were scorned. The Company (as it came to be known then) had to take care of the winners, who could not cash in their prizes if almost the total amount of the fines was unpaid. It started a lawsuit against the losers. The judge condemned them to pay the original fine and costs or spend several days in jail. All chose jail in order to defraud the Company. The bravado of a few is the source of the omnipotence of the Company and of its metaphysical and ecclesiastical power.

A little while afterward the lottery lists omitted the amounts of fines and limited themselves to publishing the days of imprisonment that each unfavorable number indicated. That laconic spirit, almost unnoticed at the time, was of capital importance. *It was the first appearance in the lottery of nonmonetary elements.* The success was tremendous. Urged by the clientele, the Company was obliged to increase the unfavorable numbers.

Everyone knows that the people of Babylon are fond of logic and even of symmetry. It was illogical for the lucky numbers to be computed in round coins and the unlucky ones in days and nights of imprisonment. Some moralists reasoned that the possession of money does not always determine happiness and that other forms of happiness are perhaps more direct.

Another concern swept the quarters of the poorer classes. The members of the college of priests multiplied their stakes and enjoyed all the vicissitudes of terror and hope; the poor (with reasonable or unavoidable envy) knew that they were excluded from that notoriously delicious rhythm. The just desire that all, rich and poor, should participate equally in the lottery, inspired an indignant agitation, the memory of which the years have not erased. Some obstinate people did not understand (or pretended not to understand) that it was a question of a new order, of a necessary historical stage. A slave stole a crimson ticket, which in the drawing credited him with the burning of his tongue. The legal code fixed that same penalty for the one who stole a ticket. Some Babylonians argued that he deserved the burning irons in his status of a thief; others, generously, that the executioner should apply it to him because chance had determined it that way. There were disturbances, there were lamentable drawings of blood, but the masses of Babylon finally imposed their will against the opposition of the rich. The people achieved amply its generous purposes. In the first place, it caused the Company to accept total power. (That unification was necessary, given the vastness and complexity of the new operations.) In the second place, it made the lottery secret, free and general. The mercenary sale of chances was abolished. Once initiated in the mysteries of Baal, every free man automatically participated in the sacred drawings, which took place in the labyrinths of the god every sixty nights and which determined his destiny until the next drawing. The consequences were incalculable. A fortunate play could bring about his promotion to the council of wise men or the imprisonment of an enemy (public or private) or finding, in the peaceful darkness of his room, the woman who begins to excite him and whom he never expected to see again. A bad play: mutilation, different kinds of infamy, death. At times one single fact—the vulgar murder of C, the mysterious apotheosis of B—was the happy solution of thirty or forty drawings. To combine the plays was difficult, but one must remember that the individuals of the Company were (and are) omnipotent and astute. In many cases the knowledge that certain happinesses were the simple product of chance would have diminished their virtue. To avoid that obstacle, the agents of the Company made use of the power of suggestion and magic. Their steps, their maneuverings, were secret. To find out about the intimate hopes and terrors of each individual, they had astrologers and spies. There were certain stone lions, there was a sacred latrine called Qaphqa, there were fissures in a dusty aqueduct which, according to general opinion, *led to the Company*; malignant or benevolent persons deposited information in these places. An alphabetical file collected these items of varying truthfulness.

Incredibly, there were complaints. The Company, with its usual discretion, did not answer directly. It preferred to scrawl in the rubbish of a mask factory a brief statement which now figures in the sacred scriptures. This doctrinal item observed that the lottery is an interpolation of chance in the order of the world and that to accept errors is not to contradict chance: it is to corroborate it. It likewise observed that those lions and that sacred receptacle, although not disavowed by the Company (which did not abandon the right to consult them), functioned without official guarantee.

This declaration pacified the public's restlessness. It also produced other effects, perhaps unforeseen by its writer. It deeply modified the spirit and the operations of the Company. I don't have much time left; they tell us that the ship is about to weigh anchor. But I shall try to explain it.

However unlikely it might seem, no one had tried out before then a general theory of chance. Babylonians are not very speculative. They revere the judgments of fate, they deliver to them their lives, their hopes, their panic, but it does not occur to them to investigate fate's labyrinthine laws nor the gyratory spheres which reveal it. Nevertheless, the *unofficial* declaration that I have mentioned inspired many discussions of judicial-mathematical character. From some one of them the following conjecture was born: if the lottery is an intensification of chance, a periodical infusion of chaos in the cosmos, would it not be right for chance to intervene in all stages of the drawing and not in one alone? Is it not ridiculous for chance to dictate someone's death and have the circumstances of that death—secrecy, publicity, the fixed time of an hour or a century—not subject to chance? These just scruples finally caused a considerable reform, whose complexities (aggravated by centuries' practice) only a few specialists understand, but which I shall try to summarize, at least in a symbolic way.

Let us imagine a first drawing, which decrees the death of a man. For its fulfillment one proceeds to another drawing, which proposes (let us say) nine possible executors. Of these executors, four can initiate a third drawing which will tell the name of the executioner, two can replace the adverse order with a fortunate one (finding a treasure, let us say), another will intensify the death penalty (that is, will make it infamous or enrich it with tortures), others can refuse to fulfill it. This is the symbolic scheme. In reality *the number of drawings is infinite*. No decision is final, all branch into others. Ignorant people suppose that infinite drawings require an infinite time; actually it is sufficient for time to be infinitely subdivisible, as the famous parable of the contest with the tortoise teaches. This infinity harmonizes admirably with the sinuous numbers of Chance and with the Celestial Archetype of the Lottery, which the Platonists adore. Some warped echo of our rites seems to have resounded on the Tiber: Ellus Lampridius, in the *Life of Antoninus Heliogabalus*, tells that this emperor wrote on shells the lots that were destined for his guests, so that one received ten pounds of gold and another ten flies, ten dormice, ten bears. It is permissible to recall that Heliogabalus was brought up in Asia Minor, among the priests of the eponymous god.

There are also impersonal drawings, with an indefinite purpose. One decrees that a sapphire of Taprobana be thrown into the waters of the Euphrates; another, that a bird be released from the roof of a tower; another, that each century there be withdrawn (or added) a grain of sand from the innumerable ones on the beach. The consequences are, at times, terrible.

Under the beneficent influence of the Company, our customs are saturated with chance. The buyer of a dozen amphoras of Damascene wine will not be surprised if one of them contains a talisman or a snake. The scribe who writes a contract almost never fails to introduce some erroneous information. I myself, in this hasty declaration, have falsified some splendor, some atrocity. Perhaps, also, some mysterious monotony . . . Our historians, who are the most penetrating on the globe, have invented a method to correct chance. It is well known that the operations of this method are (in general) reliable, although, naturally, they are not divulged without some portion of deceit. Furthermore, there is nothing so contaminated with fiction as the history of the Company. A paleographic document, exhumed in a temple, can be the result of yesterday's lottery or of an age-old lottery. No book is published without some discrepany in each one of the copies. Scribes take a secret oath to omit, to interpolate, to change. The indirect lie is also cultivated.

The Company, with divine modesty, avoids all publicity. Its agents, as is natural, are secret. The orders which it issues continually (perhaps incessantly) do not differ from those lavished by imposters. Moreover, who can brag about being a mere imposter? The drunkard who improvises an absurd order, the dreamer who awakens suddenly and strangles the woman who sleeps at his side, do they not execute, perhaps, a secret decision of the Company? That silent functioning, comparable to God's, gives rise to all sorts of conjectures. One abominably insinuates that the Company has not existed for centuries and that the sacred disorder of our lives is purely hereditary, traditional. Another judges it eternal and teaches that it will last until the last night, when the last god annihilates the world. Another declares that the Company is omnipotent, but that it only has influence in tiny things: in a bird's call, in the shadings of rust and of dust, in the half dreams of dawn. Another, in the words of masked heresiarchs, *that it has never existed and will not exist*. Another, no less vile, reasons that it is indifferent to affirm or deny the reality of the shadowy corporation, because Babylon is nothing else than an infinite game of chance.

BERNARD MALAMUD
1914–

A city boy, of Jewish background, Malamud was born and raised in Brooklyn, New York. He went to City College, for his B.A. and to Columbia University for his M.A. He taught in night school for almost ten years before taking a job at Oregon State University. His experiences in Oregon from 1949 to 1961 became the basis for his novel *A New Life* (1961). As a short story writer he has continued the tradition of Babel and Singer. Since 1961 he has taught at Bennington College in Vermont. Among his most admired works are a novel, *The Assistant* (1957), and the stories in *The Magic Barrel* (1958).

The Magic Barrel

Not long ago there lived in uptown New York, in a small, almost meager room, though crowded with books, Leo Finkle, a rabbinical student in the Yeshivah University. Finkle, after six years of study, was to be ordained in June and had been advised by an acquaintance that he might find it easier to win himself a congregation if he were married. Since he had no present prospects of marriage, after two tormented days of turning it over in his mind, he called in Pinye Salzman, a marriage broker whose two-line advertisement he had read in the *Forward*.

The matchmaker appeared one night out of the dark fourth-floor hallway of the graystone rooming house where Finkle lived, grasping a black, strapped portfolio that had been worn thin with use. Salzman, who had been long in the business, was of slight but dignified build, wearing an old hat, and an overcoat too short and tight for him. He smelled frankly of fish, which he loved to eat, and although he was missing a few teeth, his presence was not displeasing, because of an amiable manner curiously contrasted with mournful eyes. His voice, his lips, his wisp of beard, his bony fingers were animated, but give him a moment of repose and his mild blue eyes revealed a depth of sadness, a characteristic that put Leo a little at ease although the situation, for him, was inherently tense.

He at once informed Salzman why he had asked him to come, explaining that his home was in Cleveland, and that but for his parents, who had married comparatively late in life, he was alone in the world. He had for six years devoted himself almost entirely to his studies, as a result of which, understandably, he had found himself without time for a social life and the company of young women. Therefore he thought it the better part of trial and error—of embarrassing fumbling—to call in an experienced person to advise him on these matters. He remarked in passing that the function of the marriage broker was ancient and honorable, highly approved in the Jewish community, because it made practical the necessary without hindering joy. Moreover, his own parents had been brought together by a matchmaker. They had made, if not a financially profitable marriage—since neither had possessed any worldly goods to speak of—at least a successful one in the sense of their everlasting devotion to each other. Salzman listened in embarrassed surprise, sensing a sort of apology. Later, however, he experienced a glow of pride in his work, an emotion that had left him years ago, and he heartily approved of Finkle.

The two went to their business. Leo had led Salzman to the only clear place in the room, a table near a window that overlooked the lamp-lit city. He seated himself at the matchmaker's side but facing him, attempting by an act of will to suppress the unpleasant tickle in his throat. Salzman eagerly unstrapped his portfolio and removed a loose rubber band from a thin packet of much-handled cards. As he flipped through them, a gesture and sound that physically hurt Leo, the student pretended not to see and gazed steadfastly out the window. Although it was still February, winter was on its last legs, signs of which he had for the first time in years begun to notice. He now observed the round white moon, moving high in the sky through a cloud menagerie, and watched with half-open mouth as it penetrated a huge hen, and dropped out of her like an egg laying itself. Salzman, though pretending through eyeglasses he had just slipped on, to be engaged in scanning the writing on the cards, stole occasional glances at the young man's distinguished face, noting with pleasure the long, severe scholar's nose, brown eyes heavy with learning, sensitive yet ascetic lips, and a certain, almost hollow quality of the dark cheeks. He gazed around at shelves upon shelves of books and let out a soft, contented sigh.

When Leo's eyes fell upon the cards, he counted six spread out in Salzman's hand.

"So few?" he asked in disappointment.

"You wouldn't believe me how much cards I got in my office," Salzman replied. "The drawers are already filled to the top, so I keep them now in a barrel, but is every girl good for a new rabbi?"

Leo blushed at this, regretting all he had revealed of himself in a curriculum vitae he had sent to Salzman. He had thought it best to acquaint him with his strict standards and specifications, but in having done so, felt he had told the marriage broker more than was absolutely necessary.

He hesitantly inquired, "Do you keep photographs of your clients on file?"

"First comes family, amount of dowry, also what kind promises," Salzman replied, unbuttoning his tight coat and settling himself in the chair. "After comes pictures, rabbi."

"Call me Mr. Finkle. I'm not yet a rabbi."

Salzman said he would, but instead called him doctor, which he changed to rabbi when Leo was not listening too attentively.

Salzman adjusted his horn-rimmed spectacles, gently cleared his throat and read in an eager voice the contents of the top card:

"Sophie P. Twenty four years. Widow one year. No children. Educated high school and two years college. Father promises eight thousand dollars. Has wonderful wholesale business. Also real estate. On the mother's side comes teachers, also one actor. Well known on Second Avenue."

Leo gazed up in surprise. "Did you say a widow?"

"A widow don't mean spoiled, rabbi. She lived with her husband maybe four months. He was a sick boy she made a mistake to marry him."

"Marrying a widow has never entered my mind."

"This is because you have no experience. A widow, especially if she is young and healthy like this girl, is a wonderful person to marry. She will be thankful to you the rest of her life. Believe me, if I was looking now for a bride, I would marry a widow."

Leo reflected, then shook his head.

Salzman hunched his shoulders in an almost imperceptible gesture of disappointment. He placed the card down on the wooden table and began to read another:

"Lily H. High school teacher. Regular. Not a substitute. Has savings and new Dodge car. Lived in Paris one year. Father is successful dentist thirty-five years. Interested in professional man. Well Americanized family. Wonderful opportunity."

"I knew her personally," said Salzman. "I wish you could see this girl. She is a doll. Also very intelligent. All day you could talk to her about books and theyater and what not. She also knows current events."

"I don't believe you mentioned her age?"

"Her age?" Salzman said, raising his brows. "Her age is thirty-two years."

Leo said after a while, "I'm afraid that seems a little too old."

Salzman let out a laugh. "So how old are you, rabbi?"

"Twenty-seven."

"So what is the difference, tell me, between twenty-seven and thirty-two? My own wife is seven years older than me. So what did I suffer?—Nothing. If Rothschild's daughter wants to marry you, would you say on account her age, no?"

"Yes," Leo said dryly.

Salzman shook off the no in the yes. "Five years don't mean a thing. I give you my word that when you will live with her for one week you will forget her age. What does it mean five years—that she lived more and knows more than somebody who is younger? On this girl, God bless her, years are not wasted. Each one that it comes makes better the bargain."

"What subject does she teach in high school?"

"Languages. If you heard the way she speaks French, you will think it is music. I am in the business twenty-five years, and I recommend her with my whole heart. Believe me, I know what I'm talking, rabbi."

"What's on the next card?" Leo said abruptly.

Salzman reluctantly turned up the third card:

"Ruth K. Nineteen years. Honor student. Father offers thirteen thousand cash to the right bridegroom. He is a medical doctor. Stomach specialist with marvelous practice. Brother in law owns own garment business. Particular people."

Salzman looked as if he had read his trump card.

"Did you say nineteen?" Leo asked with interest.

"On the dot."

"Is she attractive?" He blushed. "Pretty?"

Salzman kissed his finger tips. "A little doll. On this I give you my word. Let me call the father tonight and you will see what means pretty."

But Leo was troubled. "You're sure she's that young?"

"This I am positive. The father will show you the birth certificate."

"Are you positive there isn't something wrong with her?" Leo insisted.

"Who says there is wrong?"

"I don't understand why an American girl her age should go to a marriage broker."

A smiled spread over Salzman's face.

"So for the same reason you went, she comes."

Leo flushed. "I am pressed for time."

Salzman, realizing he had been tactless, quickly explained. "The father came, not her. He wants she should have the best, so he looks around himself. When we will locate the right boy he will introduce him and encourage. This makes a better marriage than if a young girl without experience takes for herself. I don't have to tell you this."

"But don't you think this young girl believes in love?" Leo spoke uneasily.

Salzman was about to guffaw but caught himself and said soberly, "Love comes with the right person, not before."

Leo parted dry lips but did not speak. Noticing that Salzman had snatched a glance at the next card, he cleverly asked, "How is her health?"

"Perfect," Salzman said, breathing with difficulty. "Of course, she is a little lame on her right foot from an auto accident that it happened to her when she was twelve years, but nobody notices on account she is so brilliant and also beautiful."

Leo got up heavily and went to the window. He felt curiously bitter and upbraided himself for having called in the marriage broker. Finally, he shook his head.

"Why not?" Salzman persisted, the pitch of his voice rising.

"Because I detest stomach specialists."

"So what do you care what is his business? After you marry her do you need him? Who says he must come every Friday night in your house?"

Ashamed of the way the talk was going, Leo dismissed Salzman, who went home with heavy, melancholy eyes.

Though he had felt only relief at the marriage broker's departure, Leo was in low spirits the next day. He explained it as arising from Salzman's failure to produce a suitable bride for him. He did not care for his type of clientele. But when Leo found himself hesitating whether to seek out another matchmaker, one more polished than Pinye, he wondered if it could be—his protestations to the contrary, and although he honored his father and mother—that he did not, in essence, care for the matchmaking institution? This thought he quickly put out of mind yet found himself still upset. All day he ran around in the woods—missed an important appointment, forgot to give out his laundry, walked out of a Broadway cafeteria without paying and had to run back with the ticket in his hand; had even not recognized his landlady in the street when she passed with a friend and courteously called out, "A good evening to you, Doctor Finkle." By nightfall, however, he had regained sufficient calm to sink his nose into a book and there found peace from his thoughts.

Almost at once there came a knock on the door. Before Leo could say enter, Salzman, commercial cupid, was standing in the room. His face was gray and meager, his expression hungry, and he looked as if he would expire on his feet. Yet the marriage broker managed, by some trick of the muscles, to display a broad smile.

"So good evening. I am invited?"

Leo nodded, disturbed to see him again, yet unwilling to ask the man to leave.

Beaming still, Salzman laid his portfolio on the table. "Rabbi, I got for you tonight good news."

"I've asked you not to call me rabbi. I'm still a student."

"Your worries are finished. I have for you a first-class bride."

"Leave me in peace concerning this subject." Leo pretended lack of interest.

"The world will dance at your wedding."

"Please, Mr. Salzman, no more."

"But first must come back my strength," Salzman said weakly. He fumbled with the portfolio straps and took out of the leather case an oily paper bag, from which he extracted a hard, seeded roll and a small, smoked white fish. With a quick motion of his hand he stripped the fish out of its skin and began ravenously to chew. "All day in a rush," he muttered.

Leo watched him eat.

"A sliced tomato you have maybe?" Salzman hesitantly inquired.

"No."

The marriage broker shut his eyes and ate. When he had finished he carefully cleaned up the crumbs and rolled up the remains of the fish, in the paper bag. His spectacled eyes roamed the room until he discovered, amid some piles of books, a one-burner gas stove. Lifting his hat he humbly asked, "A glass tea you got, rabbi?"

Conscience-stricken, Leo rose and brewed the tea. He served it with a chunk of lemon and two cubes of lump sugar, delighting Salzman.

After he had drunk his tea, Salzman's strength and good spirits were restored.

"So tell me, rabbi," he said amiably, "you considered some more the three clients I mentioned yesterday?"

"There was no need to consider."

"Why not?"

"None of them suits me."

"What then suits you?"

Leo let it pass because he could give only a confused answer.

Without waiting for a reply, Salzman asked, "You remember this girl I talked to you—the high school teacher?"

"Age thirty-two?"

But, surprisingly, Salzman's face lit in a smile. "Age twenty-nine."

Leo shot him a look. "Reduced from thirty-two?"

"A mistake," Salzman avowed. "I talked today with the dentist. He took me to his safety deposit box and showed me the birth certificate. She was twenty-nine years last August. They made her a party in the mountains where she went for her vacation. When her father spoke to me the first time I forgot to write the age and I told you thirty-two, but now I remember this was a different client, a widow."

"The same one you told me about? I thought she was twenty-four?"

"A different. Am I responsible that the world is filled with widows?"

"No, but I'm not interested in them, nor for that matter, in school teachers."

Salzman pulled his clasped hands to his breast. Looking at the ceiling he devoutly exclaimed, "Yiddishe kinder, what can I say to somebody that he is not interested in high school teachers? So what then you are interested?"

Leo flushed but controlled himself.

"In what else will you be interested," Salzman went on, "if you not interested in this fine girl that she speaks four languages and has personally in the bank ten thousand dollars? Also her father guarantees further twelve thousand. Also she has a new car, wonderful clothes, talks on all subjects, and she will give you a first-class home and children. How near do we come in our life to paradise?"

"If she's so wonderful, why wasn't she married ten years ago?"

"Why?" said Salzman with a heavy laugh. "—Why? Because she is *partikiler*. This is why. She wants the *best*."

Leo was silent, amused at how he had entangled himself. But Salzman had aroused his interest in Lily H., and he began seriously to consider calling on her. When the marriage broker observed how intently Leo's mind was at work on the facts he had supplied, he felt certain they would soon come to an agreement.

Late Saturday afternoon, conscious of Salzman, Leo Finkle walked with Lily Hirschorn along Riverside Drive. He walked briskly and erectly, wearing with distinction the black fedora he had that morning taken with trepidation out of the dusty hat box on his closet shelf, and the heavy black Saturday coat he had thoroughly whisked clean. Leo also owned a walking stick, a present from a distant relative, but quickly put temptation aside and did not use it. Lily, petite and not unpretty, had on something signifying the approach of spring. She was au courant, animatedly, with all sorts of subjects, and he weighed her words and found her surprisingly sound—score another for Salzman, whom he uneasily sensed to be somewhere around, hiding perhaps high in a tree along the street, flashing the lady signals with a pocket mirror; or perhaps a cloven-hoofed Pan, piping nuptial ditties as he danced his invisible way before them, strewing wild buds on the walk and purple grapes in their path, symbolizing fruit of a union, though there was of course still none.

Lily startled Leo by remarking, "I was thinking of Mr. Salzman, a curious figure, wouldn't you say?"

Not certain what to answer, he nodded.

She bravely went on, blushing, "I for one am grateful for his introducing us. Aren't you?"

He courteously replied, "I am."

"I mean," she said with a little laugh—and it was all in good taste, or at least gave the effect of being not in bad—"do you mind that we came together so?"

He was not displeased with her honesty, recognizing that she meant to set the relationship aright, and understanding that it took a certain amount of experience in life, and courage, to want to do it quite that way. One had to have some sort of past to make that kind of beginning.

He said that he did not mind. Salzman's function was traditional and honorable—valuable for what it might achieve, which, he pointed out, was frequently nothing.

Lily agreed with a sigh. They walked on for a while and she said after a long silence, again with a nervous laugh, "Would you mind if I asked you something a little bit personal? Frankly, I find the subject fascinating." Although Leo shrugged, she went on half embarrassedly, "How was it that you came to your calling? I mean was it a sudden passionate inspiration?"

Leo after a time, slowly replied, "I was always interested in the Law."

"You saw revealed in it the presence of the Highest?"

He nodded and changed the subject. "I understand that you spent a little time in Paris, Miss Hirschorn?"

"Oh, did Mr. Salzman tell you, Rabbi Finkle?" Leo winced but she went on, "It was ages ago and almost forgotten. I remember I had to return for my sister's wedding."

And Lily would not be put off. "When," she asked in a trembly voice, "did you become enamored of God?"

He stared at her. Then it came to him that she was talking not about Leo Finkle, but of a total stranger, some mystical figure, perhaps even passionate prophet that Salzman had dreamed up for her—no relation to the living or dead. Leo trembled with rage and weakness. The trickster had obviously sold her a bill of goods, just as he had him, who'd expected to become acquainted with a young lady of twenty-nine, only to behold, the moment he laid eyes upon her strained and anxious face, a woman past thirty-five and aging rapidly. Only his self-control had kept him this long in her presence.

"I am not," he said gravely, "a talented religious person," and in seeking words to go on, found himself possessed by shame and fear. "I think," he said in a strained manner, "that I came to God not because I loved Him, but because I did not."

This confession he spoke harshly because its unexpectedness shook him.

Lily wilted. Leo saw a profusion of loaves of bread go flying like ducks high over his head, not unlike the winged loaves by which he had counted himself to sleep last night. Mercifully, then, it snowed, which he would not put past Salzman's machinations.

He was infuriated with the marriage broker and swore he would throw him out of the room the minute he reappeared. But Salzman did not come that night, and when Leo's anger had subsided, an unaccountable despair grew in its place. At first he thought this was caused by his disappointment in Lily, but before long it became evident that he had involved himself with Salzman without a true knowledge of his own intent. He gradually realized—with an empti-ness that seized him with six hands—that he had called in the broker to find him a bride because he was incapable of doing it himself. This terrifying insight he had derived as a result of his meeting and conversation with Lily Hirschorn. Her probing questions had some-how irritated him into revealing—to himself more than her—the true nature of his relationship to God, and from that it had come upon him, with shocking force, that apart from his parents, he had never loved anyone. Or perhaps it went the other way, that he did not love God so well as he might, because he had not loved man. It seemed to Leo that his whole life stood starkly revealed and he saw himself for the first time as he truly was—unloved and loveless. This bitter but somehow not fully unexpected revelation brought him to a point of panic, controlled only by extraordinary effort. He covered his face with his hands and cried.

The week that followed was the worst of his life. He did not eat and lost weight. His beard darkened and grew ragged. He stopped attending seminars and almost never opened a book. He seriously considered leaving the Yeshivah, although he was deeply troubled at the thought of the loss of all his years of study—saw them like pages torn from a book, strewn over the city—and at the devastating effect of this decision upon his parents. But he had lived without knowledge of himself, and never in the Five Books and all the Commentaries—mea culpa—had the truth been revealed to him. He did not know where to turn, and in all this desolating loneliness there was no *to whom*, although he often thought of Lily but not once could bring himself to go downstairs and make the call. He became touchy and irritable, especially with his landlady, who asked him all manner of personal questions; on the other hand, sensing his own disagreeableness, he waylaid her on the stairs and apologized abjectly, until mortified, she ran from him. Out of this, however, he drew the consolation that he was a Jew and that a Jew suffered. But gradually, as the long and terrible week drew to a close, he regained his composure and some idea of purpose in life: to go on as planned. Although he was imperfect, the ideal was not. As for his quest of a bride, the thought of continuing afflicted him with anxiety and heartburn, yet perhaps with this new knowledge of himself he would be more successful than in the past. Perhaps love would now come to him and a bride to that love. And for this sanctified seeking who needed a Salzman?

The marriage broker, a skeleton with haunted eyes, returned that very night. He looked, withal, the picture of frustrated expectancy—as if he had steadfastly waited the week at Miss Lily Hirschorn's side for a telephone call that never came.

Casually coughing, Salzman came immediately to the point: "So how did you like her?"

Leo's anger rose and he could not refrain from chiding the matchmaker: "Why did you lie to me, Salzman?"

Salzman's pale face went dead white, the world had snowed on him.

"Did you not state that she was twenty-nine?" Leo insisted.

"I give you my word—"

"She was thirty-five, if a day. *At least* thirty-five."

"Of this don't be too sure. Her father told me—"

"Never mind. The worst of it was that you lied to her."

"How did I lie to her, tell me?"

"You told her things about me that weren't true. You made me out to be more, consequently less than I am. She had in mind a totally different person, a sort of semi-mystical Wonder Rabbi."

"All I said, you was a religious man."

"I can imagine."

Salzman sighed. "This is my weakness that I have," he confessed. "My wife says to me I shouldn't be a salesman, but when I have two fine people that they would be wonderful to be married, I am so happy that I talk too much." He smiled wanly. "This is why Salzman is a poor man."

Leo's anger left him. "Well, Salzman, I'm afraid that's all."

The marriage broker fastened hungry eyes on him.

"You don't want any more a bride?"

"I do," said Leo, "but I have decided to seek her in a different way. I am no longer interested in an arranged marriage. To be frank, I now admit the necessity of premarital love. That is, I want to be in love with the one I marry."

"Love?" said Salzman, astounded. After a moment he remarked, "For us, our love is our life, not for the ladies. In the ghetto they—"

"I know, I know," said Leo. "I've thought of it often. Love, I have said to myself, should be a by-product of living and worship rather than its own end. Yet for myself I find it necessary to establish the level of my need and fulfill it."

Salzman shrugged but answered, "Listen, rabbi, if you want love, this I can find for you also. I have such beautiful clients that you will love them the minute your eyes will see them."

Leo smiled unhappily. "I'm afraid you don't understand."

But Salzman hastily unstrapped his portfolio and withdrew a manila packet from it.

"Pictures," he said, quickly laying the envelope on the table.

Leo called after him to take the pictures away, but as if on the wings of the wind, Salzman had disappeared.

March came. Leo had returned to his regular routine. Although he felt not quite himself yet—lacked energy—he was making plans for a more active social life. Of course it would cost something, but he was an expert in cutting corners; and when there was no corners left he would make circles rounder. All the while Salzman's pictures had lain on the table, gathering dust. Occasionally as Leo sat studying, or enjoying a cup of tea, his eyes fell on the manila envelope, but he never opened it.

The days went by and no social life to speak of developed with a member of the opposite sex—it was difficult, given the circumstances of his situation. One morning Leo toiled up the stairs to his room and stared out the window at the city. Although the day was bright his view of it was dark. For some time he watched the people in the street below hurrying along and then turned with a heavy heart to his little room. On the table was the packet. With a sudden relentless gesture he tore it open. For a half-hour he stood by the table in a state of excitement, examining the photographs of the ladies Salzman had included. Finally, with a deep sigh he put them down. There were six, of varying degrees of attractiveness, but look at them long enough and they all became Lily Hirschorn: all past their prime, all starved behind bright smiles, not a true personality in the lot. Life, despite their frantic yoohooings, had passed them by; they were pictures in a brief case that stank of fish. After a while, however, as Leo attempted to return the photographs into the envelope, he found in it another, a snapshot of the type taken by a machine for a quarter. He gazed at it a moment and let out a cry.

Her face deeply moved him. Why, he could at first not say. It gave him the impression of youth—spring flowers, yet age—a sense of having been used to the bone, wasted; this came from the eyes, which were hauntingly familiar, yet absolutely strange. He had a vivid impression that he had met her before, but try as he might he could not place her although he could almost recall her name, as if he had read it in her own handwriting. No, this couldn't be; he would have remembered her. It was not, he affirmed, that she had an extraordinary beauty—no, though her face was attractive enough; it was that *something* about her moved him. Feature for feature, even some of the ladies of the photographs could do better; but she leaped forth to his heart—had *lived*, or wanted to—more than just wanted, perhaps regretted how she had lived—had somehow deeply suffered: it could be seen in the depths of those reluctant eyes, and from the way the light enclosed and shone from her, and within her, opening realms of possibility: this was her own. Her he desired. His head ached and eyes narrowed with the intensity of his gazing, then as if an obscure fog had blown up in the mind, he experienced fear of her and was aware that he had received an impression, somehow, of evil. He shuddered, saying softly, it is thus with us all. Leo brewed some tea in a small pot and sat sipping it without sugar, to calm himself. But before he had finished drinking, again with excitement he examined the face and found it good: good for Leo Finkle. Only such a one could understand him and help him seek whatever he was seeking. She might, perhaps, love him. How she had happened to be among the discards in Salzman's barrel he could never guess, but he knew he must urgently go find her.

Leo rushed downstairs, grabbed up the Bronx telephone book, and searched for Salzman's home address. He was not listed, nor was his office. Neither was he in the Manhattan book. But Leo remembered having written down the address on a slip of paper after he had read Salzman's advertisement in the "personals" column of the *Forward*. He ran up to his room and tore through his papers, without luck. It was exasperating. Just when he needed the matchmaker he was nowhere to be found. Fortunately Leo remembered to look in his wallet. There on a card he found his name written and a Bronx address. No phone number was listed, the reason—Leo now recalled—he had originally communicated with Salzman by letter. He got on his coat, put a hat on over his skull cap and hurried to the subway station. All the way to the far end of the Bronx he sat on the edge of his seat. He was more than once tempted to take out the picture and see if the girl's face was as he remembered it, but he refrained, allowing the snapshot to remain in his inside coat pocket, content to have her so close. When the train pulled into the station he was waiting at the door and bolted out. He quickly located the street Salzman had advertised.

The building he sought was less than a block from the subway, but it was not an office building, nor even a loft, nor a store in which one could rent office space. It was a very old tenement house. Leo found Salzman's name in pencil on a soiled tag under the bell and climbed three dark flights to his apartment. When he knocked, the door was opened by a thin, asthmatic, gray-haired woman, in felt slippers.

"Yes?" she said, expecting nothing. She listened without listening. He could have sworn he had seen her, too, before but knew it was an illusion.

"Salzman—does he live here? Pinye Salzman," he said, "the matchmaker?"

She stared at him a long minute. "Of course."

He felt embarrassed. "Is he in?"

"No." Her mouth, though left open, offered nothing more.

"The matter is urgent. Can you tell me where his office is?"

"In the air." She pointed upward.

"You mean he has no office?" Leo asked.

"In his socks."

He peered into the apartment. It was sunless and dingy, one large room divided by a half-open curtain, beyond which he could see a sagging metal bed. The near side of a room was crowded with rickety chairs, old bureaus, a three-legged table, racks of cooking utensils, and all the apparatus of a kitchen. But there was no sign of Salzman or his magic barrel, probably also a figment of the imagination. An odor of frying fish made Leo weak to the knees.

"Where is he?" he insisted. "I've got to see your husband."

At length she answered, "So who knows where he is? Every time he thinks a new thought he runs to a different place. Go home, he will find you."

"Tell him Leo Finkle."

She gave no sign she had heard.

He walked downstairs, depressed.

But Salzman, breathless, stood waiting at his door.

Leo was astounded and overjoyed. "How did you get here before me?"

"I rushed."

"Come inside."

They entered. Leo fixed tea, and a sardine sandwich for Salzman. As they were drinking he reached behind him for the packet of pictures and handed them to the marriage broker.

Salzman put down his glass and said expectantly, "You found somebody you like?"

"Not among these."

The marriage broker turned away.

"Here is the one I want." Leo held forth the snapshot.

Salzman slipped on his glasses and took the picture into his trembling hand. He turned ghastly and let out a groan.

"What's the matter?" cried Leo.

"Excuse me. Was an accident this picture. She isn't for you."

Salzman frantically shoved the manila packet into his portfolio. He thrust the snapshot into his pocket and fled down the stairs.

Leo, after momentary paralysis, gave chase and cornered the marriage broker in the vestibule. The landlady made hysterical outcries but neither of them listened.

"Give me back the picture, Salzman."

"No." The pain in his eyes was terrible.

"Tell me who she is then."

"This I can't tell you. Excuse me."

He made to depart, but Leo, forgetting himself, seized the match-maker by his tight coat and shook him frenziedly.

"Please," sighed Salzman. *"Please."*

Leo ashamedly let him go. "Tell me who she is," he begged. "It's very important for me to know."

"She is not for you. She is a wild one—wild, without shame. This is not a bride for a rabbi."

"What do you mean wild?"

"Like an animal. Like a dog. For her to be poor was a sin. This is why to me she is dead now."

"In God's name, what do you mean?"

"Her I can't introduce to you," Salzman cried.

"Why are you so excited?"

"Why, he asks," Salzman said, bursting into tears. "This is my baby, my Stella, she should burn in hell."

Leo hurried up to bed and hid under the covers. Under the covers he thought his life through. Although he soon fell asleep he could not sleep her out of his mind. He woke, beating his breast. Though he prayed to be rid of her, his prayers went unanswered. Through days of torment he endlessly struggled not to love her; fearing success, he escaped it. He then concluded to convert her to goodness, himself to God. The idea alternately nauseated and exalted him.

He perhaps did not know that he had come to a final decision until he encountered Salzman in a Broadway cafeteria. He was sitting alone at a rear table, sucking the bony remains of a fish. The marriage broker appeared haggard, and transparent to the point of vanishing.

Salzman looked up at first without recognizing him. Leo had grown a pointed beard and his eyes were weighted with wisdom.

"Salzman," he said, "love has at last come to my heart."

"Who can love from a picture?" mocked the marriage broker.

"It is not impossible."

"If you can love her, then you can love anybody. Let me show you some new clients that they just sent me their photographs. One is a little doll."

"Just her I want," Leo murmured.

"Don't be a fool, doctor. Don't bother with her."

"Put me in touch with her, Salzman," Leo said humbly. "Perhaps I can be of service."

Salzman had stopped eating and Leo understood with emotion that it was now arranged.

Leaving the cafeteria, he was, however, afflicted by a tormenting suspicion that Salzman had planned it all to happen this way.

Leo was informed by letter that she would meet him on a certain corner, and she was there one spring night, waiting under a street lamp. He appeared, carrying a small bouquet of violets and rosebuds. Stella stood by the lamp post, smoking. She wore white with red shoes, which fitted his expectations, although in a troubled moment he had imagined the dress red, and only the shoes white. She waited uneasily and shyly. From afar he saw that her eyes—clearly her father's—were filled with desperate innocence. He pictured, in her, his own redemption. Violins and lit candles revolved in the sky. Leo ran forward with flowers outthrust.

Around the corner, Salzman, leaning against a wall, chanted prayers for the dead.

JOHN CHEEVER
1912–

He was born in Quincy, Massachusetts, where his father owned a shoe factory until the economic disaster of 1929 wiped him out. His father's ancestors were seafarers, going back to the Revolution. His mother was English. After the crash she opened a gift shop that was quite successful. He went to school in Massachusetts until he was expelled from Thayer Academy for bad behavior. His first story, "Expelled," appeared in the *New Republic* a few months later in 1930. He was a writer from the beginning, living and working in Boston, New York, and the Yaddo writer's colony in Saratoga Springs. He was poor, surviving with help from his brother and by doing odd jobs. But he had published almost forty stories when he joined the U.S. Army for World War II. His first collection of stories was published during the war, but his first real success came with his second collection, *The Enormous Radio*, in 1953. By then he was writing for the *New Yorker*, where he has placed well over a hundred stories since his first acceptance in 1940. He married in 1941 and is the father of three children. He lives in upstate New York. His reputation as a writer has grown steadily, so that the publication of his collected *Stories of John Cheever* in 1979 was a major literary event. He has written novels, but the short story is his form.

The Swimmer

It was one of those midsummer Sundays when everyone sits around saying, "I *drank* too much last night." You might have heard it whispered by the parishioners leaving church, heard it from the lips of the priest himself, struggling with his cassock in the *vestiarium*, heard it from the golf links and the tennis courts, heard it from the wild-life preserve where the leader of the Audubon group was suffering from a terrible hangover. "I *drank* too much," said Donald Westerhazy. "We all *drank* too much," said Lucinda Merrill. "It must have been the wine," said Helen Westerhazy. "I *drank* too much of that claret."

This was at the edge of the Westerhazy's pool. The pool, fed by an artesian well with a high iron content, was a pale shade of green. It was a fine day. In the west there was a massive stand of cumulus cloud so like a city seen from a distance—from the bow of an approaching ship—that it might have had a name. Lisbon. Hackensack. The sun was hot. Neddy Merrill sat by the green water, one hand in it, one around a glass of gin. He was a slender man—he seemed to have the especial slenderness of youth—and while he was far from young he had slid down his banister that morning and given the bronze backside of Aphrodite on the hall table a smack, as he jogged toward the smell of coffee in his dining room. He might have been compared to a summer's day, particularly the last hours of one, and while he lacked a tennis racket or a sail bag the impression was definitely one of youth, sport, and clement weather. He had been swimming and now he was breathing deeply, stertorously as if he could gulp into his lungs the components of that moment, the heat of the sun, the intenseness of his pleasure. It all seemed to flow into his chest. His own house stood in Bullet Park, eight miles to the south, where his four beautiful daughters would have had their lunch and might be playing tennis. Then it occurred to him that by taking a dogleg to the southwest he could reach his home by water.

His life was not confining and the delight he took in this observation could not be explained by its suggestion of escape. He seemed to see, with a cartographer's eye, that string of swimming pools, that quasi-subterranean stream that curved across the county. He had made a discovery, a contribution to modern geography; he

would name the stream Lucinda after his wife. He was not a practical joker nor was he a fool but he was determinedly original and had
a vague and modest idea of himself as a legendary figure. The day
was beautiful and it seemed to him that a long swim might enlarge
and celebrate its beauty.

He took off a sweater that was hung over his shoulders and dove
in. He had an inexplicable contempt for men who did not hurl
themselves into pools. He swam a choppy crawl, breathing either
with every stroke or every fourth stroke and counting somewhere
well in the back of his mind the one-two one-two of a flutter kick. It
was not a serviceable stroke for long distances but the domestication
of swimming had saddled the sport with some customs and in his
part of the world a crawl was customary. To be embraced and sustained by the light green water was less a pleasure, it seemed, than
the resumption of a natural condition, and he would have liked to
swim without trunks, but this was not possible, considering his
project. He hoisted himself up on the far curb—he never used the
ladder—and started across the lawn. When Lucinda asked where he
was going he said he was going to swim home.

The only maps and charts he had to go by were remembered or
imaginary but these were clear enough. First there were the Grahams, the Hammers, the Lears, the Howlands, and the Crosscups.
He would cross Ditmar Street to the Bunkers and come, after a short
portage, to the Levys, the Welvhers, and the public pool in Lancaster. Then there were the Hallorans, the Sachses, the Biswangers,
Shirley Adams, the Gilmartins, and the Clydes. The day was lovely,
and that he lived in a world so generously supplied with water
seemed like a clemency, a beneficence. His heart was high and he
ran across the grass. Making his way home by an uncommon route
gave him the feeling that he was a pilgrim, an explorer, a man with
a destiny, and he knew that he would find friends all along the way;
friends would line the banks of the Lucinda River.

He went through a hedge that separated the Westerhazy's land
from the Grahams', walked under some flowering apple trees,
passed the shed that housed their pump and filter, and came out at
the Grahams' pool. "Why, Neddy," Mrs. Graham said, "what a
marvelous surprise. I've been trying to get you on the phone all
morning. Here, let me get you a drink." He saw then, like any
explorer, that the hospitable customs and traditions of the natives
would have to be handled with diplomacy if he was ever going to
reach his destination. He did not want to mystify or seem rude to
the Grahams nor did he have the time to linger there. He swam the
length of their pool and joined them in the sun and was rescued, a
few minutes later, by the arrival of two carloads of friends from

Connecticut. During the uproarious reunions he was able to slip away. He went down by the front of the Graham's house, stepped over a thorny hedge, and crossed a vacant lot to the Hammers'. Mrs. Hammer, looking up from her roses, saw him swim by although she wasn't quite sure who it was. The Lears heard him splashing past the open windows of their living room. The Howlands and the Crosscups were away. After leaving the Howlands' he crossed Ditmar Street and started for the Bunkers', where he could hear, even at that distance, the noise of a party.

The water refracted the sound of voices and laughter and seemed to suspend it in midair. The Bunkers' pool was on a rise and he climbed some stairs to a terrace where twenty-five or thirty men and women were drinking. The only person in the water was Rusty Towers, who floated there on a rubber raft. Oh, how bonny and lush were the banks of the Lucinda River! Prosperous men and women gathered by the sapphire-colored waters while caterer's men in white coats passed them cold gin. Overhead a red de Haviland trainer was circling around and around and around in the sky with something like the glee of a child in a swing. Ned felt a passing affection for the scene, a tenderness for the gathering, as if it was something he might touch. In the distance he heard thunder. As soon as Enid Bunker saw him she began to scream: "Oh, look who's here! What a marvelous surprise! When Lucinda said that you couldn't come I thought I'd *die*." She made her way to him through the crowd, and when they had finished kissing she led him to the bar, a progress that was slowed by the fact that he stopped to kiss eight or ten other women and shake the hands of as many men. A smiling bartender he had seen at a hundred parties gave him a gin and tonic and he stood by the bar for a moment, anxious not to get stuck in any conversation that would delay his voyage. When he seemed about to be surrounded he dove in and swam close to the side to avoid colliding with Rusty's raft. At the far end of the pool he bypassed the Tomlinsons with a broad smile and jogged up the garden path. The gravel cut his feet but this was the only unpleasantness. The party was confined to the pool, and as he went toward the house he heard the brilliant, watery sound of voices fade, heard the noise of a radio from the Bunkers' kitchen, where someone was listening to a ball game. Sunday afternoon. He made his way through the parked cars and down the grassy border of their driveway to Alewives Lane. He did not want to be seen on the road in his bathing trunks but there was no traffic and he made the short distance to the Levys' driveway, marked with a PRIVATE PROPERTY sign and a green tube for *The New York Times*. All the doors and windows of the big house were open but there were no signs of life; not even a dog barked. He went around the side of the house to the pool and saw that the Levys had only recently left. Glasses and bottles and dishes of nuts were on a table at the deep end, where there was a bathhouse or gazebo, hung with Japanese lanterns. After swimming the pool he got himself a glass and poured a drink. It was his fourth or fifth drink and he had swum nearly half the length of the Lucinda River. He felt tired, clean, and pleased at that moment to be alone; pleased with everything.

It would storm. The stand of cumulus cloud—that city—had risen and darkened, and while he sat there he heard the percussiveness of thunder again. The de Haviland trainer was still circling overhead and it seemed to Ned that he could almost hear the pilot laugh with pleasure in the afternoon; but when there was another peal of thunder he took off for home. A train whistle blew and he wondered what time it had gotten to be. Four? Five? He thought of the provincial station at that hour, where a waiter, his tuxedo concealed by a raincoat, a dwarf with some flowers wrapped in newspaper, and a woman who had been crying would be waiting for the local. It was suddenly growing dark; it was that moment when the pinheaded birds seemed to organize their song into some acute and knowledgeable recognition of the storm's approach. Then there was a fine noise of rushing water from the crown of an oak at his back, as if a spigot there had been turned. Then the noise of fountains came from the crowns of all the tall trees. Why did he love storms, what was the meaning of his excitement when the door sprang open and the rain wind fled rudely up the stairs, why had the simple task of shutting the windows of an old house seemed fitting and urgent, why did the first watery notes of a storm wind have for him the unmistakable sound of good news, cheer, glad tidings? Then there was an explosion, a smell of cordite, and rain lashed the Japanese lanterns that Mrs. Levy had bought in Kyoto the year before last, or was it the year before that?

He stayed in the Levys gazebo until the storm had passed. The rain had cooled the air and he shivered. The force of the wind had stripped a maple of its red and yellow leaves and scattered them over the grass and the water. Since it was midsummer the tree must be blighted, and yet he felt a peculiar sadness at this sign of autumn. He braced his shoulders, emptied his glass, and started for the Welchers' pool. This meant crossing the Lindleys' riding ring and he was surprised to find it overgrown with grass and all the jumps dismantled. He wondered if the Lindleys had sold their horses or gone away for the summer and put them out to board. He seemed to remember having heard something about the Lindleys and their horses but the memory was unclear. On he went, barefoot through the wet grass, to the Welchers', where he found their pool was dry.

This breach in his chain of water disappointed him absurdly, and he felt like some explorer who seeks a torrential headwater and finds a dead stream. He was disappointed and mystified. It was common enough to go away for the summer but no one ever drained his pool. The Welchers had definitely gone away. The pool furniture was folded, stacked, and covered with a tarpaulin. The bathhouse was locked. All the windows of the house were shut, and when he went around to the driveway in front he saw a FOR SALE sign nailed to a tree. When had he last heard from the Welchers—when, that is, had he and Lucinda last regretted an invitation to dine with them? It seemed only a week or so ago. Was his memory failing or had he so disciplined it in the repression of unpleasant facts that he had damaged his sense of the truth? Then in the distance he heard the sound of a tennis game. This cheered him, cleared away all his apprehensions and let him regard the overcast sky and the cold air with indifference. This was the day that Neddy Merrill swam across the county. That was the day! He started off then for his most difficult portage.

Had you gone for a Sunday afternoon ride that day you might have seen him, close to naked, standing on the shoulders of Route 424, waiting for a chance to cross. You might have wondered if he was the victim of foul play, had his car broken down, or was he merely a fool. Standing barefoot in the deposits of the highway—beer cans, rags, and blowout patches—exposed to all kinds of ridicule, he seemed pitiful. He had known when he started that this was a part of his journey—it had been on his maps—but confronted with the lines of traffic, worming through the summery light, he found himself unprepared. He was laughed at, jeered at, a beer can was thrown at him, and he had no dignity or humor to bring to the situation. He could have gone back, back to the Westerhayzys', where Lucinda would still be sitting in the sun. He had signed nothing, vowed nothing, pledged nothing, not even to himself. Why, believing as he did, that all human obduracy was susceptible to common sense, was he unable to turn back? Why was he determined to complete his journey even if it meant putting his life in danger? At what point had this prank, this joke, this piece of horseplay become serious? He could not go back, he could not even recall with any clearness the green water at the Westerhazys', the sense of inhaling the day's components, the friendly and relaxed voices saying that they had *drunk* too much. In the space of an hour, more or less, he had covered a distance that made his return impossible.

An old man, tooling down the highway at fifteen miles an hour, let him get to the middle of the road, where there was a grass divider. Here he was exposed to the ridicule of the northbound traffic, but after ten or fifteen minutes he was able to cross. From here he had only a short walk to the Recreation Center at the edge of the village of Lancaster, where there were some handball courts and a public pool.

The effect of the water on voices, the illusion of brilliance and suspense, was the same here as it has been at the Bunkers' but the sounds here were louder, harsher, and more shrill, and as soon as he entered the crowded enclosure he was confronted with regimentation. "ALL SWIMMERS MUST TAKE A SHOWER BEFORE USING THE POOL. ALL SWIMMERS MUST USE THE FOOTBATH. ALL SWIMMERS MUST WEAR THEIR IDENTIFICATION DISKS." He took a shower, washed his feet in a cloudy and bitter solution, and made his way to the edge of the water. It stank of chlorine and looked to him like a sink. A pair of lifeguards in a pair of towers blew police whistles at what seemed to be regular intervals and abused the swimmers through a public address system. Neddy remembered the sapphire water at the Bunkers' with longing and thought that he might contaminate himself—damage his own prosperousness and charm—by swimming in this murk, but he reminded himself that he was an explorer, a pilgrim, and that this was merely a stagnant bend in the Lucinda River. He dove, scowling with distaste, into the chlorine and had to swim with his head above water to avoid collisions, but even so he was bumped into, splashed, and jostled. When he got to the shallow end both lifeguards were shouting at him: "Hey, you, you without the identification disk, get outa the water." He did, but they had no way of pursuing him and he went through the reek of suntan oil and chlorine out through the hurricane fence and passed the handball courts. By crossing the road he entered the wooded part of the Halloran estate. The woods were not cleared and the footing was treacherous and difficult until he reached the lawn and the clipped beech hedge that encircled their pool.

The Hallorans were friends, an elderly couple of enormous wealth who seemed to bask in the suspicion that they might be Communists. They were zealous reformers but they were not Communists, and yet when they were accused, as they sometimes were, of subversion, it seemed to gratify and excite them. Their beech hedge was yellow and he guessed this had been blighted like the Levys' maple. He called hullo, hullo, to warn the Hallorans of his approach, to palliate his invasion of their privacy. The Hallorans, for reasons that had never been explained to him, did not wear bathing suits. No explanations were in order, really. Their nakedness was a detail in their uncompromising zeal for reform and he stepped politely out of his trunks before he went through the opening in the hedge.

Mrs. Halloran, a stout woman with white hair and a serene face, was reading the *Times*. Mr. Halloran was taking beech leaves out of the water with a scoop. They seemed not surprised or displeased to see him. Their pool was perhaps the oldest in the country, a field-stone rectangle, fed by a brook. It had no filter or pump and its waters were the opaque gold of the stream.

"I'm swimming across the county," Ned said.

"Why, I didn't know one could," exclaimed Mrs. Halloran.

"Well, I've made it from the Westerhazys'," Ned said. "That must be about four miles."

He left his trunks at the deep end, walked to the shallow end, and swam this stretch. As he was pulling himself out of the water he heard Mrs. Halloran say, "We've been *terribly* sorry to hear about all your misfortunes, Neddy."

"My misfortunes?" Ned asked. "I don't know what you mean."

"Why, we heard that you'd sold the house and that your poor children . . ."

"I don't recall having sold the house," Ned said, "and the girls are at home."

"Yes," Mrs. Halloran sighed. "Yes . . ." Her voice filled the air with an unseasonable melancholy and Ned spoke briskly. "Thank you for the swim."

"Well, have a nice trip," said Mrs. Halloran.

Beyond the hedge he pulled on his trunks and fastened them. They were loose and he wondered if, during the space of an afternoon, he could have lost some weight. He was cold and he was tired and the naked Hallorans and their dark water had depressed him. The swim was too much for his strength but how could he have guessed this, sliding down the banister that morning and sitting in the Westerhazys' sun? His arms were lame. His legs felt rubbery and ached at the joints. The worst of it was the cold in his bones and the feeling that he might never be warm again. Leaves were falling down around him and he smelled wood smoke on the wind. Who would be burning wood at this time of year?

He needed a drink. Whiskey would warm him, pick him up, carry him through the last of his journey, refresh his feeling that it was original and valorous to swim across the county. Channel swimmers took brandy. He needed a stimulant. He crossed the lawn in front of the Hallorans' house and went down a little path to where they had built a house for their only daughter, Helen, and her husband, Eric Sachs. The Sachses' pool was small and he found Helen and her husband there.

"Oh, *Neddy*," Helen said. "Did you lunch at Mother's?"

"Not *really*," Ned said. "I *did* stop to see your parents." This seemed to be explanation enough. "I'm terribly sorry to break in on you like this but I've taken a chill and I wonder if you'd give me a drink."

"Why, I'd *love* to," Helen said, "but there hasn't been anything in this house to drink since Eric's operation. That was three years ago."

Was he losing his memory, had his gift for concealing painful facts let him forget that he had sold his house, that his children were in trouble, and that his friend had been ill? His eyes slipped from Eric's face to his abdomen, where he saw three pale, sutured scars, two of them at least a foot long. Gone was his navel, and what, Neddy thought, would the roving hand, bed-checking one's gifts at 3 A.M., make of a belly with no navel, no link to birth, this breach in the succession?

"I'm sure you can get a drink at the Biswangers'," Helen said. "They're having an enormous do. You can hear it from here. Listen!"

She raised her head and from across the road, the lawns, the gardens, the woods, the fields, he heard again the brilliant noise of voices over water. "Well, I'll get wet," he said, still feeling that he had no freedom of choice about his means of travel. He dove into the Sachses' cold water and, gasping, close to drowning, made his way from one end of the pool to the other. "Lucinda and I want *terribly* to see you," he said over his shoulder, his face set toward the Biswangers'. "We're sorry it's been so long and we'll call you *very* soon."

He crossed some fields to the Biswangers' and the sounds of revelry there. They would be honored to give him a drink, they would be happy to give him a drink. The Biswangers invited him and Lucinda for dinner four times a year, six weeks in advance. They were always rebuffed and yet they continued to send out their invitations, unwilling to comprehend the rigid and undemocratic realities of their society. They were the sort of people who discussed the price of things at cocktails, exchanged market tips during dinner, and after dinner told dirty stories to mixed company. They did not belong to Neddy's set—they were not even on Lucinda's Christmas card list. He went toward their pool with feelings of indifference, charity, and some unease, since it seemed to be getting dark and these were the longest days of the year. The party when he joined it was noisy and large. Grace Biswanger was the kind of hostess who asked the optometrist, the veterinarian, the real-estate dealer, and the dentist. No one was swimming and the twilight, reflected on the water of the pool, had a wintry gleam. There was a bar and he started for this. When Grace Biswanger saw him she came toward him, not affectionately as he had every right to expect, but bellicosely.

"Why, this party has everything," she said loudly, "including a gate crasher."

She could not deal him a social blow—there was no question

about this and he did not flinch. "As a gate crasher," he asked politely, "do I rate a drink?"

"Suit yourself," she said. "You don't seem to pay much attention to invitations."

She turned her back on him and joined some guests, and he went to the bar and ordered a whiskey. The bartender served him but he served him rudely. His was a world in which the caterer's men kept the social score, and to be rebuffed by a part-time barkeep meant that he had suffered some loss of social esteem. Or perhaps the man was new and uninformed. The he heard Grace at his back say: "They went for broke overnight—nothing but income—and he showed up drunk one Sunday and asked us to loan him five thousand dollars. . . ." She was always talking about money. It was worse than eating your peas off a knife. He dove into the pool, swam its length and went away.

The next pool on his list, the last but two, belonged to his old mistress, Shirley Adams. If he had suffered any injuries at the Biswangers' they would be cured here. Love—sexual roughhouse in fact—was the supreme elixir, the pain killer, the brightly colored pill that would put the spring back into his step, the joy of life in his heart. They had had an affair last week, last month, last year. He couldn't remember. It was he who had broken it off, his was the upper hand, and he stepped through the gate of the wall that surrounded her pool with nothing so considered as self-confidence. It seemed in a way to be his pool, as the lover, particularly the illicit lover, enjoys the possessions of his mistress with an authority unknown to holy matrimony. She was there, her hair the color of brass, but her figure, at the edge of the lighted, cerulean water, excited in him no profound memories. It had been, he thought, a lighthearted affair, although she had wept when he broke it off. She seemed confused to see him and he wondered if she was still wounded. Would she, God forbid, weep again?

"What do you want?" she asked.

"I'm swimming across the county."

"Good Christ. Will you ever grow up?"

"What's the matter?"

"If you've come here for money," she said, "I won't give you another cent."

"You could give me a drink."

"I could but I won't. I'm not alone."

"Well, I'm on my way."

He dove in and swam the pool, but when he tried to haul himself up onto the curb he found that the strength in his arms and shoulders had gone, and he paddled to the ladder and climbed out.

Looking over his shoulder he saw, in the lighted bathhouse, a young man. Going out onto the dark lawn he smelled chrysanthemums or marigolds—some stubborn autumnal fragrance—on the night air, strong as gas. Looking overhead he saw that the stars had come out, but why should he seem to see Andromeda, Cepheus, and Cassiopeia? What had become of the constellations of midsummer? He began to cry.

It was probably the first time in his adult life that he had ever cried, certainly the first time in his life that he had ever felt so miserable, cold, tired, and bewildered. He could not understand the rudeness of the caterer's barkeep or the rudeness of a mistress who had come to him on her knees and showered his trousers with tears. He had swum too long, he had been immersed too long, and his nose and his throat were sore from the water. What he needed then was a drink, some company, and some clean, dry clothes, and while he could have cut directly across the road to his home he went on to the Gilmartins' pool. Here, for the first time in his life, he did not dive but went down the steps into the icy water and swam a hobbled sidestroke that he might have learned as a youth. He staggered with fatigue on his way to the Clydes' and paddled the length of their pool, stopping again and again with his hand on the curb to rest. He climbed up the ladder and wondered if he had the strength to get home. He had done what he wanted, he had swum the county, but he was so stupefied with exhaustion that his triumph seemed vague. Stooped, holding on to the gateposts for support, he turned up the driveway of his own house.

The place was dark. Was it so late that they had all gone to bed? Had Lucinda stayed at the Westerhazys' for supper? Had the girls joined her there or gone someplace else? Hadn't they agreed, as they usually did on Sunday, to regret all their invitations and stay at home? He tried the garage doors to see what cars were in but the doors were locked and rust came off the handles onto his hands. Going toward the house, he saw that the force of the thunderstorm had knocked one of the rain gutters loose. It hung down over the front door like an umbrella rib, but it could be fixed in the morning. The house was locked, and he thought that the stupid cook or the stupid maid must have locked the place up until he remembered that it had been some time since they had employed a maid or a cook. He shouted, pounded on the door, tried to force it with his shoulder, and then, looking in at the windows, saw that the place was empty.

KURT VONNEGUT, JR.

1922–

He was born in Indianapolis, Indiana, where his father and grandfather were architects. At Shortridge High School he wrote for the *Daily Echo,* and at Cornell University he wrote a humor column for the *Daily Sun.* World War II interrupted Vonnegut's studies in chemistry. Conscious of his German heritage, he had been an advocate of neutrality, but, when the call came, he went. He fought against the Germans, was captured and imprisoned in Dresden, where he lived through the Allied fire-bombing of the city. After the war he married a childhood friend, studied anthropology at the University of Chicago, and worked as a police reporter for the Chicago City News Bureau. When his M.A. thesis was rejected, he left Chicago and went to work for General Electric in Schenectady, N.Y. as a public relations man. He began to publish fiction at this time and was able to leave G.E. in 1950 to eke out a living as a writer. During the next two decades he supported his family, including three children of his own and three of his sister's (after her death from cancer), by writing and occasionally teaching. In the late 1960's he began to be successful commercially and to receive serious recognition as a writer. Among his finest works are *Mother Night* (1962) and *Cat's Cradle* (1963). In 1971 the University of Chicago gave him that belated M.A. degree.

Harrison Bergeron

The year was 2081, and everybody was finally equal. They weren't only equal before God and the law. They were equal every which way. Nobody was smarter than anybody else. Nobody was better looking than anybody else. Nobody was stronger or quicker than anybody else. All this equality was due to the 211th, 212, and 213th Amendments to the Constitution, and to the unceasing vigilance of agents of the United States Handicapper General.

Some things about living still weren't quite right, though. April, for instance, still drove people crazy by not being springtime. And it was in that clammy month that the H-G men took George and Hazel Bergeron's fourteen-year-old son, Harrison, away.

It was tragic, all right, but George and Hazel couldn't think about it very hard. Hazel had a perfectly average intelligence, which meant she couldn't think about anything except in short bursts. And George, while his intelligence was way above normal, had a little mental handicap radio in his ear. He was required by law to wear it at all times. It was tuned to a government transmitter. Every twenty seconds or so, the transmitter would send out some sharp noise to keep people like George from taking unfair advantage of their brains.

George and Hazel were watching television. There were tears on Hazel's cheeks, but she's forgotten for the moment what they were about.

On the television screen were ballerinas.

A buzzer sounded in George's head. His thoughts fled in panic, like bandits from a burglar alarm.

"That was a real pretty dance, that dance they just did," said Hazel.

"Huh?" said George.

"That dance—it was nice," said Hazel.

"Yup," said George. He tried to think a little about the ballerinas. They weren't really very good—no better than anybody else would have been, anyway. They were burdened with sashweights and bags of birdshot, and their faces were masked, so that no one, seeing a free and graceful gesture or a pretty face, would feel like something the cat drug in. George was toying with the vague notion that maybe dancers shouldn't be handicapped. But he didn't get very far with it before another noise in his ear radio scattered his thoughts.

George winced. So did two out of the eight ballerinas.

Hazel saw him wince. Having no mental handicap herself, she had to ask George what the latest sound had been.

"Sounded like somebody hitting a milk bottle with a ball peen hammer," said George.

"I'd think it would be real interesting, hearing all the different sounds," said Hazel, a little envious. "All the things they think up."

"Um," said George.

"Only, if I was Handicapper General, you know what I would do?" said Hazel. Hazel, as a matter of fact, bore a strong resemblance to the Handicapper General, a woman named Diana Moon Glampers. "If I was Diana Moon Glampers," said Hazel, "I'd have chimes on Sunday—just chimes. Kind of in honor of religion."

"I could think, if it was just chimes," said George.

"Well—maybe make 'em real loud," said Hazel. "I think I'd make a good Handicapper General."

"Good as anybody else," said George.

"Who knows better'n I do what normal is?" said Hazel.

"Right," said George. He began to think glimmeringly about his abnormal son who was now in jail, about Harrison, but a twenty-one-gun salute in his head stopped that.

"Boy!" said Hazel, "That was a doozy, wasn't it?"

It was such a doozy that George was white and trembling, and tears stood on the rims of his red eyes. Two of the eight ballerinas had collapsed to the studio floor, were holding their temples.

"All of a sudden you look so tired," said Hazel. "Why don't you stretch out on the sofa, so's you can rest your handicap bag on the pillows, honeybunch." She was referring to the forty-seven pounds of birdshot in a canvas bag, which was padlocked around George's neck. "Go on and rest the bag for a little while," she said. "I don't care if you're not equal to me for a while."

George weighed the bag with his hands. "I don't mind it," he said. "I don't notice it any more. It's just a part of me."

"You been so tired lately—kind of wore out," said Hazel. "If there was just some way we could make a little hole in the bottom of the bag, and just take out a few of them lead balls. Just a few."

"Two years in prison and two thousand dollars fine for every ball I took out," said George. "I don't call that a bargain."

"If you could just take a few out when you came home from work," said Hazel. "I mean—you don't compete with anybody around here. You just set around."

"If I tried to get away with it," said George, "then other people'd get away with it—and pretty soon we'd be right back to the dark ages again, with everybody competing against everybody else. You wouldn't like that, would you?"

"I'd hate it," said Hazel.

"There you are," said George. "The minute people start cheating on laws, what do you think happens to society?"

If Hazel hadn't been able to come up with an answer to this question, George couldn't have supplied one. A siren was going off in his head.

"Reckon it'd fall all apart," said Hazel.

"What would?" said George blankly.

"Society," said Hazel uncertainly. "Wasn't that what you just said?"

"Who knows?" said George.

The television program was suddenly interrupted for a news bulletin. It wasn't clear at first as to what the bulletin was about, since the announcer, like all announcers, had a serious speech impediment. For about half a minute, and in a state of high excitement, the announcer tried to say, "Ladies and gentlemen—"

He finally gave up, handed the bulletin to a ballerina to read.

"That's all right—" Hazel said of the announcer, "he tried. That's the big thing. He tried to do the best he could with what God gave him. He should get a nice raise for trying so hard."

"Ladies and gentlemen—" said the ballerina, reading the bulletin. She must have been extraordinarily beautiful, because the mask she wore was hideous. And it was easy to see that she was the strongest and most graceful of all the dancers, for her handicap bags were as big as those worn by two-hundred-pound men.

And she had to apologize at once for her voice, which was a very unfair voice for a woman to use. Her voice was a warm, luminous, timeless melody. "Excuse me—" she said, and she began again, making her voice absolutely uncompetitive.

"Harrison Bergeron, age fourteen," she said in a grackle squawk, "has just escaped from jail, where he was held on suspicion of plotting to overthrow the government. He is a genius and an athlete, is under-handicapped, and should be regarded as extremely dangerous."

A police photograph of Harrison Bergeron was flashed on the screen-upside down, then sideways, upside down again, then right side up. The picture showed the full length of Harrison against a background calibrated in feet and inches. He was exactly seven feet tall.

The rest of Harrison's appearance was Halloween and hardware. Nobody had ever borne heavier handicaps. He had outgrown hindrances faster than the H-G men could think them up. Instead of a little ear radio for a mental handicap, he wore a tremendous pair of earphones, and spectacles with thick wavy lenses. The spectacles were intended to make him not only half blind, but to give him whanging headaches besides.

Scrap metal was hung all over him. Ordinarily, there was a certain symmetry, a military neatness to the handicaps issued to strong people, but Harrison looked like a walking junkyard. In the race of life, Harrison carried three hundred pounds.

And to offset his good looks, the H-G men required that he wear at all times a red rubber ball for a nose, keep his eyebrows shaved off, and cover his even white teeth with black caps at snaggle-tooth random.

"If you see this boy," said the ballerina, "do not—I repeat, do not—try to reason with him."

There was the shriek of a door being torn from its hinges.

Screams and barking cries of consternation came from the television set. The photograph of Harrison Bergeron on the screen jumped again and again, as though dancing to the tune of an earthquake.

George Bergeron correctly identified the earthquake, and well he might have—for many was the time his own home had danced to the same crashing tune. "My God—" said George, "that must be Harrison!"

The realization was blasted from his mind instantly by the sound of an atuomobile collision in his head.

When George could open his eyes again, the photograph of Harrison was gone. A living, breathing Harrison filled the screen.

Clanking, clownish, and huge, Harrison stood in the center of the studio. The knob of the uprooted studio door was still in his hand. Ballerinas, technicians, musicians, and announcers cowered on their knees before him, expecting to die.

"I am the Emperor!" cried Harrison. "Do you hear? I am the Emperor! Everybody must do what I say at once!" He stamped his foot and the studio shook.

"Even as I stand here—" he bellowed, "crippled, hobbled, sickened—I am a greater ruler than any man who ever lived! Now watch me become what I *can* become!"

Harrison tore the straps of his handicap harness like wet tissue paper, tore straps guaranteed to support five thousand pounds.

Harrison's scrap-iron handicaps crashed to the floor.

Harrison thrust his thumbs under the bar of the padlock that secured his head harness. The bar snapped like celery. Harrison smashed his headphones and spectacles against the wall.

He flung away his rubber-ball nose, revealed a man that would have awed Thor, the god of thunder.

"I shall now select my Empress!" he said, looking down on the cowering people. "Let the first woman who dares rise to her feet claim her mate and her throne!"

A moment passed, and then a ballerina arose, swaying like a willow.

Harrison plucked the mental handicap from her ear, snapped off her physical handicaps with marvelous delicacy. Last of all, he removed her mask.

She was blindingly beautiful.

"Now—" said Harrison, taking her hand "shall we show the people the meaning of the word dance? Music!" he commanded.

The musicians scrambled back into their chairs, and Harrison stripped them of their handicaps, too. "Play your best," he told them, "and I'll make you barons and dukes and earls."

The music began. It was normal at first—cheap, silly, false. But Harrison snatched two musicians from their chairs, waved them like batons as he sang the music as he wanted it played. He slammed them back into their chairs.

The music began again and was much improved.

Harrison and his Empress merely listened to the music for a while—listened gravely, as though synchronizing their heartbeats with it.

They shifted their weights to their toes.

Harrison placed his big hands on the girl's tiny waist, letting her sense the weightlessness that would soon be hers.

And then, in an explosion of joy and grace, into the air they sprang!

Not only were the laws of the land abandoned, but the law of gravity and the laws of motion as well.

They reeled, whirled, swiveled, flounced, capered, gamboled, and spun.

They leaped like deer on the moon.

The studio ceiling was thirty feet high, but each leap brought the dancers nearer to it.

It became their obvious intention to kiss the ceiling.

They kissed it.

And then, neutralizing gravity with love and pure will, they remained suspended in air inches below the ceiling, and they kissed each other for a long, long time.

It was then that Diana Moon Glampers, the Handicapper General, came into the studio with a double-barreled ten-gauge shotgun. She fired twice, and the Emperor and the Empress were dead before they hit the floor.

Diana Moon Glampers loaded the gun again. She aimed it at the musicians and told them they had ten seconds to get their handicaps back on.

It was then that the Bergerons' television tube burned out.

Hazel turned to comment about the blackout to George. But George had gone out into the kitchen for a can of beer.

George came back in with the beer, paused while a handicap signal shook him up. And then he sat down again. "You been crying?" he said to Hazel.

"Yup," she said.

"What about?" he said.

"I forget," she said. "Something real sad on television."

"What was it?" he said.

"It's all kind of mixed up in my mind," said Hazel.

"Forget sad things," said George.

"I always do," said Hazel.

"That's my girl," said George. He winced. There was the sound of a rivetting gun in his head.

"Gee—I could tell that one was a doozy," said Hazel.

"You can say that again," said George.

"Gee—" said Hazel. "I could tell that one was a doozy."

URSULA K. LE GUIN
1929–

Ursula Kroeber was born in Berkeley, California. Her father was a professor of Anthropology at the University of California and her mother was a writer. She graduated from Radcliffe College in 1951 and married Charles Le Guin, a historian. In 1952 she received her M.A. from Columbia University. She had three children before she began to publish science fiction in the mid-1960's. She quickly established herself as one of the best writers in the field with *The Left Hand of Darkness* (1969), her fantastic *Earthsea Trilogy* (1968, 71, 73), and *The Dispossessed* (1974).

The Ones Who Walk Away from Omelas

(Variations on a theme by William James)

With a clamor of bells that set the swallows soaring, the Festival of Summer came to the city Omelas, bright-towered by the sea. The rigging of the boats in harbor sparkled with flags. In the streets between houses with red roofs and painted walls, between old moss-grown gardens and under avenues of trees, past great parks and public buildings, processions moved. Some were decorous: old people in long stiff robes of mauve and grey, grave master workmen, quiet, merry women carrying their babies, and chatting as they walked. In other streets the music beat faster, a shimmering of gong and tambourine, and the people went dancing, the procession was a dance. Children dodged in and out, their high calls rising like the swallows' crossing flights over the music and the singing. All the processions wound towards the north side of the city, where on the great water-meadow called the Green Fields boys and girls, naked in the bright air, with mud-stained feet and ankles and long, lithe arms, exercised their restive horses before the race. The horses wore no gear at all but a halter without bit. Their manes were braided with streamers of silver, gold, and green. They flared their nostrils and pranced and boasted to one another; they were vastly excited, the horse being the only animal who has adopted our ceremonies as his own. Far off to the north and west the mountains stood up half encircling Omelas on her bay. The air of morning was so clear that the snow still crowning the Eighteen Peaks burned with white-gold fire across the miles of sunlit air, under the dark blue of the sky. There was just enough wind to make the banners that marked the racecourse snap and flutter now and then. In the silence of the broad green meadows one could hear the music winding through the city streets, farther and nearer and ever approaching, a cheerful faint sweetness of the air that from time to time trembled and gathered together and broke out into the great joyous clanging of the bells.

Joyous! How is one to tell about joy? How describe the citizens of Omelas?

They were not simple folk, you see, though they were happy. But we do not say the words of cheer much any more. All smiles have become archaic. Given a description such as this one tends to make certain assumptions. Given a description such as this one tends to look next for the King, mounted on a splendid stallion and surrounded by his noble knights, or perhaps in a golden litter borne by great-muscled slaves. But there was no king. They did not use swords, or keep slaves. They were not barbarians. I do not know the rules and laws of their society, but I suspect that they were singularly few. As they did without monarchy and slavery, so they also got on without the stock exchange, the advertisement, the secret police, and the bomb. Yet I repeat that these were not simple folk, not dulcet shepherds, noble savages, bland utopians. They were not less complex than us. The trouble is that we have a bad habit, encouraged by pedants and sophisticates, of considering happiness as something rather stupid. Only pain is intellectual, only evil interesting. This is the treason of the artist: a refusal to admit the banality of evil and the terrible boredom of pain. If you can't lick 'em, join 'em. If it hurts, repeat it. But to praise despair is to condemn delight, to embrace violence is to lose hold of everything else. We have almost lost hold; we can no longer describe a happy man, nor make any celebration of joy. How can I tell you about the people of Omelas? They were not naïve and happy children—though their children were, in fact, happy. They were mature, intelligent, passionate adults whose lives were not wretched. O miracle! but I wish I could describe it better. I wish I could convince you. Omelas sounds in my words like a city in a fairy tale, long ago and far away, once upon a time. Perhaps it would be best if you imagined it as your own fancy bids, assuming it will rise to the occasion, for certainly I cannot suit you all. For instance, how about technology? I think that there would be no cars or helicopters in and above the streets; this follows from the fact that the people of Omelas are happy people. Happiness is based on a just discrimination of what is necessary, what is neither necessary nor destructive, and what is destructive. In the middle category, however—that of the unnecessary but undestructive, that of comfort, luxury, exuberance, etc.—they could perfectly well have central heating, subway trains, washing machines, and all kinds of marvelous devices not yet invented here, floating light-sources, fuelless power, a cure for the common cold. Or they could have none of that: it doesn't matter. As you like it. I incline to think that people from towns up and down the coast have been coming in to Omelas during the last days before the Festival on very fast little trains and double-decked trams, and that the train station of Omelas is actually the handsomest building in town, though plainer than the magnificent Farmers' Market. But even granted trains, I fear that Omelas so far strikes some of you as goody-goody. Smiles, bells, parades, horses, bleh. If so, please add an orgy. If an orgy would help, don't hesitate. Let us not, however, have temples from which issue beautiful nude priests and priestesses already half in ecstasy and ready to copulate with any man or woman, lover or stranger, who desires union with the deep godhead of the blood, although that was my first idea. But really it would be better not to have any temples in Omelas—at least, not manned temples. Religion yes, clergy no. Surely the beautiful nudes can just wander about, offering themselves like divine soufflés to the hunger of the needy and the rapture of the flesh. Let them join the processions. Let tambourines be struck above the copulations, and the glory of desire be proclaimed upon the gongs, and (a not unimportant point) let the offspring of these delightful rituals be beloved and looked after by all. One thing I know there is none of in Omelas is guilt. But what else should there be? I thought at first there were no drugs, but that is puritanical. For those who like it, the faint insistent sweetness of *drooz* may perfume the ways of the city, *drooz* which first brings a great lightness and brilliance to the mind and limbs, and then after some hours a dreamy languor, and wonderful visions at last of the very arcana and inmost secrets of the Universe, as well as exciting the pleasure of sex beyond all belief; and it is not habit-forming. For more modest tastes I think there ought to be beer. What else, what else belongs in the joyous city? The sense of victory, surely, the celebration of courage. But as we did without clergy, let us do without soldiers. The joy built upon successful slaughter is not the right kind of joy; it will not do; it is fearful and it is trivial. A boundless and generous contentment, a magnanimous triumph felt not against some outer enemy but in communion with the finest and fairest in the souls of all men everywhere and the splendor of the world's summer: this is what swells the hearts of the people of Omelas, and the victory they celebrate is that of life. I really don't think many of them need to take *drooz*.

Most of the processions have reached the Green Fields by now. A marvelous smell of cooking goes forth from the red and blue tents of the provisioners. The faces of small children are amiably sticky; in the benign grey beard of a man a couple of crumbs of rich pastry are entangled. The youths and girls have mounted their horses and are beginning to group around the starting line of the course. An old woman, small, fat, and laughing, is passing out flowers from a basket, and tall young men wear her flowers in their shining hair. A child of nine or ten sits at the edge of the crowd, alone, playing on a wooden flute. People pause to listen, and they smile, but they do not speak to him, for he never ceases playing and never sees them, his dark eyes wholly rapt in the sweet, thin magic of the tune.

He finishes, and slowly lowers his hands holding the wooden flute.

As if that little private silence were the signal, all at once a trumpet sounds from the pavilion near the starting line: imperious, melancholy, piercing. The horses rear on their slender legs, and some of them neigh in answer. Sober-faced, the young riders stroke the horses' necks and soothe them, whispering, "Quiet, quiet, there my beauty, my hope. . . ." They begin to form in rank along the starting line. The crowds along the racecourse are like a field of grass and flowers in the wind. The Festival of Summer has begun.

Do you believe? Do you accept the festival, the city, the joy? No? Then let me describe one more thing.

In a basement under one of the beautiful public buildings of Omelas, or perhaps in the cellar of one of its spacious private homes, there is a room. It has one locked door, and no window. A little light seeps in dustily between cracks in the boards, secondhand from a cobwebbed window somewhere across the cellar. In one corner of the little room a couple of mops, with stiff, clotted, foul-smelling heads, stand near a rusty bucket. The floor is dirt, a little damp to the touch, as cellar dirt usually is. The room is about three paces long and two wide: a mere broom closet or disused tool room. In the room a child is sitting. It could be a boy or a girl. It looks about six, but actually is nearly ten. It is feeble-minded. Perhaps it was born defective, or perhaps it has become imbecile through fear, malnutrition, and neglect. It picks its nose and occasionally fumbles vaguely with its toes or genitals, as it sits hunched in the corner farthest from the bucket and the two mops. It is afraid of the mops. It finds them horrible. It shuts its eyes, but it knows the mops are still standing there; and the door is locked; and nobody will come. The door is always locked; and nobody ever comes, except that sometimes—the child has no understanding of time or interval—sometimes the door rattles terribly and opens, and a person, or several people, are there. One of them may come in and kick the child to make it stand up. The others never come close, but peer in at it with frightened, disgusted eyes. The food bowl and the water jug are hastily filled, the door is locked, the eyes disappear. The people at the door never say anything, but the child, who has not always lived in the tool room, and can remember sunlight and its mother's voice, sometimes speaks. "I will be good," it says. "Please let me out. I will be good!" They never answer. The child used to scream for help at night, and cry a good deal, but now it only makes a kind of whining, "eh-haa, eh-haa," and it speaks less and less often. It is so thin there are no calves to its legs; its belly protrudes; it lives on a half-bowl of corn meal and grease a day. It is naked. Its buttocks and thighs are a mass of festered sores, as it sits in its own excrement continually.

They all know it is there, all the people of Omelas. Some of them have come to see it, others are content merely to know it is there. They all know that it has to be there. Some of them understand why, and some do not, but they all understand that their happiness, the beauty of their city, the tenderness of their friendships, the health of their children, the wisdom of their scholars, the skill of their makers, even the abundance of their harvest and the kindly weathers of their skies, depends wholly on this child's abominable misery.

This is usually explained to children when they are between eight and twelve, whenever they seem capable of understanding; and most of those who come to see the child are young people, though often enough an adult comes, or comes back, to see the child. No matter how well the matter has been explained to them, these young spectators are always shocked and sickened at the sight. They feel disgust, which they had thought themselves superior to. They feel anger, outrage, impotence, despite all the explanations. They would like to do something for the child. But there is nothing they can do. If the child were brought up into the sunlight out of that vile place, if it were cleaned and fed and comforted, that would be a good thing, indeed; but if it were done, in that day and hour all the prosperity and beauty and delight of Omelas would wither and be destroyed. Those are the terms. To exchange all the goodness and grace of every life in Omelas for that single, small improvement: to throw away the happiness of thousands for the chance of the happiness of one: that would be to let guilt within the walls indeed.

The terms are strict and absolute; there may not even be a kind word spoken to the child.

Often the young people go home in tears, or in a tearless rage, when they have seen the child and faced this terrible paradox. They may brood over it for weeks or years. But as time goes on they begin to realize that even if the child could be released, it would not get much good of its freedom: a little vague pleasure of warmth and food, no doubt, but little more. It is too degraded and imbecile to know any real joy. It has been afraid too long even to be free of fear. Its habits are too uncouth for it to respond to humane treatment. Indeed, after so long it would probably be wretched without walls about it to protect it, and darkness for its eyes, and its own excrement to sit in. Their tears at the bitter injustice dry when they begin to perceive the terrible justice of reality, and to accept it. Yet it is their tears and anger, the trying of their generosity and the acceptance of their helplessness, which are perhaps the true source of the splendor of their lives. Theirs is no vapid, irresponsible happiness. They know that they, like the child, are not free. They know compassion. It is the existence of the child, and their knowledge of its existence, that makes possible the nobility of their architecture, and poignancy of their music, the profundity of their science. It is because of the child that they are so gentle with children. They know that if the wretched one were not there snivelling in the dark, the other one, the flute-player, could make no joyful music as the young riders line up in their beauty for the race in the sunlight of the first morning of summer.

Now do you believe in them? Are they not more credible? But there is one more thing to tell, and this is quite incredible.

At times one of the adolescent girls or boys who go to see the child does not go home to weep or rage, does not, in fact, go home at all.

Sometimes also a man or woman much older falls silent for a day or two, and then leaves home. These people go out into the street, and walk down the street alone. They keep walking, and walk straight out of the city of Omelas, through the beautiful gates. They keep walking across the farmlands of Omelas. Each one goes alone, youth or girl, man or woman. Night falls; the traveler must pass down village streets, between the houses with yellow-lit windows, and on out into the darkness of the fields. Each alone, they go west or north, towards the mountains. They go on. They leave Omelas, they walk ahead into the darkness, and they do not come back. The place they go towards is a place even less imaginable to most of us than the city of happiness. I cannot describe it at all. It is possible that it does not exist. But they seem to know where they are going, the ones who walk away from Omelas.

ANGELA CARTER
1940–

Angela Stalker was born in Sussex, England, in 1940. Her father was a journalist based in London. She grew up in South London and went to state schools in that city until she was eighteen, when she got a job with a newspaper in the suburb of Croyden. At twenty she had completed an unpublished novel, when she married Paul Carter and moved to Bristol with him. At Bristol she attended the University, studying English literature from its beginnings to modern times. In 1966, her first novel, *Shadow Dance*, was published. She was divorced in 1969, but kept the name Angela Carter, as she was beginning to make her reputation as a writer under that name. Since then she has published eight more volumes of fiction and a critical study of the Marquis de Sade. She has written fiction in the full range from fantasy to realism, including several novels that belong to the British "New Wave" of Science Fiction. Her transformations of fairy tales into "adult tales" in *The Bloody Chamber* (1979) have contributed to her growing reputation as a unique voice in contemporary fiction.

The Snow Child

Midwinter—invincible, immaculate. The Count and his wife go riding, he on a grey mare and she on a black one, she wrapped in the glittering pelts of black foxes; and she wore high, black, shining boots with scarlet heels, and spurs. Fresh snow fell on snow already fallen; when it ceased, the whole world was white. "I wish I had a girl as white as snow," says the Count. They ride on. They come to a hole in the snow; this hole is filled with blood. He says: "I wish I had a girl as red as blood." So they ride on again; here is a raven, perched on a bare bough. "I wish I had a girl as black as that bird's feather."

As soon as he completed her description, there she stood, beside the road, white skin, red mouth, black hair and stark naked; she was the child of his desire and the Countess hated her. The Count lifted her up and sat her in front of him on his saddle but the Countess had only one thought: how shall I be rid of her?

The Countess dropped her glove in the snow and told the girl to get down to look for it; she meant to gallop off and leave her there but the Count said: "I'll buy you new gloves." At that, the furs sprang off the Countess's shoulders and twined round the naked girl. Then the Countess threw her diamond brooch through the ice of a frozen pond: "Dive in and fetch it for me," she said; she thought the girl would drown. But the Count said: "Is she a fish, to swim in such cold weather?" Then her boots leapt off the Countess's feet and on to the girl's legs. Now the Countess was bare as a bone and the girl furred and booted; the Count felt sorry for his wife. They came to a bush of roses, all in flower. "Pick me one," said the Countess to the girl. "I can't deny you that," said the Count.

So the girl picks a rose; pricks her finger on the thorn; bleeds; screams; falls.

Weeping, the Count got off his horse, unfastened his breeches and thrust his virile member into the dead girl. The Countess reined in her stamping mare and watched him narrowly; he was soon finished.

Then the girl began to melt. Soon there was nothing left of her but a feather a bird might have dropped; a bloodstain, like the trace of a fox's kill on the snow; and the rose she had pulled off the bush. Now the Countess had all her clothes on again. With her long hand, she stroked her furs. The Count picked up the rose, bowed and handed it to his wife; when she touched it, she dropped it.

"It bites!" she said.

REALISM: *INTRODUCTION*

Even the wildest fantasy has something real about it. But works of fiction that we call "realistic" are real in a particular way. They present a world defined by certain ideas about the way social forces work upon individual human beings, and they show us characters whose inner lives conform to certain notions about human psychology. It would be impossible to define exactly what these "certain" ideas and notions are, but it is necessary to say something about them—at least in a rough and tentative way.

In earlier literature, individual characters are often shown struggling against fate or chance to achieve fame or happiness. Realism begins when writers can identify "society" as the thing against which individuals must struggle. When the romantic ideal of a unique and free personality confronts a deterministic view of social forces, realism is born. In realistic fictions we see individuals in conflict with social groups, with the class structure, the family structure, the political system. The short story—as opposed to the larger novel—specializes in loneliness, in the need for love and companionship that is seldom adequately achieved; and in the desire to retain an individual free will in the face of the enormous pressures of an indifferent or actively hostile world.

In a very definite way, realistic writers are the historians of their times—not chroniclers of the deeds of the great and powerful but witnesses to the quality of ordinary life. Two European writers showed the rest of the Western world how realism in short fiction could be achieved: Guy de Maupassant in France and Anton Chekhov in Russia. English, Irish, and American short story writers learned from them. And the Americans, in particular, learned well.

In the short story, skill with language itself counts for more than it needs to in longer fiction. The shorter a story is, the more closely it can draw upon the resources of poetry in its language. But a story, especially a realistic one, is not a poem. It must have a strong narrative structure or design, and it must get to the roots of human feeling and behavior in a way that convinces us of its human truth: truth to the way things are, to the surface of life, as well as truth to the inner lives of individuals, and the social structures in which individual lives grow or are stifled.

The range of tones and techniques employed by the writers represented here is in fact extraordinary. The interaction of individuals which is at the heart of realism can be presented in the detached, behavioral report of a Hemingway—with no interpretive commentary—or in the rich, engaged recital of a Lawrence, in which the commentary explores emotions that the characters feel but could never articulate for themselves. There are light stories with comic touches here, and heavy stories that bring us close to tears. But all these works of realistic fiction are designed to enlarge our sympathies by broadening our understanding. The end of realism is compassion.

GUY DE MAUPASSANT
1850–1893

Born Henri René Albert Guy de Maupassant, he grew up in Normandy, not far from Rouen, and went to school at the Rouen Lycée before entering government service. At the age of twenty he served in the Franco-Prussian War, and many of his finest stories came out of that experience. After the war he apprenticed himself to the older Flaubert. His greatest gifts were for the realistic short story, and he virtually perfected the form, producing nearly three hundred stories in a dozen years. Early in life he had contracted syphilis, for which there was no effective treatment at the time. In his forties he could no longer work, as the disease attacked his brain, ultimately reducing him to insanity before he died at the age of forty-three. His final condition is described in the story by Isaac Babel in this collection, called "Guy de Maupassant."

The Diamond Necklace

She was one of those pretty, charming young ladies, born, as if through an error of destiny, into a family of clerks. She had no dowry, no hopes, no means of becoming known, appreciated, loved, and married by a man either rich or distinguished; and she allowed herself to marry a petty clerk in the office of the Board of Education.

She was simple, not being able to adorn herself; but she was unhappy, as one out of her class; for women belong to no caste, no race; their grace, their beauty, and their charm serving them in the place of birth and family. Their inborn finesse, their instinctive elegance, their suppleness of wit are their only aristocracy, making some daughters of the people the equal of great ladies.

She suffered incessantly, feeling herself born for all delicacies and luxuries. She suffered from the poverty of her apartment, the shabby walls, the worn chairs, and the faded stuffs. All these things, which another woman of her station would not have noticed, tortured and angered her. The sight of the little Breton, who made this humble home, awoke in her sad regrets and desperate dreams. She thought of quiet antechambers, with their Oriental hangings, lighted by high, bronze torches, and of the two great footmen in short trousers who sleep in the large armchairs, made sleepy by the heavy air from the heating apparatus. She thought of large drawing-rooms, hung in old silks, of graceful pieces of furniture carrying bric-à-brac of inestimable value, and of the little perfumed coquettish apartments, made for five o'clock chats with most intimate friends, men known and sought after, whose attention all women envied and desired.

When she seated herself for dinner, before the round table where the tablecloth had been used three days, opposite her husband who uncovered the tureen with a delighted air, saying: "Oh! the good potpie! I know nothing better than that—" she would think of the elegant dinners, of the shining silver, of the tapestries peopling the walls with ancient personages and rare birds in the midst of fairy forests; she thought of the exquisite food served on marvelous dishes, of the whispered gallantries, listened to with the smile of the sphinx, while eating the rose-colored flesh of the trout or a chicken's wing.

She had neither frocks nor jewels, nothing. And she loved only those things. She felt that she was made for them. She had such a desire to please, to be sought after, to be clever, and courted.

She had a rich friend, a schoolmate at the convent, whom she did not like to visit, she suffered so much when she returned. And she wept for whole days from chagrin, from regret, from despair, and disappointment.

One evening her husband returned elated bearing in his hand a large envelope.

"Here," he said, "here is something for you."

She quickly tore open the wrapper and drew out a printed card on which were inscribed these words:

> The Minister of Public Instruction and Madame George Ramponneau ask the honor of Mr. and Mrs. Loisel's company Monday evening, January 18, at the Minister's residence.

Instead of being delighted, as her husband had hoped, she threw the invitation spitefully upon the table murmuring:

"What do you suppose I want with that?"

"But, my dearie, I thought it would make you happy. You never go out, and this is an occasion, and a fine one! I had a great deal of trouble to get it. Everybody wishes one, and it is very select; not many are given to employees. You will see the whole official world there."

She looked at him with an irritated eye and declared impatiently:

"What do you suppose I have to wear to such a thing as that?"

He had not thought of that; he stammered:

"Why, the dress you wear when we go to the theater. It seems very pretty to me—"

He was silent, stupefied, in dismay, at the sight of his wife weeping. Two great tears fell slowly from the corners of his eyes toward the corners of his mouth; he stammered:

"What is the matter? What is the matter?"

By a violent effort, she had controlled her vexation and responded in a calm voice, wiping her moist cheeks:

"Nothing. Only I have no dress and consequently I cannot go to this affair. Give your card to some colleague whose wife is better fitted out than I."

He was grieved, but answered:

"Let us see, Matilda. How much would a suitable costume cost, something that would serve for other occasions, something very simple?"

She reflected for some seconds, making estimates and thinking of a sum that she could ask for without bringing with it an immediate refusal and a frightened exclamation from the economical clerk.

Finally she said, in a hesitating voice:

"I cannot tell exactly, but it seems to me that four hundred francs ought to cover it."

He turned a little pale, for he had saved just this sum to buy a gun that he might be able to join some hunting parties the next summer, on the plains at Nanterre, with some friends who went to shoot larks up there on Sunday. Nevertheless, he answered:

"Very well. I will give you four hundred francs. But try to have a pretty dress."

The day of the ball approached and Mme. Loisel seemed sad, disturbed, anxious. Nevertheless, her dress was nearly ready. Her husband said to her one evening:

"What is the matter with you? You have acted strangely for two or three days."

And she responded: "I am vexed not to have a jewel, not one stone, nothing to adorn myself with. I shall have such a poverty-laden look. I would prefer not to go to this party."

He replied: "You can wear some natural flowers. At this season they look very *chic*. For ten francs you can have two or three magnificent roses."

She was not convinced. "No," she replied, "there is nothing more humiliating than to have a shabby air in the midst of rich women."

Then her husband cried out: "How stupid we are! Go and find your friend Mrs. Forestier and ask her to lend you her jewels. You are well enough acquainted with her to do this."

She uttered a cry of joy: "It is true!" she said. "I had not thought of that."

The next day she took herself to her friend's house and related her story of distress. Mrs. Forestier went to her closet with the glass doors, took out a large jewel-case, brought it, opened it, and said: "Choose, my dear."

She saw at first some bracelets, then a collar of pearls, then a

Venetian cross of gold and jewels and of admirable workmanship. She tried the jewels before the glass, hesitated, but could neither decide to take them nor leave them. Then she asked:

"Have you nothing more?"

"Why, yes. Look for yourself. I do not know what will please you."

Suddenly she discovered, in a black satin box, a superb necklace of diamonds, and her heart beat fast with an immoderate desire. Her hands trembled as she took them up. She placed them about her throat against her dress, and remained in ecstasy before them. Then she asked, in a hesitating voice, full of anxiety:

"Could you lend me this? Only this?"

"Why, yes, certainly."

She fell upon the neck of her friend, embraced her with passion, then went away with her treasure.

The day of the ball arrived. Mme. Loisel was a great success. She was the prettiest of all, elegant, gracious, smiling, and full of joy. All the men noticed her, asked her name, and wanted to be presented. All the members of the Cabinet wished to waltz with her. The Minister of Education paid her some attention.

She danced with enthusiasm, with passion, intoxicated with pleasure, thinking of nothing, in the triumph of her beauty, in the glory of her success, in a kind of cloud of happiness that came of all this homage, and all this admiration, of all these awakened desires, and this victory so complete and sweet to the heart of woman.

She went home toward four o'clock in the morning. Her husband had been half asleep in one of the little salons since midnight, with three other gentlemen whose wives were enjoying themselves very much.

He threw around her shoulders the wraps they had carried for the coming home, modest garments of everyday wear, whose poverty clashed with the elegance of the ball costume. She felt this and wished to hurry away in order not to be noticed by the other women who were wrapping themselves in rich furs.

Loisel retained her: "Wait," said he. "You will catch cold out there. I am going to call a cab."

But she would not listen and descended the steps rapidly. When they were in the street, they found no carriage; and they began to seek for one, hailing the coachmen whom they saw at a distance.

They walked along toward the Seine, hopeless and shivering. Finally they found on the dock one of those old, noctural *coupés* that one sees in Paris after nightfall, as if they were ashamed of their misery by day.

It took them as far as their door in Martyr street, and they went wearily up to their apartment. It was all over for her. And on his part, he remembered that he would have to be at the office by ten o'clock.

She removed the wraps from her shoulders before the glass, for a final view of herself in her glory. Suddenly she uttered a cry. Her necklace was not around her neck.

Her husband, already half undressed, asked: "What is the matter?"

She turned toward him excitedly:

"I have—I have—I no longer have Mrs. Forestier's necklace."

He arose in dismay: "What! How is that? It is not possible."

And they looked in the folds of the dress, in the folds of the mantle, in the pockets, everywhere. They could not find it.

He asked: "You are sure you still had it when we left the house?"

"Yes, I felt it in the vestibule as we came out."

"But if you had lost it in the street, we should have heard it fall. It must be in the cab."

"Yes. It is probable. Did you take the number?"

"No. And you, did you notice what it was?"

"No."

They looked at each other utterly cast down. Finally, Loisel dressed himself again.

"I am going," said he, "over the track where we went on foot, to see if I can find it."

And he went. She remained in her evening gown, not having the force to go to bed, stretched upon a chair, without ambition or thoughts.

Toward seven o'clock her husband returned. He had found nothing.

He went to the police and to the cab offices, and put an advertisement in the newspapers, offering a reward; he did everything that afforded them a suspicion of hope.

She waited all day in a state of bewilderment before this frightful disaster. Loisel returned at evening with his face harrowed and pale; and had discovered nothing.

"It will be necessary," said he, "to write to your friend that you have broken the clasp of the necklace and that you will have it repaired. That will give us time to turn around."

She wrote as he dictated.

At the end of a week, they had lost all hope. And Loisel, older by five years, declared:

"We must take measures to replace this jewel."

The next day they took the box which had inclosed it, to the jeweler whose name was on the inside. He consulted his books:

"It is not I, Madame," said he, "who sold this necklace; I only furnished the casket."

Then they went from jeweler to jeweler seeking a necklace like the other one, consulting their memories, and ill, both of them, with chagrin and anxiety.

In a shop of the Palais-Royal, they found a chaplet of diamonds which seemed to them exactly like the one they had lost. It was valued at forty thousand francs. They could get it for thirty-six thousand.

They begged the jeweler not to sell it for three days. And they made an arrangement by which they might return it for thirty-four thousand francs if they found the other one before the end of February.

Loisel possessed eighteen thousand francs which his father had left him. He borrowed the rest.

He borrowed it, asking for a thousand francs of one, five hundred of another, five louis of this one, and three louis of that one. He gave notes, made ruinous promises, took money of usurers and the whole race of lenders. He compromised his whole existence, in fact, risked his signature, without even knowing whether he could make it good or not, and, harassed by anxiety for the future, by the black misery which surrounded him, and by the prospect of all physical privations and moral torture, he went to get the new necklace, depositing on the merchant's counter thirty-six thousand francs.

When Mrs. Loisel took back the jewels to Mrs. Forestier, the latter said to her in a frigid tone:

"You should have returned them to me sooner, for I might have needed them."

She did open the jewel-box as her friend feared she would. If she should perceive the substitution, what would she think? What should she say? Would she take her for a robber?

Mrs. Loisel now knew the horrible life of necessity. She did her part, however, completely heroically. It was necessary to pay this frightful debt. She would pay it. They sent away the maid; they changed their lodgings; they rented some rooms under a mansard roof.

She learned the heavy cares of a household, the odious work of a kitchen. She washed the dishes, using her rosy nails upon the greasy pots and the bottoms of the stewpans. She washed the soiled linen, the chemises and dishcloths, which she hung on the line to dry; she took down the refuse to the street each morning and brought up the water, stopping at each landing to breathe. And, clothed like a woman of the people she went to the grocer's, the butcher's, and the fruiterer's, with her basket on her arm, shopping, haggling to the last sou her miserable money.

Every month it was necessary to renew some notes, thus obtaining time, and to pay others.

The husband worked evenings, putting the books of some merchants in order, and nights he often did copying at five sous a page.

And this life lasted for ten years.

At the end of ten years, they had restored all, all, with interest of the usurer, and accumulated interest besides.

Mrs. Loisel seemed old now. She had become a strong, hard woman, the crude woman of the poor household. Her hair badly dressed, her skirts awry, her hands red, she spoke in a loud tone, and washed the floors with large pails of water. But sometimes, when her husband was at the office, she would seat herself before the window and think of that evening party of former times, of that ball where she was so beautiful and so flattered.

How would it have been if she had not lost that necklace? Who knows? Who knows? How singular is life, and how full of changes! How small a thing will ruin or save one!

One Sunday, as she was taking a walk in the Champs-Elysées to rid herself of the cares of the week, she suddenly perceived a woman walking with a child. It was Mrs. Forestier, still young, still pretty, still attractive. Mrs. Loisel was affected. Should she speak to her? Yes, certainly. And now that she had paid, she would tell her all. Why not?

She approached her. "Good morning, Jeanne."

Her friend did not recognize her and was astonished to be so familiarly addressed by this common personage. She stammered:

"But, Madame—I do not know— You must be mistaken—"

"No, I am Matilda Loisel."

Her friend uttered a cry of astonishment: "Oh! my poor Matilda! How you have changed—"

"Yes, I have had some hard days since I saw you; and some miserable ones—and all because of you—"

"Because of me? How is that?"

"You recall the diamond necklace that you loaned me to wear to the Commissioner's ball?"

"Yes, very well."

"Well, I lost it."

"How is that, since you returned it to me?"

"I returned another to you exactly like it. And it has taken us ten years to pay for it. You can understand that it was not easy for us who have nothing. But it is finished and I am decently content."

Madame Forestier stopped short. She said:

"You say that you bought a diamond necklace to replace mine?"

"Yes. You did not perceive it then? They were just alike."

And she smiled with a proud and simple joy. Madame Forestier was touched and took both her hands as she replied:

"Oh! my poor Matilda! Mine were false. They were not worth over five hundred francs!"

KATE CHOPIN
1851–1904

Kate O'Flaherty was born in St. Louis, Missouri, to an Irish immigrant father and a French mother. She was educated in a Catholic convent school in St. Louis, and married a Louisiana banker named Oscar Chopin when she was nineteen. In Louisiana she had six children before her husband's death in 1882, after which she returned to St. Louis and began writing to help support herself and her family. Her fine novel, *The Awakening*, which has been called an American *Madame Bovary*, was published in 1899 and instantly became the object of attacks by reviewers. It was actually removed from the shelves of the Mercantile Library in St. Louis, and Chopin was denied membership in the Fine Arts Club because the book was, as a local magazine said, "too strong drink for moral babes and should be labeled 'poison.'" Like many another writer, Chopin is getting her due appreciation after her death. Her story reprinted here is the shortest one of this collection, but it is, if not "poison," strong medicine.

The Story of an Hour

Knowing that Mrs. Mallard was afflicted with a heart trouble, great care was taken to break to her as gently as possible the news of her husband's death.

It was her sister Josephine who told her, in broken sentences; veiled hints that revealed in half concealing. Her husband's friend Richards was there, too, near her. It was he who had been in the newspaper office when intelligence of the railroad disaster was received, with Brently Mallard's name leading the list of "killed." He had only taken the time to assure himself of its truth by a second telegram, and had hastened to forestall any less careful, less tender friend in bearing the sad message.

She did not hear the story as many women have heard the same, with a paralyzed inability to accept its significance. She wept at once, with sudden, wild abandonment, in her sister's arms. When the storm of grief had spent itself she went away to her room alone. She would have no one follow her.

There stood, facing the open window, a comfortable, roomy armchair. Into this she sank, pressed down by a physical exhaustion that haunted her body and seemed to reach into her soul.

She could see in the open square before her house the tops of trees that were all aquiver with the new spring life. The delicious breath of rain was in the air. In the street below a peddler was crying his wares. The notes of a distant song which some one was singing reached her faintly, and countless sparrows were twittering in the eaves.

There were patches of blue sky showing here and there through the clouds that had met and piled one above the other in the west facing her window.

She sat with her head thrown back upon the cushion of the chair, quite motionless, except when a sob came up into her throat and shook her, as a child who has cried itself to sleep continues to sob in its dreams.

She was young, with a fair, calm face, whose lines bespoke repression and even a certain strength. But now there was a dull stare in her eyes, whose gaze was fixed away off yonder on one of those patches of blue sky. It was not a glance of reflection, but rather indicated a suspension of intelligent thought.

There was something coming to her and she was waiting for it, fearfully. What was it? She did not know; it was too subtle and elusive to name. But she felt it, creeping out of the sky, reaching toward her through the sounds, the scents, the color that filled the air.

Now her bosom rose and fell tumultuously. She was beginning to recognize this thing that was approaching to possess her, and she was striving to beat it back with her will—as powerless as her two white slender hands would have been.

When she abandoned herself a little whispered word escaped her slightly parted lips. She said it over and over under her breath: "free, free, free!" The vacant stare and the look of terror that had followed it went from her eyes. They stayed keen and bright. Her pulses beat fast, and the coursing blood warmed and relaxed every inch of her body.

She did not stop to ask if it were or were not a monstrous joy that held her. A clear and exalted perception enabled her to dismiss the suggestion as trivial.

She knew that she would weep again when she saw the kind, tender hands folded in death; the face that had never looked save with love upon her, fixed and gray and dead. But she saw beyond that bitter moment a long procession of years to come that would belong to her absolutely. And she opened and spread her arms out to them in welcome.

There would be no one to live for during those coming years; she would live for herself. There would be no powerful will bending hers in that blind persistence with which men and women believe they have a right to impose a private will upon a fellow-creature. A kind intention or a cruel intention made the act seem no less a crime as she looked upon it in that brief moment of illumination.

And yet she had loved him—sometimes. Often she had not. What did it matter! What could love, the unsolved mystery, count for in face of this possession of self-assertion which she suddenly recognized as the strongest impulse of her being!

"Free! Body and soul free!" she kept whispering.

Josephine was kneeling before the closed door with her lips to the keyhole, imploring for admission. "Louise, open the door! I beg; open the door—you will make yourself ill. What are you doing, Louise? For heaven's sake open the door."

"Go away. I am not making myself ill." No; she was drinking in a very elixir of life through that open window.

Her fancy was running riot along those days ahead of her. Spring days, and summer days, and all sorts of days that would be her own. She breathed a quick prayer that life might be long. It was only yesterday she had thought with a shudder that life might be long.

She arose at length and opened the door to her sister's importunities. There was a feverish triumph in her eyes, and she carried herself unwittingly like a goddess of Victory. She clasped her sister's waist, and together they descended the stairs. Richards stood waiting for them at the bottom.

Some one was opening the front door with a latchkey. It was Brently Mallard who entered, a little travel-stained, composedly carrying his grip-sack and umbrella. He had been far from the scene of accident, and did not even know there had been one. He stood amazed at Josephine's piercing cry; at Richards' quick motion to screen him from the view of his wife.

But Richards was too late.

When the doctors came they said she had died of heart disease— of joy that kills.

ANTON CHEKHOV

1860–1904

Born in Taganrog, Russia, Chekhov was the son of a tradesman and grandson of a serf (peasant slave). After attending a local school, he went in 1879 to study medicine at the University of Moscow, where he supported himself by writing comic sketches for newspapers and magazines. After taking his medical degree in 1884, he began writing more seriously, publishing both stories and plays. When he married a young actress in 1901, he was already dying of tuberculosis. He moved to Yalta in the south and continued to write, finishing his dramatic masterpiece *The Cherry Orchard* in the year of his death. His hundreds of short stories made him, along with Maupassant, one of the two masters of the realistic short story in the nineteenth century.

Heartache

"To whom shall I tell my sorrow?"[1]

Evening twilight. Large flakes of wet snow are circling lazily about the street lamps which have just been lighted, settling in a thin soft layer on roofs, horses' backs, peoples' shoulders, caps. Iona Potapov, the cabby, is all white like a ghost. As hunched as a living body can be, he sits on the box without stirring. If a whole snowdrift were to fall on him, even then, perhaps he would not find it necessary to shake it off. His nag, too, is white and motionless. Her immobility, the angularity of her shape, and the sticklike straightness of her legs make her look like a penny gingerbread horse. She is probably lost in thought. Anyone who has been torn away from the plow, from the familiar gray scenes, and cast into this whirlpool full of monstrous lights, of ceaseless uproar and hurrying people, cannot help thinking.

Iona and his nag have not budged for a long time. They had driven out of the yard before dinnertime and haven't had a single fare yet. But now evening dusk is descending upon the city. The pale light of the street lamps changes to a vivid color and the bustle of the street grows louder.

"Sleigh to the Vyborg District!" Iona hears. "Sleigh!"

Iona starts, and through his snow-plastered eyelashes sees an officer in a military overcoat with a hood.

"To the Vyborg District!" repeats the officer. "Are you asleep, eh? To the Vyborg District!"

As a sign of assent Iona gives a tug at the reins, which sends layers of snow flying from the horse's back and from his own shoulders. The officer gets into the sleigh. The driver clucks to the horse, cranes his neck like a swan, rises in his seat and, more from habit than necessity, flourishes his whip. The nag, too, stretches her neck, crooks her sticklike legs and irresolutely sets off.

"Where are you barging in, damn you?" Iona is promptly assailed by shouts from the massive dark wavering to and fro before him. "Where the devil are you going? Keep to the right!"

"Don't you know how to drive? Keep to the right," says the officer with vexation.

A coachman driving a private carriage swears at him; a pedestrian who was crossing the street and brushed against the nag's nose with his shoulder, looks at him angrily and shakes the snow off his sleeve. Iona fidgets on the box as if sitting on needles and pins, thrusts out his

1. From an old Russian song comparable to a Negro Spiritual.

elbows and rolls his eyes like a madman, as though he did not know where he was or why he was there.

"What rascals they all are," the officer jokes. "They are doing their best to knock into you or be trampled by the horse. It's a conspiracy."

Iona looks at his fare and moves his lips. He wants to say something, but the only sound that comes out is a wheeze.

"What is it?" asks the officer.

Iona twists his mouth into a smile, strains his throat and croaks hoarsely: "My son, sir . . . er, my son died this week."

"H'm, what did he die of?"

Iona turns his whole body around to his fare and says, "Who can tell? It must have been a fever. He lay in the hospital only three days and then he died. . . . It is God's will."

"Get over, you devil!" comes out of the dark. "Have you gone blind, you old dog? Keep your eyes peeled!"

"Go on, go on," says the officer. "We shan't get there until tomorrow at this rate. Give her the whip!"

The driver cranes his neck again, rises in his seat, and with heavy grace swings his whip. Then he looks around at the officer several times, but the latter keeps his eyes closed and is apparently indisposed to listen. Letting his fare off in the Vyborg District, Iona stops by a teahouse and again sits motionless and hunched on the box. Again the wet snow paints him and his nag white. One hour passes, another . . .

Three young men, two tall and lanky, one short and hunchbacked, come along swearing at each other and loudly pound the pavement with their galoshes.

"Cabby, to the Police Bridge!" the hunchback shouts in a cracked voice. "The three of us . . . twenty kopecks!"

Iona tugs at the reins and clucks to his horse. Twenty kopecks is not fair, but his mind is not on that. Whether it is a ruble or five kopecks, it is all one to him now, so long as he has a fare. . . . The three young men, jostling each other and using foul language, go up to the sleigh and all three try to sit down at once. They start arguing about which two are to sit and who shall be the one to stand. After a long ill-tempered and abusive altercation, they decide that the hunchback must stand up because he is the shortest.

"Well, get going," says the hunchback in his cracked voice, taking up his station and breathing down Iona's neck. "On your way! What a cap you've got, brother! You won't find a worse one in all Petersburg—"

"Hee, hee . . . hee, hee . . ." Iona giggles, "as you say—"

"Well, then, 'as you say,' drive on. Are you going to crawl like this all the way, eh? D'you want to get it in the neck?"

"My head is splitting," says one of the tall ones. "At the Duk-masovs' yesterday, Vaska and I killed four bottles of cognac between us."

"I don't get it, why lie?" says the other tall one angrily. "He is lying like a trouper."

"Strike me dead, it's the truth!"

"It is about as true as that a louse sneezes."

"Hee, hee," giggles Iona. "The gentlemen are feeling good!"

"Faugh, the devil take you!" cries the hunchback indignantly. "Will you get a move on, you old pest, or won't you? Is that the way to drive? Give her a crack of the whip! Giddap, devil! Giddap! Let her feel it!"

Iona feels the hunchback's wriggling body and quivering voice behind his back. He hears abuse addressed to him, sees people, and the feeling of loneliness begins little by little to lift from his heart. The hunchback swears till he chokes on an elaborate three-decker oath and is overcome by cough. The tall youths begin discussing a certain Nadezhda Petrovna. Iona looks round at them. When at last there is a lull in the conversation for which he has been waiting, he turns around and says: "This week . . . er . . . my son died."

"We shall all die," says the hunchback, with a sigh wiping his lips after his coughing fit. "Come, drive on, drive on. Gentlemen, I simply cannot stand this pace! When will he get us there?"

"Well, you give him a little encouragement. Biff him in the neck!"

"Do you hear, you old pest? I'll give it to you in the neck. If one stands on ceremony with fellows like you, one may as well walk. Do you hear, you old serpent? Or don't you give a damn what we say?"

And Iona hears rather than feels the thud of a blow on his neck.

"Hee, hee," he laughs. "The gentlemen are feeling good. God give you health!"

"Cabby, are you married?" asks one of the tall ones.

"Me? Hee, hee! The gentlemen are feeling good. The only wife for me now is the damp earth . . . Hee, haw, haw! The grave, that is! . . . Here my son is dead and me alive . . . It is a queer thing, death comes in at the wrong door . . . It don't come for me, it comes for my son. . . ."

And Iona turns round to tell them how his son died, but at that point the hunchback gives a sigh of relief and announces that, thank God, they have arrived at last. Having received his twenty kopecks, for a long while Iona stares after the revelers, who disappear into a dark entrance. Again he is alone and once more silence envelops him. The grief which has been allayed for a brief space comes back again and wrenches his heart more cruelly than ever. There is a look of anxiety and torment in Iona's eyes as they wander restlessly over the crowds moving to and fro on both sides of the street. Isn't there someone among those thousands who will listen to him? But the crowds hurry past, heedless of him and his grief. His grief is immense, boundless. If his heart were to burst and his grief to pour out, it seems that it would flood the whole world, and yet no one sees it. It has found a place for itself in such an insignificant shell that no one can see it in broad daylight.

Iona notices a doorkeeper with a bag and makes up his mind to speak to him.

"What time will it be, friend?" he asks.

"Past nine. What have you stopped here for? On your way!"

Iona drives a few steps away, hunches up and surrenders himself to his grief. He feels it is useless to turn to people. But before five minutes are over, he draws himself up, shakes his head as though stabbed by a sharp pain and tugs at the reins . . . He can bear it no longer.

"Back to the yard!" he thinks. "To the yard!"

And his nag, as though she knew his thoughts, starts out at a trot. An hour and a half later, Iona is sitting beside a large dirty stove. On the stove, on the floor, on benches are men snoring. The air is stuffy and foul. Iona looks at the sleeping figures, scratches himself and regrets that he has come home so early.

"I haven't earned enough to pay for the oats," he reflects. "That's what's wrong with me. A man that knows his job . . . who has enough to eat and has enough for his horse don't need to fret."

In one of the corners a young driver gets up, hawks sleepily and reaches for the water bucket.

"Thirsty?" Iona asks him.

"Guess so."

"H'm, may it do you good, but my son is dead, brother . . . did you hear? This week in the hospital. . . . What a business!"

Iona looks to see the effect of his words, but he notices none. The young man has drawn his cover over his head and is already asleep. The old man sighs and scratches himself. Just as the young man was thirsty for water so he thirsts for talk. It will soon be a week since his son died and he hasn't talked to anybody about him properly. He ought to be able to talk about it, taking his time, sensibly. He ought to tell how his son was taken ill, how he suffered, what he said before he died, how he died. . . . He ought to describe the funeral, and how he went to the hospital to fetch his son's clothes. His daughter Anisya is still in the country. . . . And he would like to talk about her, too. Yes, he has plenty to talk about now. And his listener should gasp and moan and keen. . . . It would be even better to talk to women. Though they are foolish, two words will make them blubber.

"I must go out and have a look at the horse," Iona thinks. "There will be time enough for sleep. You will have enough sleep, no fear. . . ."

He gets dressed and goes into the stable where his horse is standing. He thinks about oats, hay, the weather. When he is alone, he dares not think of his son. It is possible to talk about him with someone, but to think of him when one is alone, to evoke his image is unbearably painful.

"You chewing?" Iona asks his mare seeing her shining eyes. "There, chew away, chew away. . . . If we haven't earned enough for oats, we'll eat hay. . . . Yes. . . . I've grown too old to drive. My son had ought to be driving, not me. . . . He was a real cabby. . . . He had ought to have lived. . . ."

Iona is silent for a space and then goes on: "That's how it is, old girl. . . . Kuzma Ionych is gone. . . . Departed this life. . . . He went and died to no purpose. . . . Now let's say you had a little colt, and you were that little colt's own mother. And suddenly, let's say, that same little colt departed this life. . . . You'd be sorry, wouldn't you?"

The nag chews, listens and breathes on her master's hands. Iona is carried away and tells her eveything.

STEPHEN CRANE
1871–1900

Born in Newark, New Jersey, Crane was the fourteenth child of a methodist minister, who named him after an ancestor who had signed the Declaration of Independence. He was a delicate child, whose health improved when his family moved to Port Jervis, New York, in 1879. After his father died he went to the Hudson River Institute at Caverack, New York, and then to Lafayette College and Syracuse University, shifting his interests from engineering to literature. He was an excellent baseball player—once considering a professional career—and a good boxer as well. While in school he began work as a journalist, a profession which he pursued for most of his life. But his reporting always suffered from an excess of art. A poetic image would distract him from journalistic details. He wrote an ironic novel (Maggie: A Girl of the Streets) when he was twenty-two, and a masterful novel of the Civil War (The Red Badge of Courage) two years later. He had not been to war but had heard the accounts of soldiers and he had read Tolstoy. Later, he became a war correspondent and confirmed his guesses first hand. Like many of America's best writers, he was cynical and sentimental at the same time. His blunt manner and indifference to public opinion offended many of his contemporaries, but Henry James and Joseph Conrad admired his work and came to pay their respects to the younger man as he was dying in England of tuberculosis.

The Bride Comes to Yellow Sky

I

The great Pullman was whirling onward with such dignity of motion that a glance from the window seemed simply to prove that the plains of Texas were pouring eastward. Vast flats of green grass, dull-hued spaces of mesquit and cactus, little groups of frame houses, woods of light and tender trees, all were sweeping into the east, sweeping over the horizon, a precipice.

A newly married pair had boarded this coach at San Antonio. The man's face was reddened from many days in the wind and sun, and a direct result of his new black clothes was that his brick-coloured hands were constantly performing in a most conscious fashion. From time to time he looked down respectfully at his attire. He sat with a hand on each knee, like a man waiting in a barber's shop. The glances he devoted to other passengers were furtive and shy.

The bride was not pretty, nor was she very young. She wore a dress of blue cashmere, with small reservations of velvet here and there, and with steel buttons abounding. She continually twisted her head to regard her puff sleeves, very stiff, straight, and high. They embarrassed her. It was quite apparent that she had cooked, and that she expected to cook, dutifully. The blushes caused by the careless scrutiny of some passengers as she had entered the car were strange to see upon this plain, under-class countenance, which was drawn in placid, almost emotionless lines.

They were evidently very happy. "Ever been in a parlour-car before?" he asked, smiling with delight.

"No," she answered; "I never was. It's fine, ain't it?"

"Great! And then after a while we'll go forward to the diner, and get a big lay-out. Finest meal in the world. Charge a dollar."

'Oh, do they?'' cried the bride. "Charge a dollar? Why, that's too much—for us—ain't it, Jack?"

"Not this trip, anyhow," he answered bravely. "We're going to go the whole thing."

Later he explained to her about the trains. "You see, it's a thousand miles from one end of Texas to the other; and this train runs right across it, and never stops but four times." He had the pride of an owner. He pointed out to her the dazzling fittings of the coach; and in truth her eyes opened wider as she contemplated the sea-green figured velvet, the shining brass, silver, and glass, the wood that gleamed as darkly brilliant as the surface of a pool of oil. At one end a bronze figure sturdily held a support for a separated chamber, and at convenient places on the ceiling were frescos in olive and silver.

To the minds of the pair, their surroundings reflected the glory of their marriage that morning in San Antonio; this was the environment of their new estate; and the man's face in particular beamed with an elation that made him appear ridiculous to the negro porter. This individual at times surveyed them from afar with an amused and superior grin. On other occasions he bullied them with skill in ways that did not make it exactly plain to them that they were being bullied. He subtly used all the manners of the most unconquerable kind of snobbery. He oppressed them; but of this oppression they had small knowledge, and they speedily forgot that infrequently a number of travellers covered them with stares of derisive enjoyment. Historically there was supposed to be something infinitely humorous in their situation.

"We are due in Yellow Sky at 3:42," he said, looking tenderly into her eyes.

"Oh, are we?" she said, as if she had not been aware of it. To evince surprise at her husband's statement was part of her wifely amiability. She took from a pocket a little silver watch; and as she held it before her, and stared at it with a frown of attention, the new husband's face shone.

"I bought it in San Anton' from a friend of mine," he told her gleefully.

"It's seventeen minutes past twelve," she said, looking up at him with a kind of shy and clumsy coquetry. A passenger, noting this play, grew excessively sardonic, and winked at himself in one of the numerous mirrors.

At last they went to the dining-car. Two rows of negro waiters, in glowing white suits, surveyed their entrance with the interest, and also the equanimity, of men who had been forewarned. The pair fell to the lot of a waiter who happened to feel pleasure in steering them through their meal. He viewed them with the manner of a fatherly pilot, his countenance radiant with benevolence. The patronage, entwined with the ordinary deference, was not plain to them. And yet, as they returned to their coach, they showed in their faces a sense of escape.

To the left, miles down a long purple slope, was a little ribbon of mist where moved the keening Rio Grande. The train was approaching it at an angle, and the apex was Yellow Sky. Presently it was apparent that, as the distance from Yellow Sky grew shorter, the husband became commensurately restless. His brick-red hands were more insistent in their prominence. Occasionally he was even rather absent-minded and far-away when the bride leaned forward and addressed him.

As a matter of truth, Jack Potter was beginning to find the shadow of a deed weigh upon him like a leaden slab. He, the town marshal of Yellow Sky, a man known, liked, and feared in his corner, a prominent person, had gone to San Antonio to meet a girl he believed he loved, and there, after the usual prayers, had actually induced her to marry him, without consulting Yellow Sky for any part of the transaction. He was now bringing his bride before an innocent and unsuspecting community.

Of course people in Yellow Sky married as it pleased them in accordance with a general custom; but such was Potter's thought of his duty to his friends, or of their idea of his duty, or of an unspoken form which does not control men in these matters, that he felt he was heinous. He had committed an extraordinary crime. Face to face with this girl in San Antonio, and spurred by his sharp impulse, he had gone headlong over all the social hedges. At San Antonio he was like a man hidden in the dark. A knife to sever any friendly duty, any form, was easy to his hand in that remote city. But the hour of Yellow Sky—the hour of daylight—was approaching.

He knew full well that his marriage was an important thing to his town. It could only be exceeded by the burning of the new hotel. His friends could not forgive him. Frequently he had reflected on the advisability of telling them by telegraph, but a new cowardice had been upon him. He feared to do it. And now the train was hurrying him toward a scene of amazement, glee, and reproach. He glanced out of the window at the line of haze swinging slowly in toward the train.

Yellow Sky had a kind of brass band, which played painfully, to the delight of the populace. He laughed without heart as he thought of it. If the citizens could dream of his prospective arrival with his bride, they would parade the band at the station and escort them, amid cheers and laughing congratulations, to his adobe home.

He resolved that he would use all the devices of speed and plainscraft in making the journey from the station to his house. Once within that safe citadel, he could issue some sort of vocal bulletin, and then not go among the citizens until they had time to wear off a little of their enthusiasm.

The bride looked anxiously at him. "What's worrying you, Jack?"

He laughed again. "I'm not worrying, girl; I'm only thinking of Yellow Sky."

She flushed in comprehension.

A sense of mutual guilt invaded their minds and developed a finer tenderness. They looked at each other with eyes softly aglow. But Potter often laughed the same nervous laugh; the flush upon the bride's face seemed quite permanent.

The traitor to the feelings of Yellow Sky narrowly watched the speeding landscape. "We're nearly there," he said.

Presently the porter came and announced the proximity of Potter's home. He held a brush in his hand, and, with all his airy superiority gone, he brushed Potter's new clothes as the latter slowly turned this way and that way. Potter fumbled out a coin and gave it to the porter, as he had seen others do. It was a heavy and muscle-bound business, as that of a man shoeing his first horse.

The porter took their bag, and as the train began to slow they moved forward to the hooded platform of the car. Presently the two engines and their long string of coaches rushed into the station of Yellow Sky.

"They have to take water here," said Potter, from a constricted throat and in mournful cadence, as one announcing death. Before the train stopped his eye had swept the length of the platform, and he was glad and astonished to see there was none upon it but the station-agent, who, with a slightly hurried and anxious air, was walking toward the water-tanks. When the train had halted, the porter alighted first, and placed in position a little temporary step.

"Come on, girl," said Potter, hoarsely. As he helped her down they each laughed on a false note. He took the bag from the negro, and bade his wife cling to his arm. As they slunk rapidly away, his hang-dog glance perceived that they were unloading the two trunks, and also that the station-agent, far ahead near the baggage-car, had turned and was running toward him, making gestures. He laughed, and groaned as he laughed, when he noted the first effect of his marital bliss upon Yellow Sky. He gripped his wife's arm firmly to his side, and they fled. Behind them the porter stood, chuckling fatuously.

II

The California express on the Southern Railway was due at Yellow Sky in twenty-one minutes. There were six men at the bar of the Weary Gentleman saloon. One was a drummer who talked a great deal and rapidly; three were Texans who did not care to talk at that time; and two were Mexican sheep-herders, who did not talk as a general practice in the Weary Gentleman saloon. The barkeeper's dog lay on the board walk that crossed in front of the door. His head was on his paws, and he glanced drowsily here and there with the constant vigilance of a dog that is kicked on occasion. Across the sandy street were some vivid green grass-plots, so wonderful in appearance, amid the sands that burned near them in a blazing sun, that they caused a doubt in the mind. They exactly resembled the grass mats used to represent lawns on the stage. At the cooler end of the railway station, a man without a coat sat in a tilted chair and smoked his pipe. The fresh-cut bank of the Rio Grande circled near the town, and there could be seen beyond it a great plum-coloured plain of mesquit.

Save for the busy drummer and his companions in the saloon, Yellow Sky was dozing. The new-comer leaned gracefully upon the bar, and recited many tales with the confidence of a bard who has come upon a new field.

"—and at the moment that the old man fell downstairs with the bureau in his arms, the old woman was coming up with two scuttles of coal, and of course—"

The drummer's tale was interrupted by a young man who suddenly appeared in the open door. He cried: "Scratchy Wilson's drunk, and has turned loose with both hands." The two Mexicans at once set down their glasses and faded out of the rear entrance of the saloon.

The drummer, innocent and jocular, answered: "All right, old man. S'pose he has? Come in and have a drink, anyhow."

But the information had made such an obvious cleft in every skull in the room that the drummer was obliged to see its importance. All had become instantly solemn. "Say," said he, mystified, "what is this?" His three companions made the introductory genture of eloquent speech; but the young man at the door forestalled them.

"It means, my friend," he answered, as he came into the saloon, "that for the next two hours this town won't be a health resort."

The barkeeper went to the door, and locked and barred it; reaching out of the window, he pulled in heavy wooden shutters, and barred them. Immediately a solemn, chapel-like gloom was upon the place. The drummer was looking from one to another.

"But say," he cried, "what is this, anyhow? You don't mean there is going to be a gun-fight?"

"Don't know whether there'll be a fight or not," answered one man, grimly; "but there'll be some shootin'—some good shootin'."

The young man who had warned them waved his hand. "Oh, there'll be a fight fast enough, if any one wants it. Anybody can get a fight out there in the street. There's a fight just waiting."

The drummer seemed to be swayed between the interest of a foreigner and a perception of personal danger.

"What did you say his name was?" he asked.

"Scratchy Wilson," they answered in chorus.

"And will he kill anybody? What are you going to do? Does this happen often? Does he rampage around like this once a week or so? Can he break in that door?"

"No; he can't break down that door," replied the barkeeper. "He's tried it three times. But when he comes you'd better lay down on the floor, stranger. He's dead sure to shoot at it, and a bullet may come through."

Thereafter the drummer kept a strict eye upon the door. The time had not yet called for him to hug the floor, but, as a minor precaution, he sidled near the wall. "Will he kill anybody?" he said again.

The men laughed low and scornfully at the question.

"He's out to shoot, and he's out for trouble. Don't see any good in experimentin' with him."

"But what do you do in a case like this? What do you do?"

A man responded: "Why, he and Jack Potter—"

"But," in chorus the other men interrupted, "Jack Potter's in San Anton."

"Well, who is he? What's he got to do with it?"

"Oh, he's the town marshal. He goes out and fights Scratchy when he gets on one of these tears."

"Wow!" said the drummer, mopping his brow. "Nice job he's got."

The voices had toned away to mere whisperings. The drummer wished to ask further questions, which were born of an increasing anxiety and bewilderment; but when he attempted them, the men merely looked at him in irritation and motioned him to remain silent. A tense waiting hush was upon them. In the deep shadows of the room their eyes shone as they listened for sounds from the street. One man made three gestures at the barkeeper; and the latter, moving like a ghost, handed him a glass and a bottle. The man poured a full glass of whisky, and set down the bottle noiselessly. He gulped the whisky in a swallow, and turned again toward the door in immovable silence. The drummer saw that the barkeeper, without a sound, had taken a Winchester from beneath the bar. Later he saw this individual beckoning to him, so he tiptoed across the room.

"You better come with me back of the bar."

"No, thanks," said the drummer, perspiring; "I'd rather be where I can make a break for the back door."

Whereupon the man of bottles made a kindly but peremptory gesture. The drummer obeyed it, and, finding himself seated on a box with his head below the level of the bar, balm was laid upon his soul at sight of various zinc and copper fittings that bore a resemblance to armour-plate. The barkeeper took a seat comfortably upon an adjacent box.

"You see," he whispered, "this here Scratchy Wilson is a wonder with a gun—a perfect wonder; and when he goes on the war-trail, we hunt our holes—naturally. He's about the last one of the old gang that used to hang out along the river here. He's a terror when he's drunk. When he's sober he's all right—kind of simple—wouldn't hurt a fly—nicest fellow in town. But when he's drunk—whoo!"

There were periods of stillness. "I wish Jack Potter was back from

San Anton'," said the barkeeper. "He shot Wilson up once—in the leg—and he would sail in and pull out the kinks in this thing."

Presently they heard from a distance the sound of a shot, followed by three wild yowls. It instantly removed a bond from the men in the darkened saloon. There was a shuffling of feet. They looked at each other. "Here he comes," they said.

III

A man in a maroon-coloured flannel shirt, which had been purchased for purposes of decoration, and made principally by some Jewish women on the East Side of New York, rounded a corner and walked into the middle of the main street of Yellow Sky. In either hand the man held a long, heavy, blue-black revolver. Often he yelled, and these cries rang through a semblance of a deserted village, shrilly flying over the roofs in a volume that seemed to have no relation to the ordinary vocal strength of a man. It was as if the surrounding stillness formed the arch of a tomb over him. These cries of ferocious challenge rang against walls of silence. And his boots had red tops with gilded imprints, of the kind beloved in winter by little sledding boys on the hillsides of New England.

The man's face flamed in a rage begot of whisky. His eyes, rolling, and yet keen for ambush, hunted the still doorways and windows. He walked with the creeping movement of the midnight cat. As it occurred to him, he roared menacing information. The long revolvers in his hands were as easy as straws; they were removed with an electric swiftness. The little fingers of each hand played sometimes in a musician's way. Plain from the low collar of the shirt, the cords of his neck straightened and sank, straightened and sank, as passion moved him. The only sounds were his terrible invitations. The calm adobes preserved their demeanour at the passing of this small thing in the middle of the street.

There was no offer of fight—no offer of fight. The man called to the sky. There were no attractions. He bellowed and fumed and swayed his revolvers here and everywhere.

The dog of the barkeeper of the Weary Gentleman saloon had not appreciated the advance of events. He yet lay dozing in front of his master's door. At sight of the dog, the man paused and raised his revolver humorously. At sight of the man, the dog sprang up and walked diagonally away, with a sullen head, and growling. The man yelled, and the dog broke into a gallop. As it was about to enter the alley, there was a loud noise, a whistling, and something spat the ground directly before it. The dog screamed, and, wheeling in terror, galloped headlong in a new direction. Again there was a noise, a whistling, and sand was kicked viciously before it. Fear-stricken, the dog turned and flurried like an animal in a pen. The man stood laughing, his weapons at his hips.

Ultimately the man was attracted by the closed door of the Weary Gentleman saloon. He went to it and, hammering with a revolver, demanded drink.

The door remaining imperturbable, he picked a bit of paper from the walk, and nailed it to the framework with a knife. He then turned his back contemptuously upon this popular resort and, walking to the opposite side of the street and spinning there on his heel quickly and lithely, fired at the bit of paper. He missed it by a half inch. He swore at himself, and went away. Later he comfortably fusilladed the windows of his most intimate friend. The man was playing with this town; it was a toy for him.

But still there was no offer of fight. The name of Jack Potter, his ancient antagonist, entered his mind, and he concluded that it would be a glad thing if he should go to Potter's house, and by bombardment induce him to come out and fight. He moved in the direction of his desire, chanting Apache scalp-music.

When he arrived at it, Potter's house presented the same still front as had the other adobes. Taking up a strategic position, the man howled a challenge. But this house regarded him as might a great stone god. It gave no sign. After a decent wait, the man howled further challenges, mingling with them wonderful epithets.

Presently there came the spectacle of a man churning himself into deepest rage over the immobility of a house. He fumed at it as the winter wind attacks a prairie cabin in the North. To the distance there should have gone the sound of a tumult like the fighting of two hundred Mexicans. As necessity bade him, he paused for breath or to reload his revolvers.

IV

Potter and his bride walked sheepishly and with speed. Sometimes they laughed together shamefacedly and low.

"Next corner, dear," he said finally.

They put forth the efforts of a pair walking bowed against a strong wind. Potter was about to raise a finger to point the first appearance of the new home when, as they circled the corner, they came face to face with a man in a maroon-coloured shirt, who was feverishly pushing cartridges into a large revolver. Upon the instant the man dropped his revolver to the ground and, like lightning, whipped another from its holster. The second weapon was aimed at the bridegroom's chest.

There was a silence. Potter's mouth seeemed to be merely a grave for his tongue. He exhibited an instinct to at once loosen his arm from the woman's grip, and he dropped the bag to the sand. As for the bride, her face had gone as yellow as old cloth. She was a slave to hideous rites, gazing at the apparitional snake.

The two men faced each other at a distance of three paces. He of the revolver smiled with a new and quiet ferocity.

"Tried to sneak up on me," he said. "Tried to sneak up on me!" His eyes grew more baleful. As Potter made a slight movement, the man thrust his revolver venomously forward "No; don't you do it, Jack Potter. Don't you move a finger toward a gun just yet. Don't you move an eyelash. The time has come for me to settle with you and I'm goin' to do it my own way, and loaf along with no inter-ferin'. So if you don't want a gun bent on you, just mind what I tell you."

Potter looked at his enemy. "I ain't got a gun on me Scratchy," he said. "Honest, I ain't." He was stiffening and steadying, but yet somewhere at the back of his mind a vision of the Pullman floated: the sea-green figured velvet, the shining brass, silver, and glass, the wood that gleamed as darkly brilliant as the surface of a pool of oil— all the glory of marriage, the environment of the new estate. "You know I fight when it comes to fighting, Scratchy Wilson; but I ain't got a gun on me. You'll have to do all the shootin' yourself."

His enemy's face went livid. He stepped forward, and lashed his weapon to and fro before Potter's chest. "Don't you tell me you ain't got no gun on you, you whelp. Don't tell me no lie like that. There ain't a man in Texas ever seen you without no gun. Don't take me for no kid." His eyes blazed with light, and his throat worked like a pump.

"I ain't takin' you for no kid," answered Potter. His heels had not moved an inch backward. "I'm takin' you for a damn fool. I tell you I ain't got a gun, and I ain't. If you're goin' to shoot me up, you better begin now; you'll never get a chance like this again."

So much enforced reasoning had told on Wilson's rage; he was calmer. "If you ain't got a gun, why ain't you got a gun?" he sneered. "Been to Sunday-school?"

"I ain't got a gun because I've just come fron San Anton' with my wife. I'm married," said Potter. "And if I'd thought there was going to be any galoots like you prowling around when I brought my wife home, I'd had a gun, and don't you forget it."

"Married!" said Scratchy, not at all comprehending.

"Yes, married. I'm married," said Potter, distinctly.

"Married?" said Scratchy. Seemingly for the first time, he saw the drooping, drowning woman at the other man's side. "No!" he said. He was like a creature allowed a glimpse of another world. He moved a pace backward, and his arm, with the revolver, dropped to his side. "Is this the lady?" he asked.

"Yes; this is the lady," answered Potter.

There was another period of silence.

"Well," said Wilson at last, slowly, "I s'pose it's all off now."

"It's all off if you say so, Scratchy. You know I didn't make the trouble." Potter lifted his valise.

"Well, I 'low it's off, Jack," said Wilson. He was looking at the ground. "Married!" He was not a student of chivalry; it was merely that in the presence of this foreign condition he was a simple child of the earlier plains. He picked up his starboard revolver, and, placing both weapons in their holsters, he went away. His feet made funnel-shaped tracks in the heavy sand.

SHERWOOD ANDERSON
1876–1941

Born in Camden, Ohio, Anderson grew up in a variety of small towns, as his talkative, unreliable father moved from job to job. The boy also did odd jobs, and was known for a while as "Jobby." He worked in the fields and at race tracks before serving in the Army—in Cuba—during the Spanish American war. Afterward he wrote advertising copy and ran a paint factory before turning seriously to the writing of fiction. After 1912 essays, poems, and stories by Anderson began appearing regularly, but today his reputation rests upon the stories of small-town America that appeared in *Winesburg, Ohio* (1919) and *Horses and Men* (1923). In his later years he influenced and befriended such younger writers as Hemingway and Faulkner, who parodied him for his pains.

I'm a Fool

It was a hard jolt for me, one of the most bitterest I ever had to face. And it all came about through my own foolishness, too. Even yet sometimes, when I think of it, I want to cry or swear or kick myself. Perhaps, even now, after all this time, there will be a kind of satisfaction in making myself look cheap by telling of it.

It began at three o'clock one October afternoon as I sat in the grandstand at the fall trotting and pacing meet at Sandusky, Ohio.

To tell the truth, I felt a little foolish that I should be sitting in the grandstand at all. During the summer before I had left my home town with Harry Whitehead and, with a nigger named Burt, had taken a job as swipe with one of the two horses Harry was campaigning through the fall race meets that year. Mother cried and my sister Mildred, who wanted to get a job as a school teacher in our town that fall, stormed and scolded about the house all during the week before I left. They both thought it something disgraceful that one of our family should take a place as a swipe with race horses. I've an idea Mildred thought my taking the place would stand in the way of her getting the job she'd been working so long for.

But after all I had to work, and there was no other work to be got. A big lumbering fellow of nineteen couldn't just hang around the house and I had got too big to mow people's lawns and sell newspapers. Little chaps who could get next to people's sympathies by their sizes were always getting jobs away from me. There was one fellow who kept saying to everyone who wanted a lawn mowed or a cistern cleaned, that he was saving money to work his way through college, and I used to lay awake nights thinking up ways to injure him without being found out. I kept thinking of wagons running over him and bricks falling on his head as he walked along the street. But never mind him.

I got the place with Harry and I liked Burt fine. We got along splendid together. He was a big nigger with a lazy sprawling body and soft, kind eyes, and when it came to a fight he could hit like Jack Johnson. He had Bucephalus, a big black pacing stallion that could do 2.09 or 2.10, if he had to, and I had a little gelding named Doctor Fritz that never lost a race all fall when Harry wanted him to win.

We set out from home late in July in a box car with the two horses and after that, until late November, we kept moving along to the race meets and the fairs. It was a peachy time for me, I'll say that. Sometimes now I think that boys who are raised regular in houses, and never have a fine nigger like Burt for best friend, and go to high schools and college, and never steal anything, or get drunk a little, or learn to swear from fellows who know how, or come walking up in front of a grandstand in their shirt sleeves and with dirty horsey pants on when the races are going on and the grandstand is full of people all dressed up—What's the use of talking about it? Such fellows don't know nothing at all. They've never had no opportunity.

But I did. Burt taught me how to rub down a horse and put the bandages on after a race and steam a horse out and a lot of valuable things for any man to know. He could wrap a bandage on a horse's leg so smooth that if it had been the same color you would think it was his skin, and I guess he'd have been a big driver, too, and got to the top like Murphy and Walter Cox and the others if he hadn't been black.

Gee whizz, it was fun. You got to a county seat town, maybe say on a Saturday or Sunday, and the fair began the next Tuesday and lasted until Friday afternoon. Doctor Fritz would be, say in the 2.25 trot on Tuesday afternoon and on Thursday afternoon Bucephalus would knock 'em cold in the "free-for-all" pace. It left you a lot of time to hang around and listen to horse talk, and see Burt knock some yap cold that got too gay, and you'd find out about horses and men and pick up a lot of stuff you could use all the rest of your life, if you had some sense and salted down what you heard and felt and saw.

And then at the end of the week when the race meet was over, and Harry had run home to tend up to his livery stable business, you and Burt hitched the two horses to carts and drove slow and steady across the country, to the place for the next meeting, so as to not overheat the horses, etc., etc., you know.

Gee whiz, Gosh amighty, the nice hickorynut and beechnut and oaks and other kinds of trees along the roads, all brown and-red, and the good smells, and Burt singing a song that was called Deep River, and the country girls at the windows of houses and everything. You can stick your colleges up your nose for all me. I guess I know where I got my education.

Why, one of those little burgs of towns you come to on the way, say now on a Saturday afternoon, and Burt says, "let's lay up here." And you did.

And you took the horses to a livery stable and fed them, and you got your good-clothes out of a box and put them on.

And the town was full of farmers gaping, because they could see you were race-horse people, and the kids maybe never see a nigger before and was afraid and run away when the two of us walked down their main street.

And that was before prohibition and all that foolishness, and so you went into a saloon, the two of you, and all the yaps come and stood around, and there was always someone pretended he was horsey and knew things and spoke up and began asking questions, and all you did was to lie and lie all you could about what horses you had, and I said I owned them, and then some fellow said, "will you have a drink of whisky," and Burt knocked his eye out the way he could say, offhandlike, "Oh well, all right, I'm agreeable to a little nip. I'll split a quart with you." Gee whizz.

But that isn't what I want to tell my story about. We got home late in November and I promised mother I'd quit the race horses for good. There's a lot of things you've got to promise a mother because she don't know any better.

And so, there not being any work in our town any more than

when I left there to go to the races, I went off to Sandusky and got a pretty good place taking care of horses for a man who owned a teaming and delivery and storage coal and real estate business there. It was a pretty good place with good eats, and a day off each week, and sleeping on a cot in a big barn, and mostly just shoveling in hay and oats to a lot of big good-enough skates of horses, that couldn't have trotted a race with a toad. I wasn't dissatisfied and I could send money home.

And then, I started to tell you, the fall races comes to Sandusky and I got the day off and I went. I left the job at noon and had on my good clothes and my new brown derby hat, I'd just bought the Saturday before, and a stand-up collar.

First of all I went downtown and walked about with the dudes. I've always thought to myself, "put up a good front" and so I did it. I had forty dollars in my pocket and so I went into the West House, a big hotel, and walked up to the cigar stand. "Give me three twenty-five cent cigars," I said. There was a lot of horsemen and strangers and dressed-up people from other towns standing around in the lobby and in the bar, and I mingled amongst them. In the bar there was a fellow with a cane and a Windsor tie on, that it made me sick to look at him. I like a man to be a man and dress up, but not to go put on that kind of airs. So I pushed him aside, kind of rough, and had me a drink of whisky. And then he looked at me, as though he thought maybe he'd get gay, but he changed his mind and didn't say anything. And then I had another drink of whisky, just to show him something, and went out and had a hack out to the races, all to myself, and when I got there I bought myself the best seat I could get up in the grandstand, but didn't go in for any of these boxes. That's putting on too many airs.

And so there I was, sitting up in the grandstand as gay as you please and looking down on the swipes coming out with their horses, and with their dirty horsey pants on and the horse blankets swung over their shoulders, same as I had been doing all the year before. I liked one thing about the same as the other, sitting up there and feeling grand and being down there and looking up at the yaps and feeling grander and more important, too. One thing's about as good as another, if you take it just right. I've often said that.

Well, right in front of me, in the grandstand that day, there was a fellow with a couple of girls and they was about my age. The young fellow was a nice guy all right. He was the kind maybe that goes to college and then comes to be a lawyer or maybe a newspaper editor or something like that, but he wasn't stuck on himself. There are some of that kind are all right and he was one of the ones.

He had his sister with him and another girl and the sister looked around over his shoulder, accidental at first, not intending to start anything—she wasn't that kind—and her eyes and mine happened to meet.

You know how it is. Gee, she was a peach! She had on a soft dress, kind of a blue stuff and it looked carelessly made, but was well sewed and made and everything. I knew that much. I blushed when she looked right at me and so did she. She was the nicest girl I've ever seen in my life. She wasn't stuck on herself and she could talk proper grammar without being like a school teacher or something like that. What I mean is she was O.K. I think maybe her father was well-to-do, but not rich to make her chesty because she was his daughter, as some are. Maybe he owned a drugstore or a drygoods store in their home town, or something like that. She never told me and I never asked.

My own people are all O.K. too, when you come to that. My grandfather was Welsh and over in the old country, in Wales he was—But never mind that.

The first heat of the first race come off and the young fellow setting there with the two girls left them and went down to make a bet. I knew what he was up to, but he didn't talk big and noisy and let everyone around know he was a sport, as some do. He wasn't that kind. Well, he come back and I heard him tell the two girls what horse he'd bet on, and when the heat was trotted they all half got to their feet and acted in the excited, sweaty way people do when they've got money down on a race, and the horse they bet on is up there pretty close at the end, and they think maybe he'll come on with a rush, but he never does because he hasn't got the old juice in him, come right down to it.

And then, pretty soon, the horses came out for the 2.18 pace and there was a horse in it I knew. He was a horse Bob French had in his string but Bob didn't own him. He was a horse owned by a Mr. Mathers down at Marietta, Ohio.

This Mr. Mathers had a lot of money and owned some coal mines or something, and he had a swell place out in the country, and he was stuck on race horses, but was a Presbyterian or something, and I think more than likely his wife was one, too, maybe a stiffer one than himself. So he never raced his horses hisself, and the story round the Ohio race tracks was that when one of his horses got ready to go to the races he turned him over to Bob French and pretended to his wife he was sold.

So Bob had the horses and he did pretty much as he pleased and you can't blame Bob, at least, I never did. Sometimes he was out to win and sometimes he wasn't. I never cared much about that when I was swiping a horse. What I did want to know was that my horse had the speed and could go out in front, if you wanted him to.

And, as I'm telling you, there was Bob in this race with one of Mr. Mather's horses, was named "About Ben Ahem" or something like that, and was fast as a streak. He was a gelding and had a mark of 2.21, but could step in .08 or .09.

Because when Burt and I were out, as I've told you, the year before, there was a nigger, Burt knew, worked for Mr. Mathers and we went out there one day when we didn't have no race on at the Marietta Fair and our boss Harry was gone home.

And so everyone was gone to the fair but just this one nigger and he took us all through Mr. Mather's swell house and he and Burt tapped a bottle of wine Mr. Mathers had hid in his bedroom, back in a closet, without his wife knowing, and he showed us this Ahem horse. Burt was always stuck on being a driver but didn't have much chance to get to the top, being a nigger, and he and the other nigger gulped that whole bottle of wine and Burt got a little lit up.

So the nigger let Burt take this About Ben Ahem and step him a mile in a track Mr. Mathers had all to himself, right there on the farm. And Mr. Mathers had one child, a daughter, kinda sick, and not very good-looking, and she came home and we had to hustle to get About Ben Ahem stuck back in the barn.

I'm only telling you to get everything straight. At Sandusky, that afternoon I was at the fair, this young fellow with the two girls was fussed, being with the girls and losing his bet. You know how a fellow is that way. One of them was his girl and the other his sister. I had figured that out.

"Gee whiz," I says to myself, "I'm going to give him the dope."

He was mighty nice when I touched him on the shoulder. He and the girls were nice to me right from the start and clear to the end. I'm not blaming them.

And so he leaned back and I give him the dope on About Ben Ahem. "Don't bet a cent on this first heat because he'll go like an oxen hitched to a plow, but when the first heat is over go right down and lay on your pile." That's what I told him.

Well, I never saw a fellow treat anyone sweller. There was a fat man sitting beside the little girl, that had looked at me twice by this time, and I at her , and both blushing, and what did he do but have the nerve to turn and ask the fat man to get up and change places with me so I could set with his crowd.

Gee whizz, craps amighty. There I was. What a chump I was to go and get gay up there in West House bar, and just because that dude was standing there with a cane and that kind of a necktie on, to go and get all balled up and drink that whisky just to show off.

Of course she would know, me setting right beside her and letting her smell of my breath. I could have kicked myself right down out of that grandstand and all around that race track and made a faster record than most of the skates of horses they had there that year.

Because that girl wasn't any mutt of a girl. What wouldn't I have give right then for a stick of chewing gum to chew, or a lozenger, or some liquorice, or most anything. I was glad I had those twenty-five cent cigars in my pocket and right away I give that fellow one and lit one myself. Then that fat man got up and we changed places and there I was, plunked right down beside her.

They introduced themselves and the fellow's best girl, he had with him, was named Miss Elinor Woodbury, and her father was a manufacturer of barrels from a place called Tiffin, Ohio. And the fellow himself was named Wilbur Wessen and his sister was Miss Lucy Wessen.

I suppose it was their having such swell names got me off my trolley. A fellow, just because he has been a swipe with a race horse, and works taking care of horses for a man in the teaming, delivery, and storage business, isn't any better or worse than anyone else. I've often thought that, and said it too.

But you know how a fellow is. There's something in that kind of nice clothes, and the kind of nice eyes she had, and the way she looked at me, awhile before, over her brother's shoulder, and me looking back at her, and both of us blushing.

I couldn't show her up for a boob, could I?

I made a fool of myself, that's what I did. I said my name was Walter Mathers from Marietta, Ohio, and then I told all three of them the smashingest lie you ever heard. What I said was that my father owned the horse About Ben Ahem and that he had let him out to this Bob French for racing purposes, because our family was proud and had never gone into racing that way, in our own name, I mean. Then I had got started and they were all leaning over and listening, and Miss Lucy Wessen's eyes were shining and I went the whole hog.

I told about our place down at Marietta, and about the big stables and the grand brick house we had on a hill, up above the Ohio River, but I knew enough not to do it in no bragging way. What I did was to start things and then let them drag the rest out of me. I acted just as reluctant to tell as I could. Our family hasn't got any barrel factory, and, since I've known us, we've always been pretty

poor, but not asking anything of anyone at that, and my grandfather, over in Wales—But never mind that.

We set there talking like we had known each other for years and
years, and I went and told them that my father had been expecting
maybe this Bob French wasn't on the square, and had sent me up to
Sandusky on the sly to find out what I could.

And I bluffed it through I had found out all about the 2.18 pace, in
which About Ben Ahem was to start.

I said he would lose the first heat by pacing like a lame cow and
then he would come back and skin 'em alive after that. And to back
up what I said I took thirty dollars out of my pocket and handed it to
Mr. Wilbur Wessen and asked him, would he mind, after the first
heat, to go down and place it on About Ben Ahem for whatever
odds he could get. What I said was that I didn't want Bob French to
see me and none of the swipes.

Sure enough the first heat come off and About Ben Ahem went off
his stride, up the back stretch, and looked like a wooden horse or a
sick one, and come in to be last. Then this Wilbur Wessen went
down to the betting place under the grandstand and there I was
with the two girls, and when that Miss Woodbury was looking the
other way once, Lucy Wessen kinda, with her shoulder you know,
kinda touched me. Not just tucking down, I don't mean. You know
how a woman can do. They get close, but not getting gay either.
You know what they do. Gee whizz.

And then they give me a jolt. What they had done, when I didn't
know, was to get together, and they had decided Wilbur Wessen
would bet fifty dollars, and the two girls had gone and put in ten
dollars each, of their own money, too. I was sick then, but I was
sicker later.

About the gelding, About Ben Ahem, and their winning their
money, I wasn't worried a lot about that. It come out O.K. Ahem
stepped the next three heats like a bushel of spoiled eggs going to
market before they could be found out, and Wilbur Wessen had got
nine to two for the money. There was something else eating me.

Because Wilbur come back, after he had bet the money, and after
that he spent most of his time talking to that Miss Woodbury, and
Lucy Wessen and I was left alone together like on a desert island.
Gee, if I'd only been on the square or if there had been any way of
getting myself on the square. There ain't any Walter Mathers, like I
said to her and them, and there hasn't ever been one, but if there
was, I bet I'd go to Marietta, Ohio, and shoot him tomorrow.

There I was, big boob that I am. Pretty soon the race was over, and Wilbur had gone down and collected our money, and we had a hack downtown, and he stood us a swell supper at the West House, and a bottle of champagne beside.

And I was with that girl and she wasn't saying much, and I wasn't saying much either. One thing I know. She wasn't stuck on me because of the lie about my father being rich and all that. There's a way you know. . . . Craps amighty. There's a kind of girl, you see just once in your life, and if you don't get busy and make hay, then you're gone for good and all, and might as well go jump off a bridge. They give you a look from inside of them somewhere, and it ain't no vamping, and what it means is—you want that girl to be your wife, and you want nice things around her like flowers and swell clothes, and you want her to have the kids you're going to have, and you want good music played and no rag-time. Gee whizz.

There's a place over near Sandusky, across a kind of bay, and it's called Cedar Point. And after we had supper we went over to it in a launch, all by ourselves. Wilbur and Miss Lucy and that Miss Woodbury had to catch a ten o'clock train back to Tiffin, Ohio, because, when you're out with girls like that you can't get careless like with some kinds of Janes.

And Wilbur blowed himself to the launch and it cost him fifteen cold plunks, but I wouldn't never have knew if I hadn't listened. He wasn't no tin horn kind of a sport.

Over at Cedar Point place, we didn't stay around where there was a gang of common kind of cattle at all.

There was big dance halls and dining places for yaps, and there was a beach you could walk along and get where it was dark, and we went there.

She didn't talk hardly at all and neither did I, and I was thinking how glad I was my mother was all right, and always made us kids learn to eat with a fork at table, and not swill soup, and not be noisy and rough like a gang you see around a race track that way.

Then Wilbur and his girl went away up the beach and Lucy and I sat down in a dark place, where there was some roots of old trees, the water had washed up, and after that the time, till we had to go back in the launch and they had to catch their trains, wasn't nothing at all. It went like winking your eye.

Here's how it was. The place we were setting in was dark, like I said, and there was the roots from that old stump sticking up like arms, and there was a watery smell, and the night was like—as if you could put your hand out and feel it—so warm and soft and dark and sweet like an orange.

I most cried and I most swore and I most jumped up and danced I was so mad and happy and sad.

When Wilbur come back from being alone with his girl, and she saw him coming, Lucy she says, "we got to go to the train now", and she was most crying too, but she never knew nothing I knew, and she couldn't be so all busted up. And then, before Wilbur and Miss Woodbury got up to where we was, she put her face up and kissed me quick and put her head up against me and she was all quivering and—Gee whizz.

Sometimes I hope I have cancer and die. I guess you know what I mean. We went in the launch across the bay to the train like that, and it was dark, too. She whispered and said it was like she and I could get out of the boat and walk on the water, and it sounded foolish, but I knew what she meant.

And then quick we were right at the depot, and there was a big gang of yaps, the kind that goes to the fairs, and crowded and milling around like cattle, and how could I tell her? "It won't be long because you'll write and I'll write to you." That's all she said.

I got a chance like a hay barn afire. A swell chance I got.

And maybe she would write me, down at Marietta that way, and the letter would come back, and stamped on the front of it by the U.S.A. "there ain't any such guy," or something like that, whatever they stamp on a letter that way.

And me trying to pass myself off for a bigbug and a swell—to her, as decent a little body as God ever made. Craps amighty—a swell chance I got!

And then the train come in, and she got on it, and Wilbur Wessen he come and shook hands with me, and that Miss Woodbury was nice too and bowed to me, and I at her, and the train went and I busted out and cried like a kid.

Gee, I could have run after that train and made Dan Patch look like a freight train after a wreck but, socks amighty, what was the use? Did you ever see such a fool?

I'll bet you what—if I had an arm broke right now or a train had run over my foot—I wouldn't go to no doctor at all. I'd go set down and let her hurt and hurt—that's what I'd do.

I'll bet you what—if I hadn't a drunk that booze I'd a never been such a boob as to go tell such a lie—that couldn't never be made straight to a lady like her.

I wish I had that fellow right here that had on a Windsor tie and carried a cane. I'd smash him for fair. Gosh darn his eyes. He's a big fool—that's what he is.

And if I'm not another you just go find me one and I'll quit working and be a bum and give him my job. I don't care nothing for working, and earning money, and saving it for no such boob as myself.

JAMES JOYCE

1882–1941

Joyce was born near Dublin, Ireland, and educated by the Jesuits at Belvedere and University College. He went into self-imposed exile in 1904, taking with him a young woman named Nora Barnacle. "She'll never leave him," said Joyce's father, and she didn't. In Italy and Switzerland Joyce earned a precarious living teaching English while trying to become a great writer. His short stories were all designed for a collection called *Dubliners*, which spent ten years finding a publisher and then sold less than five hundred copies in 1914. His autobiographical novel, *A Portrait of the Artist as a Young Man* (1916) attracted the attention of T. S. Eliot and Ezra Pound, who helped him get support for his major project, *Ulysses* (1922), which took realism to its logical conclusion and beyond. *Finnegans Wake* (1939) is all beyond—a book to keep the professors busy, as Joyce observed, and busy they are. But, as Joyce's work becomes more familiar, the technical breakthroughs and the difficulties seem less noticeable and the comic spirit and humanity come through more clearly.

The Boarding House

Mrs Mooney was a butcher's daughter. She was a woman who was quite able to keep things to herself: a determined woman. She had married her father's foreman and opened a butcher's shop near Spring Gardens. But as soon as his father-in-law was dead Mr Mooney began to go to the devil. He drank, plundered the till, ran headlong into debt. It was no use making him take the pledge: he was sure to break out again a few days after. By fighting his wife in the presence of customers and by buying bad meat he ruined his business. One night he went for his wife with the cleaver and she had to sleep in a neighbour's house.

After that they lived apart. She went to the priest and got a separation from him with care of the children. She would give him neither money nor food nor house-room; and so he was obliged to enlist himself as a sheriff's man. He was a shabby stooped little drunkard with a white face and a white moustache and white eyebrows, pencilled above his little eyes, which were pink-veined and raw; and all day long he sat in the bailiff's room, waiting to be put on a job. Mrs Mooney, who had taken what remained of her money out of the butcher business and set up a boarding house in Hardwicke Street, was a big imposing woman. Her house had a floating population made up of tourists from Liverpool and the Isle of Man and, occasionally, *artistes* from the music halls. Its resident population was made up of clerks from the city. She governed the house cunningly and firmly, knew when to give credit, when to be stern and when to let things pass. All the resident young men spoke of her as *The Madam.*

Mrs Mooney's young men paid fifteen shillings a week for board and lodgings (beer or stout at dinner excluded). They shared in common tastes and occupations and for this reason they were very chummy with one another. They discussed with one another the chances of favourites and outsiders. Jack Mooney, the Madam's son, who was clerk to a commission agent in Fleet Street, had the reputation of being a hard case. He was fond of using soldiers' obscenities: usually he came home in the small hours. When he met his friends he had always a good one to tell them and he was always sure to be on to a good thing—that is to say, a likely horse or a likely *artiste.* He was also handy with the mits and sang comic songs. On Sunday nights there would often be a reunion in Mrs Mooney's front drawing-room. The music-hall *artistes* would oblige; and Sheridan played waltzes and polkas and vamped accompaniments. Polly Mooney, the Madam's daughter, would also sing. She sang:

> *I'm a . . . naughty girl.*
> *You needn't sham:*
> *You know I am.*

Polly was a slim girl of nineteen; she had light soft hair and a small full mouth. Her eyes, which were grey with a shade of green through them, had a habit of glancing upwards when she spoke with anyone, which made her look like a little perverse madonna. Mrs Mooney had first sent her daughter to be a typist in a corn-factor's office but, as a disreputable sheriff's man used to come every other day to the office, asking to be allowed to say a word to his daughter, she had taken her daughter home again and set her to do housework. As Polly was very lively the intention was to give her the run of the young men. Besides, young men like to feel that there is a young woman not very far away. Polly, of course, flirted with the young men but Mrs Mooney, who was a shrewd judge, knew that the young men were only passing the time away: none of them meant business. Things went on so for a long time and Mrs Mooney began to think of sending Polly back to typewriting when she noticed that something was going on between Polly and one of the young men. She watched the pair and kept her own counsel.

Polly knew that she was being watched, but still her mother's persistent silence could not be misunderstood. There had been no open complicity between mother and daughter, no open understanding but, though people in the house began to talk of the affair, still Mrs Mooney did not intervene. Polly began to grow a little strange in her manner and the young man was evidently perturbed. At last, when she judged it to be the right moment, Mrs Mooney intervened. She dealt with moral problems as a cleaver deals with meat: and in this case she had made up her mind.

It was a bright Sunday morning of early summer, promising heat, but with a fresh breeze blowing. All the windows of the boarding house were open and the lace curtains ballooned gently towards the street beneath the raised sashes. The belfry of George's Church sent out constant peals and worshippers, singly or in groups, traversed the little circus before the church, revealing their purpose by their self-contained demeanour no less than by the little volumes in their gloved hands. Breakfast was over in the boarding house and the table of the breakfast-room was covered with plates on which lay yellow streaks of eggs with morsels of bacon-fat and bacon-rind. Mrs Mooney sat in the straw arm-chair and watched the servant Mary remove the breakfast things. She made Mary collect the crusts and pieces of broken bread to help to make Tuesday's bread-pudding. When the table was cleared, the broken bread collected, the sugar and butter safe under lock and key, she began to reconstruct the interview which she had had the night before with Polly. Things were as she had suspected: she had been frank in her questions and Polly had been frank in her answers. Both had been somewhat awkward, of course. She had been made awkward by her not wishing to receive the news in too cavalier a fashion or to seem to have connived and Polly had been made awkward not merely because allusions of that kind always made her awkward but also because she did not wish it to be thought that in her wise innocence she had divined the intention behind her mother's tolerance.

Mrs Mooney glanced instinctively at the little gilt clock on the mantelpiece as soon as she had become aware through her revery that the bells of George's Church had stopped ringing. It was seventeen minutes past eleven: she would have lots of time to have the matter out with Mr Doran and then catch short twelve at Marlborough Street. She was sure she would win. To begin with she had all the weight of social opinion on her side: she was an outraged mother. She had allowed him to live beneath her roof, assuming that he was a man of honour, and he had simply abused her hospitality. He was thirty-four or thirty-five years of age, so that youth could not be pleaded as his excuse; nor could ignorance be his excuse since he was a man who had seen something of the world. He had simply taken advantage of Polly's youth and inexperience: that was evident. The question was: What reparation would he make?

There must be reparation made in such cases. It is all very well for the man: he can go his ways as if nothing had happened, having had his moment of pleasure, but the girl has to bear the brunt. Some mothers would be content to patch up such an affair for a sum of money; she had known cases of it. But she would not do so. For her only one reparation could make up for the loss of her daughter's honour: marriage.

She counted all her cards again before sending Mary up to Mr Doran's room to say that she wished to speak with him. She felt sure she would win. He was a serious young man, not rakish or loud-voiced like the others. If it had been Mr Sheridan or Mr Meade or Bantam Lyons her task would have been much harder. She did not think he would face publicity. All the lodgers in the house knew something of the affair; details had been invented by some. Besides, he had been employed for thirteen years in a great Catholic wine-merchant's office and publicity would mean for him, perhaps, the loss of his sit. Whereas if he agreed all might be well. She knew he had a good screw for one thing and she suspected he had a bit of stuff put by.

Nearly the half-hour! She stood up and surveyed herself in the pier-glass. The decisive expression of her great florid face satisfied her and she thought of some mothers she knew who could not get their daughters off their hands.

Mr Doran was very anxious indeed this Sunday morning. He had made two attempts to shave but his hand had been so unsteady that he had been obliged to desist. Three days' reddish beard fringed his jaws and every two or three minutes a mist gathered on his glasses so that he had to take them off and polish them with his pocket-handkerchief. The recollection of his confession of the night before was a cause of acute pain to him; the priest had drawn out every ridiculous detail of the affair and in the end had so magnified his sin that he was almost thankful at being afforded a loophole of reparation. The harm was done. What could he do now but marry her or run away? He could not brazen it out. The affair would be sure to be talked of and his employer would be certain to hear of it. Dublin is such a small city: everyone knows everyone else's business. He felt his heart leap warmly in his throat as he heard in his excited imagination old Mr Leonard calling out in his rasping voice: *Send Mr Doran here, please.*

All his long years of service gone for nothing! All his industry and diligence thrown away! As a young man he had sown his wild oats, of course; he had boasted of his free-thinking and denied the existence of God to his companions in public-houses. But that was all passed and done with . . . nearly. He still bought a copy of *Reynolds's Newspaper* every week but he attended to his religious duties and for nine-tenths of the year lived a regular life. He had money enough to settle down on; it was not that. But the family would look down on her. First of all there was her disreputable father and then her mother's boarding house was beginning to get a certain fame. He had a notion that he was being had. He could imagine his friends talking of the affair and laughing. She *was* a little vulgar; some times she said *I seen* and *If I had've known.* But what would grammar matter if he really loved her? He could not make up his mind whether to like her or despise her for what she had done. Of course he had done it too. His instinct urged him to remain free, not to marry. Once you are married you are done for, it said.

While he was sitting helplessly on the side of the bed in shirt and trousers she tapped lightly at his door and entered. She told him all, that she had made a clean breast of it to her mother and that her mother would speak with him that morning. She cried and threw her arms round his neck, saying:

—O Bob! Bob! What am I to do? What am I to do at all?

She would put an end to herself, she said.

He comforted her feebly, telling her not to cry, that it would be all right, never fear. He felt against his shirt the agitation of her bosom.

It was not altogether his fault that it had happened. He remembered well, with the curious patient memory of the celibate, the first casual caresses her dress, her breath, her fingers had given him. Then late one night as he was undressing for bed she had tapped at his door, timidly. She wanted to relight her candle at his for hers had been blown out by a gust. It was her bath night. She wore a loose open combing-jacket of printed flannel. Her white instep shone in the opening of her furry slippers and the blood glowed warmly behind her perfumed skin. From her hands and wrists too as she lit and steadied her candle a faint perfume arose.

On nights when he came in very late it was she who warmed up his dinner. He scarcely knew what he was eating, feeling her beside him alone, at night, in the sleeping house. And her thoughtfulness! If the night was anyway cold or wet or windy there was sure to be a little tumbler of punch ready for him. Perhaps they could be happy together. . . .

They used to go upstairs together on tiptoe, each with a candle, and on the third landing exchange reluctant goodnights. They used to kiss. He remembered well her eyes, the touch of her hand and his delirium. . . .

But delirium passes. He echoed her phrase, applying it to himself: *What am I to do?* The instinct of the celibate warned him to hold back. But the sin was there; even his sense of honour told him that reparation must be made for such a sin.

While he was sitting with her on the side of the bed Mary came to the door and said that the missus wanted to see him in the parlour. He stood up to put on his coat and waistcoat, more helpless than ever. When he was dressed he went over to her to comfort her. It would be all right, never fear. He left her crying on the bed and moaning softly: *O my God!*

Going down the stairs his glasses became so dimmed with moisture that he had to take them off and polish them. He longed to ascend through the roof and fly away to another country where he would never hear again of his trouble, and yet a force pushed him downstairs step by step. The implacable faces of his employer and of the Madam stared upon his discomfiture. On the last flight of stairs he passed Jack Mooney who was coming up from the pantry nursing two bottles of *Bass*. They saluted coldly; and the lover's eyes rested for a second or two on a thick bulldog face and a pair of thick short arms. When he reached the foot of the staircase he glanced up and saw Jack regarding him from the door of the return-room.

Suddenly he remembered the night when one of the music-hall *artistes*, a little blond Londoner, had made a rather free allusion to Polly. The reunion had been almost broken up on account of Jack's violence. Everyone tried to quiet him. The music-hall *artiste*, a little paler than usual, kept smiling and saying that there was no harm meant: but Jack kept shouting at him that if any fellow tried that sort of a game on with *his* sister he'd bloody well put his teeth down his throat, so he would.

. . . .

Polly sat for a little time on the side of the bed, crying. Then she dried her eyes and went over to the looking-glass. She dipped the end of the towel in the water-jug and refreshed her eyes with the cool water. She looked at herself in profile and readjusted a hairpin above her ear. Then she went back to the bed again and sat at the foot. She regarded the pillows for a long time and the sight of them awakened in her mind secret, amiable memories. She rested the nape of her neck against the cool iron bed-rail and fell into a revery. There was no longer any perturbation visible on her face.

She waited on patiently, almost cheerfully, without alarm, her memories gradually giving place to hopes and visions of the future. Her hopes and visions were so intricate that she no longer saw the white pillows on which her gaze was fixed or remembered that she was waiting for anything.

At last she heard her mother calling. She started to her feet and ran to the banisters.

—Polly! Polly!

—Yes, mamma?

—Come down, dear. Mr Doran wants to speak to you.

Then she remembered what she had been waiting for.

D. H. LAWRENCE
1885–1930

David Herbert Lawrence was born at Eastwood, a coal-mining village in the English Midlands. His father was a miner, his mother a woman from the middle class who never accepted her husband's way of life. Lawrence was torn between them: close to his mother during her life, appreciating his father only after his death. The story of this family struggle is told in one of Lawrence's finest works, his novel *Sons and Lovers* (1913). In 1901 Lawrence nearly died of pneumonia. His health was delicate after this until his death of tuberculosis at the age of forty-five. In 1904 he took the King's Scholarship examination and came out first in all England and Wales. He seems to have been good at all academic subjects from mathematics to botany, painting, and writing. He began a career as a teacher, but trouble with his health and his early success as a writer took him away from teaching. In 1912 he ran off with the wife of a former professor of his at Nottingham University, and in 1914, when her divorce became final, he married her. From then on the Lawrences traveled, staying in England at times, but also living in Germany, Italy, Ceylon, Australia, the United States, and Mexico. After Lawrence died in southern France, his body was cremated and the ashes were brought to the United States and buried on a hill near Taos, New Mexico.

Lawrence's personality has drawn almost as much attention as his books. He spoke and wrote informally with the same vitality that animates all his literary work. And some of the informality of talk and personal correspondence can be found in his poetry and fiction. For a time censorship of his works and controversy over the supposed immorality of his views on sex obscured the seriousness and beauty of his work for many readers. But now his books are in print and his place in English letters is secure.

The Christening

The mistress of the British School stepped down from her school gate, and instead of turning to the left as usual, she turned to the right. Two women who were hastening home to scramble their husbands' dinners together—it was five minutes to four—stopped to look at her. They stood gazing after her for a moment; then they glanced at each other with a woman's little grimace.

To be sure, the retreating figure was ridiculous: small and thin, with a black straw hat, and a rusty cashmere dress hanging full all round the skirt. For so small and frail and rusty a creature to sail with slow, deliberate stride was also absurd. Hilda Rowbotham was less than thirty, so it was not years that set the measure of her pace; she had heart disease. Keeping her face, that was small with sickness, but not uncomely, firmly lifted and fronting ahead, the young woman sailed on past the market-place, like a black swan of mournful disreputable plumage.

She turned into Berryman's, the bakers. The shop displayed bread and cakes, sacks of flour and oatmeal, flitches of bacon, hams, lard and sausages. The combination of scents was not unpleasing. Hilda Rowbotham stood for some minutes nervously tapping and pushing a large knife that lay on the counter, and looking at the tall, glittering brass scales. At last a morose man with sandy whiskers came down the step from the house-place.

"What is it?" he asked, not apologising for his delay.

"Will you give me sixpennyworth of assorted cakes and pastries— and put in some macaroons, please?" she asked, in remarkably rapid and nervous speech. Her lips fluttered like two leaves in a wind, and her words crowded and rushed like a flock of sheep at a gate.

"We've got no macaroons," said the man churlishly.   surly

He had evidently caught that word. He stood waiting.

"Then I can't have any, Mr. Berryman. Now I do feel disappointed. I like those macaroons, you know, and it's not often I treat myself. One gets so tired of trying to spoil oneself, don't you think? It's less profitable even than trying to spoil somebody else." She laughed a quick little nervous laugh, putting her hand to her face.

"Then what'll you have?" asked the man, without the ghost of an answering smile. He evidently had not followed, so he looked more glum than ever.

"Oh, anything you've got," replied the schoolmistress, flushing slightly. The man moved slowly about, dropping the cakes from various dishes one by one into a paper bag.

"How's that sister o' yours getting on?" he asked, as if he were talking to the flour-scoop.

"Whom do you mean?" snapped the schoolmistress.

"The youngest," answered the stooping, pale-faced man, with a note of sarcasm.

"Emma! Oh, she's very well, thank you!" The schoolmistress was very red, but she spoke with sharp, ironical defiance. The man grunted. Then he handed her the bag, and watched her out of the shop without bidding her "Good afternoon."

She had the whole length of the main street to traverse, a half-mile of slow-stepping torture, with shame flushing over her neck. But she carried her white bag with an appearance of steadfast unconcern. When she turned into the field she seemed to droop a little. The wide valley opened out from her, with the far woods withdrawing into twilight, and away in the centre the great pit steaming its white smoke and chuffing as the men were being turned up. A full rose-coloured moon, like a flamingo flying low under the far, dusky east, drew out of the mist. It was beautiful, and it made her irritable sadness soften, diffuse.

Across the field, and she was at home. It was a new, substantial cottage, built with unstinted hand, such a house as an old miner could build himself out of his savings. In the rather small kitchen a woman of dark, saturnine complexion sat nursing a baby in a long white gown; a young woman of heavy, brutal cast stood at the table, cutting bread and butter. She had a downcast, humble mien that sat unnaturally on her, and was strangely irritating. She did not look round when her sister entered. Hilda put down the bag of cakes and left the room, not having spoken to Emma, nor to the baby, nor to Mrs. Carlin, who had come in to help for the afternoon.

Almost immediately the father entered from the yard with a dust-pan full of coals. He was a large man, but he was going to pieces. As he passed through, he gripped the door with his free hand to steady himself, but turning, he lurched and swayed. He began putting the coals on the fire, piece by piece. One lump fell from his hands and smashed on the white hearth. Emma Rowbotham looked round, and began in a rough, loud voice of anger: "Look at you!" Then she consciously moderated her tones. "I'll sweep it up in a minute—don't you bother; you'll only be going head-first into the fire."

Her father bent down nevertheless to clear up the mess he had made, saying, articulating his words loosely and slavering in his speech:

"The lousy bit of a thing, it slipped between my fingers like a fish."

As he spoke he went tilting towards the fire. The dark-browed woman cried out; he put his hand on the hot stove to save himself; Emma swung round and dragged him off.

"Didn't I tell you!" she cried roughly. "Now, have you burnt yourself?"

She held tight hold of the big man, and pushed him into his chair.

"What's the matter?" cried a sharp voice from the other room. The speaker appeared, a hard well-favoured woman of twenty-eight. "Emma, don't speak like that to father." Then, in a tone not so cold, but just as sharp: "Now, father, what have you been doing?"

Emma withdrew to her table sullenly.

"It's nöwt," said the old man, vainly protesting. "It's nöwt at a'. Get on wi' what you're doin'."

"I'm afraid 'e's burnt 'is 'and," said the black-browed woman, speaking of him with a kind of hard pity, as if he were a cumbersome child. Bertha took the old man's hand and looked at it, making a quick tut-tutting noise of impatience.

"Emma, get that zinc ointment—and some white rag," she commanded sharply. The younger sister put down her loaf with the knife in it, and went. To a sensitive observer, this obedience was more intolerable than the most hateful discord. The dark woman bent over the baby and made silent, gentle movements of motherliness to it. The little one smiled and moved on her lap. It continued to move and twist.

"I believe this child's hungry," she said. "How long is it since he had anything?"

"Just afore dinner," said Emma dully.

"Good gracious!" exclaimed Bertha. "You needn't starve the child now you've got it. Once every two hours it ought to be fed, as I've told you; and now it's three. Take him, poor little mite—I'll cut the bread." She bent and looked at the bonny baby. She could not help herself: she smiled, and pressed its cheek with her finger, and nodded to it, making little noises. Then she turned and took the loaf from her sister. The woman rose and gave the child to its mother. Emma bent over the little sucking mite. She hated it when she looked at it, and saw it as a symbol, but when she felt it, her love was like fire in her blood.

"I should think 'e canna be comin'," said the father uneasily, looking up at the clock.

"Nonsense, father—the clock's fast! It's but half-past four! Don't fidget!" Bertha continued to cut the bread and butter.

"Open a tin of pears," she said to the woman, in a much milder tone. Then she went into the next room. As soon as she was gone, the old man said again: "I should ha'e thought he'd 'a' been 'ere by now, if he means comin'."

Emma, engrossed, did not answer. The father had ceased to consider her, since she had become humbled.

"'E'll come—'e'll come!" assured the stranger.

A few minutes later Bertha hurried into the kitchen, taking off her apron. The dog barked furiously. She opened the door, commanded the dog to silence, and said: "He will be quiet now, Mr. Kendal."

"Thank you," said a sonorous voice, and there was the sound of a bicycle being propped against a wall. A clergyman entered, a big-boned, thin, ugly man of nervous manner. He went straight to the father.

"Ah—how are you—" he asked musically, peering down on the great frame of the miner, ruined by locomotor ataxy.

His voice was full of gentleness, but he seemed as if he could not see distinctly, could not get things clear.

"Have you hurt your hand?" he said comfortingly, seeing the white rag.

"It wor nöwt but a pestered bit o' coal as dropped, an' I put my hand on th' hub. I thought tha worna commin'."

The familiar "tha", and the reproach, were unconscious retaliation on the old man's part. The minister smiled, half wistfully, half indulgently. He was full of vague tenderness. Then he turned to the young mother, who flushed sullenly because her dishonoured breast was uncovered.

"How are *you*?" he asked, very softly and gently, as if she were ill and he were mindful of her.

"I'm all right," she replied, awkwardly taking his hand without rising, hiding her face and the anger that rose in her.

"Yes—yes"—he peered down at the baby, which sucked with distended mouth upon the firm breast. "Yes, yes." He seemed lost in a dim musing.

Coming to, he shook hands unseeingly with the woman.

Presently they all went into the next room, the minister hesitating to help his crippled old deacon.

"I can go by myself, thank yer," testily replied the father.

Soon all were seated. Everybody was separated in feeling and isolated at table. High tea was spread in the middle kitchen, a large, ugly room kept for special occasions.

Hilda appeared last, and the clumsy, raw-boned clergyman rose to meet her. He was afraid of this family, the well-to-do old collier, and the brutal, self-willed children. But Hilda was queen among them. She was the clever one, and had been to college. She felt responsible for the keeping up of a high standard of conduct in all the members of the family. There *was* a difference between the Rowbothams and the common collier folk. Woodbine Cottage was a superior house to most—and was built in pride by the old man. She, Hilda, was a college-trained schoolmistress; she meant to keep up the prestige of her house in spite of blows.

She had put on a dress of green voile for this special occasion. But she was very thin; her neck protruded painfully. The clergyman, however, greeted her almost with reverence, and, with some assumption of dignity, she sat down before the tray. At the far end of the table sat the broken, massive frame of her father. Next to him was the youngest daughter, nursing the restless boy. The minister sat between Hilda and Bertha, hulking his bony frame uncomfortably.

There was a great spread on the table of tinned fruits and tinned salmon, ham and cakes. Miss Rowbotham kept a keen eye on everything: she felt the importance of the occasion. The young mother who had given rise to all this solemnity ate in sulky discomfort, snatching sullen little smiles at her child, smiles which came, in spite of her, when she felt its little limbs stirring vigorously on her lap. Bertha, sharp and abrupt, was chiefly concerned with the baby. She scorned her sister, and treated her like dirt. But the infant was a streak of light to her. Miss Rowbotham concerned herself with the function and the conversation. Her hands fluttered; she talked in little volleys, exceedingly nervous. Towards the end of the meal, there came a pause. The old man wiped his mouth with his red handkerchief, then, his blue eyes going fixed and staring, he began to speak, in a loose, slobbering fashion, charging his words at the clergyman.

"Well, mester—we'n axed you to come here ter christen this childt, an' you'n come, an' I'm sure we're very thankful. I can't see lettin' the poor blessed childt miss baptizing, an' they aren't for goin' to church wi't——" He seemed to lapse into a muse. "So," he resumed, "we'n axed you to come here to do the job. I'm not sayin' as it's not 'ard on us, it is. I'm breakin' up, an' mother's gone. I don't like leavin' a girl o' mine in a situation like 'ers is, but what the Lord's done, He's done, an' it's no matter murmuring. . . . There's one thing to be thankful for, an' we *are* thankful for it: they never need know the want of bread."

Miss Rowbotham, the lady of the family, sat very stiff and pained during this discourse. She was sensitive to so many things that she was bewildered. She felt her young sister's shame, then a kind of swift protecting love for the baby, a feeling that included the mother; she was at a loss before her father's religious sentiment, and she felt and resented bitterly the mark upon the family, against which the common folk could lift their fingers. Still she winced from the sound of her father's words. It was a painful ordeal.

"It is hard for you," began the clergyman in his soft, lingering, unworldly voice. "It is hard for you to-day, but the Lord gives comfort in His time. A man child is born unto us, therefore let us rejoice and be glad. If sin has entered in among us, let us purify our hearts before the Lord. . . ."

He went on with his discourse. The young mother lifted the whimpering infant, till its face was hid in her loose hair. She was hurt, and a little glowering anger shone in her face. But nevertheless her fingers clasped the body of the child beautifully. She was stupefied with anger against this emotion let loose on her account.

Miss Bertha rose and went to the little kitchen, returning with water in a china bowl. She placed it there among the tea-things.

"Well, we're all ready," said the old man, and the clergyman began to read the service. Miss Bertha was godmother, the two men godfathers. The old man sat with bent head. The scene became impressive. At last Miss Bertha took the child and put it in the arms of the clergyman. He, big and ugly, shone with a kind of unreal love. He had never mixed with life, and women were all unliving, Biblical things to him. When he asked for the name, the old man lifted his head fiercely. "Joseph William, after me," he said, almost out of breath.

"Joseph William, I baptise thee . . ." resounded the strange, full, chanting voice of the clergyman. The baby was quite still.

"Let us pray!" It came with relief to them all. They knelt before their chairs, all but the young mother, who bent and hid herself over her baby. The clergyman began his hesitating, struggling prayer.

Just then heavy footsteps were heard coming up the path, ceasing at the window. The young mother, glancing up, saw her brother, black in his pit dirt, grinning in through the panes. His red mouth curved in a sneer; his fair hair shone above his blackened skin. He caught the eye of his sister and grinned. Then his black face disappeared. He had gone on into the kitchen. The girl with the child sat still and anger filled her heart. She herself hated now the praying clergyman and the whole emotional business; she hated her brother bitterly. In anger and bondage she sat and listened.

Suddenly her father began to pray. His familiar, loud, rambling voice made her shut herself up and become even insentient. Folks said his mind was weakening. She believed it to be true, and kept herself always disconnected from him.

"We ask Thee, Lord," the old man cried, "to look after this childt. Fatherless he is. But what does the earthly father matter before Thee? The childt is Thine, he is Thy childt. Lord, what father has a man but Thee? Lord, when a man says he is a father, he is wrong from the first word. For Thou art the Father, Lord. Lord, take away from us the conceit that our children are ours. Lord, Thou art Father of this childt as is fatherless here. O God, Thou bring him up. For I have stood between Thee and my children; I've had *my* way with them, Lord; I've stood between Thee and my children; I've cut 'em off from Thee because they were mine. And they've grown twisted, because of me. Who is their father, Lord, but Thee? But I put myself in the way, they've been plants under a stone, because of me. Lord, if it hadn't been for me, they might ha' been trees in the sunshine. Let me own it, Lord. I've done 'em mischief. It would ha' been better if they'd never known no father. No man is a father, Lord: only Thou art. They can never grow beyond Thee, but I hampered them. Lift 'em up again, and undo what I've done to my children. And let this young childt be like a willow tree beside the waters, with no father but Thee, O God. Aye, an' I wish it had been so with my children, that they'd had no father but Thee. For I've been like a stone upon them, and they rise up and curse me in their wickedness. But let me go, an' lift Thou them up, Lord . . ."

The minister, unaware of the feelings of a father, knelt in trouble, hearing without understanding the special language of fatherhood. Miss Rowbotham alone felt and understood a little. Her heart began to flutter; she was in pain. The two younger daughters kneeled unhearing, stiffened and impervious. Bertha was thinking of the baby; and the young mother thought of the father of her child, whom she hated. There was a clatter outside in the scullery. There the youngest son made as much noise as he could, pouring out the water for his wash, muttering in deep anger:

"Blortin', slaverin' old fool!"

And while the praying of his father continued, his heart was burning with rage. On the table was a paper bag. He picked it up and read: "John Berryman—Bread, Pastries, etc." Then he grinned with a grimace. The father of the baby was baker's man at Berryman's. The prayer went on in the middle kitchen. Laurie Rowbotham gathered together the mouth of the bag, inflated it, and burst it with his fist. There was a loud report. He grinned to himself. But he writhed at the same time with shame and fear of his father.

The father broke off from his prayer; the party shuffled to their feet. The young mother went into the scullery.

"What art doin', fool?" she said.

The collier youth tipped the baby under the chin, singing:

> "Pat-a-cake, pat-a-cake, baker's man,
> Bake me a cake as fast as you can. . . ."

The mother snatched the child away. "Shut thy mouth," she said, the colour coming into her cheek.

> "Prick it and stick it and mark it with P,
> And put it i' th' oven for baby an' me. . . ."

He grinned, showing a grimy, and jeering and unpleasant red mouth, and white teeth.

"I s'll gi'e thee a dab ower th' mouth," said the mother of the baby grimly. He began to sing again, and she struck out at him.

"Now what's to do?" said the father, staggering in.

The youth began to sing again. His sister stood sullen and furious.

"Why does *that* upset you?" asked the eldest Miss Rowbotham, sharply, of Emma the mother. "Good gracious, it hasn't improved your temper."

Miss Bertha came in, and took the bonny baby.

The father sat big and unheeding in his chair, his eyes vacant, his physique wrecked. He let them do as they would, he fell to pieces. And yet some power, involuntary, like a curse, remained in him. The very ruin of him was like a lodestone that held them in its control. The wreck of him still dominated the house, in his dissolution even he compelled their being. They had never lived; his life, his will had always been upon them and contained them. They were only half-individuals.

The day after the christening he staggered in at the doorway declaring, in a loud voice, with joy in life still: "The daisies light up the earth, they clap their hands in multitudes, in praise of the morning." And his daughters shrank, sullen.

KATHERINE ANNE PORTER
1890-1980

She was born in Indian Creek, Texas, and educated both at home and in a series of girls' schools in Texas and Louisiana. She was married at sixteen, but it didn't take, and she began to support herself by doing newspaper work in Chicago. Her unusual beauty enabled her to play small parts in films as a means of support while she wrote, destroyed, and rewrote stories without seeking to publish them. She began publishing fiction when she was thirty and achieved recognition with her first collection, *Flowering Judas*, in 1930. Since then a slow, steady output of polished fiction has solidified a reputation that has fluctuated little for fifty years.

Rope

On the third day after they moved to the country he came walking back from the village carrying a basket of groceries and a twenty-four-yard coil of rope. She came out to meet him, wiping her hands on her green smock. Her hair was tumbled, her nose was scarlet with sunburn; he told her that already she looked like a born country woman. His gray flannel shirt stuck to him, his heavy shoes were dusty. She assured him he looked like a rural character in a play.

Had he brought the coffee? She had been waiting all day long for coffee. They had forgot it when they ordered at the store the first day.

Gosh, no, he hadn't. Lord, now he'd have to go back. Yes, he would if it killed him. He thought, though, he had everything else. She reminded him it was only because he didn't drink coffee himself. If he did he would remember it quick enough. Suppose they ran out of cigarettes? Then she saw the rope. What was that for? Well, he thought it might do to hang clothes on, or something. Naturally she asked him if he thought they were going to run a laundry? They already had a fifty-foot line hanging right before his eyes? Why, hadn't he noticed it, really? It was a blot on the landscape to her.

He thought there were a lot of things a rope might come in handy for. She wanted to know what, for instance. He thought a few seconds, but nothing occurred. They could wait and see, couldn't they? You need all sorts of strange odds and ends around a place in the country. She said, yes, that was so; but she thought just at that time when every penny counted, it seemed funny to buy more rope. That was all. She hadn't meant anything else. She hadn't just seen, not at first, why he felt it was necessary.

Well, thunder, he had bought it because he wanted to, and that was all there was to it. She thought that was reason enough, and couldn't understand why he hadn't said so, at first. Undoubtedly it would be useful, twenty-four yards of rope, there were hundreds of things, she couldn't think of any at the moment, but it would come in. Of course. As he had said, things always did in the country.

But she was a little disappointed about the coffee, and oh, look, look, look at the eggs! Oh, my, they're all running! What had he put on top of them? Hadn't he known eggs mustn't be squeezed? Squeezed, who had squeezed them, he wanted to know. What a silly thing to say. He had simply brought them along in the basket with the other things. If they got broke it was the grocer's fault. He should know better than to put heavy things on top of eggs.

She believed it was the rope. That was the heaviest thing in the pack, she saw him plainly when he came in from the road, the rope was a big package on top of everything. He desired the whole wide world to witness that this was not a fact. He had carried the rope in one hand and the basket in the other, and what was the use of her having eyes if that was the best they could do for her?

Well, anyhow, she could see one thing plain: no eggs for breakfast. They'd have to scramble them now, for supper. It was too damned bad. She had planned to have steak for supper. No ice, meat wouldn't keep. He wanted to know why she couldn't finish breaking the eggs in a bowl and set them in a cool place.

Cool place! if he could find one for her, she'd be glad to set them there. Well, then, it seemed to him they might very well cook the meat at the same time they cooked the eggs and then warm up the meat for tomorrow. The idea simply choked her. Warmed-over meat, when they might as well have had it fresh. Second best and scraps and makeshifts, even to the meat! He rubbed her shoulder a little. It doesn't really matter so much, does it, darling? Sometimes when they were playful, he would rub her shoulder and she would arch and purr. This time she hissed and almost clawed. He was getting ready to say that they could surely manage somehow when she turned on him and said, if he told her they could manage somehow she would certainly slap his face.

He swallowed the words red hot, his face burned. He picked up the rope and started to put it on the top shelf. She would not have it on the top shelf, the jars and tins belonged there; positively she would not have the top shelf cluttered up with a lot of rope. She had borne all the clutter she meant to bear in the flat in town, there was space here at least and she meant to keep things in order.

Well, in that case, he wanted to know what the hammer and nails were doing up there? And why had she put them there when she knew very well he needed that hammer and those nails upstairs to fix the window sashes? She simply slowed down everything and made double work on the place with her insane habit of changing things around and hiding them.

She was sure she begged his pardon, and if she had had any reason to believe he was going to fix the sashes this summer she would have left the hammer and nails right where he put them; in the middle of the bedroom floor where they could step on them in the dark. And now if he didn't clear the whole mess out of there she would throw them down the well.

Oh, all right, all right—could he put them in the closet? Naturally not, there were brooms and mops and dustpans in the closet, and why couldn't he find a place for his rope outside her kitchen? Had he stopped to consider there were seven God-forsaken rooms in the house, and only one kitchen?

He wanted to know what of it? And did she realize she was making a complete fool of herself? And what did she take him for, a three-year-old idiot? The whole trouble with her was she needed something weaker than she was to heckle and tyrannize over. He wished to God now they had a couple of children she could take it out on. Maybe he'd get some rest.

Her face changed at this, she reminded him he had forgot the coffee and had bought a worthless piece of rope. And when she thought of all the things they actually needed to make the place even decently fit to live in, well, she could cry, that was all. She looked so forlorn, so lost and despairing he couldn't believe it was only a piece of rope that was causing all the racket. What *was* the matter, for God's sake?

Oh, would he please hush and go away, and *stay* away, if he could, for five minutes? By all means, yes, he would. He'd stay away indefinitely if she wished. Lord, yes, there was nothing he'd like better than to clear out and never come back. She couldn't for the life of her see what was holding him, then. It was a swell time. Here she was, stuck, miles from a railroad, with a half-empty house on her hands, and not a penny in her pocket, and everything on earth to do; it seemed the God-sent moment for him to get out from under. She was surprised he hadn't stayed in town as it was until she had come out and done the work and got things straightened out. It was his usual trick.

It appeared to him that this was going a little far. Just a touch out of bounds, if she didn't mind his saying so. Why the hell had he stayed in town the summer before? To do a half-dozen extra jobs to get the money he had sent her. That was it. She knew perfectly well they couldn't have done it otherwise. She had agreed with him at the time. And that was the only time so help him he had ever left her to do anything by herself.

Oh, he could tell that to his great-grandmother. She had her notion of what had kept him in town. Considerably more than a notion, if he wanted to know. So, she was going to bring all that up again, was she?

Well, she could just think what she pleased. He was tired of explaining. It may have looked funny but he had simply got hooked in, and what could he do? It was impossible to believe that she was going to take it seriously. Yes, yes, she knew how it was with a man: if he was left by himself a minute, some woman was certain to kidnap him. And naturally he couldn't hurt her feelings by refusing!

Well, what was she raving about? Did she forget she had told him those two weeks alone in the country were the happiest she had known for four years? And how long had they been married when she said that? All right, shut up! If she thought that hadn't stuck in his craw.

She hadn't meant she was happy because she was away from him. She meant she was happy getting the devilish house nice and ready for him. That was what she had meant, and now look! Bringing up something she had said a year ago simply to justify himself for forgetting her coffee and breaking the eggs and buying a wretched piece of rope they couldn't afford. She really thought it was time to drop the subject, and now she wanted only two things in the world. She wanted him to get that rope from underfoot, and go back to the village and get her coffee, and if he could remember it, he might bring a metal mitt for the skillets, and two more curtain rods, and if there were any rubber gloves in the village, her hands were simply raw, and a bottle of milk of magnesia from the drugstore.

He looked out at the dark blue afternoon sweltering on the slopes, and mopped his forehead and sighed heavily and said, if only she could wait a minute for *anything*, he was going back. He had said so, hadn't he, the very instant they found he had overlooked it?

Oh, yes, well . . . run along. She was going to wash windows. The country was so beautiful! She doubted they'd have a moment to enjoy it. He meant to go, but he could not until he had said that if she wasn't such a hopeless melancholiac she might see that this was only for a few days. Couldn't she remember anything pleasant about the other summers? Hadn't they ever had any fun? She hadn't time to talk about it, and now would he please not leave that rope lying around for her to trip on? He picked it up, somehow it had toppled off the table, and walked out with it under his arm.

Was he going this minute? He certainly was. She thought so. Sometimes it seemed to her he had second sight about the precisely perfect moment to leave her ditched. She had meant to put the mattresses out to sun, if they put them out this minute they would get at least three hours, he must have heard her say that morning she meant to put them out. So of course he would walk off and leave her to it. She supposed he thought the exercise would do her good.

Well, he was merely going to get her coffee. A four-mile walk for two pounds of coffee was ridiculous, but he was perfectly willing to do it. The habit was making a wreck of her, but if she wanted to wreck herself there was nothing he could do about it. If he thought it was coffee that was making a wreck of her, she congratulated him: he must have a damned easy conscience.

Conscience or no conscience, he didn't see why the mattresses couldn't very well wait until tomorrow. And anyhow, for God's sake, were they living *in* the house, or were they going to let the house ride them to death? She paled at this, her face grew livid about the mouth, she looked quite dangerous, and reminded him that housekeeping was no more her work than it was his: she had other work to do as well, and when did he think she was going to find time to do it at this rate?

Was she going to start on that again? She knew as well as he did that his work brought in the regular money, hers was only occasional, if they depended on what *she* made—and she might as well get straight on this question once for all!

That was positively not the point. The question was, when both of them were working on their own time, was there going to be a division of the housework, or wasn't there? She merely wanted to know, she had to make her plans. Why, he thought that was all arranged. It was understood that he was to help. Hadn't he always, in summers?

Hadn't he, though? Oh, just hadn't he? And when, and where, and doing what? Lord, what an uproarious joke!

It was such a very uproarious joke that her face turned slightly purple, and she screamed with laughter. She laughed so hard she had to sit down, and finally a rush of tears spurted from her eyes and poured down into the lifted corners of her mouth. He dashed towards her and dragged her up to her feet and tried to pour water on her head. The dipper hung by a string on a nail and he broke it loose. Then he tried to pump water with one hand while she struggled in the other. So he gave it up and shook her instead.

She wrenched away, crying out for him to take his rope and go to hell, she had simply given him up: and ran. He heard her high-heeled bedroom slippers clattering and stumbling on the stairs.

He went out around the house and into the lane; he suddenly realized he had a blister on his heel and his shirt felt as if it were on fire. Things broke so suddenly you didn't know where you were. She could work herself into a fury about simply nothing. She was terrible, damn it: not an ounce of reason. You might as well talk to a sieve as that woman when she got going. Damned if he'd spend his life humoring her! Well, what to do now? He would take back the rope and exchange it for something else. Things accumulated, things were mountainous, you couldn't move them or sort them out or get rid of them. They just lay and rotted around. He'd take it back. Hell, why should he? He wanted it. What was it anyhow? A piece of rope. Imagine anybody caring more about a piece of rope than about a man's feelings. What earthly right had she to say a word about it? He remembered all the useless, meaningless things she bought for herself: Why? because I wanted it, that's why! He stopped and selected a large stone by the road. He would put the rope behind it. He would put it in the tool-box when he got back. He'd heard enough about it to last him a life-time.

When he came back she was leaning against the post box beside the road waiting. It was pretty late, the smell of broiled steak floated nose high in the cooling air. Her face was young and smooth and fresh-looking. Her unmanageable funny black hair was all on end. She waved to him from a distance, and he speeded up. She called out that supper was ready and waiting, was he starved?

You bet he was starved. Here was the coffee. He waved it at her. She looked at his other hand. What was that he had there?

Well, it was the rope again. He stopped short. He had meant to exchange it but forgot. She wanted to know why he should exchange it, if it was something he really wanted. Wasn't the air sweet now, and wasn't it fine to be here?

She walked beside him with one hand hooked into his leather belt. She pulled and jostled him a little as he walked, and leaned against him. He put his arm clear around her and patted her stomach. They exchanged wary smiles. Coffee, coffee for the Ootsum-Wootsums! He felt as if he were bringing her a beautiful present.

He was a love, she firmly believed, and if she had had her coffee in the morning, she wouldn't have behaved so funny . . . . There was a whippoorwill still coming back, imagine, clear out of season, sitting in the crab-apple tree calling all by himself. Maybe his girl stood him up. Maybe she did. She hoped to hear him once more, she loved whippoorwills . . . He knew how she was, didn't he?

Sure, he knew how she was.

DOROTHY PARKER
1893–1967

Born the daughter of J. Henry and Eliza Rothschild in West End, New Jersey, she went to school at Blessed Sacrament Convent in New York City and Miss Dana's School in Morristown, N.J. At twenty she had a job with *Vogue* magazine and had begun to publish light verse. A few years later she married Edwin Parker, keeping his name though divorcing him eleven years later. Writing was her trade from the beginning, and New York City was her territory. She worked for sophisticated magazines like *Vanity Fair* and the *New Yorker*. She wrote plays for Broadway and film scripts for Hollywood. In her youth she was the only woman who belonged to a select circle of New York wits, whose base was a table in the bar of the Algonquin Hotel. She squandered her talent collaborating with clever men who were not her equals. In her later years, she stopped writing and drank too much. But for a brief period in the twenties and thirties she was the talk of the town, and her stories, verse, and even casual remarks will go on being remembered.

You Were Perfectly Fine

The pale young man eased himself carefully into the low chair, and rolled his head to the side, so that the cool chintz comforted his cheek and temple.

"Oh, dear," he said. "Oh, dear, oh, dear, oh, dear. Oh."

The clear-eyed girl, sitting light and erect on the couch, smiled brightly at him.

"Not feeling so well today?" she said.

"Oh, I'm great," he said. "Corking, I am. Know what time I got up? Four o'clock this afternoon, sharp. I kept trying to make it, and every time I took my head off the pillow, it would roll under the bed. This isn't my head I've got on now. I think this is something that used to belong to Walt Whitman. Oh, dear, oh, dear, oh, dear."

"Do you think maybe a drink would make you feel better?" she said.

"The hair of the mastiff that bit me?" he said. "Oh, no, thank you. Please never speak of anything like that again. I'm through. I'm all, all through. Look at that hand; steady as a humming-bird. Tell me, was I very terrible last night?"

"Oh, goodness," she said, "everybody was feeling pretty high. You were all right."

"Yeah," he said. "I must have been dandy. Is everybody sore at me?"

"Good heavens, no," she said. "Everyone thought you were terribly funny. Of course, Jim Pierson was a little stuffy, there for a minute at dinner. But people sort of held him back in his chair, and got him calmed down. I don't think anybody at the other tables noticed it at all. Hardly anybody."

"He was going to sock me?" he said. "Oh, Lord. What did I do to him?"

"Why, you didn't do a thing," she said. "You were perfectly fine. But you know how silly Jim gets, when he thinks anybody is making too much fuss over Elinor."

"Was I making a pass at Elinor?" he said. "Did I do that?"

"Of course you didn't," she said. "You were only fooling, that's all.

She thought you were awfully amusing. She was having a marvelous time. She only got a little tiny bit annoyed just once, when you poured the clam-juice down her back."

"My God," he said. "Clam-juice down that back. And every vertebra a little Cabot. Dear God. What'll I ever do?"

"Oh, she'll be all right," she said. "Just send her some flowers, or something. Don't worry about it. It isn't anything."

"No, I won't worry," he said. "I haven't got a care in the world. I'm sitting pretty. Oh, dear, oh, dear. Did I do any other fascinating tricks at dinner?"

"You were fine," she said. "Don't be so foolish about it. Everybody was crazy about you. The maître d'hôtel was a little worried because you wouldn't stop singing, but he really didn't mind. All he said was, he was afraid they'd close the place again, if there was so much noise. But he didn't care a bit, himself. I think he loved seeing you have such a good time. Oh, you were just singing away, there, for about an hour. It wasn't so terribly loud, at all."

"So I sang," he said. "That must have been a treat. I sang."

"Don't you remember?" she said. "You just sang one song after another. Everybody in the place was listening. They loved it. Only you kept insisting that you wanted to sing some song about some kind of fusiliers or other, and everybody kept shushing you, and you'd keep trying to start it again. You were wonderful. We were all trying to make you stop singing for a minute, and eat something, but you wouldn't hear of it. My, you were funny."

"Didn't I eat any dinner?" he said.

"Oh, not a thing," she said. "Every time the waiter would offer you something, you'd give it right back to him, because you said that he was your long-lost brother, changed in the cradle by a gypsy band, and that anything you had was his. You had him simply roaring at you."

"I bet I did," he said. "I bet I was comical. Society's Pet, I must have been. And what happened then, after my overwhelming success with the waiter?"

"Why, nothing much," she said. "You took a sort of dislike to some old man with white hair, sitting across the room, because you didn't like his necktie and you wanted to tell him about it. But we got you out, before he got really mad."

"Oh, we got out," he said. "Did I walk?"

"Walk? Of course you did," she said. "You were absolutely all right. There was that nasty stretch of ice on the sidewalk, and you did sit down awfully hard, you poor dear. But good heavens, that might have happened to anybody."

"Oh, surely," he said. "Mrs. Hoover or anybody. So I fell down on the sidewalk. That would explain what's the matter with my— Yes. I see. And then what, if you don't mind?"

"Ah, now, Peter!" she said. "You can't sit there and say you don't remember what happened after that! I did think that maybe you were just a little tight at dinner—oh, you were perfectly all right, and all that, but I did know you were feeling pretty gay. But you were so serious, from the time you fell down—I never knew you to be that way. Don't you know, how you told me I had never seen your real self before? Oh, Peter, I just couldn't bear it, if you didn't remember that lovely long ride we took together in the taxi! Please, you do remember that, don't you? I think it would simply kill me, if you didn't."

"Oh, yes," he said. "Riding in the taxi. Oh, yes, sure. Pretty long ride, hmm?"

"Round and round and round the park," she said. "Oh, and the trees were shining so in the moonlight. And you said you never knew before that you really had a soul."

"Yes," he said. "I said that. That was me."

"You said such lovely, lovely things," she said. "And I'd never known, all this time, how you had been feeling about me, and I'd never dared to let you see how I felt about you. And then last night—oh, Peter dear, I think that taxi ride was the most important thing that ever happened to us in our lives."

"Yes," he said. "I guess it must have been."

"And we're going to be so happy," she said. "Oh, I just want to tell everybody! But I don't know—I think maybe it would be sweeter to keep it all to ourselves."

"I think it would be," he said.

"Isn't it lovely?" she said.

"Yes," he said. "Great."

"Lovely!" she said.

"Look here," he said, "do you mind if I have a drink? I mean, just medicinally, you know. I'm off the stuff for life, so help me. But I think I feel a collapse coming on."

"Oh, I think it would do you good," she said. "You poor boy, it's a shame you feel so awful. I'll go make you a highball."

"Honestly," he said, "I don't see how you could ever want to speak to me again, after I made such a fool of myself, last night. I think I'd better go join a monastery in Tibet."

"You crazy idiot!" she said. "As if I could ever let you go away now! Stop talking like that. You were perfectly fine."

She jumped up from the couch, kissed him quickly on the forehead, and ran out of the room.

The pale young man looked after her and shook his head long and slowly, then dropped it in his damp and trembling hands.

"Oh, dear," he said. "Oh, dear, oh, dear, oh dear."

F. SCOTT FITZGERALD
1896–1940

Francis Scott Key Fitzgerald was born in St. Paul, Minnesota, to a genteel but ineffectual father and a doting and eccentric mother. A delicate child, he was reluctant to go to school but finally went to a small Catholic school, then to St. Paul Academy, to Newman, and finally to Princeton. He was unpopular at most of these places for most of the time, and unhappy as well, but his talent for writing and his remarkable good looks began to count for more as he grew up; so that at college he received much of the adulation for which he hungered so deeply. He was concerned to the point of obsession with social standing and prestige. Only his gift for writing and his capacity for ruthless self-criticism prevented him from sliding into a life of empty snobbery. He had to marry a beautiful girl, and he did. He had to become rich and famous—and he did. But his wife's mental health was precarious, and the fame and riches were more than he could handle. After a breakdown and painful recovery, that he described with a typical lack of self-protectiveness, he lived and worked in Hollywood, never quite recapturing the grace and beauty of his early work. He was the poet laureate of the jazz age, and in his finest novels *(The Great Gatsby, 1925, and Tender is the Night, 1934)* and his remarkable short stories, we can find the best epitaph for that era as well as for Fitzgerald himself.

Babylon Revisited

"And where's Mr. Campbell?" Charlie asked.

"Gone to Switzerland. Mr. Campbell's a pretty sick man, Mr. Wales."

"I'm sorry to hear that. And George Hardt?" Charlie inquired.

"Back in America, gone to work."

"And where is the Snow Bird?"

"He was in here last week. Anyway, his friend, Mr. Schaeffer, is in Paris."

Two familiar names from the long list of a year and a half ago. Charlie scribbled an address in his notebook and tore out the page.

"If you see Mr. Schaeffer, give him this," he said. "It's my brother-in-law's address. I haven't settled on a hotel yet."

He was not really disappointed to find Paris was so empty. But the stillness in the Ritz bar was strange and portentous. It was not an American bar any more—he felt polite in it, and not as if he owned it. It had gone back into France. He felt the stillness from the moment he got out of the taxi and saw the doorman, usually in a frenzy of activity at this hour, gossiping with a *chasseur* by the servants' entrance.

Passing through the corridor, he heard only a single, bored voice in the once-clamorous women's room. When he turned into the bar he traveled the twenty feet of green carpet with his eyes fixed straight ahead by old habit; and then, with his foot firmly on the rail, he turned and surveyed the room, encountering only a single pair of eyes that fluttered up from a newspaper in the corner. Charlie asked for the head barman, Paul, who in the latter days of the bull market had come to work in his own custom-built car—disembarking, however, with due nicety at the nearest corner. But Paul was at his country house today and Alix giving him information.

"No, no more," Charlie said, "I'm going slow these days."

Alix congratulated him: "You were going pretty strong a couple of years ago."

"I'll stick to it all right," Charlie assured him. "I've stuck to it for over a year and a half now."

"How do you find conditions in America?"

"I haven't been to America for months. I'm in business in Prague, representing a couple of concerns there. They don't know about me down there."

Alix smiled.

"Remember the night of George Hardt's bachelor dinner here?" said Charlie. "By the way, what's become of Claude Fessenden?"

Alix lowered his voice confidentially: "He's in Paris, but he doesn't come here any more. Paul doesn't allow it. He ran up a bill of thirty thousand francs, charging all his drinks and his lunches, and usually his dinner, for more than a year. And when Paul finally told him he had to pay, he gave him a bad check."

Alix shook his head sadly.

"I don't understand it, such a dandy fellow. Now he's all bloated up—" He made a plump apple of his hands.

Charlie watched a group of strident queens installing themselves in a corner.

"Nothing affects them," he thought. "Stocks rise and fall, people loaf or work, but they go on forever." The place oppressed him. He called for the dice and shook with Alix for the drink.

"Here for long, Mr. Wales?"

"I'm here for four or five days to see my little girl."

"Oh-h! You have a little girl?"

Outside, the fire-red, gas-blue, ghost-green signs shone smokily through the tranquil rain. It was late afternoon and the streets were in movement; the *bistros* gleamed. At the corner of the Boulevard des Capucines he took a taxi. The Place de la Concorde moved by in pink majesty; they crossed the logical Seine, and Charlie felt the sudden provincial quality of the Left Bank.

Charlie directed his taxi to the Avenue de l'Opéra, which was out of his way. But he wanted to see the blue hour spread over the magnificent façade, and imagine that the cab horns, playing endlessly

charlie is just seeing Paris as it really is for the first time

the first few bars of *Le Plus que Lent*, were the trumpets of the Second
Empire. They were closing the iron grill in front of Brentano's
Book-store, and people were already at dinner behind the trim little
bourgeois hedge of Duval's. He had never eaten at a really cheap
restaurant in Paris. Five-course dinner, four francs fifty, eighteen
cents, wine included. For some odd reason he wished that he had.

As they rolled on to the Left Bank and he felt its sudden provin-
cialism, he thought, "I spoiled this city for myself. I didn't realize it,
but the days came along one after another, and then two years were
gone, and everything was gone, and I was gone."

He was thirty-five, and good to look at. The Irish mobility of his face
was sobered by a deep wrinkle between his eyes. As he rang his
brother-in-law's bell in the Rue Palatine, the wrinkle deepened till it
pulled down his brows; he felt a cramping sensation in his belly. From
behind the maid who opened the door darted a lovely little girl of nine
who shrieked "Daddy!" and flew up, struggling like a fish, into his
arms. She pulled his head around by one ear and set her cheek against
his.

"My old pie," he said.

"Oh, daddy, daddy, daddy, daddy, dads, dads, dads!"

She drew him into the salon, where the family waited, a boy and a
girl his daughter's age, his sister-in-law and her husband. He greeted
Marion with his voice pitched carefully to avoid either feigned
enthusiasm or dislike, but her response was more frankly tepid,
though she minimized her expression of unalterable distrust by
directing her regard toward his child. The two men clasped hands in a
friendly way and Lincoln Peters rested his for a moment on Charlie's
shoulder.

The room was warm and comfortably American. The three children
moved intimately about, playing through the yellow oblongs that led
to other rooms; the cheer of six o'clock spoke in the eager smacks of
the fire and the sounds of French activity in the kitchen. But Charlie
did not relax; his heart sat up rigidly in his body and he drew confidence from his daughter, who from time to time came close to him,
holding in her arms the doll he had brought.

"Really extremely well," he declared in answer to Lincoln's question. "There's a lot of business there that isn't moving at all, but we're
doing even better than ever. In fact, damn well. I'm bringing my sister
over from America next month to keep house for me. My income last
year was bigger than it was when I had money. You see, the Czechs—"

His boasting was for a specific purpose; but after a moment, seeing a
faint restiveness in Lincoln's eye, he changed the subject:

"Those are fine children of yours, well brought up, good manners."

"We think Honoria's a great little girl too."

Marion Peters came back from the kitchen. She was a tall woman with worried eyes, who had once possessed a fresh American loveliness. Charlie had never been sensitive to it and was always surprised when people spoke of how pretty she had been. From the first there had been an instinctive antipathy between them. *strong dislike*

"Well, how do you find Honoria?" she asked.

"Wonderful. I was astonished how much she's grown in ten months. All the children are looking well."

"We haven't had a doctor for a year. How do you like being back in Paris?"

"It seems very funny to see so few Americans around."

"I'm delighted," Marion said vehemently. "Now at least you can go into a store without their assuming you're a millionaire. We've suffered like everybody, but on the whole it's a good deal pleasanter."

"But it was nice while it lasted," Charlie said. "We were a sort of royalty, almost infallible, with a sort of magic around us. In the bar this afternoon"—he stumbled, seeing his mistake—"there wasn't a man I knew."

She looked at him keenly. "I should think you'd have had enough of bars."

"I only stayed a minute. I take one drink every afternoon, and no more."

"Don't you want a cocktail before dinner?" Lincoln asked.

"I take only one drink every afternoon, and I've had that."

"I hope you keep to it," said Marion.

Her dislike was evident in the coldness with which she spoke, but Charlie only smiled; he had larger plans. Her very aggressiveness gave him an advantage, and he knew enough to wait. He wanted them to  initiate the discussion of what they knew had brought him to Paris.

At dinner he couldn't decide whether Honoria was most like him or her mother. Fortunate if she didn't combine the traits of both that had brought them to disaster. A great wave of protectiveness went over him. He thought he knew what to do for her. He believed in character; he wanted to jump back a whole generation and trust in character again as the eternally valuable element. Everything else wore out.

He left soon after dinner, but not to go home. He was curious to see Paris by night with clearer and more judicious eyes than those of other days. He bought a *strapontin* for the Casino and watched Josephine Baker go through her chocolate arabesques.

After an hour he left and strolled toward Montmartre, up the Rue Pigalle into the Place Blanche. The rain had stopped and there were a few people in evening clothes disembarking from taxis in front of cabarets, and *cocottes* prowling singly or in pairs, and many Negroes. He passed a lighted door from which issued music, and stopped with the sense of familiarity; it was Bricktop's, where he had parted with so many hours and so much money. A few doors farther on he found another ancient rendezvous and incautiously put his head inside. Immediately an eager orchestra burst into sound, a pair of professional dancers leaped to their feet and a maître d'hôtel swooped toward him, crying, "Crowd just arriving, sir!" But he withdrew quickly.

"You have to be damn drunk," he thought.

Zelli's was closed, the bleak and sinister cheap hotels surrounding it were dark; up in the Rue Blanche there was more light and a local, colloquial French crowd. The Poet's Cave had disappeared, but the two great mouths of the Café of Heaven and the Café of Hell still yawned—even devoured, as he watched, the meager contents of a tourist bus—a German, a Japanese, and an American couple who glanced at him with frightened eyes.

So much for the effort and ingenuity of Montmartre. All the catering to vice and waste was on an utterly childish scale, and he suddenly realized the meaning of the word "dissipate"—to dissipate into thin air; to make nothing out of something. In the little hours of the night every move from place to place was an enormous human jump, an increase of paying for the privilege of slower and slower motion.

He remembered thousand-franc notes given to an orchestra for playing a single number, hundred-franc notes tossed to a doorman for calling a cab.

But it hadn't been given for nothing.

It had been given, even the most wildly squandered sum, as an offering to destiny that he might not remember the things most worth remembering, the things that now he would always remember—his child taken from his control, his wife escaped to a grave in Vermont.

In the glare of a *brasserie* a woman spoke to him. He bought her some eggs and coffee, and then, eluding her encouraging stare, gave her a twenty-franc note and took a taxi to his hotel.

II

He woke upon a fine fall day—football weather. The depression of yesterday was gone and he liked the people on the streets. At noon he sat opposite Honoria at Le Grand Vatel, the only restaurant he could think of not reminiscent of champagne dinners and long luncheons that began at two and ended in a blurred and vague twilight.

"Now, how about vegetables? Oughtn't you to have some vegetables?"

"Well, yes."

"Here's *épinards* and *chou-fleur* and carrots and *haricots*."

"I'd like *chou-fleur*."

"Wouldn't you like to have two vegetables?"

"I usually only have one at lunch."

The waiter was pretending to be inordinately fond of children. *"Qu'elle est mignonne la petite! Elle parle exactement comme une Française."*

"How about dessert? Shall we wait and see?"

The waiter disappeared. Honoria looked at her father expectantly.

"What are we going to do?"

"First, we're going to that toy store in the Rue Saint-Honoré and buy you anything you like. And then we're going to the vaudeville at the Empire."

She hesitated. "I like it about the vaudeville, but not the toy store."

"Why not?"

"Well, you brought me this doll." She had it with her. "And I've got lots of things. And we're not rich any more, are we?"

"We never were. But today you are to have anything you want."

"All right," she agreed resignedly.

When there had been her mother and a French nurse he had been inclined to be strict; now he extended himself, reached out for a new tolerance; he must be both parents to her and not shut any of her out of communication.

"I want to get to know you," he said gravely. "First let me introduce myself. My name is Charles J. Wales, of Prague."

"Oh, daddy!" her voice cracked with laughter.

"And who are you, please?" he persisted, and she accepted a rôle immediately: "Honoria Wales, Rue Palatine, Paris."

"Married or single?"

"No, not married. Single."

He indicated the doll. "But I see you have a child, madame."

Unwilling to disinherit it, she took it to her heart and thought quickly: "Yes, I've been married, but I'm not married now. My husband is dead."

He went on quickly, "And the child's name?"

"Simone. That's after my best friend at school."

"I'm very pleased that you're doing so well at school."

"I'm third this month," she boasted. "Elsie"—that was her cousin—"is only about eighteenth, and Richard is about at the bottom."

"You like Richard and Elsie, don't you?"

"Oh, yes. I like Richard quite well and I like her all right."

Cautiously and casually he asked: "And Aunt Marion and Uncle Lincoln—which do you like best?"

"Oh, Uncle Lincoln, I guess."

He was increasingly aware of her presence. As they came in, a murmur of ". . . adorable" followed them, and now the people at the next table bent all their silences upon her, staring as if she were something no more conscious than a flower.

"Why don't I live with you?" she asked suddenly. "Because mamma's dead?"

"You must stay here and learn more French. It would have been hard for daddy to take care of you so well."

"I don't really need much taking care of any more. I do everything for myself."

Going out of the restaurant, a man and a woman unexpectedly hailed him.

"Well, the old Wales!"

"Hello there, Lorraine. . . . Dunc."

Sudden ghosts out of the past: Duncan Schaeffer, a friend from college. Lorraine Quarrles, a lovely, pale blonde of thirty; one of a crowd who had helped them make months into days in the lavish times of three years ago.

"My husband couldn't come this year," she said, in answer to his question. "We're poor as hell. So he gave me two hundred a month and told me I could do my worst on that. . . . This your little girl?"

"What about coming back and sitting down?" Duncan asked.

"Can't do it." He was glad for an excuse. As always, he felt Lorraine's passionate, provocative attraction, but his own rhythm was different now.

"Well, how about dinner?" she asked.

"I'm not free. Give me your address and let me call you."

"Charlie, I believe you're sober," she said judicially. "I honestly believe he's sober, Dunc. Pinch him and see if he's sober."

Charlie indicated Honoria with his head. They both laughed.

"What's your address?" said Duncan skeptically.

He hesitated, unwilling to give the name of his hotel.

"I'm not settled yet. I'd better call you. We're going to see the vaudeville at the Empire."

"There! That's what I want to do," Lorraine said. "I want to see some clowns and acrobats and jugglers. That's just what we'll do, Dunc."

"We've got to do an errand first," said Charlie. "Perhaps we'll see you there."

"All right, you snob. . . . Good-by, beautiful little girl."

"Good-by."

Honoria bobbed politely.

Somehow, an unwelcome encounter. They liked him because he was functioning, because he was serious; they wanted to see him, because he was stronger than they were now, because they wanted to draw a certain sustenance from his strength.

At the Empire, Honoria proudly refused to sit upon her father's folded coat. She was already an individual with a code of her own, and Charlie was more and more absorbed by the desire of putting a little of himself into her before she crystallized utterly. It was hopeless to try to know her in so short a time.

Between the acts they came upon Duncan and Lorraine in the lobby where the band was playing.

"Have a drink?"

"All right, but not up at the bar. We'll take a table."

"The perfect father."

Listening abstractedly to Lorraine, Charlie watched Honoria's eyes leave their table, and he followed them wistfully about the room, wondering what they saw. He met her glance and she smiled.

"I liked that lemonade," she said.

What had she said? What had he expected? Going home in a taxi afterward, he pulled her over until her head rested against his chest.

"Darling, do you ever think about your mother?"

"Yes, sometimes," she answered vaguely.

"I don't want you to forget her. Have you got a picture of her?"

"Yes, I think so. Anyhow, Aunt Marion has. Why don't you want me to forget her?"

"She loved you very much."

"I loved her too."

They were silent for a moment.

"Daddy, I want to come and live with you," she said suddenly.

His heart leaped; he had wanted it to come like this.

"Aren't you perfectly happy?"

"Yes, but I love you better than anybody. And you love me better than anybody, don't you, now that mummy's dead?"

"Of course I do. But you won't always like me best, honey. You'll grow up and meet somebody your own age and go marry him and forget you ever had a daddy."

"Yes, that's true," she agreed tranquilly.

He didn't go in. He was coming back at nine o'clock and he wanted to keep himself fresh and new for the thing he must say then.

"When you're safe inside, just show yourself in that window."

"All right. Good-by, dads, dads, dads, dads."

He waited in the dark street until she appeared, all warm and glowing, in the window above and kissed her fingers out into the night.

III

They were waiting. Marion sat behind the coffee service in a dignified black dinner dress that just faintly suggested mourning. Lincoln was walking up and down with the animation of one who had already been talking. They were as anxious as he was to get into the question. He opened it almost immediately:

"I suppose you know what I want to see you about—why I really came to Paris."

Marion played with the black stars on her necklace and frowned.

"I'm awfully anxious to have a home," he continued. "And I'm awfully anxious to have Honoria in it. I appreciate your taking in Honoria for her mother's sake, but things have changed now"—he hesitated and then continued more forcibly—"changed radically with me, and I want to ask you to reconsider the matter. It would be silly for me to deny that about three years ago I was acting badly—"

Marion looked up at him with hard eyes.

"—but all that's over. As I told you, I haven't had more than a drink a day for over a year, and I take that drink deliberately, so that the idea of alcohol won't get too big in my imagination. You see the idea?"

"No," said Marion succinctly.

"It's a sort of stunt I set myself. It keeps the matter in proportion."

"I get you," said Lincoln. "You don't want to admit it's got any attraction for you."

"Something like that. Sometimes I forget and don't take it. But I try to take it. Anyway, I couldn't afford to drink in my position. The people I represent are more than satisfied with what I've done, and I'm bringing my sister over from Burlington to keep house for me, and I want awfully to have Honoria too. You know that even when her mother and I weren't getting along well we never let anything that happened touch Honoria. I know she's fond of me and I know I'm able to take care of her and—well, there you are. How do you feel about it?"

He knew that now he would have to take a beating. It would last an hour or two hours, and it would be difficult, but if he modulated his inevitable resentment to the chastened attitude of the reformed sinner, he might win his point in the end.

Keep your temper, he told himself. You don't want to be justified. You want Honoria.

Lincoln spoke first: "We've been talking it over ever since we got your letter last month. We're happy to have Honoria here. She's a dear little thing, and we're glad to be able to help her, but of course that isn't the question—"

Marion interrupted suddenly. "How long are you going to stay sober, Charlie?" she asked.

"Permanently, I hope."

"How can anybody count on that?"

"You know I never did drink heavily until I gave up business and came over here with nothing to do. Then Helen and I began to run around with—"

"Please leave Helen out of it. I can't bear to hear you talk about her like that."

He stared at her grimly; he had never been certain how fond of each other the sisters were in life.

"My drinking only lasted about a year and a half—from the time we came over until I—collapsed."

"It was time enough."

"It was time enough," he agreed.

"My duty is entirely to Helen," she said. "I try to think what she would have wanted me to do. Frankly, from the night you did that terrible thing you haven't really existed for me. I can't help that. She was my sister."

"Yes."

"When she was dying she asked me to look out for Honoria. If you hadn't been in a sanitarium then, it might have helped matters."

He had no answer.

"I'll never in my life be able to forget that morning when Helen knocked at my door, soaked to the skin and shivering and said you'd locked her out."

Charlie gripped the sides of the chair. This was more difficult than he expected; he wanted to launch out into a long expostulation and explanation, but he only said: "The night I locked her out—" and she interrupted, "I don't feel up to going over that again."

After a moment's silence Lincoln said: "We're getting off the subject. You want Marion to set aside her legal guardianship and give you Honoria. I think the main point for her is whether she has confidence in you or not."

"I don't blame Marion," Charlie said slowly, "but I think she can have entire confidence in me. I had a good record up to three years ago. Of course, it's within human possibilities I might go wrong any time. But if we wait much longer I'll lose Honoria's childhood and my chance for a home." He shook his head, "I'll simply lose her, don't you see?"

"Yes, I see," said Lincoln.

"Why didn't you think of all this before?" Marion asked.

"I suppose I did, from time to time, but Helen and I were getting along badly. When I consented to the guardianship, I was flat on my back in a sanitarium and the market had cleaned me out. I knew I'd acted badly, and I thought if it would bring any peace to Helen, I'd agree to anything. But now it's different. I'm functioning, I'm behaving damn well, so far as—"

"Please don't swear at me," Marion said.

He looked at her, startled. With each remark the force of her dislike became more and more apparent. She had built up all her fear of life into one wall and faced it toward him. This trivial reproof was possibly the result of some trouble with the cook several hours before. Charlie became increasingly alarmed at leaving Honoria in this atmosphere of hostility against himself; sooner or later it would come out, in a word here, a shake of the head there, and some of that distrust would be irrevocably implanted in Honoria. But he pulled his temper down out of his face and shut it up inside him; he had won a point, for Lincoln realized the absurdity of Marion's remark and asked her lightly since when she had objected to the word "damn."

"Another thing," Charlie said: "I'm able to give her certain advantages now. I'm going to take a French governess to Prague with me. I've got a lease on a new apartment—"

He stopped, realizing that he was blundering. They couldn't be expected to accept with equanimity the fact that his income was again twice as large as their own.

"I suppose you can give her more luxuries than we can," said Marion. "When you were throwing away money we were living along watching every ten francs. . . . I suppose you'll start doing it again."

"Oh, no," he said. "I've learned. I worked hard for ten years, you know—until I got lucky in the market, like so many people. Terribly lucky. It won't happen again."

There was a long silence. All of them felt their nerves straining, and for the first time in a year Charlie wanted a drink. He was sure now that Lincoln Peters wanted him to have his child.

Marion shuddered suddenly; part of her saw that Charlie's feet were planted on the earth now, and her own maternal feeling recognized the naturalness of his desire; but she had lived for a long time with a prejudice—a prejudice founded on a curious disbelief in her sister's happiness, and which, in the shock of one terrible night, had turned to hatred for him. It had all happened at a point in her life where the discouragement of ill health and adverse circumstances made it necessary for her to believe in tangible villainy and a tangible villain.

"I can't help what I think!" she cried out suddenly. "How much you were responsible for Helen's death, I don't know. It's something you'll have to square with your own conscience."

An electric current of agony surged through him; for a moment he was almost on his feet, an unuttered sound echoing in his throat. He hung on to himself for a moment, another moment.

"Hold on there," said Lincoln uncomfortably. "I never thought you were responsible for that."

"Helen died of heart trouble," Charlie said dully.

"Yes, heart trouble." Marion spoke as if the phrase had another meaning for her.

Then, in the flatness that followed her outburst, she saw him plainly and she knew he had somehow arrived at control over the situation. Glancing at her husband, she found no help from him, and as abruptly as if it were a matter of no importance, she threw up the sponge.

"Do what you like!" she cried, springing up from her chair. "She's your child. I'm not the person to stand in your way. I think if it were my child I'd rather see her—" She managed to check herself. "You two decide it. I can't stand this. I'm sick. I'm going to bed."

She hurried from the room; after a moment Lincoln said:

"This has been a hard day for her. You know how strongly she feels—" His voice was almost apologetic: "When a woman gets an idea in her head."

"Of course."

"It's going to be all right. I think she sees now that you—can provide for the child, and so we can't very well stand in your way or Honoria's way."

"Thank you, Lincoln."

"I'd better go along and see how she is."

"I'm going."

He was still trembling when he reached the street, but a walk down the Rue Bonaparte to the *quais* set him up, and as he crossed the Seine, fresh and new by the *quai* lamps, he felt exultant. But back in his room he couldn't sleep. The image of Helen haunted him. Helen whom he had loved so until they had senselessly begun to abuse each other's love, tear it into shreds. On that terrible February night that Marion remembered so vividly, a slow quarrel had gone on for hours. There was a scene at the Florida, and then he attempted to take her home, and then she kissed young Webb at a table; after that there was what she had hysterically said. When he arrived home alone he turned the key in the lock in wild anger. How could he know she would arrive an hour later alone, that there would be a snowstorm in which she wandered about in slippers, too confused to find a taxi? Then the aftermath, her escaping pneumonia by a miracle, and all the attendant horror. They were "reconciled," but that was the beginning of the end, and Marion, who had seen with her own eyes and who imagined it to be one of many scenes from her sister's martyrdom, never forgot.

Going over it again brought Helen nearer, and in the white, soft light that steals upon half sleep near morning he found himself talking to her again. She said that he was perfectly right about Honoria and that she wanted Honoria to be with him. She said she was glad he was being good and doing better. She said a lot of other things—very friendly things—but she was in a swing in a white dress, and swinging faster and faster all the time, so that at the end he could not hear clearly all that she said.

IV

He woke up feeling happy. The door of the world was open again. He made plans, vistas, futures for Honoria and himself, but suddenly he grew sad, remembering all the plans he and Helen had made. She had not planned to die. The present was the thing—work to do and someone to love. But not to love too much, for he knew the injury that a father can do to a daughter or a mother to a son by attaching them too closely: afterward, out in the world, the child would seek in the marriage partner the same blind tenderness and, failing probably to find it, turn against love and life.

It was another bright, crisp day. He called Lincoln Peters at the bank where he worked and asked if he could count on taking Honoria when he left for Prague. Lincoln agreed that there was no reason for delay. One thing—the legal guardianship. Marion wanted to retain that a while longer. She was upset by the whole matter, and it would oil things if she felt that the situation was still in her control for another year. Charlie agreed, wanting only the tangible, visible child.

Then the question of a governess. Charles sat in a gloomy agency and talked to a cross Béarnaise and to a buxom Breton peasant, neither of whom he could have endured. There were others whom he would see tomorrow.

He lunched with Lincoln Peters at Griffons, trying to keep down his exultation.

"There's nothing quite like your own child," Lincoln said. "But you understand how Marion feels too."

"She's forgotten how hard I worked for seven years there," Charlie said. "She just remembers one night."

"There's another thing." Lincoln hesitated. "While you and Helen were tearing around Europe throwing money away, we were just getting along. I didn't touch any of the prosperity because I never got ahead enough to carry anything but my insurance. I think Marion felt there was some kind of injustice in it—you not even working toward the end, and getting richer and richer."

"It went just as quick as it came," said Charlie.

"Yes, a lot of it stayed in the hands of *chasseurs* and saxophone players and maîtres d'hôtel—well, the big party's over now. I just said that to explain Marion's feeling about those crazy years. If you drop in about six o'clock tonight before Marion's too tired, we'll settle the details on the spot."

Back at his hotel, Charlie found a *pneumatique* that had been redirected from the Ritz bar where Charlie had left his address for the purpose of finding a certain man.

DEAR CHARLIE: You were so strange when we saw you the other day that I wondered if I did something to offend you. If so, I'm not conscious of it. In fact, I have thought about you too much for the last year, and it's always been in the back of my mind that I might see you if I came over here. We *did* have such good times that crazy spring, like the night you and I stole the butcher's tricycle, and the time we tried to call on the president and you had the old derby rim and the wire cane. Everybody seems so old lately, but I don't feel old a bit. Couldn't we get together some time today for old time's sake? I've got a vile hang-over for the moment, but will be feeling better this afternoon and will look for you about five in the sweatshop at the Ritz.

Always devotedly,

LORRAINE.

His first feeling was one of awe that he had actually, in his mature years, stolen a tricycle and pedaled Lorraine all over the Étoile between the small hours and dawn. In retrospect it was a nightmare. Locking out Helen didn't fit in with any other act of his life, but the tricycle incident did—it was one of many. How many weeks or months of dissipation to arrive at that condition of utter irresponsibility?

He tried to picture how Lorraine had appeared to him then—very attractive; Helen was unhappy about it, though she said nothing. Yesterday, in the restaurant, Lorraine had seemed trite, blurred, worn away. He emphatically did not want to see her, and he was glad Alix had not given away his hotel address. It was a relief to think, instead, of Honoria, to think of Sundays spent with her and of saying good morning to her and of knowing she was there in his house at night, drawing her breath in the darkness.

At five he took a taxi and bought presents for all the Peters—a piquant cloth doll, a box of Roman soldiers, flowers for Marion, big linen handkerchiefs for Lincoln.

He saw, when he arrived in the apartment, that Marion had accepted the inevitable. She greeted him now as though he were a recalcitrant member of the family, rather than a menacing outsider. Honoria had been told she was going; Charlie was glad to see that her tact made her conceal her excessive happiness. Only on his lap did she whisper her delight and the question "When?" before she slipped away with the other children.

He and Marion were alone for a minute in the room, and on an impulse he spoke out boldly:

"Family quarrels are bitter things. They don't go according to any rules. They're not aches or wounds; they're more like splits in the skin that won't heal because there's not enough material. I wish you and I could be on better terms."

"Some things are hard to forget," she answered. "It's a question of confidence." There was no answer to this and presently she asked, "When do you propose to take her?"

"As soon as I can get a governess. I hoped the day after tomorrow."

"That's impossible. I've got to get her things in shape. Not before Saturday."

He yielded. Coming back into the room, Lincoln offered him a drink.

"I'll take my daily whisky," he said.

It was warm here, it was a home, people together by a fire. The children felt very safe and important; the mother and father were serious, watchful. They had things to do for the children more important than his visit here. A spoonful of medicine was, after all, more important than the strained relations between Marion and himself. They were not dull people, but they were very much in the grip of life and circumstances. He wondered if he couldn't do something to get Lincoln out of his rut at the bank.

A long peal at the door-bell; the *bonne à tout faire* passed through and went down the corridor. The door opened upon another long ring, and then voices, and the three in the salon looked up expectantly; Richard moved to bring the corridor within his range of vision, and Marion rose. Then the maid came back along the corridor, closely followed by the voices, which developed under the light into Duncan Schaeffer and Lorraine Quarrles.

They were gay, they were hilarious, they were roaring with laughter. For a moment Charlie was astounded; unable to understand how they ferreted out the Peters' address.

"Ah-h-h-!" Duncan wagged his finger roguishly at Charlie. "Ah-h-h!"

They both slid down another cascade of laughter. Anxious and at a loss, Charlie shook hands with them quickly and presented them to Lincoln and Marion. Marion nodded, scarcely speaking. She had drawn back a step toward the fire; her little girl stood beside her, and Marion put an arm about her shoulder.

With growing annoyance at the intrusion, Charlie waited for them to explain themselves. After some concentration Duncan said:

"We came to invite you out to dinner. Lorraine and I insist that all this shishi, cagy business 'bout your address got to stop."

Charlie came closer to them, as if to force them backward down the corridor.

"Sorry, but I can't. Tell me where you'll be and I'll phone you in half an hour."

This made no impression. Lorraine sat down suddenly on the side of a chair, and focusing her eyes on Richard, cried, "Oh, what a nice little boy! Come here, little boy." Richard glanced at his mother, but did not move. With a perceptible shrug of her shoulders, Lorraine turned back to Charlie:

"Come and dine. Sure your cousins won' mine. See you so sel'om. Or solemn."

"I can't," said Charlie sharply. "You two have dinner and I'll phone you."

Her voice became suddenly unpleasant. "All right, we'll go. But I remember once when you hammered on my door at four .A.M. I was enough of a good sport to give you a drink. Come on, Dunc."

Still in slow motion, with blurred, angry faces, with uncertain feet, they retired along the corridor.

"Good night," Charlie said.

"Good night!" responded Lorraine emphatically.

When he went back into the salon Marion had not moved, only now her son was standing in the circle of her other arm. Lincoln was still swinging Honoria back and forth like a pendulum from side to side.

"What an outrage!" Charlie broke out. "What an absolute outrage!"

Neither of them answered. Charlie dropped into an armchair, picked up his drink, set it down again and said:

"People I haven't seen for two years having the colossal nerve—"

He broke off. Marion had made the sound "Oh!" in one swift, furious breath, turned her body from him with a jerk and left the room.

Lincoln set down Honoria carefully.

"You children go in and start your soup," he said, and when they obeyed, he said to Charlie:

"Marion's not well and she can't stand shocks. That kind of people make her really physically sick."

"I didn't tell them to come here. They wormed your name out of somebody. They deliberately—"

"Well, it's too bad. It doesn't help matters. Excuse me a minute."

Left alone, Charlie sat tense in his chair. In the next room he could hear the children eating, talking in monosyllables, already oblivious to the scene between their elders. He heard a murmur of conversation from a farther room and then the ticking bell of a telephone receiver picked up, and in a panic he moved to the other side of the room and out of earshot.

In a minute Lincoln came back. "Look here, Charlie. I think we'd better call off dinner for tonight. Marion's in bad shape."

"Is she angry with me?"

"Sort of," he said, almost roughly. "She's not strong and—"

"You mean she's changed her mind about Honoria?"

"She's pretty bitter right now. I don't know. You phone me at the bank tomorrow."

"I wish you'd explain to her I never dreamed these people would come here. I'm just as sore as you are."

"I couldn't explain anything to her now."

Charlie got up. He took his coat and hat and started down the corridor. Then he opened the door of the dining room and said in a strange voice, "Good night, children."

Honoria rose and ran around the table to hug him.

"Good night, sweetheart," he said vaguely, and then trying to make his voice more tender, trying to conciliate something, "Good night, dear children."

v

Charlie went directly to the Ritz bar with the furious idea of finding Lorraine and Duncan, but they were not there, and he realized that in any case there was nothing he could do. He had not touched his drink at the Peters, and now he ordered a whisky-and-soda. Paul came over to say hello.

"It's a great change," he said sadly. "We do about half the business we did. So many fellows I hear about back in the States lost everything, maybe not in the first crash, but then in the second. Your friend George Hardt lost every cent, I hear. Are you back in the States?"

"No, I'm in business in Prague."

"I heard that you lost a lot in the crash."

"I did," and he added grimly, "but I lost everything I wanted in the boom."

"Selling short."

"Something like that."

Again the memory of those days swept over him like a nightmare— the people they had met travelling; then people who couldn't add a row of figures or speak a coherent sentence. The little man Helen had consented to dance with at the ship's party, who had insulted her ten feet from the table; the women and girls carried screaming with drink or drugs out of public places—

—The men who locked their wives out in the snow, because the snow of twenty-nine wasn't real snow. If you didn't want it to be snow, you just paid some money.

He went to the phone and called the Peters' apartment; Lincoln answered.

"I called up because this thing is on my mind. Has Marion said anything definite?"

"Marion's sick," Lincoln answered shortly. "I know this thing isn't altogether your fault, but I can't have her go to pieces about it. I'm afraid we'll have to let it slide for six months; I can't take the chance of working her up to this state again."

"I see."

"I'm sorry, Charlie."

He went back to his table. His whisky glass was empty, but he shook his head when Alix looked at it questioningly. There wasn't much he could do now except send Honoria some things; he would send her a lot of things tomorrow. He thought rather angrily that this was just money—he had given so many people money. . . .

"No, no more," he said to another waiter. "What do I owe you?"

He would come back some day; they couldn't make him pay forever. But he wanted his child, and nothing was much good now, beside that fact. He wasn't young any more, with a lot of nice thoughts and dreams to have by himself. He was absolutely sure Helen wouldn't have wanted him to be so alone.

WILLIAM FAULKNER
1897–1962

Faulkner was born in Union County, Mississippi. His family had been important in the political, economic, and cultural life of northern Mississippi for three generations, but their power and influence were declining, and for a time it looked as if young William might be its least distinguished member. He spent most of his youth hunting, fishing, and playing baseball. But he was gifted at drawing and telling stories, and maintained from an early age that he wanted to be a writer like his great-grandfather, William Cuthbert Faulkner, whose White Rose of Memphis had gone through thirty-five editions after its publication in 1880. During World War I Faulkner was turned down by the U.S. Army Air Corps because he was too short, but was accepted for flight training in the Royal Canadian Air Force. He wanted to fly in combat, but the war ended too soon, and he was injured when he and a friend celebrated Armistice Day by stunting over the field and crashing through a hangar roof.

Returning to Oxford, Mississippi, he continued to read and to write, and took courses at the University of Mississippi. But he was neither a regular nor a successful student. Nor was he having any luck trying to place his fiction and poetry with magazines. Finally, a friend subsidized a private printing of a volume of Faulkner's poetry, The Marble Faun, in 1924. In later life Faulkner spoke of himself as a "failed poet," who had turned to fiction only because his poetry was not good enough.

In 1925 he moved to New Orleans, where he was admitted to the circle of writers that gathered around Sherwood Anderson, and began to publish sketches in the Sunday feature section of the New Orleans *Times-Picayune*. Then, with the help of Anderson, he was able to get his first novel, *Soldier's Pay*, published in 1926. In his third novel, *Sartoris* (1929), he began to find his proper material and realize his strength as a writer. With this work he began his immense chronicle of an imaginary Mississippi county, based on the history of the area around his home in Oxford, Mississippi. His Yoknapatawpha County has become a permanent feature in the international literary landscape. Among his most highly regarded works are *Light in August* (1932) and *Absalom, Absalom!* (1936), and two collections of short fiction which have the shape and movement of a novel: *The Unvanquished* (1938) and *Go Down, Moses* (1942). In 1950 he received the Nobel Prize for literature.

A Rose for Emily

I

When Miss Emily Grierson died, our whole town went to her funeral: the men through a sort of respectful affection for a fallen monument, the women mostly out of curiosity to see the inside of her house, which no one save an old manservant—a combined gardener and cook—had seen in at least ten years.

It was a big, squarish frame house that had once been white, decorated with cupolas and spires and scrolled balconies in the heavily lightsome style of the seventies, set on what had once been our most select street. But garages and cotton gins had encroached and obliterated even the august names of that neighborhood; only Miss Emily's house was left, lifting its stubborn and coquettish decay above the cotton wagons and the gasoline pumps—an eyesore among eyesores. And now Miss Emily had gone to join the representatives of those august names where they lay in the cedar-bemused cemetery among the ranked and anonymous graves of Union and Confederate soldiers who fell at the battle of Jefferson.

Alive, Miss Emily had been a tradition, a duty, and a care; a sort of hereditary obligation upon the town, dating from that day in 1894 when Colonel Sartoris, the mayor—he who fathered the edict that no Negro woman should appear on the streets without an apron—remitted her taxes, the dispensation dating from the death of her father on into perpetuity. Not that Miss Emily would have accepted charity. Colonel Sartoris invented an involved tale to the effect that Miss Emily's father had loaned money to the town, which the town, as a matter of business, preferred this way of repaying. Only a man of Colonel Sartoris' generation and thought could have invented it, and only a woman could have believed it.

When the next generation, with its more modern ideas, became mayors and aldermen, this arrangement created some little dissatisfaction. On the first of the year they mailed her a tax notice. February came, and there was no reply. They wrote her a formal letter, asking her to call at the sheriff's office at her convenience. A week later the mayor wrote her himself, offering to call or to send his car for her, and received in reply a note on paper of an archaic shape, in a thin, flowing calligraphy in faded ink, to the effect that she no longer went out at all. The tax notice was also enclosed, without comment.

They called a special meeting of the Board of Aldermen. A deputation waited upon her, knocked at the door through which no visitor had passed since she ceased giving china-painting lessons eight or ten years earlier. They were admitted by the old Negro into a dim hall from which a stairway mounted into still more shadow. It smelled of dust and disuse—a close, dank smell. The Negro led them into the parlor. It was furnished in heavy, leather-covered furniture. When the Negro opened the blinds of one window, they could see that the leather was cracked; and when they sat down, a faint dust rose sluggishly about their thighs, spinning with slow motions in the single sun-ray. On a tarnished gilt easel before the fireplace stood a crayon portrait of Miss Emily's father.

They rose when she entered—a small, fat woman in black, with a thin gold chain descending to her waist and vanishing into her belt, leaning on an ebony cane with a tarnished gold head. Her skeleton was small and spare; perhaps that was why what would have been merely plumpness in another was obesity in her. She looked bloated, like a body long submerged in motionless water, and of that pallid hue. Her eyes, lost in the fatty ridges of her face, looked like two small pieces of coal pressed into a lump of dough as they moved from one face to another while the visitors stated their errand.

She did not ask them to sit. She just stood in the door and listened quietly until the spokesman came to a stumbling halt. Then they could hear the invisible watch ticking at the end of the gold chain.

Her voice was dry and cold. "I have no taxes in Jefferson. Colonel Sartoris explained it to me. Perhaps one of you can gain access to the city records and satisfy yourselves."

"But we have. We are the city authorities, Miss Emily. Didn't you get a notice from the sheriff, signed by him?"

"I received a paper, yes," Miss Emily said. "Perhaps he considers himself the sheriff . . . I have no taxes in Jefferson."

"But there is nothing on the books to show that, you see. We must go by the—"

"See Colonel Sartoris." (Colonel Sartoris had been dead almost ten years.) "I have no taxes in Jefferson. Tobe!" The Negro appeared. "Show these gentlemen out."

II

So she vanquished them, horse and foot, just as she had vanquished
their fathers thirty years before about the smell. That was two years
after her father's death and a short time after her sweetheart—the one
we believed would marry her—had deserted her. After her father's
death she went out very little; after her sweetheart went away, people
hardly saw her at all. A few of the ladies had the temerity to call, but
were not received, and the only sign of life about the place was the
Negro man—a young man then—going in and out with a market
basket.

"Just as if a man—any man—could keep a kitchen properly," the
ladies said; so they were not surprised when the smell developed. It
was another link between the gross, teeming world and the high and
mighty Griersons.

A neighbor, a woman, complained to the mayor, Judge Stevens,
eighty years old.

"But what will you have me do about it, madam?" he said.

"Why, send her word to stop it," the woman said. "Isn't there a
law?"

"I'm sure that won't be necessary," Judge Stevens said. "It's
probably just a snake or a rat that nigger of hers killed in the yard. I'll
speak to him about it."

The next day he received two more complaints, one from a man who
came in diffident deprecation. "We really must do something about it,
Judge. I'd be the last one in the world to bother Miss Emily, but we've
got to do something." That night the Board of Aldermen met—three
graybeards and one younger man, a member of the rising generation.

"It's simple enough," he said. "Send her word to have her place
cleaned up. Give her a certain time to do it in, and if she don't . . ."

"Dammit, sir," Judge Stevens said, "will you accuse a lady to her
face of smelling bad?"

So the next night, after midnight, four men crossed Miss Emily's
lawn and slunk about the house like burglars, sniffing along the base
of the brickwork and at the cellar openings while one of them
performed a regular sowing motion with his hand out of a sack slung
from his shoulder. They broke open the cellar door and sprinkled lime
there, and in all the outbuildings. As they recrossed the lawn, a
window that had been dark was lighted and Miss Emily sat in it, the
light behind her, and her upright torso motionless as that of an idol.
They crept quietly across the lawn and into the shadow of the locusts
that lined the street. After a week or two the smell went away.

That was when people had begun to feel really sorry for her. People
in our town, remembering how old lady Wyatt, her great-aunt, had
gone completely crazy at last, believed that the Griersons held

themselves a little too high for what they really were. None of the young men were quite good enough for Miss Emily and such. We had long thought of them as a tableau, Miss Emily a slender figure in white in the background, her father a spraddled silhouette in the foreground, his back to her and clutching a horsewhip, the two of them framed by the back-flung front door. So when she got to be thirty and was still single, we were not pleased exactly, but vindicated; even with insanity in the family she wouldn't have turned down all of her chances if they had really materialized.

When her father died, it got about that the house was all that was left to her; and in a way, people were glad. At last they could pity Miss Emily. Being left alone, and a pauper, she had become humanized. Now she too would know the old thrill and the old despair of a penny more or less.

The day after his death all the ladies prepared to call at the house and offer condolence and aid, as is our custom. Miss Emily met them at the door, dressed as usual and with no trace of grief on her face. She told them that her father was not dead. She did that for three days, with the ministers calling on her, and the doctors, trying to persuade her to let them dispose of the body. Just as they were about to resort to law and force, she broke down, and they buried her father quickly.

We did not say she was crazy then. We believed she had to do that. We remembered all the young men her father had driven away, and we knew that with nothing left, she would have to cling to that which had robbed her, as people will.

III

She was sick for a long time. When we saw her again, her hair was cut short, making her look like a girl, with a vague resemblance to those angels in colored church windows—sort of tragic and serene.

The town had just let the contracts for paving the sidewalks, and in the summer after her father's death they began the work. The construction company came with niggers and mules and machinery, and a foreman named Homer Barron, a Yankee—a big, dark, ready man, with a big voice and eyes lighter than his face. The little boys would follow in groups to hear him cuss the niggers, and the niggers singing in time to the rise and fall of picks. Pretty soon he knew everybody in town. Whenever you heard a lot of laughing anywhere about the square, Homer Barron would be in the center of the group. Presently we began to see him and Miss Emily on Sunday afternoons driving in the yellow-wheeled buggy and the matched team of bays from the livery stable.

At first we were glad that Miss Emily would have an interest, because the ladies all said, "Of course a Grierson would not think seriously of a Northerner, a day laborer." But there were still others,

literally means—mobility obliges — people of high birth should behave nobally toward others.

older people, who said that even grief could not cause a real lady to forget _noblesse oblige_—without calling it _noblesse oblige_. They just said, "Poor Emily. Her kinsfolk should come to her." She had some kin in Alabama; but years ago her father had fallen out with them over the estate of old lady Wyatt, the crazy woman, and there was no communication between the two families. They had not even been represented at the funeral.

And as soon as the old people said, "Poor Emily," the whispering began. "Do you suppose it's really so?" they said to one another. "Of course it is. What else could . . ." This behind their hands; rustling of craned silk and satin behind jalousies closed upon the sun of Sunday afternoon as the thin, swift clop-clop-clop of the matched team passed: "Poor Emily."

She carried her head high enough—even when we believed that she was fallen. It was as if she demanded more than ever the recognition of her dignity as the last Grierson; as if it had wanted that touch of earthiness to reaffirm her imperviousness. Like when she bought the rat poison, the arsenic. That was over a year after they had begun to say "Poor Emily," and while the two female cousins were visiting her.

"I want some poison," she said to the druggist. She was over thirty then, still a slight woman, though thinner than usual, with cold, haughty black eyes in a face the flesh of which was strained across the temples and about the eye-sockets as you imagine a lighthouse-keeper's face ought to look. "I want some poison," she said.

"Yes, Miss Emily. What kind? For rats and such? I'd recom—"

"I want the best you have. I don't care what kind."

The druggist named several. "They'll kill anything up to an elephant. But what you want is—"

"Arsenic," Miss Emily said. "Is that a good one?"

"Is . . . arsenic? Yes, ma'am. But what you want—"

"I want arsenic."

The druggist looked down at her. She looked back at him, erect, her face like a strained flag. "Why, of course," the druggist said. "If that's what you want. But the law requires you to tell what you are going to use it for."

Miss Emily just stared at him, her head tilted back in order to look him eye for eye, until he looked away and went and got the arsenic and wrapped it up. The Negro delivery boy brought her the package; the druggist didn't come back. When she opened the package at home there was written on the box, under the skull and bones: "For rats."

IV

So the next day we all said, "She will kill herself"; and we said it would be the best thing. When she had first begun to be seen with Homer Barron, we had said, "She will marry him." Then we said, "She will persuade him yet," because Homer himself had remarked—he liked men, and it was known that he drank with the younger men in the Elks' Club—that he was not a marrying man. Later we said, "Poor Emily" behind the jalousies as they passed on Sunday afternoon in the glittering buggy, Miss Emily with her head high and Homer Barron with his hat cocked and a cigar in his teeth, reins and whip in a yellow glove.

Then some of the ladies began to say that it was a disgrace to the town and a bad example to the young people. The men did not want to interfere, but at last the ladies forced the Baptist minister—Miss Emily's people were Episcopal—to call upon her. He would never divulge what happened during that interview, but he refused to go back again. The next Sunday they again drove about the streets, and the following day the minister's wife wrote to Miss Emily's relations in Alabama.

So she had blood-kin under her roof again and we sat back to watch developments. At first nothing happened. Then we were sure that they were to be married. We learned that Miss Emily had been to the jeweler's and ordered a man's toilet set in silver, with the letters H.B. on each piece. Two days later we learned that she had bought a complete outfit of men's clothing, including a nightshirt, and we said, "They are married." We were really glad. We were glad because the two female cousins were even more Grierson than Miss Emily had ever been.

So we were not surprised when Homer Barron—the streets had been finished some time since—was gone. We were a little disappointed that there was not a public blowing-off, but we believed that he had gone on to prepare for Miss Emily's coming, or to give her a chance to get rid of the cousins. (By that time it was a cabal, and we were all Miss Emily's allies to help circumvent the cousins.) Sure enough, after another week they departed. And, as we had expected all along, within three days Homer Barron was back in town. A neighbor saw the Negro man admit him at the kitchen door at dusk one evening.

And that was the last we saw of Homer Barron. And of Miss Emily for some time. The Negro man went in and out with the market basket, but the front door remained closed. Now and then we would see her at a window for a moment, as the men did that night when they sprinkled the lime, but for almost six months she did not appear on the streets. Then we knew that this was to be expected too; as if that quality of her father which had thwarted her woman's life so many times had been too virulent and too furious to die.

When we next saw Miss Emily, she had grown fat and her hair was turning gray. During the next few years it grew grayer and grayer until it attained an even pepper-and-salt iron-gray, when it ceased turning. Up to the day of her death at seventy-four it was still that vigorous iron-gray, like the hair of an active man.

From that time on her front door remained closed, save for a period of six or seven years, when she was about forty, during which she gave lessons in china-painting. She fitted up a studio in one of the downstairs rooms, where the daughters and granddaughters of Colonel Sartoris' contemporaries were sent to her with the same regularity and in the same spirit that they were sent to church on Sundays with a twenty-five-cent piece for the collection plate. Meanwhile her taxes had been remitted.

Then the newer generation became the backbone and the spirit of the town, and the painting pupils grew up and fell away and did not send their children to her with boxes of color and tedious brushes and pictures cut from the ladies' magazines. The front door closed upon the last one and remained closed for good. When the town got free postal delivery, Miss Emily alone refused to let them fasten the metal numbers above her door and attach a mailbox to it. She would not listen to them.

Daily, monthly, yearly we watched the Negro grow grayer and more stooped, going in and out with the market basket. Each December we sent her a tax notice, which would be returned by the post office a week later, unclaimed. Now and then we would see her in one of the downstairs windows—she had evidently shut up the top floor of the house—like the carven torso of an idol in a niche, looking or not looking at us, we could never tell which. Thus she passed from generation to generation—dear, inescapable, impervious, tranquil, and perverse.

And so she died. Fell ill in the house filled with dust and shadows, with only a doddering Negro man to wait on her. We did not even know she was sick; we had long since given up trying to get any information from the Negro. He talked to no one, probably not even to her, for his voice had grown harsh and rusty, as if from disuse.

She died in one of the downstairs rooms, in a heavy walnut bed with a curtain, her gray head propped on a pillow yellow and moldy with age and lack of sunlight.

V

The Negro met the first of the ladies at the front door and let them in, with their hushed, sibilant voices and their quick, curious glances, and then he disappeared. He walked right through the house and out the back and was not seen again.

The two female cousins came at once. They held the funeral on the second day, with the town coming to look at Miss Emily beneath a

platform on which a coffin sits

mass of bought flowers, with the crayon face of her father musing profoundly above the bier and the ladies sibilant and macabre; and the very old men—some in their brushed Confederate uniforms—on the porch and the lawn, talking of Miss Emily as if she had been a contemporary of theirs, believing that they had danced with her and courted her perhaps, confusing time with its mathematical progression, as the old do, to whom all the past is not a diminishing road but, instead, a huge meadow which no winter ever quite touches, divided from them now by the narrow bottle-neck of the most recent decade of years.

time

Already we knew that there was one room in that region above stairs which no one had seen in forty years, and which would have to be forced. They waited until Miss Emily was decently in the ground before they opened it.

The violence of breaking down the door seemed to fill this room with pervading dust. A thin, acrid pall as of the tomb seemed to lie everywhere upon this room decked and furnished as for a bridal: upon the valance curtains of faded rose color, upon the rose-shaded lights, upon the dressing table, upon the delicate array of crystal and the man's toilet things backed with tarnished silver, silver so tarnished that the monogram was obscured. Among them lay a collar and tie, as if they had just been removed, which, lifted, left upon the surface a pale crescent in the dust. Upon a chair hung the suit, carefully folded; beneath it the two mute shoes and the discarded socks.

The man himself lay in the bed.

For a long while we just stood there, looking down at the profound and fleshless grin. The body had apparently once lain in the attitude of an embrace, but now the long sleep that outlasts love, that conquers even the grimace of love, had cuckolded him. What was left of him, rotted beneath what was left of the nightshirt, had become inextricable from the bed in which he lay; and upon him and upon the pillow beside him lay that even coating of the patient and biding dust.

Then we noticed that in the second pillow was the indentation of a head. One of us lifted something from it, and leaning forward, that faint and invisible dust dry and acrid in the nostrils, we saw a long strand of iron-gray hair.

ERNEST HEMINGWAY
1899–1961

Born in Oak Park, Illinois, the son of a doctor and a music teacher, Ernest Hemingway went to school in Oak Park and spent his summers in the upper peninsula of Michigan, where his father taught him early to hunt and fish. He was a physically active and popular boy, good at writing but bored with school. A couple of times he simply left and went on the road, but he worked on the school newspaper, graduated, and tried to enlist in the Army for World War I. A bad eye prevented that, so he went into newspaper work and then enlisted as an ambulance driver for the Red Cross in Italy, where he saw plenty of combat, was badly wounded and showed genuine heroism under fire. After the war and some newspaper work in Chicago and Toronto, Hemingway moved to Europe where he lived with his first wife, mostly in Paris. There he met Ezra Pound and Gertrude Stein, who christened Hemingway and his young friends a "lost generation." There, too, Hemingway began to write the stories and novels that made his reputation, beginning with *In Our Time* (1925) and *The Sun Also Rises* (1926). In later years he became more of a public figure and less of a writer, as he hardened into a symbol of patriarchal machismo known as "Papa." But he had a fine success with *The Old Man and the Sea* (1952) and won the Nobel Prize in 1954. In 1961, in ill health and unable to write, he loaded his silver-inlaid double-barreled shotgun, put both barrels in his mouth and pulled the triggers.

Hills Like White Elephants

The hills across the valley of the Ebro were long and white. On this side there was no shade and no trees and the station was between two lines of rails in the sun. Close against the side of the station there was the warm shadow of the building and a curtain, made of strings of bamboo beads, hung across the open door into the bar, to keep out flies. The American and the girl with him sat at a table in the shade, outside the building. It was very hot and the express from Barcelona would come in forty minutes. It stopped at this junction for two minutes and went on to Madrid.

"What should we drink?" the girl asked. She had taken off her hat and put it on the table.

"It's pretty hot," the man said.

"Let's drink beer."

"Dos cervezas," the man said into the curtain.

"Big ones?" a woman asked from the doorway.

"Yes. Two big ones."

The woman brought two glasses of beer and two felt pads. She put the felt pads and the beer glasses on the table and looked at the man and the girl. The girl was looking off at the line of hills. They were white in the sun and the country was brown and dry.

"They look like white elephants," she said.

"I've never seen one," the man drank his beer.

"No, you wouldn't have."

"I might have," the man said. "Just because you say I wouldn't have doesn't prove anything."

The girl looked at the bead curtain. "They've painted something on it," she said. "What does it say?"

"Anis del Toro. It's a drink."

"Could we try it?"

The man called "Listen" through the curtain. The woman came out from the bar.

"Four reales."

"We want two Anis del Toro."

"With water?"

"Do you want it with water?"

"I don't know," the girl said. "Is it good with water?"

"It's all right."

"You want them with water?" asked the woman.

"Yes, with water."

"It tastes like licorice," the girl said and put the glass down.

"That's the way with everything."

"Yes," said the girl. "Everything tastes of licorice. Especially all the things you've waited so long for, like absinthe."

"Oh, cut it out."

"You started it," the girl said. "I was being amused. I was having a fine time."

"Well, let's try and have a fine time."

"All right. I was trying. I said the mountains looked like white elephants. Wasn't that bright?"

"That was bright."

"I wanted to try this new drink. That's all we do, isn't it—look at things and try new drinks?"

"I guess so."

The girl looked across at the hills.

"They're lovely hills," she said. "They don't really look like white elephants. I just meant the coloring of their skin through the trees."

"Should we have another drink?"

"All right."

The warm wind blew the bead curtain against the table.

"The beer's nice and cool," the man said.

"It's lovely," the girl said.

"It's really an awfully simple operation, Jig," the man said. "It's not really an operation at all."

The girl looked at the ground the table legs rested on.

"I know you wouldn't mind it, Jig. It's really not anything. It's just to let the air in."

The girl did not say anything.

"I'll go with you and I'll stay with you all the time. They just let the *R*
air in and then it's all perfectly natural."

"Then what will we do afterward?"

"We'll be fine afterward. Just like we were before."

"What makes you think so?"

"That's the only thing that bothers us. It's the only thing that's made
us unhappy."

The girl looked at the bead curtain, put her hand out and took hold
of two of the strings of beads.

"And you think then we'll be all right and be happy."

"I know we will. You don't have to be afraid. I've known lots of
people that have done it."

"So have I," said the girl. "And afterward they were all so happy." *ironic sarcasm*

"Well," the man said, "if you don't want to you don't have to. I *R*
wouldn't have you do it if you didn't want to. But I know it's perfectly *R*
simple."

"And you really want to?"

"I think it's the best thing to do. But I don't want you to do it if you *R*
don't really want to."

"And if I do it you'll be happy and things will be like they were and
you'll love me?"

"I love you now. You know I love you."

"I know. But if I do it, then it will be nice again if I say things are like
white elephants, and you'll like it?"

"I'll love it. I love it now but I just can't think about it. You know how
I get when I worry."

"If I do it you won't ever worry?"

"I won't worry about that because it's perfectly simple." *ironic R*

"Then I'll do it. Because I don't care about me." *Sarcasm — she cares, knows he doesn't*

"What do you mean?"

"I don't care about me."

"Well, I care about you."

"Oh, yes. But I don't care about me. And I'll do it and then
everything will be fine."

"I don't want you to do it if you feel that way." *R*

The girl stood up and walked to the end of the station. Across, on the
other side, were fields of grain and trees along the banks of the Ebro.
Far away, beyond the river, were mountains. The shadow of a cloud
moved across the field of grain and she saw the river through the trees.

"And we could have all this," she said. "And we could have
everything and every day we make it more impossible."

"What did you say?"

"I said we could have everything."

"We can have everything."

"No, we can't."

he "We can have the whole world."

"No, we can't."

he "We can go everywhere."

"No, we can't. It isn't ours any more."

he "It's ours."

"No, it isn't. And once they take it away, you never get it back."

he "But they haven't taken it away."

she "We'll wait and see."

he "Come on back in the shade," he said. "You mustn't feel that way."

"I don't feel any way," the girl said. "I just know things."

R   "I don't want you to do anything that you don't want to do—"

ironic sarcasm "Nor that isn't good for me," she said. "I know. Could we have another beer?"

"All right. But you've got to realize—"

"I realize," the girl said. "Can't we maybe stop talking?"

They sat down at the table and the girl looked across at the hills on the dry side of the valley and the man looked at her and at the table.

R   "You've got to realize," he said, "that I don't want you to do it if you don't want to. I'm perfectly willing to go through with it if it means anything to you."

"Doesn't it mean anything to you? We could get along."

"Of course it does. But I don't want anybody but you. I don't want any one else. And I know it's perfectly simple."

"Yes, you know it's perfectly simple."

"It's all right for you to say that, but I do know it."

"Would you do something for me now?"

"I'd do anything for you."

"Would you please please please please please please please stop talking?"

He did not say anything but looked at the bags against the wall of the station. There were labels on them from all the hotels where they had spent nights.

"But I don't want you to," he said, "I don't care anything about it."

"I'll scream," the girl said.

The woman came out through the curtains with two glasses of beer and put them down on the damp felt pads. "The train comes in five minutes," she said.

"What did she say?" asked the girl.

"That the train is coming in five minutes."

The girl smiled brightly at the woman, to thank her.

"I'd better take the bags over to the other side of the station," the man said. She smiled at him.

"All right. Then come back and we'll finish the beer."

He picked up the two heavy bags and carried them around the station to the other tracks. He looked up the tracks but could not see the train. Coming back, he walked through the barroom, where people waiting for the train were drinking. He drank an Anis at the bar and looked at the people. They were all waiting reasonably for the train. He went out through the bead curtain. She was sitting at the table and smiled at him.

"Do you feel better?" he asked.

"I feel fine," she said. "There's nothing wrong with me. I feel fine."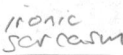

ironic
sarcasm

LANGSTON HUGHES
1902–1967

On his father's side he was descended from African slaves, a Jewish slave trader, and a Scottish distiller. On his mother's side there was French, English, and Cherokee blood. His maternal grandmother went to Oberlin College and married a man who was killed in John Brown's raid on Harper's Ferry. A granduncle had been a congressman from Virginia during the Reconstruction, and later Dean of the Law School at Howard University. But Langston Hughes's immediate family was less prominent and poorer. He was born in Joplin, Missouri, but raised in Lawrence, Kansas, by his grandmother, since his parents were separated. His mother was a stenographer; his father owned a ranch in Mexico. He went to Central High School in Cleveland, Ohio, where he began seriously writing poetry and for the first time read Maupassant in French. He taught English in Mexico for a time; then his father sent him to Columbia University. After a year he left on a ship, dumping his books over the stern. For five years he worked on ships, saw the world, got jobs as doorman, cook, waiter, and busboy at restaurants in Europe and America. One night at a hotel in Washington, D. C., where he was a busboy, he gave some poems to Vachel Lindsay, who helped him get literary recognition. He went to Lincoln College in Pennsylvania, then, where the black students were taught by a white faculty. By the time he graduated he had published two books of poetry and had finished a novel. He settled in New York, continued to travel widely and to write plays, stories, songs, and especially poems. He became both a model and an active helper in the careers of other black writers.

On the Road

He was not interested in the snow. When he got off the freight, one early evening during the depression, Sargeant never even noticed the snow. But he must have felt it seeping down his neck, cold, wet, sopping in his shoes. But if you had asked him, he wouldn't have

known it was snowing. Sargeant didn't see the snow, not even
under the bright lights of the main street, falling white and flaky
against the night. He was too hungry, too sleepy, too tired.

The Reverend Mr. Dorset, however, saw the snow when he
switched on his porch light, opened the front door of his parsonage,
and found standing there before him a big black man with snow on
his face, a human piece of night with snow on his face—obviously
unemployed.

Said the Reverend Mr. Dorset before Sargeant even realized he'd
opened his mouth: "I'm sorry. No! Go right on down this street four
blocks and turn to your left, walk up seven and you'll see the Relief
Shelter. I'm sorry. No!" He shut the door.

Sargeant wanted to tell the holy man that he had already been to
the Relief Shelter, been to hundreds of relief shelters during the
depression years, the beds were always gone and supper was over,
the place was full, and they drew the color line anyhow. But the
minister said, "No," and shut the door. Evidently he didn't want to
hear about it. And he *had* a door to shut.

The big black man turned away. And even yet he didn't see the
snow, walking right into it. Maybe he sensed it, cold, wet, sticking
to his jaws, wet on his black hands, sopping in his shoes. He
stopped and stood on the sidewalk hunched over—hungry, sleepy,
cold—looking up and down. Then he looked right where he was—
in front of a church. Of course! A church! Sure, right next to a
parsonage, certainly a church.

It had *two* doors.

Broad, white steps in the night all snowy white. Two high arched
doors with slender stone pillars on either side. And way up, a round
lacy window with a stone crucifix in the middle and Christ on the
crucifix in stone. All this was pale in the street lights, solid and
stony pale in the snow.

Sargeant blinked. When he looked up the snow fell into his eyes.
For the first time that night he *saw* the snow. He shook his head. He
shook the snow from his coat sleeves, felt hungry, felt lost, felt not
lost, felt cold. He walked up the steps of the church. He knocked at
the door. No answer. He tried the handle. Locked. He put his
shoulder against the door and his long black body slanted like a
ramrod. He pushed. With loud rhythmic grunts, like the grunts in a
chain-gang song, he pushed against the door.

"I'm tired . . . Huh! . . . Hongry . . . Uh! . . . I'm sleepy . . .
Huh! I'm cold . . . I got to sleep somewheres," Sargeant said. "This
here is a church, ain't it? Well, uh!"

He pushed against the door.

Suddenly, with an undue cracking and squeaking, the door began to give way to the tall black Negro who pushed ferociously against the door.

By now two or three white people had stopped in the street, and Sargeant was vaguely aware of some of them yelling at him concerning the door. Three or four more came running, yelling at him.

"Hey!" they said. "Hey!"

"Un-huh," answered the big tall Negro, "I know it's a white folks' church, but I got to sleep somewhere." He gave another lunge at the door. "Huh!"

And the door broke open.

But just when the door gave way, two white cops arrived in a car, ran up the steps with their clubs and grabbed Sargeant. But Sargeant for once had no intention of being pulled or pushed away from the door.

Sargeant grabbed, but not for anything so weak as a broken door. He grabbed for one of the tall stone pillars beside the door, grabbed at it and caught it. And held it. The cops pulled and Sargeant pulled. Most of the people in the street got behind the cops and helped them pull.

"A big black unemployed Negro holding onto our church!" thought the people. "The idea!"

The cops began to beat Sargeant over the head, and nobody protested. But he held on.

And then the church fell down.

Gradually, the big stone front of the church fell down, the walls and the rafters, the crucifix and the Christ. Then the whole thing fell down, covering the cops and the people with bricks and stones and debris. The whole church fell down in the snow.

Sargeant got out from under the church and went walking on up the street with the stone pillar on his shoulder. He was under the impression that he had buried the parsonage and the Reverend Mr. Dorset who said, "No!" So he laughed, and threw the pillar six blocks up the street and went on.

Sargeant thought he was alone, but listening to the crunch, crunch, crunch on the snow of his own footsteps, he heard other footsteps, too, doubling his own. He looked around and there was Christ walking along beside him, the same Christ that had been on the cross on the church—still stone with a rough stone surface, walking along beside him just like he was broken off the cross when the church fell down.

"Well, I'll be dogged," said Sargeant. "This here's the first time I ever seed you off the cross."

"Yes," said Christ, crunching his feet in the snow. "You had to pull the church down to get me off the cross."

"You glad?" said Sargeant.

"I sure am," said Christ.

They both laughed.

"I'm a hell of a fellow, ain't I?" said Sargeant. "Done pulled the church down!"

"You did a good job," said Christ. "They have kept me nailed on a cross for nearly two thousand years."

"Whee-ee-e!" said Sargeant. "I know you are glad to get off."

"I sure am," said Christ.

They walked on in the snow. Sargeant looked at the man of stone.

"And you been up there two thousand years?"

"I sure have," Christ said.

"Well, if I had a little cash," said Sargeant, "I'd show you around a bit."

"I been around," said Christ.

"Yeah, but that was a long time ago."

"All the same," said Christ, "I've been around."

They walked on in the snow until they came to the railroad yards. Sargeant was tired, sweating and tired.

"Where you goin'?" Sargeant said, stopping by the tracks. He looked at Christ. Sargeant said, "I'm just a bum on the road. How about you? Where you going'?"

"God knows," Christ said, "but I'm leavin' here."

They saw the red and green lights of the railroad yard half veiled by the snow that fell out of the night. Away down the track they saw a fire in a hobo jungle.

"I can go there and sleep," Sargeant said.

"You can?"

"Sure," said Sargeant. "That place ain't got no doors."

Outside the town, along the tracks, there were barren trees and bushes below the embankment, snow-gray in the dark. And down among the trees and bushes there were make-shift houses made out of boxes and tin and old pieces of wood and canvas. You couldn't see them in the dark, but you knew they were there if you'd ever been on the road, if you had ever lived with the homeless and hungry in a depression.

"I'm side-tracking," Sargeant said. "I'm tired."

"I'm gonna make it on to Kansas City," said Christ.

"O.K.," Sargeant said. "So long!"

He went down into the hobo jungle and found himself a place to sleep. He never did see Christ no more. About six A.M. a freight came by. Sargeant scrambled out of the jungle with a dozen or so more hoboes and ran along the track, grabbing at the freight. It was dawn, early dawn, cold and gray.

"Wonder where Christ is by now?" Sargeant thought. "He must-a gone on way on down the road. He didn't sleep in this jungle."

Sargeant grabbed the train and started to pull himself up into a moving coal car, over the edge of a wheeling coal car. But strangely enough, the car was full of cops. The nearest cop rapped Sargeant soundly across the knuckles with his night stick. Wham! Rapped his big black hands for clinging to the top of the car. Wham! But Sargeant did not turn loose. He clung on and tried to pull himself into the car. He hollered at the top of his voice, "Damn it, lemme in this car!"

"Shut up," barked the cop. "You crazy coon!" He rapped Sargeant across the knuckles and punched him in the stomach. "You ain't out in no jungle now. This ain't no train. You in jail."

Wham! across his bare black fingers clinging to the bars of his cell. Wham! between the steel bars low down against his shins.

Suddenly Sargeant realized that he really was in jail. He wasn't on no train. The blood of the night before had dried on his face, his head hurt terribly, and a cop outside in the corridor was hitting him across the knuckles for holding onto the door, yelling and shaking the cell door.

"They must-a took me to jail for breaking down the door last night," Sargeant thought, "that church door."

Sargeant went over and sat on a wooden bench against the cold stone wall. He was emptier than ever. His clothes were wet, clammy cold wet, and shoes sloppy with snow water. It was just about dawn. There he was, locked up behind a cell door, nursing his bruised fingers.

The bruised fingers were his, but not the *door*.

Not the *club*, but the fingers.

"You wait," mumbled Sargeant, black against the jail wall. "I'm gonna break down this door, too."

"Shut up—or I'll paste you one," said the cop.

"I'm gonna break down this door," yelled Sargeant as he stood up in his cell.

Then he must have been talking to himself because he said, "I wonder where Christ's gone? I wonder if he's gone to Kansas City?"

FRANK O'CONNOR
1903–1966

Michael Francis O'Donovan was born in the city of Cork, Ireland, where he lived in slum tenements on Blarney Lane and Summerhill and went to St. Patrick's National School until he was fourteen, when he left school permanently. He fought with the Irish Republican Army during the Irish Revolution and stood with the Republicans in the Civil War that followed the Irish victory. For this he was interned in a prison camp during 1923. After his release he held jobs as a librarian and, for a time, as manager of Dublin's famous Abbey Theatre. In the late 1920's his poems and essays began appearing in Irish magazines, over the name "Frank O'Connor." His first volume of stories, *Guests of the Nation*, appeared in 1931. He continued to publish, though never at ease financially, politically, or personally until his last years, when success in the U.S., divorce and remarriage, and finally honors in his own country came to him before his death in Dublin.

Guests of the Nation

I

At dusk the big Englishman, Belcher, would shift his long legs out of the ashes and say "Well, chums, what about it?" and Noble or me would say "All right, chum" (for we had picked up some of their curious expressions), and the little Englishman, Hawkins, would light the lamp and bring out the cards. Sometimes Jeremiah Donovan would come up and supervise the game and get excited over Hawkins's cards, which he always played badly, and shout at him as if he was one of our own, "Ah, you divil, you, why didn't you play the tray?"

But ordinarily Jeremiah was a sober and contented poor devil like the big Englishman, Belcher, and was looked up to only because he was a fair hand at documents, though he was slow enough even with them. He wore a small cloth hat and big gaiters over his long pants, and you seldom saw him with his hands out of his pockets. He reddened when you talked to him, tilting from toe to heel and back, and looking down all the time at his big farmer's feet. Noble and me used to make fun of his broad accent, because we were from the town.

I couldn't at the time see the point of me and Noble guarding Belcher and Hawkins at all, for it was my belief that you could have planted that pair down anywhere from this to Claregalway and they'd have taken root there like a native weed. I never in my short experience seen two men to take to the country as they did.

They were handed on to us by the Second Battalion when the search for them became too hot, and Noble and myself, being young, took over with a natural feeling of responsibility, but Hawkins made us look like fools when he showed that he knew the country better than we did.

"You're the bloke they calls Bonaparte," he says to me. "Mary Brigid O'Connell told me to ask you what you done with the pair of her brother's socks you borrowed."

For it seemed, as they explained it, that the Second used to have little evenings, and some of the girls of the neighborhood turned in, and, seeing they were such decent chaps, our fellows couldn't leave the two Englishmen out of them. Hawkins learned to dance "The Walls of Limerick," "The Siege of Ennis," and "The Waves of Tory" as well as any of them, though, naturally, we couldn't return the compliment, because our lads at that time did not dance foreign dances on principle.

So whatever privileges Belcher and Hawkins had with the Second they just naturally took with us, and after the first day or two we gave up all pretense of keeping a close eye on them. Not that they could have got far, for they had accents you could cut with a knife and wore khaki tunics and overcoats with civilian pants and boots. But it's my belief that they never had any idea of escaping and were quite content to be where they were.

It was a treat to see how Belcher got off with the old woman of the house where we were staying. She was a great warrant to scold, and cranky even with us, but before ever she had a chance of giving our guests, as I may call them, a lick of her tongue, Belcher had made her his friend for life. She was breaking sticks, and Belcher, who hadn't been more than ten minutes in the house, jumped up from his seat and went over to her.

"Allow me, madam," he says, smiling his queer little smile, "please allow me"; and he takes the bloody hatchet. She was struck too paralytic to speak, and after that, Belcher would be at her heels, carrying a bucket, a basket, or a load of turf, as the case might be. As Noble said, he got into looking before she leapt, and hot water, or any little thing she wanted, Belcher would have it ready for her. For such a huge man (and though I am five foot ten myself I had to look up at him) he had an uncommon shortness—or should I say lack?—of speech. It took us some time to get used to him, walking in and out, like a ghost, without a word. Especially because Hawkins talked enough for a platoon, it was strange to hear big Belcher with his toes in the ashes come out with a solitary "Excuse me, chum," or "That's right, chum." His one and only passion was cards, and I will say for him that he was a good cardplayer. He could have fleeced myself and Noble, but whatever we lost to him Hawkins lost to us, and Hawkins played with the money Belcher gave him.

Hawkins lost to us because he had too much old gab, and we probably lost to Belcher for the same reason. Hawkins and Noble would spit at one another about religion into the early hours of the morning, and Hawkins worried the soul out of Noble, whose brother was a priest, with a string of questions that would puzzle a cardinal. To make it worse, even in treating of holy subjects, Hawkins had a deplorable tongue. I never in all my career met a man who could mix such a variety of cursing and bad language into an argument. He was a terrible man, and a fright to argue. He never did a stroke of work, and when he had no one else to talk to, he got stuck in the old woman.

He met his match in her, for one day when he tried to get her to complain profanely of the drought, she gave him a great come-down by blaming it entirely on Jupiter Pluvius (a deity neither Hawkins nor I had ever heard of, though Noble said that among the pagans it was believed that he had something to do with the rain). Another day he was swearing at the capitalists for starting the German war when the old lady laid down her iron, puckered up her little crab's mouth, and said: "Mr. Hawkins, you can say what you like about the war, and think you'll deceive me because I'm only a simple poor country-woman, but I know what started the war. It was the Italian Count that stole the heathen divinity out of the temple in Japan. Believe me, Mr. Hawkins, nothing but sorrow and want can follow the people that disturb the hidden powers."

old womans prophecy

A queer old girl, all right.

II

We had our tea one evening, and Hawkins lit the lamp and we all sat into cards. Jeremiah Donovan came in too, and sat down and watched us for a while, and it suddenly struck me that he had no great love for the two Englishmen. It came as a great surprise to me, because I hadn't noticed anything about him before.

Late in the evening a really terrible argument blew up between Hawkins and Noble, about capitalists and priests and love of your country.

"The capitalists," says Hawkins with an angry gulp, "pays the priests to tell you about the next world so as you won't notice what the bastards are up to in this."

"Nonsense, man!" says Noble, losing his temper. "Before ever a capitalist was thought of, people believed in the next world."

Hawkins stood up as though he was preaching a sermon.

"Oh, they did, did they?" he says with a sneer. "They believed all the things you believe, isn't that what you mean? And you believe that God created Adam, and Adam created Shem, and Shem created Jehoshaphat. You believe all that silly old fairytale about Eve and Eden and the apple. Well, listen to me, chum. If you're entitled to hold a silly belief like that, I'm entitled to hold my silly belief—which is that the first thing your God created was a bleeding capitalist, with morality and Rolls-Royce complete. Am I right, chum?" he says to Belcher.

"You're right, chum," says Belcher with his amused smile, and got up from the table to stretch his long legs into the fire and stroke his moustache. So, seeing that Jeremiah Donovan was going, and that there was no knowing when the argument about religion would be over, I went out with him. We strolled down to the village together, and then stopped and started blushing and mumbling and saying I ought to be behind, keeping guard on the prisoners. I didn't like the tone he took with me, and anyway I was bored with life in the cottage, so I replied by asking him what the hell we wanted guarding them at all for. I told him I'd talked it over with Noble, and that we'd both rather be out with a fighting column.

"What use are those fellows to us?" says I.

He looked at me in surprise and said: "I thought you knew we were keeping them as hostages."

"Hostages?" I said.

"The enemy have prisoners belonging to us," he says, "and now they're talking of shooting them. If they shoot our prisoners, we'll shoot theirs."

"Shoot them?" I said.

"What else did you think we were keeping them for?" he says.

"Wasn't it very unforeseen of you not to warn Noble and myself of that in the beginning?" I said.

"How was it?" says he. "You might have known it."

"We couldn't know it, Jeremiah Donovan," says I. "How could we when they were on our hands so long?"

"The enemy have our prisoners as long and longer," says he.

"That's not the same thing at all," says I.

"What difference is there?" says he.

I couldn't tell him, because I knew he wouldn't understand. If it was only an old dog that was going to the vet's, you'd try and not get too fond of him, but Jeremiah Donovan wasn't a man that would ever be in danger of that.

"And when is this thing going to be decided?" says I.

"We might hear tonight," he says. "Or tomorrow or the next day at latest. So if it's only hanging round here that's a trouble to you, you'll be free soon enough."

It wasn't the hanging round that was a trouble to me at all by this time. I had worse things to worry about. When I got back to the cottage the argument was still on. Hawkins was holding forth in his best style, maintaining that there was no next world, and Noble was maintaining that there was; but I could see that Hawkins had had the best of it.

"Do you know what, chum?" he was saying with a saucy smile. "I think you're just as big a bleeding unbeliever as I am. You say you believe in the next world, and you know just as much about the next world as I do, which is sweet damn-all. What's heaven? You don't know. Where's heaven? You don't know. You know sweet damn-all! I ask you again, do they wear wings?"

"Very well, then," says Noble, "they do. Is that enough for you? They do wear wings."

"Where do they get them, then? Who makes them? Have they a factory for wings? Have they a sort of store where you hands in your chit and takes your bleeding wings?"

"You're an impossible man to argue with," says Noble. "Now, listen to me—" And they were off again.

It was long after midnight when we locked up and went to bed. As I blew out the candle I told Noble what Jeremiah Donovan was after telling me. Noble took it very quietly. When we'd been in bed about an hour he asked me did I think we ought to tell the Englishmen. I didn't think we should, because it was more than likely that the English wouldn't shoot our men, and even if they did, the brigade officers, who were always up and down with the Second Battalion and knew the Englishmen well, wouldn't be likely to want them plugged. "I think so too," says Noble. "It would be great cruelty to put the wind up them now."

"It was very unforeseen of Jeremiah Donovan anyhow," says I.

It was next morning that we found it so hard to face Belcher and Hawkins. We went about the house all day scarcely saying a word. Belcher didn't seem to notice; he was stretched into the ashes as usual, with his usual look of waiting in quietness for something unforeseen to happen, but Hawkins noticed and put it down to Noble's being beaten in the argument of the night before.

"Why can't you take a discussion in the proper spirit?" he says severely. "You and your Adam and Eve! I'm a Communist, that's what I am. Communist or anarchist, it all comes to much the same thing." And for hours he went round the house, muttering when the fit took him. "Adam and Eve! Adam and Eve! Nothing better to do with their time than picking bleeding apples!"

III

I don't know how we got through that day, but I was very glad when it was over, the tea things were cleared away, and Belcher said in his peaceable way: "Well, chums, what about it?" We sat round the table and Hawkins took out the cards, and just then I heard Jeremiah Donovan's footstep on the path and a dark presentiment crossed my mind. I rose from the table and caught him before he reached the door.

"What do you want?" I asked.

"I want those two soldier friends of yours," he says, getting red.

"Is that the way, Jeremiah Donovan?" I asked.

"That's the way. There were four of our lads shot this morning, one of them a boy of sixteen."

"That's bad," I said.

At that moment Noble followed me out, and the three of us walked down the path together, talking in whispers. Feeney, the local intelligence officer, was standing by the gate.

"What are you going to do about it?" I asked Jeremiah Donovan.

"I want you and Noble to get them out; tell them they're being shifted again; that'll be the quietest way."

"Leave me out of that," says Noble under his breath.

Jeremiah Donovan looks at him hard.

"All right," he says. "You and Feeney get a few tools from the shed and dig a hole by the far end of the bog. Bonaparte and myself will be after you. Don't let anyone see you with the tools. I wouldn't like it to go beyond ourselves."

We saw Feeney and Noble go round to the shed and went in ourselves. I left Jeremiah Donovan to do the explanations. He told them that he had orders to send them back to the Second Battalion. Hawkins let out a mouthful of curses, and you could see that though Belcher didn't say anything, he was a bit upset too. The old woman was for having them stay in spite of us, and she didn't stop advising them until Jeremiah Donovan lost his temper and turned on her. He had a nasty temper, I noticed. It was pitch-dark in the cottage by this time, but no one thought of lighting the lamp, and in the darkness the two Englishmen fetched their topcoats and said good-bye to the old woman.

"Just as a man makes a home of a bleeding place, some bastard at headquarters thinks you're too cushy and shunts you off," says Hawkins, shaking her hand.

"A thousand thanks, madam," says Belcher. "A thousand thanks for everything"—as though he'd made it up.

We went round to the back of the house and down towards the bog. It was only then that Jeremiah Donovan told them. He was shaking with excitement.

"There were four of our fellows shot in Cork this morning and now you're to be shot as a reprisal."

"What are you talking about?" snaps Hawkins. "It's bad enough being mucked about as we are without having to put up with your funny jokes."

"It isn't a joke," says Donovan. "I'm sorry, Hawkins, but it's true," and begins on the usual rigmarole about duty and how unpleasant it is.

I never noticed that people who talk a lot about duty find it much of a trouble to them.

"Oh, cut it out!" says Hawkins.

"Ask Bonaparte," says Donovan, seeing that Hawkins isn't taking him seriously. "Isn't it true, Bonaparte?"

"It is," I say, and Hawkins stops.

"Ah, for Christ's sake, chum."

"I mean it, chum," I say.

"You don't sound as if you meant it."

"If he doesn't mean it, I do," says Donovan, working himself up. "What have you against me, Jeremiah Donovan?"

"I never said I had anything against you. But why did your people take out four of our prisoners and shoot them in cold blood?"

He took Hawkins by the arm and dragged him on, but it was impossible to make him understand that we were in earnest. I had the Smith and Wesson in my pocket and I kept fingering it and wondering what I'd do if they put up a fight for it or ran, and wishing to God they'd do one or the other. I knew if they did run for it, that I'd never fire on them. Hawkins wanted to know was Noble in it, and when we said yes, he asked us why Noble wanted to plug him. Why did any of us want to plug him? What had he done to us? Weren't we all chums? Didn't we understand him and didn't he understand us? Did we imagine for an instant that he'd shoot us for all the so-and-so officers in the so-and-so British Army?

By this time we'd reached the bog, and I was so sick I couldn't even answer him. We walked along the edge of it in the darkness, and every now and then Hawkins would call a halt and begin all over again, as if he was wound up, about our being chums, and I knew that nothing but the sight of the grave would convince him that we had to do it. And all the time I was hoping that something would happen; that they'd run for it or that Noble would take over the responsibility from me. I had the feeling that it was worse on Noble than on me.

IV

At last we saw the lantern in the distance and made towards it. Noble was carrying it, and Feeney was standing somewhere in the darkness behind him, and the picture of them so still and silent in the bogland brought it home to me that we were in earnest, and banished the last bit of hope I had.

Belcher, on recognizing Noble, said: "Hallo, chum," in his quiet way, but Hawkins flew at him at once, and the argument began all over again, only this time Noble had nothing to say for himself and stood with his head down, holding the lantern between his legs.

It was Jeremiah Donovan who did the answering. For the twentieth time, as though it was haunting his mind, Hawkins asked if anybody thought he'd shoot Noble.

"Yes, you would," says Jeremiah Donovan.

"No, I wouldn't, damn you!"

"You would, because you'd know you'd be shot for not doing it."

"I wouldn't, not if I was to be shot twenty times over. I wouldn't shoot a pal. And Belcher wouldn't—isn't that right, Belcher?"

"That's right, chum," Belcher said, but more by way of answering the question than of joining in the argument. Belcher sounded as though whatever unforeseen thing he'd always been waiting for had come at last.

"Anyway, who says Noble would be shot if I wasn't? What do you think I'd do if I was in his place, out in the middle of a blasted bog?"

"What would you do?" asks Donovan.

"I'd go with him wherever he was going, of course. Share my last bob with him and stick by him through thick and thin. No one can ever say of me that I let down a pal."

"We had enough of this," says Jeremiah Donovan, cocking his revolver. "Is there any message you want to send?"

"No, there isn't."

"Do you want to say your prayers?"

Hawkins came out with a cold-blooded remark that even shocked me and turned on Noble again.

"Listen to me, Noble," he says. "You and me are chums. You can't come over to my side, so I'll come over to your side. That show you I mean what I say? Give me a rifle and I'll go along with you and the other lads."

Nobody answered him. We knew that was no way out.

"Hear what I'm saying?" he says. "I'm through with it. I'm a deserter or anything else you like. I don't believe in your stuff, but it's no worse then mine. That satisfy you?"

Noble raised his head, but Donovan began to speak and he lowered it again without replying.

"For the last time, have you any messages to send?" says Donovan in a cold, excited sort of voice.

"Shut up, Donovan! You don't understand me, but these lads do. They're not the sort to make a pal and kill a pal. They're not the tools of any capitalist."

I alone of the crowd saw Donovan raise his Webley to the back of Hawkins's neck, and as he did so I shut my eyes and tried to pray. Hawkins had begun to say something else when Donovan fired, and as I opened my eyes at the bang, I saw Hawkins stagger at the knees and lie out flat at Noble's feet, slowly and as quiet as a kid falling asleep, with the lantern-light on his lean legs and bright farmer's boots. We all stood very still, watching him settle out in the last agony.

Then Belcher took out a handkerchief and began to tie it about his own eyes (in our excitement we'd forgotten to do the same for Hawkins), and, seeing it wasn't big enough, turned and asked for the loan of mine. I gave it to him and he knotted the two together and pointed with his foot at Hawkins.

"He's not quite dead," he says. "Better give him another."

Sure enough, Hawkins's left knee is beginning to rise. I bend down and put my gun to his head; then, recollecting myself, I get up again. Belcher understands what's in my mind.

"Give him his first," he says. "I don't mind. Poor bastard, we don't know what's happening to him now."

I knelt and fired. By this time I didn't seem to know what I was doing. Belcher, who was fumbling a bit awkwardly with the handkerchiefs, came out with a laugh as he heard the shot. It was the first time I heard him laugh and it sent a shudder down my back; it sounded so unnatural.

"Poor bugger!" he said quietly. "And last night he was so curious about it all. It's very queer, chums, I always think. Now he knows as much about it as they'll ever let him know, and last night he was all in the dark."

Donovan helped him to tie the handkerchiefs about his eyes. "Thanks, chum," he said. Donovan asked if there were any messages he wanted sent.

"No, chum," he says. "Not for me. If any of you would like to write to Hawkins's mother, you'll find a letter from her in his pocket. He and his mother were great chums. But my missus left me eight years ago. Went away with another fellow and took the kid with her. I like the feeling of a home, as you may have noticed, but I couldn't start again after that."

It was an extraordinary thing, but in those few minutes Belcher said more than in all the weeks before. It was just as if the sound of the shot had started a flood of talk in him and he could go on the whole night like that, quite happily, talking about himself. We stood round like fools now that he couldn't see us any longer. Donovan looked at Noble, and Noble shook his head. Then Donovan raised his Webley, and at that moment Belcher gives his queer laugh again. He may have thought we were talking about him, or perhaps he noticed the same thing I'd noticed and couldn't understand it.

"Excuse me, chums," he says. "I feel I'm talking the hell of a lot, and so silly, about my being so handy about a house and things like that. But this thing came on me suddenly. You'll forgive me, I'm sure."

"You don't want to say a prayer?" asked Donovan.

"No, chum," he says. "I don't think it would help. I'm ready, and you boys want to get it over."

"You understand that we're only doing our duty?" says Donovan.

Belcher's head was raised like a blind man's, so that you could only see his chin and the tip of his nose in the lantern-light.

"I never could make out what duty was myself," he said. "I think you're all good lads, if that's what you mean. I'm not complaining."

Noble, just as if he couldn't bear any more of it, raised his fist at Donovan, and in a flash Donovan raised his gun and fired. The big man went over like a sack of meal, and this time there was no need of a second shot.

I don't remember much about the burying, but that it was worse than all the rest because we had to carry them to the grave. It was all mad lonely with nothing but a patch of lantern-light between ourselves and the dark, and birds hooting and screeching all round, disturbed by the guns. Noble went through Hawkins's belongings to find the letter from his mother, and then joined his hands together. He did the same with Belcher. Then, when we'd filled in the grave, we separated from Jeremiah Donovan and Feeney and took our tools back to the shed. All the way we didn't speak a word. The kitchen was dark and cold as we'd left it, and the old woman was sitting over the hearth, saying her beads. We walked past her into the room, and Noble struck a match to light the lamp. She rose quietly and came to the doorway with all her cantankerousness gone.

"What did ye do with them?" she asked in a whisper, and Noble started so that the match went out in his hand.

"What's that?" he asked without turning round.

"I heard ye," she said.

"What did you hear?" asked Noble.

"I heard ye. Do ye think I didn't hear ye, putting the spade back in the houseen?"

Noble struck another match and this time the lamp lit for him.

"Was that what ye did to them?" she asked.

Then, by God, in the very doorway, she fell on her knees and began praying, and after looking at her for a minute or two Noble did the same by the fireplace. I pushed my way out past her and left them at it. I stood at the door, watching the stars and listening to the shrieking of the birds dying out over the bogs. It is so strange what you feel at times like that you can't describe it. Noble says he saw everything ten times the size, as though there were nothing in the whole world but that little patch of bog with the two Englishmen stiffening into it, but with me it was as if the patch of bog where the Englishmen were was a million miles away, and even Noble and the old woman, mumbling behind me, and the birds and the bloody stars were all far away, and I was somehow very small and very lost and lonely like a child astray in the snow. And anything that happened me afterwards, I never felt the same about again.

KAY BOYLE

1903–

Born in St. Paul, Minnesota, Kay Boyle left there at the age of six months and travelled in Europe with her parents and her sister. Later she went to school in Washington, D.C. When her father suffered business reverses and opened a garage in Cincinnati, she moved there and studied violin at the Cincinnati Conservatory and architecture at the Ohio Mechanics Institute. Then she worked as a telephone operator in her father's garage, living in the building, writing poems and stories steadily. She married a French student in 1921 and went to live with him in Le Havre in 1922. When she was threatened by tuberculosis she moved south to a gentler climate. Her first daughter was born in Nice and her second in Paris in 1929, the year her first collection of stories was published. She continued to live abroad, in Austria and England as well as France, marrying a second time in 1932. After a stay in the U.S. during World War II, she returned to Europe and lived in Germany before coming back to this country. Since then she has held a number of positions teaching creative writing. She has written many novels and some poetry, but she is best known for her carefully crafted short stories. A volume of her collected stories was published in 1980.

Winter Night

There is a time of apprehension which begins with the beginning of darkness, and to which only the speech of love can lend security. It is there, in abeyance, at the end of every day, not urgent enough to be given the name of fear but rather of concern for how the hours are to be reprieved from fear, and those who have forgotten how it was when they were children can remember nothing of this. It may begin around five o'clock on a winter afternoon when the light outside is dying in the windows. At that hour the New York apartment in which Felicia lived was filled with shadows, and the little girl would wait alone in the living room, looking out at the winter-stripped trees that stood black in the park against the isolated ovals of unclean snow. Now it was January, and the day had been a cold one; the water of the artificial lake was frozen fast, but because of the cold and the coming darkness, the skaters had ceased to move across its surface. The street that lay between the park and the apartment house was wide, and the two-way streams of cars and busses, some with their headlamps already shining, advanced and halted, halted and poured swiftly on to the tempo of the traffic signals' altering lights. The time of apprehension had set in, and Felicia, who was seven, stood at the window in the evening and waited before she asked the question. When the signals below would change from red to green again, or when the double-decker bus would turn the corner below, she would ask it. The words of it were already there, tentative in her mouth, when the answer came from the far end of the hall.

"Your mother," said the voice among the sound of kitchen things, "she telephoned up before you came in from nursery school. She won't be back in time for supper. I was to tell you a sitter was coming in from the sitting parents' place."

Felicia turned back from the window into the obscurity of the living room, and she looked toward the open door, and into the hall beyond it where the light from the kitchen fell in a clear yellow angle across the wall and onto the strip of carpet. Her hands were cold, and she put them in her jacket pockets as she walked carefully across the living-room rug and stopped at the edge of light.

"Will she be home late?" she said.

For a moment there was the sound of water running in the kitchen, a long way away, and then the sound of the water ceased, and the high, Southern voice went on:

"She'll come home when she gets ready to come home. That's all I have to say. If she wants to spend two dollars and fifty cents and ten cents' carfare on top of that three or four nights out of the week for a sitting parent to come in here and sit, it's her own business. It certainly ain't nothing to do with you or me. She makes her money, just like the rest of us does. She works all day down there in the office, or whatever it is, just like the rest of us works, and she's entitled to spend her money like she wants to spend it. There's no law in the world against buying your own freedom. Your mother and me, we're just buying our own freedom, that's all we're doing. And we're not doing nobody no harm."

"Do you know who she's having supper with?" said Felicia from the edge of dark. There was one more step to take, and then she would be standing in the light that fell on the strip of carpet, but she did not take the step.

"Do I know who she's having supper with?" the voice cried out in what might have been derision, and there was the sound of dishes striking the metal ribs of the drainboard by the sink. "Maybe it's Mr. Van Johnson, or Mr. Frank Sinatra, or maybe it's just the Duke of Wincers for the evening. All I know is you're having soft-boiled egg and spinach and applesauce for supper, and you're going to have it quick now because the time is getting away."

The voice from the kitched had no name. It was as variable as the faces and figures of the women who came and sat in the evenings. Month by month the voice in the kitchen altered to another voice, and the sitting parents were no more than lonely aunts of an evening or two who sometimes returned and sometimes did not to this apartment in which they had sat before. Nobody stayed anywhere very long any more, Felicia's mother told her. It was part of the time in which you lived, and part of the life of the city, but when the fathers came back, all this would be miraculously changed. Perhaps you would live in a house again, a small one, with fir trees on either side of the short brick walk, and Father would drive up every night from the station just after darkness set in. When Felicia thought of this, she stepped quickly into the clear angle of light, and she left the dark of the living room behind her and ran softly down the hall.

The drop-leaf table stood in the kitchen between the refrigerator and the sink, and Felicia sat down at the place that was set. The voice at the sink was speaking still, and while Felicia ate it did not cease to speak until the bell of the front door rang abruptly. The girl walked around the table and went down the hall, wiping her dark palms in her apron, and, from the drop-leaf table, Felicia watched her step from the angle of light into darkness and open the door.

"You put in an early appearance," the girl said, and the woman who had rung the bell came into the hall. The door closed behind her, and the girl showed her into the living room, and lit the lamp on the bookcase, and the shadows were suddenly bleached away. But when the girl turned, the woman turned from the living room too and followed her, humbly and in silence, to the threshold of the kitchen. "Sometimes they keep me standing around waiting after it's time for me to be getting on home, the sitting parents do," the girl said, and she picked up the last two dishes from the table and put them in the sink. The woman who stood in the doorway was a small woman, and when she undid the white silk scarf from around her head, Felicia saw that her hair was black. She wore it parted in the middle, and it had not been cut, but was drawn back loosely into a knot behind her head. She had very clean white gloves on, and her face was pale, and there was a look of sorrow in her soft black eyes. "Sometimes I have to stand out there in the hall with my hat and coat on, waiting for the sitting parents to turn up," the girl said, and, as she turned on the water in the sink, the contempt she had for them hung on the kitchen air. "But you're ahead of time," she said, and she held the dishes, first one and then the other, under the flow of steaming water.

The woman in the doorway wore a neat black coat, not a new-looking coat, and it had no fur on it, but it had a smooth velvet collar and velvet lapels. She did not move, or smile, and she gave no sign that she had heard the girl speaking above the sound of water at the sink. She simply stood looking at Felicia, who sat at the table with the milk in her glass not finished yet.

"Are you the child?" she said at last, and her voice was low, and the pronunciation of the words a little strange.

"Yes, this here's Felicia," the girl said, and the dark hands dried the dishes and put them away. "You drink up your milk quick now, Felicia, so's I can rinse your glass."

"I will wash the glass," said the woman. "I would like to wash the glass for her," and Felicia sat looking across the table at the face in the doorway that was filled with such unspoken grief. "I will wash the glass for her and clean off the table," the woman was saying quietly. "When the child is finished, she will show me where her night things are."

"The others, they wouldn't do anything like that," the girl said, and she hung the dishcloth over the rack. "They wouldn't put their hand to housework, the sitting parents. That's where they got the name for them," she said.

Whenever the front door closed behind the girl in the evening, it would usually be that the sitting parent who was there would take up a book of fairy stories and read aloud for a while to Felicia; or else would settle herself in the big chair in the living room and begin to tell the words of a story in drowsiness to her, while Felicia took off her clothes in the bedroom, and folded them, and put her pajamas on, and brushed her teeth, and did her hair. But this time, that was not the way it happened. Instead, the woman sat down on the other chair at the kitchen table, and she began at once to speak, not of good fairies or bad, or of animals endowed with human speech, but to speak quietly, in spite of the eagerness behind her words, of a thing that seemed of singular importance to her.

"It is strange that I should have been sent here tonight," she said, her eyes moving slowly from feature to feature of Felicia's face, "for you look like a child that I knew once, and this is the anniversary of that child."

"Did she have hair like mine?" Felicia asked quickly, and she did not keep her eyes fixed on the unfinished glass of milk in shyness any more.

"Yes, she did. She had hair like yours," said the woman, and her glance paused for a moment on the locks which fell straight and thick on the shoulders of Felicia's dress. It may have been that she thought to stretch out her hand and touch the ends of Felicia's hair, for her fingers stirred as they lay clasped together on the table, and then they relapsed into passivity again. "But it is not the hair alone, it is the delicacy of your face, too, and your eyes the same, filled with the same spring lilac color," the woman said, pronouncing the words carefully. "She had little coats of golden fur on her arms and legs," she said, "and when we were closed up there, the lot of us in the cold, I used to make her laugh when I told her that the fur that was so pretty, like a little fawn's skin on her arms, would always help to keep her warm."

"And did it keep her warm?" asked Felicia, and she gave a little jerk of laughter as she looked down at her own legs hanging under the table, with the bare calves thin and covered with a down of hair.

"It did not keep her warm enough," the woman said, and now the mask of grief had come back upon her face. "So we used to take everything we could spare from ourselves, and we would sew them into cloaks and other kinds of garments for her and for the other children. . . ."

"Was it a school?" said Felicia when the woman's voice had ceased to speak.

"No," said the woman softly, "it was not a school, but still there were a lot of children there. It was a camp—that was the name the place had; it was a camp. It was a place where they put people until they could decide what was to be done with them." She sat with her hands clasped, silent a moment, looking at Felicia. "That little dress you have on," she said, not saying the words to anybody, scarcely saying them aloud. "Oh, she would have liked that little dress, the little buttons shaped like hearts, and the white collar——"

"I have four school dresses," Felicia said. "I'll show them to you. How many dresses did she have?"

"Well, there, you see, there in the camp," said the woman, "she did not have any dresses except the little skirt and the pullover. That was all she had. She had brought just a handkerchief of her belongings with her, like everybody else—just enough for three days away from home was what they told us, so she did not have enough to last the winter. But she had her ballet slippers," the woman said, and her clasped fingers did not move. "She had brought them because she thought during her three days away from home she would have the time to practice her ballet."

"I've been to the ballet," Felicia said suddenly, and she said it so eagerly that she stuttered a little as the words came out of her mouth. She slipped quickly down from the chair and went around the table to where the woman sat. Then she took one of the woman's hands away from the other that held it fast, and she pulled her toward the door. "Come into the living room and I'll do a pirouette for you," she said, and then she stopped speaking, her eyes halted on the woman's face. "Did she—did the little girl—could she do a pirouette very well?" she said.

"Yes, she could. At first she could," said the woman, and Felicia felt uneasy now at the sound of sorrow in her words. "But after that she was hungry. She was hungry all winter," she said in a low voice. "We were all hungry, but the children were the hungriest. Even now," she said, and her voice went suddenly savage, "when I see milk like that, clean, fresh milk standing in a glass, I want to cry out loud, I want to beat my hands on the table, because it did not have to be . . ." She had drawn her fingers abruptly away from Felicia now, and Felicia stood before her, cast off, forlorn, alone again in the time of apprehension. "That was three years ago," the woman was saying, and one hand was lifted, as in weariness, to shade her face. "It was somewhere else, it was in another country," she said, and behind her hand her eyes were turned upon the substance of a world in which Felicia had played no part.

"Did—did the little girl cry when she was hungry?" Felicia asked, and the woman shook her head.

"Sometimes she cried," she said, "but not very much. She was very quiet. One night when she heard the other children crying, she said to me, 'You know, they are not crying because they want something to eat. They are crying because their mothers have gone away.' "

Did the mothers have to go out to supper?" Felicia asked, and she watched the woman's face for the answer.

"No," said the woman. She stood up from her chair, and now that she put her hand on the little girl's shoulder, Felicia was taken into the sphere of love and intimacy again. "Shall we go into the other room, and you will do your pirouette for me?" the woman said, and they went from the kitchen and down the strip of carpet on which the clear light fell. In the front room, they paused hand in hand in the glow of the shaded lamp, and the woman looked about her, at the books, the low tables with the magazines and ash trays on them, the vase of roses on the piano, looking with dark, scarcely seeing eyes at these things that had no reality at all. It was only when she saw the little white clock on the mantelpiece that she gave any sign, and then she said quickly: "What time does your mother put you to bed?"

Felicia waited a moment, and in the interval of waiting the woman lifted one hand and, as if in reverence, touched Felicia's hair.

"What time did the little girl you knew in the other place go to bed?" Felicia asked.

"Ah, God, I do not know, I do not remember," the woman said.

"Was she your little girl?" said Felicia softly, stubbornly.

"No," said the woman. "She was not mine. At least, at first she was not mine. She had a mother, a real mother, but the mother had to go away."

"Did she come back late?" asked Felicia.

"No, ah, no, she could not come back, she never came back," the woman said, and now she turned, her arm around Felicia's shoulders, and she sat down in the low soft chair. "Why am I saying all this to you, why am I doing it?" she cried out in grief, and she held Felicia close against her. "I had thought to speak of the anniversary

to you, and that was all, and now I am saying these other things to
you. Three years ago today, exactly, the little girl became my little
girl because her mother went away. That is all there is to it. There is
nothing more."

Felicia waited another moment, held close against the woman,
and listening to the swift, strong heartbeats in the woman's breast.

"But the mother," she said then in the small, persistent voice,
"did she take a taxi when she went?"

"This is the way it used to happen," said the woman, speaking in
hopelessness and bitterness in the softly lighted room. "Every week
they used to come into the place where we were and they would
read a list of names out. Sometimes it would be the names of children they would read out, and then a little later they would have to
go away. And sometimes it would be the grown people's names, the
names of the mothers or big sisters, or other women's names. The
men were not with us. The fathers were somewhere else, in another
place."

"Yes," Felicia said. "I know."

"We had been there only a little while, maybe ten days or maybe
not so long," the woman went on, holding Felicia against her still,
"when they read the name of the little girl's mother out, and that
afternoon they took her away."

"What did the little girl do?" Felicia said.

"She wanted to think up the best way of getting out so that she
could go find her mother," said the woman, "but she could not
think of anything good enough until the third or fourth day. And
then she tied her ballet slippers up in the handkerchief again, and
she went up to the guard standing at the door." The woman's voice
was gentle, controlled now. "She asked the guard please to open the
door so that she could go out. 'This is Thrusday,' she said, 'and
every Tuesday and Thursday I have my ballet lessons. If I miss a
ballet lesson, they do not count the money off, so my mother would
be just paying for nothing, and she cannot afford to pay for nothing.
I missed my ballet lesson on Tuesday,' she said to the guard, 'and I
must not miss it again today.' "

Felicia lifted her head from the woman's shoulder, and she shook
her hair back and looked in question and wonder at the woman's
face.

"And did the man let her go?" she said.

"No, he did not. He could not do that," said the woman. "He was
a soldier and he had to do what he was told. So every evening after
her mother went, I used to brush the little girl's hair for her," the
woman went on saying. "And while I brushed it, I used to tell her
the stories of the ballets. Sometimes I would begin with *Narcissus*,"
the woman said, and she parted Felicia's locks with her fingers, "so

if you will go and get your brush now, I will tell it while I brush your hair."

"Oh, yes," said Felicia, and she made two whirls as she went quickly to the bedroom. On the way back, she stopped and held on to the piano with the fingers of one hand while she went up on her toes. "Did you see me? Did you see me standing on my toes?" she called the woman, and the woman sat smiling in love and contentment at her.

"Yes, wonderful, really wonderful," she said. "I am sure I have never seen anyone do it so well." Felicia came spinning toward her, whirling in pirouette after pirouette, and she flung herself down in the chair close to her, with her thin bones pressed against the woman's soft, wide hip. The woman took the silver-backed, monogrammed brush and the tortoise-shell comb in her hands, and now she began to brush Felicia's hair. "We did not have any soap at all and not very much water to wash in, so I never could fix her as nicely and prettily as I wanted to," she said, and the brush stroked regularly, carefuly down, caressing the shape of Felicia's head.

"If there wasn't very much water, then how did she do her teeth?" Felicia said.

"She did not do her teeth," said the woman, and she drew the comb through Felicia's hair. "There were not any toothbrushes or tooth paste, or anything like that."

Felicia waited a moment, constructing the unfamiliar scene of it in silence, and then she asked the tentative question.

"Do I have to do my teeth tonight?" she said.

"No," said the woman, and she was thinking of something else, "you do not have to do your teeth."

"If I am your little girl tonight, can I pretend there isn't enough water to wash?" said Felicia.

"Yes," said the woman, "you can pretend that if you like. You do not have to wash," she said, and the comb passed lightly through Felicia's hair.

"Will you tell me the story of the ballet?" said Felicia, and the rhythm of the brushing was like the soft, slow rocking of sleep.

"Yes," said the woman. "In the first one, the place is a forest glade with little pale birches growing in it, and they have green veils over their faces and green veils drifting from their fingers, because it is the springtime. There is the music of a flute," said the woman's voice softly, softly, "and creatures of the wood are dancing——"

"But the mother," Felicia said as suddenly as if she had been awaked from sleep. "What did the little girl's mother say when she didn't do her teeth and didn't wash at night?"

"The mother was not there, you remember," said the woman, and the brush moved steadily in her hand. "But she did send one little letter back. Sometimes the people who went away were able to do that. The mother wrote it in a train, standing up in a car that had no seats," she said, and she might have been telling the story of the ballet still, for her voice was gentle and the brush did not falter on Felicia's hair. "There were perhaps a great many other people standing up in the train with her, perhaps all trying to write their little letters on the bits of paper they had managed to hide on them, or that they had found in forgotten corners as they traveled. When they had written their letters, then they must try to slip them out through the boards of the car in which they journeyed, standing up," said the woman, "and these letters fell down on the tracks under the train, or they were blown into the fields or onto the country roads, and if it was a kind person who picked them up, he would seal them in envelopes and send them to where they were addressed to go. So a letter came back like this from the little girl's mother," the woman said, and the brush followed the comb, the comb the brush in steady pursuit through Felicia's hair. "It said good-by to the little girl, and it said please to take care of her. It said: 'Whoever reads this letter in the camp, please take good care of my little girl for me, and please have her tonsils looked at by a doctor if this is possible to do.' "

"And then," said Felicia softly, persistently, "what happened to the little girl?"

"I do not know. I cannot say," the woman said. But now the brush and comb had ceased to move, and in the silence Felicia turned her thin, small body on the chair, and she and the woman suddenly put their arms around each other. "They must all be asleep now, all of them," the woman said, and in the silence that fell on them again, they held each other closer. "They must be quietly asleep somewhere, and not crying all night because they are hungry and because they are cold. For three years I have been saying 'They must all be asleep, and the cold and the hunger and the seasons or night or day or nothing matters to them——' "

It was after midnight when Felicia's mother put her key in the lock of the front door, and pushed it open, and stepped into the hallway. She walked quickly to the living room, and just across the threshold she slipped the three blue foxskins from her shoulders and dropped them, with her little velvet bag, upon the chair. The room was quiet, so quiet that she could hear the sound of breathing in it, and no one spoke to her in greeting as she crossed toward the bedroom door. And then, as startling as a slap across her delicately tinted face, she saw the woman lying sleeping on the divan, and Felicia, in her school dress still, asleep within the woman's arms.

EUDORA WELTY

1909–

Born in Jackson, Mississippi, where her father was president of an insurance company, she went to schools there, then to the Mississippi College for Women. She broke out of her home region to finish college at the University of Wisconsin in 1929, after which she studied at the Columbia University School of Advertising in 1930 and 1931. She returned to Mississippi and worked for various radio stations and newspapers, as well as for the WPA. She began writing fiction in the 1930's, publishing her first collection, *A Curtain of Green*, in 1941. Since then she has led a quiet life in Mississippi, writing and publishing her uniquely perceptive and humorous stories and novels at regular intervals.

Why I Live at the P.O.

I was getting along fine with Mama, Papa-Daddy and Uncle Rondo until my sister Stella-Rondo just separated from her husband and came back home again. Mr. Whitaker! Of course I went with Mr. Whitaker first, when he first appeared here in China Grove, taking "Pose Yourself" photos, and Stella-Rondo broke us up. Told him I was one-sided. Bigger on one side than the other, which is a deliberate, calculated falsehood: I'm the same. Stella-Rondo is exactly twelve months to the day younger than I am and for that reason she's spoiled.

She's always had anything in the world she wanted and then she'd throw it away. Papa-Daddy gave her this gorgeous Add-a-Pearl necklace when she was eight years old and she threw it away playing baseball when she was nine, with only two pearls.

So as soon as she got married and moved away from home the first thing she did was separate! From Mr. Whitaker! This photographer with the popeyes she said she trusted. Came home from one of those towns up in Illinois and to our complete surprise brought this child of two.

Mama said she like to make her drop dead for a second. "Here you had this marvelous blond child and never so much as wrote your mother a word about it," says Mamma. "I'm thoroughly ashamed of you." But of course she wasn't.

Stella-Rondo just calmly takes off this *hat*, I wish you could see it. She says, "Why, Mama, Shirley-T.'s adopted, I can prove it."

"How?" says Mama, but all I says was, "H'm!" There I was over the hot stove, trying to stretch two chickens over five people and a completely unexpected child into the bargain, without one moment's notice.

"What do you mean—'H'm!'?" says Stella-Rondo, and Mama says, "I heard that, Sister."

I said that oh, I didn't mean a thing, only that whoever Shirley-T. was, she was the spit-image of Papa-Daddy if he'd cut off his beard, which of course he'd never do in the world. Papa-Daddy's Mama's papa and sulks.

Stella-Rondo got furious! She said, "Sister, I don't need to tell you you got a lot of nerve and always did have and I'll thank you to make no future reference to my adopted child whatsoever."

"Very well," I said. "Very well, very well. Of course I noticed at once she looks like Mr. Whitaker's side too. That frown. She looks like a cross between Mr. Whitaker and Papa-Daddy."

"Well, all I can say is she isn't."

"She looks exactly like Shirley Temple to me," says Mama, but Shirley-T. just ran away from her.

So the first thing Stella-Rondo did at the table was turn Papa-Daddy against me.

"Papa-Daddy," she says. He was trying to cut up his meat. "Papa-Daddy!" I was taken completely by surprise. Papa-Daddy is about a million years old and's got this long-long beard. "Papa-Daddy, Sister says she fails to understand why you don't cut off your beard."

So Papa-Daddy l-a-y-s down his knife and fork! He's real rich. Mama says he is, he says he isn't. So he says, "Have I heard correctly? You don't understand why I don't cut off my beard?"

"Why," I says, "Papa-Daddy, of course I understand, I did not say any such of a thing, the idea!"

He says, "Hussy!"

I says, "Papa-Daddy, you know I wouldn't any more want you to cut off your beard than the man in the moon. It was the farthest thing from my mind! Stella-Rondo sat there and made that up while she was eating breast of chicken."

But he says, "So the postmistress fails to understand why I don't cut off my beard. Which job I got you through my influence with the government. 'Bird's nest'—is that what you call it?"

Not that it isn't the next to smallest P.O. in the entire state of Mississippi.

I says, "Oh, Papa-Daddy," I says, "I didn't say any such of a thing, I never dreamed it was a bird's nest, I have always been grateful though this is the next to smallest P.O. in the state of Mississippi, and I do not enjoy being referred to as a hussy by my own grandfather."

But Stella-Rondo says, "Yes, you did say it too. Anybody in the world could of heard you, that had ears."

"Stop right there," says Mama, looking at *me*.

So I pulled my napkin straight back through the napkin ring and left the table.

As soon as I was out of the room Mama says, "Call her back, or she'll starve to death," but Papa-Daddy says, "This is the beard I started growing on the Coast when I was fifteen years old." He would of gone on till nightfall if Shirley-T. hadn't lost the Milky Way she ate in Cairo.

So Papa-Daddy says, "I am going out and lie in the hammock, and you can all sit here and remember my words: I'll never cut off my beard as long as I live, even one inch, and I don't appreciate it in you at all." Passed right by me in the hall and went straight out and got in the hammock.

It would be a holiday. It wasn't five minutes before Uncle Rondo suddenly appeared in the hall in one of Stella-Rondo's flesh-colored kimonos, all cut on the bias, like something Mr. Whitaker probably thought was gorgeous.

"Uncle Rondo!" I says. "I didn't know who that was! Where are you going?"

"Sister," he says, "get out of my way, I'm poisoned."

"If you're poisoned stay away from Papa-Daddy," I says. "Keep out of the hammock, Papa-Daddy will certainly beat you on the head if you come within forty miles of him. He thinks I deliberately said he ought to cut off his beard after he got me the P.O., and I've told him and told him and told him, and he acts like he just don't hear me. Papa-Daddy must of gone stone deaf."

"He picked a fine day to do it then," says Uncle Rondo, and before you could say "Jack Robinson" flew out in the yard.

What he'd really done, he'd drunk another bottle of that prescription. He does it every single Fourth of July as sure as shooting, and it's horribly expensive. Then he falls over in the hammock and snores. So he insisted on zigzagging right on out to the hammock, looking like a half-wit.

Papa-Daddy woke up with this horrible yell and right there without moving an inch he tried to turn Uncle Rondo against me. I heard every word he said. Oh, he told Uncle Rondo I didn't learn to read till I was eight years old and he didn't see how in the world I ever got the mail put up at the P.O., much less read it all, and he said if Uncle Rondo could only fathom the lengths he had gone to to get me that job! And he said on the other hand he thought Stella-Rondo had a brilliant mind and deserved credit for getting out of town. All the time he was just lying there swinging as pretty as you please and looping out his beard, and poor Uncle Rondo was *pleading* with him to slow down the hammock, it was making him as dizzy as a witch to watch it. But that's what Papa-Daddy likes about a hammock. So Uncle Rondo was too dizzy to get turned against me for the time being. He's Mama's only brother and is a good case of a one-track mind. Ask anybody. A certified pharmacist.

Just then I heard Stella-Rondo raising the upstairs window. While she was married she got this peculiar idea that it's cooler with the windows shut and locked. So she has to raise the window before she can make a soul hear her outdoors.

So she raises the window and says, "*Oh!*" You would have thought she was mortally wounded.

Uncle Rondo and Papa-Daddy didn't even look up, but kept right on with what they were doing. I had to laugh.

I flew up the stairs and threw the door open! I says, "What in the wide world's the matter, Stella-Rondo? You mortally wounded?"

"No," she says, "I'm not mortally wounded but I wish you would do me the favor of looking out that window there and telling me what you see."

So I shade my eyes and look out the window.

"I see the front yard," I says.

"Don't you see any human beings?" she says.

"I see Uncle Rondo trying to run Papa-Daddy out of the hammock," I says. "Nothing more. Naturally, it's so suffocating-hot in the house, with all the windows shut and locked, everybody who cares to stay in their right mind will have to go out and get in the hammock before the Fourth of July is over."

"Don't you notice anything different about Uncle Rondo?" asks Stella-Rondo.

"Why, no, except he's got on some terrible-looking flesh-colored contraption I wouldn't be found dead in, is all I can see," I says.

"Never mind, you won't be found dead in it, because it happens to be part of my trousseau, and Mr. Whitaker took several dozen photographs of me in it," says Stella-Rondo. "What on earth could Uncle Rondo *mean* by wearing part of my trousseau out in the broad open daylight without saying so much as 'Kiss my foot,' *knowing* I only got home this morning after my separation and hung my negligee up on the bathroom door, just as nervous as I could be?"

"I'm sure I don't know, and what do you expect me to do about it?" I says. "Jump out the window?"

"No, I expect nothing of the kind. I simply declare that Uncle Rondo looks like a fool in it, that's all," she says. "It makes me sick to my stomach."

"Well, he looks as good as he can," I says. "As good as anybody in reason could." I stood up for Uncle Rondo, please remember. And I said to Stella-Rondo, "I think I would do well not to criticize so freely if I were you and came home with a two-year-old child I had never said a word about, and no explanation whatever about my separation."

"I asked you the instant I entered this house not to refer one more time to my adopted child, and you gave me your word of honor you would not," was all Stella-Rondo would say, and started pulling out every one of her eyebrows with some cheap Kress tweezers.

So I merely slammed the door behind me and went down and made some green-tomato pickle. Somebody had to do it. Of course Mama had turned both the niggers loose; she always said no earthly power could hold one anyway on the Fourth of July, so she wouldn't even try. It turned out that Jaypan fell in the lake and came within a very narrow limit of drowning.

So Mama trots in. Lifts up the lid and says, "H'm! Not very good for your Uncle Rondo in his precarious condition, I must say. Or poor little adopted Shirley-T. Shame on you!"

That made me tired. I says, "Well, Stella-Rondo had better thank her lucky stars it was her instead of me came trotting in with that very peculiar-looking child. Now if it had been me that trotted in from Illinois and brought a peculiar-looking child of two, I shudder to think of the reception I'd of got, much less controlled the diet of an entire family."

"But you must remember, Sister, that you were never married to Mr. Whitaker in the first place and didn't go up to Illinois to live," says Mama, shaking a spoon in my face. "If you had I would of been just as overjoyed to see you and your little adopted girl as I was to see Stella-Rondo, when you wound up with your separation and came on back home."

"You would not," I says.

"Don't contradict me, I would," says Mama.

But I said she couldn't convince me though she talked till she was blue in the face. Then I said, "Besides, you know as well as I do that that child is not adopted."

"She most certainly is adopted," says Mama, stiff as a poker.

I says, "Why, Mama, Stella-Rondo had her just as sure as anything in this world, and just too stuck up to admit it."

"Why, Sister," said Mama. "Here I thought we were going to have a pleasant Fourth of July, and you start right out not believing a word your own baby sister tells you!"

"Just like Cousin Annie Flo. Went to her grave denying the facts of life," I remind Mama.

"I told you if you ever mentioned Annie Flo's name I'd slap your face," says Mama, and slaps my face.

"All right, you wait and see," I says.

"I," says Mama, "*I* prefer to take my children's word for anything when it's humanly possible." You ought to see Mama, she weighs two hundred pounds and has real tiny feet.

Just then something perfectly horrible occurred to me.

"Mama," I says, "can that child talk?" I simply had to whisper! "Mama, I wonder if that child can be—you know—in any way? Do you realize," I says, "that she hasn't spoken one single, solitary word to a human being up to this minute? This is the way she looks," I says, and I looked like this.

Well, Mama and I just stood there and stared at each other. It was horrible!

"I remember well that Joe Whitaker frequently drank like a fish," says Mama. "I believed to my soul he drank *chemicals*." And without another word she marches to the foot of the stairs and calls Stella-Rondo.

"Stella-Rondo? O-o-o-o-o! Stella-Rondo!"

"What?" says Stella-Rondo from upstairs. Not even the grace to get up off the bed.

"Can that child of yours talk?" asks Mama.

Stella-Rondo says, "Can she what?"

"Talk! Talk!" says Mama. "Burdyburdyburdyburdy!"

So Stella-Rondo yells back, "Who says she can't talk?"

"Sister says so," says Mama

"You didn't have to tell me, I know whose word of honor don't mean a thing in this house," says Stella-Rondo.

And in a minute the loudest Yankee voice I ever heard in my life yells out, "OE'm Pop-OE the Sailor-r-r-r Ma-a-an!" and then somebody jumps up and down in the upstairs hall. In another second the house would of fallen down.

"Not only talks, she can tap-dance!" calls Stella-Rondo. "Which is more than some people I won't name can do."

"Why, the little precious darling thing!" Mama says, so surprised. "Just as smart as she can be!" Starts talking baby talk right there. Then she turns on me. "Sister, you ought to be thoroughly ashamed! Run upstairs this instant and apologize to Stella-Rondo and Shirley-T."

"Apologize for what?" I says. "I merely wondered if the child was normal, that's all. Now that she's proved she is, why, I have nothing further to say."

But Mama just turned on her heel and flew out, furious. She ran right upstairs and hugged the baby. She believed it was adopted. Stella-Rondo hadn't done a thing but turn her against me from upstairs while I stood there helpless over the hot stove. So that made Mama, Papa-Daddy and the baby all on Stella-Rondo's side.

Next, Uncle Rondo.

I must say that Uncle Rondo has been marvelous to me at various times in the past and I was completely unprepared to be made to jump out of my skin, the way it turned out. Once Stella-Rondo did something perfectly horrible to him—broke a chain letter from Flanders Field—and he took the radio back he had given her and gave it to me. Stella-Rondo was furious! For six months we all had to call her Stella instead of Stella-Rondo, or she wouldn't answer. I always thought Uncle Rondo had all the brains of the entire family. Another time he sent me to Mammoth Cave, with all expenses paid.

But this would be the day he was drinking that prescription, the Fourth of July.

So at supper Stella-Rondo speaks up and says she thinks Uncle Rondo ought to try to eat a little something. So finally Uncle Rondo said he would try a little cold biscuits and ketchup, but that was all. So *she* brought it to him.

"Do you think it wise to disport with ketchup in Stella-Rondo's flesh-colored kimono?" I says. Trying to be considerate! If Stella-Rondo couldn't watch out for her trousseau, somebody had to.

"Any objections?" asks Uncle Rondo, just about to pour out all the ketchup.

"Don't mind what she says, Uncle Rondo," says Stella-Rondo. "Sister has been devoting this solid afternoon to sneering out my bedroom window at the way you look."

"What's that?" says Uncle Rondo. Uncle Rondo has got the most terrible temper in the world. Anything is liable to make him tear the house down if it comes at the wrong time.

So Stella-Rondo says, "Sister says, 'Uncle Rondo certainly does look like a fool in that pink kimono!' "

Do you remember who it was really said that?

Uncle Rondo spills out all the ketchup and jumps out of his chair and tears off the kimono and throws it down on the dirty floor and puts his foot on it. It had to be sent all the way to Jackson to the cleaners and re-pleated.

"So that's your opinion of your Uncle Rondo, is it?" he says. "I look like a fool, do I? Well, that's the last straw. A whole day in this house with nothing to do, and then to hear you come out with a remark like that behind my back!"

"I didn't say any such of a thing, Uncle Rondo," I says, "and I'm not saying who did, either. Why, I think you look all right. Just try to take care of yourself and not talk and eat at the same time," I says. "I think you better go lie down."

"Lie down my foot," says Uncle Rondo. I ought to of known by that he was fixing to do something perfectly horrible.

So he didn't do anything that night in the precarious state he was in—just played Casino with Mama and Stella-Rondo and Shirley-T. and gave Shirley-T. a nickel with a head on both sides. It tickled her nearly to death, and she called him "Papa." But at 6:30 A.M. the next morning, he threw a whole five-cent package of some unsold one-inch firecrackers from the store as hard as he could into my bedroom and they every one went off. Not one bad one in the string. Anybody else, there'd be one that wouldn't go off.

Well, I'm just terribly susceptible to noise of any kind, the doctor has always told me I was the most sensitive person he had ever seen in his whole life, and I was simply prostrated. I couldn't eat! People tell me they heard it as far as the cemetery, and old Aunt Jep Patterson, that had been holding her own so good, thought it was Judgment Day and she was going to meet her whole family. It's usually so quiet here.

And I'll tell you it didn't take me any longer than a minute to make up my mind what to do. There I was with the whole entire house on Stella-Rondo's side and turned against me. If I have anything at all I have pride.

So I just decided I'd go straight down to the P.O. There's plenty of room there in the back, I says to myself.

Well! I made no bones about letting the family catch on to what I was up to. I didn't try to conceal it.

The first thing they knew, I marched in where they were all playing Old Maid and pulled the electric oscillating fan out by the plug, and everything got real hot. Next I snatched the pillow I'd done the needlepoint on right off the davenport from behind Papa-Daddy. He went "Ugh!" I beat Stella-Rondo up the stairs and finally found my charm bracelet in her bureau drawer under a picture of Nelson Eddy.

"So that's the way the land lies," says Uncle Rondo. There he was, piecing on the ham. "Well, Sister, I'll be glad to donate my army cot if you got any place to set it up, providing you'll leave right this minute and let me get some peace." Uncle Rondo was in France.

"Thank you kindly for the cot and 'peace' is hardly the word I would select if I had to resort to firecrackers at 6:30 A.M. in a young girl's bedroom," I says back to him. "And as to where I intend to go, you seem to forget my position as postmistress of China Grove, Mississippi," I says. "I've always got the P.O."

Well, that made them all sit up and take notice.

I went out front and started digging up some four-o'clocks to plant around the P.O.

"Ah-ah-ah!" says Mama, raising the window. "Those happen to be my four-o'clocks. Everything planted in that star is mine. I've never known you to make anything grow in your life."

"Very well," I says. "But I take the fern. Even you, Mama, can't stand there and deny that I'm the one watered that fern. And I happen to know where I can send in a box top and get a packet of one thousand mixed seeds, no two the same kind, free."

"Oh, where?" Mama wants to know.

But I says, "Too late. You 'tend to your house, and I'll 'tend to mine. You hear things like that all the time if you know how to listen to the radio. Perfectly marvelous offers. Get anything you want free."

So I hope to tell you I marched in and got that radio, and they could of all bit a nail in two, especially Stella-Rondo, that it used to belong to, and she well knew she couldn't get it back, I'd sue for it like a shot. And I very politely took the sewing-machine motor I helped pay the most on to give Mama for Christmas back in 1929, and a good big calendar, with the first-aid remedies on it. The thermometer and the Hawaiian ukulele certainly were rightfully mine, and I stood on the step-ladder and got all my watermelon-rind preserves and every fruit and vegetable I'd put up, every jar. Then I began to pull the tacks out of the bluebird wall vases on the archway to the dining room.

"Who told you you could have those, Miss Priss?" says Mama, fanning as hard as she could.

"I bought 'em and I'll keep track of 'em," I says. "I'll tack 'em up one on each side the post-office window, and you can see 'em when you come to ask me for your mail, if you're so dead to see 'em."

"Not I! I'll never darken the door to that post office again if I live to be a hundred," Mama says. "Ungrateful child! After all the money we spent on you at the Normal."

"Me either," says Stella-Rondo. "You can just let my mail lie there and *rot*, for all I care. I'll never come and relieve you of a single, solitary piece."

"I should worry," I says. "And who you think's going to sit down and write you all those big fat letters and postcards, by the way? Mr. Whitaker? Just because he was the only man ever dropped down in China Grove and you got him—unfairly—is he going to sit down and write you a lengthy correspondence after you come home giving no rhyme nor reason whatsoever for your separation and no explanation for the presence of that child? I may not have your brilliant mind, but I fail to see it."

So Mama says, "Sister, I've told you a thousand times that Stella-Rondo simply got homesick, and this child is far too big to be hers," and she says, "Now, why don't you all just sit down and play Casino?"

Then Shirley-T. sticks out her tongue at me in this perfectly horrible way. She has no more manners than the man in the moon. I told her she was going to cross her eyes like that some day and they'd stick.

"It's too late to stop me now," I says. "You should have tried that yesterday. I'm going to the P.O. and the only way you can possibly see me is to visit me there."

So Papa-Daddy says, "You'll never catch me setting foot in that post office, even if I should take a notion into my head to write a letter some place." He says, "I won't have you reachin' out of that little old window with a pair of shears and cuttin' off any beard of mine. I'm too smart for you!"

"We all are," says Stella-Rondo.

But I said, "If you're so smart, where's Mr. Whitaker?"

So then Uncle Rondo says, "I'll thank you from now on to stop reading all the orders I get on postcards and telling everybody in China Grove what you think is the matter with them," but I says, "I draw my own conclusions and will continue in the future to draw them." I says, "If people want to write their inmost secrets on penny postcards, there's nothing in the wide world you can do about it, Uncle Rondo."

"And if you think we'll ever *write* another postcard you're sadly mistaken," says Mama.

"Cutting off your nose to spite your face then," I says. "But if you're all determined to have no more to do with the U.S. mail, think of this: What will Stella-Rondo do now, if she wants to tell Mr. Whitaker to come after her?"

"Wah!" says Stella-Rondo. I knew she'd cry. She had a conniption fit right there in the kitchen.

"It will be interesting to see how long she holds out," I says. "And now—I am leaving."

"Good-bye," says Uncle Rondo.

"Oh, I declare," says Mama, "to think that a family of mine should quarrel on the Fourth of July, or the day after, over Stella-Rondo leaving old Mr. Whitaker and having the sweetest little adopted child! It looks like we'd all be glad!"

"Wah!" says Stella-Rondo, and has a fresh conniption fit.

"*He* left *her*—you mark my words," I says. "That's Mr. Whitaker. I know Mr. Whitaker. After all, I knew him first. I said from the beginning he'd up and leave her. I foretold every single thing that's happened."

"Where did he go?" asks Mama.

"Probably to the North Pole, if he knows what's good for him," I says.

But Stella-Rondo just bawled and wouldn't say another word. She flew to her room and slammed the door.

"Now look what you've gone and done, Sister," says Mama. "You go apologize."

"I haven't got time, I'm leaving," I says.

"Well, what are you waiting around for?" asks Uncle Rondo.

So I just picked up the kitchen clock and marched off, without saying "Kiss my foot" or anything, and never did tell Stella-Rondo good-bye.

There was a nigger girl going along on a little wagon right in front.

"Nigger girl," I says, "come help me haul these things down the hill, I'm going to live in the post office."

Took her nine trips in her express wagon. Uncle Rondo came out on the porch and threw her a nickel.

And that's the last I've laid eyes on any of my family or my family laid eyes on me for five solid days and nights. Stella-Rondo may be telling the most horrible tales in the world about Mr. Whitaker, but I haven't heard them. As I tell everybody, I draw my own conclusions.

But oh, I like it here. It's ideal, as I've been saying. You see, I've got everything cater-cornered, the way I like it. Hear the radio? All the war news. Radio, sewing machine, book ends, ironing board and that great big piano lamp—peace, that's what I like. Butter-bean vines planted all along the front where the strings are.

Of course, there's not much mail. My family are naturally the main people in China Grove, and if they prefer to vanish from the face of the earth, for all the mail they get or the mail they write, why, I'm not going to open my mouth. Some of the folks here in town are taking up for me and some turned against me. I know which is which. There are always people who will quit buying stamps just to get on the right side of Papa-Daddy.

But here I am, and here I'll stay. I want the world to know I'm happy.

And if Stella-Rondo should come to me this minute, on bended knees, and *attempt* to explain the incidents of her life with Mr. Whitaker, I'd simply put my fingers in both my ears and refuse to listen.

TILLIE OLSEN
1912–

She was born in Omaha, Nebraska, and lived there until her twenties. When she was nineteen she began a novel about a poor family living through the depression, working on the book as she lived through the depression herself, moving to California, working in factories and offices. She left it unfinished in 1936 or 1937. She married, had children, and found it difficult to write until the 1950's, when she published four extraordinary stories, collected in *Tell Me a Riddle* (1961). The publication of this volume established her as an important American writer. In 1974 she published what could be salvaged of the novel she had been forced to abandon in the 1930's, *Yonnondio*.

I Stand Here Ironing

I stand here ironing, and what you asked me moves tormented back and forth with the iron.

"I wish you would manage the time to come in and talk with me about your daughter. I'm sure you can help me understand her. She's a youngster who needs help and whom I'm deeply interested in helping."

"Who needs help." Even if I came, what good would it do? You think because I am her mother I have a key, or that in some way you could use me as a key? She has lived for nineteen years. There is all that life that has happened outside of me, beyond me.

And when is there time to remember, to sift, to weigh, to estimate, to total? I will start and there will be an interruption and I will have to gather it all together again. Or I will become engulfed with all I did or did not do, with what should have been and what cannot be helped.

She was a beautiful baby. The first and only one of our five that was beautiful at birth. You do not guess how new and uneasy her tenancy in her now-loveliness. You did not know her all those years she was thought homely, or see her poring over her baby pictures, making me tell her over and over how beautiful she had been—and would be, I would tell her—and was now, to the seeing eye. But the seeing eyes were few or non-existent. Including mine.

I nursed her. They feel that's important nowadays. I nursed all the children, but with her, with all the fierce rigidity of first motherhood, I did like the books then said. Though her cries battered me to trembling and my breasts ached with swollenness, I waited till the clock decreed.

Why do I put that first? I do not even know if it matters, or if it explains anything.

She was a beautiful baby. She blew shining bubbles of sound. She loved motion, loved light, loved color and music and textures. She would lie on the floor in her blue overalls patting the surface so hard in ecstasy her hands and feet would blur. She was a miracle to me, but when she was eight months old I had to leave her daytimes with the woman downstairs to whom she was no miracle at all, for I worked or looked for work and for Emily's father, who "could no longer endure" (he wrote in his good-bye note) "sharing want with us."

I was nineteen. It was the pre-relief, pre-WPA world of the depression. I would start running as soon as I got off the streetcar, running up the stairs, the place smelling sour, and awake or asleep to startle awake, when she saw me she would break into a clogged weeping that could not be comforted, a weeping I can hear yet.

After a while I found a job hashing at night so I could be with her days, and it was better. But it came to where I had to bring her to his family and leave her.

It took a long time to raise the money for her fare back. Then she got chicken pox and I had to wait longer. When she finally came, I hardly knew her, walking quick and nervous like her father, looking like her father, thin, and dressed in a shoddy red that yellowed her skin and glared at the pockmarks. All the baby loveliness gone.

She was two. Old enough for nursery school they said, and I did not know then what I know now—the fatigue of the long day, and the lacerations of group life in the kinds of nurseries that are only parking places for children.

Except that it would have made no difference if I had known. It was the only place there was. It was the only way we could be together, the only way I could hold a job.

And even without knowing, I knew. I knew the teacher that was evil because all these years it has curdled into my memory, the little boy hunched in the corner, her rasp, "why aren't you outside, because Alvin hits you? that's no reason, go out, scaredy." I knew Emily hated it even if she did not clutch and implore "don't go Mommy" like the other children, mornings.

She always had a reason why we should stay home. Momma, you look sick, Momma. I feel sick. Momma, the teachers aren't there today, they're sick. Momma, we can't go, there was a fire there last night. Momma, it's a holiday today, no school, they told me.

But never a direct protest, never rebellion. I think of our others in their three, four-year-oldness—the explosions, the tempers, the denunciations, the demands—and I feel suddenly ill. I put the iron down. What in me demanded that goodness in her? And what was the cost, the cost to her of such goodness?

The old man living in the back once said in his gentle way: "You should smile at Emily more when you look at her." What *was* in my face when I looked at her? I loved her. There were all the acts of love.

It was only with the others I remembered what he said, and it was the face of joy, and not of care or tightness or worry I turned to them—too late for Emily. She does not smile easily, let alone almost always as her brothers and sisters do. Her face is closed and sombre, but when she wants, how fluid. You must have seen it in her pantomimes, you spoke of her rare gift for comedy on the stage that rouses a laughter out of the audience so dear they applaud and applaud and do not want to let her go.

Where does it come from, that comedy? There was none of it in her when she came back to me that second time, after I had had to send her away again. She had a new daddy now to learn to love, and I think perhaps it was a better time.

Except when we left her alone nights, telling ourselves she was old enough.

"Can't you go some other time, Mommy, like tomorrow?" she would ask. "Will it be just a little while you'll be gone? Do you promise?"

The time we came back, the front door open, the clock on the floor in the hall. She rigid awake. "It wasn't just a little while. I didn't cry. Three times I called you, just three times, and then I ran downstairs to open the door so you could come faster. The clock talked loud. I threw it away, it scared me what it talked."

She said the clock talked loud again that night I went to the hospital to have Susan. She was delirious with the fever that comes before red measles, but she was fully conscious all the week I was gone and the week after we were home when she could not come near the new baby or me.

She did not get well. She stayed skeleton thin, not wanting to eat, and night after night she had nightmares. She would call for me, and I would rouse from exhaustion to sleepily call back: "You're all right, darling, go to sleep, it's just a dream," and if she still called, in a sterner voice, "now go to sleep, Emily, there's nothing to hurt you." Twice, only twice, when I had to get up for Susan anyhow, I went in to sit with her.

Now when it is too late (as if she would let me hold and comfort her like I do the others) I get up and go to her at once at her moan or restless stirring. "Are you awake, Emily? Can I get you something?" And the answer is always the same: "No, I'm all right, go back to sleep, Mother."

They persuaded me at the clinic to send her away to a convalescent home in the country where "she can have the kind of food and care you can't manage for her, and you'll be free to concentrate on the new baby." They still send children to that place. I see pictures on the society page of sleek young women planning affairs to raise money for it, or dancing at the affairs, or decorating Easter eggs or filling Christmas stockings for the children.

They never have a picture of the children so I do not know if the girls still wear those gigantic red bows and the ravaged looks on the every other Sunday when parents can come to visit "unless otherwise notified"—as we were notified the first six weeks.

Oh it is a handsome place, green lawns and tall trees and fluted flower beds. High up on the balconies of each cottage the children stand, the girls in their red bows and white dresses, the boys in white suits and giant red ties. The parents stand below shrieking up to be heard and the children shriek down to be heard, and between them the invisible wall "Not To Be Contaminated by Parental Germs or Physical Affection."

There was a tiny girl who always stood hand in hand with Emily. Her parents never came. One visit she was gone. "They moved her to Rose College," Emily shouted in explanation. "They don't like you to love anybody here."

She wrote once a week, the labored writing of a seven-year-old. "I am fine. How is the baby. If I write my leter nicly I will have a star. Love." There never was a star. We wrote every other day, letters she could never hold or keep but only hear read—once. "We simply do not have room for children to keep any personal possessions," they patiently explained when we pieced one Sunday's shrieking together to plead how much it would mean to Emily, who loved so to keep things, to be allowed to keep her letters and cards.

Each visit she looked frailer. "She isn't eating," they told us.

(They had runny eggs for breakfast or mush with lumps, Emily said later, I'd hold it in my mouth and not swallow. Nothing ever tasted good, just when they had chicken.)

It took us eight months to get her released home, and only the fact that she gained back so little of her seven lost pounds convinced the social worker.

I used to try to hold and love her after she came back, but her body would stay stiff, and after a while she'd push away. She ate little. Food sickened her, and I think much of life too. Oh she had physical lightness and brightness, twinkling by on skates, bouncing like a ball up and down up and down over the jump rope, skimming over the hill; but these were momentary.

She fretted about her appearance, thin and dark and foreign-looking at a time when every little girl was supposed to look or thought she should look a chubby blonde replica of Shirley Temple. The doorbell sometimes rang for her, but no one seemed to come and play in the house or be a best friend. Maybe because we moved so much.

There was a boy she loved painfully through two school semesters. Months later she told me how she had taken pennies from my purse to buy him candy. "Licorice was his favorite and I brought him some every day, but he still liked Jennifer better'n me. Why, Mommy?" The kind of question for which there is no answer.

School was a worry to her. She was not glib or quick in a world where glibness and quickness were easily confused with ability to learn. To her overworked and exasperated teachers she was an over-conscientious "slow learner" who kept trying to catch up and was absent entirely too often.

I let her be absent, though sometimes the illness was imaginary.

How different from my now-strictness about attendance with the others. I wasn't working. We had a new baby, I was home anyhow. Sometimes, after Susan grew old enough, I would keep her home from school, too, to have them all together.

Mostly Emily had asthma, and her breathing, harsh and labored, would fill the house with a curiously tranquil sound. I would bring the two old dresser mirrors and her boxes of collections to her bed. She would select beads and single earrings, bottle tops and shells, dried flowers and pebbles, old postcards, and scraps, all sorts of oddments; then she and Susan would play Kingdom, setting up landscapes and furniture, peopling them with action.

Those were the only times of peaceful companionship between her and Susan. I have edged away from it, that poisonous feeling between them, that terrible balancing of hurts and needs I had to do between the two, and did so badly, those earlier years.

Oh there are conflicts between the others too, each one human, needing, demanding, hurting, taking—but only between Emily and Susan, no, Emily toward Susan that corroding resentment. It seems so obvious on the surface, yet it is not obvious. Susan, the second child, Susan, golden- and curly-haired and chubby, quick and articulate and assured, everything in appearance and manner Emily was not; Susan, not able to resist Emily's precious things, losing or sometimes clumsily breaking them; Susan telling jokes and riddles to company for applause while Emily sat silent (to say to me later: that was *my* riddle, Mother, I told it to Susan); Susan, who for all the five years' difference in age was just a year behind Emily in developing physically.

I am glad for that slow physical development that widened the difference between her and her contemporaries, though she suffered over it. She was too vulnerable for that terrible world of youthful competition, of preening and parading, of constant measuring of yourself against every other, of envy, "If I had that copper hair," "If I had that skin . . . " She tormented herself enough about not looking like the others, there was enough of the unsureness, the having to be conscious of words before you speak, the constant caring— what are they thinking of me? without having it all magnified by the merciless physical drives.

Ronnie is calling. He is wet and I change him. It is rare there is such a cry now. That time of motherhood is almost behind me when the ear is not one's own but must always be racked and listening for the child cry, the child call. We sit for a while and I hold him, looking out over the city spread in charcoal with its soft aisles of light. "*Shoogily*," he breathes and curls closer. I carry him back to bed, asleep. *Shoogily*. A funny word, a family word, inherited from

Emily, invented by her to say: *comfort.*

In this and other ways she leaves her seal, I say aloud. And startle at my saying it. What do I mean? What did I start to gather together, to try and make coherent? I was at the terrible, growing years. War years. I do not remember them well. I was working, there were four smaller ones now, there was not time for her. She had to help be a mother, and housekeeper, and shopper, She had to set her seal. Mornings of crisis and near hysteria trying to get lunches packed, hair combed, coats and shoes found, everyone to school or Child Care on time, the baby ready for transportation. And always the paper scribbled on by a smaller one, the book looked at by Susan then mislaid, the homework not done. Running out to that huge school where she was one, she was lost, she was a drop; suffering over the unpreparedness, stammering and unsure in her classes.

There was so little time left at night after the kids were bedded down. She would struggle over books, always eating (it was in those years she developed her enormous appetite that is legendary in our family) and I would be ironing, or preparing food for the next day, or writing V-mail to Bill, or tending the baby. Sometimes, to make me laugh, or out of her despair, she would imitate happenings or types at school.

I think I said once: "Why don't you do something like this in the school amateur show?" One morning she phoned me at work, hardly understandable through the weeping: "Mother, I did it. I won, I won; they gave me first prize; they clapped and clapped and wouldn't let me go."

Now suddenly she was Somebody, and as imprisoned in her difference as she had been in anonymity.

She began to be asked to perform at other high schools, even in colleges, then at city and statewide affairs. The first one we went to, I only recognized her that first moment when thin, shy, she almost drowned herself into the curtains. Then: Was this Emily? The control, the command, the convulsing and deadly clowning, the spell, then the roaring, stamping audience, unwilling to let this rare and precious laughter out of their lives.

Afterwards: You ought to do something about her with a gift like that—but without money or knowing how, what does one do? We have left it all to her, and the gift has as often eddied inside, clogged and clotted, as been used and growing.

She is coming. She runs up the stairs two at a time with her light graceful step; and I know she is happy tonight. Whatever it was that occasioned your call did not happen today.

"Aren't you ever going to finish the ironing, Mother? Whistler painted his mother in a rocker. I'd have to paint mine standing over an ironing board." This is one of her communicative nights and she tells me everything and nothing as she fixes herself a plate of food out of the icebox.

She is so lovely. Why did you want me to come in at all? Why were you concerned? She will find her way.

She starts up the stairs to bed. "Don't get me up with the rest in the morning." "But I thought you were having midterms." "Oh, those," she comes back in, kisses me, and says quite lightly," in a couple of years when we'll all be atom-dead they won't matter a bit."

She has said it before. She *believes* it. But because I have been developing the past, and all that compounds a human being is so heavy and meaningful in me, I cannot endure it tonight.

I will never total it all. I will never come in to say: She was a child seldom smiled at. Her father left me before she was a year old. I had to work her first six years when there was work, or I sent her home and to his relatives. There were years she had care she hated. She was dark and thin and foreign-looking in a world where the prestige went to blondeness and curly hair and dimples, she was slow where glibness was prized. She was a child of anxious, not proud, love. We were poor and could not afford for her the soil of easy growth. I was a young mother, I was a distracted mother. There were the other children pushing up, demanding. Her younger sister seemed all that she was not. There were years she did not let me touch her. She kept too much in herself, her life was such she had to keep too much in herself. My wisdom came too late. She has much to her and probably little will come of it. She is a child of her age, of depression, of war, of fear.

Let her be. So all that is in her will not bloom—but in how many does it? There is still enough left to live by. Only help her to know—help make it so there is cause for her to know—that she is more than this dress on the ironing board, helpless before the iron.

RALPH ELLISON
1914–

Ralph Waldo Ellison was born in Oklahoma City, Oklahoma. His father, who died when he was three, had named him after the great American transcendental philosopher Ralph Waldo Emerson—and the name influenced his life. He went to the segregated Negro schools in Omaha, where music was stressed, and grew up in one of the capitals of Southwestern jazz and blues music. He also read widely and uncritically in the Negro library there. After high school he went to Tuskegee to study music, but learned more about literature instead. Then he went to New York and met Richard Wright, who started him on his literary career, and Langston Hughes, who gave him suggestions about reading. He then calmly proceeded to write the one novel, *Invisible Man* (1952), which has put him permanently next to Twain and Melville in the ranks of American literature.

Battle Royal

It goes a long way back, some twenty years. All my life I had been looking for something, and everywhere I turned someone tried to tell me what it was. I accepted their answers too, though they were often in contradiction and even self-contradictory. I was naïve. I was looking for myself and asking everyone except myself questions which I, and only I, could answer. It took me a long time and much painful boomeranging of my expectations to achieve a realization everyone else appears to have been born with: That I am nobody but myself. But first I had to discover that I am an invisible man!

And yet I am no freak of nature, nor of history. I was in the cards, other things having been equal (or unequal) eighty-five years ago. I am not ashamed of my grandparents for having been slaves. I am only ashamed of myself for having at one time been ashamed. About eighty-five years ago they were told that they were free, united with others of our country in everything pertaining to the common good, and, in everything social, separate like the fingers of the hand. And they believed it. They exulted in it. They stayed in their place, worked hard, and brought up my father to do the same. But my grandfather is the one. He was an odd old guy, my grandfather, and I am told I take after him. It was he who caused the trouble. On his deathbed he called my father to him and said, "Son, after I'm gone I want you to keep up the good fight. I never told you, but our life is a war and I have been a traitor all my born days, a spy in the enemy's country ever since I give up my gun back in the Reconstruction. Live with your head in the lion's mouth. I want you to overcome 'em with yeses, undermine 'em with grins, agree 'em to death and destruction, let 'em swoller you till they vomit or bust wide open." They thought the old man had gone out of his mind. He had been the meekest of men. The younger children were rushed from the room, the shades drawn and the flame of the lamp turned so low that it sputtered on the wick like the old man's breathing. "Learn it to the younguns," he whispered fiercely; then he died.

But my folks were more alarmed over his last words than over his dying. It was as though he had not died at all, his words caused so much anxiety. I was warned emphatically to forget what he had said and, indeed, this is the first time it has been mentioned outside the family circle. It had a tremendous effect upon me, however. I could never be sure of what he meant. Grandfather had been a quiet old man who never made any trouble, yet on his deathbed he had called himself a traitor and a spy, and he had spoken of his meekness as a dangerous activity. It became a constant puzzle which lay unanswered in the back of my mind. And whenever things went well for me I remembered my grandfather and felt guilty and uncomfortable. It was as though I was carrying out his advice in spite of myself. And to make it worse, everyone loved me for it. I was praised by the most lily-white men of the town. I was considered an example of desirable conduct— just as my grandfather had been. And what puzzled me was that the old man had defined it as *treachery*. When I was praised for my conduct I felt a guilt that in some way I was doing something that was really against the wishes of the white folks, that if they had understood they would have desired me to act just the opposite, that I should have been sulky and mean, and that that really would have been what they wanted, even though they were fooled and thought they wanted me to act as I did. It made me afraid that some day they would look upon me as a traitor and I would be lost. Still I was more afraid to act any other way because they didn't like that at all. The old man's words were like a curse. On my graduation day I delivered an oration in which I showed that humility was the secret, indeed, the very essence of progress. (Not that I believed this—how could I, remembering my grandfather?—I only believed that it worked.) It was a great success. Everyone praised me and I was invited to give the speech at a gathering of the town's leading white citizens. It was a triumph for our whole community.

It was in the main ballroom of the leading hotel. When I got there I discovered that it was on the occasion of a smoker, and I was told that since I was to be there anyway I might as well take part in the battle royal to be fought by some of my schoolmates as part of the entertainment. The battle royal came first.

All of the town's big shots were there in their tuxedoes, wolfing down the buffet foods, drinking beer and whiskey and smoking black cigars. It was a large room with a high ceiling. Chairs were arranged in neat rows around three sides of a portable boxing ring. The fourth side was clear, revealing a gleaming space of polished floor. I had some misgivings over the battle royal, by the way. Not from a distaste for fighting, but because I didn't care too much for the other fellows who were to take part. They were tough guys who seemed to have no grandfather's curse worrying their minds. No one could mistake their toughness. And besides, I suspected that fighting a battle royal might detract from the dignity of my speech. In those pre-invisible days I visualized myself as a potential Booker T. Washington. But the other fellows didn't care too much for me either, and there were nine of them. I felt superior to them in my way, and I didn't like the manner in which we were all crowded together into the servants' elevator. Nor did they like my being there. In fact, as the warmly lighted floors flashed past the elevator we had words over the fact that I, by taking part in the fight, had knocked one of their friends out of a night's work.

We were led out of the elevator through a rococo hall into an anteroom and told to get into our fighting togs. Each of us was issued a pair of boxing gloves and ushered out into the big mirrored hall, which we entered looking cautiously about us and whispering, lest we might accidentally be heard above the noise of the room. It was foggy with cigar smoke. And already the whiskey was taking effect. I was shocked to see some of the most important men of the town quite tipsy. They were all there—bankers, lawyers, judges, doctors, fire chiefs, teachers, merchants. Even one of the more fashionable pastors. Something we could not see was going on up front. A clarinet was vibrating sensuously and the men were standing up and moving eagerly forward. We were a small tight group, clustered together, our bare upper bodies touching and shining with anticipatory sweat; while up front the big shots were becoming increasingly excited over something we still could not see. Suddenly I heard the school superintendent, who had told me to come, yell, "Bring up the shines gentlemen! Bring up the little shines!"

We were rushed up to the front of the ballroom, where it smelled even more strongly of tobacco and whiskey. Then we were pushed into place. I almost wet my pants. A sea of faces, some hostile, some amused, ringed around us, and in the center, facing us, stood a magnificent blonde—stark naked. There was dead silence. I felt a blast of cold air chill me. I tried to back away, but they were behind me and around me. Some of the boys stood with lowered heads, trembling. I felt a wave of irrational guilt and fear. My teeth chattered, my skin turned to goose flesh, my knees knocked. Yet I was strongly attracted and looked in spite of myself. Had the price of looking been blindness, I would have looked. The hair was yellow like that of a circus kewpie doll, the face heavily powdered and rouged, as though to form an abstract mask, the eyes hollow and smeared a cool blue, the color of a baboon's butt. I felt a desire to spit upon her as my eyes brushed slowly over her body. Her breasts were firm and round as the domes of East Indian temples, and I stood so close as to see the fine skin texture and beads of pearly perspiration glistening like dew around the pink and erected buds of her nipples. I wanted at one and the same time to run from the room, to sink through the floor, or go to her and cover her from my eyes and the eyes of the others with my body; to feel the soft thighs, to caress her and destroy her, to love her and murder her, to hide from her, and yet to stroke where below the small American flag tatooed upon her belly her thighs formed a capital V. I had a notion that of all in the room she saw only me with her impersonal eyes.

And then she began to dance, a slow sensuous movement; the smoke of a hundred cigars clinging to her like the thinnest of veils. She seemed like a fair bird-girl girdled in veils calling to me from the angry surface of some gray and threatening sea. I was transported. Then I became aware of the clarinet playing and the big shots yelling at us. Some threatened us if we looked and others if we did not. On my right I saw one boy faint. And now a man grabbed a silver pitcher from a table and stepped close as he dashed ice water upon him and stood him up and forced two of us to support him as his head hung and moans issued from his thick bluish lips. Another boy began to plead to go home. He was the largest of the group, wearing dark red fighting trunks much too small to conceal the erection which projected from him as though in answer to the insinuating low-registered moaning of the clarinet. He tried to hide himself with his boxing gloves.

And all the while the blonde continued dancing, smiling faintly at the big shots who watched her with fascination, and faintly smiling at our fear. I noticed a certain merchant who followed her hungrily, his lips loose and drooling. He was a large man who wore diamond studs in a shirtfront which swelled with the ample paunch underneath, and each time the blonde swayed her undulating hips he ran his hand through the thin hair of his bald head and, with his arms upheld, his posture clumsy like that of an intoxicated panda, wound his belly in a slow and obscene grind. This creature was completely hypnotized. The music had quickened. As the dancer flung herself about with a detached expression on her face, the men began reaching out to touch her. I could see their beefy fingers sink into the soft flesh. Some of the others tried to stop them and she began to move around the floor in graceful circles, as they gave chase, slipping and sliding over the polished floor. It was mad. Chairs went crashing, drinks were spilt, as they ran laughing and howling after her. They caught her just as she reached a door, raised her from the floor, and tossed her as college boys are tossed at a hazing, and above her red, fixed-smiling lips I saw the terror and disgust in her eyes, almost like my own terror and that which I saw in some of the other boys. As I watched, they tossed her twice and her soft breasts seemed to flatten against the air and her legs flung wildly as she spun. Some of the more sober ones helped her to escape. And I started off the floor, heading for the anteroom with the rest of the boys.

Some were still crying and in hysteria. But as we tried to leave we were stopped and ordered to get into the ring. There was nothing to do but what we were told. All ten of us climbed under the ropes and allowed ourselves to be blindfolded with broad bands of white cloth. One of the men seemed to feel a bit sympathetic and tried to cheer us up as we stood with our backs against the ropes. Some of us tried to grin. "See that boy over there?" one of the men said. "I want you to run across at the bell and give it to him right in the belly. If you don't get him, I'm going to get you. I don't like his looks." Each of us was told the same. The blindfolds were put on. Yet even then I had been going over my speech. In my mind each word was as bright as flame. I felt the cloth pressed into place, and frowned so that it would be loosened when I relaxed.

But now I felt a sudden fit of blind terror. I was unused to darkness. It was as though I had suddenly found myself in a dark room filled with poisonous cottonmouths. I could hear the bleary voices yelling insistently for the battle royal to begin.

"Get going in there!"

"Let me at that big nigger!"

I strained to pick up the school superintendent's voice, as though to squeeze some security out of that slightly more familiar sound.

"Let me at those black sonsabitches!" someone yelled.

"No, Jackson, no!" another voice yelled. "Here, somebody, help me hold Jack."

"I want to get at that ginger-colored nigger. Tear him limb from limb," the first voice yelled.

I stood against the ropes trembling. For in those days I was what they called ginger-colored, and he sounded as though he might crunch me between his teeth like a crisp ginger cookie.

Quite a struggle was going on. Chairs were being kicked about and I could hear voices grunting as with a terrific effort. I wanted to see, to see more desperately than ever before. But the blindfold was as tight as a thick skin-puckering scab and when I raised my gloved hands to push the layers of white aside a voice yelled, "Oh, no you don't, black bastard! Leave that alone!"

"Ring the bell before Jackson kills him a coon!" someone boomed in the sudden silence. And I heard the bell clang and the sound of the feet scuffling forward.

A glove smacked against my head. I pivoted, striking out stiffly as someone went past, and felt the jar ripple along the length of my arm to my shoulder. Then it seemed as though all nine of the boys had turned upon me at once. Blows pounded me from all sides while I struck out as best I could. So many blows landed upon me that I wondered if I were not the only blindfolded fighter in the ring, or if the man called Jackson hadn't succeeded in getting me after all.

Blindfolded, I could no longer control my motions. I had no dignity. I stumbled about like a baby or a drunken man. The smoke had become thicker and with each new blow it seemed to sear and further restrict my lungs. My saliva became like hot bitter glue. A glove connected with my head, filling my mouth with warm blood. It was everywhere. I could not tell if the moisture I felt upon my body was sweat or blood. A blow landed hard against the nape of my neck. I felt myself going over, my head hitting the floor. Streaks of blue light filled the black world behind the blindfold. I lay prone, pretending that I was knocked out, but felt myself seized by hands and yanked to my feet. "Get going, black boy! Mix it up!" My arms were like lead, my head smarting from blows. I managed to feel my way to the ropes and held on, trying to catch my breath. A glove landed in my mid-section and I went over again, feeling as though the smoke had become a knife jabbed into my guts. Pushed this way and that by the legs milling around me, I finally pulled erect and discovered that I could see the black, sweat-washed forms weaving in the smoky-blue atmosphere like drunken dancers weaving to the rapid drum-like thuds of blows.

Everyone fought hysterically. It was complete anarchy. Everybody fought everybody else. No group fought together for long. Two, three, four, fought one, then turned to fight each other, were themselves attacked. Blows landed below the belt and in the kidney, with the gloves open as well as closed, and with my eye partly opened now there was not so much terror. I moved carefully, avoiding blows, although not too many to attract attention, fighting from group to group. The boys groped about like blind, cautious crabs crouching to protect their mid-sections, their heads pulled in short against their shoulders, their arms stretched nervously before them, with their fists testing the smoke-filled air like the knobbed feelers of hypersensitive snails. In one corner I glimpsed a boy violently punching the air and heard him scream in pain as he smashed his hand against a ring post. For a second I saw him bent over holding his hand, then going down as a blow caught his unprotected head. I played one group against the other, slipping in and throwing a punch then stepping out of range while pushing the others into the melee to take the blows blindly aimed at me. The smoke was agonizing and there were no rounds, no bells at three minute intervals to relieve our exhaustion. The room spun round me, a swirl of lights, smoke, sweating bodies surrounded by tense white faces. I bled from both nose and mouth, the blood spattering upon my chest.

The men kept yelling, "Slug him, black boy! Knock his guts out!" "Uppercut him! Kill him! Kill that big boy!"

Taking a fake fall, I saw a boy going down heavily beside me as though we were felled by a single blow, saw a sneaker-clad foot shoot into his groin as the two who had knocked him down stumbled upon him. I rolled out of range, feeling a twinge of nausea.

The harder we fought the more threatening the men became. And yet, I had begun to worry about my speech again. How would it go? Would they recognize my ability? What would they give me?

I was fighting automatically when suddenly I noticed that one after another of the boys was leaving the ring. I was surprised, filled with panic, as though I had been left alone with an unknown danger. Then I understood. The boys had arranged it among themselves. It was the custom for the two men left in the ring to slug it out for the winner's prize. I discovered this too late. When the bell sounded two men in tuxedoes leaped into the ring and removed the blindfold. I found myself facing Tatlock, the biggest of the gang. I felt sick at my stomach. Hardly had the bell stopped ringing in my ears than it clanged again and I saw him moving swiftly toward me. Thinking of nothing else to do I hit him smash on the nose. He kept coming, bringing the rank sharp violence of stale sweat. His face was a black blank of a face, only his eyes alive—with hate of me and aglow with a feverish terror from what had happened to us all. I became anxious. I wanted to deliver my speech and he came at me as though he meant to beat it out of me. I smashed him again and again, taking his blows as they came. Then on a sudden impulse I struck him lightly and as we clinched, I whispered, "Fake like I knocked you out, you can have the prize."

"I'll break your behind," he whispered hoarsely.

"For *them?*"

"For *me*, sonofabitch!"

They were yelling for us to break it up and Tatlock spun me half around with a blow, and as a joggled camera sweeps in a reeling scene, I saw the howling red faces crouching tense beneath the cloud of blue-gray smoke. For a moment the world wavered, unraveled, flowed, then my head cleared and Tatlock bounced before me. That fluttering shadow before my eyes was his jabbing left hand. Then falling forward, my head against his damp shoulder, I whispered,

"I'll make it five dollars more."

"Go to hell!"

But his muscles relaxed a trifle beneath my pressure and I breathed, "Seven?"

"Give it to your ma," he said, ripping me beneath the heart.

And while I still held him I butted him and moved away. I felt myself bombarded with punches. I fought back with hopeless desperation. I wanted to deliver my speech more than anything else in the world, because I felt that only these men could judge truly my ability, and now this stupid clown was ruining my chances. I began fighting carefully now, moving in to punch him and out again with my greater speed. A lucky blow to his chin and I had him going too—until I heard a loud voice yell, "I got my money on the big boy."

Hearing this, I almost dropped my guard. I was confused: Should I try to win against the voice out there? Would not this go against my speech, and was not this a moment for humility, for nonresistance? A blow to my head as I danced about sent my right eye popping like a jack-in-the-box and settled my dilemma. The room went red as I fell. It was a dream fall, my body languid and fastidious as to where to land, until the floor became impatient and smashed up to meet me. A moment later I came to. An hypnotic voice said FIVE emphatically. And I lay there, hazily watching a dark red spot of my own blood shaping itself into a butterfly, glistening and soaking into the soiled gray world of the canvas.

When the voice drawled TEN I was lifted up and dragged to a chair. I sat dazed. My eye pained and swelled with each throb of my pounding heart and I wondered if now I would be allowed to speak. I was wringing wet, my mouth still bleeding. We were grouped along the wall now. The other boys ignored me as they congratulated Tatlock and speculated as to how much they would be paid. One boy whimpered over his smashed hand. Looking up front, I saw attendants in white jackets rolling the portable ring away and placing a small square rug in the vacant space surrounded by chairs. Perhaps, I thought, I will stand on the rug to deliver my speech.

Then the M.C. called to us, "Come on up here boys and get your money."

We ran forward to where the men laughed and talked in their chairs, waiting. Everyone seemed friendly now.

"There it is on the rug," the man said. I saw the rug covered with coins of all dimensions and a few crumpled bills. But what excited me, scattered here and there, were the gold pieces.

"Boys, it's all yours," the man said. "You get all you grab."

"That's right, Sambo," a blond man said, winking at me confidentially.

I trembled with excitement, forgetting my pain. I would get the gold and the bills, I thought. I would use both hands. I would throw my body against the boys nearest me to block them from the gold.

"Get down around the rug now," the man commanded, "and don't anyone touch it until I give the signal."

"This ought to be good," I heard.

As told, we got around the square rug on our knees. Slowly the man raised his freckled hand as we followed it upward with our eyes.

I heard, "These niggers look like they're about to pray!"

Then, "Ready," the man said. "Go!"

I lunged for a yellow coin lying on the blue design of the carpet, touching it and sending a surprised shriek to join those rising around me. I tried frantically to remove my hand but could not let go. A hot, violent force tore through my body, shaking me like a wet rat. The rug was electrified. The hair bristled up on my head as I shook myself free. My muscles jumped, my nerves jangled, writhed. But I saw that this was not stopping the other boys. Laughing in fear and embarrassment, some were holding back and scooping up the coins knocked off by the painful contortions of the others. The men roared above us as we struggled.

"Pick it up, goddamnit, pick it up!" someone called like a bass-voiced parrot. "Go on, get it!"

I crawled rapidly around the floor, picking up the coins, trying to avoid the coppers and to get greenbacks and the gold. Ignoring the shock by laughing, as I brushed the coins off quickly, I discovered that I could contain the electricity—a contradiction, but it works. Then the men began to push us onto the rug. Laughing embarrassedly, we struggled out of their hands and kept after the coins. We were all wet and slippery and hard to hold. Suddenly I saw a boy lifted into the air, glistening with sweat like a circus seal, and dropped, his wet back landing flush upon the charged rug, heard him yell and saw him literally dance upon his back, his elbows beating a frenzied tatoo upon the floor, his muscles twitching like the flesh of a horse stung by many flies. When he finally rolled off, his face was gray and no one stopped him when he ran from the floor amid booming laughter.

"Get the money," the M.C. called. "That's good hard American cash!"

And we snatched and grabbed, snatched and grabbed. I was careful not to come too close to the rug now, and when I felt the hot whiskey breath descend upon me like a cloud of foul air I reached out and grabbed the leg of a chair. It was occupied and I held on desperately.

"Leggo, nigger! Leggo!"

The huge face wavered down to mine as he tried to push me free. But my body was slippery and he was too drunk. It was Mr. Colcord, who owned a chain of movie houses and "entertainment palaces." Each time he grabbed me I slipped out of his hands. It became a real struggle. I feared the rug more than I did the drunk, so I held on, surprising myself for a moment by trying to topple *him* upon the rug. It was such an enormous idea that I found myself actually carrying it out. I tried not to be obvious, yet when I grabbed his leg, trying to tumble him out of the chair, he raised up roaring with laughter, and, looking at me with soberness dead in the eye, kicked me viciously in the chest. The chair leg flew out of my hand I felt myself going and rolled. It was as though I had rolled through a bed of hot coals. It seemed a whole century would pass before I would roll free, a century in which I was seared through the deepest levels of my body to the fearful breath within me and the breath seared and heated to the point of explosion. It'll all be over in a flash, I thought as I rolled clear It'll all be over in a flash.

But not yet, the men on the other side were waiting, red faces swollen as though from apoplexy as they bent forward in their chairs. Seeing their fingers coming toward me I rolled away as a fumbled football rolls off the receiver's fingertips, back into the coals. That time I luckily sent the rug sliding out of place and heard the coins ringing against the floor and the boys scuffling to pick them up and the M.C. calling, "All right, boys, that's all. Go get dressed and get your money."

I was limp as a dish rag. My back felt as though it had been beaten with wires.

When we had dressed the M.C. came in and gave us each five dollars, except Tatlock, who got ten for being last in the ring. Then he told us to leave. I was not to get a chance to deliver my speech, I thought. I was going out into the dim alley in despair when I was stopped and told to go back. I returned to the ballroom, where the men were pushing back their chairs and gathering in groups to talk.

The M.C. knocked on a table for quiet. "Gentlemen," he said, "we almost forgot an important part of the program. A most serious part, gentlemen. This boy was brought here to deliver a speech which he made at his graduation yesterday . . ."

"Bravo!"

"I'm told that he is the smartest boy we've got out there in Greenwood. I'm told that he knows more big words than a pocket-sized dictionary."

Much applause and laughter.

"So now, gentlemen, I want you to give him your attention."

There was still laughter as I faced them, my mouth dry, my eye throbbing. I began slowly, but evidently my throat was tense, because they began shouting, "Louder! Louder!"

"We of the younger generation extol the wisdom of that great leader and educator," I shouted, "who first spoke these flaming words of wisdom: 'A ship lost at sea for many days suddenly sighted a friendly vessel. From the mast of the unfortunate vessel was seen a signal: "Water, water; we die of thirst!" The answer from the friendly vessel came back: "Cast down your bucket where you are." The captain of the distressed vessel, at last heeding the injunction, cast down his bucket, and it came up full of fresh sparkling water from the mouth of the Amazon River.' And like him I say, and in his words, 'To those of my race who depend upon bettering their condition in a foreign land, or who underestimate the importance of cultivating friendly relations with the Southern white man, who is his next-door neighbor, I would say: "Cast down your bucket where you are"—cast it down in making friends in every manly way of the people of all races by whom we are surrounded . . .' "

I spoke automatically and with such fervor that I did not realize that the men were still talking and laughing until my dry mouth, filling up with blood from the cut, almost strangled me. I coughed, wanting to stop and go to one of the tall brass, sand-filled spittoons to relieve myself, but a few of the men, especially the superintendent, were listening and I was afraid. So I gulped it down, blood, saliva and all, and continued. (What powers of endurance I had during those days! What enthusiasm! What a belief in the rightness of things!) I spoke even louder in spite of the pain. But still they talked and still they laughed, as though deaf with cotton in dirty ears. So I spoke with greater emotional emphasis. I closed my ears and swallowed blood until I was nauseated. The speech seemed a hundred times as long as before, but I could not leave out a single word. All had to be said, each memorized nuance considered, rendered. Nor was that all. Whenever I uttered a word of three or more syllables a group of voices would yell for me to repeat it. I used the phrase "social responsibility" and they yelled:

"What's the word you say, boy?"

"Social responsibility," I said.

"What?"

"Social . . ."

"Louder."

". . . responsibility."

"More!"

"Respon—"

"Repeat!"

"—sibility."

The room filled with the uproar of laughter until, no doubt, distracted by having to gulp down my blood, I made a mistake and yelled a phrase I had often seen denounced in newspaper editorials, heard debated in private.

"Social . . ."

"What?" they yelled.

". . .equality—"

The laughter hung smokelike in the sudden stillness. I opened my eyes, puzzled. Sounds of displeasure filled the room. The M.C. rushed forward. They shouted hostile phrases at me. But I did not understand.

A small dry mustached man in the front row blared out, "Say that slowly, son!"

"What sir?"

"What you just said!"

"Social responsibility, sir," I said.

"You weren't being smart, were you, boy?" he said, not unkindly.

"No, sir!"

"You sure that about 'equality' was a mistake?'

"Oh, yes, sir," I said. "I was swallowing blood."

"Well, you had better speak more slowly so we can understand. We mean to do right by you, but you've got to know your place at all times. All right, now, go on with your speech."

I was afraid. I wanted to leave but I wanted also to speak and I was afraid they'd snatch me down.

"Thank you sir," I said, beginning where I had left off, and having them ignore me as before.

Yet when I finished there was a thunderous applause. I was surprised to see the superintendent come forth with a package wrapped in white tissue paper, and, gesturing for quiet, address the men.

"Gentlemen, you see that I did not overpraise this boy. He makes a good speech and some day he'll lead his people in the proper paths. And I don't have to tell you that that is important in these days and times. This is a good, smart boy, and so to encourage him in the right direction, in the name of the Board of Education I wish to present him a prize in the form of this . . ."

He paused, removing the tissue paper and revealing a gleaming calfskin brief case.

". . . in the form of this first-class article from Shad Whitmore's shop."

"Boy," he said, addressing me, "take this prize and keep it well. Consider it a badge of office. Prize it. Keep developing as you are and some day it will be filled with important papers that will help shape the destiny of your people."

I was so moved that I could hardly express my thanks. A rope of bloody saliva forming a shape like an undiscovered continent drooled upon the leather and I wiped it quickly away. I felt an importance that I had never dreamed.

"Open it and see what's inside," I was told.

My fingers a-tremble, I complied, smelling the fresh leather and finding an official-looking document inside. It was a scholarship to the state college for Negroes. My eyes filled with tears and I ran awkwardly off the floor.

I was overjoyed; I did not even mind when I discovered that the gold pieces I had scrambled for were brass pocket tokens advertising a certain make of automobile.

When I reached home everyone was excited. Next day the neighbors came to congratulate me. I even felt safe from grandfather, whose deathbed curse usually spoiled my triumphs. I stood beneath his photograph with my brief case in hand and smiled triumphantly into his stolid black peasant's face. It was a face that fascinated me. The eyes seemed to follow everywhere I went.

That night I dreamed I was at a circus with him and that he refused to laugh at the clowns no matter what they did. Then later he told me to open my brief case and read what was inside and I did, finding an official envelope stamped with the state seal; and inside the envelope I found another and another, endlessly, and I thought I would fall of weariness. "Them's years," he said. "Now open that one." And I did and in it I found an engraved document containing a short message in letters of gold. "Read it," my grandfather said. "Out loud."

"To Whom It May Concern," I intoned. "Keep This Nigger-Boy Running."

I awoke with the old man's laughter ringing in my ears.

(It was a dream I was to remember and dream again for many years after. But at that time I had no insight into its meaning. First I had to attend college.)

DORIS LESSING
1919–

Doris Tayler was born in Kermanshah, Persia (now Iran), where her father had a managerial post in the Imperial Bank of Persia. He was an Englishman who had lost a leg in World War I and married his nurse. In 1925 the family moved to Southern Rhodesia (now Zimbabwe), where Alfred Taylor got a loan from the government land bank to buy 3,000 acres of land recently taken away from Africans, who had been put onto reservations. With cheap native labor the Taylers raised corn on the land and never made enough money to get off it. Doris Tayler went to a Catholic convent school and Girls' High School in the small city of Salisbury, but left school at fourteen and worked as a nursemaid and then as a secretary. She was married twice (acquiring the name of Lessing) and had children, before deciding that marriage was not one of her talents. She had been writing for some time but got serious about it only in her late twenties. She left Rhodesia with her first novel and some stories complete, and moved to England, where she joined the Communist Party briefly and began her five-volume sequence of autobiographical novels, *Children of Violence*. Her most ambitious book is *The Golden Notebook* (1962). Recently, her concern for the human future has led her to writing science fiction. She is one of England's most important writers at the present time.

Sunrise on the Veld

Every night that winter he said aloud into the dark of the pillow: Half-past four! Half-past four! till he felt his brain had gripped the words and held them fast. Then he fell asleep at once, as if a shutter had fallen; and lay with his face turned to the clock so that he could see it first thing when he woke.

It was half-past four to the minute, every morning. Triumphantly pressing down the alarm-knob of the clock, which the dark half of his mind had outwitted, remaining vigilant all night and counting the hours as he lay relaxed in sleep, he huddled down for a last warm moment under the clothes, playing with the idea of lying abed for this once only. But he played with it for the fun of knowing that it was a weakness he could defeat without effort; just as he set the alarm each night for the delight of the moment when he woke and stretched his limbs, feeling the muscles tighten, and thought: Even my brain— even that! I can control every part of myself.

Luxury of warm rested body, with the arms and legs and fingers waiting like soldiers for a word of command! Joy of knowing that the precious hours were given to sleep voluntarily!—for he had once stayed awake three nights running, to prove that he could, and then worked all day, refusing even to admit that he was tired; and now sleep seemed to him a servant to be commanded and refused.

The boy stretched his frame full-length, touching the wall at his head with his hands, and the bedfoot with his toes; then he sprang out, like a fish leaping from water. And it was cold, cold.

He always dressed rapidly, so as to try and conserve his night-warmth till the sun rose two hours later; but by the time he had on his clothes his hands were numbed and he could scarcely hold his shoes. These he could not put on for fear of waking his parents, who never came to know how early he rose.

As soon as he stepped over the lintel, the flesh of his soles contracted on the chilled earth, and his legs began to ache with cold. It was night: the stars were glittering, the trees standing black and still. He looked for signs of day, for the greying of the edge of a stone, or a lightening in the sky where the sun would rise, but there was nothing yet. Alert as an animal he crept past the dangerous window, standing poised with his hand on the sill for one proudly fastidious moment, looking in at the stuffy blackness of the room where his parents lay.

Feeling for the grass-edge of the path with his toes, he reached inside another window further along the wall, where his gun had been set in readiness the night before. The steel was icy, and numbed fingers slipped along it, so that he had to hold it in the crook of his arm for safety. Then he tiptoed to the room where the dogs slept, and was fearful that they might have been tempted to go before him; but they were waiting, their haunches crouched in reluctance at the cold, but ears and swinging tails greeting the gun ecstatically. His warning undertone kept them secret and silent till the house was a hundred yards back: then they bolted off into the bush, yelping excitedly. The boy imagined his parents turning in their beds and muttering: Those dogs again! before they were dragged back in sleep; and he smiled scornfully. He always looked back over his shoulder at the house before he passed a wall of trees that shut it from sight. It looked so low and small, crouching there under a tall and brilliant sky. Then he turned his back on it, and on the frowsting sleepers, and forgot them.

He would have to hurry. Before the light grew strong he must be four miles away; and already a tint of green stood in the hollow of a leaf, and the air smelled of morning and the stars were dimming.

He slung the shoes over his shoulder, veld *skoen* that were crinkled and hard with the dews of a hundred mornings. They would be necessary when the ground became too hot to bear. Now he felt the chilled dust push up between his toes, and he let the muscles of his feet spread and settle into the shapes of the earth; and he thought: I could walk a hundred miles on feet like these! I could walk all day, and never tire!

He was walking swiftly through the dark tunnel of foliage that in day-time was a road. The dogs were invisibly ranging the lower travelways of the bush, and he heard them panting. Sometimes he felt a cold muzzle on his leg before they were off again, scouting for a trail to follow. They were not trained, but free-running companions of the hunt, who often tired of the long stalk before the final shots, and went off on their own pleasure. Soon he could see them, small and wild-looking in a wild strange light, now that the bush stood trembling on the verge of colour, waiting for the sun to paint earth and grass afresh.

The grass stood to his shoulders; and the trees were showering a faint silvery rain. He was soaked; his whole body was clenched in a steady shiver.

Once he bent to the road that was newly scored with animal trails, and regretfully straightened, reminding himself that the pleasure of tracking must wait till another day.

He began to run along the edge of a field, noting jerkily how it was filmed over with fresh spiderweb, so that the long reaches of great black clods seemed netted in glistening grey. He was using the steady lope he had learned by watching the natives, the run that is a dropping of the weight of the body from one foot to the next in a slow balancing movement that never tires, nor shortens the breath; and he felt the blood pulsing down his legs and along his arms, and the exultation and pride of body mounted in him till he was shutting his teeth hard against a violent desire to shout his triumph.

Soon he had left the cultivated part of the farm. Behind him the bush was low and black. In front was a long vlei, acres of long pale grass that sent back a hollowing gleam of light to a satiny sky. Near him thick swathes of grass were bent with the weight of water, and diamond drops sparkled on each frond.

The first bird woke at his feet and at once a flock of them sprang into the air calling shrilly that day had come; and suddenly, behind him, the bush woke into song, and he could hear the guinea fowl calling far ahead of him. That meant they would now be sailing down from their trees into thick grass, and it was for them he had come: he was too late. But he did not mind. He forgot he had come to shoot. He set his legs wide, and balanced from foot to foot, and swung his gun up and down in both hands horizontally, in a kind of improvised exercise, and let his head sink back till it was pillowed in his neck muscles, and watched how above him small rosy clouds floated in a lake of gold.

Suddenly it all rose in him: it was unbearable. He leapt up into the air, shouting and yelling wild, unrecognisable noises. Then he began to run, not carefully, as he had before, but madly, like a wild thing. He was clean crazy, yelling mad with the joy of living and a superfluity of youth. He rushed down the vlei under a tumult of crimson and gold, while all the birds of the world sang about him. He ran in great leaping strides, and shouted as he ran, feeling his body rise into the crisp rushing air and fall back surely on to sure feet; and thought briefly, not believing that such a thing could happen to him, that he could break his ankle any moment, in this thick tangled grass. He cleared bushes like a duiker, leapt over rocks; and finally came to a dead stop at a place where the ground fell abruptly away below him to the river. It had been a two-mile-long dash through waist-high growth, and he was breathing hoarsely and could no longer sing. But he poised on a rock and looked down at stretches of water that gleamed through stooping trees, and thought suddenly, I am fifteen! Fifteen! The words came new to him; so that he kept repeating them wonderingly, with swelling excitement; and he felt the years of his life with his hands, as if he were counting marbles, each one hard and separate and compact, each one a wonderful shining thing. That was what he was: fifteen years of this rich soil, and this slow-moving water, and air that smelt like a challenge whether it was warm and sultry at noon, or as brisk as cold water, like it was now.

There was nothing he couldn't do, nothing! A vision came to him, as he stood there, like when a child hears the word "eternity" and tries to understand it, and time takes possession of the mind. He felt his life ahead of him as a great and wonderful thing, something that was his; and he said aloud, with the blood rising to his head: all the great men of the world have been as I am now, and there is nothing I can't become, nothing I can't do; there is no country in the world I cannot make part of myself, if I choose. I contain the world. I can make of it what I want. If I choose, I can change everything that is going to happen: it depends on me, and what I decide now.

The urgency, and the truth and the courage of what his voice was saying exulted him so that he began to sing again, at the top of his voice, and the sound went echoing down the river gorge. He stopped for the echo, and sang again: stopped and shouted. That was what he was!—he sang, if he chose; and the world had to answer him.

And for minutes he stood there, shouting and singing and waiting for the lovely eddying sound of the echo; so that his own new strong thoughts came back and washed round his head, as if someone were answering him and encouraging him; till the gorge was full of soft voices clashing back and forth from rock to rock over the river. And then it seemed as if there was a new voice. He listened, puzzled, for it was not his own. Soon he was leaning forward, all his nerves alert, quite still: somewhere close to him there was a noise that was no joyful bird, nor tinkle of falling water, nor ponderous movement of cattle.

There it was again. In the deep morning hush that held his future and his past, was a sound of pain, and repeated over and over: it was a kind of shortened scream, as if someone, something, had no breath to scream. He came to himself, looked about him, and called for the dogs. They did not appear: they had gone off on their own business, and he was alone. Now he was clean sober, all the madness gone. His heart beating fast, because of that frightened screaming, he stepped carefully off the rock and went towards a belt of trees. He was moving cautiously, for not so long ago he had seen a leopard in just this spot.

At the edge of the trees he stopped and peered, holding his gun ready; he advanced, looking steadily about him, his eyes narrowed. Then, all at once, in the middle of a step, he faltered, and his face was puzzled. He shook his head impatiently, as if he doubted his own sight.

There, between two trees, against a background of gaunt black rocks, was a figure from a dream, a strange beast that was horned and drunken-legged, but like something he had never even imagined. It seemed to be ragged. It looked like a small buck that had black ragged tufts of fur standing up irregularly all over it, with patches of raw flesh beneath . . . but the patches of rawness were disappearing under moving black and came again elsewhere; and all the time the creature screamed, in small gasping screams, and leaped drunkenly from side to side, as if it were blind.

Then the boy understood: it *was* a buck. He ran closer, and again stood still, stopped by a new fear. Around him the grass was whispering and alive. He looked wildly about, and then down. The ground was black with ants, great energetic ants that took no notice of him, but hurried and scurried towards the fighting shape, like glistening black water flowing through the grass.

And, as he drew in his breath and pity and terror seized him, the beast fell and the screaming stopped. Now he could hear nothing but one bird singing, and the sound of the rustling, whispering ants.

He peered over at the writhing blackness that jerked convulsively with the jerking nerves. It grew quieter. There were small twitches from the mass that still looked vaguely like the shape of a small animal.

It came into his mind that he should shoot it and end its pain; and he raised the gun. Then he lowered it again. The buck could no longer feel; its fighting was a mechanical protest of the nerves. But it was not that which made him put down the gun. It was a swelling feeling of rage and misery and protest that expressed itself in the thought: if I had not come it would have died like this: so why should I interfere? All over the bush things like this happen; they happen all the time; this is how life goes on, by living things dying in anguish. He gripped the gun between his knees and felt in his own limbs the myriad swarming pain of the twitching animal that could no longer feel, and set his teeth, and said over and over again under his breath: I can't stop it. I can't stop it. There is nothing I can do.

He was glad that the buck was unconscious and had gone past suffering so that he did not have to make a decision to kill it even when he was feeling with his whole body: this is what happens, this is how things work.

It was right—that was what he was feeling. *It was right and nothing could alter it.*

The knowledge of fatality, of what has to be, had gripped him and for the first time in his life; and he was left unable to make any movement of brain or body, except to say: "Yes, yes. That is what living is." It had entered his flesh and his bones and grown in to the furthest corners of his brain and would never leave him. And at that moment he could not have performed the smallest action of mercy, knowing as he did, having lived on it all his life, the vast unalterable, cruel veld, where at any moment one might stumble over a skull or crush the skeleton of some small creature.

Suffering, sick, and angry, but also grimly satisfied with his new stoicism, he stood there leaning on his rifle, and watched the seething black mound grow smaller. At his feet, now, were ants trickling back with pink fragments in their mouths, and there was a fresh acid smell in his nostrils. He sternly controlled the uselessly convulsing muscles of his empty stomach, and reminded himself: the ants must eat too! At the same time he found that the tears were streaming down his face, and his clothes were soaked with the sweat of that other creature's pain.

The shape had grown small. Now it looked like nothing recognisable. He did not know how long it was before he saw the blackness thin, and bits of white showed through, shining in the sun—yes, there was the sun, just up, glowing over the rocks. Why, the whole thing could not have taken longer than a few minutes.

He began to swear, as if the shortness of the time was in itself unbearable, using the words he had heard his father say. He strode forward, crushing ants with each step, and brushing them off his clothes, till he stood above the skeleton, which lay sprawled under a small bush. It was clean-picked. It might have been lying there years, save that on the white bone were pink fragments of gristle. About the bones ants were ebbing away, their pincers full of meat.

The boy looked at them, big black ugly insects. A few were standing and gazing up at him with small glittering eyes.

"Go away!" he said to the ants, very coldly. "I am not for you—not just yet, at any rate. Go away." And he fancied that the ants turned and went away.

He bent over the bones and touched the sockets in the skull; that was where the eyes were, he thought incredulously, remembering the liquid dark eyes of a buck. And then he bent the slim foreleg bone, swinging it horizontally in his palm.

That morning, perhaps an hour ago, this small creature had been stepping proud and free through the bush, feeling the chill on its hide even as he himself had done, exhilarated by it. Proudly stepping the earth, tossing its horns, frisking a pretty white tail, it had sniffed the cold morning air. Walking like kings and conquerors it had moved throug this free-held bush, where each blade of grass grew for it alone, and where the river ran pure sparkling water for its slaking.

And then—what had happened? Such a swift surefooted thing could surely not be trapped by a swarm of ants?

The boy bent curiously to the skeleton. Then he saw that the back leg that lay uppermost and strained out in the tension of death, was snapped midway in the thigh, so that broken bones jutted over each other uselessly. So that was it! Limping into the ant-masses it could not escape, once it had sensed the danger. Yes, but how had the leg been broken? Had it fallen, perhaps? Impossible, a buck was too light and graceful. Had some jealous rival horned it?

What could possibly have happened? Perhaps some Africans had thrown stones at it, as they do, trying to kill it for meat, and had broken its leg. Yes, that must be it.

Even as he imagined the crowd of running, shouting natives, and the flying stones, and the leaping buck, another picture came into his mind. He saw himself, on any one of these bright ringing mornings, drunk with excitement, taking a snap shot at some half-seen buck. He saw himself with the gun lowered, wondering whether he had missed or not; and thinking at last that it was late, and he wanted his breakfast, and it was not worth while to track miles after an animal that would very likely get away from him in any case.

For a moment he would not face it. He was a small boy again, kicking sulkily at the skeleton, hanging his head, refusing to accept the responsibility.

Then he straightened up, and looked down at the bones with an odd expression of dismay, all the anger gone out of him. His mind went quite empty: all around him he could see trickles of ants disappearing into the grass. The whispering noise was faint and dry, like the rustling of a cast snakeskin.

At last he picked up his gun and walked homewards. He was telling himself half defiantly that he wanted his breakfast. He was telling himself that it was getting very hot, much too hot to be out roaming the bush.

Really, he was tired. He walked heavily, not looking where he put his feet. When he came within sight of his home he stopped, knitting his brows. There was something he had to think out. The death of that small animal was a thing that concerned him, and he was by no means finished with it. It lay at the back of his mind uncomfortably.

Soon, the very next morning, he would get clear of everybody and go to the bush and think about it.

JAMES BALDWIN
1924–

James Jones was born in Harlem Hospital, New York City. Three years later his mother married David Baldwin, a laborer and storefront preacher. David Baldwin lived until 1943, adding eight children to the family. James Baldwin went to Frederick Douglass Junior High School in Harlem, where he edited the school magazine,, and then to De Witt Clinton High School in the Bronx, where he edited their literary magazine, *The Magpie*. After a religious experience when he was sixteen, he preached at Fireside Pentecostal Assembly for several years. Upon graduation from high school he worked in New Jersey, where he first experienced the force of white racism. He moved to Greenwich Village in 1943 and began publishing his writing with the encouragement of Richard Wright. In 1948 he moved to Europe, living in Paris, Switzerland, and the south of France for ten years, writing and struggling with his racial and sexual identity. His first novel, *Go Tell It On the Mountain*, appeared in 1953. In 1957 he returned to the

United States to live. In the years since then he has become a major spokesman for black Americans and has written eloquently about sexual and racial matters. His long essay *The Fire Next Time* (1963) is a major document of the civil rights movement.

Sonny's Blues

I read about it in the paper, in the subway, on my way to work. I read it, and I couldn't believe it, and I read it again. Then perhaps I just stared at it, at the newsprint spelling out his name, spelling out the story. I stared at it in the swinging lights of the subway car, and in the faces and bodies of the people, and in my own face, trapped in the darkness which roared outside.

It was not to be believed, and I kept telling myself that as I walked from the subway station to the high school. And at the same time I couldn't doubt it. I was scared, scared for Sonny. He became real to me again. A great block of ice got settled in my belly and kept melting there slowly all day long, while I taught my classes algebra. It was a special kind of ice. It kept melting, sending trickles of ice water all up and down my veins, but it never got less. Sometimes it hardened and seemed to expand until I felt my guts were going to come spilling out or that I was going to choke or scream. This would always be at a moment when I was remembering some specific thing Sonny had once said or done.

When he was about as old as the boys in my classes, his face had been bright and open, there was a lot of copper in it; and he'd had wonderfully direct brown eyes, and great gentleness and privacy. I wondered what he looked like now. He had been picked up, the evening before, in a raid on an apartment downtown, for peddling and using heroin.

I couldn't believe it: but what I mean by that is that I couldn't find any room for it anywhere inside me. I had kept it outside me for a long time. I hadn't wanted to know. I had had suspicions, but I didn't name them, I kept putting them away. I told myself that Sonny was wild, but he wasn't crazy. And he'd always been a good boy, he hadn't ever turned hard or evil or disrespectful, the way kids can, so quick, so quick, especially in Harlem. I didn't want to believe that I'd ever see my brother going down, coming to nothing, all that light in his face gone out, in the condition I'd already seen so many others. Yet it had happened and here I was, talking about algebra to a lot of boys who might, every one of them for all I knew, be popping off needles every time they went to the head. Maybe it did more for them than algebra could.

I was sure that the first time Sonny had ever had horse, he couldn't have been much older than these boys were now. These boys, now, were living as we'd been living then, they were growing up with a rush and their heads bumped abruptly against the low ceiling of their actual possibilities. They were filled with rage. All they really knew were two darknesses, the darkness of their lives, which was now closing in on them, and the darkness of the movies, which had blinded them to that other darkness, and in which they now, vindictively, dreamed, at once more together than they were at any other time, and more alone.

When the last bell rang, the last class ended, I let out my breath. It seemed I'd been holding it for all that time. My clothes were set—I may have looked as though I'd been sitting in a steam bath, all dressed up, all afternoon. I sat alone in the classroom a long time. I listened to the boys outside, downstairs, shouting and cursing and laughing. Their laughter struck me for perhaps the first time. It was not the joyous laughter which—God knows why—one associates with children. It was mocking and insular, its intent was to denigrate. It was disenchanted, and in this, also, lay the authority of their curses. Perhaps I was listening to them because I was thinking about my brother and in them I heard my brother. And myself.

One boy was whistling a tune, at once very complicated and very simple, it seemed to be pouring out of him as though he were a bird, and it sounded very cool and moving through all that harsh, bright air, only just holding its own through all those other sounds.

I stood and walked over to the window and looked down into the courtyard. It was the beginning of the spring, and the sap was rising in the boys. A teacher passed through them every now and again, quickly, as though he or she couldn't wait to get out of that courtyard, to get those boys out of their sight and off their minds. I started collecting my stuff. I thought I'd better get home and talk to Isabel.

The courtyard was almost deserted by the time I got downstairs. I saw this boy standing in the shadow of a doorway, looking just like Sonny. I almost called his name. Then I saw that it wasn't Sonny, but somebody we used to know, a boy from around our block. He'd been Sonny's friend. He'd never been mine, having been too young for me, and, anyway, I'd never liked him. And now, even though he was a grown-up man, he still hung around that block, still spent hours on the street corner, was always high and raggy. I used to run into him from time to time, and he'd often work around to asking me for a quarter or fifty cents. He always had some real good excuse, too, and I always gave it to him, I don't know why.

But now, abruptly, I hated him. I couldn't stand the way he looked at me, partly like a dog, partly like a cunning child. I wanted to ask him what the hell he was doing in the school courtyard.

He sort of shuffled over to me, and he said, "I see you got the papers. So you already know about it."

"You mean about Sonny? Yes, I already know about it. How come they didn't get you?"

He grinned. It made him repulsive and it also brought to mind what he'd looked like as a kid. "I wasn't there. I stay away from them people."

"Good for you." I offered him a cigarette and I watched him through the smoke. "You come all the way down here just to tell me about Sonny?"

"That's right." He was sort of shaking his head and his eyes looked strange, as though they were about to cross. The bright sun deadened his damp dark brown skin and it made his eyes look yellow and showed up the dirt in his conked hair. He smelled funky. I moved a little away from him and I said, "Well, thanks. But I already know about it and I got to get home."

"I'll walk you a little ways," he said. We started walking. There were a couple of kids still loitering in the courtyard and one of them said good night to me and looked strangely at the boy beside me.

"What're you going to do?" he asked me. "I mean, about Sonny?"

"Look. I haven't seen Sonny for over a year, I'm not sure I'm going to do anything. Anyway, what the hell can I do?"

"That's right," he said quickly, "ain't nothing you can do. Can't much help old Sonny no more, I guess."

It was what I was thinking and so it seemed to me he had no right to say it.

"I'm surprised at Sonny, though," he went on—he had a funny way of talking, he looked straight ahead as though he were talking to himself—"I thought Sonny was a smart boy, I thought he was too smart to get hung."

"I guess he thought so, too," I said sharply, "and that's how he got hung. And how about you? You're pretty goddamn smart, I bet."

Then he looked directly at me, just for a minute. "I ain't smart," he said. "If I was smart, I'd have reached for a pistol a long time ago."

"Look. Don't tell *me* your sad story, if it was up to me, I'd give you one." Then I felt guilty—guilty probably, for never having supposed that the poor bastard *had* a story of his own, much less a sad one, and I asked, quickly, "What's going to happen to him now?"

He didn't answer this. He was off by himself someplace. "Funny thing," he said, and from his tone we might have been discussing the quickest way to get to Brooklyn, "when I saw the papers this morning, the first thing I asked myself was if I had anything to do with it. I felt sort of responsible."

I began to listen more carefully. The subway station was on the corner, just before us, and I stopped. He stopped, too. We were in front of a bar and he ducked slightly, peering in, but whoever he was looking for didn't seem to be there. The juke box was blasting away with something black and bouncy, and I half watched the barmaid as she danced her way from the juke box to her place behind the bar. And I watched her face as she laughingly responded to something someone said to her, still keeping time to the music. When she smiled one saw the little girl, one sensed the doomed, still-struggling woman beneath the battered face of the semi-whore.

"I never *give* Sonny nothing," the boy said finally, "but a long time ago I come to school high and Sonny asked me how it felt." He paused, I couldn't bear to watch him, I watched the barmaid, and I listened to the music which seemed to be causing the pavement to shake. "I told him it felt great." The music stopped, the barmaid paused and watched the juke box until the music began again. "It did."

All this was carrying me someplace I didn't want to go. I certainly didn't want to know how it felt. It filled everything, the people, the houses, the music, the dark, quick-silver barmaid, with menace; and this menace was their reality.

"What's going to happen to him now?" I asked again.

"They'll send him away someplace and they'll try to cure him." He shook his head. "Maybe he'll even think he's kicked the habit. Then they'll let him loose"—He gestured, throwing his cigarette into the gutter. "That's all."

"What do you mean, that's *all?*"

But I knew what he meant.

"I *mean*, that's *all*." He turned his head and looked at me, pulling down the corners of his mouth. "Don't you know what I mean?" he asked, softly.

"How the hell *would* I know what you mean?" I almost whispered it, I don't know why.

"That's right," he said to the air, "how would *he* know what I mean?" He turned toward me again, patient and calm, and yet I somehow felt him shaking, shaking as though he were going to fall apart. I felt that ice in my guts again, the dread I'd felt all afternoon; and again I watched the barmaid, moving about the bar, washing glasses, and singing. "Listen. They'll let him out and then it'll just start over again. That's what I mean."

"You mean—they'll let him out. And then he'll just start working his way back in again. You mean he'll never kick the habit. Is that what you mean?"

"That's right," he said, cheerfully. "*You* see what I mean."

"Tell me," I said at last, "why does he want to die? He must want to die, he's killing himself, why does he want to die?"

He looked at me in surprise. He licked his lips. "He don't want to die. He wants to live. Don't nobody want to die, ever."

Then I wanted to ask him—too many things. He could not have answered, or if he had, I could not have borne the answers. I started walking. "Well, I guess it's none of my business."

"It's going to be rough on old Sonny," he said. We reached the subway station. "This is your station?" he asked. I nodded. I took one step down. "Damn!" he said, suddenly. I looked up at him. He grinned again. "Damn if I didn't leave all my money home. You ain't got a dollar on you, have you? Just for a couple of days, is all."

All at once something inside gave and threatened to come pouring out of me. I didn't hate him any more. I felt that in another moment I'd start crying like a child.

"Sure," I said. "Don't sweat." I looked in my wallet and didn't have a dollar, I only had a five. "Here," I said. "That hold you?"

He didn't look at it—he didn't want to look at it. A terrible, closed look came over his face, as though he were keeping the number on the bill a secret from him and me. "Thanks," he said, and now he was dying to see me go. "Don't worry about Sonny. Maybe I'll write him or something."

"Sure," I said. "You do that. So long."

"Be seeing you," he said. I went on down the steps.

And I didn't write Sonny or send him anything for a long time. When I finally did, it was just after my little girl died, he wrote me back a letter which made me feel like a bastard.

Here's what he said:

Dear brother,
    You don't know how much I needed to hear from you. I wanted to write you many a time but I dug how much I must have hurt you and so I didn't write. But now I feel like a man who's been trying to climb up out of some deep, real deep and funky hole and just saw the sun up there, outside. I got to get outside.
    I can't tell you much about how I got here. I mean I don't know how to tell you. I guess I was afraid of something or I was trying to escape from something and you know I have never been very strong in the head (smile). I'm glad Mama and Daddy are dead and can't see what's happened to their son and I swear if I'd known what I was doing I would never have hurt you so, you and a lot of other fine people who were nice to me and who believed in me.
    I don't want you to think it had anything to do with me being a

musician. It's more than that. Or maybe less than that. I can't get anything straight in my head down here and I try not to think about what's going to happen to me when I get outside again. Sometimes I think I'm going to flip and *never* get outside and sometime I think I'll come straight back. I tell you one thing, though, I'd rather blow my brains out than go through this again. But that's what they all say, so they tell me. If I tell you when I'm coming to New York and if you could meet me, I sure would appreciate it. Give my love to Isabel and the kids and I was sure sorry to hear about little Gracie. I wish I could be like Mama and say the Lord's will be done, but I don't know it seems to me that trouble is the one thing that never does get stopped and I don't know what good it does to blame it on the Lord. But maybe it does some good if you believe it.

Your brother,
SONNY

Then I kept in constant touch with him and I sent him whatever I could and I went to meet him when he came back to New York. When I saw him, many things I thought I had forgotten came flooding back to me. This was because I had begun, finally, to wonder about Sonny, about the life that Sonny lived inside. This life, whatever it was, had made him older and thinner and it had deepened the distant stillness in which he had always moved. He looked very unlike my baby brother. Yet, when he smiled, when we shook hands, the baby brother I'd never known looked out from the depths of his private life, like an animal waiting to be coaxed into the light.

"How you been keeping?" he asked me.

"All right. And you?"

"Just fine." He was smiling all over his face. "It's good to see you again."

"It's good to see you."

The seven years' difference in our ages lay between us like a chasm: I wondered if these years would ever operate between us as a bridge. I was remembering, and it made it hard to catch my breath, that I had been there when he was born; and I had heard the first words he had ever spoken. When he started to walk, he walked from our mother straight to me. I caught him just before he fell when he took the first steps he ever took in this world.

"How's Isabel?"

"Just fine. She's dying to see you."

"And the boys?"

"They're fine, too. They're anxious to see their uncle."

"Oh, come on. You know they don't remember me."

"Are you kidding? Of course they remember you."

He grinned again. We got into a taxi. We had a lot to say to each other, far too much to know how to begin.

As the taxi began to move, I asked, "You still want to go to India?"

He laughed. "You still remember that. Hell, no. This place is Indian enough for me."

"It used to belong to them," I said.

And he laughed again. "They damn sure knew what they were doing when they got rid of it."

Years ago, when he was around fourteen, he'd been all hipped on the idea of going to India. He read books about people sitting on rocks, naked, in all kinds of weather, but mostly bad, naturally, and walking barefoot through hot coals and arriving at wisdom. I used to say that it sounded to me as though they were getting away from wisdom as fast as they could. I think he sort of looked down on me for that.

"Do you mind," he asked, "if we have the driver drive alongside the park? On the west side—I haven't seen the city in so long."

"Of course not," I said. I was afraid that I might sound as though I were humoring him, but I hoped he wouldn't take it that way.

So we drove along, between the green of the park and the stony, lifeless elegance of hotels and apartment buildings, toward the vivid, killing streets of our childhood. These streets hadn't changed, though housing projects jutted up out of them now like rocks in the middle of a boiling sea. Most of the houses in which we had grown up had vanished, as had the stores from which we had stolen, the basements in which we had first tried sex, the rooftops from which we had hurled tin cans and bricks. But houses exactly like the houses of our past yet dominated the landscape, boys exactly like the boys we once had been found themselves smothering in these houses, came down into the streets for light and air and found themselves encircled by disaster. Some escaped the trap, most didn't. Those who got out always left something of themselves behind, as some animals amputate a leg and leave it in the trap. It might be said, perhaps, that I had escaped, after all, I was a schoolteacher; or that Sonny had, he hadn't lived in Harlem for years. Yet, as the cab moved uptown through streets which seemed, with a rush, to darken with dark people, and as I covertly studied Sonny's face, it came to me that what we both were seeking through our separate cab windows was that part of ourselves which had been left behind. It's always at the hour of trouble and confrontation that the missing member aches.

We hit 110th Street and started rolling up Lenox Avenue. And I'd known this avenue all my life, but it seemed to me again, as it had seemed on the day I'd first heard about Sonny's trouble, filled with a hidden menace which was its very breath of life.

"We almost there," said Sonny.

"Almost." We were both too nervous to say anything more.

We live in a housing project. It hasn't been up long. A few days after it was up it seemed uninhabitably new, now, of course, it's already rundown. It looked like a parody of the good, clean, faceless life—God knows the people who live in it do their best to make it a parody. The beat-looking grass lying around isn't enough to make their lives green, the hedges will never hold out the streets, and they know it. The big windows fool no one, they aren't big enough to make space out of no space. They don't bother with the windows, they watch the TV screen instead. The playground is most popular with the children who don't play at jacks, or skip rope, or roller skate, or swing, and they can be found in it after dark. We moved in partly because it's not too far from where I teach, and partly for the kids; but it's really just like the houses in which Sonny and I grew up. The same things happen, they'll have the same things to remember. The moment Sonny and I started into the house I had the feeling that I was simply bringing him back into the danger he had almost died trying to escape.

Sonny has never been talkative. So I don't know why I was sure he'd be dying to talk to me when supper was over the first night. Everything went fine, the oldest boy remembered him, and the youngest boy liked him, and Sonny had remembered to bring something for each of them; and Isabel, who is really much nicer than I am, more open and giving, had gone to a lot of trouble about dinner and was genuinely glad to see him. And she'd always been able to tease Sonny in a way that I haven't. It was nice to see her face so vivid again and to hear her laugh and watch her make Sonny laugh. She wasn't, or, anyway, she didn't seem to be, at all uneasy or embarrassed. She chatted as though there were no subject which had to be avoided and she got Sonny past his first, faint stiffness. And thank God she was there, for I was filled with that icy dread again. Everything I did seemed awkward to me, and everything I said sounded freighted with hidden meaning. I was trying to remember everything I'd heard about dope addiction and I couldn't help watching Sonny for signs. I wasn't doing it out of malice. I was trying to find out something about my brother. I was dying to hear him tell me he was safe.

"Safe!" my father grunted, whenever Mama suggested trying to move to a neighborhood which might be safer for children. "Safe, hell! Ain't no place safe for kids, nor nobody."

He always went on like this, but he wasn't, ever, really as bad as he sounded, not even on weekends, when he got drunk. As a matter of fact, he was always on the lookout for "something a little better," but he died before he found it. He died suddenly, during a drunken weekend in the middle of the war, when Sonny was fifteen. He and Sonny hadn't ever got on too well. And this was partly because Sonny was the apple of his father's eye. It was because he loved Sonny so much and was frightened for him, that he was always fighting with him. It doesn't do any good to fight with Sonny. Sonny just moves back, inside himself, where he can't be reached. But the principal reason that they never hit it off is that they were so much alike. Daddy was big and rough and loud-talking, just the opposite of Sonny, but they both had—that same privacy.

Mama tried to tell me something about this, just after Daddy died. I was home on leave from the army.

This was the last time I ever saw my mother alive. Just the same, this picture gets all mixed up in my mind with pictures I had of her when she was younger. The way I always see her is the way she used to be on a Sunday afternoon, say, when the old folks were talking after the big Sunday dinner. I always see her wearing pale blue. She'd be sitting on the sofa. And my father would be sitting in the easy chair, not far from her. And the living room would be full of church folks and relatives. There they sit, in chairs all around the living room, and the night is creeping up outside, but nobody knows it yet. You can see the darkness growing against the windowpanes and you hear the street noises every now and again, or maybe the jangling beat of a tambourine from one of the churches close by, but it's real quiet in the room. For a moment nobody's talking, but every face looks darkening, like the sky outside. And my mother rocks a little from the waist, and my father's eyes are closed. Everyone is looking at something a child can't see. For a minute they've forgotten the children. Maybe a kid is lying on the rug, half asleep. Maybe somebody's got a kid in his lap and is absent-mindedly stroking the kid's head. Maybe there's a kid, quiet and big-eyed, curled up in a big chair in the corner. The silence, the darkness coming, and the darkness in the faces frighten the child obscurely. He hopes that the hand which strokes his forehead will never stop—will never die. He hopes that there will never come a time when the old folks won't be sitting around the living room, talking about where they've come from, and what they've seen, and what's happened to them and their kinfolk.

But something deep and watchful in the child knows that this is bound to end, is already ending. In a moment someone will get up and turn on the light. Then the old folks will remember the children and they won't talk any more that day. And when light fills the room, the child is filled with darkness. He knows that every time this happens he's moved just a little closer to that darkness outside. The darkness outside is what the old folks have been talking about. It's what they've come from. It's what they endure. The child knows that they won't talk any more because if he knows too much about what's happened to *them*, he'll know too much too soon, about what's going to happen to *him*.

The last time I talked to my mother, I remember I was restless. I wanted to get out and see Isabel. We weren't married then and we had a lot to straighten out between us.

There Mama sat, in black, by the window. She was humming an old church song, *Lord, you brought me from a long ways off*. Sonny was out somewhere. Mama kept watching the streets.

"I don't know," she said, "If I'll ever see you again, after you go off from here. But I hope you'll remember the things I tried to teach you."

"Don't talk like that," I said, and smiled. "You'll be here a long time yet."

She smiled, too, but she said nothing. She was quiet for a long time. And I said, "Mama, don't you worry about nothing. I'll be writing all the time, and you be getting the checks. . . ."

"I want to talk to you about your brother," she said, suddenly. "If anything happens to me, he ain't going to have nobody to look out for him."

"Mama," I said, "ain't nothing going to happen to you *or* Sonny. Sonny's all right. He's a good boy and he's got good sense."

"It ain't a question of his being a good boy," Mama said, "nor of his having good sense. It ain't only the bad ones, nor yet the dumb ones that gets sucked under." She stopped, looking at me. "Your Daddy once had a brother," she said, and she smiled in a way that made me feel she was in pain. "You didn't never know that, did you?"

"No," I said. "I never knew that," and I watched her face.

"Oh, yes," she said, "your Daddy had a brother." She looked out of the window again. "I know you never saw your Daddy cry. But *I* did—many a time, through all these years."

I asked her, "What happened to his brother? How come nobody's ever talked about him?"

This was the first time I ever saw my mother look old.

"His brother got killed," she said, "when he was just a little younger than you are now. I knew him. He was a fine boy. He was maybe a little full of the devil, but he didn't mean nobody no harm."

Then she stopped, and the room was silent, exactly as it had sometimes been on those Sunday afternoons. Mama kept looking out into the streets.

"He used to have a job in the mill," she said, "and, like all young folks, he just liked to perform on Saturday nights. Saturday nights, him and your father would drift around to different places, go to dances and things like that, or just sit around with people they knew, and your father's brother would sing, he had a fine voice, and play along with himself on his guitar. Well, this particular Saturday night, him and your father was coming home from some place, and they were both a little drunk and there was a moon that night, it was bright like day. Your father's brother was feeling kind of good, and he was whistling to himself, and he had his guitar slung over his shoulder. They was coming down a hill, and beneath them was a road that turned off from the highway. Well, your father's brother, being always kind of frisky, decided to run down this hill, and he did, with that guitar banging and clanging behind him, and he ran across the road, and he was making water behind a tree. And your father was sort of amused at him and he was still coming down the hill, kind of slow. Then he heard a car motor and that same minute his brother stepped from behind the tree, into the road, in the moonlight. And he started to cross the road. And your father started to run down the hill, he says he don't know why. This car was full of white men. They was all drunk, and when they seen your father's brother they let out a great whoop and holler and they aimed the car straight at him. They was having fun, they just wanted to scare him, the way they do sometimes, you know. But they was drunk. And I guess the boy, being drunk, too, and scared, kind of lost his head. By the time he jumped it was too late. Your father says he heard his brother scream when the car rolled over him, and he heard the wood of that guitar when it give, and he heard them strings go flying, and he heard them white men shouting, and the car kept on a-going and it ain't stopped till this day. And, time your father got down the hill, his brother weren't nothing but blood and pulp."

Tears were gleaming on my mother's face. There wasn't anything I could say.

"He never mentioned it," she said, "because I never let him mention it before you children. Your Daddy was like a crazy man that night and for many a night thereafter. He says he never in his life seen anything as dark as that road after the lights of that car had gone away. Weren't nothing, weren't nobody on that road, just your Daddy and his brother and that busted guitar. Oh, yes. Your Daddy never did really get right again. Till the day he died he weren't sure but that every white man he saw was the man that killed his brother."

She stopped and took out her handkerchief and dried her eyes and looked at me.

"I ain't telling you all this," she said, "to make you scared or bitter or to make you hate nobody. I'm telling you this because you got a brother. And the world ain't changed."

I guess I didn't want to believe this. I guess she saw this in my face. She turned away from me, toward the window again, searching those streets.

"But I praise my Redeemer," she said at last, "that he called your Daddy home before me. I ain't saying it to throw no flowers at myself, but, I declare, it keeps me from feeling too cast down to know I helped your father get safely through this world. Your father always acted like he was the roughest, strongest man on earth. And everybody took him to be like that. But if he hadn't had *me* there—to see his tears!"

She was crying again. Still, I couldn't move. I said, "Lord, Lord, Mama, I didn't know it was like that."

"Oh, honey," she said, "there's a lot that you don't know. But you are going to find it out." She stood up from the window and came over to me. "You got to hold on to your brother," she said, "and don't let him fall, no matter what it looks like is happening to him and no matter how evil you gets with him. You going to be evil with him many a time. But don't you forget what I told you, you hear?"

"I won't forget," I said. "Don't you worry, I won't forget. I won't let nothing happen to Sonny."

My mother smiled as though she were amused at something she saw in my face. Then, "You may not be able to stop nothing from happening. But you got to let him know you's *there*."

Two days later I was married, and then I was gone. And I had a lot of things on my mind and I pretty well forgot my promise to Mama until I got shipped home on a special furlough for her funeral.

And, after the funeral, with just Sonny and me alone in the empty kitchen, I tried to find out something about him.

"What do you want to do?" I asked him.

"I'm going to be a musician," he said.

For he had graduated, in the time I had been away, from dancing to the juke box to finding out who was playing what, and what they were doing with it, and he had bought himself a set of drums.

"You mean, you want to be a drummer?" I somehow had the feeling that being a drummer might be all right for other people but not for my brother Sonny.

"I don't think," he said, looking at me very gravely, "that I'll ever be a good drummer. But I think I can play a piano."

I frowned. I'd never played the role of the older brother quite so seriously before, had scarcely ever, in fact, *asked* Sonny a damn thing. I sensed myself in the presence of something I didn't really know how to handle, didn't understand. So I made my frown a little deeper as I asked: "What kind of musician do you want to be?"

He grinned. "How many kinds do you think there are?"

"Be *serious*," I said.

He laughed, throwing his head back, and then looked at me. "I *am* serious."

"Well, then, for Christ's sake, stop kidding around and answer a serious question. I mean, do you want to be a concert pianist, you want to play classical music and all that, or—or, what?" Long before I finished he was laughing again. "For Christ's *sake*, Sonny!"

He sobered, but with difficulty. "I'm sorry. But you sound so— *scared!*" And he was off again.

"Well, you may think it's funny now, baby, but it's not going to be so funny when you have to make your living at it, let me tell you *that*." I was furious because I knew he was laughing at me and I didn't know why.

"No," he said, very sober now, and afraid, perhaps, that he'd hurt me, "I don't want to be a classical pianist. That isn't what interests me. I mean"—he paused, looking hard at me, as though his eyes would help me to understand, and then gestured helplessly, as though perhaps his hand would help—"I mean, I'll have a lot of studying to do, and I'll have to study *everything*, but I mean, I want to play *with*—jazz musicians." He stopped. "I want to play jazz," he said.

Well, the word had never before sounded as heavy, as real, as it sounded that afternoon in Sonny's mouth. I just looked at him and I was probably frowning a real frown by this time. I simply couldn't see why on earth he'd want to spend his time hanging around night clubs, clowning around on bandstands, while people pushed each other around a dance floor. It seemed—beneath him, somehow. I had never thought about it before, had never been forced to, but I suppose I had always put jazz musicians in a class with what Daddy called "good-time people."

"Are you *serious?*"

"Hell, *yes*, I'm serious."

He looked more helpless than ever, and annoyed, and deeply hurt.

I suggested, helpfully: "You mean—like Louis Armstrong?"

His face closed as though I'd struck him. "No. I'm not talking about none of that old-time, down home crap."

"Well, look, Sonny, I'm sorry, don't get mad. I just don't altogether get it, that's all. Name somebody—you know, a jazz musician you admire."

"Bird."

"Who?"

"Bird! Charlie Parker! Don't they teach you nothing in the goddamn army?"

I lit a cigarette. I was surprised and then a little amused to discover that I was trembling. "I've been out of touch," I said. "You'll have to be patient with me. Now. Who's this Parker character?"

"He's just one of the greatest jazz musicians alive," said Sonny, sullenly, his hands in his pockets, his back to me. "Maybe *the* greatest," he added, bitterly, "that's probably why *you* never heard of him."

"All right," I said, "I'm ignorant. I'm sorry. I'll go out and buy all the cat's records right away, all right?"

"It don't," said Sonny, with dignity, "make any difference to me. I don't care what you listen to. Don't do me no favors."

I was beginning to realize that I'd never seen him so upset before. With another part of my mind I was thinking that this would probably turn out to be one of those things kids go through and that I shouldn't make it seem important by pushing it too hard. Still, I didn't think it would do any harm to ask: "Doesn't all this take a lot of time? Can you make a living at it?"

He turned back to me and half leaned, half sat, on the kitchen table. "Everything takes time," he said, "and—well, yes, sure, I can make a living at it. But what I don't seem to be able to make you understand is that it's the only thing I want to do."

"Well, Sonny," I said gently, "you know people can't always do exactly what they want to do—"

"*No*, I don't know that," said Sonny, surprising me. "I think people *ought* to do what they want to do, what else are they alive for?"

"You getting to be a big boy," I said desperately, "it's time you started thinking about your future."

"I'm thinking about my future," said Sonny, grimly. "I think about it all the time."

I gave up. I decided, if he didn't change his mind, that we could always talk about it later. "In the meantime," I said, "you got to finish school." We had already decided that he'd have to move in with Isabel and her folks. I knew this wasn't the ideal arrangement because Isabel's folks are inclined to be dicty and they hadn't especially wanted Isabel to marry me. But I didn't know what else to do. "And we have to get you fixed up at Isabel's."

There was a long silence. He moved from the kitchen table to the window. "That's a terrible idea. You know it yourself."

"Do you have a *better* idea?"

He just walked up and down the kitchen for a minute. He was as tall as I was. He had started to shave. I suddenly had the feeling that I didn't know him at all.

He stopped at the kitchen table and picked up my cigarettes. Looking at me with a kind of mocking, amused defiance, he put one between his lips. "You mind?"

"You smoking already?"

He lit the cigarette and nodded, watching me through the smoke. "I just wanted to see if I'd have the courage to smoke in front of you." He grinned and blew a great cloud of smoke to the ceiling. "It was easy." He looked at my face. "Come on, now. I bet you was smoking at my age, tell the truth."

I didn't say anything but the truth was on my face, and he laughed. But now there was something very strained in his laugh. "Sure. And I bet that ain't all you was doing."

He was frightening me a little. "Cut the crap," I said. "We already decided that you was going to go and live at Isabel's. Now what's got into you all of a sudden?"

"*You* decided it," he pointed out. "*I* didn't decide nothing." he stopped in front of me, leaning against the stove, arms loosely folded. "Look, brother. I don't want to stay in Harlem no more, I really don't." He was very earnest. He looked at me, then over toward the kitchen window. There was something in his eyes I'd never seen before, some thoughtfulness, some worry all his own. He rubbed the muscle of one arm. "It's time I was getting out of here."

"Where do you want to *go*, Sonny?"

"I want to join the army. Or the navy, I don't care. If I say I'm old enough, they'll believe me."

Then I got mad. It was because I was so scared. "You must be crazy. You goddamn fool, what the hell do you want to go and join the *army* for?"

"I just told you. To get out of Harlem."

"Sonny, you haven't even finished *school*. And if you really want to be a musician, how do you expect to study if you're in the *army?*"

He looked at me, trapped, and in anguish. "There's ways. I might be able to work out some kind of deal. Anyway, I'll have the G.I. Bill when I come out."

"*If* you come out." We stared at each other. "Sonny, please. Be reasonable. I know the setup is far from perfect. But we got to do the best we can."

"I ain't learning nothing in school," he said. "Even when I go." He turned away from me and opened the window and threw his cigarette out into the narrow alley. I watched his back. "At least, I ain't learning nothing you'd want me to learn." He slammed the window so hard I thought the glass would fly out, and turned back to me. "And I'm sick of the stink of these garbage cans!"

"Sonny, I said, "I know how you feel. But if you don't finish school now, you're going to be sorry later that you didn't." I grabbed him by the shoulders. "And you only got another year. It ain't so bad. And I'll come back and I swear I'll help you do *whatever* you want to do. Just try to put up with it till I come back. Will you please do that? For me?"

He didn't answer and he wouldn't look at me.

"Sonny. You hear me?"

He pulled away. "I hear you. But you never hear anything *I* say."

I didn't know what to say to that. He looked out of the window and then back at me. "OK," he said, and sighed. "I'll try."

Then I said, trying to cheer him up a little, "They got a piano at Isabel's. You can practice on it."

And as a matter of fact, it did cheer him up for a minute. "That's right," he said to himself. "I forgot that." His face relaxed a little. But the worry, the thoughtfulness, played on it still, the way shadows play on a face which is staring into the fire.

But I thought I'd never hear the end of that piano. At first, Isabel would write me, saying how nice it was that Sonny was so serious about his music and how, as soon as he came in from school, or wherever he had been when he was supposed to be at school, he went straight to that piano and stayed there until suppertime. And, after supper, he went back to that piano and stayed there until everybody went to bed. He was at that piano all day Saturday and all day Sunday. Then he bought a record player and started playing records. He'd play one record over and over again, all day long sometimes, and he'd improvise along with it on the piano. Or he'd play one section of the record, one chord, one change, one progression, then he'd do it on the piano. Then back to the record. Then back to the piano.

Well, I really don't know how they stood it. Isabel finally confessed that it wasn't like living with a person at all, it was like living with sound. And the sound didn't make any sense to her, didn't make any sense to any of them—naturally. They began, in a way, to be afflicted by this presence that was living in their home. It was as though Sonny were some sort of god, or monster. He moved in an atmosphere which wasn't like theirs at all. They fed him and he ate, he washed himself, he walked in and out of their door; he certainly wasn't nasty or unpleasant or rude, Sonny isn't any of those things; but it was as though he were all wrapped up in some cloud, some fire, some vision all his own; and there wasn't any way to reach him.

At the same time, he wasn't really a man yet, he was still a child, and they had to watch out for him in all kinds of ways. They certainly couldn't throw him out. Neither did they dare to make a great scene about that piano because even they dimly sensed, as I sensed, from so many thousands of miles away, that Sonny was at that piano playing for his life.

But he hadn't been going to school. One day a letter came from the school board, and Isabel's mother got it—there had, apparently, been other letters but Sonny had torn them up. This day, when Sonny came in, Isabel's mother showed him the letter and asked where he'd been spending his time. And she finally got it out of him that he'd been down in Greenwich Village, with musicians and other characters, in a white girl's apartment. And this scared her and she started to scream at him, and what came up, once she began—though she denies it to this day—was what sacrifices they were making to give Sonny a decent home and how little he appreciated it.

Sonny didn't play the piano that day. By evening, Isabel's mother had calmed down but then there was the old man to deal with, and Isabel herself. Isabel says she did her best to be calm but she broke down and started crying. She says she just watched Sonny's face. She could tell, by watching him, what was happening with him. And what was happening was that they penetrated his cloud, they had reached him. Even if their fingers had been a thousand times more gentle than human fingers ever are, he could hardly help feeling that they had stripped him naked and were spitting on that nakedness. For he also had to see that his presence, that music, which was life or death to him, had been torture for them and that they had endured it, not at all for his sake, but only for mine. And Sonny couldn't take that. He can take it a little better today than he could then but he's still not very good at it and, frankly, I don't know anybody who is.

The silence of the next few days must have been louder than the sound of all the music ever played since time began. One morning, before she went to work, Isabel was in his room for something and she suddenly realized that all of his records were gone. And she knew for certain that he was gone. And he was. He went as far as the navy would carry him. He finally sent me a postcard from someplace in Greece, and that was the first I knew that Sonny was still alive. I didn't see him any more until we were both back in New York and the war had long been over.

He was a man by then, of course, but I wasn't willing to see it. He came by the house from time to time, but we fought almost every time we met. I didn't like the way he carried himself, loose and dreamlike all the time, and I didn't like his friends, and his music seemed to be merely an excuse for the life he led. It sounded just that weird and disordered.

Then we had a fight, a pretty awful fight, and I didn't see him for months. By and by I looked him up, where he was living, in a furnished room in the Village, and I tried to make it up. But there were lots of other people in the room, and Sonny just lay on his bed, and he wouldn't come downstairs with me, and he treated these other people as though they were his family and I weren't. So I got mad and then he got mad, and then I told him that he might just as well be dead as live the way he was living. Then he stood up and he told me not to worry about him any more in life, that he *was* dead as far as I was concerned. Then he pushed me to the door, and the other people looked on as though nothing were happening, and he slammed the door behind me. I stood in the hallway, staring at the door. I heard somebody laugh in the room and then the tears came to my eyes. I started down the steps, whistling to keep from crying, I kept whistling to myself, *You going to need me, baby, one of these cold, rainy days.*

I read about Sonny's trouble in the spring. Little Grace died in the fall. She was a beautiful little girl. But she only lived a little over two years. She died of polio and she suffered. She had a slight fever for a couple of days, but it didn't seem like anything and we just kept her in bed. And we would certainly have called the doctor, but the fever dropped, she seemed to be all right. So we thought it had just been a cold. Then, one day, she was up, playing, Isabel was in the kitchen fixing lunch for the two boys when they'd come in from school, and she heard Grace fall down in the living room. When you have a lot of children you don't always start running when one of them falls, unless they start screaming or something. And, this time, Grace was quiet. Yet, Isabel says that when she heard that *thump* and then that silence, something happened in her to make her afraid. And she ran to the living room and there was little Grace on the floor, all twisted up, and the reason she hadn't screamed was that she couldn't get her breath. And when she did scream, it was the worst sound, Isabel says, that she's ever heard in all her life, and she still hears it sometimes in her dreams. Isabel will sometimes wake me up with a low, moaning, strangled sound, and I have to be quick to awaken her and hold her to me and where Isabel is weeping against me seems a mortal wound.

I think I may have written Sonny the very day that little Grace was buried. I was sitting in the living room in the dark, by myself, and I suddenly thought of Sonny. My trouble made his real.

One Saturday afternoon, when Sonny had been living with us, or, anyway, been in our house, for nearly two weeks, I found myself wandering aimlessly about the living room, drinking from a can of beer, and trying to work up the courage to search Sonny's room. He was out, he was usually out whenever I was home, and Isabel had taken the children to see their grandparents. Suddenly I was standing still in front of the living-room window, watching Seventh Avenue. The idea of searching Sonny's room made me still. I scarcely dared to admit to myself what I'd be searching for. I didn't know what I'd do if I found it. Or if I didn't.

On the sidewalk across from me, near the entrance to a barbecue joint, some people were holding an old-fashioned revival meeting. The barbecue cook, wearing a dirty white apron, his conked hair reddish and metallic in the pale sun, and a cigarette between his lips, stood in the doorway, watching them. Kids and older people paused in their errands and stood there, along with some older men and a couple of very tough-looking women who watched everything that happened on the avenue, as though they owned it, or were maybe owned by it. Well, they were watching this, too. The revival was being carried on by three sisters in black, and a brother. All they had were their voices and their Bibles and a tambourine. The brother was testifying and while he testified two of the sisters stood together, seeming to say, Amen, and the third sister walked around with the tambourine outstretched and a couple of people dropped coins into it. Then the brother's testimony ended, and the sister who had been taking up the collection dumped the coins into her palm and transferred them to the pocket of her long black robe. Then she raised both hands, striking the tambourine against the air, and then against one hand, and she started to sing. And the two other sisters and the brother joined in.

It was strange, suddenly, to watch, though I had been seeing these street meetings all my life. So, of course, had everybody else down there. Yet, they paused and watched and listened and I stood still at the window. " 'Tis the old ship of Zion," they sang, and the sister with the tambourine kept a steady, jangling beat, "it has rescued many a thousand!" Not a soul under the sound of their voices was hearing this song for the first time, not one of them had been rescued. Nor had they seen much in the way of rescue work being done around them. Neither did they especially believe in the holiness of the three sisters and the brother, they knew too much about them, knew where they lived, and how. The woman with the tambourine, whose voice dominated the air, whose face was bright with joy, was divided by very little from the woman who stood watching her, a cigarette between her heavy, chapped lips, her hair a cuckoo's nest, her face scarred and swollen from many beatings, and her black eyes glittering like coal. Perhaps they both knew this, which was why, when, as rarely, they addressed each other, they addressed each other as Sister. As the singing filled the air, the watching, listening faces underwent a change, the eyes focusing on something within; the music seemed to soothe a poison out of them; and time seemed, nearly, to fall away from the sullen, belligerent, battered faces, as though they were fleeing back to their first condition, while dreaming of their last. The barbecue cook half shook his head and smiled, and dropped his cigarette and disappeared into his joint. A man fumbled in his pockets for change and stood holding it in his hand impatiently, as though he had just remembered a pressing appointment further up the avenue. He looked furious. Then I saw Sonny, standing on the edge of the crowd. He was carrying a wide, flat notebook with a green cover, and it made him look, from where I was standing, almost like a schoolboy.

The coppery sun brought out the copper in his skin, he was very faintly smiling, standing very still. Then the singing stopped, the tambourine turned into a collection plate again. The furious man dropped in his coins and vanished, so did a couple of the women, and Sonny dropped some change in the plate, looking directly at the woman with a little smile. He started across the avenue, toward the house. He has a slow, loping walk, something like the way Harlem hipsters walk, only he's imposed on this his own half-beat. I had never really noticed it before.

I stayed at the window, both relieved and apprehensive. As Sonny disappeared from my sight, they began singing again. And they were still singing when his key turned in the lock.

"Hey," he said.

"Hey, yourself. You want some beer?"

"No. Well, maybe." But he came up to the window and stood beside me, looking out. "What a warm voice," he said.

They were singing *If I could only hear my mother pray again!*

"Yes," I said, "and she can sure beat that tambourine."

"But what a terrible song," he said, and laughed. He dropped his notebook on the sofa and disappeared into the kitchen. "Where's Isabel and the kids?"

"I think they went to see their grandparents. You hungry?"

"No." He came back into the living room with his can of beer. "You want to come someplace with me tonight?"

I sensed, I don't know how, that I couldn't possibly say no. "Sure. Where?"

He sat down on the sofa and picked up his notebook and started leafing through it. "I'm going to sit in with some fellows in a joint in the Village."

"You mean, you're going to play, tonight?"

"That's right." He took a swallow of his beer and moved back to the window. He gave me a sidelong look. "If you can stand it."

"I'll try," I said.

He smiled to himself, and we both watched as the meeting across the way broke up. The three sisters and the brother, heads bowed, were singing *God be with you till we meet again*. The faces around them were very quiet. Then the song ended. The small crowd dispersed. We watched the three women and the one man walk slowly up the avenue.

"When she was singing before," said Sonny, abruptly, "her voice reminded me for a minute of what heroin feels like sometimes—when it's in your veins. It makes you feel sort of warm and cool at the same time. And distant. And—and sure." He sipped his beer, very deliberately not looking at me. I watched his face. "It makes you feel—in control. Sometimes you've got to have that feeling."

"Do you?" I sat down slowly in the easy chair.

"Sometimes." He went to the sofa and picked up his notebook again. "Some people do."

"In order," I asked, "to play?" And my voice was very ugly, full of contempt and anger.

"Well"—he looked at me with great, troubled eyes, as though, in fact, he hoped his eyes would tell me things he could never otherwise say—"they *think* so. And *if* they think so—!"

"And what do *you* think?" I asked.

He sat on the sofa and put his can of beer on the floor. "I don't know," he said, and I couldn't be sure if he were answering my question or pursuing his thoughts. His face didn't tell me. "It's not so much to *play*. It's to *stand* it, to be able to make it at all. On any level." He frowned and smiled: "In order to keep from shaking to pieces."

"But these friends of yours," I said, "they seem to shake themselves to pieces pretty goddamn fast."

"Maybe." He played with the notebook. And something told me that I should curb my tongue, that Sonny was doing his best to talk, and I should listen. "But of course you only know the ones that've gone to pieces. Some don't—or at least they haven't *yet* and that's just about all *any* of us can say." He paused. "And then there are some who just live, really, in hell, and they know it and they see what's happening and they go right on. I don't know." He sighed, dropped the notebook, folded his arms. "Some guys, you can tell from the way they play, they on something *all* the time. And you can see that, well, it makes something real for them. But of course," he picked up his beer from the floor and sipped it and put the can down again, "they *want* to, too, you've got to see that. Even some of them that say they don't—*some*, not all."

"And what about you?" I asked—I couldn't help it. "What about you? Do *you* want to?"

He stood up and walked to the window and remained silent for a long time. Then he sighed. "Me," he said. Then: "While I was downstairs before, on my way here, listening to that woman sing, it struck me all of a sudden how much suffering she must have had to go through—to sing like that. It's *repulsive* to think you have to suffer that much."

I said: "But there's no way not to suffer—is there, Sonny?"

"I believe not," he said, and smiled, "but that's never stopped anyone from trying." He looked at me. "Has it?" I realized, with this mocking look, that there stood between us, forever, beyond the power of time or forgiveness, the fact that I had held silence—so long!—when he had needed human speech to help him. He turned back to the window. "No, there's no way not to suffer. But you try all kinds of ways to keep from drowning in it, to keep on top of it, and to make it seem—well, like *you*. Like you did something, all right, and now you're suffering for it. You know?" I said nothing. "Well you know," he said, impatiently, "why *do* people suffer? Maybe it's better to do something to give it a reason, *any* reason."

"But we just agreed," I said, "that there's no way not to suffer. Isn't it better, then, just to—take it?"

"But nobody just takes it," Sonny cried, "that's what I'm telling you! *Everybody* tries not to. You're just hung up on the *way* some people try—it's not *your* way!"

The hair on my face began to itch, my face felt wet. "That's not true," I said, "that's not true. I don't give a damn what other people do, I don't even care how they suffer. I just care how *you* suffer." And he looked at me. "Please believe me," I said, "I don't want to see you—die—trying not to suffer."

"I won't," he said, flatly, "die trying not to suffer. At least, not any faster than anybody else."

"But there's no need," I said, trying to laugh, "is there, in killing yourself?"

I wanted to say more, but I couldn't. I wanted to talk about will power and how life could be—well, beautiful. I wanted to say that it was all within; but was it? Or, rather, wasn't that exactly the trouble? And I wanted to promise that I would never fail him again. But it would all have sounded—empty words and lies.

So I made the promise to myself and prayed that I would keep it.

"It's terrible sometimes, inside," he said, "that's what's the trouble. You walk these streets, black and funky and cold, and there's not really a living ass to talk to, and there's nothing shaking, and there's no way of getting it out—that storm inside. You can't talk it and you can't make love with it, and when you finally try to get with it and play it, you realize *nobody's* listening. So *you've* got to listen. You got to find a way to listen."

And then he walked away from the window and sat on the sofa again, as though all the wind had suddenly been knocked out of him. "Sometimes you'll do *anything* to play, even cut your mother's throat." He laughed and looked at me. "Or your brother's." Then he sobered "Or your own." Then: "Don't worry. I'm all right now and I think I'll *be* all right. But I can't forget—where I've been. I don't mean just the physical place I've been, I mean where I've *been*. And *what* I've been."

"What have you been, Sonny?" I asked.

He smiled—but sat sideways on the sofa, his elbow resting on the back, his fingers playing with his mouth and chin, not looking at me. "I've been something I didn't recognize, didn't know I could be. Didn't know anybody could be." He stopped, looking inward, looking helplessly young, looking old. "I'm not talking about it now because I feel *guilty* or anything like that—maybe it would be better if I did. I don't know. Anyway, I can't really talk about it. Not to you, not to anybody." And now he turned and faced me. "Sometimes, you know, and it was actually when I was most out of the world, I felt that I was in it, that I was *with* it, really, and I could play or I didn't really have to *play*, it just came out of me, it was there. And I don't know how I played, thinking about it now, but I know I did awful things, those times, sometimes, to people. Or it wasn't that I *did* anything to them—it was that they weren't real." He picked up the beer can; it was empty; he rolled it between his palms: "And other times—well, I needed a fix, I needed to find a place to lean, I needed to clear a space to *listen*—and I couldn't find it, and I—went crazy, I did terrible things to *me*, I was terrible *for* me." He began pressing the beer can between his hands, I watched the metal begin to give. It glittered, as he played with it, like a knife, and I was afraid he would cut himself, but I said nothing. "Oh well. I can never tell you. I was all by myself at the bottom of something, stinking and sweating and crying and shaking, and I smelled it, you know? *My* stink, and I thought I'd die if I couldn't get away from it and yet, all the same, I knew that everything I was doing was just locking me in with it. And I didn't know," he paused, still flattening the beer can, "I didn't know, I still *don't* know, something kept telling me that maybe it was good to smell your own stink, but I didn't think that *that* was what I'd been trying to do—and—who can stand it?" And he abruptly dropped the ruined beer can, looking at me with a small, still smile, and then rose, walking to the window as though it were the lodestone rock. I watched his face, he watched the avenue. "I couldn't tell you when Mama died—but the reason I wanted to leave Harlem so bad was to get away from drugs. And then, when I ran away, that's what I was running from—really. When I came back, nothing had changed, I hadn't changed, I was just—older." And he stopped, drumming with his fingers on the windowpane. The sun had vanished, soon darkness would fall. I watched his face. "It can come again," he said, almost as though speaking to himself. Then he turned to me. "It can come again," he repeated. "I just want you to know that."

"All right," I said at last. "So it can come again. All right."

He smiled, but the smile was sorrowful. "I had to try to tell you," he said.

"Yes," I said. "I understand that."

"You're my brother," he said, looking straight at me, and not smiling at all.

"Yes," I repeated, "yes. I understand that."

He turned back to the window, looking out. "All that hatred down there," he said, "all that hatred and misery and love. It's a wonder it doesn't blow the avenue apart."

We went to the only night club on a short, dark street, downtown. We squeezed through the narrow, chattering, jam-packed bar to the entrance of the big room, where the bandstand was. And we stood there for a moment, for the lights were very dim in this room and we couldn't see. Then, "Hello, boy," said a voice, and an enormous black man, much older than Sonny or myself, erupted out of all that atmospheric lighting and put an arm around Sonny's shoulder. "I been sitting right here," he said, "waiting for you."

He had a big voice, too, and heads in the darkness turned toward us.

Sonny grinned and pulled a little away, and said, "Creole, this is my brother. I told you about him."

Creole shook my hand. "I'm glad to meet you, son," he said, and it was clear that he was glad to meet me *there*, for Sonny's sake. And he smiled. "You got a real musician in *your* family," and he took his arm from Sonny's shoulder and slapped him, lightly, affectionately, with the back of his hand.

"Well. Now I've heard it all," said a voice behind us. This was another musician, and a friend of Sonny's, a coal-black, cheerful-looking man, built close to the ground. He immediately began confiding to me, at the top of his lungs, the most terrible things about Sonny, his teeth gleaming like a lighthouse and his laugh coming up out of him like the beginning of an earthquake. And it turned out that everyone at the bar knew Sonny, or almost everyone; some were musicians, working there, or nearby, or not working, some were simply hangers-on, and some were there to hear Sonny play. I was introduced to all of them and they were all very polite to me. Yet, it was clear that, for them, I was only Sonny's brother. Here, I was in Sonny's world. Or, rather: his kingdom. Here, it was not even a question that his veins bore royal blood.

They were going to play soon, and Creole installed me, by myself, at a table in a dark corner. Then I watched them, Creole, and the little black man, and Sonny, and the others, while they horsed around, standing just below the bandstand. The light from the bandstand spilled just a little short of them and, watching them laughing and gesturing and moving about, I had the feeling that they, nevertheless, were being most careful not to step into that circle of light too suddenly: that if they moved into the light too suddenly, without thinking, they would perish in flame. Then, while I watched, one of them, the small, black man, moved into the light and crossed the bandstand and started fooling around with his drums. Then—being funny and being, also, extremely ceremonious—Creole took Sonny by the arm and led him to the piano. A woman's voice called Sonny's name, and a few hands started clapping. And Sonny, also being funny and being ceremonious, and so touched, I think, that he could have cried, but neither hiding it nor showing it, riding it like a man, grinned, and put both hands to his heart and bowed from the waist.

Creole then went to the bass fiddle and a lean, very bright-skinned brown man jumped up on the bandstand and picked up his horn. So there they were, and the atmosphere on the bandstand and in the room began to change and tighten. Someone stepped up to the microphone and announced them. Then there were all kinds of murmurs. Some people at the bar shushed others. The waitress ran around, frantically getting in the last orders, guys and chicks got closer to each other, and the lights on the bandstand, on the quartet, turned to a kind of indigo. Then they all looked different there. Creole looked about him for the last time, as though he were making certain that all his chickens were in the coop, and then he—jumped and struck the fiddle. And there they were.

All I know about music is that not many people ever really hear it. And even then, on the rare occasions when something opens within, and the music enters, what we mainly hear, or hear corroborated, are personal, private, vanishing evocations. But the man who creates the music is hearing something else, is dealing with the roar rising from the void and imposing order on it as it hits the air. What is evoked in him, then, is of another order, more terrible because it has no words, and triumphant, too, for that same reason. And his triumph, when he triumphs, is ours. I just watched Sonny's face. His face was troubled, he was working hard, but he wasn't with it. And I had the feeling that, in a way, everyone on the bandstand was waiting for him, both waiting for him and pushing him along. But as I began to watch Creole, I realized that it was Creole who held them all back. He had them on a short rein. Up there, keeping the beat with his whole body, wailing on the fiddle, with his eyes half closed, he was listening to everything, but he was listening to Sonny. He was having a dialogue with Sonny. He wanted Sonny to leave the shore line and strike out for the deep water. He was Sonny's witness that deep water and drowning were not the same thing—he had been there, and he knew. And he wanted Sonny to know. He was waiting for Sonny to do the things on the keys which would let Creole know that Sonny was in the water.

And, while Creole listened, Sonny moved, deep within, exactly like someone in torment. I had never before thought of how awful the relationship must be between the musician and his instrument. He has to fill it, this instrument, with the breath of life, his own. He has to make it do what he wants it to do. And a piano is just a piano. It's made out of so much wood and wires and little hammers and big ones, and ivory. While there's only so much you can do with it, the only way to find this out is to try to try and make it do everything.

And Sonny hadn't been near a piano for over a year. And he wasn't on much better terms with his life, not the life that stretched before him now. He and the piano stammered, started one way, got scared, stopped; started another way, panicked, marked time, started again; then seemed to have found a direction, panicked again, got stuck. And the face I saw on Sonny I'd never seen before. Everything had been burned out of it, and, at the same time, things usually hidden were being burned in, by the fire and fury of the battle which was occurring in him up there.

Yet, watching Creole's face as they neared the end of the first set, I had the feeling that something had happened, something I hadn't heard. Then they finished, there was scattered applause, and then, without an instant's warning, Creole started into something else, it was almost sardonic, it was *Am I Blue*. And, as though he commanded, Sonny began to play. Something began to happen. And Creole let out the reins. The dry, low, black man said something awful on the drums, Creole answered, and the drums talked back. Then the horn insisted, sweet and high, slightly detached perhaps, and Creole listened, commenting now and then, dry, and driving, beautiful and calm and old. Then they all came together again, and Sonny was part of the family again. I could tell this from his face. He seemed to have found, right there beneath his fingers, a damn brand-new piano. It seemed that he couldn't get over it. Then, for a while, just being happy with Sonny, they seemed to be agreeing with him that brand-new pianos certainly were a gas.

Then Creole stepped forward to remind them that what they were playing was the blues. He hit something in all of them, he hit something in me, myself, and the music tightened and deepened, apprehension began to beat the air. Creole began to tell us what the blues were all about. They were not about anything very new. He and his boys up there were keeping it new, at the risk of ruin, destruction, madness, and death, in order to find new ways to make us listen. For, while the tale of how we suffer, and how we are delighted, and how we may triumph is never new, it always must be heard. There isn't any other tale to tell, it's the only light we've got in all this darkness.

And this tale, according to that face, that body, those strong hands on those strings, has another aspect in every country, and a new depth in every generation. Listen, Creole seemed to be saying, listen. Now these are Sonny's blues. He made the little black man on the drums know it, and the bright, brown man on the horn. Creole wasn't trying any longer to get Sonny in the water. He was wishing him Godspeed.

Then he stepped back, very slowly, filling the air with the immense suggestion that Sonny speak for himself.

Then they all gathered around Sonny, and Sonny played. Every now and again one of them seemed to say, Amen. Sonny's fingers filled the air with life, his life. But that life contained so many others. And Sonny went all the way back, he really began with the spare, flat statement of the opening phrase of the song. Then he began to make it his. It was very beautiful because it wasn't hurried and it was no longer a lament. I seemed to hear with what burning he had made it his, with what burning we had yet to make it ours, how we could cease lamenting. Freedom lurked around us and I understood, at last, that he could help us to be free if we would listen, that he would never be free until we did. Yet, there was no battle in his face now. I heard what he had gone through, and would continue to go through until he came to rest in earth. He had made it his: that long line, of which we knew only Mama and Daddy. And he was giving it back, as everything must be given back, so that, passing through death, it can live forever. I saw my mother's face again, and felt, for the first time, how the stones of the road she had walked on must have bruised her feet. I saw the moonlit road where my father's brother died. And it brought something else back to me, and carried me past it. It saw my little girl again and felt Isabel's tears again, and I felt my own tears begin to rise. And I was yet aware that this was only a moment, that the world waited outside, as hungry as a tiger, and that trouble stretched above us, longer than the sky.

Then it was over. Creole and Sonny let out their breath, both soaking wet, and grinning. There was a lot of applause and some of it was real. In the dark, the girl came by and I asked her to take drinks to the bandstand. There was a long pause, while they talked up there in the indigo light and after a while I saw the girl put a Scotch and milk on top of the piano for Sonny. He didn't seem to notice it, but just before they started playing again, he sipped from it and looked toward me, and nodded. Then he put it back on top of the piano. For me, then, as they began to play again, it glowed and shook above my brother's head like the very cup of trembling.

FLANNERY O'CONNOR
1925–1964

Mary Flannery O'Connor was born in Savannah, Georgia. Her parents were Roman Catholics from families that had lived in the south for generations. She went to parochial schools in Savannah. When the girls were taught to sew and told to make clothes for dolls, she made a fancy coat for a pet chicken and brought him to school to show off his new outfit. When she was thirteen her father developed a fatal disease called "disseminated lupus," in which antibodies attack the blood vessels, joints, and internal organs. The family moved to Milledgeville, Georgia, to live with relatives, and Mary went to Peabody High School and Georgia State College for Women. She drew cartoons for the college paper and her yearbook. She also edited the literary magazine and won a fellowship to the Writers Workshop at the University of Iowa. At Iowa she began to publish her fiction, deciding to drop the "Mary" from her name. After receiving her MFA she went to Yaddo, a writers' colony at Saratoga Springs, New York, where she met people who encouraged her and helped her arrange publication for more of her work. In 1950 she was stricken with the disease that had killed her father nine years earlier. She moved to a farm near Milledgeville and continued writing there until her death in 1964, with her reputation growing steadily, even after her death. Most of her fiction can be found in *Collected Stories* (1971), which includes early versions of her two novels.

Everything That Rises Must Converge

Her doctor had told Julian's mother that she must lose twenty pounds on account of her blood pressure, so on Wednesday nights Julian had to take her downtown on the bus for a reducing class at the Y. The reducing class was designed for working girls over fifty, who weighed from 165 to 200 pounds. His mother was one of the slimmer ones, but she said ladies did not tell their age or weight. She would not ride the buses by herself at night since they had been integrated, and because the reducing class was one of her few pleasures, necessary for her health, and *free*, she said Julian could at least put himself out to take her, considering all she did for him. Julian did not like to consider all she did for him, but every Wednesday night he braced himself and took her.

She was almost ready to go, standing before the hall mirror, putting on her hat, while he, his hands behind him, appeared pinned to the door frame, waiting like Saint Sebastian for the arrows to begin piercing him. The hat was new and had cost her seven dollars and a half. She kept saying, "Maybe I shouldn't have paid that for it. No, I shouldn't have. I'll take it off and return it tomorrow. I shouldn't have bought it."

Julian raised his eyes to heaven. "Yes, you should have bought it," he said. "Put it on and let's go." It was a hideous hat. A purple velvet flap came down on one side of it and stood up on the other; the rest of it was green and looked like a cushion with the stuffing out. He decided it was less comical than jaunty and pathetic. Everything that gave her pleasure was small and depressed him.

She lifted the hat one more time and set it down slowly on top of her head. Two wings of gray hair protruded on either side of her florid face, but her eyes, sky-blue, were as innocent and untouched by experience as they must have been when she was ten. Were it not that she was a widow who had struggled fiercely to feed and clothe and put him through school and who was supporting him still, "until he got on his feet," she might have been a little girl that he had to take to town.

"It's all right, it's all right," he said. "Let's go." He opened the door himself and started down the walk to get her going. The sky was a dying violet and the houses stood out darkly against it, bulbous liver-colored monstrosities of a uniform ugliness though no two were alike. Since this had been a fashionable neighborhood forty years ago, his mother persisted in thinking they did well to have an apartment in it. Each house had a narrow collar of dirt around it in which sat, usually, a grubby child. Julian walked with his hands in his pockets, his head down and thrust forward and his eyes glazed with the determination to make himself completely numb during the time he would be sacrificed to her pleasure.

The door closed and he turned to find the dumpy figure, surmounted by the atrocious hat, coming toward him. "Well," she said, "you only live once and paying a little more for it, I at least won't meet myself coming and going."

"Some day I'll start making money," Julian said gloomily—he knew he never would—"and you can have one of those jokes whenever you take the fit." But first they would move. He visualized a place where the nearest neighbors would be three miles away on either side.

"I think you're doing fine," she said, drawing on her gloves. "You've only been out of school a year. Rome wasn't built in a day."

She was one of the few members of the Y reducing class who arrived in hat and gloves and who had a son who had been to college. "It takes time," she said, "and the world is in such a mess. This hat looked better on me than any of the others, though when she brought it out I said, 'Take that thing back. I wouldn't have it on my head,' and she said, 'Now wait till you see it on,' and when she put it on me, I said, 'We-ull,' and she said, 'If you ask me, that hat does something for you and you do something for the hat, and besides,' she said, 'with that hat, you won't meet yourself coming and going.' "

Julian thought he could have stood his lot better if she had been selfish, if she had been an old hag who drank and screamed at him. He walked along, saturated in depression, as if in the midst of his martyrdom he had lost his faith. Catching sight of his long, hopeless, irritated face, she stopped suddenly with a grief-stricken look, and pulled back on his arm. "Wait on me," she said. "I'm going back to the house and take this thing off and tomorrow I'm going to return it. I was out of my head. I can pay the gas bill with the seven-fifty."

He caught her arm in a vicious grip. "You are not going to take it back," he said. "I like it."

"Well," she said, "I don't think I ought . . ."

"Shut up and enjoy it," he muttered, more depressed than ever.

"With the world in the mess it's in," she said, "it's a wonder we can enjoy anything. I tell you, the bottom rail is on the top."

Julian sighed.

"Of course," she said, "if you know who you are, you can go anywhere." She said this every time he took her to the reducing class. "Most of them in it are not our kind of people," she said, "but I can be gracious to anybody. I know who I am."

"They don't give a damn for your graciousness," Julian said savagely. "Knowing who you are is good for one generation only. You haven't the foggiest idea where you stand now or who you are."

She stopped and allowed her eyes to flash at him. "I most certainly do know who I am," she said, "and if you don't know who you are, I'm ashamed of you."

"Oh hell," Julian said.

"Your great-grandfather was a former governor of this state," she said. "Your grandfather was a prosperous landowner. Your grandmother was a Godhigh."

"Will you look around you," he said tensely, "and see where you are now?" and he swept his arm jerkily out to indicate the neighborhood, which the growing darkness at least made less dingy.

"You remain what you are," she said. "Your great-grandfather had a plantation and two hundred slaves."

"There are no more slaves," he said irritably.

"They were better off when they were," she said. He groaned to see that she was off on that topic. She rolled onto it every few days like a train on an open track. He knew every stop, every junction, every swamp along the way, and knew the exact point at which her conclusion would roll majestically into the station: "It's ridiculous. It's simply not realistic. They should rise, yes, but on their own side of the fence."

"Let's skip it," Julian said.

"The ones I feel sorry for," she said, "are the ones that are half white. They're tragic."

"Will you skip it?"

"Suppose we were half white. We would certainly have mixed feelings."

"I have mixed feelings now," he groaned.

"Well let's talk about something pleasant," she said. "I remember going to Grandpa's when I was a little girl. Then the house had double stairways that went up to what was really the second floor—all the cooking was done on the first. I used to like to stay down in the kitchen on account of the way the walls smelled. I would sit with my nose pressed against the plaster and take deep breaths. Actually the place belonged to the Godhighs but your grandfather Chestny paid the mortgage and saved it for them. They were in reduced circumstances," she said, "but reduced or not, they never forgot who they were."

"Doubtless that decayed mansion reminded them," Julian muttered. He never spoke of it without contempt or thought of it without longing. He had seen it once when he was a child before it had been sold. The double stairways had rotted and been torn down. Negroes were living in it. But it remained in his mind as his mother had known it. It appeared in his dreams regularly. He would stand on the wide porch, listening to the rustle of oak leaves, then wander through the high-ceilinged hall into the parlor that opened onto it and gaze at the worn rugs and faded draperies. It occurred to him that it was he, not she, who could have appreciated it. He preferred its threadbare elegance to anything he could name and it was because of it that all the neighborhoods they had lived in had been a torment to him—whereas she had hardly known the difference. She called her insensitivity "being adjustable."

"And I remember the old darky who was my nurse, Caroline. There was no better person in the world. I've always had a great respect for my colored friends," she said. "I'd do anything in the world for them and they'd . . ."

"Will you for God's sake get off that subject?" Julian said. When he got on a bus by himself, he made it a point to sit down beside a Negro, in reparation as it were for his mother's sins.

"You're mighty touchy tonight," she said. "Do you feel all right?"

"Yes I feel all right," he said. "Now lay off."

She pursed her lips. "Well, you certainly are in a vile humor," she observed. "I just won't speak to you at all."

They had reached the bus stop. There was no bus in sight and Julian, his hands still jammed in his pockets and his head thrust forward, scowled down the empty street. The frustration of having to wait on the bus as well as ride on it began to creep up his neck like a hot hand. The presence of his mother was borne in upon him as she gave a pained sigh. He looked at her bleakly. She was holding herself very erect under the preposterous hat, wearing it like a banner of her imaginary dignity. There was in him an evil urge to break her spirit. He suddenly unloosened his tie and pulled it off and put it in his pocket.

She stiffened. "Why must you look like *that* when you take me to town?" she said. "Why must you deliberately embarrass me?"

"If you'll never learn where you are," he said, "you can at least learn where I am."

"You look like a—thug," she said.

"Then I must be one," he murmured.

"I'll just go home," she said. "I will not bother you. If you can't do a little thing like that for me . . ."

Rolling his eyes upward, he put his tie back on. "Restored to my class," he muttered. He thrust his face toward her and hissed, "True culture is in the mind, the *mind*," he said, and tapped his head, "the mind."

"It's in the heart," she said, "and in how you do things and how you do things is because of who you *are*."

"Nobody in the damn bus cares who you are."

"I care who I am," she said icily.

The lighted bus appeared on top of the next hill and as it approached, they moved out into the street to meet it. He put his hand under her elbow and hoisted her up on the creaking step. She entered with a little smile, as if she were going into a drawing room where everyone had been waiting for her. While he put in the tokens, she sat down on one of the broad front seats for three which faced the aisle. A thin woman with protruding teeth and long yellow hair was sitting on the end of it. His mother moved up beside her and left room for Julian besides herself. He sat down and looked at the floor across the aisle where a pair of thin feet in red and white canvas sandals were planted.

His mother immediately began a general conversation meant to attract anyone who felt like talking. "Can it get any hotter?" she said and removed from her purse a folding fan, black with a Japanese scene on it, which she began to flutter before her.

"I reckon it might could," the woman with the protruding teeth said, "but I know for a fact my apartment couldn't get no hotter."

"It must get the afternoon sun," his mother said. She sat forward and looked up and down the bus. It was half filled. Everybody was white. "I see we have the bus to ourselves," she said. Julian cringed.

"For a change," said the woman across the aisle, the owner of the red and white canvas sandals. "I come on one the other day and they were thick as fleas—up front and all through."

"The world is in a mess everywhere," his mother said. "I don't know how we've let it get in this fix."

"What gets my goat is all those boys from good families stealing automobile tires," the woman with the protruding teeth said. "I told my boy, I said you may not be rich but you been raised right and if I ever catch you in any such mess, they can send you on to the reformatory. Be exactly where you belong."

"Training tells," his mother said. "Is your boy in high school?"

"Ninth grade," the woman said.

"My son just finished college last year. He wants to write but he's selling typewriters until he gets started," his mother said.

The woman leaned forward and peered at Julian. He threw her such a malevolent look that she subsided against the seat. On the floor across the aisle there was an abandoned newspaper. He got up and got it and opened it out in front of him. His mother discreetly continued the conversation in a lower tone but the woman across the aisle said in a loud voice, "Well that's nice. Selling typewriters is close to writing. He can go right from one to the other."

"I tell him," his mother said, "that Rome wasn't built in a day."

Behind the newspaper Julian was withdrawing into the inner compartment of his mind where he spent most of his time. This was a kind of mental bubble in which he established himself when he could not bear to be a part of what was going on around him. From it he could see out and judge but in it he was safe from any kind of penetration from without. It was the only place where he felt free of the general idiocy of his fellows. His mother had never entered it but from it he could see her with absolute clarity.

The old lady was clever enough and he thought that if she had started from any of the right premises, more might have been expected of her. She lived according to the laws of her own fantasy world, outside of which he had never seen her set foot. The law of it was to sacrifice herself for him after she had first created the necessity to do so by making a mess of things. If he had permitted her sacrifices, it was only because her lack of foresight had made them necessary. All of her life had been a struggle to act like a Chestny without the Chestny goods, and to give him everything she thought a Chestny ought to have; but since, said she, it was fun to struggle, why complain? And when you had won, as she had won, what fun to look back on the hard times! He could not forgive her that she had enjoyed the struggle and that she thought *she* had won.

What she meant when she said she had won was that she had brought him up successfully and had sent him to college and that he had turned out so well—good looking (her teeth had gone unfilled so that his could be straightened), intelligent (he realized he was too intelligent to be a success), and with a future ahead of him (there was of course no future ahead of him). She excused his gloominess on the grounds that he was still growing up and his radical ideas on his lack of practical experience. She said he didn't yet know a thing about "life," that he hadn't even entered the real world—when already he was as disenchanted with it as a man of fifty.

The further irony of all this was that in spite of her, he had turned out so well. In spite of going to only a third-rate college, he had, on his own initiative, come out with a first-rate education; in spite of growing up dominated by a small mind, he had ended up with a large one; in spite of all her foolish views, he was free of prejudice and unafraid to face facts. Most miraculous of all, instead of being blinded by love for her as she was for him, he had cut himself emotionally free of her and could see her with complete objectivity. He was not dominated by his mother.

The bus stopped with a sudden jerk and shook him from his meditation. A woman from the back lurched forward with little steps and barely escaped falling in his newspaper as she righted herself. She got off and a large Negro got on. Julian kept his paper lowered to watch. It gave him a certain satisfaction to see injustice in daily operation. It confirmed his view that with a few exceptions there was no one worth knowing within a radius of three hundred miles. The Negro was well dressed and carried a briefcase. He looked around and then sat down on the other end of the seat where the woman with the red and white canvas sandals was sitting. He immediately unfolded a newspaper and obscured himself behind it. Julian's mother's elbow at once prodded insistently into his ribs. "Now you see why I won't ride on these buses by myself," she whispered.

The woman with the red and white canvas sandals had risen at the same time the Negro sat down and had gone further back in the bus and taken the seat of the woman who had got off. His mother leaned forward and cast her an approving look.

Julian rose, crossed the aisle, and sat down in the place of the woman with the canvas sandals. From this position, he looked serenely across at his mother. Her face had turned an angry red. He stared at her, making his eyes the eyes of a stranger. He felt his tension suddenly lift as if he had openly declared war on her.

He would have liked to get in conversation with the Negro and to talk with him about art or politics or any subject that would be above the comprehension of those around them, but the man remained entrenched behind his paper. He was either ignoring the change of seating or had never noticed it. There was no way for Julian to convey his sympathy.

His mother kept her eyes fixed reproachfully on his face. The woman with the protruding teeth was looking at him avidly as if he were a type of monster new to her.

"Do you have a light?" he asked the Negro.

Without looking away from his paper, the man reached in his pocket and handed him a packet of matches.

"Thanks," Julian said. For a moment he held the matches foolishly. A NO SMOKING sign looked down upon him from over the door. This alone would not have deterred him; he had no cigarettes. He had quit smoking some months before because he could not afford it. "Sorry," he muttered and handed back the matches. The Negro lowered the paper and gave him an annoyed look. He took the matches and raised the paper again.

His mother continued to gaze at him but she did not take advantage of his momentary discomfort. Her eyes retained their battered look. Her face seemed to be unnaturally red, as if her blood pressure had risen. Julian allowed no glimmer of sympathy to show on his face. Having got the advantage, he wanted desperately to keep it and carry it through. He would have liked to teach her a lesson that would last her a while, but there seemed no way to continue the point. The Negro refused to come out from behind his paper.

Julian folded his arms and looked stolidly before him, facing her but as if he did not see her, as if he had ceased to recognize her existence. He visualized a scene in which the bus having reached their stop, he would remain in his seat and when she said, "Aren't you going to get off?" he would look at her as at a stranger who had rashly addressed him. The corner they got off on was usually deserted, but it was well lighted and it would not hurt her to walk by herself the four blocks to the Y. He decided to wait until the time came and then decide whether or not he would let her get off by herself. He would have to be at the Y at ten to bring her back, but he could leave her wondering if he was going to show up. There was no reason for her to think she could always depend on him.

He retired again into the high-ceilinged room sparsely settled with large pieces of antique furniture. His soul expanded momentarily but then he became aware of his mother across from him and the vision shriveled. He studied her coldly. Her feet in little pumps dangled like a child's and did not quite reach the floor. She was training on him an exaggerated look of reproach. He felt completely detached from her. At that moment he could with pleasure have slapped her as he would have slapped a particularly obnoxious child in his charge.

He began to imagine various unlikely ways by which he could teach her a lesson. He might make friends with some distinguished Negro professor or lawyer and bring him home to spend the evening. He would be entirely justified but her blood pressure would rise to 300. He could not push her to the extent of making her have a stroke, and moreover, he had never been successful at making any Negro friends. He had tried to strike up an acquaintance on the bus with some of the better types, with ones that looked like professors or ministers or lawyers. One morning he had sat down next to a distinguished-looking dark brown man who had answered his questions with a sonorous solemnity but who had turned out to be an undertaker. Another day he had sat down beside a cigar-smoking Negro with a diamond ring on his finger, but after a few stilted pleasantries, the Negro had rung the buzzer and risen, slipping two lottery tickets into Julian's hand as he climbed over him to leave.

He imagined his mother lying desperately ill and his being able to secure only a Negro doctor for her. He toyed with that idea for a few minutes and then dropped it for a momentary vision of himself participating as a sympathizer in a sit-in demonstration. This was possible but he did not linger with it. Instead, he approached the ultimate horror. He brought home a beautiful suspiciously Negroid woman. Prepare yourself, he said. There is nothing you can do about it. This is the woman I've chosen. She's intelligent, dignified, even good, and she's suffered and she hasn't thought it *fun*. Now persecute us, go ahead and persecute us. Drive her out of here, but remember, you're driving me too. His eyes were narrowed and through the indignation he had generated, he saw his mother across the aisle, purple-faced, shrunken to the dwarf-like proportions of her moral nature, sitting like a mummy beneath the ridiculous banner of her hat.

He was tilted out of his fantasy again as the bus stopped. The door opened with a sucking hiss and out of the dark a large, gaily dressed, sullen-looking colored woman got on with a little boy. The child, who might have been four, had on a short plaid suit and a Tyrolean hat with a blue feather in it. Julian hoped that he would sit down beside him and that the woman would push in beside his mother. He could think of no better arrangement.

As she waited for her tokens, the woman was surveying the seating possibilities—he hoped with the idea of sitting where she was least wanted. There was something familiar-looking about her but Julian could not place what it was. She was a giant of a woman. Her face was set not only to meet opposition but to seek it out. The downward tilt of her large lower lip was like a warning sign: DON'T TAMPER WITH ME. Her bulging figure was encased in a green crepe dress and her feet overflowed in red shoes. She had on a hideous hat. A purple velvet flap came down on one side of it and stood up on the other; the rest of it was green and looked like a cushion with the stuffing out. She carried a mammoth red pocketbook that bulged throughout as if it were stuffed with rocks.

To Julian's disappointment, the little boy climbed up on the empty seat beside his mother. His mother lumped all children, black and white, into the common category, "cute," and she thought little

Negroes were on the whole cuter than little white children. She smiled at the little boy as he climbed on the seat.

Meanwhile the woman was bearing down upon the empty seat beside Julian. To his annoyance, she squeezed herself into it. He saw his mother's face change as the woman settled herself next to him and he realized with satisfaction that this was more objectionable to her than it was to him. Her face seemed almost gray and there was a look of dull recognition in her eyes, as if suddenly she had sickened at some awful confrontation. Julian saw that it was because she and the woman had, in a sense, swapped sons. Though his mother would not realize the symbolic significance of this, she would feel it. His amusement showed plainly on his face.

The woman next to him muttered something unintelligible to herself. He was conscious of a kind of bristling next to him, muted growling like that of an angry cat. He could not see anything but the red pocketbook upright on the bulging green thighs. He visualized the woman as she had stood waiting for her tokens—the ponderous figure, rising from the red shoes upward over the solid hips, the mammoth bosom, the haughty face, to the green and purple hat.

His eyes widened.

The vision of the two hats, identical, broke upon him with the radiance of a brilliant sunrise. His face was suddenly lit with joy. He could not believe that Fate had thrust upon his mother such a lesson. He gave a loud chuckle so that she would look at him and see that he saw. She turned her eyes on him slowly. The blue in them seemed to have turned a bruised purple. For a moment he had an uncomfortable sense of her innocence, but it lasted only a second before principle rescued him. Justice entitled him to laugh. His grin hardened until it said to her as plainly as if he were saying aloud: Your punishment exactly fits your pettiness. This should teach you a permanent lesson.

Her eyes shifted to the woman. She seemed unable to bear looking at him and to find the woman preferable. He became conscious again of the bristling presence at his side. The woman was rumbling like a volcano about to become active. His mother's mouth began to twitch slightly at one corner. With a sinking heart, he saw incipient signs of recovery on her face and realized that this was going to strike her suddenly as funny and was going to be no lesson at all. She kept her eyes on the woman and an amused smile came over her face as if the woman were a monkey that had stolen her hat. The little Negro was looking up at her with large fascinated eyes. He had been trying to attract her attention for some time.

"Carver!" the woman said suddenly. "Come heah!"

When he saw that the spotlight was on him at last, Carver drew his feet up and turned himself toward Julian's mother and giggled.

"Carver!" the woman said. "You heah me? Come heah!"

Carver slid down from the seat but remained squatting with his back against the base of it, his head turned slyly around toward Julian's mother, who was smiling at him. The woman reached a hand across the aisle and snatched him to her. He righted himself and hung backwards on her knees, grinning at Julian's mother. "Isn't he cute?" Julian's mother said to the woman with the protruding teeth.

"I reckon he is," the woman said without conviction.

The Negress yanked him upright but he eased out of her grip and shot across the aisle and scrambled, giggling wildly, onto the seat beside his love.

"I think he likes me," Julian's mother said, and smiled at the woman. It was the smile she used when she was being particularly gracious to an inferior. Julian saw everything lost. The lesson had rolled off her like rain on a roof.

The woman stood up and yanked the little boy off the seat as if she were snatching him from contagion. Julian could feel the rage in her at having no weapon like his mother's smile. She gave the child a sharp slap across his leg. He howled once and then thrust his head into her stomach and kicked his feet against her shins. "Behave," she said vehemently.

The bus stopped and the Negro who had been reading the newspaper got off. The woman moved over and set the little boy down with a thump between herself and Julian. She held him firmly by the knee. In a moment he put his hands in front of his face and peeped at Julian's mother through his fingers.

"I see yoooooooo!" she said and put her hand in front of her face and peeped at him.

The woman slapped his hand down. "Quit yo' foolishness," she said, "before I knock the living Jesus out of you!"

Julian was thankful that the next stop was theirs. He reached up and pulled the cord. The woman reached up and pulled it at the same time. Oh my God, he thought. He had the terrible intuition that when they got off the bus together, his mother would open her purse and give the little boy a nickel. The gesture would be as natural to her as breathing. The bus stopped and the woman got up and lunged to the front, dragging the child, who wished to stay on, after her. Julian and his mother got up and followed. As they neared the door, Julian tried to relieve her of her pocketbook.

"No," she murmured, "I want to give the little boy a nickel."

"No!" Julian hissed. "No!"

She smiled down at the child and opened her bag. The bus door opened and the woman picked him up by the arm and descended with him, hanging at her hip. Once in the street she set him down and shook him.

Julian's mother had to close her purse while she got down the bus step but as soon as her feet were on the ground, she opened it again and began to rummage inside. "I can't find but a penny," she whispered, "but it looks like a new one."

"Don't do it!" Julian said fiercely between his teeth. There was a streetlight on the corner and she hurried to get under it so that she could better see into her pocketbook. The woman was heading off rapidly down the street with the child still hanging backward on her hand.

"Oh little boy!" Julian's mother called and took a few quick steps and caught up with them just beyond the lamppost. "Here's a bright new penny for you," and she held out the coin, which shone bronze in the dim light.

The huge woman turned and for a moment stood, her shoulders lifted and her face frozen with frustrated rage, and stared at Julian's mother. Then all at once she seemed to explode like a piece of machinery that had been given one ounce of pressure too much. Julian saw the black fist swing out with the red pocketbook. He shut his eyes and cringed as he heard the woman shout, "He don't take nobody's pennies!" When he opened his eyes, the woman was disappearing down the street with the little boy staring wide-eyed over her shoulder. Julian's mother was sitting on the sidewalk.

"I told you not to do that," Julian said angrily. "I told you not to do that!"

He stood over her for a minute, gritting his teeth. Her legs were stretched out in front of her and her hat was on her lap. He squatted down and looked her in the face. It was totally expressionless. "You got exactly what you deserved," he said. "Now get up."

He picked up her pocketbook and put what had fallen out back in it. He picked the hat up off her lap. The penny caught his eye on the sidewalk and he picked that up and let it drop before her eyes into the purse. Then he stood up and leaned over and held his hands out to pull her up. She remained immobile. He sighed. Rising about them on either side were black apartment buildings, marked with irregular rectangles of light. At the end of the block a man came out of a door and walked off in the opposite direction. "All right," he said, "suppose somebody happens by and wants to know why you're sitting on the sidewalk?"

She took the hand and, breathing hard, pulled heavily up on it and then stood for a moment, swaying slightly as if the spots of light in the darkness were circling around her. Her eyes, shadowed and confused, finally settled on his face. He did not try to conceal his irritation. "I hope this teaches you a lesson," he said. She leaned forward and her eyes raked his face. She seemed trying to determine his identity. Then, as if she found nothing familiar about him, she started off with a headlong movement in the wrong direction.

"Aren't you going on to the Y?" he asked.

"Home," she muttered.

"Well, are we walking?"

For answer she kept going. Julian followed along, his hands behind him. He saw no reason to let the lesson she had had go without backing it up with an explanation of its meaning. She might as well be made to understand what had happened to her. "Don't think that was just an uppity Negro woman," he said. "That was the whole colored race which will no longer take your condescending pennies. That was your black double. She can wear the same hat as you, and to be sure," he added gratuitously (because he thought it was funny), "it looked better on her than it did on you. What all this means," he said, "is that the old world is gone. The old manners are obsolete and your graciousness is not worth a damn." He thought bitterly of the house that had been lost for him. "You aren't who you think you are," he said.

She continued to plow ahead, paying no attention to him. Her hair had come undone on one side. She dropped her pocketbook and took no notice. He stooped and picked it up and handed it to her but she did not take it.

"You needn't act as if the world had come to an end," he said, "because it hasn't. From now on you've got to live in a new world and face a few realities for a change. Buck up," he said, "it won't kill you."

She was breathing fast.

"Let's wait on the bus," he said.

"Home," she said thickly.

"I hate to see you behave like this," he said. "Just like a child. I should be able to expect more of you." He decided to stop where he was and make her stop and wait for a bus. "I'm not going any farther," he said, stopping. "We're going on the bus."

She continued to go on as if she had not heard him. He took a few steps and caught her arm and stopped her. He looked into her face and caught his breath. He was looking into a face he had never seen before. "Tell Grandpa to come get me," she said.

He stared, stricken.

"Tell Caroline to come get me," she said.

Stunned, he let her go and she lurched forward again, walking as if one leg were shorter than the other. A tide of darkness seemed to be sweeping her from him. "Mother!" he cried. "Darling, sweetheart, wait!" Crumpling, she fell to the pavement. He dashed forward and fell at her side, crying, "Mamma, Mamma!" He turned her over. Her face was fiercely distorted. One eye, large and staring, moved slightly on the left as if it had become unmoored. The other remained fixed on him, raked his face again, found nothing and closed.

"Wait here, wait here!" he cried and jumped up and began to run for help toward a cluster of lights he saw in the distance ahead of him. "Help, help!" he shouted, but his voice was thin, scarcely a thread of sound. The lights drifted farther away the faster he ran and his feet moved numbly as if they carried him nowhere. The tide of darkness seemed to sweep him back to her, postponing from moment to moment his entry into the world of guilt and sorrow.

METAFICTION: *INTRODUCTION*

Metafiction is really a special case of fabulation. A work of *meta*-fiction is a fictional experiment that either explores or questions the nature and conventions of fiction itself. The very elements of fiction—the relationship of the writer to the text or the text to the world, the concepts of plot, character, setting, and point-of-view—all these are taken not as givens but as questionable or problematic in metafiction.

Though practiced earlier, metafiction is very much a contemporary mode of the short story. The three examples presented here are all by writers whose reputations have been made in the past three decades. Cortázar in "Blow-Up" explores the relationship between the time of events and the time of writing—the "then" of the tale and the "now" of the teller—as well as the relationships between the place of events and the place of composition. He contrasts the delicacy of life with the crudeness of the machinery (cameras, typewriters, words themselves) through which we may try to capture it. He sets the mysteries of human motivation against the spurious certainties of language.

Barth considers some of the same problems, but he is especially attentive to the conflict between the instructions provided for students of creative writing in American classrooms and the problems of capturing real experience in verbal formulas. He is also exploring the relationship between art and life in another way. What kind of experience, he asks, is likely to turn a person into a writer? "Lost in the Funhouse" is a "Portrait of the Artist as a Boy."

In "The Hat Act" Robert Coover explores the connections between representation and reaction, language and emotion. In a theatrical setting, the magician performing his tricks becomes a version of the writer performing *his* tricks. Stock situations produce stock responses; but things begin to go wrong; the impossible happens before the audience's eyes (but not before ours—there are only words before ours) and we are left to puzzle out the curious ways of representation through language, the strange connections between inked shapes on the page and strong emotions in the human frame.

These experiments in metafiction make an appropriate place to conclude—at least temporarily—a study of the workings of fiction, for they turn the powers of fiction on fiction itself and force us to reconsider fiction, not as something natural and given but as one of humanity's many tools for ordering and shaping the world in human ways.

JULIO CORTÁZAR

1914–

He was born in Brussels, Belgium, of Argentinian parents. When he was four, the family returned to Buenos Aires, where he was raised by his mother and an aunt after his father left home. His ancestors were Basques on his father's side, French and German on his mother's. In Argentina he read fantasy and dutifully attended schools, earning qualification as an elementary school teacher in 1932 and a high school teacher in 1935. While teaching in Bolívar he began to write stories and poems. In 1945 he was invited to teach French at the University of Cuya. There he was arrested briefly for participating in a protest against Perónism. After working as a public translator he received a scholarship for study in Paris. He left Argentina for France in 1951 and has remained there ever since, writing in Spanish his surrealistic novels and stories. He has continued to travel and translate. He is six feet six inches tall and collects Charlie Parker records.

Blow-Up

It'll never be known how this has to be told, in the first person or in the second, using the third person plural or continually inventing modes that will serve for nothing. If one might say: I will see the moon rose, or: we hurt me at the back of my eyes, and especially: you the blond woman was the clouds that race before my your his our yours their faces. What the hell.

Seated ready to tell it, if one might go to drink a bock over there, and the typewriter continue by itself (because I use the machine), that would be perfection. And that's not just a manner of speaking. Perfection, yes, because here is the aperture which must be counted also as a machine (of another sort, a Contax 1.1.2) and it is possible that one machine may know more about another machine than I, you, she—the blond—and the clouds. But I have the dumb luck to know that if I go this Remington will sit turned to stone on top of the table with the air of being twice as quiet that mobile things have when they are not moving. So, I have to write. One of us all has to write, if this is going to get told. Better that it be me who am dead, for I'm less compromised than the rest; I who see only the clouds and can think without being distracted, write without being distracted (there goes another, with a grey edge) and remember without being distracted, I who am dead (and I'm alive, I'm not trying to fool anybody, you'll see when we get to the moment, because I have to begin some way and

Translated by Paul Blackburn.

I've begun with this period, the last one back the one at the beginning, which in the end is the best of the periods when you want to tell something).

All of a sudden I wonder why I have to tell this, but if one begins to wonder why he does all he does do, if one wonders why he accepts an invitation to lunch (now a pigeon's flying by and it seems to me a sparrow), or why when someone has told us a good joke immediately there starts up something like a tickling in the stomach and we are not at peace until we've gone into the office across the hall and told the joke over again; then it feels good immediately, one is fine, happy, and can get back to work. For I imagine that no one has explained this, that really the best thing is to put aside all decorum and tell it, because, after all's done, nobody is ashamed of breathing or of putting on his shoes; they're things that you do, and when something weird happens, when you find a spider in your shoe or if you take a breath and feel like a broken window, then you have to tell what's happening, tell it to the guys at the office or to the doctor. Oh, doctor, every time I take a breath . . . Always tell it, always get rid of that tickle in the stomach that bothers you.

And now that we're finally going to tell it, let's put things a little bit in order, we'd be walking down the staircase in this house as far as Sunday, November 7, just a month back. One goes down five floors and stands then in the Sunday in the sun one would not have suspected of Paris in November, with a large appetite to walk around, to see things, to take photos (because we were photographers, I'm a photographer). I know that the most difficult thing is going to be finding a way to tell it, and I'm not afraid of repeating myself. It's going to be difficult because nobody really knows who it is telling it, if I am I or what actually occurred or what I'm seeing (clouds, and once in a while a pigeon) or if, simply, I'm telling a truth which is only my truth, and then is the truth only for my stomach, for this impulse to go running out and to finish up in some manner with this, whatever it is.

We're going to tell it slowly, what happens in the middle of what I'm writing is coming already. If they replace me, if, so soon, I don't know what to say, if the clouds stop coming and something else starts (because it's impossible that this keep coming, clouds passing continually and occasionally a pigeon), if something out of all this . . . And after the "if" what am I going to put if I'm going to close the sentence structure correctly? But if I begin to ask questions, I'll never tell anything, maybe to tell would be like an answer, at least for someone who's reading it.

Roberto Michel, French-Chilean, translator and in his spare time an amateur photographer, left number 11, rue Monsieur-le-Prince Sunday November 7 of the current year (now there're two small ones passing, with silver linings). He had spent three weeks working on the French version of a treatise on challenges and appeals by José Norberto Allende, professor at the University of Santiago. It's rare that there's wind in Paris, and even less seldom a wind like this that swirled around corners and rose up to whip at old wooden venetian blinds behind what astonished ladies commented variously on how unreliable the weather had been these last few years. But the sun was out also, riding the wind and friend of the cats, so there was nothing that would keep me from taking a walk along the docks of the Seine and taking photos of the Conservatoire and Sainte-Chapelle. It was hardly ten o'clock, and I figured that by eleven the light would be good, the best you can get in the fall; to kill some time I detoured around by the Isle Saint-Louis and started to walk along the quai d'Anjou. I stared for a bit at the hôtel de Lauzun, I recited bits from Apollinaire which always get into my head whenever I pass in front of the hôtel de Lauzun (and at that I ought to be remembering the other poet, but Michel is an obstinate beggar), and when the wind stopped all at once and the sun came out at least twice as hard (I mean warmer, but really it's the same thing), I sat down on the parapet and felt terribly happy in the Sunday morning.

One of the many ways of contesting level-zero, and one of the best, is to take photographs, an activity in which one should start becoming an adept very early in life, teach it to children since it requires discipline, aesthetic education, a good eye and steady fingers. I'm not talking about waylaying the lie like any old reporter, snapping the stupid silhouette of the VIP leaving number 10 Downing Street, but in all ways when one is walking about with a camera, one has almost a duty to be attentive, to not lose that abrupt and happy rebound of sun's rays off an old stone, or the pigtails-flying run of a small girl going home with a loaf of bread or a bottle of milk. Michel knew that the photographer always worked as a permutation of his personal way of seeing the world as other than the camera insidiously imposed upon it (now a large cloud is by, almost black), but he lacked no confidence in himself, knowing that he had only to go out without the Contax to recover the keynote of distraction, the sight without a frame around it, light without the diaphragm aperture or 1/250 sec. Right now (what a word, now, what a dumb lie) I was able to sit quietly on the railing overlooking the river watching the red and black motorboats passing below without it occurring to me to think photographically of the scenes, nothing more than letting myself go in the letting go of objects, running immobile in the stream of time. And then the wind was not blowing.

After, I wandered down the quai de Bourbon until getting to the end of the isle where the intimate square was (intimate because it was small, not that it was hidden, it offered its whole breast to the river and the sky), I enjoyed it, a lot. Nothing there but a couple and, of course, pigeons; maybe even some of those which are flying past now so that I'm seeing them. A leap up and I settled on the wall, and let myself turn about and be caught and fixed by the sun, giving it my face and ears and hands (I kept my gloves in my pocket). I had no desire to shoot pictures, and lit a cigarette to be doing something; I think it was that moment when the match was about to touch the tobacco that I saw the young boy for the first time.

What I'd thought was a couple seemed much more now a boy with his mother, although at the same time I realized that it was not a kid and his mother, and that it was a couple in the sense that we always allegate to couples when we see them leaning up against the parapets or embracing on the benches in the squares. As I had nothing else to do, I had more than enough time to wonder why the boy was so nervous, like a young colt or a hare, sticking his hands into his pockets, taking them out immediately, one after the other, running his fingers through his hair, changing his stance, and especially why was he afraid, well, you could guess that from every gesture, a fear suffocated by his shyness, an impulse to step backwards which he telegraphed, his body standing as if it were on the edge of flight, holding itself back in a final, pitiful decorum.

All this was so clear, ten feet away—and we were alone against the parapet at the tip of the island—that at the beginning the boy's fright didn't let me see the blond very well. Now, thinking back on it, I see her much better at that first second when I read her face (she'd turned around suddenly, swinging like a metal weathercock, and the eyes, the eyes were there), when I vaguely understood what might have been occurring to the boy and figured it would be worth the trouble to stay and watch (the wind was blowing their words away and they were speaking in a low murmur). I think that I know how to look, if it's something I know, and also that every looking oozes with mendacity, because it's that which expels us furthest outside ourselves, without the least guarantee, whereas to smell, or (but Michel rambles on to himself easily enough, there's no need to let him harangue on this way). In any case, if the likely inaccuracy can be seen beforehand, it becomes possible again to look; perhaps it suffices to choose between looking and the reality looked at, to strip things of all their unnecessary clothing. And surely all this is difficult besides.

As for the boy I remember the image before his actual body (that will clear itself up later), while now I am sure that I remember the woman's body much better than the image. She was thin and willowy, two unfair words to describe what she was, and was wearing an almost-black fur coat, almost long, almost handsome. All the morning's wind (now it was hardly a breeze and it wasn't cold) had blown through her blond hair which pared away her white, bleak face—two unfair words—and put the world at her feet and horribly alone in front of her dark eyes, her eyes fell on things like two eagles, two leaps into nothingness, two puffs of greem slime. I'm not describing anything, it's more a matter of trying to understand it. And I said two puffs of green slime.

Let's be fair, the boy was well enough dressed and was sporting yellow gloves which I would have sworn belonged to his older brother, a student of law or sociology; it was pleasant to see the fingers of the gloves sticking out of his jacket pocket. For a long time I didn't see his face, barely a profile, not stupid—a terrified bird, a Fra Filippo angel, rice pudding with milk—and the back of an adolescent who wants to take up judo and has had a scuffle or two in defense of an idea or his sister. Turning fourteen, perhaps fifteen, one would guess that he was dressed and fed by his parents but without a nickel in his pocket, having to debate with his buddies before making up his mind to buy a coffee, a cognac, a pack of cigarettes. He'd walk through the streets thinking of the girls in his class, about how good it would be to go to the movies and see the latest film, or to buy novels or neckties or bottles of liquor with green and white labels on them. At home (it would be a respectable home, lunch at noon and romantic landscapes on the walls, with a dark entryway and a mahogany umbrella stand inside the door) there'd be the slow rain of time, for studying, for being mama's hope, for looking like dad, for writing to his aunt in Avignon. So that there was a lot of walking the streets, the whole of the river for him (but without a nickel) and the mysterious city of fifteen-year-olds with its signs in doorways, its terrifying cats, a paper of fried potatoes for thirty francs, the pornographic magazine folded four ways, a solitude like the emptiness of his pockets, the eagerness for so much that was incomprehensible but illumined by a total love, by the availability analogous to the wind and the streets.

This biography was of the boy and of any boy whatsoever, but this particular one now, you could see he was insular, surrounded solely by the blond's presence as she continued talking with him. (I'm tired of insisting, but two long ragged ones just went by. That morning I don't think I looked at the sky once, because what was happening with the boy and the woman appeared so soon I could do nothing but look at them and wait, look at them and . . .) To cut it short, the boy was agitated and one could guess without too much trouble what had just occurred a few minutes before, at most half-an-hour. The boy had come onto the tip of the island, seen the woman and thought her marvelous. The woman was waiting for that because she was there waiting for that, or maybe the boy arrived before her and she saw him from one of the balconies or from a car and got out to meet him, starting the conversation with whatever, from the beginning she was sure that he was going to be afraid and want to run off, and that, naturally, he'd stay, stiff and sullen, pretending experience and the pleasure of the adventure. The rest was easy because it was happening ten feet away from me, and anyone could have gauged the stages of the game, the derisive, competitive fencing; its major attraction was not that it was happening but in foreseeing its denouement. The boy would try to end it by pretending a date, an obligation, whatever, and would go stumbling off disconcerted, wishing he were walking with some assurance, but naked under the mocking glance which would follow him until he was out of sight. Or rather, he would stay there, fascinated or simply incapable of taking the initiative, and the woman would begin to touch his face gently, muss his hair, still talking to him voicelessly, and soon would take him by the arm to lead him off, unless he, with an uneasiness beginning to tinge the edge of desire, even his stake in the adventure, would rouse himself to put his arm around her waist and to kiss her. Any of this could have happened, though it did not, and perversely Michel waited, sitting on the railing, making the settings almost without looking at the camera, ready to take a picturesque shot of a corner of the island with an uncommon couple talking and looking at one another.

Strange how the scene (almost nothing: two figures there mismatched in their youth) was taking on a disquieting aura. I thought it was I imposing it, and that my photo, if I shot it, would reconstitute things in their true stupidity. I would have liked to know what he was thinking, a man in a grey hat sitting at the wheel of a car parked on the dock which led up to the footbridge, and whether he was reading the paper or asleep. I had just discovered him because people inside a parked car have a tendency to disappear, they get lost in that wretched, private cage stripped of the beauty that motion and danger give it. And nevertheless, the car had been there the whole time, forming part (or deforming that part) of the isle. A car: like saying a lighted streetlamp, a park bench. Never like saying wind, sunlight, those elements always new to the skin and the eyes, and also the boy and the woman, unique, put there to change the island, to show it to me in another way. Finally, it may have been that the man with the newspaper also became aware of what was happening and would, like me, feel that malicious sensation of waiting for everything to happen. Now the woman had swung around smoothly, putting the young boy between herself and the wall, I saw them almost in profile, and he was taller, though not much taller, and yet she dominated him, it seemed like she was hovering over him (her laugh, all at once, a whip of feathers), crushing him just by being there, smiling, one hand taking a stroll through the air. Why wait any longer? Aperture at sixteen, a sighting which would not include the horrible black car, but yes, that tree, necessary to break up too much grey space . . .

I raised the camera, pretended to study a focus which did not include them, and waited and watched closely, sure that I would finally catch the revealing expression, one that would sum it all up, life that is rhythmed by movement but which a stiff image destroys, taking time in cross section, if we do not choose the essential imperceptible fraction of it. I did not have to wait long. The woman was getting on with the job of handcuffing the boy smoothly, stripping from him what was left of his freedom a hair at a time, in an incredibly slow and delicious torture. I imagined the possible endings (now a small fluffy cloud appears, almost alone in the sky), I saw their arrival at the house (a basement apartment probably, which she would have filled with large cushions and cats) and conjectured the boy's terror and his desperate decision to play it cool and to be led off pretending there was nothing new in it for him. Closing my eyes, if I did in fact close my eyes, I set the scene: the teasing kisses, the woman mildly repelling the hands which were trying to undress her, like in novels, on a bed that would have a lilac-colored comforter, on the other hand she taking off his clothes, plainly mother and son under a milky yellow light, and everything would end up as usual, perhaps, but maybe everything would go otherwise, and the initiation of the adolescent would not happen, she would not let it happen, after a long prologue wherein the awkwardnesses, the exasperating caresses, the running of hands over bodies would be resolved in who knows what, in a separate and solitary pleasure, in a petulant denial mixed with the art of tiring and disconcerting so much poor innocence. It might go like that, it might very well go like that; that woman was not looking for the boy as a lover, and at the same time she was dominating him toward some end impossible to understand if you do not imagine it as a cruel game, the desire to desire without satisfaction, to excite herself for someone else, someone who in no way could be that kid.

Michel is guilty of making literature, of indulging in fabricated unrealities. Nothing pleases him more than to imagine exceptions to the rule, individuals outside the species, not-always-repugnant monsters. But that woman invited speculation, perhaps giving clues enough for the fantasy to hit the bullseye. Before she left, and now that she would fill my imaginings for several days, for I'm given to ruminating, I decided not to lose a moment more. I got it all into the view-finder (with the tree, the railing, the eleven-o'clock sun) and took the shot. In time to realize that they both had noticed and stood there looking at me, the boy surprised and as though questioning, but she was irritated, her face and body flat-footedly hostile, feeling robbed, ignominiously recorded on a small chemical image.

i might be able to tell it in much greater detail but it's not worth the trouble. The woman said that no one had the right to take a picture without permission, and demanded that I hand her over the film. All this in a dry, clear voice with a good Parisian accent, which rose in color and tone with every phrase. For my part, it hardly mattered whether she got the roll of film or not, but anyone who knows me will tell you, if you want anything from me, ask nicely. With the result that I restricted myself to formulating the opinion that not only was photography in public places not prohibited, but it was looked upon with decided favor, both private and official. And while that was getting said, I noticed on the sly how the boy was falling back, sort of actively backing up though without moving, and all at once (it seemed almost incredible) he turned and broke into a run, the poor kid, thinking that he was walking off and in fact in full flight, running past the side of the car, disappearing like a gossamer filament of angel-spit in the morning air.

But filaments of angel-spittle are also called devil-spit, and Michel had to endure rather particular curses, to hear himself called meddler and imbecile, taking great pains meanwhile to smile and to abate with simple movements of his head such a hard sell. As I was beginning to get tired, I heard the car door slam. The man in the grey hat was there, looking at us. It was only at that point that I realized he was playing a part in the comedy.

He began to walk toward us, carrying in his hand the paper he had been pretending to read. What I remember best is the grimace that twisted his mouth askew, it covered his face with wrinkles, changed somewhat both in location and shape because his lips trembled and the grimace went from one side of his mouth to the other as though it were on wheels, independent and involuntary. But the rest stayed fixed, a flour-powdered clown or bloodless man, dull dry skin, eyes deepset, the nostrils black and prominently visible, blacker than the eyebrows or hair or the black necktie. Walking cautiously as though the pavement hurt his feet; I saw patent-leather shoes with such thin soles that he must have felt every roughness in the pavement. I don't know why I got down off the railing, nor very well why I decided to not give them the photo, to refuse that demand in which I guessed at their fear and cowardice. The clown and the woman consulted one another in silence: we made a perfect and unbearable triangle, something I felt compelled to break with a crack of a whip. I laughed in their faces and began to walk off, a little more slowly, I imagine, than the boy. At the level of the first houses, beside the iron footbridge, I turned around to look at them. They were not moving, but the man had dropped his newspaper; it seemed to me that the woman, her back to the parapet, ran her hands over the stone with the classical and absurd gesture of someone pursued looking for a way out.

What happened after that happened here, almost just now, in a room on the fifth floor. Several days went by before Michel developed the photos he'd taken on Sunday; his shots of the Conservatoire and of Sainte-Chapelle were all they should be. Then he found two or three proof-shots he'd forgotten, a poor attempt to catch a cat perched astonishingly on the roof of a rambling public urinal, and also the shot of the blond and the kid. The negative was so good that he made an enlargement; the enlargement was so good that he made one very much larger, almost the size of a poster. It did not occur to him (now one wonders and wonders) that only the shots of the Conservatoire were worth so much work. Of the whole series, the snapshot of the tip of the island was the only one which interested him; he tacked up the enlargement on one wall of the room, and the first day he spent some time looking at it and remembering, that gloomy operation of comparing the memory with the gone reality; a frozen memory, like any photo, where nothing is missing, not even, and especially, nothingness, the true solidifier of the scene. There was the woman, there was the boy, the tree rigid above their heads, the sky as sharp as the stone of the parapet, clouds and stones melded into a single substance and inseparable (now one with sharp edges is going by, like a thunderhead). The first two days I accepted what I had done, from the photo itself to the enlargement on the wall, and didn't even question that every once in a while I would interrupt my translation of José Norberto Allende's treatise to encounter once more the woman's face, the dark splotches on the railing. I'm such a jerk; it had never occurred to me that when we look at a photo from the front, the eyes reproduce exactly the position and the vision of the lens; it's these things that are taken for granted and it never occurs to anyone to think about them. From my chair, with the typewriter directly in front of me, I looked at the photo ten feet away, and then it occurred to me that I had hung it exactly at the point of view of the lens. It looked very good that way; no doubt, it was the best way to appreciate a photo, though the angle from the diagonal doubtless has its pleasures and might even divulge different aspects. Every few minutes, for example when I was unable to find the way to say in good French what José Norberto Allende was saying in very good Spanish, I raised my eyes and looked at the photo; sometimes the woman would catch my eye, sometimes the boy, sometimes the pavement where a dry leaf had fallen admirably situated to heighten a lateral section. Then I rested a bit from my labors, and I enclosed myself again happily in that morning in which the photo was drenched, I recalled ironically the angry picture of the woman demanding I give her the photograph, the boy's pathetic and ridiculous flight, the entrance on the scene of the man with the white face. Basically, I was satisfied with myself; my part had not been too brilliant, and since the French have been given the gift of the sharp response, I did not see very well why I'd chosen to leave without a complete demonstration of the rights, privileges and prerogatives of citizens. The important thing, the really important thing was having helped the kid to escape in time (this in case my theorizing was correct, which was not sufficiently proven, but the running away itself seemed to show it so). Out of plain meddling, I had given him the opportunity finally to take advantage of his fright to do something useful; now he would be regretting it, feeling his honor impaired, his manhood diminished. That was better than the attentions of a woman capable of looking as she had looked at him on that island. Michel is something of a puritan at times, he believes that one should not seduce someone from a position of strength. In the last analysis, taking that photo had been a good act.

Well, it wasn't because of the good act that I looked at it between paragraphs while I was working. At that moment I didn't know the reason, the reason I had tacked the enlargement onto the wall; maybe all fatal acts happen that way, and that is the condition of their fulfillment. I don't think the almost-furtive trembling of the leaves on the tree alarmed me. I was working on a sentence and rounded it out successfully. Habits are like immense herbariums, in the end an enlargement of 32 x 28 looks like a movie screen, where, on the tip of the island, a woman is speaking with a boy and a tree is shaking its dry leaves over their heads.

But her hands were just too much. I had just translated: "In that case, the second key resides in the intrinsic nature of difficulties which societies . . ." —when I saw the woman's hand beginning to stir slowly, finger by finger. There was nothing left of me, a phrase in French which I would never have to finish, a typewriter on the floor, a chair that squeaked and shook, fog. The kid had ducked his head like boxers do when they've done all they can and are waiting for the final blow to fall; he had turned up the collar of his overcoat and seemed more a prisoner than ever, the perfect victim helping promote the catastrophe. Now the woman was talking into his ear, and her hand opened again to lay itself against his cheekbone, to caress and caress it, burning it, taking her time. The kid was less startled than he was suspicious, once or twice he poked his head over the woman's shoulder and she continued talking, saying something that made him look back every few minutes toward that area where Michel knew the car was parked and the man in the grey hat, carefully eliminated from the photo but present in the boy's eyes (how doubt that now) in the words of the woman, in the woman's hands, in the vicarious presence of the woman. When I saw the man come up, stop near them and look at them, his hands in his pockets and a stance somewhere between disgusted and demanding, the master who is about to whistle in his dog after a frolic in the square, I understood, if that was to understand, what had to happen now, what had to have happened then, what would have to happen at that moment, among these people, just where I had poked my nose in to upset an established order, interfering innocently in that which had not happened, but which was now going to happen, now was going to be fulfilled. And what I had imagined earlier was much less horrible than the reality, that woman, who was not there by herself, she was not caressing or propositioning or encouraging for her own pleasure, to lead the angel away with his tousled hair and play the tease with his terror and his eager grace. The real boss was waiting there, smiling petulantly, already certain of the business; he was not the first to send a woman in the vanguard, to bring him the prisoners manacled with flowers. The rest of it would be so simple, the car, some house or another, drinks, stimulating engravings, tardy tears, the awakening in hell. And there was nothing I could do, this time I could do absolutely nothing. My strength had been a photograph, that, there, where they were taking their revenge on me, demonstrating clearly what was going to happen. The photo had been taken, the time had run out, gone; we were so far from one another, the abusive act had certainly already taken place, the tears already shed, and the rest conjecture and sorrow. All at once the order was inverted, they were alive, moving, they were deciding and had decided, they were going to their future; and I on this side, prisoner of another time, in a room on the fifth floor, to not know who they were, that woman, that man, and that boy, to be only the lens of my camera, something fixed, rigid, incapable of intervention. It was horrible, their mocking me, deciding it before my impotent eye, mocking me, for the boy again was looking at the flour-faced clown and I had to accept the fact that he was going to say yes, that the proposition carried money with it or a gimmick, and I couldn't yell for him to run, or even open the road to him again with a new photo, a small and almost meek intervention which would ruin the framework of drool and perfume. Everything was going to resolve itself right there, at that moment; there was like an immense silence which had nothing to do with physical silence. It was stretching it out, setting itself up. I think I screamed, I screamed terribly, and that at that exact second I realized that I was beginning to move toward them, four inches, a step, another step, the tree swung its branches rhythmically in the foreground, a place where the railing was tarnished emerged from the frame, the woman's face turned toward me as though surprised, was enlarging, and then I turned a bit, I mean that the camera turned a little, and without losing sight of the woman, I began to close in on the man who was looking at me with the black holes he had in places of eyes, surprised and angered both, he looked, wanting to nail me onto the air, and at that instant I happened to see something like a large bird outside the focus that was flying in a single swoop in front of the picture, and I leaned up against the wall of my room and was happy because the boy had just managed to escape, I saw him running off, in focus again, sprinting with his hair flying in the wind, learning finally to fly across the island, to arrive at the footbridge, return to the city. For the second time he'd escaped them, for the second time I was helping him to escape, returning him to his precarious paradise. Out of breath, I stood in front of them; no need to step closer, the game was played out. Of the woman you could see just maybe a shoulder and a bit of the hair, brutally cut off by the frame of the picture; but the man was directly center, his mouth half open, you could see a shaking black tongue, and he lifted his hands slowly, bringing them into the foreground, an instant still in perfect focus, and then all of him a lump that blotted out the island, the tree, and I shut my eyes, I didn't want to see any more, and I covered my face and broke into tears like an idiot.

Now there's a big white cloud, as on all these days, all this untellable time. What remains to be said is always a cloud, two clouds, or long hours of a sky perfectly clear, a very clean, clear rectangle tacked up with pins on the wall of my room. That was what I saw when I opened my eyes and dried them with my fingers: the clear sky, and then a cloud that drifted in from the left, passed gracefully and slowly across and disappeared on the right. And then another, and for a change sometimes, everything gets grey, all one enormous cloud, and suddenly the splotches of rain cracking down, for a long spell you can see it raining over the picture, like a spell of weeping reversed, and little by little, the frame becomes clear, perhaps the sun comes out, and again the clouds begin to come, two at a time, three at a time. And the pigeons once in a while, and a sparrow or two.

JOHN BARTH

1930–

John Barth and his twin sister Jill were born in Cambridge, on the eastern shore of Maryland. As a boy he was a serious musician, organizing his own band and starting study at the Juliard School of Music. His interest shifted to literature and he transferred to Johns Hopkins, where he received his M.A. in 1952. He supported himself, his wife, and children by his music until he got his first teaching job in 1953. He has taught ever since, publishing his first novel in 1956 and establishing himself as a major writer with *The Sot-Weed Factor* in 1960 and his collection of short fiction *Lost in the Funhouse* in 1968.

Lost in the Funhouse

For whom is the funhouse fun? Perhaps for lovers. For Ambrose it is *a place of fear and confusion.* He has come to the seashore with his family for the holiday, *the occasion of their visit is Independence Day, the most important secular holiday of the United States of America.* A single straight underline is the manuscript mark for italic type, *which in turn* is the printed equivalent to oral emphasis of words and phrases as well as the customary type for titles of complete works, not to mention. Italics are also employed, in fiction stories especially, for "outside," intrusive, or artificial voices, such as radio announcements, the texts of telegrams and newspaper articles, et cetera. They should be used *sparingly.* If passages originally in roman type are italicized by someone repeating them, it's customary to acknowledge the fact. *Italics mine.*

Ambrose was "at that awkward age." His voice came out high-pitched as a child's if he let himself get carried away; to be on the safe side, therefore, he moved and spoke with *deliberate calm* and *adult gravity.* Talking soberly of unimportant or irrelevant matters and listening consciously to the sound of your own voice are useful habits for maintaining control in this difficult interval. *Enroute* to Ocean City he sat in the back seat of the family car with his brother Peter, age fifteen, and Magda G——, age fourteen, a pretty girl and exquisite young lady, who lived not far from them on B—— Street in the town of D——, Maryland. Initials, blanks, or both were often substituted for proper names in nineteenth-century fiction to enhance the illusion of reality. It is as if the author felt it necessary to delete the names for reasons of tact or legal liability. Interestingly, as with other aspects of realism, it is an *illusion* that is being enhanced, by purely artificial means. Is it likely, does it violate the principle of verisimilitude, that a thirteen-year-old boy could make such a sophisticated observation? A girl of fourteen is *the psychological coeval* of a boy of fifteen or sixteen; a thirteen-year-old boy, therefore, even one precocious in some other respects, might be three years *her emotional junior.*

Thrice a year—on Memorial, Independence, and Labor Days—the family visits Ocean City for the afternoon and evening. When Ambrose and Peter's father was their age, the excursion was made by train, as mentioned in the novel *The 42nd Parallel* by John Dos Passos.

Many families from the same neighborhood used to travel together, with dependent relatives and often with Negro servants; schoolfuls of children swarmed through the railway cars; everyone shared everyone else's Maryland fried chicken, Virginia ham, deviled eggs, potato salad, beaten biscuits, iced tea. Nowadays (that is, in 19—, the year of our story) the journey is made by automobile—more comfortably and quickly though without the extra fun though without the *camaraderie* of a general excursion. It's all part of the deterioration of American life, their father declares; Uncle Karl supposes that when the boys take *their* families to Ocean City for the holidays they'll fly in Autogiros. Their mother, sitting in the middle of the front seat like Magda in the second, only with her arms on the seat-back behind the men's shoulders, wouldn't want the good old days back again, the steaming trains and stuffy long dresses; on the other hand she can do without Autogiros, too, if she has to become a grandmother to fly in them.

Description of physical appearance and mannerisms is one of several standard methods of characterization used by writers of fiction. It is also important to "keep the senses operating"; when a detail from one of the five senses, say visual, is "crossed" with a detail from another, say auditory, the reader's imagination is oriented to the scene, perhaps unconsciously. This procedure may be compared to the way surveyors and navigators determine their positions by two or more compass bearings, a process known as triangulation. The brown hair on Ambrose's mother's forearms gleamed in the sun like. Though right-handed, she took her left arm from the seat-back to press the dashboard cigar lighter for Uncle Karl. When the glass bead in its handle glowed red, the lighter was ready for use. The smell of Uncle Karl's cigar smoke reminded one of. The fragrance of the ocean came strong to the picnic ground where they always stopped for lunch, two miles inland from Ocean City. Having to pause for a full hour almost within sound of the breakers was difficult for Peter and Ambrose when they were younger; even at their present age it was not easy to keep their anticipation, *stimulated by the briny spume*, from turning into short temper. The Irish author James Joyce, in his unusual novel entitled *Ulysses*, now available in this country, uses the adjectives *snot-green* and *scrotum-tightening* to describe the sea. Visual; auditory; tactile; olfactory; gustatory. Peter and Ambrose's father, while steering their black 1936 LaSalle sedan with one hand, could with the other remove the first cigarette from a white pack of Lucky Strikes and, more remarkably, light it with a match forefingered from its book and thumbed against the flint paper without being detached. The matchbook cover merely advertised U. S. War Bonds and Stamps. A fine metaphor, simile, or other figure of speech, in addition to its obvious "first-order" relevance to the thing it describes, will be seen upon reflection to have a second order of significance: it may be drawn from the *milieu* of the action, for example, or be particularly appropriate to the sensibility of the narrator, even hinting to the reader things of which the narrator is unaware; or it may cast further and subtler lights upon the things it describes, sometimes ironically qualifying the more evident sense of the comparison.

To say that Ambrose's and Peter's mother was *pretty* is to accomplish nothing; the reader may acknowledge the proposition, but his imagination is not engaged. Besides, Magda was also pretty, yet in an altogether different way. Although she lived on B—— Street she had very good manners and did better than average in school. Her figure was very well developed for her age. Her right hand lay casually on the plush upholstery of the seat, very near Ambrose's left leg, on which his own hand rested. The space between their legs, between her right and his left leg, was out of the line of sight of anyone sitting on the other side of Magda, as well as anyone glancing into the rear-view mirror. Uncle Karl's face resembled Peter's—rather, vice versa. Both had dark hair and eyes, short husky statures, deep voices. Magda's left hand was probably in a similar position on her left side. The boys' father is difficult to describe; no particular feature of his appearance or manner stood out. He wore glasses and was principal of a T—— County grade school. Uncle Karl was a masonry contractor.

Although Peter must have known as well as Ambrose that the latter, because of his position in the car, would be the first to see the electrical towers of the power plant at V——, the halfway point of their trip, he leaned forward and slightly toward the center of the car and pretended to be looking for them through the flat pinewoods and tuckahoe creeks along the highway. For as long as the boys could remember, "looking for the Towers" had been a feature of the first half of their excursions to Ocean City, "looking for the standpipe" of the second. Though the game was childish, their mother preserved the tradition of rewarding the first to see the Towers with a candy-bar or piece of fruit. She insisted now that Magda play the game; the prize, she said, was "something hard to get nowadays." Ambrose decided not to join in; he sat far back in his seat. Magda, like Peter, leaned forward. Two sets of straps were discernible through the shoulders of her sun dress; the inside right one, a brassiere-strap, was fastened or shortened with a small safety pin. The right armpit of her dress, presumably the left as well, was damp with perspiration. The simple strategy for being first to espy the Towers, which Ambrose had understood by the age of four, was to sit on the right-hand side of the car. Whoever sat there, however, had also to put up with the worst of the sun, and so Ambrose, without mentioning the matter, chose sometimes the one and sometimes the other. Not impossibly Peter had never caught on to the trick, or thought that his brother hadn't simply because Ambrose on occasion preferred shade to a Baby Ruth or tangerine.

The shade-sun situation didn't apply to the front seat, owing to the windshield; if anything the driver got more sun, since the person on the passenger side not only was shaded below by the door and dashboard but might swing down his sunvisor all the way too.

"Is that them?" Magda asked. Ambrose's mother teased the boys for letting Magda win, insinuating that "somebody [had] a girlfriend." Peter and Ambrose's father reached a long thin arm across their mother to butt his cigarette in the dashboard ashtray, under the lighter. The prize this time for seeing the Towers first was a banana. Their mother bestowed it after chiding their father for wasting a half-smoked cigarette when everything was so scarce. Magda, to take the prize, moved her hand from so near Ambrose's that he could have touched it as though accidentally. She offered to share the prize, things like that were so hard to find; but everyone insisted it was hers alone. Ambrose's mother sang an iambic trimeter couplet from a popular song, femininely rhymed:

> "What's good is in the Army;
> What's left will never harm me."

Uncle Karl tapped his cigar ash out the ventilator window; some particles were sucked by the slipstream back into the car through the rear window on the passenger side. Magda demonstrated her ability to hold a banana in one hand and peel it with her teeth. She still sat forward; Ambrose pushed his glasses back onto the bridge of his nose with his left hand, which he then negligently let fall to the seat cushion immediately behind her. He even permitted the single hair, gold, on the second joint of his thumb to brush the fabric of her skirt. Should she have sat back at that instant, his hand would have been caught under her.

Plush upholstery prickles uncomfortably through gabardine slacks in the July sun. The function of the *beginning* of a story is to introduce the principal characters, establish their initial relationships, set the scene for the main action, expose the background of the situation if necessary, plant motifs and foreshadowings where appropriate, and initiate the first complication or whatever of the "rising action." Actually, if one imagines a story called "The Funhouse," or "Lost in the Funhouse," the details of the drive to Ocean City don't seem especially relevant. The *beginning* should recount the events between Ambrose's first sight of the funhouse early in the afternoon and his entering it with Magda and Peter in the evening. The *middle* would narrate all relevant events from the time he goes in to the time he loses his way; middles have the double and contradictory function of delaying the climax while at the same time preparing the reader for it and fetching him to it. Then the *ending* would tell what Ambrose does while he's lost, how he finally finds his way out, and what everybody makes of the experience. So far there's been no real dialogue, very little sensory detail, and nothing in the way of a *theme*. And a long time has gone by already without anything happening; it makes a person wonder. We haven't even reached Ocean City yet: we will never get out of the funhouse.

The more closely an author identifies with the narrator, literally or metaphorically, the less advisable it is, as a rule, to use the first-person narrative viewpoint. Once three years previously the young people *aforementioned* played Niggers and Masters in the backyard; when it was Ambrose's turn to be Master and theirs to be Niggers Peter had to go serve his evening papers; Ambrose was afraid to punish Magda alone, but she led him to the whitewashed Torture Chamber between the woodshed and the privy in the Slaves Quarters; there she knelt sweating among bamboo rakes and dusty Mason jars, pleadingly embraced his knees, and while bees droned in the lattice as if on an ordinary summer afternoon, purchased clemency at a surprising price set by herself. Doubtless she remembered nothing of this event; Ambrose on the other hand seemed unable to forget the least detail of his life. He even recalled how, standing beside himself with awed impersonality in the reeky heat, he'd stared the while at an empty cigar box in which Uncle Karl kept stone-cutting chisels: beneath the words *El Producto*; a laureled, loose-toga'd lady regarded the sea from a marble bench; beside her, forgotten or not yet turned to, was a five-stringed lyre. Her chin reposed on the back of her right hand; her left depended negligently from the bench-arm. The lower half of the scene and lady was peeled away; the words EXAMINED BY ___ were inked there into the wood. Nowadays cigar boxes are made of pasteboard. Ambrose wondered what Magda would have done, Ambrose wondered what Magda would do when she sat back on his hand as he resolved she should. Be angry. Make a teasing joke of it. Give no sign at all. For a long time she leaned forward, playing cow-poker with Peter against Uncle Karl and Mother and watching for the first sign of Ocean City. At nearly the same instant, picnic ground and Ocean City standpipe hove into view; an Amoco filling station on their side of the road cost Mother and Uncle Karl fifty cows and the game; Magda bounced back, clapping her right hand on Mother's right arm; Ambrose moved clear "in the nick of time."

At this rate our hero, at this rate our protagonist will remain in the funhouse forever. Narrative ordinarily consists of alternating dramatization and summarization. One symptom of nervous tension, paradoxically, is repeated and violent yawning; neither Peter nor Magda nor Uncle Karl nor Mother reacted in this manner. Although they were no longer small children, Peter and Ambrose were each given a dollar to spend on boardwalk amusements in addition to what money of their own they'd brought along. Magda too, though she protested she had ample spending money. The boys' mother made a little scene out of distributing the bills; she pretended that her sons and Magda were small children and cautioned them not to spend the sum too quickly or in one place. Magda promised with a merry laugh and, having both hands free, took the bill with her left. Peter laughed also and pledged in a falsetto to be a good boy. His imitation of a child was not clever. The boys' father was tall and thin, balding, fair-complexioned. Assertions of that sort are not effective; the reader may acknowledge the proposition, but. We should be much farther along than we are; something has gone wrong; not much of this preliminary rambling seems relevant. Yet everyone begins in the same place; how is it that most go along without difficulty but a few lose their way?

"Stay out from under the boardwalk," Uncle Karl growled from the side of his mouth. The boys' mother pushed his shoulder *in mock annoyance.* They were all standing before Fat May the Laughing Lady who advertised the funhouse. Larger than life, Fat May mechanically shook, rocked on her heels, slapped her thighs, while recorded laughter—uproarious, female—came amplified from a hidden loudspeaker. It chuckled, wheezed, wept; tried in vain to catch its breath; tittered, groaned, exploded raucous and anew. You couldn't hear it without laughing yourself, no matter how you felt. Father came back from talking to a Coast-Guardsman on duty and reported that the surf was spoiled with crude oil from tankers recently torpedoed offshore. Lumps of it, difficult to remove, made tarry tidelines on the beach and stuck on swimmers. Many bathed in the surf nevertheless and came out speckled; others paid to use a municipal pool and only sunbathed on the beach. We would do the latter. We would do the latter. We would do the latter.

Under the boardwalk, matchbook covers, grainy other things. What is the story's theme? Ambrose is ill. He perspires in the dark passages; candied apples-on-a-stick, delicious-looking, disappointing to eat. Funhouses need men's and ladies' rooms at intervals. Others perhaps have also vomited in corners and corridors; may even have had bowel movements liable to be stepped in in the dark. The word *fuck* suggests suction and/or and/or flatulence. Mother and Father; grandmothers and grandfathers on both sides; great-grandmothers and great-grandfathers on four sides, et cetera. Count a generation as thirty years: in approximately the year when Lord Baltimore was granted charter to the province of Maryland by Charles I, five hundred twelve

women—English, Welsh, Bavarian, Swiss—of every class and character, received into themselves the penises the intromittent organs of
five hundred twelve men, ditto, in every circumstance and posture, to
conceive the five hundred twelve ancestors of the two hundred
fifty-six ancestors of the et cetera et cetera et cetera et cetera et cetera et
cetera et cetera et cetera of the author, of the narrator, of this story,
Lost in the Funhouse. In alleyways, ditches, canopy beds, pinewoods,
bridal suites, ship's cabins, coach-and-fours, coaches-and-four, sultry toolsheds; on the cold sand under boardwalks, littered with El
Producto cigar butts, treasured with Lucky Strike cigarette stubs,
Coca-Cola caps, gritty turds, cardboard lollipop sticks, matchbook
covers warning that A Slip of the Lip Can Sink a Ship. The shluppish
whisper, continuous as seawash round the globe, tidelike falls and
rises with the circuit of dawn and dusk.

Magda's teeth. She was left-handed. Perspiration. They've gone all
the way, through, Magda and Peter, they've been waiting for hours
with Mother and Uncle Karl while Father searches for his lost son; they
draw french-fried potatoes from a paper cup and shake their heads.
They've named the children they'll one day have and bring to Ocean
City on holidays. Can spermatozoa properly be thought of as male
animalcules when there are no female spermatozoa? They grope
through hot, dark windings, past Love's Tunnel's fearsome obstacles.
Some perhaps lose their way.

Peter suggested then and there that they do the funhouse; he had
been through it before, so had Magda, Ambrose hadn't and
suggested, his voice cracking on account of Fat May's laughter, that
they swim first. All were chuckling, couldn't help it; Ambrose's father,
Ambrose's and Peter's father came up grinning like a lunatic with two
boxes of syrup-coated popcorn, one for Mother, one for Magda; the
men were to help themselves. Ambrose walked on Magda's right;
being by nature left-handed, she carried the box in her left hand. Up
front the situation was reversed.

"What are you limping for?" Magda inquired of Ambrose. He
supposed in a husky tone that his foot had gone to sleep in the car. Her
teeth flashed. "Pins and needles?" It was the honeysuckle on the
lattice of the former privy that drew the bees. Imagine being stung
there. How long is this going to take?

The adults decided to forego the pool; but Uncle Karl insisted they
change into swimsuits and do the beach. "He wants to watch the
pretty girls," Peter teased, and ducked behind Magda from Uncle
Karl's pretended wrath. "You've got all the pretty girls you need right
here," Magda declared, and Mother said: "Now that's the gospel
truth." Magda scolded Peter, who reached over her shoulder to sneak
some popcorn. "Your brother and father aren't getting any." Uncle

Karl wondered if they were going to have fireworks that night, what with the shortages. It wasn't the shortages, Mr. M——— replied; Ocean City had fireworks from pre-war. But it was too risky on account of the enemy submarines, some people thought.

"Don't seem like Fourth of July without fireworks," said Uncle Karl. The inverted tag in dialogue writing is still considered permissible with proper names or epithets, but sounds old-fashioned with personal pronouns. "We'll have 'em again soon enough," predicted the boys' father. Their mother declared she could do without fireworks: they reminded her too much of the real thing. Their father said all the more reason to shoot off a few now and again. Uncle Karl asked *rhetorically* who needed reminding, just look at people's hair and skin.

"The oil, yes," said Mrs. M———.

Ambrose had a pain in his stomach and so didn't swim but enjoyed watching the others. He and his father burned red easily. Magda's figure was exceedingly well developed for her age. She too declined to swim, and got mad, and became angry when Peter attempted to drag her into the pool. She always swam, he insisted; what did she mean not swim? Why did a person come to Ocean City?

"Maybe I want to lay here with Ambrose," Magda teased.

Nobody likes a pedant.

"Aha," said Mother. Peter grabbed Magda by one ankle and ordered Ambrose to grab the other. She squealed and rolled over on the beach blanket. Ambrose pretended to help hold her back. Her tan was darker than even Mother's and Peter's. "Help out, Uncle Karl!" Peter cried. Uncle Karl went to seize the other ankle. Inside the top of her swimsuit, however, you could see the line where the sunburn ended and, when she hunched her shoulders and squealed again, one nipple's auburn edge. Mother made them behave themselves. *"You* should certainly know," she said to Uncle Karl. Archly. "That when a lady says she doesn't feel like swimming, a gentleman doesn't ask questions." Uncle Karl said excuse *him;* Mother winked at Magda; Ambrose blushed; stupid Peter kept saying "Phooey on *feel like!"* and tugging at Magda's ankle; then even he got the point, and cannon-balled with a holler into the pool.

"I swear," Magda said, in mock *in feigned* exasperation.

The diving would make a suitable literary symbol. To go off the high board you had to wait in a line along the poolside and up the ladder. Fellows tickled girls and goosed one another and shouted to the ones at the top to hurry up, or razzed them for bellyfloppers. Once on the springboard some took a great while posing or clowning or deciding on a dive or getting up their nerve; others ran right off. Especially among the younger fellows the idea was to strike the funniest pose or do the craziest stunt as you fell; a thing that got harder to do as you kept on and kept on. But whether you hollered *Geronimo!* or *Sieg heil!*, held your nose or "rode a bicycle," pretended to be shot or did a perfect jacknife or changed your mind halfway down and ended up with nothing, it was over in two seconds, after all that wait. Spring, pose, splash. Spring, neat-o, splash. Spring, aw fooey, splash.

The grown-ups had gone on; Ambrose wanted to converse with Magda; she was remarkably well developed for her age; it was said that that came from rubbing with a turkish towel, and there were other theories. Ambrose could think of nothing to say except how good a diver Peter was, who was showing off for her benefit. You could pretty well tell by looking at their bathing suits and arm muscles how far along the different fellows were. Ambrose was glad he hadn't gone in swimming, the cold water shrank you up so. Magda pretended to be uninterested in the diving; she probably weighed as much as he did. If you knew your way around in the funhouse like your own bedroom, you could wait until a girl came along and then slip away without ever getting caught, even if her boyfriend was right with her. She'd think *he* did it! It would be better to be the boyfriend, and act outraged, and tear the funhouse apart.

Not act; *be*.

"He's a master diver," Ambrose said. In feigned admiration. "You really have to slave away at it to get that good." What would it matter anyhow if he asked her right out whether she remembered, even teased her with it as Peter would have?

There's no point in going farther; this isn't getting anybody anywhere; they haven't even come to the funhouse yet. Ambrose is off the track, in some new or old part of the place that's not supposed to be used; he strayed into it by some one-in-a-million chance, like the time the roller coaster car left the tracks in the nineteen-teens against all the laws of physics and sailed over the boardwalk in the dark. And they can't locate him because they don't know where to look. Even the designer and operator have forgotten this other part, that winds around on itself like a whelk shell. That winds around the right part like the snakes on Mercury's caduceus. Some people, perhaps, don't "hit their stride" until their twenties, when the growing-up business is over and women appreciate other things besides wisecracks and teasing and strutting. Peter didn't have one-tenth the imagination *he* had, not one-tenth. Peter did this naming-their-children thing as a joke, making up names like Aloysius and Murgatroyd, but Ambrose knew *exactly* how it would feel to be married and have children of your own, and be a loving husband and father, and go comfortably to work in the mornings and to bed with your wife at night, and wake up with her there. With a breeze coming through the sash and birds and mockingbirds singing in the Chinese-cigar trees. His eyes watered, there aren't enough ways to say that. He would be quite famous in his line of work. Whether Magda was his wife or not, one evening when he was wise-lined and gray at the temples he'd smile gravely, at a fashionable dinner party, and remind her of his youthful passion. The time they went with his family to Ocean City; the *erotic fantasies* he used to have about her. How long ago it seemed, and childish! Yet tender, too, *n'est-ce pas?* Would she have imagined that the world-famous whatever remembered how many strings were on the lyre on the bench beside the girl on the label of the cigar box he'd stared at in the toolshed at age ten while she, age eleven. Even then he had felt *wise beyond his years;* he'd stroked her hair and said in his deepest voice and correctest English, as to a dear child: "I shall never forget this moment."

But though he had breathed heavily, groaned as if ecstatic, what he'd really felt throughout was an odd detachment, as though some one else were Master. Strive as he might to be transported, he heard his mind take notes upon the scene: *This is what they call* passion. *I am experiencing it.* Many of the digger machines were out of order in the penny arcades and could not be repaired or replaced for the duration. Moreover the prizes, made now in USA, were less interesting than formerly, pasteboard items for the most part, and some of the machines wouldn't work on white pennies. The gypsy fortune-teller machine might have provided a foreshadowing of the climax of this story if Ambrose had operated it. It was even dilapidateder than most: the silver coating was worn off the brown metal handles, the glass windows around the dummy were cracked and taped, her kerchiefs and silks long-faded. If a man lived by himself, he could take a department-store mannequin with flexible joints and modify her in certain ways. *However:* by the time he was that old he'd have a real woman. There was a machine that stamped your name around a white-metal coin with a star in the middle: *A_____.* His son would be the second, and when the lad reached thirteen or so he would put a strong arm around his shoulder and tell him calmly: "It is perfectly normal. We have all been through it. It will not last forever." Nobody knew how to be what they were right. He'd smoke a pipe, teach his son how to fish and softcrab, assure him he needn't worry about himself. Magda would certainly give, Magda would certainly yield a great deal of milk, although guilty of occasional solecisms. It don't taste so bad. Suppose the lights came on now!

The day wore on. You think you're yourself, but there are other persons in you. Ambrose gets hard when Ambrose doesn't want to, *and obversely.* Ambrose watches them disagree; Ambrose watches him watch. In the funhouse mirror-room you can't see yourself go on forever, because no matter how you stand, your head gets in the way.

Even if you had a glass periscope, the image of your eye would cover up the thing you really wanted to see. The police will come; there'll be a story in the papers. That must be where it happened. Unless he can find a surprise exit, an unofficial backdoor or escape hatch opening on an alley, say, and then stroll up to the family in front of the funhouse and ask where everybody's been; *he's* been out of the place for ages. That's just where it happened, in that last lighted room: Peter and Magda found the right exit; he found one that you weren't supposed to find and strayed off into the works somewhere. In a perfect funhouse you'd be able to go only one way, like the divers off the highboard; getting lost would be impossible; the doors and halls would work like minnow traps or the valves in veins.

On account of German U-boats, Ocean City was "browned out": streetlights were shaded on the seaward side; shop-windows and boardwalk amusement places were kept dim, not to silhouette tankers and Liberty-ships for torpedoing. In a short story about Ocean City, Maryland, during World War II, the author could make use of the image of sailors on leave in the penny arcades and shooting galleries, sighting through the crosshairs of toy machine guns at swastika'd subs, while out in the black Atlantic a U-boat skipper squints through his periscope at real ships outlined by the glow of penny arcades. After dinner the family strolled back to the amusement end of the boardwalk. The boys' father had burnt red as always and was masked with Noxema, a minstrel in reverse. The grown-ups stood at the end of the boardwalk where the Hurricane of '33 had cut an inlet from the ocean to Assawoman Bay.

"Pronounced with a long *o*," Uncle Karl reminded Magda with a wink. His shirt sleeves were rolled up; Mother punched his brown biceps with the arrowed heart on it and said his mind was naughty. Fat May's laugh came suddenly from the funhouse, as if she'd just got the joke; the family laughed too at the coincidence. Ambrose went under the boardwalk to search for out-of-town matchbook covers with the aid of his pocket flashlight; he looked out from the edge of the North American continent and wondered how far their laughter carried over the water. Spies in rubber rafts; survivors in lifeboats. If the joke had been beyond his understanding, he could have said: "*The laughter was over his head.*" And let the reader see the serious wordplay on second reading.

He turned the flashlight on and then off at once even before the woman whooped. He sprang away, heart athud, dropping the light. What had the man grunted? Perspiration drenched and chilled him by the time he scrambled up to the family. "See anything?" his father asked. His voice wouldn't come; he shrugged and violently brushed sand from his pants legs.

"Let's ride the old flying horses!" Magda cried. I'll never be an author. It's been forever already, everybody's gone home, Ocean City's deserted, the ghost-crabs are tickling across the beach and down the littered cold streets. And the empty halls of clapboard hotels and abandoned funhouses. A tidal wave; an enemy air raid; a monster-crab swelling like an island from the sea. *The inhabitants fled in terror.* Magda clung to his trouser leg; he alone knew the maze's secret. "He gave his life that we might live," said Uncle Karl with a scowl of pain, as he. The fellow's hands had been tattooed; the woman's legs, the woman's fat white legs had. *An astonishing coincidence.* He yearned to tell Peter. He wanted to throw up for excitement. They hadn't even chased him. He wished he were dead.

One possible ending would be to have Ambrose come across another lost person in the dark. They'd match their wits together against the funhouse, struggle like Ulysses past obstacle after obstacle, help and encourage each other. Or a girl. By the time they found the exit they'd be closest friends, sweethearts if it were a girl; they'd know each other's inmost souls, be bound together *by the cement of shared adventure;* then they'd emerge into the light and it would turn out that his friend was a Negro. A blind girl. President Roosevelt's son. Ambrose's former archenemy.

Shortly after the mirror room he'd groped along a musty corridor, his heart already misgiving him at the absence of phosphorescent arrows and other signs. He's found a crack of light—not a door, it turned out, but a seam between the plyboard wall panels—and squinting up to it, espied a small old man, *in appearance not unlike* the photographs at home of Ambrose's late grandfather, nodding upon a stool beneath a bare, speckled bulb. A crude panel of toggle- and knife-switches hung beside the open fuse box near his head; elsewhere in the little room were wooden levers and ropes belayed to boat cleats. At the time, Ambrose wasn't lost enough to rap or call; later he couldn't find that crack. Now it seemed to him that he'd possibly dozed off for a few minutes somewhere along the way; certainly he was exhausted from the afternoon's sunshine and the evening's problems; he couldn't be sure he hadn't dreamed part or all of the sight. Had an old black wall fan droned like bees and shimmied two flypaper streamers? Had the funhouse operator—gentle, somewhat sad and tired-appearing, in expression not unlike the photographs at home of Ambrose's late Uncle Konrad—murmured in his sleep? Is there really such a person as Ambrose, or is he a figment of the author's imagination? Was it Assawoman Bay or Sinepuxent? Are there other errors of fact in this fiction? Was there another sound besides the little slap slap of thigh on ham, like water sucking at the chine-boards of a skiff?

When you're lost, the smartest thing to do is stay put till you're found, hollering if necessary. But to holler guarantees humiliation as well as rescue; keeping silent permits some saving of face—you can act surprised at the fuss when your rescuers find you and swear you weren't lost, if they do. What's more you might find your own way yet, *however belatedly*.

"Don't tell me your foot's still asleep!" Magda exclaimed as the three young people walked from the inlet to the area set aside for ferris wheels, carrousels, and other carnival rides, they having decided in favor of the vast and ancient merry-go-round instead of the funhouse. What a sentence, everything was wrong from the outset. People don't know what to make of him, he doen't know what to make of himself, he's only thirteen, *athletically and socially inept*, not astonishingly bright, but there are antennae; he has . . . some sort of receivers in his head; things speak to him, he understands more than he should, the world winks at him through its objects, grabs grinning at his coat. Everybody else is in on some secret he doesn't know; they've forgotten to tell him. Through simple *procrastination* his mother put off his baptism until this year. Everyone else had it done as a baby; he'd assumed the same of himself, as had his mother, so she claimed, until it was time for him to join Grace Methodist-Protestant and the oversight came out. He was mortified, but pitched sleepless through his private catechizing, intimidated by the ancient mysteries, a thirteen year old would never say that, resolved to experience conversion like St. Augustine. When the water touched his brow and Adam's sin left him, he contrived by a strain like defecation to bring tears into his eyes—but felt nothing. There was some simple, radical difference about him; he hoped it was genius, feared it was madness, devoted himself to amiability and inconspicuousness. Alone on the seawall near his house he was seized by the terrifying transports he'd thought to find in toolshed, in Communion-cup. The grass was alive! The town, the river, himself, were not imaginary; time roared in his ears like wind; the world was *going on!* This part ought to be dramatized. The Irish author James Joyce once wrote. Ambrose M____ is going to scream.

There is no *texture of rendered sensory detail,* for one thing. The faded distorting mirrors beside Fat May; the impossibility of choosing a mount when one had but a single ride on the great carrousel; the *vertigo attendant on his recognition* that Ocean City was worn out, the place of fathers and grandfathers, straw-boatered men and parasoled ladies survived by their amusements. Money spent, the three paused at Peter's insistence beside Fat May to watch the girls get their skirts blown up. The object was to tease Magda, who said: "I swear, Peter M____, you've got a one-track mind! Amby and me aren't *interested* in such things." In the tumbling-barrel, too, just inside the Devil's-mouth entrance to the funhouse, the girls were upended and their boyfriends and others could see up their dresses if they cared to. Which was the whole point, Ambrose realized. Of the entire funhouse! If you looked around, you noticed that almost all the people on the boardwalk were paired off into couples except the small children; in a way, that was the whole point of Ocean City! If you had X-ray eyes and could see everything going on at that instant under the boardwalk and in all the hotel rooms and cars and alleyways, you'd realize that all that normally *showed,* like restaurants and dance halls and clothing and test-your-strength machines, was merely preparation and intermission. Fat May screamed.

Because he watched the goings-on from the corner of his eye, it was Ambrose who spied the half-dollar on the boardwalk near the tumbling-barrel. Losers weepers. The first time he'd heard some people moving through a corridor not far away, just after he'd lost sight of the crack of light, he'd decided not to call to them, for fear they'd guess he was scared and poke fun; it sounded like roughnecks; he'd hoped they'd come by and he could follow in the dark without their knowing. Another time he'd heard just one person, unless he imagined it, bumping along as if on the other side of the plywood; perhaps Peter coming back for him, or Father, or Magda lost too. Or the owner and operator of the funhouse. He'd called out once, as though merrily: "Anybody know where the heck we are?" But the query was too stiff, his voice cracked, when the sounds stopped he was terrified: maybe it was a queer who waited for fellows to get lost, or a longhaired filthy monster that lived in some cranny of the funhouse. He stood rigid for hours it seemed like, scarcely respiring. His future was shockingly clear, in outline. He tried holding his breath to the point of unconsciousness. There ought to be a button you could push to end your life absolutely without pain; disappear in a flick, like turning out a light. He would push it instantly! He despised Uncle Karl. But he despised his father too, for not being what he was supposed to be. Perhaps his father hated *his* father, and so on, and his son would hate him, and so on. Instantly!

Naturally he didn't have nerve enough to ask Magda to go through the funhouse with him. With incredible nerve and to everyone's surprise he invited Magda, quietly and politely, to go through the funhouse with him. "I warn you, I've never been through it before," he added, *laughing easily;* "but I reckon we can manage somehow. The important thing to remember, after all, is that it's meant to be a *fun*house; that is, a place of amusement. If people really got lost or injured or too badly frightened in it, the owner'd go out of business. There'd even be lawsuits. No character in a work of fiction can make a speech this long without interruption or acknowledgment from the other characters."

Mother teased Uncle Karl: "Three's a crowd, I always heard." But actually Ambrose was relieved that Peter now had a quarter too. Nothing was what it looked like. Every instant, under the surface of the Atlantic Ocean, millions of living animals devoured one another. Pilots were falling in flames over Europe; women were being forcibly raped in the South Pacific. His father should have taken him aside and said: "There is a simple secret to getting through the funhouse, as simple as being first to see the Towers. Here it is. Peter does not know it; neither does your Uncle Karl. You and I are different. Not surprisingly, you've often wished you weren't. Don't think I haven't noticed how unhappy your childhood has been! But you'll understand, when I tell you, why it had to be kept secret until now. And you won't regret not being like your brother and your uncle. *On the contrary!*" If you knew all the stories behind all the people on the boardwalk, you'd see that *nothing* was what it looked like. Husbands and wives often hated each other; parents didn't necessarily love their children; et cetera. A child took things for granted because he had nothing to compare his life to and everybody acted as if things were as they should be. Therefore each saw himself as the hero of the story, when the truth might turn out to be that he's the villain, or the coward. And there wasn't one thing you could do about it!

Hunchbacks, fat ladies, fools—that no one chose what he was was unbearable. In the movies he'd meet a beautiful young girl in the funhouse; they'd have hairs-breadth escapes from real dangers; he'd do and say the right things; she also; in the end they'd be lovers; their dialogue lines would match up; he'd be perfectly at ease; she'd not only like him well enough, she'd think he was *marvelous*; she'd lie awake thinking about *him,* instead of vice versa—the way *his* face looked in different lights and how he stood and exactly what he'd said—and yet that would be only one small episode in his wonderful life, among many many others. Not a *turning point* at all. What had happened in the toolshed was nothing. He hated, he loathed his parents! One reason for not writing a lost-in-the-funhouse story is that either everybody's felt what Ambrose feels, in which case it goes without saying, or else no normal person feels such things, in which case Ambrose is a freak. "Is anything more tiresome, in fiction, than the problems of sensitive adolescents?" And it's all too long and rambling, as if the author. For all a person knows the first time through, the end could be just around any corner; perhaps, *not impossibly* it's been within reach any number of times. On the other hand he may be scarcely past the start, with everything yet to get through, an intolerable idea.

Fill in: His father's raised eyebrows when he announced his decision to do the funhouse with Magda. Ambrose understands now, but didn't then, that his father was wondering whether he knew what the funhouse was *for*—especially since he didn't object, as he should have, when Peter decided to come along too. The ticket-woman, witchlike, mortifying him when inadvertently he gave her his name-coin instead of the half-dollar, then unkindly calling Magda's attention to the birthmark on his temple: "Watch out for him, girlie, he's a marked man!" She wasn't even cruel, he understood, only vulgar and insensitive. Somewhere in the world there was a young woman with such splendid understanding that she'd see him entire, like a poem or story, and find his words so valuable after all that when he confessed his apprehensions she would explain why they were in fact the very things that made him precious to her . . . and to Western Civilization! There was no such girl, the simple truth being. Violent yawns as they approached the mouth. Whispered advice from an old-timer on a bench near the barrel: "Go crabwise and ye'll get an eyeful without upsetting!" Composure vanished at the first pitch: Peter hollered joyously, Magda tumbled, shrieked, clutched her skirt; Ambrose scrambled crabwise, tight-lipped with terror, was soon out, watched his dropped name-coin slide among the couples. Shamefaced he saw that to get through expeditiously was not the point; Peter feigned assistance in order to trip Magda up, shouted "I see Christmas!" when her legs went flying. The old man, his latest betrayer, cackled approval. A dim hall then of black-thread cobwebs and recorded gibber: he took Magda's elbow to steady her against revolving discs set in the slanted floor to throw your feet out from under, and explained to her in a calm, deep voice his theory that each phase of the funhouse was triggered either automatically, by a series of photoelectric devices, or else manually by operators stationed at peepholes. But he lost his voice thrice as the discs unbalanced him; Magda was anyhow squealing; but at one point she clutched him about the waist to keep from falling, and her right cheek pressed for a moment against his belt-buckle. Heroically he drew her up, it was his chance to clutch her close as if for support and say: "I love you." He even put an arm lightly about the small of her back before a sailor-and-girl pitched into them from behind, sorely treading his left big toe and knocking Magda asprawl with them. The sailor's girl was a string-haired hussy with a loud laugh and light blue drawers; Ambrose realized that he wouldn't have said "I love you" anyhow, and was smitten with self-contempt. How much better it would be to be that common sailor! A wiry little Seaman 3rd, the fellow squeezed a girl to each side and stumbled hilarious into the mirror room, closer to Magda in thirty seconds than Ambrose had got in thirteen years. She giggled at something the fellow said to Peter; she drew her hair from her eyes with a movement so womanly it struck Ambrose's heart; Peter's smacking her backside then seemed particularly coarse. But

Magda made a pleased indignant face and cried, "All right for *you*, mister!" and pursued Peter into the maze without a backward glance. The sailor followed after, leisurely, drawing his girl against his hip; Ambrose understood not only that they were all so relieved to be rid of his burdensome company that they didn't even notice his absence, but that he himself shared their relief. Stepping from the treacherous passage at last into the mirror-maze, he saw once again, more clearly than ever, how readily he deceived himself into supposing he was a person. He even foresaw, wincing at his dreadful self-knowledge, that he would repeat the deception, at ever-rarer intervals, all his wretched life, so fearful were the alternatives. Fame, madness, suicide; perhaps all three. It's not believable that so young a boy could articulate that reflection, and in fiction the merely true must always yield to the plausible. Moreover, the symbolism is in places heavy-footed. Yet Ambrose M___ understood, as few adults do, that the famous loneliness of the great was no popular myth but a general truth—furthermore, that it was as much cause as effect.

All the preceding except the last few sentences is exposition that should've been done earlier or interspersed with the present action instead of lumped together. No reader would put up with so much with such *prolixity*. It's interesting that Ambrose's father, though presumably an intelligent man (as indicated by his role as grade-school principal), neither encouraged nor discouraged his sons at all in any way—as if he either didn't care about them or cared all right but didn't know how to act. If this fact should contribute to one of them's becoming a celebrated but wretchedly unhappy scientist, was it a good thing or not? He too might someday face the question; it would be useful to know whether it had tortured his father for years, for example, or never once crossed his mind.

In the maze two important things happened. First, our hero found a name-coin someone else had lost or discarded: *AMBROSE*, suggestive of the famous lightship and of his late grandfather's favorite dessert, which his mother used to prepare on special occasions out of coconut, oranges, grapes, and what else. Second, as he wondered at the endless replication of his image in the mirrors, second, as he *lost himself in the reflection* that the necessity for an observer makes perfect observation impossible, better make him eighteen at least, yet that would render other things unlikely, he heard Peter and Magda chuckling somewhere together in the maze. "Here!" "No, here!" they shouted to each other; Peter said, "Where's Amby?" Magda murmured. "Amb?" Peter called. In a pleased, friendly voice. He didn't reply. The truth was, his brother was a *happy-go-lucky youngster* who'd've been better off with a regular brother of his own, but who seldom complained of his lot and was generally cordial. Ambrose's throat ached; there aren't enough different ways to say that. He stood quietly while the two young people giggled and thumped through the glittering maze, hurrah'd their discovery of its exit, cried out in joyful alarm at what next beset them. Then he set his mouth and followed after, as he supposed, took a wrong turn, strayed into the pass *wherein he lingers yet*.

The action of conventional dramatic narrative may be represented by a diagram called Freitag's Triangle:

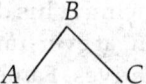

or more accurately by a variant of that diagram:

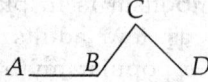

in which *AB* represents the exposition, *B* the introduction of conflict, *BC* the "rising action," complication, or development of the conflict, *C* the climax, or turn of the action, *CD* the dénouement, or resolution of the conflict. While there is no reason to regard this pattern as an absolute necessity, like many other conventions it became conventional because great numbers of people over many years learned by trial and error that it was effective; one ought not to forsake it, therefore, unless one wishes to forsake as well the effect of drama or has clear cause to feel that deliberate violation of the "normal" pattern can better can better effect that effect. This can't go on much longer; it can go on forever. He died telling stories to himself in the dark; years later, when that vast unsuspected area of the funhouse came to light, the first expedition found his skeleton in one of its labyrinthine corridors and mistook it for part of the entertainment. He died of starvation telling himself stories in the dark; but unbeknownst unbeknownst to him, an assistant operator of the funhouse, happening to overhear him, crouched just behind the plyboard partition and wrote down his every word. The operator's daughter, an exquisite young woman with a figure unusually well developed for her age, crouched just behind the partition and transcribed his every word. Though she had never laid eyes on him, she recognized that here was one of Western Culture's truly great imaginations, the eloquence of whose suffering would be an inspiration to unnumbered. And her heart was torn between her love for the misfortunate young man (yes, she loved him, though she had never laid though she knew him only—but how well!—through his words, and the deep, calm voice in which he spoke them) between her love et cetera and her womanly intuition that only in suffering and isolation could he give voice et cetera. Lone dark dying. Quietly she kissed the rough plyboard, and a tear fell upon the page. Where she had written in shorthand *Where she had written in shorthand* Where she had written in shorthand *Where she* et cetera. A long time ago we should have passed the apex of Freitag's Triangle and made brief work of the *dénouement;* the plot doesn't rise by meaningful steps but winds upon itself, digresses, retreats, hesitates, sighs, collapses, expires. The climax of the story must be it's protagonist's discovery of a way to get through the funhouse. But he has found none, may have ceased to search.

What relevance does the war have to the story? Should there be fireworks outside or not?

Ambrose wandered, languished, dozed. Now and then he fell into his habit of rehearsing to himself the unadventurous story of his life, narrated from the third-person point of view, from his earliest memory parenthesis of maple leaves stirring in the summer breath of tidewater Maryland end of parenthesis to the present moment. Its principle events, on this telling, would appear to have been *A, B, C,* and *D.*

He imagined himself years hence, successful, married, at ease in the world, the trials of his adolescence far behind him. He has come to the seashore with his family for the holiday: how Ocean City has changed! But at one seldom at one ill-frequented end of the boardwalk a few derelict amusements survive from times gone by: the great carrousel from the turn of the century, with its monstrous griffins and mechanical concert band; the roller coaster rumored since 1916 to have been condemned; the mechanical shooting gallery in which only the image of our enemies changed. His own son laughs with Fat May and wants to know what a funhouse is; Ambrose hugs the sturdy lad close and smiles around his pipestem at his wife.

The family's going home. Mother sits between Father and Uncle Karl, who teases him good-naturedly who chuckles over the fact that the comrade with whom he'd fought his way shoulder to shoulder through the funhouse had turned out to be a blind Negro girl—to their mutual discomfort, as they'd opened their souls. But such are the walls of custom, which even. Whose arm is where? How must it feel. He dreams of a funhouse vaster by far than any yet constructed; but by then they may be out of fashion, like steamboats and excursion trains. Already quaint and seedy: the draperied ladies on the frieze of the carrousel are his father's father's mooncheeked dreams; if he thinks of it more he will vomit his apple-on-a-stick.

He wonders: will he become a regular person? Something has gone wrong; his vaccination didn't take; at the Boy-Scout initiation campfire he only pretended to be deeply moved, as he pretends to this hour that it is not so bad after all in the funhouse, and that he has a little limp. How long will it last? He envisions a truly astonishing funhouse, incredibly complex yet utterly controlled from a great central switchboard like the console of a pipe organ. Nobody had enough imagination. He could design such a place himself, wiring and all, and he's only thirteen years old. He would be its operator: panel lights would show what was up in every cranny of its cunning of its multifarious vastness; a switch-flick would ease this fellow's way, complicate that's, to balance things out; if anyone seemed lost or frightened, all the operator had to do was.

He wishes he had never entered the funhouse. But he has. Then he wishes he were dead. But he's not. Therefore he will construct funhouses for others and be their secret operator—though he would rather be among the lovers for whom funhouses are designed.

ROBERT COOVER
1932–

Robert Coover was born in Charles City, Iowa, but spent most of his youth in southern Illinois and Indiana, where his father worked on newspapers. As a boy he developed an elaborate baseball game, played with dice, for which he invented players, leagues, and a whole world. This later bacame the basis for his metaphysical novel *The Universal Baseball Association, J. Henry Waugh, Prop.*, published in 1968. He graduated from Indiana University in 1953 and went to Officers Candidate School in the U.S. Navy, serving in Europe. In Spain he met and married a doctor's daughter from Tarragona. They have three children. He returned to the United States, did some teaching in Illinois, graduate work at the University of Chicago, and began to publish experimental short fiction. His first success was an award-winning novel about a mining disaster, *The Origin of the Brunists* (1966), but his collection of experiments in short fiction, *Pricksongs and Descants* (1969), has received the most critical attention and acclaim. He lived and worked in England for ten years after that but has recently returned to the United States.

The Hat Act

In the middle of the stage: a plain table.

A man enters, dressed as a magician with black cape and black silk hat. Doffs hat in wide sweep to audience, bows elegantly.

Applause.

He displays inside of hat. It is empty. He thumps it. It is clearly empty. Places hat on table, brim up. Extends both hands over hat, tugs back sleeves exposing wrists, snaps fingers. Reaches in, extracts a rabbit.

Applause.

Pitches rabbit into wings. Snaps fingers over hat again, reaches in, extracts a dove.

Applause.

Pitches dove into wings. Snaps fingers over hat, reaches in, extracts another rabbit. No applause. Stuffs rabbit hurriedly back in hat, snaps fingers, reaches in, extracts another hat, precisely like the one from which it came.

Applause.

Places second hat alongside first one. Snaps fingers over new hat, withdraws a third hat, exactly like the first two.

Light applause.

Snaps fingers over third hat, withdraws a fourth hat, again identical. No applause. Does not snap fingers. Peers into fourth hat, extracts a fifth one. In fifth, he finds a sixth. Rabbit appears in third hat. Magician extracts seventh hat from sixth. Third hat rabbit withdraws a second rabbit from first hat. Magician withdraws eighth hat from seventh, ninth from eighth, as rabbits extract other rabbits from other hats. Rabbits and hats are everywhere. Stage is one mad turmoil of hats and rabbits.

Laughter and applause.

Frantically, magician gathers up hats and stuffs them into each other, bowing, smiling at audience, pitching rabbits three and four at a time into wings, smiling, bowing. It is a desperate struggle. At first, it is difficult to be sure he is stuffing hats and pitching rabbits faster than they are reappearing. Bows, stuffs, pitches, smiles, perspires.

Laughter mounts.

Slowly the confusion diminishes. Now there is one small pile of hats and rabbits. Now there are no rabbits. At last there are only two hats. Magician, perspiring from overexertion, gasping for breath, staggers to table with two hats.

Light applause, laughter.

Magician, mopping brow with silk handkerchief, stares in perplexity at two remaining hats. Pockets handkerchief. Peers into one hat, then into other. Attempts tentatively to stuff first into second, but in vain. Attempts to fit second into first, but also without success. Smiles weakly at audience. No applause. Drops first hat to floor, leaps on it until crushed. Wads crushed hat in fist, attempts once more to stuff it into second hat. Still, it will not fit.

Light booing, impatient applause.

Trembling with anxiety, magician pressed out first hat, places it brim up on table, crushes second hat on floor. Wads second hat, tries desperately to jam it into first hat. No, it will not fit. Turns irritably to pitch second hat into wings.

Loud booing.

Freezes. Pales. Returns to table with both hats, first in fair condition brim up, second still in a crumpled wad. Faces hats in defeat. Bows head as though to weep silently.

Hissing and booing.

Smile suddenly lights magician's face. He smoothes out second hat and places it firmly on his head, leaving first hat bottomside-up on table. Crawls up on table and disappears feet first into hat.

Surprised applause.

Moments later, magician's feet poke up out of hat on table, then legs, then torso. Last part to emerge is magician's head, which, when lifted from table, brings first hat with it. Magician doffs first hat to audience, shows it is empty. Second hat has disappeared. Bows deeply.

Enthusiastic and prolonged applause, cheers.

Magician returns hat to head, thumps it, steps behind table. Without removing hat, reaches up, snaps fingers, extracts rabbit from top of hat.

Applause.

Pitches rabbit into wings. Snaps fingers, withdraws dove from top of hat.

Sprinkling of applause.

Pitches dove into wings. Snaps fingers, extracts lovely assistant from top of hat.

Astonished but enthusiastic applause and whistles.

Lovely assistant wears high feathery green hat, tight green halter, little green shorts, black net stockings, high green heels. Smiles coyly at whistles and applause, scampers bouncily offstage.

Whistling and shouting, applause.

Magician attempts to remove hat, but it appears to be stuck. Twists and writhes in struggle with stuck hat.

Mild laughter.

Struggle continues. Contortions. Grimaces.

Laughter.

Finally, magician requests two volunteers from audience. Two large brawny men enter stage from audience, smiling awkwardly.

Light applause and laughter.

One large man grasps hat, other clutches magician's legs. They pull cautiously. The hat does not come off. They pull harder. Still, it is stuck. They tug now with great effort, their heavy faces reddening, their thick neck muscles taut and throbbing. Magician's neck stretches, snaps in two: POP! Large men tumble apart, rolling to opposite sides of stage, one with body, other with hat containing magician's severed head.

Screams of terror.

Two large men stand, stare aghast at handiwork, clutch mouths.

Shrieks and screams.

Decapitated body stands.

Shrieks and screams.

Zipper in front of decapitated body opens, magician emerges. He is as before, wearing same black cape and same black silk hat. Pitches deflated decapitated body into wings. Pitches hat and head into wings. Two large men sigh with immense relief, shake heads as though completely baffled, smile faintly, return to audience. Magician doffs hat and bows.

Wild applause, shouts, cheers.

Lovely assistant, still in green costume, enters, carrying glass of water.

Applause and whistling.

Lovely assistant acknowledges whistling with coy smile, sets glass of water on table, stands dutifully by. Magician hands her his hat, orders her by gesture to eat it.

Whistling continues.

Lovely assistant smiles, bites into hat, chews slowly.

Laughter and much whistling.

She washes down each bit of hat with water from glass she has brought in. Hat at last is entirely consumed, except for narrow silk band left on table. Sighs, pats slender exposed tummy.

Laughter and applause, excited whistling.

Magician invites young country boy in audience to come to stage. Young country boy steps forward shyly, stumbling clumsily over own big feet. Appears confused and utterly abashed.

Loud laughter and catcalls.

Young country boy stands with one foot on top of other, staring down redfaced at his hands, twisting nervously in front of him.

Laughter and catcalls increase.

Lovely assistant sidles up to boy, embraces him in motherly fashion. Boy ducks head away, steps first on foot, then on other, wrings hands.

More laughter and catcalls, whistles.

Lovely assistant winks broadly at audience, kisses young country boy on cheek. Boy jumps as though scalded, trips over own feet, and falls to floor.

Thundering laughter.

Lovely assistant helps boy to his feet, lifting him under armpits. Boy, ticklish, struggles and giggles helplessly.

Laughter (as before).

Magician raps table with knuckles. Lovely assistant releases hysterical country boy, returns smiling to table. Boy resumes awkward stance, wipes his runny nose with back of his hand, sniffles.

Mild laughter and applause.

Magician hands lovely assistant narrow silk band of hat she has eaten. She stuffs band into her mouth, chews thoughtfully, swallows with some difficulty, shudders. She drinks from glass. Laughter and shouting have fallen away to expectant hush. Magician grasps nape of lovely assistant's neck, forces her head with its feathered hat down between her stockinged knees. He releases grip and her head springs back to upright position. Magician repeats action slowly. Then repeats action rapidly four or five times. Looks inquiringly at lovely assistant. Her face is flushed from exertion. She meditates, then shakes head: no. Magician again forces her head to her knees, releases grip, allowing head to snap back to upright position. Repeats this two or three times. Looks inquiringly at lovely assistant. She smiles and nods. Magician drags abashed young country boy over behind lovely assistant and invites him to reach into lovely assistant's tight green shorts. Young country boy is flustered beyound belief.

Loud laughter and whistling resumes.

Young country boy, in desperation, tries to escape. Magician captures him and drags him once more behind lovely assistant.

Laughter etc. (as before).

Magician grasps country boy's arm and thrusts it forcibly into assistant's shorts. Young country boy wets pants.

Hysterical laughter and catcalls.

Lovely assistant grimaces once. Magician, smiling, releases grip on agonizingly embarrassed country boy. Boy withdraws hand. In it, he finds he is holding magician's original black silk hat, entirely whole, narrow silk band and all.

Wild applause and footstamping, laughter and cheers.

Magician winks broadly at audience, silencing them momentarily, invites young country boy to don hat. Boy ducks head shyly. Magician insists. Timidly, grinning foolishly, country boy lifts hat to head. Water spills out, runs down over his head, and soaks young country boy.

Laughter, applause, wild catcalls.

Young country boy, utterly humiliated, drops hat and turns to run offstage, but lovely assistant is standing on his foot. He trips and falls to his face.

Laughter, etc. (as before).

Country boy crawls abjectly offstage on his stomach. Magician, laughing heartily with audience, pitches lovely assistant into wings, picks up hat from floor. Brushes hat on sleeve, thumps it two or three times, returns it with elegant flourish to his head.

Appreciative applause.

Magician steps behind table. Carefully brushes off one space on table. Blows away dust. Reaches for hat. But again, it seems to be stuck. Struggles feverishly with hat.

Mild laughter.

Requests volunteers. Same two large men as before enter. One quickly grasps hat, other grasps magician's legs. They tug furiously, but in vain.

Laughter and applause.

First large man grabs magician's head under jaw. Magician appears to be protesting. Second large man wraps magician's legs around his waist. Both pull apart with terrific strain, their faces reddening, the veins in their temples throbbing. Magician's tongue protrudes, hands flutter hopelessly.

Laughter and applause.

Magician's neck stretches. But it does not snap. It is now several feet long. Two large men strain mightily.

Laughter and applause.

Magician's eyes pop like bubbles from their sockets.

Laughter and applause.

Neck snaps at last. Large men tumble head over heels with respective bloody burdens to opposite sides of stage. Expectant amused hush falls over audience. First large man scrambles to his feet, pitches head and hat into wings, rushes to assist second large man. Together they unzip decapitated body. Lovely assistant emerges.

Surprised laughter and enthusiastic applause, whistling.

Lovely assistant pitches deflated decapitated body into wings. Large men ogle her and make mildly obscene gestures for audience.

Mounting laughter and friendly catcalls.

Lovely assistant invites one of two large men to reach inside her tight green shorts.

Wild whistling.

Both large men jump forward eagerly, tripping over each other and tumbling to floor in angry heap. Lovely assistant winks broadly at audience.

Derisive catcalls.

Both men stand, face each other, furious. First large man spits at second. Second pushes first. First returns push, toppling second to floor. Second leaps to feet, smashes first in nose. First reels, wipes blood from nose, drives fist into second's abdomen.

Loud cheers.

Second weaves confusedly, crumples miserably to floor clutching abdomen. First kicks second brutally in face.

Cheers and mild laughter.

Second staggers blindly to feet, face a mutilated mess. First smashes second back against wall, knees him in groin. Second doubles over, blinded with pain. First clips second with heel of hand behind ear. Second crumples to floor, dead.

Prolonged cheering and applause.

First large man acknowledges applause with self-conscious bow. Flexes knuckles. Lovely assistant approaches first large man, embraces him in motherly fashion, winks broadly at audience.

Prolonged applause and whistling.

Large man grins and embraces lovely assistant in unmotherly fashion, as she makes faces of mock astonishment for audience.

Shouting and laughter, wild whistling.

Lovely assistant frees self from large man, turns plump hindquarters to him, and bends over, her hands on her knees, her shapely legs straight. Large man grins at audience, pats lovely assistant's green clad rear.

Wild shouting, etc. (as before).

Large man reaches inside lovely assistant's tight green shorts, rolls his eyes, and grins obscenely. She grimaces and wiggles rear briefly.

Wild shouting, etc. (as before).

Large man withdraws hand from inside lovely assistant's shorts, extracting magician in black cape and black silk hat.

Thunder of astonished applause.

Magician bows deeply, doffing hat to audience.

Prolonged enthusiastic applause, cheering.

Magician pitches lovely assistant and first large man into wings. Inspects second large man, lying dead on stage. Unzips him and young country boy emerges, flushed and embarrassed. Young country boy creeps abjectly offstage on stomach.

Laughter and catcalls, more applause.

Magician pitches deflated corpse of second large man into wings. Lovely assistant reenters, smiling, dressed as before in high feathery hat, tight green halter, green shorts, net stockings, high heels.

Applause and whistling.

Magician displays inside of hat to audience as lovely assistant points to magician. He thumps hat two or three times. It is empty. Places hat on table, and invites lovely assistant to enter it. She does so.

Vigorous applause.

Once she has entirely disappeared, magician extends both hands over hat, tugs back sleeves exposing wrists, snaps fingers. Reaches in, extracts one green high-heeled shoe.

Applause.

Pitches shoe into wings. Snaps fingers over hat again. Reaches in, withdraws a second shoe.

Applause.

Pitches shoe into wings. Snaps finger over hat. Reaches in, withdraws one long net stocking.

Applause and scattered whistling.

Pitches stocking into wings. Snaps fingers over hat. Reaches in, extracts a second black net stocking.

Applause and scattered whistling.

Pitches stocking into wings. Snaps fingers over hat. Reaches in, pulls out high feathery hat.

Increased applause and whistling, rhythmic stamping of feet.

Pitches hat into wings. Snaps fingers over hat. Reaches in, fumbles briefly.

Light laughter.

Withdraws green halter, displays it with grand flourish.

Enthusiastic applause, shouting, whistling, stamping of feet.

Pitches halter into wings. Snaps fingers over hat. Reaches in, fumbles. Distant absorbed gaze.

Burst of laughter.

Withdraws green shorts, displays them with elegant flourish.

Tremendous crash of applause and cheering, whistling.

Pitches green shorts into wings. Snaps fingers over hat. Reaches in. Prolonged fumbling. Sound of a slap. Withdraws hand hastily, a look of astonished pain on his face. Peers inside.

Laughter.

Head of lovely assistant pops out of hat, pouting indignantly.

Laughter and applause.

With difficulty, she extracts one arm from hat, then other arm. Pressing hands down against hat brim, she wriggles and twists until one naked breast pops out of hat.

Applause and wild whistling.

The other breast: POP!

More applause and whistling.

She wriggles free to the waist. She grunts and struggles, but is unable to free her hips. She looks pathetically, but uncertainly at magician. He tugs and pulls but she seems firmly stuck.

Laughter.

He grasps lovely assistant under armpits and plants feet against hat brim. Strains. In vain.

Laughter.

Thrusts lovely assistant forcibly back into hat. Fumbles again. Loud slap.

Laughter increases.

Magician returns slap soundly.

Laughter ceases abruptly, some scattered booing.

Magician reaches into hat, withdraws one unstockinged leg. He reaches in again, pulls out one arm. He tugs on arm and leg, but for all his effort cannot extract the remainder.

Scattered booing, Some whistling.

Magician glances uneasily at audience, stuffs arm and leg back into hat. He is perspiring. Fumbles inside hat. Withdraws nude hindquarters of lovely assistant.

Burst of cheers and wild whistling.

Smiles uncomfortably at audience. Tugs desperately on plump hindquarters, but rest will not follow.

Whistling diminishes, increased booing.

Jams hindquarters back into hat, mops brow with silk handkerchief.

Loud unfriendly booing.

Pockets handkerchief. Is becoming rather frantic. Grasps hat and thumps it vigorously, shakes it. Places it once more on table, brim up. Closes eyes as though in incantations, hands extended over hat. Snaps fingers several times, reaches in tenuously. Fumbles. Loud slap. Withdraws hand hastily in angry astonishment. Grasps hat. Gritting teeth, enfuriated, hurls hat to floor, leaps on it with both feet. Something crunches. Hideous piercing shriek.

Screams and shouts.

Magician, aghast, picks up hat, stares into it. Pales.

Violent screaming and shouting.

Magician gingerly sets hat on floor, and kneels, utterly appalled and grief-stricken, in front of it. Weeps silently.

Weeping, moaning, shouting.

Magician huddles miserably over crushed hat, weeping convulsively. First large man and young country boy enter timidly, soberly, from wings. They are pale and frightened. They peer uneasily into hat. They start back in horror. They clutch their mouths, turn away, and vomit.

Weeping, shouting, vomiting, accusations of murder.

Large man and country boy tie up magician, drag him away.

Weeping, retching.

Large man and country boy return, lift crushed hat gingerly, and trembling uncontrollably, carry it at arms's length into wings.

Momentary increase of weeping, retching, moaning, then dying away of sound of silence.

Country boy creeps onto stage, alone, sets up placard against table and facing audience, then creeps abjectly away.

THIS ACT IS CONCLUDED
THE MANAGEMENT REGRETS THERE
WILL BE NO REFUND

2
POETRY

The Elements of Poetry

INTRODUCTION

The Poetry Game

If you ask a poet, "What good is it? I mean, what earthly good is it?" you may get an answer like Marianne Moore's "I, too, dislike it," or W. H. Auden's "Poetry makes nothing happen." The modern poet is not likely to make grandiose claims for his craft. And we shall try not to betray that honest and tough-minded attitude. Poetry is essentially a game, with artificial rules, and it takes two—a writer and a reader—to play it. If the reader is reluctant, the game will not work.

Physical games have their practical aspects. They help make sound bodies to go with the sound minds so much admired by philosophers of education. A language game like poetry also has uses, but they are by-products rather than its proper ends. Poetry exercises a valuable though perhaps "unsound" side of the mind: imagination. (It takes an exercise of the imagination, for example, to get at what Bob Dylan means by a "hard rain.") Poetry can also be used to develop the student's ability to control and respond to language. But it is a game first of all, where—as Robert Frost said—"the work is play for mortal stakes."

A game can require great exertion, but it must reward that exertion with pleasure or there is no playing it. Anyone who has ever responded to a nursery rhyme, or to a Beatles record, or to Pete Seeger singing a ballad, has experienced the fundamental pleasure of poetry. More complicated and sophisticated poems offer essentially the same kind of pleasure. We labor to understand the rules of the game so that we need not think about them when we are playing. We master technique to make our execution easier. When we are really proficient the work becomes play.

The Qualities of Poetry

Part of the pleasure of poetry lies in its relation to music. It awakens in us a fundamental response to rhythmic repetitions of various kinds. Learning to read poetry is partly a matter of learning to respond to subtle and delicate rhythmic patterns as well as to the most obvious and persistant ones. But poetry is not just a kind of music. It is a special combination of musical and linguistic qualities—of sounds regarded both as pure sound and as meaningful speech. In particular, poetry is expressive language. It does for us what Samuel Beckett's character Watt wanted done for him:

> Not that Watt desired information, for he did not. But he desired words to be applied to his situation, to Mr Knott, to the house, to the grounds, to his duties, to the stairs, to his bedroom, to the kitchen, and in a general way to the conditions of being in which he found himself.

Poetry applies words to our situations, to the conditions of being in which we find ourselves. By doing so, it gives us pleasure because it helps us articulate our states of mind. The poets we value are important because they speak for us and help us learn to speak for ourselves. A revealing instance of a poet's learning to apply words to his own situation, and finding in their order and symmetry a soothing pleasure, has been recorded by James Joyce. Here we see a child of nine years making an important discovery about the nature and uses of poetry:

[Bray: in the parlour of the house in Martello Terrace]
MR VANCE (comes in with a stick) . . . O, you know, he'll have to apologise, Mrs Joyce.
MRS JOYCE O yes . . . Do you hear that, Jim?
MR VANCE Or else—if he doesn't—the eagles'll come and pull out his eyes.
MRS JOYCE O, but I'm sure he will apologise.
JOYCE (under the table, to himself)
—Pull out his eyes,
Apologise,
Apologise,
Pull out his eyes.

Apologise,
Pull out his eyes,
Pull out his eyes,
Apologise.

The coincidence of sound that links the four-word phrase "pull-out-his-eyes" with the four-syllable word "apologise" offers the child a refuge from Mr Vance far more secure than the table under which he is hiding. In his novel *A Portrait of the Artist as a Young Man,* Joyce used this moment from his own life to illustrate Stephen's vocation for verbal art.

As a poem the child's effort is of course a simple one, but it achieves a real effect because of the contrast between the meanings of its two basic lines that sound so much alike. Gentle "apologise" and fierce "pull out his eyes" ought not to fit together so neatly, the poem implies; and in doing so it makes an ethical criticism of Mr Vance, who, after all, coupled them in the first place. Young Joyce's deliberate wit has made a poem from the old man's witless tirade.

Marianne Moore qualifies her dislike of poetry this way:

> I, too, dislike it: there are things that are important beyond
>   all this fiddle.
> Reading it, however, with a perfect contempt of it, one
>   discovers in
> it after all, a place for the genuine.
>   Hands that can grasp, eyes
>   that can dilate, hair that can rise
>   if it must, these things are important not because a
>
> high-sounding interpretation can be put upon them but
>   because they are
> useful. . . .

And Auden adds,

> . . . poetry makes nothing happen: it survives
> In the valley of its making where executives
> Would never want to tamper: flows on south
> From ranches of isolation and the busy griefs,
> Raw towns that we believe and die in; it survives,
> A way of happening, a mouth.

He concludes the poem "In Memory of W. B. Yeats," from which these lines are taken, with some advice to poets that suggests the kinds of thing poetry can do:

> Follow, poet, follow right
> To the bottom of the night,
> With your unconstraining voice
> Still persuade us to rejoice;
>
> With the farming of a verse
> Make a vineyard of the curse,
> Sing of human unsuccess
> In a rapture of distress;
>
> In the deserts of the heart
> Let the healing fountain start,
> In the prison of his days
> Teach the free man how to praise.

10

Poetry, then, is a kind of musical word game that we value because of its expressive qualities. Not all poems are equally musical, or equally playful, or equally expressive. Nor are they necessarily musical, playful, or expressive in the same way. But we may consider these three qualities as the basic constituents of poetry so that we may examine some of the various ways in which poets combine and modify them in making different kinds of poems. Recognizing various poetic possibilities is important to the student of poetry because the greatest single problem for the reader of a poem is the problem of tact.

Tact

Tact acknowledges the diversity of poetry. A tactful approach to a poem must be appropriate to the special nature of the poem under consideration. Reading a poem for the first time ought to be a little like meeting a person for the first time. An initial exploratory conversation may lead to friendship, dislike, indifference, or any of dozens of other shades of attitude from love to hate. If the relation progresses, it will gain in intimacy as surface politeness is replaced by exchange of ideas and feelings at a deeper level.

We need, of course, to speak the same language if we are to communicate in any serious way. For most of us, this means we make friends with people who speak English and we read poems written in English. But speaking the same language means more than just inheriting or acquiring the same linguistic patterns. Some poems, like some people, seem to talk to us not merely in our native language but in our own idiom as well. We understand them easily and naturally. Others speak in ways that seem strange and puzzling. With poems, as with people, our first response to the puzzling should be a polite effort to eliminate misunderstanding. We need not adopt any false reverence before the poems of earlier ages. An old poem may be as much of a bore as an old person. But we should treat the aged with genuine politeness, paying attention to their words, trying to adjust to their idiom. This may turn out to be very rewarding, or it may not. But only after we have understood are we entitled to reject—or accept—any utterance.

Since the English language itself has changed considerably over the centuries and continues to change, we must often make a greater effort to understand an older poem than a modern one. Also, notions of what poetry is and should be have changed in the past and continue to change. The poetry game has not always been played with the same linguistic equipment or under the same rules. The difference between a love lyric by an Elizabethan sonneteer and a contemporary poem of love may be as great as the difference between Elizabethan tennis and modern tennis. The Elizabethans played tennis indoors, in an intricately walled court which required great finesse to master all its angles. The modern game is flat and open, all power serves and rushes to the net. Which ought to remind us that Robert Frost likened free verse (verse with unrhymed, irregular lines) to playing tennis with the net down. Such a game would make points easy to score but would not be much fun to play. Poetry, like tennis, depends on artificial rules and hindrances. These arbitrary restrictions are what give it its game-like quality.

Unlike the rules of tennis, however, the rules of poetry have never really been written down. Although critics have frequently tried to produce a "poetics" that would operate like a code of rules, they have always failed because poetry is always changing. In fact poetic "rules" are not really rules but conventions that change perpetually and must change perpetually to prevent poems from being turned out on a mass scale according to formulas. Every poet learns from his predecessors, but any poet who merely imitates them produces flat, stale poems. A poet is above all a man who finds a unique idiom, a special voice for his own poetry. The tactful reader quickly picks up the conventions operating in any particular poem and pays careful attention to the idiom of every poet, so that he can understand and appreciate or criticize each separate poetic performance.

The following parts of this discussion are designed to help the student of poetry to acquire tact. They are arranged to present certain basic elements drawn from the whole system of poetic conventions. Tact itself cannot be taught because it is of the spirit. But if the instinct for it is there, tact can be developed and refined through conscious effort. In the pages that follow, the student may consider consciously and deliberately the kinds of intellectual and emotional adjustments that the expert reader of poetry makes effortlessly and instantaneously.

EXPRESSION

Drama and Narration

Drama usually implies actors on a stage impersonating characters who speak to one another in a sequence of situations or scenes. A short poem with a single speaker, thus, is dramatic only in a limited sense. Nevertheless, *some* poems are very dramatic; the element of drama in them must be grasped if we are to understand them at all. And *all* poems are dramatic to some extent, however slight.

We approach the dramatic element in poetry by assuming that every poem shares some qualities with a speech in a play: that it is spoken aloud by a "speaker" who is a character in a situation which implies a certain relationship with other characters; and we assume that this speech is "overheard" by an audience. We may have to modify these assumptions. The poem may finally be more like a soliloquy or unspoken thought than like a part of a dialogue. Or it may seem more like a letter or a song than a speech. Still, in approaching our poem we must make a tentative decision about who the speaker is, what his situation is, and whom he seems to be addressing. In poems that are especially dramatic, the interest of the poem will depend on the interest of the character and situation presented. But because dramatic poems are very short and compressed in comparison with plays, the reader must usually do a good deal of guessing or inferring in order to grasp the elements of character and situation. The good reader will make plausible inferences; the inadequate reader will guess wildly, breaking the rules of plausibility and spoiling the inferential game.

Consider the following lines from the beginning of a dramatic poem. This imaginary speech is assigned by the title of the poem to a painter who lived in Renaissance Italy. Brother Filippo Lippi was a Carmelite friar and an important painter, whose work was sponsored by the rich and powerful Florentine banker Cosimo di Medici.

Fra Lippo Lippi

I am poor brother Lippo, by your leave!
You need not clap your torches to my face.
Zooks, what's to blame? you think you see a monk!
What, 't is past midnight, and you go the rounds,
And here you catch me at an alley's end
Where sportive ladies leave their doors ajar?
The Carmine's my cloister: hunt it up,
Do,—harry out, if you must show your zeal,
Whatever rat, there, haps on his wrong hole,
10   And nip each softling of a wee white mouse,
Weke, weke, that's crept to keep him company!
Aha, you know your betters! Then, you'll take
Your hand away that 's fiddling on my throat,
And please to know me likewise. Who am I?
Why, one, sir, who is lodging with a friend
Three streets off—he 's a certain . . . how d' ye call?
Master—a . . . Cosimo of the Medici,
I' the house that caps the corner. Boh! you were best!
Remember and tell me, the day you 're hanged,
20   How you affected such a gullet's-gripe!
But you, sir, it concerns you that your knaves
Pick up a manner nor discredit you:
Zooks, are we pilchards, that they sweep the streets
And count fair prize what comes into their net?
He 's Judas to a tittle, that man is!
Just such a face! Why, sir, you make amends.
Lord, I 'm not angry! Bid your hangdogs go
Drink out this quarter-florin to the health
Of the munificent House that harbours me
30   (And many more beside, lads! more beside!)
And all 's come square again. I 'd like his face—
His, elbowing on his comrade in the door
With the pike and lantern,—for the slave that holds

John Baptist's head a-dangle by the hair
With one hand ("Look, you, now," as who should say)
And his weapon in the other, yet unwiped!
It 's not your chance to have a bit of chalk,
A wood-coal or the like? or you should see!
Yes, I'm the painter, since you style me so.

Now consider, in order, each of these questions:

1. From these lines, what can we infer about the situation and its development?

2. Who is Lippo speaking to in the opening lines?

3. At what time of day and in what sort of neighborhood does this scene take place?

4. Would we be justified in making an inference about what Lippo has been up to? What inference might we make?

5. What is Lippo talking about when he says in line 18, "Boh! you were best!"? And whom does he say it to? What produced the action which Lippo refers to here?

6. In line 21 he addresses a different person in "you, sir." Who is he addressing?

7. What kind of man do the details in these lines suggest is speaking in this poem?

8. How would you describe the whole progress of the situation? How might the events presented in these 39 lines be re-told in the form of a story narrated by an observer of the action?

This series of questions—and their answers—should suggest the kind of inferential activity that many dramatic poems require of their readers. The words of such a poem are points of departure, and the actual poem is the one we create with our imaginative but logical response to the poet's words. The poet—Robert Browning—offers us the pleasure of helping to create his poem, and also the pleasure of entering a world remote from our own in time and space. Dramatic poems like Browning's do not so much apply words to our situations as take us out of ourselves into situations beyond our experience. When we speak Lippo's words aloud, or read them imaginatively, we are refreshed by this assumption of a strange role and this expression of a personality other than our own. In a sense, our minds are expanded, and we return to ourselves enriched by the experience. Yet even the strangest characters will often express ideas and attitudes that we recognize as related to our own, related to certain moods or conditions of being in which we have found ourselves. Every citizen who has had to explain an awkward situation to a policeman has something in common with Lippo Lippi as he begins to speak.

The line between the dramatic and narrative elements in a poem is not always clear. But a narrative poem gives us a story as told by a narrator from a perspective outside the action, while a dramatic poem presents a fragment of an action (or story) through the voice (or point of view) of a character involved in that action. The principal speaker in a narrative poem addresses us—the audience—directly, telling us about the situation and perhaps offering us introductions to characters who function as dramatic elements in the poem. In the days when long stories were recited aloud by bardic poets, verse was the natural form for narration, because it provided easily memorizable units of composition and a regular, flowing rhythm into which these units might be fitted. But now that printing has converted most of the audience for fiction from listeners to readers, most stories are told in prose. The only narrative verse form that is really alive today is the ballad, which justifies its use of rhyme and rhythm by being set to music and sung. Verse meant to be sung has its own rules or conventions, which will be discussed later on. But here we can talk about the narrative element in ballads and other forms of fiction in verse, and how versified fiction differs from the kind of story we expect to find in prose.

If we think of a dramatic poem as something like a self-sufficient fragment torn from a play, which through its compression encourages us to fill out its dramatic frame by acts of inference and imagination—then we may think of a narrative poem as related to prose fiction in a similar way. In comparison to stories, narrative poems are compressed and elliptical, shifting their focus, concentrating on striking details, and leaving us to make appropriate connections and draw appropriate conclusions. In fact, there is a strong tendency toward the dramatic in short verse narratives—a tendency to present more dialogue or action in relation to description than we would expect to find in prose fiction dealing with the same subject matter.

Actually, we find poetic elements in much prose fiction and fictional elements in many poems. Here we are concerned mainly with the special problems posed by the compressed and elliptical form taken by fiction in short poems such as this one, by E. A. Robinson:

Reuben Bright

Because he was a butcher and thereby
Did earn an honest living (and did right)
I would not have you think that Reuben Bright
Was any more a brute than you or I;
For when they told him that his wife must die,

He stared at them, and shook with grief and fright,
And cried like a great baby half that night,
And made the women cry to see him cry.

10 And after she was dead, and he had paid
The singers and the sexton and the rest,
He packed a lot of things that she had made
Most mournfully away in an old chest
Of hers, and put some chopped-up cedar boughs
In with them, and tore down the slaughter-house.

The poem is narrative for the reason that the speaker addresses us from a perspective outside the action and undertakes to comment for our benefit on the character and situation presented: Reuben earns an "honest" living; he did "right." Yet the narrator presents just two incidents from the whole of Bright's life, and he makes no final interpretation or commentary on Bright's climactic act. It is left for us to conclude that only by destroying the place of butchery could this butcher express his anguish at the death of his beloved wife. And it is left for us to note the irony involved in this presentation of an act of destructive violence as evidence that the butcher is not "any more a brute than you or I." It is also left for us to note the pathos of this gesture by which the butcher tries to dissociate himself from that death which has claimed his wife. The compactness and brevity characteristic of poetry often move narration in the direction of drama.

Consider the combination of drama and narration in the following poem by D. H. Lawrence:

Piano

Softly, in the dusk, a woman is singing to me;
Taking me back down the vista of years, till I see
A child sitting under the piano, in the boom of the tingling strings
And pressing the small, poised feet of a mother who smiles as she sings.

In spite of myself, the insidious mastery of song
Betrays me back, till the heart of me weeps to belong
To the old Sunday evenings at home, with winter outside
And hymns in the cosy parlour, the tinkling piano our guide.
So now it is vain for the singer to burst into clamour
10 With the great black piano appassionato. The glamour
Of childish days is upon me, my manhood is cast
Down in the flood of remembrance, I weep like a child for the past.

Here the speaker seems to be addressing us directly as a narrator. But he is describing a scene in which he is the central character, and describing it in the present tense as something in progress. Drama is always *now*. Narrative is always *then*. But this scene mingles now *and* then, bringing together two pianos, and two pianists; linking the speaker's childish self with his present manhood. In a sense, the poem depends on its combination of now and then, drama and narration, for its effect—uniting now and then, man and child, in its last clause: "I weep like a child for the past."

Because this is a poem, tightly compressed, it is possible for us to miss an essential aspect of the dramatic situation it presents. Why is it "vain" for the singer to play the piano "appassionato"? Why does he say that his "manhood" is cast down? What does this phrase mean? These elliptical references seem intended to suggest that the woman at the piano is in some sense wooing the man who listens, attempting to arouse his passion through her performance. But ironically, she only reminds him of his mother, casting down his manhood, reducing him from a lover to a son, from a man to a child.

It is interesting to compare this poem by D. H. Lawrence to an early version. Looking at the early draft, we might consider Lawrence's revisions as an attempt to achieve a more satisfactory combination of narrative and drama, and a more intense poem. The early version tells quite a different story from the later one—almost the opposite story. And it contains much that Lawrence eliminated. Examine the revisions in detail. What does each change accomplish? Which changes are most important, most effective?

The Piano
(*Early version*)

Somewhere beneath that piano's superb sleek black
Must hide my mother's piano, little and brown, with the back
That stood close to the wall, and the front's faded silk both torn,
And the keys with little hollows, that my mother's fingers had worn.

Softly, in the shadows, a woman is singing to me
Quietly, through the years I have crept back to see
A child sitting under the piano, in the boom of the shaking strings
Pressing the little poised feet of the mother who smiles as she sings.

The full throated woman has chosen a winning, living song
10   And surely the heart that is in me must belong
To the old Sunday evenings, when darkness wandered outside
And hymns gleamed on our warm lips, as we watched mother's fingers glide.

Or this is my sister at home in the old front room
Singing love's first surprised gladness, alone in the gloom.
She will start when she sees me, and blushing, spread out her hands
To cover my mouth's raillery, till I'm bound in her shame's heartspun bands.

A woman is singing me a wild Hungarian air
And her arms, and her bosom, and the whole of her soul is bare,
And the great black piano is clamouring as my mother's never could clamour
20   And my mother's tunes are devoured of this music's ravaging glamour.

Description and Meditation

Description is the element in poetry closest to painting and sculpture. Poets like Edmund Spenser, Keats, and Tennyson have been very sensitive to this relationship: Spenser maintained that the Poet's wit "passeth Painter farre," while Keats admitted that a painted piece of Greek pottery could "express a flowery tale more sweetly than our rhyme." In fact, describing with words has both advantages and disadvantages in comparison to plastic representation. Words are rich in meaning and suggestion but weak for rendering precise spatial relations and shades of color. Therefore, what descriptive words do best is convey an attitude or feeling through the objects that they describe.

Take a very simple description from a short poem by William Carlos Williams:

a red wheel
barrow

glazed with rain
water

beside the white
chickens.

We sense a word game here in the arbitrary arrangement of the words in lines, as they lead us to consider a visual image dominated by contrasting colors and textures—feathery white and glazed red, animate and inanimate things. But it is hard to sense distinctly any attitude conveyed by the description, which seems like a poor substitute for a painting.

Here is the entire poem:

so much depends
upon

a red wheel
barrow

glazed with rain
water

beside the white
chickens.

Now we can see how the description itself depends upon the assertion "so much depends" for its animation. The assertion directs our search for meaning, and conveys the speaker's attitude toward the objects described. We may wonder how anything at all can "depend" on such insignificant objects, and yet this very response is a response not just to a description but to a poem as well. The poem is created by the distance between this sweeping statement and the apparent insignificance of the objects it refers to. We understand, finally, that the poet is using this distance to make us feel his concern for trivial things, his sense that there is beauty in humble objects; and beyond that, he is encouraging us to share his alertness to the beautiful in things that are neither artful nor conventionally pretty. He is advising us to keep our eyes open, and he does it not with a direct admonition but with a description charged with the vigor of his own response to the visible world.

It is of the essence of poetic description that it come to us charged with the poet's feelings and attitudes. Sometimes these will be made explicit by statement or commentary in the poem. Sometimes they will remain implicit, matters of tone, rhythm, and metaphor. Consider these four opening lines from a poem by Tennyson. What attitudes or emotions are conveyed by them, and how are they conveyed?

The woods decay, the woods decay and fall,
The vapours weep their burthen to the ground,
Man comes and tills the field and lies beneath,
And after many a summer dies the swan.

The topic is decay and death, presented in terms of generalized natural description. In line 1 the continuing process of decay is emphasized by the exact repetition of a whole clause. In line 2 the vapors are presented as sentient creatures who weep. In line 3 the whole adult life of man is compressed into just nine words, few seconds, a patch of earth. In the climactic position, reserved by an inversion of normal syntax for the very last place in the sentence, comes the death of the swan. The life and death of man is thus surrounded by decay and death in other natural things, and in this way is reduced, distanced. It is not horrible but natural, and characterized by a melancholy beauty.

These lines of description serve in the poem as the beginning of a dramatic monologue. The nature of the speaker and his situation (as we come to understand them) help us to refine our grasp of the tone and the attitude these lines convey toward the objects they describe. Here is the opening verse-paragraph of the poem:

Tithonus

The woods decay, the woods decay and fall,
The vapours weep their burthen to the ground,
Man comes and tills the field and lies beneath,
And after many a summer dies the swan.
Me only cruel immortality
Consumes: I wither slowly in thine arms,
Here at the quiet limit of the world,

A white-haired shadow roaming like a dream
The ever-silent spaces of the East,
10   Far-folded mists, and gleaming halls of morn.

The speaker is Tithonus, a mythological prince who became the lover of the dawn goddess; she made him immortal but could not prevent him from growing older throughout eternity. In the light of lines 5 and 6, the first four lines are enriched with the wistful envy of one who is unable to die. At the close of the poem (some seventy lines later) the speaker returns to the images of line 3 in speaking of "happy men that have the power to die" and of "the grassy barrows of the happier dead." He asks for release so that he can become "earth in earth" and forget his unhappy existence.

The melancholy beauty of the opening lines becomes more lovely and less sad as we move toward the conclusion of the poem with its powerful projection of man's return to earth as the most desirable of consummations. Behind the dramatic speaker in the poem—the mythological Tithonus— stands the poet, reminding us that death is natural and the appropriate end of life. In this poem, description and drama collaborate to suggest rather than state a meaning.

Serious English poetry has often embodied in particular poems a movement from description to overt meditation. This movement is frequently found in religious poetry, as poets move from contemplation of created things to an awareness of the Creator. William Wordsworth was a master— prehaps *the* master—of this kind of poetic movement in English. Thus, a selection from Wordsworth makes a fitting conclusion to this discussion of description and meditation. The poem is a sonnet (see the note on this form in the introduction to Shakespeare in our Selection of Poets), in which the first eight lines (the *octet*) are devoted to description of nature and the last six (the *sestet*) take the form of a meditation on Wordsworth's daughter Caroline. The expression "Abraham's bosom" in the poem refers of course to heaven. In the New Testament (Luke 16:22) we are told that the righteous will join the patriarch Abraham in heaven after death.

It is a beauteous evening, calm and free,
The holy time is quiet as a Nun
Breathless with adoration; the broad sun
Is sinking down in its tranquillity;
The gentleness of heaven broods o'er the Sea:
Listen! the mighty Being is awake,
And doth with his eternal motion make
A sound like thunder—everlastingly.
Dear Child! dear Girl! that walkest with me here,
10   If thou appear untouched by solemn thought,
Thy nature is not therefore less divine:
Thou liest in Abraham's bosom all the year;
And worshipp'st at the Temple's inner shrine,
God being with thee when we know it not.

WORD GAMES

Language can be used to help us perceive relations that connect disparate things, or to help us make discriminations that separate similar things. In poetry these two aspects of language take the form of metaphorical comparison and ironic contrast. Metaphor and irony are the twin bases of poetical language. This means that a good reader of poetry must be especially alert and tactful in his responses to metaphorical and ironic language.

It is because poetry places such stress on these crucial dimensions of language that it is of such great use in developing linguistic skills in its readers. It makes unusual demands and offers unusual rewards. The kind of skill it takes to be a first-rate reader of poetry cannot be acquired by reading a textbook like this one, any more than the ability to play the piano can be acquired in a few lessons. Continuing practice is the most important factor in a performing art like piano playing—and reading poetry (even silently, to oneself) has many of the qualities and satisfactions of a performing art.

In the sections that follow on metaphoric and ironic language we have not tried to present an exhaustive list of poetical devices to be carefully noted and memorized. We have tried to examine some of the main varieties of metaphoric and ironic language, with a view toward establishing an awareness of these two crucial varieties of poetical word-play. To move from awareness to expertise, the student must read many poems and consider them carefully.

Some Varieties of Metaphorical Language

SIMILE

This is the easiest form of metaphor to perceive because in it both of the images or ideas being joined are stated and explicity linked by the word *as* or *like* or a similar linking-word. Similes are often quite simple:

O my Love's like a red, red rose

But even a statement of resemblance as simple and direct as this one of Robert Burns's asks us to consider the ways in which his beloved is like a rose—and not a white or yellow rose, but a red rose. And not just a red rose but a "red, red" rose. What the redness of the rose has to do with the qualities of the speaker's beloved is the first question this simile poses for us. In the poem, the simile is further complicated by a second line:

O my Love's like a red, red rose,
   That's newly sprung in June;

Here we are asked to associate the freshness of the flower and its early blooming with the qualities of the speaker's beloved. In the poem, the next two lines add a second image, compounding the simile:

O my Love's like the melodie
    That's sweetly played in tune.

The first image emphasizes the spontaneous naturalness of the beloved, the second her harmonious composure. Both roses and sweet melodies are pleasing; so that, in a sense, the poet is using his similes to make the simple statement that his beloved is pleasing to behold. But the simile is also saying that she has a complicated kind of appeal: like the rose, to sight and smell; like the melody, to the sense of sound; like the rose, a natural fresh quality; like the melody, a deliberate artfulness which intends to please. The simile also conveys to us the strength of the poet's feeling; his choice of images tells us something about the qualities of his feeling for her, because it is *he* who has found these words—which themselves have some of the qualities of spontaneous freshness and tuneful order.

A single simile can also be elaborated: as in the traditional epic simile, in which the illustrative image is often extensive enough to require the construction *as . . . so,* or *like . . . thus.* An extended simile, by multiplying possible points of contact between the thing presented and the illustrative image, can often become very complicated indeed, with the illustrative image itself becoming a thing to be illustrated or developed with other images still. Consider, for example, this epic simile from Book IV of Spenser's *Faerie Queene:*

27

Like as the tide that comes from th' Ocean main,
Flows up the Shanon with contrary force,
And overruling him in his own reign,
Drives back the current of his kindly course,
And makes it seem to have some other source:
But when the flood is spent, then back again
His borrowed waters forced to redisbourse
He sends the sea his own with double gain
And tribute eke withall, as to his Soveraine.

28

Thus did the battle vary to and fro . . .

METAPHOR

The word "metaphor" is used both as a general term for all kinds of poetic linking of images and ideas, and as a specific term for such linking when the thing and image are not presented as a direct analogy (A is *like* B) but by discussing one in terms of the other (A *is* B-ish, or A B's; Albert *is* a dog or Albert *barked* at me). For example, within the epic simile from Spenser, we can find metaphor at work. The simile involves describing a hand-to-hand combat in terms of the ebb and flow of tides where the River Shannon meets the Atlantic Ocean. The ebb and flow of the waters illustrates the shifting tide of battle (as this metaphor become a cliché usually puts it). But this basic simile in Spenser is enriched by the idea of Shannon and Ocean as hostile potentates engaged in a struggle, with the Ocean tide invading the river and "overruling him in his own reign."

The struggle of potentates is itself further complicated by a financial metaphor. The phrase "when the flood is spent" means literally when the incoming tide has expended its force and lost its momentum. But Spenser chooses to use the financial overtones in the word "spent" to further adorn his metaphor. From "spent" he moves to "borrowed" and "redisburse," and the concept of repayment with 100 percent interest in the expression "double gain." This transaction between Ocean and Shannon can be seen as a combat or a loan. Finally, Spenser merges these two metaphors in the last line of the stanza, by calling this double payment the "tribute" of a lesser feudal power to a higher. And here Spenser actually turns his metaphor into a simile within the basic simile, with the expression "*as to his Soveraine.*"

This kind of interweaving of similes and metaphors is playful and decorative in its intent. The metaphors seem to emerge naturally and blend easily with one another. But these graceful arabesques tell us nothing much about the course of the combat of the two warriors, beyond the suggestion that the fight ebbs and flows. Their struggle is not so much described as dignified by this heroic comparison to two sovereign forces of nature.

In poems that depend heavily on metaphoric processes for their interest, the subtle interaction of images and ideas almost defies analysis; yet such poems may depend upon our attempts to follow their metaphoric threads. For us to understand such a poem, to feel it, we must start our thoughts along the lines indicated by the metaphors. Consider Shakespeare's sonnet 73 as an example of this kind of poem:

That time of year thou may'st in me behold
When yellow leaves, or none, or few, do hang
Upon those boughs which shake against the cold—
Bare ruin'd choirs where late the sweet birds sang.
In me thou see'st the twilight of such day
As after Sunset fadeth in the West,
Which by and by black night doth take away,
Death's second self, that seals up all in rest.
In me thou see'st the glowing of such fire
That on the ashes of his youth doth lie,
As the death-bed whereon it must expire,

Consumed with that which it was nourish'd by.
This thou perceiv'st, which makes thy love more strong
To love that well which thou must leave ere long.

The images of the first twelve lines are all elaborations of the simple
notion that the speaker is getting old. The last two lines are a dramatic
assertion, also rather simple. The speaker tells his listener that the listener
will love him all the more, precisely because old age and death threaten their
relationship. We can infer that the speaker is older than the listener, and in
terms of the dramatic situation we are entitled to wonder whether these
self-assured words are merely wishful thinking, or an appraisal of the
listener's attitude. How does the imagery of the first twelve lines contribute
to the situation and to our understanding of it? We have in these lines three
separate but related metaphors, each developed for four lines. The speaker
says, in effect, "You see in me—autumn; you see in me—twilight; you see
in me—embers."

These three metaphors for aging have in common certain qualities: a
growing coldness and darkness; suggestions of finality and impending
extinction. But each image generates its own attitude and emphasizes a
different aspect of the aging process. The first four lines suggest an analogy
between an aging person and trees whose leaves have fallen, leaving them
exposed to cold winds. And the bare trees suggest, by a further reach of
metaphor, a ruined and desolate church. Above all, this complex metaphor
generates sympathy for the speaker, a sympathy based on our concern for
lost beauty, for destruction of spiritual things, and for victims of the forces
of nature.

The next four lines, focusing on the twilight after sunset, emphasize the
threat of coming darkness. By another extension of metaphor, "black night"
is called "Death's second self." The brevity of the time between sunset and
night increases our sense of sympathetic urgency, and the introduction of
"Death" takes us full circle through the metaphors back to their object, an
aging man. The next four lines also introduce a complex metaphor. The
speaker compares himself to the glowing embers of a dying fire which lies
upon "the ashes of his youth." The fire becomes human, here, and returns
us again to the life of the speaker.

This image is the most intense of the three, because it likens the arrival of
age not merely to a seasonal change, worked by the passage of time, but to
the consumption or destruction of matter which can never be restored to its
original state. The ashes of the fire lying upon its deathbed are forcible
reminders that the speaker's body will soon lie upon a deathbed, and will
become ashes, to be returned to the ashes and dust of the grave. It is the
emotional force of all "This" which the speaker maintains in the next-to-last
line that the listener must perceive. And the confidence of the assertion is

partly the confidence of a poet who still has his poetical power. He can still sing like a sweet bird and move his hearer with his poetry. The imagery justifies the dramatic situation, and the situation intensifies the significance of the imagery.

THE CONCEIT

It is useful to think of the conceit as an extension of the simile in which aspects of the basic analogy are developed with a kind of relentless ingenuity. The "metaphysical" poets of the late sixteenth and the seventeenth century specialized in witty conceits. Here, for example, John Donne combines a dramatic situation with development of a conceit so that the images become an argument persuading his lady listener to give in.

The Flea

Mark but this flea, and mark in this,
How little that which thou deny'st me is;
Me it sucked first, and now sucks thee,
And in this flea, our two bloods mingled be;
Confess it, this cannot be said
A sin, or shame, or loss of maidenhead,
　　Yet this enjoys before it woo,
　　And pampered swells with one blood made of two,
　　And this, alas, is more than we would do.

10　Oh stay, three lives in one flea spare,
Where we almost, nay more than married are.
This flea is you and I, and this
Our marriage bed, and marriage temple is;
Though parents grudge, and you, we are met,
And cloistered in these living walls of jet.
　　Though use make you apt to kill me,
　　Let not to this, self murder added be,
　　And sacrilege, three sins in killing three.

Cruel and sudden, hast thou since
20　Purpled thy nail, in blood of innocence?
In what could this flea guilty be,
Except in that drop which it sucked from thee?
Yet thou triumph'st, and say'st that thou
Find'st not thyself, nor me the weaker now;
　　'Tis true, then learn how false, fears be;
　　Just so much honour, when thou yield'st to me,
　　Will waste, as this flea's death took life from thee.

In the first two lines the speaker makes the basic analogy between the flea's having bitten both himself and the lady, and the act of love-making to which he would like to persuade her. In the rest of the poem he develops the analogy as an argument in a changing dramatic context. At the start of stanza two, the lady has threatened to kill the flea. By stanza three she has done so. And meanwhile the speaker has imaginatively transformed the flea into a marriage bed, a temple, a cloister, and a figure of the Holy Trinity (three in one); so that the flea's destruction can be hyperbolically described as murder, suicide, and sacrilege. All in preparation for the turn of the argument in the last three lines of the poem. Donne's conceit is both ingenious and playful in this poem. It is witty in more than one sense.

THE SYMBOL

The symbol can be seen as an extension of the metaphor. In it, instead of saying that A is B-ish, or calling an A a B, the poet presents us with one half of the analogy only, and requires us to supply the missing part. This invites the reader to be creative and imaginative in a situation controlled by the poet. Bob Dylan's "Hard Rain" is a symbolic poem. And here is a symbolic poem by W. B. Yeats:

The Dolls

A doll in the doll-maker's house
Looks at the cradle and bawls:
'That is an insult to us.'
But the oldest of all the dolls,
Who had seen, being kept for show,
Generations of his sort,
Out-screams the whole shelf: 'Although
There's not a man can report
Evil of this place,
10   The man and the woman bring
Hither, to our disgrace,
A noisy and filthy thing.'
Hearing him groan and stretch
The doll-maker's wife is aware
Her husband has heard the wretch,
And crouched by the arm of his chair,
She murmurs into his ear,
Head upon shoulder leant:
'My dear, my dear, O dear,
20   It was an accident.'

This whole incident stands in a metaphoric relation to something else. In other words, the poem is only apparently about dolls and doll-makers. It is really about something symbolized by the incident narrated. What? And how do we go about determining what? We must work very carefully from the situation toward possible analogies in the world of ideas and experience, first exploring the situation and images in the poem. The situation derives from the doll-maker's unique role as creator of two kinds of small, man-shaped objects: dolls and children. The dolls in their lifeless perfection resent the noise and filth produced by an actual human child. The human baby is, in fact, as the doll-maker's wife apologetically points out, not "made" in the same sense as dolls are made. Birth is an "accident"; dolls are deliberately constructed. The situation leads us outward until we see it as an illustration of the opposition between art and life, between the ideal and the real. The doll-maker himself thus symbolizes any artist who is obliged to live in the real world but create idealized objects, or any person who faces the impossible problem of realizing his ideas—or idealizing reality.

Having got this far from the concrete situation of the poem, the reader is in a position to return and consider the ways in which Yeats has used language to control his tone and charge the scene with emotion. How should we react to the various characters in this little drama? What, finally, should our attitude be toward the real/ideal conflict that the drama illustrates?

THE PUN

Often subjected to abuse as a "low" form of wit, the pun is essentially a kind of metaphor that can be used lightly and facetiously or for more serious purposes. Consider some verses by Thomas Hood (selected by William Empson to exemplify punning techniques):

How frail is our uncertain breath!
The laundress seems full hale, but death
Shall her 'last linen' bring;
The groom will die, like all his kind;
And even the stable boy will find
This life no stable thing. . . .

Cook, butler, Susan, Jonathan,
The girl that scours the pot and pan
And those that tend the steeds,
10   All, all shall have another sort
Of service after this—in short
The one the parson reads.

These puns on "stable" and "service" are playful but not funny. They use the basic device of the pun—dissimilar meanings for the same "word" or rather the same sound—to convey an attitude toward an idea. That both the life of a servant and his funeral are somehow included in that one piece of language—"service"—brings home to us the interconnection of life and death—which is the point of the poem.

Shakespeare was a master of the pun as of other metaphorical devices. Hamlet's bitter, punning responses to his uncle's smooth speeches are deadly serious and powerfully dramatic in their witty compression of his resentment.

KING   . . . But now, my cousin Hamlet, and my son—
HAMLET [*Aside*]   A little more than kin and less than kind!
KING   How is it that the clouds still hang on you?
HAMLET   Not so, my lord. I am too much i' the sun.

Hamlet and the King are more than *kin* (twice related: uncle/nephew and stepfather/son) but Hamlet feels they are not kindred spirits, not the same *kind*. And being called *son* by his father's murderer rouses all Hamlet's bitterness, causing him to return the King's metaphorical question about Hamlet's emotional weather with a pun that brings the metaphor back to the literal with a sarcastic bite: I am too much in the *son*.

The Language of Animation and Personification

In addition to their playful or ingenious aspects, the various metaphorical devices help to generate the qualities of compression and intensity that we value in much poetry. Similar qualities are often achieved by other means, such as animation and personification.

ANIMATION

Animation confers on objects or creatures a greater degree of awareness or purposefulness than we normally credit them with. When Tennyson writes, "The vapours weep their burthen to the ground," he gives life to the vapours, animating them with an emotion, sadness, that only living creatures experience. Less lovely scenes can also be intensified by animation. Consider these lines from Samuel Johnson's "Vanity of Human Wishes," which describe the treatment accorded the portraits of a statesman whose power has waned. Those who were honored to gaze at his features, now that no more is to be gained from the man, suddenly find the likeness ugly:

From every room descends the painted face,
That hung the bright palladium of the place;
And, smoked in kitchens, or in auctions sold,
To better features yields the frame of gold;
For now no more we trace in every line
Heroic worth, benevolence divine;
The form distorted justifies the fall,
And detestation rids th' indignant wall.

In that last line Johnson intensifies his satire by animating the very wall on which the picture hangs—it, even, is indignant and wishes to be rid of these odious features. The removal itself is effected by a person who has dwindled into an attitude—"detestation."

PERSONIFICATION

In this example from Dr. Johnson, we have a kind of reverse personification—as a human being becomes an abstract idea. Personification usually works the other way, clothing abstractions with the attributes of personality. Of all the ideas presented as sentient beings, Love has been most frequently selected. In mythology, Love figures as the boy-god Cupid or Eros, offering poets a ready-made personification which they have often used. The mechanical use of traditional personification can be a dull and dreary thing. But observe Sir Philip Sidney as he personifies Love in this sonnet, and finds ways to make concrete a whole range of other abstractions such as reverence, fear, hope, will, memory, and desire. If Love is personified here, these other notions are objectified—turned into material objects.

I on my horse, and Love on me doth try
    Our horsemanships, while by strange work I prove
    A horseman to my horse, a horse to Love;
    And now man's wrongs in me, poor beast, descry.

The reins wherewith my rider doth me tie,
    Are humbled thoughts, which bit of reverence move,
    Curb'd in with fear, but with gilt boss above
    Of hope, which makes it seem fair to the eye.

The wand is will; thou, fancy, saddle art,
10   Girt fast by memory, and while I spur
    My horse, he spurs with sharp desire my heart:

He sits me fast, however I do stir:
    And now hath made me to his hand so right,
    That in the manage my self takes delight.

The dominant image of Love as horseman provides the subordinate imagery for making concrete the other abstractions which serve to amplify this picture of a love-ridden man. The effectiveness of the poem depends on the ingenuity with which the poet has matched the objects and ideas to one another, relating all to the dominant personification of Love. Like Spenser's epic simile, Sidney's personification seems to breed subordinate metaphors easily, gracefully, and naturally.

The Anti-Metaphorical Language of Irony

Verbal irony may be said to start with simple negation of resemblance in situations where resemblance is customarily insisted upon: as in Shakespeare's sonnet 130, which begins,

My mistress' eyes are nothing like the sun;
Coral is far more red than her lips red:
If snow be white, why then her breasts are dun;
If hairs be wires, black wires grow on her head.

The anti-similes of the first three lines serve the same function as the ugly metaphor in line 4. All four lines present attacks on what the speaker will name in the last line as "false compare"—the misuse by poets of the metaphorical dimension of poetical language.

Usually, however, irony is not so straightforward. In fact, we normally think of it as involving some indirection or misleading of the reader—some gap between what the words *seem* to be saying and what they *are* saying. Thus, in this Shakespearean sonnet, after eight more lines of plain speaking about an ordinary human female, the speaker concludes,

And yet, by heaven, I think my love as rare
As any she belied by false compare.

What we might have taken as disparagement of the lady turns out to be praise after all. She is not uglier than the others; she just has a lover who won't exaggerate her beauty with the usual clichés. Thus, there is an irony in the disparity between the apparent disparagement of the lady in the first part of the poem and the praise of her at the end. We can see, then, in those opening lines, a kind of understatement, which works finally to convince us of the lady's beauty more effectively than a conventionally exaggerated simile of "false compare" would have done. (The entire sonnet may be found in our Selection of Poets.)

Understatement and overstatement are two of the most frequently used kinds of verbal irony. When Swift causes a character to observe (in prose), "Last Week I saw a Woman *flay'd*, and you will hardly believe, how much it altered her Person for the worse"—the main thing that strikes us is the awful inadequacy of the sentiment for the event. Disparity, contrast, incongruity—these things are at the heart of verbal irony. And, perhaps at the heart of that heart lies the notion that all words are inadequate for the representation of things. The poet as maker of metaphors may be seen as a genuine magician, bringing new things into the world, or as a charlatan pretending with feeble words to unite things that are essentially separate. Metaphor emphasizes the creative dimension of language, irony its tricky dimension.

For example, in Marvell's "To His Coy Mistress" the exaggerated protestations of the extent that the speaker's love would require "Had we but world enough and time" are all based on the view that of course we do *not* have world enough and time. Even before we get there, we sense the presence of the "But" on which the poem will make its turn:

But at my back I always hear
Time's winged chariot hurrying near;

The contrast between what the speaker *would* do:

Two hundred years should go to praise
Thine eyes, and on thy forehead gaze:
Two hundred to adore each breast:
And thirty thousand to the rest;

and what he *does* urge:

Now let us sport us while we may,

is an ironic one, enhanced by the extreme distance in time between hundreds or thousands of years and "Now." (Marvell's poem may be found in our Selection of Poets.)

Irony can also take the form of metaphorical overstatement, as it does in Alexander Pope's description of coffee being poured into a China cup:

From silver spouts the grateful liquors glide,
While China's earth receives the smoking tide.

These lines are metaphorical in that they present one thing (pouring a cup of coffee) in terms of another image (a kind of burning flood pouring over the mainland of China); but they are ironic in that the equation is made mainly so that we will perceive the disparity between the two images and enjoy their incongruity. Something of this reverse anti-metaphorical wit is present in many metaphors. John Donne's "The Flea" has a witty, ironic dimension derived from the inappropriateness of his basic image. To call a flea a temple is to establish a very far-fetched metaphor. The conceits used by Donne and other "metaphysical" poets of his time often have an ironic dimension.

Samuel Johnson characterized the metaphysical poets precisely in terms of this dimension—a special and extreme form of "wit" based on the "discovery of occult resemblances in things apparently unlike," and resulting in poems in which "the most heterogeneous ideas are yoked by violence together." Johnson's description emphasizes ("yoked by violence") the tension between metaphoric comparison and ironic contrast in many metaphysical conceits. Conceits tend to be witty, cerebral, unnatural; while metaphors are serious, imaginative, and natural. The metaphors of Romantic poetry are perceptions of relationships felt actually to exist. Metaphysical conceits often establish powerful but artificial relationships where one would least expect to find them.

Linking incongruous things is a feature of most kinds of witty poetry. A simple list with one incongruous element can serve to indict a whole way of life, as when Alexander Pope surveys the debris on a lady's dressing table:

Puffs, Powders, Patches, Bibles, Billet-doux

The inclusion of Bibles among love letters and cosmetics suggests a confusion between worldly and spiritual values—a failure to distinguish between true and false worth. The list is funny, but in an ironic and satiric way—as is this list of possible calamities from the same poem:

Whether the nymph shall break Diana's law,
Or some frail China jar receive a flaw;
Or stain her honour or her new brocade;
Forget her prayers or miss a masquerade;
Or lose her heart or necklace at a ball; . . .

Here Pope mixes several serious matters of the spirit with trivial and worldly items. The breaking of Diana's law of chastity is equated with damage to a jar. A single verb, "stain," governs two objects—"honour" and "brocade"—of different qualities and intensities. By this manipulation of grammar Pope makes us forcibly aware of the frivolousness of an attitude toward life which equates things that properly should have different values. He brings those two objects under that one verb so that we will feel a powerful urge to part them in our minds, resolving the incongruity by separating the elements he has brought together.

Another kind of incongruity is that achieved by Byron in such passages as this one, which presents a romantic lover trying to keep his mind on his beloved while his stomach is attacked by seasickness;

"Sooner shall heaven kiss earth—(here he fell sicker)
    Oh, Julia! what is every other woe?—
(For God's sake let me have a glass of liquor;
    Pedro, Battista, help me down below.)
Julia my love—(you rascal, Pedro, quicker)—
    Oh, Julia—(this curst vessel pitches so)—
Beloved Julia, hear me still beseeching!"
(Here he grew inarticulate with retching.)

The irony here is more a matter of drama than of language; but the difference between the language of the speaker's romantic assertions and his cries to his servants, supports the dramatic irony. The narrator points up the contrast by mis-rhyming "retching" with "beseeching" in the last two lines.

Beyond Metaphor and Irony

Much of the best contemporary poetry presents combinations of images and ideas so stretched and disconnected that they go beyond metaphor and yet so serious and appropriate they transcend irony also. The difficulty in understanding many modern poems stems from a profusion of images that seem ironically disconnected, but nevertheless suggest genuine metaphorical connection. We can find a relatively simple illustration in a few lines from a ballad by W. H. Auden entitled "As I Walked Out One Evening":

The glacier knocks in the cupboard,
  The desert sighs in the bed
And the crack in the tea-cup opens
  A lane to the land of the dead.

Here Auden seems to be operating with ironic incongruities—the glacier in the cupboard and so on—but this collection of incongruities adds up to a quite coherent statement about the absurd and empty horror that threatens much of modern life. Such a collection of images seems to combine qualities of conceit and symbol with ironic incongruity, leaving us to resolve the problem of whether these assertions are ironic overstatements or powerful metaphors for our condition.

A poem composed of a number of these high-tension ironic metaphors can be immediately intelligible in a general way and still difficult to reduce to prose sense at every point. But we should make the effort to establish prose sense—or possible prose senses—for each image and situation in such a poem, because even if we do not succeed entirely, we will be testing the ultimate intelligibility of the poem, the durability of its interest. As with certain kinds of modern art, it is sometimes hard to separate the fraudulent from the real in contemporary poetry. If we cannot discover intelligibility and coherence in a poem, if its images and situations do not enhance one another, we are confronted by either a fraudulent poem or a poem that is beyond us—one that we have not as yet learned how to read. Differences in poetic quality cannot be demonstrated conclusively, yet they exist. The following poem by a young American poet, William Knott, is offered as a problem in intelligibility and evaluation. Does it make sense? Does it work? Is it good?

Survival of the Fittest Groceries

The violence in the newspapers is pure genius
A daily gift to the reader
From some poet who wants to keep in good with us
Brown-noser wastepaperbasket-emptier

I shot 437 people that day
2 were still alive when I killed them
Why do people want to be exhumed movie-stars
I mean rats still biting them, the flesh of comets, why do they walk around like that?

I'm going to throw all of you into the refrigerator
10   And leave you to claw it out with the vegetables and meats

MUSIC

The musical element in poetry is the hardest to talk about because it is non-verbal. Our responses to rhythm and to pleasing combinations of sounds are in a sense too immediate, too fundamental to be comprehended in words. Yet music is important in all poetry, and for most poetry written before the last half-century it is crucial. Therefore, we must try to get some sort of verbal grasp of this poetical element, simply in order to do justice to most poetic achievement. Students generally prefer discussing one aspect of poetry to another in an order something like this:

1. ideas
2. situations
3. language
4. metrics

But if we are concerned about what makes poetry poetry rather than another kind of composition, we should probably reverse this order. If a piece of writing is neither especially rhythmical nor especially ironic or metaphorical in its language, it is not poetry, regardless of its dramatic situations or the ideas it presents.

In our experience, students are not only least interested in metrics of all the elements of poetry; they are also least competent in it. To demonstrate this, one need only ask them to translate a few sentences of prose into a simple, versified equivalent. Most will find this very difficult to do. No wonder they don't like poetry. They can't hear it properly. Fortunately, the fundamentals of versification are teachable to some extent, and should be part of any poetical curriculum. In the pages that follow, these fundamentals are presented in a fairly simple way, with a minimum of special terminology.

Metrics

Metrics has to do with all rhythmical effects in poetry. In English versification this means that it is largely a matter of accents and pauses. The pauses are determined by the usual grammatical principles that govern our speech and writing, and are indicated by the usual grammatical symbols: periods, commas, and so on. But one new factor is added. The end of a line of verse is itself a mark of punctuation. If a line ends with a regular mark of punctuation we call it *end-stopped*. If the last word of a line is followed by no punctuation and is part of a continuing grammatical unit like a prepositional phrase, we call the line *run-on*, or *enjambed*. In end-stopped lines, the line-end works *with* the punctuation and reinforces it, making each line a tight unit of thought. In enjambed lines the line-end works *against* the punctuation, throwing certain words into a prominence that they would not ordinarily have. The enjambed line really adds a special kind of poetical punctuation to the language: something at once more and less than a comma. Poets who use free verse forms with no regular rhythm are very dependent on enjambment to give their words a special poetical quality.

Reconsider the little poem by Williams:

so much depends
upon

a red wheel
barrow

glazed with rain
water

beside the white
chickens.

If we write this out as prose we get

So much depends upon a red wheelbarrow, glazed
with rainwater, beside the white chickens.

This is a simple, declarative prose sentence, with a couple of adjectival phrases tacked on, set off with commas. Has anything been lost by this rearrangement of the poem on the page? Decidedly so. The assertion being made is much less convincing in plain prose. The free-verse form of the sentence uses its line-endings to work against the prose movement, slowing it up, and providing a metrical equivalent for the visual highlighting of the images. Just where we would bring the words closest together in prose—making single words out of "wheel" and "barrow," "rain" and "water"—Williams has pulled them apart by breaking the line in mid-word.

The poem may or may not carry us to final agreement with its assertion, but in the free-verse form it certainly convinces us of the speaker's earnestness. We get a sense of how much he cares about what he is saying from the care with which he has spaced out his words. And when we read the poem aloud, with little pauses at line-ends, it carries us further toward conviction than the same sentence in its prosaic form.

That is a simple illustration of how poetry's special line-end punctuation can group words in a rhythm different from the rhythm of normal speech or prose. Here is a further illustration of how a poet can use the line-end to achieve an ironic effect virtually unduplicatable in prose. E. E. Cummings begins a poem this way:

pity this busy monster, manunkind,
not.

The first word of the second line absolutely reverses the meaning of the first line. We pause, with a comma, at the end of line 1. We stop entirely, with a period, after the first word of line 2. We hover, thus, with the wrong meaning until we are given the word that changes it, whereupon we stop to contemplate the admonition offered us in the whole opening sentence. Consider it rearranged as plain prose:

Pity this busy monster, manunkind, not.

or more prosaically,

Do not pity this busy monster, manunkind.

or still more prosaically,

Do not pity this busy, unkind monster, man.

By unraveling the poetical arrangement and combination of the words, we have destroyed the force of the admonition, taking away its suspense and eliminating the recoil in the original last word.

In verse that is not markedly rhythmical, unusual pauses and arrangements of words are the principal metrical device. In verse that is regularly rhythmical, however, the rhythm or meter itself is the crucial metrical element. Poetical arrangement does something to prosaic language, but not so much as does rhythm, which lifts an utterance and moves it in the direction of music. Just as the line-end pauses in a poem can work with or against the normal grammatical pauses of speech and prose, poetic rhythm can work both with and against our normal patterns of pronunciation.

In speech we begin with standard grammatical pronunciations for words. Take the word "defense." Normally we pronounce this word by accenting the first syllable lightly and the second syllable heavily. Indicating light accent by $\cup$ and heavy accent by —, we pronounce the word this way:

$\overset{\cup}{}\ \overset{\text{—}}{}$
defense. That is grammatical accent or grammatical stress. But in certain situations we might change this pronunciation for purposes of emphasis, as in, "It's not offense that's important, it's defense." Here we pronounce the

word defense. This is not grammatical stress but rhetorical stress. We have altered the usual pattern of light and heavy accent in order to make a point. (Grammar, or course, keeps changing, and the repeated use of one particular rhetorical pattern can eventually alter standard pronunciation. Broadcasts of football and basketball games, for instance, are helping to make defense the standard way to accent the word.)

Both grammatical and rhetorical stress operate in poetry, where they are complicated by a third kind of accent, which we may call poetical stress. Poetical stress is a regular system of accents which establishes the basic rhythm of a poem. There are only two fundamental systems of poetic stress in English verse, though they have many variations. Most frequently, English verse simply alternates light and heavy accents, giving every other syllable the same stress. Like this:

The woods decay, the woods decay and fall

Less frequently, English verse uses two light syllables between each heavy stress. Like this:

The Assyrian came down like the wolf on the fold
And his cohorts were gleaming in purple and gold

The rhythm of this second metrical pattern is more insistent than that of the first. The simple da-dum, da-dum of "The woods decay" is more like the spoken language than the da-da-dum, da-da-dum of "like the wolf on the fold."

When discussing metrics it is useful to have a term for the units that are repeated to make the pattern. It is customary to call these units *feet*. In the first example above, we have five repeated units in the line, five feet divided this way:

The woods | decay, | the woods | decay | and fall

In the second example each line has four feet, divided like this:

And his co | horts were gleam | ing in pur | ple and gold

In describing metrical patterns we usually state the number of feet in the basic line and name the standard foot in each line. The traditional name for the foot used in the first example (da-dum) is the *iamb*. The traditional name for the foot used in the second example (da-da-dum) is the *anapest*. In referring to the number of feet in the basic line of a poem, it is customary to use numerical prefixes derived from the Greek. Thus,

one-foot line =	mono	+ meter =	monometer
two-foot line =	di	+ meter =	dimeter
three-foot line =	tri	+ meter =	trimeter
four-foot line =	tetra	+ meter =	tetrameter
five-foot line =	penta	+ meter =	pentameter
six-foot line =	hexa	+ meter =	hexameter

We could skip the Greek and talk about such things as "lines with ten syllables that go da-dum" and so on, but it is finally easier to learn the accepted terms and say simply "iambic pentameter."

The iamb and the anapest each have a variant foot which is made by placing the accented syllable at the beginning of each foot rather than at the end. These are called the *trochee* (dum-da) and the *dactyl* (dum-da-da). They are not used very consistenly for one good reason. Rhyme in poetry is pleasing only if it includes the last accented syllable in a line *and all the unaccented syllables that follow it*. Thus, if you write,

Upon a mid | night drear | y once

You need find only a one-syllable rhyme for your rhyming line, such as:

Upon a midnight dreary once
I tried my hand at kicking punts

But if you use the trochee, and write

Once u | pon a | midnight | dreary

then you must rhyme

Once upon a midnight dreary
Of kicking punts my foot was weary.

The trochaic foot can, in fact, grow quite wearisome if carried through to the rhyme word consistently; so we often get a variation that looks like this:

Tiger, Tiger burning bright
In the forests of the night

These lines first appear trochaic (dum-da) and end by looking iambic (da-dum). (Though, actually the second line is more complicated in a way we will consider later on.) The two lines could be made fully iambic by a very slight change in each:

Ŏ, Tīgĕr, Tīgĕr būrnĭng brīght

Wĭthīn thĕ fōrĕst ŏf thĕ nīght

or we could make them fully trochaic by this kind of alteration:

Tīgĕr, Tīgĕr būrnĭng brīghtlў,

Rōamĭng thrŏugh thĕ fōrĕst nīghtlў

In order to name the metrical pattern of "Tiger, Tiger" we must supply an imaginary unaccented syllable at one end of the line or the other, like this:

x̆ Tī | gĕr, Tī | gĕr, būrn | ĭng brīght

or this:

Tīgĕr, | Tīgĕr, | būrnĭng | brīght x̆ |

These maneuverings strongly suggest that the special terminology of metrical analysis is not important in itself, and that beyond the major distinction between the two-syllable foot and the three-syllable foot, we need not be terribly fussy in classifying. What, then, is the use of all these special terms?

The art of metrics involves a poet's ability to generate and maintain a consistent meter without destroying normal patterns of grammar and syntax. To succeed metrically a poet must make language dance without making it unnatural. And a really crucial aspect of this art is perceptible only when we have the terminology to recognize it. Any absolutely regular meter quickly becomes boring through repetition. But a totally irregular poem is totally without the kind of interest and pleasure that rhythm provides.

All good poets who work in regular meters introduce metrical variations into their poems. The simplest way to understand this is to see the variations as substitutions of a different sort of foot for the one called for by the established meter of the poem. (The second line of Blake's "The Tyger," is not quite the same as the first. Can you devise alternative ways to describe its rhythm? The whole poem may be found in our Selection of Poets.) As an example of metrical variation, consider this stanza from a poem by A. E. Housman:

ˇ — ˇ — ˇ—ˇ
With rue my heart is laden
  ˇ — ˇ — ˇ —
  For golden friends I had
ˇ — ˇ ˇ — ˇ — ˇ
For many a rose-lipt maiden
  ˇ — ˇ ˇ—ˇ —
  And many a lightfoot lad.

The meter is basically iambic, complicated a little by the extra syllable of a feminine rhyme in alternate lines (laden, maiden—two-syllable rhymes are called *feminine*). But the basic meter is varied by the addition of one anapestic foot in lines three and four.

The second (and last) stanza of that poem goes like this:

By brooks too broad for leaping
  The lightfoot boys are laid;
The rose-lipt girls are sleeping
  In fields where roses fade.

This looks almost absolutely regular—iambic trimeter with alternate feminine rhyme—but it is not quite. Both grammar and rhetoric urge us to accent and elongate the sound of the word "too" in the first line. Thus the line must be scanned (analyzed metrically) this way:

ˇ — — — ˇ — (ˇ)
by brooks | too broad | for leaping

The second foot of this line has two accented syllables and no unaccented one. This is a kind of foot that is often used as a substitute but never as the metrical basis for a whole poem. Its technical name is *spondee*. Housman has used the spondee here for a slight variation of his rhythm—one that is almost unnoticeable to the analytic eye but works subtly on the ear to prevent the rhythm from becoming monotonous.

Having noticed that substitution, we might notice also that in both stanzas the words "lightfoot" and "rose-lipt" work gently in a spondaic direction. In both stanzas these words appear so that the heavy accent of the iamb falls on their first syllable. But that second syllable is a word in its own right, and one that might well take a heavy accent in another metrical situation, such as this:

˘ — ˘ — ˘
My foot is weary,

˘ — ˘ — ˘
My eye is teary,

˘ — ˘ — ˘
My lip is beery.

"Foot" and "lip" (or "lipt") can both take heavy accents. In Housman's stanzas the syllables "foot" and "lipt," falling where we would expect light accents, actually result in something between heavy and light.

The basic terminology of metrical analysis establishes only the simple distinction between heavy and light, thus it cannot take us too far into any metrical subtleties. In scansion, however, we need to consider subtleties, and should probably be ready to use at least one more symbol to indicate a stress between heavy and light. Using a combination of the two stress marks we already have in operation to indicate an intermediate stress, we might re-scan the first stanza this way:

˘ — ˘ — ˘ — ˘
With rue my heart is laden

˘ — ˘ — ˘ —
for golden friends I had,

˘ — ˘˘ — ˘ — ˘
For many a rose-lipt maiden

˘ — ˘˘ — ˘ —
And many a lightfoot lad.

Then we could point out that the intermediate accents on lipt and foot make the last feet of lines 3 and 4 partially spondaic.

Thus far we have considered the metrics of this little poem only in terms of its pleasing variation within a firmly established pattern. We can see how the pattern is established in the first two lines of the first stanza, and then varies subtly in most of the succeeding lines, until the pattern reasserts itself in the perfectly regular last line. Now, we are in a position to deal with the question of the relation of the metrics to the meaning of the poem. The poem makes a simple statement about sadness felt for the death of those who were once agile and pretty. But death is never mentioned. It is evoked metaphorically through words like "laid" and "sleeping." These metaphors are very gentle, suggesting more the peace of the grave than any decay or destruction. In the second stanza the speaker also suggests delicately the frustration and sadness felt by those in the world of the living. The unleapable brooks symbolize things unachievable in life; the fading roses symbolize the impermanence of living things. The peace of the dead is ironically contrasted with the sadness of the living. The speaker is finally rueful not just because his golden friends are dead but because *he* is alive.

How does the meter relate to all this? Iambic trimeter calls for a good deal of rhyme—a rhyming sound every third foot. The addition of feminine rhymes in alternate lines makes for even more rhyming syllables. If we compare this metrical situation with that in another poem (by Ben Jonson) about death and decay, we should notice something about the effect of meter.

Slow, slow, fresh fount, keep time with my salt tears;
  Yet slower, yet; O faintly gentle springs;
List to the heavy part the music bears,
   Woe weeps out her division when she sings:
    Droop herbs and flowers;
    Fall grief in showers;
    Our beauties are not ours.
     O, I could still,
Like melting snow upon some craggy hill,
    Drop, drop, drop, drop,
Since nature's pride is now a withered daffodil.

How should this first line be scanned? Something like this:

$$\text{—} \quad \text{—} \quad | \quad \text{—} \quad \text{—} \quad | \quad \breve{} \; \text{—} \quad | \quad \breve{} \; \breve{} \quad | \quad \text{—} \quad \text{—}$$
Slow, slow, | fresh fount, | keep time | with my | salt tears;

Here we have that rarity, a line almost completely spondaic—with only a suggestion of iambs in the third and fourth feet. An iambic pattern establishes itself gradually in the poem, but the verse is dominated by spondees, even in the short lines:

$$\text{—} \quad \text{—} \quad \breve{} \; \text{—} \; (\breve{})$$
Droop herbs and flowers;

$$\text{—} \quad \text{—} \; \breve{} \; \text{—} \; (\breve{})$$
Fall grief in showers;

$$\text{—} \quad \text{—} \; \breve{} \; \text{—} \; \text{—} \; \text{-} (\breve{})$$
Our beauties are not ours.[1]

In addition to this spondaic domination, the lines are frequently broken by pauses—those indicated by the punctuation, as well as those which naturally follow imperatives like "droop" and "fall." These pauses and the spondees work together to give the poem a slow, hesitant, funereal movement like the sound of muffled drums. This meter works in a metaphoric or harmonious relation to the sense of the poem, which is a direct utterance of grief over seasonal decay and the death it symbolizes.

Now, how does this compare to the movement of the Housman poem? Housman's iambic trimeter, virtually pauseless except for line-ends, is a much lighter, almost gay meter. The stresses bounce regularly, the lines

1. These rhyme words can all be scanned as either one or two syllables.

flow smoothly, the rhymes chime insistently. This pattern establishes an ironic or contrasting relation to the mournful sense of the words, but is perfectly appropriate because the words themselves are finally ironic. Housman deals with death lightly, easily, if wryly. Jonson works hard to make us respond seriously and sadly. The frequent pauses, the heavy spondees, the varying length of the lines—all these work to reinforce the sadness and seriousness of Jonson's words. Both poems have a pronounced musical dimension, but Housman's is like a spritely ballad meter and Jonson's is like a funeral dirge.

Before considering rhyme and other sound effects further, we need to look at one last important dimension of metrics. The standard line of English verse which is meant to be spoken rather than sung is a line of five iambic feet—iambic pentameter. This is the basic line of Chaucer's *Canterbury Tales*, of Spenser's *Faerie Queene*, of Shakespeare's plays, of Milton's *Paradise Lost*, of the satires of Dryden and Pope, of Byron's *Don Juan*, of Wordsworth's *Prelude*, of Browning's *The Ring and the Book*. This line often appears unrhymed, as in Shakespeare's plays (for the most part), *Paradise Lost*, and *The Prelude*; or in pairs of rhymed lines. Technically, the unrhymed iambic pentameter line is called blank verse; the paired rhymes are called couplets. In both these iambic pentameter lines, an important element is the mid-line pause or *caesura*. Varying the location of the *caesura* is an important way of preventing monotony in blank verse and pentameter couplets. Consider, for example, these opening lines of Book II of *Paradise Lost:*

High on a Throne of Royal State, which far
Outshone the wealth of *Ormus* and of *Ind*,
Or where the gorgeous East with richest hand
Show'rs on her Kings *Barbaric* Pearl and Gold,
Satan exalted sat, by merit rais'd
To that bad eminence; and from despair
Thus high uplifted beyond hope, aspires
Beyond thus high, insatiate to pursue
Vain war with Heav'n, and by success untaught
10 His proud imaginations thus display'd.

If we locate the obvious *caesurae*—those indicated by internal punctuation marks—we find this situation:

line 1 . . . end of 4th foot
line 2 . . . none
line 3 . . . none
line 4 . . . none
line 5 . . . end of 3rd foot
line 6 . . . end of 3rd foot

line 7 . . . end of 4th foot
line 8 . . . end of 2nd foot
line 9 . . . end of 2nd foot
line 10 . . . none

In reading the poem aloud, we will find ourselves pausing slightly, at some point in nearly every line, whether a pause is indicated by punctuation or not. Thus, we can mark the whole passage this way, using a single slash for a slight pause and two for a noticeable one, three for a full stop.

High on a throne of Royal State,// which far
Outshone/ the wealth of *Ormus*/ and of *Ind*,
Or where the gorgeous East/ with richest hand
Show'rs on her kings/ *Barbaric* Pearl and Gold,
Satan exalted sat,// by merit rais'd
To that bad eminence;/// and from despair
Thus high uplifted beyond hope,// aspires
Beyond thus high,// insatiate to pursue
Vain war with Heav'n,// and by success untaught
10 His proud imaginations/ thus display'd.

By varying end-stopped lines with enjambed, and deploying caesurae of varying strengths at different points in his line, Milton continually shifts his pauses to prevent the march of his lines from growing wearisome. He also uses substitute feet frequently—especially a trochee or spondee in the first foot of a line. We count three trochees and one spondee in the first feet of these ten lines. Check this count yourself.

Now consider Alexander Pope's use of enjambment, caesura, and substitution of feet in the following lines. Pope uses a tight form, with punctuation coming nearly always at the end of each couplet. These closed couplets (as opposed to enjambed or open couplets) in iambic pentameter are called "heroic" couplets because they were the standard verse form of Restoration heroic drama (but they might better be called satiric, because they have been most successful in the satiric poems of Dryden, Pope, and Samuel Johnson).

In such a tight form as the heroic couplet, great skill is needed to avoid monotony. When we read only the real masters of such a form, we tend to take such skill for granted, but it is far from easy. Here we find Pope talking about poetic blunders and poetic skill, modulating his own verse deftly to illustrate the points he is making. (The *Alexandrine* referred to is an iambic hexameter line, occasionally used for variety in English iambic pentameter forms.) These two passages from Pope's "Essay on Criticism" are printed here widely spaced, to allow the student to write in his or her own scansion.

These equal syllables alone require,

Though oft the ear the open vowels tire;

While expletives their feeble aid do join;

And ten low words oft creep in one dull line:

While they ring round the same unvaried chimes,

With sure returns of still expected rhymes;

Where'er you find "the cooling western breeze,"

In the next line, it "whispers through the trees:"

If crystal streams "with pleasing murmurs creep,"

10   The reader's threatened (not in vain) with "sleep:"

Then, at the last and only couplet fraught

With some unmeaning thing they call a thought,

A needless Alexandrine ends the song

That, like a wounded snake, drags its slow length along.

True ease in writing comes from art, not chance,

As those move easiest who have learned to dance.

'Tis not enough no harshness gives offence,

The sound must seem an Echo to the sense:

Soft is the strain when Zephyr gently blows,

And the smooth stream in smoother numbers flows;

But when loud surges lash the sounding shore,

The hoarse, rough verse should like the torrent roar:

When Ajax strives some rock's vast weight to throw,

10   The line too labours, and the words move slow;

Not so, when swift Camilla scours the plain,

Flies o'er th' unbending corn, and skims along the main.

Rhyme is an important element in musical poetry, but much less so in dramatic poetry—where it can be too artificial—or in meditative poetry. Associated with rhyme as elements designed to generate a pleasure in sound which is almost purely aesthetic are such devices as alliteration and assonance. Alliteration is the repetition of the same sound at the beginning of words in the same line or adjacent lines. Assonance is the repetition of vowel sounds in the same or adjacent lines. For full rhyme we require the same vowel sounds which end in the same consonantal sounds. "Fight" and "foot" are alliterative. "Fight" and "bike" are assonant. "Fight" and "fire" are both assonant and alliterative but do not make a rhyme. "Fight" and "bite" make a rhyme. Consider the metrical and sonic effects in this stanza of a poem by Swinburne:

Till the slow sea rise and the sheer cliff crumble,
  Till terrace and meadow the deep gulfs drink,
Till the strength of the waves of the high tides humble
  The fields that lessen, the rocks that shrink,
Here now in his triumph where all things falter,
  Stretched out on the spoils that his own hand spread,
As a god self-slain on his own strange altar,
    Death lies dead.

The meter is mainly a mixture of anapests and spondees—an exotic combination of rapid and slow feet. Can you discern any particular pattern in the way the feet are combined? Is there variation in the pattern? What do rhyme, assonance, and alliteration contribute to the pattern?

In addition to its purely aesthetic or decorative effect, designed to charm the reader out of a critical posture and into a receptive one, rhyme can be used for just the opposite effect. In satiric or comic verse, strained rhymes are often used to awaken the reader's wits and give him a comic kind of pleasure. Ogden Nash often combines strained rhymes with lines of awkwardly unequal length for especially absurd effects. But something similar can be achieved within fairly strict formal limits. In the following stanza from Byron's *Don Juan*, we find the poet using feminine and even triple rhyme with deliberate clumsiness:

'Tis pity learned virgins ever wed
  With persons of no sort of education,
Or gentlemen, who, though well born and bred,
  Grow tired of scientific conversation:
I don't choose to say much upon this head,
  I'm a plain man, and in a single station,
But—Oh! ye lords of ladies intellectual,
Inform us truly, have they not hen-peck'd you all?

The last rhyme in particular is surprising, audacious, and deliberately strained—echoing in this way the sense of the stanza. Like imagery and metrics, rhyme can be used harmoniously or ironically, to establish or to break a mood.

Before closing, we should note that it is customary to indicate the rhyme scheme of any given poetic selection by assigning letters of the alphabet to each rhyming sound, repeating each letter as the sound is repeated. The rhyme scheme of the Byron stanza we just considered would be designated this way: *abababcc*, with *a* standing for the sounds in *wed, bred,* and *head; b,* for . . . *ation;* and *c,* for . . . *ectual* and . . . *eck'd you all.* And in the Swinburne quoted just above, the rhyme scheme is simply *ababcdcd.*

Approaching a Poem

We do not, if we are honest, keep in readiness a number of different approaches to poems or to people. We try to keep our integrity. But at the same time we must recognize and accept the otherness that we face. In getting to know a person or a poem we make the kind of accommodation that we have called tact. But we do not pretend, we do not emote falsely, and we try not to make stock responses to surface qualities. We do not judge a man by his clothes or even by his skin. We do not judge a poem by words or ideas taken out of their full poetic context. We do not consider a statement in a poem without attention to its dramatic context, the overtones generated by its metaphors and ironies, the mood established by its metrics. And we try to give each element of every poem its proper weight.

Obviously, there can be no single method for treating every poem with tact. What is required is a flexible procedure through which we can begin to understand the nature of any poem. The suggestions below are intended to facilitate such a procedure. Like everything else in this book they should serve as a scaffolding only—a temporary structure inside of which the real building takes shape. Like any scaffolding, this one must be discarded as soon as it becomes constricting or loses its usefulness. Like good manners learned by rote, this procedure will never amount to anything until it is replaced by naturally tactful behavior. Then it will have served its purpose.

1. Try to grasp the expressive dimension of the poem first. This means especially getting a clear sense of the nature and situation of the speaker. What are the circumstances under which he or she says, writes, or thinks these words? Who hears them? Are they part of an ongoing action which is implied by them?

2. Consider the relative importance of the narrative-dramatic dimension and the descriptive-meditative dimension in the poem. Is the main interest psychological or philosophical—in character or in idea? Or is the poem's verbal playfulness or music its main reason for being? How do the nature of the speaker and the situation in which he speaks color the ideas and attitudes presented?

3. After you have a sense of the poem's larger, expressive dimension, re-read it with particular attention to the play of language. Consider the way that metaphor and irony color the ideas and situations. How does the language work to characterize the speaker or to color the ideas presented with shadings of attitude? How important is sheer word-play

or verbal wit in the poem? How well do the images and ideas fit together and reinforce one another in a metaphoric or ironic way?

4. Re-read the poem yet again with special attention to its musical dimension. To the extent that it seems important, analyze the relation of rhythm and rhyme to the expressive dimension of the poem.

5. Throughout this process, reading the poem aloud can be helpful in establishing emphases and locating problems. Parts of a poem that are not fully understood will prove troublesome in the reading. Questions of tone and attitude will become more insistent in oral performance. Thus, it is advisable to work toward a reading performance as a final check on the degree to which we have mastered situation, ideas, images, attitudes, and music. An expert may be able to read through a piece of piano music and hear in his mind a perfect performance of it. Most of us need to tap out the notes before we can grasp melodies, harmonies, and rhythms with any sureness. Reading poetry aloud helps us to establish our grasp of it—especially if a patient and knowledgeable teacher is there to correct our performance and encourage us to try again.

One last piece of advice, in the form of some lines by the Spanish poet Antonio Machado, translated by Robert Bly:

People possess four things
that are no good at sea
anchor, rudder, oars
and the fear of going down.

A Selection of Poets

INTRODUCTION

The poems collected here are intended as an introduction to the work of twenty-nine poets. For each we have provided at least four poems: enough for a student to get some sense of how that poet uses the English language to create poetry. We have not attempted to provide translations from other languages, since a translation into English must either become a new poem or fail utterly. Poetry, as Robert Frost remarked, is what gets lost in translation.

The poets are presented in the chronological order of their birth dates. They range in time and place from William Shakespeare, who wrote his sonnets in England before the year 1590, to Rosmarie Waldrop, whose first volume of poetry was published in 1972. Still, this is not a "history of poetry in English." What this collection is and what it is not should be clarified here.

These selections do not constitute anyone's choice of the greatest English and American poets. Some of the greatest, indeed, have been excluded here. Spenser, Milton, and Pope—to name but three—were omitted for the reason that most of their best work is found in long poems, and even their shorter works are inaccessible to the beginning student of poetry without a deadening amount of annotation. (Along with others not anthologized here, these three poets are, however, represented in the discussion of poetic elements just completed; and all poets represented are listed in the Index.)

BALLADS

A Note on the Ballad

The ballad comes down to us from a time when few people knew how to read and write. Because ballads were transmitted orally by ballad singers, they had to be easy to remember. Consequently, in most ballads we find a four-line stanza with a simple *abcb* rhyme scheme and regular metrical pattern: usually the first and third lines are iambic tetrameter and the second and fourth are iambic trimeter, as in this stanza from "The Demon Lover":

> They had not sailed a league, a league,
>   A League but scarcely three,
> Till altered grew his countenance,
>   And raging grew the sea.

Of the older ballads here, "The Demon Lover" and "The Unquiet Grave" follow this scheme with but few variations, while "Edward" has a more complex rhyme scheme of *aabaab*, with refrains interspersed after the first and fourth lines of each stanza.

   The ballad is a narrative about a single event, which is presented in a straightforward manner with attention to action. The most popular themes of the older ballads were tragic love affairs, supernatural events, and various forms of violence usually resulting in death. Some humorous ballads exist, as well as some with religious themes, but these are far outnumbered by the tragic and mournful ballads. Then as now, the news of most interest, and therefore the most likely to be remembered and passed on to be savored by others, tended to be violent or tragic. The story is presented simply and chronologically with each stanza repeating the previous one and adding another new piece to the narrative strand. This characteristic feature is called *incremental repetition*. Dialogue is frequently used to forward the action. Here, "Edward" provides the most dramatic example of the question and answer form of dialogue, while "The Unquiet Grave" and "The Demon Lover" combine narrative and dialogue. In some ballads, such as "The Streets of Laredo," we find a first-person narrator introducing the action, but this "I" is not any one particular person. Rather, this is a communal "I," an objective voice speaking for a group of people. So while the subject of a ballad may deal with a moral issue, very little moralizing occurs; and while the subject may be an emotional one, such as a tragic love affair, we find little expression of feeling.

   The question of authorship of early ballads has provoked lively debate. Is "Anonymous" one author, or a group of authors? The answer might well be both; however, it's more likely that a ballad was created by one person, but in its oral transmission from place to place and person to person, each new singer added to, subtracted from, or rearranged the original material.

Consequently, in the most definitive collection of ballads we have, Francis Child's *The English and Scottish Popular Ballads*, we find that most ballads exist in more than one version. For example, there are seven versions of "The Demon Lover" ranging in length from thirty-two stanzas (Version A) to nine stanzas (Versions D and G).

The American folk ballad, represented here by "The Streets of Laredo" and "John Henry," has its roots in the many lands from which America's settlers came, bringing their musical heritages with them. As these groups settled and mingled, their music mingled as well, and the variety of ballad versions increased. Americanized versions of British or continental ballads tended to be a bit more strait-laced than their ancestors, perhaps because of the Puritan heritage of this country. For example, "The Streets of Laredo" is taken from an eighteenth-century English ballad, "The Sailor Cut Down in His Prime." In the American ballad, the dying young cowboy who has been shot knows he's "done wrong," and we can assume that his trips to "the dram house and then to the card house" mean that he got involved in a drunken barroom brawl about gambling, but the ballad is not specific about details here. The cowboy requests a romanticized funeral:

Get six jolly cowboys to carry my coffin,
Get six pretty maidens to bear up my pall,
Put bunches of roses all over my coffin,
Put roses to deaden the sods as they fall.

The English version is more specific about the young sailor's ruin and about his funeral:

His poor old father, his good old mother,
Oft-times had told him about his past life,
When along with those flash girls his money he'd squander,
And along with those flash girls he took his delight.

And now he's dead and he lies in his coffin,
Six jolly sailors shall carry him along,
And six jolly maidens shall carry white roses,
Not for to smell him as they pass him by.

While both ballads use the universal and poignant theme of the untimely death of a young person, the English version takes a more ironically humorous view toward the facts of life than does the more sentimental and melancholy American version, which is based on a very American story, one fairly common in the early West: that of the feisty young cowboy hitting town after some months on the trail, and his search for fun ending in disaster.

Where "The Streets of Laredo" refers to a general theme, "John Henry," on the other hand, has its roots in an actual event: a contest between man and machine at the Big Bend Tunnel in West Virginia about 1870. John Henry, a tall strong black railroad worker, won the contest and achieved legendary status thereby. The original form of this ballad was derived from a Scottish ballad, but in the version we have chosen here (and it is one of many), we can see the influence of West African rhythms transforming the original structure. "Eleanor Rigby" provides a twentieth-century example of the commercial popular ballad. Like its ancestors, it is meant to be sung, and like them, it makes use of a refrain. But we leave it to you to consider whether the narrative here is as simple and straightforward as in the older ballads.

After you have studied this group of ballads, you might look at A. E. Housman's "Is My Team Ploughing" and W. H. Auden's "As I Walked Out One Evening" as examples of modern poets who have been influenced by the ballad form. Their use of this form is called the *literary ballad*, and its most noticeable difference lies in the reader's awareness of the shaping imagination of a single poet who is addressing a message to an educated audience.

Edward

"Why does your brand[1] sae drap wi' bluid,
  Edward, Edward,
Why does your brand sae drap wi' bluid,
  And why sae sad gang[2] ye, O?"
"O I ha'e killed my hawke sae guid,
  Mither, Mither,
O I ha'e killed my hawke sae guid,
  And I had nae mair but he, O."

"Your hawke's bluid was never sae reid,
10 Edward, Edward,
Your hawke's bluid was never sae reid,
  My dear son I tell thee, O."
"O I ha'e killed my reid-roan steed,
  Mither, Mither,
O I ha'e killed my reid-roan steed,
  That erst was sae fair and free, O."

1. sword
2. go

"Your steed was auld, and ye ha'e got mair,
    Edward, Edward,
Your steed was auld, and ye ha'e got mair,
20   Some other dule ye drie,[3] O."
"O I ha'e killed my fader dear,
    Mither, Mither,
O I ha'e killed my fader dear,
    Alas, and wae is me, O!"

"And whatten penance wul ye drie for that,
    Edward, Edward,
And whatten penance wul ye drie for that,
    My dear son, now tell me, O?"
"I'll set my feet in yonder boat,
30   Mither, Mither,
"I'll set my feet in yonder boat,
    And I'll fare over the sea, O."

"And what wul ye do wi' your towers and your ha',
    Edward, Edward,
And what wul ye do wi' your tower and your ha',
    That were sae fair to see, O?"
"I'll let them stand tul down they fa',
    Mither, Mither,
I'll let them stand tul down they fa',
40   For here never mair maun[4] I be, O."

"And what wul ye leave to your bairns[5] and your wife,
    Edward, Edward,
And what wul ye leave to your bairns and your wife,
    When ye gang over the sea, O?"
"The warldes room,[6] let them beg thrae life,
    Mither, Mither,
The warldes room, let them beg thrae life,
    For them never mair wul I see, O."

"And what wul ye leave to your ain mither dear,
50   Edward, Edward,
And what wul ye leave to your ain mither dear,
    My dear son, now tell me, O."

3. grief you suffer
4. must
5. children
6. world's space

"The curse of hell frae me sall ye bear,
  Mither, Mither,
The curse of hell frae me sall ye bear,
  Sic⁷ counsels ye gave to me, O."

7. such

The Unquiet Grave

"The wind doth blow today, my love,
  And a few small drops of rain:
I never had but one true-love,
  In cold grave she was lain.

"I'll do as much for my true-love
  As any young man may;
I'll sit and mourn all at her grave
  For a twelvemonth and a day."

The twelvemonth and a day being up,
10 The dead began to speak:
"Oh who sits weeping on my grave,
  And will not let me sleep?"

" 'Tis I, my love, sits on your grave,
  And will not let you sleep;
For I crave one kiss of your clay-cold lips,
  And that is all I seek."

"You crave one kiss of my clay-cold lips;
  But my breath smells earthy strong;
If you have one kiss of my clay-cold lips,
20 Your time will not be long.

" 'Tis down in yonder garden green,
  Love, where we used to walk,
The finest flower that ere was seen
  Is withered to a stalk.

"The stalk is withered dry, my love,
  So will our hearts decay;
So make yourself content, my love,
  Till God calls you away."

The Demon Lover

"Where have you been, my long lost lover,
   This seven long years and more?"
"I've been seeking gold for thee, my love,
   And riches of great store.

"Now I've come for the vows you promised me,
   You promised me long ago;"
"My former vows you must forgive,
   For I'm a wedded wife."

"I might have been married to a king's daughter,
10   Far, far ayont the sea;
But I refused the crown of gold,
   And it's all for love of thee."

"If you might have married a king's daughter,
   Yourself you have to blame;
For I'm married to a ship's carpenter,
   And to him I have a son.

"Have you any place to put me in,
   If I with you should gang?"[1]
"I've seven brave ships upon the sea,
20   All laden to the brim.

"I'll build my love a bridge of steel,
   All for to help her o'er;
Likewise webs of silk down her side,
   To keep my love from the cold."

She took her eldest son into her arms,
   And sweetly did him kiss;
"My blessing go with you, and your father too,
   For little does he know of this."

As they were walking up the street,
30   Most beautiful for to behold,
He cast a glamour[2] o'er her face,
   And it shone like brightest gold.

1. go
2. enchantment, magic spell

As they were walking along the sea-side,
   Where his gallant ship lay in,
So ready was the chair of gold
   To welcome this lady in.

They had not sailed a league, a league,
   A league but scarcely three,
Till altered grew his countenance,
40   And raging grew the sea.

When they came to yon sea-side,
   She set her down to rest;
It's then she spied his cloven foot,
   Most bitterly she wept.

"O is it for gold that you do weep?
   Or is it for fear?
Or is it for the man you left behind
   When that you did come here?"

"It is not for gold that I do weep,
50   O no, nor yet for fear;
But it is for the man I left behind
   When that I did come here.

"O what a bright, bright hill is yon,
   That shines so clear to see?"
"O it is the hill of heaven," he said,
   "Where you shall never be."

"O what a black, dark hill is yon,
   That looks so dark to me?"
"O it is the hill of hell," he said,
60   "Where you and I shall be.

"Would you wish to see the fishes swim
   In the bottom of the sea,
Or wish to see the leaves grow green
   On the banks of Italy?"

"I hope I'll never see the fishes swim
   On the bottom of the sea,
But I hope to see the leaves grow green
   On the banks of Italy."

He took her up to the topmast high,
70   To see what she could see;
He sunk the ship in a flash of fire,
    To the bottom of the sea.

The Streets of Laredo

As I walked out in the streets of Laredo,
As I walked out in Laredo one day,
I spied a poor cowboy wrapped up in white linen,
Wrapped in white linen as cold as the clay.

Oh, beat the drums slowly, and play the fife lowly,
Play the dead march as you carry me along,
Take me to the green valley, there lay the sod o'er me,
For I'm a young cowboy, and I know I've done wrong.

Let sixteen gamblers come handle my coffin,
10   Let sixteen cowboys come sing me a song,
Take me to the graveyard, and lay the sod o'er me,
For I'm a poor cowboy, and I know I've done wrong.

It was once in the saddle I used to go dashing,
It was once in the saddle I used to go gay,
First to the dram house, and then to the card house,
Got shot in the breast, and I'm dying today.

Get six jolly cowboys to carry my coffin,
Get six pretty maidens to bear up my pall,
Put bunches of roses all over my coffin,
20   Put roses to deaden the sods as they fall.

Oh, bury me beside my knife and my six-shooter,
My spurs on my heel, my rifle by my side,
And over my coffin put a bottle of brandy,
That's the cowboy's drink, and carry me along.

We beat the drums slowly and played the fife lowly,
And bitterly wept as we bore him along,
For we all loved our comrade, so brave, young, and handsome,
We all loved our comrade, although he'd done wrong.

John Henry

When John Henry was a little babe,
    A-holding to his mama's hand,
Says, "If I live till I'm twenty-one,
    I'm going to make a steel-driving man, my babe,
    I'm going to make a steel-driving man."

When John Henry was a little boy,
    A-sitting on his father's knee,
Says, "The Big Bend Tunnel on the C. & O. Road
    Is going to be the death of me, my babe,
10   Is going to be the death of me."

John he made a steel-driving man,
    They took him to the tunnel to drive;
He drove so hard he broke his heart,
    He laid down his hammer and he died, my babe,
    He laid down his hammer and he died.

O now John Henry is a steel-driving man,
    He belongs to the steel-driving crew,
And every time his hammer comes down,
    You can see that steel walking through, my babe,
20   You can see that steel walking through.

The steam drill standing on the right-hand side,
    John Henry standing on the left;
He says, "I'll beat that steam drill down,
    Or I'll die with my hammer in my breast, my babe,
    Or I'll die with my hammer in my breast."

He placed his drill on the top of the rock,
    The steam drill standing close at hand;
He beat it down one inch and a half
    And laid down his hammer like a man, my babe,
30   And laid down his hammer like a man.

Johnny looked up to his boss-man and said,
    "O boss-man, how can it be?
For the rock is so hard and the steel is so tough,
    I can feel my muscles giving way, my babe,
    I can feel my muscles giving way."

Johnny looked down to his turner and said,
    "O turner, how can it be?

The rock is so hard and the steel is so tough
   That everybody's turning after me, my babe,
40   That everybody's turning after me."

They took poor Johnny to the steep hillside,
   He looked to his heavens above;
He says, "Take my hammer and wrap it in gold
   And give it to the girl I love, my babe,
   And give it to the girl I love."

They took his hammer and wrapped it in gold
   And gave it to Julia Ann;
And the last word John Henry said to her
   Was, "Julia, do the best you can, my babe,"
50   Was, "Julia, do the best you can."

"If I die a railroad man,
   Go bury me under the tie,
So I can hear old Number Four,
   As she goes rolling by, my babe,
   As she goes rolling by.

"If I die a railroad man,
   Go bury me under the sand,
With a pick and shovel at my head and feet,
   And a nine-pound hammer in my hand, my babe,
60   And a nine-pound hammer in my hand."

JOHN LENNON and PAUL McCARTNEY
1940–1980   1942—

Eleanor Rigby

Ah, look at all the lonely people!
Ah, look at all the lonely people!
Eleanor Rigby picks up the rice
   in the church
Where a wedding has been.
Lives in a dream.
Waits at the window, wearing the face
   that she keeps in a jar by the door.
Who is it for?

10   All the lonely people,
         where do they all come from?
      All the lonely people,
         where do they all belong?

      Father McKenzie writing the words
         of a sermon that no one will hear—
      No one comes near. Look at him
         working, darning his socks in the night
         when there's nobody there.
      What does he care?

20   All the lonely people,
         where do they all come from?
      All the lonely people,
         where do they all belong?

      Ah, look at all the lonely people!
      Ah, look at all the lonely people!
      Eleanor Rigby died in the church and
         was buried along with her name.
      Nobody came.
      Father McKenzie wiping the dirt from
30   his hands as he walks from the grave.
      No one was saved.

      All the lonely people,
         where do they all come from?
      All the lonely people,
         where do they all belong?

WILLIAM SHAKESPEARE
1564–1616

William Shakespeare was born into a middle-class family in the Warwick-shire market town of Stratford-on-Avon. His father, a glover by trade, was a leading citizen, holding the office of bailiff, a position equivalent to mayor. As a boy, Shakespeare attended the very strict Stratford Grammar School, where the curriculum consisted of grammar, reading, writing, and recita-tion done almost entirely in Latin. In 1582, when he was eighteen, Shake-speare married Anne Hathaway, but not much else is known of him until 1592, by which time he had established himself as author and playwright in the London theater world. He turned to writing poetry when an outbreak of the plague closed the London theaters from the summer of 1592 until June, 1594. Most of Shakespeare's 154 sonnets were written between 1593 and 1599, and about ten were written between then and 1609, the year of their publication. The sonnets were dedicated "To the Onlie Begetter of these ensving Sonnets Mr. W.H.," who was probably Shakespeare's patron but whose identity is not known. Nor have scholars been able to establish identities for the characters found in the sonnets: the poet's young friend of high social position who is addressed in sonnets 1–126; the "dark lady" of sonnets 127–154 who causes joy and pain for the poet; and a rival poet. Though the autobiographical mystery is tantalizing, it is probably wiser to read and enjoy the sonnets for the mastery of language and form which was to inspire so many other poets.

A Note on the Sonnet

The sonnet was invented by Italians to plague Englishmen—or so some poets have maintained. It is a special form of verse that requires a good deal of intricate rhyming—which is easier to do in Italian than in English. Nevertheless, once domesticated in the sixteenth century, the sonnet form has persisted in English poetry with surprising vigor and is still alive today, though at its lowest ebb in four hundred years. Its rules are relatively few. A fourteen-line sequence of iambic pentameter verse has become the norm, even though the early sonneteers did not always adhere to this measure. The tightest rhyme schemes require just four or five sounds, in one combination or another, at the end of all fourteen lines.

In structure, most sonnets may be seen as variations on two basic patterns—and these are patterns of thought as well as of grammar and rhyme. One pattern is called *Italian* (or *Petrarchan* after its first important practitioner), the other *English* (or *Shakespearean*). In the Petrarchan structure the poem is divided into two major units of thought, syntax, and rhyme: the first eight lines, called the *octave*, and the last six, called the *sestet.* Here is an example of a Petrarchan sonnet by an American poet of the nineteenth century: Henry Wadsworth Longfellow's "Milton."

I pace the sounding sea-beach and behold
How the voluminous billows roll and run,
Upheaving and subsiding, while the sun
Shines through their sheeted emerald far unrolled
And the ninth wave, slow gathering fold by fold
All its loose-flowing garments into one,
Plunges upon the shore, and floods the dun
Pale reach of sands, and changes them to gold.
So in majestic cadence rise and fall
The mighty undulations of thy song,
O sightless Bard, England's Mæonides!
And ever and anon, high over all
Uplifted, a ninth wave superb and strong,
Floods all the soul with its melodious seas.

Longfellow uses the octet for a single sentence that flows on—barely slowed by punctuation (a few commas)—until the mighty wave it describes breaks in the seventh and eighth lines. The sestet then turns the wave into an epic simile describing the epic poet Milton's verse. Actually, the sestet is composed of two sentences, each of three lines. The rhyme scheme is very strict: *a b b a a b b a* for the octet, and *c e d c e d* for the sestet. Thus, the rhymes, the sentence-structure, and the thought patterns all reinforce one another.

John Milton (1608–1674) himself tended to work in a quite different way. Although he composed sonnets in both Italian and English, following a variety of rhyme schemes, he did not work often or comfortably in this form. His most regular sonnets are on subjects of trivial consequence, and when he wrote on a subject of great importance to him he was apt to set his syntax working against the sonnet form, just as he breaks the iambic line with heavy pauses when writing long narrative poems (as our discussion of a passage from *Paradise Lost* on pp. 458–59 indicates). Here is a sonnet that Milton wrote on his own blindness. While it is less regular than Longfellow's, it concludes with one of those "ninth wave" lines of which Longfellow wrote—a line so memorable that it has become a permanent part of the language.

When I consider how my light is spent
Ere half my days, in this dark world and wide,
And that one talent which is death to hide,
Lodged with me useless, though my soul more bent

To serve therewith my Maker, and present
My true account, lest he returning chide,
"Doth God exact day-labour, light denied?"
I fondly ask; but Patience, to prevent
That murmur, soon replies, "God doth not need
Either man's work or his own gifts; who best
Bear his mild yoke, they serve him best. His state
Is kingly. Thousands at his bidding speed
And post o'er land and ocean without rest:
They also serve who only stand and wait."

In the Shakespearean sonnet the poem's fourteen lines are divided into twelve and two, and end with a rhymed couplet. In the hands of Shakespeare himself the couplet is a potent force: the whole meaning of a poem may turn on it. The first twelve lines, as we saw in sonnet 73 (discussed on pp. 438–39 above) may be subdivided in various ways, often into three quatrains, so that the whole poem will rhyme *abab cdcd efef gg,* and each of the four rhyming units will be a separate grammatical and conceptual unit as well—either a whole sentence or a major independent clause.

When the English borrowed (or stole) the sonnet from Italy they acquired a special "Petrarchan" subject matter along with the form. A true Petrarchan sonneteer might produce a whole sequence of sonnets—a hundred or more—devoted to a single subject matter: the poet's love for a lady who refuses to accept him as her lover. (See, for example, Sidney's sonnet 49 from *Astrophil and Stella,* quoted above, p. 444.) The poet describes his sufferings at great length—his fever, chills, pallor—and the lady's beauties at similar length. Often this description takes the form of a "blazon," which is a formal recounting of said beauties, one by one: eyes, nose, lips, teeth, bosom, and so on. Relics of the blazon are found in many love poems written after the English poets had escaped the domination of Italy. Shakespeare himself toyed with the Petrarchan conventions, writing to a man about his "beauties" and refusing to depict his "mistress" in the conventional way.

The Shakespearean form has been the most popular among English poets, and they have turned it to a variety of uses, serious and frivolous. We shall give one of these poets the last word on the sonnet at this point, after a reminder to watch for the progress of the sonnet throughout this anthology, noting its transformations in the modern poets. Gerard Manley Hopkins wrote sonnets in a slightly disguised form, as the attentive reader will discover. Here is William Wordsworth's view of the sonnet, expressed in Shakespearean form. The names mentioned by Wordsworth include some Italian poets of the Middle Ages and Renaissance, and the Portugese poet Camöens, as well as England's Shakespeare, Spenser, and Milton.

Scorn not the Sonnet; Critic, you have frowned,
Mindless of its just honours; with this key
Shakespeare unlocked his heart; the melody
Of this small lute gave ease to Petrarch's wound;
A thousand times this pipe did Tasso sound;
With it Camöens soothed an exile's grief;
The Sonnet glittered a gay myrtle leaf
Amid the cypress with which Dante crowned
His visionary brow: a glow-worm lamp,
It cheered mild Spenser, called from Faery-land
To struggle through dark ways; and when a damp
Fell round the path of Milton, in his hand
The Thing became a trumpet; whence he blew
Soul-animating strains—alas, too few!

Sonnets

18

Shall I compare thee to a summer's day?
Thou art more lovely and more temperate.
Rough winds do shake the darling buds of May,
And summer's lease hath all too short a date.
Sometime too hot the eye of heaven shines,
And often is his gold complexion dimmed;
And every fair from fair sometimes declines,
By chance, or nature's changing course, untrimmed:
But thy eternal summer shall not fade
10   Nor lose possession of that fair thou ow'st,
Nor shall Death brag thou wand'rest in his shade
When in eternal lines to time thou grow'st.
　So long as men can breathe or eyes can see,
　So long lives this, and this gives life to thee.

29

When, in disgrace with Fortune and men's eyes,
I all alone beweep my outcast state,
And trouble deaf heaven with my bootless cries
And look upon myself and curse my fate,
Wishing me like to one more rich in hope,
Featured like him, like him with friends possessed,

Desiring this man's art, and that man's scope,
With what I most enjoy contented least;
Yet in these thoughts myself almost despising,
10 Haply I think on thee, and then my state,
Like to the lark at break of day arising
From sullen earth, sings hymns at heaven's gate;
    For thy sweet love remembered such wealth brings
    That then I scorn to change my state with kings.

55

Not marble nor the gilded monuments
Of princes shall outlive this powerful rime,
But you shall shine more bright in these contents
Than unswept stone, besmeared with sluttish time.
When wasteful war shall statues overturn,
And broils root out the work of masonry,
Nor Mars his sword nor war's quick fire shall burn
The living record of your memory.
'Gainst death and all oblivious enmity
10 Shall you pace forth; your praise shall still find room
Even in the eyes of all posterity
That wear this world out to the ending doom.
    So, till the judgment that yourself arise,
    You live in this, and dwell in lovers' eyes.

65

Since brass, nor stone, nor earth, nor boundless sea,
But sad mortality o'ersways their power,
How with this rage shall beauty hold a plea,
Whose action is no stronger than a flower?
O, how shall summer's honey breath hold out
Against the wrackful siege of batt'ring days,
When rocks impregnable are not so stout,
Nor gates of steel so strong but Time decays?
O fearful meditation: where, alack,
10 Shall Time's best jewel from Time's chest lie hid?
Or what strong hand can hold his swift foot back,
Or who his spoil of beauty can forbid?
    O, none, unless this miracle have might,
    That in black ink my love may still shine bright.

94

They that have power to hurt and will do none,
That do not do the thing they most do show,
Who, moving others, are themselves as stone,
Unmovèd, cold, and to temptation slow;
They rightly do inherit heaven's graces
And husband nature's riches from expense;
They are the lords and owners of their faces,
Others but stewards of their excellence.
The summer's flower is to the summer sweet,
10 Though to itself it only live and die;
But if that flower with base infection meet,
The basest weed outbraves his dignity:
    For sweetest things turn sourest by their deeds;
    Lilies that fester smell far worse than weeds.

130

My mistress' eyes are nothing like the sun;
Coral is far more red than her lips' red;
If snow be white, why then her breasts are dun;
If hairs be wires, black wires grow on her head.
I have seen roses damasked, red and white,
But no such roses see I in her cheeks;
And in some perfumes is there more delight
Than in the breath that from my mistress reeks.
I love to hear her speak; yet well I know
10 That music hath a far more pleasing sound:
I grant I never saw a goddess go;
My mistress, when she walks, treads on the ground.
    And yet, by heaven, I think my love as rare
    As any she belied with false compare.

JOHN DONNE
1572–1631

As a young man, Donne appears to have pursued knowledge and women with equal passion—or so his earlier lyrics would have us believe. However, he may well have been more interested in flouting Elizabethan poetic conventions than in displaying his amorous adventures. Certainly he had his share of the latter, when as a young law student he was using his personal charm, wit, and learning to gain preferment in Elizabethan court circles. But his career in state affairs ended abruptly in 1601 when he eloped with the sixteen-year-old niece of Sir Thomas Egerton, whose secretary he was. Elopement was unlawful, Donne hadn't the means to support a wife and family, and until 1615, when Donne's fine sermons had made him well known, he lived on the edge of poverty. At the urging of King James, he became an Anglican priest and was one of the greatest preachers of his time. Though he achieved material security, he was not a happy man. We see in his poetry and devotional writing his constant spiritual struggle worsened by frequent illness. During his lifetime, his eloquent devotional writing was widely read, but the genius of his amorous poetry, published after his death in 1633, with its stunningly unconventional metaphors and the strong, irregular rhythms of ordinary speech, was considered "rough," and not fully appreciated until Herbert Grierson's edition of his poems appeared in 1912.

A Note on Metaphysical Poetry

We have learned to call a certain group of seventeenth-century English poets "metaphysical" because of Dr. Samuel Johnson, the eighteenth-century critic, poet, and lexicographer, who complained that these poets used strained and unnatural language in which heterogeneous ideas were "yoked by violence together." Johnson's adjective has stuck to these poets, even though his criticism of them is not always accepted. Donne, in particular, has been a favorite of modern readers, perhaps because in his work the metaphysical impulse is always colored by strong erotic or religious feeling. His love poetry is no Petrarchan ritual, nor is his religious poetry in any way perfunctory. In Donne's view, God himself, as Creator of this world and Author of the Bible, was a kind of "metaphysical" poet, too, as we can see in this quotation from one of Donne's *Devotions*, a sequence of prose meditations he wrote during a serious illness. Donne's words describe the metaphysical impulse perfectly. They are worth the close attention they require.

From **Devotion 19**

My God, my God, thou art a direct God, may I not say a literal God, a God that wouldst be understood literally and according to the plain sense of all that thou sayest? but thou art also (Lord, I intend it to thy glory, and let no profane misinterpreter abuse it to thy diminution), thou art a figurative, a metaphorical God too; a God in whose words there is such a height of figures, such voyages, such peregrinations to fetch remote and precious metaphors, such extensions, such spreadings, such curtains of allegories, such third heavens of hyperboles, so harmonious elocutions, so retired and so reserved expressions, so commanding persuasions, so persuading commandments, such sinews even in thy milk, and such things in thy words, as all profane authors seem of the seed of the serpent that creeps, thou art the Dove that flies. O, what words but thine can express the inexpressible texture and composition of thy word, in which to one man that argument that binds his faith to believe that to be the word of God, is the reverent simplicity of the word, and to another the majesty of the word; and in which two men equally pious may meet, and one wonder that all should not understand it, and the other as much that any man should. So, Lord, thou givest us the same earth to labour on and to lie in, a house and a grave of the same earth; so, Lord, thou givest us the same word for our satisfaction and for our inquisition, for our instruction and for our admiration too; for there are places that thy servants Hierom[1] and Augustine would scarce believe (when they grew warm by mutual letters) of one another, that they understood them, and yet both Hierom and Augustine call upon persons whom they knew to be far weaker than they thought one another (old women and young maids) to read the Scriptures, without confining them to these or those places. Neither art thou thus a figurative, a metaphorical God in thy word only, but in thy works too. The style of thy works, the phrase of thine actions, is metaphorical. The institution of thy whole worship in the old law was a continual allegory; types and figures overspread all, and figures flowed into figures, and poured themselves out into farther figures; circumcision carried a figure of baptism, and baptism carries a figure of that purity which we shall have in perfection in the new Jerusalem. Neither didst thou speak and work in this language only in the time of thy prophets; but since thou spokest in thy Son it is so too. How often, how much more often, doth thy Son call himself a way, and a light, and a gate, and a vine, and bread, than the Son of God, or of man? How much oftener doth he exhibit a metaphorical Christ, than a real, a literal? This hath occasioned thine ancient servants, whose delight it was to write after thy copy, to proceed the same way in their expositions of the Scriptures, and in their composing both of public liturgies and of private prayers to thee, to make their accesses to thee in such a kind of language as thou wast pleased to speak to them, in a figurative, in a metaphorical language, in which manner I am bold to call the comfort which I receive now in this sickness in the indication of the concoction and maturity thereof, in certain clouds and recidences, which the physicians observe, a discovering of land from sea after a long and tempestuous voyage.

1. St. Jerome, like St. Augustine, one of the early Fathers of the Church

Love Poems

The Good Morrow

I wonder, by my troth, what thou and I
Did, till we loved? Were we not weaned till then,
But sucked on country pleasures, childishly?
Or snorted we in the seven sleepers' den?
'Twas so; but this, all pleasures fancies be.
If ever any beauty I did see,
Which I desired, and got, 'twas but a dream of thee.

And now good morrow to our waking souls,
Which watch not one another out of fear;
10   For love all love of other sights controls,
And makes one little room an everywhere.
Let sea-discoverers to new worlds have gone,
Let maps to other, worlds on worlds have shown,
Let us possess one world; each hath one, and is one.

My face in thine eye, thine in mine appears,
And true plain hearts do in the faces rest;
Where can we find two better hemispheres
Without sharp North, without declining West?
Whatever dies was not mixed equally;
20   If our two loves be one, or thou and I
Love so alike that none do slacken, none can die.

The Sun Rising

Busy old fool, unruly sun,
    Why doest thou thus
Through windows and through curtains call on us?
Must to thy motions lovers' seasons run?
    Saucy pedantic wretch, go chide
    Late schoolboys and sour prentices,
Go tell court-huntsmen that the king will ride,
    Call country ants to harvest offices;
Love, all alike, no season knows, nor clime,
10   Nor hours, days, months, which are the rags of time.

Thy beams, so reverend, and strong
    Why shouldst thou think?
I could eclipse and cloud them with a wink,

But that I would not lose her sight so long;
   If her eyes have not blinded thine,
   Look, and tomorrow late tell me
  Whether both the Indias of spice and mine
  Be where thou left'st them, or lie here with me.
Ask for those kings whom thou saw'st yesterday,
20 And thou shalt hear, all here in one bed lay.

   She is all states, and all princes I;
    Nothing else is.
Princes do but play us; compared to this,
All honor's mimic, all wealth alchemy.
   Thou, sun, art half as happy as we,
   In that the world's contracted thus;
  Thine age asks ease, and since thy duties be
  To warm the world, that's done in warming us.
Shine here to us, and thou art everywhere;
30 This bed thy center is, these walls thy sphere.

The Canonization

For God's sake hold your tongue and let me love;
   Or chide my palsy or my gout,
My five gray hairs or ruined fortune flout,
  With wealth your state, your mind with arts improve,
   Take you a course, get you a place,
   Observe His Honour, or His Grace,
Or the King's real, or his stamped face
  Contemplate; what you will, approve,
  So you will let me love.

10 Alas, alas, who's injured by my love?
  What merchant's ships have my sighs drown'd?
Who says my tears have overflow'd his ground?
  When did my colds a forward spring remove?
   When did the heats which my veins fill
   Add one more to the plaguey Bill?[1]
Soldiers find wars, and Lawyers find out still
  Litigious men, which quarrels move,
  Though she and I do love.

1. List of those dead of the plague

Call us what you will, we are made such by love;
  Call her one, me another fly,
We are tapers too, and at our own cost die,
  And we in us find th' Eagle and the Dove.
    The Phoenix[2] riddle hath more wit
    By us: we two being one, are it.
So to one neutral thing both sexes fit;
  We die and rise the same, and prove
  Mysterious by this love.

We can die by it, if not live by love,
  And if unfit for tombs and hearse
Our legend be, it will be fit for verse;
  And if no piece of Chronicle we prove,
    We'll build in sonnets pretty rooms;
    As well a well-wrought urn becomes
The greatest ashes, as half-acre tombs,
  And by these hymns, all shall approve
  Us *Canonized* for Love;

And thus invoke us: You whom reverend love
  Made one another's hermitage;
You, to whom love was peace, that now is rage;
  Who did the whole world's soul contract, and drove
    Into the glasses of your eyes
    (So made such mirrors and such spies
That they did all to you epitomize);
  Countries, Towns, Courts: Beg from above
  A pattern of your love!

2. Mythical bird of no sex that lived a thousand years,
then burned itself and was reborn from the ashes

The Relic

    When my grave is broke up again
    Some second guest to entertain
    (For graves have learned that womanhead
    To be to more than one a bed)
      And he that digs it spies
A bracelet of bright hair about the bone,
      Will he not let us alone,
And think that there a loving couple lies,

Who thought that this device might be some way
10   To make their souls at the last busy day
Meet at this grave, and make a little stay?

If this fall in a time or land
Where mis-devotion doth command,
Then he that digs us up will bring
Us to the bishop and the king
To make us relics; then
Thou shalt be a Mary Magdalen,[1] and I
A something else thereby.
All women shall adore us, and some men;
20   And since at such time miracles are sought,
I would have that age by this paper taught
What miracles we harmless lovers wrought.

First, we loved well and faithfully,
Yet knew not what we loved, nor why;
Difference of sex no more we knew
Than our guardian angels do;
Coming and going, we
Perchance might kiss, but not between those meals;
Our hands ne'er touched the seals
30   Which nature, injured by late law, sets free.
These miracles we did; but now, alas,
All measure and all language I should pass,
Should I tell what a miracle she was.

1. In Christian tradition Mary Magdalene was a prostitute
who reformed to follow Jesus—which suggests that
the "something else" in the next line refers to Christ.

Holy Sonnets

5

I am a little world made cunningly
Of elements, and an angelic sprite;
But black sin hath betrayed to endless night
My world's both parts, and O, both parts must die.
You which beyond that heaven which was most high
Have found new spheres, and of new lands can write,
Pour new seas in mine eyes, that so I might

Drown my world with my weeping earnestly,
Or wash it if it must be drowned no more.
10   But O, it must be burnt! Alas, the fire
Of lust and envy have burnt it heretofore,
And made it fouler; let their flames retire,
And burn me, O Lord, with a fiery zeal
Of Thee and Thy house, which doth in eating heal.

10

Death, be not proud, though some have callèd thee
Mighty and dreadful, for thou are not so;
For those whom thou think'st thou dost overthrow
Die not, poor Death, nor yet canst thou kill me.
From rest and sleep, which but thy pictures be,
Much pleasure; then from thee much more must flow,
And soonest our best men with thee do go,
Rest of their bones, and soul's delivery.
Thou'art slave to fate, chance, kings, and desperate men,
10   And dost with poison, war, and sickness dwell,
And poppy'or charms can make us sleep as well
And better than thy stroke; why swell'st thou then?
One short sleep past, we wake eternally
And death shall be no more; Death, thou shalt die.

ROBERT HERRICK
1591–1674

Born the son of a prosperous London goldsmith, Robert Herrick was apprenticed to this trade at the age of twelve. Ten years later, however, he went to Cambridge and received his B.A. degree in 1617. He returned to London to pursue a literary life as admirer and pupil of the popular playwright Ben Jonson with whom he enjoyed "lyrick Feasts" (conversing and drinking) in such taverns as The Sun and The Dog. In 1627 he entered the priesthood of the Church of England, a common career for younger sons of good family. Two years later, Herrick was named Vicar of Dean Priory in Devonshire, a locale noted for its brutish peasantry, who lived mostly in hovels, changed their clothes infrequently, and provided unpleasant subject matter for Herrick's satirical poetry. Pleasanter subjects were such inhabitants of the vicarage as Herrick's maid Prudence, his pet sparrow Phill, and his beloved spaniel Tracie. But out of this bachelor's imagination

emerged his best subjects: the bewitching and beribboned Julias and Co-
rinnas who grace his most lyrical poetry. They dance through a pastoral
world of happy pagan ritual, gathering rosebuds and strewing them
through the dewy grass in celebration of the joys of this life, a life made the
more poignant by an awareness of the next life fast approaching.

Ousted from his vicarage in 1647 by the Puritans, Herrick returned to
London and published *Hesperides* and *Noble Numbers*. But his light, playful lyrics went unappreciated in such parlous times. When the monarchy
was restored in 1660, Herrick returned to Devonshire to quietly live out his
final years.

A Note on Cavalier Poetry

England in the seventeenth century was deeply divided both politically and
religiously. The same impulse that brought Puritans to the American
Colonies seeking religious freedom led to a Puritan rebellion against the
King and the Church of England. Commanded by Oliver Cromwell, the
Puritans deposed the King of England, Charles I, and later executed him. But
after a few decades his son, who had been in exile in France, returned to be
crowned as Charles II in 1660.

The wars of this era were aspects of a class struggle as well as of a religious
one, and they anticipated the revolutions that came a century later in
America and France. The King's strongest defenders were members of the
hereditary aristocracy, of conservative and Catholic tendencies. His opponents were drawn mainly from the rising middle class, and were more
radically Protestant, often Puritan. The greatest poet of the era was the
Puritan John Milton, but the other side was neither mute nor inglorious
when it came to verse. Those who sympathized with the King, whether they
went into exile or stayed home in England, were called "Cavaliers." Some of
them wrote elegant verse, more light than serious, so that the term
"Cavalier Poetry" came to refer to a kind of light lyric, often advocating a
carpe diem attitude.

Carpe diem, a Latin phrase meaning literally "seize the day," is a familiar
theme in poetry from ancient times to the present. To "seize the day"
means to disregard the future, including any "hereafter," so that one might
expect the poets of this theme to ignore religion. But life is not so simple.
Some Cavalier poets were also men of strong religious faith, though they
wrote neither religious epics nor holy sonnets.

Robert Herrick was such a poet. And the last seventeenth-century poet
included in this anthology, Andrew Marvell, managed a blend of Metaphysical and Cavalier attitudes and techniques so neat and elegant that he has
been classified under both headings. There is a lesson in this about
classification of poetic schools in general. Such conceptual guides must

never be applied too rigidly. No good poet will stay put calmly in a box. But let Herrick sum up for us his own approach to poetry, in a little poem he used as preface to a volume of his verse.

I sing of Brooks, of Blossoms, Birds, and Bowers:
Of April, May, of June, and July-Flowers.
I sing of May-poles, Hock-carts, Wassails, Wakes,
Of Bride-grooms, Brides, and of their Bridal-cakes.
I write of Youth, of Love, and have access
By these, to sing of cleanly-wantonness.
I sing of Dews, of Rains, and piece by piece
Of Balm, of Oil, of Spice, and Amber-Greece.
I sing of Times trans-shifting; and I write
10   How Roses first came red, and Lilies white.
I write of Groves, of Twilights, and I sing
The Court of Mab, and of the Fairy-King.
I write of Hell; I sing (and ever shall)
Of Heaven, and hope to have it after all.

Delight in Disorder

A sweet disorder in the dress
Kindles in clothes a wantonness.
A lawn[1] about the shoulders thrown
Into a fine distraction;
An erring lace, which here and there
Enthralls the crimson stomacher[2];
A cuff neglectful, and thereby
Ribbons to flow confusedly;
A winning wave, deserving note,
10   In the tempestuous petticoat;
A careless shoestring, in whose tie
I see a wild civility
Do more bewitch me than when art
Is too precise in every part.

1. Fine linen (as a scarf)
2. Separate piece for the center front of a bodice

Upon Julia's Clothes

Whenas in silks my Julia goes
Then, then (methinks) how sweetly flows
That liquefaction of her clothes.

Next, when I cast mine eyes and see
That brave vibration each way free;
O how that glittering taketh me!

To the Virgins, to Make Much of Time

Gather ye rosebuds while ye may,
  Old time is still a-flying,
And this same flower that smiles to-day,
  To-morrow will be dying.

The glorious lamp of heaven, the sun,
  The higher he's a-getting,
The sooner will his race be run,
  And nearer he's to setting.

That age is best which is the first,
10   When youth and blood are warmer;
But being spent, the worse, and worst
  Times still succeed the former.

Then be not coy, but use your time,
  And while ye may, go marry;
For having lost but once your prime,
  You may for ever tarry.

Corinna's Going A-Maying[1]

Get up, get up for shame, the blooming morn
Upon her wings presents the god unshorn.[2]
    See how Aurora[3] throws her fair
    Fresh-quilted colors through the air:

1. May Day observances go back to pagan times, when they
related to fertility rites. In Herrick's time they continued to
have a religious or ritual overtone.
2. Apollo's locks were never cut.
3. The dawn

Get up, sweet-slug-a-bed, and see
The dew bespangling herb and tree.
Each flower has wept, and bowed toward the east,
Above an hour since; yet you not drest,
    Nay! not so much as out of bed?
10   When all the birds have matins said,
    And sung their thankful hymns: 'tis sin,
    May, profanation to keep in,
When as a thousand virgins on this day
Spring, sooner than the lark, to fetch in May.

Rise; and put on your foliage, and be seen
To come forth, like the springtime, fresh and green;
    And sweet as Flora.[4] Take no care
    For jewels for your gown, or hair:
    Fear not; the leaves will strew
20   Gems in abundance upon you:
Besides, the childhood of the day has kept,
Against[5] you come, some orient pearls[6] unwept:
    Come, and receive them while the light
    Hangs on the dew-locks of the night:
    And Titan[7] on the eastern hill
    Retires himself, or else stands still
Till you come forth. Wash, dress, be brief in praying:
Few beads[8] are best, when once we go a-Maying.

Come, my Corinna, come; and coming, mark
30 How each field turns a street; each street a park
    Made green, and trimmed with trees: see how
    Devotion gives each house a bough,
    Or branch: each porch, each door, ere this,
    An ark,[9] a tabernacle is
Made up of white-thorn neatly interwove;
As if here were those cooler shades of love.
    Can such delights be in the street,
    And open fields, and we not see 't?
    Come, we'll abroad; and let's obey
40   The proclamation made for May:
And sin no more, as we have done, by staying;
But my Corinna, come, let's go a-Maying.

---

4. Goddess of flowers   7. Sun
5. Until   8. Rosary beads, prayers
6. Dew   9. Hebrew Ark of the Covenant (see Ex. 25: 10–21)

There's not a budding boy, or girl, this day,
But is got up, and gone to bring in May.
    A deal of youth, ere this, is come
    Back, and with white-thorn laden home.
    Some have dispatched their cakes and cream,
    Before that we have left to dream:[10]
And some have wept, and wooed, and plighted troth,
50   And chose their priest, ere we can cast off sloth:
    Many a green[11] gown has been given;
    Many a kiss, both odd and even:
    Many a glance too has been sent
    From out the eye, Love's firmament:
Many a jest told of the keys betraying
This night, and locks picked, yet we're not a-Maying.

Come, let us go, while we are in our prime;
And take the harmless folly of the time.
    We shall grow old apace, and die
60   Before we know our liberty.
    Our life is short; and our days run
    As fast away as does the sun:
And as a vapor, or a drop of rain
Once lost, can ne'er be found again:
    So when or you or I are made
    A fable, song, or fleeting shade;
    All love, all liking, all delight
    Lies drowned with us in endless night.
Then while time serves, and we are but decaying;
70   Come, my Corinna, come, let's go a-Maying.

10. Left off dreaming
11. From lying in the grass

ANDREW MARVELL
1621–1678

Andrew Marvell is an elusive figure whose life presents as many paradoxes as his poetry does. During his lifetime he was known as a public servant and politician, but not as a poet. However, during this public career he was writing a private kind of poetry, extolling pastoral solitude and the inner life of the mind. He was a Puritan, yet he wrote one of the most erotic proposals of all time, "To His Coy Mistress." Marvell was born in Winestead, near Hull, where his father was rector of the parish church. He went to Trinity

College, Cambridge, at the age of twelve, and mastered six ancient languages. After his father died in 1641, we know that Marvell was a clerk in a Hull business house, and that he later travelled to Europe for four years before becoming tutor to the twelve-year-old daughter of Lord Fairfax whose garden at Nun Appleton House probably inspired the "green thoughts" of Marvell's lyrics, for he wrote prolifically during this period. In 1657, Marvell was an assistant to the blind poet John Milton, Cromwell's Latin Secretary, and in 1659, Marvell was elected to Parliament and represented Hull for the rest of his life. When his poems were published in 1681, three years after his death, they were ignored and felt to be out of date. Though his work was appreciated by later poets such as Blake, Wordsworth, and Tennyson, Marvell did not receive full critical attention until the twentieth century.

To His Coy Mistress

Had we but world enough, and time,
This coyness, lady, were no crime.
We would sit down, and think which way
To walk, and pass our long love's day.
Thou by the Indian Ganges' side
Should'st rubies find: I by the tide
Of Humber would complain. I would
Love you ten years before the Flood,
And you should, if you please, refuse
10   Till the conversion of the Jews.
My vegetable love should grow
Vaster than empires, and more slow.
An hundred years should go to praise
Thine eyes, and on thy forehead gaze;
Two hundred to adore each breast,
But thirty thousand to the rest;
An age at least to every part,
And the last age should show your heart.
For, lady, you deserve this state,
20   Nor would I love at lower rate.
    But at my back I always hear
Time's wingèd chariot hurrying near:
And yonder all before us lie
Deserts of vast eternity.
Thy beauty shall no more be found;
Nor, in thy marble vault, shall sound
My echoing song: then worms shall try
That long-preserved virginity.

And your quaint honor turn to dust,
30   And into ashes all my lust.
The grave's a fine and private place,
But none, I think, do there embrace.
    Now, therefore, while the youthful hue
Sits on thy skin like morning dew,
And while thy willing soul transpires
At every pore with instant fires,
Now let us sport us while we may;
And now, like amorous birds of prey,
Rather at once our Time devour,
40   Than languish in his slow-chapt power.
Let us roll all our strength and all
Our sweetness up into one ball,
And tear our pleasures with rough strife
Thorough the iron gates of life.
Thus, though we cannot make our sun
Stand still, yet we will make him run.

The Garden

How vainly men themselves amaze
To win the palm, the oak, or bays;
And their incessant labors see
Crowned from some single herb, or tree,
Whose short and narrow-vergèd shade
Does prudently their toils upbraid;
While all flowers and all trees do close
To weave the garlands of repose!

Fair Quiet, have I found thee here,
10   And Innocence, thy sister dear!
Mistaken long, I sought you then
In busy companies of men.
Your sacred plants, if here below,
Only among the plants will grow;
Society is all but rude
To this delicious solitude.

No white nor red was ever seen
So amorous as this lovely green.
Fond lovers, cruel as their flame,
20   Cut in these trees their mistress' name:
Little, alas! they know or heed
How far these beauties hers exceed!

Fair trees! wheres'e'er your barks I wound
No name shall but your own be found.

When we have run our passion's heat,
Love hither makes his best retreat.
The gods, that mortal beauty chase,
Still in a tree did end their race;
Apollo hunted Daphne so,
30 Only that she might laurel grow;
And Pan did after Syrinx speed,
Not as a nymph, but for a reed.

What wondrous life is this I lead!
Ripe apples drop about my head;
The luscious clusters of the vine
Upon my mouth do crush their wine;
The nectarine, and curious peach,
Into my hands themselves do reach;
Stumbling on melons, as I pass,
40 Ensnar'd with flowers, I fall on grass.

Meanwhile, the mind, from pleasure less,
Withdraws into its happiness:
The mind, that ocean where each kind
Does straight its own resemblance find;
Yet it creates, transcending these,
Far other worlds, and other seas;
Annihilating all that's made
To a green thought in a green shade.

Here at the fountain's sliding foot,
50 Or at some fruit-tree's mossy root,
Casting the body's vest aside,
My soul into the boughs does glide:
There like a bird it sits, and sings,
Then whets and combs its silver wings;
And, till prepared for longer flight,
Waves in its plumes the various light.

Such was that happy garden-state,
While man there walked without a mate:
After a place so pure and sweet,
60 What other help could yet be meet?
But 'twas beyond a mortal's share
To wander solitary there:

Two paradises 'twere in one,
To live in paradise alone.

How well the skillful gardener drew
Of flowers, and herbs, this dial new;
Where, from above, the milder sun
Does through a fragrant zodiac run;
And, as it works, the industrious bee
70   Computes its time as well as we.
How could such sweet and wholesome hours
Be reckoned but with herbs and flowers!

The Fair Singer

To make a final conquest of all me,
Love did compose so sweet an enemy,
In whom both beauties to my death agree,
Joyning themselves in fatal harmony;
That while she with her eyes my heart does bind,
She with her voice might captivate my mind.

I could have fled from one but singly fair:
My dis-intangled soul itself might save,
Breaking the curléd trammels of her hair.
10   But how should I avoid to be her slave,
Whose subtle art invisibly can wreath
My fetters of the very air I breath?

It had been easie fighting in some plain,
Where victory might hang in equal choice.
But all resistance against her is vain,
Who has th' advantage both of eyes and voice.
And all my forces needs must be undone,
She having gainéd both the wind and sun.

The Coronet

When for the thorns with which I long, too long,
    With many a piercing wound,
    My Saviour's head have crown'd
I seek with garlands to redress that wrong:
    Through every garden, every mead,
I gather flow'rs (my fruits are only flow'rs)

Dismantling all the fragrant tow'rs
That once adorn'd my shepherdess's head.
And now when I have summed up all my store,
10   Thinking (so I my self deceive)
So rich a chaplet thence to weave
As never yet the King of glory wore:
Alas I find the serpent old
That, twining in his speckled breast,
About the flow'rs disguised does fold,
With wreaths of fame and interest.
Ah, foolish man, that would'st debase with them,
And mortal glory, heaven's diadem!
But Thou who only could'st the serpent tame
20   Either his slippery knots at once untie,
And disentangle all his winding snare:
Or shatter too with him my curious frame:
And let these wither, so that he may die,
Though set with skill and chosen out with care.
That they, while Thou on both their spoils dost tread,
May crown Thy feet, that could not crown Thy head.

WILLIAM BLAKE

1757–1827

Blake's wife once said, "I have very little of Mr. Blake's company. He is always in Paradise." Living with a visionary genius was probably not easy, especially for a woman who had been illiterate until her marriage, when her husband taught her to read and write. Blake, the son of a tradesman interested in the mystical ideas of Swedenborg and Jacob Boehme, was mostly self-taught, and formally schooled only in drawing. At the age of fourteen, he was apprenticed to an engraver for seven years and later supported himself with engraving and printing work. He lived most of his life in London, whose dull and ugly streets infused him with the sense of social injustice so poignantly expressed in such poems as "The Chimney-Sweeper" and "London." For Blake, the world of senses was full of symbols and a source of the metaphors in his poetry. In his earlier poetry, he turned to forms such as the ballad as inspiration for new forms and techniques. Utterly unorthodox in his religious and moral beliefs, he developed a complete mythology of his own, a radically spiritual interpretation of the Bible. He was seeking a vision which would transfigure the natural, or fallen world, revealing its correspondence with an eternal form (see "Auguries of Innocence," below). Much of his poetry was accompanied by his engravings, for he made little distinction between these two expressive forms. In his art, he refused to cater to popular taste, and his work was largely ignored by the public. Like many geniuses, he seemed not to belong to his time or place, and though he battled with poverty much of his life, he died serene and full of joy.

A Note on Romantic Poetry

England's Romantic poets (of whom the greatest are Blake, Wordsworth, Coleridge, Byron, Keats, and Shelley) constitute the most important single influence on later poetry in English. Though the poetic style and the values of each poet may show striking differences, the Romantic poets as a group tended to be radical in their politics (in sympathy with the American and French revolutions, against royalty and slavery) and transcendental in their philosophy, seeing nature as symbolic of the Creator's presence, and natural creation as analogous to the lesser creations of imaginative human beings.

These poets were part of a larger Romantic or transcendental movement, with philosophical roots in Germany and political roots in France. In America, poets and men of letters like Emerson, Bryant, and Thoreau were a part of this same movement of mind, which strongly influenced Whitman and through him most later American poetry. We are all children of the Romantic movement, no matter how rebellious we may be.

The Clod and the Pebble

"Love seeketh not itself to please,
  Nor for itself hath any care,
  But for another gives its ease,
  And builds a heaven in hell's despair."

  So sung a little clod of clay,
  Trodden with the cattle's feet,
  But a pebble of the brook
  Warbled out these metres meet:

"Love seeketh only self to please,
10 To bind another to its delight,
  Joys in another's loss of ease,
  And builds a hell in heaven's despite."

The Chimney-Sweeper

A little black thing among the snow,
Crying "weep, weep" in notes of woe!
"Where are thy father and mother, say?"—
"They are both gone up to church to pray.

"Because I was happy upon the heath,
And smiled among the winter's snow,
They clothed me in the clothes of death,
And taught me to sing the notes of woe.

"And because I am happy, and dance and sing,
10 They think they have done me no injury,
And are gone to praise God and his Priest and King,
Who make up a heaven of our misery."

The Sick Rose

O Rose, thou art sick:
The invisible worm,
That flies in the night,
In the howling storm,

Has found out thy bed
Of crimson joy;
And his dark secret love
Does thy life destroy.

The Tyger

Tyger! Tyger! burning bright
In the forests of the night,
What immortal hand or eye
Could frame thy fearful symmetry?

In what distant deeps or skies
Burnt the fire of thine eyes?
On what wings dare he aspire?
What the hand dare seize the fire?

And what shoulder, and what art,
10 Could twist the sinews of thy heart?
And when thy heart began to beat,
What dread hand? and what dread feet?

What the hammer? what the chain?
In what furnace was thy brain?
What the anvil? what dread grasp
Dare its deadly terrors clasp?

When the stars threw down their spears,
And water'd heaven with their tears,
Did he smile his work to see?
20 Did he who made the Lamb make thee?

Tyger! Tyger! burning bright
In the forests of the night,
What immortal hand or eye,
Dare frame thy fearful symmetry?

London

I wander through each charter'd¹ street,
Near where the charter'd Thames does flow,
And mark in every face I meet
Marks of weakness, marks of woe.

In every cry of every man,
In every infant's cry of fear,
In every voice in every ban,
The mind-forg'd manacles I hear.

How the chimney-sweeper's cry
10 Every blackening church appalls;
And the hapless soldier's sigh
Runs in blood down palace walls.

But most through midnight streets I hear
How the youthful harlot's curse
Blasts the new born infant's tear,
And blights with plagues the marriage hearse.

1. Pre-empted or rented

Auguries of Innocence

To see a world in a grain of sand
And a heaven in a wild flower,
Hold infinity in the palm of your hand,
And eternity in an hour.

A robin redbreast in a cage
Puts all heaven in a rage.
A dove-house filled with doves and pigeons
Shudders hell through all its regions.
A dog starved at his master's gate
10   Predicts the ruin of the state.
A horse misused upon the road
Calls to heaven for human blood.
Each outcry of the hunted hare
A fiber from the brain does tear.
A skylark wounded in the wing,
A cherubim does cease to sing;
The game cock clipped and armed for fight
Does the rising sun affright.
Every wolf's and lion's howl
20   Raises from hell a human soul.
The wild deer wandering here and there,
Keeps the human soul from care.
The lamb misused breeds public strife
And yet forgives the butcher's knife.
The bat that flits at close of eve
Has left the brain that won't believe.
The owl that calls upon the night
Speaks the unbeliever's fright.
He who shall hurt the little wren
30   Shall never be beloved by men.
He who the ox to wrath has moved
Shall never be by woman loved.
The wanton boy that kills the fly
Shall feel the spider's enmity.
He who torments the chafer's sprite
Weaves a bower in endless night.
The caterpillar on the leaf
Repeats to thee thy mother's grief.
Kill not the moth nor butterfly,
40   For the last judgment draweth nigh.
He who shall train the horse to war
Shall never pass the polar bar.

The beggar's dog and widow's cat,
Feed them and thou wilt grow fat.
The gnat that sings his summer's song
Poison gets from slander's tongue.
The poison of the snake and newt
Is the sweat of envy's foot.
The poison of the honey bee
50 Is the artist's jealousy.
The prince's robes and beggar's rags
Are toadstools on the miser's bags.
A truth that's told with bad intent
Beats all the lies you can invent.
It is right it should be so;
Man was made for joy and woe;
And when this we rightly know,
Through the world we safely go.
Joy and woe are woven fine,
60 A clothing for the soul divine;
Under every grief and pine
Runs a joy with silken twine.
The babe is more than swadling bands,
Throughout all these human lands;
Tools were made, and born were hands,
Every farmer understands.
Every tear from every eye
Becomes a babe in eternity;
This is caught by females bright,
70 And returned to its own delight.
The bleat, the bark, bellow, and roar
Are waves that beat on heaven's shore.
The babe that weeps the rod beneath
Writes revenge in realms of death.
The beggar's rags, fluttering in air,
Does to rags the heavens tear.
The soldier, armed with sword and gun,
Palsied strikes the summer's sun.
The poor man's farthing is worth more
80 Than all the gold on Afric's shore.
One mite wrung from the lab'rer's hands
Shall buy and sell the miser's lands;
Or, if protected from on high,
Does that whole nation sell and buy.
He who mocks the infant's faith
Shall be mocked in age and death.
He who shall teach the child to doubt

The rotting grave shall never get out.
He who respects the infant's faith
90 Triumphs over hell and death.
The child's toys and the old man's reasons
Are the fruits of the two seasons.
The questioner, who sits so sly
Shall never know how to reply.
He who replies to words of doubt
Doth put the light of knowledge out.
The strongest poison ever known
Came from Caesar's laurel crown.
Naught can deform the human race
100 Like to the armour's iron brace.
When gold and gems adorn the plow
To peaceful arts shall envy bow.
A riddle, or the cricket's cry,
Is to doubt a fit reply.
The emmet's inch and eagle's mile
Make lame philosophy to smile.
He who doubts from what he sees
Will ne'er believe, do what you please.
If the sun and moon should doubt,
110 They'd immediately go out.
To be in a passion you good may do,
But no good if a passion is in you.
The whore and gambler, by the state
Licensed, build that nation's fate.
The harlot's cry from street to street
Shall weave Old England's winding sheet.
The winner's shout, the loser's curse,
Dance before dead England's hearse.
Every night and every morn
120 Some to misery are born.
Every morn and every night
Some are born to sweet delight.
Some are born to sweet delight,
Some are born to endless night.
We are led to believe a lie
When we see not through the eye,
Which was born in a night to perish in a night,
When the soul slept in beams of light.
God appears, and God is light,
130 To those poor souls who dwell in night,
But does a human form display
To those who dwell in realms of day.

WILLIAM WORDSWORTH

1770–1850

Wordsworth was born and educated at the edge of the Lake District in Cumberland, England, and spent his youthful days roaming the countryside, absorbing the sights and sounds that would inspire his greatest poetry. The headmaster of his boarding school encouraged Wordsworth's early interest in poetry, an interest which deepened when he attended St. John's College, Cambridge. In 1791, after graduation, he travelled the continent, excited by the possibilities of the French Revolution. In France he met Annette Vallon, on whom he fathered a child. Forced to return to England because of financial problems, and unable to get back to France because war had broken out, his ardor for Vallon eventually cooled, and they never married. Wordsworth settled with his sister Dorothy in a cottage at Racedown, and then moved to Alfoxden, Somerset, to be near Samuel Taylor Coleridge, with whom he wrote the *Lyrical Ballads*. The *Ballads* signalled a new trend in poetry, a break with the neoclassical tradition. Subjects for poetry, according to Wordsworth, should be "incidents and situations from common life," and they should be written in language "really used by men," rather than in the elevated diction found in eighteenth-century poetry. Wordsworth and Dorothy eventually moved back to the Lake District, settling in Grasmere in a little house named Dove Cottage. Wordsworth married a woman he had known since childhood, and steadily acquired a reputation as an outstanding poet, as well as financial security. For the young Wordsworth, nature was invested with an almost divine radiance, but such vision was lost as he grew older, and in the *Immortality Ode*, Wordsworth mourns this loss and tries to take comfort "In years that bring the philosophic mind." It is generally agreed that Wordsworth's best poetry was written before 1807 when his youthful experience was the source of his poetry. Much of his later poetry is prosaic, reflecting the orthodoxy which had replaced his earlier revolutionary fervor. He was named poet laureate of England in 1843.

To My Sister

It is the first mild day of March;
Each minute sweeter than before,
The redbreast sings from the tall larch
That stands beside our door.

There is a blessing in the air,
Which seems a sense of joy to yield
To the bare trees, and mountains bare,
And grass in the green field.

My sister! ('tis a wish of mine)
10 Now that our morning meal is done,
Make haste, your morning task resign;
Come forth and feel the sun.

Edward will come with you; —and, pray,
Put on with speed your woodland dress;
And bring no book: for this one day
We'll give to idleness.

No joyless forms shall regulate
Our living calendar:
We from to-day, my Friend, will date
20 The opening of the year.

Love, now a universal birth,
From heart to heart is stealing.
From earth to man, from man to earth:
—It is the hour of feeling.

One moment now may give us more
Than years of toiling reason:
Our minds shall drink at every pore
The spirit of the season.

Some silent laws our hearts will make,
30 Which they shall long obey:
We for the year to come may take
Our temper from to-day.

And from the blessèd power that rolls
About, below, above,
We'll frame the measure of our souls:
They shall be tuned to love.

Then come, my Sister! come, I pray,
With speed put on your woodland dress;
And bring no book: for this one day
40 We'll give to idleness.

I Wandered Lonely as a Cloud

I wandered lonely as a cloud
That floats on high o'er vales and hills,
When all at once I saw a crowd,
A host, of golden daffodils;
Beside the lake, beneath the trees,
Fluttering and dancing in the breeze.

Continuous as the stars that shine
And twinkle on the milky way,
They stretched in never-ending line
10   Along the margin of a bay:
Ten thousand saw I at a glance,
Tossing their heads in sprightly dance.

The waves beside them danced; but they
Out-did the sparkling waves in glee:
A poet could not but be gay,
In such a jocund company:
I gazed—and gazed—but little thought
What wealth the show to me had brought:

For oft, when on my couch I lie
20   In vacant or in pensive mood,
They flash upon that inward eye
Which is the bliss of solitude;
And then my heart with pleasure fills,
And dances with the daffodils.

Ode

*Intimations of Immortality from Recollections
of Early Childhood*

> The Child is father of the Man;
> And I could wish my days to be
> Bound each to each by natural piety.

I

There was a time when meadow, grove, and stream,
The earth, and every common sight,
    To me did seem
    Apparelled in celestial light,

The glory and the freshness of a dream.
It is not now as it hath been of yore;—
  Turn whereso'er I may,
   By night or day,
The things which I have seen I now can see no more.

   II

The Rainbow comes and goes,
  And lovely is the Rose,
  The Moon doth with delight
Look round her when the heavens are bare,
  Waters on a starry night
  Are beautiful and fair;
 The sunshine is a glorious birth;
 But yet I know, where'er I go,
That there hath past away a glory from the earth.

   III

Now, while the birds thus sing a joyous song,
 And while the young lambs bound
  As to the tabor's sound,
To me alone there came a thought of grief:
A timely utterance gave that thought relief,
  And I again am strong:
The cataracts blow their trumpets from the steep;
No more shall grief of mine the season wrong;
I hear the Echoes through the mountains throng,
The Winds come to me from the fields of sleep,
  And all the earth is gay;
   Land and sea
  Give themselves up to jollity.
  And with the heart of May
 Doth every Beast keep holiday;—
  Thou Child of Joy,
Shout round me, let me hear thy shouts, thou happy Shepherd-boy!

   IV

Ye blessèd Creatures, I have heard the call
 Ye to each other make; I see
The heavens laugh with you in your jubilee;
 My heart is at your festival,
 My head hath its coronal,

The fulness of your bliss, I feel—I feel it all.
        Oh evil day! if I were sullen
        While Earth herself is adorning,
            This sweet May-morning,
        And the Children are culling
            On every side,
        In a thousand valleys far and wide,
        Fresh flowers; while the sun shines warm,
And the Babe leaps up on his Mother's arm:—
50   I hear, I hear, with joy I hear!
        —But there's a Tree, of many, one,
A single Field which I have looked upon,
Both of them speak of something that is gone:
        The Pansy at my feet
        Doth the same tale repeat:
Whither is fled the visionary gleam?
Where is it now, the glory and the dream?

                    V

Our birth is but a sleep and a forgetting:
The Soul that rises with us, our life's Star,
60   Hath had elsewhere its setting,
            And cometh from afar:
        Not in entire forgetfulness,
        And not in utter nakedness,
But trailing clouds of glory do we come
        From God, who is our home:
Heaven lies about us in our infancy!
Shades of the prison-house begin to close
        Upon the growing Boy,
But He beholds the light, and whence it flows,
70   He sees it in his joy;
The Youth, who daily farther from the east
        Must travel, still is Nature's Priest,
        And by the vision splendid
        Is on his way attended;
At length the Man perceives it die away,
And fade into the light of common day.

                    VI

Earth fills her lap with pleasures of her own;
Yearnings she hath in her own natural kind,

And, even with something of a Mother's mind,
80   And no unworthy aim,
     The homely Nurse doth all she can
To make her Foster-child, her Inmate Man,
     Forget the glories he hath known,
And that imperial palace whence he came.

               VII

Behold the Child among his new-born blisses,
A six years' Darling of a pigmy size!
See, where 'mid work of his own hand he lies,
Fretted by sallies of his mother's kisses,
With light upon him from his father's eyes!
90 See, at his feet, some little plan or chart,
Some fragment from his dream of human life,
Shaped by himself with newly-learned art;
          A wedding or a festival,
          A mourning or a funeral;
          And this hath now his heart,
          And unto this he frames his song.
               Then will he fit his tongue
To dialogues of business, love, or strife;
          But it will not be long
100   Ere this be thrown aside,
          And with new joy and pride
The little Actor cons another part;
Filling from time to time his "humorous stage"
With all the Persons, down to palsied Age,
That Life brings with her in her equipage;
          As if his whole vocation
          Were endless imitation.

               VIII

Thou, whose exterior semblance doth belie
          Thy Soul's immensity;
110 Thou best Philosopher, who yet dost keep
Thy heritage, thou Eye among the blind,
That, deaf and silent, read'st the eternal deep,
Haunted for ever by the eternal mind, —
          Mighty Prophet! Seer blest!
          On whom those truths do rest,
Which we are toiling all our lives to find,

In darkness lost, the darkness of the grave,
Thou, over whom thy Immortality
Broods like the Day, a Master o'er a Slave,
120   A Presence which is not to be put by;
Thou little Child, yet glorious in the might
Of heaven-born freedom on thy being's height,
Why with such earnest pains dost thou provoke
The years to bring the inevitable yoke,
Thus blindly with thy blessedness at strife?
Full soon thy Soul shall have her earthly freight,
And custom lie upon thee with a weight,
Heavy as frost, and deep almost as life!

IX

O joy! that in our embers
130   Is something that doth live,
That nature yet remembers
What was so fugitive!
The thought of our past years in me doth breed
Perpetual benediction: not indeed
For that which is most worthy to be blest;
Delight and liberty, the simple creed
Of Childhood, whether busy or at rest,
With new-fledged hope still fluttering in his breast:—
Not for these I raise
140   The song of thanks and praise:
But for those obstinate questionings
Of sense and outward things,
Fallings from us, vanishings;
Blank misgivings of a Creature
Moving about in worlds not realised,
High instincts before which our mortal Nature
Did tremble like a guilty Thing surprised:
But for those first affections,
Those shadowy recollections,
150   Which, be they what they may,
Are yet the fountain-light of all our day,
Are yet a master-light of all our seeing;
Uphold us, cherish, and have power to make
Our noisy years seem moments in the being
Of the eternal Silence: truths that wake,
To perish never:
Which neither listlessness, nor mad endeavour,
Nor Man nor Boy,

Nor all that is at enmity with joy,
160 Can utterly abolish or destroy!
        Hence in a season of calm weather
            Though inland far we be,
Our Souls have sight of that immortal sea
            Which brought us hither,
        Can in a moment travel thither,
And see the Children sport upon the shore,
And hear the mighty waters rolling evermore.

        x

Then sing, ye Birds, sing, sing a joyous song!
        And let the young Lambs bound
170   As to the tabor's sound!
We in thought will join your throng,
        Ye that pipe and ye that play,
        Ye that through your hearts today
        Feel the gladness of the May!
What though the radiance which was once so bright
Be now for ever taken from my sight,
        Though nothing can bring back the hour
Of splendour in the grass, of glory in the flower;
        We will grieve not, rather find
180   Strength in what remains behind;
        In the primal sympathy
        Which having been must ever be;
        In the soothing thoughts that spring
        Out of human suffering;
        In the faith that looks through death,
In years that bring the philosophic mind.

        XI

And O, ye Fountains, Meadows, Hills, and Groves,
Forebode not any severing of our loves!
Yet in my heart of hearts I feel your might;
190 I only have relinquished one delight
To live beneath your more habitual sway.
I love the Brooks which down their channels fret,
Even more than when I tripped lightly as they;
The innocent brightness of a new-born Day
        Is lovely yet;
The Clouds that gather round the setting sun
Do take a sober colouring from an eye

That hath kept watch o'er man's mortality;
Another race hath been, and other palms are won.
200 Thanks to the human heart by which we live,
Thanks to its tenderness, its joys, and fears,
To me the meanest flower that blows can give
Thoughts that do often lie too deep for tears.

Sonnets

4

Composed upon Westminster Bridge,
September 3, 1802

Earth has not anything to show more fair:
Dull would he be of soul who could pass by
A sight so touching in its majesty:
This City now doth, like a garment, wear
The beauty of the morning; silent, bare,
Ships, towers, domes, theatres, and temples lie
Open unto the fields, and to the sky;
All bright and glittering in the smokeless air.
Never did sun more beautifully steep
10   In his first splendour, valley, rock, or hill;
Ne'er saw I, never felt, a calm so deep!
The river glideth at his own sweet will:
Dear God! the very houses seem asleep;
And all that mighty heart is lying still!

14

The world is too much with us; late and soon,
Getting and spending, we lay waste our powers:
Little we see in Nature that is ours;
We have given our hearts away, a sordid boon!
This Sea that bares her bosom to the moon;
The winds that will be howling at all hours,
And are up-gathered now like sleeping flowers;
For this, for everything, we are out of tune;
It moves us not.—Great God! I'd rather be
10   A Pagan suckled in a creed outworn;
So might I, standing on this pleasant lea,

Have glimpses that would make me less forlorn;
Have sight of Proteus rising from the sea;
Or hear old Triton blow his wreathèd horn.

JOHN KEATS
1795–1821

"Here lies one whose name was writ in water," is the epitaph Keats chose for his gravestone. Though his life was pitifully brief, his name survives as one of the greatest of English poets. Perhaps his creative fire burned the more intensely because he knew he would be doomed by the tuberculosis that had killed other members of his family. His father had died when Keats was nine; his mother when he was fifteen, and at that time his formal schooling came to an end. At his school in Enfield, the handsome, small but tough boy was well-liked by his classmates, and it was during this period that he became fascinated with the classical mythology that was to structure much of his poetry. He was apprenticed to an apothecary-surgeon and then continued his medical studies and was licensed to practice. But his love for literature made him give up medicine for poetry and what was to be a difficult life. Yet during the terrible period when he was deeply in love with Fanny Brawne but too poor to marry her, when his brother Tom had just died of tuberculosis and when the symptoms of that awful disease appeared in him, he produced some of his finest poetry: the Odes and his verse romances. He died at the age of twenty-five in Rome, where he had gone in a desperate search for health in a warmer climate.

Bright Star

Bright star! would I were steadfast as thou art—
    Not in lone splendor hung aloft the night
And watching, with eternal lids apart
    Like Nature's patient sleepless Eremite,[1]
The moving waters at their priestlike task
    Of pure ablution round earth's human shores,
Or gazing on the new soft fallen mask
    Of snow upon the mountains and the moors—
No—yet still steadfast, still unchangeable,
10   Pillowed upon my fair love's ripening breast,
To feel forever its soft fall and swell,
    Awake forever in a sweet unrest,
Still, still to hear her tender-taken breath,
And so live ever—or else swoon to death.

1. Religious hermit

On the Sonnet

If by dull rhymes our English must be chained,
    And, like Andromeda,[1] the Sonnet sweet
Fettered, in spite of painèd loveliness;
Let us find out, if we must be constrained,
    Sandals more interwoven and complete
To fit the naked foot of poesy;
Let us inspect the lyre, and weigh the stress
Of every chord, and see what may be gained
    By ear industrious, and attention meet;
10 Misers of sound and syllable, no less
Than Midas of his coinage, let us be
    Jealous of dead leaves in the bay-wreath crown;
So, if we may not let the Muse be free,
    She will be bound with garlands of her own.

1. Ethiopian princess chained as prey for a monster
   and rescued by Perseus, who then married her

Ode to a Nightingale

1

My heart aches, and a drowsy numbness pains
    My sense, as though of hemlock I had drunk,
Or emptied some dull opiate to the drains
    One minute past, and Lethe-wards[1] had sunk:
'Tis not through envy of thy happy lot,
    But being too happy in thine happiness,—
        That thou, light-wingèd Dryad[2] of the trees,
            In some melodious plot
Of beechen green, and shadows numberless,
10   Singest of summer in full-throated ease.

2

O, for a draught of vintage! that hath been
    Cool'd a long age in the deep-delved earth,
Tasting of Flora[3] and the country green,
    Dance, and Provençal song, and sunburnt mirth!
O for a beaker full of the warm South,
    Full of the true, the blushful Hippocrene,[4]

1. Toward Lethe, the river of Hades whose waters cause forgetfulness
2. Wood nymph
3. Goddess of flowers: personification for flowers
4. Fountain of the Muses on Mt. Helicon

With beaded bubbles winking at the brim,
   And purple-stained mouth;
That I might drink, and leave the world unseen,
20   And with thee fade away into the forest dim:

3

Fade far away, dissolve, and quite forget
   What thou among the leaves hast never known,
The weariness, the fever, and the fret
   Here, where men sit and hear each other groan;
Where palsy shakes a few, sad, last gray hairs,
   Where youth grows pale, and spectre-thin, and dies;
    Where but to think is to be full of sorrow
     And leaden-eyed despairs,
Where Beauty cannot keep her lustrous eyes,
30   Or new Love pine at them beyond tomorrow.

4

Away! away! for I will fly to thee,
   Not charioted by Bacchus[5] and his pards,
But on the viewless wings of Poesy,
   Though the dull brain perplexes and retards:
Already with thee! tender is the night,
   And haply the Queen-Moon is on her throne,
    Cluster'd around by all her starry fays;
     But here there is no light,
Save what from heaven is with the breezes blown
40   Through verdurous glooms and winding mossy ways.

5

I cannot see what flowers are at my feet,
   Nor what soft incense hangs upon the boughs,
But, in embalmèd darkness, guess each sweet
   Wherewith the seasonable month endows
The grass, the thicket, and the fruit-tree wild;
   White hawthorn, and the pastoral eglantine;
    Fast fading violets cover'd up in leaves;
     And mid-May's eldest child.
The coming musk-rose, full of dewy wine,
50   The murmurous haunt of flies on summer eves.

6

Darkling I listen; and, for many a time
   I have been half in love with easeful Death,

5. God of wine, whose chariot is drawn by leopards

Call'd him soft names in many a musèd rhyme,
　　To take into the air my quiet breath;
Now more than ever seems it rich to die,
　　To cease upon the midnight with no pain,
　　　While thou art pouring forth thy soul abroad
　　　　In such an ecstasy!
Still wouldst thou sing, and I have ears in vain—
60　　To thy high requiem become a sod.

7

Thou wast not born for death, immortal Bird!
　　No hungry generations tread thee down;
The voice I hear this passing night was heard
　　In ancient days by emperor and clown:
Perhaps the self-same song that found a path
　　Through the sad heart of Ruth,[6] when, sick for home,
　　　She stood in tears amid the alien corn;
　　　　The same that oft-times hath
Charm'd magic casements, opening on the foam
70　　Of perilous seas, in faery lands forlorn.

8

Forlorn! the very word is like a bell
　　To toll me back from thee to my sole self!
Adieu! the fancy cannot cheat so well
　　As she is fam'd to do, deceiving elf.
Adieu! adieu! thy plaintive anthem fades
Past the near meadows, over the still stream,
　　Up the hill-side; and now 'tis buried deep
　　　In the next valley-glades:
Was it a vision, or a waking dream?
80　　Fled is that music:—Do I wake or sleep?

6. In the Bible, Ruth forsook her native land to live in Israel with Naomi, her mother-in-law.

Ode on a Grecian Urn

1

Thou still unravish'd bride of quietness,
　　Thou foster-child of silence and slow time,
Sylvan historian, who canst thus express
　　A flowery tale more sweetly than our rhyme:

What leaf-fring'd legend haunts about thy shape
  Of deities or mortals, or of both,
    In Tempe[1] or the dales of Arcady?[1]
What men or gods are these? What maidens loth?
  What mad pursuit? What struggle to escape?
10   What pipes and timbrels?[2] What wild ecstasy?

2

Heard melodies are sweet, but those unheard
  Are sweeter; therefore, ye soft pipes, play on;
Not to the sensual ear, but, more endear'd,
  Pipe to the spirit ditties of no tone;
Fair youth, beneath the trees, thou canst not leave
  Thy song, nor ever can those trees be bare;
    Bold Lover, never, never canst thou kiss,
Though winning near the goal—yet, do not grieve;
  She cannot fade, though thou hast not thy bliss,
20   For ever wilt thou love, and she be fair!

3

Ah, happy, happy boughs! that cannot shed
  Your leaves, nor ever bid the Spring adieu;
And, happy melodist, unwearièd,
  For ever piping songs for ever new;
More happy love! more happy, happy love!
  For ever warm and still to be enjoy'd,
    For ever panting, and for ever young;
All breathing human passion far above,
  That leaves a heart high-sorrowful and cloy'd,
30   A burning forehead, and a parching tongue.

4

Who are these coming to the sacrifice?
  To what green altar, O mysterious priest,
Lead'st thou that heifer lowing at the skies,
  And all her silken flanks with garlands drest?
What little town by river or sea shore,
  Or mountain-built with peaceful citadel,
    Is emptied of this folk, this pious morn?
And, little town, thy streets for evermore
  Will silent be; and not a soul to tell
40   Why thou art desolate, can e'er return.

1. In Greek poetry, symbols of pastoral beauty
2. Tambourines

5

O Attic shape! Fair attitude! with brede
    Of marble men and maidens overwrought,
With forest branches and the trodden weed;
    Thou, silent form, dost tease us out of thought
As doth eternity: Cold Pastoral!
    When old age shall this generation waste,
      Thou shalt remain, in midst of other woe
Than ours, a friend to man, to whom thou say'st,
    "Beauty is truth, truth beauty,"—that is all
50   Ye know on earth, and all ye need to know.

Ode to Autumn

1

Season of mists and mellow fruitfulness!
    Close bosom-friend of the maturing sun;
Conspiring with him how to load and bless
    With fruit the vines that round the thatch-eaves run;
To bend with apples the moss'd cottage-trees,
    And fill all fruit with ripeness to the core;
      To swell the gourd, and plump the hazel shells
With a sweet kernel; to set budding more
And still more, later flowers for the bees,
10 Until they think warm days will never cease;
    For summer has o'er-brimm'd their clammy cells.

2

Who hath not seen thee oft amid thy store?
    Sometimes whoever seeks abroad may find
Thee sitting careless on a granary floor,
    Thy hair soft-lifted by the winnowing wind;
Or on a half-reap'd furrow sound asleep,
    Drowsed with the fume of poppies, while thy hook
      Spares the next swath and all its twinèd flowers;
And sometimes like a gleaner thou dost keep
20 Steady thy laden head across a brook;
Or by a cider-press, with patient look,
    Thou watchest the last oozings, hours by hours.

3

Where are the songs of Spring? Aye, where are they?
    Think not of them,—thou hast thy music too,

While barred clouds bloom the soft-dying day
   And touch the stubble-plains with rosy hue;
Then in a wailful choir the small gnats mourn
   Among the river-sallows, borne aloft
     Or sinking as the light wind lives or dies;
30   And full-grown lambs loud bleat from hilly bourn;
Hedge-crickets sing, and now with treble soft
The redbreast whistles from a garden-croft:
   And gathering swallows twitter in the skies.

ALFRED, LORD TENNYSON
1809–1892

Tennyson was the fourth son born into an eccentric but loving family in Lincolnshire, England. Eleven children and many pets, including an owl and a monkey, filled Somersby Rectory, which was presided over by George Clayton Tennyson, a clergyman of erratic moods, and his wife Elizabeth, a gentle and beautiful woman who was so casual a housekeeper that she often forgot to order food for family meals. The house was full of books, and both parents loved poetry and often read it to their children, who at very tender ages started composing their own. Tennyson spent four miserable years at Louth Grammar School, an institution which featured thrashing as an incentive to learning. At the age of eleven he returned home to be tutored by his father. Because George Tennyson was frequently ill, Alfred escaped to roam the countryside, composing and reciting his poetry aloud, a habit he kept for the rest of his life. He went to Trinity College, Cambridge, where he became close friends with Arthur Henry Hallam, whose lively wit complemented Tennyson's shyness and melancholy humor. Hallam's sudden death at the age of twenty-two was a shock from which Tennyson never fully recovered. Some of his greatest poetry, including "Ulysses" and *In Memoriam* resulted from his struggle with grief, and with faith and doubt. After leaving Cambridge, Tennyson, who never wanted to be anything but a poet, assumed a sort of nomadic existence, inviting himself to the homes of friends in London and in the countryside. He would stay for weeks or months at a time, filling the rooms with pungent pipesmoke, composing aloud, and consuming large amounts of port. By 1850, when *In Memoriam* was published to great acclaim, and when he became poet laureate, he finally felt himself financially secure enough to marry Emily Sellwood after a fourteen-year courtship. When he died he was the most popular poet in Victorian England and America, and he was buried with his head crowned with laurel from Virgil's tomb, and a copy of Shakespeare's *Cymbeline*, the last thing he read, in his hand.

Ulysses

It little profits that an idle king,
By this still hearth, among these barren crags,
Match'd with an aged wife, I mete and dole
Unequal laws unto a savage race,
That hoard, and sleep, and feed, and know not me.
I cannot rest from travel: I will drink
Life to the lees: all times I have enjoy'd
Greatly, have suffer'd greatly, both with those
That loved me, and alone; on shore, and when
10   Thro' scudding drifts the rainy Hyades
Vext the dim sea: I am become a name;
For always roaming with a hungry heart
Much have I seen and known: cities of men,
And manners, climates, councils, governments,
Myself not least, but honour'd of them all;
And drunk delight of battle with my peers,
Far on the ringing plains of windy Troy.
I am a part of all that I have met;
Yet all experience is an arch wherethro'
20   Gleams that untravell'd world, whose margin fades
For ever and for ever when I move.
How dull it is to pause, to make an end,
To rust unburnish'd, not to shine in use!
As tho' to breathe were life. Life piled on life
Were all too little, and of one to me
Little remains: but every hour is saved
From that eternal silence, something more,
A bringer of new things; and vile it were
For some three suns to store and hoard myself,
30   And this gray spirit yearning in desire
To follow knowledge like a sinking star,
Beyond the utmost bound of human thought.
    This is my son, mine own Telemachus,
To whom I leave the sceptre and the isle—
Well-lov'd of me, discerning to fulfil
This labour, by slow prudence to make mild
A rugged people, and thro' soft degrees
Subdue them to the useful and the good.
Most blameless is he, centred in the sphere
40   Of common duties, decent not to fail
In offices of tenderness, and pay
Meet adoration to my household gods,

When I am gone. He works his work, I mine.
   There lies the port; the vessel puffs her sail:
There gloom the dark broad seas. My mariners,
Souls that have toil'd, and wrought, and thought with me—
That ever with a frolic welcome took
The thunder and the sunshine, and opposed
Free hearts, free foreheads—you and I are old;
50 Old age hath yet his honour and his toil;
Death closes all: but something ere the end,
Some work of noble note, may yet be done,
Not unbecoming men that strove with Gods.
The lights begin to twinkle from the rocks:
The long day wanes: the slow moon climbs: the deep
Moans round with many voices. Come, my friends,
'Tis not too late to seek a newer world.
Push off, and sitting well in order smite
The sounding furrows; for my purpose holds
60 To sail beyond the sunset, and the baths
Of all the western stars, until I die.
It may be that the gulfs will wash us down:
It may be we shall touch the Happy Isles,
And see the great Achilles, whom we knew.
Tho' much is taken, much abides; and tho'
We are not now that strength which in old days
Moved earth and heaven; that which we are, we are;
One equal temper of heroic hearts,
Made weak by time and fate, but strong in will
70 To strive, to seek, to find, and not to yield.

The Eagle

Fragment

He clasps the crag with crooked hands;
Close to the sun in lonely lands,
Ring'd with the azure world, he stands.
The wrinkled sea beneath him crawls;
He watches from his mountain walls,
And like a thunderbolt he falls.

Tears, Idle Tears

Tears, idle tears, I know not what they mean,
Tears from the depth of some divine despair
Rise in the heart, and gather to the eyes,
In looking on the happy Autumn-fields,
And thinking of the days that are no more.

Fresh as the first beam glittering on a sail,
That brings our friends up from the underworld,
Sad as the last which reddens over one
That sinks with all we love below the verge;
10   So sad, so fresh, the days that are no more.

Ah, sad and strange as in dark summer dawns
The earliest pipe of half-awaken'd birds
To dying ears, when unto dying eyes
The casement slowly grows a glimmering square;
So sad, so strange, the days that are no more.

Dear as remember'd kisses after death,
And sweet as those by hopeless fancy feign'd
On lips that are for others; deep as love,
Deep as first love, and wild with all regret;
20   O Death in Life, the days that are no more.

From **In Memoriam**

7

Dark house, by which once more I stand
    Here in the long unlovely street,
    Doors, where my heart was used to beat
So quickly, waiting for a hand,

A hand that can be clasp'd no more—
    Behold me, for I cannot sleep,
    And like a guilty thing I creep
At earliest morning to the door.

He[1] is not here; but far away
10   The noise of life begins again,

And ghastly thro' the drizzling rain
On the bald street breaks the blank day.

8

A happy lover who has come
   To look on her that loves him well,
   Who 'lights and rings the gateway bell,
And learns her gone and far from home;

He saddens, all the magic light
   Dies off at once from bower and hall,
   And all the place is dark, and all
The chambers emptied of delight:

So find I every pleasant spot
   In which we two were wont to meet,
   The field, the chamber and the street,
For all is dark where thou are not.

Yet as that other, wandering there
   In those deserted walks, may find
   A flower beat with rain and wind,
Which once she foster'd up with care;

So seems it in my deep regret,
   O my forsaken heart, with thee
   And this poor flower of poesy
Which little cared for fades not yet.

But since it pleased a vanish'd eye,
   I go to plant it on his tomb,
   That if it can it there may bloom,
Or dying, there at least may die.

115

Now fades the last long streak of snow,
   Now burgeons every maze of quick

1. Arthur Henry Hallam, Tennyson's friend,
   whose death inspired a sequence of poems
   entitled *In Memoriam A. H. H.*

About the flowering squares, and thick
By ashen roots the violets blow.

Now rings the woodland loud and long,
    The distance takes a lovelier hue,
    And drown'd in yonder living blue
The lark becomes a sightless song.

Now dance the lights on lawn and lea,
10   The flocks are whiter down the vale,
    And milkier every milky sail
On winding stream or distant sea;

Where now the seamew pipes, or dives
    In yonder greening gleam, and fly
    The happy birds, that change their sky
To build and brood; that live their lives

From land to land; and in my breast
    Spring wakens too; and my regret
    Becomes an April violet,
20 And buds and blossoms like the rest.

ROBERT BROWNING
1812–1889

Browning is a poet of masks. While we know a lot about his life, we don't ever feel that we really know him. He hides behind the faces of the rogues' gallery in his dramatic monologues, allowing his characters to present psychological portraits of themselves, but not of him. His greatest work, *The Ring and the Book*, is a seventeenth-century Roman murder mystery featuring the despicable Count Guido Franceschini, recounted through dramatic monologues in which each character presents a contrasting point of view. Browning's interest in things Italian started when he was a boy living in the London suburb of Camberwell. Largely educated at home by tutors, he all but devoured his father's 6000-volume library, from which he acquired much of his wide knowledge of Italian history, art, and literature. He lived happily with his parents until the age of thirty-four, when he eloped to Italy with the semi-invalid poet, Elizabeth Barrett, rescuing her from her jealous, tyrannical father and a life of languishing on divans covered with lap robes. This love affair was the great romance of its time, and continued for fifteen idyllic years spent mostly in Italy, until Elizabeth Barrett Browning's death in

1861. Like Tennyson, Browning was enormously productive, and also like Tennyson, he was an extremely popular poet. Shortly before his death, the Browning Society was formed. These literary groups blossomed throughout the English-speaking world, revering Browning as the great affirmative voice of the age, a voice which, they sincerely believed, would refute Tennysonian doubt.

Soliloquy of the Spanish Cloister

Gr-r-r—there go, my heart's abhorrence!
    Water your damned flower-pots, do!
If hate killed men, Brother Lawrence,
    God's blood, would not mine kill you!
What? your myrtle-bush wants trimming?
    Oh, that rose has prior claims—
Needs its leaden vase filled brimming?
    Hell dry you up with its flames!

At the meal we sit together;
10   *Salve tibi!*[1] I must hear
Wise talk of the kind of weather,
    Sort of season, time of year:
Not a plenteous cork-crop: scarcely
    Dare we hope oak-galls, I doubt;
What's the Latin name for "parsley"?
    What's the Greek name for Swine's Snout?

Whew! We'll have our platter burnished,
    Laid with care on our own shelf!
With a fire-new spoon we're furnished,
20   And a goblet for ourself,
Rinsed like something sacrificial
    Ere 'tis fit to touch our chaps—
Marked with L. for our initial!
    (He-he! There his lily snaps!)

Saint, forsooth! While brown Dolores
    Squats outside the Convent bank
With Sanchicha, telling stories,
    Steeping tresses in the tank,

1. Greetings to you!

Blue-black, lustrous, thick like horsehairs,
30   —Can't I see his dead eye glow,
Bright as 'twere a Barbary corsair's?
    (That is, if he'd let it show!)

When he finishes refection,
    Knife and fork he never lays
Cross-wise, to my recollection,
    As do I, in Jesu's praise.
I, the Trinity illustrate,
    Drinking watered orange-pulp—
In three sips the Arian[2] frustrate;
40   While he drains his at one gulp!

Oh, those melons! if he's able
    We're to have a feast; so nice!
One goes to the Abbot's table,
    All of us get each a slice.
How go on your flowers? None double?
    Not one fruit-sort can you spy?
Strange!—And I, too, at such trouble,
    Keep them close-nipped on the sly!

There's a great text in Galatians,[3]
50   Once you trip on it, entails
Twenty-nine distinct damnations,
    One sure, if another fails;
If I trip him just a-dying,
    Sure of heaven as sure can be,
Spin him round and send him flying
    Off to hell, a Manichee?[4]

Or, my scrofulous French novel
    On grey paper with blunt type!
Simply glance at it, you grovel
60   Hand and foot in Belial's[5] gripe;
If I double down its pages
    At the woeful sixteenth print,

2. Follower of the heretic Arius, who denied the Trinity
3. One of St. Paul's Epistles
4. Follower of the heretic Mani
5. A devil

When he gathers his greengages,
  Ope a sieve and slip it in't?

Or, there's Satan!—one might venture
  Pledge one's soul to him, yet leave
Such a flaw in the indenture
  As he'd miss till, past retrieve,
Blasted lay that rose-acacia
70   We're so proud of! Hy, Zy, Hine....
'St, there's Vespers!⁶ *Plena gratia*
  Ave, Virgo! Gr-r-r—you swine!

6. Evening prayers. The speaker intones "Hail Virgin, full of grace."

My Last Duchess

Ferrara

[handwritten: not last as in final – but last in that she]

That's my last Duchess painted on the wall,
Looking as if she were alive. I call
That piece a wonder, now: Frà Pandolf's hands
Worked busily a day, and there she stands.
Will't please you sit and look at her? I said
"Frà Pandolf" by design, for never read
Strangers like you that pictured countenance,
The depth and passion of its earnest glance,
But to myself they turned (since none puts by
10 The curtain I have drawn for you, but I)
And seemed as they would ask me, if they durst,
How such a glance came there; so, not the first
Are you to turn and ask thus. Sir, 'twas not
Her husband's presence only, called that spot
Of joy into the Duchess' cheek; perhaps
Frà Pandolf chanced to say, "Her mantle laps
Over my lady's wrist too much," or "Paint
Must never hope to reproduce the faint
Half-flush that dies along her throat": such stuff
20 Was courtesy, she thought, and cause enough
For calling up that spot of joy. She had
A heart—how shall I say?—too soon made glad,
Too easily impressed: she liked whate'er
She looked on, and her looks went everywhere.
Sir, 'twas all one! My favour at her breast,
The dropping of the daylight in the West,

The bough of cherries some officious fool
Broke in the orchard for her, the white mule
She rode with round the terrace—all and each
30   Would draw from her alike the approving speech.
Or blush, at least. She thanked men,—good! but thanked
Somehow—I know not how—as if she ranked
My gift of a nine-hundred-years-old name
With anybody's gift. Who'd stoop to blame
This sort of trifling? Even had you skill
In speech—(which I have not)—to make your will
Quite clear to such an one, and say, "Just this
Or that in you disgusts me; here you miss,
Or there exceed the mark"—and if she let
40   Herself be lessoned so, nor plainly set
Her wits to yours, forsooth, and made excuse,
—E'en then would be some stooping; and I choose
Never to stoop. Oh sir, she smiled, no doubt,
Whene'er I passed her; but who passed without
Much the same smile? This grew; I gave commands;
Then all smiles stopped together. There she stands
As if alive. Will't please you rise? We'll meet
The company below, then. I repeat,
The Count your master's known munificence
50   Is ample warrant that no just pretence
Of mine for dowry will be disallowed;
Though his fair daughter's self, as I avowed
At starting, is my object. Nay, we'll go
Together down, sir. Notice Neptune, though,
Taming a sea-horse, thought a rarity,
Which Claus of Innsbruck cast in bronze for me!

The Bishop Orders His Tomb at Saint Praxed's Church

Rome, 15—

Vanity, saith the preacher, vanity!
Draw round my bed: is Anselm keeping back?
Nephews—sons mine . . . ah God, I know not! Well—
She, men would have to be your mother once,
Old Gandolf envied me, so fair she was!
What's done is done, and she is dead beside,
Dead long ago, and I am Bishop since,
And as she died so must we die ourselves,

And thence ye may perceive the world's a dream.
10   Life, how and what is it? As here I lie
In this state-chamber, dying by degrees,
Hours and long hours in the dead night, I ask,
"Do I live, am I dead?" Peace, peace seems all.
Saint Praxed's ever was the church for peace;
And so, about this tomb of mine. I fought
With tooth and nail to save my niche, ye know:
—Old Gandolf cozened me, despite my care;
Shrewd was that snatch from out the corner South
He graced his carrion with, God curse the same!
20   Yet still my niche is not so cramped but thence
One sees the pulpit o' the epistle-side,
And somewhat of the choir, those silent seats,
And up into the aery dome where live
The angels, and a sunbeam's sure to lurk:
And I shall fill my slab of basalt there,
And 'neath my tabernacle take my rest,
With those nine columns round me, two and two,
The odd one at my feet where Anselm stands:
Peach-blossom marble all, the rare, the ripe
30   As fresh-poured red wine of a mighty pulse.
—Old Gandolf with his paltry onion-stone,
Put me where I may look at him! True peach,
Rosy and flawless: how I earned the prize!
Draw close: that conflagration of my church
—What then? So much was saved if aught were missed!
My sons, ye would not be my death? Go dig
The white-grape vineyard where the oil-press stood,
Drop water gently till the surface sink,
And if ye find . . . Ah God, I know not, I! . . .
40   Bedded in store of rotten fig-leaves soft,
And corded up in a tight olive-frail,
Some lump, ah God, of *lapis lazuli*,
Big as a Jew's head cut off at the nape,
Blue as a vein o'er the Madonna's breast . . .
Sons, all have I bequeathed you, villas, all,
That brave Frascati villa with its bath,
So, let the blue lump poise between my knees,
Like God the Father's globe on both his hands
Ye worship in the Jesu Chruch so gay,
50   For Gandolf shall not choose but see and burst!
Swift as a weaver's shuttle fleet our years:
Man goeth to the grave, and where is he?

Did I say basalt for my slab, sons? Black—
'Twas ever antique-black I meant! How else
Shall ye contrast my frieze to come beneath?
The bas-relief in bronze ye promised me,
Those Pans and Nymphs ye wot of, and perchance
Some tripod, thyrsus, with a vase or so,
The Savior at his sermon on the mount,
60   Saint Praxed in a glory, and one Pan
Ready to twitch the Nymph's last garment off,
And Moses with the tables . . . but I know
Ye mark me not! What do they whisper thee,
Child of my bowels, Anselm? Ah, ye hope
To revel down my villas while I gasp
Bricked o'er with beggar's moldy travertine
Which Gandolf from his tomb-top chuckles at!
Nay, boys, ye love me—all of jasper, then!
'Tis jasper ye stand pledged to, lest I grieve.
70   My bath must needs be left behind, alas!
One block, pure green as a pistachio-nut,
There's plenty jasper somewhere in the world—
And have I not Saint Praxed's ear to pray
Horses for ye, and brown Greek manuscripts,
And mistresses with great smooth marbly limbs?
—That's if ye carve my epitaph aright,
Choice Latin, picked phrase, Tully's every word,
No gaudy ware like Gandolf's second line—
Tully, my masters? Ulpian serves his need!
80   And then how I shall lie through centuries,
And hear the blessed mutter of the mass,
And see God made and eaten all day long,
And feel the steady candle-flame, and taste
Good, strong, thick, stupefying incense-smoke!
For as I lie here, hours of the dead night,
Dying in state and by such slow degrees,
I fold my arms as if they clasped a crook,
And stretch my feet forth straight as stone can point,
And let the bedclothes, for a mortcloth, drop
90   Into great laps and folds of sculptor's-work:
And as yon tapers dwindle, and strange thoughts
Grow, with a certain humming in my ears,
About the life before I lived this life,
And this life too, popes, cardinals and priests,
Saint Praxed at his sermon on the mount,
Your tall pale mother with her talking eyes,
And new-found agate urns as fresh as day,

And marble's language, Latin pure, discreet,
—Aha, ELUCESCEBAT[1] quoth our friend?
100 No Tully, said I, Ulpian at the best!
Evil and brief hath been my pilgrimage.
All *lapis*, all, sons! Else I give the Pope
My villas! Will ye ever eat my heart?
Ever your eyes were as a lizard's quick,
They glitter like your mother's for my soul,
Or ye would heighten my impoverished frieze,
Piece out its starved design, and fill my vase
With grapes, and add a visor and a Term,
And to the tripod ye would tie a lynx
110 That in his struggle throws the thyrsus down,
To comfort me on my entablature
Whereon I am to lie till I must ask,
"Do I live, am I dead?" There, leave me, there!
For ye have stabbed me with ingratitude
To death—ye wish it—God, ye wish it! Stone—
Gritstone, a-crumble! Clammy squares which sweat
As if the corpse they keep were oozing through—
And no more *lapis* to delight the world!
Well, go! I bless ye. Fewer tapers there,
120 But in a row: and, going, turn your backs
—Aye, like departing altar-ministrants,
And leave me in my church, the church for peace,
That I may watch at leisure if he leers—
Old Gandolf—at me, from his onion-stone,
As still he envied me, so fair she was!

1. He was famous: not in the pure Latin of Cicero (Tully)
   but in the debased style of Ulpian.

The Lost Mistress

I

All's over, then: does truth sound bitter
    As one at first believes?
Hark, 'tis the sparrows' good-night twitter
    About your cottage eaves!

II

And the leaf-buds on the vine are wooly,
    I noticed that, to-day;

One day more bursts them open fully
  —You know the red turns grey.

III

To-morrow we meet the same then, dearest?
10   May I take your hand in mine?
Mere friends are we,—well, friends the merest
  Keep much that I resign:

IV

For each glance of the eye so bright and black,
  Though I keep with heart's endeavour,—
Your voice, when you wish the snowdrops back,
  Though it stay in my soul for ever!—

V

Yet I will but say what mere friends say,
  Or only a thought stronger;
I will hold your hand but as long as all may,
20   Or so very little longer!

WALT WHITMAN
1819–1892

In 1844, Ralph Waldo Emerson called for a truly American poet who would see that "America is a poem in our eyes; its ample geography dazzles the imagination, and it will not wait long for metres." Eleven years later Walt Whitman's "barbaric yawp," as he himself called it, gave answer to Emerson's request. The voice was distinctly American and the form broke away from conventional metrical regularity, its lines swelling and undulating with oceanic rhythm, echoing the biblical psalmists, or declaiming oratorically in the best American political tradition. It was an expansive voice for an expanding America, and Whitman saw himself as prophet and seer celebrating individualism and democratic idealism as it manifested itself in all experience. Whitman would "let nature speak, without check, with original energy," and this energy was sexual, "the procreant urge" of nature and of man and woman. He would speak for all people, and not just for privileged literary circles: "I am your voice—it was tied in you—in me it begins to talk." Emerson was impressed with the first edition of Leaves of Grass, but though he realized that Whitman was indeed the poet he sought, he was somewhat shocked at some of Whitman's subject matter. Whitman in his time was not considered respectable, and each new edition of *Leaves of Grass* was inevitably pronounced "obscene."

Whitman was born on Long Island, New York, and grew up in Brooklyn, returning frequently to Long Island and his beloved ocean. Mostly self-educated, he attended school only six years, and then worked variously as an office boy, schoolteacher, newspaper editor, or carpenter. He would roam the streets of the city absorbing sights and sounds, a friend of both artists and laborers. During the Civil War he was a wound dresser in a Washington army hospital, and after the war he lost his job in the Office of Indian Affairs when it was discovered he had written an "indecent" book. Never financially secure, Whitman supported himself as he could, continuing to expand and rearrange the poetry of *Leaves of Grass*. Toward the end of his life, his poetry was becoming accepted, and when he addressed "Poets to come," he could be confident in the immortality of his vision. And rightly so, for it was these poets who would answer him affirmatively, as those of his own time could not.

Poets to Come

Poets to come! orators, singers, musicians to come!
Not to-day is to justify me and answer what I am for,
But you, a new brood, native, athletic, continental, greater than before known,
Arouse! for you must justify me.

I myself but write one or two indicative words for the future,
I but advance a moment only to wheel and hurry back in the darkness.

I am a man who, sauntering along without fully stopping, turns a casual look upon
     you and then averts his face,
Leaving it to you to prove and define it,
Expecting the main things from you.

Crossing Brooklyn Ferry

1

Flood-tide below me! I see you face to face!
Clouds of the west—sun there half an hour high—I see you also face to face.

Crowds of men and women attired in the usual costumes, how curious you are to
     me!
On the ferry-boats the hundreds and hundreds that cross, returning home, are
     more curious to me than you suppose,
And you that shall cross from shore to shore years hence are more to me, and more
     in my meditations, than you might suppose.

2

The impalpable sustenance of me from all things at all hours of the day,
The simple, compact, well-join'd scheme, myself disintegrated, every one
    disintegrated yet part of the scheme,
The similitudes of the past and those of the future,
The glories strung like beads on my smallest sights and hearings, on the walk in
    the street and the passage over the river,
10 The current rushing so swiftly and swimming with me far away,
The others that are to follow me, the ties between me and them,
The certainty of others, the life, love, sight, hearing of others.
Others will enter the gates of the ferry and cross from shore to shore,
Others will watch the run of the flood-tide,
Others will see the shipping of Manhattan north and west, and the heights of
    Brooklyn to the south and east,
Others will see the islands large and small;
Fifty years hence, others will see them as they cross, the sun half an hour high,
A hundred years hence, or ever so many hundred years hence, others will see
    them,
Will enjoy the sunset, the pouring-in of the flood-tide, the falling-back to the sea of
    the ebb-tide.

3

20 It avails not, time nor place—distance avails not,
I am with you, you men and women of a generation, or ever so many generations
    hence,
Just as you feel when you look on the river and sky, so I felt,
Just as any of you is one of a living crowd, I was one of a crowd,
Just as you are refresh'd by the gladness of the river and the bright flow, I was
    refresh'd,
Just as you stand and lean on the rail, yet hurry with the swift current, I stood yet
    was hurried,
Just as you look on the numberless masts of ships and the thick-stemm'd pipes of
    steamboats, I look'd.

I too many and many a time cross'd the river of old,
Watched the Twelfth-month sea-gulls, saw them high in the air floating with
    motionless wings, oscillating their bodies,
Saw how the glistening yellow lit up parts of their bodies and left the rest in strong
    shadow,
30 Saw the slow-wheeling circles and the gradual edging toward the south,
Saw the reflection of the summer sky in the water,
Had my eyes dazzled by the shimmering track of beams,

Look'd at the fine centrifugal spokes of light round the shape of my head in the
    sunlit water,
Look'd on the haze on the hills southward and south-westward,
Look'd on the vapor as it flew in fleeces tinged with violet,
Look'd toward the lower bay to notice the vessels arriving,
Saw their approach, saw aboard those that were near me,
Saw the white sails of schooners and sloops, saw the ships at anchor,
The sailors at work in the rigging or out astride the spars,
40 The round masts, the swinging motion of the hulls, the slender serpentine
    pennants,
The large and small steamers in motion, the pilots in their pilot-houses,
The white wake left by the passage, the quick tremulous whirl of the wheels,
The flags of all nations, the falling of them at sunset,
The scallop-edged waves in the twilight, the ladled cups, the frolicsome crests and
    glistening,
The stretch afar growing dimmer and dimmer, the gray walls of the granite
    storehouses by the docks,
On the river the shadowy group, the big steam-tug closely flank'd on each side by
    the barges, the hay-boat, the belated lighter,
On the neighboring shore the fires from the foundry chimneys burning high and
    glaringly into the night,
Casting their flicker of black contrasted with wild red and yellow light over the
    tops of houses and down into the clefts of streets.

4

These and all else were to me the same as they are to you,
50 I loved well those cities, loved well the stately and rapid river,
The men and women I saw were all near to me,
Others the same—others who look back on me because I look'd forward to them,
(The time will come, though I stop here to-day and to-night.)

5

What is it then between us?
What is the count of the scores or hundreds of years between us?

Whatever it is, it avails not—distance avails not, and place avails not,
I too lived, Brooklyn of ample hills was mine,
I too walk'd the streets of Manhattan island, and bathed in the waters around it,
I too felt the curious abrupt questionings stir within me,
60 In the day among crowds of people sometimes they came upon me,
In my walks home late at night or as I lay in my bed they came upon me,
I too had been struck from the float forever held in solution,

I too had receiv'd identity by my body,
That I was I knew was of my body, and what I should be I knew I should be of my
    body.

                6

It is not upon you alone the dark patches fall,
The dark threw its patches down upon me also,
The best I had done seem'd to me blank and suspicious,
My great thoughts as I supposed them, were they not in reality meagre?
Nor is it you alone who know what it is to be evil,
70   I am he who knew what it was to be evil,
I too knitted the old knot of contrariety,
Blabb'd, blush'd, resented, lied, stole, grudg'd,
Had guile, anger, lust, hot wishes I dared not speak,
Was wayward, vain, greedy, shallow, sly, cowardly, malignant,
The wolf, the snake, the hog, not wanting in me,
The cheating look, the frivolous word, the adulterous wish, not wanting,
Refusals, hates, postponements, meanness, laziness, none of these wanting,
Was one with the rest, the days and haps of the rest,
Was call'd by my nighest name by clear loud voices of young men as they saw me
    approaching or passing,
80   Felt their arms on my neck as I stood, or the negligent leaning of their flesh against
    me as I sat,
Saw many I loved in the street or ferry-boat or public assembly, yet never told
    them a word,
Lived the same life with the rest, the same old laughing, gnawing, sleeping,
Play'd the part that still looks back on the actor or actress,
The same old role, the role that is what we make it, as great as we like,
Or as small as we like, or both great and small.

                7

Closer yet I approach you,
What thought you have of me now, I had as much of you—I laid in my stores in
    advance,
I consider'd long and seriously of you before you were born.

Who was to know what should come home to me?
90   Who knows but I am enjoying this?
Who knows, for all the distance, but I am as good as looking at you now, for all you
    cannot see me?

8

Ah, what can ever be more stately and admirable to me than mast-hemm'd
  Manhattan?
River and sunset and scallop-edg'd waves of flood-tide?
The sea-gulls oscillating their bodies, the hay-boat in the twilight, and the belated
  lighter?
What gods can exceed these that clasp me by the hand, and with voices I love call
  me promptly and loudly by my nighest name as I approach?
What is more subtle than this which ties me to the woman or man that looks in my
  face?
Which fuses me into you now, and pours my meaning into you?
We understand then do we not?
What I promis'd without mentioning it, have you not accepted?
100 What the study could not teach—what the preaching could not accomplish is
  accomplish'd, is it not?

9

Flow on, river! flow with the flood-tide, and ebb with the ebb-tide!
Frolic on, crested and scallop-edg'd waves!
Gorgeous clouds of the sunset! drench with your splendor me, or the men and
  women generations after me!
Cross from shore to shore, countless crowds of passengers!
Stand up, tall masts of Mannahatta! stand up, beautiful hills of Brooklyn!
Throb, baffled and curious brain! throw out questions and answers!
Suspend here and everywhere, eternal float of solution!
Gaze, loving and thirsty eyes, in the house or street or public assembly!
Sound out, voices of young men! loudly and musically call me by my nighest
  name!
110 Live, old life! play the part that looks back on the actor or actress!
Play the old role, the role that is great or small according as one makes it!
Consider, you who peruse me, whether I may not in unknown ways be looking
  upon you;
Be firm, rail over the river, to support those who lean idly, yet haste with the
  hasting current;
Fly on, sea-birds! fly sideways, or wheel in large circles high in the air;
Receive the summer sky, you water, and faithfully hold it till all downcast eyes
  have time to take it from you!
Diverge, fine spokes of light, from the shape of my head, or any one's head, in the
  sunlit water!
Come on, ships from the lower bay! pass up or down, white-sail'd schooners,
  sloops, lighters!

Flaunt away, flags of all nations! be duly lower'd at sunset!
Burn high your fires, foundry chimneys! cast black shadows at nightfall! cast red
    and yellow light over the tops of the houses!
120 Appearances, now or henceforth, indicate what you are,
You necessary film, continue to envelop the soul,
About my body for me, and your body for you, be hung out divinest aromas,
Thrive, cities—bring your freight, bring your shows, ample and sufficient rivers,
Expand, being than which none else is perhaps more spiritual,
Keep your places, objects than which none else is more lasting.

You have waited, you always wait, you dumb, beautiful ministers,
We receive you with free sense at last, and are insatiate henceforward,
Not you any more shall be able to foil us, or withhold yourselves from us,
We use you, and do not cast you aside—we plant you permanently within us,
130 We fathom you not—we love you—there is perfection in you also,
You furnish your parts toward eternity,
Great or small, you furnish your parts toward the soul.

I Hear America Singing

I hear America singing, the varied carols I hear,
Those of mechanics, each one singing his as it should be blithe and strong,
The carpenter singing his as he measures his plank or beam,
The mason singing his as he makes ready for work, or leaves off work,
The boatman singing what belongs to him in his boat, the deckhand singing on
    the steamboat deck,
The shoemaker singing as he sits on his bench, the hatter singing as he stands,
The wood-cutter's song, the ploughboy's on his way in the morning, or at noon
    intermission or at sundown,
The delicious singing of the mother, or of the young wife at work, or of the girl
    sewing or washing,
Each singing what belongs to him or her and to none else,
10 The day what belongs to the day—at night the party of young fellows, robust,
    friendly,
Singing with open mouths their strong melodious songs.

The World below the Brine

The world below the brine,
Forests at the bottom of the sea, the branches and leaves,
Sea-lettuce, vast lichens, strange flowers and seeds, the thick tangle, openings,
    and pink turf,

Different colors, pale gray and green, purple, white, and gold, the play of light
    through the water,
Dumb swimmers there among the rocks, coral, gluten, grass, rushes, and the
    aliment of the swimmers,
Sluggish existences grazing there suspended, or slowly crawling close to the
    bottom,
The sperm-whale at the surface blowing air and spray, or disporting with his
    flukes,
The leaden-eyed shark, the walrus, the turtle, the hairy sea-leopard, and the
    sting-ray,
Passions there, wars, pursuits, tribes, sight in those ocean-depths, breathing that
    thick-breathing air, as so many do,
10   The change thence to the sight here, and to the subtle air breathed by beings like
    us who walk this sphere,
The change onward from ours to that of beings who walk other spheres.

The Dalliance of the Eagles

Skirting the river road, (my forenoon walk, my rest,)
Skyward in air a sudden muffled sound, the dalliance of the eagles,
The rushing amorous contact high in space together,
The clinching interlocking claws, a living, fierce, gyrating wheel,
Four beating wings, two beaks, a swirling mass tight grappling,
In tumbling turning clustering loops, straight downward falling,
Till o'er the river pois'd, the twain yet one, a moment's lull,
A motionless still balance in the air, then parting, talons loosing,
Upward again on slow-firm pinions slanting, their separate diverse flight,
10   She hers, he his, pursuing.

A Sight in Camp in the Daybreak Gray and Dim

A sight in camp in the daybreak gray and dim,
As from my tent I emerge so early sleepless,
As slow I walk in the cool fresh air the path near by the hospital tent,
Three forms I see on stretchers lying, brought out there untended lying,
Over each the blanket spread, ample brownish woolen blanket,
Gray and heavy blanket, folding, covering all.

Curious I halt and silent stand,
Then with light fingers I from the face of the nearest the first just lift the blanket;
Who are you elderly man so gaunt and grim, with well-gray'd hair, and flesh all
    sunken about the eyes?
10   Who are you my dear comrade?

Then to the second I step—and who are you my child and darling?
Who are you sweet boy with cheeks yet blooming?

Then to the third—a face nor child nor old, very calm, as of beautiful yellow-white
    ivory;
Young man I think I know you—I think this face is the face of the Christ himself,
Dead and divine and brother of all, and here again he lies.

Who Learns My Lesson Complete?

Who learns my lesson complete?
Boss, journeyman, apprentice, churchman and atheist,
The stupid and the wise thinker, parents and offspring, merchant, clerk, porter
    and customer,
Editor, author, artist, and schoolboy—draw nigh and commence;
It is no lesson—it lets down the bars to a good lesson,
And that to another, and every one to another still.

The great laws take and effuse without argument,
I am of the same style, for I am their friend,
I love them quits and quits, I do not halt and make salaams.

10   I lie abstracted and hear beautiful tales of things and the reasons of things.
They are so beautiful I nudge myself to listen.

I cannot say to any person what I hear—I cannot say it to myself—it is very
    wonderful.

It is no small matter, this round and delicious globe moving so exactly in its orbit
    for ever and ever, without one jolt or the untruth of a single second,
I do not think it was made in six days, nor in ten thousand years, nor ten billions
    of years,
Nor plann'd and built one thing after another as an architect plans and builds a
    house.

I do not think seventy years is the time of a man or woman,
Nor that seventy millions of years is the time of a man or woman,
Nor that years will ever stop the existence of me, or any one else.

Is it wonderful that I should be immortal? as every one is immortal;
20   I know it is wonderful, but my eyesight is equally wonderful, and how I was
    conceived in my mother's womb is equally wonderful,

And pass'd from a babe in the creeping trance of a couple of summers and winters
    to articulate and walk—all this is equally wonderful.

And that my soul embraces you this hour, and we affect each other without ever
    seeing each other, and never perhaps to see each other, is every bit as
    wonderful.

And that I can think such thoughts as these is just as wonderful,
And that I can remind you, and you think them and know them to be true, is just
    as wonderful.

And that the moon spins round the earth and on with the earth, is equally
    wonderful,
And that they balance themselves with the sun and stars is equally wonderful.

The Ox-Tamer

In a far-away northern county in the placid pastoral region,
Lives my farmer friend, the theme of my recitative, a famous tamer of oxen,
There they bring him the three-year-olds and the four-year-olds to break them,
He will take the wildest steer in the world and break him and tame him,
He will go fearless without any whip where the young bullock chafes up and down
    the yard,
The bullock's head tosses restless high in the air with raging eyes,
Yet see you! how soon his rage subsides—how soon this tamer tames him;
See you! on the farms hereabout a hundred oxen young and old, and he is the man
    who has tamed them,
They all know him, all are affectionate to him;
10 See you! some are such beautiful animals, so lofty looking;
Some are buff-color'd, some mottled, one has a white line running along his back,
    some are brindled,
Some have wide flaring horns (a good sign)—see you! the bright hides,
See, the two with stars on their foreheads—see, the round bodies and broad backs,
How straight and square they stand on their legs—what fine sagacious eyes!
How they watch their tamer—they wish him near them—how they turn to look
    after him!
What yearning expression! how uneasy they are when he moves away from them;
Now I marvel what it can be he appears to them, (books, politics, poems,
    depart—all else departs,)
I confess I envy only his fascination—my silent, illiterate friend,
Whom a hundred oxen love there in his life on farms,
20 In the northern county far, in the placid pastoral region.

As I Sit Writing Here

As I sit writing here, sick and grown old,
Not my least burden is that dulness of the years, querilities,
Ungracious glooms, aches, lethargy, constipation, whimpering *ennui*,
May filter in my daily songs.

EMILY DICKINSON

1830–1886

Emily Dickinson provided another new voice for American poetry, but one quite the opposite of that of her contemporary, Walt Whitman. She is as coiled and condensed as he is loose and expansive; as private as he is public. She was born in Amherst, Massachusetts, the daughter of a highly respected lawyer. She graduated from Amherst Academy and entered nearby Mount Holyoke Female Seminary. However, less than a year later she returned home because she could not accept the Seminary's rigid brand of Christianity, and because she was homesick. She lived the rest of her life in her father's house, rarely leaving Amherst, and eventually becoming a recluse, seeing only a few visitors a year. Though some biographers have characterized Dickinson as a frail, highly eccentric spinster, hiding from the world and frustrated in life and in love, the power of her poetry and the sheer amount of her literary output belies such a picture. Rather, we might consider her withdrawal from society a choice for the freedom to pursue the career of poet. And poet she was, producing over 1700 poems, of which only seven were published during her lifetime. Though the form of her poetry looks simple, with its patterns of meter and rhyme suggesting her use of nineteenth-century hymnals as models of prosody, there is nothing simplistic in what she says, and her unconventional punctuation forces us to pause with her thoughts as she examines faith and doubt, death, nature, and varieties of love.

[Success Is Counted Sweetest]

Success is counted sweetest
By those who ne'er succeed.
To comprehend a nectar
Requires sorest need.

Not one of all the purple Host
Who took the Flag today
Can tell the definition
So clear of Victory

As he defeated—dying—
10   On whose forbidden ear
The distant strains of triumph
Burst agonized and clear!

[I Never Hear the Word]

I never hear the word "escape"
Without a quicker blood,
A sudden expectation,
A flying attitude!

I never hear of prisons broad
By soldiers battered down,
But I tug childish at my bars
Only to fail again!

[I'm "Wife"—I've Finished That]

I'm "wife"—I've finished that—
That other state—
I'm Czar—I'm "Woman" now—
It's safer so—

How odd the Girl's life looks
Behind this soft Eclipse—
I think that Earth feels so
To folks in Heaven—now—

This being comfort—then
10   That other kind—was pain—
But why compare?
I'm "Wife"! Stop there!

[What Is—"Paradise"]

What is—"Paradise"—
Who live there—
Are they "Farmers"—
Do they "hoe"—
Do they know that this is "Amherst"—
And that I—am coming—too—

Do they wear "new shoes"—in "Eden"—
Is it always pleasant—there—
Won't they scold us—when we're hungry—
10 Or tell God—how cross we are—

You are sure there's such a person
As "a Father"—in the sky—
So if I get lost—there—ever—
Or do what the nurse calls "die"—
I shan't walk the "Jasper"—barefoot—
Ransomed folks—won't laugh at me—
Maybe—"Eden" a'nt so lonesome
As New England used to be!

[I Heard a Fly Buzz]

I heard a Fly buzz—when I died—
The Stillness in the Room
Was like the Stillness in the Air—
Between the Heaves of Storm—

The Eyes around—had wrung them dry—
And Breaths were gathering firm
For that last Onset—when the King
Be witnessed—in the Room—

I willed my Keepsakes—Signed away
10 What portion of me be
Assignable—and then it was
There interposed a Fly—

With Blue—uncertain stumbling Buzz—
Between the light—and me—
And then the Windows failed—and then
I could not see to see—

[The Heart Asks Pleasure—First]

The Heart asks Pleasure—first—
And then—Excuse from Pain—
And then—those little Anodynes
That deaden suffering—

And then—to go to sleep—
And then—if it should be
The will of its Inquisitor
The privilege to die—

[Because I Could Not Stop for Death]

Because I could not stop for Death—
He kindly stopped for me—
The Carriage held but just Ourselves—
And Immortality.

We slowly drove—He knew no haste
And I had put away
My labor and my leisure too,
For His Civility—

We passed the School, where Children strove
10   At Recess—in the Ring—
We passed the Fields of Gazing Grain—
We passed the Setting Sun—

Or rather—He passed Us—
The Dews drew quivering and chill—
For only Gossamer, my Gown—
My Tippet—only Tulle—

We paused before a House that seemed
A Swelling of the Ground—
The Roof was scarcely visible—
20   The Cornice—in the Ground—

Since then—'tis Centuries—and yet
Feels shorter than the Day
I first surmised the Horses' Heads
Were toward Eternity—

[A Narrow Fellow in the Grass]

A narrow Fellow in the Grass
Occasionally rides—
You may have met Him—did you not
His notice sudden is—

The Grass divides as with a Comb—
A spotted shaft is seen—
And then it closes at your feet
And opens further on—

He likes a Boggy Acre
10   A Floor too cool for Corn—
Yet when a Boy, and Barefoot—
I more than once at Noon

Have passed, I thought, a Whip lash
Unbraiding in the Sun
When stooping to secure it
It wrinkled, and was gone—

Several of Nature's People
I know, and they know me—
I feel for them a transport
20   Of cordiality—

But never met this Fellow
Attended, or alone
Without a tighter breathing
And Zero at the Bone—

GERARD MANLEY HOPKINS
1844–1889

Born in Stratford, Essex, the son of a London marine insurance adjuster,
Hopkins showed an early interest in poetry, winning a poetry prize at Highgate School in London. He then went on to Balliol College, Oxford, but at
this time, he wanted to become a painter. Caught up in the Oxford Movement, a revival of ritualistic Christianity, he converted to Catholicism in
1866. Two years later he joined the Jesuits, was ordained as a priest in 1877,
and served as a missionary in the squalid slums of Liverpool. He later took
a church at Oxford, and near the end of his life was professor of Greek at
University College, Dublin. While studying for the priesthood, Hopkins had
burned all his poetry, but in 1875, still struggling with the demands of his
faith and with his aesthetic interests, he began writing again, exploring this
struggle in his poetry. An intense observer of the natural world, Hopkins
saw patterns, which he called "inscapes," in natural phenomena, and his
poetry attempts to convey the complex unity of his sensual observation. Yet

his is primarily a poetry for the ear. Experimenting in prosody, he drew on rhythms of early English poetry, modeling his "sprung rhythm" on ordinary speech. Wrenching and straining syntax into original and startling forms, he presents us with an inspired vision of the beauty of nature infused with the glory of God.

God's Grandeur

The world is charged with the grandeur of God.
  It will flame out, like shining from shook foil;
  It gathers to a greatness, like the ooze of oil
Crushed. Why do men then now not reck his rod?
Generations have trod, have trod, have trod;
  And all is seared with trade; bleared, smeared with toil;
  And wears man's smudge and shares man's smell: the soil
Is bare now, nor can foot feel, being shod.

And for all this, nature is never spent;
  There lives the dearest freshness deep down things;
And though the last lights off the black West went
  Oh, morning, at the brown brink eastward, springs—
Because the Holy Ghost over the bent
  World broods with warm breast and with ah! bright wings.

The Windhover

To Christ Our Lord

I caught this morning morning's minion, king-
  dom of daylight's dauphin, dapple-dawn-drawn Falcon, in his riding
  Of the rolling level underneath him steady air, and striding
High there, how he rung upon the rein of a wimpling wing
In his ecstasy! then off, off forth on swing,
  As a skate's heel sweeps smooth on a bow-bend: the hurl and gliding
  Rebuffed the big wind. My heart in hiding
Stirred for a bird,—the achieve of, the mastery of the thing!

Brute beauty and valour and act, oh, air, pride, plume, here
  Buckle! AND the fire that breaks from thee then, a billion
Times told lovelier, more dangerous, O my chevalier!

  No wonder of it: shéer plód makes plough down sillion
Shine, and blue-bleak embers, ah my dear,
  Fall, gall themselves, and gash gold-vermilion.

Pied Beauty

Glory be to God for dappled things—
    For skies of couple-colour as a brinded cow;
      For rose-moles all in stipple upon trout that swim;
Fresh-firecoal chestnut-falls; finches' wings;
    Landscape plotted and pieced—fold, fallow, and plough;
      And áll trádes, their gear and tackle and trim.
All things counter, original, spare, strange;
    Whatever is fickle, freckled (who knows how?)
      With swift, slow; sweet, sour; adazzle, dim;
10 He fathers-forth whose beauty is past change:
                       Praise him.

Spring and Fall: To a Young Child

Márgarét, are you gríeving
Over Goldengrove unleaving?
Leáves, líke the things of man, you
With your fresh thoughts care for, can you?
Áh! ás the heart grows older
It will come to such sights colder
By and by, nor spare a sigh
Though worlds of wanwood leafmeal lie;
And yet you *will* weep and know why.
10 Now no matter, child, the name:
Sórrow's spríngs áre the same.
Nor mouth had, no nor mind, expressed
What heart heard of, ghost guessed:
It ís the blight man was born for,
It is Margaret you mourn for.

[Thou Art Indeed Just, Lord]

      Justus quidem tu es, Domine, si disputem tecum: verumtamen
      justa loquar ad te: Quare via impiorum prosperatur? &c.[1]

Thou are indeed just, Lord, if I contend
With thee; but, sir, so what I plead is just.
Why do sinners' ways prosper? and why must
Disappointment all I endeavor end?

1. Quoted from the Biblical prophet Jeremiah, and translated
   in the first three lines of the poem.

Wert thou my enemy, O thou my friend,
How wouldst thou worse, I wonder, than thou dost
Defeat, thwart me? Oh, the sots and thralls of lust
Do in spare hours more thrive than I that spend,

Sir, life upon thy cause. See, banks and brakes
10   Now, leavèd how thick! lacèd they are again
With fretty chervil, look, and fresh wind shakes

Them; birds build—but not I build; no, but strain,
Time's eunuch, and not breed one work that wakes.
Mine, O thou lord of life, send my roots rain.

A. E. HOUSMAN
1859–1936

He is a poet of deceptive simplicity, who presents a paradox in his life as
well as in his art. Alfred Edward Housman was born in the Shropshire border country he was to use as background for his poetry, and went on to
study classics and philosophy at Oxford, but flunked his final examinations.
After a boring ten-year stretch as a clerk in the British Patent Office, he
resumed his classical studies, becoming a great Latin scholar, and teaching
at University College London and then at Cambridge. Though he presented
himself as a very shy person, in his scholarly writing he was known for his
scathing criticism of inept or careless scholars. In his carefully modeled
poetry, he masked himself as well, expressing a negative philosophy of
doomed youth in brisk rhythms and deceptively simple language. Influenced by classical lyrics and the traditional English ballad, he sings of the
natural beauty of the countryside, but at the same time expresses the in-
humanity of nature. When A Shropshire Lad appeared in 1896, it was enthusiastically received and gained Housman an international reputation,
presumably from those who were believers in such philosophy as "Luck's a
chance, but trouble's sure,/ I'd face it as a wise man would,/ And train for ill
and not for good."

From **A Shropshire Lad**

2

Loveliest of trees, the cherry now
Is hung with bloom along the bough,
And stands about the woodland ride
Wearing white for Eastertide.

Now, of my threescore years and ten,
Twenty will not come again,
And take from seventy springs a score,
It only leaves me fifty more.

And since to look at things in bloom
10 Fifty springs are little room,
About the woodlands I will go
To see the cherry hung with snow.

13

When I was one-and-twenty
    I heard a wise man say,
"Give crowns and pounds and guineas
    But not your heart away;
Give pearls away and rubies
    But keep your fancy free."
But I was one-and-twenty,
    No use to talk to me.

When I was one-and-twenty
10   I heard him say again,
"The heart out of the bosom
    Was never given in vain;
'Tis paid with sighs a plenty
    And sold for endless rue."
And I am two-and-twenty,
    And oh, 'tis true, 'tis true.

19

To an Athlete Dying Young

The time you won your town the race
We chaired you through the market-place;
Man and boy stood cheering by,
And home we brought you shoulder-high.

To-day, the road all runners come,
Shoulder-high we bring you home,
And set you at your threshold down,
Townsman of a stiller town.

Smart lad, to slip betimes away
From fields where glory does not stay
And early though the laurel grows
It withers quicker than the rose.

Eyes the shady night has shut
Cannot see the record cut,
And silence sounds no worse than cheers
After earth has stopped the ears:

Now you will not swell the rout
Of lads that wore their honours out,
Runners whom renown outran
And the name died before the man.

So set, before its echoes fade,
The fleet foot on the sill of shade,
And hold to the low lintel up
The still-defended challenge-cup.

And round that early-laurelled head
Will flock to gaze the strengthless dead,
And find unwithered on its curls
The garland briefer than a girl's.

27

"Is my team ploughing,
    That I was used to drive
And hear the harness jingle
    When I was man alive?"

Ay, the horses trample,
    The harness jingles now;
No change though you lie under
    The land you used to plough.

"Is football playing
    Along the river shore,
With lads to chase the leather,
    Now I stand up no more?"

Ay, the ball is flying,
    The lads play heart and soul;

The goal stands up, the keeper
   Stands up to keep the goal.

"Is my girl happy,
   That I thought hard to leave,
And has she tired of weeping
20   As she lies down at eve?"

Ay, she lies down lightly,
   She lies not down to weep:
Your girl is well contented.
   Be still, my lad, and sleep.

"Is my friend hearty,
   Now I am thin and pine,
And has he found to sleep in
   A better bed than mine?"

Yes, lad, I lie easy,
30   I lie as lads would choose;
I cheer a dead man's sweetheart,
   Never ask me whose.

                62

   "Terence, this is stupid stuff:
You eat your victuals fast enough;
There can't be much amiss, 'tis clear,
To see the rate you drink your beer.
But oh, good Lord, the verse you make,
It gives a chap the belly-ache.
The cow, the old cow, she is dead;
It sleeps well, the horned head:
We poor lads, 'tis our turn now
10   To hear such tunes as killed the cow.
Pretty friendship 'tis to rhyme
Your friends to death before their time
Moping melancholy mad:
Come, pipe a tune to dance to, lad."

   Why, if 'tis dancing you would be,
There's brisker pipes than poetry.
Say, for what were hop-yards meant,
Or why was Burton built on Trent?

Oh many a peer of England brews
20 Livelier liquor than the Muse,
And malt does more than Milton can
To justify God's ways to man.
Ale, man, ale's the stuff to drink
For fellows whom it hurts to think:
Look into the pewter pot
To see the world as the world's not.
And faith, 'tis pleasant till 'tis past:
The mischief is that 'twill not last.
Oh I have been to Ludlow fair
30 And left my necktie God knows where,
And carried half-way home, or near,
Pints and quarts of Ludlow beer:
Then the world seemed none so bad,
And I myself a sterling lad;
And down in lovely muck I've lain,
Happy till I woke again.
Then I saw the morning sky:
Heigho, the tale was all a lie;
The world, it was the old world yet,
40 I was I, my things were wet,
And nothing now remained to do
But begin the game anew.

Therefore, since the world has still
Much good, but much less good than ill,
And while the sun and moon endure
Luck's a chance, but trouble's sure,
I'd face it as a wise man would,
And train for ill and not for good.
'Tis true the stuff I bring for sale
50 Is not so brisk a brew as ale:
Out of a stem that scored the hand
I wrung it in a weary land.
But take it: if the smack is sour,
The better for the embittered hour;
It should do good to heart and head
When your soul is in my soul's stead;
And I will friend you, if I may,
In the dark and cloudy day.

There was a king reigned in the East:
60 There, when kings will sit to feast,

They get their fill before they think
With poisoned meat and poisoned drink.
He gathered all that springs to birth
From the many-venomed earth;
First a little, thence to more,
He sampled all her killing store;
And easy, smiling, seasoned sound,
Sate the king when healths went round.
They put arsenic in his meat
70 And stared aghast to watch him eat;
They poured strychnine in his cup
And shook to see him drink it up:
They shook, they stared as white's their shirt:
Them it was their poison hurt.
—I tell the tale that I heard told.
Mithridates, he died old.

Eight O'Clock

He stood, and heard the steeple
　Sprinkle the quarters on the morning town.
One, two, three, four, to market-place and people
　It tossed them down.

Strapped, noosed, nighing his hour,
　He stood and counted them and cursed his luck;
And then the clock collected in the tower
　Its strength, and struck.

WILLIAM BUTLER YEATS
1865–1939

Yeats was born at Sandymount, near Dublin, Ireland. His father, John Butler
Yeats, was a well-known artist. Yeats was educated at schools in London and
Dublin, but was never an outstanding scholar. He went to art school, but
left after two years to devote himself to poetry. As a boy, he loved to roam
the countryside of County Sligo, listening to folk tales told around peat fires
and absorbing the "symbols, popular beliefs, and old scraps of verse that
made Ireland romantic to herself." His early poems are full of Irish mythology, with the poet striking a romantic pose and musically intoning in archaic
diction. Yeats grew out of this phase, influenced by the movement for Irish
nationalism, and he turned to actual events and real people to speak for

"the new Ireland, overwhelmed by responsibility, [which] begins to long for psychological truth." In 1899, with the help of Lady Gregory, herself a writer and promoter of Irish literature, he founded the Irish National Theater. He went on to become a public figure, serving from 1922–1928 as Senator of the Irish Free State, and he was at the same time achieving worldwide recognition as a great poet. In 1917, he married Georgie Hyde-Lees, who claimed to have powers as a spiritualist medium. She would fall into trances, and through automatic writing, she produced many of the symbols Yeats used in *A Vision*, a work which presents his theories of the cyclical patterns of history, human psychology, and the soul's migrations after death. After his death, he was buried as he requested in County Sligo near the mountain that had figured so much both in Irish legend and in Yeats's poetry: "Under bare Ben Bulben's head/ In Drumcliff churchyard Yeats is laid."

The Lake Isle of Innisfree

I will arise and go now, and go to Innisfree,
And a small cabin build there, of clay and wattles made:
Nine bean-rows will I have there, a hive for the honeybee,
And live alone in the bee-loud glade.

And I shall have some peace there, for peace comes dropping slow,
Dropping from the veils of the morning to where the cricket sings;
There midnight's all a glimmer, and noon a purple glow,
And evening full of the linnet's wings.

I will arise and go now, for always night and day
10   I hear lake water lapping with low sounds by the shore;
While I stand on the roadway, or on the pavements grey,
I hear it in the deep heart's core.

The Song of Wandering Aengus

I went out to the hazel wood,
Because a fire was in my head,
And cut and peeled a hazel wand,
And hooked a berry to a thread;
And when white moths were on the wing,
And moth-like stars were flickering out,
I dropped the berry in a stream
And caught a little silver trout.

When I had laid it on the floor
10 I went to blow the fire aflame,
But something rustled on the floor,
And some one called me by my name:
It had become a glimmering girl
With apple blossom in her hair
Who called me by my name and ran
And faded through the brightening air.

Though I am old with wandering
Through hollow lands and hilly lands,
I will find out where she has gone,
20 And kiss her lips and take her hands;
And walk among long dappled grass,
And pluck till time and times are done
The silver apples of the moon,
The golden apples of the sun.

The Wild Swans at Coole

The trees are in their autumn beauty,
The woodland paths are dry,
Under the October twilight the water
Mirrors a still sky;
Upon the brimming water among the stones
Are nine-and-fifty swans.

The nineteenth autumn has come upon me
Since I first made my count;
I saw, before I had well finished,
10 All suddenly mount
And scatter wheeling in great broken rings
Upon their clamorous wings.

I have looked upon those brilliant creatures,
And now my heart is sore.
All's changed since I, hearing at twilight,
The first time on this shore,
The bell-beat of their wings above my head,
Trod with a lighter tread.

Unwearied still, lover by lover,
20 They paddle in the cold
Companionable streams or climb the air;

Their hearts have not grown old;
Passion or conquest, wander where they will,
Attend upon them still.

But now they drift on the still water,
Mysterious, beautiful;
Among what rushes will they build,
By what lake's edge or pool
Delight men's eyes when I awake some day
30   To find they have flown away?

The Fisherman

Although I can see him still,
The freckled man who goes
To a grey place on a hill
In grey Connemara clothes
At dawn to cast his flies,
It's long since I began
To call up to the eyes
This wise and simple man.

All day I'd looked in the face
10   What I had hoped 'twould be
To write for my own race
And the reality;
The living men that I hate,
The dead man that I loved,
The craven man in his seat,
The insolent unreproved,
And no knave brought to book
Who has won a drunken cheer,
The witty man and his joke
20   Aimed at the commonest ear,
The clever man who cries
The catch-cries of the clown,
The beating down of the wise
And great Art beaten down.

Maybe a twelvemonth since
Suddenly I began,
In scorn of this audience,
Imagining a man,
And his sun-freckled face,

30   And grey Connemara cloth,
     Climbing up to a place
     Where stone is dark under froth,
     And the down-turn of his wrist
     When the flies drop in the stream;
     A man who does not exist,
     A man who is but a dream;
     And cried, "Before I am old
     I shall have written him one
     Poem maybe as cold
40   And passionate as the dawn."

Leda and the Swan[1]

A sudden blow: the great wings beating still
Above the staggering girl, her thighs caressed
By the dark webs, her nape caught in his bill
He holds her helpless breast upon his breast.

How can those terrified vague fingers push
The feathered glory from her loosening thighs?
And how can body, laid in that white rush,
But feel the strange heart beating where it lies?

A shudder in the loins engenders there
10   The broken wall, the burning roof and tower
And Agamemnon dead.
                              Being so caught up,
So mastered by the brute blood of the air,
Did she put on his knowledge with his power
Before the indifferent beak could let her drop?

1. Zeus, in the form of a swan, ravished Leda, who gave birth to Helen,
   whose desertion of her husband, King Menelaus, caused the Trojan War.
   Another offspring of this union, Clytemnestra, murdered her husband
   Agamemnon.

Sailing to Byzantium[1]

That is no country for old men. The young
In one another's arms, birds in the trees
—Those dying generations—at their song,
The salmon-falls, the mackerel-crowded seas,

1. Now Istanbul

Ancient City on the Bosporus; made the capital of the Roman Empire in 330 A.D.

Fish, flesh, or fowl, commend all summer long
Whatever is begotten, born, and dies.
Caught in that sensual music all neglect
Monuments of unaging intellect.

An aged man is but a paltry thing,
10   A tattered coat upon a stick, unless
Soul clap its hands and sing, and louder sing
For every tatter in its mortal dress,
Nor is there singing school but studying
Monuments of its own magnificence;
And therefore I have sailed the seas and come
To the holy city of Byzantium.

O sages standing in God's holy fire
As in the gold mosaic of a wall,
Come from the holy fire, perne in a gyre,[2]
20   And be the singing-masters of my soul.
Consume my heart away; sick with desire
And fastened to a dying animal
It knows not what it is; and gather me
Into the artifice of eternity.

Once out of nature I shall never take
My bodily form from any natural thing,
But such a form as Grecian goldsmiths make
Of hammered gold and gold enamelling
To keep a drowsy emperor awake;
30   Or set upon a golden bough to sing
To lords and ladies of Byzantium
Of what is past, or passing, or to come.

2. Revolve in a spiral

For Anne Gregory

"Never shall a young man,
Thrown into despair
By those great honey-coloured
Ramparts at your ear,
Love you for yourself alone
And not your yellow hair."

"But I can get a hair-dye
And set such colour there,
Brown, or black, or carrot,
That young men in despair
May love me for myself alone
And not my yellow hair."

"I heard an old religious man
But yesternight declare
That he had found a text to prove
That only God, my dear,
Could love you for yourself alone
And not your yellow hair."

After Long Silence

Speech after long silence; it is right,
All other lovers being estranged or dead,
Unfriendly lamplight hid under its shade,
The curtains drawn upon unfriendly night,
That we descant and yet again descant
Upon the supreme theme of Art and Song:
Bodily decrepitude is wisdom; young
We loved each other and were ignorant.

The Circus Animals' Desertion

I

I sought a theme and sought for it in vain,
I sought it daily for six weeks or so.
Maybe at last, being but a broken man,
I must be satisfied with my heart, although
Winter and summer till old age began
My circus animals[1] were all on show,

---

1. In the course of the poem, Yeats alludes to much of
   his previous work, especially his mythological
   and symbolic figures.

Those stilted boys, that burnished chariot,
Lion and woman and the Lord knows what.

II

What can I but enumerate old themes?
First that sea-rider Oisin led by the nose
Through three enchanted islands, allegorical dreams,
Vain gaiety, vain battle, vain repose,
Themes of the embittered heart, or so it seems,
That might adorn old songs or courtly shows;
But what cared I that set him on to ride,
I, starved for the bosom of his faery bride?

And then a counter-truth filled out its play,
The Countess Cathleen was the name I gave it;
She, pity-crazed, had given her soul away,
But masterful Heaven had intervened to save it.
I thought my dear must her own soul destroy,
So did fanaticism and hate enslave it,
And this brought forth a dream and soon enough
This dream itself had all my thought and love.

And when the Fool and Blind Man stole the bread
Cuchulain fought the ungovernable sea;
Heart-mysteries there, and yet when all is said
It was the dream itself enchanted me:
Character isolated by a deed
To engross the present and dominate memory.
Players and painted stage took all my love,
And not those things that they were emblems of.

III

Those masterful images because complete
Grew in pure mind, but out of what began?
A mound of refuse or the sweeping of a street,
Old kettles, old bottles, and a broken can,
Old iron, old bones, old rags, that raving slut
Who keeps the till. Now that my ladder's gone,
I must lie down where all the ladders start,
In the foul rag-and-bone shop of the heart.

EDWIN ARLINGTON ROBINSON

1869–1935

The youngest of three sons, Robinson was born in Head Tide, Maine, to a well-to-do family. His father, who had made his fortune buying and selling timber and keeping a store, moved the family to Gardiner, Maine, then a bustling mill town, because he wanted better schooling for his children. After finishing high school, Robinson was not allowed to go to college. He joined a small poetry circle consisting of a homeopathic physician, a judge, and Robinson's former high school English teacher. They encouraged his writing, and when Robinson finally convinced his father to send him to Harvard, he returned after two years to follow the only career he wanted: being a poet. He used the town of Gardiner and its people as subjects for his poetry, which at first was appreciated by only a very small audience. However, the quiet, laconic Robinson continued to write, supporting himself with such employment as time checker on the New York subway construction. After his poetry came to the attention of President Theodore Roosevelt, he was given a position in the New York Customs Office. Robinson was a loner who never married, and even when he became well known, refused to seek popularity through poetry readings. "People are rather interesting after all, if you don't have to talk with them," was his attitude. His *Collected Poems* won the Pulitzer Prize in 1921, bringing him both recognition and financial security. Though he won the Pulitzer twice more, he kept to the same quiet life, writing his clear, quiet but powerful poetry in solitude.

Richard Cory

Whenever Richard Cory went down town,
We people on the pavement looked at him:
He was a gentleman from sole to crown,
Clean favored, and imperially slim.

And he was always quietly arrayed,
And he was always human when he talked;
But still he fluttered pulses when he said,
"Good-morning," and he glittered when he walked.

And he was rich—yes, richer than a king—
10 And admirably schooled in every grace:
In fine, we thought that he was everything
To make us wish that we were in his place.

So on we worked, and waited for the light,
And went without the meat, and cursed the bread;
And Richard Cory, one calm summer night,
Went home and put a bullet through his head.

The Pity of the Leaves

Vengeful across the cold November moors,
Loud with ancestral shame there came the bleak
Sad wind that shrieked, and answered with a shriek,
Reverberant through lonely corridors.

The old man heard it; and he heard, perforce,
Words out of lips that were no more to speak—
Words of the past that shook the old man's cheek
Like dead, remembered footsteps on old floors.

And then there were the leaves that plagued him so!
10   The brown, thin leaves that on the stones outside
Skipped with a freezing whisper. Now and then
They stopped, and stayed there—just to let him know
How dead they were, but if the old man cried,
They fluttered off like withered souls of men.

Eros Turannos[1]

She fears him, and will always ask
    What fated her to choose him;
She meets in his engaging mask
    All reasons to refuse him;
But what she meets and what she fears
Are less than are the downward years,
Drawn slowly to the foamless weirs
    Of age, were she to lose him.

Between a blurred sagacity
10   That once had power to sound him,
And Love, that will not let him be
    The Judas that she found him,
Her pride assuages her almost,
As if it were alone the cost.—

1. Love, the tyrant.

He sees that he will not be lost,
   And waits and looks around him.

A sense of ocean and old trees
   Envelops and allures him;
Tradition, touching all he sees,
20   Beguiles and reassures him;
And all her doubts of what he says
Are dimmed with what she knows of days—
Till even prejudice delays
   And fades, and she secures him.

The falling leaf inaugurates
   The reign of her confusion;
The pounding wave reverberates
   The dirge of her illusion;
And home, where passion lived and died,
30 Becomes a place where she can hide,
While all the town and harbor side
   Vibrate with her seclusion.

We tell you, tapping on our brows,
   The story as it should be,—
As if the story of a house
   Were told, or ever could be;
We'll have no kindly veil between
Her visions and those we have seen,—
As if we guessed what hers have been,
40   Or what they are or would be.

Meanwhile we do no harm; for they
   That with a god have striven,
Not hearing much of what we say,
   Take what the god has given;
Though like waves breaking it may be
Or like a changed familiar tree,
Or like a stairway to the sea
   Where down the blind are driven.

Mr. Flood's Party

Old Eben Flood, climbing alone one night
Over the hill between the town below
And the forsaken upland hermitage

That held as much as he should ever know
On earth again of home, paused warily.
The road was his with not a native near;
And Eben, having leisure, said aloud,
For no man else in Tilbury Town to hear:

"Well, Mr. Flood, we have the harvest moon
10   Again, and we may not have many more;
The bird is on the wing, the poet says,
And you and I have said it here before.
Drink to the bird." He raised up to the light
The jug that he had gone so far to fill,
And answered huskily: "Well, Mr. Flood,
Since you propose it, I believe I will."

Alone, as if enduring to the end
A valiant armor of scarred hopes outworn,
He stood there in the middle of the road
20   Like Roland's ghost winding a silent horn.
Below him, in the town among the trees,
Where friends of other days had honored him,
A phantom salutation of the dead
Rang thinly till old Eben's eyes were dim.

Then, as a mother lays her sleeping child
Down tenderly, fearing it may awake,
He set the jug down slowly at his feet
With trembling care, knowing that most things break;
And only when assured that on firm earth
30   It stood, as the uncertain lives of men
Assuredly did not, he paced away,
And with his hand extended paused again:

"Well, Mr. Flood, we have not met like this
In a long time; and many a change has come
To both of us, I fear, since last it was
We had a drop together. Welcome home!"
Convivially returning with himself,
Again he raised the jug up to the light;
And with an acquiescent quaver said:
40   "Well, Mr. Flood, if you insist, I might.

"Only a very little, Mr. Flood—
For auld lang syne. No more, sir; that will do."
So, for the time, apparently it did,

And Eben evidently thought so too;
For soon amid the silver loneliness
Of night he lifted up his voice and sang,
Secure, with only two moons listening,
Until the whole harmonious landscape rang—

"For auld lang syne." The weary throat gave out,
50   The last word wavered, and the song was done.
He raised again the jug regretfully
And shook his head, and was again alone.
There was not much that was ahead of him,
And there was nothing in the town below—
Where strangers would have shut the many doors
That many friends had opened long ago.

ROBERT FROST

1874–1963

Robert Frost was born in San Francisco where his father was a journalist and an aspiring politician. Frost's mother wrote poetry and introduced her son to Scottish poetry and to such poets as Wordsworth, Bryant, and Emerson, whose use of nature in their work undoubtedly influenced Frost. After his father died, the family moved to New England, where Frost's mother taught school. After graduating from high school in Lawrence, Massachusetts, where he was class poet and where he shared the post of valedictorian with Elinor White, whom he later married, Frost attended Dartmouth and Harvard. He did not graduate, but returned home to marry Elinor. They moved to a farm in Derry, New Hampshire, where Frost taught school, wrote poetry, and tried to run a farm. These were years of hardship for the growing family, and discouraged by his inability to interest American publishers in his poetry, Frost sold the farm and the family moved to England. Shortly after his arrival, his first collection of poetry, A Boy's Will, was accepted for publication; North of Boston followed soon after. Frost met Ezra Pound, who introduced Frost's poetry to American publishers, and three years later, when the family returned because of the outbreak of World War I, Frost had achieved recognition as a major poetic talent. He has always had a wide audience of readers; there are those who read him as a New England nature poet who extols the values of rural America and its work ethic, and those who read him as one who sees nature as other, as a sometimes barren landscape against which human dramas are played out, as they so effectively are in Frost's dramatic narratives. Frost described poetry as "a momentary stay against confusion," but he also said: "The figure a poem makes. It begins in delight and ends in wisdom. The figure is the same as for love."

Mending Wall

Something there is that doesn't love a wall,
That sends the frozen-ground-swell under it
And spills the upper boulders in the sun,
And makes gaps even two can pass abreast.
The work of hunters is another thing:
I have come after them and made repair
Where they have left not one stone on a stone,
But they would have the rabbit out of hiding,
To please the yelping dogs. The gaps I mean,
No one has seen them made or heard them made,
But at spring mending-time we find them there.
I let my neighbor know beyond the hill;
And on a day we meet to walk the line
And set the wall between us once again.
We keep the wall between us as we go.
To each the boulders that have fallen to each.
And some are loaves and some so nearly balls
We have to use a spell to make them balance:
'Stay where you are until our backs are turned!'
We wear our fingers rough with handling them.
Oh, just another kind of outdoor game,
One on a side. It comes to little more:
There where it is we do not need the wall:
He is all pine and I am apple orchard.
My apple trees will never get across
And eat the cones under his pines, I tell him.
He only says, 'Good fences make good neighbors.'
Spring is the mischief in me, and I wonder
If I could put a notion in his head:
'Why do they make good neighbors? Isn't it
Where there are cows? But here there are no cows.
Before I built a wall I'd ask to know
What I was walling in or walling out,
And to whom I was like to give offense.
Something there is that doesn't love a wall,
That wants it down.' I could say 'Elves' to him,
But it's not elves exactly, and I'd rather
He said it for himself. I see him there

Bringing a stone grasped firmly by the top
40   In each hand, like an old-stone savage armed.
He moves in darkness as it seems to me,
Not of woods only and the shade of trees.
He will not go behind his father's saying,
And he likes having thought of it so well
He says again, 'Good fences make good neighbors.'

After Apple-picking

My long two-pointed ladder's sticking through a tree
Toward heaven still,
And there's a barrel that I didn't fill
Beside it, and there may be two or three
Apples I didn't pick upon some bough.
But I am done with apple-picking now.
Essence of winter sleep is on the night,
The scent of apples: I am drowsing off.
I cannot rub the strangeness from my sight
10   I got from looking through a pane of glass
I skimmed this morning from the drinking trough
And held against the world of hoary grass.
It melted, and I let it fall and break.
But I was well
Upon my way to sleep before it fell,
And I could tell
What form my dreaming was about to take.
Magnified apples appear and disappear,
Stem end and blossom end,
20   And every fleck of russet showing clear.
My instep arch not only keeps the ache,
It keeps the pressure of a ladder-round.
I feel the ladder sway as the boughs bend.
And I keep hearing from the cellar bin
The rumbling sound
Of load on load of apples coming in.
For I have had too much
Of apple-picking: I am overtired
Of the great harvest I myself desired.
30   There were ten thousand thousand fruit to touch,
Cherish in hand, lift down, and not let fall.
For all
That struck the earth,
No matter if not bruised or spiked with stubble,

Went surely to the cider-apple heap
As of no worth.
One can see what will trouble
This sleep of mine, whatever sleep it is.
Were he not gone,
40 The woodchuck could say whether it's like his
Long sleep, as I describe its coming on,
Or just some human sleep.

Stopping by Woods on a Snowy Evening

Whose woods these are I think I know.
His house is in the village, though;
He will not see me stopping here
To watch his woods fill up with snow.

My little horse must think it queer
To stop without a farmhouse near
Between the woods and frozen lake
The darkest evening of the year.
He gives his harness bells a shake
10 To ask if there is some mistake.
The only other sound's the sweep
Of easy wind and downy flake.

The woods are lovely, dark, and deep,
But I have promises to keep,
And miles to go before I sleep,
And miles to go before I sleep.

Two Tramps in Mud Time

Out of the mud two strangers came
And caught me splitting wood in the yard.
And one of them put me off my aim
By hailing cheerily "Hit them hard!"
I knew pretty well why he dropped behind
And let the other go on a way.
I knew pretty well what he had in mind:
He wanted to take my job for pay.

Good blocks of oak it was I split,
10 As large around as the chopping block;

And every piece I squarely hit
Fell splinterless as a cloven rock.
The blows that a life of self-control
Spares to strike for the common good,
That day, giving a loose to my soul,
I spent on the unimportant wood.

The sun was warm but the wind was chill.
You know how it is with an April day
When the sun is out and the wind is still,
20   You're one month on in the middle of May.
But if you so much as dare to speak,
A cloud comes over the sunlit arch,
A wind comes off a frozen peak,
And you're two months back in the middle of March.

A bluebird comes tenderly up to alight
And turns to the wind to unruffle a plume,
His song so pitched as not to excite
A single flower as yet to bloom.
It is snowing a flake: and he half knew
30   Winter was only playing possum.
Except in color he isn't blue,
But he wouldn't advise a thing to blossom.

The water for which we may have to look
In summertime with a witching wand,
In every wheelrut's now a brook,
In every print of a hoof a pond.
Be glad of water, but don't forget
The lurking frost in the earth beneath
That will steal forth after the sun is set
40   And show on the water its crystal teeth.

The time when most I loved my task
These two must make me love it more
By coming with what they came to ask.
You'd think I never had felt before
The weight of an ax-head poised aloft,
The grip on earth of outspread feet,
The life of muscles rocking soft
And smooth and moist in vernal heat.

Out of the woods two hulking tramps
50   (From sleeping God knows where last night,

But not long since in the lumber camps).
They thought all chopping was theirs of right.
Men of the woods and lumberjacks,
They judged me by their appropriate tool.
Except as a fellow handled an ax,
They had no way of knowing a fool.

Nothing on either side was said.
They knew they had but to stay their stay
And all their logic would fill my head:
60   As that I had no right to play
With what was another man's work for gain.
My right might be love but theirs was need.
And where the two exist in twain
Theirs was the better right—agreed.

But yield who will to their separation,
My object in living is to unite
My avocation and my vocation
As my two eyes make one in sight.
Only where love and need are one,
70   And the work is play for mortal stakes,
Is the deed ever really done
For Heaven and the future's sakes.

Design

I found a dimpled spider, fat and white,
On a white heal-all, holding up a moth
Like a white piece of rigid satin cloth—
Assorted characters of death and blight
Mixed ready to begin the morning right,
Like the ingredients of a witches' broth—
A snow-drop spider, a flower like a froth,
And dead wings carried like a paper kite.

What had that flower to do with being white,
10   The wayside blue and innocent heal-all?
What brought the kindred spider to that height,
Then steered the white moth thither in the night?
What but design of darkness to appall?—
If design govern in a thing so small.

Provide, Provide

The witch that came (the withered hag)
To wash the steps with pail and rag,
Was once the beauty Abishag,[1]

The picture pride of Hollywood.
Too many fall from great and good
For you to doubt the likelihood.

Die early and avoid the fate.
Or if predestined to die late,
Make up your mind to die in state.

10   Make the whole stock exchange your own!
If need be occupy a throne,
Where nobody can call *you* crone.

Some have relied on what they knew;
Others on simply being true.
What worked for them might work for you.

No memory of having starred
Atones for later disregard,
Or keeps the end from being hard.

Better to go down dignified
20   With boughten friendship at your side
Than none at all. Provide, provide!

1. Biblical beauty brought in to warm dying King David

The Silken Tent

She is as in a field a silken tent
At midday when a sunny summer breeze
Has dried the dew and all its ropes relent,
So that in guys it gently sways at ease,
And its supporting central cedar pole,
That is its pinnacle to heavenward
And signifies the sureness of the soul,
Seems to owe naught to any single cord,
But strictly held by none, is loosely bound
10   By countless silken ties of love and thought

To everything on earth the compass round,
And only by one's going slightly taut
In the capriciousness of summer air
Is of the slightest bondage made aware.

WALLACE STEVENS
1879–1955

Stevens was born in Reading, Pennsylvania, where his father was an attorney and a schoolteacher with an interest in poetry. After graduating from high school, Stevens attended Harvard for three years as a special student. He was writing poetry at this time, some of which was published in the Harvard *Advocate*, and when he left Harvard, his intention was to pursue a literary career in New York City. He became a reporter for the *Herald Tribune*, but didn't like this job, so he entered law school, was admitted to the bar, but was unsuccessful in private practice. He then joined the legal staff of a bonding company, and feeling himself sufficiently settled, he married Elsie Moll, a young woman from his home town. Seven years later, he joined the Hartford Accident and Insurance Company and in 1916 moved to Hartford, Connecticut, where he lived the rest of his life. Stevens wrote his poetry during his spare time, and though he had some literary friends such as William Carlos Williams and Marianne Moore, his business activities kept him at some remove from literary circles. *Harmonium*, his first volume of poems, appeared in 1923, and though Stevens began to acquire a reputation as one of the outstanding poets of the twentieth century, his coworkers at the insurance company were not aware of this until he won the Bollingen Prize in 1950. This was partly because of Stevens's natural reticence about himself, and partly because he doubtless felt they would not understand. Certainly, it is difficult to reconcile the pragmatics of Stevens's business activities with the gaiety of language and the celebration of the imagination in his poetry.

Sunday Morning

I

Complacencies of the peignoir, and late
Coffee and oranges in a sunny chair,
And the green freedom of a cockatoo
Upon a rug mingle to dissipate
The holy hush of ancient sacrifice.
She dreams a little, and she feels the dark
Encroachment of that old catastrophe,

As a calm darkens among water-lights.
The pungent oranges and bright, green wings
10 Seem things in some procession of the dead,
Winding across wide water, without sound.
The day is like wide water, without sound,
Stilled for the passing of her dreaming feet
Over the seas, to silent Palestine,
Dominion of the blood and sepulchre.

                    II

Why should she give her bounty to the dead?
What is divinity if it can come
Only in silent shadows and in dreams?
Shall she not find in comforts of the sun,
20 In pungent fruit and bright, green wings, or else
In any balm or beauty of the earth,
Things to be cherished like the thought of heaven?
Divinity must live within herself:
Passions of rain, or moods in falling snow;
Grievings in loneliness, or unsubdued
Elations when the forest blooms; gusty
Emotions on wet roads on autumn nights;
All pleasures and all pains, remembering
The bough of summer and the winter branch.
30 These are the measures destined for her soul.

                    III

Jove in the clouds had his inhuman birth.
No mother suckled him, no sweet land gave
Large-mannered motions to his mythy mind.
He moved among us, as a muttering king,
Magnificent, would move among his hinds,
Until our blood, commingling, virginal,
With heaven, brought such requital to desire
The very hinds discerned it, in a star.
Shall our blood fail? Or shall it come to be
40 The blood of paradise? And shall the earth
Seem all of paradise that we shall know?
The sky will be much friendlier then than now,
A part of labor and a part of pain,
And next in glory to enduring love,
Not this dividing and indifferent blue.

IV

She says, "I am content when wakened birds,
Before they fly, test the reality
Of misty fields, by their sweet questionings;
But when the birds are gone, and their warm fields
50 Return no more, where, then, is paradise?"
There is not any haunt of prophecy,
Nor any old chimera of the grave,
Neither the golden underground, nor isle
Melodious, where spirits gat them home,
Nor visionary south, nor cloudy palm
Remote on heaven's hill, that has endured
As April's green endures; or will endure
Like her remembrance of awakened birds,
Or her desire for June and evening, tipped
60 By the consummation of the swallow's wings.

V

She says, "But in contentment I still feel
The need of some imperishable bliss."
Death is the mother of beauty; hence from her,
Alone, shall come fulfilment to our dreams
And our desires. Although she strews the leaves
Of sure obliteration on our paths,
The path sick sorrow took, the many paths
Where triumph rang its brassy phrase, or love
Whispered a little out of tenderness,
70 She makes the willow shiver in the sun
For maidens who were wont to sit and gaze
Upon the grass, relinquished to their feet.
She causes boys to pile new plums and pears
On disregarded plate. The maidens taste
And stray impassioned in the littering leaves.

VI

Is there no change of death in paradise?
Does ripe fruit never fall? Or do the boughs
Hang always heavy in that perfect sky,
Unchanging, yet so like our perishing earth,
80 With rivers like our own that seek for seas
They never find, the same receding shores

That never touch with inarticulate pang?
Why set the pear upon those river-banks
Or spice the shores with odors of the plum?
Alas, that they should wear out colors there,
The silken weavings of our afternoons,
And pick the strings of our insipid lutes!
Death is the mother of beauty, mystical,
Within whose burning bosom we devise
90 Our earthly mothers waiting, sleeplessly.

VII

Supple and turbulent, a ring of men
Shall chant in orgy on a summer morn
Their boisterous devotion to the sun,
Not as a god, but as a god might be,
Naked among them, like a savage source.
Their chant shall be a chant of paradise,
Out of their blood, returning to the sky;
And in their chant shall enter, voice by voice,
The windy lake wherein their lord delights,
100 The trees, like serafin, and echoing hills,
That choir among themselves long afterward.
They shall know well the heavenly fellowship
Of men that perish and of summer morn.
And whence they came and whither they shall go
The dew upon their feet shall manifest.

VIII

She hears, upon that water without sound,
A voice that cries, "The tomb in Palestine
Is not the porch of spirits lingering.
It is the grave of Jesus, where he lay."
110 We live in an old chaos of the sun,
Or old dependency of day and night,
Or island solitude, unsponsored, free,
Of that wide water, inescapable.
Deer walk upon our mountains, and the quail
Whistle about us their spontaneous cries;
Sweet berries ripen in the wilderness;
And, in the isolation of the sky,
At evening, casual flocks of pigeons make
Ambiguous undulations as they sink,
120 Downward to darkness, on extended wings.

Anecdote of the Jar

I placed a jar in Tennessee,
And round it was, upon a hill.
It made the slovenly wilderness
Surround that hill.

The wilderness rose up to it,
And sprawled around, no longer wild.
The jar was round upon the ground
And tall and of a port in air.

It took dominion everywhere.
The jar was gray and bare.
It did not give of bird or bush,
Like nothing else in Tennessee.

Thirteen Ways of Looking at a Blackbird

I
Among twenty snowy mountains,
The only moving thing
Was the eye of the blackbird.

II
I was of three minds,
Like a tree
In which there are three blackbirds.

III
The blackbird whirled in the autumn winds.
It was a small part of the pantomime.

IV
A man and a woman
Are one.
A man and a woman and a blackbird
Are one.

V
I do not know which to prefer,
The beauty of inflections

Or the beauty of innuendoes,
The blackbird whistling
Or just after.

VI

Icicles filled the long window
With barbaric glass.
The shadow of the blackbird
Crossed it, to and fro.
The mood
Traced in the shadow
An indecipherable cause.

VII

O thin men of Haddam,
Why do you imagine golden birds?
Do you not see how the blackbird
Walks around the feet
Of the women about you?

VIII

I know noble accents
And lucid, inescapable rhythms;
But I know, too,
That the blackbird is involved
In what I know.

IX

When the blackbird flew out of sight,
It marked the edge
Of one of many circles.

X

At the sight of blackbirds
Flying in a green light,
Even the bawds of euphony
Would cry out sharply.

XI

He rode over Connecticut
In a glass coach.
Once, a fear pierced him,

In that he mistook
The shadow of his equipage
For blackbirds.

XII

The river is moving.
The blackbird must be flying.

XIII

50 It was evening all afternoon.
It was snowing
And it was going to snow.
The blackbird sat
In the cedar-limbs.

The Snow Man

One must have a mind of winter
To regard the frost and the boughs
Of the pine-trees crusted with snow;

And have been cold a long time
To behold the junipers shagged with ice,
The spruces rough in the distant glitter

Of the January sun; and not to think
Of any misery in the sound of the wind,
In the sound of a few leaves,

10 Which is the sound of the land
Full of the same wind
That is blowing in the same bare place

For the listener, who listens in the snow,
And, nothing himself, beholds
Nothing that is not there and the nothing that is.

A High-Toned Old Christian Woman

Poetry is the supreme fiction, madame.
Take the moral law and make a nave of it
And from the nave build haunted heaven. Thus,

The conscience is converted into palms,
Like windy citherns hankering for hymns.
We agree in principle. That's clear. But take
The opposing law and make a peristyle,
And from the peristyle project a masque
Beyond the planets. Thus, our bawdiness,
10   Unpurged by epitaph, indulged at last,
Is equally converted into palms,
Squiggling like saxophones. And palm for palm,
Madame, we are where we began. Allow,
Therefore, that in the planetary scene
Your disaffected flagellants, well-stuffed,
Smacking their muzzy bellies in parade,
Proud of such novelties of the sublime,
Such tink and tank and tunk-a-tunk-tunk,
May, merely may, madame, whip from themselves
20   A jovial hullabaloo among the spheres.
This will make widows wince. But fictive things
Wink as they will. Wink most when widows wince.

Of Modern Poetry

The poem of the mind in the act of finding
What will suffice. It has not always had
To find: the scene was set; it repeated what
Was in the script.
             Then the theatre was changed
To something else. Its past was a souvenir.
It has to be living, to learn the speech of the place.
It has to face the men of the time and to meet
The women of the time. It has to think about war
And it has to find what will suffice. It has
10   To construct a new stage. It has to be on that stage
And, like an insatiable actor, slowly and
With meditation, speak words that in the ear,
In the delicatest ear of the mind, repeat,
Exactly, that which it wants to hear, at the sound
Of which, an invisible audience listens,
Not to the play, but to itself, expressed
In an emotion as of two people, as of two
Emotions becoming one. The actor is
A metaphysician in the dark, twanging

20 An instrument, twanging a wiry string that gives
Sounds passing through sudden rightness, wholly
Containing the mind, below which it cannot descend,
Beyond which it has no will to rise.
                              It must
Be the finding of a satisfaction, and may
Be of a man skating, a woman dancing, a woman
Combing. The poem of the act of the mind.

Of Mere Being

The palm at the end of the mind,
Beyond the last thought, rises
In the bronze decor,

A gold-feathered bird
Sings in the palm, without human meaning,
Without human feeling, a foreign song.

You know then that it is not the reason
That makes us happy or unhappy.
The bird sings. Its feathers shine.

10 The palm stands on the edge of space.
The wind moves slowly in the branches.
The bird's fire-fangled feathers dangle down.

WILLIAM CARLOS WILLIAMS

1883–1963

Born in Rutherford, New Jersey to an English father and a Puerto Rican
mother, Williams attended preparatory schools in Switzerland and Paris,
and after graduating from Horace Mann High School in New York went to
medical school at the University of Pennsylvania. There he was friendly with
poets Ezra Pound and Hilda Doolittle and met painter Charles Demuth, with
whom he shared a keen interest in modernist painting, over a dish of
prunes in a Philadelphia boarding house. Williams did further pediatric
study in Leipzig, Germany, and in 1912 he married and began his medical
practice in Rutherford, a practice in which he was fully active until he suffered a stroke in 1952. Williams wrote his poetry at night and between
professional appointments, for while he was "determined to be a poet," he

was convinced that "only medicine, a job I enjoyed, would make it possible for me to live and write as I wanted to." And write he did: in addition to numerous volumes of poetry, he published short stories, essays, novels, and an autobiography. Energetic and feisty, he railed against T. S. Eliot's poetry of literary allusion, stressing that American poets should break with traditional conventions and use the diction and rhythms of American speech. Like Whitman, he celebrated the "vitality of the body" as he saw and felt it in his everyday life as a physician. His most ambitious work, *Paterson*, is an epic giving metaphoric expression to an American city and its people, past and present. *Paterson* also presented new poetic forms which have greatly influenced other American poets.

The Widow's Lament in Springtime

Sorrow is my own yard
where the new grass
flames as it has flamed
often before but not
with the cold fire
that closes round me this year.
Thirtyfive years
I lived with my husband.
The plumtree is white today
10   with masses of flowers.
Masses of flowers
load the cherry branches
and color some bushes
yellow and some red
but the grief in my heart
is stronger than they
for though they were my joy
formerly, today I notice them
and turned away forgetting.
20   Today my son told me
that in the meadows,
at the edge of the heavy woods
in the distance, he saw
trees of white flowers.
I feel that I would like
to go there
and fall into those flowers
and sink into the marsh near them.

Spring and All

By the road to the contagious hospital
under the surge of the blue
mottled clouds driven from the
northeast—a cold wind. Beyond, the
waste of broad, muddy fields
brown with dried weeds, standing and fallen

patches of standing water
the scattering of tall trees

All along the road the reddish
10 purplish, forked, upstanding, twiggy
stuff of bushes and small trees
with dead, brown leaves under them
leafless vines—

Lifeless in appearance, sluggish
dazed spring approaches—

They enter the new world naked,
cold, uncertain of all
save that they enter. All about them
the cold, familiar wind—

20 Now the grass, tomorrow
the stiff curl of wildcarrot leaf
One by one objects are defined—
It quickens: clarity, outline of leaf

But now the stark dignity of
entrance—Still, the profound change
has come upon them: rooted, they
grip down and begin to awaken

Nantucket

Flowers through the window
lavender and yellow

changed by white curtains—
Smell of cleanliness—

Sunshine of late afternoon—
On the glass tray

a glass pitcher, the tumbler
turned down, by which

a key is lying—And the
10   immaculate white bed

This Is Just to Say

I have eaten
the plums
that were in
the icebox

and which
you were probably
saving
for breakfast

Forgive me
10   they were delicious
so sweet
and so cold

Flowers by the Sea

When over the flowery, sharp pasture's
edge, unseen, the salt ocean

lifts its form—chicory and daisies
tied, released, seem hardly flowers alone

but color and the movement—or the shape
perhaps—of restlessness, whereas

the sea is circled and sways
peacefully upon its plantlike stem

The Yachts

contend in a sea which the land partly encloses
shielding them from the too-heavy blows
of an ungoverned ocean which when it chooses

tortures the biggest hulls, the best man knows
to pit against its beatings, and sinks them pitilessly.
Mothlike in mists, scintillant in the minute

brilliance of cloudless days, with broad bellying sails
they glide to the wind tossing green water
from their sharp prows while over them the crew crawls

10   ant-like, solicitously grooming them, releasing,
making fast as they turn, lean far over and having
caught the wind again, side by side, head for the mark.

In a well guarded arena of open water surrounded by
lesser and greater craft which, sycophant, lumbering
and flittering follow them, they appear youthful, rare

as the light of a happy eye, live with the grace
of all that in the mind is fleckless, free and
naturally to be desired. Now the sea which holds them

is moody, lapping their glossy sides, as if feeling
20   for some slightest flaw but fails completely.
Today no race. Then the wind comes again. The yachts

move, jockeying for a start, the signal is set and they
are off. Now the waves strike at them but they are too
well made, they slip through, though they take in canvas.

Arms with hands grasping seek to clutch at the prows.
Bodies thrown recklessly in the way are cut aside.
It is a sea of faces about them in agony, in despair

until the horror of the race dawns staggering the mind,
the whole sea become an entanglement of watery bodies
30   lost to the world bearing what they cannot hold. Broken,

beaten, desolate, reaching from the dead to be taken up
they cry out, failing, failing! their cries rising
in waves still as the skillful yachts pass over.

The Last Words of My English Grandmother

There were some dirty plates
and a glass of milk
beside her on a small table
near the rank, disheveled bed—

Wrinkled and nearly blind
she lay and snored
rousing with anger in her tones
to cry for food,

10   Gimme something to eat—
They're starving me—
I'm all right I won't go
to the hospital. No, no, no

Give me something to eat
Let me take you
to the hospital, I said
and after you are well

you can do as you please.
She smiled, Yes
you do what you please first
20   then I can do what I please—

Oh, oh, oh! she cried
as the ambulance men lifted
her to the stretcher—
Is this what you call

making me comfortable?
By now her mind was clear—
Oh you think you're smart
you young people,

she said, but I'll tell you
30   you don't know anything.
Then we started.
On the way

we passed a long row
of elms. She looked at them
awhile out of
the ambulance window and said,

What are all those
fuzzy-looking things out there?
Trees? Well, I'm tired
40   of them and rolled her head away.

Landscape with the Fall of Icarus[1]

According to Brueghel
when Icarus fell
it was spring

a farmer was ploughing
his field
the whole pageantry

of the year was
awake tingling
near

10   the edge of the sea
concerned
with itself

sweating in the sun
that melted
the wings' wax

unsignificantly
off the coast
there was

a splash quite unnoticed
20   this was
Icarus drowning

1. Second poem from a series based on the paintings
   of the Flemish artist Pieter Brueghel. This painting
   shows the mythical youth Icarus, son of Daedalus,
   falling into the sea after the wings made for him by
   his father had melted. W. H. Auden has also based a
   poem on this painting.

MARIANNE MOORE
1887–1972

She was born in Kirkwood, Missouri, to a very devout Presbyterian family. Her father abandoned the family after he had suffered a mental breakdown and the collapse of his business. She and her mother moved to Carlisle, Pennsylvania, and Moore attended Metzger Institute, where her mother taught. She went on to Bryn Mawr College, and though she was getting better grades in biology than in literature, she was trying to write poetry. After her graduation in 1909, she taught at the U.S. Indian School in Carlisle, and starting in 1915, her poetry began to be accepted by literary journals. The Moores were a very close family, and when her brother, a Presbyterian minister, took a position in Brooklyn, she and her mother joined him. Moore worked as a tutor and secretary in a girls' school, and as an assistant in a branch library. She was at this time enjoying the company of artists and writers, as well as writing and publishing her poetry. She was editor of *The Dial*, a literary magazine, for three years. After that, she concentrated solely on her writing. In later years, Moore was renowned as probably the most literate baseball fan the Brooklyn Dodgers ever had.

Poetry

I, too, dislike it: there are things that are important beyond
      all this fiddle.
  Reading it, however, with a perfect contempt for it, one
      discovers in
it after all, a place for the genuine.
    Hands that can grasp, eyes
    that can dilate, hair that can rise
      if it must, these things are important not because a

high-sounding interpretation can be put upon them but
      because they are
  useful. When they become so derivative as to become
      unintelligible,
the same thing may be said for all of us, that we
    do not admire what
    we cannot understand: the bat
      holding on upside down or in quest of something to

eat, elephants pushing, a wild horse taking a roll, a tireless
      wolf under
  a tree, the immovable critic twitching his skin like a

horse that feels a flea, the baseball fan, the statistician—
    nor is it valid
        to discriminate against 'business documents and

school-books';[1] all these phenomena are important. One
        must make a distinction
however: when dragged into prominence by half poets,
        the result is not poetry,
20   nor till the poets among us can be
        'literalists of
        the imagination'[2]—above
           insolence and triviality and can present

for inspection, imaginary gardens with real toads in them,
        shall we have
it. In the meantime, if you demand on the one hand,
the raw material of poetry in
        all its rawness and
        that which is on the other hand
           genuine, then you are interested in poetry.

1. Tolstoy in his *Diary* writes: "Where the boundary between prose and
poetry lies, I shall never be able to understand. . . . Poetry is verse:
prose is not verse. Or else poetry is everything with the exception
of business documents and school books."—*From Miss Moore's notes*
2. W. B. Yeats in his essay "William Blake and the Imagination"
speaks of Blake as a "too literal realist of the imagination, as
others are of nature."—*From Miss Moore's notes*

The Fish

wade
through black jade.
    Of the crow-blue mussel-shells, one keeps
    adjusting the ash-heaps;
        opening and shutting itself like

an
injured fan.
    The barnacles which encrust the side
    of the wave, cannot hide
10   there for the submerged shafts of the

sun,
split like spun
   glass, move themselves with spotlight swiftness
   into the crevices—
      in and out, illuminating

the
turquoise sea
   of bodies. The water drives a wedge
   of iron through the iron edge
20   of the cliff; whereupon the stars,

pink
rice-grains, ink-
   bespattered jelly-fish, crabs like green
   lilies, and submarine
      toadstools, slide each on the other.

All
external
   marks of abuse are present on this
   defiant edifice—
30   all the physical features of

ac-
cident—lack
   of cornice, dynamite grooves, burns, and
   hatchet strokes, these things stand
      out on it; the chasm-side is

dead.
Repeated
   evidence has proved that it can live
   on what can not revive
40   its youth. The sea grows old in it.

A Jellyfish

Visible, invisible,
   a fluctuating charm
an amber-tinctured amethyst
   inhabits it, your arm

approaches and it opens
    and it closes; you had meant
to catch it and it quivers;
    you abandon your intent.

Nevertheless

you've seen a strawberry
        that's had a struggle; yet
        was, where the fragments met,

a hedgehog or a star-
        fish for the multitude
        of seeds. What better food

than apple-seeds—the fruit
        within the fruit—locked in
        like counter-curved twin

10 hazel-nuts? Frost that kills
        the little rubber-plant-
        leaves of *kok-saghyz* stalks, can't

harm the roots; they still grow
        in frozen ground. Once where
        there was a prickly-pear-

leaf clinging to barbed wire,
        a root shot down to grow
        in earth two feet below;

as carrots form mandrakes
20   or a ram's-horn root some-
        times. Victory won't come

to me unless I go
        to it; a grape-tendril
        ties a knot in knots till

knotted thirty times,—so
        the bound twig that's under-
        gone and over-gone, can't stir.

The weak overcomes its
    menace, the strong over-
30   comes itself. What is there

like fortitude! What sap
    went through that little thread
    to make the cherry red!

T.S. ELIOT
1888–1965

Thomas Stearns Eliot was born in St. Louis, Missouri, the youngest of seven children of a well-to-do family with deep roots in New England. Both parents were cultivated and well-read, and Eliot showed an early interest in literature; his first published poem, an imitation of Ben Jonson, appeared in Smith Academy's literary journal when Eliot was fifteen. Eliot went on to Harvard for his undergraduate and graduate work, absorbing Dante, Donne, and discovering the French symbolist poets who would have a strong influence on his early poetry. He went on to Oxford to do further work in Greek and philosophy, finally completing his dissertation on philosopher F. H. Bradley in 1916. But by then he wished to pursue a literary rather than an academic career, and he was achieving a reputation in literary circles with the publication of his "Preludes" and "J. Alfred Prufrock." In 1915, he had entered into what was to prove a disastrous marriage, and was supporting himself and his wife by working in Lloyd's Bank, writing book reviews, and editing journals. Somehow he found time to write, and in 1922, after a struggle with a mental breakdown, and with the editorial help of Ezra Pound, The Waste Land was published. This was the most influential poem of its time, partly because of its innovative fragmented structure, and partly because to many it symbolized the enervation and spiritual emptiness of the post-World War I period. The poetry Eliot wrote after The Waste Land is generated from a spiritual struggle which culminated in Eliot's joining the Anglican church. He considered the meditative poetry of The Four Quartets his finest work, though some critics feel that his Christian orthodoxy dulled his poetic edge. Nevertheless, he was considered the major poet of his generation, and won the Nobel Prize for Literature in 1948.

The Love Song of J. Alfred Prufrock

S'io credessi che mia risposta fosse
A persona che mai tornasse al mondo,
Questa fiamma staria senza più scosse.
Ma per ciò che giammai de questo fondo
Non tornò vivo alcun, s'i'odo il vero
Senza tema d'infamia ti rispondo.[1]

Let us go then, you and I,
When the evening is spread out against the sky
Like a patient etherized upon a table;
Let us go, through certain half-deserted streets,
The muttering retreats
Of restless nights in one-night cheap hotels
And sawdust restaurants with oyster-shells:
Streets that follow like a tedious argument
Of insidious intent
10 To lead you to an overwhelming question....
Oh, do not ask, 'What is it?'
Let us go and make our visit.

In the room the women come and go
Talking of Michelangelo.

The yellow fog that rubs its back upon the window-panes,
The yellow smoke that rubs its muzzle on the window-panes,
Licked its tongue into the corners of the evening,
Lingered upon the pools that stand in drains,
Let fall upon its back the soot that falls from chimneys,
20 Slipped by the terrace, made a sudden leap,
And seeing that it was a soft October night,
Curled once about the house, and fell asleep.

And indeed there will be time
For the yellow smoke that slides along the street
Rubbing its back upon the window-panes;
There will be time, there will be time
To prepare a face to meet the faces that you meet;

1. "If I believed that my answer were to a person who should ever return
   to the world, this flame would stand without further movement;
   but since never one returns alive from this deep, if I hear true,
   I answer you without fear of infamy." *Inferno*, xxvii, 61–66. These words
   are the response a damned soul in Hell makes when a question is put to him.

There will be time to murder and create,
And time for all the works and days of hands
30 That lift and drop a question on your plate;
Time for you and time for me,
And time yet for a hundred indecisions,
And for a hundred visions and revisions,
Before the taking of a toast and tea.

In the room the women come and go
Talking of Michelangelo.

And indeed there will be time
To wonder, 'Do I dare?' and, 'Do I dare?'
Time to turn back and descend the stair,
40 With a bald spot in the middle of my hair—
(They will say: 'How his hair is growing thin!')
My morning coat, my collar mounting firmly to the chin,
My necktie rich and modest, but asserted by a simple pin—
(They will say: 'But how his arms and legs are thin!')
Do I dare
Disturb the universe?
In a minute there is time
For decisions and revisions which a minute will reverse.

For I have known them all already, known them all—
50 Have known the evenings, mornings, afternoons,
I have measured out my life with coffee spoons;
I know the voices dying with a dying fall
Beneath the music from a farther room.
    So how should I presume?

And I have known the eyes already, known them all—
The eyes that fix you in a formulated phrase,
And when I am formulated, sprawling on a pin,
When I am pinned and wriggling on the wall,
Then how should I begin
60 To spit out all the butt-ends of my days and ways?
    And how should I presume?

And I have known the arms already, known them all—
Arms that are braceleted and white and bare
(But in the lamplight, downed with light brown hair!)
Is it perfume from a dress

That makes me so digress?
Arms that lie along a table, or wrap about a shawl.
    And should I then presume?
    And how should I begin?

    . . .

70 Shall I say, I have gone at dusk through narrow streets
And watched the smoke that rises from the pipes
Of lonely men in shirt-sleeves, leaning out of the windows? . . .

    I should have been a pair of ragged claws
Scuttling across the floors of silent seas.

    . . .

And the afternoon, the evening, sleeps so peacefully!
Smoothed by long fingers,
Asleep . . . tired . . . or it malingers,
Stretched on the floor, here beside you and me.
Should I, after tea and cakes and ices,
80 Have the strength to force the moment to its crisis?
But though I have wept and fasted, wept and prayed,
Though I have seen my head (grown slightly bald) brought
        in upon a platter,[2]
I am no prophet—and here's no great matter;
I have seen the moment of my greatness flicker,
And I have seen the eternal Footman hold my coat, and
    snicker,
And in short, I was afraid.

    And would it have been worth it, after all,
After the cups, the marmalade, the tea,
Among the porcelain, among some talk of you and me,
90 Would it have been worth while,
To have bitten off the matter with a smile,
To have squeezed the universe into a ball
To roll it toward some overwhelming question,
To say: 'I am Lazarus, come from the dead,
Come back to tell you all, I shall tell you all'—

2. The head of John the Baptist was "brought in upon a platter" at
   the request of Salome as a reward for her dancing before Herod.

If one, settling a pillow by her head,
    Should say: 'That is not what I meant at all.
    That is not it, at all.'

    And would it have been worth it, after all,
Would it have been worth while,
After the sunsets and the dooryards and the sprinkled streets,
After the novels, after the teacups, after the skirts that trail
       along the floor—
And this, and so much more?—
It is impossible to say just what I mean!
But as if a magic lantern threw the nerves in patterns on a
      screen:
Would it have been worth while
If one, settling a pillow or throwing off a shawl,
And turning toward the window, should say:
    'That is not it at all,
    That is not what I meant, at all.'

      . . .

No! I am not Prince Hamlet, nor was meant to be;
Am an attendant lord, one that will do
To swell a progress,[3] start a scene or two,
Advise the prince; no doubt, an easy tool,
Deferential, glad to be of use,
Politic, cautious, and meticulous;
Full of high sentence, but a bit obtuse;
At times, indeed, almost ridiculous—
Almost, at times, the Fool.

    I grow old. . . . I grow old. . . .
I shall wear the bottoms of my trousers rolled.

    Shall I part my hair behind? Do I dare to eat a peach?
I shall wear white flannel trousers, and walk upon the beach.
I have heard the mermaids singing, each to each.

    I do not think that they will sing to me.

    I have seen them riding seaward on the waves
Combing the white hair of the waves blown back
When the wind blows the water white and black.

3. Ceremonial procession at a royal court

We have lingered in the chambers of the sea
130   By sea-girls wreathed with seaweed red and brown
Till human voices wake us, and we drown.

Morning at the Window

They are rattling breakfast plates in basement kitchens,
And along the trampled edges of the street
I am aware of the damp souls of housemaids
Sprouting despondently at area gates.

   The brown waves of fog toss up to me
Twisted faces from the bottom of the street,
And tear from a passer-by with muddy skirts
An aimless smile that hovers in the air
And vanishes along the level of the roofs.

The Hollow Men

Mistah Kurtz — he dead.
A penny for the Old Guy

I

We are the hollow men
We are the stuffed men
Leaning together
Headpiece filled with straw. Alas!
Our dried voices, when
We whisper together
Are quiet and meaningless
As wind in dry grass
Or rats' feet over broken glass
10   In our dry cellar

   Shape without form, shade without colour,
Paralysed force, gesture without motion;

   Those who have crossed
With direct eyes, to death's other Kingdom
Remember us—if at all—not as lost
Violent souls, but only
As the hollow men
The stuffed men.

II

Eyes I dare not meet in dreams
20 In death's dream kingdom
These do not appear:
There, the eyes are
Sunlight on a broken column
There, is a tree swinging
And voices are
In the wind's singing
More distant and more solemn
Than a fading star.

Let me be no nearer
30 In death's dream kingdom
Let me also wear
Such deliberate disguises
Rat's coat, crowskin, crossed staves
In a field
Behaving as the wind behaves
No nearer—

Not that final meeting
In the twilight kingdom

III

This is the dead land
40 This is cactus land
Here the stone images
Are raised, here they receive
The supplication of a dead man's hand
Under the twinkle of a fading star.

Is it like this
In death's other kingdom
Waking alone
At the hour when we are
Trembling with tenderness
50 Lips that would kiss
Form prayers to broken stone.

IV

The eyes are not here
There are no eyes here

In this valley of dying stars
In this hollow valley
This broken jaw of our lost kingdoms

   In this last of meeting places
We grope together
And avoid speech
60 Gathered on this beach of the tumid river

   Sightless, unless
The eyes reappear
As the perpetual star
Multifoliate rose
Of death's twilight kingdom
The hope only
Of empty men.

       v

Here we go round the prickly pear
Prickly pear prickly pear
70 *Here we go round the prickly pear*
At five o'clock in the morning.

   Between the idea
And the reality
Between the motion
And the act
Falls the Shadow
          For Thine is the Kingdom

   Between the conception
And the creation
80 Between the emotion
And the response
Falls the Shadow
         Life is very long

   Between the desire
And the spasm
Between the potency
And the existence
Between the essence
And the descent
90 Falls the Shadow
          For Thine is the Kingdom

For Thine is
Life is
For Thine is the

This is the way the world ends
This is the way the world ends
This is the way the world ends
Not with a bang but a whimper.

Journey of the Magi

"A cold coming we had of it,
Just the worst time of the year
For a journey, and such a long journey:
The ways deep and the weather sharp,
The very dead of winter."
And the camels galled, sore-footed, refractory,
Lying down in the melting snow.
There were times we regretted
The summer palaces on slopes, the terraces,
And the silken girls bringing sherbet.
Then the camel men cursing and grumbling
And running away, and wanting their liquor and women,
And the night-fires going out, and the lack of shelters,
And the cities hostile and the towns unfriendly
And the villages dirty and charging high prices:
A hard time we had of it.
At the end we preferred to travel all night,
Sleeping in snatches,
With the voices singing in our ears, saying
That this was all folly.

Then at dawn we came down to a temperate valley,
Wet, below the snow line, smelling of vegetation;
With a running stream and a water-mill beating the darkness,
And three trees on the low sky,
And an old white horse galloped away in the meadow.
Then we came to a tavern with vine-leaves over the lintel,
Six hands at an open door dicing for pieces of silver,
And feet kicking the empty wine-skins.
But there was no information, and so we continued
And arrived at evening, not a moment too soon
Finding the place; it was (you may say) satisfactory.

All this was a long time ago, I remember,

And I would do it again, but set down
This set down
This: were we led all that way for
Birth or Death? There was a Birth, certainly,
We had evidence and no doubt. I had seen birth and death,
But had thought they were different; this Birth was
Hard and bitter agony for us, like Death, our death.
40 We returned to our places, these Kingdoms,
But no longer at ease here, in the old dispensation,
With an alien people clutching their gods.
I should be glad of another death.

Macavity: The Mystery Cat

Macavity's a Mystery Cat: he's called the Hidden Paw—
For he's the master criminal who can defy the Law.
He's the bafflement of Scotland Yard, the Flying Squad's despair:
For when they reach the scene of the crime—*Macavity's not there!*

Macavity, Macavity, there's no one like Macavity,
He's broken every human law, he breaks the law of gravity.
His powers of levitation would make a fakir stare,
And when you reach the scene of crime—*Macavity's not there!*
You may seek him in the basement, you may look up in the air—
10 But I tell you once and once again, *Macavity's not there!*

Macavity's a ginger cat, he's very tall and thin;
You would know him if you saw him, for his eyes are sunken in.
His brow is deeply lined with thought, his head is highly domed;
His coat is dusty from neglect, his whiskers are uncombed.
He sways his head from side to side, with movements like a snake;
And when you think he's half asleep, he's always wide awake.

Macavity, Macavity, there's no one like Macavity,
For he's a fiend in feline shape, a monster of depravity.
You may meet him in a by-street, you may see him in the square—
20 But when a crime's discovered, then *Macavity's not there!*

He's outwardly respectable. (They say he cheats at cards.)
And his footprints are not found in any file of Scotland Yard's.
And when the larder's looted, or the jewel-case is rifled,
Or when the milk is missing, or another Peke's been stifled,
Or the greenhouse glass is broken, and the trellis past repair—
Ay, there's the wonder of the thing! *Macavity's not there!*

And when the Foreign Office find a Treaty's gone astray,
Or the Admiralty lose some plans and drawings by the way,
There may be a scrap of paper in the hall or on the stair—
30   But it's useless to investigate—*Macavity's not there!*
And when the loss has been disclosed, the Secret Service say:
"It *must* have been Macavity!"—but he's a mile away.
You'll be sure to find him resting, or a-licking of his thumbs,
Or engaged in doing complicated long division sums.

Macavity, Macavity, there's no one like Macavity,
There never was a Cat of such deceitfulness and suavity.
He always has an alibi, and one or two to spare:
At whatever time the deed took place—MACAVITY WASN'T THERE!
And they say that all the Cats whose wicked deeds are widely known
40   (I might mention Mungojerrie, I might mention Griddlebone)
Are nothing more than agents for the Cat who all the time
Just controls their operations: the Napoleon of Crime!

E. E. CUMMINGS
1894–1962

He was born Edward Estlin Cummings, the son of an English professor at
Harvard who was later pastor of the Old South Church in Boston. Cummings took his B.A. and M.A. at Harvard, and then joined the Norton Harje
Ambulance Corps in France during World War I. Because of the wrongheaded suspicions of a censor regarding "unpatriotic" letters, Cummings
was imprisoned in a French concentration camp for three months, a period
which is memorably evoked in his novel, *The Enormous Room*, which made
him famous. After the war, he lived in Paris and studied painting, then
settled in New York's Greenwich Village with other writers and artists, continuing to paint and to write poetry. He developed an innovative, playful
poetic style, flaunting the rules of syntax, grammar, and punctuation in order to make us see words and their relationships in a new way. In the form
of his poetry and in his themes, he strikes out against conformity, and cele-
brates the vitality of human love. He is not a poet of ideas, but he is one of
our most joyful singers of the traditional themes of love and spring, as well
as one of the sharpest satirists in modern poetry.

Buffalo Bill's

Buffalo Bill's
defunct

who used to
ride a watersmooth-silver
                          stallion
and break onetwothreefourfive pigeonsjustlikethat
                                            Jesus

he was a handsome man
                          and what i want to know is
10   how do you like your blueeyed boy
Mister Death

Spring is like a perhaps hand

Spring is like a perhaps hand
(which comes carefully
out of Nowhere)arranging
a window,into which people look(while
people stare
arranging and changing placing
carefully there a strange
thing and a known thing here)and

changing everything carefully

10   spring is like a perhaps
Hand in a window
(carefully to
and fro moving New and
Old things,while
people stare carefully
moving a perhaps
fraction of flower here placing
an inch of air there)and

without breaking anything.

"next to of course god america i

"next to of course god america i
love you land of the pilgrims' and so forth oh
say can you see by the dawn's early my
country 'tis of centuries come and go
and are no more what of it we should worry

in every language even deafanddumb
thy sons acclaim your glorious name by gorry
by jingo by gee by gosh by gum
why talk of beauty what could be more beautiful than these heroic happy dead
who rushed like lions to the roaring slaughter
they did not stop to think they died instead
then shall the voice of liberty be mute?"

He spoke. And drank rapidly a glass of water

somewhere i have never travelled

somewhere i have never travelled,gladly beyond
any experience,your eyes have their silence:
in your most frail gesture are things which enclose me,
or which i cannot touch because they are too near

your slightest look easily will unclose me
though i have closed myself as fingers,
you open always petal by petal myself as Spring opens
(touching skilfully,mysteriously)her first rose

or if your wish be to close me,i and
my life will shut very beautifully,suddenly,
as when the heart of this flower imagines
the snow carefully everywhere descending;

nothing which we are to perceive in this world equals
the power of your intense fragility:whose texture
compels me with the colour of its countries,
rendering death and forever with each breathing

(i do not know what it is about you that closes
and opens; only something in me understands
the voice of your eyes is deeper than all roses)
nobody,not even the rain,has such small hands

r-p-o-p-h-e-s-s-a-g-r

                              r-p-o-p-h-e-s-s-a-g-r
                    who
a)s w(e loo)k

upnowgath
                                PPEGORHRASS
                                                eringint(o-

aThe):l
                eA
                        !p:
10   S   a

                        (r
rIvInG   .gRrEaPsPhOs)
                                                                to

rea(be)rran(com)gi(e)ngly
,grasshopper;

my father moved through dooms of love

my father moved through dooms of love
through sames of am through haves of give,
singing each morning out of each night
my father moved through depths of height

this motionless forgetful where
turned at his glance to shining here;
that if(so timid air is firm)
under his eyes would stir and squirm

newly as from unburied which
10   floats the first who,his april touch
drove sleeping selves to swarm their fates
woke dreamers to their ghostly roots

and should some why completely weep
my father's fingers brought her sleep:
vainly no smallest voice might cry
for he could feel the mountains grow.

Lifting the valleys of the sea
my father moved through griefs of joy;
praising a forehead called the moon
20   singing desire into begin

joy was his song and joy so pure
a heart of star by him could steer
and pure so now and now so yes
the wrists of twilight would rejoice

keen as midsummer's keen beyond
conceiving mind of sun will stand,
so strictly(over utmost him
so hugely)stood my father's dream

his flesh was flesh his blood was blood:
30   no hungry man but wished him food;
no cripple wouldn't creep one mile
uphill to only see him smile.

Scorning the pomp of must and shall
my father moved through dooms of feel;
his anger was as right as rain
his pity was as green as grain

septembering arms of year extend
less humbly wealth to foe and friend
than he to foolish and to wise
40   offered immeasurable is

proudly and(by octobering flame
beckoned)as earth will downward climb,
so naked for immortal work
his shoulders marched against the dark

his sorrow was as true as bread:
no liar looked him in the head;
if every friend became his foe
he'd laugh and build a world with snow.

My father moved through theys of we,
50   singing each new leaf out of each tree
(and every child was sure that spring
danced when she heard my father sing)

then let men kill which cannot share,
let blood and flesh be mud and mire,
scheming imagine,passion willed,
freedom a drug that's bought and sold

giving to steal and cruel kind,
a heart to fear,to doubt a mind,
to differ a disease of same,
60   conform the pinnacle of am

though dull were all we taste as bright,
bitter all utterly things sweet,
maggoty minus and dumb death
all we inherit,all bequeath

and nothing quite so least as truth
—i say though hate were why men breathe—
because my father lived his soul
love is the whole and more than all

pity this busy monster

pity this busy monster,manunkind,

not. Progress is a comfortable disease:
your victim(death and life safely beyond)

plays with the bigness of his littleness
—electrons deify one razorblade
into a mountainrange;lenses extend

unwish through curving wherewhen till unwish
returns on its unself.
                              A world of made
10   is not a world of born—pity poor flesh

and trees,poor stars and stones,but never this
fine specimen of hypermagical

ultraomnipotence. We doctors know

a hopeless case if—listen:there's a hell
of a good universe next door;let's go

W. H. AUDEN
1907–1973

Wystan Hugh Auden was born in York, England, the third son of a physician of comfortable means, who was also interested in archaeology, classical literature, and Icelandic sagas. Auden developed an early interest in geology during family outings on the Limestone moors of Yorkshire, and evocations of those barren simple landscapes can be found in much of his poetry.

These outings also took him to the Roman Wall, and to investigations of pre-Norman churches and crosses. It seems natural that when he was at Oxford he should study Anglo-Saxon poetry, whose rhythms and allitera-tion he later emulated. He experimented with many other forms, including the folk ballad, and was an extremely talented versifier. His first book of poetry appeared in 1928; this was followed by *September Poems*, and in 1932, *The Orators*. Auden became well-known as one of the major voices of the thirties, an "age of anxiety" resulting from worldwide depression and the growing threat of another war. Influenced by Freud, Auden wrote of the guilt and fears of the human heart; but he wrote just as strongly of the power of love as the only force which could overcome anxiety. He came to America in 1939, and taught at a number of colleges and universities, be-coming an American citizen in 1946. A prolific writer, he produced a large number of reviews and essays in addition to his poetry. He also wrote plays with Christopher Isherwood and opera librettos with Chester Kallmann. In 1957, he bought a farmhouse in Kirchstetten, Austria, where he spent springs and summers until his death there in 1973.

Who's Who

A shilling life will give you all the facts:
How Father beat him, how he ran away,
What were the struggles of his youth, what acts
Made him the greatest figure of his day:
Of how he fought, fished, hunted, worked all night,
Though giddy, climbed new mountains; named a sea:
Some of the last researchers even write
Love made him weep his pints like you and me.

With all his honours on, he sighed for one
10 Who, say astonished critics, lived at home;
Did little jobs about the house with skill
And nothing else; could whistle; would sit still
Or potter round the garden; answered some
Of his long marvellous letters but kept none.

On This Island

Look, stranger, on this island now
The leaping light for your delight discovers,
Stand stable here
And silent be,

That through the channels of the ear
May wander like a river
The swaying sound of the sea.

Here at the small field's ending pause
When the chalk wall falls to the foam and its tall ledges
10 Oppose the pluck
And knock of the tide,
And the shingle scrambles after the suck-
-ing surf,
And the gull lodges
A moment on its sheer side.

Far off like floating seeds the ships
Diverge on urgent voluntary errands,
And the full view
Indeed may enter
20 And move in memory as now these clouds do,
That pass the harbour mirror
And all the summer through the water saunter.

As I Walked Out One Evening

As I walked out one evening,
　　Walking down Bristol Street,
The crowds upon the pavement
　　Were fields of harvest wheat.

And down by the brimming river
　　I heard a lover sing
Under an arch of the railway:
　　'Love has no ending.

'I'll love you, dear, I'll love you
10 　　Till China and Africa meet,
And the river jumps over the mountain
　　And the salmon sing in the street,

'I'll love you till the ocean
　　Is folded and hung up to dry
And the seven stars go squawking
　　Like geese about the sky.

'The years shall run like rabbits,
    For in my arms I hold
The Flower of the Ages,
20   And the first love of the world.'

But all the clocks in the city
    Began to whirr and chime:
'O let not Time deceive you,
    You cannot conquer Time.

'In the burrows of the Nightmare
    Where Justice naked is,
Time watches from the shadow
    And coughs when you would kiss.

'In headaches and in worry
30   Vaguely life leaks away,
And Time will have his fancy
    To-morrow or to-day.

'Into many a green valley
    Drifts the appalling snow;
Time breaks the threaded dances
    And the diver's brilliant bow.

'O plunge your hands in water,
    Plunge them in up to the wrist;
Stare, stare in the basin
40   And wonder what you've missed.

'The glacier knocks in the cupboard,
    The desert sighs in the bed,
And the crack in the tea-cup opens
    A lane to the land of the dead.

'Where the beggars raffle the banknotes
    And the Giant is enchanting to Jack,
And the Lily-white Boy is a Roarer,
    And Jill goes down on her back.

'O look, look in the mirror,
50   O look in your distress;
Life remains a blessing
    Although you cannot bless.

'O stand, stand at the window
  As the tears scald and start;
You shall love your crooked neighbour
  With your crooked heart.'

It was late, late in the evening,
  The lovers they were gone;
The clocks had ceased their chiming,
60 And the deep river ran on.

Lullaby

Lay your sleeping head, my love,
Human on my faithless arm;
Time and fevers burn away
Individual beauty from
Thoughtful children, and the grave
Proves the child ephemeral:
But in my arms till break of day
Let the living creature lie,
Mortal, guilty, but to me
10 The entirely beautiful.

Soul and body have no bounds:
To lovers as they lie upon
Her tolerant enchanted slope
In their ordinary swoon,
Grave the vision Venus sends
Of supernatural sympathy,
Universal love and hope;
While an abstract insight wakes
Among the glaciers and the rocks
20 The hermit's carnal ecstasy.

Certainty, fidelity
On the stroke of midnight pass
Like vibrations of a bell
And fashionable madmen raise
Their pedantic boring cry:
Every farthing of the cost,
All the dreaded cards foretell,
Shall be paid, but from this night
Not a whisper, not a thought,
30 Not a kiss nor look be lost.

Beauty, midnight, vision dies:
Let the winds of dawn that blow
Softly round your dreaming head
Such a day of welcome show
Eye and knocking heart may bless,
Find our mortal world enough;
Noons of dryness find you fed
By the involuntary powers,
Nights of insult let you pass
40   Watched by every human love.

Musée des Beaux Arts[1]

About suffering they were never wrong,
The Old Masters: how well they understood
Its human position; how it takes place
While someone else is eating or opening a window or just walking dully along;
How, when the aged are reverently, passionately waiting
For the miraculous birth, there always must be
Children who did not specially want it to happen, skating
On a pond at the edge of the wood:
They never forgot
10   That even the dreadful martyrdom must run its course
Anyhow in a corner, some untidy spot
Where the dogs go on with their doggy life and the torturer's horse
Scratches its innocent behind on a tree.

In Brueghel's *Icarus,* for instance: how everything turns away
Quite leisurely from the disaster; the ploughman may
Have heard the splash, the forsaken cry,
But for him it was not an important failure; the sun shone
As it had to on the white legs disappearing into the green
Water; and the expensive delicate ship that must have seen
20   Something amazing, a boy falling out of the sky,
Had somewhere to get to and sailed calmly on.

1. Museum of Fine Arts. See also note to William Carlos Williams's poem
    on Brueghel's "Icarus," above.

In Memory of W. B. Yeats

(d. Jan. 1939)

I

He disappeared in the dead of winter:
The brooks were frozen, the airports almost deserted,
And snow disfigured the public statues;
The mercury sank in the mouth of the dying day.
What instruments we have agree
The day of his death was a dark cold day.

Far from his illness
The wolves ran on through the evergreen forests,
The pleasant river was untempted by the fashionable quays;
By mourning tongues
The death of the poet was kept from his poems.

But for him it was his last afternoon as himself,
An afternoon of nurses and rumours;
The provinces of his body revolted,
The squares of his mind were empty,
Silence invaded the suburbs,
The current of his feeling failed; he became his admirers.

Now he is scattered among a hundred cities
And wholly given over to unfamiliar affections,
To find his happiness in another kind of wood
And be punished under a foreign code of conscience.
The words of a dead man
Are modified in the guts of the living.

But in the importance and noise of to-morrow
When the brokers are roaring like beasts on the floor of the Bourse,
And the poor have the sufferings to which they are fairly
        accustomed,
And each in the cell of himself is almost convinced of his freedom,
A few thousand will think of this day
As one thinks of a day when one did something slightly unusual.
What instruments we have agree
The day of his death was a dark cold day.

II

You were silly like us; your gift survived it all:
The parish of rich women, physical decay,
Yourself. Mad Ireland hurt you into poetry.
Now Ireland has her madness and her weather still,
For poetry makes nothing happen: it survives
In the valley of its making where executives
Would never want to tamper, flows on south
From ranches of isolation and the busy griefs,
Raw towns that we believe and die in; it survives,
A way of happening, a mouth.

III

Earth, receive an honoured guest:
William Yeats is laid to rest.
Let the Irish vessel lie
Emptied of its poetry.

In the nightmare of the dark
All the dogs of Europe bark,
And the living nations wait,
Each sequestered in its hate;

Intellectual disgrace
Stares from every human face,
And the seas of pity lie
Locked and frozen in each eye.

Follow, poet, follow right
To the bottom of the night,
With your unconstraining voice
Still persuade us to rejoice;

With the farming of a verse
Make a vineyard of the curse,
Sing of human unsuccess
In a rapture of distress;

In the deserts of the heart
Let the healing fountain start,
In the prison of his days
Teach the free man how to praise.

The Unknown Citizen

To JS/07/M/378
This Marble Monument
Is Erected by the State

He was found by the Bureau of Statistics to be
One against whom there was no official complaint,
And all the reports on his conduct agree
That, in the modern sense of an old-fashioned word, he was a saint,
For in everything he did he served the Greater Community.
Except for the War till the day he retired
He worked in a factory and never got fired,
But satisfied his employers, Fudge Motors Inc.
Yet he wasn't a scab or odd in his views,
For his Union reports that he paid his dues,
(Our report on his Union shows it was sound)
And our Social Psychology workers found
That he was popular with his mates and liked a drink.
The Press are convinced that he bought a paper every day
And that his reactions to advertisements were normal in every way.
Policies taken out in his name prove that he was fully insured,
And his Health-card shows he was once in hospital but left it cured.
Both Producers Research and High-Grade Living declare
He was fully sensible to the advantages of the Instalment Plan
And had everything necessary to the Modern Man,
A phonograph, a radio, a car and a frigidaire.
Our researchers into Public Opinion are content
That he held the proper opinions for the time of year;
When there was peace, he was for peace; when there was war, he went.
He was married and added five children to the population,
Which our Eugenist says was the right number for a parent of his generation,
And our teachers report that he never interfered with their education.
Was he free? Was he happy? The question is absurd:
Had anything been wrong, we should certainly have heard.

THEODORE ROETHKE

1908–1963

Roethke was born in Saginaw, Michigan, where his father owned green-
houses. Much of Roethke's poetry springs from this greenhouse world in
which he grew up, developing a deep love of nature. As a boy, he read
Emerson, Thoreau, Stevenson, Pater, and "anthologies of great thoughts"

in an effort to learn to write "chiseled" prose. He graduated from the University of Michigan, did some graduate work at Harvard, and then taught at several colleges and universities. Renowned as a great teacher of poetry and of aspiring young poets, he became poet-in-residence at the University of Washington. Nature was his major subject, and he paralleled its rhythms to those of human life, emphasizing that "we think by feeling. What is there to know?" He also produced some of the finest love poems of this century, though his personal life was not a happy one as he struggled with alcoholism and depression.

The Premonition

Walking this field I remember
Days of another summer.
Oh that was long ago! I kept
Close to the heels of my father,
Matching his stride with half-steps
Until we came to a river.
He dipped his hand in the shallow:
Water ran over and under
Hair on a narrow wrist bone;
His image kept following after,—
Flashed with the sun in the ripple.
But when he stood up, that face
Was lost in a maze of water.

My Papa's Waltz

The whiskey on your breath
Could make a small boy dizzy;
But I hung on like death:
Such waltzing was not easy.

We romped until the pans
Slid from the kitchen shelf;
My mother's countenance
Could not unfrown itself.

The hand that held my wrist
Was battered on one knuckle;
At every step you missed
My right ear scraped a buckle.

You beat time on my head
With a palm caked hard by dirt,
Then waltzed me off to bed
Still clinging to your shirt.

Old Florist

That hump of a man bunching chrysanthemums
Or pinching-back asters, or planting azaleas,
Tamping and stamping dirt into pots,—
How he could flick and pick
Rotten leaves or yellowy petals,
Or scoop out a weed close to flourishing roots,
Or make the dust buzz with a light spray,
Or drown a bug in one spit of tobacco juice,
Or fan life into wilted sweet-peas with his hat,
10   Or stand all night watering roses, his feet blue in rubber boots.

Dolor

I have known the inexorable sadness of pencils,
Neat in their boxes, dolor of pad and paper-weight,
All the misery of manilla folders and mucilage,
Desolation in immaculate public places,
Lonely reception room, lavatory, switchboard,
The unalterable pathos of basin and pitcher,
Ritual of multigraph, paper-clip, comma,
Endless duplication of lives and objects.
And I have seen dust from the walls of institutions,
10   Finer than flour, alive, more dangerous than silica,
Sift, almost invisible, through long afternoons of tedium,
Dropping a fine film on nails and delicate eyebrows,
Glazing the pale hair, the duplicate grey standard faces.

Elegy for Jane

My Student, Thrown by a Horse

I remember the neckcurls, limp and damp as tendrils;
And her quick look, a sidelong pickerel smile;
And how, once startled into talk, the light syllables leaped for her,
And she balanced in the delight of her thought,

A wren, happy, tail into the wind,
Her song trembling the twigs and small branches.
The shade sang with her;
The leaves, their whispers turned to kissing;
And the mold sang in the bleached valleys under the rose.

10 Oh, when she was sad, she cast herself down into such a pure depth,
Even a father could not find her:
Scraping her cheek against straw;
Stirring the clearest water.

My sparrow, you are not here,
Waiting like a fern, making a spiny shadow.
The sides of wet stones cannot console me,
Nor the moss, wound with the last light.

If only I could nudge you from this sleep,
My maimed darling, my skittery pigeon.
20 Over this damp grave I speak the words of my love:
I, with no rights in this matter,
Neither father nor lover.

The Waking[1]

I wake to sleep, and take my waking slow.
I feel my fate in what I cannot fear.
I learn by going where I have to go.

We think by feeling. What is there to know?
I hear my being dance from ear to ear.
I wake to sleep, and take my waking slow.

Of those so close beside me, which are you?
God bless the Ground! I shall walk softly there,
And learn by going where I have to go.

10 Light takes the Tree; but who can tell us how?
The lowly worm climbs up a winding stair;
I wake to sleep, and take my waking slow.

1. This poem is a villanelle, a strict form with only two rhyming sounds,
   in which the last two lines of the poem are also the last lines of alternate stanzas.
   Roethke loosens the form just a bit.

Great Nature has another thing to do
To you and me; so take the lively air,
And, lovely, learn by going where to go.

This shaking keeps me steady. I should know.
What falls away is always. And is near.
I wake to sleep, and take my waking slow.
I learn by going where I have to go.

I Knew a Woman

I knew a woman, lovely in her bones,
When small birds sighed, she would sigh back at them;
Ah, when she moved, she moved more ways than one:
The shapes a bright container can contain!
Of her choice virtues only gods should speak,
Or English poets who grew up on Greek
(I'd have them sing in chorus, cheek to cheek).

How well her wishes went! She stroked my chin,
She taught me Turn, and Counter-turn, and Stand;
10   She taught me Touch, that undulant white skin;
I nibbled meekly from her proffered hand;
She was the sickle; I, poor I, the rake,
Coming behind her for her pretty sake
(But what prodigious mowing we did make).

Love likes a gander, and adores a goose:
Her full lips pursed, the errant note to seize;
She played it quick, she played it light and loose;
My eyes, they dazzled at her flowing knees;
Her several parts could keep a pure repose,
20   Or one hip quiver with a mobile nose
(She moved in circles, and those circles moved).

Let seed be grass, and grass turn into hay:
I'm martyr to a motion not my own;
What's freedom for? To know eternity.
I swear she cast a shadow white as stone.
But who would count eternity in days?
These old bones live to learn her wanton ways:
(I measure time by how a body sways).

DYLAN THOMAS

1914–1953

Born in Swansea, Wales, Thomas attended the Swansea Grammar School where his father was Senior English Master. Never much of a scholar, Thomas did well only in English, and loved to act in school plays and little theater productions. When he left school in 1931, he worked for two newspapers, writing on books and theater, and his explorations of the pubs and streets of his seaport town provided him with material for the short stories he was writing at this time. He was also writing poems in penny exercise books, composing much of his carefully crafted syllabic verse in pubs, with a glass of beer by his notebook. Much of his finest poetry was written before he was twenty, and from 1933 on, he was published regularly. Thomas, who enjoyed playing the role of poet, became known as an extraordinarily fine reader of poetry, doing regular poetry readings for BBC radio. Though he was popular and making a good income, he was always in debt and incapable of managing his money. On his tours to the United States, he was renowned not only for his readings, but for his wild drinking bouts. He died suddenly and prematurely in New York after downing eighteen straight whiskies.

The Force That through the Green Fuse Drives the Flower

The force that through the green fuse drives the flower
Drives my green age; that blasts the roots of trees
Is my destroyer.
And I am dumb to tell the crooked rose
My youth is bent by the same wintry fever.

The force that drives the water through the rocks
Drives my red blood; that dries the mouthing streams
Turns mine to wax.
And I am dumb to mouth unto my veins
10 How at the mountain spring the same mouth sucks.

The hand that whirls the water in the pool
Stirs the quicksand; that ropes the blowing wind
Hauls my shroud sail.
And I am dumb to tell the hanging man
How of my clay is made the hangman's lime.

The lips of time leech to the fountain head;
Love drips and gathers, but the fallen blood

622

Shall calm her sores.
And I am dumb to tell a weather's wind
20   How time has ticked a heaven round the stars.

And I am dumb to tell the lover's tomb
How at my sheet goes the same crooked worm.

This Bread I Break

This bread I break was once the oat,
This wine upon a foreign tree
Plunged in its fruit;
Man in the day or wind at night
Laid the crops low, broke the grape's joy.

Once in this wine the summer blood
Knocked in the flesh that decked the vine,
Once in this bread
The oat was merry in the wind;
10   Man broke the sun, pulled the wind down.

This flesh you break, this blood you let
Make desolation in the vein,
Were oat and grape
Born of the sensual root and sap;
My wine you drink, my bread you snap.

A Refusal to Mourn the Death, By Fire, of a Child in London

Never until the mankind making
Bird beast and flower
Fathering and all humbling darkness
Tells with silence the last light breaking
And the still hour
Is come of the sea tumbling in harness

And I must enter again the round
Zion of the water bead
And the synagogue of the ear of corn
10   Shall I let pray the shadow of a sound
Or sow my salt seed
In the least valley of sackcloth to mourn

The majesty and burning of the child's death.
I shall not murder
The mankind of her going with a grave truth
Nor blaspheme down the stations of the breath
With any further
Elegy of innocence and youth.

Deep with the first dead lies London's daughter,
20 Robed in the long friends,
The grains beyond age, the dark veins of her mother,
Secret by the unmourning water
Of the riding Thames.
After the first death, there is no other.

Do Not Go Gentle into That Good Night[1]

Do not go gentle into that good night,
Old age should burn and rave at close of day;
Rage, rage against the dying of the light.

Though wise men at their end know dark is right,
Because their words had forked no lightning they
Do not go gentle into that good night.

Good men, the last wave by, crying how bright
Their frail deeds might have danced in a green bay,
Rage, rage against the dying of the light.

10 Wild men who caught and sang the sun in flight,
And learn, too late, they grieved it on its way,
Do not go gentle into that good night.

Grave men, near death, who see with blinding sight
Blind eyes could blaze like meteors and be gay,
Rage, rage against the dying of the light.

And you, my father, there on the sad height,
Curse, bless, me now with your fierce tears, I pray.
Do not go gentle into that good night.
Rage, rage against the dying of the light.

1. Like Roethke's "The Waking," this is a villanelle. See above, p. 620.

Fern Hill

Now as I was young and easy under the apple boughs
About the lilting house and happy as the grass was green,
    The night above the dingle starry,
        Time let me hail and climb
    Golden in the heydays of his eyes,
And honoured among wagons I was prince of the apple towns
And once below a time I lordly had the trees and leaves
        Trail with daisies and barley
    Down the rivers of the windfall light.

10 And as I was green and carefree, famous among the barns
About the happy yard and singing as the farm was home,
    In the sun that is young once only,
        Time let me play and be
    Golden in the mercy of his means,
And green and golden I was huntsman and herdsman, the calves
Sang to my horn, the foxes on the hills barked clear and cold,
        And the sabbath rang slowly
    In the pebbles of the holy streams.

All the sun long it was running, it was lovely, the hay
20 Fields high as the house, the tunes from the chimneys, it was air
      And playing, lovely and watery
        And fire green as grass.
      And nightly under the simple stars
As I rode to sleep the owls were bearing the farm away,
All the moon long I heard, blessed among stables, the night-jars
      Flying with the ricks, and the horses
        Flashing into the dark.

And then to awake, and the farm, like a wanderer white
With the dew, come back, the cock on his shoulder: it was all
30   Shining, it was Adam and maiden,
      The sky gathered again
      And the sun grew round that very day.
So it must have been after the birth of the simple light
In the first, spinning place, the spellbound horses walking warm
    Out of the whinnying green stable
      On to the fields of praise.

And honoured among foxes and pheasants by the gay house
Under the new made clouds and happy as the heart was long,

In the sun born over and over,
40   I ran my heedless ways,
My wishes raced through the house high hay
And nothing I cared, at my sky blue trades, that time allows
In all his tuneful turning so few and such morning songs
          Before the children green and golden
                    Follow him out of grace,

Nothing I cared, in the lamb white days, that time would take me
Up to the swallow thronged loft by the shadow of my hand,
          In the moon that is always rising,
                    Nor that riding to sleep
50   I should hear him fly with the high fields
And wake to the farm forever fled from the childless land.
Oh as I was young and easy in the mercy of his means,
          Time held me green and dying
          Though I sang in my chains like the sea.

ROBERT LOWELL
1917–1977

Robert Lowell's poetry is primarily autobiographical, revealing his deep interest in his family's New England history, as well as his reactions to his
lineage. He was born in Boston, the son of a naval officer, attended St.
Mark's School (founded by his grandfather), and, as was proper for young
men of good family in Boston, he went on to Harvard. But after two years
he left and went to study with poet and critic John Crowe Ransom at Kenyon
College. He converted to Catholicism in 1940, and during World War II, he
tried unsuccessfully to enlist in the navy. He refused to be drafted into the
army, and as a conscientious objector, was jailed for six months. His first
book of poetry was published in 1944, and in 1947 he won the Pulitzer Prize
for *Lord Weary's Castle* and became Consultant in Poetry at the Library of
Congress. *Life Studies* (1959) reveals some influence of the self-revelatory
mode of the Beat poets, and of William Carlos Williams' colloquial American diction. Lowell's form is highly controlled as he strives for a tone of
"heightened conversation" in these complex and personal portraits which
many consider his finest poetry. During his career, Lowell taught at several
universities, including Harvard, wrote for the theater, and translated European poetry. In his last book, *Day by Day*, he returned to an exploration of
his childhood.

"To Speak of Woe That Is in Marriage"

"It is the future generation that presses into being by means of these exuberant feelings and supersensible soap bubbles of ours."

SCHOPENHAUER

"The hot night makes us keep our bedroom windows open.
Our magnolia blossoms. Life begins to happen.
My hopped up husband drops his home disputes,
and hits the streets to cruise for prostitutes,
free-lancing out along the razor's edge.
This screwball might kill his wife, then take the pledge.
Oh the monotonous meanness of his lust. . . .
It's the injustice . . . he is so unjust—
whiskey-blind, swaggering home at five.
My only thought is how to keep alive.
What makes him tick? Each night now I tie
ten dollars and his car key to my thigh. . . .
Gored by the climacteric of his want,
he stalls above me like an elephant."

Skunk Hour

[FOR ELIZABETH BISHOP]

Nautilus Island's hermit
heiress still lives through winter in her Spartan cottage;
her sheep still graze above the sea.
Her son's a bishop. Her farmer
is first selectman in our village;
she's in her dotage.

Thirsting for
the hierarchic privacy
of Queen Victoria's century,
she buys up all
the eyesores facing her shore,
and lets them fall.

The season's ill—
we've lost our summer millionaire,
who seemed to leap from an L. L. Bean
catalogue. His nine-knot yawl
was auctioned off to lobstermen.
A red fox stain covers Blue Hill.

And now our fairy
20 decorator brightens his shop for fall;
his fishnet's filled with orange cork,
orange, his cobbler's bench and awl;
there is no money in his work,
he'd rather marry.

One dark night,
my Tudor Ford climbed the hill's skull;
I watched for love-cars. Lights turned down,
they lay together, hull to hull,
where the graveyard shelves on the town. . . .
30 My mind's not right.

A car radio bleats,
"Love, O careless Love. . . ." I hear
my ill-spirit sob in each blood cell,
as if my hand were at its throat. . . .
I myself am hell;
nobody's here—

only skunks, that search
in the moonlight for a bite to eat.
They march on their soles up Main Street:
40 white stripes, moonstruck eyes' red fire
under the chalk-dry and spar spire
of the Trinitarian Church.

I stand on top
of our back steps and breathe the rich air—
a mother skunk with her column of kittens swills the garbage pail.
She jabs her wedge-head in a cup
of sour cream, drops her ostrich tail,
and will not scare.

Water

It was a Maine lobster town—
each morning boatloads of hands
pushed off for granite
quarries on the islands,

and left dozens of bleak
white frame houses stuck

like oyster shells
on a hill of rock,

and below us, the sea lapped
10   the raw little match-stick
mazes of a weir,
where the fish for bait were trapped.

Remember? We sat on a slab of rock.
From this distance in time,
it seems the color
of iris, rotting and turning purpler,

but it was only
the usual gray rock
turning the usual green
20   when drenched by the sea.

The sea drenched the rock
at our feet all day,
and kept tearing away
flake after flake.

One night you dreamed
you were a mermaid clinging to a wharf-pile,
and trying to pull
off the barnacles with your hands.

We wished our two souls
30   might return like gulls
to the rock. In the end,
the water was too cold for us.

For the Union Dead

"Relinquunt Omnia Servare Rem Publicam."[1]

The old South Boston Aquarium stands
in a Sahara of snow now. Its broken windows are boarded.
The bronze weathervane cod has lost half its scales.
The airy tanks are dry.

1. "They give up everything to serve the republic."

Once my nose crawled like a snail on the glass;
my hand tingled
to burst the bubbles
drifting from the noses of the cowed, compliant fish.

My hand draws back. I often sigh still
10   for the dark downward and vegetating kingdom
of the fish and reptile. One morning last March,
I pressed against the new barbed and galvanized

fence on the Boston Common. Behind their cage,
yellow dinosaur steamshovels were grunting
as they cropped up tons of mush and grass
to gouge their underworld garage.

Parking spaces luxuriate like civic
sandpiles in the heart of Boston.
A girdle of orange, Puritan-pumpkin colored girders
20   braces the tingling Statehouse,

shaking over the excavations, as it faces Colonel Shaw[2]
and his bell-cheeked Negro infantry
on St. Gaudens' shaking Civil War relief,
propped by a plank splint against the garage's earthquake.

Two months after marching through Boston,
half the regiment was dead;
at the dedication,
William James could almost hear the bronze Negroes breathe.

Their monument sticks like a fishbone
30   in the city's throat.
Its Colonel is as lean
as a compass-needle.

He has an angry wrenlike vigilance,
a greyhound's gentle tautness;
he seems to wince at pleasure,
and suffocate for privacy.

2. Robert Gould Shaw led the first northern Negro regiment, the Massachusetts 54th.
   He and many of his men were killed leading an attack on Fort Wagner, South
   Carolina.

He is out of bounds now. He rejoices in man's lovely,
peculiar power to choose life and die—
when he leads his black soldiers to death,
40   he cannot bend his back.

On a thousand small town New England greens,
the old white churches hold their air
of sparse, sincere rebellion; frayed flags
quilt the graveyards of the Grand Army of the Republic.

The stone statues of the abstract Union Soldier
grow slimmer and younger each year—
wasp-waisted, they doze over muskets
and muse through their sideburns . . .

Shaw's father wanted no monument
50   except the ditch,
where his son's body was thrown
and lost with his "niggers."

The ditch is nearer.
There are no statues for the last war here;
on Boylston Street, a commercial photograph
shows Hiroshima boiling

over a Mosler Safe, the "Rock of Ages"
that survived the blast. Space is nearer.
When I crouch to my television set,
60   the drained faces of Negro school-children rise like balloons.

Colonel Shaw
is riding on his bubble,
he waits
for the blesséd break.

The Aquarium is gone. Everywhere,
giant finned cars nose forward like fish;
a savage servility
slides by on grease.

GWENDOLYN BROOKS

1917–

She was born in Topeka, Kansas, but grew up in Chicago, where she attended Englewood High School and graduated from Wilson Junior College. She started writing poetry when she was seven, with her mother encouraging her and predicting that she would be "the *lady* Paul Dunbar" (1872–1906). But Brooks did not become a dialect poet like Dunbar; rather, the strong lines of her poetry speak with equal facility in cultivated rhythms, or black rhythms of Chicago streets and storefront churches of "Bronzeville," as the black ghetto was called in Chicago. She began her professional career as a poet in the South Side Community Art Center's poetry workshop in 1941, and published her first book, *A Street in Bronzeville*, in 1945. In 1950, she became the first black to win the Pulitzer Prize for poetry, and in 1969, she was named "Poet Laureate of the State of Illinois." Her latest work is directed more specifically to a black audience, and especially to the problems of black women.

The Mother

Abortions will not let you forget.
You remember the children you got that you did not get,
The damp small pulps with a little or with no hair,
The singers and workers that never handled the air.
You will never neglect or beat
Them, or silence or buy with a sweet.
You will never wind up the sucking-thumb
Or scuttle off ghosts that come.
You will never leave them, controlling your luscious sigh,
10 Return for a snack of them, with gobbling mother-eye.
I have heard in the voices of the wind the voices of my dim killed children.
I have contracted. I have eased
My dim dears at the breasts they could never suck.
I have said, Sweets, if I sinned, if I seized
Your luck
And your lives from your unfinished reach,
If I stole your births and your names,
Your straight baby tears and your games,
20 Your stilted or lovely loves, your tumults, your marriages, aches, and your deaths,
If I poisoned the beginnings of your breaths,
Believe that even in my deliberateness I was not deliberate.

Though why should I whine,
Whine that the crime was other than mine?—
Since anyhow you are dead.
Or rather, or instead,
You were never made.
But that too, I am afraid,
30   Is faulty: oh, what shall I say, how is the truth to be said?
You were born, you had body, you died.
It is just that you never giggled or planned or cried.

Believe me, I loved you all.
Believe me, I knew you, though faintly, and I loved, I loved you
All.

Kitchenette Building

We are things of dry hours and the involuntary plan,
Grayed in, and gray. "Dream" makes a giddy sound, not strong
Like "rent," "feeding a wife," "satisfying a man."

But could a dream send up through onion fumes
Its white and violet, fight with fried potatoes
And yesterday's garbage ripening in the hall,
Flutter, or sing an aria down these rooms

Even if we were willing to let it in,
Had time to warm it, keep it very clean,
10   Anticipate a message, let it begin?

We wonder. But not well! not for a minute!
Since Number Five is out of the bathroom now,
We think of lukewarm water, hope to get in it.

The Rites for Cousin Vit

Carried her unprotesting out the door.
Kicked back the casket-stand. But it can't hold her,
That stuff and satin aiming to enfold her,
The lid's contrition nor the bolts before.
Oh oh. Too much. Too much. Even now, surmise,
She rises in the sunshine. There she goes,

Back to the bars she knew and the repose
In love-rooms and the things in people's eyes.
Too vital and too squeaking. Must emerge.
10   Even now she does the snake-hips with a hiss,
Slops the bad wine across her shantung, talks
Of pregnancy, guitars and bridgework, walks
In parks or alleys, comes haply on the verge
Of happiness, haply hysterics. Is.

We Real Cool

> The Pool Players.
> Seven at the Golden Shovel.

We real cool. We
Left school. We

Lurk late. We
Strike straight. We

Sing sin. We
Thin gin. We

Jazz June. We
Die soon.

The Lovers of the Poor

                    arrive. The Ladies from the Ladies' Betterment League
Arrive in the afternoon, the late light slanting
In diluted gold bars across the boulevard brag
Of proud, seamed faces with mercy and murder hinting
Here, there, interrupting, all deep and debonair,
The pink paint on the innocence of fear;
Walk in a gingerly manner up the hall.
Cutting with knives served by their softest care,
Served by their love, so barbarously fair.
10   Whose mothers taught: You'd better not be cruel!
You had better not throw stones upon the wrens!
Herein they kiss and coddle and assault

Anew and dearly in the innocence
With which they baffle nature. Who are full,
Sleek, tender-clad, fit, fiftyish, a-glow, all
Sweetly abortive, hinting at fat fruit,
Judge it high time that fiftyish fingers felt
Beneath the lovelier planes of enterprise.
To resurrect. To moisten with milky chill.
20   To be a random hitching-post or plush.
To be, for wet eyes, random and handy hem.
    Their guild is giving money to the poor.
The worthy poor. The very very worthy
And beautiful poor. Perhaps just not too swarthy?
Perhaps just not too dirty nor too dim
Nor—passionate. In truth, what they could wish
Is—something less than derelict or dull.
Not staunch enough to stab, though, gaze for gaze!
God shield them sharply from the beggar-bold!
30   The noxious needy ones whose battle's bald
Nonetheless for being voiceless, hits one down.
    But it's all so bad! and entirely too much for them.
The stench; the urine, cabbage, and dead beans,
Dead porridges of assorted dusty grains,
The old smoke, *heavy* diapers, and, they're told,
Something called chitterlings. The darkness. Drawn
Darkness, or dirty light. The soil that stirs.
The soil that looks the soil of centuries.
And for that matter the *general* oldness. Old
40   Wood. Old marble. Old tile. Old old old.
Not homekind Oldness! Not Lake Forest, Glencoe.
Nothing is sturdy, nothing is majestic,
There is no quiet drama, no rubbed glaze, no
Unkillable infirmity of such
A tasteful turn as lately they have left,
Glencoe, Lake Forest, and to which their cars
Must presently restore them. When they're done
With dullards and distortions of this fistic
Patience of the poor and put-upon.
50   They've never seen such a make-do-ness as
Newspaper rugs before! In this, this "flat,"
Their hostess is gathering up the oozed, the rich
Rugs of the morning (tattered! the bespattered. . . .)
Readies to spread clean rugs for afternoon.
Here is a scene for you. The Ladies look,

In horror, behind a substantial citizeness
Whose trains clank out across her swollen heart.
Who, arms akimbo, almost fills a door.
All tumbling children, quilts dragged to the floor
60 And tortured thereover, potato peelings, soft-
Eyed kitten, hunched-up, haggard, to-be-hurt.
    Their League is alloting largesse to the Lost.
But to put their clean, their pretty money, to put
Their money collected from delicate rose-fingers
Tipped with their hundred flawless rose-nails seems . . .
    They own Spode, Lowestoft, candelabra,
Mantels, and hostess gowns, and sunburst clocks,
Turtle soup, Chippendale, red satin "hangings,"
Aubussons and Hattie Carnegie. They Winter
70 In Palm Beach; cross the Water in June; attend,
When suitable, the nice Art Institute;
Buy the right books in the best bindings; saunter
On Michigan, Easter mornings, in sun or wind.
Oh Squalor! This sick four-story hulk, this fibre
With fissures everywhere! Why, what are bringings
Of loathe-love largesse? What shall peril hungers
So old old, what shall flatter the desolate?
Tin can, blocked fire escape and chitterling
And swaggering seeking youth and the puzzled wreckage
80 Of the middle-passage, and urine and stale shames
And, again, the porridges of the underslung
And children children children. Heavens! That
Was a rat, surely, off there, in the shadows? Long
And long-tailed? Gray? The Ladies from the Ladies'
Betterment League agree it will be better
To achieve the outer air that rights and steadies,
To hie to a house that does not holler, to ring
Bells elsetime, better presently to cater
To no more Possibilities, to get
90 Away. Perhaps the money can be posted.
Perhaps they two may choose another Slum!
Some serious sooty half-unhappy home!—
Where loathe-love likelier may be invested.
    Keeping their scented bodies in the center
Of the hall as they walk down the hysterical hall,
They allow their lovely skirts to graze no wall,
Are off at what they manage of a canter,
And, resuming all the clues of what they were,
Try to avoid inhaling the laden air.

W. S. MERWIN

1927–

William Stanley Merwin grew up in Union City, New Jersey, and Scranton, Pennsylvania. He claims that a strong early influence on his poetry was hearing his father, a Presbyterian minister, read from the King James Version of the Bible. He went to Princeton, where he tended to spend too much time reading, horseback riding, and trying "with abiding desperation" to write poetry. He did further studies in Romance languages at McGill University, and then traveled abroad, earning his living as a tutor in France and Portugal. He then lived in England for five years, doing translations for the British Broadcasting Company Third Programme. He is as well known as a translator as he is as a poet, and considers translation "practice," much "as a dancer practices," for his own poetry. In 1971 he won the Pulitzer Prize for *The Carrier of Ladders*, and he now lives and writes on the island of Maui, Hawaii, with his wife and his collie, Koa. He likes to read books on animal behavior, and is fascinated that "we are beginning to be able to talk to animals just as our language is dissolving."

Separation

Your absence has gone through me
Like thread through a needle.
Everything I do is stitched with its color.

Things

Possessor
At the approach of winter we are there.
Better than friends, in your sorrows we take no pleasure,
We have none of our own and no memory but yours.
We are the anchor of your future.
Patient as a border of beggars, each hand holding out its whole treasure,

We will be all the points on your compass.
We will give you interest on yourself as you deposit yourself with us.
Be a gentleman: you acquired us when you needed us,
10   We do what we can to please, we have some beauty, we are helpless,
Depend on us.

Economy

No need to break the mirror.
Here is the face shattered,
Good for seven years of sorrow.

Departure's Girl-Friend

Loneliness leapt in the mirrors, but all week
I kept them covered like cages. Then I thought
Of a better thing.

And though it was late night in the city
There I was on my way
To my boat, feeling good to be going, hugging
This big wreath with the words like real
Silver: *Bon Voyage.*

          The night
Was mine but everyone's, like a birthday.
10   Its fur touched my face in passing. I was going
Down to my boat, my boat,
To see it off, and glad at the thought.
Some leaves of the wreath were holding my hands
And the rest waved good-bye as I walked, as though
They were still alive.

And all went well till I came to the wharf, and no one.

I say no one, but I mean
There was this young man, maybe
Out of the merchant marine,
20   In some uniform, and I knew who he was; just the same
When he said to me where do you think you're going,
I was happy to tell him.

But he said to me, it isn't your boat,
You don't have one. I said, it's mine, I can prove it:
Look at this wreath I'm carrying to it,
Bon Voyage. He said, this is the stone wharf, lady,
You don't own anything here.

And as I
Was turning away, the injustice of it
Lit up the buildings, and there I was
30 In the other and hated city
Where I was born, where nothing is moored, where
The lights crawl over the stone like flies, spelling now,
Now, and the same fat chances roll
Their many eyes; and I step once more
Through a hoop of tears and walk on, holding this
Buoy of flowers in front of my beauty,
Wishing myself the good voyage.

When You Go Away

When you go away the wind clicks around to the north
The painters work all day but at sundown the paint falls
Showing the black walls
The clock goes back to striking the same hour
That has no place in the years

And at night wrapped in the bed of ashes
In one breath I wake
It is the time when the beards of the dead get their growth
I remember that I am falling
10 That I am the reason
And that my words are the garment of what I shall never be
Like the tucked sleeve of a one-armed boy

Tale

After many winters the moss
finds the sawdust crushed bark chips
and says old friend
old friend

Elegy

Who would I show it to

The Morning

The first morning
I woke in surprise to your body
for I had been dreaming it
as I do

all around us white petals had never slept
leaves touched the early light
your breath warm as your skin on my neck
your eyes opening

smell of dew

PHILIP LEVINE

1928–

Levine was born in Detroit, Michigan, and educated in the public schools
there. He graduated from Wayne State University, and then went on to the
University of Iowa for his M.F.A. He began writing poetry at the age of
nineteen, and pursued careers as "an industrial worker and a bum." Tired
of urban life, he left Detroit in 1958 to teach at California State University in
Fresno. He is not a poet who fits neatly into any one particular mold, nor
does he wish to be: "to settle into any role, philosophy, world-view, faith
would be a betrayal of who I was put on earth to be and what my poetry
should be about." His subjects are often street people, blue collar workers,
young toughs; he writes of abattoirs, dirt and sweat, and hopeless causes.
Yet he writes also of love, of his Jewish boyhood, his family and his children. He combines a delicacy of touch, a controlled energy in whatever he
writes. His rhythms range from incantatory to lyrical, and the voice is very
human.

For Fran

She packs the flower beds with leaves,
Rags, dampened papers, ties with twine
The lemon tree, but winter carves
Its features on the uprooted stem.

I see the true vein in her neck
And where the smaller ones have broken
Blueing the skin, and where the dark
Cold lines of weariness have eaten

Out through the winding of the bone.
10   On the hard ground where Adam strayed,
Where nothing but his wants remain,
What do we do to those we need,

To those whose need of us endures
Even the knowledge of what we are?
I turn to her whose future bears
The promise of the appalling air,

My living wife, Frances Levine,
Mother of Theodore, John, and Mark,
Out of whatever we have been
20   We will make something for the dark.

Hold Me

The table is cleared of my place
and cannot remember. The bed sags
where I turned to death, the earth fills
my first footsteps, the sun drowns my sight.

A woman turns from the basket
of dried white laundry and sees the room
flooding with the rays of my eyes,
the burning of my hair and tongue.

I enter your bedroom, you look up
10   in the dark from tying your shoes
and see nothing, your boney shoulders
stiffen and hold, your fingers stop.

Was I dust that I should fall?
Was I silence that the cat heard?
Was I anger the jay swallowed?
The black elm choking on leaves?

In May, like this May, long ago
my tiny Russian Grandpa—the bottle king—
cupped a stained hand under my chin
20   and ran his comb through my golden hair.

Sweat, black shag, horse turds on the wind,
the last wooden cart rattling down

the alleys, the clop of his great gray mare,
green glass flashing in December sun . . .

I am the eye filled with salt,
his child climbing the rain, we are
all the moon, the one planet, the hand
of five stars flung on the night river.

No One Remembers

A soft wind
off the stones of the dead.
I pass by, stop the car,
and walk among none
of my own, to say
something useless
for them, something
that will calm me under
the same old beaten sky,
10   something to let me
go on with this day
that began so badly
alone in a motel 10 miles
from where I was born.

I say *Goodbye* finally
because nothing else is here,
because it is Goodbye,
Uncle Joe, big cigar, fist
on the ear, nodding *sure*
20   *bitch* and coming at me.
You can't touch me now,
and she's a thousand miles
from here, hell, she may be
dancing long past dawn
across the river
from Philly. It's morning
there too, even in Philly,
it's morning on Lake St. Clair
where we never went fishing,
30   along the Ohio River, the Detroit,
morning breaking on
the New York Central Express
crashing through the tunnel
and the last gasp of steam

before the entrance into hell
or Baltimore, but it's not
morning where you are, Joe,
unless you come with me.

I'm going to see her today.
40   She'll cry like always
when you raised your voice
or your fist, she'll
be robed near the window
of the ward when I come in.
No, she won't be dancing.
It's my hand she'll take
in hers and spread on her lap,
it's me she'll feel
slowly finger by finger
50   like so many threads back
to where the blood died
and our lives met
and went wrong, back
to all she said she'd be,
woman, promise, sigh,
dark hair in the mirror
of a car window all night
on the way back from Georgia.

You think because I
60   was a boy, I didn't hear,
you think because you had
a pocketful of loose change,
your feet on the desk,
your own phone, a yellow car
on credit, I didn't see
you open your hands
like a prayer and die
into them the way a child
dies into a razor, black hair,
70   into a tire iron, a chain.
You think I didn't smell
the sweat that rose
from your bed, didn't
know you on the stairs
in the dark, grunting
into a frightened girl.
Because you could push me

aside like a kitchen chair
and hit where you wanted,
80   you think I was a wren,
a mourning dove
surrendering the nest.

The earth is asleep, Joe,
it's rock, steel, ice,
the earth doesn't care
or forgive. No one remembers
your eyes before they tired,
the way you fought weeping.
No one remembers how much
90   it cost to drive all night
to Chicago, how much
to sleep all night in a car,
to have it all except
the money. No one remembers
your hand, opened, warm
and sweating on the back
of my neck when you first
picked me up and said
my name, *Philip,* and held
100   the winter sun up
for me to see outside
the French windows of
the old house on Pingree,
no one remembers.

Ricky

I go into the back yard
and arrange some twigs
and a few flowers. I go alone
and speak to you as I never could
when you lived, when you
smiled back at me shyly.
Now I can talk to you as I talked
to a star when I was a boy,
expecting no answer, as I talked
10   to my father who had become
the wind, particles of rain
and fire, these few twigs
and flowers that have no name.

*

Last night they said a rosary
and my boys went, awkward
in slacks and sport shirts,
and later sitting under the hidden
stars they were attacked and beaten.
You are dead, and a nameless rage
20   is loose. It is 105,
the young and the old burn
in the fields, and though they cry
enough the sun hangs on
bloodying the dust above the aisles
of cotton and grape.

*

This morning they will say a mass
and then the mile-long line of cars.
Teddy and John, their faces swollen,
and four others will let you
30   slowly down into the fresh earth
where you go on. Scared now,
they will understand some of it.
Not the mass or the rosary
or the funeral, but the rage.
Not you falling through the dark
moving underwater like a flower
no one could find until
it was too late and you had gone out,
your breath passing through dark water
40   never to return to the young man,
pigeon-breasted, who rode
his brother's Harley up the driveway.

*

Wet grass sticks to my feet, bright
marigold and daisy burst in the new day.
The bees move at the clumps
of clover, the carrots—
almost as tall as I—
have flowered, pale lacework.
Hard dark buds

50 of next year's oranges, new green
of slick leaves, yellow grass
tall and blowing by the fence. The grapes
are slow, climbing the arbor,
but some day there will be shade
here where the morning sun whitens
everything and punishes my eyes.

*

Your people worked so hard
for some small piece of earth,
for a home, adding a room
60 a boy might want. Butchie said
you could have the Harley
if only you would come back,
anything that was his.

*

A dog barks down the block
and it is another day. I hear
the soft call of the dove,
screech of mockingbird and jay.
A small dog picks up the tune,
and then *tow-weet tow-weet*
70 of hidden birds, and two finches
darting over the low trees—
there is no end.

*

What can I say to this mound
of twigs and dry flowers, what
can I say now that I would speak
to you? Ask the wind, ask
the absence or the rose burned
at the edges and still blood red.
And the answer is you
80 falling through black water
into the stillness that fathers
the moon, the bees ramming into
the soft cups, the eucalyptus
swaying like grass under water.

My John told me your cousin
punched holes in the wall
the night you died and was afraid
to be alone. Your brother
walks staring at the earth.
90   I am afraid of water.

*

And the earth goes on
in blinding sunlight.
I hold your image
a moment, the long
Indian face
the brown almond eyes
your dark skin full
and glowing as you grew
into the hard body
100   of a young man.

*

And now it is bird screech
and a tree rat suddenly
parting the tall grass
by the fence, lumbering
off, and in the distance
the crashing of waves
against some shore
maybe only in memory.

*

We lived by the sea.
110   Remember, my boys wrote
postcards and missed you
and your brother. I slept
and wakened to the sea,
I remember in my dreams
water pounded the windows
and walls, it seeped
through everything,
and like your spirit,
Ricky, like your breath,
120   nothing could contain it.

Let Me Begin Again

Let me begin again as a speck
of dust caught in the night winds
sweeping out to sea. Let me begin
this time knowing the world is
salt water and dark clouds, the world
is grinding and sighing all night, and dawn
comes slowly and changes nothing. Let
me go back to land after a lifetime
of going nowhere. This time lodged
10 in the feathers of some scavenging gull
white above the black ship that docks
and broods upon the oily waters of
your harbor. This leaking freighter
has brought a hold full of hayforks
from Spain, great jeroboams of dark
Algerian wine and quill pens that can't
write English. The sailors have stumbled
off toward the bars or the bright houses.
The captain closes his log and falls asleep.
20 1/10'28. Tonight I shall enter my life
after being at sea for ages, quietly,
in a hospital named for an automobile.
The one child of millions of children
who has flown alone by the stars
above the black wastes of moonless waters
that stretched forever, who has turned
golden in the full sun of a new day.
A tiny wise child who this time will love
his life because it is like no other.

ADRIENNE RICH
1929–

Born the daughter of a physician in Baltimore, Maryland, Adrienne Rich
completed her first book of poetry, *A Change of World* (1952), while still an
undergraduate at Radcliffe. W. H. Auden, who had chosen her book for
publication in the Yale Series of Younger Poets, described her poems as
"very neatly and modestly dressed," as poems which "respect their elders
but are not cowed by them." Rich had indeed learned her craft well from
her elders: Frost, Thomas, Auden, Stevens, Yeats—all male poets. "I had
been taught that poetry should be 'universal,' which meant of course, non-

female." In her poetry, one sees her moving from the split between "the
girl who wrote poems, who defined herself in writing poems, and the girl
who was to define herself by her relationship with men," until she was "able
to write for the first time, directly about experiencing myself as a woman."
Much of her poetry deals with the separation between men and women,
between self and others, though her latest poetry emphasizes the possibility of a "common language" which will transcend such separation. She
was married in 1953 to Alfred Conrad, an economist who died in 1970, and
with whom she had three sons. She has taught at a number of colleges and
universities, and presently teaches at Douglass College, Rutgers.

The Afterwake

Nursing your nerves
to rest, I've roused my own; well,
now for a few bad hours!
Sleep sees you behind closed doors.
Alone, I slump in his front parlor.
You're safe inside. Good. But I'm
like a midwife who at dawn
has all in order: bloodstains
washed up, teapot on the stove,
10   and starts her five miles home
walking, the birthyell still
exploding in her head.

Yes, I'm with her now: here's
the streaked, livid road
edged with shut houses
breathing night out and in.
Legs tight with fatigue,
we move under morning's coal-blue star,
colossal as this load
20   of unexpired purpose, which drains
slowly, till scissors of cockcrow snip the air.

Novella

Two people in a room, speaking harshly.
One gets up, goes out to walk.
(That is the man.)
The other goes into the next room
and washes the dishes, cracking one.
(That is the woman.)

It gets dark outside.
The children quarrel in the attic.
She has no blood left in her heart.
10   The man comes back to a dark house.
The only light is in the attic.
He has forgotten his key.
He rings at his own door
and hears sobbing on the stairs.
The lights go on in the house.
The door closes behind him.
Outside, separate as minds,
the stars too come alight.

Night-Pieces: For a Child

1. *The Crib*

You sleeping I bend to cover.
Your eyelids work. I see
your dream, cloudy as a negative,
swimming underneath.
You blurt a cry. Your eyes
spring open, still filmed in dream.
Wider, they fix me—
—death's head, sphinx, medusa?
You scream.
10   Tears lick my cheeks, my knees
droop at your fear.
Mother I no more am,
but woman, and nightmare.

2. *Her Waking*

Tonight I jerk astart in a dark
hourless as Hiroshima,
almost hearing you breathe
in a cot three doors away.

You still breathe, yes—
and my dream with its gift of knives,
its murderous hider and seeker,
ebbs away, recoils

back into the egg of dreams,
10   the vanishing point of mind.
All gone.

But you and I—
swaddled in a dumb dark
old as sickheartedness,
modern as pure annihilation—

we drift in ignorance.
If I could hear you now
mutter some gentle animal sound!
If milk flowed from my breast again. . . .

5:30 A.M.

Birds and periodic blood.
Old recapitulations.
The fox, panting, fire-eyed,
gone to earth in my chest.
How beautiful we are,
she and I, with our auburn
pelts, our trails of blood,
our miracle escapes,
our whiplash panic flogging us on
10   to new miracles!
They've supplied us with pills
for bleeding, pills for panic.
Wash them down the sink.
This is truth, then:
dull needle groping in the spinal fluid,
weak acid in the bottom of the cup,
foreboding, foreboding.
No one tells the truth about truth,
that it's what the fox
20   sees from her scuffled burrow:
dull-jawed, onrushing
killer, being that
inanely single-minded
will have our skins at last.

Moving in Winter

Their life, collapsed like unplayed cards,
is carried piecemeal through the snow:
Headboard and footboard now, the bed
where she has lain desiring him
where overhead his sleep will build
its canopy to smother her once more;

their table, by four elbows worn
evenings after evening while the wax runs down;
mirrors grey with reflecting them,
10   bureaus coffining from the cold
things that can shuffle in a drawer,
carpets rolled up around those echoes
which, shaken out, take wing and breed
new altercations, the old silences.

Rape

There is a cop who is both prowler and father:
he comes from your block, grew up with your brothers,
had certain ideals.
You hardly know him in his boots and silver badge,
on horseback, one hand touching his gun.

You hardly know him but you have to get to know him:
he has access to machinery that could kill you.
He and his stallion clop like warlords among the trash,
his ideals stand in the air, a frozen cloud
10   from between his unsmiling lips.

And so, when the time comes, you have to turn to him,
the maniac's sperm still greasing your thighs,
your mind whirling like crazy. You have to confess
to him, you are guilty of the crime
of having been forced.

And you see his blue eyes, the blue eyes of all the family
whom you used to know, grow narrow and glisten,
his hand types out the details
and he wants them all
20   but the hysteria in your voice pleases him best.

You hardly know him but now he thinks he knows you:
he has taken down your worst moment
on a machine and filed it in a file.
He knows, or thinks he knows, how much you imagined;
he knows, or thinks he knows, what you secretly wanted.

He has access to machinery that could get you put away;
and if, in the sickening light of the precinct,

and if, in the sickening light of the precinct,
your details sound like a portrait of your confessor,
30   will you swallow, will you deny them, will you lie your way home?

Amnesia

I almost trust myself to know
when we're getting to that scene—
call it the snow-scene in *Citizen Kane:*

the mother handing over her son
the earliest American dream
shot in a black-and-white

where every flake of snow
is incandescent
with its own burden, adding-

10   up, always adding-up to the
cold blur of the past
But first there is the picture of the past

simple and pitiless as the deed
truly was
the putting-away of a childish thing

Becoming a man means leaving
someone, or something—
still, why

must the snow-scene blot itself out
20   the flakes come down so fast
so heavy, so unrevealing

over the something that gets left behind?

GARY SNYDER
1930–

Gary Snyder was born in San Francisco and grew up on a farm just north of
Seattle, Washington. His mother stimulated his early interest in poetry. She
herself wrote poetry, read poetry to her boy every night, and wrote down

the poems that he made up before he could read and write. After graduating from Reed College, Snyder studied linguistics at Indiana, Oriental culture at Berkeley, and Zen Buddhism in Kyoto, Japan, with the aid of a Bollingen grant. He has worked as a logger, forest ranger, and merchant seaman, and claims that his impulse to write often comes from working with his hands, feeling "very close to the rhythms of whatever my work is." His poems reflect both his closeness to nature and his meditations on it as a "nonverbal world, which is nature as nature is itself."

Mid-August at Sourdough Mountain Lookout

Down valley a smoke haze
Three days heat, after five days rain
Pitch glows on the fir-cones
Across rocks and meadows
Swarms of new flies.

I cannot remember things I once read
A few friends, but they are in cities.
Drinking cold snow-water from a tin cup
Looking down for miles
10   Through high still air.

Riprap[1]

Lay down these words
Before your mind like rocks.
        placed solid, by hands
In choice of place, set
Before the body of the mind
        in space and time:
Solidity of bark, leaf, or wall
        riprap of things:
Cobble of milky way,
10   straying planets,
These poems, people,
        lost ponies with
Dragging saddles—
        and rocky sure-foot trails.

1. In trail-building some places are reinforced with a "riprap"
   of stones to retard erosion.

The worlds like an endless
        four-dimensional
Game of *Go*.
        ants and pebbles
In the thin loam, each rock a word
        a creek-washed stone
Granite: ingrained
        with torment of fire and weight
Crystal and sediment linked hot
        all change, in thoughts,
As well as things.

20

An Autumn Morning in Shokoku-ji

Last night watching the Pleiades,
Breath smoking in the moonlight,
Bitter memory like vomit
Choked my throat.
I unrolled a sleeping bag
On mats on the porch
Under the thick autumn stars.
In dream you appeared
(Three times in nine years)
Wild, cold, and accusing.
I woke shamed and angry:
The pointless wars of the heart.
Almost dawn. Venus and Jupiter.
The first time I have
Ever seen them close.

10

Looking at Pictures
to Be Put Away

Who was this girl
In her white night gown
Clutching a pair of jeans

On a foggy redwood deck.
She looks up at me tender,
Calm, surprised,

What will we remember
Bodies thick with food and lovers
After twenty years.

It Was When

We harked up the path in the dark
    to the bamboo house
        green strokes down my back
        arms over your doubled hips
  under cow-breath thatch
      bent   cool
              breasts brush my chest
—and Naga walked in with a candle,
    "I'm sleepy"

10 Or jungle ridge by a snag—
      banyan canyon—a Temminck's Robin
        whirled down the waterfall gorge
    in zazen, a poncho spread out on the stones.
      below us the overturning
        silvery
      brush-bamboo slopes—
rainsqualls came up on us naked
    brown nipples in needles of ocean-
        cloud
20   rain.

Or the night in the farmhouse
    with Franco on one side, or Pon
    Miko's head against me, I swung you
      around and came into you
  careless and joyous,
        late
        when Antares had set

Or out on the boulders
    south beach at noon
30   rockt by surf
    burnd under by stone
    burnd over by sun
        saltwater caked
  skin swing
      hips on my eyes
          burn   between;

That we caught: sprout
    took grip in your womb and it held.

40

new power in your breath called its place.
blood of the moon   stoppt;
you pickt your steps well.

Waves
    and the
        prevalent easterly
            breeze.
        whispering into you,
            through us,
                the grace.

SYLVIA PLATH
1932–1963

She was the daughter of Aurelia Plath, a high school teacher of Austrian parentage, and Otto Plath, who had come from Prussia at the age of sixteen, was a professor of biology at Boston University, and an authority on bees. After her father's death in 1940, the family moved to Wellesley, where Aurelia Plath taught high school and encouraged Sylvia and her brother in their literary pursuits. By the time Plath entered Smith College, she was beginning to have her poems and short stories published. She graduated from Smith in 1955 and won a Fulbright Scholarship to Newnham College, Cambridge. There she met, and in 1956 married, British poet Ted Hughes. Except for a year during which Plath taught freshman English at Smith College, the couple lived in England. In 1960, Plath published her first book of poems, *Colossus*, and her first child was born. After the birth of a second child in 1962, Plath and Hughes separated. Plath was frequently ill, working to support herself and her children, and waking before daybreak to write her poetry, turning out two to three poems a day. The strain proved too great, and she took her life in February, 1963.

Sheep in Fog

The hills step off into whiteness.
People or stars
Regard me sadly, I disappoint them.

The train leaves a line of breath.
O slow
Horse the colour of rust,

Hooves, dolorous bells—
All morning the
Morning has been blackening,

10 A flower left out.
My bones hold a stillness, the far
Fields melt my heart.

They threaten
To let me through to a heaven
Starless and fatherless, a dark water.

Daddy

You do not do, you do not do
Any more, black shoe
In which I have lived like a foot
For thirty years, poor and white,
Barely daring to breathe or Achoo.

Daddy, I have had to kill you.
You died before I had time—
Marble-heavy, a bag full of God,
Ghastly statue with one grey toe
10 Big as a Frisco seal

And a head in the freakish Atlantic
Where it pours bean green over blue
In the waters off beautiful Nauset.
I used to pray to recover you.
Ach, du.

In the German tongue, in the Polish town
Scraped flat by the roller
Of wars, wars, wars.
But the name of the town is common.
20 My Polack friend

Says there are a dozen or two.
So I never could tell where you
Put your foot, your root,
I never could talk to you.
The tongue stuck in my jaw.

It stuck in a barb wire snare.
Ich, ich, ich, ich,
I could hardly speak.
I thought every German was you.
30 And the language obscene

An engine, an engine
Chuffing me off like a Jew.
A Jew to Dachau, Auschwitz, Belsen.
I began to talk like a Jew.
I think I may well be a Jew.

The snows of the Tyrol, the clear beer of Vienna
Are not very pure or true.
With my gypsy ancestress and my weird luck
And my Taroc pack and my Taroc pack
40 I may be a bit of a Jew.

I have always been scared of *you*,
With your Luftwaffe, your gobbledygoo.
And your neat mustache
And your Aryan eye, bright blue.
Panzer-man, panzer-man, O You—

Not God but a swastika
So black no sky could squeak through.
Every woman adores a Fascist,
The boot in the face, the brute
50 Brute heart of a brute like you.

You stand at the blackboard, daddy,
In the picture I have of you,
A cleft in your chin instead of your foot
But no less a devil for that, no not
Any less the black man who

Bit my pretty red heart in two.
I was ten when they buried you.
At twenty I tried to die
And get back, back, back to you.
60 I thought even the bones would do.

But they pulled me out of the sack,
And they stuck me together with glue.
And then I knew what to do.
I made a model of you,
A man in black with a Meinkampf look

And a love of the rack and the screw.
And I said I do, I do.
So daddy, I'm finally through.
The black telephone's off at the root,
70   The voices just can't worm through.

If I've killed one man, I've killed two—
The vampire who said he was you
And drank my blood for a year,
Seven years, if you want to know.
Daddy, you can lie back now.

There's a stake in your fat black heart
And the villagers never liked you.
They are dancing and stamping on you.
They always *knew* it was you.
80   Daddy, daddy, you bastard, I'm through.

Kindness

Kindness glides about my house.
Dame Kindness, she is so nice!
The blue and red jewels of her rings smoke
In the windows, the mirrors
Are filling with smiles.

What is so real as the cry of a child?
A rabbit's cry may be wilder
But it has no soul.
Sugar can cure everything, so Kindness says.
10   Sugar is a necessary fluid,

Its crystals a little poultice.
O kindness, kindness
Sweetly picking up pieces!
My Japanese silks, desperate butterflies,
May be pinned any minute, anaesthetized.

And here you come, with a cup of tea
Wreathed in steam.
The blood jet is poetry,
There is no stopping it.
20   You hand me two children, two roses.

Edge

The woman is perfected.
Her dead

Body wears the smile of accomplishment,
The illusion of a Greek necessity

Flows in the scrolls of her toga,
Her bare

Feet seem to be saying:
We have come so far, it is over.

Each dead child coiled, a white serpent,
10   One at each little

Pitcher of milk, now empty.
She has folded

Them back into her body as petals
Of a rose close when the garden

Stiffens and odours bleed
From the sweet, deep throats of the night flower.

The moon has nothing to be sad about,
Staring from her hood of bone.

She is used to this sort of thing.
20   Her blacks crackle and drag.

Words

Axes
After whose stroke the wood rings,
And the echoes!
Echoes travelling
Off from the centre like horses.

The sap
Wells like tears, like the
Water striving
To re-establish its mirror
10   Over the rock

That drops and turns,
A white skull,
Eaten by weedy greens.
Years later I
Encounter them on the road—

Words dry and riderless,
The indefatigable hoof-taps.
While
From the bottom of the pool, fixed stars
20   Govern a life.

IMAMU AMIRI BARAKA (LEROI JONES)
1934–

He was born LeRoi Jones in Newark, New Jersey, where his father was a postal superintendent and his mother was a social worker. His early attempts at writing were comic strips and science fiction. At the age of nineteen, he graduated from Howard University, where he had first majored in pre-medical studies but had switched to an English major. From 1954 to 1957, he served in the Strategic Air Command as an aerial gunner and climatographer, and then settled in New York's Greenwich Village, becoming known as a jazz critic. He returned to graduate work, studying German literature and philosophy at Columbia University and the New School for Social Research. Caught up in the growing civil rights movement, he moved to Harlem in 1965, and then to Newark, where he founded the Black Community Development and Defense Organization. He was arrested during the Newark riots in 1967, but was later acquitted. One of the strongest voices of the Afro-American community, he has won many awards as a poet, dramatist, essayist, and novelist.

The Turncoat

The steel fibrous slant & ribboned glint
of water. The Sea. Even my secret speech is moist
with it. When I am alone & brooding, locked in
with dull memories & self hate, & the terrible disorder
of a young man.

I move slowly. My cape spread stiff & pressing cautiously
in the first night wind off the Hudson. I glide down
onto my own roof, peering in at the pitiful shadow of myself.

How can it mean anything? The stop & spout, the
10   wind's dumb shift. Creak of the house & wet smells
coming in. Night forms on my left. The blind still
up to admit a sun that no longer exists. Sea move.

I dream long bays & towers . . . & soft steps on moist sand.
I become them, sometimes. Pure flight. Pure fantasy. Lean.

Ka 'Ba

A closed window looks down
on a dirty courtyard, and black people
call across or scream across or walk across
defying physics in the stream of their will

Our world is full of sound
Our world is more lovely than anyone's
tho we suffer, and kill each other
and sometimes fail to walk the air

We are beautiful people
10   with african imaginations
full of masks and dances and swelling chants
with african eyes, and noses, and arms,
though we sprawl in grey chains in a place
full of winters, when what we want is sun.

We have been captured,
brothers. And we labor
to make our getaway, into
the ancient image, into a new

correspondence with ourselves
20   and our black family. We need magic
now we need the spells, to raise up
return, destroy, and create. What will be

the sacred words?

Legacy

(For Blues People)

In the south, sleeping against
the drugstore, growling under

the trucks and stoves, stumbling
through and over the cluttered eyes
of early mysterious night. Frowning
drunk waving moving a hand or lash.
Dancing kneeling reaching out, letting
a hand rest in shadows. Squatting
to drink or pee. Stretching to climb
10   pulling themselves onto horses near
where there was sea (the old songs
lead you to believe). Riding out
from this town, to another, where
it is also black. Down a road
where people are asleep. Towards
the moon or the shadows of houses.
Towards the songs' pretended sea.

An Agony. As Now.

I am inside someone
who hates me. I look
out from his eyes. Smell
what fouled tunes come in
to his breath. Love his
wretched women.

Slits in the metal, for sun. Where
my eyes sit turning, at the cool air
the glance of light, or hard flesh
10   rubbed against me, a woman, a man,
without shadow, or voice, or meaning.

This is the enclosure (flesh,
where innocence is a weapon. An
abstraction. Touch. (Not mine.
Or yours, if you are the soul I had
and abandoned when I was blind and had
my enemies carry me as a dead man
(if he is beautiful, or pitied.

It can be pain. (As now, as all his
20   flesh hurts me.) It can be that. Or

pain. As when she ran from me into
that forest.
   Or pain, the mind
silver spiraled whirled against the
sun, higher than even old men thought
God would be. Or pain. And the other. The
yes. (Inside his books, his fingers. They
are withered yellow flowers and were never
beautiful.) The yes. You will, lost soul, say
30   'beauty.' Beauty, practiced, as the tree. The
slow river. A white sun in its wet sentences.

Or, the cold men in their gale. Ecstasy. Flesh
or souls. The yes. (Their robes blown. Their bowls
empty. They chant at my heels, not at yours.) Flesh
or soul, as corrupt. Where the answer moves too quickly.
Where the God is a self, after all.)

Cold air blown through narrow blind eyes. Flesh,
white hot metal. Glows as the day with its sun.
It is a human love, I live inside. A bony skeleton
40   you recognize as words or simple feeling.

But it has no feeling. As the metal, is hot, it is not,
given to love.

It burns the thing
inside it. And that thing
screams.

ROSMARIE WALDROP

1935–

She was born in Kitzingen am Main, Germany, and studied comparative
literature in Würzburg, Aix-en-Provence, and took her Ph.D. at the University of Michigan. She combines teaching with writing, and with her husband
Keith Waldrop is an editor and printer of poetry for Burning Deck Press in
Providence, Rhode Island. She also translates French and German poetry,
her largest project being Edmund Jabès' seven-volume *Book of Questions*.
Some of the poems here are from a sequence inspired in part by a tedious
year of commuting between teaching at Wesleyan University in Middle-
town, Connecticut, and living in Providence. She has since given up driving
and has turned her car in for a bicycle.

Deflecting Forces

We try to make ourselves at home
in our lives
horses
in their stable
rubbing cheeks against security
and it takes effort
leaves our arteries dry
caked
with the cult of
10 all that's solid
but it takes wind
the always restless air
washes against the
PROVIDENCE HURRICANE BARRIER
to tell us rest
is a peculiar kind of movement
on the moving earth
our element's
unstable
20 it takes sky swept lengthwise
by gusts and squalls
cut into lines of energy
tensed
to breaking
furrows like
strata of tin and
lead
it takes whirling
widdershins towards the pole
30 and I'll sway like elms
their arms raised
witnesses
of terrifying visions
and scream
and scream

Stroke

Your leg won't
let you stand on it
you think it's out of place
somewhere

disconnected
at the ankle or the knee
everybody looks like
someone you know
this nurse or that
10   strange lady with
the alligator purse
this is march '66
your wife
took all your things from you
her needle's watching
you have nothing now but it's
because you're religious
lights and flashes
on the wall you see them now
20   also you have no elbow
in your right arm
this doesn't look like your hand
doesn't feel like it either
and it just won't

From **The Road Is Everywhere or Stop This Body**

76

as drowsiness mists lines
into contagious surfaces
swallow the steep
horizon straight ahead where
I'm going.
ahead is behind me in the grey
dizzy swerves and screws on an assembly
line up endlessly repeated
gestures flatten out
10   as this corvair will in a year
unless I keep its hulk
a monument:
THE VICTORY OF MICHIGAN

77

the body's angle at a
tilt downhill surrenders its
shadow falls back behind

the metal's pull
swings space out into
the face in the next car held in
by its profile
as gestures fold back against trying
to leave in sudden bolts of legs and wrists
10   eddies
uneven glints

78

the cigarette still burning
a voice says "we must go beyond
the surface"
withdraws from scrutiny
into the turmoil our code
makes head or tail of
all the orifices of the body
ears vulva penis nostrils mouth
anus heedless of

10   the duration of a word until
the now discounts desire into
being seen and
seeing intervals
step out of line
into solidity

79

it's not enough to think to see

shock of the "outside" at our
fingertips

radiate a cone of attention
through the steering wheel out into
points of space my body
haunts from inside
the "world" is not ahead where I'm
launched into the gap
10   of mind ahead of body
widens with the metal lining of
my skin
flaunts its refusal
to harden into
durability

                    80

the signs
of course I want this sequence

won't get me out I
participate in spite
of me
if I look back
there's no trace
of my passage
no improbable footprint
10   or tire mark
sitting in my own obstacle
eyes open on
the constant disappearing
translating
one measurement
into another

3
DRAMA

Contexts of Drama

DRAMA, LITERATURE, AND REPRESENTATIONAL ART

Drama begins in make-believe, in the play acting of children, in the ritual of primitive religion. And it never forsakes its primitive beginnings, for imitative action is its essence. When an actor appears on stage, he makes believe he is someone other than himself, much as a child does, much as primitive people still do. Thus, like play-acting and ritual, drama creates its experience by doing things that can be heard and seen. "Drama," in fact, comes from a Greek word meaning "thing done." And the things it does, as with play-acting and ritual, create a world apart—a world modeled on ours yet leading its own charmed existence.

Drama, of course, is neither primitive ritual nor child's play, but it does share with them the essential quality of *enactment*. This quality should remind us that drama is not solely a form of literature. It is at once literary art *and* representational art. As literary art, a play is a fiction made out of words. It has a plot, characters, and dialogue. But it is a special kind of fiction—a fiction *acted out* rather than narrated. In a novel or short story, we learn about characters and events through the words of a narrator who stands between us and them, but in a play nothing stands between us and the total make-up of its world. Characters appear and events happen without any intermediate comment or explanation. Drama, then, offers us a *direct* presentation of its imaginative reality. In this sense it is representational art.

As students of drama, we are faced with something of a paradox. Because it is literature, a play can be read. But because it is representational art, a play is meant to be witnessed. We can see this problem in other terms. The text of a play is something like the score of a symphony—a finished work, yet only a potentiality until it is performed. Most plays, after all, are written to be performed. Those eccentric few that are not—that are written only to

673

be read—we usually refer to as *closet dramas*. Very little can take place in a closet, but anything is possible in the theater. For most of us, however, the experience of drama is usually confined to plays in print rather than in performance. This means that we have to be unusually resourceful in our study of drama. Careful reading is not enough. We have to be creative readers as well. We have to imagine drama on the stage: not only must we attend to the meanings and implications of words—we also have to envision the words in performance. By doing so, we can begin to experience the understanding *and* pleasure that spectators gain when they attend a play. Their place, of course, is the theater, where our study properly begins.

DRAMA AND THEATRICAL PERFORMANCE

The magic of theater, its ability to conjure up even such incredible characters as the Ghost in *Hamlet,* or the Witches in *Macbeth,* or Death in *Everyman,* depends on the power of *spectacle.* And by spectacle we mean all the sights and sounds of performance—the slightest twitch or the boldest thrust of a sword, the faintest whisper or the loudest cry. Spectacle, in short, is the means by which the fictional world of a play is brought to life in the theater. When we witness a play, our thoughts and feelings are provoked as much by the spectacle as by the words themselves. Thus in reading a play, we should continually seek to create its spectacle in the imaginative theater of our minds. To do so, we must take a special approach to the text of a play.

It is not enough to read the text as simply a sequence of statements made by characters talking to one another or to themselves. We must also read the text as a *script* for performance, as if we were directors and actors involved in staging the play. Once we interpret it as a script, we can then see that the text contains innumerable cues from which we can construct a spectacle in our mind's eye. If we are attentive to those cues, they will tell us about the various elements that make up the total spectacle: *setting, costuming, props, blocking* (the arrangement of characters on the stage), *movement, gestures, intonation,* and *pacing* (the tempo and coordination of performance). By keeping those elements continuously in mind, we can imagine what the play looks and sounds like on stage. Then we will truly be entering into the world of the play, and by doing so we will not only understand, but also experience, its meaning.

Some dramatists, such as Ibsen, Shaw, and Williams, provide extensive and explicit directions for performance in parenthetical remarks preceding the dialogue and interspersed with it. But no matter how extensive their remarks may be, they are never complete guides to production. They still require us to infer elements of the spectacle from the dialogue itself. Other dramatists such as Sophocles, Shakespeare, and Molière provide little, if any, explicit guidance about staging. When we read their plays, we must gather our cues almost entirely from the dialogue. Thus we have chosen a passage from Shakespeare both to illustrate how the text of a play can embody a script for performance, and to demonstrate the analytic method appropriate for discovering its implicit cues. In the next paragraph we will provide a brief explanation of the context for the passage. With that background in hand, you should then examine the dialogue carefully to see what details you can infer on your own about the arrangement, gestures, and physical interaction of the characters.

The following passage from Act I, Scene 2, of *Othello* depicts a confrontation between Othello, leader of the Venetian military forces, and Brabantio, a Venetian senator. The confrontation is occasioned by the fact that Othello has secretly courted and married Brabantio's daughter Desdemona—a fact revealed to Brabantio in the previous scene by Roderigo, a jealous suitor of Desdemona, and Iago, the duplicitous subordinate of Othello. As the passage begins, Othello and his officers Cassio and Iago are on their way to meet with the Duke of Venice, who has sent messengers to summon Othello to a military planning session.

IAGO   Come, captain, will you go?
OTHELLO   Have with you.
CASSIO   Here comes another troop to seek for you.

Enter Brabantio, Roderigo, and others with lights and weapons.

IAGO   It is Brabantio. General, be advised.
   He comes to bad intent.
OTHELLO   Holla! stand there!
RODERIGO   Signior, it is the Moor.
BRABANTIO   Down with him, thief!

They draw on both sides.

IAGO   You, Roderigo! Come, sir, I am for you.
OTHELLO   Keep up your bright swords, for the dew will rust them.
   Good signior, you shall more command with years
   Than with your weapons.
BRABANTIO   O thou foul thief, where hast thou stowed my daughter?
   Damned as thou art, thou hast enchanted her!
   For I'll refer me to all things of sense,
   If she in chains of magic were not bound,
   Whether a maid so tender, fair, and happy,
   So opposite to marriage that she shunned
   The wealthy curlèd darlings of our nation,
   Would ever have, t'incur a general mock,
   Run from her guardage to the sooty bosom
   Of such a thing as thou—to fear, not to delight.
   Judge me the world if 'tis not gross in sense
   That thou hast practiced on her with foul charms,

Abused her delicate youth with drugs or minerals
That weaken motion. I'll have't disputed on;
'Tis probable, and palpable to thinking.
I therefore apprehend and do attach thee
For an abuser of the world, a practicer
Of arts inhibited and out of warrant.
Lay hold upon him. If he do resist,
Subdue him at his peril.
OTHELLO   Hold your hands,
Both you of my inclining and the rest.
Were it my cue to fight, I should have known it
Without a prompter.

This passage depicts a confrontation that twice threatens to erupt into a pitched sword battle between Brabantio's followers and those of Othello. Thus it is a highly dramatic moment in the play, and our purpose should be to envision the performance as fully and as precisely as possible. From the initial remarks of Iago and Othello, it appears that they must be moving to exit from one side of the stage, while Cassio, who is standing nearby, has not yet turned to depart and thus sees a group of people with torches entering from the opposite side of the stage. Cassio does not identify them—presumably because they are still some distance away and the light of their torches obscures their faces. But Cassio's announcement of "another troop" must cause Iago and Othello to reverse their direction, by which time Brabantio and his followers have moved close enough to be recognized by Iago.

Iago, of course, is directly responsible for Brabantio's appearance on the scene, having previously aroused his anger with the revelation of Othello's elopement. But since Othello and his followers are unaware of Iago's double-dealing, they can only take his warning about Brabantio's "bad intent" as the straightforward advice of a loyal officer. Thus, when Iago utters his warning, we should imagine Cassio and the other attendants of Othello moving forward and unsheathing their swords as though to make ready for a battle with Brabantio and his troop. Once we do so, we can recognize that Othello's command—"stand there!"—which might seem to be addressed to Brabantio and his followers, is in fact addressed to his own men. Even though Othello is a military man, he does not wish to settle this personal matter by force of arms, as is clear from his subsequent remarks to Brabantio. We might, then, even imagine Othello raising his arm at this point to accentuate that command of restraint to his troops.

Brabantio, however, responding to Roderigo's recognition of Othello—"Signior, it is the Moor"—incites his own followers to attack Othello and his men. Thus, at the moment that Brabantio makes his command to attack—"Down with him, thief!"—we should picture the two groups of men not only drawing their swords but also moving toward one another. Iago's challenge to Roderigo—"You, Roderigo! Come, sir, I am for you"—should cause us to see him as leading the charge of Othello's men. He is, of course, simply feigning an attack to sustain the impression of being Othello's loyal officer.

At this point Othello gives his second command of the scene—"Keep up your bright swords." When he does so, we should not only hear the authority of his voice but also envision the authority of his movement. We should imagine Othello, without any sword at all, stepping between the two groups of men, raising his arms to quell the movement on both sides, and then turning to address Brabantio face to face with a courtly but gentle reproof—"Good signior, you shall more command with years/Than with your weapons." At the same time that Othello is turning to address Brabantio, we should also visualize the two groups of men responding to his command by stepping back and away from one another, as well as relaxing their sword arms, so that Othello and Brabantio become the exclusive focus in the foreground of the scene.

Othello's attempt to calm the two sides does not by any means subdue Brabantio's anger. Brabantio instead delivers a lengthy attack on Othello's character, uttering a series of insults and accusations so extreme that we might well expect them to arouse Othello to defend his honor with his sword. But Othello, we notice, is silent throughout the harangue—which is a powerful dramatic statement in itself. That restraint should also lead us to see Othello as standing in a dignified posture, arms by his sides, while Brabantio accentuates his insults with physical gestures and movements, first pointing his finger accusingly at him, then raising his arm in self-righteous judgment, and probably even moving back and forth in front of him as he gives voice to his accusations. Then, at the conclusion of his harangue, we should imagine Brabantio as once again turning to his troop of men to issue his second command—"Lay hold upon him. If he do resist,/Subdue him at his peril."

Once again we should imagine the two groups of men raising their swords and moving to attack one another. And once again, when Othello gives his third command—"Hold your hands,/Both you of my inclining and the rest"—we should see him moving between the two groups to prevent a battle from taking place. That visual image of the action is important for us to keep in mind, because it is a definitive spectacle. It embodies above all the exceptional authority and restraint of Othello: twice in this brief passage he is faced with a potentially explosive situation, and twice he subdues the situation and himself with extraordinary grace.

Our discussion has thus far treated the passage as a script to guide us in imagining the physical interaction of the characters. We have examined each bit of the dialogue with an eye to the cues it contains about the gestures, movements, and spatial relations of the characters at every moment in the scene. Our approach has emphasized the theatrical, rather than the literary, implications of the passage. Detailed as it is, however, our analysis has not yet envisioned the action *on* stage *in* a theater. And we must do that too, if we wish to experience and understand the total spectacle of the scene. At this point, then, it might be tempting to imagine the action on a modern stage, equipped with machinery for sets and special lighting effects. We might imagine the characters arranged in front of a set depicting, for example, houses and public buildings, for we know from earlier cues in the text that the scene takes place on a street in Venice. We might, in turn, imagine the stage as completely darkened, except for the torches carried by the attendants of Othello and Brabantio, for we know also from earlier cues in the text, as well as from the torches themselves, that the scene takes place at about midnight. And we might, finally, imagine ourselves sitting in a darkened theater and witnessing the scene, which is framed like a picture by the arch of the stage.

Then we would have a vividly dramatic image and experience of the potential conflict between Brabantio's men and the supporters of Othello. Then, for example, the space initially dividing the two groups of men would be dramatically set off by the darkness engulfing it. Then their aggressive movements toward each other would be dramatically accentuated by the fiery movement of their torches. Then their weapons, reflecting the light of their torches, would truly appear to be "bright swords," as Othello calls them, particularly by contrast with the surrounding darkness. And then, each time Othello stepped between them, their response to his command would be visible in the subduing of that fiery brightness. All in all, the spectacle would be as dazzling as the authority of Othello himself.

But that spectacle is not what Shakespeare's seventeenth-century audiences would have seen when they witnessed the play. The Globe Theater, where Shakespeare's plays were originally produced, was an open-air structure without sets or lights of any kind. Thus the spectators of Shakespeare's time could not have witnessed the "realistic" illusion of a midnight street scene such as we have imagined in the previous paragraph. They would have seen the action take place in broad daylight on a bare stage without a backdrop. Thus they would have depended wholly upon the language, the actors, and their torches to evoke a sense of that dark Venetian street suddenly lighted up by those two fiery groups of men. Even so, they would have had a more intimate involvement with the characters and the action, for the Globe stage, rather than being set behind an arch, extended out into the audience itself. Their experience of the scene would thus have been quite different from that provided by our modern stage version. In light of that difference, we might well ask which version is valid. Both, in fact, are valid, but for different reasons. The modern version is valid, primarily because it is true to the theatrical conditions of our own time. Most modern theaters, after all, are not designed like the Globe, and if we attend a performance of *Othello* we should not expect it to duplicate the scene as produced in Shakespeare's time. But when we are reading the play we *can* imagine how it would have been produced in the Globe and thus be true to the theatrical conditions for which Shakespeare created it.

Once we have imagined any play in the context of the theater for which it was written, we can also bring that understanding to any production we may happen to witness. We can compare our imagined production with the production on stage, and by doing so we can recognize how the director and actors have adapted the original context of the play to their own theatrical circumstances. If, for example, we were to attend a production of *Othello*, we might see that scene with Brabantio, Othello, and their followers performed on a bare stage, without sets or props of any kind. Having imagined the scene in its original theatrical context, we would then not be surprised or puzzled by that bare stage, but would recognize that the director was attempting to incorporate an important element of seventeenth-century theater in a contemporary production. By being histor- ically informed play-readers, we can also become critically enlightened play-goers. With this in mind, we shall preface each of the plays in the "Classical to Neoclassical Drama" section with a description of the theater for which it was written. Those descriptions will provide a context for imagining the plays in their original theatrical setting. For this reason we recommend that before reading any play in that section, you read the theatrical description preceding it.

DRAMA AND OTHER LITERARY FORMS

In the preceding section we considered drama primarily as a theatrical event—a representational art to be performed and witnessed. In doing so, we were concerned with the uniquely dramatic experience created by a play in performance. But any performance, moving as it may be, is an *interpretation*—of how the lines should be enacted and delivered. Thus every production of a play stresses some words and minimizes others, includes some meanings and excludes others. No single production can possibly convey all the implications in the language of a play. This should remind us that drama is also a form of literature—an art made out of words—and should be understood in relation not only to the theater but also to the other literary forms: story, poem, and essay.

In relating drama to the other literary forms, we might first look again at the diagram in the general introduction to this book. That diagram, you will recall, locates and defines each form according to the unique way it uses words and communicates them to the reader. Drama in its pure form uses words to create action through the dialogue of characters talking to one another rather than to the reader: its essential quality is *interaction*. But the diagram, as we noted earlier, also represents the proximity of the forms to each other. Like a story, drama is concerned with plot and character. Like a poem, it is overheard rather than being addressed to a reader. Like an essay, it is capable of being used to explore issues and propose ideas. Using these relationships as points of departure, we can now examine some of the ways in which drama takes on the characteristics and devices of the other forms.

Drama and Narration

A play is at its most dramatic, of course, when it uses the give-and-take of dialogue to create interaction. But the interaction always takes place within a specific context—a background in time and place without which it cannot be properly understood. To bring about this understanding, drama turns to the narrative techniques of the story. This is not to say that we should expect to find storytellers addressing us directly in plays. Occasionally they do turn up (like the Stage Manager in *Our Town*), but more often the characters become storytellers in their dialogue with one another. The most obvious form of this storytelling occurs at the beginning of plays, and is appropriately called *exposition* because it sets forth and explains in a manner typical of narrative.

Exposition is important not only because it establishes the mood of a play but also because it conveys information about the world of that play. Through expository dialogue the dramatist may reveal information about the public state of affairs, as in the opening of *Oedipus Rex;* or exposition may disclose information about past actions and private relations of the characters, as in the opening of *Othello*. Often the information comes in bits and pieces of dialogue, as in life itself, so that we must put it together on our own. But once we have done so, we have a background for understanding the action that takes place during the play.

Related to exposition is another narrative device, called *retrospection*. Often, during the process of action, characters look back and survey significant events that took place well before the time of the play; and when this happens, drama is again using an element of narration. Sometimes retrospection may lead to major revelations about the characters and the motivations for their behavior, as in the lengthy conversation between Brick and Big Daddy toward the end of Act II of *Cat on a Hot Tin Roof*. Sometimes retrospection may be the principal activity of the play, as in *Oedipus Rex* and *The Stronger*. In both these plays the chief characters become preoccupied with piecing together elements from their past, and in each case the climax occurs when their retrospection leads them to discoveries about their past which totally reverse their view of themselves and their world.

Thus far we have looked at narrative elements referring to pre-play action, but there are also occasions when narration is used to convey the action of the play itself—when narration replaces interaction. Occasions such as these are produced when offstage action is reported rather than represented—for even when characters are offstage they are still doing things that we must know about in order to have a total view of the action. When offstage action is reported, a play becomes most nearly like a story. Words then are being used to develop a view of character and situation rather than to create action through dialogue. This process can be seen most clearly in *Oedipus Rex*, when the Second Messenger tells the Choragus about the death of Iokastê and the self-blinding of Oedipus. The interaction on stage ceases entirely for the length of almost fifty lines, and what we get instead has all the features of a miniature story.

The Messenger first establishes his narrative authority, then moves into his tale, supplying detailed information, offering explanations for facts he cannot provide, reporting dialogue, and concluding with a general reflection on the fate of Oedipus and Iokastê, whose experience he sees as epitomizing the "misery of mankind." In trying to explain why Sophocles has these events reported rather than showing them on stage, we might simply conclude that they are too gruesome to be displayed. But it is also true that through the Messenger's report Sophocles is able to provide a comment on the meaning of the events.

The Messenger's commentary brings us to the last important element of narration in drama—*choric commentary*. When the narrator of a story wishes to comment on characters and events, he can do so at will. But the dramatist, of course, cannot suddenly appear in the play—or on stage—to provide a point of view on the action. The dramatist's alternative is the *chorus*, or *choric characters*—personages, that is, who are relatively detached from the action and can thus stand off from it, somewhat like a narrator, to reflect on the significance of events. In Greek drama the chorus performed this function.

The existence of a chorus, however, is no guarantee that its opinions are always to be trusted. Sometimes it can be as wrongheaded as any of the more involved characters. Sometimes it is completely reliable, as in its concluding remarks in *Oedipus Rex* about the frailty of the human condition. Choric commentary, then, provides a point of view, but not necessarily an authoritative one, or one to be associated necessarily with the dramatist. In each case it has to be judged in the context of the entire play. But whether it is valid, or partially reliable, or completely invalid, the chorus does provoke us to reflect on the meaning of events by providing commentary for us to assess.

After the classical Greek period the formal chorus disappeared almost entirely from drama. Remnants of the chorus can, of course, be found in later plays—even in modern drama. In *The Threepenny Opera*, for example, several of the songs, particularly the three finales, explicitly comment on the social and political implications of the play. But for us as readers the important matter is to recognize that choric characters persist in drama despite the absence of a formally designated chorus. Minor characters such as messengers, servants, clowns, or others not directly involved in the action, can carry out the functions of a chorus, as does the Doctor at the end of *Everyman*. Characters involved in the action can also function as choric commentators, particularly if they are, like Eliante in *The Misanthrope*, endowed with a highly reasonable disposition. Ultimately, any character is capable of becoming a commentator of a sort, simply by standing off from the action and viewing it as a spectator rather than as a participant. And their reflections should be taken no less seriously than those of a chorus. After all, like Nora in the last scene of *A Doll's House*, or Othello in his last speech of the play, characters can be the most discerning judges of their world.

Drama and Meditation

When we recall that interaction through dialogue is the basis of drama, we can readily see that a play is committed by its very nature to showing us the public side of its characters. Realizing this, we can see as well the artistic problem a dramatist faces when trying to reveal the private side of such characters. The narrator of a story can solve this problem simply by telling us the innermost thoughts of the characters. But a dramatist must turn to the conventions of the poem, using words addressed by a speaker talking or thinking to himself.

When reading a purely lyric poem, we automatically assume that the situation is private rather than public and that we can overhear the words even though they might never be spoken aloud. In reading or witnessing a play, we must make a similar imaginative effort. To assist our efforts, dramatists have traditionally organized their plays so as to make sure that a character thinking to himself is seen in private. That special situation is implied by our term *soliloquy*, which means (literally) to speak alone. But it is also true that we have private thoughts even in the presence of others, and this psychological reality has been recognized by modern dramatists whose characters may often be seen thinking to themselves in the most public situations. Whatever the circumstances, private or public, the soliloquy makes unusual demands on both actors and audience.

As readers we should be aware that the soliloquy can perform a variety of functions, and, since it is so unusual an element in drama, it achieves its purposes with great effectiveness. Customarily, the soliloquy is a means of giving expression to a complex state of mind and feeling, and in most cases the speaker is seen struggling with problems of the utmost consequence. This accounts for the intensity we often find in the soliloquy. We are all familiar, for example, with Hamlet's predicaments—to be or not to be, to kill or not to kill the king—and these are typical of the weighty issues that usually burden the speaker of a soliloquy. In soliloquy, then, the interaction among characters is replaced by the interaction of a mind with itself.

When a play shifts from dramatic interaction to meditation, its process of events is temporarily suspended, and the soliloquizing character necessarily becomes a spectator of his world. In this way the soliloquy, like choric commentary, offers the dramatist a means of providing a point of view on the action of the play. In reading a soliloquy, then, we should examine it not only as the private revelation of a character but also as a significant form of commentary on other characters and events. Even the soliloquies of a villain such as Iago can offer us valuable points of view, especially when the villain happens, like Iago, to be a discerning judge of his world.

In considering the soliloquy, we have been examining only an element of meditation in drama. It is also possible for plays to become primarily or even exclusively meditative—though at first this probably sounds like a contradiction of dramatic form. If drama depends on the interaction of dialogue, how is it possible for internalized thought and feeling to be the principal subject of a play? Actually, this can happen in a number of ways. One way—a very traditional way—is to create a cast of characters who represent not persons but abstractions—who embody aspects, or qualities, or thoughts, or feelings of a single mind. In *Everyman*, for example, the title character is shown in conversation with other characters named Beauty, Strength, Discretion, and Five Wits. Interaction among characters of that sort is clearly meant to represent the interaction of a mind with itself, and so it constitutes the dramatization of a meditative experience achieved through what we might call an allegory of the mind.

We can also recognize plays dramatizing the life of the mind through methods other than allegory. Many modern plays, such as *Death of a Salesman*, or *A Streetcar Named Desire*, or *Equus*, include not only soliloquies and other kinds of monologue but also imaginary sequences depicting dreams and fantasies. And some contemporary plays, such as *Krapp's Last Tape*, consist exclusively of a single character talking to himself. Plays such as these reflect the influence of modern psychological theories about the behavior of the mind. Writing in 1932, for example, Eugene O'Neill defined the "modern dramatist's problem" as discovering how to "express those profound hidden conflicts of the mind which the probings of psychology continue to disclose to us." Almost fifty years earlier, in 1888, the Swedish dramatist Strindberg anticipated the same idea: "I have noticed that what interests people most nowadays is the psychological action." Looking at their statements side by side, we can see that they share the same concern. O'Neill speaks of "hidden conflicts of the mind," and Strindberg of "psychological action." We might also call it *meditative drama*.

Whatever form a meditative drama may take, we as readers must be alert to the "hidden conflicts" it aims to dramatize. To recognize such conflicts we must be attentive not only to the external action but also to what we might call the internal action. We should examine both plot and dialogue for what they can tell us about the mental life of the characters. And rather than looking for a clearly defined sequence of events, we should expect to find a kind of movement as irregular and hazy as the workings of the mind itself.

Drama and Persuasion

A play could be exclusively a piece of persuasion only if it consisted of a single character—the dramatist!—addressing ideas directly to the audience. In such an event, of course, it would be difficult to distinguish the play from a lecture. This extreme case should remind us that drama is rarely, if ever, simply an exposition or assertion of ideas. Ideas can, of course, be found throughout the dialogue of almost any play, but, as we have seen in the preceding sections, it is best to assume that those ideas are sentiments of the characters rather than the opinions of the dramatist. A character is a character. A dramatist is a dramatist. And dramatists are never present to speak for themselves, except in prefaces, prologues, epilogues, stage directions—and other statements outside the framework of the play.

Although dramatists cannot speak for themselves, their plays can. The essential quality of drama—interaction—may be made to serve the purposes of an essay. Dialogue, plot, and character may be used to expound ideas and sway the opinions of an audience. The desire to persuade usually implies the existence of conflicting ideas, and plays with a persuasive intention customarily seek to demonstrate the superiority of one idea, or set of attitudes, over another. Thus characters may become spokesmen for ideas, dialogue a form of debating ideas, and action a form of testing ideas. Plays of this kind inevitably force audiences and readers to examine the merits of each position and align themselves with one side or the other. In reading such plays, we must be attentive not only to the motives and personalities of characters but also to the ideas they espouse. Similarly, we must be interested not only in the fate of the characters but also in the success or failure of their ideas. Ultimately, then, these plays do not allow us the pleasure of simply witnessing the interaction of characters. Like essays, they seek to challenge our ideas and change our minds.

Because they focus on conflicting beliefs and ideas, plays with a persuasive intention often embody elements similar to a formal argument or debate. Like *The Misanthrope* or *Major Barbara*, they usually set up opposing values in their opening scenes. In the first scene of *The Misanthrope*, for example, Philinte espouses social conformity, Alceste opposes him by defending personal integrity; and their disagreement produces a debate that continues throughout the play. In much the same way, the opening act of *Major Barbara* establishes a conflict between the Salvation Army philosophy of Barbara and the economic-political vision of Undershaft. In defending their ideas, these characters behave so much like contestants in a debate that their dialogue sounds like disputation rather than conversation. And in the process of reading or witnessing each debate, we are clearly invited to take a stand ourselves, to side with one view or the other. The choice, of course, is not an easy one, and each play is designed to keep us from making a simple choice.

Modes of Drama

DRAMA, THE WORLD, AND IMITATION

Drama, as we said at the start, creates a world modeled on our own: its essence is imitative action. But drama is not imitative in the ordinary sense of the word. It does not offer us a literal copy of reality, for the truth of drama does not depend upon reproducing the world exactly as it is. Drama is true to life by being false to our conventional notions of reality.

The sexual sit-down strike in *Lysistrata* is outlandish. The abstract characters of *Everyman* are fantastic. The dialogue in *Krapp's Last Tape* is frequently bizarre. Yet each of these plays creates a world that we recognize as being in some sense like our own. Our problem then is to define the special sense in which drama is imitative. We can begin by recognizing that its mode of imitation must be selective rather than all-inclusive, intensive rather than extensive. It has to be, since time is short and space is limited in the theater. Faced with limitations in stage size and performance time, the dramatist obviously cannot hope to reproduce the world exactly as it is. By selecting and intensifying things, however, the dramatist can emphasize the dominant patterns and essential qualities of human experience. Thus, our understanding of any play requires that we define the principle of emphasis that determines the make-up of its world and the experience of its characters.

In defining the emphasis of any play, we can ask ourselves whether the dramatist has focused on the beautiful or the ugly, on the orderly or the chaotic, on what is best or on what is worst in the world. A play that emphasizes the beautiful and the orderly tends toward an idealized vision of the world—which is the mode we call *romance*. A play focusing on the ugly and chaotic tends toward a debased view of the world, and this we call *satire*. Both these emphases depend for their effect upon extreme views of human nature and existence.

In contrast to the extreme conditions of romance and satire, another pair of dramatic processes takes place in a world neither so beautiful as that of romance nor so ugly as that of satire—in a world more nearly like our own. Rather than focusing on essential qualities in the world, these processes—*comedy* and *tragedy*—emphasize the dominant patterns of experience that characters undergo in the world. In comedy the principal characters ordinarily begin in a state of opposition either to one another or to their world—often both. By the end of the play, their opposition is replaced by harmony. Thus the characters are integrated with one another and with their world. In tragedy, however, the hero and his world begin in a condition of harmony that subsequently disintegrates, leaving him by the end of the play completely isolated or destroyed.

With these four possibilities in mind, we might draw a simple diagram such as this:

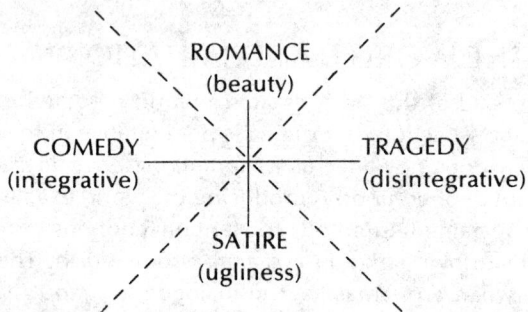

ROMANCE
(beauty)

COMEDY   TRAGEDY
(integrative)   (disintegrative)

SATIRE
(ugliness)

The vertical pair emphasize the essential qualities in the world; the horizontal pair emphasize the dominant patterns of human experience; the point of intersection—the absence of emphasis—refers to the world as it is. In this way we can immediately visualize each of the emphases, its distinguishing characteristics, and its relation to each of the others. Once we have recognized these possibilities, we might be tempted simply to categorize plays in terms of the characteristics we have identified with each emphasis. Yet it should be kept in mind that each emphasis is at best an abstraction—a definition formulated in order to generalize about a great number of plays, not an explanation of any one play in particular. Thus, when we turn to individual plays we should not necessarily expect that they can be accurately described and understood simply by labeling them comedy or tragedy, satire or romance.

As a way of anticipating some of the complexities, we can see in the diagram that each emphasis borders on two others. Comedy, for example, tends toward romance, on the one hand, and satire, on the other. The same is true of tragedy, and the others. Even the antithetical possibilities, as we will see, can interact. But this should hardly surprise us: if the world can incorporate both the beautiful and the ugly, so can a play. Ultimately, then, these categories will serve us best if we use them tactfully as guides to understanding rather than as a rigid system of classification. But before they can serve us as guides, we must familiarize ourselves with their characteristics in greater detail.

TRAGEDY AND COMEDY

Tragedies usually end in death and mourning, comedies in marriage and dancing. That difference accounts for the two familiar masks of drama, one expressing sorrow, the other joy, one provoking tears, the other laughter. That difference also accounts for the commonly held notion that tragedy is serious, and comedy frivolous. But when we consider that both modes are probably descended from primitive fertility rites—tragedy from ritual sacrifice, comedy from ritual feasting—we can recognize that they dramatize equally important dimensions of human experience. Tragedy embodies the inevitability of individual death, comedy the irrepressibility of social rebirth. So, like autumn and spring, tragedy and comedy are equally significant phases in a natural cycle of dramatic possibilities. Indeed, like the seasons of the year and the nature of human experience, they are inextricably bound up with one another.

Every comedy contains a potential tragedy—the faint possibility that harmony may not be achieved, that the lovers may not come together to form a new society. And every tragedy contains a potential comedy—the faint possibility that disaster may be averted, that the hero or heroine may survive. This in turn should remind us that we must be concerned not only with the distinctive endings of tragedy and of comedy, but also with the means by which each brings about its end. Catastrophe in and of itself does not constitute tragedy, nor does marriage alone make for comedy. The unique experience of each mode is produced by the design of its plot and the nature of the characters who take part in it. We can grasp this principle most clearly by looking first at the elements of tragedy, then at the elements of comedy.

Tragedy was first defined by the Greek philosopher Aristotle (384–322 B.C.), who inferred its essential elements from witnessing the plays of his own time. His observations, which he set down in the *Poetics,* cannot be expected to explain all the tragedies that have ever been written; no single theory could possibly do so. But Aristotle's theory has influenced more dramatists—and critics—than any other propounded since his time, and thus it remains the best guide we have to the nature of tragedy.

Aristotle considered *plot* to be the most important element of tragedy, because he believed that "all human happiness or misery takes the form of action," that "it is in our actions—what we do—that we are happy or the reverse." Thus, in discussing tragedy, he emphasized the design of the plot and established several important qualities that contribute to its effect. First, he stressed the *unity* of a tragic plot. By unity he meant that the plot represents a single action, or story, with a definite beginning, middle, and end, and further that all its incidents are "so closely connected that the transposal or withdrawal of any one of them will disjoin or dislocate the whole." By close connection he also meant that the incidents are causally related to one another, so that their sequence is probable and necessary. Ultimately, then, we can see that, in emphasizing the unity of a tragic plot, Aristotle was calling attention to the quality of the inevitable that we associate with tragedy. Thus in reading a tragedy we should attempt to define the chain of cause and effect linking each incident in the plot. In this way we will understand the process that makes its catastrophe inevitable, and thus gain insight into the meaning of the catastrophe.

In examining the plot of a tragedy such as *Oedipus Rex,* we may be tempted to regard its catastrophe as not only inevitable but also inescapable. Aristotle, however, did not see the inevitable change in the fortunes of the tragic hero as being the result of chance, or coincidence, or fate, or even of some profound flaw in the character of the hero. Rather, he saw the change of fortune as being caused by "some error of judgment," a "great error," on the part of the hero. In defining this element of tragedy, Aristotle clearly regarded the hero or heroine, and not some condition beyond human control, as responsible for initiating the chain of events leading to the change of fortune. Even a profound flaw in character, after all, is beyond human control. Accordingly, Aristotle described the tragic hero as an "intermediate kind of personage" in moral character, neither "preeminently virtuous and just," nor afflicted "by vice and depravity"—as someone morally "like ourselves," in whom we can engage our emotional concern. Thus, when we read tragedies such as *Oedipus Rex* or *Othello,* we should not regard their protagonists as victims of absurd circumstances, but rather should seek to identify the sense in which they are agents of their undoing.

While we seek to understand the nature of their error, we should not forget that most tragic heroes are genuinely admirable characters—persons, as Aristotle tells us, who deservedly enjoy "great reputation and prosperity." And their reputation is a function not simply of their social rank but also of their commitment to noble purposes. Oedipus is not merely a king but also a man committed to discovering the truth and ridding his city of the plague. Othello is not only a military leader but also a man committed to moral purity in all his actions as well as in all his personal relations. Romeo and Juliet are not simply the children of aristocratic families but also persons committed to a love that transcends the pettiness of family squabbles and political factions. Our response to them should thus combine judgment with sympathy and admiration.

Once we make the effort to discover their error, we shall find that we undergo an experience parallel to that of the protagonists themselves. We shall find that we are compelled by the process of events—by the turn of the plot—to recognize how they have undone themselves. The protagonist's act of recognition is defined by Aristotle as the *discovery*, because it entails "a change from ignorance to knowledge." And the discovery, as Aristotle recognized, is caused inevitably by a *reversal*, an incident or sequence of incidents that go contrary to the protagonist's expectations. Reversal and discovery are crucial elements of the tragic experience, because they crystalize its meaning for the protagonist—and for us. When events go contrary to their expectations, when the irony of their situation becomes evident, they—and we—have no choice but to recognize exactly how the noblest intentions can bring about the direst consequences. Thus, in its discovery, as in its entire plot, tragedy affirms both the dignity and the frailty of man.

Discovery scenes take place in comedy as well, but, rather than accounting for an inevitable disaster, comic discoveries reveal information that enables characters to avoid a probable catastrophe. Lost wills may be found, or mistaken identities corrected, or some other fortuitous circumstance may be revealed. Somehow comedy always manages to bring about a happy turn of events for its heroes and heroines—and thus those heroes and heroines are rarely the sole or primary agents of their success. Usually, in fact, they get a large helping hand from chance, or coincidence, or some other lucky state of affairs. Comedy thrives on improbability. And in doing so it defies the mortal imperatives of tragedy.

In this sense comedy embodies the spirit of spring with its eternal promise of rebirth and renewal, and it embodies, too, the festive air and festive activities we associate with spring. The term *comedy*, in fact, is derived from a Greek word, *komoidia*, meaning revel-song, and revelry always finds its way into comedy, whether in the form of feasts and dancing, tricks and joking, sex and loving—or all of them combined, as in *Lysistrata*. So the perils that develop in the world of comedy rarely seem very perilous to us. Although the characters themselves may feel temporarily threatened, the festive air makes us sense that ultimately no permanent damage will be done, and thus we share the perspective of Puck in *A Midsummer Night's Dream*, when he says:

> Jack shall have Jill,
> Naught shall go ill,
> The man shall have his mare again, and all shall be well.

Though comedy avoids the experience of death, it does not evade the significance of life. Comic plots, in fact, usually arise out of conflicts that embody opposing values and beliefs. Thus the conflicts among characters inevitably pit one set of attitudes against another, one kind of social vision against another. In reading comedies, therefore, we should attempt to identify the attitudes that bring characters into conflict. In *Lysistrata*, for example, the wives are committed to peace, their husbands to political honor. In *A Midsummer Night's Dream* the young lovers, Hermia and Ly-sander, are committed to their vows of true love, but Hermia's father is com-mitted to his parental authority. In *Major Barbara*, Lady Britomart is committed to social tradition, Barbara to social philanthropy, and Under-shaft to social engineering. Once we have identified those conflicting val-ues, we will discover that they can help us to understand the meaning of a comic plot.

Comedy usually begins with a state of affairs dominated by one kind of social idea, and thus the resolution of a comic plot—achieved through its scenes of discovery—embodies the triumph of a new social order. Whoever wins out in comedy is invariably on the right side, no matter how improb-able the victory may seem. Thus it is that the characters who oppose the new order of things—the blocking figures—are usually subjected to comic ridicule throughout the play. Comedy, after all, expresses an irreverent at-titude toward old and inflexible ideas, toward any idea that stifles natural and reasonable impulses in the human spirit. But comedy, as we said earlier, also embodies the generous and abundant spirit of spring. Its heroes and heroines—the proponents of the new society—always seek to include their opponents in the final comic festivities. Comedy seeks not to destroy the old, but rather to reclaim it. And therein is to be seen the ultimate expres-sion of its exuberant faith in life.

SATIRE AND ROMANCE

Satire and romance, rather than dramatizing the dominant patterns of hu-man experience, embody the essential qualities and potentialities of human nature. Romance bears witness to what humanity can be at its best, satire to what it can be at its worst. Romance offers us an idealized vision of hu-man potentiality, satire a spectacle of inferior human conduct. Thus, when we encounter plays in these modes, we should not expect to find the mor-ally "intermediate kind" of character of whom Aristotle speaks in his dis-cussion of tragedy. Rather we should expect to encounter characters who tend toward moral, social, or psychological extremes of behavior. For the same reason, we should not expect finely detailed personalities with com-plex motivations. Rather, we should expect characters who represent types of human nature dominated by clear-cut attitudes and impulses.

Satire and romance are intended ultimately to produce clear-cut images of good or evil, virtue or vice, wisdom or folly; and those images may be embodied most vividly in characters who are boldly outlined rather than finely detailed. Such qualities may also be highlighted through *contrast*. Thus, the plots of satire and romance often bring together characters from both extremes, using their interaction to create emphatic contrasts. We can best understand these elements by looking first at satire, then at romance.

Satiric drama always expresses a critical attitude toward a particular aspect of human conduct and affairs. The satire may focus on morality, society, politics, or some other dimension of human nature and culture. Our first purpose in reading a satiric play should thus be to identify the focus of its criticism, as we can do by examining the characters themselves to see what particular types of behavior predominate among them. In Ben Jonson's *Volpone*, for example, all the leading characters in the first act—Volpone, Mosca, Corvino, Corbaccio, and Voltore—are obsessed by material greed. The principal character, Volpone, is motivated additionally by lust and pride. In short, the world of *Volpone* impresses us as being morally corrupt. In *The Misanthrope*, most of the characters are motivated by social ambitiousness. Célimène is a malicious gossip and an incurable coquette, Arsinoe a jealous and hypocritical prude, Oronte a vain poet and officious lover, Acaste and Clitandre a matched pair of pretentious fops. Even Alceste, the "misanthrope," the self-proclaimed enemy of social pretensions, is badly flawed by his extraordinary egotism. The world of these characters thus strikes us as a false and shallow society.

Once we have identified the dominant vices of the characters, we should explore the consequences of their behavior, and we can do so by examining the incidents of the plot. In *Volpone*, for example, the greed of the characters is shown to threaten the ethical and legal foundations of their society. In *The Misanthrope* the social pretensions of the characters are shown to make them incapable of loving one another or feeling genuine affection for one another. Thus in each case the plot is designed to dramatize not only the vice but also its moral or social implications. Satiric plots incorporate discovery scenes as well, and the discoveries of satire inevitably bring about the public exposure of the principal characters. Volpone, for example, is exposed in court and legally punished. Célimène is exposed in her own house and subjected to social ridicule.

As those discovery scenes indicate, satiric drama does not necessarily offer us a completely pessimistic spectacle of human affairs. Indeed, we will usually find that a satire incorporates at least a few virtuous characters. Celia and Bonario in *Volpone* are completely generous and trusting individuals— so much so that they are almost helpless to prevent themselves from being victimized by the others. And in *The Misanthrope*, Philinte and particularly Eliante are sensible enough to transcend the shallowness of their society. These characters, by representing the virtuous potentiality of human nature, not only highlight the ugliness surrounding them in the satiric world but also remind us in the end that humanity is not—and need not be—depraved. In other words, satire offers us an intensified but not completely negative view of human imperfection.

Romance, by analogy, offers us an intensified but not completely idealized vision of human excellence. The heroes of romance, for example, are typically shown in conflict with characters representing aspects of human imperfection or depravity. Prospero in *The Tempest* is threatened by his malign brother Antonio, who embodies the sin of pride; Everyman is tempted by Fellowship and Goods, who embody the evils of worldliness. Although these heroes triumph over the malign forces in their world, the struggle is perilous, and their success inevitably requires the assistance of miraculous events or supernatural powers. Prospero depends on his magic wand and on Ariel, the spirit who performs extraordinary deeds for him. And Everyman can redeem his soul only through the miraculous power of the sacraments. In this respect the heroes of dramatic romance resemble their counterparts in a well-known narrative form of romance, the medieval tale of chivalric love and adventure, which portrays virtuous knights doing battle with evil monsters and triumphing over them through the power of a magic sword or some other kind of talisman. Their miraculous power, of course, is derived from, and symbolic of, their commitment to the forces of goodness and truth in their world. And that condition should remind us that romance typically assumes the existence of a divinely ordered world, in which the hero succeeds because he recognizes that order and is obedient to it.

In reading or witnessing a romance play, such as *The Tempest* or *Everyman,* we must make a similar commitment ourselves. We must be willing to believe in the possibility of a supernatural power. That act of belief, however, is nothing more than an extension of our willingness to accept the imaginative premises of any story or play. Once we do so, we can see that romance drama develops plausibly within its special premises, that the miraculous achievements of its heroes are genuinely deserved. Prospero in the end is able to redeem his kingdom because he recognizes the persistence of evil in his world and the necessity to be eternally vigilant against it. And Everyman at last is able to redeem his soul because he recognizes the futility of clinging to bodily life, as well as the necessity to accept its inevitable demise. Thus the discovery scenes of romance, which reveal the hero's miraculous achievement, are prepared for by the hero's heightened state of moral or spiritual awareness. And that awareness always includes a recognition of human frailty. In this sense, as in its plot and characters, the idealized vision of romance never completely ignores the actual conditions of the world.

TRAGICOMEDY, NATURALISM, AND ABSURDIST DRAMA

Tragedy, comedy, satire, and romance—each of those primary modes embodies its own unique pattern of dramatic experience. As we have seen, each incorporates distinctly different kinds of plots and characters, distinctly different kinds of conflicts and discovery scenes, and each achieves a distinctly different view of human existence. Thus, when we read or witness a tragedy or comedy, a satire or romance, we undergo an experience that is more or less clear-cut. We feel sorrow or joy, scorn or admiration. We know, in short, exactly how we feel, exactly what we think.

But some plays—many modern plays, especially—do not arouse such clear-cut responses. As we read or witness them, our feelings and judgments may well be confused, or ambiguous, or mixed in one way or another. We may well feel torn between sorrow and joy, scorn and admiration. Indeed, we may not know exactly how we feel, or exactly what we think. When we find ourselves experiencing such mixed feelings, we will probably also discover that the play itself has been designed to leave us in an unresolved state of mind—that it does not embody a clear-cut pattern of catastrophe or rebirth (as in tragedy or comedy) or present clear-cut images of good or evil (as in romance or satire). Many plays, rather than being dominated by a single mode, actually combine differing or opposing modes of dramatic experience. In describing such works we use the term *tragicomedy*—not as a value judgment but as a means of defining the ambiguous experience that we witness in the play and feel within ourselves. Tragicomedy, then, leaves us with a complex reaction, similar to the uncertainty we often feel in response to life itself.

Uncertainty—about the nature of human existence—is a fundamental source of the tragicomic quality we find in many modern and contemporary plays. In some, that quality is produced by a *naturalistic* view of human nature and experience—a view of men and women as influenced by psychological, social, and economic forces so complex that their character and behavior cannot be easily judged or explained. That view of human nature led Strindberg, for example, to create characters whom he describes as being "somewhat 'characterless'"—characters, that is, who are influenced by "a whole series of motives," rather than by any single, or simple, purpose. Like other naturalistic dramatists, Strindberg is unwilling to offer us simple explanations to account for human behavior:

> A suicide is committed. Business troubles, says the man of affairs. Unrequited love, say the women. Sickness, says the invalid. Despair, says the down-and out. But it is possible that the motive lay in all or none of these directions, or that the dead man concealed his actual motive by revealing quite another, likely to reflect more to his glory.

Just as we cannot definitely account for their actions, so too the characters in naturalistic drama cannot themselves perceive, much less control, all the forces influencing their behavior. Typically, then, the protagonists of naturalistic drama, such as Mrs. X in *The Stronger*, or Nora in *A Doll's House*, or Brick in *Cat on a Hot Tin Roof*, or the women in *Mother and Child*, are placed in dramatic situations portraying them as being in some sense victims of their environment. They may wilfully deceive themselves about the nature of their circumstances, as does Mrs. X, or they may attempt to alter their circumstances, as does Nora, or they may acquiesce in them, as does Brick, or they may sit in judgment upon them, as do the women; but whatever action they take, it does not lead to a clear-cut resolution of the kind we associate with tragedy and comedy. Nor does their situation allow us to make the clear-cut moral judgment that we do of characters in satire and romance. "Vice has a reverse side very much like virtue," as Strindberg reminds us. Thus, naturalistic drama leaves us with a problematic view of human experience, and the most we can hope for is to understand, to the degree that we humanly can, the psychological, social, and economic circumstances that are contributing to the problematic situations of its characters.

In some contemporary plays the problematic situation is produced by conditions that transcend even naturalistic explanations. In these plays we sense the presence of some profound situation that afflicts the characters but is in the end indefinable. In Beckett's *Endgame*, for example, we find the principal characters existing in a world where all the elements of nature seem to be on the verge of extinction; yet the cause of that condition remains a mystery. In *Krapp's Last Tape*, we are faced with a single character, namely Krapp, whose existence is defined almost exclusively by an insatiable appetite for bananas, an unquenchable thirst for soda-water, and an obsessive fixation on his tape-recorded diary. These mysterious, even ridiculous, circumstances lead us to wonder whether there is *any* ultimate source of meaning *at all* in the world of those plays, or for that matter whether there is *any* rational source of explanation *at all* for the experience of the characters. For this reason, such plays are known as *absurdist* drama.

Their absurdity is usually evident not only in plot but in dialogue as well. Often, for example, the conversation of characters in absurdist drama does not make perfect sense, either because they are talking at cross purposes, or because their language has no clear point of reference to anything in their world. Yet even as we read the dialogue we will find it to be at once laughably out of joint and terrifyingly uncommunicative. In much the same way we may be puzzled by the resolution of these plays—wondering whether the characters' situation at the end is in any significant respect different from what it was at the beginning, wondering whether the play is tragic or comic, wondering even whether there is any single word, or concept, such as *tragicomedy*, that can adequately express the possibility that human existence may be meaningless. Ultimately, then, absurdist drama like the other modes does embody a view of human existence; but rather than perceiving existence as dominated by one pattern or another, one quality or another, that view implies that existence may have no pattern or meaning at all.

Elements of Drama

CONTEXTS, MODES, AND THE ELEMENTS OF DRAMA

Characters, dialogue, plot—these are the indispensable elements of drama. Together they make possible the imitative world of every play, for characters are like people, dialogue and plot like the things they say and do. But likeness does not mean identicalness. As we indicated in our discussion of dramatic modes, the truth of drama does not depend upon reproducing the world exactly as it is. For this reason, we should not expect to find characters who talk and act in just the same way that people do, nor should we expect to find plots that develop in just the same way that ordinary events do. The characters who populate romance and satire, for example, are modeled less on specific people than on human potentialities. Similarly, the plots elaborated in comedy and tragedy are based less on real occurrences than on basic patterns of human experience. The elements of drama, then, are highly specialized versions of the elements that make up the world as it is. The particular version we encounter in any single play will be determined by a variety of circumstances—by the mode of the play, the purpose of the play, the literary form of the play, and the design of the theater for which it was written. Thus we should always keep these circumstances in mind when we study the elements of drama.

DIALOGUE

The give-and-take of dialogue is a specialized form of conversation. Designed as it is to serve the needs created by the various contexts and modes of drama, it can hardly be expected to sound like our customary patterns of speech. In ordinary conversation, for example, we adjust our style to meet the needs of the people with whom we are talking, and we reinforce our words with a wide range of facial expressions, bodily gestures, and vocal inflections, many of which we perform unconsciously. If we recognize that we are not being understood, we may stammer momentarily while trying to rephrase our feelings and ideas. Then, before we can get the words out, someone may have interrupted us and completely changed the topic of conversation. Whatever the case, we find ourselves continually adjusting to circumstances that are as random as our thoughts and the thoughts of those with whom we are talking. If we were to transcribe and then listen to the tape of an ordinary conversation, even one that we considered coherent and orderly, we would probably find it far more erratic and incoherent than we had imagined.

Drama cannot afford to reproduce conversation as faithfully as a tape recorder. To begin with, the limitations of performance time require that characters express their ideas and feelings much more economically than we do in the leisurely course of ordinary conversation. The conditions of theatrical performance demand also that dialogue be formulated so that it can be not only heard by characters talking to one another but also overheard and understood by the audience in the theater. Thus the continuity of dialogue must be very clearly marked out at every point. On the basis of what is overheard, the audience—or the reader—must be able to develop a full understanding of the characters and the plot.

Dialogue, then, is an extraordinarily significant form of conversation, for it is the means by which every play conveys the total make-up of its imaginative world. And this is not all. Dialogue must fulfill the needs of not only the audience but also the director, the set designer, and the actors. This means that the dialogue must serve as a script for all the elements of production and performance—for the entire theatrical realization of a play.

Because it has to serve so many purposes all at once, dialogue is necessarily a more artificial form of discourse than ordinary conversation. Thus, in reading any segment of dialogue, we should always keep in mind its special purposes. It is a script for theatrical production, and that means that we should see what it can tell us about the total spectacle: the setting, the arrangement of characters on the stage, their physical movements, gestures, facial expressions, and inflections. It is also a text for conveying the imaginative world of the play, which means that we should see what it can tell us about the character speaking, the character listening, and the other characters not present; about the public and private relations among the characters, the past as well as present circumstances of the characters, and the quality of the world they inhabit; about the events that have taken place prior to the play, the events that have taken place offstage during the play, the events that have caused the interaction of the characters during the dialogue itself, and the events that are likely to follow from their interaction. If we read the dialogue with all these concerns in mind, we will find in the end that it takes us out of ourselves and leads us into the imaginative experience of the play.

PLOT

Plot is a specialized form of experience. We can see just how specialized it is if we consider for a moment what happens during the ordinary course of our daily experience. Between waking and sleeping, we probably converse with a number of people and perform a variety of actions. But most of these events have very little to do with one another, and they usually serve no purpose other than our pleasure, our work, or our bodily necessities. In general, the events that take place in our daily existence do not embody a significant pattern or process. If they have any pattern at all, it is merely the product of habit and routine.

In drama, however, every event is part of a carefully designed pattern and process. And this is what we call plot. Plot, then, is not at all like the routine, and often random, course of our daily existence. Rather it is a wholly interconnected system of events, deliberately selected and arranged for the purpose of fulfilling a complex set of imaginative and theatrical purposes. Plot is thus an extremely artificial element, and it has to be so. Within the limits of a few hours the interest of spectators—and readers—has to be deeply engaged and continuously sustained. That requires a system of events that quickly develops complications and suspense, and leads in turn to a climax and resolution. Interest must also be aroused by events that make up a process capable of being represented on stage. And the totality of events must create a coherent imitation of the world.

In order to understand how plot fulfills these multiple purposes, we should first recognize that it comprises *everything* that takes place in the imaginative world of a play. In other words, plot is not confined to what takes place on stage: it includes off-stage as well as on-stage action, reported as well as represented action. In *The Misanthrope,* for example, we witness a process that includes among other events a lawsuit brought against Alceste, tried in court, and judged in favor of his enemy. Yet we never actually see his enemy, nor do we hear the case being tried. We only hear *about* it—before and after it takes place—from the dialogue of Alceste and Philinte. Obviously the lawsuit does take place within the imaginative world of the play. It is part of the plot. But it is not part of what we call the *scenario*—the action occurring on stage. Thus, if we wish to identify the plot of a play, we have to distinguish it from the scenario. The scenario embodies the plot and presents it to us, but it is not itself the plot.

We can understand this distinction in another way if we realize that in a plot all the events are necessarily arranged *chronologically.* whereas in a scenario events are arranged *dramatically*—that is, in an order that will create the greatest impact on the audience. In some cases that may result in non-chronological order. We may well reach the end of a scenario before we learn about events that took place years before. For this reason, in studying the plot of a play, we must consider not only the events of which it consists but also the order in which those events are presented by the scenario.

The ordering of events can best be grasped if we think of the scenario as being constructed of a series of *dramatic units:* each time a character enters or leaves the stage a new dramatic unit begins. The appearance or departure of a character or group of characters is thus like a form of punctuation that we should take special note of whenever we are reading or witnessing a play. As one grouping of characters gives way to another, the dramatic situation necessarily changes—sometimes slightly, sometimes very perceptibly—to carry the play forward in the evolution of its process and the fulfillment of its plot. Thus we should examine each unit individually, to discover not only what on-stage action takes place within it but also what off-stage action is revealed within it. Then we should determine how the off-stage action that is reported affects the on-stage action, as well as how it shapes our own understanding of the characters and the plot.

In the opening dramatic unit of *Oedipus Rex,* for example, we witness a conversation between Oedipus and a Priest, in which the Priest pleads with Oedipus to rid Thebes of the plague, while Oedipus assures the Priest that he is eager to cure the city of its sickness. During that conversation we also learn from the Priest that, in years past, Oedipus had through his wisdom and knowledge liberated the city from the domination of the Sphinx, and we learn from Oedipus that he has recently sent his brother-in-law, Creon, to seek advice from the oracle at Delphi. These two reports of off-stage action establish the heroic stature of Oedipus, revealing him to be an exceptionally effective and responsible leader. The dramatic unit leads the Priest and Oedipus—and us as spectators—to expect that he will be equally successful in this crisis. In examining the unit we thus see that it not only identifies the motivating problem of the plot but also establishes Oedipus as the hero of the play; and that, moreover, it creates a set of positive expectations about his ability to overcome the problem. (He does, of course, overcome the problem but not without undoing himself in the process.) The unit, then, is crucial in creating a complicated mixture of true and false expectations within both the characters—and us.

In addition to examining dramatic units individually, we should also examine them in relation to one another—in context. Context is important because it is one of the dramatist's major techniques for influencing our perception and understanding of characters and plot. Dramatists usually select and arrange events so as to produce significant parallels or contrasts between them. Thus, if we look at the units in context, we will be able to perceive those relationships and their implications. Finally, of course, we must move beyond pairs and series of units to an overview of all the units together. By doing that we will be able to recognize the dominant process of the play. We will, that is, be able to perceive how it sets up the complications and works toward the discoveries and resolutions of tragedy, comedy, satire, romance, or tragicomedy. By examining the over-all design of the plot, we can thus recognize the dominant view of experience embodied in the play.

On the basis of our discussion, it should be obvious that plot is an extremely complicated element, one that can be understood only through a detailed analysis of dramatic units. Here, then, are some reminders and suggestions to follow in analyzing the plot of any play. Identify *all* the events that take place within the plot and the chronological order in which they occur. In order to do this, examine the scenario closely, paying attention to instances of implied and reported action. Once the details and make-up of the plot have been established, then examine how the plot is presented by the scenario. In order to do this, examine each dramatic unit in detail, beginning with the first and proceeding consecutively through the play. Remember that a single dramatic unit can serve a variety of purposes. Remember, too, that every unit exists within a context of units: within the context of units that immediately precede and follow it, and within the context of all the units of the play.

CHARACTER

Although characters in a play are like real people in some respects, they are by no means identical to people in real life. Real people, after all, exist in the world as it is, whereas characters exist in an imaginative world shaped by the theatrical contexts and imitative purposes of drama. In the classical Greek theater, for example, a character was defined visually by the fixed expression of his or her facial mask. Clearly, it would have been impossible for spectators to regard such characters as identical to complex human personalities. And if we look at Oedipus, we can see that he is conceived in terms of a few dominant traits that could be projected through the bold acting required by the enormous size of the ancient Greek theater.

Even when production conditions allow for greater psychological detail, as in the relatively intimate theaters of seventeenth-century France, there are usually other circumstances that work against the formation of completely lifelike characters. In *The Misanthrope*, for example, detailed characterization is less important than the essayistic form and satiric purpose of the play. Thus Alceste and Philinte have personality traits consistent with the ideas they espouse, and the other characters are exaggerated versions of objectionable human tendencies that show up in high society. They are character types consistent with Moliere's satiric purpose.

Because of its sustained interest in psychological behavior, modern drama tends to put a great deal of emphasis on character. Yet even plays—such as *A Doll's House* and *Cat on a Hot Tin Roof*—that are concerned specifically with the workings of the human mind, do not embody characters who can be taken as identical to real people. It would be misleading to think of Nora or Brick, for example, or any other principal characters in these plays, as fully developed personalities. Although they do represent complex studies in human psychology, they are conceived to dramatize specific ideas about the impact of the family and society upon the individual. In other words, they exhibit patterns of behavior that are *typical* rather than *actual*.

Although dramatic characters are not real people, they are endowed with human capacities. They talk and act and interact with one another. They experience pleasure and endure pain. They feel, and they act on their feelings. They believe, and they act according to their beliefs. It would thus be inhuman of us not to respond to their humanity. But we can only respond appropriately if we know what we are responding to: we have to consider all of the ways in which characters are revealed and defined by dialogue and plot.

The most immediate way to understand a character is to examine in detail everything the character says, in order to identify the important attitudes, beliefs, and feelings of that character. Examine not only the content but also the style of such utterances. Look, for example, at the kinds of words, and images, and sentence structures that mark the character's dialogue, for often these elements of style provide insight into subtle aspects of character. A further source of information is what others in the play say about the character. Since characters, like real people, are repeatedly talking about one another—to their faces and behind their backs—what they have to say often will provide valuable insights into the character. The things a character does may reveal as much as what the character says and what others have to say.

In examining their actions, pay careful attention to context, for characters are likely to behave differently in different situations. The problem in such a case is to determine whether the character has actually changed, for what appears to be a change in character may simply be the result of our knowing the character more fully. Another important key to understanding is to compare and contrast a character with others in the play. A study of this kind often sharpens and intensifies the perceptions we have gained from examining the character in isolation.

Character analysis can be a source of pleasure and understanding in its own right, but it should ultimately lead us more deeply into the play as a whole. For that reason, when we analyze characters, we should always keep in mind the theatrical contexts and imaginative purposes that shape their being. In this way we shall be truly able to appreciate the dramatic imitation of a world created by the wedding of literary and of representational art.

A Collection of Plays

1. *Classical to Neoclassical Drama*

TRAGEDY IN THE CLASSICAL GREEK THEATER

The theater of Dionysus at Athens, where *Oedipus Rex* was first produced (c. 425 B.C.), could accommodate an audience of almost fifteen
thousand. So vast a structure could not, of course, be roofed over, but had
to be open-air. This fact alone will take us a long way toward understanding
the nature of a Greek dramatic performance. To begin with, we can see
that the experience must have been very public and communal—nothing at
all like the coziness of our fully enclosed modern theaters, where no more
than five hundred—or a thousand at most—gather in darkened rows of
cushioned seats. The size of the theater also required the drama to be
conceived on a monumental scale and performed in a correspondingly
emphatic style of acting. When Oedipus accused Teiresias of treason, his
impetuous judgment had to be heard and seen by thousands of spectators.
Facial expression obviously would not serve the purpose, nor would a
conversational tone of voice. Instead, the actors wore large, stylized masks
and costumes—an inheritance from primitive ritual—representing character
types; and as their fortunes and emotions changed, they changed their
masks to suit the situation. Further, those masks were probably equipped
with a mouthpiece to aid in projecting the dialogue. In short, we should not
imagine a style of performance corresponding in any way to that of our
present-day ideas about dramatic realism. Exaggerated gestures, bold
movements, declamatory utterances—everything was larger than life and
highly formalized, if only to ensure a clear theatrical impression.

Size alone was not responsible for the highly formal style of Greek drama.

The design of the theater, and the religious origin of its design, also had a great deal to do with the ceremonial quality of the production. The Greek theater evolved from places of ritual celebration consisting of a circular area for dancers and singers, surrounded by a hillside to accommodate worshipers. A modified version of that arrangement is what we have in the classical Greek theater illustrated here. The theater consisted of three parts. Its focal element was the *orchestra* (literally, the dancing place), a circular space sixty-four feet in diameter. The *orchestra* was surrounded by the *theatron* (literally, the seeing place), a semicircular terraced hillside equipped with benches. Facing the *theatron* was the *skene* (literally, the hut), a one-story building with three openings entering on to the *orchestra,* wings projecting toward the *orchestra,* and a slightly raised stage-like platform extending between the wings. The classic simplicity of that design is unparalleled in the history of the theater.

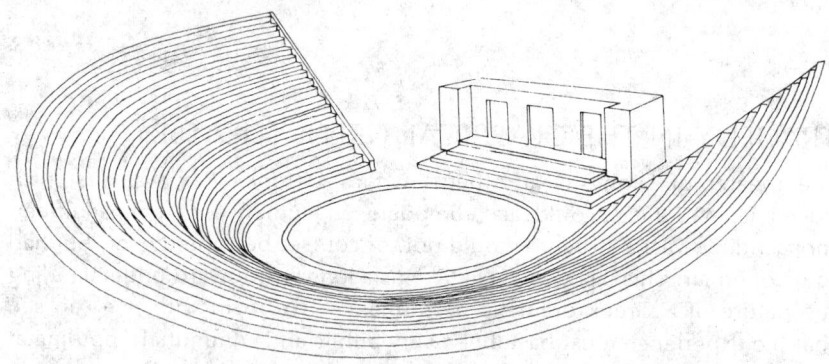

The *skene* was used for storing properties, changing costumes, providing entrances and exits, and serving as a scenic background. Stylized scenes were painted on the areas between the doors to suggest the outlines of a location, and the *skene* itself was understood to represent any structure central to the action (such as the palace in *Oedipus Rex*). Beyond these few hints, the Greek theater provided very little in the way of scenery or props to assist the spectator's imagination. At most, a chariot might be driven in to the *orchestra* to represent the arrival of a hero, or an actor lowered by machine from the roof of the *skene* to depict the intervention of a god, or a tableau wheeled out of the *skene* to suggest off-stage action.

The most important part of the theater was the *orchestra,* for it served as the primary acting area. Within that area the performance of a tragedy such as *Oedipus Rex* adhered to a highly formalized structure. The actors made their initial entrance to the *orchestra* from the *skene* and then performed a brief expository episode, the *prologos.* Then the chorus (of fifteen members) made its entrance—the *parados*—by marching in a stately rhythm through the passageways between the *theatron* and the *skene*. When all the members of the tragic chorus had entered the orchestra, they arranged themselves in rectangular formation and began their choral song and dance to the accompaniment of a flute. The chorus remained in the *orchestra* throughout the play, performing not only during its odes but also during the episodes, sometimes exchanging dialogue with the characters through its leader (the *choragos*), sometimes, no doubt, making gestures and movements in sympathetic response to the action. In this way the chorus provided a sustained point of reference, a source of mediation between the audience and the actors, who moved back and forth between the *orchestra* and the *skene* as their parts dictated.

In imagining the effect produced by the simultaneous presence of actors and chorus, we should remember that the chorus retained the skills inherited from the ritual celebrations of an earlier time, so that its members, like the actors, were accomplished dancers and singers. When we read *Oedipus Rex*, therefore, we should visualize the chorus as moving through a slow and graceful dance appropriate to tragedy. And we should try to hear how it sounded as it chanted its parts accompanied by a flute player. Musically and visually, the total performance must have been as complex as a modern opera—though by no means similar in emphasis, for in opera everything is subordinated to the music, whereas in Greek tragedy everything is subordinated to the action. Taken all in all—the choric singing and dancing, the simplified setting, the bold acting—dramatic productions in ancient Greece must have matched the grand dimensions of the theater and of the tragedies written for it by Sophocles.

SOPHOCLES

496–406 B.C.

Born in Athens, where his father was a wealthy and influential businessman, Sophocles himself became a very influential and admired public figure in Athens during the remarkable century of its rise and fall as a great city-state. During the course of his lifetime, he served his country as an ambassador, general, and treasurer; he served its religion as a priest of the god of healing; and he served its culture as a pre-eminent tragic dramatist. His plays, like those of his Greek contemporaries, were written and produced for an extraordinary drama competition that was held in Athens each spring as the major event in a festival celebrating Dionysus, the Greek god who embodied the power and fertility of nature. Each tragic dramatist who chose to compete submitted a set of three or four plays, known as trilogies or tetralogies, and Sophocles won the contest twenty-four times. He reportedly wrote more than 120 plays, but only 7 of them have survived, all of which show him to have been a masterful dramatist in the conception and elaboration of tragically compelling plots and characters. His best known plays— *Antigone* (c. 440), *Oedipus Rex* (c. 425), and *Oedipus at Colonus* (406)— though written more than thirty years apart, all deal with related characters and themes from the haunting myth of Oedipus and Thebes.

Oedipus Rex

PERSONS REPRESENTED

OEDIPUS	MESSENGER
A PRIEST	SHEPHERD OF LAÏOS
KREON	SECOND MESSENGER
TEIRESIAS	CHORUS OF THEBAN ELDERS
IOKASTE	

The Scene. Before the palace of Oedipus, King of Thebes. A central door and two lateral doors open onto a platform which runs the length of the façade. On the platform, right and left, are altars; and three steps lead down into the "orchestra," or chorus-ground. At the beginning of the action these steps are crowded

An English version by Dudley Fitts and Robert Fitzgerald

by suppliants who have brought branches and chaplets of olive leaves and who sit
in various attitudes of despair.

Oedipus enters.

PROLOGUE

OEDIPUS   My children, generations of the living
    In the line of Kadmos, nursed at his ancient hearth:
    Why have you strewn yourselves before these altars
    In supplication, with your boughs and garlands?
    The breath of incense rises from the city
    With a sound of prayer and lamentation.
                       Children,
    I would not have you speak through messengers,
    And therefore I have come myself to hear you—
    I, Oedipus, who bear the famous name.

To a Priest

10   You, there, since you are eldest in the company,
    Speak for them all, tell me what preys upon you,
    Whether you come in dread, or crave some blessing:
    Tell me, and never doubt that I will help you
    In every way I can; I should be heartless
    Were I not moved to find you suppliant here.
PRIEST   Great Oedipus, O powerful King of Thebes!
    You see how all the ages of our people
    Cling to your altar steps: here are boys
    Who can barely stand alone, and here are priests
20   By weight of age, as I am a priest of God,
    And young men chosen from those yet unmarried;
    As for the others, all that multitude,
    They wait with olive chaplets in the squares,
    At the two shrines of Pallas, and where Apollo
    Speaks in the glowing embers.
                    Your own eyes
    Must tell you: Thebes is tossed on a murdering sea
    And can not lift her head from the death surge.
    A rust consumes the buds and fruits of the earth;

The herds are sick; children die unborn,
And labor is vain. The god of plague and pyre
Raids like detestable lightning through the city,
And all the house of Kadmos is laid waste,
All emptied, and all darkened: Death alone
Battens upon the misery of Thebes.

You are not one of the immortal gods, we know;
Yet we have come to you to make our prayer
As to the man surest in mortal ways
And wisest in the ways of God. You saved us
From the Sphinx, that flinty singer, and the tribute
We paid to her so long; yet you were never
Better informed than we, nor could we teach you:
A god's touch, it seems, enabled you to help us.

Therefore, O mighty power, we turn to you:
Find us our safety, find us a remedy,
Whether by counsel of the gods or of men.
A king of wisdom tested in the past
Can act in a time of troubles, and act well.
Noblest of men, restore
Life to your city! Think how all men call you
Liberator for your boldness long ago;
Ah, when your years of kingship are remembered,
Let them not say *We rose, but later fell—*
Keep the State from going down in the storm!
Once, years ago, with happy augury,
You brought us fortune; be the same again!
No man questions your power to rule the land:
But rule over men, not over a dead city!
Ships are only hulls, high walls are nothing,
When no life moves in the empty passageways.

OEDIPUS Poor children! You may be sure I know
All that you longed for in your coming here.
I know that you are deathly sick; and yet,
Sick as you are, not one is as sick as I.
Each of you suffers in himself alone
His anguish, not another's; but my spirit
Groans for the city, for myself, for you.

I was not sleeping, you are not waking me.

No, I have been in tears for a long while
And in my restless thought walked many ways.
70   In all my search I found one remedy,
And I have adopted it: I have sent Kreon,
Son of Menoikeus, brother of the Queen,
To Delphi, Apollo's place of revelation,
To learn there, if he can,
What act or pledge of mine may save the city.
I have counted the days, and now, this very day,
I am troubled, for he has overstayed his time.
What is he doing? He has been gone too long.
Yet whenever he comes back, I should do ill
80   Not to take any action the god orders.
PRIEST It is a timely promise. At this instant
They tell me Kreon is here.
OEDIPUS   O Lord Apollo!
May his news be fair as his face is radiant!
PRIEST   Good news, I gather: he is crowned with bay,
The chaplet is thick with berries.
OEDIPUS   We shall soon know;
He is near enough to hear us now.

Enter Kreon.

O Prince:

Brother: son of Menoikeus:
What answer do you bring us from the God?
KREON   A strong one. I can tell you, great afflictions
90   Will turn out well, if they are taken well.
OEDIPUS   What was the oracle? These vague words
Leave me still hanging between hope and fear.
KREON   Is it your pleasure to hear me with all these
Gathered around us? I am prepared to speak,
But should we not go in?
OEDIPUS   Speak to them all.
It is for them I suffer, more than for myself.
KREON   Then I will tell you what I heard at Delphi.

In plain words
The god commands us to expel from the land of Thebes

100   An old defilement we are sheltering.
It is a deathly thing, beyond cure;
We must not let it feed upon us longer.
OEDIPUS   What defilement? How shall we rid ourselves of it?
KREON   By exile or death, blood for blood. It was
Murder that brought the plague-wind on the city.
OEDIPUS   Murder of whom? Surely the god has named him?
KREON   My lord: Laïos once ruled this land,
Before you came to govern us.
OEDIPUS   I know;
I learned of him from others; I never saw him.
110   KREON   He was murdered; and Apollo commands us now
To take revenge upon whoever killed him.
OEDIPUS   Upon whom? Where are they? Where shall we find a clue
To solve that crime, after so many years?
KREON   Here in this land, he said. Search reveals
Things that escape an inattentive man.
OEDIPUS   Tell me: Was Laïos murdered in his house,
Or in the fields, or in some foreign country?
KREON   He said he planned to make a pilgrimage.
He did not come home again.
OEDIPUS   And was there no one,
120   No witness, no companion, to tell what happened?
KREON   They were all killed but one, and he got away
So frightened that he could remember one thing only.
OEDIPUS   What was that one thing? One may be the key
To everything, if we resolve to use it.
KREON   He said that a band of highwaymen attacked them,
Outnumbered them, and overwhelmed the King.
OEDIPUS   Strange, that a highwayman should be so daring—
Unless some faction here bribed him to do it.
KREON   We thought of that. But after Laïos' death
130   New troubles arose and we had no avenger.
OEDIPUS   What troubles could prevent your hunting down the killers?
KREON   The riddling Sphinx's song
Made us deaf to all mysteries but her own.
OEDIPUS   Then once more I must bring what is dark to light.
It is most fitting that Apollo shows,
As you do, this compunction for the dead.
You shall see how I stand by you, as I should,
Avenging this country and the god as well,
And not as though it were for some distant friend,
140   But for my own sake, to be rid of evil.

Whoever killed King Laïos might—who knows?—
Lay violent hands even on me—and soon.
I act for the murdered king in my own interest.

Come, then, my children: leave the altar steps,
Lift up your olive boughs!
                    One of you go
And summon the people of Kadmos to gather here.
I will do all that I can; you may tell them that.

Exit a Page.

So, with the help of God.
We shall be saved—or else indeed we are lost.

150   PRIEST   Let us rise, children. It was for this we came,
And now the King has promised it.
Phoibos has sent us an oracle; may he descend
Himself to save us and drive out the plague.

Exeunt Oedipus and Kreon into the palace by the central door. The Priest and the Suppliants disperse right and left. After a short pause the Chorus enters the orchêstra.

PÁRODOS

CHORUS   What is God singing in his profound   STROPHE I
     Delphi of gold and shadow?
     What oracle for Thebes, the sunwhipped city?

Fear unjoints me, the roots of my heart tremble.

Now I remember, O Healer, your power and wonder:
Will you send doom like a sudden cloud, or weave it
Like nightfall of the past?

Speak, speak to us, issue of holy sound;
Dearest to our Expectancy: be tender!

10   Let me pray to Athenê, the immortal daughter of Zeus, ANTISTROPHE I
     And to Artemis her sister
     Who keeps her famous throne in the market ring,

And to Apollo, archer from distant heaven—

O gods, descend! Like three streams leap against
The fires of our grief, the fires of darkness;
Be swift to bring us rest!

As in the old time from the brilliant house
Of air you stepped to save us, come again!

Now our afflictions have no end   STROPHE 2
20   Now all our stricken host lies down
And no man fights off death with his mind;

The noble plowland bears no grain,
And groaning mothers can not bear—

See, how our lives like birds take wing,
Like sparks that fly when a fire soars,
To the shore of the god of evening.

The plague burns on, it is pitiless,   ANTISTROPHE 2
Though pallid children laden with death
Lie unwept in the stony ways,

30   And old gray women by every path
Flock to the strand about the altars

There to strike their breasts and cry
Worship of Phoibos in wailing prayers:
Be kind, God's golden child!

There are no swords in this attack by fire,   STROPHE 3
No shields, but we are ringed with cries.

Send the besieger plunging from our homes
Into the vast sea-room of the Atlantic
40   Or into the waves that foam eastward of Thrace—
For the day ravages what the night spares—

Destroy our enemy, lord of the thunder!
Let him be riven by lightning from heaven!

Phoibos Apollo, stretch the sun's bowstring,   ANTISTROPHE 3
That golden cord, until it sing for us,
Flashing arrows in heaven!
                              Artemis, Huntress,
Race with flaring lights upon our mountains!

O scarlet god, O golden-banded brow,
O Theban Bacchos in a storm of Maenads,

Enter Oedipus, center.

Whirl upon Death, that all the Undying hate!
50   Come with blinding torches, come in joy!

SCENE I

OEDIPUS   Is this your prayer? It may be answered. Come,
   Listen to me, act as the crisis demands,
   And you shall have relief from all these evils.

   Until now I was a stranger to this tale,
   As I had been a stranger to the crime.
   Could I track down the murderer without a clue?
   But now, friends,
   As one who became a citizen after the murder,
   I make this proclamation to all Thebans:

10   If any man knows by whose hand Laïos, son of Labdakos,
   Met his death, I direct that man to tell me everything,
   No matter what he fears for having so long withheld it.
   Let it stand as promised that no further trouble
   Will come to him, but he may leave the land in safety.

   Moreover: If anyone knows the murderer to be foreign,
   Let him not keep silent: he shall have his reward from me.
   However, if he does conceal it; if any man
   Fearing for his friend or for himself disobeys this edict,
   Hear what I propose to do:

20 I solemnly forbid the people of this country,
Where power and throne are mine, ever to receive that man
Or speak to him, no matter who he is, or let him
Join in sacrifice, lustration, or in prayer.
I decree that he be driven from every house,
Being, as he is, corruption itself to us: the Delphic
Voice of Apollo has pronounced this revelation.
Thus I associate myself with the oracle
And take the side of the murdered king.

As for the criminal, I pray to God—
30 Whether it be a lurking thief, or one of a number—
I pray that that man's life be consumed in evil and wretchedness.
And as for me, this curse applies no less
If it should turn out that the culprit is my guest here,
Sharing my hearth.
                    You have heard the penalty.

I lay it on you now to attend to this
For my sake, for Apollo's, for the sick
Sterile city that heaven has abandoned.
Suppose the oracle had given you no command:
Should this defilement go uncleansed for ever?
40 You should have found the murderer: your king,
A noble king, had been destroyed!
                              Now I,
Having the power that he held before me,
Having his bed, begetting children there
Upon his wife, as he would have, had he lived—
Their son would have been my children's brother,
If Laïos had had luck in fatherhood!
(And now his bad fortune has struck him down)—
I say I take the son's part, just as though
I were his son, to press the fight for him
50 And see it won! I'll find the hand that brought
Death to Labdakos' and Polydoros' child,
Heir of Kadmos' and Agenor's line.
And as for those who fail me,
May the gods deny them the fruit of the earth,
Fruit of the womb, and may they rot utterly!
Let them be wretched as we are wretched, and worse!
For you, for loyal Thebans, and for all

Who find my actions right, I pray the favor
Of justice, and of all the immortal gods.

60   CHORAGOS   Since I am under oath, my lord, I swear
I did not do the murder, I can not name
The murderer. Phoibos ordained the search;
Why did he not say who the culprit was?

OEDIPUS   An honest question. But no man in the world
Can make the gods do more than the gods will.

CHORAGOS   There is an alternative, I think—
OEDIPUS   Tell me.
Any or all, you must not fail to tell me.

CHORAGOS   A lord clairvoyant to the lord Apollo,
As we all know, is the skilled Teiresias.

70   One might learn much about this from him, Oedipus.

OEDIPUS   I am not wasting time:
Kreon spoke of this, and I have sent for him—
Twice, in fact; it is strange that he is not here.

CHORAGOS   The other matter—that old report—seems useless.

OEDIPUS   What was that? I am interested in all reports.

CHORAGOS   The King was said to have been killed by highwaymen.

OEDIPUS   I know. But we have no witnesses to that.

CHORAGOS   If the killer can feel a particle of dread,
Your curse will bring him out of hiding!

OEDIPUS   No.

80   The man who dared that act will fear no curse.

Enter the blind seer Teiresias, led by a Page.

CHORAGOS   But there is one man who may detect the criminal.
This is Teiresias, this is the holy prophet
In whom, alone of all men, truth was born.

OEDIPUS   Teiresias: seer: student of mysteries,
Of all that's taught and all that no man tells,
Secrets of Heaven and secrets of the earth:
Blind though you are, you know the city lies
Sick with plague; and from this plague, my lord,
We find that you alone can guard or save us.

90   Possibly you did not hear the messengers?
Apollo, when we sent to him,
Sent us back word that this great pestilence
Would lift, but only if we established clearly
The identity of those who murdered Laïos.

They must be killed or exiled.
                        Can you use
Birdflight or any art of divination
To purify yourself, and Thebes, and me
From this contagion? We are in your hands.
There is no fairer duty

100   Than that of helping others in distress.
TEIRESIAS How dreadful knowledge of the truth can be
When there's no help in truth! I knew this well
But did not act on it: else I should not have come.
OEDIPUS What is troubling you? Why are your eyes so cold?
TEIRESIAS Let me go home. Bear your own fate, and I'll
Bear mine. It is better so: trust what I say.
OEDIPUS What you say is ungracious and unhelpful
To your native country. Do not refuse to speak.
TEIRESIAS When it comes to speech, your own is neither temperate

110   Nor opportune. I wish to be more prudent.
OEDIPUS In God's name, we all beg you—
TEIRESIAS   You are all ignorant.
No; I will never tell you what I know.
Now it is my misery; then, it would be yours.
OEDIPUS What! You do know something, and will not tell us?
You would betray us all and wreck the State?
TEIRESIAS I do not intend to torture myself, or you.
Why persist in asking? You will not persuade me.
OEDIPUS What a wicked old man you are! You'd try a stone's
Patience! Out with it! Have you no feeling at all?

120 TEIRESIAS You call me unfeeling. If you could only see
The nature of your own feelings . . .
OEDIPUS   Why,
Who would not feel as I do? Who could endure
Your arrogance toward the city?
TEIRESIAS   What does it matter?
Whether I speak or not, it is bound to come.
OEDIPUS Then, if 'it' is bound to come, you are bound to tell me.
TEIRESIAS No, I will not go on. Rage as you please.
OEDIPUS Rage? Why not!
                  And I'll tell you what I think:
You planned it, you had it done, you all but
Killed him with your own hands: if you had eyes,

130   I'd say the crime was yours, and yours alone.
TEIRESIAS So? I charge you, then,
Abide by the proclamation you have made:
From this day forth

Never speak again to these men or to me;
You yourself are the pollution of this country.
OEDIPUS   You dare say that! Can you possibly think you have
Some way of going free, after such insolence?
TEIRESIAS   I have gone free. It is the truth sustains me.
OEDIPUS   Who taught you shamelessness? It was not your craft.
140   TEIRESIAS   You did. You made me speak. I did not want to.
OEDIPUS   Speak what? Let me hear it again more clearly.
TEIRESIAS   Was it not clear before? Are you tempting me?
OEDIPUS   I did not understand it. Say it again.
TEIRESIAS   I say that you are the murderer whom you seek.
OEDIPUS   Now twice you have spat out infamy. You'll pay for it!
TEIRESIAS   Would you care for more? Do you wish to be really angry?
OEDIPUS   Say what you will. Whatever you say is worthless.
TEIRESIAS   I say you live in hideous shame with those
Most dear to you. You can not see the evil.
150   OEDIPUS   Can you go on babbling like this for ever?
TEIRESIAS   I can, if there is power in truth.
OEDIPUS   There is:
But not for you, not for you,
You sightless, witless, senseless, mad old man!
TEIRESIAS   You are the madman. There is no one here
Who will not curse you soon, as you curse me.
OEDIPUS   You child of total night! I would not touch you;
Neither would any man who sees the sun.
TEIRESIAS   True: it is not from you my fate will come.
That lies within Apollo's competence,
As it is his concern.
160   OEDIPUS   Tell me, who made
These fine discoveries? Kreon? or someone else?
TEIRESIAS   Kreon is no threat. You weave your own doom.
OEDIPUS   Wealth, power, craft of statesmanship!
Kingly position, everywhere admired!
What savage envy is stored up against these,
If Kreon, whom I trusted, Kreon my friend,
For this great office which the city once
Put in my hands unsought—if for this power
Kreon desires in secret to destroy me!

170   He has bought this decrepit fortune-teller, this
Collector of dirty pennies, this prophet fraud—
Why, he is no more clairvoyant than I am!
                                        Tell us:
Has your mystic mummery ever approached the truth?

When that hellcat the Sphinx was performing here,
What help were you to these people?
Her magic was not for the first man who came along:
It demanded a real exorcist. Your birds—
What good were they? or the gods, for the matter of that?
But I came by,
180 Oedipus, the simple man, who knows nothing—
I thought it out for myself, no birds helped me!
And this is the man you think you can destroy.
That you may be close to Kreon when he's king!
Well, you and your friend Kreon, it seems to me,
Will suffer most. If you were not an old man,
You would have paid already for your plot.

CHORAGOS   We can not see that his words or yours
Have been spoken except in anger, Oedipus,
And of anger we have no need. How to accomplish
190 The god's will best: that is what most concerns us.

TEIRESIAS   You are a king. But where argument's concerned
I am your man, as much a king as you.
I am not your servant, but Apollo's
I have no need of Kreon's name.

Listen to me. You mock my blindness, do you?
But I say that you, with both your eyes, are blind:
You can not see the wretchedness of your life,
Nor in whose house you live, no, nor with whom.
Who are your father and mother? Can you tell me?
200 You do not even know the blind wrongs
That you have done them, on earth and in the world below.
But the double lash of you parents' curse will whip you
Out of this land some day, with only night
Upon your precious eyes.
Your cries then—where will they not be heard?
What fastness of Kithairon will not echo them?
And that bridal-descant of yours—you'll know it then,
The song they sang when you came here to Thebes
And found your misguided berthing.
210 All this, and more, that you can not guess at now,
Will bring you to yourself among your children.

Be angry, then. Curse Kreon. Curse my words.
I tell you, no man that walks upon the earth
Shall be rooted out more horribly than you.

OEDIPUS   Am I to bear this from him?—Damnation
    Take you! Out of this place! Out of my sight!
TEIRESIAS   I would not have come at all if you had not asked me.
OEDIPUS   Could I have told that you'd talk nonsense, that
    You'd come here to make a fool of yourself, and of me?
220   TEIRESIAS   A fool? Your parents thought me sane enough.
OEDIPUS   My parents again!—Wait: who were my parents?
TEIRESIAS   This day will give you a father, and break your heart.
OEDIPUS   Your infantile riddles! Your damned abracadabra!
TEIRESIAS   You were a great man once at solving riddles.
OEDIPUS   Mock me with that if you like; you will find it true.
TEIRESIAS   It was true enough. It brought about your ruin.
OEDIPUS   But if it saved this town?
TEIRESIAS   *To the Page*   Boy, give me your hand.
OEDIPUS   Yes, boy; lead him away.
                —While you are here
    We can do nothing. Go; leave us in peace.
230   TEIRESIAS   I will go when I have said what I have to say.
    How can you hurt me? And I tell you again:
    The man you have been looking for all this time,
    The damned man, the murderer of Laïos,
    That man is in Thebes. To your mind he is foreign-born,
    But it will soon be shown that he is a Theban,
    A revelation that will fail to please.
                A blind man,
    Who has his eyes now; a penniless man, who is rich now;
    And he will go tapping the strange earth with his staff.
    To the children with whom he lives now he will be
240   Brother and father—the very same; to her
    Who bore him, son and husband—the very same
    Who came to his father's bed, wet with his father's blood.

    Enough. Go think that over.
    If later you find error in what I have said,
    You may say that I have no skill in prophecy.

Exit Teiresias, led by his Page. Oedipus goes into the palace.

ODE I

CHORUS   The Delphic stone of prophecies   STROPHE 1
    Remembers ancient regicide
    And a still bloody hand.

That killer's hour of flight has come.
He must be stronger than riderless
Coursers of untiring wind,
For the son of Zeus armed with his father's thunder
Leaps in lightning after him;
And the Furies hold his track, the sad Furies.

10   Holy Parnassos' peak of snow   ANTISTROPHE 1
Flashes and blinds that secret man,
That all shall hunt him down:
Though he may roam the forest shade
Like a bull gone wild from pasture
To rage through glooms of stone.
Doom comes down on him; flight will not avail him;
For the world's heart calls him desolate,
And the immortal voices follow, for ever follow.

But now a wilder thing is heard   STROPHE 2
20   From the old man skilled at hearing Fate in the wing-beat of a bird.
Bewildered as a blown bird, my soul hovers and can not find
Foothold in this debate, or any reason or rest of mind.
But no man ever brought—none can bring
Proof of strife between Thebes' royal house,
Labdakos' line, and the son of Polybos;
And never until now has any man brought word
Of Laïos' dark death staining Oedipus the King.

Divine Zeus and Apollo hold   ANTISTROPHE 2
Perfect intelligence alone of all tales ever told;
30   And well though this diviner works, he works in his own night;
No man can judge that rough unknown or trust in second sight,
For wisdom changes hands among the wise.
Shall I believe my great lord criminal
At a raging word that a blind old man let fall?
I saw him, when the carrion woman faced him of old,
Prove his heroic mind. These evil words are lies.

SCENE II

KREON   Men of Thebes:
    I am told that heavy accusations
    Have been brought against me by King Oedipus.

I am not the kind of man to bear this tamely.

If in these present difficulties
He holds me accountable for any harm to him
Through anything I have said or done—why, then,
I do not value life in this dishonor.

It is not as though this rumor touched upon
10   Some private indiscretion. The matter is grave.
The fact is that I am being called disloyal
To the State, to my fellow citizens, to my friends.
CHORAGOS He may have spoken in anger, not from his mind.
KREON But did you not hear him say I was the one
Who seduced the old prophet into lying?
CHORAGOS The thing was said; I do not know how seriously.
KREON But you were watching him! Were his eyes steady?
Did he look like a man in his right mind?
CHORAGOS   I do not know.
I can not judge the behavior of great men.
But here is the King himself.

Enter Oedipus.

20   OEDIPUS   So you dared come back.
Why? How brazen of you to come to my house,
You murderer!
                Do you think I do not know
That you plotted to kill me, plotted to steal my throne?
Tell me, in God's name: am I coward, a fool,
That you should dream you could accomplish this?
A fool who could not see your slippery game?
A coward, not to fight back when I saw it?
You are the fool, Kreon, are you not? hoping
Without support or friends to get a throne?
30   Thrones may be won or bought: you could do neither.
KREON Now listen to me. You have talked; let me talk, too.
You can not judge unless you know the facts.
OEDIPUS You speak well: there is one fact; but I find it hard
To learn from the deadliest enemy I have.
KREON That above all I must dispute with you.
OEDIPUS That above all I will not hear you deny.
KREON If you think there is anything good in being stubborn
Against all reason, then I say you are wrong.

OEDIPUS   If you think a man can sin against his own kind
40   And not be punished for it, I say you are mad.

KREON   I agree. But tell me: what have I done to you?

OEDIPUS   You advised me to send for that wizard, did you not?

KREON   I did. I should do it again.

OEDIPUS   Very well. Now tell me:
       How long has it been since Laïos—

KREON   What of Laïos?

OEDIPUS   Since he vanished in that onset by the road?

KREON   It was long ago, a long time.

OEDIPUS   And this prophet,
       Was he practicing here then?

KREON   He was; and with honor, as now.

OEDIPUS   Did he speak of me at that time?

KREON   He never did;
       At least, not when I was present.

OEDIPUS   But . . . the enquiry?
       I suppose you held one?

50   KREON   We did, but we learned nothing.

OEDIPUS   Why did the prophet not speak against me then?

KREON   I do not know; and I am the kind of man
       Who holds his tongue when he has no facts to go on.

OEDIPUS   There's one fact that you know, and you could tell it.

KREON   What fact is that? If I know it, you shall have it.

OEDIPUS   If he were not involved with you, he could not say
       That it was I who murdered Laïos.

KREON   If he says that, you are the one that knows it!—
       But now it is my turn to question you.

60   OEDIPUS   Put your questions. I am no murderer.

KREON   First, then: You married my sister?

OEDIPUS   I married your sister.

KREON   And you rule the kingdom equally with her?

OEDIPUS   Everything that she wants she has from me.

KREON   And I am the third, equal to both of you?

OEDIPUS   That is why I call you a bad friend.

KREON   No. Reason it out, as I have done.
       Think of this first: Would any sane man prefer
       Power, with all a king's anxieties,
       To that same power and the grace of sleep?
70   Certainly not I.
       I have never longed for the king's power—only his rights.
       Would any wise man differ from me in this?
       As matters stand, I have my way in everything
       With your consent, and no responsibilities.

If I were king, I should be a slave to policy.
How could I desire a sceptre more
Than what is now mine—untroubled influence?
No, I have not gone mad; I need no honors,
Except those with the perquisites I have now.
80   I am welcome everywhere; every man salutes me,
And those who want your favor seek my ear,
Since I know how to manage what they ask.
Should I exchange this ease for that anxiety?
Besides, no sober mind is treasonable.
I hate anarchy
And never would deal with any man who likes it.

Test what I have said. Go to the priestess
At Delphi, ask if I quoted her correctly.
And as for this other thing: if I am found
90   Guilty of treason with Teiresias,
Then sentence me to death. You have my word
It is a sentence I should cast my vote for—
But not without evidence!
                    You do wrong
When you take good men for bad, bad men for good.
A true friend thrown aside—why, life itself
Is not more precious!
                    In time you will know this well:
For time, and time alone, will show the just man,
Though scoundrels are discovered in a day.
CHORAGOS   This is well said, and a prudent man would ponder it.
100   Judgments too quickly formed are dangerous.
OEDIPUS   But is he not quick in his duplicity?
And shall I not be quick to parry him?
Would you have me stand still, holding my peace, and let
This man win everything, through my inaction?
KREON   And you want—what is it, then? To banish me?
OEDIPUS   No, not exile. It is your death I want,
So that all the world may see what treason means.
KREON   You will persist, then? You will not believe me?
OEDIPUS   How can I believe you?
KREON   Then you are a fool.
OEDIPUS   To save myself?
110   KREON   In justice, think of me.
OEDIPUS   You are evil incarnate.   *the embodyment of evil*
KREON   But suppose that you are wrong?
OEDIPUS   Still I must rule.

KREON   But not if you rule badly.

OEDIPUS   O city, city!

KREON   It is my city, too!

CHORAGOS   Now, my lords, be still. I see the Queen,
   Iokastê, coming from her palace chambers;
   And it is time she came, for the sake of you both.
   This dreadful quarrel can be resolved through her.

Enter Iokastê.

IOKASTÊ   Poor foolish men, what wicked din is this?
   With Thebes sick to death, is it not shameful
120   That you should rake some private quarrel up?

To Oedipus

   Come into the house
                —And you, Kreon, go now:
   Let us have no more of this tumult over nothing.

KREON   Nothing? No, sister: what your husband plans for me
   Is one of two great evils: exile or death.

OEDIPUS   He is right.
                    Why, woman I have caught him squarely
   Plotting against my life.

KREON   No! Let me die
   Accurst if ever I have wished you harm!

IOKASTÊ   Ah, believe it, Oedipus!
   In the name of the gods, respect this oath of his
130   For my sake, for the sake of these people here!

CHORAGOS   STROPHE 1
   Open your mind to her, my lord. Be ruled by her, I beg you!

OEDIPUS   What would you have me do?

CHORAGOS   Respect Kreon's word. He has never spoken like a fool,
   And now he has sworn an oath.

OEDIPUS   You know what you ask?

CHORAGOS   I do.

OEDIPUS   Speak on, then.

CHORAGOS   A friend so sworn should not be baited so,
   In blind malice, and without final proof.

OEDIPUS   You are aware, I hope, that what you say
   Means death for me, or exile at the least.

CHORAGOS

140   No, I swear by Helios, first in Heaven!   STROPHE 2
           May I die friendless and accurst,
        The worst of deaths, if ever I meant that!
           It is the withering fields
             That hurt my sick heart:
        Must we bear all these ills,
             And now your bad blood as well?

OEDIPUS   Then let him go. And let me die, if I must,
        Or be driven by him in shame from the land of Thebes.
        It is your unhappiness, and not his talk,
        That touches me.
150   As for him—
        Wherever he goes, hatred will follow him.
KREON   Ugly in yielding, as you were ugly in rage!
        Natures like yours chiefly torment themselves.
OEDIPUS   Can you not go? Can you not leave me?
KREON   I can.
        You do not know me; but the city knows me,
        And in its eyes I am just, if not in yours.

                                              Exit Kreon.

CHORAGOS   ANTISTROPHE 1
        Lady Iokastê, did you not ask the King to go to his chambers?
IOKASTÊ   First tell me what has happened.
CHORAGOS   There was suspicion without evidence; yet it rankled
160   As even false charges will.
IOKASTÊ   On both sides?
CHORAGOS   On both.
IOKASTÊ   But what was said?

CHORAGOS   Oh let it rest, let it be done with!
        Have we not suffered enough?
OEDIPUS   You see to what your decency has brought you:
        You have made difficulties where my heart saw none.

CHORAGOS
        Oedipus, it is not once only I have told you—   ANTISTROPHE 2
           You must know I should count myself unwise
        To the point of madness, should I now forsake you—
             You, under whose hand,

170   In the storm of another time,
                  Our dear land sailed out free.
                  But now stand fast at the helm!

IOKASTÊ   In God's name, Oedipus, inform your wife as well:
    Why are you so set in this hard anger?

OEDIPUS   I will tell you, for none of these men deserves
    My confidence as you do. It is Kreon's work,
    His treachery, his plotting against me.

IOKASTÊ   Go on, if you can make this clear to me.

OEDIPUS   He charges me with the murder of Laïos.

180 IOKASTÊ   Has he some knowledge? Or does he speak from hearsay?

OEDIPUS   He would not commit himself to such a charge,
    But he has brought in that damnable soothsayer
    To tell his story.

IOKASTÊ   Set your mind at rest.
    If it is a question of soothsayers, I tell you
    That you will find no man whose craft gives knowledge
    Of the unknowable.

                       Here is my proof:
    An oracle was reported to Laïos once
    (I will not say from Phoibos himself, but from
    His appointed ministers, at any rate)
190   That his doom would be death at the hands of his own son—
    His son, born of his flesh and of mine!

    Now, you remember the story: Laïos was killed
    By marauding strangers where three highways meet;
    But his child had not been three days in this world
    Before the King had pierced the baby's ankles
    And left him to die on a lonely mountainside.

    Thus, Apollo never caused that child
    To kill his father, and it was not Laïos' fate
    To die at the hands of his son, as he had feared.
200   This is what prophets and prophecies are worth!
    Have no dread of them.
                       It is God himself
    Who can show us what he wills, in his own way.

OEDIPUS   How strange a shadowy memory crossed my mind,
    Just now while you were speaking; it chilled my heart.

IOKASTÊ   What do you mean? What memory do you speak of?

OEDIPUS   If I understand you, Laïos was killed
    At a place where three roads meet.

IOKASTÊ   So it was said:
We have no later story.

OEDIPUS   Where did it happen?

IOKASTÊ   Phokis, it is called: at a place where the Theban Way
210   Divides into the roads toward Delphi and Daulia.

OEDIPUS   When?

IOKASTÊ   We had the news not long before you came
And proved the right to your succession here.

OEDIPUS   Ah, what net has God been weaving for me?

IOKASTÊ   Oedipus! Why does this trouble you?

OEDIPUS   Do not ask me yet.
First, tell me how Laïos looked, and tell me
How old he was.

OEDIPUS   He was tall, his hair just touched
With white; his form was not unlike your own.

OEDIPUS   I think that I myself may be accurst
By my own ignorant edict.

IOKASTÊ   You speak strangely.
220   It makes me tremble to look at you, my King.

OEDIPUS   I am not sure that the blind man can not see.
But I should know better if you were to tell me—

IOKASTÊ   Anything—though I dread to hear you ask it.

OEDIPUS   Was the King lightly escorted, or did he ride
With a large company, as a ruler should?

IOKASTÊ   There were five men with him in all: one was a herald;
And a single chariot, which he was driving.

OEDIPUS   Alas, that makes it plain enough!
                                    But who—
Who told you how it happened?

IOKASTÊ   A household servant,
The only one to escape.

230   OEDIPUS   And is he still
A servant of ours?

IOKASTÊ   No; for when he came back at last
And found you enthroned in the place of the dead king,
He came to me, touched my hand with his, and begged
That I would send him away to the frontier district
Where only the shepherds go—
As far away from the city as I could send him.
I granted his prayer; for although the man was a slave,
He had earned more than this favor at my hands.

OEDPIUS   Can he be called back quickly?

IOKASTÊ   Easily.
But why?

240   OEDIPUS   I have taken too much upon myself
           Without enquiry; therefore I wish to consult him.
      IOKASTÊ   Then he shall come.
                                  But am I not one also
           To whom you might confide these fears of yours?
      OEDIPUS   That is your right; it will not be denied you,
           Now least of all; for I have reached a pitch
           Of wild foreboding. Is there anyone
           To whom I should sooner speak?

           Polybos of Corinth is my father.
           My mother is a Dorian: Meropê.
250   I grew up chief among the men of Corinth
           Until a strange thing happened—
           Not worth my passion, it may be, but strange.

           At a feast, a drunken man maundering in his cups
           Cries out that I am not my father's son!
           I contained myself that night, though I felt anger
           And a sinking heart. The next day I visited
           My father and mother, and questioned them. They stormed,
           Calling it all the slanderous rant of a fool;
           And this relieved me. Yet the suspicion
260   Remained always aching in my mind;
           I knew there was talk; I could not rest;
           And finally, saying nothing to my parents,
           I went to the shrine at Delphi.

           The god dismissed my question without reply;
           He spoke of other things.
                                  Some were clear,
           Full of wretchedness, dreadful, unbearable:
           As that I should lie with my own mother, breed
           Children from whom all men would turn their eyes;
           And that I should be my father's murderer.

270   I heard all this, and fled. And from that day
           Corinth to me was only in the stars
           Descending in that quarter of the sky,
           As I wandered farther and farther on my way
           To a land where I should never see the evil
           Sung by the oracle. And I came to this country
           Where, so you say, King Laïos was killed.

I will tell you all that happened there, my lady.

There were three highways
Coming together at a place I passed;
280   And there a herald came towards me, and a chariot
Drawn by horses, with a man such as you describe
Seated in it. The groom leading the horses
Forced me off the road at his lord's command;
But as this charioteer lurched over towards me
I struck him in my rage. The old man saw me
And brought his double goad down upon my head
As I came abreast.

He was paid back, and more!
Swinging my club in this right hand I knocked him
Out of his car, and he rolled on the ground.

I killed him.
290   I killed them all.
Now if that stranger and Laïos were—kin,
Where is a man more miserable than I?
More hated by the gods? Citizen and alien alike
Must never shelter me or speak to me—
I must be shunned by all.

And I myself
Pronounced this malediction upon myself!

Think of it: I have touched you with these hands,
These hands that killed your husband. What defilement!

Am I all evil, then? It must be so,
300   Since I must flee from Thebes, yet never again
See my own countrymen, my own country,
For fear of joining my mother in marriage
And killing Polybos, my father.

Ah,
If I was created so, born to this fate,
Who could deny the savagery of God?

O holy majesty of heavenly powers!
May I never see that day! Never!
Rather let me vanish from the race of men
Than know the abomination destined me!
310   CHORAGOS   We too, my lord, have felt dismay at this.
But there is hope: you have yet to hear the shepherd.

OEDIPUS   Indeed, I fear no other hope is left me.

IOKASTÊ   What do you hope from him when he comes?

OEDIPUS   This much:
    If his account of the murder tallies with yours,
    Then I am cleared.

IOKASTÊ   What was it that I said
    Of such importance?

OEDIPUS   Why, "marauders," you said,
    Killed the King, according to this man's story.
    If he maintains that still, if there were several,
    Clearly the guilt is not mine: I was alone.
320   But if he says one man, singlehanded, did it,
    Then the evidence all points to me.

IOKASTÊ   You may be sure that he said there were several;
    And can he call back that story now? He cán not.
    The whole city heard it as plainly as I.
    But suppose he alters some detail of it:
    He can not ever show that Laïos' death
    Fulfilled the oracle: for Apollo said
    My child was doomed to kill him; and my child—
    Poor baby!—it was my child that died first.

330   No. From now on, where oracles are concerned,
    I would not waste a second thought on any.

OEDIPUS   You may be right.
                   But come: let someone go
    For the shepherd at once. This matter must be settled.

IOKASTÊ   I will send for him.
    I would not wish to cross you in anything,
    And surely not in this.—Let us go in.

Exeunt into the palace.

ODE II

CHORUS   Let me be reverent in the ways of right,   STROPHE 1
    Lowly the paths I journey on;
    Let all my words and actions keep
    The laws of the pure universe
    From highest Heaven handed down.
    For Heaven is their bright nurse,
    Those generations of the realms of light;
    Ah, never of mortal kind were they begot,

Nor are they slaves of memory, lost in sleep:
10   Their Father is greater than Time, and ages not.

The tyrant is a child of Pride   ANTISTROPHE 1
Who drinks from his great sickening cup
Recklessness and vanity,
Until from his high crest headlong
He plummets to the dust of hope.
That strong man is not strong.
But let no fair ambition be denied;
May God protect the wrestler for the State
In government, in comely policy,
20   Who will fear God, and on His ordinance wait.

Haughtiness and the high hand of disdain   STROPHE 2
Tempt and outrage God's holy law;
And any mortal who dares hold
No immortal Power in awe
Will be caught up in a net of pain:
The price for which his levity is sold.
Let each man take due earnings, then,
And keep his hands from holy things,
And from blasphemy stand apart—
30   Else the crackling blast of heaven
Blows on his head, and on his desperate heart.
Though fools will honor impious men,
In their cities no tragic poet sings.

Shall we lose faith in Delphi's obscurities,   ANTISTROPHE 2
We who have heard the world's core
Discredited, and the sacred wood
Of Zeus at Elis praised no more?
The deeds and the strange prophecies
Must make a pattern yet to be understood.
40   Zeus, if indeed you are lord of all,
Throned in light over night and day,
Mirror this in your endless mind:
Our masters call the oracle
Words on the wind, and the Delphic vision blind!
Their hearts no longer know Apollo,
And reverence for the gods has died away.

SCENE III

Enter Iokastê.

IOKASTÊ   Princes of Thebes, it has occurred to me
　　　To visit the altars of the gods, bearing
　　　These branches as a suppliant, and this incense.
　　　Our King is not himself: his noble soul
　　　Is overwrought with fantasies of dread,
　　　Else he would consider
　　　The new prophecies in the light of the old.
　　　He will listen to any voice that speaks disaster,
　　　And my advice goes for nothing.

She approaches the altar, right.

　　　　　　　　　　　To you, then, Apollo,
10　　　Lycéan lord, since you are nearest, I turn in prayer.

　　　Receive these offerings, and grant us deliverance
　　　From defilement. Our hearts are heavy with fear
　　　When we see our leader distracted, as helpless sailors
　　　Are terrified by the confusion of their helmsman.

Enter Messenger.

MESSENGER   Friends, no doubt you can direct me:
　　　Where shall I find the house of Oedipus,
　　　Or, better still, where is the King himself?
CHORAGOS   It is this very place, stranger; he is inside.
　　　This is his wife and mother of his children.
20　MESSENGER   I wish her happiness in a happy house,
　　　Blest in all the fulfillment of her marriage.
IOKASTÊ   I wish as much for you: your courtesy
　　　Deserves a like good fortune. But now, tell me:
　　　Why have you come? What have you to say to us?
MESSENGER   Good news, my lady, for your house and your husband.
IOKASTÊ   What news? Who sent you here?
MESSENGER   　　　　　　　　　　　　　　I am from Corinth.
　　　The news I bring ought to mean joy for you,
　　　Though it may be you will find some grief in it.
IOKASTÊ   What is it? How can it touch us in both ways?

30 MESSENGER   The word is that the people of the Isthmus
        Intend to call Oedipus to be their king.
    IOKASTÊ   But old King Polybos—is he not reigning still?
    MESSENGER   No. Death holds him in his sepulchre.
    IOKASTÊ   What are you saying? Polybos is dead?
    MESSENGER   If I am not telling the truth, may I die myself.
    IOKASTÊ   *To a Maidservant*
        Go in, go quickly; tell this to your master.

        O riddlers of God's will, where are you now!
        This was the man whom Oedipus, long ago,
        Feared so, fled so, in dread of destroying him—
40   But it was another fate by which he died.

Enter Oedipus, center.

    OEDIPUS   Dearest Iokastê, why have you sent for me?
    IOKASTÊ   Listen to what this man says, and then tell me
        What has become of the solemn prophecies.
    OEDIPUS   Who is this man? What is his news for me?
    IOKASTÊ   He has come from Corinth to announce your father's death!
    OEDIPUS   Is it true, stranger? Tell me in your own words.
    MESSENGER   I can not say it more clearly: the King is dead.
    OEDIPUS   Was it by treason? Or by an attack of illness?
    MESSENGER   A little thing brings old men to their rest.
    OEDIPUS   It was sickness, then?
50 MESSENGER   Yes, and his many years.
    OEDIPUS   Ah!
        Why should a man respect the Pythian hearth, or
        Give heed to the birds that jangle above his head?
        They prophesied that I should kill Polybos,
        Kill my own father; but he is dead and buried,
        And I am here—I never touched him, never,
        Unless he died of grief for my departure,
        And thus, in a sense, through me. No. Polybos
        Has packed the oracles off with him underground.
        They are empty words.
    IOKASTÊ   Had I not told you so?
60 OEDIPUS   You had; it was my faint heart that betrayed me.
    IOKASTÊ   From now on never think of those things again.
    OEDIPUS   And yet—must I not fear my mother's bed?
    IOKASTÊ   Why should anyone in this world be afraid,
        Since Fate rules us and nothing can be foreseen?
        A man should live only for the present day.

Have no more fear of sleeping with your mother:
How many men, in dreams, have lain with their mothers!
No reasonable man is troubled by such things.

OEDIPUS   That is true; only—

70   If only my mother were not still alive!
But she is alive. I can not help my dread.

IOKASTÊ   Yet this news of your father's death is wonderful.

OEDIPUS   Wonderful. But I fear the living woman.

MESSENGER   Tell me, who is this woman that you fear?

OEDIPUS   It is Meropê, man; the wife of King Polybos.

MESSENGER   Meropê? Why should you be afraid of her?

OEDIPUS   An oracle of the gods, a dreadful saying.

MESSENGER   Can you tell me about it or are you sworn to silence?

OEDIPUS   I can tell you, and I will.

80   Apollo said through his prophet that I was the man
Who should marry his own mother, shed his father's blood
With his own hands. And so, for all these years
I have kept clear of Corinth, and no harm has come—
Though it would have been sweet to see my parents again.

MESSENGER   And is this the fear that drove you out of Corinth?

OEDIPUS   Would you have me kill my father?

MESSENGER   As for that
You must be reassured by the news I gave you.

OEDIPUS   If you could reassure me, I would reward you.

MESSENGER   I had that in mind, I will confess: I thought

90   I could count on you when you returned to Corinth.

OEDIPUS   No: I will never go near my parents again.

MESSENGER   Ah, son, you still do not know what you are doing—

OEDIPUS   What do you mean? In the name of God tell me!

MESSENGER   —If these are your reasons for not going home.

OEDIPUS   I tell you, I fear the oracle may come true.

MESSENGER   And guilt may come upon you through your parents?

OEDIPUS   That is the dread that is always in my heart.

MESSENGER   Can you not see that all your fears are groundless?

OEDIPUS   Groundless? Am I not my parents' son?

MESSENGER   Polybos was not your father.

100   OEDIPUS   Not my father?

MESSENGER   No more your father than the man speaking to you.

OEDIPUS   But you are nothing to me!

MESSENGER   Neither was he.

OEDIPUS   Then why did he call me son?

MESSENGER   I will tell you:
Long ago he had you from my hands, as a gift.

OEDIPUS   Then how could he love me so, if I was not his?

MESSENGER   He had no children, and his heart turned to you.

OEDIPUS   What of you? Did you buy me? Did you find me by chance?

MESSENGER   I came upon you in the woody vales of Kithairon.

OEDIPUS   And what were you doing there?

MESSENGER   Tending my flocks.

OEDIPUS   A wandering shepherd?

110 MESSENGER   But your savior, son, that day.

OEDIPUS   From what did you save me?

MESSENGER   Your ankles should tell you that.

OEDIPUS   Ah, stranger, why do you speak of that childhood pain?

MESSENGER   I pulled the skewer that pinned your feet together.

OEDIPUS   I have had the mark as long as I can remember.

MESSENGER   That was why you were given the name you bear.

OEDIPUS   God! Was it my father or my mother who did it?
　　Tell me!

MESSENGER   I do not know. The man who gave you to me
　　Can tell you better than I.

OEDIPUS   It was not you that found me, but another?

120 MESSENGER   It was another shepherd gave you to me.

OEDIPUS   Who was he? Can you tell me who he was?

MESSENGER   I think he was said to be one of Laïos' people.

OEDIPUS   You mean the Laïos who was king here years ago?

MESSENGER   Yes; King Laïos; and the man was one of his herdsmen.

OEDIPUS   Is he still alive? Can I see him?

MESSENGER   These men here
　　Know best about such things.

OEDIPUS   Does anyone here
　　Know this shepherd that he is talking about?
　　Have you seen him in the fields, or in the town?
　　If you have, tell me. It is time things were made plain.

130 CHORAGOS   I think the man he means is that same shepherd
　　You have already asked to see. Iokastê perhaps
　　Could tell you something.

OEDIPUS   Do you know anything
　　About him, Lady? Is he the man we have summoned?
　　Is that the man this shepherd means?

IOKASTÊ   Why think of him?
　　Forget this herdsman. Forget it all.
　　This talk is a waste of time.

OEDIPUS   How can you say that,
　　When the clues to my true birth are in my hands?

IOKASTÊ   For God's love, let us have no more questioning!
　　Is your life nothing to you?

140 　　My own is pain enough for me to bear.

OEDIPUS   You need not worry. Suppose my mother a slave,
        And born of slaves: no baseness can touch you.
IOKASTÊ   Listen to me, I beg you: do not do this thing!
OEDIPUS   I will not listen; the truth must be made known.
IOKASTÊ   Everything that I say is for your own good!
OEDIPUS   My own good
        Snaps my patience, then; I want none of it.
IOKASTÊ   You are fatally wrong! May you never learn who you are!
OEDIPUS   Go, one of you, and bring the shepherd here.
        Let us leave this woman to brag of her royal name.
150   IOKASTÊ   Ah, miserable!
        That is the only word I have for you now.
        That is the only word I can ever have.

                                        Exit into the palace.

CHORAGOS   Why has she left us, Oedipus? Why has she gone
        In such a passion of sorrow? I fear this silence:
        Something dreadful may come of it.
OEDIPUS   Let it come!
        However base my birth, I must know about it.
        The Queen, like a woman, is perhaps ashamed
        To think of my low origin. But I
        Am a child of Luck; I can not be dishonored.
160   Luck is my mother; the passing months, my brothers,
        Have seen me rich and poor.
                              If this is so,
        How could I wish that I were someone else?
        How could I not be glad to know my birth?

ODE III

CHORUS   If ever the coming time were known   STROPHE
        To my heart's pondering,
        Kithairon, now by Heaven I see the torches
        At the festival of the next full moon,
        And see the dance, and hear the choir sing
        A grace to your gentle shade:
        Mountain where Oedipus was found,
        O mountain guard of a noble race!
        May the god who heals us lend his aid,
10   And let that glory come to pass
        For our king's cradling-ground.

Of the nymphs that flower beyond the years,   ANTISTROPHE
Who bore you, royal child,
To Pan of the hills or the timberline Apollo,
Cold in delight where the upland clears,
Or Hermês for whom Kyllenê's heights are piled?
Or flushed as evening cloud,
Great Dionysos, roamer of mountains,
He—was it he who found you there,
20   And caught you up in his own proud
Arms from the sweet god-ravisher
Who laughed by the Muses' fountains?

SCENE IV

OEDIPUS   Sirs: though I do not know the man,
I think I see him coming, this shepherd we want:
He is old, like our friend here, and the men
Bringing him seem to be servants of my house.
But you can tell, if you have ever seen him.

Enter Shepherd escorted by servants.

CHORAGOS   I know him, he was Laïos' man. You can trust him.
OEDIPUS   Tell me first, you from Corinth: is this the shepherd
We were discussing?
MESSENGER   This is the very man.
OEDIPUS   *To Shepherd*
Come here. No, look at me. You must answer
10   Everything I ask.—You belonged to Laïos?
SHEPHERD   Yes: born his slave, brought up in his house.
OEDIPUS   Tell me: what kind of work did you do for him?
SHEPHERD   I was a shepherd of his, most of my life.
OEDIPUS   Where mainly did you go for pasturage?
SHEPHERD   Sometimes Kithairon, sometimes the hills near-by.
OEDIPUS   Do you remember ever seeing this man out there?
SHEPHERD   What would he be doing there? This man?
OEDIPUS   This man standing here. Have you ever seen him before?
SHEPHERD   No. At least, not to my recollection.
20   MESSENGER   And that is not strange, my lord. But I'll refresh
His memory: he must remember when we two
Spent three whole seasons together, March to September,
On Kithairon or thereabouts. He had two flocks;
I had one. Each autumn I'd drive mine home

And he would go back with his to Laïos' sheepfold.—
Is this not true, just as I have described it?

SHEPHERD True, yes; but it was all so long ago.

MESSENGER Well, then: do you remember, back in those days,
That you gave me a baby boy to bring up as my own?

30 SHEPHERD What if I did? What are you trying to say?

MESSENGER King Oedipus was once that little child.

SHEPHERD Damn you, hold your tongue!

OEDIPUS   No more of that!
It is your tongue needs watching, not this man's.

SHEPHERD My King, my Master, what is it I have done wrong?

OEDIPUS You have not answered his question about the boy.

SHEPHERD He does not know . . . He is only making trouble . . .

OEDIPUS Come, speak plainly, or it will go hard with you.

SHEPHERD In God's name, do not torture an old man!

OEDIPUS Come here, one of you; bind his arms behind him.

40 SHEPHERD Unhappy king! What more do you wish to learn?

OEDIPUS Did you give this man the child he speaks of?

SHEPHERD   I did.
And I would to God I had died that very day.

OEDIPUS You will die now unless you speak the truth.

SHEPHERD Yet if I speak the truth, I am worse than dead.

OEDIPUS *To Attendant*
He intends to draw it out, apparently—

SHEPHERD No! I have told you already that I gave him the boy.

OEDIPUS Where did you get him? From your house? From somewhere else?

SHEPHERD Not from mine, no. A man gave him to me.

OEDIPUS Is that man here? Whose house did he belong to?

50 SHEPHERD For God's love, my King, do not ask me any more!

OEDIPUS You are a dead man if I have to ask you again.

SHEPHERD Then . . . Then the child was from the palace of Laïos.

OEDIPUS A slave child? or a child of his own line?

SHEPHERD Ah, I am on the brink of dreadful speech!

OEDIPUS And I of dreadful hearing. Yet I must hear.

SHEPHERD If you must be told, then . . .
                              They said it was Laïos' child:
But it is your wife who can tell you about that.

OEDIPUS My wife!—Did she give it to you?

SHEPHERD   My Lord, she did.

OEDIPUS Do you know why?

SHEPHERD   I was told to get rid of it.

OEDIPUS Oh heartless mother!

60 SHEPHERD   But in dread of prophecies . . .

OEDIPUS Tell me.

SHEPHERD   It was said that the boy would kill his own father.
OEDIPUS   Then why did you give him over to this old man?
SHEPHERD   I pitied the baby, my King,
    And I thought that this man would take him far away
    To his own country.
                     He saved him—but for what a fate!
    For if you are what this man says you are,
    No man living is more wretched than Oedipus.
OEDIPUS   Ah God!
    It was true!
             All the prophecies!
                    —Now,
70   O Light, may I look on you for the last time!
    I, Oedipus,
    Oedipus, damned in his birth, in his marriage damned,
    Damned in the blood he shed with his own hand!

He rushes into the palace.

ODE IV

CHORUS   Alas for the seed of men.   STROPHE 1

    What measure shall I give these generations
    That breathe on the void and are void
    And exist and do not exist?

    Who bears more weight of joy
    Than mass of sunlight shifting in images,
    Or who shall make his thought stay on
    That down time drifts away?

    Your splendor is all fallen.

10   O naked brow of wrath and tears,
    O change of Oedipus!
    I who saw your days call no man blest—
    Your great days like ghósts góne.

    That mind was a strong bow.   ANTISTROPHE 1

    Deep, how deep you drew it then, hard archer,
    At a dim fearful range,

And brought dear glory down!

You overcame the stranger—
The virgin with her hooking lion claws—
And though death sang, stood like a tower
To make pale Thebes take heart.

Fortress against our sorrow!

True king, giver of laws,
Majestic Oedipus!
No prince in Thebes had ever such renown,
No prince won such grace of power.

And now of all men ever known   STROPHE 2
Most pitiful is this man's story:
His fortunes are most changed, his state
Fallen to a low slave's
Ground under bitter fate.

O Oedipus, most royal one!
The great door that expelled you to the light
Gave at night—ah, gave night to your glory:
As to the father, to the fathering son.

All understood too late.

How could that queen whom Laïos won,
The garden that he harrowed at his height,
Be silent when that act was done?

But all eyes fail before time's eye,   ANTISTROPHE 2
All actions come to justice there.
Though never willed, though far down the deep past,
Your bed, your dread sirings,
Are brought to book at last.

Child by Laïos doomed to die,
Then doomed to lose that fortunate little death,
Would God you never took breath in this air
That with my wailing lips I take to cry:

For I weep the world's outcast.

50   I was blind, and now I can tell why:
        Asleep, for you had given ease of breath
        To Thebes, while the false years went by.

ÉXODOS

Enter, from the palace, Second Messenger.

SECOND MESSENGER Elders of Thebes, most honored in this land,
        What horrors are yours to see and hear, what weight
        Of sorrow to be endured, if, true to your birth,
        You venerate the line of Labdakos!
        I think neither Istros nor Phasis, those great rivers,
        Could purify this place of all the evil
        It shelters now, or soon must bring to light—
        Evil not done unconsciously, but willed.

        The greatest griefs are those we cause ourselves
10 CHORAGOS Surely, friend, we have grief enough already;
        What new sorrow do you mean?
SECOND MESSENGER   The Queen is dead.
CHORAGOS O miserable Queen! But at whose hand?
SECOND MESSENGER   Her own.
        The full horror of what happened you can not know,
        For you did not see it; but I, who did, will tell you
        As clearly as I can how she met her death.

        When she had left us,
        In passionate silence, passing through the court,
        She ran to her apartment in the house,
        Her hair clutched by the fingers of both hands.
20   She closed the doors behind her; then, by that bed
        Where long ago the fatal son was conceived—
        That son who should bring about his father's death—
        We heard her call upon Laïos, dead so many years,
        And heard her wail for the double fruit of her marriage,
        A husband by her husband, children by her child.

        Exactly how she died I do not know:
        For Oedipus burst in moaning and would not let us
        Keep vigil to the end: it was by him
        As he stormed about the room that our eyes were caught.
30   From one to another of us he went, begging a sword,
        Hunting the wife who was not his wife, the mother

Whose womb had carried his own children and himself.
I do not know: it was none of us aided him,
But surely one of the gods was in control!
For with a dreadful cry
He hurled his weight, as though wrenched out of himself,
At the twin doors: the bolts gave, and he rushed in.
And there we saw her hanging, her body swaying
From the cruel cord she had noosed about her neck.
40   A great sob broke from him, heartbreaking to hear,
As he loosed the rope and lowered her to the ground.

I would blot out from my mind what happened next!
For the King ripped from her gown the golden brooches
That were her ornament, and raised them, and plunged them down
Straight into his own eyeballs, crying, "No more,
No more shall you look on the misery about me,
The horrors of my own doing! Too long you have known
The faces of those whom I should never have seen,
Too long been blind to those for whom I was searching!
50   From this hour, go in darkness!" And as he spoke,
He struck at his eyes—not once, but many times;
And the blood spattered his beard,
Bursting from his ruined sockets like red hail.

So from the unhappiness of two this evil has sprung,
A curse on the man and woman alike. The old
Happiness of the house of Labdakos
Was happiness enough: where is it today?
It is all wailing and ruin, disgrace, death—all
The misery of mankind that has a name—
60   And it is wholly and for ever theirs.
CHORAGOS   Is he in agony still? Is there no rest for him?
SECOND MESSENGER   He is calling for someone to open the doors wide
So that all the children of Kadmos may look upon
His father's murderer, his mother's—no,
I can not say it!
                  And then he will leave Thebes,
Self-exiled, in order that the curse
Which he himself pronounced may depart from the house.
He is weak, and there is none to lead him,
So terrible is his suffering.
                           But you will see:
70   Look, the doors are opening; in a moment
You will see a thing that would crush a heart of stone.

The central door is opened; Oedipus, blinded, is led in.

CHORAGOS   Dreadful indeed for men to see.
    Never have my own eyes
    Looked on a sight so full of fear.

    Oedipus!
    What madness came upon you, what daemon
    Leaped on your life with heavier
    Punishment than a mortal man can bear?
    No: I can not even
80   Look at you, poor ruined one.
    And I would speak, question, ponder,
    If I were able. No.
    You make me shudder.
OEDIPUS   God. God.
    Is there a sorrow greater?
    Where shall I find harbor in this world?
    My voice is hurled far on a dark wind.
    What has God done to me?
CHORAGOS   Too terrible to think of, or to see.

90 OEDIPUS   O cloud of night,   STROPHE 1
    Never to be turned away: night coming on,
    I can not tell how: night like a shroud!

    My fair winds brought me here.
                    O God. Again
    The pain of the spikes where I had sight,
    The flooding pain
    Of memory, never to be gouged out.

CHORAGOS   This is not strange.
    You suffer it all twice over, remorse in pain,
    Pain in remorse.

100 OEDIPUS   Ah dear friend   ANTISTROPHE 1
    Are you faithful even yet, you alone?
    Are you still standing near me, will you stay here,
    Patient, to care for the blind?
                    The blind man!
    Yet even blind I know who it is attends me,
    By the voice's tone—
    Though my new darkness hide the comforter.

CHORAGOS   Oh fearful act!
    What god was it drove you to rake black
    Night across your eyes?

110   OEDIPUS   Apollo. Apollo. Dear   STROPHE 2
    Children, the god was Apollo.
    He brought my sick, sick fate upon me.
    But the blinding hand was my own!
    How could I bear to see
    When all my sight was horror everywhere?

CHORAGOS   Everywhere; that is true.

OEDIPUS   And now what is left?
    Images? Love? A greeting even,
    Sweet to the senses? Is there anything?
120   Ah, no, friends: lead me away.
    Lead me away from Thebes.
                  Lead the great wreck
    And hell of Oedipus, whom the gods hate.

CHORAGOS   Your misery, you are not blind to that.
    Would God you had never found it out!

OEDIPUS   Death take the man who unbound   ANTISTROPHE 2
    My feet on that hillside
    And delivered me from death to life! What life?
    If only I had died,
    This weight of monstrous doom
130   Could not have dragged me and my darlings down.

CHORAGOS   I would have wished the same.

OEDIPUS   Oh never to have come here
    With my father's blood upon me! Never
    To have been the man they call his mother's husband!
    Oh accurst! Oh child of evil,
    To have entered that wretched bed—
                     the selfsame one!
    More primal than sin itself, this fell to me.

CHORAGOS   I do not know what words to offer you.
    You were better dead than alive and blind.

140   OEDIPUS   Do not counsel me any more. This punishment

That I have laid upon myself is just.
If I had eyes,
I do not know how I could bear the sight
Of my father, when I came to the house of Death,
Or my mother; for I have sinned against them both
So vilely that I could not make my peace
By strangling my own life.

                     Or do you think my children,
Born as they were born, would be sweet to my eyes?
Ah never, never! Nor this town with its high walls,
Nor the holy images of the gods.

150   For I,
Thrice miserable!—Oedipus, noblest of all the line
Of Kadmos, have condemned myself to enjoy
These things no more, by my own malediction
Expelling that man whom the gods declared
To be a defilement in the house of Laïos.
After exposing the rankness of my own guilt,
How could I look men frankly in the eyes?
No, I swear it,
If I could have stifled my hearing at its source,
160 I would have done it and made all this body
A tight cell of misery, blank to light and sound:
So I should have been safe in my dark mind
Beyond external evil.

                  Ah Kithairon!
Why did you shelter me? When I was cast upon you,
Why did I not die? Then I should never
Have shown the world my execrable birth.

Ah Polybos! Corinth, city that I believed
The ancient seat of my ancestors: how fair
I seemed, your child! And all the while this evil
Was cancerous within me!
170   For I am sick
In my own being, sick in my origin.

O three roads, dark ravine, woodland and way
Where three roads met: you, drinking my father's blood,
My own blood, spilled by my own hand: can you remember
The unspeakable things I did there, and the things
I went on from there to do?

                  O marriage, marriage!
The act that engendered me, and again the act

Performed by the son in the same bed—

Ah, the net

Of incest, mingling fathers, brothers, sons,

180   With brides, wives, mothers: the last evil

That can be known by men: no tongue can say

How evil!

No. For the love of God, conceal me

Somewhere far from Thebes; or kill me; or hurl me

Into the sea, away from men's eyes for ever.

Come, lead me. You need not fear to touch me.

Of all men, I alone can bear this guilt.

Enter Kreon.

CHORAGOS   Kreon is here now. As to what you ask,

He may decide the course to take. He only

Is left to protect the city in your place.

190   OEDIPUS   Alas, how can I speak to him? What right have I

To beg his courtesy whom I have deeply wronged?

KREON   I have not come to mock you, Oedipus,

Or to reproach you, either.

To Attendants   —You standing there:

If you have lost all respect for man's dignity,

At least respect the flame of Lord Helios:

Do not allow this pollution to show itself

Openly here, an affront to the earth

And Heaven's rain and the light of day. No, take him

Into the house as quickly as you can.

200   For it is proper

That only the close kindred see his grief.

OEDIPUS   I pray you in God's name, since your courtesy

Ignores my dark expectation, visiting

With mercy this man of all men most execrable:

Give me what I ask—for your good, not for mine.

KREON   And what is it that you turn to me begging for?

OEDIPUS   Drive me out of this country as quickly as may be

To a place where no human voice can ever greet me.

KREON   I should have done that before now—only,

210   God's will had not been wholly revealed to me.

OEDIPUS   But his command is plain: the parricide

Must be destroyed. I am that evil man.

KREON   That is the sense of it, yes; but as things are,

We had best discover clearly what is to be done.

OEDIPUS   You would learn more about a man like me?

KREON   You are ready now to listen to the god.

OEDIPUS I will listen. But it is to you
    That I must turn for help. I beg you, hear me.

    The woman in there—
220   Give her whatever funeral you think proper:
    She is your sister.
                —But let me go, Kreon!
    Let me purge my father's Thebes of the pollution
    Of my living here, and go out to the wild hills,
    To Kithairon, that has won such fame with me,
    The tomb my mother and father appointed for me,
    And let me die there, as they willed I should.
    And yet I know
    Death will not ever come to me through sickness
    Or in any natural way: I have been preserved
230   For some unthinkable fate. But let that be.

    As for my sons, you need not care for them.
    They are men, they will find some way to live.
    But my poor daughters, who have shared my table,
    Who never before have been parted from their father—
    Take care of them, Kreon; do this for me.
    And will you let me touch them with my hands
    A last time, and let us weep together?
    Be kind, my lord,
    Great prince, be kind!
                  Could I but touch them,
240   They would be mine again, as when I had my eyes.

Enter Antigone and Ismene, attended.

    Ah, God!
    Is it my dearest children I hear weeping?
    Has Kreon pitied me and sent my daughters?
KREON Yes, Oedipus: I knew that they were dear to you
    In the old days, and know you must love them still.
OEDIPUS May God bless you for this—and be friendlier
    Guardian to you than he has been to me!

    Children, where are you?
    Come quickly to my hands: they are your brother's—
250   Hands that have brought your father's once clear eyes
    To this way of seeing—
               Ah dearest ones,

I had neither sight nor knowledge then, your father
By the woman who was the source of his own life!
And I weep for you—having no strength to see you—,
I weep for you when I think of the bitterness
That men will visit upon you all your lives.
What homes, what festivals can you attend
Without being forced to depart again in tears?
And when you come to marriageable age,
Where is the man, my daughters, who would dare
Risk the bane that lies on all my children?
Is there any evil wanting? Your father killed
His father; sowed the womb of her who bore him;
Engendered you at the fount of his own existence!

That is what they will say of you.

Then, whom
Can you ever marry? There are no bridegrooms for you,
And your lives must wither away in sterile dreaming.

O Kreon, son of Menoikeus!
You are the only father my daughters have,
Since we, their parents, are both of us gone for ever.
They are your own blood: you will not let them
Fall into beggary and loneliness;
You will keep them from the miseries that are mine!
Take pity on them; see, they are only children,
Friendless except for you. Promise me this,
Great Prince, and give me your hand in token of it.

Kreon clasps his right hand.

Children:
I could say much, if you could understand me,
But as it is, I have only this prayer for you:
Live where you can, be as happy as you can—
Happier, please God, than God has made your father.
KREON   Enough. You have wept enough. Now go within.
OEDIPUS   I must; but it is hard.
KREON   Time eases all things.
OEDIPUS   You know my mind, then?
KREON   Say what you desire.
OEDIPUS   Send me from Thebes!
KREON   God grant that I may!

OEDIPUS   But since God hates me . . .

KREON   No, he will grant your wish.

OEDIPUS   You promise?

KREON   I can not speak beyond my knowledge.

OEDIPUS   Then lead me in.

KREON   Come now, and leave your children.

OEDIPUS   No! Do not take them from me!

KREON   Think no longer

290   That you are in command here, but rather think
      How, when you were, you served your own destruction.

Exeunt into the house all but the Chorus; the Choragos chants directly to the audience.

CHORAGOS   Men of Thebes: look upon Oedipus.

        This is the king who solved the famous riddle
        And towered up, most powerful of men.
        No mortal eyes but looked on him with envy,
        Yet in the end ruin swept over him.

        Let every man in mankind's frailty
        Consider his last day; and let none
        Presume on his good fortune until he find
300   Life, at his death, a memory without pain.

COMEDY IN THE CLASSICAL GREEK THEATER

Lysistrata was first staged in 411 B.C. at the theater of Dionysus in Athens, where *Oedipus Rex* had been produced some fifteen years earlier. (A description of that theater can be found in our introduction to *Oedipus Rex*.) The method of staging, however, was quite different for the two plays—as different as tragedy and comedy. If we recall that classical Greek comedy developed from primitive fertility rites and masquerades, in which people wore fantastic costumes and went throughout the streets singing, dancing, carousing, and even jesting with bystanders, we can begin to sense the bizarre quality of the spectacle created in the original performance of *Lysistrata*. We can get an even more particular sense of its outlandishness when we realize that the male characters would have been costumed in extremely short tunics and flesh-colored tights padded to suggest comic deformity, and that between their legs they would have been sporting large leather phalluses so as to ridicule their sexual frustration. Their masks, too, would have been ridiculously ugly and contorted so as to suggest the lewd grimace of a coarse peasant type.

In their physical movements as in their costumes, they would have aimed to accentuate the bawdy element of the comedy. They would not have limited themselves simply to reciting their lines, but would also have performed ribald dance movements, kicking their buttocks, slapping their thighs, and possibly even pummeling one another. And the same would have been true of the choral dancing and singing.

The chorus, in fact, had a major role in the performance of *Lysistrata*, as in all Greek comedies. Its function can best be appreciated when seen within the typical structure of Greek comedy. Comedy always began with a short scene, a *prologos*, in which the comic protagonist proposed a fantastic solution to a pressing social or political issue. Lysistrata, for example, opens the play by gathering her cohorts together and proposing that they go on a sex strike against their husbands as a means of ending the war that was then literally consuming Athenian life.

Immediately after the *prologos*, the chorus entered in two groups, one group siding with the protagonist, the other with the antagonists; and a contest, or *agon*, developed between the two groups as they debated the fantastic proposal. Thus, immediately after Lysistrata and her cohorts depart, the chorus of old men appears carrying logs and torches, then the chorus of old women carrying pitchers of water; and soon the old women are dousing the old men with water. Indeed, the *agon* typically developed into a knock-down drag-out struggle, one that involved not only bawdy words and slapstick action but also a series of ridiculously complicated patter songs, the last of which was sung rapidly without drawing a single breath. The *agon* also included a debate between the protagonist and a single antagonist. Thus Lysistrata is shown humiliating the Athenian magistrate in word and in deed.

The climax of the *agon* took place only after the protagonist and supporting chorus had literally beaten down all opposition to their proposal. Then all the actors departed and the chorus supporting the protagonist stepped forward and addressed the spectators directly, exhorting them to side with the idea of the play. In this section, known as the *parabasis,* the dramatist actually had his say, as does Aristophanes when the Chorus of Women implore the citizens of Athens to "hear useful words for the state." After the *parabasis* the actors returned, and in a series of short scenes the fantastic proposal was put into action and shown to be successful. Thus *Lysistrata* concludes with the raucous festivities that might have taken place had Athens and Sparta actually made peace in 411 B.C.

Though *Lysistrata* was occasioned by the immediate circumstances of the war between Athens and Sparta, it makes a statement about war that has been true for all times. It makes that statement through the fantastic idea dreamed up by Lysistrata—to force the Athenian men to make peace by refusing to make love to them so long as they continue the war. Nearly twenty-five centuries ago, Aristophanes was pleading with his audience to make love not war. And he showed his audience that truth by staging a war of the sexes—and celebrating the peace that might follow such a war.

ARISTOPHANES

c. 445–385 B.C.

Born in Athens, where his father was a wealthy and very conservative businessman, Aristophanes grew up during the period that was marked by the
onset of the Peloponnesian Wars, which began in 431 B.C., continued for
more than twenty years, and led to the collapse of Athens and its surrender
to Sparta in 404. The cultural and political convulsions produced by the war
evidently provoked Aristophanes very early in his career to become a satiric
dramatist, for in 426 he devoted his second play, *Babylonians,* to a reportedly scathing satire of Cleon, the leading spokesman for the war against
Sparta. This non-extant play led Cleon to accuse Aristophanes of "slander-
ing the state," and though the accusation did not lead to a conviction, it did
foment a lifelong struggle between the two, from which Aristophanes never
flinched, despite the extraordinary power and influence of Cleon. Three of
Aristophanes' eleven extant comedies are explicitly antiwar plays: *Acharni-
ans* (425), *Peace* (421), and *Lysistrata* (411). Two others, though not explicitly
antiwar plays, do reflect cultural disasters occasioned by the war: *The Birds*
(414) and *The Frogs* (404). Altogether, Aristophanes reportedly wrote more
than forty comedies, most of them dealing with the educational, philosophical, political, and social issues of his time. His mastery of satiric
comedy may be judged from the fact that he won the first prize for comedy
more often than any of his contemporaries.

Lysistrata

CHARACTERS

LYSISTRATA ⎫
CALONICE ⎬ Athenian women
MYRRHINE ⎭
LAMPITO, a Spartan woman
LEADER of Chorus of Old Men
CHORUS of Old Men
LEADER of Chorus of Old Women
CHORUS of Old Women
ATHENIAN MAGISTRATE

THREE ATHENIAN WOMEN
CINESIAS, an Athenian, husband
  of Myrrhine
SPARTAN HERALD
SPARTAN AMBASSADORS
ATHENIAN AMBASSADORS
TWO ATHENIAN CITIZENS
CHORUS of Athenians
CHORUS of Spartans

Translated by Charles T. Murphy

Scene. In Athens, beneath the Acropolis. In the center of the stage is the propylaea, or gate-way to the Acropolis; to one side is a small grotto, sacred to Pan. The orchestra represents a slope leading up to the gate-way.

It is early in the morning. Lysistrata is pacing impatiently up and down.

LYSISTRATA   If they'd been summoned to worship the God of Wine, or Pan, or to visit the Queen of Love, why, you couldn't have pushed your way through the streets for all the timbrels. But now there's not a single woman here—except my neighbour; here she comes.

Enter Calonice.

Good day to you, Calonice.

CALONICE   And to you, Lysistrata. [*Noticing Lysistrata's impatient air*] But what ails you? Don't scowl, my dear; it's not becoming to you to knit your brows like that.

LYSISTRATA [*sadly*]   Ah, Calonice, my heart aches; I'm so annoyed at us women. For among men we have a reputation for sly trickery—

CALONICE   And rightly too, on my word!

LYSISTRATA   —but when they were told to meet here to consider a matter of no small importance, they lie abed and don't come.

CALONICE   Oh, they'll come all right, my dear. It's not easy for a woman to get out, you know. One is working on her husband, another is getting up the maid, another has to put the baby to bed, or wash and feed it.

LYSISTRATA   But after all, there are other matters more important than all that.

CALONICE   My dear Lysistrata, just what is this matter you've summoned us women to consider? What's up? Something big?

LYSISTRATA   Very big.

CALONICE [*interested*]   Is it stout, too?

LYSISTRATA [*smiling*]   Yes indeed—both big and stout.

CALONICE   What? And the women still haven't come?

LYSISTRATA   It's not what you suppose; they'd have come soon enough for *that*. But I've worked up something, and for many a sleepless night I've turned it this way and that.

CALONICE [*in mock disappointment*]   Oh, I guess it's pretty fine and slender, if you've turned it this way and that.

LYSISTRATA   So fine that the safety of the whole of Greece lies in us women.

CALONICE   In us women? It depends on a very slender reed then.

LYSISTRATA   Our country's fortunes are in our hands; and whether the Spartans shall perish—

CALONICE   Good! Let them perish, by all means.

LYSISTRATA   —and the Boeotians shall be completely annihilated.

CALONICE   Not completely! Please spare the eels.

LYSISTRATA   As for Athens, I won't use any such unpleasant words. But you understand what I mean. But if the women will meet here—the Spartans, the Boeotians, and we Athenians—then all together we will save Greece.

CALONICE   But what could women do that's clever or distinguished? We just sit around all dolled up in silk robes, looking pretty in our sheer gowns and evening slippers.

LYSISTRATA   These are just the things I hope will save us: these silk robes, perfumes, evening slippers, rouge, and our chiffon blouses.

CALONICE   How so?

LYSISTRATA   So never a man alive will lift a spear against the foe—

CALONICE   I'll get a silk gown at once.

LYSISTRATA   —or take up his shield—

CALONICE   I'll put on my sheerest gown!

LYSISTRATA   —or sword.

CALONICE   I'll buy a pair of evening slippers.

LYSISTRATA   Well then, shouldn't the women have come?

CALONICE   Come? Why, they should have *flown* here.

LYSISTRATA   Well, my dear, just watch: they'll act in true Athenian fashion—everything too late! And now there's not a woman here from the shore or from Salamis.

CALONICE   They're coming, I'm sure; at daybreak they were laying—to their oars to cross the straits.

LYSISTRATA   And those I expected would be the first to come—the women of Acharnae—they haven't arrived.

CALONICE   Yet the wife of Theagenes means to come: she consulted Hecate about it. [*Seeing a group of women approaching*] But look! Here come a few. And there are some more over here. Hurrah! Where do they come from?

LYSISTRATA   From Anagyra.

CALONICE   Yes indeed! We've raised up quite a stink from Anagyra anyway.

Enter Myrrhine in haste, followed by several other women.

MYRRHINE [*breathlessly*]   Have we come in time, Lysistrata? What do you say? Why so quiet?

LYSISTRATA   I can't say much for you, Myrrhine, coming at this hour on such important business.

MYRRHINE   Why, I had trouble finding my girdle in the dark. But if it's so important, we're here now; tell us.

LYSISTRATA   No. Let's wait a little for the women from Boeotia and the Peloponnesus.

MYRRHINE   That's a much better suggestion. Look! Here comes Lampito now.

Enter Lampito with two other women.

LYSISTRATA   Greetings, my dear Spartan friend. How pretty you look, my dear. What a smooth complexion and well-developed figure! You could throttle an ox.

LAMPITO   Faith, yes, I think I could. I take exercises and kick my heels against my bum. [*She demonstrates with a few steps of the Spartan "bottom-kicking" dance.*]

LYSISTRATA   And what splendid breasts you have.

LAMPITO   La! You handle me like a prize steer.

LYSISTRATA   And who is this young lady with you?

LAMPITO   Faith, she's an Ambassadress from Boeotia.

LYSISTRATA   Oh yes, a Boeotian, and blooming like a garden too.

CALONICE [*lifting up her skirt*]   My word! How neatly her garden's weeded!

LYSISTRATA   And who is the other girl?

LAMPITO   Oh, she's a Corinthian swell.

MYRRHINE [*after a rapid examination*]   Yes indeed. She swells very nicely [*pointing*] here and here.

LAMPITO   Who has gathered together this company of women?

LYSISTRATA   I have.

LAMPITO   Speak up, then. What do you want?

MYRRHINE   Yes, my dear, tell us what this important matter is.

LYSISTRATA   Very well, I'll tell you. But before I speak, let me ask you a little question.

MYRRHINE   Anything you like.

LYSISTRATA [*earnestly*]   Tell me: don't you yearn for the fathers of your children, who are away at the wars? I know you all have husbands abroad.

CALONICE   Why, yes; mercy me! my husband's been away for five months in Thrace keeping guard on—Eucrates.

MYRRHINE   And mine for seven whole months in Pylus.

LAMPITO   And mine, as soon as ever he returns from the fray, readjusts his shield and flies out of the house again.

LYSISTRATA   And as for lovers, there's not even a ghost of one left. Since the Milesians revolted from us, I've not even seen an eight-inch dingus to be a leather consolation for us widows. Are you willing, if I can find a way, to help me end the war?

MYRRHINE   Goodness, yes! I'd do it, even if I had to pawn my dress and— get drunk on the spot!

CALONICE   And I, even if I had to let myself be split in two like a flounder.

LAMPITO   I'd climb up Mt. Taygetus if I could catch a glimpse of peace.

LYSISTRATA   I'll tell you, then, in plain and simple words. My friends, if we are going to force our men to make peace, we must do without—

MYRRHINE   Without what? Tell us.

LYSISTRATA   Will you do it?

MYRRHINE   We'll do it, if it kills us.

LYSISTRATA   Well then, we must do without sex altogether. [General consternation.] Why do you turn away? Where go you? Why turn so pale? Why those tears? Will you do it or not? What means this hesitation?

MYRRHINE   I won't do it! Let the war go on.

CALONICE   Nor I! Let the war go on.

LYSISTRATA   So, my little flounder? Didn't you say just now you'd split yourself in half?

CALONICE   Anything else you like. I'm willing, even if I have to walk through fire. Anything rather than sex. There's nothing like it, my dear.

LYSISTRATA   [to Myrrhine]   What about you?

MYRRHINE   [sullenly]   I'm willing to walk through fire, too.

LYSISTRATA   Oh vile and cursed breed! No wonder they make tragedies about us: we're naught but "love-affairs and bassinets." But you, my dear Spartan friend, if you alone are with me, our enterprise might yet succeed. Will you vote with me?

LAMPITO   'Tis cruel hard, by my faith, for a woman to sleep alone without her nooky; but for all that, we certainly do need peace.

LYSISTRATA   O my dearest friend! You're the only real woman here.

CALONICE [wavering]   Well, if we do refrain from—[shuddering] what you say (God forbid!), would that bring peace?

LYSISTRATA   My goodness, yes! If we sit at home all rouged and powdered, dressed in our sheerest gowns, and neatly depilated, our men will get excited and want to take us; but if you don't come to them and keep away, they'll soon make a truce.

LAMPITO   Aye; Menelaus caught sight of Helen's naked breast and dropped his sword, they say.

CALONICE   What if the men give us up?

LYSISTRATA   "Flay a skinned dog," as Pherecrates says.

CALONICE   Rubbish! These make-shifts are no good. But suppose they grab us and drag us into the bedroom?

LYSISTRATA   Hold on to the door.

CALONICE   And if they beat us?

LYSISTRATA   Give in with a bad grace. There's no pleasure in it for them when they have to use violence. And you must torment them in every possible way. They'll give up soon enough; a man gets no joy if he doesn't get along with his wife.

MYRRHINE   If this is your opinion, we agree.

LAMPITO   As for our own men, we can persuade them to make a just and fair peace; but what about the Athenian rabble? Who will persuade them not to start any more monkey-shines?

LYSISTRATA   Don't worry. We guarantee to convince them.

LAMPITO   Not while their ships are rigged so well and they have that mighty treasure in the temple of Athene.

LYSISTRATA   We've taken good care for that too: we shall seize the Acropolis today. The older women have orders to do this, and while we are making our arrangements, they are to pretend to make a sacrifice and occupy the Acropolis.

LAMPITO   All will be well then. That's a very fine idea.

LYSISTRATA   Let's ratify this, Lampito, with the most solemn oath.

LAMPITO   Tell us what oath we shall swear.

LYSISTRATA   Well said. Where's our Policewoman? [to a Scythian slave] What are you gaping at? Set a shield upside-down here in front of me, and give me the sacred meats.

CALONICE   Lysistrata, what sort of an oath are we to take?

LYSISTRATA   What oath? I'm going to slaughter a sheep over the shield, as they do in Aeschylus.

CALONICE   Don't, Lysistrata! No oaths about peace over a shield.

LYSISTRATA   What shall the oath be, then?

CALONICE   How about getting a white horse somewhere and cutting out its entrails for the sacrifice?

LYSISTRATA   White horse indeed!

CALONICE   Well then, how shall we swear?

MYRRHINE   I'll tell you: let's place a large black bowl upside-down and then slaughter—a flask of Thasian wine. And then let's swear—not to pour in a single drop of water.

LAMPITO   Lord! How I like that oath!

LYSISTRATA   Someone bring out a bowl and a flask.

A slave brings the utensils for the sacrifice.

CALONICE   Look, my friends! What a big jar! Here's a cup that 'twould give me joy to handle. [She picks up the bowl.]

LYSISTRATA Set it down and put your hands on our victim. [*As Calonice places her hands on the flask*] O Lady of Persuasion and dear Loving Cup, graciously vouchsafe to receive this sacrifice from us women. [*She pours the wine into the bowl.*]

CALONICE The blood has a good colour and spurts out nicely.

LAMPITO Faith, it has a pleasant smell, too.

MYRRHINE Oh, let me be the first to swear, ladies!

CALONICE No, by our Lady! Not unless you're allotted the first turn.

LYSISTRATA Place all your hands on the cup, and one of you repeat on behalf of all what I say. Then all will swear and ratify the oath. *I will suffer no man, be he husband or lover,*

CALONICE *I will suffer no man, be he husband or lover,*

LYSISTRATA *To approach me all hot and horny.* [*As Calonice hesitates*] Say it!

CALONICE [*slowly and painfully*] *To approach me all hot and horny.* O Lysistrata, I feel so weak in the knees!

LYSISTRATA *I will remain at home unmated,*

CALONICE *I will remain at home unmated,*

LYSISTRATA *Wearing my sheerest gown and carefully adorned,*

CALONICE *Wearing my sheerest gown and carefully adorned,*

LYSISTRATA *That my husband may burn with desire for me,*

CALONICE *That my husband may burn with desire for me,*

LYSISTRATA *And if he takes me by force against my will,*

CALONICE *And if he takes me by force against my will,*

LYSISTRATA *I shall do it badly and keep from moving.*

CALONICE *I shall do it badly and keep from moving.*

LYSISTRATA *I will not stretch my slippers toward the ceiling,*

CALONICE *I will not stretch my slippers toward the ceiling,*

LYSISTRATA *Nor will I take the posture of the lioness on the knife-handle.*

CALONICE *Nor will I take the posture of the lioness on the knife-handle.*

LYSISTRATA *If I keep this oath, may I be permitted to drink from this cup,*

CALONICE *If I keep this oath, may I be permitted to drink from this cup,*

LYSISTRATA *But if I break it, may the cup be filled with water.*

CALONICE *But if I break it, may the cup be filled with water.*

LYSISTRATA Do you all swear to this?

ALL I do, so help me!

LYSISTRATA Come then, I'll just consummate this offering.

She takes a long drink from the cup.

CALONICE [*snatching the cup away*] Shares, my dear! Let's drink to our continued friendship.

A shout is heard from off-stage.

LAMPITO   What's that shouting?

LYSISTRATA   That's what I was telling you: the women have just seized the
Acropolis. Now, Lampito, go home and arrange matters in Sparta; and
leave these two ladies here as hostages. We'll enter the Acropolis to join
our friends and help them lock the gates.

CALONICE   Don't you suppose the men will come to attack us?

LYSISTRATA   Don't worry about them. Neither threats nor fire will suffice to
open the gates, except on the terms we've stated.

CALONICE   I should say not! Else we'd belie our reputation as unmanageable
pests.

*Lampito leaves the stage. The other women retire and enter the Acropolis through
the Propylaea.*
Enter the Chorus of Old Men, carrying fire-pots and a load of heavy sticks.

LEADER OF MEN   Onward, Draces, step by step, though your shoulder's
aching.

Cursèd logs of olive-wood, what a load you're making!

FIRST SEMI-CHORUS OF OLD MEN [*singing*]
Aye, many surprises await a man who lives to a ripe old age;
For who could suppose, Strymodorus my lad, that the women we've
nourished (alas!),
  Who sat at home to vex our days,
  Would seize the holy image here,
  And occupy this sacred shrine,
  With bolts and bars, with fell design,
  To lock the Propylaea?

LEADER OF MEN   Come with speed, Philourgus, come! to the temple hast'n-
ing.

There we'll heap these logs about in a circle round them,
And whoever has conspired, raising this rebellion,
Shall be roasted, scorched, and burnt, all without exception,
Doomed by one unanimous vote—but first the wife of Lycon.

SECOND SEMI-CHORUS [*singing*]
No, no! by Demeter, while I'm alive, no woman shall mock at me.
Not even the Spartan Cleomenes, our citadel first to seize,
  Got off unscathed; for all his pride
  And haughty Spartan arrogance,

He left his arms and sneaked away,
Stripped to his shirt, unkempt, unshav'd,
With six years' filth still on him.

LEADER OF MEN   I besieged that hero bold, sleeping at my station,
Marshalled at these holy gates sixteen deep against him.
Shall I not these cursèd pests punish for their daring,
Burning these Euripides-and-God-detested women?
Aye! or else may Marathon overturn my trophy.

FIRST SEMI-CHORUS [singing]   There remains of my road
Just this brow of the hill;
There I speed on my way.
Drag the logs up the hill, though we've got no ass to help.
(God! my shoulder's bruised and sore!)
Onward still must we go.
Blow the fire! Don't let it go out
Now we're near the end of our road.

ALL [blowing on the fire-pots]   Whew! Whew! Drat the smoke!

SECOND SEMI-CHORUS [singing]   Lord, what smoke rushing forth
From the pot, like a dog
Running mad, bites my eyes!
This must be Lemnos-fire. What a sharp and stinging smoke!
Rushing onward to the shrine
Aid the gods. Once for all
Show your mettle, Laches my boy!
To the rescue hastening all!

ALL [blowing on the fire-pots]   Whew! Whew! Drat the smoke!

The chorus has now reached the edge of the Orchestra nearest the stage, in front of the propylaea. They begin laying their logs and fire-pots on the ground.

LEADER OF MEN   Thank heaven, this fire is still alive. Now let's first put
down these logs here and place our torches in the pots to catch; then
let's make a rush for the gates with a battering-ram. If the women don't
unbar the gate at our summons, we'll have to smoke them out.
   Let me put down my load. Ouch! That hurts! [*To the audience*] Would
any of the generals in Samos like to lend a hand with this log? [*Throwing
down a log*] Well, *that* won't break my back any more, at any rate.
[*Turning to his fire-pot*] Your job, my little pot, is to keep those coals alive
and furnish me shortly with a red-hot torch.
   O mistress Victory, be my ally and grant me to rout these audacious
women in the Acropolis.

While the men are busy with their logs and fires, the Chorus of Old Women enters,
carrying pitchers of water.

LEADER OF WOMEN   What's this I see? Smoke and flames? Is that a fire
    ablazing?
  Let's rush upon them. Hurry up! They'll find us women ready.
FIRST SEMI-CHORUS OF OLD WOMEN [*singing*]
    With wingèd foot onward I fly,
    Ere the flames consume Neodice;
    Lest Critylla be overwhelmed
  By a lawless, accurst herd of old men.
  I shudder with fear. Am I too late to aid them?
  At break of the day filled we our jars with water
  Fresh from the spring, pushing our way straight through the crowds.
    Oh, what a din!
  Mid crockery crashing, jostled by slave-girls,
  Sped we to save them, aiding our neighbours,
  Bearing this water to put out the flames.
SECOND SEMI-CHORUS OF OLD WOMEN [*singing*]
    Such news I've heard; doddering fools
    Come with logs, like furnace-attendants,
    Loaded down with three hundred pounds,
  Breathing many a vain, blustering threat,
  That all these abhorred sluts will be burnt to charcoal.
  O goddess, I pray never may they be kindled;
  Grant them to save Greece and our men, madness and war help them to
    end.
  With this as our purpose, golden-plumed Maiden,
  Guardian of Athens, seized we thy precinct.
  Be my ally, Warrior-maiden,
  'Gainst these old men, bearing water with me.

The women have now reached their position in the Orchestra, and their Leader
advances toward the Leader of the Men.

LEADER OF WOMEN   Hold on there! What's this, you utter scoundrels? No
    decent, God-fearing citizens would act like this.
LEADER OF MEN   Oho! Here's something unexpected: a swarm of women
    have come out to attack us.
LEADER OF WOMEN   What, do we frighten you? Surely you don't think we're

too many for you. And yet there are ten thousand times more of us whom you haven't even seen.

LEADER OF MEN   What say, Phaedria? Shall we let these women wag their tongues? Shan't we take our sticks and break them over their backs?

LEADER OF WOMEN   Let's set our pitchers on the ground; then if anyone lays a hand on us, they won't get in our way.

LEADER OF MEN   By God! If someone gave them two or three smacks on the jaw, like Bupalus, they wouldn't talk so much!

LEADER OF WOMEN   Go on, hit me, somebody! Here's my jaw! But no other bitch will bite a piece out of you before me.

LEADER OF MEN   Silence! or I'll knock out your—senility!

LEADER OF WOMEN   Just lay one finger on Stratyllis, I dare you!

LEADER OF MEN   Suppose I dust you off with this fist? What will you do?

LEADER OF WOMEN   I'll tear the living guts out of you with my teeth.

LEADER OF MEN   No poet is more clever than Euripides: "There is no beast so shameless as a woman."

LEADER OF WOMEN   Let's pick up our jars of water, Rhodippe.

LEADER OF MEN   Why have you come here with water, you detestable slut?

LEADER OF WOMEN   And why have you come with fire, you funeral vault? To cremate yourself?

LEADER OF MEN   To light a fire and singe your friends.

LEADER OF WOMEN   And I've brought water to put out your fire.

LEADER OF MEN   What? You'll put out my fire?

LEADER OF WOMEN   Just try and see!

LEADER OF MEN   I wonder: shall I scorch you with this torch of mine?

LEADER OF WOMEN   If you've got any soap, I'll give you a bath.

LEADER OF MEN   Give *me* a bath, you stinking hag?

LEADER OF WOMEN   Yes—a bridal bath!

LEADER OF MEN   Just listen to her! What crust!

LEADER OF WOMEN   Well, I'm a free citizen.

LEADER OF MEN   I'll put an end to your brawling.

The men pick up their torches.

LEADER OF WOMEN   You'll never do jury-duty again.

The women pick up their pitchers.

LEADER OF MEN   Singe her hair for her!

LEADER OF WOMEN   Do your duty, water!

The women empty their pitchers on the men.

LEADER OF MEN   Ow! Ow! For heaven's sake!

LEADER OF WOMEN   Is it too hot?

LEADER OF MEN   What do you mean "hot"? Stop! What are you doing?

LEADER OF WOMEN   I'm watering you, so you'll be fresh and green.

LEADER OF MEN   But I'm all withered up with shaking.

LEADER OF WOMEN   Well, you've got a fire; why don't you dry yourself?

Enter an Athenian Magistrate, accompanied by four Scythian policemen.

MAGISTRATE   Have these wanton women flared up again with their timbrels
and their continual worship of Sabazius? Is this another Adonis-dirge
upon the roof-tops—which we heard not long ago in the Assembly?
That confounded Demostratus was urging us to sail to Sicily, and the
whirling women shouted, "Woe for Adonis!" And then Demostratus
said we'd best enroll the infantry from Zacynthus, and a tipsy woman
on the roof shrieked, "Beat your breasts for Adonis!" And that vile and
filthy lunatic forced his measure through. Such license do our women
take.

LEADER OF MEN   What if you heard of the insolence of these women here?
Besides their other violent acts, they threw water all over us, and we
have to shake out our clothes just as if we'd leaked in them.

MAGISTRATE   And rightly, too, by God! For we ourselves lead the women
astray and teach them to play the wanton; from these roots such notions
blossom forth. A man goes into the jeweler's shop and says, "About
that necklace you made for my wife, goldsmith: last night, while she
was dancing, the fastening-bolt slipped out of the hole. I have to sail
over to Salamis today; if you're free, do come around tonight and fit in a
new bolt for her." Another goes to the shoe-maker, a strapping young
fellow with manly parts, and says, "See here, cobbler, the sandal-strap
chafes my wife's little—toe; it's so tender. Come around during the
siesta and stretch it a little, so she'll be more comfortable." Now we see
the results of such treatment: here I'm a special Councillor and need
money to procure oars for the galleys; and I'm locked out of the Treasury
by these women.

   But this is no time to stand around. Bring up crow-bars there! I'll put
an end to their insolence. [*To one of the policemen*] What are you gaping
at, you wretch? What are you staring at? Got an eye out for a tavern, eh?
Set your crow-bars here to the gates and force them open. [*Retiring to a
safe distance*] I'll help from over here.

*The gates are thrown open and Lysistrata comes out followed by several other
women.*

LYSISTRATA   Don't force the gates; I'm coming out of my own accord. We don't need crow-bars here; what we need is good sound common-sense.

MAGISTRATE   Is that so, you strumpet? Where's my policeman? Officer, arrest her and tie her arms behind her back.

LYSISTRATA   By Artemis, if he lays a finger on me, he'll pay for it, even if he is a public servant.

The policeman retires in terror.

MAGISTRATE   You there, are you afraid? Seize her round the waist—and you, too. Tie her up, both of you!

FIRST WOMAN *(as the second policeman approaches Lysistrata)*   By Pandrosus, if you but touch her with your hand, I'll kick the stuffings out of you.

The second policeman retires in terror.

MAGISTRATE   Just listen to that: "kick the stuffings out." Where's another policeman? Tie *her* up first, for her chatter.

SECOND WOMAN   By the Goddess of the Light, if you lay the tip of your finger on her, you'll soon need a doctor.

The third policeman retires in terror.

MAGISTRATE   What's this? Where's my policemen? Seize *her* too. I'll soon stop your sallies.

THIRD WOMAN   By the Goddess of Tauros, if you go near her, I'll tear out your hair until it shrieks with pain.

The fourth policeman retires in terror.

MAGISTRATE   Oh, damn it all! I've run out of policemen. But women must never defeat us. Officers, let's charge them all together. Close up your ranks!

The policemen rally for a mass attack.

LYSISTRATA   By heaven, you'll soon find out that we have four companies of warrior-women, all fully equipped within!

MAGISTRATE [*advancing*]   Twist their arms off, men!

LYSISTRATA [*shouting*]   To the rescue, my valiant women!
  O sellers-of-barley-green-stuffs-and-eggs,
  O sellers-of-garlic, ye keepers-of-taverns, and vendors-of-bread,
    Grapple! Smite! Smash!
  Won't you heap filth on them? Give them a tongue-lashing!

The women beat off the policemen.

Halt! Withdraw! No looting on the field.

MAGISTRATE   Damn it! My police-force has put up a very poor show.

LYSISTRATA   What did you expect? Did you think you were attacking slaves?
Didn't you know that women are filled with passion?

MAGISTRATE   Aye, passion enough—for a good strong drink!

LEADER OF MEN   O chief and leader of this land, why spend your words in
vain?
Don't argue with these shameless beasts. You know not how we've
fared:
A soapless bath they've given us; our clothes are soundly soaked.

LEADER OF WOMEN   Poor fool! You never should attack or strike a peaceful
girl.
But if you do, your eyes must swell. For I am quite content
To sit unmoved, like modest maids, in peace and cause no pain;
But let a man stir up my hive, he'll find me like a wasp.

CHORUS OF MEN [*singing*]
O God, whatever shall we do with creatures like Womankind?
This can't be endured by any man alive. Question them!
    Let us try to find out what this means.
    To what end have they seized on this shrine,
        This steep and rugged, high and holy,
            Undefiled Acropolis?

LEADER OF MEN   Come, put your questions; don't give in, and probe her
every statement.
For base and shameful it would be to leave this plot untested.

MAGISTRATE   Well then, first of all I wish to ask her this: for what purpose
have you barred us from the Acropolis?

LYSISTRATA   To keep the treasure safe, so you won't make war on account of
it.

MAGISTRATE   What? Do we make war on account of the treasure?

LYSISTRATA   Yes, and you cause all our other troubles for it, too. Peisander
and those greedy office-seekers keep things stirred up so they can find
occasions to steal. Now let them do what they like: they'll never again
make off with any of this money.

MAGISTRATE   What will you do?

LYSISTRATA   What a question! We'll administer it ourselves.

MAGISTRATE   *You* will administer the treasure?

LYSISTRATA   What's so strange in that? Don't we administer the household
money for you?

MAGISTRATE   That's different.

LYSISTRATA   How is it different?

MAGISTRATE   We've got to make war with this money.

LYSISTRATA   But that's the very first thing: you mustn't make war.

MAGISTRATE   How else can we be saved?

LYSISTRATA   We'll save you.

MAGISTRATE   *You?*

LYSISTRATA   Yes, we!

MAGISTRATE   God forbid!

LYSISTRATA   We'll save you, whether you want it or not.

MAGISTRATE   Oh! This is terrible!

LYSISTRATA   You don't like it, but we're going to do it none the less.

MAGISTRATE   Good God! it's illegal!

LYSISTRATA   We *will* save you, my little man!

MAGISTRATE   Suppose I don't want you to?

LYSISTRATA   That's all the more reason.

MAGISTRATE   What business have you with war and peace?

LYSISTRATA   I'll explain.

MAGISTRATE   [*shaking his fist*]   Speak up, or you'll smart for it.

LYSISTRATA   Just listen, and try to keep your hands still.

MAGISTRATE   I can't. I'm so mad I can't stop them.

FIRST WOMAN   Then you'll be the one to smart for it.

MAGISTRATE   Croak to yourself, old hag! [*To Lysistrata*] Now then, speak up.

LYSISTRATA   Very well. Formerly we endured the war for a good long time
    with our usual restraint, no matter what you men did. You wouln't let
    us say "boo," although nothing you did suited us. But we watched you
    well, and though we stayed at home we'd often hear of some terribly
    stupid measure you'd proposed. Then, though grieving at heart, we'd
    smile sweetly and say, "What was passed in the Assembly today about
    writing on the treaty-stone?" "What's that to you?" my husband would
    say. "Hold your tongue!" And I held my tongue.

FIRST WOMAN   But I wouldn't have—not I!

MAGISTRATE   You'd have been soundly smacked, if you hadn't kept still.

LYSISTRATA   So I kept still at home. Then we'd hear of some plan still worse
    than the first; we'd say, "Husband, how could you pass such a stupid
    proposal!" He'd scowl at me and say, "If you don't mind your spinning,
    your head will be sore for weeks. *War shall be the concern of men.*"

MAGISTRATE   And he was right, upon my word!

LYSISTRATA   Why right, you confounded fool, when your proposals were so
    stupid and we weren't allowed to make any suggestions?
        "There's not a *man* left in the country," says one. "No, not one," says
    another. Therefore all we women have decided in council to make a
    common effort to save Greece. How long should we have waited? Now,
    if you're willing to listen to our excellent proposals and keep silence for
    us in your turn, we still may save you.

MAGISTRATE   We men keep silence for you? That's terrible; I won't endure it!

LYSISTRATA   Silence!

MAGISTRATE   Silence for *you*, you wench, when you're wearing a snood? I'd rather die!

LYSISTRATA   Well, if that's all that bothers you—here! take my snood and tie it round your head. [*During the following words the women dress up the Magistrate in women's garments.*] And *now* keep quiet! Here, take this spinning-basket, too, and card your wool with robes tucked up, munching on beans. *War shall be the concern of Women!*

LEADER OF WOMEN   Arise and leave your pitchers, girls; no time is this to falter.

We too must aid our loyal friends; our turn has come for action.

CHORUS OF WOMEN [*singing*]

I'll never tire of aiding them with song and dance; never may
Faintness keep my legs from moving to and fro endlessly.
    For I yearn to do all for my friends;
    They have charm, they have wit, they have grace,
        With courage, brains, and best of virtues—
            Patriotic sapience.

LEADER OF WOMEN   Come, child of manliest ancient dames, offspring of stinging nettles,

Advance with rage unsoftened; for fair breezes speed you onward.

LYSISTRATA   If only sweet Eros and the Cyprian Queen of Love shed charm over our breasts and limbs and inspire our men with amorous longing and priapic spasms, I think we may soon be called Peacemakers among the Greeks.

MAGISTRATE   What will you do?

LYSISTRATA   First of all, we'll stop those fellows who run madly about the Marketplace in arms.

FIRST WOMAN   Indeed we shall, by the Queen of Paphos.

LYSISTRATA   For now they roam about the market, amid the pots and greenstuffs, armed to the teeth like Corybantes.

MAGISTRATE   That's what manly fellows ought to do!

LYSISTRATA   But it's so silly: a chap with a Gorgon-emblazoned shield buying pickled herring.

FIRST WOMAN   Why, just the other day I saw one of those long-haired dandies who command our cavalry ride up on horseback and pour into his bronze helmet the egg-broth he'd bought from an old dame. And there was a Thracian slinger too, shaking his lance like Tereus; he'd scared the life out of the poor fig-peddler and was gulping down all her ripest fruit.

MAGISTRATE   How can you stop all the confusion in the various states and bring them together?

LYSISTRATA   Very easily.

MAGISTRATE   Tell me how.

LYSISTRATA   Just like a ball of wool, when it's confused and snarled: we take it thus, and draw out a thread here and a thread there with our spindles; thus we'll unsnarl this war, if no one prevents us, and draw together the various states with embassies here and embassies there.

MAGISTRATE   Do you suppose you can stop this dreadful business with balls of wool and spindles, you nit-wits?

LYSISTRATA   Why, if *you* had any wits, you'd manage all affairs of state like our wool-working.

MAGISTRATE   How so?

LYSISTRATA   First you ought to treat the city as we do when we wash the dirt out of a fleece: stretch it out and pluck and thrash out of the city all those prickly scoundrels; aye, and card out those who conspire and stick together to gain office, pulling off their heads. Then card the wool, all of it, into one fair basket of goodwill, mingling in the aliens residing here, any loyal foreigners, and anyone who's in debt to the Treasury; and consider that all our colonies lie scattered round about like remnants; from all of these collect the wool and gather it together here, wind up a great ball, and then weave a good stout cloak for the democracy.

MAGISTRATE   Dreadful! Talking about thrashing and winding balls of wool, when you haven't the slightest share in the war!

LYSISTRATA   Why, you dirty scoundrel, we bear more than twice as much as you. First, we bear children and send off our sons as soldiers.

MAGISTRATE   Hush! Let bygones be bygones!

LYSISTRATA   Then, when we ought to be happy and enjoy our youth, we sleep alone because of your expeditions abroad. But never mind us married women: I grieve most for the maids who grow old at home unwed.

MAGISTRATE   Don't men grow old, too?

LYSISTRATA   For heaven's sake! That's not the same thing. When a man comes home, no matter how grey he is, he soon finds a girl to marry. But woman's bloom is short and fleeting; if she doesn't grasp her chance, no man is willing to marry her and she sits at home a prey to every fortune-teller.

MAGISTRATE   [*coarsely*]   But if a man can still get it up—

LYSISTRATA   See here, you: what's the matter? Aren't you dead yet? There's plenty of room for you. Buy yourself a shroud and I'll bake you a honey-cake. [*Handing him a copper coin for his passage across the Styx*] Here's your fare! Now get yourself a wreath.

During the following dialogue the women dress up the Magistrate as a corpse.

FIRST WOMAN   Here, take these fillets.

SECOND WOMAN   Here, take this wreath.

LYSISTRATA   What do you want? What's lacking? Get moving; off to the ferry! Charon is calling you; don't keep him from sailing.

MAGISTRATE   Am I to endure these insults? By God! I'm going straight to the magistrates to show them how I've been treated.

LYSISTRATA   Are you grumbling that you haven't been properly laid out? Well, the day after tomorrow we'll send around all the usual offerings early in the morning.

The Magistrate goes out still wearing his funeral decorations. Lysistrata and the women retire into the Acropolis.

LEADER OF MEN   Wake, ye sons of freedom, wake! 'Tis no time for sleeping. Up and at them, like a man! Let us strip for action.

The Chorus of Men remove their outer cloaks.

CHORUS OF MEN [*singing*]
Surely there is something here greater than meets the eye;
For without a doubt I smell Hippias' tyrany.
Dreadful fear assails me lest certain bands of Spartan men,
Meeting here with Cleisthenes, have inspired through treachery
All these god-detested women secretly to seize
Athens' treasure in the temple, and to stop that pay
    Whence I live at my ease.

LEADER OF MEN   Now isn't it terrible for them to advise the state and chatter about shields, being mere women?
    And they think to reconcile us with the Spartans—men who hold nothing sacred any more than hungry wolves. Surely this is a web of deceit, my friends, to conceal an attempt at tyranny. But they'll never lord it over me; I'll be on my guard and from now on,
    "The blade I bear   A myrtle spray shall wear."
I'll occupy the market under arms and stand next to Aristogeiton.
    Thus I'll stand beside him [*He strikes the pose of the famous statue of the tyrannicides, with one arm raised.*] And here's my chance to take this accurst old hag and—[*striking the Leader of Women*] smack her on the jaw!

LEADER OF WOMEN   You'll go home in such a state your Ma won't recognize you!
Ladies all, upon the ground let us place these garments.

The Chorus of Women remove their outer garments.

CHORUS OF WOMEN [*singing*]
Citizens of Athens, hear useful words for the state.
Rightly; for it nurtured me in my youth royally.
As a child of seven years carried I the sacred box;

Then I was a Miller-maid, grinding at Athene's shrine;
Next I wore the saffron robe and played Brauronia's Bear;
And I walked as a Basket-bearer, wearing chains of figs,
    As a sweet maiden fair.

LEADER OF WOMEN   Therefore, am I not bound to give good advice to the city?

Don't take it ill that I was born a woman, if I contribute something better than our present troubles. I pay my share; for I contribute MEN. But you miserable old fools contribute nothing, and after squandering our ancestral treasure, the fruit of the Persian Wars, you make no contribution in return. And now, all on account of you, we're facing ruin.

What, muttering, are you? If you annoy me, I'll take this hard, rough slipper and—[striking the Leader of Men] smack you on the jaw!

CHORUS OF MEN [singing]

This is outright insolence! Things go from bad to worse.
If you're men with any guts, prepare to meet the foe.
Let us strip our tunics off! We need the smell of male
Vigour. And we cannot fight all swaddled up in clothes.

They strip off their tunics.

Come then, my comrades, on to the battle, ye once to Leipsydrion came;
    Then ye were MEN. Now call back your youthful vigour.
With light, wingèd footstep advance,
    Shaking old age from your frame.

LEADER OF MEN   If any of us give these wenches the slightest hold, they'll stop at nothing; such is their cunning.

They will even build ships and sail against us, like Artemisia. Or if they turn to mounting, I count our Knights as done for: a woman's such a tricky jockey when she gets astraddle, with a good firm seat for trotting. Just look at those Amazons that Micon painted, fighting on horseback against men!

But we must throw them all in the pillory—[seizing and choking the Leader of Women] grabbing hold of yonder neck!

CHORUS OF WOMEN [singing]

'Ware my anger! Like a boar 'twill rush upon you men.
Soon you'll bawl aloud for help, you'll be so soundly trimmed!
Come, my friends, let's strip with speed, and lay aside these robes;
Catch the scent of women's rage. Attack with tooth and nail!

They strip off their tunics.

Now then, come near me, you miserable man! You'll never eat garlic or
　　black beans again.
And if you utter a single hard word, in rage I will "nurse" you as once
　　The beetle requited her foe.

LEADER OF WOMEN   For you don't worry me; no, not so long as my Lampito
　　lives and our Theban friend, the noble Ismenia.

　　You can't do anything, not even if you pass a dozen—decrees! You
miserable fool, all our neighbours hate you. Why, just the other day
when I was holding a festival for Hecate, I invited as playmate from our
neighbours the Boeotians a charming, wellbred Copaic—eel. But they
refused to send me one on account of your decrees.

　　And you'll never stop passing decrees until I grab your foot and—
[tripping up the Leader of Men] toss you down and break your neck!

*Here an interval of five days is supposed to elapse. Lysistrata comes out from the
Acropolis.*

LEADER OF WOMEN [*dramatically*]   Empress of this great emprise and under-
　　taking,
　　Why come you forth, I pray, with frowning brow?
LYSISTRATA   Ah, these cursèd women! Their deeds and female notions make
　　me pace up and down in utter despair.
LEADER OF WOMEN   Ah, what sayest thou?
LYSISTRATA   The truth, alas! the truth.
LEADER OF WOMEN   What dreadful tale hast thou to tell thy friends?
LYSISTRATA   'Tis shame to speak, and not to speak is hard.
LEADER OF WOMEN   Hide not from me whatever woes we suffer.
LYSISTRATA   Well then, to put it briefly, we want—laying!
LEADER OF WOMEN   O Zeus, Zeus!
LYSISTRATA   Why call on Zeus? That's the way things are. I can no longer
　　keep them away from the men, and they're all deserting. I caught one
　　wriggling through a hole near the grotto of Pan, another sliding down
　　a rope, another deserting her post; and yesterday I found one getting on
　　a sparrow's back to fly off to Orsilochus, and had to pull her back by the
　　hair. They're digging up all sorts of excuses to get home. Look, here
　　comes one of them now.

A woman comes hastily out of the Acropolis.

　　Here you! Where are you off to in such a hurry?
FIRST WOMAN   I want to go home. My very best wool is being devoured by
　　moths.
LYSISTRATA   Moths? Nonsense! Go back inside.

FIRST WOMAN   I'll come right back; I swear it. I just want to lay it out on the
    bed.
LYSISTRATA   Well, you won't lay it out, and you won't go home, either.
FIRST WOMAN   Shall I let my wool be ruined?
LYSISTRATA   If necessary, yes.

Another woman comes out.

SECOND WOMAN   Oh dear! Oh dear! My precious flax! I left it at home all
    unpeeled.
LYSISTRATA   Here's another one, going home for her "flax." Come back
    here!
SECOND WOMAN   But I just want to work it up a little and then I'll be right
    back.
LYSISTRATA   No indeed! If you start this, all the other women will want to do
    the same.

A third woman comes out.

THIRD WOMAN   O Eilithyia, goddess of travail, stop my labour till I come to a
    lawful spot!
LYSISTRATA   What's this nonsense?
THIRD WOMAN   I'm going to have a baby—right now!
LYSISTRATA   But you weren't even pregnant yesterday.
THIRD WOMAN   Well, I am today. O Lysistrata, do send me home to see a
    midwife, right away.
LYSISTRATA   What are you talking about? [*Putting her hand on her stomach*]
    What's this hard lump here?
THIRD WOMAN   A little boy.
LYSISTRATA   My goodness, what have you got there? It seems hollow; I'll just
    find out. [*Pulling aside her robe*] Why, you silly goose, you've got
    Athene's sacred helmet there. And you said you were having a baby!
THIRD WOMAN   Well, I *am* having one, I swear!
LYSISTRATA   Then what's this helmet for?
THIRD WOMAN   If the baby starts coming while I'm still in the Acropolis, I'll
    creep into this like a pigeon and give birth to it there.
LYSISTRATA   Stuff and nonsense! It's plain enough what you're up to. You
    just wait here for the christening of this—helmet.
THIRD WOMAN   But I can't sleep in the Acropolis since I saw the sacred
    snake.
FIRST WOMAN   And I'm dying for lack of sleep: the hooting of the owls keep
    me awake.
LYSISTRATA   Enough of these shams, you wretched creatures. You want your
    husbands, I suppose. Well, don't you think they want us? I'm sure

they're spending miserable nights. Hold out, my friends, and endure for just a little while. There's an oracle that we shall conquer, if we don't split up. [*Producing a roll of paper*] Here it is.

FIRST WOMAN   Tell us what it says.

LYSISTRATA   Listen.

"When in the length of time the Swallows shall gather together,
Fleeing the Hoopoe's amorous flight and the Cockatoo shunning,
Then shall your woes be ended and Zeus who thunders in heaven
Set what's below on top—"

FIRST WOMAN   What? Are we going to be on top?

LYSISTRATA   "But if the Swallows rebel and flutter away from the temple,
Never a bird in the world shall seem more wanton and worthless."

FIRST WOMAN   That's clear enough, upon my word!

LYSISTRATA   By all that's holy, let's not give up the struggle now. Let's go back inside. It would be a shame, my dear friends, to disobey the oracle.

The women all retire to the Acropolis again.

CHORUS OF MEN [*singing*]
I have a tale to tell,
Which I know full well.
    It was told me
    In the nursery.

Once there was a likely lad,
    Melanion they name him;
The thought of marriage made him mad,
    For which I cannot blame him.

So off he went to mountains fair;
    (No women to upbraid him!)
A mighty hunter of the hare,
    He had a dog to aid him.

He never came back home to see
    Detested women's faces.
He showed a shrewd mentality.
    With him I'd fain change places!

ONE OF THE MEN [*to one of the women*]   Come here, old dame; give me a kiss.

WOMAN   You'll ne'er eat garlic, if you dare!

MAN   I want to kick you—just like this!

WOMAN   Oh, there's a leg with bushy hair!

MAN   Myronides and Phormio
      Were hairy—and they thrashed the foe.

CHORUS OF WOMEN [*singing*]
          I have another tale,
          With which to assail
              Your contention
              'Bout Melanion.

          Once upon a time a man
              Named Timon left our city,
          To live in some deserted land.
              (We thought him rather witty.)

          He dwelt alone amidst the thorn;
              In solitude he brooded.
          From some grim Fury he was born:
              Such hatred he exuded.

          He cursed you men, as scoundrels through
              And through, till life he ended.
          He couldn't stand the sight of you!
              But women he befriended.

WOMAN [*to one of the men*]   I'll smash your face in, if you like.
MAN   Oh no, please don't! You frighten me.
WOMAN   I'll lift my foot—and thus I'll strike.
MAN   Aha! Look there! What's that I see?
WOMAN   Whate'er you see, you cannot say
      That I'm not neatly trimmed today.

Lysistrata appears on the wall of the Acropolis.

LYSISTRATA   Hello! Hello! Girls, come here quick!

Several women appear beside her.

WOMAN   What is it? Why are you calling?
LYSISTRATA   I see a man coming: he's in a dreadful state. He's mad with
      passion. O Queen of Cyprus, Cythera, and Paphos, just keep on this
      way!
WOMAN   Where is the fellow?
LYSISTRATA   There, beside the shrine of Demeter.

WOMAN   Oh yes, so he is. Who is he?

LYSISTRATA   Let's see. Do any of you know him?

MYRRHINE   Yes indeed. That's my husband, Cinesias.

LYSISTRATA   It's up to you, now: roast him, rack him, fool him, love him—
and leave him! Do everything, except what our oath forbids.

MYRRHINE   Don't worry; I'll do it.

LYSISTRATA   I'll stay here to tease him and warm him up a bit. Off with you.

*The other women retire from the wall. Enter Cinesias followed by a slave carrying
a baby. Cinesias is obviously in great pain and distress.*

CINESIAS [*groaning*]   Oh-h! Oh-h-h! This is killing me! O God, what tortures
I'm suffering!

LYSISTRATA [*from the wall*]   Who's that within our lines?

CINESIAS   Me.

LYSISTRATA   A *man*?

CINESIAS [*pointing*]   A *man*, indeed!

LYSISTRATA   Well, go away!

CINESIAS   Who are you to send me away?

LYSISTRATA   The captain of the guard.

CINESIAS   Oh, for heaven's sake, call out Myrrhine for me.

LYSISTRATA   Call Myrrhine? Nonsense! Who are you?

CINESIAS   Her husband, Cinesias of Paionidai.

LYSISTRATA [*appearing much impressed*]   Oh, greetings, friend. Your name is
not without honour here among us. Your wife is always talking about
you, and whenever she takes an egg or an apple, she says, "Here's to
my dear Cinesias!"

CINESIAS [*quivering with excitement*]   Oh, ye gods in heaven!

LYSISTRATA   Indeed she does! And whenever our conversations turn to men,
your wife immediately says, "All others are mere rubbish compared
with Cinesias."

CINESIAS [*groaning*]   Oh! Do call her for me.

LYSISTRATA   Why should I? What will you give me?

CINESIAS   Whatever you want. All I have is yours—and you see what I've
got.

LYSISTRATA   Well then, I'll go down and call her. [*She descends.*]

CINESIAS   And hurry up! I've had no joy of life ever since she left home.
When I go in the house, I feel awful: everything seems so empty and I
can't enjoy my dinner. I'm in such a state all the time!

MYRRHINE [*from behind the wall*]   I *do* love him so. But he won't let me love
him. No, no! Don't ask me to see him!

CINESIAS   O my darling, O Myrrhine honey, why do you do this to me?

Myrrhine appears on the wall.

Come down here!

MYRRHINE   No, I won't come down.

CINESIAS   Won't you come, Myrrhine, when I call you?

MYRRHINE   No; you don't want me.

CINESIAS   *Don't want you?* I'm in agony!

MYRRHINE   I'm going now.

CINESIAS   Please don't. At least, listen to your baby. [*To the baby*] Here you, call your mamma! [*Pinching the baby*]

BABY   Ma-ma! Ma-ma! Ma-ma!

CINESIAS [*to Myrrhine*]   What's the matter with you? Have you no pity for your child, who hasn't been washed or fed for five whole days?

MYRRHINE   Oh, poor child; your father pays no attention to you.

CINESIAS   Come down then, you heartless wretch, for the baby's sake.

MYRRHINE   Oh, what it is to be a mother! I've got to come down, I suppose.

She leaves the wall and shortly reappears at the gate.

CINESIAS [*to himself*]   She seems much younger, and she has such a sweet look about her. Oh, the way she teases me! And her pretty, provoking ways make me burn with longing.

MYRRHINE [*coming out of the gate and taking the baby*]   O my sweet little angel. Naughty papa! Here, let Mummy kiss you, Mamma's little sweetheart!

She fondles the baby lovingly.

CINESIAS [*in despair*]   You heartless creature, why do you do this? Why follow these other women and make both of us suffer so?

He tries to embrace her.

MYRRHINE   Don't touch me!

CINESIAS   You're letting all our things at home go to wrack and ruin.

MYRRHINE   I don't care.

CINESIAS   You don't care that your wool is being plucked to pieces by the chickens?

MYRRHINE   Not in the least.

CINESIAS   And you haven't celebrated the rites of Aphrodite for ever so long. Won't you come home?

MYRRHINE   Not on your life, unless you men make a truce and stop the war.

CINESIAS   Well, then, if that pleases you, we'll do it.

MYRRHINE   Well then, if that pleases *you*, I'll come home—afterwards! Right now I'm on oath not to.

CINESIAS   Then just lie down here with me for a moment.

MYRRHINE   No—[*in a teasing voice*] and yet I won't say I don't love you.

CINESIAS   You love me? Oh, do lie down here, Myrrhine dear!

MYRRHINE   What, you silly fool! in front of the baby?

CINESIAS   [*hastily thrusting the baby at the slave*]   Of course not. Here—home! Take him, Manes! [*The slave goes off with the baby.*] See, the baby's out of the way. Now won't you lie down?

MYRRHINE   But where, my dear?

CINESIAS   Where? The grotto of Pan's a lovely spot.

MYRRHINE   How could I purify myself before returning to the shrine?

CINESIAS   Easily: just wash here in the Clepsydra.

MYRRHINE   And then, shall I go back on my oath?

CINESIAS   On my head be it! Don't worry about the oath.

MYRRHINE   All right, then. Just let me bring out a bed.

CINESIAS   No, don't. The ground's all right.

MYRRHINE   Heavens, no! Bad as you are, I won't let you lie on the bare ground.

She goes into the Acropolis.

CINESIAS   Why, she really loves me; it's plain to see.

MYRRHINE   [*returning with a bed*]   There! Now hurry up and lie down. I'll just slip off this dress. But—let's see: oh yes, I must fetch a mattress.

CINESIAS   Nonsense! No mattress for me.

MYRRHINE   Yes indeed! It's not nice on the bare springs.

CINESIAS   Give me a kiss.

MYRRHINE   [*giving him a hasty kiss*]   There!

She goes.

CINESIAS   [*in mingled distress and delight*]   Oh-h! Hurry back!

MYRRHINE   [*returning with a mattress*]   Here's the mattress; lie down on it. I'm taking my things off now—but—let's see: you have no pillow.

CINESIAS   I don't *want* a pillow.

MYRRHINE   But I do.

She goes.

CINESIAS   Cheated again, just like Heracles and his dinner!

MYRRHINE   [*returning with a pillow*]   Here, lift your head. [*To herself, wondering how else to tease him*] Is that all?

CINESIAS Surely that's all! Do come here, precious!

MYRRHINE I'm taking off my girdle. But remember: don't go back on your promise about the truce.

CINESIAS I hope to die, if I do.

MYRRHINE You don't have a blanket.

CINESIAS [shouting in exasperation] I don't want one! I WANT TO—

MYRRHINE Sh-h! There, there, I'll be back in a minute.

She goes.

CINESIAS She'll be the death of me with these bed-clothes.

MYRRHINE [returning with a blanket] Here, get up.

CINESIAS I've got *this* up!

MYRRHINE Would you like some perfume?

CINESIAS Good heavens, no! I won't have it!

MYRRHINE Yes, you shall, whether you want it or not.

She goes.

CINESIAS O lord! Confound all perfumes anyway!

MYRRHINE [returning with a flask] Stretch out your hand and put some on.

CINESIAS [suspiciously] By God, I don't much like this perfume. It smacks of shilly-shallying, and has no scent of the marriage-bed.

MYRRHINE Oh dear! This is Rhodian perfume I've brought.

CINESIAS It's quite all right, dear. Never mind.

MYRRHINE Don't be silly!

She goes out with the flask.

CINESIAS Damn the man who first concocted perfumes!

MYRRHINE [returning with another flask] Here, try this flask.

CINESIAS I've got another one all ready for you. Come, you wretch, lie down and stop bringing me things.

MYRRHINE All right; I'm taking off my shoes. But, my dear, see that you vote for peace.

CINESIAS [absently] I'll consider it.

Myrrhine runs away to the Acropolis.

I'm ruined! The wench has skinned me and run away! [chanting, in tragic style] Alas! Alas! Deceived, deserted by this fairest of women, whom shall I—lay? Ah, my poor little child, how shall I nurture thee? Where's Cynalopex? I needs must hire a nurse!

LEADER OF MEN [chanting] Ah, wretched man, in dreadful wise beguiled, bewrayed, thy soul is sore distressed. I pity thee, alas! alas! What soul, what loins, what liver could stand this strain? How firm and unyielding he stands, with naught to aid him of a morning.

CINESIAS   O lord! O Zeus! What tortures I endure!

LEADER OF MEN   This is the way she's treated you, that vile and cursèd wanton.

LEADER OF WOMEN   Nay, not vile and cursèd, but sweet and dear.

LEADER OF MEN   Sweet, you say? Nay, hateful, hateful!

CINESIAS   Hateful indeed! O Zeus, Zeus!
    Seize her and snatch her away,
    Like a handful of dust, in a mighty,
    Fiery tempest! Whirl her aloft, then let her drop
    Down to the earth, with a crash, as she falls—
    On the point of this waiting
        Thingummybob!

He goes out.
Enter a Spartan Herald, in an obvious state of excitement, which he is doing his best to conceal.

HERALD   Where can I find the Senate or the Prytanes? I've got an important message.

The Athenian Magistrate enters.

MAGISTRATE   Say there, are you a man or Priapus?

HERALD [*in annoyance*]   I'm a herald, you lout! I've come from Sparta about the truce.

MAGISTRATE   Is that a spear you've got under your cloak?

HERALD   No, of course not!

MAGISTRATE   Why do you twist and turn so? Why hold your cloak in front of you? Did you rupture yourself on the trip?

HERALD   By gum, the fellow's an old fool.

MAGISTRATE [*pointing*]   Why, you dirty rascal, you're all excited.

HERALD   Not at all. Stop this tom-foolery.

MAGISTRATE   Well, what's that I see?

HERALD   A Spartan message-staff.

MAGISTRATE   Oh, certainly! That's just the kind of message-staff I've got. But tell me the honest truth: how are things going in Sparta?

HERALD   All the land of Sparta is up in arms—and our allies are up, too. We need Pellene.

MAGISTRATE   What brought this trouble on you? A sudden Panic?

HERALD   No, Lampito started it and then all the other women in Sparta with one accord chased their husbands out of their beds.

MAGISTRATE   How do you feel?

HERALD   Terrible. We walk around the city bent over like men lighting matches in a wind. For our women won't let us touch them until we all agree and make peace throughout Greece.

MAGISTRATE   This is a general conspiracy of the women; I see it now. Well, hurry back and tell the Spartans to send ambassadors here with full powers to arrange a truce. And I'll go tell the Council to choose ambassadors from here; I've got something here that will soon persuade them!

HERALD   I'll fly there; for you've made an excellent suggestion.

The Herald and the Magistrate depart on opposite sides of the stage.

LEADER OF MEN   No beast or fire is harder than womankind to tame,
Nor is the spotted leopard so devoid of shame.

LEADER OF WOMEN   Knowing this, you dare provoke us to attack?
I'd be your steady friend, if you'd but take us back.

LEADER OF MEN   I'll never cease my hatred keen of womankind.

LEADER OF WOMEN   Just as you will. But now just let me help you find
That cloak you threw aside. You look so silly there
Without your clothes. Here, put it on and don't go bare.

LEADER OF MEN   That's very kind, and shows you're not entirely bad.
But I threw off my things when I was good and mad.

LEADER OF WOMEN   At last you seem a man, and won't be mocked, my lad.
If you'd been nice to me, I'd take this little gnat
That's in your eye and pluck it out for you, like that.

LEADER OF MEN   So that's what's bothered me and bit my eye so long!
Please dig it out for me. I own that I've been wrong.

LEADER OF WOMEN   I'll do so, though you've been a most ill-natured brat.
Ye gods! See here! A huge and monstrous little gnat!

LEADER OF MEN   Oh, how that helps! For it was digging wells in me.
And now it's out, my tears can roll down hard and free.

LEADER OF WOMEN   Here, let me wipe them off, although you're such a knave,
And kiss me.

LEADER OF MEN   No!

LEADER OF WOMEN   Whate'er you say, a kiss I'll have.

She kisses him.

LEADER OF MEN   Oh, confound these women! They've a coaxing way about them.
He was wise and never spoke a truer word, who said,
"We can't live with women, but we cannot live without them."
Now I'll make a truce with you. We'll fight no more; instead,

I will not injure you if you do me no wrong.
And now let's join our ranks and then begin a song.
COMBINED CHORUS [*singing*]
    Athenians, we're not prepared,
    To say a single ugly word
    About our fellow-citizens.
Quite the contrary: we desire but to say and to do
Naught but good. Quite enough are the ills now on hand.

    Men and women, be advised:
        If anyone requires
    Money—minae two or three—
        We've got what he desires.

    My purse is yours, on easy terms:
        When Peace shall reappear,
    Whate'er you've borrowed will be due.
        So speak up without fear.

    You needn't pay me back, you see,
    If you can get a cent from me!

    We're about to entertain
        Some foreign gentlemen;
    We've soup and tender, fresh-killed pork.
        Come round to dine at ten.

    Come early; wash and dress with care,
        And bring the children, too.
    Then step right in, no "by your leave."
        We'll be expecting you.

    Walk in as if you owned the place.
    You'll find the door—shut in your face!

Enter a group of Spartan Ambassadors; they are in the same desperate condition as the Herald in the previous scene.

LEADER OF CHORUS   Here comes the envoys from Sparta, sprouting long beards and looking for the world as if they were carrying pig-pens in front of them.
    Greetings, gentlemen of Sparta. Tell me, in what state have you come?

SPARTAN   Why waste words? You can plainly see what state we've come in!

LEADER OF CHORUS   Wow! You're in a pretty high-strung condition, and it seems to be getting worse.

SPARTAN   It's indescribable. Won't someone please arrange a peace for us—in any way you like.

LEADER OF CHORUS   Here come our own, native ambassadors, crouching like wrestlers and holding their clothes in front of them; this seems an athletic kind of malady.

Enter several Athenian Ambassadors.

ATHENIAN   Can anyone tell us where Lysistrata is? You see our condition.

LEADER OF CHORUS   Here's another case of the same complaint. Tell me, are the attacks worse in the morning?

ATHENIAN   No, we're always afflicted this way. If someone doesn't soon arrange this truce, you'd better not let me get my hands on— Cleisthenes!

LEADER OF CHORUS   If you're smart, you'll arrange your cloaks so none of these fellows who smashed the Hermae can see you.

ATHENIAN   Right you are; a very good suggestion.

SPARTAN   Aye, by all means. Here, let's hitch up our clothes.

ATHENIAN   Greetings, Spartan. We've suffered dreadful things.

SPARTAN   My dear fellow, we'd have suffered still worse if one of those fellows had seen us in this condition.

ATHENIAN   Well, gentlemen, we must get down to business. What's your errand here?

SPARTAN   We're ambassadors about peace.

ATHENIAN   Excellent; so are we. Only Lysistrata can arrange things for us; shall we summon her?

SPARTAN   Aye, and Lysistratus too, if you like.

LEADER OF CHORUS   No need to summon her, it seems. She's coming out of her own accord.

Enter Lysistrata accompanied by a statue of a nude female figure, which represents Reconciliation.

> Hail, noblest of women; now must thou be
> A judge shrewd and subtle, mild and severe,
> Be sweet yet majestic: all manners employ.
> The leaders of Hellas, caught by thy love-charms,
> Have come to thy judgment, their charges submitting.

LYSISTRATA   This is no difficult task, if one catch them still in amorous passion, before they've resorted to each other. But I'll soon find out. Where's Reconciliation? Go, first bring the Spartans here, and don't seize them rudely and violently, as our tactless husbands used to do, but as befits a woman, like an old, familiar friend; if they won't give you their hands, take them however you can. Then go fetch these Athenians here, taking hold of whatever they offer you. Now then, men of Sparta, stand here beside me, and you Athenians on the other side, and listen to my words.

I am a woman, it is true, but I have a mind; I'm not badly off in native wit, and by listening to my father and my elders, I've had a decent schooling.

Now I intend to give you a scolding which you both deserve. With one common font you worship at the same altars, just like brothers, at Olympia, at Thermopylae, at Delphi—how many more might I name, if time permitted;—and the Barbarians stand by waiting with their armies; yet you are destroying the men and towns of Greece.

ATHENIAN   Oh, this tension is killing me!

LYSISTRATA   And now, men of Sparta,—to turn to you—don't you remember how the Spartan Pericleidas came here once as a suppliant, and sitting at our altar, all pale with fear in his crimson cloak, begged us for an army? For all Messene had attacked you and the god sent an earthquake too? Then Cimon went forth with four thousand hoplites and saved all Lacedaemon. Such was the aid you received from Athens, and now you lay waste the country which once treated you so well.

ATHENIAN   [hotly]   They're in the wrong, Lysistrata, upon my word, they are!

SPARTAN   [absently, looking at the statue of Reconciliation]   We're in the wrong. What hips! How lovely they are!

LYSISTRATA   Don't think I'm going to let you Athenians off. Don't you remember how the Spartans came in arms when you were wearing the rough, sheepskin cloak of slaves and slew the host of Thessalians, the comrades and allies of Hippias? Fighting with you on that day, alone of all the Greeks, they set you free and instead of a sheepskin gave your folk a handsome robe to wear.

SPARTAN   [looking at Lysistrata]   I've never seen a more distinguished woman.

ATHENIAN   [looking at Reconciliation]   I've never seen a more voluptuous body!

LYSISTRATA   Why then, with these many noble deeds to think of, do you fight each other? Why don't you stop this villany? Why not make peace? Tell me, what prevents it?

SPARTAN   [waving vaguely at Reconciliation]   We're willing, if you're willing to give up your position on yonder flank.

LYSISTRATA   What position, my good man?

SPARTAN   Pylus; we've been panting for it for ever so long.

ATHENIAN   No, by God! You shan't have it!

LYSISTRATA Let them have it, my friend.

ATHENIAN Then what shall we have to rouse things up?

LYSISTRATA Ask for another place in exchange.

ATHENIAN Well, let's see: first of all [*pointing to various parts of Reconcilia-tion's anatomy*] give us Echinus here, this Maliac Inlet in back there, and these two Megarian legs.

SPARTAN No, by heavens! You can't have *everything*, you crazy fool!

LYSISTRATA Let it go. Don't fight over a pair of legs.

ATHENIAN [*taking off his cloak*] I think I'll strip and do a little planting now.

SPARTAN [*following suit*] And I'll just do a little fertilizing, by gosh!

LYSISTRATA Wait until the truce is concluded. Now if you've decided on this course, hold a conference and discuss the matter with your allies.

ATHENIAN Allies? Don't be ridiculous! They're in the same state we are. Won't all our allies want the same thing we do—to jump in bed with their women?

SPARTAN Ours will, I know.

ATHENIAN Especially the Carystians, by God!

LYSISTRATA Very well. Now purify yourselves, that your wives may feast and entertain you in the Acropolis; we've provisions by the basketfull. Exchange your oaths and pledges there, and then each of you may take his wife and go home.

ATHENIAN Let's go at once.

SPARTAN Come on, where you will.

ATHENIAN For God's sake, let's hurry!

They all go into the Acropolis.

CHORUS [*singing*]
>Whate'er I have of coverlets
>>And robes of varied hue
>And golden trinkets,—without stint
>>I offer them to you.

>Take what you will and bear it home,
>>Your children to delight,
>Or if your girl's a Basket-maid;
>>Just choose whate'er's in sight.

>There's naught within so well secured
>>You cannot break the seal
>And bear it off; just help yourselves;
>>No hesitation feel.

But you'll see nothing, though you try,
Unless you've sharper eyes than I!

If anyone needs bread to feed
  A growing family,
I've lots of wheat and full-grown loaves;
  So just apply to me.

Let every poor man who desires
  Come round and bring a sack
To fetch the grain; my slave is there
  To load it on his back.

But don't come near my door, I say:
Beware the dog, and stay away!

An Athenian enters carrying a torch; he knocks at the gate.

ATHENIAN   Open the door! [*To the Chorus, which is clustered around the gate*]
Make way, won't you! What are you hanging around for? Want me to
singe you with this torch? [*To himself*] No; it's a stale trick, I won't do it!
[*To the audience*] Still if I've got to do it to please *you*, I suppose I'll have
to take the trouble.

A Second Athenian comes out of the gate.

SECOND ATHENIAN   And I'll help you.
FIRST ATHENIAN [*waving his torch at the Chorus*]   Get out! Go bawl your
heads off! Move on there, so the Spartans can leave in peace when the
banquet's over.

They brandish their torches until the Chorus leaves the Orchestra.

SECOND ATHENIAN   I've never seen such a pleasant banquet: the Spartans are
charming fellows, indeed they are! And we Athenians are very witty in
our cups.
FIRST ATHENIAN   Naturally: for when we're sober we're never at our best. If
the Athenians would listen to me, we'd always get a little tipsy on our
embassies. As things are now, we go to Sparta when we're sober and
look around to stir up trouble. And then we don't hear what they say—
and as for what they *don't* say, we have all sorts of suspicions. And then
we bring back varying reports about the mission. But this time every-

thing is pleasant; even if a man should sing the Telamon-song when he ought to sing "Cleitagorus," we'd praise him and swear it was excellent.

The two Choruses return, as a Chorus of Athenians and a Chorus of Spartans.

Here they come back again. Go to the devil, you scoundrels!
SECOND ATHENIAN   Get out, I say! They're coming out from the feast.

Enter the Spartan and Athenian envoys, followed by Lysistrata and all the women.

SPARTAN [*to one of his fellow-envoys*]   My good fellow, take up your pipes; I want to do a fancy two-step and sing a jolly song for the Athenians.
ATHENIAN   Yes, do take your pipes, by all means. I'd love to see you dance.
SPARTAN [*singing and dancing with the Chorus of Spartans*]
     These youths inspire
To song and dance, O Memory;
Stir up my Muse, to tell how we
And Athens' men, in our galleys clashing
At Artemisium, 'gainst foemen dashing
     In godlike ire,
Conquered the Persian and set Greece free.

     Leonidas
Led on his valiant warriors
Whetting their teeth like angry boars.
Abundant foam on their lips was flow'ring,
A stream of sweat from their limbs was show'ring.
     The Persian was
Numberless as the sand on the shores.

O Huntress who slayest the beasts in the glade,
O Virgin divine, hither come to our truce,
Unite us in bonds which all time will not loose.
Grant us to find in this treaty, we pray,
An unfailing source of true friendship today,
And all of our days, helping us to refrain
From weaseling tricks which bring war in their train.
     Then hither, come hither! O huntress maid.

LYSISTRATA   Come then, since all is fairly done, men of Sparta, lead away your wives, and you, Athenians, take yours. Let every man stand beside his wife, and every wife beside her man, and then, to celebrate our fortune, let's dance. And in the future, let's take care to avoid these misunderstandings.

CHORUS OF ATHENIANS [*singing and dancing*]
> Lead on the dances, your graces revealing.
> Call Artemis hither, call Artemis' twin,
> Leader of dances, Apollo the Healing,
> Kindly God—hither! let's summon him in!
>
> Nysian Bacchus call,
> Who with his Maenads, his eyes flashing fire,
> Dances, and last of all
> Zeus of the thunderbolt flaming, the Sire,
> And Hera in majesty,
> Queen of prosperity.
> Come, ye Powers who dwell above
> Unforgetting, our witnesses be
> Of Peace with bonds of harmonius love—
> The Peace which Cypris has wrought for me.
> Alleluia! Io Paean!
> Leap in joy—hurrah! hurrah!
> 'Tis victory—hurrah! hurrah!
> Euoi! Euoi! Euai! Euai!

LYSISTRATA [*to the Spartans*]   Come now, sing a new song to cap ours.

CHORUS OF SPARTANS [*singing and dancing*]
> Leaving Taygetus fair and renown'd
> Muse of Laconia, hither come:
> Amyclae's god in hymns resound,
> Athene of the Brazen Home,
> And Castor and Pollux, Tyndareus' sons,
> Who sport where Eurotas murmuring runs.
>
> On with the dance! Heia! Ho!
> All leaping along,
> Mantles a-swinging as we go!
> Of Sparta our song.
> There the holy chorus ever gladdens,
> There the beat of stamping feet,
> As our winsome fillies, lovely maidens,
> Dance, beside Eurotas, banks a-skipping,—
> Nimbly go to and fro
> Hast'ning, leaping feet in measures tripping,

Like the Bacchae's revels, hair a-streaming.
Leda's child, divine and mild,
Leads the holy dance, her fair face beaming.
  On with the dance! as your hand
    Presses the hair
  Streaming away unconfined.
    Leap in the air
  Light as the deer; footsteps resound
  Aiding our dance, beating the ground.
Praise Athene, Maid divine, unrivalled in her might,
Dweller in the Brazen Home, unconquered in the fight.

All go out singing and dancing.

MORALITY DRAMA ON THE MEDIEVAL STAGE

Permanent theaters did not exist in England during the medieval period. When the morality play *Everyman* was first produced sometime near the end of the fifteenth century, it was probably performed on a makeshift platform set up in a village square or in the great dining hall of a castle. On the platform a couple of small set-like structures known as *mansions* (literally, dwelling places) would have been set up to stand for the two specific locations where action takes place—namely, heaven, from which God speaks at the opening of the play, and the house of salvation, to which Everyman goes in the middle of the play for confession and penance. As the action moved from one mansion to the other, the stage was understood to be an extension of one location and then of the other.

Sometimes, of course, the location of the action was neither specified nor implied, as when Everyman encounters Death, or Fellowship, or Kindred and Cousin. In such instances the stage would have been understood to represent a street or some other open area. And at the end of the play, when Everyman is about to die, he would have moved to the front of the stage, so that after his last speech he could step down from the stage to indicate that he had entered his grave. Thus the medieval method of staging *Everyman* was fundamentally symbolic in its use of space and processional in its movement from one mansion or location to another.

Costuming was also symbolic rather than realistic, and yet at the same time highly vivid. God, for example, might be dressed in the imperial vestments of a Pope, and Goods might be got up in a costume decorated with jewels or gold and silver coins. The audience, then, would have been treated to a spectacle that was at once visually appealing and spiritually significant.

The medieval method of staging brought actors and spectators closer to one another than ever before or since. They were not separated either by distance or by the architecture of a theater. Spectators witnessed the play from only a few feet away, and on occasion—as when Everyman enters his grave—an actor literally moved into the area of the audience. Although that movement into the audience may strike us today as being a violation of theatrical conventions, it would have affected medieval spectators quite differently: it would have shown them the imminence of their own death and the futility of clinging to their worldly possessions. That vision of *Everyman* would have been especially meaningful to medieval spectators, for they had also endured the bubonic plague, the so-called Black Death, which had ravaged England and the Continent during the fourteenth century.

Although we have not witnessed the Black Death, we all know the inescapable facts of death—the physical decay, the loss of consciousness, the end of being in the world—and *Everyman* does show us how those facts might affect a representative human being like ourselves. Everyman's initial denial of death, his desire to postpone it, his attempt to bargain with it, his final acceptance of it, and his ultimate recognition that it can be transcended only by the knowledge of having lived a decent life—the spectacle of these events makes the play as relevant for us as it must have been for its medieval audience.

ANONYMOUS

c. 1485

Everyman

CHARACTERS

MESSENGER	GOOD DEEDS
GOD	KNOWLEDGE
DEATH	CONFESSION
EVERYMAN	BEAUTY
FELLOWSHIP	STRENGTH
KINDRED	DISCRETION
COUSIN	FIVE WITS
GOODS	ANGEL
DOCTOR	

Here beginneth a treatise how the High Father of Heaven sendeth Death to summon every creature to come and give account of their lives in this world, and is in manner of a moral play.

Enter Messenger

MESSENGER   I pray you all give your audience
    And hear this matter with reverence,
    By figure a moral play:
    The Summoning of Everyman called it is,
    That of our lives and ending shows
    How transitory we be all day.
    This matter is wondrous precious,
    But the intent of it is more gracious
    And sweet to bear away.
10   The story saith: Man, in the beginning
    Look well, and take good heed to the ending,
    Be you never so gay!
    Ye think sin in the beginning full sweet,
    Which in the end causeth the soul to weep,
    When the body lieth in clay.
    Here shall you see how Fellowship and Jollity
    Both, Strength, Pleasure and Beauty
    Will fade from thee as flower in May;

Edited by Kate Franks

20   For ye shall hear how our Heaven's King
         Calleth Everyman to a general reckoning.
         Give audience, and hear what he doth say.

Exit Messenger

God speaks.

GOD   I perceive, here in my majesty,
         How that all creatures be to me unkind,
         Living without dread in worldly prosperity.
         Of ghostly sight[1] the people be so blind,
         Drowned in sin, they know me not for their God.
         In worldly riches is all their mind;
         They fear not my righteousness, the sharp rod.
         My law that I showed when I for them died
30   They forget clean, and shedding of my blood red.
         I hanged between two thieves, it cannot be denied;
         To get them life I suffered to be dead;
         I healed their feet, with thorns hurt was my head.
         I could do no more than I did, truly;
         And now I see the people do clean forsake me.
         They use the seven deadly sins damnable,
         As pride, covetise, wrath, and lechery
         Now in the world be made commendable;
         And thus they leave of angels the heavenly company.
40   Every man liveth so after his own pleasure,
         And yet of their life they be nothing sure.
         I see the more that I them forbear
         The worse they be from year to year.
         All that liveth appaireth[2] fast;
         Therefore I will, in all the haste,
         Have a reckoning of every man's person;
         For, if I leave the people thus alone
         In their life and wicked tempests,
         Verily they will become much worse than beasts;
50   For now one would by envy another up eat;
         Charity they do all clean forget.
         I hoped well that every man
         In my glory should make his mansion,
         And thereto I had them all elect;
         But now I see, like traitors deject,

1. Spiritual sight; knowledge of God
2. Worsens

They thank me not for the pleasure that I to them meant,
Nor yet for their being that I them have lent.
I proffered the people great multitude of mercy,
And few there be that asketh it heartily.
60   They be so cumbered with worldly riches
That needs on them I must do justice,
On every man living without fear.
Where art thou, Death, thou mighty messenger?

Enter Death

DEATH   Almighty God, I am here at your will,
Your commandment to fulfill.
GOD   Go thou to Everyman
And show him, in my name,
A pilgrimage he must on him take,
Which he in no wise may escape;
70   And that he bring with him a sure reckoning
Without delay or any tarrying.
DEATH   Lord, I will in the world go run over all
And cruelly search out both great and small.
Every man will I beset that liveth beastly
Out of God's laws, and dreadeth not folly.
He that loveth riches I will strike with my dart,
His sight to blind, and from Heaven to depart—
Except that alms be his good friend—
In hell for to dwell, world without end.

Enter Everyman.

80   Lo, yonder I see Everyman walking.
Full little he thinketh on my coming;
His mind is on fleshly lusts and his treasure,
And great pain it shall cause him to endure
Before the Lord, Heaven's King.
Everyman, stand still! Whither art thou going
Thus gaily? Hast thou thy Maker forgot?
EVERYMAN   Why askest thou?
Wouldest thou know?
DEATH   Yea, sir. I will you show:
90   In great haste I am sent to thee
From God out of his majesty.
EVERYMAN   What, sent to me?

DEATH   Yea, certainly.
    Though thou have forgot him here,
    He thinketh on thee in the heavenly sphere,
    As, ere we depart, thou shalt know.

EVERYMAN   What desireth God of me?

DEATH   That I shall show to thee:
    A reckoning he will needs have
100   Without any longer respite.

EVERYMAN   To give a reckoning longer leisure I crave;
    This blind[3] matter troubleth my wit.

DEATH   On thee thou must take a long journey;
    Therefore thy book of account with thee thou bring,
    For turn again thou cannot, by no way.
    And look thou be sure of thy reckoning,
    For before God thou shalt answer and show
    Thy many bad deeds, and good but a few;
    How thou hast spent thy life, and in what wise,
110   Before the Chief Lord of Paradise.
    Have ado that thou were in that way,
    For know thou well, thou shalt make no attorney.[4]

EVERYMAN   Full unready I am, such reckoning to give.
    I know thee not. What messenger art thou?

DEATH   I am Death that no man dreadeth,[5]
    For every man I rest and no man spareth;
    For it is God's commandment
    That all to me should be obedient.

EVERYMAN   O Death, thou comest when I had thee least in mind!
120   In thy power it lieth me to save;
    Yet of my goods will I give thee, if thou will be kind—
    Yea, a thousand pound shalt thou have!—
    And defer this matter till another day.

DEATH   Everyman, it may not be, by no way.
    I set not by gold, silver, nor riches,
    Nor by pope, emperor, king, duke, nor princes;
    For, if I would receive gifts great,
    All the world I might get;
    But my custom is clean contrary:
130   I give thee no respite. Come hence, and not tarry!

EVERYMAN   Alas, shall I have no longer respite?
    I may say Death giveth no warning!

3. Unknown, obscure
4. You won't be able to plead your case
5. Who fears no man

To think on thee, it maketh my heart sick,
For all unready is my book of reckoning.
But twelve years if I might have abiding,
My accounting book I would make so clear
That my reckoning I should not need to fear.
Wherefore, Death, I pray thee, for God's mercy,
Spare me till I be provided of remedy.

DEATH   Thee availeth not to cry, weep and pray;
But haste thee lightly[6] that thou were gone that journey,
And prove thy friends if thou can.
For know thou well the tide abideth no man,
And in the world each living creature
For Adam's sin must die of nature.

EVERYMAN   Death, if I should this pilgrimage take
And my reckoning surely make,
Show me, for sainted charity,
Should I not come again shortly?

DEATH   No, Everyman. If thou be once there
Thou mayst never more come here,
Trust me verily.

EVERYMAN   O gracious God in the high seat celestial,
Have mercy on me in this most need!
Shall I have no company from this vale terrestial
Of mine acquaintance, that way me to lead?

DEATH   Yea, if any be so hardy
That would go with thee and bear thee company.
Hie thee that thou were gone to God's magnificence,
Thy reckoning to give before his presence.
What, thinkest thou thy life is given thee
And thy worldly goods also?

EVERYMAN   I had thought so, verily.

DEATH   Nay, nay, it was but lent thee;
For as soon as thou art gone,
Another a while shall have it and then go therefrom,
Even as thou hast done.
Everyman, thou art mad! Thou hast thy wits five
And here on earth will not amend thy life;
For suddenly I do come.

EVERYMAN   O wretchéd caitiff, whither shall I flee,
That I might escape this endless sorrow?
Now, gentle Death, spare me till tomorrow,

6. Quickly

That I may amend me
With good advisement.
DEATH   Nay, thereto I will not consent,
Nor no man will I respite;
But to the heart suddenly I shall smite
Without any advisement.
180   And now out of thy sight I will me hie.
See thou make thee ready shortly;
For thou mayst say this is the day
That no man living may escape away.

Exit Death.

EVERYMAN   Alas, I may well weep with sighs deep!
Now have I no manner of company
To help me in my journey and me to keep;
And also my writing is full unready.
How shall I do now for to excuse me?
I would to God I had never been begot!
190   To my soul a full great profit it had been;
For now I fear pains huge and great.
The time passeth. Lord, help, that all wrought!
For though I mourn it availeth naught.
The day passeth and is almost ago;
I know not well what for to do.
To whom were I best my complaint to make?
What if I to Fellowship thereof spake
And showed him of this sudden chance?
For in him is all mine affiance;[7]
200   We have in the world so many a day
Been good friends in sport and play.

Enter Fellowship.

I see him yonder, certainly.
I trust that he will bear me company;
Therefore to him will I speak to ease my sorrow.
Well met, good Fellowship, and good morrow!
FELLOWSHIP   Everyman, good morrow, by this day!
Sir, why lookest thou so piteously?
If anything be amiss, I pray thee me say,
That I may help to remedy.
210   EVERYMAN   Yea, good Fellowship, yea,
I am in great jeopardy.

7. Faith or trust

FELLOWSHIP   My true friend, show to me your mind.
　　I will not forsake thee to my life's end
　　In the way of good company.
EVERYMAN   That was well spoken and lovingly.
FELLOWSHIP   Sir, I must needs know your heaviness;
　　I have pity to see you in any distress.
　　If any have you wronged, ye shall revenged be,
　　Though I on the ground be slain for thee,
220　　Though that I know before that I should die.
EVERYMAN   Verily, Fellowship, gramercy.
FELLOWSHIP   Tush! By thy thanks I set not a straw.
　　Show me your grief, and say no more.
EVERYMAN   If I my heart should to you break,
　　And then you to turn your mind from me
　　And would not me comfort when ye hear me speak,
　　Then should I ten times sorrier be.
FELLOWSHIP   Sir, I say as I will do in deed.
EVERYMAN   Then be you a good friend in need.
230　　I have found you true herebefore.
FELLOWSHIP   And so ye shall evermore;
　　For, in faith, if thou go to hell,
　　I will not forsake thee by the way.
EVERYMAN   Ye speak like a good friend; I believe you well.
　　I shall deserve it, if I may.
FELLOWSHIP   I speak of no deserving, by this day!
　　For he that will say and nothing do
　　Is not worthy with good company to go;
　　Therefore show me the grief of your mind,
240　　As to your friend most loving and kind.
EVERYMAN   I shall show you how it is:
　　Commanded I am to go a journey,
　　A long way hard and dangerous,
　　And give a straight account without delay
　　Before the high judge, Adonai.[8]
　　Wherefore, I pray you, bear me company,
　　As ye have promised, in this journey.
FELLOWSHIP   That is matter indeed! Promise is duty;
　　But if I should take such a voyage on me,
250　　I know it well, it should be to my pain;
　　Also it maketh me afeared, certain.
　　But let us take counsel here as well as we can,
　　For your words would fear a strong man.

8. Hebrew name for God

EVERYMAN   Why, ye said if I had need
  Ye would me never forsake, quick nor dead,
  Though it were to hell, truly.
FELLOWSHIP   So I said, certainly,
  But such pleasures be set aside, the sooth to say;
  And also, if we took such a journey
260 When should we again come?
EVERYMAN   Nay, never again till the day of doom.
FELLOWSHIP   In faith, then will not I come there!
  Who hath you these tidings brought?
EVERYMAN   Indeed, Death was with me here.
FELLOWSHIP   Now, by God that all hath bought,
  If Death were the messenger,
  For no man that is living today
  I will not go that loath journey—
  Not for the father that begat me!
270 EVERYMAN   Ye promised otherwise, pardie.
FELLOWSHIP   I know well I said so, truly;
  And yet, if thou wilt eat and drink and make good cheer,
  Or haunt to women the lusty company[9]
  I would not forsake you while the day is clear,
  Trust me verily.
EVERYMAN   Yea, thereto ye would be ready!
  To go to mirth, solace and play
  Your mind will sooner apply
  Than to bear me company in my long journey.
280 FELLOWSHIP   Now, in good faith, I will not that way;
  But if thou will murder or any man kill,
  In that I will help thee with a good will.
EVERYMAN   O, that is a simple advice indeed.
  Gentle fellow, help me in my necessity!
  We have loved long, and now I need;
  And now, gentle Fellowship, remember me.
FELLOWSHIP   Whether ye have loved me or no,
  By Saint John, I will not with thee go!
EVERYMAN   Yet, I pray thee, take the labor and do so much for me
290 To bring me forward, for sainted charity,
  And comfort me till I come without the town.
FELLOWSHIP   Nay, if thou would give me a new gown,
  I will not a foot with thee go;
  But if thou had tarried, I would not have left thee so.

9. Seek women's company for pleasure; go a-whoring

And as now, God speed thee in thy journey,
For from thee I will depart as fast as I may.
EVERYMAN   Wither away, Fellowship? Will thou forsake me?
FELLOWSHIP   Yea, by my faith! To God I betake[10] thee.
EVERYMAN   Farewell, good Fellowship! For thee my heart is sore.
300   Adieu forever! I shall see thee no more.
FELLOWSHIP   In faith, Everyman, farewell now at the ending!
For you I will remember that parting is mourning.

Exit Fellowship.

EVERYMAN   Alack, shall we thus depart indeed—
Ah, Lady, help!—without any more comfort?
Lo, Fellowship forsaketh me in my most need.
For help in this world whither shall I resort?
Fellowship herebefore with me would merry make,
And now little sorrow for me doth he take.
It is said, "In prosperity men friends may find,
310   Which in adversity be full unkind."
Now whither for succor shall I flee,
Since that Fellowship hath forsaken me?
To my kinsmen I will, truly,
Praying them to help me in my necessity.
I believe that they will do so,
For kind will creep where it may not go.[11]

Enter Kindred and Cousin.

I will go say, for yonder I see them.
Where be ye now, my friends and kinsmen?
KINDRED   Here be we now at your commandment.
320   Cousin, I pray you show us your intent
In any wise and not spare.
COUSIN   Yea, Everyman, and to us declare
If ye be disposed to go anywhither;
For know you well, we will live and die together.
KINDRED   In wealth and woe we will with you hold,
For over his kin a man may be bold.
EVERYMAN   Gramercy, my friends and kinsmen kind.
Now shall I show you the grief of my mind:
I was commanded by a messenger,
330   That is a high king's chief officer;

10. Entrust
11. One's kin will crawl where they may not walk;
     i.e., will do what they can.

He bade me go a pilgrimage, to my pain,
And I know well I shall never come again.
Also I must give a reckoning strait,
For I have a great enemy that hath me in wait,
Which intendeth me for to hinder.

KINDRED   What account is that which ye must render?
That would I know.

EVERYMAN   Of all my works I must show
How I have lived and my days spent;
340   Also of ill deeds that I have used
In my time, since life was me lent;
And of all virtues that I have refused.
Therefore, I pray you, go thither with me
To help to make mine account, for saint charity.

COUSIN   What, to go thither? Is that the matter?
Nay, Everyman, I had liefer fast bread and water
All this five years and more.

EVERYMAN   Alas, that ever I was born!
For now shall I never be merry
350   If that you forsake me.

KINDRED   Ah, sir, but ye be a merry man!
Take good heart to you, and make no moan.
But one thing I warn you, by Saint Anne—
As for me, ye shall go alone.

EVERYMAN   My Cousin, will you not with me go?

COUSIN   No, by our Lady! I have the cramp in my toe.
Trust not to me; for, so God me speed,
I will deceive you in your most need.

KINDRED   It availeth not us to entice.
360   Ye shall have my maid with all my heart;
She loveth to go to feasts, there to be nice,
And to dance and abroad to start.
I will give her leave to help you in that journey,
If that you and she may agree.

EVERYMAN   Now show me the very effect of your mind:
Will you go with me, or abide behind?

KINDRED   Abide behind? Yea, that will I, if I may!
Therefore farewell till another day.

Exit Kindred.

EVERYMAN   How should I be merry or glad?
370   For fair promises men to me make,
But when I have most need they me forsake.
I am deceived; that maketh me sad.

COUSIN   Cousin Everyman, farewell now,

For verily I will not go with you.
Also of mine own an unready reckoning
I have to account; therefore I make tarrying.
Now God keep thee, for now I go.

Exit Cousin.

EVERYMAN   Ah, Jesus, is all come hereto?
Lo, fair words maketh fools fain;
380 They promise and nothing will do, certain.
My kinsmen promised me faithfully
For to abide with me steadfastly,
And now fast away do they flee,
Even so Fellowship promised me.
What friend were best me of to provide?
I lose my time here longer to abide.
Yet in my mind a thing there is:
All my life I have loved riches;
If that my Goods now help me might,
390 He would make my heart full light.
I will speak to him in this distress.
Where art thou, my Goods and riches?

Goods revealed in a corner.

GOODS   Who calleth me? Everyman? What, hast thou haste?
I lie here in corners, trussed and piled so high,
And in chests I am locked so fast,
Also sacked in bags. Thou mayst see with thine eye
I cannot stir; in packs, low I lie.
What would ye have? Lightly me say.
EVERYMAN   Come hither, Goods, in all the haste thou may,
400 For of counsel I must desire thee.
GOODS   Sir, if ye in the world have sorrow or adversity,
That can I help you to remedy shortly.
EVERYMAN   It is another disease that grieveth me;
In this world it is not, I tell thee so.
I am sent for, another way to go,
To give a strait account general
Before the highest Jupiter of all;
And all my life I have had joy and pleasure in thee.
Therefore, I pray thee, go with me;
410 For, peradventure, thou mayst before God Almighty
My reckoning help to clean and purify;
For it is said ever among
That "money maketh all right that is wrong."

GOODS Nay, Everyman, I sing another song.
　　　I follow no man in such voyages; ·
　　　For if I went with thee,
　　　Thou shouldst fare much the worse for me.
　　　For because on me thou did set thy mind,
　　　Thy reckoning I have made blotted and blind,
420　　That thine account thou cannot make truly—
　　　And that hast thou for the love of me!
EVERYMAN That would grieve me full sore,
　　　When I should come to that fearful answer.
　　　Up, let us go thither together.
GOODS Nay, not so! I am too brittle, I may not endure.
　　　I will follow no man one foot, be ye sure.
EVERYMAN Alas, I have thee loved, and had great pleasure
　　　All my life-days in goods and treasure.
GOODS That is to thy damnation, without lying,
430　　For my love is contrary to the love everlasting.
　　　But if thou had me loved moderately during,
　　　As to the poor given part of me,
　　　Then shouldst thou not in this dolor be,
　　　Nor in this great sorrow and care.
EVERYMAN Lo, now was I deceived ere I was aware,
　　　And all I may lay to my spending of time.
GOODS What, thinkest thou that I am thine?
EVERYMAN I had thought so.
GOODS Nay, Everyman, I say no.
440　　As for a while I was lent thee;
　　　A season thou hast had me in prosperity.
　　　My condition is a man's soul to kill;
　　　If I save one, a thousand I do spill.
　　　Thinkest thou that I will follow thee?
　　　Nay, from this world not, verily.
EVERYMAN I had thought otherwise.
GOODS Therefore to thy soul Goods is a thief;
　　　For when thou art dead, this is my guise—
　　　Another to deceive in this same wise
450　　As I have done thee, and all to his soul's reprief.[12]
EVERYMAN O false Goods, cursed thou be,
　　　Thou traitor to God, that hast deceived me
　　　And caught me in thy snare!
GOODS Marry, thou brought thyself in care,

12. Harm

Whereof I am glad.
I must needs laugh; I cannot be sad.
EVERYMAN   Ah, Goods, thou hast had long my hearty love;
    I gave thee that which should be the Lord's above.
    But wilt thou not go with me indeed?
460   I pray thee truth to say.
GOODS   No, so God me speed!
    Therefore farewell, and have good day.

Exit Goods.

EVERYMAN   O, to whom shall I make my moan
    For to go with me in that heavy journey?
    First Fellowship said he would with me go;
    His words were very pleasant and gay,
    But afterward he left me alone.
    Then spake I to my kinsmen, all in despair,
    And also they gave me words fair;
470   They lacked no fair speaking,
    But all forsook me in the ending.
    Then went I to my Goods that I loved best,
    In hope to have comfort; but there had I least,
    For my Goods sharply did me tell
    That he bringeth many into Hell.
    Then of myself I was ashamed,
    And so I am worthy to be blamed;
    Thus may I well myself hate.
    Of whom shall I now counsel take?
480   I think that I shall never speed
    Till that I go to my Good Deeds.
    But, alas, she is so weak
    That she can neither go nor speak;
    Yet will I venture on her now.
    My Good Deeds, where be you?

Good Deeds revealed on the ground.

GOOD DEEDS   Here I lie, cold in the ground.
    Thy sins hath me so sore bound
    That I cannot stir.
EVERYMAN   O Good Deeds, I stand in fear!
490   I must you pray of counsel,
    For help now should come right well.
GOOD DEEDS   Everyman, I have understanding

That ye be summoned account to make
Before Messiah, of Jerusalem King;
If you do by me, that journey with you will I take.
EVERYMAN   Therefore I come to you my moan to make.
I pray you that ye will go with me.
GOOD DEEDS   I would full fain, but I cannot stand, verily.
EVERYMAN   Why, is there anything on you fallen?
500   GOOD DEEDS   Yea, sir, I may thank you of all.
If ye had perfectly cheered me,
Your book of account full ready would be.
Look, the books of your works and deeds eke,[13]
As how they lie under the feet
To your soul's heaviness.
EVERYMAN   Our Lord Jesus help me!
For one letter here I cannot see.
GOOD DEEDS   There is a blind reckoning in time of distress.
EVERYMAN   Good Deeds, I pray you help me in this need,
510   Or else I am forever damned indeed;
Therefore help me to make reckoning
Before the Redeemer of all things,
That King is, and was, and ever shall.
GOOD DEEDS   Everyman, I am sorry of your fall,
And fain would I help you if I were able.
EVERYMAN   Good Deeds, your counsel I pray you give me.
GOOD DEEDS   That shall I do verily.
Though that on my feet I may not go,
I have a sister that shall with you also,
520   Called Knowledge, which shall with you abide
To help you to make that dreadful reckoning.

Enter Knowledge.

KNOWLEDGE   Everyman, I will go with thee and be thy guide,
In thy most need to go by thy side.
EVERYMAN   In good condition I am now in everything
And am wholly content with this good thing;
Thanked be God my Creator.
GOOD DEEDS   And when she hath brought you there,
Where thou shalt heal thee of thy smart,
Then go you with your reckoning and your Good Deeds together
530   For to make you joyful at heart
Before the Blesséd Trinity.

13. Also

EVERYMAN My Good Deeds, gramercy!
   I am well content, certainly,
   With your words sweet.

Everyman and Knowledge leave Good Deeds.

KNOWLEDGE Now go we together lovingly
   To Confession, that cleansing river.
EVERYMAN For joy I weep; I would we were there!
   But, I pray you, give me cognition
   Where dwelleth that holy man, Confession.
540 KNOWLEDGE In the house of salvation;
   We shall find him in that place
   That shall us comfort, by God's grace.

Knowledge leads Everyman to Confession.

   Lo, this is Confession. Kneel down and ask mercy,
   For he is in good esteem with God Almighty.
EVERYMAN O glorious fountain, that all uncleaness doth clarify,
   Wash from me the spots of vice unclean,
   That on me no sin may be seen.
   I come with Knowledge for my redemption,
   Redempt with hearty and full contrition;
550 For I am commanded a pilgrimage to take
   And great accounts before God to make.
   Now I pray you, Shrift, mother of salvation,
   Help my Good Deeds for my piteous exclamation.
CONFESSION I know your sorrow well, Everyman.
   Because with Knowledge ye come to me,
   I will you comfort as well as I can,
   And a precious jewel I will give thee,
   Called penance, voider of adversity;
   Therewith shall your body chastised be,
560 With abstinence and perseverance in God's serviture.
   Here shall you receive that scourge of me
   Which is penance strong that ye must endure,
   To remember thy Saviour was scourged for thee
   With sharp scourges and suffered it patiently;
   So must thou, ere thou escape that painful pilgrimage.

Confession gives scourge to Knowledge.

   Knowledge, keep him in this voyage,

And by that time Good Deeds will be with thee.
But in any wise be sure of mercy,
For your time draweth fast; if ye will saved be,
570   Ask God mercy, and he will grant truly.
When with the scourge of penance man doth him bind,
The oil of forgiveness then shall he find.

Everyman and Knowledge leave Confession.

EVERYMAN   Thanked be God for his gracious work!
For now I will my penance begin.
This hath rejoiced and lighted my heart,
Though the knots be painful and hard within.
KNOWLEDGE   Everyman, look your penance that ye fulfill,
What pain that ever it to you be;
And Knowledge shall give you counsel at will
580   How your account ye shall make clearly.
EVERYMAN   O eternal God, O heavenly figure,
O way of righteousness, O goodly vision,
Which descended down in a virgin pure
Because he would every man redeem,
Which Adam forfeited by his disobedience;
O blesséd Godhead, elect and high divine,
Forgive me my grievous offence!
Here I cry thee mercy in this presence.
O ghostly[14] treasure, O ransomer and redeemer,
590   Of all the world hope and conductor,
Mirror of joy, foundation of mercy,
Which illumineth Heaven and earth thereby,
Hear my clamorous complaint though it late be;
Receive my prayers unworthy in this heavy life!
Though I be a sinner most abominable,
Yet let my name be written in Moses' table.
O Mary, pray to the Maker of all things,
Me for to help at my ending;
And save me from the power of my enemy,
600   For Death assaileth me strongly.
And, Lady, that I may by means of thy prayer
Of your Son's glory to be partner,
By the means of his passion, I it crave;
I beseech you, help my soul to save.

14. Spiritual, as in Holy Ghost

Knowledge, give me the scourge of penance;
My flesh therewith shall give acquittance.
I will now begin if God give me grace.

Knowledge gives scourge to Everyman.

KNOWLEDGE   Everyman, God give you time and space!
Thus I bequeath you in the hands of our Saviour;
610   Now may you make your reckoning sure.
EVERYMAN   In the name of the Holy Trinity,
My body sore punishéd shall be:
Take this, body, for the sins of the flesh!
Also thou delightest to go gay and fresh,
And in the way of damnation thou did me bring;
Therefore suffer now strokes of punishing.
Now of penance I will wade the water clear
To save me from Purgatory, that sharp fire.

Good Deeds rises from the ground.

GOOD DEEDS   I thank God, now I can walk and go
620   And am delivered of my sickness and woe.
Therefore with Everyman I will go and not spare;
His good works I will help him to declare.
KNOWLEDGE   Now, Everyman, be merry and glad!
Your Good Deeds cometh now; ye may not be sad.
Now is your Good Deeds whole and sound,
Going upright upon the ground.
EVERYMAN   My heart is light and shall be evermore;
Now will I smite faster than I did before.
GOOD DEEDS   Everyman, pilgrim, my special friend,
630   Blessed be thou without end!
For thee is prepared the eternal glory.
Ye have me made whole and sound,
Therefore I will bide by thee in every stound.[15]
EVERYMAN   Welcome, my Good Deeds! Now I hear thy voice
I weep for very sweetness of love.
KNOWLEDGE   Be no more sad, but ever rejoice;
God seeth thy living in his throne above.

Knowledge gives Everyman the garment of contrition.

15. Instance, occasion

Put on this garment to thy behove,[16]
Which is wet with your tears,
640   Or else before God you may it miss
When you to your journey's end come shall.
EVERYMAN   Gentle knowledge, what do ye it call?
KNOWLEDGE   It is the garment of sorrow;
From pain it will you borrow.
Contrition it is
That getteth forgiveness;
It pleaseth God passing well.
GOOD DEEDS   Everyman, will you wear it for your heal?[17]

Everyman puts on the garment of contrition.

EVERYMAN   Now blesséd be Jesu, Mary's Son,
650   For now have I on true contrition;
And let us go now without tarrying.
Good Deeds, have we clear our reckoning?
GOOD DEEDS   Yea, indeed, I have it here.
EVERYMAN   Then I trust we need not fear.
Now, friends, let us not part in twain.
KNOWLEDGE   Nay, Everyman, that will we not, certain.
GOOD DEEDS   Yet must thou lead with thee
Three persons of great might.
EVERYMAN   Who should they be?
660   GOOD DEEDS   Discretion and Strength they hight,[18]
And thy Beauty may not abide behind.
KNOWLEDGE   Also ye must call to mind
Your Five Wits as for your counsellors.
GOOD DEEDS   You must have them ready at all hours.
EVERYMAN   How shall I get them hither?
KNOWLEDGE   You must call them all together,
And they will hear you incontinent.[19]
EVERYMAN   My friends, come hither and be present:
Discretion, Strength, my Five Wits, and Beauty.

Enter Discretion, Strength, Five Wits, and Beauty.

670   BEAUTY   Here at your will we be all ready.
What would ye that we should do?

16. Benefit
17. Salvation
18. Are called
19. At once

GOOD DEEDS   That ye would with Everyman go
    And help him in his pilgrimage.
    Advise you, will ye with him or not in that voyage?
STRENGTH   We will bring him all thither
    To his help and comfort, ye may believe me.
DISCRETION   So will we go with him all together.
EVERYMAN   Almighty God, loved may thou be!
    I give thee laud that I have hither brought
680   Strength, Discretion, Beauty and Five Wits. Lack I naught;
    And my Good Deeds, with Knowledge clear,
    All be in company at my will here.
    I desire no more to my business.
STRENGTH   And I, Strength, will by you stand in distress,
    Though thou would in battle fight on the ground.
FIVE WITS   And though it were through the world round,
    We will not depart for sweet nor sour.
BEAUTY   No more will I unto death's hour,
    Whatsoever thereof befall.
690 DISCRETION   Everyman, advise you first of all;
    Go with a good advisement and deliberation.
    We all give you virtuous monition
    That all shall be well.
EVERYMAN   My friends, hearken what I will tell:
    I pray God reward you in his heavenly sphere.
    Now hearken, all that be here,
    For I will make my testament
    Here before you all present:
    In alms, half my goods I will give with my hands twain
700   In the way of charity with good intent,
    And the other half still shall remain
    In queth,[20] to be returned where it ought to be.
    This I do in despite of the fiend of hell,
    To go quite out of his peril
    Ever after and this day.
KNOWLEDGE   Everyman, hearken what I say:
    Go to Priesthood, I you advise,
    And receive of him in any wise
    The holy sacrament and ointment together;
710   Then shortly see ye turn again hither.
    We will all abide you here.
FIVE WITS   Yea, Everyman, hie you that ye ready were.

---

20. As a bequest; though the remainder of the line indicates that it is
    actually a restitution of illegally acquired property.

There is no emperor, king, duke, nor baron
That of God hath commission
As hath the least priest in the world being;
For of the blessèd sacraments pure and benign,
He beareth the keys, and thereof hath the cure
For man's redemption—it is ever sure—
Which God for our soul's medicine
720   Gave us out of his heart with great pine.[21]
Here in this transitory life, for thee and me,
The blessed sacraments seven there be:
Baptism, confirmation with priesthood good,
And the sacrament of God's precious flesh and blood,
Marriage, the holy extreme unction, and penance.
These seven be good to have in remembrance,
Gracious sacraments of high divinity.

EVERYMAN   Fain would I receive that holy body,
And meekly to my ghostly[22] father I will go.

730   FIVE WITS   Everyman, that is the best that ye can do.
God will you to salvation bring,
For priesthood exceedeth all other things:
To us holy scripture they do teach
And converteth man from sin, Heaven to reach;
God hath to them more power given
Than to any angel that is in Heaven.
With five words he may consecrate,
God's body in flesh and blood to make,
And handleth his Maker between his hands.
740   The priest bindeth and unbindeth all bands,
Both in earth and in Heaven.
Thou ministers all the sacraments seven;
Though we kissed thy feet, thou were worthy.
Thou art surgeon that cureth sin deadly;
No remedy we find under God
But all only priesthood.
Everyman, God gave priests that dignity
And setteth them in his stead among us to be;
Thus be they above angels in degree.

Exit Everyman.

750   KNOWLEDGE   If priests be good, it is so, surely.
But when Jesu hanged on the cross with great smart,
There he gave, out of his blessèd heart,

21. Anguish, torment
22. Spiritual

The seven sacraments in great torment;
He sold them not to us, that Lord omnipotent;
Therefore Saint Peter the apostle doth say
That Jesu's curse hath all they
Which God their Saviour do buy or sell,
Or they for any money do take or tell.[23]
760   Sinful priests giveth the sinners example bad;
Their children sitteth by other men's fires, I have heard;
And some haunteth women's company
With unclean life, as lusts of lechery;
These be with sin made blind.
FIVE WITS I trust to God no such may we find;
Therefore let us priesthood honor
And follow their doctrine for our souls' succour.
We be their sheep, and they shepherds be
By whom we all be kept in surety.
Peace! For yonder I see Everyman come,
770   Which hath made true satisfaction.
GOOD DEEDS Methinks it is he indeed.

Re-enter Everyman.

EVERYMAN Now Jesu be your alder speed![24]
I have received the sacrament for my redemption
And then mine extreme unction.
Blessèd be all they that counselled me to take it!
And now, friends, let us go without longer respite.
I thank God that ye have tarried so long.
Now set each of you on this rood your hand
And shortly follow me.
780   I go before where I would be. God be our guide!

They go toward the grave.

STRENGTH Everyman, we will not from you go
Till ye have done this voyage long.
DISCRETION I, Discretion, will bide by you also.
KNOWLEDGE And though this pilgrimage be never so strong,
I will never part you from.
STRENGTH Everyman, I will be as sure by thee
As ever I did by Judas Maccabee.[25]

23. Count out, as in bank teller
24. Help to all of you
25. A Jewish leader of the second century B.C., known for his courage (1 Macc. 3)

They arrive at the grave.

EVERYMAN   Alas, I am so faint I may not stand;
  My limbs under me do fold.
790 Friends, let us not turn again to this land,
  Not for all the world's gold;
  For into this cave must I creep
  And turn to earth, and thereto sleep.
BEAUTY   What, into this grave? Alas!
EVERYMAN   Yea, there shall ye consume, more and less.[26]
BEAUTY   And what, should I smother here?
EVERYMAN   Yea, by my faith, and never more appear.
  In this world live no more we shall,
  But in Heaven before the highest Lord of all.
800 BEAUTY   I cross out all this. Adieu, by Saint John!
  I take my tap in my lap and am gone.[27]
EVERYMAN   What, Beauty, whither will ye?
BEAUTY   Peace! I am deaf. I look not behind me,
  Not if thou wouldest give me all the gold in thy chest.

             Exit Beauty.

EVERYMAN   Alas, whereto may I trust?
  Beauty goeth fast away from me.
  She promised with me to live and die.
STRENGTH   Everyman, I will thee also forsake and deny;
  Thy game liketh me not at all.
810 EVERYMAN   Why, then, ye will forsake me all?
  Sweet Strength, tarry a little space.
STRENGTH   Nay, sir, by the rood of grace!
  I will hie me from thee fast,
  Though thou weep till thy heart to-brast.[28]
EVERYMAN   Ye would ever bide by me, ye said.
STRENGTH   Yea, I have you far enough conveyed.
  Ye be old enough, I understand,
  Your pilgrimage to take in hand.
  I repent me that I hither came.
820 EVERYMAN   Strength, you to displease I am to blame;
  Yet promise is debt, this ye well wot.[29]
STRENGTH   In faith, I care not.

---

26. The grave devours all, both the great and the small.
27. A tap is an unspun tuft of wool or flax. Hence, like a peasant housewife, Beauty
  is saying, "I'm pocketing my spinning materials and am off."
28. Bursts in two
29. Know

Thou art but a fool to complain;
You spend your speech and waste your brain.
Go thrust thee into the ground!

Exit Strength.

EVERYMAN   I had thought surer I should you have found.
He that trusteth in his Strength,
She him deceiveth at the length.
Both Strength and Beauty forsaketh me;
830   Yet they promised me fair and lovingly.
DISCRETION   Everyman, I will after Strength be gone.
As for me, I will leave you alone.
EVERYMAN   Why, Discretion, will ye forsake me?
DISCRETION   Yea, in faith, I will go from thee;
For when Strength goeth before,
I follow after evermore.
EVERYMAN   Yet, I pray thee, for the love of the Trinity,
Look in my grave once piteously.
DISCRETION   Nay, so nigh will I not come.
840   Farewell, everyone!

Exit Discretion.

EVERYMAN   O, all things faileth, save God alone—
Beauty, Strength and Discretion;
For when Death bloweth his blast,
They all run from me full fast.
FIVE WITS   Everyman, my leave now of thee I take.
I will follow the others, for here I thee forsake.
EVERYMAN   Alas, then may I wail and weep,
For I took you for my best friend.
FIVE WITS   I will no longer thee keep.
850   Now farewell, and there an end.

Exit Five Wits.

EVERYMAN   O Jesu, help! All hath forsaken me.
GOOD DEEDS   Nay, Everyman, I will bide with thee.
I will not forsake thee in deed;
Thou shalt find me a good friend in need.
EVERYMAN   Gramercy, Good Deeds! Now may I true friends see.
They have forsaken me, every one;
I loved them better than my Good Deeds alone.
Knowledge, will ye forsake me also?
KNOWLEDGE   Yea, Everyman, when ye to Death shall go;
860   But not yet, for no manner of danger.
EVERYMAN   Gramercy, Knowledge, with all my heart.
KNOWLEDGE   Nay, yet I will not from hence depart
Till I see where ye shall be come.

EVERYMAN   Methinks, alas, that I must be gone
  To make my reckoning and my debts pay,
  For I see my time is nigh spent away.
  Take example, all ye that this do hear or see,
  How they that I loved best do forsake me,
  Except my Good Deeds that bideth truly.
870 GOOD DEEDS   All earthly things is but vanity:
  Beauty, Strength and Discretion do man forsake,
  Foolish friends and kinsmen that fair spake—
  All fleeth save Good Deeds, and that am I.
EVERYMAN   Have mercy on me, God most mighty,
  And stand by me, thou mother and maid, Holy Mary!
GOOD DEEDS   Fear not, I will speak for thee.
EVERYMAN   Here I cry God mercy.
GOOD DEEDS   Shorten our end, and diminish our pain;
  Let us go and never come again.

Good Deeds leads Everyman into grave.

880 EVERYMAN   Into thy hands, Lord, my soul I commend;
  Receive it, Lord, that it be not lost.
  As thou me boughtest, so me defend
  And save me from the fiend's boast,
  That I may appear with that blessèd host
  That shall be saved at the day of doom.
  In manus tuas, of mights most
  Forever, *commendo spiritum meum.*[30]

        Exeunt Everyman and Good Deeds.

KNOWLEDGE   Now hath he suffered that we all shall endure;
  The Good Deeds shall make all sure.
890   Now hath he made ending;
  Methinks that I hear angels sing
  And make great joy and melody
  Where Everyman's soul received shall be.

Enter Angel.

THE ANGEL   Come, excellent elect spouse, to Jesu!
  Here above thou shalt go
  Because of thy singular virtue.
  Now thy soul is taken thy body from,
  Thy reckoning is crystal clear.

---

30. *In manus tuas . . . commendo spiritum meum:* Into thy hands I commend my spirit.

Now shalt thou into the heavenly sphere,
900   Unto the which all ye shall come
That liveth well before the day of doom.

Exeunt Angel and Knowledge.

Enter Doctor.

DOCTOR   This moral men may have in mind.
Ye hearers, take it of worth, old and young,
And forsake Pride, for he deceiveth you in the end;
And remember Beauty, Five Wits, Strength, and Discretion,
They all at the last do Everyman forsake,
Save his Good Deeds there doth he take.
But beware, for if they be small,
Before God he hath no help at all:
No excuse may be there for Everyman.
910   Alas, how shall he do then?
For after death amends may no man make,
For then mercy and pity doth him forsake.
If his reckoning be not clear when he doth come,
God will say, *"Ite, maledicti, in ignem eternum."*[31]
And he that hath his account whole and sound,
High in Heaven he shall be crowned;
Unto which place God bring us all thither,
That we may live body and soul together.
Thereto help the Trinity!
920   Amen, say ye, for saint charity.

Exit Doctor.

Thus endeth this moral play of Everyman.

31. Go, sinners, into eternal fire.

TRAGEDY IN THE RENAISSANCE ENGLISH THEATER

The first recorded production of Shakespeare's tragedy *Othello* took place in 1604 in the Globe theater, a public playhouse capable of accommodating between two and three thousand spectators. Despite its large seating capacity, the Globe, like other theaters in Renaissance England, created an intimate experience of drama, as we can tell by considering its physical dimensions and design. The Globe was a circular or polygonally shaped building, approximately eighty-four feet in diameter and thirty-three feet high. Its height was sufficient to accommodate three levels of galleries for spectators. The area enclosed by the galleries was approximately fifty-five feet in diameter. Into this space extended an acting platform approximately

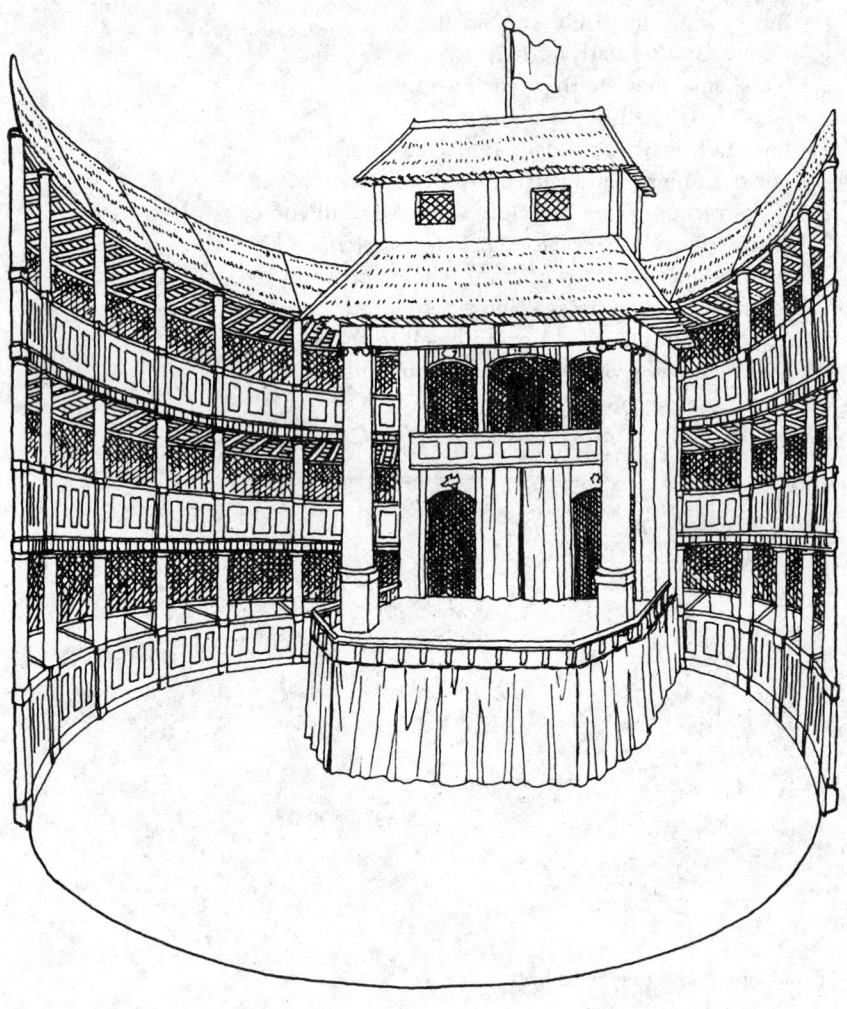

forty-three feet wide and about twenty-seven feet deep, leaving a sizable area of ground surrounding the stage for standing spectators.

We can readily see that this arrangement must have created an intimate relationship between actors and members of the audience. Since the actors were surrounded on three sides by spectators in the yard and the galleries, they were in fact much closer to one another than in our smaller modern theaters where actors and spectators are physically set off from one another by the framed and curtained stage. The Renaissance audience could see the actors up close—which meant that the actors had to pay meticulous attention to all their gestures and facial expressions. Most significantly, that physical intimacy necessarily must have aroused in the spectators a very immediate and personal engagement in the action of the play. In another respect, however, drama in the Renaissance English theater was a very public and communal affair, for the yard area was open to the sky, and plays were thus performed in full daylight. As they sat in the galleries or stood in the yard, the spectators could easily see one another, as well as the actors.

The stage itself consisted of two acting levels. The main area was the platform jutting into the yard; at the rear of the platform on each side were doors for entrances and exits. Between the doors was a curtained inner stage for use in "discoveries" and special dramatic situations, such as the bedchamber scene in the final act of *Othello*. Above this inner stage was the second acting level, a gallery, which could be used for balcony scenes, such as when Brabantio is awakened by Roderigo and Iago and appears at the window of his house in Act I of *Othello*. The gallery was used also for musicians, or even for spectators when it was not required for the performance. Directly above the gallery was a roof covering the rear half of the acting platform. As we can see from these arrangements, Shakespeare's stage was a remarkably flexible one, allowing action to be set in a number of different areas, and allowing, too, for rapid entrances and exits of the sort that take place during Cassio's drunken quarrel with Roderigo and Montano in Act II of *Othello*.

Flexibility in staging resulted also from the fact that scenery was not used in the Globe Theater. The stage was understood to stand for whatever setting was implied by the action and from whatever props were placed on stage. Thus when the Duke and Senators appeared in Act I, Scene 3, of *Othello*, the table and chairs provided for them on stage would have been enough to indicate that the scene was taking place at court. Their costuming, however, was sumptuous, and by that means the actors were able to create a vivid spectacle, particularly by contrast with their spare surroundings. In that scene at the Duke's court, for example, the actors would have been richly arrayed in Renaissance styles of dress appropriate to a Duke and his Senators.

Even though the English theater of the Renaissance did not create a realistic or by any means complete scenic illusion of the sort we are accustomed to on the modern stage, it set forth a vividly human and symbolic spectacle—a spectacle, in fact, that would have been regarded by the audience as embodying universal significance. For when the actors appeared on stage, they were also understood to be standing between the heavens implied by that roof above them and hell implied by the space beneath the stage. Thus, when the audience witnessed the action of *Othello*, they would have regarded it not only as representing the catastrophe of a particular man who is undone by an officer he trusts more than his wife, but also as presenting a spectacle of universal significance about the conflict of good and evil.

WILLIAM SHAKESPEARE
1554–1615

Born and raised in Stratford-upon-Avon, where his father was a glover, tanner, and dealer in hides, Shakespeare was educated locally at the King's New School and there acquired some familiarity with the classics, particularly in Latin language and literature, but did not go on to attend one of the universities. Instead, he went off to London, probably attracted by the touring theatrical companies of the period, to make a career for himself as an actor and dramatist. He made his way to London sometime in the late 1580s, when public theater was just beginning to become a popular enterprise in the city, and no doubt started out as an actor with one of the local companies. By 1590, his earliest plays were being produced, and during his remaining twenty-three years of involvement with the theater he wrote thirty-seven plays, as well as becoming a leading actor and shareholder in one of the major theatrical companies of the period. His plays cover a broad range of dramatic modes, extending from the comedies and history plays that figured largely in his early career, through the problem plays, tragedies, and romances that predominated in his later career. His plays reflect an equally broad range of experience, extending from the English battle scenes and tavern life of *1 Henry IV*, to the Roman and Egyptian court scenes of *Antony and Cleopatra*, to the fantastic island world of *The Tempest*. Like most of his contemporaries he borrowed ideas for many of his works from classical, continental, or native sources. But he always transformed the material that he borrowed into strikingly original plays, as when he turned a brief and rambling Italian story into one of his most tightly constructed and complexly motivated tragedies, *Othello*.

The Tragedy of Othello
The Moor of Venice

CHARACTERS

DUKE OF VENICE
BRABANTIO, a senator, father to Desdemona
SENATORS OF VENICE
GRATIANO, brother to Brabantio, a noble Venetian
LODOVICO, kinsman to Brabantio, a noble Venetian
OTHELLO, the Moor, in the military service of Venice
CASSIO, an honorable lieutenant to Othello
IAGO, Othello's ensign, a villain
RODERIGO, a gulled gentleman
MONTANO, governor of Cyprus
CLOWN, servant to Othello
DESDEMONA, daughter to Brabantio and wife to Othello
EMILIA, wife to Iago
BIANCA, a courtesan
GENTLEMEN, SAILORS, OFFICERS, MESSENGERS, HERALD, MUSICIANS, ATTENDANTS

Scene: Venice and Cyprus

ACT I

SCENE 1

Enter Roderigo and Iago.

RODERIGO   Tush, never tell me! I take it much unkindly
    That thou, Iago, who hast had my purse
    As if the strings were thine, shouldst know of this.[1]
IAGO   'Sblood, but you will not hear me!
    If ever I did dream of such a matter,
    Abhor me.
RODERIGO   Thou told'st me thou didst hold him[2] in thy hate.
IAGO   Despise me if I do not. Three great ones of the city,
    In personal suit to make me his lieutenant,

---

1. Desdemona's elopement with Othello   2. Othello

10   Off-capped to him; and, by the faith of man,
        I know my price; I am worth no worse a place.
        But he, as loving his own pride and purposes,
        Evades them with a bombast circumstance.
        Horribly stuffed with epithets of war;
        And, in conclusion,
        Nonsuits[3] my mediators; for, "Certes," says he,
        "I have already chose my officer."
        And what was he?
        Forsooth, a great arithmetician,[4]
20   One Michael Cassio, a Florentine
        (A fellow almost damned in a fair wife)[5]
        That never set a squadron in the field,
        Nor the division of a battle knows
        More than a spinster;[6] unless the bookish theoric,
        Wherein the togèd consuls[7] can propose
        As masterly as he. Mere prattle without practice
        Is all his soldiership. But he, sir, had th' election;
        And I (of whom his eyes had seen the proof
        At Rhodes, at Cyprus, and on other grounds
30   Christian and heathen) must be belee'd and calmed[8]
        By debitor and creditor; this counter-caster,[9]
        He, in good time, must his lieutenant be,
        And I—God bless the mark!—his Moorship's ancient.[10]
RODERIGO   By heaven, I rather would have been his hangman.
IAGO   Why, there's no remedy; 'tis the curse of service.
        Preferment[11] goes by letter and affection,[12]
        And not by old gradation,[13] where each second
        Stood heir to th' first. Now, sir, be judge yourself,
        Whether I in any just term am affined[14]
        To love the Moor.
40   RODERIGO   I would not follow him then.
IAGO   O, sir, content you;
        I follow him to serve my turn upon him.

---

3. Rejects
4. Person skilled in military calculations, but not in actual warfare
5. *almost . . . wife:* unexplainable phrase. Cassio is not married, nor is he about to be married. In the Italian novella that was the source for Shakespeare's play, Cassio is married, and perhaps Shakespeare intended to follow the novella when he began writing the play.
6. Spinner of thread; i.e., housewife

7. Senators dressed in togas; i.e., clothed for the council chamber, not the battlefield
8. Have the wind taken out of my sails and left becalmed
9. Accountant
10. Ensign, standard-bearer
11. Advancement
12. Personal favoritism
13. Seniority
14. Bound

We cannot all be masters, nor all masters
Cannot be truly followed. You shall mark
Many a duteous and knee-crooking knave
That, doting on his own obsequious bondage, -
Wears out his time, much like his master's ass,
For naught but provender; and when he's old, cashiered.[15]
Whip me such honest knaves! Others there are
50   Who, trimmed in forms and visages of duty,
Keep yet their hearts attending on themselves;
And, throwing but shows of service on their lords,
Do well thrive by them, and when they have lined their coats,
Do themselves homage. These fellows have some soul;
And such a one do I profess myself. For, sir,
It is as sure as you are Roderigo,
Were I the Moor, I would not be Iago. ·
In following him, I follow but myself;
Heaven is my judge, not I for love and duty,
60   But seeming so, for my own peculiar[16] end;
For when my outward action doth demonstrate
The native act and figure of my heart
In compliment extern,[17] 'tis not long after
But I will wear my heart upon my sleeve
For daws to peck at; I am not what I am.

RODERIGO   What a full fortune does the thick-lips owe[18]
If he can carry't thus!

IAGO   Call up her father,
Rouse him. Make after him, poison his delight,
Proclaim him in the streets. Incense her kinsmen,
70   And though he in a fertile climate dwell,
Plague him with flies; though that his joy be joy,
Yet throw such changes of vexation on't
As it may lose some color.

RODERIGO   Here is her father's house. I'll call aloud.

IAGO   Do, with like timorous[19] accent and dire yell
As when, by night and negligence, the fire
Is spied in populous cities.

RODERIGO   What, ho, Brabantio! Signior Brabantio, ho!

IAGO   Awake! What, ho, Brabantio! Thieves! thieves! thieves!
80   Look to your house, your daughter, and your bags!
Thieves! thieves!

15. Dismissed
16. Personal
17. External show

18. Own
19. Terrifying

Brabantio at a window.

BRABANTIO [*above*]   What is the reason of this terrible summons?
    What is the matter there?
RODERIGO   Signior, is all your family within?
IAGO   Are your doors locked?
BRABANTIO   Why, wherefore ask you this?
IAGO   Zounds, sir, y'are robbed! For shame, put on your gown!
    Your heart is burst; you have lost half your soul.
    Even now, now, very now, an old black ram
    Is tupping your white ewe. Arise, arise!
90   Awake the snorting[20] citizens with the bell,
    Or else the devil will make a grandsire of you.
    Arise, I say!
BRABANTIO   What, have you lost your wits?
RODERIGO   Most reverend signior, do you know my voice?
BRABANTIO   Not I. What are you?
RODERIGO   My name is Roderigo.
BRABANTIO   The worser welcome!
    I have charged thee not to haunt about my doors.
    In honest plainness thou hast heard me say
    My daughter is not for thee; and now, in madness,
    Being full of supper and distemp'ring[21] draughts,
100   Upon malicious bravery[22] dost thou come
    To start[23] my quiet.
RODERIGO   Sir, sir, sir—
BRABANTIO   But thou must needs be sure
    My spirit and my place have in them power
    To make this bitter to thee.
RODERIGO   Patience, good sir.
BRABANTIO   What tell'st thou me of robbing? This is Venice;
    My house is not a grange.[24]
RODERIGO   Most grave Brabantio,
    In simple and pure soul I come to you.
IAGO   Zounds, sir, you are one of those that will not serve God if the
    devil bid you. Because we come to do you service, and you think we are
110   ruffians, you'll have your daughter covered with a Barbary horse; you'll
    have your nephews[25] neigh to you; you'll have coursers for cousins,[26]
    and gennets for germans.[27]
BRABANTIO   What profane wretch art thou?

20. Snoring
21. Intoxicating
22. Bravado
23. Upset

24. Isolated farmhouse
25. Grandsons
26. Horses for kinsmen
27. Spanish horses for close relatives

IAGO   I am one, sir, that comes to tell you your daughter and the Moor
 are now making the beast with two backs.
BRABANTIO   Thou art a villain.
IAGO   You are—a senator.
120 BRABANTIO   This thou shalt answer. I know thee, Roderigo.
RODERIGO   Sir, I will answer anything. But I beseech you,
 If't be your pleasure and most wise consent,
 As partly I find it is, that your fair daughter,
 At this odd-even[28] and dull watch o' th' night,
 Transported, with no worse nor better guard
 But with a knave of common hire, a gondolier,
 To the gross clasps of a lascivious Moor—
 If this be known to you, and your allowance,
 We then have done you bold and saucy[29] wrongs;
130 But if you know not this, my manners tell me
 We have your wrong rebuke. Do not believe
 That, from the sense of[30] all civility,
 I thus would play and trifle with your reverence.
 Your daughter, if you have not given her leave,
 I say again, hath made a gross revolt,
 Tying her duty, beauty, wit, and fortunes
 In an extravagant and wheeling[31] stranger
 Of here and everywhere. Straight satisfy yourself.
 If she be in her chamber, or your house,
140 Let loose on me the justice of the state
 For thus deluding you.
BRABANTIO   Strike on the tinder, ho!
 Give me a taper! Call up all my people!
 This accident[32] is not unlike my dream.
 Belief of it oppresses me already.
 Light, I say! Light!   Exit above.
IAGO   Farewell, for I must leave you.
 It seems not meet, nor wholesome to my place,
 To be produced—as, if I stay, I shall—
 Against the Moor. For I do know the state,
 However this may gall him with some check,[33]
150 Cannot with safety cast[34] him; for he's embarked
 With such loud reason to the Cyprus wars,
 Which even now stand in act,[35] that for their souls

28. Around midnight, when the end of one
 day is indistinguishable from the beginning of the next
29. Insolent
30. Contrary to

31. Wandering and roving
32. Occurrence
33. Reprimand
34. Dismiss
35. Are underway

Another of his fathom[36] they have none
To lead their business; in which regard,
Though I do hate him as I do hell-pains,
Yet, for necessity of present life,
I must show out a flag and sign of love,
Which is indeed but sign. That you shall surely find him,
Lead to the Sagittary[37] the raisèd search;
160   And there will I be with him. So farewell.   *Exit.*

Enter, below, Brabantio, and Servants with torches.

BRABANTIO   It is too true an evil. Gone she is;
And what's to come of my despisèd time
Is naught but bitterness. Now, Roderigo,
Where didst thou see her?—O unhappy girl!—
With the Moor, say'st thou?—Who would be a father?—
How didst thou know 'twas she?—O, she deceives me
Past thought!—What said she to you?—Get more tapers!
Raise all my kindred!—Are they married, think you?
RODERIGO   Truly I think they are.
170   BRABANTIO   O heaven! How got she out? O treason of the blood!
Fathers, from hence trust not your daughters' minds
By what you see them act. Is there not charms
By which the property[38] of youth and maidhood
May be abused? Have you not read, Roderigo,
Of some such thing?
RODERIGO   Yes, sir, I have indeed.
BRABANTIO   Call up my brother.—O, would you had had her!—
Some one way, some another.—Do you know
Where we may apprehend her and the Moor?
RODERIGO   I think I can discover him, if you please
180   To get good guard and go along with me.
BRABANTIO   Pray you lead on. At every house I'll call;
I may command at most.—Get weapons, ho!
And raise some special officers of night.—
On, good Roderigo; I'll deserve[39] your pains.   *Exeunt.*

SCENE 2

Enter Othello, Iago, and Attendants with torches.

IAGO   Though in the trade of war I have slain men,

---

36. Ability   38. Nature
37. An inn   39. Reward

Yet do I hold it very stuff o' th' conscience
To do no contrived murther. I lack iniquity
Sometimes to do me service. Nine or ten times
I had thought t' have yerked[40] him here under the ribs.

OTHELLO   'Tis better as it is.

IAGO   Nay, but he prated,
And spoke such scurvy and provoking terms
Against your honor
That with the little godliness I have
10   I did full hard forbear him.[41] But I pray you, sir,
Are you fast married? Be assured of this,
That the magnifico[42] is much beloved,
And hath in his effect a voice potential
As double as the duke's.[43] He will divorce you,
Or put upon you what restraint and grievance
The law, with all his might to enforce it on,
Will give him cable.[44]

OTHELLO   Let him do his spite.
My services which I have done the signiory[45]
Shall out-tongue his complaints. 'Tis yet to know[46]—
20   Which, when I know that boasting is an honor,
I shall promulgate—I fetch my life and being
From men of royal siege;[47] and my demerits[48]
May speak unbonneted[49] to as proud a fortune
As this that I have reached. For know, Iago,
But that I love the gentle Desdemona,
I would not my unhoused[50] free condition
Put into circumscription and confine
For the sea's worth.

Enter Cassio, Officers, with torches.

                        But look, what lights come yond?

IAGO   Those are the raisèd father and his friends.
You were best go in.

30   OTHELLO   Not I; I must be found.

---

40. Stabbed
41. *did . . . him:* had great difficulty restraining myself from attacking him
42. Venetian nobleman (Brabantio)
43. *voice . . . duke's:* influence so strong it is like having two votes, as does the Duke of Venice
44. Scope
45. Venetian government
46. Still not known
47. Rank
48. Merits
49. Without taking my hat off; i.e., on equal terms
50. Unconfined

My parts,[51] my title, and my perfect soul[52]
Shall manifest me rightly. Is it they?

IAGO   By Janus, I think no.

OTHELLO   The servants of the duke, and my lieutenant.
The goodness of the night upon you, friends!
What is the news?

CASSIO   The duke does greet you, general;
And he requires your haste-post-haste appearance
Even on the instant.

OTHELLO   What's the matter, think you?

CASSIO   Something from Cyprus, as I may divine.
40   It is a business of some heat. The galleys
Have sent a dozen sequent[53] messengers
This very night at one another's heels,
And many of the consuls, raised and met,
Are at the duke's already. You have been hotly called for;
When, being not at your lodging to be found,
The Senate hath sent about three several quests
To search you out.

OTHELLO   'Tis well I am found by you.
I will but spend a word here in the house,
And go with you.   *Exit.*

CASSIO   Ancient, what makes he here?
50   IAGO   Faith, he to-night hath boarded a land carack.[54]
If it prove lawful prize, he's made for ever.

CASSIO   I do not understand.

IAGO   He's married.

CASSIO   To who?

Enter Othello.

IAGO   Marry, to—Come, captain, will you go?

OTHELLO   Have with you.

CASSIO   Here comes another troop to seek for you.

Enter Brabantio, Roderigo, and others with lights and weapons.

IAGO   It is Brabantio. General, be advised.
He comes to bad intent.

51. Personal qualities   53. Consecutive
52. Clear conscience   54. Trading ship

OTHELLO   Holla! stand there!
RODERIGO   Signior, it is the Moor.
BRABANTIO   Down with him, thief!

They draw on both sides.

IAGO   You, Roderigo! Come, sir, I am for you.
OTHELLO   Keep up your bright swords, for the dew will rust them.
60   Good signior, you shall more command with years
          Than with your weapons.
BRABANTIO   O thou foul thief, where has thou stowed my daughter?
          Damned as thou art, thou hast enchanted her!
          For I'll refer me to all things of sense,[55]
          If she in chains of magic were not bound,
          Whether a maid so tender, fair, and happy,
          So opposite to marriage that she shunned
          The wealthy curlèd darlings of our nation,
          Would ever have, t' incur a general mock,
70   Run from her guardage to the sooty bosom
          Of such a thing as thou—to fear, not to delight.
          Judge me the world if 'tis not gross in sense[56]
          That thou hast practiced on her with foul charms,
          Abused her delicate youth with drugs or minerals
          That weaken motion.[57] I'll have't disputed on;[58]
          'Tis probable, and palpable to thinking.
          I therefore apprehend and do attach[59] thee
          For an abuser of the world, a practicer
          Of arts inhibited and out of warrant.[60]
80   Lay hold upon him. If he do resist,
          Subdue him at his peril.
OTHELLO   Hold your hands,
          Both you of my inclining and the rest.
          Were it my cue to fight, I should have known it
          Without a prompter. Where will you that I go
          To answer this your charge?
BRABANTIO   To prison, till fit time
          Of law and course of direct session
          Call thee to answer.
OTHELLO   What if I do obey?

55. *refer . . . sense:* appeal to common sense   59. Arrest
56. Obvious   60. *inhibited . . . warrant:* prohibited and
57. Senses and mental powers   illegal
58. Tried in court

How may the duke be therewith satisfied,
Whose messengers are here about my side
90 Upon some present business of the state
To bring me to him?

OFFICER   'Tis true, most worthy signior.
The duke's in council, and your noble self
I am sure is sent for.

BRABANTIO   How? The duke in council?
In this time of the night? Bring him away.
Mine's not an idle[61] cause. The duke himself,
Or any of my brothers of the state,
Cannot but feel this wrong as 'twere their own;
For if such actions may have passage free,
Bondslaves and pagans shall our statesmen be.   *Exeunt.*

SCENE 3

Enter Duke and Senators, set at a table, with lights and Attendants.

DUKE   There is no composition[62] in these news
That gives them credit.

1. SENATOR   Indeed they are disproportioned.
My letters say a hundred and seven galleys.

DUKE   And mine a hundred forty.

2. SENATOR   And mine two hundred.
But though they jump[63] not on a just account—
As in these cases where the aim[64] reports
'Tis oft with difference—yet do they all confirm
A Turkish fleet, and bearing up to Cyprus.

DUKE   Nay, it is possible enough to judgment.
10 I do not so secure me in the error[65]
But the main article I do approve[66]
In fearful sense.

SAILOR [*within*]   What, ho! what, ho! what, ho!

OFFICER   A messenger from the galleys.

Enter Sailor.

DUKE   Now, what's the business?

61. Trivial   64. Conjecture
62. Consistency   65. *secure . . . error:* rely on inconsistencies
63. Agree   66. Accept

SAILOR   The Turkish preparation makes for Rhodes.
         So was I bid report here to the state
         By Signior Angelo.
DUKE   How say you by this change?
1. SENATOR   This cannot be
         By no assay[67] of reason. 'Tis a pageant
         To keep us in false gaze.[68] When we consider
20   Th' importancy of Cyprus to the Turk,
         And let ourselves again but understand
         That, as it more concerns the Turk than Rhodes,
         So may he with more facile question bear it,[69]
         For that it stands not in such warlike brace,[70]
         But altogether lacks th' abilities
         That Rhodes is dressed in—if we make thought of this,
         We must not think the Turk is so unskillful
         To leave that latest which concerns him first,
         Neglecting an attempt of ease and gain
30   To wake and wage[71] a danger profitless.
DUKE   Nay, in all confidence he's not for Rhodes.
OFFICER   Here is more news.

Enter a Messenger.

MESSENGER   The Ottomites, reverend and gracious,
         Steering with due course toward the isle of Rhodes,
         Have there injointed them with an after fleet.
1. SENATOR   Ay, so I thought. How many, as you guess?
MESSENGER   Of thirty sail; and now they do restem
         Their backward course, bearing with frank appearance
         Their purposes toward Cyprus. Signior Montano,
40   Your trusty and most valiant servitor,
         With his free duty[72] recommends[73] you thus,
         And prays you to believe him.
DUKE   'Tis certain then for Cyprus.
         Marcus Luccicos, is not he in town?
1. SENATOR   He's now in Florence.
DUKE   Write from us to him; post, post-haste dispatch.

Enter Barbantio, Othello, Cassio, Iago, Roderigo, and Officers.

67. Test
68. Looking the wrong way
69. More easily capture
70. Preparedness
71. Risk
72. Freely given expression of loyalty
73. Informs

1. SENATOR   Here comes Brabantio and the valiant Moor.

DUKE   Valiant Othello, we must straight employ you
    Against the general enemy Ottoman.
50   *[To Brabantio]* I did not see you. Welcome, gentle signior.
    We lacked your counsel and your help to-night.

BRABANTIO   So did I yours. Good your grace, pardon me.
    Neither my place, nor aught I heard of business,
    Hath raised me from my bed; nor doth the general care
    Take hold on me; for my particular grief
    Is of so floodgate[74] and o'erbearing nature
    That it engluts and swallows other sorrows,
    And it is still itself.

DUKE   Why, what's the matter?

BRABANTIO   My daughter! O, my daughter!

ALL   Dead?

BRABANTIO   Ay, to me.
60   She is abused, stol'n from me, and corrupted
    By spells and medicines bought of mountebanks;
    For nature so prepost'rously to err,
    Being not deficient, blind, or lame of sense,
    Sans[75] witchcraft could not.

DUKE   Whoe'er he be that in this foul proceeding
    Hath thus beguiled your daughter of herself,
    And you of her, the bloody book of law
    You shall yourself read in the bitter letter
    After your own sense; yea, though our proper[76] son
    Stood in your action.[77]
70 BRABANTIO   Humbly I thank your grace.
    Here is the man—this Moor, whom now, it seems,
    Your special mandate for the state affairs
    Hath hither brought.

ALL   We are very sorry for't.

DUKE *[to Othello]*   What, in your own part, can you say to this?

BRABANTIO   Nothing, but this is so.

OTHELLO   Most potent, grave, and reverend signiors,
    My very noble, and approved good masters,
    That I have ta'en away this old man's daughter,
    It is most true; true I have married her.
80   The very head and front[78] of my offending
    Hath this extent, no more. Rude am I in my speech,

---

74. Overflowing
75. Without
76. My own

77. Were accused by you
78. The utmost

And little blessed with the soft phrase of peace;
For since these arms of mine had seven years' pith[79]
Till now some nine moons wasted, they have used
Their dearest action in the tented field;
And little of this great world can I speak
More than pertains to feats of broil and battle;
And therefore little shall I grace my cause
In speaking for myself. Yet, by your gracious patience,
90   I will a round[80] unvarnished tale deliver
Of my whole course of love—what drugs, what charms,
What conjuration, and what mighty magic
(For such proceeding am I charged withal)
I won his daughter.
BRABANTIO   A maiden never bold;
Of spirit so still and quiet that her motion
Blushed at herself;[81] and she—in spite of nature,
Of years, of country, credit, everything—
To fall in love with what she feared to look on!
It is a judgment maimed and most imperfect
100   That will confess perfection so could err
Against all rules of nature, and must be driven
To find out practices of cunning hell
Why this should be. I therefore vouch again
That with some mixtures pow'rful o'er the blood,
Or with some dram, conjured to this effect,
He wrought upon her.
DUKE   To vouch this is no proof,
Without more certain and more overt test
Than these thin habits[82] and poor likelihoods
Of modern seeming[83] do prefer against him.
110 1. SENATOR   But, Othello, speak.
Did you by indirect and forcèd courses
Subdue and poison this young maid's affections?
Or came it by request, and such fair question
As soul to soul affordeth?
OTHELLO   I do beseech you,
Send for the lady to the Sagittary
And let her speak of me before her father.
If you do find me foul in her report,
The trust, the office, I do hold of you

79. Strength
80. Plain
81. *her motion . . . herself:* her own emo-
    tions made her blush

82. Slight appearing
83. Commonplace suppositions

Not only take away, but let your sentence
Even fall upon my life.
120 DUKE   Fetch Desdemona hither.
OTHELLO   Ancient, conduct them; you best know the place.

Exit Iago, with two or three Attendants.

And till she come, as truly as to heaven
I do confess the vices of my blood,
So justly to your grave ears I'll present
How I did thrive in this fair lady's love,
And she in mine.
DUKE   Say it, Othello.
OTHELLO   Her father loved me, oft invited me;
Still questioned me the story of my life
130 From year to year—the battles, sieges, fortunes
That I have passed.
I ran it through, even from my boyish days
To th' very moment that he bade me tell it.
Wherein I spake of most disastrous chances,
Of moving accidents by flood and field;
Of hairbreadth scapes i' th' imminent deadly breach;
Of being taken by the insolent foe
And sold to slavery; of my redemption thence
And portance[84] in my travel's history;
140 Wherein of anters[85] vast and deserts idle,[86]
Rough quarries, rocks, and hills whose heads touch heaven,
It was my hint to speak—such was the process;
And of the Cannibals that each other eat,
The Anthropophagi,[87] and men whose heads
Do grow beneath their shoulders. This to hear
Would Desdemona seriously incline;
But still the house affairs would draw her thence;
Which ever as she could with haste dispatch,
150 She'ld come again, and with a greedy ear
Devour up my discourse. Which I observing,
Took once a pliant[88] hour, and found good means
To draw from her a prayer of earnest heart
That I would all my pilgrimage dilate,[89]
Whereof by parcels[90] she had something heard,
But not intentively.[91] I did consent,
And often did beguile her of her tears

84. Behavior
85. Caves
86. Barren
87. Man-eaters

88. Convenient
89. Relate
90. In bits and pieces
91. With full attention

When I did speak of some distressful stroke
That my youth suffered. My story being done,
She gave me for my pains a world of sighs.
160   She swore, i' faith, 'twas strange, 'twas passing strange;
'Twas pitiful, 'twas wondrous pitiful.
She wished she had not heard it; yet she wished
That heaven had made her such a man. She thanked me;
And bade me, if I had a friend that loved her,
I should but teach him how to tell my story,
And that would woo her. Upon this hint[92] I spake.
She loved me for the dangers I had passed,
And I loved her that she did pity them.
This only is the witchcraft I have used.
170   Here comes the lady. Let her witness it.

Enter Desdemona, Iago, Attendants.

DUKE   I think this tale would win my daughter too.
Good Brabantio,
Take up this mangled matter at the best.
Men do their broken weapons rather use
Than their bare hands.
BRABANTIO   I pray you hear her speak.
If she confess that she was half the wooer,
Destruction on my head if my bad blame
Light on the man! Come hither, gentle mistress.
Do you perceive in all this noble company
Where most you owe obedience?
180   DESDEMONA   My noble father,
I do perceive here a divided duty.
To you I am bound for life and education;
My life and education[93] both do learn me
How to respect you: you are the lord of duty;
I am hitherto your daughter. But here's my husband;
And so much duty as my mother showed
To you, preferring you before her father,
So much I challenge[94] that I may profess
Due to the Moor my lord.
BRABANTIO   God b' wi' ye! I have done.
190   Please if your grace, on to the state affairs.
I had rather to adopt a child than get[95] it.

92. Opportunity
93. Upbringing
94. Claim
95. Beget

Come hither, Moor.
I here do give thee that with all my heart
Which, but thou hast already, with all my heart
I would keep from thee. For your sake,[96] jewel,
I am glad at soul I have no other child;
For thy escape would teach me tyranny,
To hang clogs on them. I have done, my lord.

DUKE   Let me speak like yourself[97] and lay a sentence[98]

200   Which, as a grise[99] or step, may help these lovers
Into your favor.
When remedies are past, the griefs are ended
By seeing the worst, which late on hopes depended.
To mourn a mischief that is past and gone
Is the next way to draw new mischief on.
What cannot be preserved when fortune takes,
Patience her injury a mock'ry makes.
The robbed that smiles steals something from the thief;
He robs himself that spends a bootless[100] grief.

210   BRABANTIO   So let the Turk of Cyprus us beguile:
We lose it not so long as we can smile.
He bears the sentence well that nothing bears
But the free comfort which from thence he hears;
But he bears both the sentence and the sorrow
That to pay grief must of poor patience borrow.
These sentences, to sugar, or to gall,
Being strong on both sides, are equivocal.
But words are words. I never yet did hear
That the bruised heart was piecèd[101] through the ear.

220   Beseech you, now to the affairs of state.

DUKE   The Turk with a most mighty preparation makes for Cyprus. Othello,
the fortitude of the place is best known to you; and though we have
there a substitute of most allowed[102] sufficiency, yet opinion, a sovereign
mistress of effects,[103] throws a more safer voice on you. You must
therefore be content to slubber[104] the gloss of your new fortunes with
this more stubborn and boisterous expedition.

230   OTHELLO   The tyrant custom, most grave senators,
Hath made the flinty and steel couch of war
My thrice-driven[105] bed of down. I do agnize[106]

---

96. Because of what you have done
97. As you should
98. Maxim
99. Degree
100. Unavailing
101. Relieved

102. Acknowledged
103. Of what should be done
104. Sully
105. Thrice-winnowed; i.e., softest
106. Recognize

A natural and prompt alacrity
I find in hardness;[107] and do undertake
These present wars against the Ottomites.
Most humbly, therefore, bending to your state,
I crave fit disposition[108] for my wife,
Due reference of place, and exhibition,[109]
With such accommodation and besort[110]
As levels with her breeding.

240   DUKE   If you please,
Be't at her father's.

BRABANTIO   I'll not have it so.

OTHELLO   Nor I.

DESDEMONA   Nor I. I would not there reside,
To put my father in impatient thoughts
By being in his eye. Most gracious duke,
To my unfolding lend your prosperous[111] ear,
And let me find a charter in your voice,
To assist my simpleness.

DUKE   What would you, Desdemona?

DESDEMONA   That I did love the Moor to live with him,
250   My downright violence, and storm of fortunes,
May trumpet to the world. My heart's subdued
Even to the very quality of my lord.
I saw Othello's visage in his mind,
And to his honors and his valiant parts
Did I my soul and fortunes consecrate.
So that, dear lords, if I be left behind,
A moth of peace, and he go to the war,
The rites for which I love him are bereft me,
And I a heavy interim shall support
260   By his dear absence. Let me go with him.

OTHELLO   Let her have your voices.
Vouch with me, heaven, I therefore beg it not
To please the palate of my appetite,
Nor to comply with heat[112]—the young affects[113]
In me defunct—and proper[114] satisfaction;
But to be free and bounteous to her mind;
And heaven defend[115] your good souls that you think

107. *alacrity . . . hardness:* readiness to en-
       dure hardship
108. Suitable provision
109. *reference . . . exhibition:* assignment of
       residence and allowance of money
110. Suitable company
111. Favorable
112. Sexual desire
113. Excesses of youthful passion
114. Personal
115. Forbid

I will your serious and great business scant
For[116] she is with me. No, when light-winged toys
270 Of feathered Cupid seel[117] with wanton dullness
My speculative and officed instruments,[118]
That[119] my disports corrupt and taint my business,
Let housewives make a skillet of my helm,
And all indign[120] and base adversities
Make head against my estimation![121]

DUKE   Be it as you shall privately determine,
Either for her stay or going. Th' affair cries haste,
And speed must answer it. You must hence to-night.

DESDEMONA   To-night, my lord?

DUKE   This night.

OTHELLO   With all my heart.

280 DUKE   At nine i' th' morning here we'll meet again.
Othello, leave some officer behind,
And he shall our commission bring to you,
With such things else of quality and respect
As doth import[122] you.

OTHELLO   So please your grace, my ancient;
A man he is of honesty and trust.
To his conveyance I assign my wife,
With what else needful your good grace shall think
To be sent after me.

DUKE   Let it be so.
Good night to every one. [*To Brabantio*] And, noble signior,
290 If virtue no delighted[123] beauty lack,
Your son-in-law is far more fair than black.

1. SENATOR   Adieu, brave Moor. Use Desdemona well.

BRABANTIO   Look to her, Moor, if thou hast eyes to see:
She has deceived her father, and may thee.

OTHELLO   My life upon her faith!

                            Exeunt Duke, Senators, Officers, &c.
                    Honest Iago,
My Desdemona must I leave to thee.
I prithee let thy wife attend on her,
And bring them after in the best advantage.[124]
Come, Desdemona. I have but an hour

---

116. Because
117. Blind
118. *My . . . instruments:* perceptual and
    mental powers
119. So that
120. Shameful
121. Reputation
122. Concern
123. Delightful
124. *in . . . advantage:* at the most opportune
    time

Of love, of worldly matters and direction,
300   To spend with thee. We must obey the time.

Exit Moor and Desdemona.

RODERIGO   Iago,—

IAGO   What say'st thou, noble heart?

RODERIGO   What will I do, think'st thou?

IAGO   Why, go to bed and sleep.

RODERIGO   I will incontinently[125] drown myself.

IAGO   If thou dost, I shall never love thee after. Why, thou silly gentleman?

RODERIGO   It is silliness to live when to live is torment; and then have we a
prescription to die when death is our physician.

IAGO   O villainous! I have looked upon the world for four times seven years;
310   and since I could distinguish betwixt a benefit and an injury, I never
found man that knew how to love himself. Ere I would say I would
drown myself for the love of a guinea hen, I would change my humanity
with a baboon.

RODERIGO   What should I do? I confess it is my shame to be so fond, but it is
not in my virtue to amend it.

IAGO   Virtue? a fig! 'Tis in ourselves that we are thus or thus. Our bodies are
our gardens, to the which our wills are gardeners; so that if we will plant
nettles or sow lettuce, set hyssop and weed up thyme, supply it with one
gender[126] of herbs or distract it with many—either to have it sterile with
320   idleness or manured with industry—why, the power and corrigible[127]
authority of this lies in our wills. If the balance of our lives had not one
scale of reason to poise another of sensuality, the blood and baseness of
our natures would conduct us to most preposterous conclusions. But we
have reason to cool our raging motions, our carnal stings, our unbitted[128]
lusts; whereof I take this that you call love to be a sect or scion.[129]

RODERIGO   It cannot be.

IAGO   It is merely a lust of the blood and a permission of the will. Come, be a
man! Drown thyself? Drown cats and blind puppies! I have professed
me thy friend, and I confess me knit to thy deserving with cables of
330   perdurable[130] toughness. I could never better stead[131] thee than now. Put
money in thy purse. Follow these wars; defeat thy favor[132] with an
usurped beard. I say, put money in thy purse. It cannot be that Desdemona should long continue her love to the Moor—put money in thy
purse—nor he his to her. It was a violent commencement, and thou shalt
see an answerable sequestration[133]—put but money in thy purse. These
Moors are changeable in their wills—fill thy purse with money. The food

125. Immediately	130. Everlasting
126. Species	131. Help
127. Corrective	132. Disguise yourself
128. Uncontrolled	133. Equally abrupt ending
129. Cutting or offshoot	

that to him now is as luscious as locusts[134] shall be to him shortly as bitter as coloquintida.[135] She must change for youth: when she is sated with his body, she will find the error of her choice. She must have
340 change, she must. Therefore put money in thy purse. If thou wilt needs damn thyself, do it a more delicate way than drowning. Make[136] all the money thou canst. If sanctimony[137] and a frail vow betwixt an erring[138] barbarian and a supersubtle[139] Venetian be not too hard for my wits and all the tribe of hell, thou shalt enjoy her. Therefore make money. A pox of drowning! 'Tis clean out of the way. Seek thou rather to be hanged in compassing thy joy than to be drowned and go without her.

RODERIGO   Wilt thou be fast[140] to my hopes, if I depend on the issue?

IAGO   Thou art sure of me. Go, make money. I have told thee often, and I retell thee again and again, I hate the Moor. My cause is hearted;[141] thine
350 hath no less reason. Let us be conjunctive in our revenge against him. If thou canst cuckold him, thou dost thyself a pleasure, me a sport. There are many events in the womb of time, which will be delivered. Traverse,[142] go, provide thy money! We have more of this to-morrow. Adieu.

RODERIGO   Where shall we meet i' th' morning?

IAGO   At my lodging.

RODERIGO   I'll be with thee betimes.

IAGO   Go to, farewell.—Do you hear, Roderigo?

RODERIGO   What say you?

360 IAGO   No more of drowning, do you hear?

RODERIGO   I am changed.

IAGO   Go to, farewell. Put money enough in your purse.

RODERIGO   I'll sell my land.   Exit.

IAGO   Thus do I ever make my fool my purse;
For I mine own gained knowledge should profane
If I would time expend with such a snipe[143]
But for my sport and profit. I hate the Moor;
And it is thought abroad that 'twixt my sheets
H'as done my office. I know not if't be true;
370 Yet I, for mere suspicion in that kind,
Will do as if for surety.[144] He holds me well;[145]
The better shall my purpose work on him.
Cassio's a proper[146] man. Let me see now:

134. Sweet Mediterranean fruit	141. Rooted in my heart; i.e., deeply felt
135. Bitter apple, used as a purgative	142. March forward
136. Raise, or get together	143. Woodcock; silly bird; i.e., fool
137. Religious ceremony	144. As if it were a proven fact
138. Vagabond	145. In high regard
139. Highly refined	146. Handsome
140. True	

To get his place, and to plume up my will[147]
In double knavery—How, how?—Let's see:—
After some time, to abuse Othello's ear
That he is too familiar with his wife.
He hath a person and a smooth dispose[148]
To be suspected—framed to make women false.
380   The Moor is of a free and open nature
That thinks men honest that but seem to be so;
And will as tenderly be led by th' nose
As asses are.
I have't! It is engendered! Hell and night
Must bring this monstrous birth to the world's light.

                                                    Exit.

147. Dress up my intentions   148. Manner

ACT II

SCENE 1

Enter Montano and two Gentlemen.

MONTANO   What from the cape can you discern at sea?
1. GENTLEMAN   Nothing at all: it is a high-wrought flood.
     I cannot 'twixt the heaven and the main
     Descry a sail.
MONTANO   Methinks the wind hath spoke aloud at land;
     A fuller blast ne'er shook our battlements.
     If it hath ruffianed so upon the sea,
     What ribs of oak, when mountains melt on them,
     Can hold the mortise?[1] What shall we hear of this?
10   2. GENTLEMAN   A segregation[2] of the Turkish fleet.
     For do but stand upon the foaming shore,
     The chidden billow seems to pelt the clouds;
     The wind-shaked surge, with high and monstrous mane,
     Seems to cast water on the burning Bear
     And quench the guards[3] of th' ever-fixèd pole.
     I never did like molestation[4] view
     On the enchafèd flood.

1. Hold the joints together   3. Stars near the North Star
2. Scattering   4. Disturbance

MONTANO   If that the Turkish fleet
     Be not ensheltered and embayed, they are drowned;
     It is impossible they bear it out.

Enter a third Gentleman.

20   3. GENTLEMAN   News, lads! Our wars are done.
     The desperate tempest hath so banged the Turks
     That their designment halts.[5] A noble ship of Venice
     Hath seen a grievous wrack and sufferance[6]
     On most part of their fleet.
     MONTANO   How? Is this true?
     3. GENTLEMAN   The ship is here put in,
     A Veronesa;[7] Michael Cassio,
     Lieutenant to the warlike Moor Othello,
     Is come on shore; the Moor himself at sea,
     And is in full commission here for Cyprus.
30   MONTANO   I am glad on't. 'Tis a worthy governor.
     3. GENTLEMAN   But this same Cassio, though he speak of comfort
     Touching the Turkish loss, yet he looks sadly
     And prays the Moor be safe, for they were parted
     With foul and violent tempest.
     MONTANO   Pray heaven he be;
     For I have served him, and the man commands
     Like a full soldier. Let's to the seaside, ho!
     As well to see the vessel that's come in
     As to throw out our eyes for brave Othello,
     Even till we make the main[8] and th' aerial blue
     An indistinct regard.[9]
40   3. GENTLEMAN   Come, let's do so;
     For every minute is expectancy
     Of more arrivance.

Enter Cassio.

CASSIO   Thanks, you the valiant of this warlike isle,
     That so approve the Moor! O, let the heavens
     Give him defense against the elements,
     For I have lost him on a dangerous sea!
     MONTANO   Is he well shipped?

5. Plan is crippled   8. Sea
6. Damage   9. Indistinguishable
7. Ship furnished by Verona

CASSIO His bark is stoutly timbered, and his pilot
    Of very expert and approved allowance;[10]
50   Therefore my hopes, not surfeited to death,
    Stand in bold cure.[11]   [Within] A sail, a sail, a sail!

Enter a Messenger.

CASSIO What noise?
MESSENGER The town is empty; on the brow o' th' sea
    Stand ranks of people, and they cry 'A sail!'
CASSIO My hopes do shape him for the governor.   [A shot.]
2. GENTLEMAN They do discharge their shot of courtesy:
    Our friends at least.
CASSIO   I pray you, sir, go forth
    And give us truth who 'tis that is arrived.
2. GENTLEMAN I shall.   *Exit.*
60 MONTANO But, good lieutenant, is your general wived?
CASSIO Most fortunately. He hath achieved a maid
    That paragons[12] description and wild fame;
    One that excels the quirks of blazoning pens,[13]
    And in th' essential vesture of creation
    Does tire the ingener.[14]

Enter Second Gentleman.

               How now? Who has put in?
2. GENTLEMAN 'Tis one Iago, ancient to the general.
CASSIO H'as had most favorable and happy speed:
    Tempests themselves, high seas, and howling winds,
    The guttered[15] rocks and congregated sands,
70   Traitors ensteeped[16] to clog the guiltless keel,
    As having sense of beauty, do omit
    Their mortal[17] natures, letting go safely by
    The divine Desdemona.
MONTANO   What is she?
CASSIO She that I spake of, our great captain's captain,

10. Skill
11. *not surfeited . . . cure:* not having been
    overindulged stand a good chance of
    being fulfilled
12. Surpasses
13. *quirks . . . pens:* ingenious descriptions
    of writers who seek to list all her
    beauties
14. *in . . . ingener:* her essential nature as it
    was created by God overwhelms the
    imagination of anyone who seeks to
    praise it
15. Jagged
16. Submerged
17. Deadly

Left in the conduct of the bold Iago,
Whose footing[18] here anticipates our thoughts
A se'nnight's[19] speed. Great Jove, Othello guard,
And swell his sail with thine own pow'rful breath,
That he may bless this bay with his tall ship,
80   Make love's quick pants in Desdemona's arms,
Give renewed fire to our extinct spirits,
And bring all Cyprus comfort!

Enter Desdemona, Iago, Roderigo, and Emilia with Attendants.

                          O, behold!
The riches of the ship is come on shore!
Ye men of Cyprus, let her have your knees.
Hail to thee, lady! and the grace of heaven,
Before, behind thee, and on every hand,
Enwheel thee round!
DESDEMONA   I thank you, valiant Cassio.
What tidings can you tell me of my lord?
CASSIO He is not yet arrived; nor know I aught
90   But that he's well and will be shortly here.
DESDEMONA O but I fear! How lost you company?
CASSIO The great contention of the sea and skies
Parted our fellowship.   [*Within*] A sail, a sail! [*A shot.*]
                    But hark. A sail!
2. GENTLEMAN They give their greeting to the citadel;
This likewise is a friend.
CASSIO   See for the news.
                                        Exit Gentleman.
Good ancient, you are welcome. [*To Emilia*] Welcome, mistress.—
Let it not gall your patience, good Iago,
That I extend[20] my manners. 'Tis my breeding
100   That gives me this bold show of courtesy. [*Kisses Emilia.*]
IAGO Sir, would she give you so much of her lips
As of her tongue she oft bestows on me,
You would have enough.
DESDEMONA   Alas, she has no speech!
IAGO In faith, too much.
I find it still when I have list[21] to sleep.
Marry, before your ladyship, I grant,

18. Landing   20. Show
19. Week's   21. Desire

She puts her tongue a little in her heart
And chides with thinking.

EMILIA   You have little cause to say so.

110 IAGO   Come on, come on! You are pictures out of doors,
Bells in your parlors, wildcats in your kitchens,
Saints in your injuries, devils being offended,
Players[22] in your housewifery, and housewives[23] in your beds.

DESDEMONA   O, fie upon thee, slanderer!

IAGO   Nay, it is true, or else I am a Turk:
You rise to play, and go to bed to work.

EMILIA   You shall not write my praise.

IAGO   No, let me not.

DESDEMONA   What wouldst thou write of me, if thou shouldst praise me?

IAGO   O gentle lady, do not put me to't,
120   For I am nothing if not critical.

DESDEMONA   Come on, assay.[24]—There's one gone to the harbor?

IAGO   Ay, madam.

DESDEMONA   I am not merry; but I do beguile
The thing I am by seeming otherwise.—
Come, how wouldst thou praise me?

IAGO   I am about it; but indeed my invention
Comes from my pate as birdlime[25] does from frieze[26]—
It plucks out brains and all. But my Muse labors,
And thus she is delivered:
130   If she be fair[27] and wise, fairness and wit—
The one's for use, the other useth it.

DESDEMONA   Well praised! How if she be black[28] and witty?

IAGO   If she be black, and thereto have a wit,
She'll find a white that shall her blackness fit.

DESDEMONA   Worse and worse!

EMILIA   How if fair and foolish?

IAGO   She never yet was foolish that was fair,
For even her folly[29] helped her to an heir.

DESDEMONA   These are old fond[30] paradoxes to make fools laugh i' th'
140   alehouse. What miserable praise hast thou for her that's foul[31] and
foolish?

IAGO   There's none so foul, and foolish thereunto,
But does foul pranks which fair and wise ones do.

DESDEMONA   O heavy ignorance! Thou praisest the worst best. But what

22. Actors
23. Hussies
24. Try
25. Sticky paste used to catch birds
26. Coarse cloth
27. Blonde
28. Brunette
29. Wantonness
30. Foolish
31. Ugly

praise couldst thou bestow on a deserving woman indeed—one that in the authority of her merit did justly put on the vouch[32] of very malice itself?

IAGO   She that was ever fair, and never proud;
150   Had tongue at will, and yet was never loud;
Never lacked gold, and yet went never gay;[33]
Fled from her wish, and yet said 'Now I may';
She that, being angered, her revenge being nigh,
Bade her wrong stay,[34] and her displeasure fly;
She that in wisdom never was so frail
To change the cod's head for the salmon's tail;[35]
She that could think, and ne'er disclose her mind;
See suitors following, and not look behind:
She was a wight[36] (if ever such wight were)—
160   DESDEMONA   To do what?

IAGO   To suckle fools[37] and chronicle small beer.[38]

DESDEMONA   O most lame and impotent conclusion! Do not learn of him, Emilia, though he be thy husband. How say you, Cassio? Is he not a most profane and liberal[39] counsellor?

CASSIO   He speaks home,[40] madam. You may relish him more in the[41] soldier than in the scholar.

IAGO [aside]   He takes her by the palm. Ay, well said, whisper! With as little
170   a web as this will I ensnare as great a fly as Cassio. Ay, smile upon her, do! I will gyve[42] thee in thine own courtship.[43]—You say true; 'tis so, indeed!—If such tricks as these strip you out of your lieutenantry, it had been better you had not kissed your three fingers so oft—which now again you are most apt to play the sir[44] in. Very good! well kissed! an excellent curtsy! 'Tis so, indeed. Yet again your fingers to your lips? Would they were clyster pipes[45] for your sake! [Trumpet within.] The
180   Moor! I know his trumpet.

CASSIO   'Tis truly so.

DESDEMONA   Let's meet him and receive him.

CASSIO   Lo, where he comes.

Enter Othello and Attendants.

---

32. *put . . . vouch:* compel the praise
33. Extravagantly dressed
34. Sense of injury cease
35. *To . . . tail:* to exchange something common but valuable for something rare but useless
36. Person
37. Babies
38. Keep petty household accounts in order

39. Free-speaking; i.e., lewd
40. Bluntly
41. In the character of
42. Trap
43. Courtly manners
44. Courtly gentleman
45. Syringes for an enema

OTHELLO   O my fair warrior!

DESDEMONA   My dear Othello!

OTHELLO   It gives me wonder great as my content
To see you here before me. O my soul's joy!
If after every tempest come such calms,
May the winds blow till they have wakened death!
And let the laboring bark climb hills of seas
190   Olympus-high, and duck again as low
As hell's from heaven! If it were now to die,
'Twere now to be most happy; for I fear
My soul hath her content so absolute
That not another comfort like to this
Succeeds in unknown fate.

DESDEMONA   The heavens forbid
But that our loves and comforts should increase
Even as our days do grow.

OTHELLO   Amen to that, sweet powers!
I cannot speak enough of this content;
It stops me here; it is too much of joy.
200   And this, and this, the greatest discords be   *They kiss.*
That e'er our hearts shall make!

IAGO   [*Aside*] O, you are well tuned now!
But I'll set down[46] the pegs that make this music,
As honest as I am.

OTHELLO   Come, let us to the castle.
News, friends! Our wars are done; the Turks are drowned.
How does my old acquaintance of this isle?—
Honey, you shall be well desired[47] in Cyprus;
I have found great love amongst them. O my sweet,
I prattle out of fashion, and I dote
In mine own comforts. I prithee, good Iago,
210   Go to the bay and disembark my coffers.
Bring thou the master to the citadel;
He is a good one, and his worthiness
Does challenge much respect.—Come, Desdemona,
Once more well met at Cyprus.

                              Exit Othello with all but Iago and Roderigo.

IAGO [*to an Attendant, who goes out*].   Do thou meet me presently at the harbor. [*To Roderigo*] Come hither. If thou be'st valiant (as they say base
men being in love have then a nobility in their natures more than is
native to them), list me. The lieutenant to-night watches on the court of

46. Loosen   47. Warmly welcomed

guard.[48] First, I must tell thee this: Desdemona is directly in love with
220   him.

RODERIGO   With him? Why, 'tis not possible.

IAGO   Lay thy finger thus,[49] and let thy soul be instructed. Mark me with
what violence she first loved the Moor, but for bragging and telling her
fantastical lies; and will she love him still for prating? Let not thy discreet heart think it. Her eye must be fed; and what delight shall she have
to look on the devil? When the blood is made dull with the act of sport,
there should be, again to inflame it and to give satiety a fresh appetite,
loveliness in favor, sympathy in years, manners, and beauties; all which
the Moor is defective in. Now for want of these required conveniences,[50]
230   her delicate tenderness will find itself abused, begin to heave the
gorge,[51] disrelish and abhor the Moor. Very nature will instruct her in it
and compel her to some second choice. Now, sir, this granted—as it is a
most pregnant and unforced position—who stands so eminent in the
degree of this fortune as Cassio does? A knave very voluble; no further
conscionable than in putting on the mere form of civil and humane[52]
seeming for the better compassing of his salt[53] and most hidden loose
affection? Why, none! why, none! A slipper[54] and subtle knave; a
finder-out of occasions; that has an eye can stamp and counterfeit advantages, though true advantage never present itself; a devilish knave! Be-
240   sides, the knave is handsome, young, and hath all those requisites in
him that folly and green[55] minds look after. A pestilent complete knave!
and the woman hath found him already.

RODERIGO   I cannot believe that in her; she's full of most blessed condition.

IAGO   Blessed fig's-end! The wine she drinks is made of grapes. If she had
been blessed, she would never have loved the Moor. Blessed pudding!
Didst thou not see her paddle with the palm of his hand? Didst not mark
that?

RODERIGO   Yes, that I did; but that was but courtesy.

IAGO   Lechery, by this hand! an index and obscure prologue to the history
250   of lust and foul thoughts. They met so near with their lips that their
breaths embraced together. Villainous thoughts, Roderigo! When these
mutualities so marshal the way, hard at hand comes the master and
main exercise, th' incorporate[56] conclusion. Pish! But, sir, be you ruled
by me: I have brought you from Venice. Watch you to-night; for the
command, I'll lay't upon you. Cassio knows you not. I'll not be far from
you: do you find some occasion to anger Cassio, either by speaking too

---

48. *watches . . . guard:* Has charge of the   52. Courteous
     watch   53. Lecherous
49. On your lips   54. Slippery
50. Compatibilities   55. Wanton and youthful
51. Be nauseated   56. Sexual

loud, or tainting[57] his discipline, or from what other course you please
which the time shall more favorably minister.

RODERIGO   Well.

260 IAGO   Sir, he is rash and very sudden in choler,[58] and haply with his trun-
cheon may strike at you. Provoke him that he may; for even out of that
will I cause these of Cyprus to mutiny; whose qualification[59] shall come
into no true taste again but by the displanting of Cassio. So shall you
have a shorter journey to your desires by the means I shall then have to
prefer[60] them; and the impediment most profitably removed without the
which there were no expectation of our prosperity.

RODERIGO   I will do this if you can bring it to any opportunity.

IAGO   I warrant thee. Meet me by and by at the citadel; I must fetch his
necessaries ashore. Farewell.

270 RODERIGO   Adieu.   *Exit.*

IAGO   That Cassio loves her, I do well believe it;
That she loves him, 'tis apt and of great credit.[61]
The Moor, howbeit that I endure him not,
Is of a constant, loving, noble nature,
And I dare think he'll prove to Desdemona
A most dear husband. Now I do love her too;
Not out of absolute lust, though peradventure
I stand accountant for as great a sin,
But partly led to diet my revenge,
280 For that I do suspect the lusty Moor
Hath leaped into my seat; the thought whereof
Doth, like a poisonous mineral, gnaw my inwards;
And nothing can or shall content my soul
Till I am evened with him, wife for wife;
Or failing so, yet that I put the Moor
At least into a jealousy so strong
That judgment cannot cure. Which thing to do,
If this poor trash of Venice, whom I trash[62]
For his quick hunting, stand the putting on,[63]
290 I'll have our Michael Cassio on the hip,[64]
Abuse him to the Moor in the rank garb[65]
(For I fear Cassio with my nightcap too),

57. Discrediting
58. Quick to anger
59. Satisfaction
60. Advance
61. *apt . . . credit:* probable and believable
62. Hang weights on, as was done to hounds to restrain them from hunting too fast
63. *stand the putting on:* performs properly in response to my command
64. In a vulnerable position (a term from wrestling)
65. Coarse manner

Make the Moor thank me, love me, and reward me
For making him egregiously an ass
And practicing upon[66] his peace and quiet
Even to madness. 'Tis here, but yet confused:
Knavery's plain face is never seen till used.   *Exit.*

SCENE 2

Enter Othello's Herald, with a proclamation.

HERALD   It is Othello's pleasure, our noble and valiant general, that, upon
certain tidings now arrived, importing the mere perdition[67] of the Turkish fleet, every man put himself into triumph; some to dance, some to
make bonfires, each man to what sport and revels his addiction leads
him. For, besides these beneficial news, it is the celebration of his nuptial. So much was his pleasure should be proclaimed. All offices[68] are
open, and there is full liberty of feasting from this present hour of five
till the bell have told eleven. Heaven bless the isle of Cyprus and our
noble general Othello!   *Exit.*

SCENE 3

Enter Othello, Desdemona, Cassio, and Attendants.

OTHELLO   Good Michael, look you to the guard to-night.
Let's teach ourselves that honorable stop,
Not to outsport discretion.
CASSIO   Iago hath direction what to do;
But not withstanding, with my personal eye
Will I look to't.
OTHELLO   Iago is most honest.
Michael, good night. To-morrow with your earliest
Let me have speech with you. [*To Desdemona*] Come, my dear love.
The purchase made, the fruits are to ensue;
10   That profit's yet to come 'tween me and you.—
Good night.
                                Exit Othello with Desdemona and Attendants.

Enter Iago.

CASSIO   Welcome, Iago. We must to the watch.

66. Plotting against
67. Complete destruction
68. Kitchens and storerooms

IAGO   Not this hour, lieutenant; 'tis not yet ten o' th' clock. Our general cast[69] us thus early for the love of his Desdemona; who let us not therefore blame. He hath not yet made wanton the night with her, and she is sport for Jove.

CASSIO   She's a most exquisite lady.

20   IAGO   And, I'll warrant her, full of game.

CASSIO   Indeed, she's a most fresh and delicate creature.

IAGO   What an eye she has! Methinks it sounds a parley to provocation.

CASSIO   An inviting eye; and yet methinks right modest.

IAGO   And when she speaks, is it not an alarum[70] to love?

CASSIO   She is indeed perfection.

30   IAGO   Well, happiness to their sheets! Come, lieutenant, I have a stoup[71] of wine, and here without are a brace of Cyprus gallants that would fain have a measure to the health of black Othello.

CASSIO   Not to-night, good Iago. I have very poor and unhappy brains for drinking; I could well wish courtesy would invent some other custom of entertainment.

IAGO   O, they are our friends. But one cup! I'll drink for you.

40   CASSIO   I have drunk but one cup to-night, and that was craftily qualified[72] too; and behold what innovation[73] it makes here. I am unfortunate in the infirmity and dare not task my weakness with any more.

IAGO   What, man! 'Tis a night of revels: the gallants desire it.

CASSIO   Where are they?

IAGO   Here at the door; I pray you call them in.

CASSIO   I'll do't, but it dislikes me.[74]   Exit.

50   IAGO   If I can fasten but one cup upon him
With that which he hath drunk to-night already,
He'll be as full of quarrel and offense
As my young mistress' dog. Now my sick fool Roderigo,
Whom love hath turned almost the wrong side out,
To Desdemona hath to-night caroused
Potations pottle-deep;[75] and he's to watch.
Three lads of Cyprus—noble swelling spirits,
That hold their honors in a wary distance,[76]
The very elements of this warlike isle—
60   Have I to-night flustered with flowing cups,
And they watch too. Now, 'mongst this flock of drunkards
Am I to put our Cassio in some action
That may offend the isle.

69. Dismissed   74. I don't want to
70. Trumpet signal   75. To the bottom of the tankard
71. Two-quart tankard   76. *hold . . . distance:* are very touchy about
72. Carefully diluted   their honor
73. Disturbing change

Enter Cassio, Montano, and Gentlemen; Servants following with wine.

But here they come.
If consequence do but approve my dream,[77]
My boat sails freely, both with wind and stream.

CASSIO 'Fore God, they have given me a rouse[78] already.

MONTANO Good faith, a little one; not past a pint, as I am a soldier.

70 IAGO Some wine, ho!

[*Sings*] And let me the canakin clink, clink;
And let me the canakin clink.
A soldier's a man;
A life's but a span,
Why then, let a soldier drink.

Some wine, boys!

CASSIO 'Fore God, an excellent song!

IAGO I learned it in England, where indeed they are most potent in potting.

80 Your Dane, your German, and your swag-bellied Hollander—Drink, ho!—are nothing to your English.

CASSIO Is your Englishman so expert in his drinking?

IAGO Why, he drinks you with facility your Dane dead drunk; he sweats not to overthrow your Almain;[79] he gives your Hollander a vomit ere the next pottle can be filled.

CASSIO To the health of our general!

90 MONTANO I am for it, lieutenant, and I'll do you justice.

IAGO O sweet England!

[*Sings*] King Stephen was a worthy peer;
His breeches cost him but a crown;
He held 'em sixpence all to dear,
With that he called the tailor lown.[80]
He was a wight of high renown,
And thou art but of low degree.
'Tis pride that pulls the country down;
Then take thine auld cloak about thee.

100 Some wine, ho!

CASSIO 'Fore God, this is a more exquisite song than the other.

IAGO Will you hear't again?

77. *If . . . dream:* if events work out as I
   hope
78. Drink

79. German
80. Rascal

CASSIO No, for I hold him to be unworthy of his place that does those
things. Well, God's above all; and there be souls must be saved, and
there be souls must not be saved.

IAGO It's true, good lieutenant.

110 CASSIO For mine own part—no offense to the general, nor any man of
quality—I hope to be saved.

IAGO And so do I too, lieutenant.

CASSIO Ay, but, by your leave, not before me. The lieutenant is to be saved
before the ancient. Let's have no more of this; let's to our affairs.—God
forgive us our sins!—Gentlemen, let's look to our business. Do not
think, gentlemen, I am drunk. This is my ancient; this is my right hand,
120 and this is my left. I am not drunk now. I can stand well enough, and
speak well enough.

ALL Excellent well!

CASSIO Why, very well then. You must not think then that I am drunk.

Exit.

MONTANO To th' platform, masters. Come, let's set the watch.

IAGO You see this fellow that is gone before.
He is a soldier fit to stand by Caesar
And give direction; and do but see his vice.
'Tis to his virtue a just equinox,[81]
130 The one as long as th' other. 'Tis pity of him.
I fear the trust Othello puts him in,
On some odd time of his infirmity,
Will shake this island.

MONTANO   But is he often thus?

IAGO 'Tis evermore the prologue to his sleep:
He'll watch the horologe a double set[82]
If drink rock not his cradle.

MONTANO   It were well
The general were put in mind of it.
Perhaps he sees it not, or his good nature
Prizes the virtue that appears in Cassio
140 And looks not on his evils. Is not this true?

Enter Roderigo.

IAGO [_aside to him_] How now, Roderigo?
I pray you after the lieutenant, go!   _Exit Roderigo._

MONTANO And 'tis great pity that the noble Moor
Should hazard such a place as his own second

81. Exact equivalent
82. _watch . . . set:_ stay awake two times
around the clock

With one of an ingraft[83] infirmity.
It were an honest action to say
So to the Moor.
IAGO   Not I, for this fair island!
I do love Cassio well and would do much
To cure him of this evil.   [*Within*] Help! help!
                But hark! What noise?

Enter Cassio, driving in Roderigo.

CASSIO   Zounds, you rogue! you rascal!
150   MONTANO   What's the matter, lieutenant?
CASSIO   A knave teach me my duty?
I'll beat the knave into a twiggen[84] bottle.
RODERIGO   Beat me?
CASSIO   Dost thou prate, rogue?   *Strikes him.*
MONTANO   Nay, good lieutenant!
                                        Stays him.

Pray, sir, hold your hand.
CASSIO   Let me go, sir.
Or I'll knock you o'er the mazzard.[85]
MONTANO   Come, come, you're drunk!
CASSIO   Drunk?   *They fight.*
IAGO [*aside to Roderigo*]   Away, I say! Go out and cry a mutiny!
                                    Exit Roderigo.

Nay, good lieutenant. God's will, gentlemen!
Help, ho!—lieutenant—sir—Montano—sir—
Help, masters!—Here's a goodly watch indeed!

A bell rung.

160   Who's that which rings the bell? Diablo, ho!
The town will rise. God's will, lieutenant, hold!
You will be shamed for ever.

Enter Othello and Gentlemen with weapons.

OTHELLO   What is the matter here?
MONTANO   Zounds, I bleed still. I am hurt to the death.
He dies!
OTHELLO   Hold for your lives!

83. Ingrained   85. Head
84. Wicker covered

IAGO   Hold, hold! Lieutenant—sir—Montano—gentlemen!
Have you forgot all sense of place and duty?
Hold! The general speaks to you. Hold, hold, for shame!

OTHELLO   Why, how now, ho? From whence ariseth this?
170   Are we turned Turks, and to ourselves do that
Which heaven hath forbid the Ottomites?
For Christian shame put by this barbarous brawl!
He that stirs next to carve for[86] his own rage
Holds his soul light; he dies upon his motion.
Silence that dreadful bell! It frights the isle
From her propriety.[87] What's the matter, masters?
Honest Iago, that looks dead with grieving,
Speak. Who began this? On thy love, I charge thee.

IAGO   I do not know. Friends all but now, even now,
180   In quarter, and in terms like bride and groom
Devesting them for bed; and then, but now—
As if some planet had unwitted men—
Swords out, and tilting one at other's breast
In opposition bloody. I cannot speak
Any beginning to this peevish odds.[88]
And would in action glorious I had lost
Those legs that brought me to a part of it!

OTHELLO   How comes it, Michael, you are thus forgot?

CASSIO   I pray you pardon me; I cannot speak.

190   OTHELLO   Worthy Montano, you were wont be civil;
The gravity and stillness of your youth
The world hath noted, and your name is great
In mouths of wisest censure.[89] What's the matter
That you unlace your reputation thus
And spend your rich opinion[90] for the name
Of a night-brawler? Give me answer to't.

MONTANO   Worthy Othello, I am hurt to danger.
Your officer, Iago, can inform you,
While I spare speech, which something now offends[91] me,
200   Of all that I do know; nor know I aught
By me that's said or done amiss this night,
Unless self-charity be sometimes a vice,
And to defend ourselves it be a sin
When violence assails us.

OTHELLO   Now, by heaven,

86. Indulge
87. Natural condition
88. Childish quarrel

89. Judgment
90. High reputation
91. Pains

My blood begins my safer guides to rule,
And passion, having my best judgment collied,[92]
Assays to lead the way. If I once stir
Or do but lift this arm, the best of you
Shall sink in my rebuke. Give me to know
210   How this foul rout began, who set it on;
And he that is approved in[93] this offense,
Though he had twinned with me, both at a birth,
Shall lose me. What! in a town of war,
Yet wild, the people's hearts brimful of fear,
To manage[94] private and domestic quarrel?
In night, and on the court and guard of safety?
'Tis monstrous. Iago, who began't?

MONTANO   If partially affined, or leagued in office,[95]
Thou dost deliver more or less than truth,
Thou art no soldier.

220   IAGO   Touch me not so near.
I had rather have this tongue cut from my mouth
Than it should do offense to Michael Cassio;
Yet I persuade myself, to speak the truth
Shall nothing wrong him. Thus it is, general.
Montano and myself being in speech,
There comes a fellow crying out for help,
And Cassio following him with determined sword
To execute[96] upon him. Sir, this gentleman
Steps in to Cassio and entreats his pause.
230   Myself the crying fellow did pursue,
Lest by his clamor—as it so fell out—
The town might fall in fright. He, swift of foot,
Outran my purpose; and I returned the rather
For that I heard the clink and fall of swords,
And Cassio high in oath; which till to-night
I ne'er might say before. When I came back—
For this was brief—I found them close together
At blow and thrust, even as again they were
When you yourself did part them.
240   More of this matter cannot I report;
But men are men; the best sometimes forget.
Though Cassio did some little wrong to him,

92. Darkened
93. Proved guilty of
94. Carry on
95. *partially . . . office:* biased because of personal or official ties
96. Work his will

As men in rage strike those that wish them best,
Yet surely Cassio I believe received
From him that fled some strange indignity,
Which patience could not pass.[97]

OTHELLO   I know, Iago,
Thy honesty and love doth mince this matter,
Making it light to Cassio. Cassio, I love thee;
But never more be officer of mine.

Enter Desdemona, attended.

250   Look if my gentle love be not raised up!
I'll make thee an example.

DESDEMONA   What's the matter?

OTHELLO   All's well now, sweeting; come away to bed.
   [*To Montano*] Sir, for your hurts, myself will be your surgeon.
   Lead him off.   *Montano is led off.*
   Iago, look with care about the town
   And silence those whom this vile brawl distracted.
   Come, Desdemona: 'tis the soldiers' life
   To have their balmy slumbers waked with strife.
                    Exit with all but Iago and Cassio.

IAGO   What, are you hurt, lieutenant?

260 CASSIO   Ay, past all surgery.

IAGO   Marry, God forbid!

CASSIO   Reputation, reputation, reputation! O, I have lost my reputation! I
   have lost the immortal part of myself, and what remains is bestial. My
   reputation, Iago, my reputation!

IAGO   As I am an honest man, I thought you had received some bodily
   wound. There is more sense in that than in reputation. Reputation is an
270 idle and most false imposition; oft got without merit and lost without
   deserving. You have lost no reputation at all unless you repute yourself
   such a loser. What, man! there are ways to recover the general again. You
   are but now cast in his mood[98]—a punishment more in policy than in
   malice, even so as one would beat his offenseless dog to affright an
   imperious lion. Sue to him again, and he's yours.

CASSIO   I will rather sue to be despised than to deceive so good a commander with so slight, so drunken, and so indiscreet an officer. Drunk!
280 and speak parrot![99] and squabble! swagger! swear! and discourse

97. Ignore   99. Talk nonsense
98. *cast . . . mood:* dismissed because of his
anger

fustian[100] with one's own shadow! O thou invisible spirit of wine, if thou hast no name to be known by, let us call thee devil!

IAGO   What was he that you followed with your sword? What had he done to you?

CASSIO   I know not.

IAGO   Is't possible?

290   CASSIO   I remember a mass of things, but nothing distinctly; a quarrel, but nothing wherefore. O God, that men should put an enemy in their mouths to steal away their brains! that we should with joy, pleasance, revel, and applause transform ourselves into beasts!

IAGO   Why, but you are now well enough. How came you thus recovered?

CASSIO   It hath pleased the devil drunkenness to give place to the devil wrath. One unperfectness shows me another, to make me frankly

300   despise myself.

IAGO   Come, you are too severe a moraler. As the time, the place, and the condition of this country stands, I could heartily wish this had not so befall'n; but since it is as it is, mend it for your own good.

CASSIO   I will ask him for my place again: he shall tell me I am a drunkard! Had I as many mouths as Hydra,[101] such an answer would stop them all. To be now a sensible man, by and by a fool, and presently a beast! O strange! Every inordinate cup is unblest, and the ingredient is a devil.

310   IAGO   Come, come, good wine is a good familiar creature if it be well used. Exclaim no more against it. And, good lieutenant, I think you think I love you.

CASSIO   I have well approved[102] it, sir. I drunk!

IAGO   You or any man living may be drunk at some time, man. I'll tell you what you shall do. Our general's wife is now the general. I may say so in this respect, for that he hath devoted and given up himself to the con-

320   templation, mark, and denotement of her parts and graces. Confess yourself freely to her; importune her help to put you in your place again. She is of so free,[103] so kind, so apt, so blessed a disposition she holds it a vice in her goodness not to do more than she is requested. This broken joint between you and her husband entreat her to splinter;[104] and my fortunes against any lay[105] worth naming, this crack of your love shall

330   grow stronger than 'twas before.

CASSIO   You advise me well.

IAGO   I protest, in the sincerity of love and honest kindness.

CASSIO   I think it freely; and betimes in the morning will I beseech the

---

100. Bombastic gibberish
101. Many-headed monster of classical mythology
102. Proved
103. Generous
104. Bind up with splints
105. Wager

virtuous Desdemona to undertake for me. I am desperate of my fortunes
if they check me here.

340 IAGO   You are in the right. Good night, lieutenant; I must to the watch.

CASSIO   Good night, honest Iago.   *Exit Cassio.*

IAGO   And what's he then that says I play the villain,
When this advice is free I give and honest,
Probal[106] to thinking, and indeed the course
To win the Moor again? For 'tis most easy
Th' inclining Desdemona to subdue[107]
In any honest suit; she's framed as fruitful[108]
As the free elements. And then for her
To win the Moor—were't to renounce his baptism,
350 All seals and symbols of redeemèd sin—
His soul is so enfettered to her love
That she may make, unmake, do what she list,[109]
Even as her appetite shall play the god
With his weak function. How am I then a villain
To counsel Cassio to this parallel course,
Directly to his good? Divinity[110] of hell!
When devils will the blackest sins put on,
They do suggest at first with heavenly shows,
As I do now. For whiles this honest fool
360 Plies Desdemona to repair his fortunes,
And she for him pleads strongly to the Moor,
I'll pour this pestilence into his ear,
That she repeals[111] him for her body's lust;
And by how much she strives to do him good,
She shall undo her credit with the Moor.
So will I turn her virtue into pitch,
And out of her own goodness make the net
That shall enmesh them all.

Enter Roderigo.

                        How, now, Roderigo?

RODERIGO   I do follow here in the chase, not like a hound that hunts, but one
370 that fills up the cry.[112] My money is almost spent; I have been to-night
exceedingly well cudgelled; and I think the issue will be—I shall have so

106. Probable
107. Persuade
108. Generous
109. Pleases

110. Theology
111. Pleads for his reinstatement
112. Pack

much experience for my pains; and so, with no money at all, and a little
more wit, return again to Venice.

IAGO   How poor are they that have not patience!
What wound did ever heal but by degrees?
Thou know'st we work by wit, and not by witchcraft;
And wit depends on dilatory time.
380   Does't not go well? Cassio hath beaten thee,
And thou by that small hurt hast cashiered[113] Cassio.
Though other things grow fair against the sun,
Yet fruits that blossom first will first be ripe.
Content thyself awhile. By the mass, 'tis morning!
Pleasure and action make the hours seem short.
Retire thee; go where thou art billeted.
Away, I say! Thou shalt know more hereafter.
Nay, get thee gone!   *Exit Roderigo.*
                         Two things are to be done:
My wife must move for Cassio to her mistress;
390   I'll set her on;
Myself the while to draw the Moor apart
And bring him jump[114] when he may Cassio find
Soliciting his wife. Ay, that's the way!
Dull not device by coldness and delay.   *Exit.*

---

113. Brought about Cassio's discharge   114. At the exact moment

ACT III

SCENE 1

Enter Cassio, with Musicians.

CASSIO   Masters, play here, I will content[1] your pains:
Something that's brief; and bid 'Good morrow, general.'

                                                    They play.

Enter the Clown.

CLOWN   Why, masters, ha' your instruments been at Naples, that they speak
i' th' nose[2] thus?

---

1. Reward you for
2. *Naples . . . nose:* Naples was reputed to
be a center of venereal disease, and ve-

nereal diseases were thought to damage
the structure of the nose, resulting in a
peculiar nasal sound.

MUSICIAN   How, sir, how?

CLOWN   Are these, I pray, called wind instruments?

MUSICIAN   Ay, marry, are they, sir.

CLOWN   O, thereby hangs a tail.

MUSICIAN   Whereby hangs a tale, sir?

CLOWN   Marry, sir, by many a wind instrument that I know. But, masters, here's money for you; and the general so likes your music that he desires you, for love's sake, to make no more noise with it.

10 MUSICIAN   Well, sir, we will not.

CLOWN   If you have any music that may not be heard, to't again: but, as they say, to hear music the general does not greatly care.

MUSICIAN   We have none such, sir.

CLOWN   Then put up your pipes in your bag, for I'll away. Go, vanish into air, away!   *Exit Musician with his fellows.*

CASSIO   Dost thou hear, my honest friend?

CLOWN   No, I hear not your honest friend. I hear you.

CASSIO   Prithee keep up thy quillets.[3] There's a poor piece of gold for thee. If the gentlewoman that attends the general's wife be stirring, tell her

20   there's one Cassio entreats her a little favor of speech. Wilt thou do this?

CLOWN   She is stirring, sir. If she will stir hither, I shall seem to notify unto her.

CASSIO   Do, good my friend.   *Exit Clown.*

Enter Iago.

                    In happy time, Iago.

IAGO   You have not been abed then!

CASSIO   Why, no; the day had broke
Before we parted. I have made bold, Iago,
To send in to your wife: my suit to her
Is that she will to virtuous Desdemona
Procure me some access.

IAGO   I'll send her to you presently;
And I'll devise a mean to draw the Moor

30   Out of the way, that your converse and business
May be more free.

CASSIO   I humbly thank you for't.   *Exit Iago.*
                    I never knew
A Florentine more kind and honest.

Enter Emilia.

3. Puns

EMILIA   Good morrow, good lieutenant. I am sorry
For your displeasure; but all will sure be well.
The general and his wife are talking of it,
And she speaks for you stoutly. The Moor replies
That he you hurt is of great fame in Cyprus
And great affinity,[4] and that in wholesome wisdom
He might not but refuse you; but he protests he loves you,
And needs no other suitor but his likings
To take the safest occasion by the front[5]
To bring you in again.
CASSIO   Yet I beseech you,
If you think fit, or that it may be done,
Give me advantage of some brief discourse
With Desdemona alone.
EMILIA   Pray you come in.
I will bestow you where you shall have time
To speak your bosom[6] freely.
CASSIO   I am much bound to you.   *Exeunt.*

SCENE 2

Enter Othello, Iago, and Gentlemen.

OTHELLO   These letters give, Iago, to the pilot
And by him do my duties[7] to the Senate.
That done, I will be walking on the works;[8]
Repair there to me.
IAGO   Well, my good lord, I'll do't.
OTHELLO   This fortification, gentlemen, shall we see't?
GENTLEMEN   We'll wait upon your lordship.   *Exeunt.*

SCENE 3

Enter Desdemona, Cassio, and Emilia.

DESDEMONA   Be thou assured, good Cassio, I will do
All my abilities in thy behalf.
EMILIA   Good madam, do. I warrant it grieves my husband
As if the cause were his.
DESDEMONA   O, that's an honest fellow. Do not doubt, Cassio,

---

4. Family connections
5. Forelock
6. Most private thoughts

7. Pay my respects
8. Fortifications

But I will have my lord and you again
As friendly as you were.

CASSIO   Bounteous madam,
Whatever shall become of Michael Cassio,
He's never anything but your true servant.

10 DESDEMONA   I know't; I thank you. You do love my lord;
You have known him long; and be you well assured
He shall in strangeness[9] stand no farther off
Than in a politic distance.

CASSIO   Ay, but, lady,
That policy may either last so long,
Or feed upon such nice[10] and waterish diet,
Or breed itself so out of circumstance,
That, I being absent, and my place supplied,
My general will forget my love and service.

DESDEMONA   Do not doubt[11] that; before Emilia here
20 I give thee warrant of thy place. Assure thee,
If I do vow a friendship, I'll perform it
To the last article. My lord shall never rest;
I'll watch him tame[12] and talk him out of patience;
His bed shall seem a school, his board a shrift;[13]
I'll intermingle everything he does
With Cassio's suit. Therefore be merry, Cassio,
For thy solicitor shall rather die
Than give thy cause away.

Enter Othello and Iago at a distance.

EMILIA   Madam, here comes my lord.
30 CASSIO   Madam, I'll take my leave.

DESDEMONA   Why, stay, and hear me speak.

CASSIO   Madam, not now: I am very ill at ease,
Unfit for mine own purposes.

DESDEMONA   Well, do your discretion.   *Exit Cassio.*

IAGO   Ha! I like not that.

OTHELLO   What dost thou say?

IAGO   Nothing, my lord; or if—I know not what.

OTHELLO   Was not that Cassio parted from my wife?

IAGO   Cassio, my lord? No, sure, I cannot think it,

---

9. Aloofness
10. Trivial
11. Fear
12. Keep him awake (hawks were tamed by being kept awake)
13. Confessional

That he would steal away so guilty-like,
Seeing you coming.

40 OTHELLO   I do believe 'twas he.

DESDEMONA How now, my lord?
I have been talking with a suitor here,
A man that languishes in your displeasure.

OTHELLO Who is't you mean?

DESDEMONA Why, your lieutenant, Cassio. Good my lord,
If I have any grace or power to move you,
His present reconciliation[14] take;
For if he be not one that truly loves you,
That errs in ignorance, and not in cunning,
50 I have no judgment in an honest face.
I prithee call him back.

OTHELLO   Went he hence now?

DESDEMONA Yes, faith; so humbled
That he hath left part of his grief with me
To suffer with him. Good love, call him back.

OTHELLO Not now, sweet Desdemon; some other time.

DESDEMONA But shall't be shortly?

OTHELLO   The sooner, sweet, for you.

DESDEMONA Shall't be to-night at supper?

OTHELLO   No, not to-night.

DESDEMONA To-morrow dinner then?

OTHELLO   I shall not dine at home;
I meet the captains at the citadel.

60 DESDEMONA Why then, to-morrow night, or Tuesday morn,
On Tuesday noon or night, or Wednesday morn.
I prithee name the time, but let it not
Exceed three days. I' faith, he's penitent;
And yet his trespass, in our common reason
(Save that, they say, the wars must make examples
Out of their best), is not almost[15] a fault
T' incur a private check.[16] When shall he come?
Tell me, Othello. I wonder in my soul
What you could ask me that I should deny
70 Or stand so mamm'ring on.[17] What? Michael Cassio,
That came a-wooing with you, and so many a time,
When I have spoke of you dispraisingly,
Hath ta'en your part—to have so much to do
To bring him in? By'r Lady, I could do much—

---

14. Accept his repentance
15. Hardly

16. Even a private reprimand
17. *stand . . . on:* be so hesitant to do

OTHELLO   Prithee no more. Let him come when he will!
  I will deny thee nothing.
DESDEMONA   Why, this is not a boon;
  'Tis as I should entreat you wear your gloves,
  Or feed on nourishing dishes, or keep you warm,
  Or sue to you to do a peculiar profit
80 To your own person. Nay, when I have a suit
  Wherein I mean to touch your love indeed,
  It shall be full of poise and difficult weight,
  And fearful to be granted.
OTHELLO   I will deny thee nothing!
  Whereon I do beseech thee grant me this,
  To leave me but a little to myself.
DESDEMONA   Shall I deny you? No. Farewell, my lord.
OTHELLO   Farewell, my Desdemon: I'll come to thee straight.
DESDEMONA   Emilia, come.—Be as your fancies teach you;
  Whate'er you be, I am obedient.   *Exit with Emilia.*
90 OTHELLO   Excellent wretch! Perdition catch my soul
  But I do love thee! and when I love thee not,
  Chaos is come again.
IAGO   My noble lord—
OTHELLO   What dost thou say, Iago?
IAGO   Did Michael Cassio, when you wooed my lady,
  Know of your love?
OTHELLO   He did, from first to last. Why dost thou ask?
IAGO   But for a satisfaction of my thought;
  No further harm.
OTHELLO   Why of thy thought, Iago?
IAGO   I did not think he had been acquainted with her.
100 OTHELLO   O, yes, and went between us very oft.
IAGO   Indeed?
OTHELLO   Indeed? Ay, indeed! Discern'st thou aught in that?
  Is he not honest?
IAGO   Honest, my lord?
OTHELLO   Honest. Ay, honest.
IAGO   My lord, for aught I know.
OTHELLO   What dost thou think?
IAGO   Think, my lord?
OTHELLO   Think, my lord?
  By heaven, he echoes me,
  As if there were some monster in his thought
  Too hideous to be shown. Thou dost mean something:
  I heard thee say but now, thou lik'st not that,
110 When Cassio left my wife. What didst not like?

And when I told thee he was of my counsel
In my whole course of wooing, thou cried'st 'Indeed?'
And didst contract and purse thy brow together,
As if thou then hadst shut up in thy brain
Some horrible conceit.[18] If thou dost love me,
Show me thy thought.

IAGO   My lord, you know I love you.

OTHELLO   I think thou dost;
And, for[19] I know thou'rt full of love and honesty
And weigh'st thy words before thou giv'st them breath,
Therefore these stops of thine fright me the more;
For such things in a false disloyal knave
Are tricks of custom; but in a man that's just
They are close dilations,[20] working from the heart
That passion cannot rule.

IAGO   For Michael Cassio,
I dare be sworn I think that he is honest.

OTHELLO   I think so too.

IAGO   Men should be what they seem;
Or those that be not, would they might seem none!

OTHELLO   Certain, men should be what they seem.

IAGO   Why then, I think Cassio's an honest man.

OTHELLO   Nay, yet there's more in this.
I prithee speak to me as to thy thinkings,
As thou dost ruminate, and give thy worst of thoughts
The worst of words.

IAGO   Good my lord, pardon me:
Though I am bound to every act of duty,
I am not bound to that all slaves are free to.
Utter my thoughts? Why, say they are vile and false,
As where's that palace whereinto foul things
Sometimes intrude not? Who has a breast so pure
But some uncleanly apprehensions
Keep leets[21] and law days, and in session sit
With meditations lawful?

OTHELLO   Thou dost conspire against thy friend, Iago,
If thou but think'st him wronged, and mak'st his ear
A stranger to thy thoughts.

IAGO   I do beseech you—
Though I perchance am vicious in my guess
(As I confess it is my nature's plague

---

18. Idea
19. Because

20. Secret feelings
21. Sessions of local courts

To spy into abuses, and oft my jealousy[22]
Shapes faults that are not), that your wisdom yet
From one that so imperfectly conjects[23]
150   Would take no notice, nor build yourself a trouble
Out of his scattering and unsure observance.
It were not for your quiet nor your good,
Nor for my manhood, honesty, or wisdom,
To let you know my thoughts.

OTHELLO   What dost thou mean?

IAGO   Good name in man and woman, dear my lord,
Is the immediate jewel of their souls.
Who steals my purse steals trash; 'tis something, nothing;
'Twas mine, 'tis his, and has been slave to thousands;
But he that filches from me my good name
160   Robs me of that which not enriches him
And makes me poor indeed.

OTHELLO   By heaven, I'll know thy thoughts!

IAGO   You cannot, if my heart were in your hand;
Nor shall not whilst 'tis in my custody.

OTHELLO   Ha!

IAGO   O, beware, my lord, of jealousy!
It is the green-eyed monster, which doth mock[24]
The meat it feeds on. That cuckold lives in bliss
Who, certain of his fate, loves not his wronger;
But O, what damnèd minutes tells he o'er
170   Who dotes, yet doubts—suspects, yet strongly loves!

OTHELLO   O misery!

IAGO   Poor and content is rich, and rich enough;
But riches fineless[25] is as poor as winter
To him that ever fears he shall be poor.
Good God, the souls of all my tribe defend
From jealousy!

OTHELLO   Why, why is this?
Think'st thou I'ld make a life of jealousy,
To follow still the changes of the moon
With fresh suspicions? No! To be once in doubt
180   Is once to be resolved. Exchange me for a goat
When I shall turn the business of my soul
To such exsufflicate and blown[26] surmises,
Matching thy inference. 'Tis not to make me jealous

22. Suspicion
23. Conjectures
24. Play with; i.e., torture
25. Boundless
26. Inflated and flyblown

To say my wife is fair, feeds well, loves company,
Is free of speech, sings, plays, and dances well;
Where virtue is, these are more virtuous.
Nor from mine own weak merits will I draw
The smallest fear or doubt of her revolt,
For she had eyes, and chose me. No, Iago;
190   I'll see before I doubt; when I doubt, prove;
And on the proof there is no more but this—
Away at once with love or jealousy!

IAGO   I am glad of this; for now I shall have reason
To show the love and duty that I bear you
With franker spirit. Therefore, as I am bound,
Receive it from me. I speak not yet of proof.
Look to your wife; observe her well with Cassio;
Wear your eye thus, not jealous nor secure:
I would not have your free and noble nature,
200   Out of self-bounty,²⁷ be abused. Look to't.
I know our country disposition well:
In Venice they do let God see the pranks
They dare not show their husbands; their best conscience
Is not to leave't undone, but keep't unknown.

OTHELLO   Dost thou say so?

IAGO   She did deceive her father, marrying you;
And when she seemed to shake and fear your looks,
She loved them most.

OTHELLO   And so she did.

IAGO   Why, go to then!
She that, so young, could give out such a seeming
210   To seel²⁸ her father's eyes up close as oak²⁹—
He thought 'twas witchcraft—but I am much to blame.
I humbly do beseech you of your pardon
For too much loving you.

OTHELLO   I am bound to thee for ever.

IAGO   I see this hath a little dashed your spirits.

OTHELLO   Not a jot, not a jot.

IAGO   I' faith, I fear it has.
I hope you will consider what is spoke
Comes from my love. But I do see y' are moved.
I am to pray you not to strain my speech
To grosser issues³⁰ nor to larger reach
220   Than to suspicion.

27. Natural goodness
28. Close; i.e., deceive
29. Close grained wood
30. Consequences

OTHELLO   I will not.

IAGO   Should you do so, my lord,
My speech should fall into such vile success[31]
As my thoughts aim not at. Cassio's my worthy friend—
My lord, I see y' are moved.

OTHELLO   No, not much moved:
I do not think but Desdemona's honest.[32]

IAGO   Long live she so! and long live you to think so!

OTHELLO   And yet, how nature erring from itself—

IAGO   Ay, there's the point! as (to be bold with you)
Not to affect[33] many proposèd matches
230   Of her own clime, complexion, and degree,
Whereto we see in all things nature tends—
Foh! one may smell in such a will[34] most rank,
Foul disproportion, thoughts unnatural—
But pardon me—I do not in position[35]
Distinctly speak of her; though I may fear
Her will, recoiling[36] to her better judgment,
May fall to match[37] you with her country forms,[38]
And happily[39] repent.

OTHELLO   Farewell, farewell!
If more thou dost perceive, let me know more.
240   Set on thy wife to observe. Leave me, Iago.

IAGO   My lord, I take my leave.   *Going.*

OTHELLO   Why did I marry? This honest creature doubtless
Sees and knows more, much more, than he unfolds.

IAGO [*returns*]   My lord, I would I might entreat your honor
To scan this thing no further: leave it to time.
Although 'tis fit that Cassio have his place,
For sure he fills it up with great ability,
Yet, if you please to hold him off awhile,
You shall by that perceive him and his means.
250   Note if your lady strain his entertainment[40]
With any strong or vehement importunity;
Much will be seen in that. In the mean time
Let me be thought too busy in my fears
(As worthy cause I have to fear I am)
And hold her free.[41] I do beseech your honor.

31. Evil outcome	37. Happen to compare
32. Chaste	38. Appearance of her countrymen
33. Desire	39. Perchance
34. Desire	40. Urge his reinstatement
35. In these assertions	41. Consider her guiltless
36. Reverting	

OTHELLO   Fear not my government.[42]

IAGO   I once more take my leave.   *Exit.*

OTHELLO   This fellow's of exceeding honesty,
And knows all qualities, with a learnèd spirit
260   Of human dealings. If I do prove her haggard,[43]
Though that her jesses[44] were my dear heartstrings,
I'd whistle her off and let her down the wind[45]
To prey at fortune. Haply, for I am black
And have not those soft parts of conversation[46]
That chamberers[47] have, or for I am declined
Into the vale of years—yet that's not much—
She's gone. I am abused, and my relief
Must be to loathe her. O curse of marriage,
That we can call these delicate creatures ours,
270   And not their appetites! I had rather be a toad
And live upon the vapor of a dungeon
Than keep a corner in the thing I love
For others' uses. Yet 'tis the plague of great ones;
Prerogatived[48] are they less than the base.
'Tis destiny unshunnable, like death.
Even then this forkèd plague[49] is fated to us
When we do quicken.[50] Look where she comes.

Enter Desdemona and Emilia.

If she be false, O, then heaven mocks itself!
I'll not believe't.

DESDEMONA   How now, my dear Othello?
280   Your dinner, and the generous[51] islanders
By you invited, do attend your presence.

OTHELLO   I am to blame.

DESDEMONA   Why do you speak so faintly?
Are you not well?

OTHELLO   I have a pain upon my forehead, here.

DESDEMONA   Faith, that's with watching;[52] 'twill away again.
Let me but bind it hard, within this hour
It will be well.

OTHELLO   Your napkin is too little

42. Self-control
43. Wild hawk
44. Straps connected to the legs of a hawk
for keeping it under control
45. *whistle . . . wind:* turn her loose and let
her fly wherever her will might take her
(presumably to her self destruction)

46. *soft . . . conversation:* polished manners
47. Courtiers
48. Privileged
49. Horns of a cuckold
50. Are born
51. Noble
52. From lack of sleep

He pushes the handkerchief from him, and it falls unnoticed.

Let it alone. Come, I'll go in with you.

DESDEMONA   I am very sorry that you are not well.   *Exit with Othello.*

290   EMILIA   I am glad I have found this napkin;
This was her first remembrance from the Moor.
My wayward husband hath a hundred times
Wooed me to steal it; but she so loves the token
(For he conjured her she should ever keep it)
That she reserves it evermore about her
To kiss and talk to. I'll have the work ta'en out⁵³
And give't Iago.
What he will do with it heaven knows, not I;
I nothing but⁵⁴ to please his fantasy.⁵⁵

Enter Iago.

300   IAGO   How now? What do you here alone?

EMILIA   Do not you chide; I have a thing for you.

IAGO   A thing for me? It is a common thing—

EMILIA   Ha?

IAGO   To have a foolish wife.

EMILIA   O, is that all? What will you give me now
For that same handkerchief?

IAGO   What handkerchief?

EMILIA   What handkerchief!
Why, that the Moor first gave to Desdemona;
That which so often you did bid me steal.

310   IAGO   Hast stol'n it from her?

EMILIA   No, faith; she let it drop by negligence,
And to th' advantage, I, being here, took't up.
Look, here it is.

IAGO   A good wench! Give it me.

EMILIA   What will you do with't, that you have been so earnest
To have me filch it?

IAGO   Why, what's that to you?   *Snatches it.*

EMILIA   If it be not for some purpose of import,
Give't me again. Poor lady, she'll run mad
When she shall lack it.

IAGO   Be not acknown on't;⁵⁶ I have use for it.

53. Pattern copied
54. My only desire is
55. Whim

56. *Be . . . it:* pretend that you know nothing about it

320 Go, leave me.   *Exit Emilia.*
    I will in Cassio's lodging lose this napkin
    And let him find it. Trifles light as air
    Are to the jealous confirmations strong
    As proofs of holy writ. This may do something.
    The Moor already changes with my poison:
    Dangerous conceits are in their natures poisons,
    Which at the first are scarce found to distaste,
    But with a little act upon the blood
    Burn like the mines of sulphur.

Enter Othello.

                              I did say so.
330 Look where he comes! Not poppy nor mandragora,[57]
    Nor all the drowsy syrups of the world,
    Shall ever med'cine thee to that sweet sleep
    Which thou owedst yesterday.
    OTHELLO   Ha! ha! false to me?
    IAGO   Why, how now, general? No more of that!
    OTHELLO   Avaunt! be gone! Thou hast set me on the rack.
        I swear 'tis better to be much abused
        Than but to know't a little.
    IAGO   How now, my lord?
    OTHELLO   What sense had I of her stol'n hours of lust?
        I saw't not, thought it not, it harmed not me;
340   I slept the next night well, fed well, was free[58] and merry;
        I found not Cassio's kisses on her lips.
        He that is robbed, not wanting what is stol'n,
        Let him not know't, and he's not robbed at all.
    IAGO   I am sorry to hear this.
    OTHELLO   I had been happy if the general camp,
        Pioneers[59] and all, had tasted her sweet body,
        So I had nothing known. O, now for ever
        Farewell the tranquil mind! farewell content!
        Farewell the plumèd troop, and the big wars
350   That make ambition virtue! O, farewell!
        Farewell the neighing steed and the shrill trump,
        The spirit-stirring drum, th' ear-piercing fife,
        The royal banner, and all quality,
        Pride, pomp, and circumstance[60] of glorious war!

57. A narcotic   59. Lowest rank of soldier
58. Carefree   60. Pageantry

And O you mortal engines[61] whose rude throats
Th' immortal Jove's dread clamors counterfeit,[62]
Farewell! Othello's occupation's gone!

IAGO   Is't possible, my lord?

OTHELLO   Villain, be sure thou prove my love a whore!
360   Be sure of it; give me the ocular proof;
Or, by the worth of man's eternal soul,
Thou hadst been better have been born a dog
Than answer my waked wrath!

IAGO   Is't come to this?

OTHELLO   Make me to see't; or at the least so prove it
That the probation[63] bear no hinge nor loop
To hang a doubt on—or woe upon thy life!

IAGO   My noble lord—

OTHELLO   If thou dost slander her and torture me,
Never pray more; abandon all remorse;
370   On horror's head horrors accumulate;
Do deeds to make heaven weep, all earth amazed;
For nothing canst thou to damnation add
Greater than that.

IAGO   O grace! O heaven forgive me!
Are you a man? Have you a soul or sense?—
God b' wi' you! take mine office. O wretched fool,
That liv'st to make thine honesty a vice!
O monstrous world! Take note, take note, O world,
To be direct and honest is not safe.
I thank you for this profit;[64] and from hence
380   I'll love no friend, sith love breed such offense.

OTHELLO   Nay, stay. Thou shouldst be honest.

IAGO   I should be wise; for honesty's a fool
And loses that it works for.

OTHELLO   By the world,
I think my wife be honest, and think she is not;
I think that thou art just, and think thou art not.
I'll have some proof. Her name, that was as fresh
As Dian's visage, is now begrimed and black
As mine own face. If there be cords, or knives,
Poison, or fire, or suffocating streams,
390   I'll not endure it. Would I were satisfied!

IAGO   I see, sir, you are eaten up with passion:

---

61. Deadly artillery   63. Proof
62. Imitate   64. Lesson

I do repent me that I put it to you.
You would be satisfied?

OTHELLO Would? Nay, I will.

IAGO And may; but how? how satisfied, my lord?
Would you, the supervisor, grossly gape on?
Behold her topped?

OTHELLO Death and damnation! O!

IAGO It were a tedious difficulty, I think,
To bring them to that prospect. Damn them then,
If ever mortal eyes do see them bolster[65]
400   More[66] than their own! What then? How then?
What shall I say? Where's satisfaction?
It is impossible you should see this,
Were they as prime[67] as goats, as hot as monkeys,
As salt[68] as wolves in pride,[69] and fools as gross
As ignorance made drunk. But yet, I say,
If imputation and strong circumstances
Which lead directly to the door of truth
Will give you satisfaction, you may have't.

OTHELLO Give me a living reason she's disloyal.

410 IAGO I do not like the office.
But sith I am entered in this cause so far,
Pricked to't by foolish honesty and love,
I will go on. I lay with Cassio lately,
And being troubled with a raging tooth,
I could not sleep.
There are a kind of men so loose of soul
That in their sleeps will mutter their affairs.
One of this kind is Cassio.
In sleep I heard him say, 'Sweet Desdemona,
420   Let us be wary, let us hide our loves!'
And then, sir, would he gripe[70] and wring my hand,
Cry 'O sweet creature!' and then kiss me hard,
As if he plucked up kisses by the roots
That grew upon my lips; then laid his leg
Over my thigh, and sighed, and kissed, and then
Cried 'Cursèd fate that gave thee to the Moor!'

OTHELLO O monstrous! monstrous!

IAGO Nay, this was but his dream.

65. Lie together
66. Other
67. Lustful

68. Lecherous
69. Heat
70. Grip

OTHELLO   But this denoted a foregone conclusion:
'Tis a shrewd doubt,[71] though it be but a dream.

430   IAGO   And this may help to thicken other proofs
That do demonstrate thinly.

OTHELLO   I'll tear her all to pieces!

IAGO   Nay, but be wise. Yet we see nothing done;
She may be honest yet. Tell me but this—
Have you not sometimes seen a handkerchief
Spotted with strawberries in your wife's hand?

OTHELLO   I gave her such a one; 'twas my first gift.

IAGO   I know not that; but such a handkerchief—
I am sure it was your wife's—did I to-day
See Cassio wipe his beard with.

OTHELLO   If't be that—

440   IAGO   If it be that, or any that was hers,
It speaks against her with the other proofs.

OTHELLO   O, that the slave had forty thousand lives!
One is too poor, too weak for my revenge.
Now do I see 'tis true. Look here, Iago:
All my fond love thus do I blow to heaven.
'Tis gone.
Arise, black vengeance, from the hollow hell!
Yield up, O love, thy crown and hearted throne
To tyrannous hate! Swell, bosom, with thy fraught,[72]
For 'tis of aspics'[73] tongues!

450   IAGO   Yet be content.

OTHELLO   O, blood, blood, blood!

IAGO   Patience, I say. Your mind perhaps may change.

OTHELLO   Never, Iago. Like to the Pontic sea,[74]
Whose icy current and compulsive course
Ne'er feels retiring ebb, but keeps due on
To the Propontic and the Hellespont,
Even so my bloody thoughts, with violent pace,
Shall ne'er look back, ne'er ebb to humble love,
Till that a capable[75] and wide revenge

460   Swallow them up. [He kneels.] Now, by yond marble heaven,
In the due reverence of a sacred vow
I here engage my words.

IAGO   Do not rise yet.   *Iago kneels.*

---

71. Strong reason for suspicion   74. Black Sea
72. Burden   75. Comprehensive
73. Asps' (deadly poisonous snakes)

Witness, you ever-burning lights above,
You elements that clip[76] us round about,
Witness that here Iago doth give up
The execution[77] of his wit, hands, heart
To wronged Othello's service! Let him command,
And to obey shall be in me remorse,[78]
What bloody business ever.   *They rise.*

OTHELLO   I greet thy love,
470   Not with vain thanks but with acceptance bounteous,
And will upon the instant put thee to't.
Within these three days let me hear thee say
That Cassio's not alive.

IAGO   My friend is dead; 'tis done at your request.
But let her live.

OTHELLO   Damn her, lewd minx! O, damn her!
Come, go with me apart. I will withdraw
To furnish me with some swift means of death
For the fair devil. Now art thou my lieutenant.

IAGO   I am your own for ever.   *Exeunt.*

SCENE 4

Enter Desdemona, Emilia, and Clown.

DESDEMONA   Do you know, sirrah, where Lieutenant Cassio lies?[79]

CLOWN   I dare not say he lies anywhere.

DESDEMONA   Why, man?

CLOWN   He's a soldier, and for me to say a soldier lies is stabbing.

DESDEMONA   Go to. Where lodges he?

CLOWN   To tell you where he lodges is to tell you where I lie.

10   DESDEMONA   Can anything be made of this?

CLOWN   I know not where he lodges; and for me to devise a lodging, and say
he lies here or he lies there, were to lie in mine own throat.[80]

DESDEMONA   Can you enquire him out, and be edified by report?

CLOWN   I will catechize the world for him; that is, make questions, and by
them answer.

DESDEMONA   Seek him, bid him come hither. Tell him I have moved my lord
20   on his behalf and hope all will be well.

CLOWN   To do this is within the compass of man's wit, and therefore I'll
attempt the doing of it.   *Exit.*

76. Encompass   79. Lodges
77. Action   80. Tell an obvious lie
78. Expression of pity (for Othello)

DESDEMONA   Where should I lose that handkerchief, Emilia?
EMILIA   I know not, madam.
DESDEMONA   Believe me, I had rather have lost my purse
    Full of crusadoes;[81] and but my noble Moor
    Is true of mind, and made of no such baseness
    As jealous creatures are, it were enough
    To put him to ill thinking.
EMILIA   Is he not jealous?
30   DESDEMONA   Who? he? I think the sun where he was born
    Drew all such humors[82] from him.

Enter Othello.

EMILIA   Look where he comes.
DESDEMONA   I will not leave him now till Cassio
    Be called to him.—How is't with you, my lord?
OTHELLO   Well, my good lady. [*Aside*] O, hardness to dissemble!—
    How do you, Desdemona?
DESDEMONA   Well, my good lord.
OTHELLO   Give me your hand. This hand is moist, my lady.
DESDEMONA   It yet hath felt no age nor known no sorrow.
OTHELLO   This argues fruitfulness and liberal heart.
    Hot, hot, and moist. This hand of yours requires
40   A sequester[83] from liberty, fasting and prayer,
    Much castigation, exercise devout;
    For here's a young and sweating devil here
    That commonly rebels. 'Tis a good hand,
    A frank one.
DESDEMONA   You may, indeed, say so;
    For 'twas that hand that gave away my heart.
OTHELLO   A liberal hand! The hearts of old gave hands;
    But our new heraldry is hands, not hearts.
DESDEMONA   I cannot speak of this. Come now, your promise!
OTHELLO   What promise, chuck?
50   DESDEMONA   I have sent to bid Cassio come speak with you.
OTHELLO   I have a salt and sorry rheum[84] offends me.
    Lend me thy handkerchief
DESDEMONA   Here, my lord.
OTHELLO   That which I gave you.
DESDEMONA   I have it not about me.
OTHELLO   Not?

81. Portuguese gold coins
82. Temperamental inclinations
83. Removal
84. Head cold

DESDEMONA   No, faith, my lord.

OTHELLO   That is a fault.
That handkerchief
Did an Egyptian[85] to my mother give.
She was a charmer,[86] and could almost read
The thoughts of people. She told her, while she kept it,
'Twould make her amiable[87] and subdue my father
60   Entirely to her love; but if she lost it
Or made a gift of it, my father's eye
Should hold her loathly, and his spirits should hunt
After new fancies. She, dying, gave it me,
And bid me, when my fate would have me wive,
To give it her. I did so; and take heed on't;
Make it a darling like your precious eye.
To lose't or give't away were such perdition
As nothing else could match.

DESDEMONA   Is't possible?

OTHELLO 'Tis true. There's magic in the web of it.
70   A sibyl[88] that had numbered in the world
The sun to course two hundred compasses,
In her prophetic fury sewed the work;
The worms were hallowed that did breed the silk;
And it was dyed in mummy[89] which the skillful
Conserved[90] of maidens' hearts.

DESDEMONA   I' faith? Is't true?

OTHELLO Most veritable. Therefore look to't well.

DESDEMONA Then would to God that I had never seen't!

OTHELLO Ha! Wherefore?

DESDEMONA Why do you speak so startingly and rash?

80 OTHELLO Is't lost? Is't gone? Speak, is it out o' th' way?

DESDEMONA Heaven bless us!

OTHELLO Say you?

DESDEMONA It is not lost. But what an if it were?

OTHELLO How?

DESDEMONA I say it is not lost.

OTHELLO   Fetch't, let me see't!

DESDEMONA Why, so I can, sir; but I will not now.
This is a trick to put me from my suit:
Pray you let Cassio be received again.

OTHELLO Fetch me the handkerchief! My mind misgives.

---

85. Gypsy
86. Magician
87. Desirable

88. Prophetess
89. Fluid derived from embalmed bodies
90. Preserved

90   DESDEMONA   Come, come!
        You'll never meet a more sufficient man.
OTHELLO   The handkerchief!
DESDEMONA   I pray talk me of Cassio.
OTHELLO   The handkerchief!
DESDEMONA   A man that all his time
        Hath founded his good fortunes on your love,
        Shared dangers with you—
OTHELLO   The handkerchief!
DESDEMONA   I'faith, you are to blame.
OTHELLO   Zounds!   *Exit.*
EMILIA   Is not this man jealous?
100   DESDEMONA   I ne'er saw this before.
        Sure there's some wonder in this handkerchief;
        I am most unhappy in the loss of it.
EMILIA   'Tis not a year or two shows us a man.
        They are all but stomachs, and we all but food;
        They eat us hungerly, and when they are full,
        They belch us.

Enter Iago and Cassio.

                        Look you—Cassio and my husband!
IAGO   There is no other way; 'tis she must do't.
        And lo the happiness![91] Go and importune her.
DESDEMONA   How now, good Cassio? What's the news with you?
110   CASSIO   Madam, my former suit. I do beseech you
        That by your virtuous means I may again
        Exist, and be a member of his love
        Whom I with all the office of my heart
        Entirely honor. I would not be delayed.
        If my offense be of such mortal kind
        That neither service past, nor present sorrows,
        Nor purposed merit in futurity,
        Can ransom me into his love again,
        But to know so must be my benefit.
120   So shall I clothe me in a forced content,
        And shut myself up in some other course,
        To fortune's alms.
DESDEMONA   Alas, thrice-gentle Cassio!
        My advocation[92] is not now in tune.
        My lord is not my lord; nor should I know him,

91. Good luck   92. Advocacy

Were he in favor[93] as in humor altered.
So help me every spirit sanctified
As I have spoken for you all my best
And stood within the blank[94] of his displeasure
For my free speech! You must awhile be patient.
130   What I can do I will; and more I will
Than for myself I dare. Let that suffice you.

IAGO   Is my lord angry?

EMILIA   He went hence but now,
And certainly in strange unquietness.

IAGO   Can he be angry? I have seen the cannon
When it hath blown his ranks into the air
And, like the devil, from his very arm
Puffed his own brother—and can he be angry?
Something of moment then. I will go meet him.
There's matter in't indeed if he be angry.

DESDEMONA   I prithee do so.   *Exit Iago.*
140   Something sure of state,
Either from Venice or some unhatched practice[95]
Made demonstrable here in Cyprus to him,
Hath puddled[96] his clear spirit; and in such cases
Men's natures wrangle with inferior things,
Though great ones are their object. 'Tis even so;
For let our finger ache, and it endues[97]
Our other, healthful members even to that sense
Of pain. Nay, we must think men are not gods,
Nor of them look for such observancy[98]
150   As fits the bridal. Beshrew me much, Emilia,
I was, unhandsome warrior as I am,
Arraigning his unkindness with my soul;
But now I find I had suborned the witness,
And he's indicted falsely.

EMILIA   Pray heaven it be state matters, as you think,
And no conception nor no jealous toy[99]
Concerning you.

DESDEMONA   Alas the day! I never gave him cause.

EMILIA   But jealous souls will not be answered so;
160   They are not ever jealous for the cause,
But jealous for they are jealous. 'Tis a monster
Begot upon itself, born on itself.

93. Appearance   97. Brings
94. Center of a target   98. Devoted attention
95. Plot in the making   99. Fancy
96. Muddied

DESDEMONA   Heaven keep that monster from Othello's mind!
EMILIA   Lady, amen.
DESDEMONA   I will go seek him. Cassio, walk here about:
    If I do find him fit, I'll move your suit
    And seek to effect it to my uttermost.
CASSIO   I humbly thank your ladyship.   *Exeunt Desdemona and Emilia.*

Enter Bianca.

BIANCA   Save you, friend Cassio!
CASSIO   What make you from home?
170   How is it with you, my most fair Bianca?
    I' faith, sweet love, I was coming to your house.
BIANCA   And I was going to your lodging, Cassio.
    What, keep a week away? seven days and nights?
    Eightscore eight hours? and lovers' absent hours,
    More tedious than the dial[100] eightscore times?
    O weary reck'ning!
CASSIO   Pardon me, Bianca:
    I have this while with leaden thoughts been pressed;
    But I shall in a more continuate[101] time
    Strike off this score of absence. Sweet Bianca,

Gives her Desdemona's handkerchief.

    Take me this work out.
180 BIANCA   O Cassio, whence came this?
    This is some token from a newer friend.
    To the felt absence now I feel a cause.
    Is't come to this? Well, well.
CASSIO   Go to, woman!
    Throw your vile guesses in the devil's teeth,
    From whence you have them. You are jealous now
    That this is from some mistress, some remembrance.
    No, by my faith, Bianca.
BIANCA   Why, whose is it?
CASSIO   I know not, sweet; I found it in my chamber.
    I like the work well; ere it be demanded,
190   As like enough it will, I'd have it copied.
    Take it and do't, and leave me for this time.
BIANCA   Leave you? Wherefore?
CASSIO   I do attend here on the general

100. Clock   101. Uninterrupted

And think it no addition, nor my wish,
To have him see me womaned.
BIANCA   Why, I pray you?
CASSIO Not that I love you not.
BIANCA   But that you do not love me!
   I pray you bring me on the way a little,
   And say if I shall see you soon at night.
CASSIO 'Tis but a little way that I can bring you,
   For I attend here; but I'll see you soon.
200 BIANCA 'Tis very good. I must be circumstanced.[102]   *Exeunt.*

102. Governed by circumstances

ACT IV

SCENE 1

Enter Othello and Iago.

IAGO Will you think so?
OTHELLO   Think so, Iago?
IAGO   What,
   To kiss in private?
OTHELLO   An unauthorized kiss.
IAGO Or to be naked with her friend in bed
   An hour or more, not meaning any harm?
OTHELLO Naked in bed, Iago, and not mean harm?
   It is hypocrisy against the devil.
   They that mean virtuously, and yet do so,
   The devil their virtue tempts, and they tempt heaven.
IAGO So they do nothing, 'tis a venial slip.
10   But if I give my wife a handkerchief—
OTHELLO What then?
IAGO Why, then 'tis hers, my lord; and being hers,
   She may, I think, bestow't on any man.
OTHELLO She is protectress of her honor too;
   May she give that?
IAGO Her honor is an essence that's not seen;
   They have it very oft[1] that have it not.
   But for the handkerchief—
OTHELLO By heaven, I would most gladly have forgot it!

1. *They . . . oft:* they often have the appearance of it

20   Thou said'st—O, it comes o'er my memory
        As doth the raven o'er the infected house,
        Boding to all!—he had my handkerchief.
IAGO   Ay, what of that?
OTHELLO   That's not so good now.
IAGO   What
        If I had said I had seen him do you wrong?
        Or heard him say—as knaves be such abroad
        Who having, by their own importunate suit,
        Or voluntary dotage of some mistress,
        Convincèd or supplied² them, cannot choose
        But they must blab—
OTHELLO   Hath he said anything?
30 IAGO   He hath, my lord; but be you well assured,
        No more than he'll unswear.
OTHELLO   What hath he said?
IAGO   Faith, that he did—I know not what he did.
OTHELLO   What? what?
IAGO   Lie—
OTHELLO   With her?
IAGO   With her, on her; what you will.
OTHELLO   Lie with her? lie on her?—We say lie on her when they belie
        her.—Lie with her! Zounds, that's fulsome.—Handkerchief—
40   confessions—handkerchief!—To confess, and be hanged for his labor—
        first to be hanged, and then to confess! I tremble at it. Nature would not
        invest herself in such shadowing³ passion without some instruction.⁴ It
        is not words that shakes me thus.—Pish! Noses, ears, and lips? Is't
        possible?—Confess?—Handkerchief?—O devil!   *Falls in a trance.*
IAGO   Work on,
        My med'cine, work! Thus credulous fools are caught,
        And many worthy and chaste dames even thus,
        All guiltless, meet reproach.—What, ho! my lord!
        My lord, I say! Othello!

Enter Cassio.

                    How now, Cassio?
50 CASSIO   What's the matter?
IAGO   My lord is fall'n into an epilepsy.
        This is his second fit; he had one yesterday.
CASSIO   Rub him about the temples.

2. Overcome or gratified   4. Prompting, or cause
3. Overwhelming

IAGO   No, forbear.
    The lethargy must have his quiet course.
    If not, he foams at mouth, and by and by
    Breaks out to savage madness. Look, he stirs.
    Do you withdraw yourself a little while.
    He will recover straight. When he is gone,
    I would on great occasion speak with you.   *Exit Cassio.*
60   How is it, general? Have you not hurt your head?
OTHELLO   Dost thou mock me?
IAGO   I mock you? No, by heaven.
    Would you would bear your fortune like a man!
OTHELLO   A hornèd man's[5] a monster and a beast.
IAGO   There's many a beast then in a populous city,
    And many a civil monster.
OTHELLO   Did he confess it?
IAGO   Good, sir, be a man.
    Think every bearded fellow that's but yoked[6]
    May draw with you. There's millions now alive
    That nightly lie in those unproper[7] beds
70   Which they dare swear peculiar:[8] your case is better.
    O, 'tis the spite of hell, the fiend's arch-mock,
    To lip a wanton in a secure[9] couch,
    And to suppose her chaste! No, let me know;
    And knowing what I am, I know what she shall be.
OTHELLO   O, thou are wise! 'Tis certain.
IAGO   Stand you awhile apart;
    Confine yourself but in a patient list.[10]
    Whilst you were here, o'erwhelmèd with your grief—
    A passion most unsuiting such a man—
    Cassio came hither. I shifted him away
80   And laid good 'scuse upon your ecstasy;[11]
    Bade him anon return, and here speak with me;
    The which he promised. Do but encave[12] yourself
    And mark the fleers,[13] the gibes, and notable scorns
    That dwell in every region of his face;
    For I will make him tell the tale anew—
    Where, how, how oft, how long ago, and when

5. Cuckold
6. Married
7. Not exclusively their own
8. Exclusively their own
9. Free from suspicion

10. Within the bounds of patience
11. Trance
12. Conceal
13. Sneers

He hath, and is again to cope[14] your wife.
I say, but mark his gesture. Marry, patience!
Or I shall say you are all in all in spleen,[15]
And nothing of a man.

90   OTHELLO   Dost thou hear, Iago?
I will be found most cunning in my patience;
But—dost thou hear?—most bloody.

IAGO   That's not amiss;
But yet keep time in all. Will you withdraw?   *Othello retires.*
Now will I question Cassio of Bianca,
A huswife[16] that by selling her desires
Buys herself bread and clothes. It is a creature
That dotes on Cassio, as 'tis the strumpet's plague
To beguile many and be beguiled by one.
He, when he hears of her, cannot refrain

100   From the excess of laughter. Here he comes.
As he shall smile, Othello shall go mad;
And his unbookish[17] jealousy must conster[18]
Poor Cassio's smiles, gestures, and light behavior
Quite in the wrong. How do you now, lieutenant?

CASSIO   The worser that you give me the addition[19]
Whose want even kills me.

IAGO   Ply Desdemona well, and you are sure on't.
Now, if this suit lay in Bianca's power,
How quickly should you speed!

CASSIO   Alas, poor caitiff![20]

110   OTHELLO   Look how he laughs already!

IAGO   I never knew a woman love man so.

CASSIO   Alas, poor rogue! I think, i' faith, she loves me.

OTHELLO   Now he denies it faintly, and laughs it out.

IAGO   Do you hear, Cassio?

OTHELLO   Now he importunes him
To tell it o'er. Go to! Well said, well said!

IAGO   She gives it out that you shall marry her.
Do you intend it?

120   CASSIO   Ha, ha, ha!

OTHELLO   Do you triumph, Roman? Do you triumph?

---

14. Meet
15. Completely overcome by emotion
16. Hussy
17. Uninstructed

18. Construe
19. Title (of lieutenant)
20. Wretch

CASSIO   I marry her? What, a customer?[21] Prithee bear some charity to my
wit; do not think it so unwholesome. Ha, ha, ha!

OTHELLO   So, so, so, so! They laugh that win!

IAGO   Faith, the cry goes that you shall marry her.

CASSIO   Prithee say true.

IAGO   I am a very villain else.

130 OTHELLO   Have you scored[22] me? Well.

CASSIO   This is the monkey's own giving out. She is persuaded I will marry
her out of her own love and flattery, not out of my promise.

OTHELLO   Iago beckons me; now he begins the story.

CASSIO   She was here even now; she haunts me in every place. I was t' other
day talking on the sea bank with certain Venetians, and thither comes
140 the bauble,[23] and, by this hand, she falls me thus about my neck—

OTHELLO   Crying 'O dear Cassio!' as it were. His gesture imports it.

CASSIO   So hangs, and lolls, and weeps upon me; so hales and pulls me! Ha,
ha, ha!

OTHELLO   Now he tells how she plucked him to my chamber.
O, I see that nose of yours, but not that dog I shall throw't to.

CASSIO   Well, I must leave her company.

Enter Bianca.

IAGO   Before me! Look where she comes.

150 CASSIO   'Tis such another fitchew![24] marry, a perfumed one. What do you
mean by this haunting of me?

BIANCA   Let the devil and his dam haunt you! What did you mean by that
same handkerchief you gave me even now? I was a fine fool to take it. I
must take out the whole work? A likely piece of work that you should
find it in your chamber and know not who left it there! This is some
minx's token, and I must take out the work? There! Give it your hobby-
160 horse.[25] Wheresoever you had it, I'll take out no work on't.

CASSIO   How now, my sweet Bianca? How now? how now?

OTHELLO   By heaven, that should be my handkerchief!

BIANCA   An you'll come to supper to-night, you may; an you will not, come
when you are next prepared for.   *Exit.*

IAGO   After her, after her!

170 CASSIO   Faith, I must; she'll rail i' th' street else.

IAGO   Will you sup there?

CASSIO   Yes, I intend so.

IAGO   Well, I may chance to see you; for I would very fain speak with you.

---

21. Prostitute   24. Polecat; slang term for a whore
22. Beaten   25. Harlot
23. Plaything

CASSIO Prithee come. Will you?

IAGO Go to! say no more.   *Exit Cassio.*

180 OTHELLO [*comes forward*] How shall I murder him, Iago?

IAGO Did you perceive how he laughed at his vice?

OTHELLO O Iago!

IAGO And did you see the handkerchief?

OTHELLO Was that mine?

IAGO Yours, by this hand! And to see how he prizes the foolish woman
your wife! She gave it him, and he hath giv'n it his whore.

OTHELLO I would have him nine years a-killing!—A fine woman! a fair
woman! a sweet woman!

190 IAGO Nay, you must forget that.

OTHELLO Ay, let her rot, and perish, and be damned to-night; for she shall
not live. No, my heart is turned to stone; I strike it, and it hurts my
hand. O, the world hath not a sweeter creature! She might lie by an
emperor's side and command him tasks.

IAGO Nay, that's not your way.

OTHELLO Hang her! I do but say what she is. So delicate with her needle! an
admirable musician! O, she will sing the savageness out of a bear! Of so
200 high and plenteous wit and invention—

IAGO She's the worse for all this.

OTHELLO O, a thousand thousand times! And then, of so gentle[26] a condition!

IAGO Ay, too gentle.[27]

OTHELLO Nay, that's certain. But yet the pity of it, Iago! O Iago, the pity of
it, Iago!

210 IAGO If you are so fond over her iniquity, give her patent[28] to offend; for if it
touch not you, it comes near nobody.

OTHELLO I will chop her into messes! Cuckold me!

IAGO O, 'tis foul in her.

OTHELLO With mine officer!

IAGO That's fouler.

OTHELLO Get me some poison, Iago, this night. I'll not expostulate with her,
lest her body and beauty unprovide[29] my mind again. This night, Iago!

IAGO Do it not with poison. Strangle her in her bed, even the bed she hath
contaminated.

OTHELLO Good, good! The justice of it pleases. Very good!

220 IAGO And for Cassio, let me be his undertaker: you shall hear more by
midnight.

OTHELLO Excellent good!   *A trumpet.*

What trumpet is that same?

---

26. Nobly born and bred   28. License
27. Generous   29. Unsettle

IAGO   Something from Venice, sure.

Enter Lodovico, Desdemona, and Attendants.

                             'Tis Lodovico,
   Come from the duke; and see, your wife is with him.
LODOVICO   God save you, worthy general!
OTHELLO   With all my heart, sir.
230   LODOVICO   The duke and senators of Venice greet you.   *Gives him a letter.*
OTHELLO   I kiss the instrument of their pleasures.

Opens the letter and reads.

DESDEMONA   And what's the news, good cousin Lodovico?
IAGO   I am very glad to see you, signior.
   Welcome to Cyprus.
LODOVICO   I thank you. How does Lieutenant Cassio?
IAGO   Lives, sir.
DESDEMONA   Cousin, there's fall'n between him and my lord
   An unkind breach; but you shall make all well.
OTHELLO   Are you sure of that?
DESDEMONA   My lord?
240   OTHELLO [*reads*]   'This fail you not to do, as you will—'
LODOVICO   He did not call; he's busy in the paper.
   Is there division 'twixt thy lord and Cassio?
DESDEMONA   A most unhappy one. I would do much
   T' atone[30] them, for the love I bear to Cassio.
OTHELLO   Fire and brimstone!
DESDEMONA   My lord?
OTHELLO   Are you wise?
DESDEMONA   What, is he angry?
LODOVICO   May be the letter moved him;
   For, as I think, they do command him home,
   Deputing Cassio in his government.
DESDEMONA   By my troth, I am glad on't.
OTHELLO   Indeed?
DESDEMONA   My lord?
OTHELLO   I am glad to see you mad.
250   DESDEMONA   Why, sweet Othello—
OTHELLO   Devil!   *Strikes her.*
DESDEMONA   I have not deserved this.
LODOVICO   My lord, this would not be believed in Venice,

30. To reconcile

Though I should swear I saw't. 'Tis very much.
Make her amends; she weeps.

OTHELLO   O devil, devil!
If that the earth could teem with[31] woman's tears,
Each drop she falls would prove a crocodile.
Out of my sight!

DESDEMONA   I will not stay to offend you.   *Going.*

LODOVICO   Truly, an obedient lady.
260   I do beseech your lordship call her back.

OTHELLO   Mistress!

DESDEMONA   My lord?

OTHELLO   What would you with her, sir?

LODOVICO   Who? I, my lord?

OTHELLO   Ay! You did wish that I would make her turn.
Sir, she can turn, and turn, and yet go on
And turn again; and she can weep, sir, weep;
And she's obedient; as you say, obedient,
Very obedient.—Proceed you in your tears.—
Concerning this, sir—O well-painted passion!—
I am commanded home.—Get you away;
270   I'll send for you anon.—Sir, I obey the mandate
And will return to Venice.—Hence, avaunt!   *Exit Desdemona.*
Cassio shall have my place. And, sir, to-night
I do entreat that we may sup together.
You are welcome, sir, to Cyprus.—Goats and monkeys!   *Exit.*

LODOVICO   Is this the noble Moor whom our full Senate
Call all in all sufficient? Is this the nature
Whom passion could not shake? whose solid virtue
The shot of accident nor dart of chance
Could neither graze nor pierce?

IAGO   He is much changed.
280   LODOVICO   Are his wits safe? Is he not light of brain?

IAGO   He's that he is; I may not breathe my censure.
What he might be (if, what he might, he is not)
I would to heaven he were!

LODOVICO   What, strike his wife?

IAGO   Faith, that was not so well; yet would I knew
That stroke would prove the worst!

LODOVICO   Is it his use?[32]
Or did the letter work upon his blood
And new-create this fault?

IAGO   Alas, alas!

31. Be made pregnant by   32. Habit

It is not honesty in me to speak
What I have seen and known. You shall observe him,
290   And his own courses will denote him so
That I may save my speech. Do but go after
And mark how he continues.

LODOVICO   I am sorry that I am deceived in him.   *Exeunt.*

SCENE 2

Enter Othello and Emilia.

OTHELLO   You have seen nothing then?

EMILIA   Nor ever heard, nor ever did suspect.

OTHELLO   Yes, you have seen Cassio and she together.

EMILIA   But then I saw no harm, and then I heard
Each syllable that breath made up between them.

OTHELLO   What, did they never whisper?

EMILIA   Never, my lord.

OTHELLO   Nor send you out o' th' way?

EMILIA   Never.

OTHELLO   To fetch her fan, her gloves, her mask, nor nothing?

10   EMILIA   Never, my lord.

OTHELLO   That's strange.

EMILIA   I durst, my lord, to wager she is honest,
Lay down my soul at stake. If you think other,
Remove your thought; it doth abuse your bosom.
If any wretch have put this in your head,
Let heaven requite it with the serpent's curse!
For if she be not honest, chaste, and true,
There's no man happy; the purest of their wives
Is foul as slander.

OTHELLO   Bid her come hither. Go.   *Exit Emilia.*

20   She says enough; yet she's a simple bawd
That cannot say as much. This is a subtle whore,
A closet lock and key of villainous secrets;
And yet she'll kneel and pray; I have seen her do't.

Enter Desdemona and Emilia.

DESDEMONA   My lord, what is your will?

OTHELLO   Pray, chuck, come hither.

DESDEMONA   What is your pleasure?

OTHELLO   Let me see your eyes.
Look in my face.

DESDEMONA   What horrible fancy's this?

OTHELLO [to Emilia]   Some of your function,[33] mistress.
  Leave procreants alone and shut the door;
  Cough or cry hem if anybody come.

30 Your mystery,[34] your mystery! Nay, dispatch!   *Exit Emilia.*

DESDEMONA   Upon my knees, what doth your speech import?
  I understand a fury in your words,
  But not the words.

OTHELLO   Why, what art thou?

DESDEMONA   Your wife, my lord; your true
  And loyal wife.

OTHELLO   Come, swear it, damn thyself;
  Lest, being like one of heaven, the devils themselves
  Should fear to seize thee. Therefore be double-damned—
  Swear thou art honest.

DESDEMONA   Heaven doth truly know it.

OTHELLO   Heaven truly knows that thou art false as hell.

40 DESDEMONA   To whom, my lord? With whom? How am I false?

OTHELLO   Ah, Desdemon! away! away! away!

DESDEMONA   Alas the heavy day! Why do you weep?
  Am I the motive[35] of these tears, my lord?
  If haply you my father do suspect
  An instrument of this your calling back,
  Lay not your blame on me. If you have lost him,
  Why, I have lost him too.

OTHELLO   Had it pleased heaven
  To try me with affliction, had they rained
  All kinds of sores and shames on my bare head,

50 Steeped me in poverty to the very lips,
  Given to captivity me and my utmost hopes,
  I should have found in some place of my soul
  A drop of patience. But, alas, to make me
  A fixèd figure for the time of scorn[36]
  To point his slow unmoving finger at!
  Yet could I bear that too; well, very well.
  But there where I have garnered up my heart,
  Where either I must live or bear no life,
  The fountain from the which my current runs

60 Or else dries up—to be discarded thence,
  Or keep it as a cistern for foul toads

---

33. Go about your business; i.e., perform   35. Cause
    your function as the madam of a brothel   36. Scornful world
34. Trade

To knot and gender in—turn thy complexion there,[37]
Patience, thou young and rose-lipped cherubin!
Ay, there look grim as hell!

DESDEMONA I hope my noble lord esteems me honest.

OTHELLO O, ay; as summer flies are in the shambles,[38]
That quicken even with blowing.[39] O thou weed,
Who art so lovely fair, and smell'st so sweet,
That the sense aches at thee, would thou hadst ne'er been born!

70 DESDEMONA Alas, what ignorant sin have I committed?

OTHELLO Was this fair paper, this most goodly book,
Made to write 'whore' upon? What committed?
Committed? O thou public commoner![40]
I should make very forges of my cheeks
That would to cinders burn up modesty,
Did I but speak thy deeds. What committed?
Heaven stops the nose at it, and the moon winks;[41]
The bawdy wind, that kisses all it meets,
Is hushed within the hollow mine of earth
80 And will not hear it. What committed?
Impudent strumpet!

DESDEMONA   By heaven, you do me wrong!

OTHELLO Are not you a strumpet?

DESDEMONA   No, as I am a Christian!
If to preserve this vessel for my lord
From any other foul unlawful touch
Be not to be a strumpet, I am none.

OTHELLO What, not a whore?

DESDEMONA   No, as I shall be saved!

OTHELLO Is't possible?

DESDEMONA O, heaven forgive us!

OTHELLO   I cry you mercy[42] then.
I took you for that cunning whore of Venice
90 That married with Othello.—[Calling] You, mistress,
That have the office opposite to Saint Peter
And keep the gate of hell!

Enter Emilia.

                You, you, ay, you!

---

37. *turn . . . there:* change your color at that
point
38. Slaughterhouses
39. *quicken . . . blowing:* come to life as soon
as their eggs are deposited
40. Whore
41. Closes her eyes
42. Beg your pardon

We have done our course; there's money for your pains:
I pray you turn the key, and keep our counsel.   *Exit.*

EMILIA   Alas, what does this gentleman conceive?
How do you, madam? How do you, my good lady?

DESDEMONA   Faith, half asleep.

EMILIA   Good madam, what's the matter with my lord?

DESDEMONA   With who?

100 EMILIA   Why, with my lord, madam.

DESDEMONA   Who is thy lord?

EMILIA   He that is yours, sweet lady.

DESDEMONA   I have none. Do not talk to me, Emilia.
I cannot weep; nor answer have I none
But what should go by water.[43] Prithee to-night
Lay on my bed my wedding sheets, remember;
And call thy husband hither.

EMILIA   Here's a change indeed!   *Exit.*

DESDEMONA   'Tis meet I should be used so, very meet.
How have I been behaved, that he might stick
The small'st opinion[44] on my least misuse?[45]

Enter Iago and Emilia.

110 IAGO   What is your pleasure, madam? How is't with you?

DESDEMONA   I cannot tell. Those that do teach young babes
Do it with gentle means and easy tasks:
He might have chid me so; for, in good faith,
I am a child to chiding.

IAGO   What is the matter, lady?

EMILIA   Alas, Iago, my lord hath so bewhored her,
Thrown such despite and heavy terms upon her
As true hearts cannot bear.

DESDEMONA   Am I that name, Iago?

IAGO   What name, fair lady?

DESDEMONA   Such as she says my lord did say I was.

120 EMILIA   He called her whore. A beggar in his drink
Could not have laid such terms upon his callet.[46]

IAGO   Why did he so?

DESDEMONA   I do not know; I am sure I am none such.

IAGO   Do not weep, do not weep. Alas the day!

EMILIA   Hath she forsook so many noble matches,

43. Tears   45. Slightest misconduct
44. Suspicion   46. Whore

Her father and her country, all her friends,
To be called whore? Would it not make one weep?

DESDEMONA It is my wretched fortune.

IAGO   Beshrew him for't!
How comes this trick[47] upon him?

DESDEMONA   Nay, heaven doth know.

130 EMILIA I will be hanged if some eternal villain,
Some busy and insinuating rogue,
Some cogging,[48] cozening slave, to get some office,
Have not devised this slander. I'll be hanged else.

IAGO Fie, there is no such man! It is impossible.

DESDEMONA If any such there be, heaven pardon him!

EMILIA A halter pardon him! and hell gnaw his bones!
Why should he call her whore? Who keeps her company?
What place? what time? what form? what likelihood?
The Moor's abused by some most villainous knave,
140 Some base notorious knave, some scurvy fellow.
O heaven, that such companions thou'dst unfold,[49]
And put in every honest hand a whip
To lash the rascals naked through the world
Even from the east to th' west!

IAGO   Speak within door.[50]

EMILIA O, fie upon them! Some such squire he was
That turned your wit the seamy side without
And made you to suspect me with the Moor.

IAGO You are a fool. Go to.

DESDEMONA   O good Iago,
What shall I do to win my lord again?
150 Good friend, go to him; for, by this light of heaven,
I know not how I lost him. Here I kneel:
If e'er my will did trespass 'gainst his love
Either in discourse of thought or actual deed,
Or that mine eyes, mine ears, or any sense
Delighted them in any other form,
Or that I do not yet, and ever did,
And ever will (though he do shake me off
To beggarly divorcement) love him dearly,
Comfort forswear[51] me! Unkindness may do much;
160 And his unkindness may defeat my life,

---

47. Strange behavior
48. Cheating
49. Expose

50. Quietly
51. Happiness forsake

But never taint my love. I cannot say "whore."
It doth abhor me now I speak the word;
To do the act that might th' addition earn
Not the world's mass of vanity could make me.
IAGO   I pray you be content. 'Tis but his humor.
The business of the state does him offense,
And he does chide with you.
DESDEMONA   If 'twere no other—
IAGO   'Tis but so, I warrant.

Trumpets within.

170   Hark how these instruments summon you to supper.
The messengers of Venice stay the meal[52]
Go in, and weep not. All things shall be well.

Exeunt Desdemona and Emilia.

Enter Roderigo.

How now, Roderigo?
RODERIGO   I do not find that thou deal'st justly with me.
IAGO   What in the contrary?
RODERIGO   Every day thou daff'st me[53] with some device, Iago, and rather,
as it seems to me now, keep'st from me all conveniency[54] than suppliest
me with the least advantage of hope. I will indeed no longer endure it;
nor am I yet persuaded to put up in peace what already I have foolishly
suffered.
180   IAGO   Will you hear me, Roderigo?
RODERIGO   Faith, I have heard too much; for your words and performance
are no kin together.
IAGO   You charge me most unjustly.
RODERIGO   With naught but truth. I have wasted myself out of means. The
jewels you have had from me to deliver to Desdemona would half have
corrupted a votarist.[55] You have told me she hath received them, and
returned me expectations and comforts of sudden respect and acquaintance; but I find none.
IAGO   Well, go to; very well.

52. Wait to eat
53. Put me off

54. Opportunities (to meet with Desdemona)
55. Nun

190 RODERIGO   Very well! go to! I cannot go to, man; nor 'tis not very well. By
this hand, I say 'tis very scurvy, and begin to find myself fopped[56] in it.

IAGO   Very well.

RODERIGO   I tell you 'tis not very well. I will make myself known to Desdemona. If she will return me my jewels, I will give over my suit and
repent my unlawful solicitation; if not, assure yourself I will seek satisfaction of you.

IAGO   You have said now.

RODERIGO   Ay, and said nothing but what I protest intendment of doing.

IAGO   Why, now I see there's mettle in thee; and even from this instant do
200   build on thee a better opinion than ever before. Give me thy hand,
Roderigo. Thou hast taken against me a most just exception; but yet I
protest I have dealt most directly in thy affair.

RODERIGO   It hath not appeared.

IAGO   I grant indeed it hath not appeared, and your suspicion is not without
wit and judgment. But, Roderigo, if thou hast that in thee indeed which
I have greater reason to believe now than ever, I mean purpose, courage,
and valor, this night show it. If thou the next night following enjoy not
Desdemona, take me from this world with treachery and devise engines
for[57] my life.

210 RODERIGO   Well, what is it? Is it within reason and compass?

IAGO   Sir, there is especial commission come from Venice to depute Cassio
in Othello's place.

RODERIGO   Is that true? Why, then Othello and Desdemona return again to
Venice.

IAGO   O, no; he goes into Mauritania and takes away with him the fair
Desdemona, unless his abode be lingered here by some accident;
wherein none can be so determinate[58] as the removing of Cassio.

RODERIGO   How do you mean removing of him?

IAGO   Why, by making him uncapable of Othello's place—knocking out his
220   brains.

RODERIGO   And that you would have me to do?

IAGO   Ay, if you dare do yourself a profit and a right. He sups to-night with
a harlotry, and thither will I go to him. He knows not yet of his honorable fortune. If you will watch his going thence, which I will fashion to
fall out between twelve and one, you may take him at your pleasure. I
will be near to second your attempt, and he shall fall between us. Come,
stand not amazed at it, but go along with me. I will show you such a
necessity in his death that you shall think yourself bound to put it on
him. It is now high suppertime, and the night grows to waste. About it!

56. Fooled   58. Effective
57. Plots against

230 RODERIGO   I will hear further reason for this.
IAGO   And you shall be satisfied.   *Exeunt.*

SCENE 3

Enter Othello, Lodovico, Desdemona, Emilia, and Attendants.

LODOVICO   I do beseech you, sir, trouble yourself no further.
OTHELLO   O, pardon me; 'twill do me good to walk.
LODOVICO   Madam, good night. I humbly thank your ladyship.
DESDEMONA   Your honor is most welcome.
OTHELLO   Will you walk, sir?
     O, Desdemona—
DESDEMONA   My lord?
OTHELLO   Get you to bed on th' instant; I will be returned forthwith. Dis-
     miss your attendant there. Look't be done.
10 DESDEMONA   I will, my lord.
                              Exit Othello, with Lodovico and Attendants.
EMILIA   How goes it now? He looks gentler than he did.
DESDEMONA   He says he will return incontinent.[59]
     He hath commanded me to go to bed,
     And bade me to dismiss you.
EMILIA   Dismiss me?
DESDEMONA   It was his bidding; therefore, good Emilia,
     Give me my nightly wearing, and adieu.
     We must not now displease him.
EMILIA   I would you had never seen him!
DESDEMONA   So would not I. My love doth so approve him
20   That even his stubbornness,[60] his checks,[61] his frowns—
     Prithee unpin me—have grace and favor in them.
EMILIA   I have laid those sheets you bade me on the bed.
DESDEMONA   All's one. Good faith, how foolish are our minds!
     If I do die before thee, prithee shroud me
     In one of those same sheets.
EMILIA   Come, come! You talk.
DESDEMONA   My mother had a maid called Barbary.
     She was in love; and he she loved proved mad[62]
     And did forsake her. She had a song of 'Willow';
     An old thing 'twas; but it expressed her fortune,
30   And she died singing it. That song to-night

59. Immediately   61. Rebukes
60. Roughness   62. Untrue

Will not go from my mind; I have much to do
But to go hang my head all at one side
And sing it like poor Barbary. Prithee dispatch.

EMILIA   Shall I go fetch your nightgown?

DESDEMONA   No, unpin me here.
This Lodovico is a proper man.

EMILIA   A very handsome man.

DESDEMONA   He speaks well.

EMILIA   I know a lady in Venice would have walked barefoot to Palestine for
40   a touch of his nether lip.

DESDEMONA [sings].

    The poor soul sat sighing by a sycamore tree,
        Sing all a green willow;
    Her hand on her bosom, her head on her knee,
        Sing willow, willow, willow.
    The fresh streams ran by her and murmured her moans;
        Sing willow, willow, willow;
    Her salt tears fell from her, and soft'ned the stones—

    Lay by these.

    Sing willow, willow, willow—

50   Prithee hie thee; he'll come anon.

    Sing all a green willow must be my garland.
    Let nobody blame him; his scorn I approve—

    Nay, that's not next. Hark! who is't that knocks?

EMILIA   It is the wind.

DESDEMONA [sings].

    I called my love false love; but what said he then?
        Sing willow, willow, willow:
    If I court moe women, you'll couch with moe men.

    So, get thee gone; good night. Mine eyes do itch.
    Doth that bode weeping?

EMILIA   'Tis neither here nor there.

60   DESDEMONA   I have heard it said so. O, these men, these men!
    Dost thou in conscience think—tell me, Emilia—
    That there be women do abuse their husbands
    In such gross kind?

EMILIA   There be some such, no question.

DESDEMONA   Wouldst thou do such a deed for all the world?

EMILIA   Why, would not you?

DESDEMONA   No, by this heavenly light!

EMILIA   Nor I neither by this heavenly light.
I might do't as well i' th' dark.

DESDEMONA   Wouldst thou do such a deed for all the world?

EMILIA   The world's a huge thing; it is a great price for a small vice.

70   DESDEMONA   Good troth, I think thou wouldst not.

EMILIA   By my troth, I think I should; and undo't when I had done it. Marry,
I would not do such a thing for a joint-ring,[63] nor for measures of lawn,[64]
nor for gowns, petticoats, nor caps, nor any petty exhibition;[65] but, for
all the whole world—'Ud's pity! who would not make her husband a
cuckold to make him a monarch? I should venture purgatory for't.

DESDEMONA   Beshrew me if I would do such a wrong
For the whole world.

80   EMILIA   Why, the wrong is but a wrong i' th' world; and having the world
for your labor, 'tis a wrong in your own world, and you might quickly
make it right.

DESDEMONA   I do not think there is any such woman.

EMILIA   Yes, a dozen; and as many to th' vantage[66] as would store[67] the
world they played for.
But I do think it is their husbands' faults
If wives do fall. Say that they slack their duties
And pour our treasures into foreign laps;

90   Or else break out in peevish jealousies,
Throwing restraint upon us; or say they strike us,
Or scant our former having[68] in despite[69]—
Why, we have galls;[70] and though we have some grace,
Yet have we some revenge. Let husbands know
Their wives have sense like them. They see, and smell,
And have their palates both for sweet and sour,
As husbands have. What is it that they do
When they change us for others? Is it sport?
I think it is. And doth affection breed it?

100   I think it doth. Is't frailty that thus errs?
It is so too. And have not we affections,
Desires for sport, and frailty, as men have?

63. Cheap ring
64. Fine linen
65. Gift
66. In addition
67. Populate
68. Allowance
69. Spite
70. Capacity to feel resentment

Then let them use us well; else let them know,
The ills we do, their ills instruct us so.

DESDEMONA   Good night, good night. God me such usage[71] send,
Not to pick bad from bad, but by bad mend!   *Exeunt.*

71. Habits

ACT V

SCENE 1

Enter Iago and Roderigo.

IAGO   Here, stand behind this bulk;[1] straight will he come.
Wear thy good rapier bare, and put it home.
Quick, quick! Fear nothing; I'll be at thy elbow.
It makes us, or it mars us—think on that,
And fix most firm thy resolution.

RODERIGO   Be near at hand; I may miscarry in't.

IAGO   Here, at thy hand. Be bold, and take thy stand.   *Stands aside.*

RODERIGO   I have no great devotion to the deed,
And yet he hath given me satisfying reasons.

10   'Tis but a man gone. Forth my sword! He dies!

IAGO   I have rubbed this young quat[2] almost to the sense,[3]
And he grows angry. Now whether he kill Cassio,
Or Cassio him, or each do kill the other,
Every way makes my gain. Live Roderigo,
He calls me to a restitution large
Of gold and jewels that I bobbed[4] from him
As gifts to Desdemona.
It must not be. If Cassio do remain,
He hath a daily beauty in his life

20   That makes me ugly; and besides, the Moor
May unfold me to him; there stand I in much peril.
No, he must die. Be't so! I hear him coming.

Enter Cassio.

RODERIGO   I know his gait. 'Tis he. Villain, thou diest!

                                      Makes a pass at Cassio.

1. Projecting store front   3. Raw
2. Pimple   4. Swindled

CASSIO   That thrust had been mine enemy indeed
　　But that my coat is better than thou know'st.
　　I will make proof of thine.　　　　　　*Draws, and wounds Roderigo.*
RODERIGO　　　　　　　　　O, I am slain!

Iago darts from concealment behind Cassio, wounds him in the leg, and exit.

CASSIO   I am maimed for ever. Help, ho! Murder! murder!　　　　*Falls.*

Enter Othello.

OTHELLO   The voice of Cassio. Iago keeps his word.
RODERIGO   O, villain that I am!
OTHELLO　　　　　　　　It is even so.
30　CASSIO   O, help, ho! light! a surgeon!
OTHELLO   'Tis he. O brave Iago, honest and just,
　　That hast such noble sense of thy friend's wrong!
　　Thou teachest me. Minion,[5] your dear lies dead,
　　And your unblest fate hies.[6] Strumpet, I come.
　　Forth of my heart those charms, thine eyes, are blotted.
　　Thy bed, lust-stained, shall with lust's blood be spotted.　　　*Exit.*

Enter Lodovico and Gratiano.

CASSIO   What, ho? No watch? No passage?[7] Murder! murder!
GRATIANO   'Tis some mischance. The cry is very direful.
CASSIO   O, help!
40　LODOVICO   Hark!
RODERIGO   O wretched villain!
LODOVICO   Two or three groan. It is a heavy[8] night.
　　These may be counterfeits. Let's think't unsafe
　　To come in to the cry without more help.
RODERIGO   Nobody come? Then shall I bleed to death.
LODOVICO   Hark!

Enter Iago, with a light.

GRATIANO   Here's one comes in his shirt, with light and weapons.
IAGO   Who's there? Whose noise is this that cries on murder?
LODOVICO   We do not know.
IAGO　　　　　　　　Did not you hear a cry?

5. Mistress　　　　　　　7. Passersby
6. Hurries on　　　　　　8. Dark

CASSIO   Here, here! For heaven's sake, help me!

50   IAGO   What's the matter?

GRATIANO   This is Othello's ancient, as I take it.

LODOVICO   The same indeed, a very valiant fellow.

IAGO   What are you here that cry so grievously?

CASSIO   Iago? O, I am spoiled, undone by villains!
    Give me some help.

IAGO   O me, lieutenant! What villains have done this?

CASSIO   I think that one of them is hereabout
    And I cannot make away.

IAGO   O treacherous villains!
    [*To Lodovico and Gratiano*] What are you there? Come in, and give some help.

60   RODERIGO   O, help me here!

CASSIO   That's one of them.

IAGO   O murd'rous slave! O villain!   *Stabs Roderigo.*

RODERIGO   O damned Iago! O inhuman dog!

IAGO   Kill men i' th' dark?—Where be these bloody thieves?—
    How silent is this town!—Ho! murder! murder!—
    What may you be? Are you of good or evil?

LODOVICO   As you shall prove us, praise us.

IAGO   Signior Lodovico?

LODOVICO   He, sir.

IAGO   I cry you mercy. Here's Cassio hurt by villains.

70   GRATIANO   Cassio?

IAGO   How is it, brother?

CASSIO   My leg is cut in two.

IAGO   Marry, heaven forbid!
    Light, gentlemen. I'll bind it with my shirt.

Enter Bianca.

BIANCA   What is the matter, ho? Who is't that cried?

IAGO   Who is't that cried?

BIANCA   O my dear Cassio! my sweet Cassio!
    O Cassio, Cassio, Cassio!

IAGO   O notable strumpet!—Cassio, may you suspect
    Who they should be that thus have mangled you?

80   CASSIO   No.

GRATIANO   I am sorry to find you thus. I have been to seek you.

IAGO   Lend me a garter. So. O for a chair
    To bear him easily hence!

BIANCA   Alas, he faints! O Cassio, Cassio, Cassio!

IAGO   Gentlemen all, I do suspect this trash
    To be a party in this injury.—

Patience awhile, good Cassio.—Come, come!
Lend me a light. Know we this face or no?
Alas, my friend and my dear countryman
90   Roderigo? No.—Yes, sure.—O heaven, Roderigo!
GRATIANO   What, of Venice?
IAGO   Even he, sir. Did you know him?
GRATIANO   Know him? Ay.
IAGO   Signior Gratiano? I cry you gentle pardon.
    These bloody accidents must excuse my manners
    That so neglected you.
GRATIANO   I am glad to see you.
IAGO   How do you, Cassio?—O, a chair, a chair!
GRATIANO   Roderigo?
IAGO   He, he, 'tis he! [A chair brought in.] O, that's well said;[9] the chair.
    Some good man bear him carefully from hence.
100   I'll fetch the general's surgeon. [To Bianca] For you, mistress,
    Save you your labor.—He that lies slain here, Cassio,
    Was my dear friend. What malice was between you?
CASSIO   None in the world; nor do I know the man.
IAGO [To Bianca]   What, look you pale?—O, bear him out o' th' air.

Cassio and Roderigo are borne off.

Stay you, good gentlemen.—Look you pale, mistress?—
Do you perceive the gastness[10] of her eye?—
Nay, if you stare, we shall hear more anon.
Behold her well; I pray you look upon her.
Do you see, gentlemen? Nay, guiltiness will speak,
110   Though tongues were out of use.

Enter Emilia.

EMILIA   'Las, what's the matter? What's the matter, husband?
IAGO   Cassio hath here been set on in the dark
    By Roderigo, and fellows that are scaped.
    He's almost slain, and Roderigo dead.
EMILIA   Alas, good gentleman! alas, good Cassio!
IAGO   This is the fruit of whoring. Prithee, Emilia,
    Go know of Cassio where he supped to-night.
    [To Bianca] What, do you shake at that?
BIANCA   He supped at my house; but I therefore shake not.
120   IAGO   O, did he so? I charge you go with me.

9. Well done   10. Terror

EMILIA   Fie, fie upon thee, strumpet!

BIANCA   I am no strumpet, but of life as honest
As you that thus abuse me.

EMILIA   As I? Foh! fie upon thee!

IAGO   Kind gentlemen, let's go see poor Cassio dressed.
[*To Bianca*] Come, mistress, you must tell's another tale.
Emilia, run you to the citadel
And tell my lord and lady what hath happed.   *Exit Emilia.*
Will you go on afore?   *Exeunt all but Iago.*
                        This is the night
That either makes me or fordoes[11] me quite.   *Exit.*

SCENE 2

Desdemona asleep in her bed. Enter Othello with a light.

OTHELLO   It is the cause,[12] it is the cause, my soul.
Let me not name it to you, you chaste stars!
It is the cause. Yet I'll not shed her blood,
Nor scar that whiter skin of hers than snow,
And smooth as monumental alabaster.
Yet she must die, else she'll betray more men.
Put out the light, and then put out the light.
If I quench thee, thou flaming minister,
I can again thy former light restore,
10   Should I repent me; but once put out thy light,
Thou cunning'st pattern of excelling nature,
I know not where is that Promethean heat[13]
That can thy light relume.[14] When I have plucked the rose,
I cannot give it vital growth again;
It needs must wither. I'll smell thee on the tree.   *He kisses her.*
O balmy breath, that dost almost persuade
Justice to break her sword! One more, one more!
Be thus when thou art dead, and I will kill thee,
And love thee after. One more, and this the last!
20   So sweet was ne'er so fatal. I must weep,
But they are cruel tears. This sorrow's heavenly;
It strikes where it doth love. She wakes.

DESDEMONA   Who's there? Othello?

OTHELLO   Ay, Desdemona.

DESDEMONA   Will you come to bed, my lord?

11. Destroys   13. Divine fire
12. Cause of justice   14. Rekindle

OTHELLO   Have you prayed to-night, Desdemona?

DESDEMONA   Ay, my lord.

OTHELLO   If you bethink yourself of any crime

Unreconciled as yet to heaven and grace,

Solicit for it straight.

DESDEMONA   Alack, my lord, what may you mean by that?

30 OTHELLO   Well, do it, and be brief; I will walk by.

I would not kill thy unprepared spirit.

No, heaven forfend!¹⁵ I would not kill thy soul.

DESDEMONA   Talk you of killing?

OTHELLO   Ay, I do.

DESDEMONA   Then heaven

Have mercy on me!

OTHELLO   Amen, with all my heart!

DESDEMONA   If you say so, I hope you will not kill me.

OTHELLO   Hum!

DESDEMONA   And yet I fear you; for you are fatal then

When your eyes roll so. Why I should fear I know not,

Since guiltiness I know not; but yet I feel I fear.

OTHELLO   Think on thy sins.

40 DESDEMONA   They are loves I bear to you.

OTHELLO   Ay, and for that thou diest.

DESDEMONA   That death's unnatural that kills for loving.

Alas, why gnaw you so your nether lip?

Some bloody passion shakes your very frame.

These are portents; but yet I hope, I hope,

They do not point on me.

OTHELLO   Peace and be still!

DESDEMONA   I will so. What's the matter?

OTHELLO   That handkerchief which I so loved and gave thee

Thou gav'st to Cassio.

DESDEMONA   No, by my life and soul!

Send for the man and ask him.

50 OTHELLO   Sweet soul, take heed,

Take heed of perjury; thou art on thy deathbed.

DESDEMONA   Ay, but not yet to die.

OTHELLO   Yes, presently.

Therefore confess thee freely of thy sin;

For to deny each article with oath

Cannot remove nor choke the strong conception¹⁶

That I do groan withal. Thou art to die.

DESDEMONA   Then Lord have mercy on me!

---

15. Forbid   16. Belief (of her being guilty)

OTHELLO   I say amen.

DESDEMONA   And have you mercy too! I never did
    Offend[17] you in my life; never loved Cassio
60   But with such general warranty of heaven
    As I might love. I never gave him token.

OTHELLO   By heaven, I saw my handkerchief in's hand!
    O perjured woman! thou dost stone[18] my heart,
    And mak'st me call what I intend to do
    A murder, which I thought a sacrifice.
    I saw the handkerchief.

DESDEMONA   He found it then.
    I never gave it him. Send for him hither.
    Let him confess a truth.

OTHELLO   He hath confessed.

DESDEMONA   What, my lord?

OTHELLO   That he hath used thee.

70 DESDEMONA   How? unlawfully?

OTHELLO   Ay.

DESDEMONA   He will not say so.

OTHELLO   No, his mouth is stopped.
    Honest Iago hath ta'en order for't.[19]

DESDEMONA   O, my fear interprets. What, is he dead?

OTHELLO   Had all his hairs been lives, my great revenge
    Had stomach for them all.

DESDEMONA   Alas, he is betrayed, and I undone!

OTHELLO   Out, strumpet! Weep'st thou for him to my face?

DESDEMONA   O, banish me, my lord, but kill me not!

OTHELLO   Down, strumpet!

80 DESDEMONA   Kill me to-morrow; let me live to-night!

OTHELLO   Nay, an you strive[20]—

DESDEMONA   But half an hour!

OTHELLO   Being done, there is no pause.

DESDEMONA   But while I say one prayer!

OTHELLO   It is too late.

                            Smothers her.

DESDEMONA   O Lord, Lord, Lord!

Emilia at the door.

17. Wrong   19. Take measures to bring it about
18. Turn to stone   20. Struggle

EMILIA [*calls within*].   My lord, my lord! What, ho, my lord, my lord!
OTHELLO   What noise is this? Not dead? Not yet quite dead?
   I that am cruel am yet merciful;
   I would not have thee linger in thy pain.
   So, so.
EMILIA [*within*].   What, ho! my lord, my lord!
OTHELLO   Who's there?
90 EMILIA [*within*].   O, good my lord, I would speak a word with you!
OTHELLO   Yes, 'tis Emilia.—By and by.—She's dead.—
   'Tis like she comes to speak of Cassio's death.
   The noise was here. Ha! no more moving?
   Still as the grave.—Shall she come in? Were't good?—
   I think she stirs again. No.—What's best to do?
   If she come in, she'll sure speak to my wife.
   My wife! my wife! what wife? I have no wife.
   O, insupportable! O heavy hour!
   Methinks it should be now a huge eclipse
100   Of sun and moon, and that th' affrighted globe
   Should yawn[21] at alteration.
EMILIA   [*within*] I do beseech you
   That I may speak with you, O good my lord!
OTHELLO   I had forgot thee. O, come in, Emilia.
   Soft, by and by.—Let me the curtains draw.—

                                     Closes the bed-curtains.
Where art thou?   *Opens the door.*
Enter Emilia.

                    What's the matter with thee now?
EMILIA   O my good lord, yonder's foul murder done!
OTHELLO   What? Now?
EMILIA   But now, my lord.
OTHELLO   It is the very error[22] of the moon.
   She comes more nearer earth than she was wont
110   And makes men mad.
EMILIA   Cassio, my lord, hath killed a young Venetian
   Called Roderigo.
OTHELLO   Roderigo killed?
   And Cassio killed?
EMILIA   No, Cassio is not killed.
OTHELLO   Not Cassio killed? Then murder's out of tune,
   And sweet revenge grows harsh.
DESDEMONA   O, falsely, falsely murdered!

---

21. Open, as in an earthquake   22. Straying from its natural course

EMILIA   O Lord! what cry is that?

OTHELLO   That? What?

EMILIA   Out and alas! that was my lady's voice.

120   Help! help, ho! help! O lady, speak again!
       Sweet Desdemona! O sweet mistress, speak!

DESDEMONA   A guiltless death I die.

EMILIA   O, who hath done this deed?

DESDEMONA   Nobody—I myself. Farewell.
       Commend me to my kind lord. O, farewell!   *She dies.*

OTHELLO   Why, how should she be murd'red?

EMILIA   Alas, who knows?

OTHELLO   You heard her say herself, it was not I.

EMILIA   She said so. I must needs report the truth.

OTHELLO   She's like a liar gone to burning hell!
       'Twas I that killed her.

130   EMILIA   O, the more angel she,
       And you the blacker devil!

OTHELLO   She turned to folly, and she was a whore.

EMILIA   Thou dost belie her, and thou art a devil.

OTHELLO   She was false as water.

EMILIA   Thou art rash as fire to say
       That she was false. O, she was heavenly true!

OTHELLO   Cassio did top her. Ask thy husband else.
       O, I were damned beneath all depth in hell
       But that I did proceed upon just grounds
       To this extremity. Thy husband knew it all.

140   EMILIA   My husband?

OTHELLO   Thy husband.

EMILIA   That she was false to wedlock?

OTHELLO   Ay, with Cassio. Nay, had she been true,
       If heaven would make me such another world
       Of one entire and perfect chrysolite,
       I'ld not have sold her for it.

EMILIA   My husband?

OTHELLO   Ay, 'twas he that told me first.
       An honest man he is, and hates the slime
       That sticks on filthy deeds.

EMILIA   My husband?

150   OTHELLO   What needs this iterance?[23] Woman, I say thy husband.

EMILIA   O mistress, villainy hath made mocks with love!
       My husband say that she was false?

OTHELLO   He, woman.

23. Repetition

I say, thy husband. Dost understand the word?

My friend, thy husband; honest, honest, Iago.

EMILIA   If he say so, may his pernicious soul

 Rot half a grain a day! he lies to th' heart.

 She was too fond of her most filthy bargain.

OTHELLO   Ha!

EMILIA   Do thy worst.

160   This deed of thine is no more worthy heaven

 Than thou wast worthy her.

OTHELLO   Peace, you were best.

EMILIA   Thou hast not half the power to do me harm

 As I have to be hurt.[24] O gull! O dolt!

 As ignorant as dirt! thou hast done a deed—

 I care not for thy sword; I'll make thee known,

 Though I lost twenty lives. Help! help! O, help!

 The Moor hath killed my mistress! Murder! murder!

Enter Montano, Gratiano, Iago, and Others.

MONTANO   What is the matter? How now, general?

EMILIA   O, are you come, Iago? You have done well,

170   That men must lay their murders on your neck.

GRATIANO   What is the matter?

EMILIA   Disprove this villain, if thou be'st a man.

 He says thou told'st him that his wife was false.

 I know thou didst not; thou'rt not such a villain.

 Speak, for my heart is full.

IAGO   I told him what I thought, and told no more

 Than what he found himself was apt and true.

EMILIA   But did you ever tell him she was false?

IAGO   I did.

180   EMILIA   You told a lie, an odious damnèd lie!

 Upon my soul, a lie! a wicked lie!

 She false with Cassio? Did you say with Cassio?

IAGO   With Cassio, mistress. Go to, charm[25] your tongue.

EMILIA   I will not charm my tongue; I am bound to speak:

 My mistress here lies murdered in her bed—

ALL   O heavens forfend!

EMILIA   And your reports have set the murder on.

OTHELLO   Nay, stare not, masters. It is true indeed.

GRATIANO   'Tis a strange truth.

MONTANO   O monstrous act!

---

24. To endure pain   25. Cast a spell on; i.e., silence

190 EMILIA   Villainy, villainy, villainy!
    I think upon't—I think I smell't!—O villainy!
    I thought so then.—I'll kill myself for grief.—
    O villainy, villainy!
IAGO What, are you mad? I charge you get you home.
EMILIA Good gentlemen, let me have leave to speak.
    'Tis proper I obey him, but not now.
    Perchance, Iago, I will ne'er go home.
OTHELLO O! O! O!   *Falls on the bed.*
EMILIA   Nay, lay thee down and roar!
    For thou hast killed the sweetest innocent
    That e'er did lift up eye.
200 OTHELLO   O, she was foul!   *Rises.*
    I scarce did know you, uncle. There lies your niece,
    Whose breath, indeed, these hands have newly stopped.
    I know this act shows horrible and grim.
GRATIANO Poor Desdemon! I am glad thy father's dead.
    Thy match was mortal to him, and pure grief
    Shore[26] his old thread in twain. Did he live now,
    This sight would make him do a desperate turn;[27]
    Yea, curse his better angel from his side,
    And fall to reprobation.[28]
210 OTHELLO 'Tis pitiful; but yet Iago knows
    That she with Cassio hath the act of shame
    A thousand times committed. Cassio confessed it;
    And she did gratify his amorous works
    With the recognizance and pledge of love
    Which I first gave her. I saw it in his hand.
    It was a handkerchief, an antique token
    My father gave my mother.
EMILIA O God! O heavenly God!
IAGO Zounds, hold your peace!
EMILIA   'Twill out, 'twill out! I peace?
220 No, I will speak as liberal[29] as the north.[30]
    Let heaven and men and devils, let them all,
    All, all, cry shame against me, yet I'll speak.
IAGO Be wise, and get you home.
EMILIA   I will not.

Iago draws and threatens Emilia.

26. Cut   29. Unrestrainedly
27. Deed   30. Blowing of the north wind
28. Be rejected by God

GRATIANO   Fie!
    Your sword upon a woman?
EMILIA   O thou dull Moor, that handkerchief thou speak'st of
    I found by fortune, and did give my husband;
    For often with a solemn earnestness—
    More than indeed belonged to such a trifle—
    He begged of me to steal't.
IAGO   Villainous whore!
230   EMILIA   She give it Cassio? No, alas, I found it,
    And I did give't my husband.
IAGO   Filth, thou liest!
EMILIA   By heaven, I do not, I do not, gentlemen.
    O murd'rous coxcomb! what should such a fool
    Do with so good a wife?
OTHELLO   Are there no stones[31] in heaven
    But what serves for the thunder? Precious villain!

The Moor runs at Iago, but is disarmed by Montano. Iago kills his wife.

GRATIANO   The woman falls. Sure he hath killed his wife.
EMILIA   Ay, ay. O, lay me by my mistress' side.   *Exit Iago.*
GRATIANO   He's gone, but his wife's killed.
MONTANO   'Tis a notorious villain. Take you this weapon,
240   Which I have here recovered from the Moor.
    Come, guard the door without. Let him not pass,
    But kill him rather. I'll after that same villain,
    For 'tis a damnèd slave.

Exit Montano, with all but Othello and Emilia.

OTHELLO   I am not valiant neither;
    But every puny whipster[32] gets my sword.
    But why should honor outlive honesty?
    Let it go all.
EMILIA   What did thy song bode, lady?
    Hark, canst thou hear me? I will play the swan,
    And die in music [*sings*] 'Willow, willow, willow.'
    Moor, she was chaste. She loved thee, cruel Moor:
250   So come my soul to bliss as I speak true.
    So speaking as I think, I die, I die.   *She dies.*
OTHELLO   I have another weapon in this chamber;

31. Thunderbolts   32. Top-whipping boy

It is a sword of Spain, the Isebrook's[33] temper.

O, here it is.—Uncle, I must come forth.

GRATIANO [within] If thou attempt it, it will cost thee dear.

Thou hast no weapon, and perforce must suffer.

OTHELLO Look in upon me then and speak with me,

Or, naked[34] as I am, I will assault thee.

Enter Gratiano.

GRATIANO What is the matter?

OTHELLO   Behold, I have a weapon;

260 A better never did itself sustain

Upon a soldier's thigh. I have seen the day

That with this little arm and this good sword

I have made my way through more impediments

Than twenty times your stop.[35] But O vain boast!

Who can control his fate? 'Tis not so now.

Be not afraid, though you do see me weaponed.

Here is my journey's end, here is my butt,[36]

And very seamark[37] of my utmost sail.

Do you go back dismayed? 'Tis a lost[38] fear.

270 Man but a rush[39] against Othello's breast,

And he retires. Where should Othello go?

Now, how dost thou look now? O ill-starred wench!

Pale as thy smock! When we shall meet at compt,[40]

This look of thine will hurl my soul from heaven,

And fiends will snatch at it. Cold, cold, my girl?

Even like thy chastity.

O cursèd, cursèd slave! Whip me, ye devils,

From the possession of this heavenly sight!

Blow me about in winds! roast me in sulphur!

280 Wash me in steep-down gulfs of liquid fire!

O Desdemona, Desdemona! dead!

O! O! O!

Enter Lodovico, Montano, Iago as prisoner, and Officers; Cassio in a chair.

LODOVICO Where is this rash and most unfortunate man?

OTHELLO That's he that was Othello. Here I am.

33. Innsbruck, where the finest steel blades
of the time were forged
34. Unarmed
35. Power to stop
36. Limit

37. Beacon
38. Wasted
39. Wield a mere reed
40. Final accounting; i.e., Day of Judgment

LODOVICO   Where is that viper? Bring the villain forth.

OTHELLO   I look down towards his feet[41]—but that's a fable.

    If that thou be'st a devil, I cannot kill thee.   *Wounds Iago.*

LODOVICO   Wrench his sword from him.   *Othello is disarmed.*

IAGO   I bleed, sir, but not killed.

OTHELLO   I am not sorry neither. I'ld have thee live;

290   For in my sense, 'tis happiness to die.

LODOVICO   O thou Othello that wert once so good,

    Fall'n in the practice[42] of a damnèd slave,

    What shall be said to thee?

OTHELLO   Why, anything:

    An honorable murderer, if you will;

    For naught did I in hate, but all in honor.

LODOVICO   This wretch hath part confessed his villainy.

    Did you and he consent in Cassio's death?

OTHELLO   Ay.

CASSIO   Dear general, I never gave you cause.

300 OTHELLO   I do believe it, and I ask your pardon.

    Will you, I pray, demand that demi-devil

    Why he hath thus ensnared my soul and body?

IAGO   Demand me nothing. What you know, you know.

    From this time forth I never will speak word.

LODOVICO   What, not to pray?

GRATIANO   Torments will ope your lips.

OTHELLO   Well, thou dost best.

LODOVICO   Sir, you shall understand what hath befall'n,

    Which, as I think, you know not. Here is a letter

    Found in the pocket of the slain Roderigo;

310   And here another. The one of them imports

    The death of Cassio to be undertook

    By Roderigo.

OTHELLO   O villain!

CASSIO   Most heathenish and most gross!

LODOVICO   Now here's another discontented paper

    Found in his pocket too; and this, it seems,

    Roderigo meant t' have sent this damnèd villain;

    But that, belike, Iago in the nick[43]

    Came in and satisfied him.

OTHELLO   O thou pernicious caitiff!—

    How came you, Cassio, by that handkerchief

    That was my wife's?

---

41. *I . . . feet:* to see if they are cloven, as the   42. Plot
    Devil's feet were believed to be   43. Nick of time

320 CASSIO   I found it in my chamber;
        And he himself confessed but even now
        That there he dropped it for a special purpose
        Which wrought to his desire.
    OTHELLO   O fool! fool! fool!
    CASSIO   There is besides in Roderigo's letter,
        How he upbraids Iago that he made him
        Brave[44] me upon the watch; whereon it came
        That I was cast;[45] and even but now he spake,
        After long seeming dead—Iago hurt him,
        Iago set him on.
330 LODOVICO   You must forsake this room and go with us.
        Your power and your command is taken off,
        And Cassio rules in Cyprus. For this slave,
        If there be any cunning cruelty
        That can torment him much and hold him long,
        It shall be his. You shall close prisoner rest
        Till that the nature of your fault be known
        To the Venetian state. Come, bring away.
    OTHELLO   Soft you! a word or two before you go.
        I have done the state some service, and they know't.
340   No more of that. I pray you, in your letters,
        When you shall these unlucky deeds relate,
        Speak of me as I am. Nothing extenuate,
        Nor set down aught in malice. Then must you speak
        Of one that loved not wisely, but too well;
        Of one not easily jealous, but, being wrought,
        Perplexed[46] in the extreme; of one whose hand,
        Like the base Indian, threw a pearl away
        Richer than all his tribe; of one whose subdued eyes,
        Albeit unusèd to the melting mood,
350   Drop tears as fast as the Arabian trees
        Their med'cinable gum. Set you down this.
        And say besides that in Aleppo once,
        Where a malignant and a turbaned Turk
        Beat a Venetian and traduced the state,
        I took by th' throat the circumcisèd dog
        And smote him—thus.   *He stabs himself.*
    LODOVICO   O bloody period![47]
    GRATIANO   All that's spoke is marred.

    44. Defy   46. Distraught
    45. Dismissed   47. Ending

OTHELLO   I kissed thee ere I killed thee. No way but this,
    Killing myself, to die upon a kiss.   *He falls upon the bed and dies.*
360 CASSIO   This did I fear, but thought he had no weapon;
    For he was great of heart.
LODOVICO   [*to Iago*] O Spartan dog,[48]
    More fell[49] than anguish, hunger, or the sea!
    Look on the tragic loading of this bed.
    This is thy work. The object[50] poisons sight;
    Let it be hid. Gratiano, keep the house,
    And seize upon[51] the fortunes of the Moor,
    For they succeed on you. To you, lord governor,
    Remains the censure[52] of this hellish villain,
    The time, the place, the torture. O, enforce it!
370   Myself will straight abroad, and to the state
    This heavy act with heavy heart relate.   *Exeunt.*

48. Type of bloodhound, noted for its silence
    and relentlessness
49. Cruel
50. Spectacle
51. Take possession
52. Legal sentencing

SATIRE IN THE NEOCLASSICAL FRENCH THEATER

Molière's *The Misanthrope* was first performed in 1666 at the theater of the Palais-Royal, a fully enclosed structure within an elegant palace that had been erected by Cardinal de Richelieu, King Louis XIII's chief minister. The play, in short, had its premiere within a building that embodied the very same aristocratic and sophisticated culture that Molière was satirizing in his work. Indeed, the audience was made up largely of members of the aristocracy and nobility, and they could hardly have failed to interpret the play as a reflection on themselves. The theater itself was elegantly decked out, with neoclassical columns on each side of the stage, decorative trim around the galleries and the moldings of the upper walls, and chandeliers suspended from the ceiling of the auditorium and from the center of the stage. Thus the actors on stage and the audience watching them were illuminated by candlelight.

Despite the shared light of candles, the actors and audience were actually

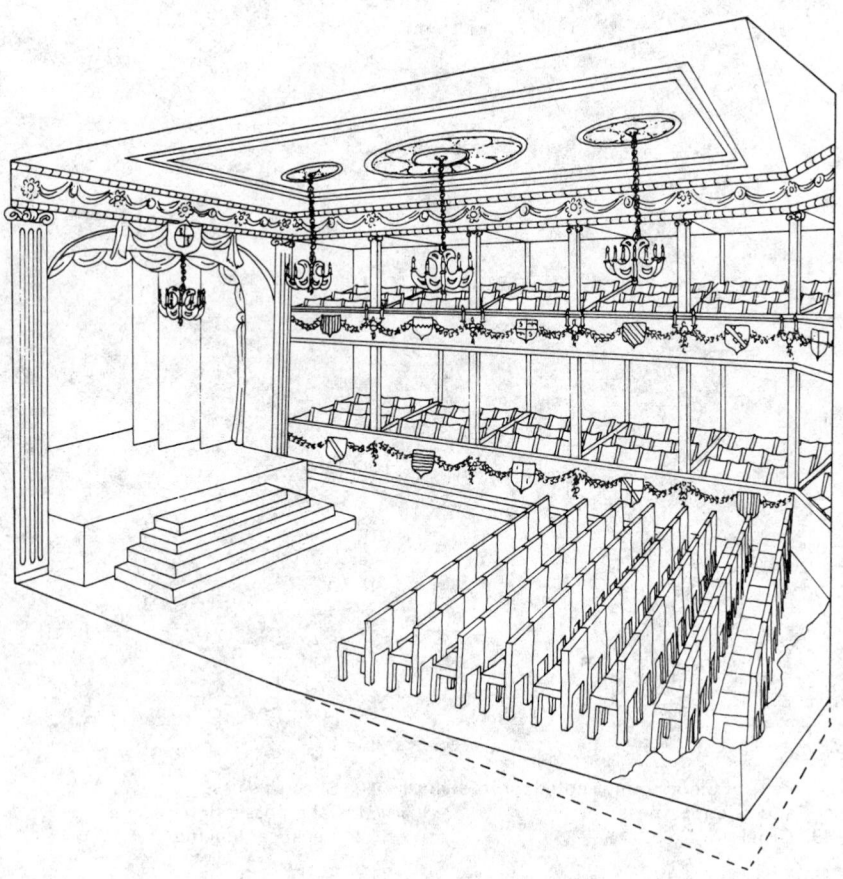

separated from one another by the physical design of the theater. The Palais-Royal theater was a long rectangle in shape, with a rather deep stage at one end. Spectators viewed the action either from the main floor or from two levels of galleries located on each side of the hall. The theater accommodated six hundred persons in all—an intimate audience whose members could see and be seen by one another under the glowing candlelight of the chandeliers.

As we can see from the design of the theater, however, the audience was distinctly separated from the actors by the proscenium arch, which framed the action like a picture. And the barrier created by the arch was reinforced by the use of a curtain to divide the separate acts of the play. The audience was thus placed in the position of looking into something like a box, one side of which had been stripped away when the curtain was pulled apart. In this respect the neoclassical audience could be said to have witnessed dramatic performances from a perspective similar to that of our modern theaters—except that spectators seated in the galleries probably had a very restricted angle from which to view the stage. And neoclassical French settings were not designed to create the kind of highly realistic illusion we associate with modern theatrical productions. The action of *The Misanthrope*, for example, was played in front of a flat piece of background scenery depicting something like the wall of a salon in Célimène's house, but it was not elaborated to create the impression of a three-dimensional space. It was, rather, a standard setting that would have been used repeatedly in comedies and satires having to do with sophisticated social experience.

Acting styles of the period were also highly formalized. If we try to imagine the style used in *The Misanthrope* we will do best to refer to *commedia dell'arte*, a popular form of drama which emerged during the Italian Renaissance (sixteenth century), and which exerted a strong influence on French actors, particularly on Molière. *Commedia* was an improvisational theater built upon an array of type characters, such as the clever servant, the braggart soldier, the ingenious maid, the foolish husband, the angry father, and so on. Associated with each type was a stylized, exaggerated mode of gesture and movement, which would have been especially appropriate to such characters as Arsinoe (the hypocritical prude), or Célimène (the flirtatious coquette), or Oronte (the vain fop). Thus the method of acting, like the theater itself, provided a stylized form of production ideally suited to the social satire dramatized in *The Misanthrope*.

MOLIÈRE
1622–1673

Jean Baptiste Poquelin, who wrote, acted, and directed under the singular name of Molière, was born and raised in Paris, where his father was master upholsterer to the court of Louis XIII, and where Molière, in turn, was expected to serve as the royal upholsterer. But after studying humanities at the Jesuit College de Clermont, where his father had sent him to prepare for the cultured life of the court, and then going on to receive training in the law, Molière became involved with a family of talented actors, joined with them to create a theatrical company in 1643, and subsequently devoted his entire life to the stage. Molière and his company initially fared so badly in Paris that he was briefly imprisoned for unpaid debts, and the group was forced to leave the city and take to the countryside, where they toured the provinces from 1645 to 1658. During that period, Molière acquired a mastery of all the elements of theater, particularly the theater of farce and comedy, and in 1658 returned to Paris as director of the company, which he had substantially improved by acquiring the best performers from other road groups. Molière immediately won the approval of Louis XIV with a farce he had prepared for performance before the court; by 1661 he had taken over the theater in the Palais-Royal; and in 1665 his group was named "The King's Company." Molière is well known for his satiric treatment of social folly and fashionable excess, which he ridiculed in all of his many farces and comedies, both for the public and for the court. But his best-known comedies, such as *The School for Wives* (1662), *The Misanthrope* (1666), *The Miser* (1668), and *Tartuffe* (1669), are not only social satires but also serious studies of individualized characters and their haunting mental obsessions.

The Misanthrope

CHARACTERS

ALCESTE, in love with Célimène
PHILINTE, Alceste's friend
ORONTE, in love with Célimène

ACASTE ⎫
CLITANDRE ⎬ marquesses
BASQUE, Célimène's servant

Translated by Richard Wilbur

CÉLIMÈNE, Alceste's beloved   A GUARD of the Marshalsea
ÉLIANTE, Célimène's cousin   DUBOIS, Alceste's valet
ARSINOÉ, a friend of Célimène's

The scene throughout is in Célimène's house at Paris.

ACT I

SCENE 1

PHILINTE, ALCESTE

PHILINTE Now, what's got into you?
ALCESTE, *seated.*   Kindly leave me alone.
PHILINTE Come, come, what is it? This lugubrious tone . . .
ALCESTE Leave me, I said; you spoil my solitude.
PHILINTE Oh, listen to me, now, and don't be rude.
ALCESTE I choose to be rude, Sir, and to be hard of hearing.
PHILINTE These ugly moods of yours are not endearing;
    Friends though we are, I really must insist . . .
ALCESTE, *abruptly rising.* "Friends? Friends, you say? Well, cross me off your
    list.
    I've been your friend till now, as you well know;
10   But after what I saw a moment ago
    I tell you flatly that our ways must part.
    I wish no place in a dishonest heart.
PHILINTE Why, what have I done, Alceste? Is this quite just?
ALCESTE My God, you ought to die of self-disgust.
    I call your conduct inexcusable, Sir,
    And every man of honor will concur.
    I see you almost hug a man to death,
    Exclaim for joy until you're out of breath,
    And supplement these loving demonstrations
20   With endless offers, vows, and protestations;
    Then when I ask you "Who was that?" I find
    That you can barely bring his name to mind!
    Once the man's back is turned, you cease to love him,
    And speak with absolute indifference of him!
    By God, I say it's base and scandalous

> To falsify the heart's affections thus;
> If I caught myself behaving in such a way,
> I'd hang myself for shame, without delay.

PHILINTE   It hardly seems a hanging matter to me;
30   I hope that you will take it graciously
> If I extend myself a slight reprieve,
> And live a little longer, by your leave.

ALCESTE   How dare you joke about a crime so grave?

PHILINTE   What crime? How else are people to behave?

ALCESTE   I'd have them be sincere, and never part
> With any word that isn't from the heart.

PHILINTE   When someone greets us with a show of pleasure,
> It's but polite to give him equal measure,
> Return his love the best that we know how,
40   And trade him offer for offer, vow for vow.

ALCESTE   No, no, this formula you'd have me follow,
> However fashionable, is false and hollow,
> And I despise the frenzied operations
> Of all these barterers of protestations,
> These lavishers of meaningless embraces,
> These utterers of obliging commonplaces,
> Who court and flatter everyone on earth
> And praise the fool no less than the man of worth.
> Should you rejoice that someone fondles you,
50   Offers his love and service, swears to be true,
> And fills your ears with praises of your name,
> When to the first damned fop he'll say the same?
> No, no: no self-respecting heart would dream
> Of prizing so promiscuous an esteem;
> However high the praise, there's nothing worse
> Than sharing honors with the universe.
> Esteem is founded on comparison:
> To honor all men is to honor none.
> Since you embrace this indiscriminate vice,
60   Your friendship comes at far too cheap a price;
> I spurn the easy tribute of a heart
> Which will not set the worthy man apart:
> I choose, Sir, to be chosen; and in fine,
> The friend of mankind is no friend of mine.

PHILINTE   But in polite society, custom decrees
> That we show certain outward courtesies. . . .

ALCESTE   Ah, no! we should condemn with all our force
> Such false and artificial intercourse.

> Let men behave like men; let them display
70   Their inmost hearts in everything they say;
> Let the heart speak, and let our sentiments
> Not mask themselves in silly compliments.

PHILINTE In certain cases it would be uncouth
> And most absurd to speak the naked truth;
> With all respect for your exalted notions,
> It's often best to veil one's true emotions.
> Wouldn't the social fabric come undone
> If we were wholly frank with everyone?
> Suppose you met with someone you couldn't bear;
80   Would you inform him of it then and there?

ALCESTE Yes.

PHILINTE   Then you'd tell old Emilie it's pathetic
> The way she daubs her features with cosmetic
> And plays the gay coquette at sixty-four?

ALCESTE I would.

PHILINTE   And you'd call Dorilas a bore,
> And tell him every ear at court is lame
> From hearing him brag about his noble name?

ALCESTE Precisely.

PHILINTE   Ah, you're joking.

ALCESTE   *Au contraire:*
> In this regard there's none I'd choose to spare.
> All are corrupt; there's nothing to be seen
90   In court or town but aggravates my spleen.
> I fall into deep gloom and melancholy
> When I survey the scene of human folly,
> Finding on every hand base flattery,
> Injustice, fraud, self-interest, treachery. . . .
> Ah, it's too much; mankind has grown so base,
> I mean to break with the whole human race.

PHILINTE This philosophic rage is a bit extreme;
> You've no idea how comical you seem;
> Indeed, we're like those brothers in the play
100   Called *School for Husbands*, one of whom was prey . . .

ALCESTE Enough, now! None of your stupid similes.

PHILINTE Then let's have no more tirades, if you please.
> The world won't change, whatever you say or do;
> And since plain speaking means so much to you,
> I'll tell you plainly that by being frank
> You've earned the reputation of a crank,
> And that you're thought ridiculous when you rage

And rant against the manners of the age.

ALCESTE   So much the better; just what I wish to hear.
110   No news could be more grateful to my ear.
All men are so detestable in my eyes,
I should be sorry if they thought me wise.

PHILINTE   Your hatred's very sweeping, is it not?

ALCESTE   Quite right: I hate the whole degraded lot.

PHILINTE   Must all poor human creatures be embraced,
Without distinction, by your vast distaste?
Even in these bad times, there are surely a few . . .

ALCESTE   No, I include all men in one dim view:
Some men I hate for being rogues; the others
120   I hate because they treat the rogues like brothers,
And, lacking a virtuous scorn for what is vile,
Receive the villain with a complaisant smile.
Notice how tolerant people choose to be
Toward that bold rascal who's at law with me.
His social polish can't conceal his nature;
One sees at once that he's a treacherous creature;
No one could possibly be taken in
By those soft speeches and that sugary grin.
The whole world knows the shady means by which
130   The low-brow's grown so powerful and rich,
And risen to a rank so bright and high
That virtue can but blush, and merit sigh.
Whenever his name comes up in conversation,
None will defend his wretched reputation;
Call him knave, liar, scoundrel, and all the rest,
Each head will nod, and no one will protest.
And yet his smirk is seen in every house,
He's greeted everywhere with smiles and bows,
And when there's any honor that can be got
140   By pulling strings, he'll get it, like as not.
My God! It chills my heart to see the ways
Men come to terms with evil nowadays;
Sometimes, I swear, I'm moved to flee and find
Some desert land unfouled by humankind.

PHILINTE   Come, let's forget the follies of the times
And pardon mankind for its petty crimes;
Let's have an end of rantings and of railings,
And show some leniency toward human failings.
This world requires a pliant rectitude;
150   Too stern a virtue makes one stiff and rude;

Good sense views all extremes with detestation,
And bids us to be noble in moderation.
The rigid virtues of the ancient days
Are not for us; they jar with all our ways
And ask of us too lofty a perfection.
Wise men accept their times without objection,
And there's no greater folly, if you ask me,
Than trying to reform society.
Like you, I see each day a hundred and one
160 Unhandsome deeds that might be better done,
But still, for all the faults that meet my view,
I'm never known to storm and rave like you.
I take men as they are, or let them be,
And teach my soul to bear their frailty;
And whether in court or town, whatever the scene,
My phlegm's as philosophic as your spleen.
ALCESTE This phlegm which you so eloquently commend,
Does nothing ever rile it up, my friend?
Suppose some man you trust should treacherously
170 Conspire to rob you of your property,
And do his best to wreck your reputation?
Wouldn't you feel a certain indignation?
PHILINTE Why, no. These faults of which you so complain
Are part of human nature, I maintain,
And it's no more a matter for disgust
That men are knavish, selfish and unjust,
Than that the vulture dines upon the dead,
And wolves are furious, and apes ill-bred.
ALCESTE Shall I see myself betrayed, robbed, torn to bits,
180 And not . . . Oh, let's be still and rest our wits.
Enough of reasoning, now. I've had my fill.
PHILINTE Indeed, you would do well, Sir, to be still.
Rage less at your opponent, and give some thought
To how you'll win this lawsuit that he's brought.
ALCESTE I assure you I'll do nothing of the sort.
PHILINTE Then who will plead your case before the court?
ALCESTE Reason and right and justice will plead for me.
PHILINTE Oh, Lord. What judges do you plan to see?
ALCESTE Why, none. The justice of my cause is clear.
190 PHILINTE Of course, man; but there's politics to fear. . . .
ALCESTE No, I refuse to lift a hand. That's flat.
I'm either right, or wrong.
PHILINTE   Don't count on that.

ALCESTE   No, I'll do nothing.

PHILINTE   Your enemy's influence
       Is great, you know . . .

ALCESTE   That makes no difference.

PHILINTE   It will; you'll see.

ALCESTE   Must honor bow to guile?
       If so, I shall be proud to lose the trial.

PHILINTE   Oh, really . . .

ALCESTE   I'll discover by this case
       Whether or not men are sufficiently base
       And impudent and villainous and perverse
200   To do me wrong before the universe.

PHILINTE   What a man!

ALCESTE   Oh, I could wish, whatever the cost,
       Just for the beauty of it, that my trial were lost.

PHILINTE   If people heard you talking so, Alceste,
       They'd split their sides. Your name would be a jest.

ALCESTE   So much the worse for jesters.

PHILINTE   May I enquire
       Whether this rectitude you so admire,
       And these hard virtues you're enamored of
       Are qualities of the lady whom you love?
       It much surprises me that you, who seem
210   To view mankind with furious disesteem,
       Have yet found something to enchant your eyes
       Amidst a species which you so despise.
       And what is more amazing, I'm afraid,
       Is the most curious choice your heart has made.
       The honest Éliante is fond of you,
       Arsinoé, the prude, admires you too;
       And yet your spirit's been perversely led
       To choose the flighty Célimène instead,
       Whose brittle malice and coquettish ways
220   So typify the manners of our days.
       How is it that the traits you most abhor
       Are bearable in this lady you adore?
       Are you so blind with love that you can't find them?
       Or do you contrive, in her case, not to mind them?

ALCESTE   My love for that young widow's not the kind
       That can't perceive defects; no, I'm not blind.
       I see her faults, despite my ardent love,
       And all I see I fervently reprove.
       And yet I'm weak; for all her falsity,

230   That woman knows the art of pleasing me,
       And though I never cease complaining of her,
       I swear I cannot manage not to love her.
       Her charm outweighs her faults; I can but aim
       To cleanse her spirit in my love's pure flame.
PHILINTE   That's no small task; I wish you all success.
       You think then that she loves you?
ALCESTE   Heavens, yes!
       I wouldn't love her did she not love me.
PHILINTE   Well, if her taste for you is plain to see,
       Why do these rivals cause you such despair?
240   ALCESTE   True love, Sir, is possessive, and cannot bear
       To share with all the world. I'm here today
       To tell her she must send that mob away.
PHILINTE   If I were you, and had your choice to make,
       Éliante, her cousin, would be the one I'd take;
       That honest heart, which cares for you alone,
       Would harmonize far better with your own.
ALCESTE   True, true: each day my reason tells me so;
       But reason doesn't rule in love, you know.
PHILINTE   I fear some bitter sorrow is in store;
250   This love . . .

SCENE 2

ORONTE, ALCESTE, PHILINTE

ORONTE, *to Alceste.*   The servants told me at the door
       That Éliante and Célimène were out,
       But when I heard, dear Sir, that you were about,
       I came to say, without exaggeration,
       That I hold you in the vastest admiration,
       And that it's always been my dearest desire
       To be the friend of one I so admire.
       I hope to see my love of merit requited,
       And you and I in friendship's bond united.
10   I'm sure you won't refuse—if I may be frank—
       A friend of my devotedness—and rank.

*During this speech of Oronte's, Alceste is abstracted, and seems unaware that he is being
spoken to. He only breaks off his reverie when Oronte says:*

It was for you, if you please, that my words were intended.

ALCESTE For me, Sir?

ORONTE   Yes, for you. You're not offended?

ALCESTE By no means. But this much surprises me. . . .
The honor comes most unexpectedly. . . .

ORONTE My high regard should not astonish you;
The whole world feels the same. It is your due.

ALCESTE Sir . . .

ORONTE   Why, in all the State there isn't one
Can match your merits; they shine, Sir, like the sun.

ALCESTE Sir . . .

20 ORONTE   You are higher in my estimation
Than all that's most illustrious in the nation.

ALCESTE Sir . . .

ORONTE   If I lie, may heaven strike me dead!
To show you that I mean what I have said,
Permit me, Sir, to embrace you most sincerely,
And swear that I will prize our friendship dearly.
Give me your hand. And now, Sir, if you choose,
We'll make our vows.

ALCESTE   Sir . . .

ORONTE   What! You refuse?

ALCESTE Sir, it's a very great honor you extend:
But friendship is a sacred thing, my friend;

30 It would be profanation to bestow
The name of friend on one you hardly know.
All parts are better played when well-rehearsed;
Let's put off friendship, and get acquainted first.
We may discover it would be unwise
To try to make our natures harmonize.

ORONTE By heaven! You're sagacious to the core;
This speech has made me admire you even more.
Let time, then, bring us closer day by day;
Meanwhile, I shall be yours in every way.

40 If, for example, there should be anything
You wish at court, I'll mention it to the King.
I have his ear, of course; it's quite well known
That I am much in favor with the throne.
In short, I am your servant. And now, dear friend,
Since you have such fine judgment, I intend
To please you, if I can, with a small sonnet
I wrote not long ago. Please comment on it,
And tell me whether I ought to publish it.

ALCESTE You must excuse me, Sir; I'm hardly fit
    To judge such matters.
ORONTE   Why not?
50   ALCESTE   I am, I fear,
    Inclined to be unfashionably sincere.
ORONTE Just what I ask; I'd take no satisfaction
    In anything but your sincere reaction.
    I beg you not to dream of being kind.
ALCESTE Since you desire it, Sir, I'll speak my mind.
ORONTE *Sonnet*. It's a sonnet. . . . *Hope* . . . The poem's addressed
    To a lady who wakened hopes within my breast.
    Hope . . . this is not the pompous sort of thing,
    Just modest little verses, with a tender ring.
ALCESTE Well, we shall see.
60   ORONTE   *Hope* . . . I'm anxious to hear
    Whether the style seems properly smooth and clear,
    And whether the choice of words is good or bad.
ALCESTE We'll see, we'll see.
ORONTE   Perhaps I ought to add
    That it took me only a quarter-hour to write it.
ALCESTE The time's irrelevant, Sir: kindly recite it.
ORONTE, *reading*.

    Hope comforts us awhile, 'tis true,
    Lulling our cares with careless laughter,
    And yet such joy is full of rue,
    My Phyllis, if nothing follows after.

70   PHILINTE I'm charmed by this already; the style's delightful.
ALCESTE, *sotto voce, to Philinte*. How can you say that? Why, the thing is
    frightful.

ORONTE Your fair face smiled on me awhile,
    But was it kindness so to enchant me?
    'Twould have been fairer not to smile,
    If hope was all you meant to grant me.

PHILINTE What a clever thought! How handsomely you phrase it!
ALCESTE, *sotto voce, to Philinte*. You know the thing is trash. How dare you
    praise it?

ORONTE If it's to be my passion's fate
    Thus everlastingly to wait,

80   Then death will come to set me free:
            For death is fairer than the fair;
            Phyllis, to hope is to despair
            When one must hope eternally.

PHILINTE   The close is exquisite—full of feeling and grace.
ALCESTE, *sotto voce, aside*.   Oh, blast the close; you'd better close your face
            Before you send your lying soul to hell.
PHILINTE   I can't remember a poem I've liked so well.
ALCESTE, *sotto voce, aside*.   Good Lord!
ORONTE, *to Philinte*.   I fear you're flattering me a bit.
PHILINTE   Oh, no!
ALCESTE, *sotto voce, aside*.
                        What else d'you call it, you hypocrite?
90 ORONTE, *to Alceste*.   But you, Sir, keep your promise now: don't shrink
            From telling me sincerely what you think.
ALCESTE   Sir, these are delicate matters; we all desire
            To be told that we've the true poetic fire.
            But once, to one whose name I shall not mention,
            I said, regarding some verse of his invention,
            That gentlemen should rigorously control
            That itch to write which often afflicts the soul;
            That one should curb the heady inclination
            To publicize one's little avocation;
100   And that in showing off one's works of art
            One often plays a very clownish part.
ORONTE   Are you suggesting in a devious way
            That I ought not . . .
ALCESTE   Oh, that I do not say.
            Further, I told him that no fault is worse
            Than that of writing frigid, lifeless verse,
            And that the merest whisper of such a shame
            Suffices to destroy a man's good name.
ORONTE   D'you mean to say my sonnet's dull and trite?
ALCESTE   I don't say that. But I went on to cite
110   Numerous cases of once-respected men
            Who came to grief by taking up the pen.
ORONTE   And am I like them? Do I write so poorly?
ALCESTE   I don't say that. But I told this person, "Surely
            You're under no necessity to compose;
            Why you should wish to publish, heaven knows.
            There's no excuse for printing tedious rot
            Unless one writes for bread, as you do not.
            Resist temptation, then, I beg of you;

Conceal your pastimes from the public view;
And don't give up, on any provocation,
Your present high and courtly reputation,
To purchase at a greedy printer's shop
The name of silly author and scribbling fop."
These were the points I tried to make him see.
ORONTE I sense that they are also aimed at me;
But now—about my sonnet—I'd like to be told . . .
ALCESTE Frankly, that sonnet should be pigeonholed.
You've chosen the worst models to imitate.
The style's unnatural. Let me illustrate:

For example, *Your fair face smiled on me awhile,*
Followed by, *'Twould have been fairer not to smile!*
Or this: *such joy is full of rue;*
Or this: *For death is fairer than the fair;*
Or, *Phyllis, to hope is to despair*
  When one must hope eternally!

This artificial style, that's all the fashion,
Has neither taste, nor honesty, nor passion;
It's nothing but a sort of wordy play,
And nature never spoke in such a way.
What, in this shallow age, is not debased?
Our fathers, though less refined, had better taste;
I'd barter all that men admire today
For one old love song I shall try to say:

If the King had given me for my own
Paris, his citadel,
And I for that must leave alone
Her whom I love so well,
I'd say then to the Crown,
Take back your glittering town;
My darling is more fair, I swear,
My darling is more fair.

The rhyme's not rich, the style is rough and old,
But don't you see that it's the purest gold
Beside the tinsel nonsense now preferred,
And that there's passion in its every word?

If the King had given me for my own
Paris, his citadel,

And I for that must leave alone
Her whom I love so well,
160   I'd say then to the Crown,
Take back your glittering town;
My darling is more fair, I swear,
My darling is more fair.

There speaks a loving heart. [*To Philinte*] You're laughing, eh?
Laugh on, my precious wit. Whatever you say,
I hold that song's worth all the bibelots
That people hail today with ah's and oh's.

ORONTE   And I maintain my sonnet's very good.
ALCESTE   It's not at all surprising that you should.
170   You have your reasons; permit me to have mine
For thinking that you cannot write a line.
ORONTE   Others have praised my sonnet to the skies.
ALCESTE   I lack their art of telling pleasant lies.
ORONTE   You seem to think you've got no end of wit.
ALCESTE   To praise your verse, I'd need still more of it.
ORONTE   I'm not in need of your approval, Sir.
ALCESTE   That's good; you couldn't have it if you were.
ORONTE   Come now, I'll lend you the subject of my sonnet;
I'd like to see you try to improve upon it.
180   ALCESTE   I might, by chance, write something just as shoddy;
But then I wouldn't show it to everybody.
ORONTE   You're most opinionated and conceited.
ALCESTE   Go find your flatterers, and be better treated.
ORONTE   Look here, my little fellow, pray watch your tone.
ALCESTE   My great big fellow, you'd better watch your own.
PHILINTE, *stepping between them.*   Oh, please, please, gentlemen! This will
never do.
ORONTE   The fault is mine, and I leave the field to you.
I am your servant, Sir, in every way.
ALCESTE   And I, Sir, am your most abject valet.

SCENE 3

PHILINTE, ALCESTE

PHILINTE   Well, as you see, sincerity in excess
Can get you into a very pretty mess;
Oronte was hungry for appreciation. . . .
ALCESTE   Don't speak to me.
PHILINTE   What?

ALCESTE   No more conversation.
PHILINTE   Really, now . . .
ALCESTE   Leave me alone.
PHILINTE   If I . . .
ALCESTE   Out of my sight!
PHILINTE   But what . . .
ALCESTE   I won't listen.
PHILINTE   But . . .
ALCESTE   Silence!
PHILINTE   Now, is it polite . . .
ALCESTE   By heaven, I've had enough. Don't follow me.
PHILINTE   Ah, you're just joking. I'll keep you company.

ACT II

SCENE 1

ALCESTE, CÉLIMÈNE

ALCESTE   Shall I speak plainly, Madam? I confess
          Your conduct gives me infinite distress,
          And my resentment's grown too hot to smother.
          Soon, I foresee, we'll break with one another.
          If I said otherwise, I should deceive you;
          Sooner or later, I shall be forced to leave you,
          And if I swore that we shall never part,
          I should misread the omens of my heart.
CÉLIMÈNE   You kindly saw me home, it would appear,
10   So as to pour invectives in my ear.
ALCESTE   I've no desire to quarrel. But I deplore
          Your inability to shut the door
          On all these suitors who beset you so.
          There's what annoys me, if you care to know.
CÉLIMÈNE   Is it my fault that all these men pursue me?
          Am I to blame if they're attracted to me?
          And when they gently beg an audience,
          Ought I to take a stick and drive them hence?
ALCESTE   Madam, there's no necessity for a stick;
20   A less responsive heart would do the trick.
          Of your attractiveness I don't complain;
          But those your charms attract, you then detain
          By a most melting and receptive manner,
          And so enlist their hearts beneath your banner.

It's the agreeable hopes which you excite
That keep these lovers round you day and night;
Were they less liberally smiled upon,
That sighing troop would very soon be gone.
But tell me, Madam, why it is that lately
30 This man Clitandre interests you so greatly?
Because of what high merits do you deem
Him worthy of the honor of your esteem?
Is it that your admiring glances linger
On the splendidly long nail of his little finger?
Or do you share the general deep respect
For the blond wig he chooses to affect?
Are you in love with his embroidered hose?
Do you adore his ribbons and his bows?
Or is it that this paragon bewitches
40 Your tasteful eye with his vast German breeches?
Perhaps his giggle, or his falsetto voice,
Makes him the latest gallant of your choice?

CÉLIMÈNE You're much mistaken to resent him so.
Why I put up with him you surely know:
My lawsuit's very shortly to be tried,
And I must have his influence on my side.

ALCESTE Then lose your lawsuit, Madam, or let it drop;
Don't torture me by humoring such a fop.

CÉLIMÈNE You're jealous of the whole world, Sir.

ALCESTE   That's true,
50 Since the whole world is well-received by you.

CÉLIMÈNE That my good nature is so unconfined
Should serve to pacify your jealous mind;
Were I to smile on one, and scorn the rest,
Then you might have some cause to be distressed.

ALCESTE Well, if I mustn't be jealous, tell me, then,
Just how I'm better treated than other men.

CÉLIMÈNE You know you have my love. Will that not do?

ALCESTE What proof have I that what you say is true?

CÉLIMÈNE I would expect, Sir, that my having said it
60 Might give the statement a sufficient credit.

ALCESTE But how can I be sure that you don't tell
The selfsame thing to other men as well?

CÉLIMÈNE What a gallant speech! How flattering to me!
What a sweet creature you make me out to be!
Well then, to save you from the pangs of doubt,
All that I've said I hereby cancel out;
Now, none but yourself shall make a monkey of you:
Are you content?

ALCESTE   Why, why am I doomed to love you?
   I swear that I shall bless the blissful hour
70   When this poor heart's no longer in your power!
   I make no secret of it: I've done my best
   To exorcise this passion from my breast;
   But thus far all in vain; it will not go;
   It's for my sins that I must love you so.
CÉLIMÈNE   Your love for me is matchless, Sir; that's clear.
ALCESTE   Indeed, in all the world it has no peer;
   Words can't describe the nature of my passion,
   And no man ever loved in such a fashion.
CÉLIMÈNE   Yes, it's a brand-new fashion, I agree:
80   You show your love by castigating me,
   And all your speeches are enraged and rude.
   I've never been so furiously wooed.
ALCESTE   Yet you could calm that fury, if you chose.
   Come, shall we bring our quarrels to a close?
   Let's speak with open hearts, then, and begin . . .

SCENE 2

CÉLIMÈNE, ALCESTE, BASQUE

CÉLIMÈNE   What is it?
BASQUE   Acaste is here.
CÉLIMÈNE   Well, send him in.

SCENE 3

CÉLIMÈNE, ALCESTE

ALCESTE   What! Shall we never be alone at all?
   You're always ready to receive a call,
   And you can't bear, for ten ticks of the clock,
   Not to keep open house for all who knock.
CÉLIMÈNE   I couldn't refuse him: he'd be most put out.
ALCESTE   Surely that's not worth worrying about.
CÉLIMÈNE   Acaste would never forgive me if he guessed
   That I consider him a dreadful pest.
ALCESTE   If he's a pest, why bother with him then?
10 CÉLIMÈNE   Heavens! One can't antagonize such men;
   Why, they're the chartered gossips of the court,

And have a say in things of every sort.
One must receive them, and be full of charm;
They're no great help, but they can do you harm,
And though your influence be ever so great,
They're hardly the best people to alienate.

ALCESTE   I see, dear lady, that you could make a case
For putting up with the whole human race;
These friendships that you calculate so nicely . . .

SCENE 4

ALCESTE, CÉLIMÈNE, BASQUE

BASQUE   Madam, Clitandre is here as well.
ALCESTE   Precisely.
CÉLIMÈNE   Where are you going?
ALCESTE   Elsewhere.
CÉLIMÈNE   Stay.
ALCESTE   No, no.
CÉLMINÈNE   Stay, Sir.
ALCESTE   I can't.
CÉLIMÈNE   I wish it.
ALCESTE   No, I must go.
I beg you, Madam, not to press the matter;
You know I have no taste for idle chatter.
CÉLIMÈNE   Stay: I command you.
ALCESTE   No, I cannot stay.
CÉLIMÈNE   Very well; you have my leave to go away.

SCENE 5

ÉLIANTE, PHILINTE, ACASTE, CLITANDRE, ALCESTE, CÉLIMÈNE, BASQUE

ÉLIANTE, *to Célimène.*   The Marquesses have kindly come to call.
Were they announced?
CÉLIMÈNE   Yes. Basque, bring chairs for all.

Basque provides the chairs, and exits.

To Alceste.   You haven't gone?
ALCESTE   No; and I shan't depart
Till you decide who's foremost in your heart.
CÉLIMÈNE   Oh, hush.
ALCESTE   It's time to choose; take them, or me.

CÉLIMÈNE   You're mad.

ALCESTE   I'm not, as you shall shortly see.

CÉLIMÈNE   Oh?

ALCESTE   You'll decide.

CÉLIMÈNE   You're joking now, dear friend.

ALCESTE   No, no; you'll choose; my patience is at an end.

CLITANDRE   Madam, I come from court, where poor Cléonte
10   Behaved like a perfect fool, as is his wont.
          Has he no friend to counsel him, I wonder,
          And teach him less unerringly to blunder?

CÉLIMÈNE   It's true, the man's a most accomplished dunce;
          His gauche behavior charms the eye at once;
          And every time one sees him, on my word,
          His manner's grown a trifle more absurd.

ACASTE   Speaking of dunces, I've just now conversed
          With old Damon, who's one of the very worst;
          I stood a lifetime in the broiling sun
20   Before his dreary monologue was done.

CÉLIMÈNE   Oh, he's a wondrous talker, and has the power
          To tell you nothing hour after hour:
          If, by mistake, he ever came to the point,
          The shock would put his jawbone out of joint.

ÉLIANTE, to Philinte.   The conversation takes its usual turn,
          And all our dear friends' ears will shortly burn.

CLITANDRE   Timante's a character, Madam.

CÉLIMÈNE   Isn't he, though?
          A man of mystery from top to toe,
          Who moves about in a romantic mist
30   On secret missions which do not exist.
          His talk is full of eyebrows and grimaces;
          How tired one gets of his momentous faces;
          He's always whispering something confidential
          Which turns out to be quite inconsequential;
          Nothing's too slight for him to mystify;
          He even whispers when he says "good-by."

ACASTE   Tell us about Géralde.

CÉLIMÈNE   That tiresome ass.
          He mixes only with the titled class,
40   And fawns on dukes and princes, and is bored
          With anyone who's not at least a lord.
          The man's obsessed with rank, and his discourses
          Are all of hounds and carriages and horses;
          He uses Christian names with all the great,
          And the word Milord, with him, is out of date.

CLITANDRE   He's very taken with Bélise, I hear.

CÉLIMÈNE   She is the dreariest company, poor dear.
     Whenever she comes to call, I grope about
     To find some topic which will draw her out,
50   But, owing to her dry and faint replies,
     The conversation wilts, and droops, and dies.
     In vain one hopes to animate her face
     By mentioning the ultimate commonplace;
     But sun or shower, even hail or frost
     Are matters she can instantly exhaust.
     Meanwhile her visit, painful though it is,
     Drags on and on through mute eternities,
     And though you ask the time, and yawn, and yawn,
     She sits there like a stone and won't be gone.

ACASTE   Now for Adraste.

60 CÉLIMÈNE   Oh, that conceited elf
     Has a gigantic passion for himself;
     He rails against the court, and cannot bear it
     That none will recognize his hidden merit;
     All honors given to others give offense
     To his imaginary excellence.

CLITANDRE   What about young Cléon? His house, they say,
     Is full of the best society, night and day.

CÉLIMÈNE   His cook has made him popular, not he:
     It's Cléon's table that people come to see.

70 ÉLIANTE   He gives a splendid dinner, you must admit.

CÉLIMÈNE   But must he serve himself along with it?
     For my taste, he's a most insipid dish
     Whose presence sours the wine and spoils the fish.

PHILINTE   Damis, his uncle, is admired no end.
     What's your opinion, Madam?

CÉLIMÈNE   Why, he's my friend.

PHILINTE   He seems a decent fellow, and rather clever.

CÉLIMÈNE   He works too hard at cleverness, however.
     I hate to see him sweat and struggle so
     To fill his conversation with bons mots.
80   Since he's decided to become a wit
     His taste's so pure that nothing pleases it;
     He scolds at all the latest books and plays,
     Thinking that wit must never stoop to praise,
     That finding fault's a sign of intellect,
     That all appreciation is abject,
     And that by damning everything in sight
     One shows oneself in a distinguished light.

He's scornful even of our conversations:
Their trivial nature sorely tries his patience;
90   He folds his arms, and stands above the battle,
And listens sadly to our childish prattle.
ACASTE Wonderful, Madam! You've hit him off precisely.
CLITANDRE No one can sketch a character so nicely.
ALCESTE How bravely, Sirs, you cut and thrust at all
These absent fools, till one by one they fall:
But let one come in sight, and you'll at once
Embrace the man you lately called a dunce,
Telling him in a tone sincere and fervent
How proud you are to be his humble servant.
100 CLITANDRE Why pick on us? *Madame's* been speaking, Sir,
And you should quarrel, if you must, with her.
ALCESTE No, no, by God, the fault is yours, because
You lead her on with laughter and applause,
And make her think that she's the more delightful
The more her talk is scandalous and spiteful.
Oh, she would stoop to malice far, far less
If no such claque approved her cleverness.
It's flatterers like you whose foolish praise
Nourishes all the vices of these days.
110 PHILINTE But why protest when someone ridicules
Those you'd condemn, yourself, as knaves or fools?
CÉLIMÈNE Why, Sir? Because he loves to make a fuss.
You don't expect him to agree with us,
When there's an opportunity to express
His heaven-sent spirit of contrariness?
What other people think, he can't abide;
Whatever they say, he's on the other side;
He lives in deadly terror of agreeing;
'Twould make him seem an ordinary being.
120 Indeed, he's so in love with contradiction,
He'll turn against his most profound conviction
And with a furious eloquence deplore it,
If only someone else is speaking for it.
ALCESTE Go on, dear lady, mock me as you please;
You have your audience in ecstasies.
PHILINTE But what she says is true: you have a way
Of bridling at whatever people say;
Whether they praise or blame, your angry spirit
Is equally unsatisfied to hear it.
130 ALCESTE Men, Sir, are always wrong, and that's the reason
That righteous anger's never out of season;

All that I hear in all their conversation
Is flattering praise or reckless condemnation.
CÉLIMÈNE But . . .
ALCESTE   No, no, Madam, I am forced to state
That you have pleasures which I deprecate,
And that these others, here, are much to blame
For nourishing the faults which are your shame.
CLITANDRE I shan't defend myself, Sir; but I vow
I'd thought this lady faultless until now.
140 ACASTE I see her charms and graces, which are many;
But as for faults, I've never noticed any.
ALCESTE I see them, Sir; and rather than ignore them,
I strenuously criticize her for them.
The more one loves, the more one should object
To every blemish, every least defect.
Were I this lady, I would soon get rid
Of lovers who approved of all I did,
And by their slack indulgence and applause
Endorsed my follies and excused my flaws.
150 CÉLIMÈNE If all hearts beat according to your measure,
The dawn of love would be the end of pleasure;
And love would find its perfect consummation
In ecstasies of rage and reprobation.
ÉLIANTE Love, as a rule, affects men otherwise,
And lovers rarely love to criticize.
They see their lady as a charming blur,
And find all things commendable in her.
If she has any blemish, fault, or shame,
They will redeem it by a pleasing name.
160 The pale-faced lady's lily-white, perforce;
The swarthy one's a sweet brunette, of course;
The spindly lady has a slender grace;
The fat one has a most majestic pace;
The plain one, with her dress in disarray,
They classify as *beauté négligée;*
The hulking one's a goddess in their eyes,
The dwarf, a concentrate of Paradise;
The haughty lady has a noble mind;
The mean one's witty, and the dull one's kind;
170 The chatterbox has liveliness and verve,
The mute one has a virtuous reserve.
So lovers manage, in their passion's cause,
To love their ladies even for their flaws.
ALCESTE But I still say . . .

CÉLIMÈNE   I think it would be nice
 To stroll around the gallery once or twice.
 What! You're not going, Sirs?
CLITANDRE AND ACASTE   No, Madam, no.
ALCESTE You seem to be in terror lest they go.
 Do what you will, Sirs; leave, or linger on,
 But I shan't go till after you are gone.
180 ACASTE I'm free to linger, unless I should perceive
 Madame is tired, and wishes me to leave.
CLITANDRE And as for me, I needn't go today
 Until the hour of the King's *coucher.*
CÉLIMÈNE, *to Alceste.*   You're joking, surely?
ALCESTE   Not in the least; we'll see
 Whether you'd rather part with them, or me.

SCENE 6

ALCESTE, CÉLIMÈNE, ÉLIANTE, ACASTE, PHILINTE, CLITANDRE, BASQUE

BASQUE, *to Alceste.*   Sir, there's a fellow here who bids me state
 That he must see you, and that it can't wait.
ALCESTE Tell him that I have no such pressing affairs.
BASQUE It's a long tailcoat that this fellow wears,
 With gold all over.
CÉLIMÈNE, *to Alceste.*   You'd best go down and see.
 Or—have him enter.

SCENE 7

ALCESTE, CÉLIMÈNE, ÉLIANTE, ACASTE, PHILINTE, CLITANDRE, GUARD

ALCESTE, *confronting the Guard.*   Well, what do you want with me?
 Come in, Sir.
GUARD   I've a word, Sir, for your ear.
ALCESTE Speak it aloud, Sir; I shall strive to hear.
GUARD The Marshals have instructed me to say
 You must report to them without delay.
ALCESTE Who? Me, Sir?
GUARD   Yes, Sir; you.
ALCESTE   But what do they want?
PHILINTE, *to Alceste.*   To scotch your silly quarrel with Oronte.
CÉLIMÈNE, *to Philinte.*   What quarrel?
PHILINTE   Oronte and he have fallen out

Over some verse he spoke his mind about;
10   The Marshals wish to arbitrate the matter.
ALCESTE   Never shall I equivocate or flatter!
PHILINTE   You'd best obey their summons; come, let's go.
ALCESTE   How can they mend our quarrel, I'd like to know?
    Am I to make a cowardly retraction,
    And praise those jingles to his satisfaction?
    I'll not recant; I've judged that sonnet rightly.
    It's bad.
PHILINTE   But you might say so more politely. . . .
ALCESTE   I'll not back down; his verses make me sick.
PHILINTE   If only you could be more politic!
    But come, let's go.
20   ALCESTE   I'll go, but I won't unsay
    A single word.
PHILINTE   Well, let's be on our way.
ALCESTE   Till I am ordered by my lord the King
    To praise that poem, I shall say the thing
    Is scandalous, by God, and that the poet
    Ought to be hanged for having the nerve to show it.

To Clitandre and Acaste, who are laughing.

    By heaven, Sirs, I really didn't know
    That I was being humorous.
CÉLIMÈNE   Go, Sir, go;
    Settle your business.
ALCESTE   I shall, and when I'm through,
    I shall return to settle things with you.

ACT III

SCENE 1

CLITANDRE, ACASTE

CLITANDRE   Dear Marquess, how contented you appear;
    All things delight you, nothing mars your cheer.
    Can you, in perfect honesty, declare
    That you've a right to be so debonair?
ACASTE   By Jove, when I survey myself, I find
    No cause whatever for distress of mind.
    I'm young and rich; I can in modesty

Lay claim to an exalted pedigree;
And owing to my name and my condition
I shall not want for honors and position.
Then as to courage, that most precious trait,
I seem to have it, as was proved of late
Upon the field of honor, where my bearing,
They say, was very cool and rather daring.
I've wit, of course; and taste in such perfection
That I can judge without the least reflection,
And at the theater, which is my delight,
Can make or break a play on opening night,
And lead the crowd in hisses or bravos,
And generally be known as one who knows.
I'm clever, handsome, gracefully polite;
My waist is small, my teeth are strong and white;
As for my dress, the world's astonished eyes
Assure me that I bear away the prize.
I find myself in favor everywhere,
Honored by men, and worshiped by the fair;
And since these things are so, it seems to me
I'm justified in my complacency.

CLITANDRE   Well, if so many ladies hold you dear,
Why do you press a hopeless courtship here?

ACASTE   Hopeless, you say? I'm not the sort of fool
That likes his ladies difficult and cool.
Men who are awkward, shy, and peasantish
May pine for heartless beauties, if they wish,
Grovel before them, bear their cruelties,
Woo them with tears and sighs and bended knees,
And hope by dogged faithfulness to gain
What their poor merits never could obtain.
For men like me, however, it makes no sense
To love on trust, and foot the whole expense.
Whatever any lady's merits be,
I think, thank God, that I'm as choice as she;
That if my heart is kind enough to burn
For her, she owes me something in return;
And that in any proper love affair
The partners must invest an equal share.

CLITANDRE   You think, then, that our hostess favors you?

ACASTE   I've reason to believe that that is true.

CLITANDRE   How did you come to such a mad conclusion?
You're blind, dear fellow. This is sheer delusion.

ACASTE   All right, then: I'm deluded and I'm blind.

CLITANDRE   Whatever put the notion in your mind?

ACASTE Delusion.

CLITANDRE   What persuades you that you're right?

ACASTE I'm blind.

CLITANDRE   But have you any proofs to cite?

ACASTE I tell you I'm deluded.

CLITANDRE   Have you, then,
   Received some secret pledge from Célimène?

ACASTE Oh, no: she scorns me.

CLITANDRE   Tell me the truth, I beg.

ACASTE She just can't bear me.

CLITANDRE   Ah, don't pull my leg.
   Tell me what hope she's given you, I pray.

60 ACASTE I'm hopeless, and it's you who win the day.
   She hates me thoroughly, and I'm so vexed
   I mean to hang myself on Tuesday next.

CLITANDRE Dear Marquess, let us have an armistice
   And make a treaty. What do you say to this?
   If ever one of us can plainly prove
   That Célimène encourages his love,
   The other must abandon hope, and yield,
   And leave him in possession of the field.

ACASTE Now, there's a bargain that appeals to me;
70   With all my heart, dear Marquess, I agree.
   But hush.

SCENE 2

CÉLIMÈNE, ACASTE, CLITANDRE

CÉLIMÈNE Still here?

CLITANDRE   'Twas love that stayed our feet.

CÉLIMÈNE I think I heard a carriage in the street.
   Whose is it? D'you know?

SCENE 3

CÉLIMÈNE, ACASTE, CLITANDRE, BASQUE

BASQUE   Arsinoé is here,
   Madame.

CÉLIMÈNE Arsinoé, you say? Oh, dear.

BASQUE Éliante is entertaining her below.

CÉLIMÈNE What brings the creature here, I'd like to know?

ACASTE   They say she's dreadfully prudish, but in fact
    I think her piety . . .
CÉLIMÈNE   It's all an act.
    At heart she's worldly, and her poor success
    In snaring men explains her prudishness.
    It breaks her heart to see the beaux and gallants
    Engrossed by other women's charms and talents,
10   And so she's always in a jealous rage
    Against the faulty standards of the age.
    She lets the world believe that she's a prude
    To justify her loveless solitude,
    And strives to put a brand of moral shame
    On all the graces that she cannot claim.
    But still she'd love a lover; and Alceste
    Appears to be the one she'd love the best.
    His visits here are poison to her pride;
    She seems to think I've lured him from her side;
20   And everywhere, at court or in the town,
    The spiteful, envious woman runs me down.
    In short, she's just as stupid as can be,
    Vicious and arrogant in the last degree,
    And . . .

SCENE 4

ARSINOÉ, CÉLIMÈNE, CLITANDRE, ACASTE

CÉLIMÈNE   Ah! What happy chance has brought you here?
    I've thought about you ever so much, my dear.
ARSINOÉ   I've come to tell you something you should know.
CÉLIMÈNE   How good of you to think of doing so!

                Clitandre and Acaste go out, laughing.

SCENE 5

ARSINOÉ, CÉLIMÈNE

ARSINOÉ   It's just as well those gentlemen didn't tarry.
CÉLIMÈNE   Shall we sit down?
ARSINOÉ   That won't be necessary.
    Madam, the flame of friendship ought to burn
    Brightest in matters of the most concern,
    And as there's nothing which concerns us more

Than honor, I have hastened to your door
To bring you, as your friend, some information
About the status of your reputation.
I visited, last night, some virtuous folk,
And, quite by chance, it was of you they spoke;
There was, I fear, no tendency to praise
Your light behavior and your dashing ways.
The quantity of gentlemen you see
And your by now notorious coquetry
Were both so vehemently criticized
By everyone, that I was much surprised.
Of course, I needn't tell you where I stood;
I came to your defense as best I could,
Assured them you were harmless, and declared
Your soul was absolutely unimpaired.
But there are some things, you must realize,
One can't excuse, however hard one tries,
And I was forced at last into conceding
That your behavior, Madam, is misleading,
That it makes a bad impression, giving rise
To ugly gossip and obscene surmise,
And that if you were more *overtly* good,
You wouldn't be so much misunderstood.
Not that I think you've been unchaste—no! no!
The saints preserve me from a thought so low!
But mere good conscience never did suffice:
One must avoid the outward show of vice.
Madam, you're too intelligent, I'm sure,
To think my motives anything but pure
In offering you this counsel—which I do
Out of a zealous interest in you.
CÉLIMÈNE   Madam, I haven't taken you amiss;
I'm very much obliged to you for this;
And I'll at once discharge the obligation
By telling you about *your* reputation.
You've been so friendly as to let me know
What certain people say of me, and so
I mean to follow your benign example
By offering you a somewhat similar sample.
The other day, I went to an affair
And found some most distinguished people there
Discussing piety, both false and true.
The conversation soon came round to you.
Alas! Your prudery and bustling zeal

50   Appeared to have a very slight appeal.
     Your affectation of a grave demeanor,
     Your endless talk of virtue and of honor,
     The aptitude of your suspicious mind
     For finding sin where there is none to find,
     Your towering self-esteem, that pitying face
     With which you contemplate the human race,
     Your sermonizings and your sharp aspersions
     On people's pure and innocent diversions—
     All these were mentioned, Madam, and, in fact,
60   Were roundly and concertedly attacked.
     "What good," they said, "are all these outward shows,
     When everything belies her pious pose?
     She prays incessantly; but then, they say,
     She beats her maids and cheats them of their pay;
     She shows her zeal in every holy place,
     But still she's vain enough to paint her face;
     She holds that naked statues are immoral,
     But with a naked *man* she'd have no quarrel."
     Of course, I said to everybody there
70   That they were being viciously unfair;
     But still they were disposed to criticize you,
     And all agreed that someone should advise you
     To leave the morals of the world alone,
     And worry rather more about your own.
     They felt that one's self-knowledge should be great
     Before one thinks of setting others straight;
     That one should learn the art of living well
     Before one threatens other men with hell,
     And that the Church is best equipped, no doubt,
80   To guide our souls and root our vices out.
     Madam, you're too intelligent, I'm sure,
     To think my motives anything but pure
     In offering you this counsel—which I do
     Out of a zealous interest in you.
ARSINOÉ   I dared not hope for gratitude, but I
     Did not expect so acid a reply;
     I judge, since you've been so extremely tart,
     That my good counsel pierced you to the heart.
CÉLIMÈNE   Far from it, Madam. Indeed, it seems to me
90   We ought to trade advice more frequently.
     One's vision of oneself is so defective
     That it would be an excellent corrective.
     If you are willing, Madam, let's arrange

Shortly to have another frank exchange
In which we'll tell each other, *entre nous,*
What you've heard tell of me, and I of you.

ARSINOÉ Oh, people never censure you, my dear;
It's me they criticize. Or so I hear.

CÉLIMÈNE Madam, I think we either blame or praise
100   According to our taste and length of days.
There is a time of life for coquetry,
And there's a season, too, for prudery.
When all one's charms are gone, it is, I'm sure,
Good strategy to be devout and pure:
It makes one seem a little less forsaken.
Some day, perhaps, I'll take the road you've taken:
Time brings all things. But I have time aplenty,
And see no cause to be a prude at twenty.

ARSINOÉ You give your age in such a gloating tone
110   That one would think I was an ancient crone;
We're not so far apart, in sober truth,
That you can mock me with a boast of youth!
Madam, you baffle me. I wish I knew
What moves you to provoke me as you do.

CÉLIMÈNE For my part, Madam, I should like to know
Why you abuse me everywhere you go.
Is it my fault, dear lady, that your hand
Is not, alas, in very great demand?
If men admire me, if they pay me court
120   And daily make me offers of the sort
You'd dearly love to have them make to you,
How can I help it? What would you have me do?
If what you want is lovers, please feel free
To take as many as you can from me.

ARSINOÉ Oh, come. D'you think the world is losing sleep
Over that flock of lovers which you keep,
Or that we find it difficult to guess
What price you pay for their devotedness?
Surely you don't expect us to suppose
130   Mere merit could attract so many beaux?
It's not your virtue that they're dazzled by;
Nor is it virtuous love for which they sigh.
You're fooling no one, Madam; the world's not blind;
There's many a lady heaven has designed
To call men's noblest, tenderest feelings out,
Who has no lovers dogging her about;
From which it's plain that lovers nowadays

Must be acquired in bold and shameless ways,
And only pay one court for such reward
140   As modesty and virtue can't afford.
Then don't be quite so puffed up, if you please,
About your tawdry little victories;
Try, if you can, to be a shade less vain,
And treat the world with somewhat less disdain.
If one were envious of your amours,
One soon could have a following like yours;
Lovers are no great trouble to collect
If one prefers them to one's self-respect.
CÉLIMÈNE   Collect them then, my dear; I'd love to see
150   You demonstrate that charming theory;
Who knows, you might . . .
ARSINOÉ   Now, Madam, that will do;
It's time to end this trying interview.
My coach is late in coming to your door,
Or I'd have taken leave of you before.
CÉLIMÈNE   Oh, please don't feel that you must rush away;
I'd be delighted, Madam, if you'd stay.
However, lest my conversation bore you,
Let me provide some better company for you;
This gentleman, who comes most apropos,
160   Will please you more than I could do, I know.

SCENE 6

ALCESTE, CÉLIMÈNE, ARSINOÉ

CÉLIMÈNE   Alceste, I have a little note to write
Which simply must go out before tonight;
Please entertain *Madame;* I'm sure that she
Will overlook my incivility.

SCENE 7

ALCESTE, ARSINOÉ

ARSINOÉ   Well, Sir, our hostess graciously contrives
For us to chat until my coach arrives;
And I shall be forever in her debt
For granting me this little tête-à-tête.
We women very rightly give our hearts

To men of noble character and parts,
And your especial merits, dear Alceste,
Have roused the deepest sympathy in my breast.
Oh, how I wish they had sufficient sense
At court, to recognize your excellence!
They wrong you greatly, Sir. How it must hurt you
Never to be rewarded for your virtue!

ALCESTE   Why, Madam, what cause have I to feel aggrieved?
What great and brilliant thing have I achieved?
What service have I rendered to the King
That I should look to him for anything?

ARSINOÉ   Not everyone who's honored by the State
Has done great services. A man must wait
Till time and fortune offer him the chance.
Your merit, Sir, is obvious at a glance,
And . . .

ALCESTE   Ah, forget my merit; I'm not neglected.
The court, I think, can hardly be expected
To mine men's souls for merit, and unearth
Our hidden virtues and our secret worth.

ARSINOÉ   *Some* virtues, though, are far too bright to hide;
Yours are acknowledged, Sir, on every side.
Indeed, I've heard you warmly praised of late
By persons of considerable weight.

ALCESTE   This fawning age has praise for everyone,
And all distinctions, Madam, are undone.
All things have equal honor nowadays,
And no one should be gratified by praise.
To be admired, one only need exist,
And every lackey's on the honors list.

ARSINOÉ   I only wish, Sir, that you had your eye
On some position at court, however high;
You'd only have to hint at such a notion
For me to set the proper wheels in motion;
I've certain friendships I'd be glad to use
To get you any office you might choose.

ALCESTE   Madam, I fear that any such ambition
Is wholly foreign to my disposition.
The soul God gave me isn't of the sort
That prospers in the weather of a court.
It's all too obvious that I don't possess
The virtues necessary for success.
My one great talent is for speaking plain;
I've never learned to flatter or to feign;

And anyone so stupidly sincere
50   Had best not seek a courtier's career.
Outside the court, I know, one must dispense
With honors, privilege, and influence;
But still one gains the right, foregoing these,
Not to be tortured by the wish to please.
One needn't live in dread of snubs and slights,
Nor praise the verse that every idiot writes,
Nor humor silly Marquesses, nor bestow
Politic sighs on Madam So-and-So.
ARSINOÉ   Forget the court, then; let the matter rest.
60   But I've another cause to be distressed
About your present situation, Sir.
It's to your love affair that I refer.
She whom you love, and who pretends to love you,
Is, I regret to say, unworthy of you.
ALCESTE   Why, Madam! Can you seriously intend
To make so grave a charge against your friend?
ARSINOÉ   Alas, I must. I've stood aside too long
And let that lady do you grievous wrong;
But now my debt to conscience shall be paid:
70   I tell you that your love has been betrayed.
ALCESTE   I thank you, Madam; you're extrmely kind.
Such words are soothing to a lover's mind.
ARSINOÉ   Yes, though she *is* my friend, I say again
You're very much too good for Célimène.
She's wantonly misled you from the start.
ALCESTE   You may be right; who knows another's heart?
But ask yourself if it's the part of charity
To shake my soul with doubts of her sincerity.
ARSINOÉ   Well, if you'd rather be a dupe than doubt her,
80   That's your affair. I'll say no more about her.
ALCESTE   Madam, you know that doubt and vague suspicion
Are painful to a man in my position;
It's most unkind to worry me this way
Unless you've some real proof of what you say.
ARSINOÉ   Sir, say no more: all doubt shall be removed,
And all that I've been saying shall be proved.
You've only to escort me home, and there
We'll look into the heart of this affair.
I've ocular evidence which will persuade you
90   Beyond a doubt, that Célimène's betrayed you.
Then, if you're saddened by that revelation,
Perhaps I can provide some consolation.

ACT IV

SCENE 1

ÉLIANTE, PHILINTE

PHILINTE   Madam, he acted like a stubborn child;
    I thought they never would be reconciled;
    In vain we reasoned, threatened, and appealed;
    He stood his ground and simply would not yield.
    The Marshals, I feel sure, have never heard
    An argument so splendidly absurd.
    "No, gentlemen," said he, "I'll not retract.
    His verse is bad: extremely bad, in fact.
    Surely it does the man no harm to know it.
10   Does it disgrace him, not to be a poet?
    A gentleman may be respected still,
    Whether he writes a sonnet well or ill.
    That I dislike his verse should not offend him;
    In all that touches honor, I commend him;
    He's noble, brave, and virtuous—but I fear
    He can't in truth be called a sonneteer.
    I'll gladly praise his wardrobe; I'll endorse
    His dancing, or the way he sits a horse;
    But, gentlemen, I cannot praise his rhyme.
20   In fact, it ought to be a capital crime
    For anyone so sadly unendowed
    To write a sonnet, and read the thing aloud."
    At length he fell into a gentler mood
    And, striking a concessive attitude,
    He paid Oronte the following courtesies:
    "Sir, I regret that I'm so hard to please,
    And I'm profoundly sorry that your lyric
    Failed to provoke me to a panegyric."
    After these curious words, the two embraced,
30   And then the hearing was adjourned—in haste.
ÉLIANTE   His conduct has been very singular lately;
    Still, I confess that I respect him greatly.
    The honesty in which he takes such pride
    Has—to my mind—its noble, heroic side.
    In this false age, such candor seems outrageous;
    But I could wish that it were more contagious.
PHILINTE   What most intrigues me in our friend Alceste
    Is the grand passion that rages in his breast.

The sullen humors he's compounded of
40   Should not, I think, dispose his heart to love;
But since they do, it puzzles me still more
That he should choose your cousin to adore.

ÉLIANTE It does, indeed, belie the theory
That love is born of gentle sympathy,
And that the tender passion must be based
On sweet accords of temper and of taste.

PHILINTE Does she return his love, do you suppose?

ÉLIANTE Ah that's a difficult question, Sir. Who knows?
How can we judge the truth of her devotion?
50   Her heart's a stranger to its own emotion.
Sometimes it thinks it loves, when no love's there;
At other times it loves quite unaware.

PHILINTE I rather think Alceste is in for more
Distress and sorrow than he's bargained for;
Were he of my mind, Madam, his affection
Would turn in quite a different direction,
And we would see him more responsive to
The kind regard which he receives from you.

ÉLIANTE Sir, I believe in frankness, and I'm inclined,
60   In matters of the heart, to speak my mind.
I don't oppose his love for her; indeed,
I hope with all my heart that he'll succeed,
And were it in my power, I'd rejoice
In giving him the lady of his choice.
But if, as happens frequently enough
In love affairs, he meets with a rebuff—
If Célimène should grant some rival's suit—
I'd gladly play the role of substitute;
Nor would his tender speeches please me less
70   Because they'd once been made without success.

PHILINTE Well, Madam, as for me, I don't oppose
Your hopes in this affair; and heaven knows
That in my conversations with the man
I plead your cause as often as I can.
But if those two should marry, and so remove
All chance that he will offer you his love,
Then I'll declare my own, and hope to see
Your gracious favor pass from him to me.
In short, should you be cheated of Alceste,
80   I'd be most happy to be second best.

ÉLIANTE Philinte, you're teasing.

PHILINTE   Ah, Madam, never fear;

No words of mine were ever so sincere,
And I shall live in fretful expectation
Till I can make a fuller declaration.

SCENE 2

ALCESTE, ÉLIANTE, PHILINTE

ALCESTE   Avenge me, Madam! I must have satisfaction,
   Or this great wrong will drive me to distraction!
ÉLIANTE   Why, what's the matter? What's upset you so?
ALCESTE   Madam, I've had a mortal, mortal blow.
   If Chaos repossessed the universe,
   I swear I'd not be shaken any worse.
   I'm ruined. . . . I can say no more. . . . My soul . . .
ÉLIANTE   Do try, Sir, to regain your self-control.
ALCESTE   Just heaven! Why were so much beauty and grace
10   Bestowed on one so vicious and so base?
ÉLIANTE   Once more, Sir, tell us . . .
ALCESTE   My world has gone to wrack;
   I'm—I'm betrayed; she's stabbed me in the back:
   Yes, Célimène (who would have thought it of her?)
   Is false to me, and has another lover.
ÉLIANTE   Are you quite certain? Can you prove these things?
PHILINTE   Lovers are prey to wild imaginings
   And jealous fancies. No doubt there's some mistake. . . .
ALCESTE   Mind your own business, Sir, for heaven's sake.
   To Éliante.
   Madam, I have the proof that you demand
20   Here in my pocket, penned by her own hand.
   Yes, all the shameful evidence one could want
   Lies in this letter written to Oronte—
   Oronte! whom I felt sure she couldn't love,
   And hardly bothered to be jealous of.
PHILINTE   Still, in a letter, appearances may deceive;
   This may not be so bad as you believe.
ALCESTE   Once more I beg you, Sir, to let me be;
   Tend to your own affairs; leave mine to me.
ÉLIANTE   Compose yourself; this anguish that you feel . . .
30   ALCESTE   Is something, Madam, you alone can heal.
   My outraged heart, beside itself with grief,
   Appeals to you for comfort and relief.
   Avenge me on your cousin, whose unjust

And faithless nature has deceived my trust;
Avenge a crime your pure soul must detest.

ÉLIANTE   But how, Sir?

ALCESTE   Madam, this heart within my breast
Is yours; pray take it; redeem my heart from her,
And so avenge me on my torturer.
Let her be punished by the fond emotion,
40   The ardent love, the bottomless devotion,
The faithful worship which this heart of mine
Will offer up to yours as to a shrine.

ÉLIANTE   You have my sympathy, Sir, in all you suffer;
Nor do I scorn the noble heart you offer;
But I suspect you'll soon be mollified,
And this desire for vengeance will subside.
When some belovèd hand has done us wrong
We thirst for retribution—but not for long;
However dark the deed that she's committed,
50   A lovely culprit's very soon acquitted.
Nothing's so stormy as an injured lover,
And yet no storm so quickly passes over.

ALCESTE   No, Madam, no—this is no lovers' spat;
I'll not forgive her; it's gone too far for that;
My mind's made up; I'll kill myself before
I waste my hopes upon her any more.
Ah, here she is. My wrath intensifies.
I shall confront her with her tricks and lies,
And crush her utterly, and bring you then
60   A heart no longer slave to Célimène.

SCENE 3

CÉLIMÉNE, ALCESTE

ALCESTE, *aside.*   Sweet heaven, help me to control my passion.
CÉLIMÉNE, *aside.*   Oh, Lord.
    To Alceste.
                            Why stand there staring in that fashion?
And what d'you mean by those dramatic sighs,
And that malignant glitter in your eyes?

ALCESTE   I mean that sins which cause the blood to freeze
Look innocent beside your treacheries;
That nothing Hell's or Heaven's wrath could do
Ever produced so bad a thing as you.

CÉLIMÈNE   Your compliments were always sweet and pretty.

10 ALCESTE   Madam, it's not the moment to be witty.
No, blush and hang your head; you've ample reason,
Since I've the fullest evidence of your treason.
Ah, this is what my sad heart prophesied;
Now all my anxious fears are verified;
My dark suspicion and my gloomy doubt
Divined the truth, and now the truth is out.
For all your trickery, I was not deceived;
It was my bitter stars that I believed.
But don't imagine that you'll go scot-free;

20 You shan't misuse me with impunity.
I know that love's irrational and blind;
I know the heart's not subject to the mind,
And can't be reasoned into beating faster;
I know each soul is free to choose its master;
Therefore had you but spoken from the heart,
Rejecting my attentions from the start,
I'd have no grievance, or at any rate
I could complain of nothing but my fate.
Ah, but so falsely to encourage me—

30 That was a treason and a treachery
For which you cannot suffer too severely,
And you shall pay for that behavior dearly.
Yes, now I have no pity, not a shred;
My temper's out of hand; I've lost my head;
Shocked by the knowledge of your double-dealings,
My reason can't restrain my savage feelings;
A righteous wrath deprives me of my senses,
And I won't answer for the consequences.

CÉLIMÈNE   What does this outburst mean? Will you please explain?

40 Have you, by any chance, gone quite insane?

ALCESTE   Yes, yes, I went insane the day I fell
A victim to your black and fatal spell,
Thinking to meet with some sincerity
Among the treacherous charms that beckoned me.

CÉLIMÈNE   Pooh. Of what treachery can you complain?

ALCESTE   How sly you are, how cleverly you feign!
But you'll not victimize me any more.
Look: here's a document you've seen before.
This evidence, which I acquired today,

50 Leaves you, I think, without a thing to say.

CÉLIMÈNE   Is this what sent you into such a fit?

ALCESTE   You should be blushing at the sight of it.

CÉLIMÈNE   Ought I to blush? I truly don't see why.

ALCESTE   Ah, now you're being bold as well as sly;
 Since there's no signature, perhaps you'll claim . . .

CÉLIMÈNE   I wrote it, whether or not it bears my name.

ALCESTE   And you can view with equanimity
 This proof of your disloyalty to me!

CÉLIMÈNE   Oh, don't be so outrageous and extreme.

60   ALCESTE   You take this matter lightly, it would seem.
 Was it no wrong to me, no shame to you,
 That you should send Oronte this billet-doux?

CÉLIMÈNE   Oronte! Who said it was for him?

ALCESTE   Why, those
 Who brought me this example of your prose.
 But what's the difference? If you wrote the letter
 To someone else, it pleases me no better.
 My grievance and your guilt remain the same.

CÉLIMÈNE   But need you rage, and need I blush for shame,
 If this was written to a *woman* friend?

70   ALCESTE   Ah! Most ingenious. I'm impressed no end;
 And after that incredible evasion
 Your guilt is clear. I need no more persuasion.
 How dare you try so clumsy a deception?
 D'you think I'm wholly wanting in perception?
 Come, come, let's see how brazenly you'll try
 To bolster up so palpable a lie:
 Kindly construe this ardent closing section
 As nothing more than sisterly affection!
 Here, let me read it. Tell me, if you dare to,
 That this is for a woman . . .

80   CÉLIMÈNE   I don't care to.
 What right have you to badger and berate me,
 And so highhandedly interrogate me?

ALCESTE   Now, don't be angry; all I ask of you
 Is that you justify a phrase or two . . .

CÉLIMÈNE   No, I shall not. I utterly refuse,
 And you may take those phrases as you choose.

ALCESTE   Just show me how this letter could be meant
 For a woman's eyes, and I shall be content.

CÉLIMÈNE   No, no, it's for Oronte; you're perfectly right.

90   I welcome his attentions with delight,
 I prize his character and his intellect,
 And everything is just as you suspect.
 Come, do your worst now; give your rage free rein;
 But kindly cease to bicker and complain.

ALCESTE, *aside.*   Good God! Could anything be more inhuman?
Was ever a heart so mangled by a woman?
When I complain of how she has betrayed me,
She bridles, and commences to upbraid me!
She tries my tortured patience to the limit;
100 She won't deny her guilt; she glories in it!
And yet my heart's too faint and cowardly
To break these chains of passion, and be free,
To scorn her as it should, and rise above
This unrewarded, mad, and bitter love.

To Célimène.

Ah, traitress, in how confident a fashion
You take advantage of my helpless passion,
And use my weakness for your faithless charms
To make me once again throw down my arms!
But do at least deny this black transgression;
110 Take back that mocking and perverse confession;
Defend this letter and your innocence,
And I, poor fool, will aid in your defense.
Pretend, pretend, that you are just and true,
And I shall make myself believe in you.

CÉLIMÈNE   Oh, stop it. Don't be such a jealous dunce,
Or I shall leave off loving you at once.
Just why should I *pretend?* What could impel me
To stoop so low as that? And kindly tell me
Why, if I loved another, I shouldn't merely
120 Inform you of it, simply and sincerely!
I've told you where you stand, and that admission
Should altogether clear me of suspicion;
After so generous a guarantee,
What right have you to harbor doubts of me?
Since women are (from natural reticence)
Reluctant to declare their sentiments,
And since the honor of our sex requires
That we conceal our amorous desires,
Ought any man for whom such laws are broken
130 To question what the oracle has spoken?
Should he not rather feel an obligation
To trust that most obliging declaration?
Enough, now. Your suspicions quite disgust me;
Why should I love a man who doesn't trust me?
I cannot understand why I continue,

Fool that I am, to take an interest in you.
I ought to choose a man less prone to doubt,
And give you something to be vexed about.

ALCESTE   Ah, what a poor enchanted fool I am;
140   These gentle words, no doubt, were all a sham;
But destiny requires me to entrust
My happiness to you, and so I must.
I'll love you to the bitter end, and see
How false and treacherous you dare to be.

CÉLIMÈNE   No, you don't really love me as you ought.

ALCESTE   I love you more than can be said or thought;
Indeed, I wish you were in such distress
That I might show my deep devotedness.
Yes, I could wish that you were wretchedly poor,
150   Unloved, uncherished, utterly obscure;
That fate had set you down upon the earth
Without possessions, rank, or gentle birth;
Then, by the offer of my heart, I might
Repair the great injustice of your plight;
I'd raise you from the dust, and proudly prove
The purity and vastness of my love.

CÉLIMÈNE   This is a strange benevolence indeed!
God grant that I may never be in need. . . .
Ah, here's Monsieur Dubois, in quaint disguise.

SCENE 4

CÉLIMÈNE, ALCESTE, DUBOIS

ALCESTE   Well, why this costume? Why those frightened eyes?
What ails you?

DUBOIS   Well, Sir, things are most mysterious.

ALCESTE   What do you mean?

DUBOIS   I fear they're very serious.

ALCESTE   What?

DUBOIS   Shall I speak more loudly?

ALCESTE   Yes; speak out.

DUBOIS   Isn't there someone here, Sir?

ALCESTE   Speak, you lout!
Stop wasting time

DUBOIS   Sir, we must slip away.

ALCESTE   How's that?

DUBOIS   We must decamp without delay.

ALCESTE   Explain yourself.

DUBOIS   I tell you we must fly.

ALCESTE   What for?

DUBOIS   We mustn't pause to say good-by.

10   ALCESTE   Now what d'you mean by all of this, you clown?

DUBOIS   I mean, Sir, that we've got to leave this town.

ALCESTE   I'll tear you limb from limb and joint from joint
If you don't come more quickly to the point.

DUBOIS   Well, Sir, today a man in a black suit,
Who wore a black and ugly scowl to boot,
Left us a document scrawled in such a hand
As even Satan couldn't understand.
It bears upon your lawsuit, I don't doubt;
But all hell's devils couldn't make it out.

20   ALCESTE   Well, well, go on. What then? I fail to see
How this event obliges us to flee.

DUBOIS   Well, Sir: an hour later, hardly more,
A gentleman who's often called before
Came looking for you in an anxious way.
Not finding you, he asked me to convey
(Knowing I could be trusted with the same)
The following message. . . . Now, what *was* his name?

ALCESTE   Forget his name, you idiot. What did he say?

DUBOIS   Well, it was one of your friends, Sir, anyway.

30   He warned you to begone, and he suggested
That if you stay, you may well be arrested.

ALCESTE   What? Nothing more specific? Think, man, think!

DUBOIS   No, Sir. He had me bring him pen and ink,
And dashed you off a letter which, I'm sure,
Will render things distinctly less obscure.

ALCESTE   Well—let me have it!

CÉLIMÈNE   What *is* this all about?

ALCESTE   God knows; but I have hopes of finding out.
How long am I to wait, you blitherer?

DUBOIS, *after a protracted search for the letter.*   I must have left it on your table,
Sir.

ALCESTE   I ought to . . .

40   CÉLIMÈNE   No, no, keep your self-control;
Go find out what's behind his rigmarole.

ALCESTE   It seems that fate, no matter what I do,
Has sworn that I may not converse with you;
But, Madam, pray permit your faithful lover
To try once more before the day is over.

ACT V

SCENE 1

ALCESTE, PHILINTE

ALCESTE   No, it's too much. My mind's made up, I tell you.
PHILINTE   Why should this blow, however hard, compel you . . .
ALCESTE   No, no, don't waste your breath in argument;
  Nothing you say will alter my intent;
  This age is vile, and I've made up my mind
  To have no further commerce with mankind.
  Did not truth, honor, decency, and the laws
  Oppose my enemy and approve my cause?
  My claims were justified in all men's sight;
10 I put my trust in equity and right;
  Yet, to my horror and the world's disgrace,
  Justice is mocked, and I have lost my case!
  A scoundrel whose dishonesty is notorious
  Emerges from another lie victorious!
  Honor and right condone his brazen fraud,
  While rectitude and decency applaud!
  Before his smirking face, the truth stands charmed,
  And virtue conquered, and the law disarmed!
  His crime is sanctioned by a court decree!
20 And not content with what he's done to me,
  The dog now seeks to ruin me by stating
  That I composed a book now circulating,
  A book so wholly criminal and vicious
  That even to speak its title is seditious!
  Meanwhile Oronte, my rival, lends his credit
  To the same libelous tale, and helps to spread it!
  Oronte! a man of honor and of rank,
  With whom I've been entirely fair and frank;
  Who sought me out and forced me, willy-nilly,
30 To judge some verse I found extremely silly;
  And who, because I properly refused
  To flatter him, or see the truth abused,
  Abets my enemy in a rotten slander!
  There's the reward of honesty and candor!
  The man will hate me to the end of time
  For failing to commend his wretched rhyme!
  And not this man alone, but all humanity

Do what they do from interest and vanity;
They prate of honor, truth, and righteousness,
40   But lie, betray, and swindle nonetheless.
Come then: man's villainy is too much to bear;
Let's leave this jungle and this jackal's lair.
Yes! treacherous and savage race of men,
You shall not look upon my face again.

PHILINTE   Oh, don't rush into exile prematurely;
Things aren't as dreadful as you make them, surely.
It's rather obvious, since you're still at large,
That people don't believe your enemy's charge.
Indeed, his tale's so patently untrue
50   That it may do more harm to him than you.

ALCESTE   Nothing could do that scoundrel any harm:
His frank corruption is his greatest charm,
And, far from hurting him, a further shame
Would only serve to magnify his name.

PHILINTE   In any case, his bald prevarication
Has done no injury to your reputation,
And you may feel secure in that regard.
As for your lawsuit, it should not be hard
To have the case reopened, and contest
This judgment . . .

60   ALCESTE   No, no, let the verdict rest.
Whatever cruel penalty it may bring,
I wouldn't have it changed for anything.
It shows the times' injustice with such clarity
That I shall pass it down to our posterity
As a great proof and signal demonstration
Of the black wickedness of this generation.
It may cost twenty thousand francs; but I
Shall pay their twenty thousand, and gain thereby
The right to storm and rage at human evil,
70   And send the race of mankind to the devil.

PHILINTE   Listen to me. . . .

ALCESTE   Why? What can you possibly say?
Don't argue, Sir; your labor's thrown away.
Do you propose to offer lame excuses
For men's behavior and the times' abuses?

PHILINTE   No, all you say I'll readily concede:
This is a low, conniving age indeed;
Nothing but trickery prospers nowadays,
And people ought to mend their shabby ways.
Yes, man's a beastly creature; but must we then

80   Abandon the society of men?
       Here in the world, each human frailty
       Provides occasion for philosophy,
       And that is virtue's noblest exercise;
       If honesty shone forth from all men's eyes,
       If every heart were frank and kind and just,
       What could our virtues do but gather dust
       (Since their employment is to help us bear
       The villainies of men without despair)?
       A heart well-armed with virtue can endure. . . .
90 ALCESTE   Sir, you're a matchless reasoner, to be sure;
       Your words are fine and full of cogency;
       But don't waste time and eloquence on me.
       My reason bids me go, for my own good.
       My tongue won't lie and flatter as it should;
       God knows what frankness it might next commit,
       And what I'd suffer on account of it.
       Pray let me wait for Célimène's return
       In peace and quiet. I shall shortly learn,
       By her response to what I have in view,
100   Whether her love for me is feigned or true.
    PHILINTE   Till then, let's visit Éliante upstairs.
    ALCESTE   No, I am too weighed down with somber cares.
       Go to her, do; and leave me with my gloom
       Here in the darkened corner of this room.
    PHILINTE   Why, that's no sort of company, my friend;
       I'll see if Éliante will not descend.

SCENE 2

CÉLIMÈNE, ORONTE, ALCESTE

   ORONTE   Yes, Madam, if you wish me to remain
       Your true and ardent lover, you must deign
       To give me some more positive assurance.
       All this suspense is quite beyond endurance.
       If your heart shares the sweet desires of mine,
       Show me as much by some convincing sign;
       And here's the sign I urgently suggest:
       That you no longer tolerate Alceste,
       But sacrifice him to my love, and sever
10   All your relations with the man forever.
    CÉLIMÈNE   Why do you suddenly dislike him so?
       You praised him to the skies not long ago.

ORONTE   Madam, that's not the point. I'm here to find
    Which way your tender feelings are inclined.
    Choose, if you please, between Alceste and me,
    And I shall stay or go accordingly.
ALCESTE, *emerging from the corner.*   Yes, Madam, choose; this gentleman's demand
    Is wholly just, and I support his stand.
    I too am true and ardent; I too am here
20   To ask you that you make your feelings clear.
    No more delays, now; no equivocation;
    The time has come to make your declaration.
ORONTE   Sir, I've no wish in any way to be
    An obstacle to your felicity.
ALCESTE   Sir, I've no wish to share her heart with you;
    That may sound jealous, but at least it's true.
ORONTE   If, weighing us, she leans in your direction . . .
ALCESTE   If she regards you with the least affection . . .
ORONTE   I swear I'll yield her to you there and then.
30 ALCESTE   I swear I'll never see her face again.
ORONTE   No, Madam, tell us what we've come to hear.
ALCESTE   Madam, speak openly and have no fear.
ORONTE   Just say which one is to remain your lover.
ALCESTE   Just name one name, and it will all be over.
ORONTE   What! Is it possible that you're undecided?
ALCESTE   What! Can your feelings possibly be divided?
CÉLIMÈNE   Enough: this inquisition's gone too far:
    How utterly unreasonable you are!
    Not that I couldn't make the choice with ease;
40   My heart has no conflicting sympathies;
    I know full well which one of you I favor,
    And you'd not see me hesitate or waver.
    But how can you expect me to reveal
    So cruelly and bluntly what I feel?
    I think it altogether too unpleasant
    To choose between two men when both are present;
    One's heart has means more subtle and more kind
    Of letting its affections be divined,
    Nor need one be uncharitably plain
50   To let a lover know he loves in vain.
ORONTE   No, no, speak plainly; I for one can stand it.
    I beg you to be frank.
ALCESTE   And I demand it.
    The simple truth is what I wish to know,
    And there's no need for softening the blow.

You've made an art of pleasing everyone,
But now your days of coquetry are done:
You have no choice now, Madam, but to choose,
For I'll know what to think if you refuse;
I'll take your silence for a clear admission
That I'm entitled to my worst suspicion.

60

ORONTE   I thank you for this ultimatum, Sir,
And I may say I heartily concur.

CÉLIMÈNE   Really, this foolishness is very wearing:
Must you be so unjust and overbearing?
Haven't I told you why I must demur?
Ah, here's Éliante; I'll put the case to her.

SCENE 3

ÉLIANTE, PHILINTE, CÉLIMÈNE, ORONTE, ALCESTE

CÉLIMÈNE   Cousin, I'm being persecuted here
By these two persons, who, it would appear,
Will not be satisfied till I confess
Which one I love the more, and which the less,
And tell the latter to his face that he
Is henceforth banished from my company.
Tell me, has ever such a thing been done?

ÉLIANTE   You'd best not turn to me; I'm not the one
To back you in a matter of this kind:

10

I'm all for those who frankly speak their mind.

ORONTE   Madam, you'll search in vain for a defender.

ALCESTE   You're beaten, Madam, and may as well surrender.

ORONTE   Speak, speak, you must; and end this awful strain.

ALCESTE   Or don't, and your position will be plain.

ORONTE   A single word will close this painful scene.

ALCESTE   But if you're silent, I'll know what you mean.

SCENE 4

ARSINOÉ, CÉLIMÈNE, ÉLIANTE, ALCESTE, PHILINTE, ACASTE, CLITANDRE, ORONTE

ACASTE, *to Célimène*.   Madam, with all due deference, we two
Have come to pick a little bone with you.

CLITANDRE, *to Oronte and Alceste*.   I'm glad you're present, Sirs; as you'll
soon learn,
Our business here is also your concern.

ARSINOÉ, *to Célimène*.   Madam, I visit you so soon again

Only because of these two gentlemen,
Who came to me indignant and aggrieved
About a crime too base to be believed.
Knowing your virtue, having such confidence in it,
I couldn't think you guilty for a minute,
In spite of all their telling evidence;
And, rising above our little difference,
I've hastened here in friendship's name to see
You clear yourself of this great calumny.

ACASTE Yes, Madam, let us see with what composure
You'll manage to respond to this disclosure.
You lately sent Clitandre this tender note.

CLITANDRE And this one, for Acaste, you also wrote.

ACASTE, *to Oronte and Alceste*. You'll recognize this writing, Sirs, I think;
The lady is so free with pen and ink
That you must know it all too well, I fear.
But listen: this is something you should hear.

"How absurd you are to condemn my lightheartedness in society,
and to accuse me of being happiest in the company of others.
Nothing could be more unjust; and if you do not come to me
instantly and beg pardon for saying such a thing, I shall never
forgive you as long as I live. Our big bumbling friend the Viscount
. . ."

What a shame that he's not here.

"Our big bumbling friend the Viscount, whose name stands first
in your complaint, is hardly a man to my taste; and ever since the
day I watched him spend three-quarters of an hour spitting into a
well, so as to make circles in the water, I have been unable to think
highly of him. As for the little Marquess . . ."

In all modesty, gentlemen, that is I.

"As for the little Marquess, who sat squeezing my hand for such a
long while yesterday, I find him in all respects the most trifling
creature alive; and the only things of value about him are his cape
and his sword. As for the man with the green ribbons . . ."

To Alceste. It's your turn now, Sir.

"As for the man with the green ribbons, he amuses me now and
then with his bluntness and his bearish ill-humor; but there are

many times indeed when I think him the greatest bore in the world. And as for the sonneteer . . ."

To Oronte.   Here's your helping.

"And as for the sonneteer, who has taken it into his head to be witty, and insists on being an author in the teeth of opinion, I simply cannot be bothered to listen to him, and his prose wearies me quite as much as his poetry. Be assured that I am not always so well-entertained as you suppose; that I long for your company, more than I dare to say, at all these entertainments to which people drag me; and that the presence of those one loves is the true and perfect seasoning to all one's pleasures."

60

CLITANDRE   And now for me.

"Clitandre, whom you mention, and who so pesters me with his saccharine speeches, is the last man on earth for whom I could feel any affection. He is quite mad to suppose that I love him, and so are you, to doubt that you are loved. Do come to your senses; exchange your suppositions for his; and visit me as often as possible, to help me bear the annoyance of his unwelcome attentions."

70

It's a sweet character that these letters show,
And what to call it, Madam, you well know.
Enough. We're off to make the world acquainted
With this sublime self-portrait that you've painted.
ACASTE   Madam, I'll make you no farewell oration;
No, you're not worthy of my indignation.
Far choicer hearts than yours, as you'll discover,
Would like this little Marquess for a lover.

80

SCENE 5

CÉLIMÈNE, ÉLIANTE, ARSINOÉ, ALCESTE, ORONTE, PHILINTE

ORONTE   So! After all those loving letters you wrote,
You turn on me like this, and cut my throat!
And your dissembling, faithless heart, I find,
Has pledged itself by turns to all mankind!
How blind I've been! But now I clearly see;
I thank you, Madam, for enlightening me.
My heart is mine once more, and I'm content;
The loss of it shall be your punishment.

To Alceste.

Sir, she is yours; I'll seek no more to stand
10   Between your wishes and this lady's hand.

SCENE 6

CÉLIMÈNE, ÉLIANTE, ARSINOÉ, ALCESTE, PHILINTE

ARSINOÉ, *to Célimène.*   Madam, I'm forced to speak. I'm far too stirred
To keep my counsel, after what I've heard.
I'm shocked and staggered by your want of morals.
It's not my way to mix in others' quarrels;
But really, when this fine and noble spirit,
This man of honor and surpassing merit,
Laid down the offering of his heart before you,
How *could* you . . .
ALCESTE   Madam, permit me, I implore you,
To represent myself in this debate.
10   Don't bother, please, to be my advocate.
My heart, in any case, could not afford
To give your services their due reward;
And if I chose, for consolation's sake,
Some other lady, 'twould not be you I'd take.
ARSINOÉ   What makes you think you could, Sir? And how dare you
Imply that I've been trying to ensnare you?
If you can for a moment entertain
Such flattering fancies, you're extremely vain.
I'm not so interested as you suppose
20   In Célimène's discarded gigolos.
Get rid of that absurd illusion, do.
Women like me are not for such as you.
Stay with this creature, to whom you're so attached;
I've never seen two people better matched.

SCENE 7

CÉLIMÈNE, ÉLIANTE, ALCESTE, PHILINTE

ALCESTE, *to Célimène.*   Well, I've been still throughout this exposé,
Till everyone but me has said his say.
Come, have I shown sufficient self-restraint?
And may I now . . .
CÉLIMÈNE   Yes, make your just complaint.

Reproach me freely, call me what you will;
You've every right to say I've used you ill.
I've wronged you, I confess it; and in my shame
I'll make no effort to escape the blame.
The anger of those others I could despise;
My guilt toward you I sadly recognize.
Your wrath is wholly justified, I fear;
I know how culpable I must appear,
I know all things bespeak my treachery,
And that, in short, you've grounds for hating me.
Do so; I give you leave.

ALCESTE   Ah, traitress—how,
How should I cease to love you, even now?
Though mind and will were passionately bent
On hating you, my heart would not consent.

To Éliante and Philinte.

Be witness to my madness, both of you;
See what infatuation drives one to;
But wait; my folly's only just begun,
And I shall prove to you before I'm done
How strange the human heart is, and how far
From rational we sorry creatures are.

To Célimène.

Woman, I'm willing to forget your shame,
And clothe your treacheries in a sweeter name;
I'll call them youthful errors, instead of crimes,
And lay the blame on these corrupting times.
My one condition is that you agree
To share my chosen fate, and fly with me
To that wild, trackless, solitary place
In which I shall forget the human race.
Only by such a course can you atone
For those atrocious letters; by that alone
Can you remove my present horror of you,
And make it possible for me to love you.

CÉLIMÈNE What! *I* renounce the world at my young age,
And die of boredom in some hermitage?

ALCESTE Ah, if you really loved me as you ought,
You wouldn't give the world a moment's thought;
Must you have me, and all the world beside?

CÉLIMÈNE   Alas, at twenty one is terrified
    Of solitude. I fear I lack the force
    And depth of soul to take so stern a course.
    But if my hand in marriage will content you,
    Why, there's a plan which I might well consent to,
    And . . .

ALCESTE   No, I detest you now. I could excuse
    Everything else, but since you thus refuse
    To love me wholly, as a wife should do,
50   And see the world in me, as I in you,
    Go! I reject your hand, and disenthrall
    My heart from your enchantments, once for all.

SCENE 8

ÉLIANTE, ALCESTE, PHILINTE

ALCESTE, *to Éliante.*   Madam, your virtuous beauty has no peer;
    Of all this world, you only are sincere;
    I've long esteemed you highly, as you know;
    Permit me ever to esteem you so,
    And if I do not now request your hand,
    Forgive me, Madam, and try to understand.
    I feel unworthy of it; I sense that fate
    Does not intend me for the married state,
    That I should do you wrong by offering you
    My shattered heart's unhappy residue,
    And that in short . . .

10 ÉLIANTE   Your argument's well taken:
    Nor need you fear that I shall feel forsaken.
    Were I to offer him this hand of mine,
    Your friend Philinte, I think, would not decline.

PHILINTE   Ah, Madam, that's my heart's most cherished goal,
    For which I'd gladly give my life and soul.

ALCESTE, *to Éliante and Philinte.*   May you be true to all you now profess,
    And so deserve unending happiness.
    Meanwhile, betrayed and wronged in everything,
    I'll flee this bitter world where vice is king,
20   And seek some spot unpeopled and apart
    Where I'll be free to have an honest heart.

PHILINTE   Come, Madam, let's do everything we can
    To change the mind of this unhappy man.

2. Modern to Contemporary Drama

SETTING AND SYMBOLISM IN MODERN AND CONTEMPORARY DRAMA

Each play in this collection of modern and contemporary drama invites us to imagine not only a particular location but also a highly detailed setting within that locale. In the stage directions preceding the first act of *A Doll's House*, for example, Ibsen is not content simply to tell us that the play takes place in the living room of Torvald Helmer's home. He gives us, rather, an elaborate description of that room and all of its furnishings:

> A comfortably and tastefully, but not expensively furnished room. Backstage right a door leads out to the hall; backstage left, another door to Helmer's study. Between these two doors stands a piano. In the middle of the left-hand wall is a door, with a window downstage of it. Near the window, a round table with armchairs and a small sofa. In the right-hand wall, slightly upstage, is a door; downstage of this, against the same wall, a stove lined with porcelain tiles, with a couple of armchairs and a rocking chair in front of it. Between the stove and the side door is a small table. Engravings on the wall. A what-not with china and other bric-à-brac; a small bookcase with leather-bound books. A carpet on the floor; a fire in the stove.

That description is so complete that it asks us even to visualize a fire burning in the stove. And why not, since the action takes place shortly before Christmas? It seems to be a perfectly logical detail for Ibsen to note. But it seems logical to us because as twentieth-century playgoers we have become accustomed to the vividly realistic stage illusions of our present-day theaters.

To Ibsen's audience (which witnessed the first production of *A Doll's*

House in 1879) that elaborately realistic set, depicting an upper-middle class interior of the nineteenth century, was almost as revolutionary as his frankly realistic approach to the marital problems of that upper-middle class family. Until the 1850s, in fact, theatrical settings of the nineteenth century consisted largely of painted flats depicting the exotic landscapes of Romantic melodrama. And before the nineteenth century, as we have seen in our introductory notes on classical-through-neoclassical theaters, there were virtually no attempts whatsoever to create a completely detailed visual illusion on stage. Shakespeare's plays were originally staged without sets at all and only a few props. And most of Molière's comedies were originally performed in front of a stock set—a flat painted to represent the wall of a drawing room with four doors cut in for entrances and exits. Thus, in a brief stage direction preceding the first act of *A Misanthrope,* Molière tells us simply that "the scene throughout is in Célimène's house at Paris."

Molière, of course, was writing two centuries before Ibsen, at a time—as we might assume—when the machinery of the theater provided him with limited opportunities for elaborately designed sets. But that is not the case at all. The theaters of Molière's time were equipped with highly sophisticated machinery capable of producing visual extravaganzas for the entertainment of the King and his court. Those visual spectacles, however, were limited to the staging of operas and ballets. Apparently, then, Molière and his contemporaries did not lack the technical means for creating detailed theatrical illusions within their plays. They simply did not choose to create them. But Ibsen and many dramatists since his time have deliberately aimed to create elaborate settings for their plays, and thus we should be aware of their purposes in doing so. We should not be content simply to attribute those sets to technical advances in the design of theaters.

In Ibsen's case that detailed setting is related directly to the naturalistic impulse of his play. Thus, in *A Doll's House* he not only portrays the psychological relationship between Helmer and Nora, but he also displays the environment in which that relationship is rooted. He is, in fact, at such pains to create a total sense of their environment that he turns the stage into a completely furnished living room with a wall at both sides as well as at the back. That box set is also crucial to an experiencing of the play. Were we to witness a production of the play, we would feel as though we were peering in on the characters, as though the space defined by the proscenium arch did not exist for them, as though they were in a room surrounded by four walls, as though they were conducting their personal lives in private.

But beyond having us experience this naturalistic illusion, Ibsen intends us also to see that elaborate set as symbolizing the impact of the Helmers' environment upon their marriage—indeed as symbolizing the very nature of that marriage. That set with all its expensive possessions embodies the profound pressures placed on Helmer and Nora by the material and social conditions of their world. Thus, when we read the play we should keep continually in our mind's eye the rich clutter of that room with its bric-à-brac and its overstuffed chairs that in the end are as stifling—and as deceiving—as the marriage of Nora and Helmer. We should be aware, for example, of how deeply attached Nora is to those possessions in the beginning of the play—like a child, she does not wish to give up the illusions of her doll's house—and thus of how much it takes for her to free herself of their very solid hold on her life: on her physical life *and* on her mental life.

Once we recognize setting as a potentially symbolic element of modern and contemporary drama, we shall find that our reading of plays is enriched when we pay close attention to all the descriptive details concerning the make-up of the set. Dramatists provide those elaborate descriptions not only for the guidance of set designers but also for the enlightenment of readers like us who may not have the opportunity to witness a production of their plays. And as we move from one play to the next, we shall find that the settings enlighten us in quite different ways. Just as dramatists write in different styles, so they use their settings for different symbolic effects. At the beginning of *Major Barbara*, for example, Shaw offers us a relatively sketchy description of the "library in Lady Britomart Undershaft's house in Wilton Crescent," noting merely that it contains a "large and comfortable settee in the middle of the room, upholstered in dark leather," a "writing table" on each side of it, a "window with a window seat," "an armchair" nearby, "books in the library," and "pictures on the walls." From these few details, Shaw does not appear to be interested in providing a naturalistic display of Lady Britomart's environment. Instead, he aims to present her library as an emblem of the traditional aristocratic social values for which she stands, as he makes clear in the remarks he offers about Lady Britomart immediately after the details about her library. He tells us, for example, that she is "a very typical managing matron of the upper class . . . limited in the oddest way with domestic and class limitations, conceiving the universe exactly as if it were a large house in Wilton Crescent." Thus her library with its few typical marks of upper-class privilege is sufficient to stand as a symbol of her aristocratic outlook.

Tennessee Williams also describes an interior setting, in this case a bedroom, at the beginning of *Cat on a Hot Tin Roof*; yet it is neither satiric like Shaw's nor completely naturalistic like Ibsen's. At one point it appears to be a naturalistically detailed set, for Williams offers a meticulous description of the furniture it includes, in particular "a *huge* console combination of radio-phonograph (Hi-Fi with three speakers) TV set *and* liquor cabinet." He even provides an interpretation of its symbolic significance:

> This piece of furniture . . . is a very complete and compact little shrine to virtually all the comforts and illusions behind which we hide from such things as the characters in the play are faced with.

Immediately after that interpretation, however, he complicates our understanding of the set by disclaiming its naturalistic connection with reality:

> The set should be far less realistic than I have so far implied. I think the wall below the ceiling should dissolve into air; the set should be roofed by the sky; stars and moon suggested by traces of milky pallor, as if they were observed through a telescope lens out of focus.

Suddenly, then, his realistic set design seems to melt into thin air, to become surrealistic, as though to imply that it is not a wholly reliable symbol of his characters' environment. Later still, he tells us that

> The designer should take as many pains to give the actors room to move about freely (to show their restlessness, their passion for breaking out) as if it were a set for a ballet.

Williams's set clearly has numerous implications—far more in fact than we have suggested by our few quotations from his description. Most settings in modern and contemporary drama are indeed just as richly significant as the actions that take place within them, but that should not surprise us, for we have come to know from our own lives that the environments in which we exist not only influence us but are in turn influenced by us. So it is with the settings and characters of the plays we have included in this collection. They are inextricably bound up with one another, and thus they can be understood only in relation to one another.

HENRIK IBSEN
1828–1906

Born in Skien, Norway, a small town where his father was then a successful merchant, Ibsen grew up amid the painful circumstances that were brought about by the decline of his father's business, which ended in bankruptcy when Ibsen was eight years old. His family was then forced to move from their large and comfortable home to a small attic apartment, and by the time Ibsen was sixteen he was sent off to another town to make his own way as a druggist's apprentice. When he was twenty-two, he moved to Christiana (now Oslo), hoping to study medicine at the University there, but his failure to gain admission led him to make a career out of the playwriting that he had begun to do several years earlier. During the next sixteen years, he was influenced largely by the nationalistic and romantic movement in Norwegian theater, and thus gave himself over mostly to writing blank verse plays on subjects drawn from Norwegian myth and history. But in 1869, with *The League of Youth*, a play exposing the corruption of provincial politics and politicians, Ibsen began to write realistic prose plays about the social problems of his time. His best-known problem plays—*A Doll's House* (1879) and *Ghosts* (1881)—were highly controversial in his own time, especially among his Norwegian countrymen, who regarded them as attacking such traditional values as marriage and the family. Social reformers then and now have hailed them as eloquent pleas in defense of women's rights. These plays may also be seen as foreshadowing his late dramatic studies of psychologically troubled men and women in *Rosmersholm* (1886) and *Hedda Gabler* (1890), and thus he has properly come to be regarded as the father of modern naturalistic drama.

A Doll's House

CHARACTERS

TORVALD HELMER, a lawyer
NORA, his wife
DR. RANK
MRS. LINDE
NILS KROGSTAD, also a lawyer

The HELMERS' three small children
ANNE-MARIE, their nurse
HELEN, the maid
A PORTER

The action takes place in the Helmers' apartment.

ACT I

A comfortably and tastefully, but not expensively furnished room. Backstage right a door leads out to the hall; backstage left, another door to Helmer's study. Between these two doors stands a piano. In the middle of the left-hand wall is a door, with a window downstage of it. Near the window, a round table with armchairs and a small sofa. In the right-hand wall, slightly upstage, is a door; downstage of this, against the same wall, a stove lined with porcelain tiles, with a couple of armchairs and a rocking-chair in front of it. Between the stove and the side door is a small table. Engravings on the wall. A what-not with china and other bric-a-brac; a small bookcase with leather-bound books. A carpet on the floor; a fire in the stove. A winter day.

  A bell rings in the hall outside. After a moment, we hear the front door being opened. Nora enters the room, humming contentedly to herself. She is wearing outdoor clothes and carrying a lot of parcels, which she puts down on the table right. She leaves the door to the hall open; through it, we can see a Porter carrying

Translated by Michael Meyer

a Christmas tree and a basket. He gives these to the Maid, who has opened the door for them.

NORA   Hide that Christmas tree away, Helen. The children mustn't see it before I've decorated it this evening. [*To the Porter, taking out her purse.*] How much—?
PORTER   A shilling.
NORA   Here's half a crown. No, keep it.

The Porter touches his cap and goes. Nora closes the door. She continues to laugh happily to herself as she removes her coat, etc. She takes from her pocket a bag containing macaroons and eats a couple. Then she tiptoes across and listens at her husband's door.

NORA   Yes, he's here. [*Starts humming again as she goes over to the table, right.*]
HELMER [*from his room*]   Is that my skylark twittering out there?
NORA [*opening some of the parcels*]   It is!
HELMER   Is that my squirrel rustling?
NORA   Yes!
HELMER   When did my squirrel come home?
NORA   Just now. [*Pops the bag of macaroons in her pocket and wipes her mouth.*] Come out here, Torvald, and see what I've bought.
HELMER   You mustn't disturb me! [*Short pause; then he opens the door and looks in, his pen in his hand.*] Bought, did you say? All that? Has my little squanderbird been overspending again?
NORA   Oh, Torvald, surely we can let ourselves go a little this year! It's the first Christmas we don't have to scrape.
HELMER   Well, you know, we can't afford to be extravagant.
NORA   Oh yes, Torvald, we can be a little extravagant now. Can't we? Just a tiny bit? You've got a big salary now, and you're going to make lots and lots of money.
HELMER   Next year, yes. But my new salary doesn't start till April.
NORA   Pooh; we can borrow till then.
HELMER   Nora! [*Goes over to her and takes her playfully by the ear.*] What a little spendthrift you are! Suppose I were to borrow fifty pounds today, and you spent it all over Christmas, and then on New Year's Eve a tile fell off a roof on to my head—
NORA [*puts her hand over his mouth*]   Oh, Torvald! Don't say such dreadful things!
HELMER   Yes, but suppose something like that did happen? What then?
NORA   If anything as frightful as that happened, it wouldn't make much difference whether I was in debt or not.
HELMER   But what about the people I'd borrowed from?

NORA   Them? Who cares about them? They're strangers.

HELMER   Oh, Nora, Nora, how like a woman! No, but seriously, Nora, you
know how I feel about this. No debts! Never borrow! A home that is
founded on debts can never be a place of freedom and beauty. We two
have stuck it out bravely up to now; and we shall continue to do so for
the short time we still have to.

NORA [goes over towards the stove]   Very well, Torvald. As you say.

HELMER [follows her]   Now, now! My little songbird mustn't droop her
wings. What's this? Is little squirrel sulking? [Takes out his purse] Nora;
guess what I've got here!

NORA [turns quickly]   Money!

HELMER   Look. [Hands her some banknotes] I know how these small expenses
crop up at Christmas.

NORA [counts them]   One—two—three—four. Oh, thank you, Torvald, thank
you! I should be able to manage with this.

HELMER   You'll have to.

NORA   Yes, yes, of course I will. But come over here, I want to show you
everything I've bought. And so cheaply! Look, here are new clothes for
Ivar—and a sword. And a horse and a trumpet for Bob. And a doll and a
cradle for Emmy—they're nothing much, but she'll pull them apart in a
few days. And some bits of material and handkerchiefs for the maids. Old
Anne-Marie ought to have had something better, really.

HELMER   And what's in that parcel?

NORA [cries]   No, Torvald, you mustn't see that before this evening!

HELMER   Very well. But now, tell me, you little spendthrift, what do you
want for Christmas?

NORA   Me? Oh, pooh, I don't want anything.

HELMER   Oh, yes, you do. Now tell me, what, within reason, would you
most like?

NORA   No, I really don't know. Oh, yes—Torvald—!

HELMER   Well?

NORA [plays with his coat-buttons; not looking at him]   If you really want to
give me something, you could—you could—

HELMER   Come on, out with it.

NORA [quickly]   You could give me money, Torvald. Only as much as you
feel you can afford; then later I'll buy something with it.

HELMER   But, Nora—

NORA   Oh yes, Torvald dear, please! Please! Then I'll wrap up the notes in
pretty gold paper and hang them on the Christmas tree. Wouldn't that
be fun?

HELMER   What's the name of that little bird that can never keep any money?

NORA   Yes, yes, squanderbird; I know. But let's do as I say, Torvald; then I'll
have time to think about what I need most. Isn't that the best way? Mm?

HELMER [smiles]   To be sure it would be, if you could keep what I give you and really buy yourself something with it. But you'll spend it on all sorts of useless things for the house, and then I'll have to put my hand in my pocket again.

NORA   Oh, but Torvald—

HELMER   You can't deny it, Nora dear. [*Puts his arm round her waist.*] The squanderbird's a pretty little creature, but she gets through an awful lot of money. It's incredible what an expensive pet she is for a man to keep.

NORA   For shame! How can you say such a thing? I save every penny I can.

HELMER   [*laughs*]   That's quite true. Every penny you can. But you can't.

NORA   [*hums and smiles, quietly gleeful*]   Hm. If you only knew how many expenses we larks and squirrels have, Torvald.

HELMER   You're a funny little creature. Just like your father used to be. Always on the look-out for some way to get money, but as soon as you have any it just runs through your fingers, and you never know where it's gone. Well, I suppose I must take you as you are. It's in your blood. Yes, yes, yes, these things are hereditary, Nora.

NORA   Oh, I wish I'd inherited more of Papa's qualities.

HELMER   And I wouldn't wish my darling little songbird to be any different from what she is. By the way, that reminds me. You look awfully—how shall I put it?—awfully guilty today.

NORA   Do I—

HELMER   Yes, you do. Look me in the eyes.

NORA   [*looks at him*]   Well?

HELMER   [*wags his finger*]   Has my little sweet-tooth been indulging herself in town today, by any chance?

NORA   No, how can you think of such a thing?

HELMER   Not a tiny little digression into a pastry shop?

NORA   No, Torvald, I promise—

HELMER   Not just a wee jam tart?

NORA   Certainly not.

HELMER   Not a little nibble at a macaroon?

NORA   No, Torvald—I promise you, honestly—

HELMER   There, there. I was only joking.

NORA   [*goes over to the table, right*]   You know I could never act against your wishes.

HELMER   Of course not. And you've given me your word—[*Goes over to her.*] Well, my beloved Nora, you keep your little Christmas secrets to yourself. They'll be revealed this evening, I've no doubt, once the Christmas tree has been lit.

NORA   Have you remembered to invite Dr. Rank?

HELMER   No. But there's no need; he knows he'll be dining with us. Anyway, I'll ask him when he comes this morning. I've ordered some good wine. Oh, Nora, you can't imagine how I'm looking forward to this evening.

NORA   So am I. And, Torvald, how the children will love it!

HELMER Yes, it's a wonderful thing to know that one's position is assured and that one has an ample income. Don't you agree? It's good to know that, isn't it?

NORA Yes, it's almost like a miracle.

HELMER Do you remember last Christmas? For three whole weeks you shut yourself away every evening to make flowers for the Christmas tree, and all those other things you were going to surprise us with. Ugh, it was the most boring time I've ever had in my life.

NORA I didn't find it boring.

HELMER [smiles] But it all came to nothing in the end, didn't it?

NORA Oh, are you going to bring that up again? How could I help the cat getting in and tearing everything to bits?

HELMER No, my poor little Nora, of course you couldn't. You simply wanted to make us happy, and that's all that matters. But it's good that those hard times are past.

NORA Yes, it's wonderful.

HELMER I don't have to sit by myself and be bored. And you don't have to tire your pretty eyes and your delicate little hands—

NORA [claps her hands] No, Torvald, that's true, isn't it—I don't have to any longer? Oh, it's really all just like a miracle. [Takes his arm] Now, I'm going to tell you what I thought we might do, Torvald. As soon as Christmas is over— [A bell rings in the hall.] Oh, there's the doorbell. [Tidies up one or two things in the room.] Someone's coming. What a bore.

HELMER I'm not at home to any visitors. Remember!

MAID [in the doorway] A lady's called, madam. A stranger.

NORA Well, ask her to come in.

MAID And the doctor's here too, sir.

HELMER Has he gone to my room?

MAID Yes, sir.

Helmer goes into his room. The Maid shows in Mrs. Linde, who is dressed in travelling clothes, and closes the door.

MRS. LINDE [shyly and a little hesitantly] Good evening, Nora.

NORA [uncertainly] Good evening—

MRS. LINDE I don't suppose you recognize me.

NORA No, I'm afraid I— Yes, wait a minute—surely— [Exclaims.] Why, Christine! Is it really you?

MRS. LINDE Yes, it's me.

NORA Christine! And I didn't recognize you! But how could I—? [More quietly] How you've changed, Christine!

MRS. LINDE Yes, I know. It's been nine years—nearly ten—

NORA Is it so long? Yes, it must be. Oh, these last eight years have been such a happy time for me!. So you've come to town? All that way in winter! How brave of you!

MRS. LINDE   I arrived by the steamer this morning.

NORA   Yes, of course—to enjoy yourself over Christmas. Oh, how splendid! We'll have to celebrate! But take off your coat. You're not cold, are you? [*Helps her off with it.*] There! Now let's sit down here by the stove and be comfortable. No, you take the armchair. I'll sit here in the rocking-chair. [*Clasps Mrs. Linde's hands.*] Yes, now you look like your old self. It was just at first that—you've got a little paler, though, Christine. And perhaps a bit thinner.

MRS. LINDE   And older, Nora. Much, much older.

NORA   Yes, perhaps a little older. Just a tiny bit. Not much. [*Checks herself suddenly and says earnestly.*] Oh, but how thoughtless of me to sit here and chatter away like this! Dear, sweet Christine, can you forgive me?

MRS. LINDE   What do you mean, Nora?

NORA   [*quietly*]   Poor Christine, you've become a widow.

MRS. LINDE   Yes. Three years ago.

NORA   I know, I know—I read it in the papers. Oh, Christine, I meant to write to you so often, honestly. But I always put it off, and something else always cropped up.

MRS. LINDE   I understand, Nora dear.

NORA   No, Christine, it was beastly of me. Oh, my poor darling, what you've gone through! And he didn't leave you anything?

MRS. LINDE   No.

NORA   No children, either?

MRS. LINDE   No.

NORA   Nothing at all, then?

MRS. LINDE   Not even a feeling of loss or sorrow.

NORA   [*looks incredulously at her*]   But, Christine, how is that possible?

MRS. LINDE   [*smiles sadly and strokes Nora's hair*]   Oh, these things happen, Nora.

NORA   All alone. How dreadful that must be for you. I've three lovely children. I'm afraid you can't see them now, because they're out with nanny. But you must tell me everything—

MRS. LINDE   No, no, no. I want to hear about you.

NORA   No, you start. I'm not going to be selfish today, I'm just going to think about you. Oh, but there's one thing I *must* tell you. Have you heard of the wonderful luck we've just had?

MRS. LINDE   No. What?

NORA   Would you believe it—my husband's just been made manager of the bank!

MRS. LINDE   Your husband? Oh, how lucky—!

NORA   Yes, isn't it? Being a lawyer is so uncertain, you know, especially if one isn't prepared to touch any case that isn't—well—quite nice. And of course Torvald's been very firm about that—and I'm absolutely with him. Oh, you can imagine how happy we are! He's joining the bank in the New Year, and he'll be getting a big salary, and lots of percentages too. From now on we'll be able to live quite differently—we'll be able to do whatever we want. Oh, Christine, it's such a relief! I feel so happy! Well, I mean, it's lovely to have heaps of money and not to have to worry about anything. Don't you think?

MRS. LINDE   It must be lovely to have enough to cover one's needs, anyway.

NORA   Not just our needs! We're going to have heaps and heaps of money!

MRS. LINDE [smiles]   Nora, Nora, haven't you grown up yet? When we were at school you were a terrible little spendthrift.

NORA [laughs quietly]   Yes, Torvald still says that. [Wags her finger.] But "Nora, Nora" isn't as silly as you think. Oh, we've been in no position for me to waste money. We've both had to work.

MRS. LINDE   You too?

NORA   Yes, little things—fancy work, crocheting, embroidery and so forth. [Casually.] And other things too. I suppose you know Torvald left the Ministry when we got married? There were no prospects of promotion in his department, and of course he needed more money. But the first year he overworked himself quite dreadfully. He had to take on all sorts of extra jobs, and worked day and night. But it was too much for him, and he became frightfully ill. The doctors said he'd have to go to a warmer climate.

MRS. LINDE   Yes, you spent a whole year in Italy, didn't you?

NORA   Yes. It wasn't easy for me to get away, you know. I'd just had Ivar. But of course we had to do it. Oh, it was a marvelous trip! And it saved Torvald's life. But it cost an awful lot of money, Christine.

MRS. LINDE   I can imagine.

NORA   Two hundred and fifty pounds. That's a lot of money, you know.

MRS. LINDE   How lucky you had it.

NORA   Well, actually, we got it from my father.

MRS. LINDE   Oh, I see. Didn't he die just about that time?

NORA   Yes, Christine, just about then. Wasn't it dreadful, I couldn't go and look after him. I was expecting little Ivar any day. And then I had my poor Torvald to care for—we really didn't think he'd live. Dear, kind Papa! I never saw him again, Christine. Oh, it's the saddest thing that's happened to me since I got married.

MRS. LINDE   I know you were very fond of him. But you went to Italy—?

NORA   Yes. Well, we had the money, you see, and the doctors said we mustn't delay. So we went the month after Papa died.

MRS. LINDE   And your husband came back completely cured?

NORA   Fit as a fiddle!

MRS. LINDE   But—the doctor?

NORA   How do you mean?

MRS. LINDE   I thought the maid said that the gentleman who arrived with me was the doctor.

NORA   Oh yes, that's Doctor Rank, but he doesn't come because anyone's ill. He's our best friend, and he looks us up at least once every day. No, Torvald hasn't had a moment's illness since we went away. And the children are fit and healthy and so am I. [*Jumps up and claps her hands.*] Oh God, oh God, Christine, isn't it a wonderful thing to be alive and happy! Oh, but how beastly of me! I'm only talking about myself. [*Sits on a footstool and rests her arms on Mrs. Linde's knee.*] Oh, please don't be angry with me! Tell me, is it really true you didn't love your husband? Why did you marry him, then?

MRS. LINDE   Well, my mother was still alive; and she was helpless and bedridden. And I had my two little brothers to take care of. I didn't feel I could say no.

NORA   Yes, well, perhaps you're right. He was rich then, was he?

MRS. LINDE   Quite comfortably off, I believe. But his business was unsound, you see, Nora. When he died it went bankrupt, and there was nothing left.

NORA   What did you do?

MRS. LINDE   Well, I had to try to make ends meet somehow, so I started a little shop, and a little school, and anything else I could turn my hand to. These last three years have been just one endless slog for me, without a moment's rest. But now it's over, Nora. My poor dear mother doesn't need me any more; she's passed away. And the boys don't need me either; they've got jobs now and can look after themselves.

NORA   How relieved you must feel—

MRS. LINDE   No, Nora. Just unspeakably empty. No one to live for any more. [*Gets up restlessly.*] That's why I couldn't bear to stay out there any longer, cut off from the world. I thought it'd be easier to find some work here that will exercise and occupy my mind. If only I could get a regular job—office work of some kind—

NORA   Oh but, Christine, that's dreadfully exhausting; and you look practically finished already. It'd be much better for you if you could go away somewhere.

MRS. LINDE   [*goes over to the window*]   I have no Papa to pay for my holidays, Nora.

NORA   [*gets up*]   Oh, please don't be angry with me.

MRS. LINDE   My dear Nora, it's I who should ask you not to be angry. That's the worst thing about this kind of situation—it makes one so bitter. One has no one to work for; and yet one has to be continually sponging for jobs. One has to live; and so one becomes completely egocentric. When you told me about this luck you've just had with Torvald's new job—can you imagine?—I was happy not so much on your account, as on my own.

NORA   How do you mean? Oh, I understand. You mean Torvald might be able to do something for you?

MRS. LINDE   Yes, I was thinking that.

NORA   He will too, Christine. Just you leave it to me. I'll lead up to it so delicately, so delicately; I'll get him in the right mood. Oh, Christine, I do so want to help you.

MRS. LINDE   It's sweet of you to bother so much about me, Nora. Especially since you know so little of the worries and hardships of life.

NORA   I! You say *I* know little of—?

MRS. LINDE   [*smiles*]   Well, good heavens—those bits of fancy work of yours—well, really—! You're a child, Nora.

NORA   [*tosses her head and walks across the room*]   You shouldn't say that so patronizingly.

MRS. LINDE   Oh?

NORA   You're like the rest. You all think I'm incapable of getting down to anything serious—

MRS. LINDE   My dear—

NORA   You think I've never had any worries like the rest of you.

MRS. LINDE   Nora dear, you've just told me about all your difficulties—

NORA   Pooh—that! [*Quietly.*] I haven't told you about the big thing.

MRS. LINDE   What big thing? What do you mean?

NORA   You patronize me, Christine; but you shouldn't. You're proud that you've worked so long and so hard for your mother.

MRS. LINDE   I don't patronize anyone, Nora. But you're right—I am both proud and happy that I was able to make my mother's last months on earth comparatively easy.

NORA   And you're also proud at what you've done for your brothers.

MRS. LINDE   I think I have a right to be.

NORA   I think so too. But let me tell you something, Christine. I too have done something to be proud and happy about.

MRS. LINDE   I don't doubt it. But—how do you mean?

NORA   Speak quietly! Suppose Torvald should hear! He mustn't, at any price—no one must know, Christine—no one but you.

MRS. LINDE   But what is this?

NORA   Come over here. [*Pulls her down on to the sofa beside her.*] Yes, Christine—I too have done something to be happy and proud about. It was I who saved Torvald's life.

MRS. LINDE   Saved his—? How did you save it?

NORA   I told you about our trip to Italy. Torvald couldn't have lived if he hadn't managed to get down there—

MRS. LINDE   Yes, well—your father provided the money—

NORA   [*smiles*]   So Torvald and everyone else thinks. But—

MRS. LINDE   Yes?

NORA   Papa didn't give us a penny. It was I who found the money.

MRS. LINDE   You? All of it?

NORA   Two hundred and fifty pounds. What do you say to that?

MRS. LINDE   But Nora, how could you? Did you win a lottery or something?

NORA [*scornfully*]   Lottery? [*Sniffs.*] What would there be to be proud of in that?

MRS. LINDE   But where did you get it from, then?

NORA [*hums and smiles secretively*]   Hm; tra-la-la-la!

MRS. LINDE   You couldn't have borrowed it.

NORA   Oh? Why not?

MRS. LINDE   Well, a wife can't borrow money without her husband's consent.

NORA [*tosses her head*]   Ah, but when a wife has a little business sense, and knows how to be clever—

MRS. LINDE   But Nora, I simply don't understand—

NORA   You don't have to. No one has said I borrowed the money. I could have got it in some other way. [*Throws herself back on the sofa.*] I could have got it from an admirer. When a girl's as pretty as I am—

MRS. LINDE   Nora, you're crazy!

NORA   You're dying of curiosity now, aren't you, Christine?

MRS. LINDE   Nora dear, you haven't done anything foolish?

NORA [*sits up again*]   Is it foolish to save one's husband's life?

MRS. LINDE   I think it's foolish if without his knowledge you—

NORA   But the whole point was that he mustn't know! Great heavens, don't you see? He hadn't to know how dangerously ill he was. I was the one they told that his life was in danger and that only going to a warm climate could save him. Do you suppose I didn't try to think of other ways of getting him down there? I told him how wonderful it would be for me to go abroad like other young wives; I cried and prayed; I asked him to remember my condition, and said he ought to be nice and tender to me; and then I suggested he might quite easily borrow the money. But then he got almost angry with me, Christine. He said I was frivolous, and that it was his duty as a husband not to pander to my moods and caprices—I think that's what he called them. Well, well, I thought, you've got to be saved somehow. And then I thought of a way—

MRS. LINDE   But didn't your husband find out from your father that the money hadn't come from him?

NORA   No, never. Papa died just then. I'd thought of letting him into the plot and asking him not to tell. But since he was so ill—! And as things turned out, it didn't become necessary.

MRS. LINDE   And you've never told your husband about this?

NORA   For heaven's sake, no! What an idea! He's frightfully strict about such matters. And besides—he's so proud of being a *man*—it'd be so painful and humiliating for him to know that he owed anything to me. It'd completely wreck our relationship. This life we have built together would no longer exist.

MRS. LINDE   Will you never tell him?

NORA [*thoughtfully, half-smiling*]   Yes—some time, perhaps. Years from now, when I'm no longer pretty. You mustn't laugh! I mean of course, when Torvald no longer loves me as he does now; when it no longer amuses him to see me dance and dress up and play the fool for him. Then it might be useful to have something up my sleeve. [*Breaks off.*] Stupid, stupid, stupid! That time will never come. Well, what do you think of my big secret, Christine? I'm not completely useless, am I? Mind you, all this has caused me a frightful lot of worry. It hasn't been easy for me to meet my obligations punctually. In case you don't know, in the world of business there are things called quarterly instalments and interest, and they're a terrible problem to cope with. So I've had to scrape a little here and save a little there as best I can. I haven't been able to save much on the housekeeping money, because Torvald likes to live well; and I couldn't let the children go short of clothes—I couldn't take anything out of what he gives me for them. The poor little angels!

MRS. LINDE   So you've had to stint yourself, my poor Nora?

NORA   Of course. Well, after all, it was my problem. Whenever Torvald gave me money to buy myself new clothes, I never used more than half of it; and I always bought what was cheapest and plainest. Thank heaven anything suits me, so that Torvald's never noticed. But it made me a bit sad sometimes, because it's lovely to wear pretty clothes. Don't you think?

MRS. LINDE   Indeed it is.

NORA   And then I've found one or two other sources of income. Last winter I managed to get a lot of copying to do. So I shut myself away and wrote every evening, late into the night. Oh, I often got so tired, so tired. But it was great fun, though, sitting there working and earning money. It was almost like being a man.

MRS. LINDE   But how much have you managed to pay off like this?

NORA   Well, I can't say exactly. It's awfully difficult to keep an exact check on these kind of transactions. I only know I've paid everything I've managed to scrape together. Sometimes I really didn't know where to turn. [*Smiles*] Then I'd sit here and imagine some rich old gentleman had fallen in love with me—

MRS. LINDE   What! What gentleman?

NORA   Silly! And that now he'd died and when they opened his will it said in big letters: "Everything I possess is to be paid forthwith to my beloved Mrs. Nora Helmer in cash."

MRS. LINDE   But, Nora dear, who was this gentleman?

NORA   Great heavens, don't you understand? There wasn't any old gentleman; he was just something I used to dream up as I sat here evening after evening wondering how on earth I could raise the money. But what does it matter? The old bore can stay imaginary as far as I'm concerned, because now I don't have to worry any longer! [*Jumps up.*] Oh, Christine, isn't it wonderful? I don't have to worry any more! No more troubles! I can play all day with the children, I can fill the house with pretty things, just the way Torvald likes. And, Christine, it'll soon be spring, and the air'll be fresh and the skies blue,—and then perhaps we'll be able to take a little trip somewhere. I shall be able to see the sun again. Oh, yes, yes, it's a wonderful thing to be alive and happy!

The bell rings in the hall.

MRS. LINDE [*gets up*]   You've a visitor. Perhaps I'd better go.

NORA   No, stay. It won't be for me. It's someone for Torvald—

MAID [*in the doorway*]   Excuse me, madam, a gentleman's called who says he wants to speak to the master. But I didn't know—seeing as the doctor's with him—

NORA   Who is this gentleman?

KROGSTAD [*in the doorway*]   It's me, Mrs. Helmer.

Mrs. Linde starts, composes herself and turns away to the window.

NORA [*takes a step towards him and whispers tensely*]   You? What is it? What do you want to talk to my husband about?

KROGSTAD   Business—you might call it. I hold a minor post in the bank, and I hear your husband is to become our new chief—

NORA   Oh—then it isn't—?

KROGSTAD   Pure business, Mrs. Helmer. Nothing more.

NORA   Well, you'll find him in his study.

Nods indifferently as she closes the hall door behind him. Then she walks across the room and sees to the stove.

MRS. LINDE   Nora, who was that man?

NORA   A lawyer called Krogstad.

MRS. LINDE   It was him, then.

NORA   Do you know that man?

MRS. LINDE   I used to know him—some years ago. He was a solicitor's clerk in our town, for a while.

NORA   Yes, of course, so he was.

MRS. LINDE   How he's changed!

NORA   He was very unhappily married, I believe.

MRS. LINDE   Is he a widower now?

NORA   Yes, with a lot of children. Ah, now it's alight.

She closes the door of the stove and moves the rocking-chair a little to one side.

MRS. LINDE   He does—various things now, I hear?

NORA   Does he? It's quite possible—I really don't know. But don't let's talk about business. It's so boring.

Dr. Rank enters from Helmer's study.

RANK [*still in the doorway*]   No, no, my dear chap, don't see me out. I'll go
and have a word with your wife. [*Closes the door and notices Mrs. Linde.*]
Oh, I beg your pardon. I seem to be *de trop* here too.

NORA   Not in the least. [*Introduces them.*] Dr. Rank. Mrs. Linde.

RANK   Ah! A name I have often heard in this house. I believe I passed you
on the stairs as I came up.

MRS. LINDE   Yes. Stairs tire me; I have to take them slowly.

RANK   Oh, have you hurt yourself?

MRS. LINDE   No, I'm just a little run down.

RANK   Ah, is that all? Then I take it you've come to town to cure yourself by
a round of parties?

MRS. LINDE   I have come here to find work.

RANK   Is that an approved remedy for being run down?

MRS. LINDE   One has to live, Doctor.

RANK   Yes, people do seem to regard it as a necessity.

NORA   Oh, really, Dr. Rank. I bet you want to stay alive.

RANK   You bet I do. However miserable I sometimes feel, I still want to go
on being tortured for as long as possible. It's the same with all my
patients; and with people who are morally sick, too. There's a moral
cripple in with Helmer at this very moment—

MRS. LINDE [*softly*]   Oh!

NORA   Whom do you mean?

RANK   Oh, a lawyer fellow called Krogstad—you wouldn't know him. He's
crippled all right; morally twisted. But even he started off by announcing, as though it were a matter of enormous importance, that he had to
live.

NORA   Oh? What did he want to talk to Torvald about?

RANK   I haven't the faintest idea. All I heard was something about the bank.

NORA   I didn't know that Krog—that this man Krogstad had any connection
with the bank.

RANK   Yes, he's got some kind of job down there. [*To Mrs. Linde.*] I wonder
if in your part of the world you too have a species of human being that
spends its time fussing around trying to smell out moral corruption?
And when they find a case they give him some nice, comfortable
position so that they can keep a good watch on him. The healthy ones
just have to lump it.

MRS. LINDE   But surely it's the sick who need care most?

RANK [*shrugs his shoulders*]   Well, there we have it. It's that attitude that's
turning human society into a hospital.

Nora, lost in her own thoughts, laughs half to herself and claps her hands.

RANK   Why are you laughing? Do you really know what society is?

NORA   What do I care about society? I think it's a bore. I was laughing at something else—something frightfully funny. Tell me, Dr. Rank—will everyone who works at the bank come under Torvald now?

RANK   Do you find that particularly funny?

NORA   [*smiles and hums*]   Never mind! Never you mind! [*Walks around the room*] Yes, I find it very amusing to think that we—I mean, Torvald—has obtained so much influence over so many people. [*Takes the paper bag from her pocket.*] Dr. Rank, would you like a small macaroon?

RANK   Macaroons! I say! I thought they were forbidden here.

NORA   Yes, well, these are some Christine gave me.

MRS. LINDE   What? I—?

NORA   All right, all right, don't get frightened. You weren't to know Torvald had forbidden them. He's afraid they'll ruin my teeth. But, dash it—for once—! Don't you agree, Dr. Rank? Here! [*Pops a macaroon into his mouth.*] You too, Christine. And I'll have one too. Just a little one. Two at the most. [*Begins to walk round again.*] Yes, now I feel really, really happy. Now there's just one thing in the world I'd really love to do.

RANK   Oh? And what is that?

NORA   Just something I'd love to say to Torvald.

RANK   Well, why don't you say it?

NORA   No, I daren't. It's too dreadful.

MRS. LINDE   Dreadful?

RANK   Well, then, you'd better not. But you can say it to us. What is it you'd so love to say to Torvald?

NORA   I've the most extraordinary longing to say: "Bloody hell!"

RANK   Are you mad?

MRS. LINDE   My dear Nora—!

RANK   Say it. Here he is.

NORA   [*hiding the bag of macaroons.*]   Ssh! Ssh!

Helmer, with his overcoat on his arm and his hat in his hand, enters from his study.

NORA   [*goes to meet him*]   Well, Torvald dear, did you get rid of him?

HELMER   Yes, he's just gone.

NORA   May I introduce you—? This is Christine. She's just arrived in town.

HELMER   Christine—? Forgive me, but I don't think—

NORA   Mrs. Linde, Torvald dear. Christine Linde.

HELMER   Ah. A childhood friend of my wife's, I presume?

MRS. LINDE   Yes, we knew each other in earlier days.

NORA   And imagine, now she's traveled all this way to talk to you.

HELMER   Oh?

MRS. LINDE   Well, I didn't really—

NORA You see, Christine's frightfully good at office work, and she's mad to come under some really clever man who can teach her even more than she knows already—

HELMER Very sensible, madam.

NORA So when she heard you'd become head of the bank—it was in her local paper—she came here as quickly as she could and—Torvald, you will, won't you? Do a little something to help Christine? For my sake?

HELMER Well, that shouldn't be impossible. You are a widow, I take it, Mrs. Linde?

MRS. LINDE Yes.

HELMER And you have experience of office work?

MRS. LINDE Yes, quite a bit.

HELMER Well then, it's quite likely I may be able to find some job for you—

NORA [claps her hands] You see, you see!

HELMER You've come at a lucky moment, Mrs. Linde.

MRS. LINDE Oh, how can I ever thank you—?

HELMER There's absolutely no need. [Puts on his overcoat.] But now I'm afraid I must ask you to excuse me—

RANK Wait. I'll come with you.

He gets his fur coat from the hall and warms it at the stove.

NORA Don't be long, Torvald dear.

HELMER I'll only be an hour.

NORA Are you going too, Christine?

MRS. LINDE [puts on her outdoor clothes] Yes, I must start to look round for a room.

HELMER Then perhaps we can walk part of the way together.

NORA [helps her] It's such a nuisance we're so cramped here—I'm afraid we can't offer to—

MRS. LINDE Oh, I wouldn't dream of it. Goodbye, Nora dear, and thanks for everything.

NORA Au revoir. You'll be coming back this evening, of course. And you too, Dr. Rank. What? If you're well enough? Of course you'll be well enough. Wrap up warmly, though.

They go out, talking, into the hall. Children's voices are heard from the stairs.

NORA Here they are! Here they are!

She runs out and opens the door. Anne-Marie, the nurse, enters with the children.

NORA Come in, come in! [Stoops down and kisses them.] Oh, my sweet darlings—! Look at them, Christine! Aren't they beautiful?

RANK Don't stand here chattering in this draught!

HELMER Come, Mrs. Linde. This is for mothers only.

Dr. Rank, Helmer, and Mrs. Linde go down the stairs. The Nurse brings the children into the room. Nora follows, and closes the door to the hall.

NORA How well you look! What red cheeks you've got! Like apples and roses! [*The children answer her inaudibly as she talks to them.*] Have you had fun? That's splendid. You gave Emmy and Bob a ride on the sledge? What, both together? I say! What a clever boy you are, Ivar! Oh, let me hold her for a moment, Anne-Marie! My sweet little baby doll! [*Takes the smallest child from the Nurse and dances with her.*] Yes, yes, Mummy will dance with Bob too. What? Have you been throwing snowballs? Oh, I wish I'd been there! No, don't—I'll undress them myself, Anne-Marie. No, please let me; it's such fun. Go inside and warm yourself; you look frozen. There's some hot coffee on the stove. [*The Nurse goes into the room on the left. Nora takes off the children's outdoor clothes and throws them anywhere while they all chatter simultaneously.*] What? A big dog ran after you? But he didn't bite you? No, dogs don't bite lovely little baby dolls. Leave those parcels alone, Ivar. What's in them? Ah, wouldn't you like to know! No, no; it's nothing nice. Come on, let's play a game. What shall we play? Hide and seek. Yes, let's play hide and seek. Bob shall hide first. You want me to? All right, let me hide first.

Nora and the children play around the room, and in the adjacent room to the left, laughing and shouting. At length Nora hides under the table. The children rush in, look, but cannot find her. Then they hear her half-stifled laughter, run to the table, lift up the cloth and see her. Great excitement. She crawls out as though to frighten them. Further excitement. Meanwhile, there has been a knock on the door leading from the hall, but no one has noticed it. Now the door is half-opened and Krogstad enters. He waits for a moment; the game continues.

KROGSTAD Excuse me, Mrs. Helmer—

NORA [*turns with a stifled cry and half jumps up*] Oh! What do you want?

KROGSTAD I beg your pardon; the front door was ajar. Someone must have forgotten to close it.

NORA [*gets up*] My husband is not at home, Mr. Krogstad.

KROGSTAD I know.

NORA Well, what do you want here, then?

KROGSTAD A word with you.

NORA With—? [*To the children, quietly.*] Go inside to Anne-Marie. What? No, the strange gentleman won't do anything to hurt Mummy. When he's gone we'll start playing again.

She takes the children into the room on the left and closes the door behind them.

NORA [*uneasy, tense*]   You want to speak to me?

KROGSTAD   Yes.

NORA   Today? But it's not the first of the month yet.

KROGSTAD   No, it is Christmas Eve. Whether or not you have a merry
Christmas depends on you.

NORA   What do you want? I can't give you anything today—

KROGSTAD   We won't talk about that for the present. There's something else.
You have a moment to spare?

NORA   Oh, yes. Yes, I suppose so; though—

KROGSTAD   Good. I was sitting in the café down below and I saw your
husband cross the street—

NORA   Yes.

KROGSTAD   With a lady.

NORA   Well?

KROGSTAD   Might I be so bold as to ask: was not that lady a Mrs. Linde?

NORA   Yes.

KROGSTAD   Recently arrived in town?

NORA   Yes, today.

KROGSTAD   She is a good friend of yours, is she not?

NORA   Yes, she is. But I don't see—

KROGSTAD   I used to know her too once.

NORA   I know.

KROGSTAD   Oh? You've discovered that. Yes, I thought you would. Well
then, may I ask you a straight question: is Mrs. Linde to be employed at
the bank?

NORA   How dare you presume to cross-examine me, Mr. Krogstad? You, one
of my husband's employees? But since you ask, you shall have an
answer. Yes, Mrs. Linde is to be employed by the bank. And I arranged
it, Mr. Krogstad. Now you know.

KROGSTAD   I guessed right, then.

NORA [*walks up and down the room*]   Oh, one has a little influence, you know.
Just because one's a woman it doesn't necessarily mean that— When one
is in a humble position, Mr. Krogstad, one should think twice before
offending someone who—hm—

KROGSTAD   —who has influence?

NORA   Precisely.

KROGSTAD [*changes his tone*]   Mrs. Helmer, will you have the kindness to use
your influence on my behalf?

NORA   What? What do you mean?

KROGSTAD   Will you be so good as to see that I keep my humble position at
the bank?

NORA   What do you mean? Who is thinking of removing you from your position?

KROGSTAD   Oh, you don't need to play the innocent with me. I realize it can't be very pleasant for your friend to risk bumping into me; and now I also realize whom I have to thank for being hounded out like this.

NORA   But I assure you—

KROGSTAD   Look, let's not beat about the bush. There's still time, and I'd advise you to use your influence to stop it.

NORA   But, Mr. Krogstad, I have no influence!

KROGSTAD   Oh? I thought you just said—

NORA   But I didn't mean it like that! I? How on earth could you imagine that I would have any influence over my husband?

KROGSTAD   Oh, I've known your husband since we were students together. I imagine he has his weaknesses like other married men.

NORA   If you speak impertinently of my husband, I shall show you the door.

KROGSTAD   You're a bold woman, Mrs. Helmer.

NORA   I'm not afraid of you any longer. Once the New Year is in, I'll soon be rid of you.

KROGSTAD   [more controlled]   Now listen to me, Mrs. Helmer. If I'm forced to, I shall fight for my little job at the bank as I would fight for my life.

NORA   So it sounds.

KROGSTAD   It isn't just the money; that's the last thing I care about. There's something else—well, you might as well know. It's like this, you see. You know of course, as everyone else does, that some years ago I committed an indiscretion.

NORA   I think I did hear something—

KROGSTAD   It never came into court; but from that day, every opening was barred to me. So I turned my hand to the kind of business you know about. I had to do something; and I don't think I was one of the worst. But now I want to give up all that. My sons are growing up; for their sake, I must try to regain what respectability I can. This job in the bank was the first step on the ladder. And now your husband wants to kick me off that ladder back into the dirt.

NORA   But my dear Mr. Krogstad, it simply isn't in my power to help you.

KROGSTAD   You say that because you don't want to help me. But I have the means to make you.

NORA   You don't mean you'd tell my husband that I owe you money?

KROGSTAD   And if I did?

NORA   That'd be a filthy trick! [Almost in tears.] This secret that is my pride and my joy—that he should hear about it in such a filthy, beastly way—hear about it from you! It'd involve me in the most dreadful unpleasantness—

KROGSTAD   Only—unpleasantness?

NORA   [vehemently]   All right, do it! You'll be the one who'll suffer. It'll show my husband the kind of man you are, and then you'll never keep your job.

KROGSTAD I asked you whether it was merely domestic unpleasantness you were afraid of.

NORA If my husband hears about it, he will of course immediately pay you whatever is owing. And then we shall have nothing more to do with you.

KROGSTAD [takes a step closer] Listen, Mrs. Helmer. Either you've a bad memory or else you know very little about financial transactions. I had better enlighten you.

NORA What do you mean?

KROGSTAD When your husband was ill, you came to me to borrow two hundred and fifty pounds.

NORA I didn't know anyone else.

KROGSTAD I promised to find that sum for you—

NORA And you did find it.

KROGSTAD I promised to find that sum for you on certain conditions. You were so worried about your husband's illness and so keen to get the money to take him abroad that I don't think you bothered much about the details. So it won't be out of place if I refresh your memory. Well—I promised to get you the money in exchange for an I.O.U., which I drew up.

NORA Yes, and which I signed.

KROGSTAD Exactly. But then I added a few lines naming your father as security for the debt. This paragraph was to be signed by your father.

NORA Was to be? He did sign it.

KROGSTAD I left the date blank for your father to fill in when he signed this paper. You remember, Mrs. Helmer?

NORA Yes, I think so—

KROGSTAD Then I gave you back this I.O.U. for you to post to your father. Is that not correct?

NORA Yes.

KROGSTAD And of course you posted it at once; for within five or six days you brought it along to me with your father's signature on it. Where-upon I handed you the money.

NORA Yes, well. Haven't I repaid the instalments as agreed?

KROGSTAD Mm—yes, more or less. But to return to what we were speaking about—that was a difficult time for you just then, wasn't it, Mrs. Helmer?

NORA Yes, it was.

KROGSTAD Your father was very ill, if I am not mistaken.

NORA He was dying.

KROGSTAD He did in fact die shortly afterwards?

NORA Yes.

KROGSTAD   Tell me, Mrs. Helmer, do you by any chance remember the date
of your father's death? The day of the month, I mean.

NORA   Papa died on the twenty-ninth of September.

KROGSTAD   Quite correct; I took the trouble to confirm it. And that leaves me
with a curious little problem— [*Takes out a paper*] —which I simply
cannot solve.

NORA   Problem? I don't see—

KROGSTAD   The problem, Mrs. Helmer, is that your father signed this paper
three days after his death.

NORA   What? I don't understand—

KROGSTAD   Your father died on the twenty-ninth of September. But look at
this. Here your father has dated his signature the second of October.
Isn't that a curious little problem, Mrs. Helmer? [*Nora is silent.*] Can you
suggest any explanation? [*She remains silent.*] And there's another
curious thing. The words "second of October" and the year are written
in a hand which is not your father's, but which I seem to know. Well,
there's a simple explanation to that. Your father could have forgotten to
write in the date when he signed, and someone else could have added it
before the news came of his death. There's nothing criminal about that.
It's the signature itself I'm wondering about. It *is* genuine, I suppose,
Mrs. Helmer? It was your father who wrote his name here?

NORA [*after a short silence, throws back her head and looks defiantly at him*]   No,
it was not. It was I who wrote Papa's name there.

KROGSTAD   Look, Mrs. Helmer, do you realize this is a dangerous admission?

NORA   Why? You'll get your money.

KROGSTAD   May I ask you a question? Why didn't you send this paper to
your father?

NORA   I couldn't. Papa was very ill. If I'd asked him to sign this, I'd have had
to tell him what the money was for. But I couldn't have told him in his
condition that my husband's life was in danger. I couldn't have done
that!

KROGSTAD   Then you would have been wiser to have given up your idea of a
holiday.

NORA   But I couldn't! It was to save my husband's life. I couldn't put it off.

KROGSTAD   But didn't it occur to you that you were being dishonest towards
me?

NORA   I couldn't bother about that. I didn't care about you. I hated you
because of all the beastly difficulties you'd put in my way when you
knew how dangerously ill my husband was.

KROGSTAD   Mrs. Helmer, you evidently don't appreciate exactly what you
have done. But I can assure you that it is no bigger nor worse a crime
than the one I once committed, and thereby ruined my whole social
position.

NORA   You? Do you expect me to believe that you would have taken a risk like that to save your wife's life?

KROGSTAD   The law does not concern itself with motives.

NORA   Then the law must be very stupid.

KROGSTAD   Stupid or not, if I show this paper to the police, you will be judged according to it.

NORA   I don't believe that. Hasn't a daughter the right to shield her father from worry and anxiety when he's old and dying? Hasn't a wife the right to save her husband's life? I don't know much about the law, but there must be something somewhere that says that such things are allowed. You ought to know about that, you're meant to be a lawyer, aren't you? You can't be a very good lawyer, Mr. Krogstad.

KROGSTAD   Possibly not. But business, the kind of business we two have been transacting—I think you'll admit I understand something about that? Good. Do as you please. But I tell you this. If I get thrown into the gutter for a second time, I shall take you with me.

He bows and goes out through the hall.

NORA   [*stands for a moment in thought, then tosses her head*]   What nonsense! He's trying to frighten me! I'm not that stupid. [*Busies herself gathering together the children's clothes; then she suddenly stops.*] But—? No, it's impossible. I did it for love, didn't I?

THE CHILDREN   [*in the doorway, left*]   Mummy, the strange gentleman's gone out into the street.

NORA   Yes, yes, I know. But don't talk to anyone about the strange gentleman. You hear? Not even to Daddy.

CHILDREN   No, Mummy. Will you play with us again now?

NORA   No, no. Not now.

CHILDREN   Oh but, Mummy, you promised!

NORA   I know, but I can't just now. Go back to the nursery. I've got a lot to do. Go away, my darlings, go away. [*She pushes them gently into the other room, and closes the door behind them. She sits on the sofa, takes up her embroidery, stitches for a few moments, but soon stops.*] No! [*Throws the embroidery aside, gets up, goes to the door leading to the hall and calls.*] Helen! Bring in the Christmas tree! [*She goes to the table on the left and opens the drawer in it; then pauses again.*] No, but it's utterly impossible!

MAID   [*enters with the tree*]   Where shall I put it, madam?

NORA   There, in the middle of the room.

MAID   Will you be wanting anything else?

NORA   No, thank you. I have everything I need.

The Maid puts down the tree and goes out.

NORA [*busy decorating the tree*]   Now—candles here—and flowers here. That loathsome man! Nonsense, nonsense, there's nothing to be frightened about. The Christmas tree must be beautiful. I'll do everything that you like, Torvald. I'll sing for you, dance for you—

Helmer, with a bundle of papers under his arm, enters.

NORA   Oh—are you back already?

HELMER   Yes. Has anyone been here?

NORA   Here? No.

HELMER   That's strange. I saw Krogstad come out of the front door.

NORA   Did you? Oh yes, that's quite right—Krogstad was here for a few minutes.

HELMER   Nora, I can tell from your face, he's been here and asked you to put in a good word for him.

NORA   Yes.

HELMER   And you were to pretend you were doing it of your own accord? You weren't going to tell me he'd been here? He asked you to do that too, didn't he?

NORA   Yes, Torvald. But—

HELMER   Nora, Nora! And you were ready to enter into such a conspiracy? Talking to a man like that, and making him promises—and then, on top of it all, to tell me an untruth!

NORA   An untruth?

HELMER   Didn't you say no one had been here? [*Wags his finger.*] My little songbird must never do that again. A songbird must have a clean beak to sing with; otherwise she'll start twittering out of tune. [*Puts his arm round her waist.*] Isn't that the way we want things? Yes, of course it is. [*Lets go of her.*] So let's hear no more about that. [*Sits down in front of the stove.*] Ah, how cosy and peaceful it is here. [*Glances for a few moments at his papers.*]

NORA [*busy with the tree; after a short silence*]   Torvald.

HELMER   Yes.

NORA   I'm terribly looking forward to that fancy dress ball at the Stenborgs on Boxing Day.

HELMER   And I'm terribly curious to see what you're going to surprise me with.

NORA   Oh, it's so maddening.

HELMER   What is?

NORA   I can't think of anything to wear. It all seems so stupid and meaningless.

HELMER   So my little Nora's come to that conclusion, has she?

NORA [*behind his chair, resting her arms on its back*]   Are you very busy, Torvald?

HELMER Oh—

NORA What are those papers?

HELMER Just something to do with the bank.

NORA Already?

HELMER I persuaded the trustees to give me authority to make certain immediate changes in the staff and organization. I want to have everything straight by the New Year.

NORA Then that's why this poor man Krogstad—

HELMER Hm.

NORA [still leaning over his chair, slowly strokes the back of his head] If you hadn't been so busy, I was going to ask you an enormous favour, Torvald.

HELMER Well, tell me. What was it to be?

NORA You know I trust your taste more than anyone's. I'm so anxious to look really beautiful at the fancy dress ball. Torvald, couldn't you help me to decide what I shall go as, and what kind of costume I ought to wear?

HELMER Aha! So little Miss Independent's in trouble and needs a man to rescue her, does she?

NORA Yes, Torvald. I can't get anywhere without your help.

HELMER Well, well, I'll give the matter thought. We'll find something.

NORA Oh, how kind of you! [Goes back to the tree. Pause.] How pretty these red flowers look! But, tell me, is it so dreadful, this thing that Krogstad's done?

HELMER He forged someone else's name. Have you any idea what that means?

NORA Mightn't he have been forced to do it by some emergency?

HELMER He probably just didn't think—that's what usually happens. I'm not so heartless as to condemn a man for an isolated action.

NORA No, Torvald, of course not!

HELMER Men often succeed in re-establishing themselves if they admit their crime and take their punishment.

NORA Punishment?

HELMER But Krogstad didn't do that. He chose to try and trick his way out of it; and that's what has morally destroyed him.

NORA You think that would—?

HELMER Just think how a man with that load on his conscience must always be lying and cheating and dissembling; how he must wear a mask even in the presence of those who are dearest to him, even his own wife and children! Yes, the children. That's the worst danger, Nora.

NORA Why?

HELMER Because an atmosphere of lies contaminates and poisons every corner of the home. Every breath that the children draw in such a house contains the germs of evil.

NORA [*comes closer behind him*]   Do you really believe that?

HELMER   Oh, my dear, I've come across it so often in my work at the bar. Nearly all young criminals are the children of mothers who are constitutional liars.

NORA   Why do you say mothers?

HELMER   It's usually the mother; though of course the father can have the same influence. Every lawyer knows that only too well. And yet this fellow Krogstad has been sitting at home all these years poisoning his children with his lies and pretences. That's why I say that, morally speaking, he is dead. [*Stretches out his hands towards her.*] So my pretty little Nora must promise me not to plead his case. Your hand on it. Come, come, what's this? Give me your hand. There. That's settled, now. I assure you it'd be quite impossible for me to work in the same building as him. I literally feel physically ill in the presence of a man like that.

NORA [*draws her hand from his and goes over to the other side of the Christmas tree*]   How hot it is in here! And I've so much to do.

HELMER [*gets up and gathers his papers*]   Yes, and I must try to get some of this read before dinner. I'll think about your costume too. And I may even have something up my sleeve to hang in gold paper on the Christmas tree. [*Lays his hand on her head.*] My precious little songbird!

He goes into his study and closes the door.

NORA [*softly, after a pause*]   It's nonsense. It must be. It's impossible. It *must* be impossible!

NURSE [*in the doorway, left*]   The children are asking if they can come in to Mummy.

NORA   No, no, no; don't let them in! You stay with them, Anne-Marie.

NURSE   Very good, madam. [*Closes the door.*]

NORA [*pale with fear*]   Corrupt my little children—! Poison my home! [*Short pause. She throws back her head.*] It isn't true! It *couldn't* be true!

ACT II

The same room. In the corner by the piano the Christmas tree stands, stripped and disheveled, its candles burned to their sockets. Nora's outdoor clothes lie on the sofa. She is alone in the room, walking restlessly to and fro. At length she stops by the sofa and picks up her coat.

NORA [*drops the coat again*]   There's someone coming! [*Goes to the door and listens*] No, it's no one. Of course—no one'll come today, it's Christmas

Day. Nor tomorrow. But perhaps—! [*Opens the door and looks out.*] No. Nothing in the letter-box. Quite empty. [*Walks across the room.*] Silly, silly. Of course he won't do anything. It couldn't happen. It isn't possible. Why, I've three small children.

The Nurse, carrying a large cardboard box, enters from the room on the left.

NURSE   I found those fancy dress clothes at last, madam.

NORA   Thank you. Put them on the table.

NURSE [*does so*]   They're all rumpled up.

NORA   Oh, I wish I could tear them into a million pieces!

NURSE   Why, madam! They'll be all right. Just a little patience.

NORA   Yes, of course. I'll go and get Mrs. Linde to help me.

NURSE   What, out again? In this dreadful weather? You'll catch a chill, madam.

NORA   Well, that wouldn't be the worst. How are the children?

NURSE   Playing with their Christmas presents, poor little dears. But—

NORA   Are they still asking to see me?

NURSE   They're so used to having their Mummy with them.

NORA   Yes, but, Anne-Marie, from now on I shan't be able to spend so much time with them.

NURSE   Well, children get used to anything in time.

NORA   Do you think so? Do you think they'd forget their mother if she went away from them—for ever?

NURSE   Mercy's sake, madam! For ever!

NORA   Tell me, Anne-Marie—I've so often wondered. How could you bear to give your child away—to strangers?

NURSE   But I had to when I came to nurse my little Miss Nora.

NORA   Do you mean you wanted to?

NURSE   When I had the chance of such a good job? A poor girl what's got into trouble can't afford to pick and choose. That good-for-nothing didn't lift a finger.

NORA   But your daughter must have completely forgotten you.

NURSE   Oh no, indeed she hasn't. She's written to me twice, once when she got confirmed and then again when she got married.

NORA [*hugs her*]   Dear old Anne-Marie, you were a good mother to me.

NURSE   Poor little Miss Nora, you never had any mother but me.

NORA   And if my little ones had no one else, I know you would—no, silly, silly, silly! [*Opens the cardboard box.*] Go back to them, Anne-Marie. Now I must—Tomorrow you'll see how pretty I shall look.

NURSE   Why, there'll be no one at the ball as beautiful as my Miss Nora.

She goes into the room, left.

NORA [*begins to unpack the clothes from the box, but soon throws them down again*]   Oh, if only I dared go out! If I could be sure no one would come and nothing would happen while I was away! Stupid, stupid! No one will come. I just mustn't think about it. Brush this muff. Pretty gloves, pretty gloves! Don't think about it, don't think about it! One, two, three, four, five, six— [*Cries*] Ah—they're coming—!

She begins to run towards the door, but stops uncertainly. Mrs. Linde enters from the hall, where she has been taking off her outdoor clothes.

NORA   Oh, it's you, Christine. There's no one else out there, is there? Oh, I'm so glad you've come.

MRS. LINDE   I hear you were at my room asking for me.

NORA   Yes, I just happened to be passing. I want to ask you to help me with something. Let's sit down here on the sofa. Look at this. There's going to be a fancy dress ball tomorrow night upstairs at Consul Stenborg's, and Torvald wants me to go as a Neapolitan fisher-girl and dance the tarantella. I learned it on Capri.

MRS. LINDE   I say, are you going to give a performance?

NORA   Yes, Torvald says I should. Look, here's the dress. Torvald had it made for me in Italy; but now it's all so torn, I don't know—

MRS. LINDE   Oh, we'll soon put that right; the stitching's just come away. Needle and thread? Ah, here we are.

NORA   You're being awfully sweet.

MRS. LINDE [*sews*]   So you're going to dress up tomorrow, Nora? I must pop over for a moment to see how you look. Oh, but I've completely forgotten to thank you for that nice evening yesterday.

NORA [*gets up and walks across the room*]   Oh, I didn't think it was as nice as usual. You ought to have come to town a little earlier, Christine. . . . Yes, Torvald understands how to make a home look attractive.

MRS. LINDE   I'm sure you do, too. You're not your father's daughter for nothing. But, tell me. Is Dr. Rank always in such low spirits as he was yesterday?

NORA   No, last night it was very noticeable. But he's got a terrible disease; he's got spinal tuberculosis, poor man. His father was a frightful creature who kept mistresses and so on. As a result Dr. Rank has been sickly ever since he was a child—you understand—

MRS. LINDE [*puts down her sewing*]   But, my dear Nora, how on earth did you get to know about such things?

NORA [*walks about the room*]   Oh, don't be silly, Christine—when one has three children, one comes into contact with women who—well, who know about medical matters, and they tell one a thing or two.

MRS. LINDE [*sews again; a short silence*]   Does Dr. Rank visit you every day?

NORA   Yes, every day. He's Torvald's oldest friend, and a good friend to me too. Dr. Rank's almost one of the family.

MRS. LINDE   But, tell me—is he quite sincere? I mean, doesn't he rather say the sort of thing he thinks people want to hear?

NORA   No, quite the contrary. What gave you that idea?

MRS. LINDE   When you introduced me to him yesterday, he said he'd often heard my name mentioned here. But later I noticed your husband had no idea who I was. So how could Dr. Rank—?

NORA   Yes, that's quite right, Christine. You see, Torvald's so hopelessly in love with me that he wants to have me all to himself—those were his very words. When we were first married, he got quite jealous if I as much as mentioned any of my old friends back home. So naturally, I stopped talking about them. But I often chat with Dr. Rank about that kind of thing. He enjoys it, you see.

MRS. LINDE   Now listen, Nora. In many ways you're still a child; I'm a bit older than you and have a little more experience of the world. There's something I want to say to you. You ought to give up this business with Dr. Rank.

NORA   What business?

MRS. LINDE   Well, everything. Last night you were speaking about this rich admirer of yours who was going to give you money—

NORA   Yes, and who doesn't exist—unfortunately. But what's that got to do with—?

MRS. LINDE   Is Dr. Rank rich?

NORA   Yes.

MRS. LINDE   And he has no dependants?

NORA   No, no one. But—

MRS. LINDE   And he comes here to see you every day?

NORA   Yes, I've told you.

MRS. LINDE   But how dare a man of his education be so forward?

NORA   What on earth are you talking about?

MRS. LINDE   Oh, stop pretending, Nora. Do you think I haven't guessed who it was who lent you that two hundred pounds?

NORA   Are you out of your mind? How could you imagine such a thing? A friend, someone who comes here every day! Why, that'd be an impossible situation!

MRS. LINDE   Then it really wasn't him?

NORA   No, of course not. I've never for a moment dreamed of—anyway, he hadn't any money to lend then. He didn't come into that till later.

MRS. LINDE   Well, I think that was a lucky thing for you, Nora dear.

NORA   No, I could never have dreamed of asking Dr. Rank— Though I'm sure that if I ever did ask him—

MRS. LINDE   But of course you won't.

NORA Of course not. I can't imagine that it should ever become necessary. But I'm perfectly sure that if I did speak to Dr. Rank—

MRS. LINDE Behind your husband's back?

NORA I've got to get out of this other business; and *that's* been going on behind his back. I've *got* to get out of it.

MRS. LINDE Yes, well, that's what I told you yesterday. But—

NORA [*walking up and down*] It's much easier for a man to arrange these things than a woman—

MRS. LINDE One's own husband, yes.

NORA Oh, bosh. [*Stops walking.*] When you've completely repaid a debt, you get your I.O.U. back, don't you?

MRS. LINDE Yes, of course.

NORA And you can tear it into a thousand pieces and burn the filthy, beastly thing!

MRS. LINDE [*looks hard at her, puts down her sewing and gets up slowly*] Nora, you're hiding something from me.

NORA Can you see that?

MRS. LINDE Something has happened since yesterday morning. Nora, what is it?

NORA [*goes towards her*] Christine! [*Listens.*] Ssh! There's Torvald. Would you mind going into the nursery for a few minutes? Torvald can't bear to see sewing around. Anne-Marie'll help you.

MRS. LINDE [*gathers some of her things together*] Very well. But I shan't leave this house until we've talked this matter out.

She goes into the nursery, left. As she does so, Helmer enters from the hall.

NORA [*runs to meet him*] Oh, Torvald dear, I've been so longing for you to come back!

HELMER Was that the dressmaker?

NORA No, it was Christine. She's helping me mend my costume. I'm going to look rather splendid in that.

HELMER Yes, that was quite a bright idea of mine, wasn't it?

NORA Wonderful! But wasn't it nice of me to give in to you?

HELMER [*takes her chin in his hand*] Nice—to give in to your husband? All right, little silly, I know you didn't mean it like that. But I won't disturb you. I expect you'll be wanting to try it on.

NORA Are you going to work now?

HELMER Yes. [*Shows her a bundle of papers.*] Look at these. I've been down to the bank— [*Turns to go into his study.*]

NORA Torvald.

HELMER [*stops*] Yes.

NORA If little squirrel asked you really prettily to grant her a wish—

HELMER Well?

NORA   Would you grant it to her?

HELMER   First I should naturally have to know what it was.

NORA   Squirrel would do lots of pretty tricks for you if you granted her wish.

HELMER   Out with it, then.

NORA   Your little skylark would sing in every room—

HELMER   My little skylark does that already.

NORA   I'd turn myself into a little fairy and dance for you in the moonlight, Torvald.

HELMER   Nora, it isn't that business you were talking about this morning?

NORA [comes closer]   Yes, Torvald—oh, please! I beg of you!

HELMER   Have you really the nerve to bring that up again?

NORA   Yes, Torvald, yes, you must do as I ask! You must let Krogstad keep his place at the bank!

HELMER   My dear Nora, his is the job I'm giving to Mrs. Linde.

NORA   Yes, that's terribly sweet of you. But you can get rid of one of the other clerks instead of Krogstad.

HELMER   Really, you're being incredibly obstinate. Just because you thoughtlessly promised to put in a word for him, you expect me to—

NORA   No, it isn't that, Helmer. It's for your own sake. That man writes for the most beastly newspapers—you said so yourself. He could do you tremendous harm. I'm so dreadfully frightened of him—

HELMER   Oh, I understand. Memories of the past. That's what's frightening you.

NORA   What do you mean?

HELMER   You're thinking of your father, aren't you?

NORA   Yes, yes. Of course. Just think what those dreadful men wrote in the papers about Papa! The most frightful slanders. I really believe it would have lost him his job if the Ministry hadn't sent you down to investigate, and you hadn't been so kind and helpful to him.

HELMER   But my dear little Nora, there's a considerable difference between your father and me. Your father was not a man of unassailable reputation. But I am; and I hope to remain so all my life.

NORA   But no one knows what spiteful people may not dig up. We could be so peaceful and happy now, Torvald—we could be free from every worry—you and I and the children. Oh, please, Torvald, please—!

HELMER   The very fact of your pleading his cause makes it impossible for me to keep him. Everyone at the bank already knows that I intend to dismiss Krogstad. If the rumor got about that the new manager had allowed his wife to persuade him to change his mind—

NORA   Well, what then?

HELMER   Oh, nothing, nothing. As long as my little Miss Obstinate gets her way—! Do you expect me to make a laughing-stock of myself before my entire staff—give people the idea that I am open to outside influence? Believe me, I'd soon feel the consequences! Besides—there's something

else that makes it impossible for Krogstad to remain in the bank while I
am its manager.

NORA   What is that?

HELMER   I might conceivably have allowed myself to ignore his moral
obloquies—

NORA   Yes, Torvald, surely?

HELMER   And I hear he's quite efficient at his job. But we—well, we were
schoolfriends. It was one of those friendships that one enters into
over-hastily and so often comes to regret later in life. I might as well
confess the truth. We—well, we're on Christian name terms. And the
tactless idiot makes no attempt to conceal it when other people are
present. On the contrary, he thinks it gives him the right to be familiar
with me. He shows off the whole time, with "Torvald this," and
"Torvald that." I can tell you, I find it damned annoying. If he stayed,
he'd make my position intolerable.

NORA   Torvald, you can't mean this seriously.

HELMER   Oh? And why not?

NORA   But it's so petty.

HELMER   What did you say? Petty? You think I am petty?

NORA   No, Torvald dear, of course you're not. That's just why—

HELMER   Don't quibble! You call my motives petty. Then I must be petty
too. Petty! I see. Well, I've had enough of this. [Goes to the door and calls
into the hall.] Helen!

NORA   What are you going to do?

HELMER   [searching among his papers]   I'm going to settle this matter once and
for all. [The Maid enters.] Take this letter downstairs at once. Find a
messenger and see that he delivers it. Immediately! The address is on
the envelope. Here's the money.

MAID   Very good, sir. [Goes out with the letter.]

HELMER   [putting his papers in order]   There now, little Miss Obstinate.

NORA   [tensely]   Torvald—what was in that letter?

HELMER   Krogstad's dismissal.

NORA   Call her back, Torvald! There's still time. Oh, Torvald, call her back!
Do it for my sake—for your own sake—for the children! Do you hear me,
Torvald? Please do it! You don't realize what this may do to us all!

HELMER   Too late.

NORA   Yes. Too late.

HELMER   My dear Nora, I forgive you this anxiety. Though it is a bit of an
insult to me. Oh, but it is! Isn't it an insult to imply that I should be
frightened by the vindictiveness of a depraved hack journalist? But I
forgive you, because it so charmingly testifies to the love you bear me.
[Takes her in his arms.] Which is as it should be, my own dearest Nora.
Let what will happen, happen. When the real crisis comes, you will not

find me lacking in strength or courage. I am man enough to bear the burden for us both.

NORA [*fearfully*]   What do you mean?

HELMER   The whole burden, I say—

NORA [*calmly*]   I shall never let you do that.

HELMER   Very well. We shall share it, Nora—as man and wife. And that is as it should be. [*Caresses her.*] Are you happy now? There, there, there; don't look at me with those frightened little eyes. You're simply imagining things. You go ahead now and do your tarantella, and get some practice on that tambourine. I'll sit in my study and close the door. Then I won't hear anything, and you can make all the noise you want. [*Turns in the doorway.*] When Dr. Rank comes, tell him where to find me. [*He nods to her, goes into his room with his papers and closes the door.*]

NORA [*desperate with anxiety, stands as though transfixed, and whispers*]   He said he'd do it. He will do it. He will do it, and nothing'll stop him. No, never that. I'd rather anything. There must be some escape—! Some way out—! [*The bell rings in the hall.*] Dr. Rank—! Anything but that! Anything, I don't care—!

She passes her hand across her face, composes herself, walks across and opens the door to the hall. Dr. Rank is standing there, hanging up his fur coat. During the following scene it begins to grow dark.

NORA   Good evening, Dr. Rank. I recognized your ring. But you mustn't go in to Torvald yet. I think he's busy.

RANK   And—you?

NORA [*as he enters the room and she closes the door behind him*]   Oh, you know very well I've always time to talk to you.

RANK   Thank you. I shall avail myself of that privilege as long as I can.

NORA   What do you mean by that? As long as you *can*?

RANK   Yes. Does that frighten you?

NORA   Well, it's rather a curious expression. Is something going to happen?

RANK   Something I've been expecting to happen for a long time. But I didn't think it would happen quite so soon.

NORA [*seizes his arm*]   What is it? Dr. Rank, you must tell me!

RANK [*sits down by the stove*]   I'm on the way out. And there's nothing to be done about it.

NORA [*sighs with relief*]   Oh, it's you—?

RANK   Who else? No, it's no good lying to oneself. I am the most wretched of all my patients, Mrs. Helmer. These last few days I've been going through the books of this poor body of mine, and I find I am bankrupt. Within a month I may be rotting up there in the churchyard.

NORA   Ugh, what a nasty way to talk!

RANK   The facts aren't exactly nice. But the worst is that there's so much else that's nasty to come first. I've only one more test to make. When that's done I'll have a pretty accurate idea of when the final disintegration is likely to begin. I want to ask you a favor. Helmer's a sensitive chap, and I know how he hates anything ugly. I don't want him to visit me when I'm in hospital—

NORA   Oh but, Dr. Rank—

RANK   I don't want him there. On any pretext. I shan't have him allowed in. As soon as I know the worst, I'll send you my visiting card with a black cross on it, and then you'll know that the final filthy process has begun.

NORA   Really, you're being quite impossible this evening. And I did hope you'd be in a good mood.

RANK   With death on my hands? And all this to atone for someone else's sin? Is there justice in that? And in every single family, in one way or another, the same merciless law of retribution is at work—

NORA   [holds her hands to her ears]   Nonsense! Cheer up! Laugh!

RANK   Yes, you're right. Laughter's all the damned thing's fit for. My poor innocent spine must pay for the fun my father had as a gay young lieutenant.

NORA   [at the table, left]   You mean he was too fond of asparagus and foie gras?

RANK   Yes; and truffles too.

NORA   Yes, of course, truffles, yes. And oysters too, I suppose?

RANK   Yes, oysters, oysters. Of course.

NORA   And all that port and champagne to wash them down. It's too sad that all those lovely things should affect one's spine.

RANK   Especially a poor spine that never got any pleasure out of them.

NORA   Oh yes, that's the saddest thing of all.

RANK   [looks searchingly at her]   Hm—

NORA   [after a moment]   Why did you smile?

RANK   No, it was you who laughed.

NORA   No, it was you who smiled, Dr. Rank!

RANK   [gets up]   You're a worse little rogue than I thought.

NORA   Oh, I'm full of stupid tricks today.

RANK   So it seems.

NORA   [puts both her hands on his shoulders]   Dear, dear Dr. Rank, you mustn't die and leave Torvald and me.

RANK   Oh, you'll soon get over it. Once one is gone, one is soon forgotten.

NORA   [looks at him anxiously]   Do you believe that?

RANK   One finds replacements, and then—

NORA   Who will find a replacement?

RANK   You and Helmer both will, when I am gone. You seem to have made a start already, haven't you? What was this Mrs. Linde doing here yesterday evening?

NORA   Aha! But surely you can't be jealous of poor Christine?

RANK   Indeed I am. She will be my successor in this house. When I have moved on, this lady will—

NORA   Ssh—don't speak so loud! She's in there!

RANK   Today again? You see!

NORA   She's only come to mend my dress. Good heavens, how unreasonable you are! [*Sits on the sofa.*] Be nice now, Dr. Rank. Tomorrow you'll see how beautifully I shall dance; and you must imagine that I'm doing it just for you. And for Torvald, of course; obviously. [*Takes some things out of the box.*] Dr. Rank, sit down here and I'll show you something.

RANK   [*sits*]   What's this?

NORA   Look here! Look!

RANK   Silk stockings!

NORA   Flesh-coloured. Aren't they beautiful? It's very dark in here now, of course, but tomorrow—! No, no, no; only the soles. Oh well, I suppose you can look a bit higher if you want to.

RANK   Hm—

NORA   Why are you looking so critical? Don't you think they'll fit me?

RANK   I can't really give you a qualified opinion on that.

NORA   [*looks at him for a moment*]   Shame on you! [*Flicks him on the ear with the stockings.*] Take that. [*Puts them back in the box.*]

RANK   What other wonders are to be revealed to me?

NORA   I shan't show you anything else. You're being naughty.

She hums a little and looks among the things in the box.

RANK   [*after a short silence*]   When I sit here like this being so intimate with you, I can't think—I cannot imagine what would have become of me if I had never entered this house.

NORA   [*smiles*]   Yes, I think you enjoy being with us, don't you?

RANK   [*more quietly, looking into the middle distance*]   And now to have to leave it all—

NORA   Nonsense. You're not leaving us.

RANK   [*as before*]   And not to be able to leave even the most wretched token of gratitude behind; hardly even a passing sense of loss; only an empty place, to be filled by the next comer.

NORA   Suppose I were to ask you to—? No—

RANK   To do what?

NORA   To give me proof of your friendship—

RANK   Yes, yes?

NORA   No, I mean—to do me a very great service—

RANK   Would you really for once grant me that happiness?

NORA   But you've no idea what it is.

RANK   Very well, tell me, then.

NORA   No, but, Dr. Rank, I can't. It's far too much—I want your help and
advice, and I want you to do something for me.

RANK   The more the better. I've no idea what it can be. But tell me. You do
trust me, don't you?

NORA   Oh, yes, more than anyone. You're my best and truest friend.
Otherwise I couldn't tell you. Well then, Dr. Rank—there's something
you must help me to prevent. You know how much Torvald loves
me—he'd never hesitate for an instant to lay down his life for me—

RANK   [leans over towards her]   Nora—do you think he is the only one—?

NORA   [with a slight start]   What do you mean?

RANK   Who would gladly lay down his life for you?

NORA   [sadly]   Oh, I see.

RANK   I swore to myself I would let you know that before I go. I shall never
have a better opportunity. . . . Well, Nora, now you know that. And now
you also know that you can trust me as you can trust nobody else.

NORA   [rises; calmly and quietly]   Let me pass, please.

RANK   [makes room for her but remains seated]   Nora—

NORA   [in the doorway to the hall]   Helen, bring the lamp. [Goes over to the
stove.] Oh, dear Dr. Rank, this was really horrid of you.

RANK   [gets up]   That I have loved you as deeply as anyone else has? Was that
horrid of me?

NORA   No—but that you should go and tell me. That was quite unnecessary—

RANK   What do you mean? Did you know, then—?

The Maid enters with the lamp, puts it on the table and goes out.

RANK   Nora—Mrs. Helmer—I am asking you, did you know this?

NORA   Oh, what do I know, what did I know, what didn't I know—I really
can't say. How could you be so stupid, Dr. Rank? Everything was so
nice.

RANK   Well, at any rate now you know that I am ready to serve you, body
and soul. So—please continue.

NORA   [looks at him]   After this?

RANK   Please tell me what it is.

NORA   I can't possibly tell you now.

RANK   Yes, yes! You mustn't punish me like this. Let me be allowed to do
what I can for you.

NORA   You can't do anything for me now. Anyway, I don't need any help. It
was only my imagination—you'll see. Yes, really. Honestly. [Sits in the
rocking chair, looks at him and smiles.] Well, upon my word you are a fine
gentleman, Dr. Rank. Aren't you ashamed of yourself, now that the
lamp's been lit?

RANK   Frankly, no. But perhaps I ought to say—adieu?

NORA   Of course not. You will naturally continue to visit us as before. You know quite well how Torvald depends on your company.

RANK   Yes, but you?

NORA   Oh, I always think it's enormous fun having you here.

RANK   That was what misled me. You're a riddle to me, you know. I'd often felt you'd just as soon be with me as with Helmer.

NORA   Well, you see, there are some people whom one loves, and others whom it's almost more fun to be with.

RANK   Oh yes, there's some truth in that.

NORA   When I was at home, of course I loved Papa best. But I always used to think it was terribly amusing to go down and talk to the servants; because they never told me what I ought to do; and they were such fun to listen to.

RANK   I see. So I've taken their place?

NORA   [jumps up and runs over to him]   Oh, dear sweet Dr. Rank, I didn't mean that at all. But I'm sure you understand—I feel the same about Torvald as I did about Papa.

MAID   [enters from the hall]   Excuse me, madam. [Whispers to her and hands her a visiting card.]

NORA   [glances at the card]   Oh! [Puts it quickly in her pocket.]

RANK   Anything wrong?

NORA   No, no, nothing at all. It's just something that—it's my new dress.

RANK   What? But your costume is lying over there.

NORA   Oh—that, yes—but there's another—I ordered it specially—Torvald mustn't know—

RANK   Ah, so that's your big secret?

NORA   Yes, yes. Go in and talk to him—he's in his study—keep him talking for a bit—

RANK   Don't worry. He won't get away from me. [Goes into Helmer's study.]

NORA   [to the Maid]   Is he waiting in the kitchen?

MAID   Yes, madam, he came up the back way—

NORA   But didn't you tell him I had a visitor?

MAID   Yes, but he wouldn't go.

NORA   Wouldn't go?

MAID   No, madam, not until he'd spoken with you.

NORA   Very well, show him in; but quietly. Helen, you mustn't tell anyone about this. It's a surprise for my husband.

MAID   Very good, madam. I understand. [Goes.]

NORA   It's happening. It's happening after all. No, no, no, it can't happen, it mustn't happen.

She walks across and bolts the door of Helmer's study. The Maid opens the door from the hall to admit Krogstad, and closes it behind him. He is wearing an overcoat, heavy boots and a fur cap.

NORA [*goes towards him.*] Speak quietly. My husband's at home.

KROGSTAD Let him hear.

NORA What do you want from me?

KROGSTAD Information.

NORA Hurry up, then. What is it?

KROGSTAD I suppose you know I've been given the sack.

NORA I couldn't stop it, Mr. Krogstad. I did my best for you, but it didn't help.

KROGSTAD Does your husband love you so little? He knows what I can do to you, and yet he dares to—

NORA Surely you don't imagine I told him?

KROGSTAD No, I didn't really think you had. It wouldn't have been like my old friend Torvald Helmer to show that much courage—

NORA Mr. Krogstad, I'll trouble you to speak respectfully of my husband.

KROGSTAD Don't worry, I'll show him all the respect he deserves. But since you're so anxious to keep this matter hushed up, I presume you're better informed than you were yesterday of the gravity of what you've done?

NORA I've learned more than you could ever teach me.

KROGSTAD Yes, a bad lawyer like me—

NORA What do you want from me?

KROGSTAD I just wanted to see how things were with you, Mrs. Helmer. I've been thinking about you all day. Even duns and hack journalists have hearts, you know.

NORA Show some heart, then. Think of my little children.

KROGSTAD Have you and your husband thought of mine? Well, let's forget that. I just wanted to tell you, you don't need to take this business too seriously. I'm not going to take any action, for the present.

NORA Oh, no—you won't, will you? I knew it.

KROGSTAD It can all be settled quite amicably. There's no need for it to become public. We'll keep it among the three of us.

NORA My husband must never know about this.

KROGSTAD How can you stop him? Can you pay the balance of what you owe me?

NORA Not immediately.

KROGSTAD Have you any means of raising the money during the next few days?

NORA None that I would care to use.

KROGSTAD Well, it wouldn't have helped anyway. However much money you offered me now I wouldn't give you back that paper.

NORA What are you going to do with it?

KROGSTAD Just keep it. No one else need ever hear about it. So in case you were thinking of doing anything desperate—

NORA I am.

KROGSTAD Such as running away—

NORA   I am.

KROGSTAD   Or anything more desperate—

NORA   How did you know?

KROGSTAD   —just give up the idea.

NORA   How did you know?

KROGSTAD   Most of us think of that at first. I did. But I hadn't the courage—

NORA [*dully*]   Neither have I.

KROGSTAD [*relieved*]   It's true, isn't it? You haven't the courage either?

NORA   No. I haven't. I haven't.

KROGSTAD   It'd be a stupid thing to do anyway. Once the first little domestic explosion is over. . . . I've got a letter in my pocket here addressed to your husband—

NORA   Telling him everything?

KROGSTAD   As delicately as possibly.

NORA [*quickly*]   He must never see that letter. Tear it up. I'll find the money somehow—

KROGSTAD   I'm sorry, Mrs. Helmer, I thought I'd explained—

NORA   Oh, I don't mean the money I owe you. Let me know how much you want from my husband, and I'll find it for you.

KROGSTAD   I'm not asking your husband for money.

NORA   What do you want, then?

KROGSTAD   I'll tell you. I want to get on my feet again, Mrs. Helmer. I want to get to the top. And your husband's going to help me. For eighteen months now my record's been clean. I've been in hard straits all that time; I was content to fight my way back inch by inch. Now I've been chucked back into the mud, and I'm not going to be satisfied with just getting back my job. I'm going to get to the top, I tell you. I'm going to get back into the bank, and it's going to be higher up. Your husband's going to create a new job for me—

NORA   He'll never do that!

KROGSTAD   Oh, yes he will. I know him. He won't dare to risk a scandal. And once I'm in there with him, you'll see! Within a year I'll be his right-hand man. It'll be Nils Krogstad who'll be running that bank, not Torvald Helmer!

NORA   That will never happen.

KROGSTAD   Are you thinking of—?

NORA   Now I *have* the courage.

KROGSTAD   Oh, you can't frighten me. A pampered little pretty like you—

NORA   You'll see! You'll see!

KROGSTAD   Under the ice? Down in the cold, black water? And then, in the spring to float up again, ugly, unrecognizable, hairless—?

NORA   You can't frighten me.

KROGSTAD   And you can't frighten me. People don't do such things, Mrs. Helmer. And anyway, what'd be the use? I've got him in my pocket.

NORA But afterwards? When I'm no longer—?

KROGSTAD Have you forgotten that then your reputation will be in my hands? [*She looks at him speechlessly.*] Well, I've warned you. Don't do anything silly. When Helmer's read my letter, he'll get in touch with me. And remember, it's your husband who's forced me to act like this. And for that I'll never forgive him. Goodbye, Mrs. Helmer. [*He goes out through the hall.*]

NORA [*runs to the hall door, opens it a few inches and listens*] He's going. He's not going to give him the letter. Oh, no, no, it couldn't possibly happen. [*Opens the door a little wider.*] What's he doing? Standing outside the front door. He's not going downstairs. Is he changing his mind? Yes, he—!

A letter falls into the letter-box. Krogstad's footsteps die away down the stairs.

NORA [*with a stifled cry, runs across the room towards the table by the sofa. A pause*] In the letter-box. [*Steals timidly over towards the hall door.*] There it is! Oh, Torvald, Torvald! Now we're lost!

MRS. LINDE [*enters from the nursery with Nora's costume*] Well, I've done the best I can. Shall we see how it looks—?

NORA [*whispers hoarsely*] Christine, come here.

MRS. LINDE [*throws the dress on the sofa*] What's wrong with you? You look as though you'd seen a ghost!

NORA Come here. Do you see that letter? There—look—through the glass of the letter-box.

MRS. LINDE Yes, yes, I see it.

NORA That letter's from Krogstad—

MRS. LINDE Nora! It was Krogstad who lent you the money!

NORA Yes. And now Torvald's going to discover everything.

MRS. LINDE Oh, believe me, Nora, it'll be best for you both.

NORA You don't know what's happened. I've committed a forgery—

MRS. LINDE But, for heaven's sake—!

NORA Christine, all I want is for you to be my witness.

MRS. LINDE What do you mean? Witness what?

NORA If I should go out of my mind—and it might easily happen—

MRS. LINDE Nora!

NORA Or if anything else should happen to me—so that I wasn't here any longer—

MRS. LINDE Nora, Nora, you don't know what you're saying!

NORA If anyone should try to take the blame, and say it was all his fault—you understand—?

MRS. LINDE Yes, yes—but how can you think—?

NORA Then you must testify that it isn't true, Christine. I'm not mad—I know exactly what I'm saying—and I'm telling you, no one else knows anything about this. I did it entirely on my own. Remember that.

MRS. LINDE All right. But I simply don't understand—

NORA Oh, how could you understand? A miracle—is—about to happen.

MRS. LINDE Miracle?

NORA Yes. A miracle. But it's so frightening, Christine. It *mustn't* happen, not for anything in the world.

MRS. LINDE I'll go over and talk to Krogstad.

NORA Don't go near him. He'll only do something to hurt you.

MRS. LINDE Once upon a time he'd have done anything for my sake.

NORA He?

MRS. LINDE Where does he live?

NORA Oh, how should I know—? Oh yes, wait a moment—! [*Feels in her pocket.*] Here's his card. But the letter, the letter—!

HELMER [*from his study, knocks on the door*] Nora!

NORA [*cries in alarm*] What is it?

HELMER Now, now, don't get alarmed. We're not coming in; you've closed the door. Are you trying on your costume?

NORA Yes, yes—I'm trying on my costume. I'm going to look so pretty for you, Torvald.

MRS. LINDE [*who has been reading the card*] Why, he lives just round the corner.

NORA Yes; but it's no use. There's nothing to be done now. The letter's lying there in the box.

MRS. LINDE And your husband has the key?

NORA Yes, he always keeps it.

MRS. LINDE Krogstad must ask him to send the letter back unread. He must find some excuse—

NORA But Torvald always opens the box at just about this time—

MRS. LINDE You must stop him. Go in and keep him talking. I'll be back as quickly as I can.

She hurries out through the hall.

NORA [*goes over to Helmer's door, opens it and peeps in*] Torvald!

HELMER [*offstage*] Well, may a man enter his own drawing room again? Come on, Rank, now we'll see what— [*In the doorway.*] But what's this?

NORA What, Torvald dear?

HELMER Rank's been preparing me for some great transformation scene.

RANK [*in the doorway*] So I understood. But I seem to have been mistaken.

NORA Yes, no one's to be allowed to see me before tomorrow night.

HELMER But, my dear Nora, you look quite worn out. Have you been practising too hard?

NORA   No, I haven't practised at all yet.

HELMER   Well, you must.

NORA   Yes, Torvald, I must, I know. But I can't get anywhere without your help. I've completely forgotten everything.

HELMER   Oh, we'll soon put that to rights.

NORA   Yes, help me, Torvald. Promise me you will? Oh, I'm so nervous. All those people—! You must forget everything except me this evening. You mustn't think of business—I won't even let you touch a pen. Promise me, Torvald?

HELMER   I promise. This evening I shall think of nothing but you—my poor, helpless little darling. Oh, there's just one thing I must see to— [Goes towards the hall door.]

NORA   What do you want out there?

HELMER   I'm only going to see if any letters have come.

NORA   No, Torvald, no!

HELMER   Why, what's the matter?

NORA   Torvald, I beg you. There's nothing there.

HELMER   Well, I'll just make sure.

He moves towards the door. Nora runs to the piano and plays the first bars of the tarantella.

HELMER [at the door, turns]   Aha!

NORA   I can't dance tomorrow if I don't practise with you now.

HELMER [goes over to her]   Are you really so frightened, Nora dear?

NORA   Yes, terribly frightened. Let me start practising now, at once—we've still time before dinner. Oh, do sit down and play for me, Torvald dear. Correct me, lead me, the way you always do.

HELMER   Very well, my dear, if you wish it.

He sits down at the piano. Nora seizes the tambourine and a long multi-coloured shawl from the cardboard box, wraps the latter hastily around her, then takes a quick leap into the center of the room.

NORA   Play for me! I want to dance!

Helmer plays and Nora dances. Dr. Rank stands behind Helmer at the piano and watches her.

HELMER [as he plays]   Slower, slower!

NORA   I can't!

HELMER   Not so violently, Nora.

NORA   I must!

HELMER [stops playing]   No, no, this won't do at all.

NORA [laughs and swings her tambourine]   Isn't that what I told you?
RANK   Let me play for her.
HELMER [gets up]   Yes, would you? Then it'll be easier for me to show her.

Rank sits down at the piano and plays. Nora dances more and more wildly. Helmer has stationed himself by the stove and tries repeatedly to correct her, but she seems not to hear him. Her hair works loose and falls over her shoulders; she ignores it and continues to dance. Mrs. Linde enters.

MRS. LINDE [stands in the doorwary as though tongue-tied]   Ah—!
NORA [as she dances]   Christine, we're having such fun!
HELMER   But, Nora darling, you're dancing as if your life depended on it.
NORA   It does.
HELMER   Rank, stop it! This is sheer lunacy. Stop it, I say!

Rank ceases playing. Nora suddenly stops dancing.

HELMER [goes over to her]   I'd never have believed it. You've forgotten everything I taught you.
NORA [throws away the tambourine]   You see!
HELMER   I'll have to show you every step.
NORA   You see how much I need you! You must show me every step of the way. Right to the end of the dance. Promise me you will, Torvald?
HELMER   Never fear. I will.
NORA   You mustn't think about anything but me—today or tomorrow. Don't open any letters—don't even open the letter-box—
HELMER   Aha, you're still worried about that fellow—
NORA   Oh, yes, yes, him too.
HELMER   Nora, I can tell from the way you're behaving, there's a letter from him already lying there.
NORA   I don't know. I think so. But you mustn't read it now. I don't want anything ugly to come between us till it's all over.
RANK [quietly, to Helmer]   Better give her her way.
HELMER [puts his arm round her]   My child shall have her way. But tomorrow night, when your dance is over—
NORA   Then you will be free.
MAID [appears in the doorway, right]   Dinner is served, madam.
NORA   Put out some champagne, Helen.
MAID   Very good, madam. [Goes.]
HELMER   I say! What's this, a banquet?
NORA   We'll drink champagne until dawn! [Calls.] And, Helen! Put out some macaroons! Lots of macaroons—for once!
HELMER [takes her hands in his]   Now, now, now. Don't get so excited. Where's my little songbird, the one I know?

NORA   All right. Go and sit down—and you too, Dr. Rank. I'll be with you in a minute. Christine, you must help me put my hair up.

RANK [*quietly, as they go*]   There's nothing wrong, is there? I mean, she isn't—er—expecting—?

HELMER   Good heavens no, my dear chap. She just gets scared like a child sometimes—I told you before—

They go out right.

NORA   Well?

MRS. LINDE   He's left town.

NORA   I saw it from your face.

MRS. LINDE   He'll be back tomorrow evening. I left a note for him.

NORA   You needn't have bothered. You can't stop anything now. Anyway, it's wonderful really, in a way—sitting here and waiting for the miracle to happen.

MRS. LINDE   Waiting for what?

NORA   Oh, you wouldn't understand. Go in and join them. I'll be with you in a moment.

Mrs. Linde goes into the dining-room.

NORA [*stands for a moment as though collecting herself. Then she looks at her watch*]   Five o'clock. Seven hours till midnight. Then another twenty-four hours till midnight tomorrow. And then the tarantella will be finished. Twenty-four and seven? Thirty-one hours to live.

HELMER [*appears in the doorway, right*]   What's happened to my little songbird?

NORA [*runs to him with her arms wide*]   Your songbird is here!

ACT III

The same room. The table which was formerly by the sofa has been moved into the centre of the room; the chairs surround it as before. The door to the hall stands open. Dance music can be heard from the floor above. Mrs. Linde is seated at the table, absent-mindedly glancing through a book. She is trying to read, but seems unable to keep her mind on it. More than once she turns and listens anxiously towards the front door.

MRS. LINDE [*looks at her watch*]   Not here yet. There's not much time left. Please God he hasn't—! [*Listens again.*] Ah, here he is. [*Goes out into the hall and cautiously opens the front door. Footsteps can be heard softly ascending the stairs. She whispers.*] Come in. There's no one here.

KROGSTAD [*in the doorway*]   I found a note from you at my lodgings. What does this mean?

MRS. LINDE   I must speak with you.

KROGSTAD   Oh? And must our conversation take place in this house?

MRS. LINDE   We couldn't meet at my place; my room has no separate entrance. Come in. We're quite alone. The maid's asleep, and the Helmers are at the dance upstairs.

KROGSTAD [*comes into the room*]   Well, well! So the Helmers are dancing this evening? Are they indeed?

MRS. LINDE   Yes, why not?

KROGSTAD   True enough. Why not?

MRS. LINDE   Well, Krogstad. You and I must have a talk together.

KROGSTAD   Have we two anything further to discuss?

MRS. LINDE   We have a great deal to discuss.

KROGSTAD   I wasn't aware of it.

MRS. LINDE   That's because you've never really understood me.

KROGSTAD   Was there anything to understand? It's the old story, isn't it—a woman chucking a man because something better turns up?

MRS. LINDE   Do you really think I'm so utterly heartless? You think it was easy for me to give you up?

KROGSTAD   Wasn't it?

MRS. LINDE   Oh, Nils, did you really believe that?

KROGSTAD   Then why did you write to me the way you did?

MRS. LINDE   I had to. Since I had to break with you, I thought it my duty to destroy all the feelings you had for me.

KROGSTAD [*clenches his fists*]   So that was it. And you did this for money!

MRS. LINDE   You mustn't forget I had a helpless mother to take care of, and two little brothers. We couldn't wait for you, Nils. It would have been so long before you'd had enough to support us.

KROGSTAD   Maybe. But you had no right to cast me off for someone else.

MRS. LINDE   Perhaps not. I've often asked myself that.

KROGSTAD [*more quietly*]   When I lost you, it was just as though all solid ground had been swept from under my feet. Look at me. Now I am a shipwrecked man, clinging to a spar.

MRS. LINDE   Help may be near at hand.

KROGSTAD   It was near. But then you came, and stood between it and me.

MRS. LINDE   I didn't know, Nils. No one told me till today that this job I'd found was yours.

KROGSTAD   I believe you, since you say so. But now you know, won't you give it up?

MRS. LINDE   No—because it wouldn't help you even if I did.

KROGSTAD   Wouldn't it? I'd do it all the same.

MRS. LINDE   I've learned to look at things practically. Life and poverty have taught me that.

KROGSTAD   And life has taught me to distrust fine words.

MRS. LINDE   Then it's taught you a useful lesson. But surely you still believe in actions?

KROGSTAD   What do you mean?

MRS. LINDE   You said you were like a shipwrecked man clinging to a spar.

KROGSTAD   I have good reason to say it.

MRS. LINDE   I'm in the same postion as you. No one to care about, no one to care for.

KROGSTAD   You made your own choice.

MRS. LINDE   I had no choice—then.

KROGSTAD   Well?

MRS. LINDE   Nils, suppose we two shipwrecked souls could join hands?

KROGSTAD   What are you saying?

MRS. LINDE   Castaways have a better chance of survival together than on their own.

KROGSTAD   Christine!

MRS. LINDE   Why do you suppose I came to this town?

KROGSTAD   You mean—you came because of me?

MRS. LINDE   I must work if I'm to find life worth living. I've always worked, for as long as I can remember; it's been the greatest joy of my life—my only joy. But now I'm alone in the world, and I feel so dreadfully lost and empty. There's no joy in working just for oneself. Oh, Nils, give me something—someone—to work for.

KROGSTAD   I don't believe all that. You're just being hysterical and romantic. You want to find an excuse for self-sacrifice.

MRS. LINDE   Have you ever known me to be hysterical?

KROGSTAD   You mean you really—? Is it possible? Tell me—you know all about my past?

MRS. LINDE   Yes.

KROGSTAD   And you know what people think of me here?

MRS. LINDE   You said just now that with me you might have become a different person.

KROGSTAD   I know I could have.

MRS. LINDE   Couldn't it still happen?

KROGSTAD   Christine—do you really mean this? Yes—you do—I see it in your face. Have you really the courage—?

MRS. LINDE   I need someone to be a mother to; and your children need a mother. And you and I need each other. I believe in you, Nils. I am afraid of nothing—with you.

KROGSTAD [clasps her hands]   Thank you, Christine—thank you! Now I shall make the world believe in me as you do! Oh—but I'd forgotten—

MRS. LINDE [listens]   Ssh! The tarantella! Go quickly, go!

KROGSTAD   Why? What is it?

MRS. LINDE   You hear that dance? As soon as it's finished, they'll be coming down.

KROGSTAD   All right, I'll go. It's no good, Christine. I'd forgotten—you don't know what I've just done to the Helmers.

MRS. LINDE   Yes, Nils. I know.

KROGSTAD   And yet you'd still have the courage to—?

MRS. LINDE   I know what despair can drive a man like you to.

KROGSTAD   Oh, if only I could undo this!

MRS. LINDE   You can. Your letter is still lying in the box.

KROGSTAD   Are you sure?

MRS. LINDE   Quite sure. But—

KROGSTAD [looks searchingly at her]   Is that why you're doing this? You want to save your friend at any price? Tell me the truth. Is that the reason?

MRS. LINDE   Nils, a woman who has sold herself once for the sake of others doesn't make the same mistake again.

KROGSTAD   I shall demand my letter back.

MRS. LINDE   No, no.

KROGSTAD   Of course I shall. I shall stay here till Helmer comes down. I'll tell him he must give me back my letter—I'll say it was only to do with my dismissal, and that I don't want him to read it—

MRS. LINDE   No, Nils, you mustn't ask for that letter back.

KROGSTAD   But—tell me—wasn't that the real reason you asked me to come here?

MRS. LINDE   Yes—at first, when I was frightened. But a day has passed since then, and in that time I've seen incredible things happen in this house. Helmer must know the truth. This unhappy secret of Nora's must be revealed. They must come to a full understanding; there must be an end of all these shiftings and evasions.

KROGSTAD   Very well. If you're prepared to risk it. But one thing I can do—and at once—

MRS. LINDE [listens]   Hurry! Go, go! The dance is over. We aren't safe here another moment.

KROGSTAD   I'll wait for you downstairs.

MRS. LINDE   Yes, do. You can see me home.

KROGSTAD   I've never been so happy in my life before!

He goes out through the front door. The door leading from the room into the hall remains open.

MRS. LINDE [tidies the room a little and gets her hat and coat]   What a change! Oh, what a change! Someone to work for—to live for! A home to bring joy into! I won't let this chance of happiness slip through my fingers. Oh, why don't they come? [*Listens.*] Ah, here they are. I must get my coat on.

She takes her hat and coat. Helmer's and Nora's voices become audible outside. A key is turned in the lock and Helmer leads Nora almost forcibly into the hall. She is dressed in an Italian costume with a large black shawl. He is in evening dress, with a black cloak.

NORA [*still in the doorway, resisting him*]   No, no, no—not in here! I want to go back upstairs. I don't want to leave so early.

HELMER   But my dearest Nora—

NORA   Oh, please, Torvald, please! Just another hour!

HELMER   Not another minute, Nora, my sweet. You know what we agreed. Come along, now. Into the drawing-room. You'll catch cold if you stay out here.

He leads her, despite her efforts to resist him, gently into the room.

MRS. LINDE   Good evening.

NORA   Christine!

HELMER   Oh, hullo, Mrs. Linde. You still here?

MRS. LINDE   Please forgive me. I did so want to see Nora in her costume.

NORA   Have you been sitting here waiting for me?

MRS. LINDE   Yes. I got here too late, I'm afraid. You'd already gone up. And I felt I really couldn't go back home without seeing you.

HELMER [*takes off Nora's shawl*]   Well, take a good look at her. She's worth looking at, don't you think? Isn't she beautiful, Mrs. Linde?

MRS. LINDE   Oh, yes, indeed—

HELMER   Isn't she unbelievably beautiful? Everyone at the party said so. But dreadfully stubborn she is, bless her pretty little heart. What's to be done about that? Would you believe it, I practically had to use force to get her away!

NORA   Oh, Torvald, you're going to regret not letting me stay—just half an hour longer.

HELMER   Hear that, Mrs. Linde? She dances her tarantella—makes a roaring success—and very well deserved—though possibly a trifle too realistic—more so than was aesthetically necessary, strictly speaking. But never mind that. Main thing is—she had a success—roaring success. Was I going to let her stay on after that and spoil the impression? No, thank you. I took my beautiful little Capri signorina—my capricious little Capricienne, what?—under my arm—a swift round of the ballroom, a curtsey to the company, and, as they say in novels, the beautiful apparition disappeared! An exit should always be dramatic, Mrs. Linde. But unfortunately that's just what I can't get Nora to realize. I say, it's hot in here. [*Throws his cloak on a chair and opens the door to his study.*] What's this? It's dark in here. Ah, yes, of course—excuse me. [*Goes in and lights a couple of candles.*]

NORA [*whispers swiftly, breathlessly*] Well?

MRS. LINDE [*quietly*] I've spoken to him.

NORA Yes?

MRS. LINDE Nora—you must tell your husband everything.

NORA [*dully*] I knew it.

MRS. LINDE You've nothing to fear from Krogstad. But you must tell him.

NORA I shan't tell him anything.

MRS. LINDE Then the letter will.

NORA Thank you, Christine. Now I know what I must do. Ssh!

HELMER [*returns*] Well, Mrs. Linde, finished admiring her?

MRS. LINDE Yes. Now I must say good night.

HELMER Oh, already? Does this knitting belong to you?

MRS. LINDE [*takes it*] Thank you, yes. I nearly forgot it.

HELMER You knit, then?

MRS. LINDE Why, yes.

HELMER Know what? You ought to take up embroidery.

MRS. LINDE Oh? Why?

HELMER It's much prettier. Watch me, now. You hold the embroidery in your left hand, like this, and then you take the needle in your right hand and go in and out in a slow, easy movement—like this. I am right, aren't I?

MRS. LINDE Yes, I'm sure—

HELMER But knitting, now—that's an ugly business—can't help it. Look—arms all huddled up—great clumsy needles going up and down—makes you look like a damned Chinaman. I say, that really was a magnificent champagne they served us.

MRS. LINDE Well, good night, Nora. And stop being stubborn. Remember!

HELMER Quite right, Mrs. Linde!

MRS. LINDE Good night, Mr. Helmer.

HELMER [*accompanies her to the door*] Good night, good night! I hope you'll manage to get home all right? I'd gladly—but you haven't far to go, have you? Good night, good night. [*She goes. He closes the door behind her and returns.*] Well, we've got rid of her at last. Dreadful bore that woman is!

NORA Aren't you very tired, Torvald?

HELMER No, not in the least.

NORA Aren't you sleepy?

HELMER Not a bit. On the contrary, I feel extraordinarily exhilarated. But what about you? Yes, you look very sleepy and tired.

NORA Yes, I am very tired. Soon I shall sleep.

HELMER You see, you see! How right I was not to let you stay longer!

NORA   Oh, you're always right, whatever you do.

HELMER [*kisses her on the forehead*]   Now my little songbird's talking just like a real big human being. I say, did you notice how cheerful Rank was this evening?

NORA   Oh? Was he? I didn't have a chance to speak with him.

HELMER   I hardly did. But I haven't seen him in such a jolly mood for ages. [*Looks at her for a moment, then comes closer.*] I say, it's nice to get back to one's home again, and be all alone with you. Upon my word, you're a distractingly beautiful young woman.

NORA   Don't look at me like that, Torvald!

HELMER   What, not look at my most treasured possession? At all this wonderful beauty that's mine, mine alone, all mine.

NORA [*goes round to the other side of the table*]   You mustn't talk to me like that tonight.

HELMER [*follows her*]   You've still the tarantella in your blood, I see. And that makes you even more desirable. Listen! Now the other guests are beginning to go. [*More quietly.*] Nora—soon the whole house will be absolutely quiet.

NORA   Yes, I hope so.

HELMER   Yes, my beloved Nora, of course you do! Do you know—when I'm out with you among other people like we were tonight, do you know why I say so little to you, why I keep so aloof from you, and just throw you an occasional glance? Do you know why I do that? It's because I pretend to myself that you're my secret mistress, my clandestine little sweetheart, and that nobody knows there's anything at all between us.

NORA   Oh, yes, yes, yes—I know you never think of anything but me.

HELMER   And then when we're about to go, and I wrap the shawl round your lovely young shoulders, over this wonderful curve of your neck— then I pretend to myself that you are my young bride, that we've just come from the wedding, that I'm taking you to my house for the first time—that, for the first time, I am alone with you—quite alone with you, as you stand there young and trembling and beautiful. All evening I've had no eyes for anyone but you. When I saw you dance the tarantella, like a huntress, a temptress, my blood grew hot, I couldn't stand it any longer! That was why I seized you and dragged you down here with me—

NORA   Leave me, Torvald! Get away from me! I don't want all this.

HELMER   What? Now, Nora, you're joking with me. Don't want, don't want—? Aren't I your husband—?

There is a knock on the front door.

NORA [*starts*]   What was that?

HELMER [*goes towards the hall*]   Who is it?

RANK [*outside*]   It's me. May I come in for a moment?

HELMER [*quietly, annoyed*]   Oh, what does he want now? [*Calls.*] Wait a moment. [*Walks over and opens the door.*] Well! Nice of you not to go by without looking in.

RANK   I thought I heard your voice, so I felt I had to say goodbye. [*His eyes travel swiftly around the room.*] Ah, yes—these dear rooms, how well I know them. What a happy, peaceful home you two have.

HELMER   You seemed to be having a pretty happy time yourself upstairs.

RANK   Indeed I did. Why not? Why shouldn't one make the most of this world? As much as one can, and for as long as one can. The wine was excellent—

HELMER   Especially the champagne.

RANK   You noticed that too? It's almost incredible how much I managed to get down.

NORA   Torvald drank a lot of champagne too, this evening.

RANK   Oh?

NORA   Yes. It always makes him merry afterwards.

RANK   Well, why shouldn't a man have a merry evening after a well-spent day?

HELMER   Well-spent? Oh, I don't know that I can claim that.

RANK [*slaps him across the back*]   I can, though, my dear fellow!

NORA   Yes, of course, Dr. Rank—you've been carrying out a scientific experiment today, haven't you?

RANK   Exactly.

HELMER   Scientific experiment! Those are big words for my little Nora to use!

NORA   And may I congratulate you on the finding?

RANK   You may indeed.

NORA   It was good, then?

RANK   The best possible finding—both for the doctor and the patient. Certainty.

NORA [*quickly*]   Certainty?

RANK   Absolute certainty. So aren't I entitled to have a merry evening after that?

NORA   Yes, Dr. Rank. You were quite right to.

HELMER   I agree. Provided you don't have to regret it tomorrow.

RANK   Well, you never get anything in this life without paying for it.

NORA   Dr. Rank—you like masquerades, don't you?

RANK   Yes, if the disguises are sufficiently amusing.

NORA   Tell me. What shall we two wear at the next masquerade?

HELMER   You little gadabout! Are you thinking about the next one already?

RANK   We two? Yes, I'll tell you. You must go as the Spirit of Happiness—

HELMER   You try to think of a costume that'll convey that.

RANK   Your wife need only appear as her normal, everyday self—

HELMER   Quite right! Well said! But what are you going to be? Have you decided that?

RANK   Yes, my dear friend. I have decided that.

HELMER   Well?

RANK   At the next masquerade, I shall be invisible.

HELMER   Well, that's a funny idea.

RANK   There's a big, black hat—haven't you heard of the invisible hat? Once it's over your head, no one can see you any more.

HELMER   [represses a smile]   Ah yes, of course.

RANK   But I'm forgetting what I came for. Helmer, give me a cigar. One of your black Havanas.

HELMER   With the greatest pleasure. [Offers him the box.]

RANK   [takes one and cuts off the tip]   Thank you.

NORA   [strikes a match]   Let me give you a light.

RANK   Thank you. [She holds out the match for him. He lights his cigar.] And now—goodbye.

HELMER   Goodbye, my dear chap, goodbye.

NORA   Sleep well, Dr. Rank.

RANK   Thank you for that kind wish.

NORA   Wish me the same.

RANK   You? Very well—since you ask. Sleep well. And thank you for the light. [He nods to them both and goes.]

HELMER   [quietly]   He's been drinking too much.

NORA   [abstractedly]   Perhaps.

Helmer takes his bunch of keys from his pocket and goes out into the hall.

NORA   Torvald, what do you want out there?

HELMER   I must empty the letter-box. It's absolutely full. There'll be no room for the newspapers in the morning.

NORA   Are you going to work tonight?

HELMER   You know very well I'm not. Hullo, what's this? Someone's been at the lock.

NORA   At the lock—?

HELMER   Yes, I'm sure of it. Who on earth—? Surely not one of the maids? Here's a broken hairpin. Nora, it's yours—

NORA   [quickly]   Then it must have been the children.

HELMER   Well, you'll have to break them of that habit. Hm, hm. Ah, that's done it. [Takes out the contents of the box and calls into the kitchen.] Helen! Helen! Put out the light on the staircase. [Comes back into the drawing room with the letters in his hand and closes the door to the hall.] Look at this! You see how they've piled up? [Glances through them.] What on earth's this?

NORA   [at the window]   The letter! Oh, no, Torvald, no!

HELMER   Two visiting cards—from Rank.

NORA   From Dr. Rank?

HELMER [*looks at them*]   Peter Rank, M.D. They were on top. He must have dropped them in as he left.

NORA   Has he written anything on them?

HELMER   There's a black cross above his name. Look. Rather gruesome, isn't it? It looks just as though he was announcing his death.

NORA   He is.

HELMER   What? Do you know something? Has he told you anything?

NORA   Yes. When these cards come, it means he's said good-bye to us. He wants to shut himself up in his house and die.

HELMER   Ah, poor fellow. I knew I wouldn't be seeing him for much longer. But so soon—! And now he's going to slink away and hide like a wounded beast.

NORA   When the time comes, it's best to go silently. Don't you think so, Torvald?

HELMER [*walks up and down*]   He was so much a part of our life. I can't realize that he's gone. His suffering and loneliness seemed to provide a kind of dark background to the happy sunlight of our marriage. Well, perhaps it's best this way. For him, anyway. [*Stops walking.*] And perhaps for us too, Nora. Now we have only each other. [*Embraces her.*] Oh, my beloved wife—I feel as though I could never hold you close enough. Do you know, Nora, often I wish some terrible danger might threaten you, so that I could offer my life and my blood, everything, for your sake.

NORA [*tears herself loose and says in a clear, firm voice*]   Read your letters now, Torvald.

HELMER   No, no. Not tonight. Tonight I want to be with you, my darling wife—

NORA   When your friend is about to die—?

HELMER   You're right. This news has upset us both. An ugliness has come between us; thoughts of death and dissolution. We must try to forget them. Until then—you go to your room; I shall go to mine.

NORA [*throws her arms round his neck*]   Good night, Torvald! Good night!

HELMER [*kisses her on the forehead*]   Good night, my darling little songbird. Sleep well, Nora. I'll go and read my letters.

He goes into the study with the letters in his hand, and closes the door.

NORA [*wild-eyed, fumbles around, seizes Helmer's cloak, throws it round herself and whispers quickly, hoarsely*]   Never see him again. Never. Never. Never. [*Throws the shawl over her head.*] Never see the children again. Them too. Never. Never. Oh—the icy black water! Oh—that bottomless—that—! Oh, if only it were all over! Now he's got it—he's reading it. Oh, no, no! Goodbye, Torvald! Goodbye, my darlings!

She turns to run into the hall. As she does so, Helmer throws open his door and stands there with an open letter in his hand.

HELMER   Nora!

NORA [*shrieks*]   Ah—!

HELMER   What is this? Do you know what is in this letter?

NORA   Yes, I know. Let me go! Let me go!

HELMER [*holds her back*]   Go? Where?

NORA [*tries to tear herself loose*]   You mustn't try to save me, Torvald!

HELMER [*staggers back*]   Is it true? Is it true, what he writes? Oh, my God! No, no—it's impossible, it can't be true!

NORA   It *is* true. I've loved you more than anything else in the world.

HELMER   Oh, don't try to make silly excuses.

NORA [*takes a step towards him*]   Torvald—

HELMER   Wretched woman! What have you done?

NORA   Let me go! You're not going to suffer for my sake. I won't let you!

HELMER   Stop being theatrical. [*Locks the front door.*] You're going to stay here and explain yourself. Do you understand what you've done? Answer me! Do you understand?

NORA [*looks unflinchingly at him and, her expression growing colder, says*]   Yes. Now I am beginning to understand.

HELMER [*walking round the room*]   Oh, what a dreadful awakening! For eight whole years—she who was my joy and my pride—a hypocrite, a liar—worse, worse—a criminal! Oh, the hideousness of it! Shame on you, shame!

Nora is silent and stares unblinkingly at him.

HELMER [*stops in front of her*]   I ought to have guessed that something of this sort would happen. I should have foreseen it. All your father's recklessness and instability—be quiet!—I repeat, all your father's recklessness and instability he has handed on to you. No religion, no morals, no sense of duty! Oh, how I have been punished for closing my eyes to his faults! I did it for your sake. And now you reward me like this.

NORA   Yes. Like this.

HELMER   Now you have destroyed all my happiness. You have ruined my whole future. Oh, it's too dreadful to contemplate! I am in the power of a man who is completely without scruples. He can do what he likes with me, demand what he pleases, order me to do anything—I dare not disobey him. I am condemned to humiliation and ruin simply for the weakness of a woman.

NORA   When I am gone from this world, you will be free.

HELMER   Oh, don't be melodramatic. Your father was always ready with that kind of remark. How would it help me if you were "gone from this world," as you put it? It wouldn't assist me in the slightest. He can still make all the facts public; and if he does, I may quite easily be suspected of having been an accomplice in your crime. People may think that I was behind it—that it was I who encouraged you! And for all this I have to thank you, you whom I have carried on my hands through all the years of our marriage! Now do you realize what you've done to me?

NORA [*coldly calm*]   Yes.

HELMER   It's so unbelievable I can hardly credit it. But we must try to find some way out. Take off that shawl. Take it off, I say! I must try to buy him off somehow. This thing must be hushed up at any price. As regards our relationship—we must appear to be living together just as before. Only *appear*, of course. You will therefore continue to reside here. That is understood. But the children shall be taken out of your hands. I dare no longer entrust them to you. Oh, to have to say this to the woman I once loved so dearly—and whom I still—! Well, all that must be finished. Henceforth there can be no question of happiness; we must merely strive to save what shreds and tatters— [*The front door bell rings. Helmer starts.*] What can that be? At this hour? Surely not—? He wouldn't—? Hide yourself, Nora. Say you're ill.

Nora does not move. Helmer goes to the door of the room and opens it. The Maid is standing half-dressed in the hall.

MAID   A letter for madam.

HELMER   Give it me. [*Seizes the letter and shuts the door.*]   Yes, it's from him. You're not having it. I'll read this myself.

NORA   Read it.

HELMER [*by the lamp*]   I hardly dare to. This may mean the end for us both. No. I must know. [*Tears open the letter hastily; reads a few lines; looks at a piece of paper which is enclosed with it; utters a cry of joy.*] Nora! [*She looks at him questioningly.*] Nora! No—I must read it once more. Yes, yes, it's true! I am saved! Nora, I am saved!

NORA   What about me?

HELMER   You too, of course. We're both saved, you and I. Look! He's returning your I.O.U. He writes that he is sorry for what has happened—a happy accident has changed his life—oh, what does it matter what he writes? We are saved, Nora! No one can harm you now. Oh, Nora, Nora—no, first let me destroy this filthy thing. Let me see—! [*Glances at the I.O.U.*] No, I don't want to look at it. I shall merely regard the whole business as a dream. [*He tears the I.O.U. and both letters into pieces, throws them into the stove and watches them burn.*] There. Now they're destroyed. He wrote that ever since Christmas Eve you've been—oh, these must have been three dreadful days for you, Nora.

NORA   Yes. It's been a hard fight.

HELMER It must have been terrible—seeing no way out except—no, we'll forget the whole sordid business. We'll just be happy and go on telling ourselves over and over again: "It's over! It's over!" Listen to me, Nora. You don't seem to realize. It's over! Why are you looking so pale? Ah, my poor little Nora, I understand. You can't believe that I have forgiven you. But I have, Nora. I swear it to you. I have forgiven you everything. I know that what you did you did for your love of me.

NORA That is true.

HELMER You have loved me as a wife should love her husband. It was simply that in your inexperience you chose the wrong means. But do you think I love you any the less because you don't know how to act on your own initiative? No, no. Just lean on me. I shall counsel you. I shall guide you. I would not be a true man if your feminine helplessness did not make you doubly attractive in my eyes. You mustn't mind the hard words I said to you in those first dreadful moments when my whole world seemed to be tumbling about my ears. I have forgiven you, Nora. I swear it to you; I have forgiven you.

NORA Thank you for your forgiveness.

She goes out through the door, right.

HELMER No, don't go— [*Looks in.*] What are you doing there?

NORA [*offstage*] Taking off my fancy dress.

HELMER [*by the open door*] Yes, do that. Try to calm yourself and get your balance again, my frightened little songbird. Don't be afraid. I have broad wings to shield you. [*Begins to walk around near the door.*] How lovely and peaceful this little home of ours is, Nora. You are safe here; I shall watch over you like a hunted dove which I have snatched unharmed from the claws of the falcon. Your wildly beating little heart shall find peace with me. It will happen, Nora; it will take time, but it will happen, believe me. Tomorrow all this will seem quite different. Soon everything will be as it was before. I shall no longer need to remind you that I have forgiven you; your own heart will tell you that it is true. Do you really think I could ever bring myself to disown you, or even to reproach you? Ah, Nora, you don't understand what goes on in a husband's heart. There is something indescribably wonderful and satisfying for a husband in knowing that he has forgiven his wife— forgiven her unreservedly, from the bottom of his heart. It means that she has become his property in a double sense; he has, as it were, brought her into the world anew; she is now not only his wife but also his child. From now on that is what you shall be to me, my poor, helpless, bewildered little creature. Never be frightened of anything again, Nora. Just open your heart to me. I shall be both your will and your conscience. What's this? Not in bed? Have you changed?

NORA [*in her everyday dress*] Yes, Torvald. I've changed.

HELMER But why now—so late—?

NORA I shall not sleep tonight.

HELMER But, my dear Nora—

NORA [*looks at her watch*] It isn't that late. Sit down here, Torvald. You and I have a lot to talk about.

She sits down on one side of the table.

HELMER Nora, what does this mean? You look quite drawn—

NORA Sit down. It's going to take a long time. I've a lot to say to you.

HELMER [*sits down on the other side of the table*] You alarm me, Nora. I don't understand you.

NORA No, that's just it. You don't understand me. And I've never understood you—until this evening. No, don't interrupt me. Just listen to what I have to say. You and I have got to face facts, Torvald.

HELMER What do you mean by that?

NORA [*after a short silence*] Doesn't anything strike you about the way we're sitting here?

HELMER What?

NORA We've been married for eight years. Does it occur to you that this is the first time that we two, you and I, man and wife, have ever had a serious talk together?

HELMER Serious? What do you mean, serious?

NORA In eight whole years—no, longer—ever since we first met—we have never exchanged a serious word on a serious subject.

HELMER Did you expect me to drag you into all my worries—worries you couldn't possibly have helped me with?

NORA I'm not talking about worries. I'm simply saying that we have never sat down seriously to try to get to the bottom of anything.

HELMER But, my dear Nora, what on earth has that got to do with you?

NORA That's just the point. You have never understood me. A great wrong has been done to me, Torvald. First by Papa, and then by you.

HELMER What? But we two have loved you more than anyone in the world!

NORA [*shakes her head*] You have never loved me. You just thought it was fun to be in love with me.

HELMER Nora, what kind of a way is this to talk?

NORA It's the truth, Torvald. When I lived with Papa, he used to tell me what he thought about everything, so that I never had any opinions but his. And if I did have any of my own, I kept them quiet, because he wouldn't have liked them. He called me his little doll, and he played with me just the way I played with my dolls. Then I came here to live in your house—

HELMER What kind of a way is that to describe our marriage?

NORA [*undisturbed*]   I mean, then I passed from Papa's hands into yours. You arranged everything the way you wanted it, so that I simply took over your taste in everything—or pretended I did—I don't really know—I think it was a little of both—first one and then the other. Now I look back on it, it's as if I've been living here like a pauper, from hand to mouth. I performed tricks for you, and you gave me food and drink. But that was how you wanted it. You and Papa have done me a great wrong. It's your fault that I have done nothing with my life.

HELMER   Nora, how can you be so unreasonable and ungrateful? Haven't you been happy here?

NORA   No; never. I used to think I was; but I haven't ever been happy.

HELMER   Not—not happy?

NORA   No. I've just had fun. You've always been very kind to me. But our home has never been anything but a playroom. I've been your doll-wife, just as I used to be Papa's doll-child. And the children have been my dolls. I used to think it was fun when you came in and played with me, just as they think it's fun when I go in and play games with them. That's all our marriage has been, Torvald.

HELMER   There may be a little truth in what you say, though you exaggerate and romanticize. But from now on it'll be different. Playtime is over. Now the time has come for education.

NORA   Whose education? Mine or the children's?

HELMER   Both yours and the children's, my dearest Nora.

NORA   Oh, Torvald, you're not the man to educate me into being the right wife for you.

HELMER   How can you say that?

NORA   And what about me? Am I fit to educate the children?

HELMER   Nora!

NORA   Didn't you say yourself a few minutes ago that you dare not leave them in my charge?

HELMER   In a moment of excitement. Surely you don't think I meant it seriously?

NORA   Yes. You were perfectly right. I'm not fitted to educate them. There's something else I must do first. I must educate myself. And you can't help me with that. It's something I must do by myself. That's why I'm leaving you.

HELMER [*jumps up*]   What did you say?

NORA   I must stand on my own feet if I am to find out the truth about myself and about life. So I can't go on living here with you any longer.

HELMER   Nora, Nora!

NORA   I'm leaving you now, at once. Christine will put me up for tonight—

HELMER   You're out of your mind! You can't do this! I forbid you!

NORA   It's no use your trying to forbid me any more. I shall take with me nothing but what is mine. I don't want anything from you, now or ever.

HELMER   What kind of madness is this?

NORA   Tomorrow I shall go home—I mean, to where I was born. It'll be easiest for me to find some kind of a job there.

HELMER   But you're blind! You've no experience of the world—

NORA   I must try to get some, Torvald.

HELMER   But to leave your home, your husband, your children! Have you thought what people will say?

NORA   I can't help that. I only know that I must do this.

HELMER   But this is monstrous! Can you neglect your most sacred duties?

NORA   What do you call my most sacred duties?

HELMER   Do I have to tell you? Your duties towards your husband, and your children.

NORA   I have another duty which is equally sacred.

HELMER   You have not. What on earth could that be?

NORA   My duty towards myself.

HELMER   First and foremost you are a wife and a mother.

NORA   I don't believe that any longer. I believe that I am first and foremost a human being, like you—or anyway, that I must try to become one. I know most people think as you do, Torvald, and I know there's something of the sort to be found in books. But I'm no longer prepared to accept what people say and what's written in books. I must think things out for myself, and try to find my own answer.

HELMER   Do you need to ask where your duty lies in your own home? Haven't you an infallible guide in such matters—your religion?

NORA   Oh, Torvald, I don't really know what religion means.

HELMER   What are you saying?

NORA   I only know what Pastor Hansen told me when I went to confirmation. He explained that religion meant this and that. When I get away from all this and can think things out on my own, that's one of the questions I want to look into. I want to find out whether what Pastor Hansen said was right—or anyway, whether it is right for me.

HELMER   But it's unheard of for so young a woman to behave like this! If religion cannot guide you, let me at least appeal to your conscience. I presume you have some moral feelings left? Or—perhaps you haven't? Well, answer me.

NORA   Oh, Torvald, that isn't an easy question to answer. I simply don't know. I don't know where I am in these matters. I only know that these things mean something quite different to me from what they do to you. I've learned now that certain laws are different from what I'd imagined them to be; but I can't accept that such laws can be right. Has a woman really not the right to spare her dying father pain, or save her husband's life? I can't believe that.

HELMER   You're talking like a child. You don't understand how society works.

NORA   No, I don't. But now I intend to learn. I must try to satisfy myself which is right, society or I.

HELMER   Nora, you're ill; you're feverish. I almost believe you're out of your mind.

NORA   I've never felt so sane and sure in my life.

HELMER   You feel sure that it is right to leave your husband and your children?

NORA   Yes. I do.

HELMER   Then there is only one possible explanation.

NORA   What?

HELMER   That you don't love me any longer.

NORA   No, that's exactly it.

HELMER   Nora! How can you say this to me?

NORA   Oh, Torvald, it hurts me terribly to have to say it, because you've always been so kind to me. But I can't help it. I don't love you any longer.

HELMER   [controlling his emotions with difficulty]   And you feel quite sure about this too?

NORA   Yes, absolutely sure. That's why I can't go on living here any longer.

HELMER   Can you also explain why I have lost your love?

NORA   Yes, I can. It happened this evening, when the miracle failed to happen. It was then that I realized you weren't the man I'd thought you to be.

HELMER   Explain more clearly. I don't understand you.

NORA   I've waited so patiently, for eight whole years—well, good heavens, I'm not such a fool as to suppose that miracles occur every day. Then this dreadful thing happened to me, and then I knew: "Now the miracle will take place!" When Krogstad's letter was lying out there, it never occurred to me for a moment that you would let that man trample over you. I knew that you would say to him: "Publish the facts to the world." And when he had done this—

HELMER   Yes, what then? When I'd exposed my wife's name to shame and scandal—

NORA   Then I was certain that you would step forward and take all the blame on yourself, and say: "I am the one who is guilty!"

HELMER   Nora!

NORA   You're thinking I wouldn't have accepted such a sacrifice from you? No, of course I wouldn't! But what would my word have counted for against yours? That was the miracle I was hoping for, and dreading. And it was to prevent it happening that I wanted to end my life.

HELMER   Nora, I would gladly work for you night and day, and endure sorrow and hardship for your sake. But no man can be expected to sacrifice his honor, even for the person he loves.

NORA   Millions of women have done it.

HELMER   Oh, you think and talk like a stupid child.

NORA   That may be. But you neither think nor talk like the man I could share my life with. Once you'd got over your fright—and you weren't frightened of what might threaten me, but only of what threatened you—once the danger was past, then as far as you were concerned it was exactly as though nothing had happened. I was your little songbird just as before—your doll whom henceforth you would take particular care to protect from the world because she was so weak and fragile. [*Gets up.*] Torvald, in that moment I realized that for eight years I had been living here with a complete stranger, and had borne him three children—! Oh, I can't bear to think of it! I could tear myself to pieces!

HELMER   [*sadly*]   I see it, I see it. A gulf has indeed opened between us. Oh, but Nora—couldn't it be bridged?

NORA   As I am now, I am no wife for you.

HELMER   I have the strength to change.

NORA   Perhaps—if your doll is taken from you.

HELMER   But to be parted—to be parted from you! No, no, Nora, I can't conceive of it happening!

NORA   [*goes into the room, right*]   All the more necessary that it should happen.

She comes back with her outdoor things and a small traveling-bag, which she puts down on a chair by the table.

HELMER   Nora, Nora, not now! Wait till tomorrow!

NORA   [*puts on her coat*]   I can't spend the night in a strange man's house.

HELMER   But can't we live here as brother and sister, then—?

NORA   [*fastens her hat*]   You know quite well it wouldn't last. [*Puts on her shawl.*] Goodbye, Torvald. I don't want to see the children. I know they're in better hands than mine. As I am now, I can be nothing to them.

HELMER   But some time, Nora—some time—?

NORA   How can I tell? I've no idea what will happen to me.

HELMER   But you are my wife, both as you are and as you will be.

NORA   Listen, Torvald. When a wife leaves her husband's house, as I'm doing now, I'm told that according to the law he is freed of any obligations towards her. In any case, I release you from any such obligations. You mustn't feel bound to me in any way, however small, just as I shall not feel bound to you. We must both be quite free. Here is your ring back. Give me mine.

HELMER   That too?

NORA   That too.

HELMER   Here it is.

NORA   Good. Well, now it's over. I'll leave the keys here. The servants know about everything to do with the house—much better than I do. Tomorrow, when I have left town, Christine will come to pack the things I brought here from home. I'll have them sent on after me.

HELMER   This is the end then! Nora, will you never think of me any more?

NORA   Yes, of course. I shall often think of you and the children and this house.

HELMER   May I write to you, Nora?

NORA   No. Never. You mustn't do that.

HELMER   But at least you must let me send you—

NORA   Nothing. Nothing.

HELMER   But if you should need help—?

NORA   I tell you, no. I don't accept things from strangers.

HELMER   Nora—can I never be anything but a stranger to you?

NORA   [picks up her bag]   Oh, Torvald! Then the miracle of miracles would have to happen.

HELMER   The miracle of miracles?

NORA   You and I would both have to change so much that—oh, Torvald, I don't believe in miracles any longer.

HELMER   But I want to believe in them. Tell me. We should have to change so much that—?

NORA   That life together between us two could become a marriage. Goodbye.

She goes out through the hall.

HELMER   [sinks down on a chair by the door and buries his face in his hands] Nora! Nora! [Looks round and gets up.] Empty! She's gone! [A hope strikes him.] The miracle of miracles—?

The street door is slammed shut downstairs.

AUGUST STRINDBERG

1849–1912

Born and raised in Stockholm, Sweden, where his father was a respectable businessman and his mother a working-class woman, Strindberg was the fourth of twelve children and the first born in wedlock. He intermittently attended Uppsala University in Stockholm from 1867 to 1872, and worked briefly as a librarian, telegraph clerk, tutor, and actor before turning full time to writing in the mid-1870s. During this period, he also became involved with Baroness Siri von Essen, an aspiring actress, who left her husband and married Strindberg in 1877. After fourteen years and countless sexual quarrels and jealousies, the marriage ended in divorce, but it evidently provided Strindberg with a rich source of material not only for a series of thinly veiled autobiographical novels, but also for a group of intensely naturalistic plays—most notably *The Father* (1887), *Miss Julie* (1888), and *The Stronger* (1890)—which depict men and women in a variety of psychological and sexual struggles. During the early 1890s, he was married and divorced again. During the mid 1890s, he suffered a prolonged and profound period of psychological and spiritual turmoil, reflected in his novel, *The Inferno* (1897). And during the late 1890s, he returned to playwriting with a series of works noted for their dark vision of human nature and experience, as well as for their highly experimental use of expressionistic and symbolic elements, such as dreams, fantasies, and nightmarish spectacles. The best known of these plays, written after the disintegration of his third marriage, is *Ghost Sonata* (1907).

The Stronger

CHARACTERS

MRS. X., actress, married
MISS Y., actress, unmarried
A WAITRESS

Scene: A corner of a ladies' café (in Stockholm in the eighteen eighties). Two small wrought-iron tables, a red plush settee and a few chairs.

Miss Y. is sitting with a half-empty bottle of beer on the table before her, reading an illustrated weekly which from time to time she exchanges for another.

Mrs. X. enters, wearing a winter hat and coat and carrying a decorative Japanese basket.

MRS. x   Why, Millie, my dear, how are you? Sitting here all alone on Christmas Eve like some poor bachelor.

Miss Y. looks up from her magazine, nods, and continues to read.

MRS. x   You know it makes me feel really sad to see you. Alone. Alone in a café and on Christmas Eve of all times. It makes me feel as sad as when once in Paris I saw a wedding party at a restaurant. The bride was reading a comic paper and the bridegroom playing billiards with the

Translated by Elizabeth Sprigge

witnesses. Ah me, I said to myself, with such a beginning how will it go, and how will it end? He was playing billiards on his wedding day! And she, you were going to say, was reading a comic paper on hers. But that's not quite the same.

A waitress brings a cup of chocolate to Mrs. X. and goes out.

MRS. X   Do you know, Amelia, I really believe now you would have done better to stick to him. Don't forget I was the first who told you to forgive him. Do you remember? Then you would be married now and have a home. Think how happy you were that Christmas when you stayed with your fiancé's people in the country. How warmly you spoke of domestic happiness! You really quite longed to be out of the theatre. Yes, Amelia dear, home is best—next best to the stage, and as for children—but you couldn't know anything about that.

Miss Y.'s expression is disdainful. Mrs. X. sips a few spoonfuls of chocolate, then opens her basket and displays some Christmas presents.

MRS. X   Now you must see what I have bought for my little chicks. [*Takes out a doll.*] Look at this. That's for Lisa. Do you see how she can roll her eyes and turn her head. Isn't she lovely? And here's a toy pistol for Maja.[1] [*She loads the pistol and shoots it at Miss Y., who appears frightened.*]
MRS. X   Were you scared? Did you think I was going to shoot you? Really, I didn't think you'd believe that of me. Now if *you* were to shoot *me* it wouldn't be so surprising, for after all I did get in your way, and I know you never forget it—although I was entirely innocent. You still think I intrigued to get you out of the Grand Theatre, but I didn't. I didn't, however much you think I did. Well, it's no good talking, you will believe it was me . . . [*Takes out a pair of embroidered slippers.*] And these are for my old man, with tulips on them that I embroidered myself. As a matter of fact I hate tulips, but he has to have tulips on everything.

Miss Y. looks up, irony and curiosity in her face.

MRS. X [*putting one hand in each slipper*]   Look what small feet Bob has, hasn't he? And you ought to see the charming way he walks—you've never seen him in slippers, have you?

Miss Y. laughs.

1. Pronounced Maya

MRS. X   Look, I'll show you. [*She makes the slippers walk across the table, and Miss Y. laughs again.*]

MRS. X.   But when he gets angry, look, he stamps his foot like this. "Those damn girls who can never learn how to make coffee! Blast! That silly idiot hasn't trimmed the lamp properly!" Then there's a draught under the door and his feet get cold. "Hell, it's freezing, and the damn fools can't even keep the stove going!" [*She rubs the sole of one slipper against the instep of the other. Miss Y. roars with laughter.*]

MRS. X.   And then he comes home and has to hunt for his slippers, which Mary has pushed under the bureau . . . Well, perhaps it's not right to make fun of one's husband like this. He's sweet anyhow, and a good, dear husband. You ought to have had a husband like him, Amelia. What are you laughing at? What is it? Eh? And, you see, I know he is faithful to me. Yes, I know it. He told me himself—what *are* you giggling at?—that while I was on tour in Norway that horrible Frederica came and tried to seduce him. Can you imagine anything more abominable? [*Pause.*] I'd have scratched her eyes out if she had come around while I was at home. [*Pause.*] I'm glad Bob told me about it himself, so I didn't just hear it from gossip. [*Pause.*] And, as a matter of fact, Frederica wasn't the only one. I can't think why, but all the women in the Company seem to be crazy about my husband. They must think his position gives him some say in who is engaged at the Theatre. Perhaps you have run after him yourself? I don't trust you very far, but I know he has never been attracted by you, and you always seemed to have some sort of grudge against him, or so I felt.

Pause. They look at one another guardedly.

MRS. X.   Do come and spend Christmas Eve with us tonight, Amelia—just to show that you're not offended with us, or anyhow not with me. I don't know why, but it seems specially unpleasant not to be friends with you. Perhaps it's because I did get in your way that time . . . [*slowly*] or—I don't know—really, I don't know at all why it is.

Pause. Miss Y. gazes curiously at Mrs. X.

MRS. X.   [*thoughtfully*]   It was so strange when we were getting to know one another. Do you know, when we first met, I was frightened of you, so frightened I didn't dare let you out of my sight. I arranged all my goings and comings to be near you. I dared not be your enemy, so I became your friend. But when you came to our home, I always had an uneasy feeling, because I saw my husband didn't like you, and that irritated me—like when a dress doesn't fit. I did all I could to make him be nice to you, but it was no good—until you went and got engaged. Then you became such tremendous friends that at first it looked as if you only dared show your real feelings then—when you were safe. And then, let me see, how was it after that? I wasn't jealous—that's queer. And I remember at the christening, when you were the godmother, I told him to kiss you. He did, and you were so upset . . . As a matter of fact I didn't notice that then . . . I didn't think about it afterwards either . . . I've never thought about it—until *now!* [*Rises abruptly.*] Why don't you say something? You haven't said a word all this time. You've just let me go on talking. You have sat there with your eyes drawing all these thoughts out of me—they were there in me like silk in a cocoon—thoughts . . . Mistaken thoughts? Let me think. Why did you break off your engagement? Why did you never come to our house after that? Why don't you want to come to us tonight?

Miss Y. makes a motion, as if about to speak.

MRS. X.   No. You don't need to say anything, for now I see it all. That was why—and why—and why. Yes. Yes, that's why it was. Yes, yes, all the pieces fit together now. That's it. I won't sit at the same table as you. [*Moves her things to the other table.*] That's why I have to embroider tulips, which I loathe, on his slippers—because you liked tulips. [*Throws the slippers on the floor.*] That's why we have to spend the summer on the lake—because you couldn't bear the seaside. That's why my son had to be called Eskil—because it was your father's name. That's why I had to wear your colours, read your books, eat the dishes you liked, drink your drinks—your chocolate, for instance. That's why—oh my God, it's terrible to think of, terrible! Everything, everything came to me from you—even your passions. Your soul bored into mine like a worm into an apple, and ate and ate and burrowed and burrowed, till nothing was left but the skin and a little black mould. I wanted to fly from you, but I couldn't. You were there like a snake, your black eyes fascinating me. When I spread my wings, they only dragged me down. I lay in the water with my feet tied together, and the harder I worked my arms, the deeper I sank—down, down, till I reached the bottom, where you lay in waiting like a giant crab to catch me in your claws—and now here I am. Oh how I hate you! I hate you, I hate you! And you just go on sitting there, silent, calm, indifferent, not caring whether the moon is new or full, if it's Christmas or New Year, if other people are happy or unhappy. You don't know how to hate or to love. You just sit there without moving—like a cat at a mouse-hole. You can't drag your prey out, you can't chase it, but you can out-stay it. Here you sit in your corner—you know they call it the rat-trap after you—reading the papers to see if anyone's ruined or wretched or been thrown out of the Company. Here you sit sizing up your victims and weighing your chances—like a pilot his shipwrecks for the salvage. [*Pause.*]Poor Amelia! Do you know, I couldn't be more sorry for you. I know you are miserable, miserable like some wounded creature, and vicious because you are wounded. I can't be angry with you. I should like to be, but after all you are the small one—and as for your affair with Bob, that doesn't worry me in the least. Why should it matter to me? And if you, or somebody else, taught me to drink chocolate, what's the difference? [*Drinks a spoonful. Smugly.*] Chocolate is very wholesome anyhow. And if I learnt from you how to dress, *tant mieux!*—that only gave me a stronger hold over my husband, and you have lost what I gained. Yes, to judge from various signs, I think you have now lost him. Of course, you meant me to walk out, as you once did, and which you're now regretting. But I won't do that, you may be sure. One shouldn't be narrow-minded, you know. And why should nobody else want what I have? [*Pause.*] Perhaps, my dear, taking everything into consideration, at this moment it is I who am the stronger. You never got anything from me, you just gave away—from yourself. And now, like the thief in the night, when you woke up I had what you had lost. Why was it then that everything you touched became worthless and sterile? You couldn't keep a man's love—for all your tulips and your passions—but I could. You couldn't learn the art of living from your books—but I learnt it. You bore no little Eskil, although that was your father's name. [*Pause.*] And why is it you are silent—everywhere, always silent? Yes, I used to think this was strength, but perhaps it was because you hadn't anything to say, because you couldn't think of anything. [*Rises and picks up the slippers.*] Now I am going home, taking the tulips with me—*your* tulips. You couldn't learn from others, you couldn't bend, and so you broke like a dry stick. I did not. Thank you, Amelia, for all your good lessons. Thank you for teaching my husband how to love. Now I am going home—to love him.

Exit.

GEORGE BERNARD SHAW

1856–1950

Born and raised in Dublin, Ireland, Shaw was the youngest child of an unhappy marriage between his drunken, joke-telling father and his artistic, undomestic mother. He dropped out of school when he was fifteen, briefly worked at an office job in Dublin, and when he was twenty moved to London, where he lived with his mother who helped to support him out of her income as a private music teacher, while he tried unsuccessfully to make his way as a novelist. During his late twenties, he discovered the economic and political theories of Karl Marx and was so inspired by them that he joined a socialist group, known as the Fabians, and quickly became one of their leading spokesmen, lecturing and writing pamphlets to reform local government, to revise the poor laws, to promote trade unions, and to support women's rights. By his mid-thirties, he had also become a well-known art, literary, and music critic through his reviews for various London newspapers, and he had published his first book, *The Quintessence of Ibsenism* (1891), a manifesto celebrating the socially conscious drama of Ibsen. Having proclaimed the English need for a "new drama" of social ideas, Shaw took up playwriting in 1892, and from then until his death wrote forty-seven full-length plays promoting his ideas and opinions about economics, politics, society, morality, religion, science, and literature. Most of his plays are comedies, which feature witty men and equally witty women who engage in lively debates that illustrate Shaw's belief in "free vitality" and the "life force" as the primary sources of "creative evolution" within human beings and their social institutions. Among his best-known plays are *Candida* (1895), *Man and Superman* (1903), *Major Barbara* (1905), *Heartbreak House* (1919), and *St. Joan* (1923).

Shaw expounded his views not only in his plays but also in prefaces that he wrote for the published versions of his plays. By means of these prefaces, which were sometimes as long as the plays themselves, Shaw used his incisive prose style to explicate his characters, plots, and themes, as well as to gain a wider audience for his ideas than was possible in the theater alone. In his lengthy "Preface to *Major Barbara*," for example, Shaw provides a detailed historical and philosophical rationale for "the gospel of Andrew Undershaft," as well as a sustained attack on "the weaknesses of the Salvation Army" and of "Popular Christianity" in meeting the needs of "real life." Copies of the "Preface to *Major Barbara*" may be purchased from Oxford University Press or it may be located in Volume 3 of the Definitive Edition of Bernard Shaw's *Collected Plays with Their Prefaces*, Dodd, Mead & Company (1975).

Major Barbara
A Discussion in Three Acts

CHARACTERS

SIR ANDREW UNDERSHAFT
LADY BRITOMART UNDERSHAFT, his wife
BARBARA, his elder daughter, a Major in the Salvation Army
SARAH, his youngest daughter
STEPHEN, his son
ADOPLPHUS CUSINS, a professor of Greek in love with Barbara
CHARLES LOMAX, young-man-about-town, engaged to Sarah
MORRISON, Lady Britomart's butler
BRONTERRE O'BRIEN ("SNOBBY") PRICE, a cobbler-carpenter down on his luck
MRS. ROMOLA ("RUMMY") MITCHENS, a worn-out lady who relies on the Salvation
   Army
JENNY HILL, a young Salvation Army worker
PETER SHIRLEY, an unemployed coal-broker
BILL WALKER, a bully
MRS. BAINES, Commissioner in the Salvation Army
BILTON, a foreman at Perivale St. Andrews

*Scene: The action of the play occurs within several days in January, 1906. ACT 1: The
library of Lady Britomart's house in Wilton Crescent, a fashionable London suburb. ACT
2: The yard of the Salvation Army shelter in West Ham, an industrial suburb in London's
East End. ACT 3: The library in Lady Britomart's house; a parapet overlooking Perivale
St. Andrews, a region in Middlesex northwest of London.*

ACT I

*It is after dinner in January 1906, in the library in Lady Britomart Undershaft's house in
Wilton Crescent. A large and comfortable settee is in the middle of the room, upholstered
in dark leather. A person sitting on it (it is vacant at present) would have, on his right,
Lady Britomart's writing table, with the lady herself busy at it; a smaller writing table
behind him on his left; the door behind him on Lady Britomart's side; and a window with a
window seat directly on his left. Near the window is an armchair.*

*Lady Britomart is a woman of fifty or thereabouts, well dressed and yet careless of
her dress, well bred and quite reckless of her breeding, well mannered and yet appall-
ingly outspoken and indifferent to the opinion of her interlocutors, amiable and yet
peremptory, arbitrary, and high-tempered to the last bearable degree, and withal a very
typical managing matron of the upper class, treated as a naughty child until she grew
into a scolding mother, and finally settling down with plenty of practical ability and*

worldly experience, limited in the oddest way with domestic and class limitations, conceiving the universe exactly as if it were a large house in Wilton Crescent, though handling her corner of it very effectively on that assumption, and being quite enlightened and liberal as to the books in the library, the pictures on the walls, the music in the portfolios, and the articles in the papers.

Her son, Stephen, comes in. He is a gravely correct young man under 25, taking himself very seriously, but still in some awe of his mother, from childish habit and bachelor shyness, rather than from any weakness of character.

STEPHEN   Whats the matter?

LADY BRITOMART   Presently, Stephen.

Stephen submissively walks to the settee and sits down. He takes up a Liberal weekly called The Speaker.

LADY BRITOMART   Dont begin to read, Stephen. I shall require all your attention.

STEPHEN   It was only while I was waiting—

LADY BRITOMART   Dont make excuses, Stephen.[*He puts down The Speaker*]. Now! [*She finishes her writing; rises; comes to the settee*]. I have not kept you waiting very long, I think.

STEPHEN   Not at all, mother.

LADY BRITOMART   Bring me my cushion. [*He takes the cushion from the chair at the desk and arranges it for her as she sits down on the settee*]. Sit down. [*He sits down and fingers his tie nervously*]. Dont fiddle with your tie, Stephen: there is nothing the matter with it.

STEPHEN   I beg your pardon. [*He fiddles with his watch chain instead*].

LADY BRITOMART   Now are you attending to me, Stephen?

STEPHEN   Of course, mother.

LADY BRITOMART   No: it's not of course. I want something much more than your everyday matter-of-course attention. I am going to speak to you very seriously, Stephen. I wish you would let that chain alone.

STEPHEN   [*hastily relinquishing the chain*]   Have I done anything to annoy you, mother? If so, it was quite unintentional.

LADY BRITOMART   [*astonished*]   Nonsense! [*With some remorse*] My poor boy, did you think I was angry with you?

STEPHEN   What is it, then, mother? You are making me very uneasy.

LADY BRITOMART   [*squaring herself at him rather aggressively*]   Stephen: may I ask how soon you intend to realize that you are a grown-up man, and that I am only a woman?

STEPHEN   [*amazed*]   Only a—

LADY BRITOMART   Dont repeat my words, please: it is a most aggravating habit. You must learn to face life seriously, Stephen. I really cannot bear the whole burden of our family affairs any longer. You must advise me: you must assume the responsibility.

STEPHEN I!

LADY BRITOMART Yes, you, of course. You were 24 last June. Youve been at Harrow and Cambridge. Youve been to India and Japan. You must know a lot of things, now; unless you have wasted your time most scandalously. Well, advise me.

STEPHEN [*much perplexed*] You know I have never interfered in the household—

LADY BRITOMART No: I should think not. I dont want you to order the dinner.

STEPHEN I mean in our family affairs.

LADY BRITOMART Well, you must interfere now; for they are getting quite beyond me.

STEPHEN [*troubled*] I have thought sometimes that perhaps I ought; but really, mother, I know so little about them; and what I do know is so painful! it is so impossible to mention some things to you—[*he stops, ashamed*].

LADY BRITOMART I suppose you mean your father.

STEPHEN [*almost inaudibly*] Yes.

LADY BRITOMART My dear: we cant go on all our lives not mentioning him. Of course you were quite right not to open the subject until I asked you to; but you are old enough now to be taken into my confidence, and to help me to deal with him about the girls.

STEPHEN But the girls are all right. They are engaged.

LADY BRITOMART [*complacently*] Yes: I have made a very good match for Sarah. Charles Lomax will be a millionaire at 35. But that is ten years ahead; and in the meantime his trustees cannot under the terms of his father's will allow him more than £800 a year.

STEPHEN But the will says also that if he increases his income by his own exertions, they may double the increase.

LADY BRITOMART Charles Lomax's exertions are much more likely to decrease his income than to increase it. Sarah will have to find at least another £800 a year for the next ten years; and even then they will be as poor as church mice. And what about Barbara? I thought Barbara was going to make the most brilliant career of all of you. And what does she do? Joins the Salvation Army; discharges her maid; lives on a pound a week; and walks in one evening with a professor of Greek whom she has picked up in the street, and who pretends to be a Salvationist, and actually plays the big drum for her in public because he has fallen head over ears in love with her.

STEPHEN I was certainly rather taken aback when I heard they were engaged. Cusins is a very nice fellow, certainly: nobody would ever guess that he was born in Australia; but—

LADY BRITOMART Oh, Adolphus Cusins will make a very good husband. After all, nobody can say a word against Greek: it stamps a man at once as an educated gentleman. And my family, thank Heaven, is not a pig-headed Tory one. We are Whigs, and believe in liberty. Let snobbish people say what they please: Barbara shall marry, not the man they like, but the man *I* like.

STEPHEN Of course I was thinking only of his income. However, he is not likely to be extravagant.

LADY BRITOMART Dont be too sure of that, Stephen. I know your quiet, simple, refined, poetic people like Adolphus: quite content with the best of everything! They cost more than your extravagant people, who are always as mean as they are second rate. No: Barbara will need at least £2000 a year. You see it means two additional households. Besides, my dear, you must marry soon. I dont approve of the present fashion of philandering bachelors and late marriages; and I am trying to arrange something for you.

STEPHEN It's very good of you, mother; but perhaps I had better arrange that for myself.

LADY BRITOMART Nonsense! you are much too young to begin matchmaking: you would be taken in by some pretty little nobody. Of course I dont mean that you are not to be consulted: you know that as well as I do. [Stephen closes his lips and is silent]. Now dont sulk, Stephen.

STEPHEN I am not sulking, mother. What has all this got to do with—with—with my father?

LADY BRITOMART My dear Stephen: where is the money to come from? It is easy enough for you and the other children to live on my income as long as we are in the same house; but I cant keep four families in four separate houses. You know how poor my father is: he has barely seven thousand a year now; and really, if he were not the Earl of Stevenage, he would have to give up society. He can do nothing for us. He says, naturally enough, that it is absurd that he should be asked to provide for the children of a man who is rolling in money. You see, Stephen, your father must be fabulously wealthy, because there is always a war going on somewhere.

STEPHEN You need not remind me of that, mother. I have hardly ever opened a newspaper in my life without seeing our name in it. The Undershaft torpedo! The Undershaft quick firer! The Undershaft ten inch! The Undershaft disappearing rampart gun! the Undershaft submarine! and now the Undershaft aerial battleship! At Harrow they called me the Woolwich Infant. At Cambridge it was the same. A little brute at King's who was always trying to get up revivals, spoilt my Bible—your first birthday present to me—by writing under my name, "Son and heir to Undershaft and Lazarus, Death and Destruction Dealers: address, Christendom and Judea." But that was not so bad as the way I was kowtowed to everywhere because my father was making millions by selling cannons.

LADY BRITOMART It is not only the cannons, but the war loans that Lazarus arranges under cover of giving credit for the cannons. You know, Stephen, it's perfectly scandalous. Those two men, Andrew Undershaft and Lazarus, positively have Europe under their thumbs. That is why your father is able to behave as he does. He is above the law. Do you think Bismarck or Gladstone or Disraeli could have openly defied every social and moral obligation all their lives as your father has? They simply wouldnt have dared. I asked Gladstone to take it up. I asked The Times to take it up. I asked the Lord Chamberlain to take it up. But it was just like asking them to declare war on the Sultan. They wouldnt. They said they couldnt touch him. I believe they were afraid.

STEPHEN   What could they do? He does not actually break the law.

LADY BRITOMART   Not break the law! He is always breaking the law. He broke the law when he was born: his parents were not married.

STEPHEN   Mother! Is that true?

LADY BRITOMART   Of course it's true: that was why we separated.

STEPHEN   He married without letting you know this!

LADY BRITOMART [*rather taken aback by this inference*]   Oh no. To do Andrew justice, that was not the sort of thing he did. Besides, you know the Undershaft motto: Unashamed. Everybody knew.

STEPHEN   But you said that was why you separated.

LADY BRITOMART   Yes, because he was not content with being a foundling himself: he wanted to disinherit you for another foundling. That was what I couldnt stand.

STEPHEN [*ashamed*]   Do you mean for—for—for

LADY BRITOMART   Dont stammer, Stephen. Speak distinctly.

STEPHEN   But this is so frightful to me, mother. To have to speak to you about such things!

LADY BRITOMART   It's not pleasant for me, either, especially if you are still so childish that you must make it worse by a display of embarrassment. It is only in the middle classes, Stephen, that people get into a state of dumb helpless horror when they find that there are wicked people in the world. In our class, we have to decide what is to be done with wicked people; and nothing should disturb our self-possession. Now ask your question properly.

STEPHEN   Mother: have you no consideration for me? For Heaven's sake either treat me as a child, as you always do, and tell me nothing at all; or tell me everything and let me take it as best I can.

LADY BRITOMART   Treat you as a child! What do you mean? It is most unkind and ungrateful of you to say such a thing. You know I have never treated any of you as children. I have always made you my companions and friends, and allowed you perfect freedom to do and say whatever you liked, so long as you liked what I could approve of.

STEPHEN [*desperately*]   I daresay we have been the very imperfect children of a very perfect mother; but I do beg you to let me alone for once, and tell me about this horrible business of my father wanting to set me aside for another son.

LADY BRITOMART [*amazed*]   Another son! I never said anything of the kind. I never dreamt of such a thing. This is what comes of interrupting me.

STEPHEN   But you said—

LADY BRITOMART [*cutting him short*]   Now be a good boy, Stephen, and listen to me patiently. The Undershafts are descended from a foundling in the parish of St Andrew Undershaft in the city. That was long ago, in the reign of James the First. Well, this foundling was adopted by an armorer and gun-maker. In the course of time the foundling succeeded to the business; and from some notion of gratitude, or some vow or something, he adopted another foundling, and left the business to him. And that foundling did the same. Ever since that, the cannon business has always been left to an adopted foundling named Andrew Undershaft.

STEPHEN   But did they never marry? Were there no legitimate sons?

LADY BRITOMART   Oh yes: they married just as your father did; and they were rich enough to buy land for their own children and leave them well provided for. But they always adopted and trained some foundling to succeed them in the business; and of course they always quarrelled with their wives furiously over it. Your father was adopted in that way; and he pretends to consider himself bound to keep up the tradition and adopt somebody to leave the business to. Of course I was not going to stand that. There may have been some reason for it when the Undershafts could only marry women in their own class, whose sons were not fit to govern great estates. But there could be no excuse for passing over my son.

STEPHEN [*dubiously*]   I am afraid I should make a poor hand of managing a cannon foundry.

LADY BRITOMART   Nonsense! you could easily get a manager and pay him a salary.

STEPHEN   My father evidently had no great opinion of my capacity.

LADY BRITOMART   Stuff, child! you were only a baby; it had nothing to do with your capacity. Andrew did it on principle, just as he did every perverse and wicked thing on principle. When my father remonstrated, Andrew actually told him to his face that history tells us of only two successful institutions: one the Undershaft firm, and the other the Roman Empire under the Antonines. That was because the Antonine emperors all adopted their successors. Such rubbish! The Stevenages are as good as the Antonines, I hope; and you are a Stevenage. But that was Andrew all over. There you have the man! Always clever and unanswerable when he was defending nonsense and wickedness: always awkward and sullen when he had to behave sensibly and decently!

STEPHEN   Then it was on my account that your home life was broken up, mother. I am sorry.

LADY BRITOMART   Well, dear, there were other differences. I really cannot bear an immoral man. I am not a Pharisee, I hope; and I should not have minded his merely doing wrong things: we are none of us perfect. But your father didnt exactly do wrong things: he said them and thought them: that was what was so dreadful. He really had a sort of religion of wrongness. Just as one doesnt mind men practising immorality so long as they own that they are in the wrong by preaching morality; so I couldnt forgive Andrew for preaching immorality while he practised morality. You would all have grown up without principles, without any knowledge of right and wrong, if he had been in the house. You know, my dear, your father was a very attractive man in some ways. Children did not dislike him; and he took advantage of it to put the wickedest ideas into their heads, and make them quite unmanageable. I did not dislike him myself: very far from it; but nothing can bridge over moral disagreement.

STEPHEN   All this simply bewilders me, mother. People may differ about matters of opinion, or even about religion; but how can they differ about right and wrong? Right is right; and wrong is wrong; and if a man cannot distinguish them properly, he is either a fool or a rascal: thats all.

LADY BRITOMART [*touched*]   Thats my own boy [*she pats his cheek*]! Your father never could answer that: he used to laugh and get out of it under cover of some affectionate nonsense. And now that you understand the situation, what do you advise me to do?

STEPHEN   Well, what can you do?

LADY BRITOMART   I must get the money somehow.

STEPHEN   We cannot take money from him. I had rather go and live in some cheap place like Bedford Square or even Hampstead than take a farthing of his money.

LADY BRITOMART   But after all, Stephen, our present income comes from Andrew.

STEPHEN [*shocked*]   I never knew that.

LADY BRITOMART   Well, you surely didnt suppose your grandfather had anything to give me. The Stevenages could not do everything for you. We gave you social position. Andrew had to contribute something. He had a very good bargain, I think.

STEPHEN [*bitterly*]   We are utterly dependent on him and his cannons, then?

LADY BRITOMART   Certainly not: the money is settled. But he provided it. So you see it is not a question of taking money from him or not: it is simply a question of how much. I dont want any more for myself.

STEPHEN   Nor do I.

LADY BRITOMART   But Sarah does; and Barbara does. That is, Charles Lomax and Adolphus Cusins will cost them more. So I must put my pride in my pocket and ask for it, I suppose. That is your advice, Stephen, is it not?

STEPHEN   No.

LADY BRITOMART [*sharply*]   Stephen!

STEPHEN   Of course if you are determined—

LADY BRITOMART   I am not determined: I ask your advice; and I am waiting for it. I will not have all the responsibility thrown on my shoulders.

STEPHEN [*obstinately*]   I would die sooner than ask him for another penny.

LADY BRITOMART [*resignedly*]   You mean that *I* must ask him. Very well, Stephen: it shall be as you wish. You will be glad to know that your grandfather concurs. But he thinks I ought to ask Andrew to come here and see the girls. After all, he must have some natural affection for them.

STEPHEN   Ask him here!!!

LADY BRITOMART   Do not repeat my words, Stephen. Where else can I ask him?

STEPHEN   I never expected you to ask him at all.

LADY BRITOMART   Now dont tease, Stephen, Come! you see that it is necessary that he should pay us a visit, dont you?

STEPHEN [*reluctantly*]   I suppose so, if the girls cannot do without his money.

LADY BRITOMART   Thank you, Stephen: I knew you would give me the right advice when it was properly explained to you. I have asked your father to come this evening. [*Stephen bounds from his seat*] Dont jump, Stephen: it fidgets me.

STEPHEN [*in utter consternation*]   Do you mean to say that my father is coming here tonight—that he may be here at any moment?

LADY BRITOMART [*looking at her watch*]   I said nine. [*He gasps. She rises*]. Ring the bell, please. [*Stephen goes to the smaller writing table; presses a button on it; and sits at it with his elbows on the table and his head in his hands, outwitted and overwhelmed*]. It is ten minutes to nine yet: and I have to prepare the girls. I asked Charles Lomax and Adolphus to dinner on purpose that they might be here. Andrew had better see them in case he should cherish any delusions as to their being capable of supporting their wives. [*The butler enters: Lady Britomart goes behind the settee to speak to him*]. Morrison: go up to the drawing room and tell everybody to come down here at once. [*Morrison withdraws. Lady Britomart turns to Stephen*]. Now remember, Stephen: I shall need all your countenance and authority. [*He rises and tries to recover some vestige of these attributes*]. Give me a chair, dear. [*He pushes a chair forward from the wall to where she stands, near the smaller writing table. She sits down; and he goes to the armchair, into which he throws himself*]. I dont know how Barbara will take it. Ever since they made her a major in the Salvation Army she has developed a propensity to have her own way and order people about which quite cows me sometimes. It's not ladylike: I'm sure I dont know where she picked it up. Anyhow, Barbara shant bully m e; but still it's just as well that your father should be here before she has time to refuse to meet him or make a fuss. Dont look nervous, Stephen: it will only encourage Barbara to make difficulties. *I* am nervous enough, goodness knows: but I dont shew it.

Sarah and Barbara come in with their respective young men, Charles Lomax and Adolphus Cusins. Sarah is slender, bored, and mundane. Barbara is robuster, jollier, much more energetic. Sarah is fashionably dressed: Barbara is in Salvation Army uniform. Lomax, a young man about town, is like many other young men about town. He is afflicted with a frivolous sense of humor which plunges him at the most inopportune moments into paroxysms of imperfectly suppressed laughter. Cusins is a spectacled student, slight, thin haired, and sweet voiced, with a more complex form of Lomax's complaint. His sense of humor is intellectual and subtle, and is complicated by an appalling temper. The lifelong struggle of a benevolent temperament and a high conscience against impulses of inhuman ridicule and fierce impatience has set up a chronic strain which has visibly wrecked his constitution. He is a most implacable, determined, tenacious, intolerant person who by mere force of character presents himself as—and indeed actually is—considerate, gentle, explanatory, even mild and apologetic, capable possibly of murder, but not of cruelty or coarseness. By the operation of some instinct which is not merciful enough to blind him with the illusions of love, he is obstinately bent on marrying Barbara. Lomax likes Sarah and thinks it will be rather a lark to marry her. Consequently he has not attempted to resist Lady Britomart's arrangements to that end.

All four look as if they had been having a good deal of fun in the drawing room. The girls enter first, leaving the swains outside. Sarah comes to the settee. Barbara comes in after her and stops at the door.

BARBARA   Are Cholly and Dolly to come in?

LADY BRITOMART [*forcibly*]   Barbara: I will not have Charles called Cholly: the vulgarity of it positively makes me ill.

BARBARA   It's all right, mother: Cholly is quite correct nowadays. Are they to come in?

LADY BRITOMART   Yes, if they will behave themselves.

BARBARA [*through the door*]   Come in, Dolly; and behave yourself.

Barbara comes to her mother's writing table. Cusins enters smiling, and wanders towards Lady Britomart.

SARAH [*calling*]   Come in, Cholly. [*Lomax enters, controlling his features very imperfectly, and places himself vaguely between Sarah and Barbara*].

LADY BRITOMART [*peremptorily*]   Sit down, all of you. [*They sit. Cusins crosses to the window and seats himself there. Lomax takes a chair. Barbara sits at the writing table and Sarah on the settee*]. I dont in the least know what you are laughing at, Adolphus. I am surprised at you, though I expected nothing better from Charles Lomax.

CUSINS [*in a remarkably gentle voice*]   Barbara has been trying to teach me the West Ham Salvation March.

LADY BRITOMART   I see nothing to laugh at in that; nor should you if you are really converted.

CUSINS [*sweetly*]   You were not present. It was really funny, I believe.

LOMAX   Ripping.

LADY BRITOMART   Be quiet, Charles. Now listen to me, children. Your father is coming here this evening.

General stupefaction. Lomax, Sarah, and Barbara rise; Sarah scared, and Barbara amused and expectant.

LOMAX [*remonstrating*]   Oh I say!

LADY BRITOMART   You are not called on to say anything, Charles.

SARAH   Are you serious, mother?

LADY BRITOMART   Of course I am serious. It is on your account, Sarah, and also on Charles's. [*Silence. Sarah sits, with a shrug. Charles looks painfully unworthy*]. I hope you are not going to object, Barbara.

BARBARA   I! why should I? My father has a soul to be saved like anybody else.

He's quite welcome as far as I am concerned. [*She sits on the table, and softly whistles 'Onward Christian Soldiers'*].

LOMAX [*still remonstrant*]   But really, dont you know! Oh I say!

LADY BRITOMART [*frigidly*]   What do you wish to convey, Charles?

LOMAX   Well, you must admit that this is a bit thick.

LADY BRITOMART [*turning with ominous suavity to Cusins*]   Adolphus: you are a professor of Greek. Can you translate Charles Lomax's remarks into reputable English for us?

CUSINS [*cautiously*]   If I may say so, Lady Brit, I think Charles has rather happily expressed what we all feel. Homer, speaking of Autolycus, uses the same phrase. πυκινὸν δόμον ἐλθῖν means a bit thick.

LOMAX [*handsomely*]   Not that I mind, you know, if Sarah dont. [*He sits*].

LADY BRITOMART [*crushingly*]   Thank you. Have I your permission, Adolphus, to invite my own husband to my own house?

CUSINS [*gallantly*]   You have my unhesitating support in everything you do.

LADY BRITOMART   Tush! Sarah: have you nothing to say?

SARAH   Do you mean that he is coming regularly to live here?

LADY BRITOMART   Certainly not. The spare room is ready for him if he likes to stay for a day or two and see a little more of you; but there are limits.

SARAH   Well, he cant eat us, I suppose. *I* dont mind.

LOMAX [*chuckling*]   I wonder how the old man will take it.

LADY BRITOMART   Much as the old woman will, no doubt, Charles.

LOMAX [*abashed*]   I didnt mean—at least—

LADY BRITOMART   You didnt think, Charles. You never do; and the result is, you never mean anything. And now please attend to me, children. Your father will be quite a stranger to us.

LOMAX   I suppose he hasnt seen Sarah since she was a little kid.

LADY BRITOMART   Not since she was a little kid, Charles, as you express it with that elegance of diction and refinement of thought that seem never to desert you. Accordingly—er—[*impatiently*] Now I have forgotten what I was going to say. That comes of your provoking me to be sarcastic, Charles. Adolphus: you will kindly tell me where I was.

CUSINS [*sweetly*]   You were saying that as Mr Undershaft has not seen his children since they were babies, he will form his opinion of the way you have brought them up from their behavior tonight, and that therefore you wish us all to be particularly careful to conduct ourselves well, especially Charles.

LADY BRITOMART [*with emphatic approval*]   Precisely.

LOMAX   Look here, Dolly: Lady Brit didnt say that.

LADY BRITOMART [*vehemently*]   I did, Charles. Adolphus's recollection is perfectly correct. It is most important that you should be good; and I do beg you for once not to pair off into opposite corners and giggle and whisper while I am speaking to your father.

BARBARA   All right, mother. We'll do you credit. [*She comes off the table, and sits in her chair with ladylike elegance*].

LADY BRITOMART Remember, Charles, that Sarah will want to feel proud of you instead of ashamed of you.

LOMAX Oh I say! theres nothing to be exactly proud of, dont you know.

LADY BRITOMART Well, try and look as if there was.

Morrison, pale and dismayed, breaks into the room in unconcealed disorder.

MORRISON Might I speak a word to you, my lady?

LADY BRITOMART Nonsense! Shew him up.

MORRISON Yes, my lady. [*He goes*].

LOMAX Does Morrison know who it is?

LADY BRITOMART Of course. Morrison has always been with us.

LOMAX It must be a regular corker for him, dont you know.

LADY BRITOMART Is this a moment to get on my nerves, Charles, with your outrageous expressions?

LOMAX But this is something out of the ordinary, really—

MORRISON [*at the door*] The—er—Mr Undershaft. [*He retreats in confusion*].

Andrew Undershaft comes in. All rise. Lady Britomart meets him in the middle of the room behind the settee.

Andrew is, on the surface, a stoutish, easygoing elderly man, with kindly patient manners, and an engaging simplicity of character. But he has a watchful, deliberate, waiting, listening face, and formidable reserves of power, both bodily and mental, in his capacious chest and long head. His gentleness is partly that of a strong man who has learnt by experience that his natural grip hurts ordinary people unless he handles them very carefully, and partly the mellowness of age and success. He is also a little shy in his present very delicate situation.

LADY BRITOMART Good evening, Andrew.

UNDERSHAFT How d'ye do, my dear.

LADY BRITOMART You look a good deal older.

UNDERSHAFT [*apologetically*] I am somewhat older. [*Taking her hand with a touch of courtship*] Time has stood still with you.

LADY BRITOMART [*throwing away his hand*] Rubbish! This is your family.

UNDERSHAFT [*surprised*] Is it so large? I am sorry to say my memory is failing very badly in some things. [*He offers his hand with paternal kindness to Lomax*].

LOMAX [*jerkily shaking his hand*] Ahdedoo.

UNDERSHAFT I can see you are my eldest. I am very glad to meet you again, my boy.

LOMAX [*remonstrating*] No, but look here dont you know—[*Overcome*] Oh I say!

LADY BRITOMART [*recovering from momentary speechlessness*] Andrew: do you mean to say that you dont remember how many children you have?

UNDERSHAFT Well, I am afraid I—. They have grown so much—er. Am I making any ridiculous mistake? I may as well confess: I recollect only one son. But so many things have happened since, of course—er—

LADY BRITOMART [*decisively*]   Andrew: you are talking nonsense. Of course you have only one son.

UNDERSHAFT   Perhaps you will be good enough to introduce me, my dear.

LADY BRITOMART   That is Charles Lomax, who is engaged to Sarah.

UNDERSHAFT   My dear sir, I beg your pardon.

LOMAX   Notatall. Delighted, I assure you.

LADY BRITOMART   This Stephen.

UNDERSHAFT [*bowing*]   Happy to make your acquaintance. Mr. Stephen. Then [*going to Cusins*] you must be my son. [*Taking Cusins' hands in his*] How are you, my young friend? [*To Lady Britomart*] He is very like you, my love.

CUSINS   You flatter me, Mr Undershaft, My name is Cusins: engaged to Barbara [*Very explicitly*] That is Major Barbara Undershaft, of the Salvation Army. That is Sarah, your second daughter. This is Stephen Undershaft, your son.

UNDERSHAFT   My dear Stephen, I beg your pardon.

STEPHEN   Not at all.

UNDERSHAFT   Mr Cusins: I am much indebted to you for explaining so precisely. [*Turning to Sarah*] Barbara, my dear—

SARAH [*prompting him*]   Sarah.

UNDERSHAFT   Sarah, of course. [*They shake hands. He goes over to Barbara*] Barbara—I am right this time, I hope?

BARBARA   Quite right. [*They shake hands*].

LADY BRITOMART [*resuming command*]   Sit down, all of you. Sit down, Andrew. [*She comes forward and sits on the settee. Cusins also brings his chair forward on her left. Barbara and Stephen resume their seats. Lomax gives his chair to Sarah and goes for another*].

UNDERSHAFT   Thank you, my love.

LOMAX [*conversationally, as he brings a chair forward between the writing table and the settee, and offers it to Undershaft*]   Takes you some time to find out exactly where you are, dont it?

UNDERSHAFT [*accepting the chair, but remaining standing*]   That is not what embarrasses me, Mr Lomax. My difficulty is that if I play the part of a father I shall produce the effect of an intrusive stranger; and if I play the part of a discreet stranger, I may appear a callous father.

LADY BRITOMART   There is no need for you to play any part at all, Andrew. You had much better be sincere and natural.

UNDERSHAFT [*submissively*]   Yes, my dear: I daresay that will be best. [*He sits down comfortably*]. Well, here I am. Now what can I do for you all?

LADY BRITOMART   You need not do anything, Andrew. You are one of the family. You can sit with us and enjoy yourself.

A painfully conscious pause. Barbara makes a face at Lomax, whose too long suppressed mirth immediately explodes in agonized neighings.

LADY BRITOMART [*outraged*]   Charles Lomax: if you can behave yourself, behave yourself. If not, leave the room.

LOMAX   I'm awfully sorry, Lady Brit; but really you know, upon my soul! [*He sits on the settee between Lady Britomart and Undershaft, quite overcome*].

BARBARA   Why dont you laugh if you want to, Cholly? It's good for your inside.

LADY BRITOMART   Barbara: you have had the education of a lady. Please let your father see that; and dont talk like a street girl.

UNDERSHAFT   Never mind me, my dear. As you know, I am not a gentleman; and I was never educated.

LOMAX [*encouragingly*]   Nobody'd know it, I assure you. You look all right, you know.

CUSINS   Let me advise you to study Greek, Mr Undershaft. Greek scholars are privileged men. Few of them know Greek; and none of them know anything else; but their position is unchallengeable. Other languages are the qualifications of waiters and commercial travellers: Greek is to a man of position what the hallmark is to silver.

BARBARA   Dolly: dont be insincere. Cholly: fetch your concertina and play something for us.

LOMAX [*jumps up eagerly, but checks himself to remark doubtfully to Undershaft*]   Perhaps that sort of thing isnt in your line, eh?

UNDERSHAFT   I am particularly fond of music.

LOMAX [*delighted*]   Are you? Then I'll get it. [*He goes upstairs for the instrument*].

UNDERSHAFT   Do you play, Barbara?

BARBARA   Only the tambourine. But Cholly's teaching me the concertina.

UNDERSHAFT   Is Cholly also a member of the Salvation Army?

BARBARA   No: he says it's bad form to be a dissenter. But I dont despair of Cholly. I made him come yesterday to a meeting at the dock gates, and take the collection in his hat.

UNDERSHAFT [*looks whimsically at his wife*]!!

LADY BRITOMART   It is not my doing, Andrew. Barbara is old enough to take her own way. She has no father to advise her.

BARBARA   Oh yes she has. There are no orphans in the Salvation Army.

UNDERSHAFT   Your father there has a great many children and plenty of experience, eh?

BARBARA [*looking at him with quick interest and nodding*]   Just so. How did you come to understand that? [*Lomax is heard at the door trying the concertina*].

LADY BRITOMART   Come in, Charles. Play us something at once.

LOMAX   Righto! [*He sits down in his former place, and preludes*].

UNDERSHAFT   One moment, Mr. Lomax. I am rather interested in the Salvation Army. Its motto might be my own: Blood and Fire.

LOMAX [*shocked*]   But not your sort of blood and fire, you know.

UNDERSHAFT   My sort of blood cleanses: my sort of fire purifies.

BARBARA   So do ours. Come down tomorrow to my shelter—the West Ham shelter—and see what we're doing. We're going to march to a great meeting in the Assembly Hall at Mile End. Come and see the shelter and then march with us: it will do you a lot of good. Can you play anything?

UNDERSHAFT In my youth I earned pennies, and even shillings occasionally, in the streets and in public parlors by my natural talent for stepdancing. Later on, I became a member of the Undershaft orchestral society, and performed passably on the tenor trombone.

LOMAX [scandalized—putting down the concertina] Oh I say!

BARBARA Many a sinner has played himself into heaven on the trombone, thanks to the Army.

LOMAX [to Barbara, still rather shocked] Yes; but what about the cannon business, dont you know? [To Undershaft] Getting into heaven is not exactly in your line, is it?

LADY BRITOMART Charles!!!

LOMAX Well; but it stands to reason, dont it? The cannon business may be necessary and all that: we cant get on without cannons; but it isnt right, you know. On the other hand, there may be a certain amount of tosh about the Salvation Army—I belong to the Established Church myself—but still you cant deny that it's religion; and you cant go against religion, can you? At least unless youre downright immoral, dont you know.

UNDERSHAFT You hardly appreciate my position, Mr Lomax—

LOMAX [hastily] I'm not saying anything against you personally—

UNDERSHAFT Quite so, quite so. But consider for a moment. Here I am, a profiteer in mutilation and murder. I find myself in a specially amiable humor just now because, this morning, down at the foundry, we blew twenty-seven dummy soldiers into fragments with a gun which formerly destroyed only thirteen.

LOMAX [leniently] Well, the more destructive war becomes, the sooner it will be abolished, eh?

UNDERSHAFT Not at all. The more destructive war becomes the more fascinating we find it. No, Mr Lomax: I am obliged to you for making the usual excuse for my trade; but I am not ashamed of it. I am not one of those men who keep their morals and their business in water-tight compartments. All the spare money my trade rivals spend on hospitals, cathedrals, and other receptacles for conscience money, I devote to experiments and researches in improved methods of destroying life and property. I have always done so; and I always shall. Therefore your Christmas card moralities of peace on earth and goodwill among men are of no use to me. Your Christianity, which enjoins you to resist not evil, and to turn the other cheek, would make me a bankrupt. My morality—my religion—must have a place for cannons and torpedoes in it.

STEPHEN [coldly—almost sullenly] You speak as if there were half a dozen moralities and religions to choose from, instead of one true morality and one true religion.

UNDERSHAFT For me there is only one true morality; but it might not fit you, as you do not manufacture aerial battleships. There is only one true morality for every man; but every man has not the same true morality.

LOMAX [*overtaxed*] Would you mind saying that again? I didnt quite follow it.

CUSINS It's quite simple. As Euripides says, one man's meat is another man's poison morally as well as physically.

UNDERSHAFT Precisely.

LOMAX Oh, that! Yes, yes, yes. True. True.

STEPHEN In other words, some men are honest and some are scoundrels.

BARBARA Bosh! There are no scoundrels.

UNDERSHAFT Indeed? Are there any good men?

BARBARA No. Not one. There are neither good men nor scoundrels: there are just children of one Father; and the sooner they stop calling one another names the better. You neednt talk to me: I know them. Ive had scores of them through my hands: scoundrels, criminals, infidels, philanthropists, missionaries, county councillors, all sorts. Theyre all just the same sort of sinner; and theres the same salvation ready for them all.

UNDERSHAFT May I ask have you ever saved a maker of cannons?

BARBARA No. Will you let me try?

UNDERSHAFT Well, I will make a bargain with you. If I go to see you tomorrow in your Salvation Shelter, will you come the day after to see me in my cannon works?

BARBARA Take care. It may end in your giving up the cannons for the sake of the Salvation Army.

UNDERSHAFT Are you sure it will not end in your giving up the Salvation Army for the sake of the cannons?

BARBARA I will take my chance of that.

UNDERSHAFT And I will take my chance of the other. [*They shake hands on it*]. Where is your shelter?

BARBARA In West Ham. At the sign of the cross. Ask anybody in Canning Town. Where are your works?

UNDERSHAFT In Perivale St Andrews. At the sign of the sword. Ask anybody in Europe.

LOMAX Hadnt I better play something?

BARBARA Yes. Give us Onward, Christian Soldiers.

LOMAX Well, thats rather a strong order to begin with, dont you know. Suppose I sing Thourt passing hence, my brother. It's much the same tune.

BARBARA It's too melancholy. You get saved, Cholly; and youll pass hence, my brother, without making such a fuss about it.

LADY BRITOMART Really, Barbara, you go on as if religion were a pleasant subject. Do have some sense of propriety.

UNDERSHAFT I do not find it an unpleasant subject, my dear. It is the only one that capable people really care for.

LADY BRITOMART [*looking at her watch*] Well, if you are determined to have it, I insist on having it in a proper and respectable way. Charles: ring for prayers. *General amazement. Stephen rises in dismay.*

LOMAX [*rising*] Oh I say!

UNDERSHAFT [*rising*] I am afraid I must be going.

LADY BRITOMART You cannot go now, Andrew: it would be most improper. Sit down. What will the servants think?

UNDERSHAFT My dear: I have conscientious scruples. May I suggest a compromise? If Barbara will conduct a little service in the drawing room, with Mr Lomax as organist, I will attend it willingly. I will even take part, if a trombone can be procured.

LADY BRITOMART Dont mock, Andrew.

UNDERSHAFT [*shocked—to Barbara*] You dont think I am mocking, my love, I hope.

BARBARA No, of course not; and it wouldnt matter if you were: half the Army came to their first meeting for a lark. [*Rising*] Come along. [*She throws her arm round her father and sweeps him out, calling to the others from the threshold*] Come, Dolly. Come, Cholly.

Cusins rises.

LADY BRITOMART I will not be disobeyed by everybody. Adolphus: sit down. [*He does not*]. Charles: you may go. You are not fit for prayers: you cannot keep your countenance.

LOMAX Oh I say! [*He goes out*].

LADY BRITOMART [*continuing*] But you, Adolphus, can behave yourself if you choose to. I insist on your staying.

CUSINS My dear Lady Brit: there are things in the family prayer book that I couldnt bear to hear you say.

LADY BRITOMART What things, pray?

CUSINS Well, you would have to say before all the servants that we have done things we ought not to have done, and left undone things we ought to have done, and that there is no health in us. I cannot bear to hear you doing yourself such an injustice, and Barbara such an injustice. As for myself, I flatly deny it: I have done my best. I shouldnt dare to marry Barbara—I couldnt look you in the face—if it were true. So I must go to the drawing room.

LADY BRITOMART [*offended*] Well, go. [*He starts for the door*]. And remember this, Adolphus [*he turns to listen*]: I have a very strong suspicion that you went to the Salvation Army to worship Barbara and nothing else. And I quite appreciate the very clever way in which you systematically humbug me. I have found you out. Take care Barbara doesnt. Thats all.

CUSINS [*with unruffled sweetness*] Dont tell on me. [*He steals out*].

LADY BRITOMART   Sarah: if you want to go, go. Anything's better than to sit there as if you wished you were a thousand miles away.

SARAH [*languidly*]   Very well, mamma. [*She goes*].

Lady Britomart, with a sudden flounce, gives way to a little gust of tears.

STEPHEN [*going to her*]   Mother: whats the matter?

LADY BRITOMART [*swishing away her tears with her handkerchief*]   Nothing! Foolishness. You can go with him, too, if you like, and leave me with the servants.

STEPHEN   Oh, you mustnt think that, mother. I—I dont like him.

LADY BRITOMART   The others do. That is the injustice of a woman's lot. A woman has to bring up her children; and that means to restrain them, to deny them things they want, to set them tasks, to punish them when they do wrong, to do all the unpleasant things. And the father, who has nothing to do but pet them and spoil them, comes in when all her work is done and steals their affection from her.

STEPHEN   He has not stolen our affection from you. It is only curiosity.

LADY BRITOMART [*violently*]   I wont be consoled, Stephen. There is nothing the matter with me. [*She rises and goes towards the door*].

STEPHEN   Where are you going, mother?

LADY BRITOMART   To the drawing room, of course [*She goes out. Onward, Christian Soldiers, on the concertina, with tambourine accompaniment, is heard when the door opens*]. Are you coming, Stephen?

STEPHEN   No. Certainly not. [*She goes. He sits down on the settee, with compressed lips and an expression of strong dislike*].

ACT II

The yard of the West Ham shelter of the Salvation Army is a cold place on a January morning. The building itself, an old warehouse, is newly whitewashed. Its gabled end projects into the yard in the middle, with a door on the ground floor, and another in the loft above it without any balcony or ladder, but with a pulley rigged over it for hoisting sacks. Those who come from this central gable end into the yard have the gateway leading to the street on their left, with a stone horse-trough just beyond it, and, on the right, a penthouse shielding a table from the weather. There are forms at the table; and on them are seated a man and a woman, both much down on their luck, finishing a meal of bread (one thick slice each, with margarine and golden syrup) and diluted milk.

The man, a workman out of employment, is young, agile, a talker, a poser, sharp enough to be capable of anything in reason except honesty or altruistic considerations of any kind. The woman is a commonplace old bundle of poverty and hard-worn humanity. She looks sixty and is probably forty-five. If they were rich people, gloved and muffed and well wrapped up in furs and overcoats, they would be numbed and miserable; for it is a grind-

ingly cold raw January day; and a glance at the background of grimy warehouses and leaden sky visible over the whitewashed walls of the yard would drive any idle rich person straight to the Mediterranean. But these two, being no more troubled with visions of the Mediterranean than of the moon, and being compelled to keep more of their clothes in the pawnshop, and less on their persons, in winter than in summer, are not depressed by the cold: rather are they stung into vivacity, to which their meal has just now given an almost jolly turn. The man takes a pull at his mug, and then gets up and moves about the yard with his hands deep in his pockets, occasionally breaking into a stepdance.

THE WOMAN   Feel better arter your meal, sir?

THE MAN   No. Call that a meal! Good enough for you, praps; but wot is it to me, an intelligent workin man.

THE WOMAN   Workin man! Wot are you?

THE MAN   Painter.

THE WOMAN [*sceptically*]   Yus, I dessay.

THE MAN   Yus, you dessay! I know. Every loafer that cant do nothink calls isself a painter. Well, I'm a real painter: grainer, finisher, thirty-eight bob a week when I can get it.

THE WOMAN   Then why dont you go and get it?

THE MAN   I'll tell you why. Fust: I'm intelligent—fffff! it's rotten cold here [*he dances a step or two*]—yes: intelligent beyond the station o life into which it has pleased the capitalists to call me; and they dont like a man that sees through em. Second, an intelligent bein needs a doo share of appiness; so I drink somethink cruel when I get the chawnce. Third, I stand by my class and do as little as I can so's to leave arf the job for me fellow workers. Fourth, I'm fly enough to know wots inside the law and wots outside it; and inside it I do as the capitalists do: pinch wot I can lay me ands on. In a proper state of society I am sober, industrious and honest: in Rome, so to speak, I do as the Romans do. Wots the consequence? When trade is bad—and it's rotten bad just now—and the employers az to sack arf their men, they generally start on me.

THE WOMAN   Whats your name?

THE MAN   Price. Bronterre O'Brien Price. Usually called Snobby Price, for short.

THE WOMAN   Snobby's a carpenter, aint it? You said you was a painter.

PRICE   Not that kind of snob, but the genteel sort. I'm too uppish, owing to my intelligence, and my father being a Chartist and a reading, thinking man: a stationer, too. I'm none of your common hewers of wood and drawers of water; and dont you forget it. [*He returns to his seat at the table, and takes up his mug*]. Wots your name?

THE WOMAN   Rummy Mitchens, sir.

PRICE [*quaffing the remains of his milk to her*]   Your elth, Miss Mitchens.

RUMMY [*correcting him*]   Missis Mitchens.

PRICE   Wot! Oh Rummy, Rummy! Respectable married woman, Rummy, gittin rescued by the Salvation Army by pretendin to be a bad un. Same old game!

RUMMY What am I to do? I cant starve. Them Salvation lasses is dear good girls; but the better you are, the worse they likes to think you were before they rescued you. Why shouldnt they av a bit o credit, poor loves? theyre worn to rags by their work. And where would they get the money to rescue us if we was to let on we're no worse than other people? You know what ladies and gentlemen are.

PRICE Thievin swine! Wish I ad their job, Rummy, all the same. Wot does Rummy stand for? Pet name praps?

RUMMY Short for Romola.

PRICE For wot!?

RUMMY Romola. It was out of a new book. Somebody me mother wanted me to grow up like.

PRICE We're companions in misfortune, Rummy. Both on us got names that nobody cawnt pronounce. Consequently I'm Snobby and youre Rummy because Bill and Sally wasnt good enough for our parents. Such is life!

RUMMY Who saved you, Mr Price? Was it Major Barbara?

PRICE No: I come here on my own. I'm going to be Bronterre O'Brien Price, the converted painter. I know wot they like. I'll tell em how I blasphemed and gambled and wopped my poor old mother—

RUMMY [shocked] Used you to beat your mother?

PRICE Not likely. She used to beat me. No matter: you come and listen to the converted painter, and youll hear how she was a pious woman that taught me me prayers at er knee, an how I used to come home drunk and drag her out o bed be er snow white airs, an lam into er with the poker.

RUMMY Thats whats so unfair to us women. Your confessions is just as big lies as ours: you dont tell what you really done no more than us; but you men can tell your lies right out at the meetins and be made much of for it; while the sort o confessions we az to make az to be wispered to one lady at a time. It aint right, spite of all their piety.

PRICE Right! Do you spose the Army'd be allowed if it went and did right? Not much. It combs our air and makes us good little blokes to be robbed and put upon. But I'll play the game as good as any of em. I'll see somebody struck by lightnin, or hear a voice sayin "Snobby Price: where will you spend eternity?" I'll av a time of it, I tell you.

RUMMY You wont be let drink, though.

PRICE I'll take it out in gorspellin, then. I dont want to drink if I can get fun enough any other way.

Jenny Hill, a pale, overwrought, pretty Salvation lass of 18, comes in through the yard gate, leading Peter Shirley, a half hardened, half worn-out elderly man, weak with hunger.

JENNY [supporting him] Come! pluck up. I'll get you something to eat. Youll be all right then.

PRICE [rising and hurrying officiously to take the old man off Jenny's hands] Poor old man! Cheer up, brother: youll find rest and peace and appiness ere. Hurry up with the food, miss: e's fair done. [*Jenny hurries into the shelter*]. Ere, buck up, daddy! she's fetchin y'a thick slice o breadn treacle, an a mug o skyblue. [*He seats him at the corner of the table*].

RUMMY [*gaily*]   Keep up your old art! Never say die!

SHIRLEY   I'm not an old man. I'm only 46. I'm as good as ever I was. The grey patch come in my hair before I was thirty. All it wants is three pennorth o hair dye: am I to be turned on the streets to starve for it? Holy God! Ive worked ten to twelve hours a day since I was thirteen, and paid my way all through; and now am I to be thrown into the gutter and my job given to a young man that can do it no better than me because Ive black hair that goes white at the first change?

PRICE [*cheerfully*]   No good jawrin about it. Youre ony a jumped-up, jerked-off, orspittle-turned-out-incurable of an ole workin man: who cares about you? Eh? Make the thievin swine give you a meal: theyve stole many a one from you. Get a bit o your own back. [*Jenny returns with the usual meal*]. There you are, brother. Awsk a blessin an tuck that into you.

SHIRLEY [*looking at it ravenously but not touching it, and crying like a child*]   I never took anything before.

JENNY [*petting him*]   Come, come! the Lord sends it to you: he wasnt above taking bread from his friends; and why should you be? Besides, when we find you a job you can pay us for it if you like.

SHIRLEY [*eagerly*]   Yes, yes: thats true. I can pay you back: it's only a loan. [*Shivering*] Oh Lord! oh Lord! [*He turns to the table and attacks the meal ravenously*].

JENNY   Well, Rummy, are you more comfortable now?

RUMMY   God bless you, lovey! youve fed my body and saved my soul, havnt you? [*Jenny, touched, kisses her*]. Sit down and rest a bit: you must be ready to drop.

JENNY   I've been going hard since morning. But theres more work than we can do. I mustnt stop.

RUMMY   Try a prayer for just two minutes. Youll work all the better after.

JENNY [*her eyes lighting up*]   Oh isnt it wonderful how a few minutes prayer revives you! I was quite lightheaded at twelve o'clock, I was so tired; but Major Barbara just sent me to pray for five minutes; and I was able to go on as if I had only just begun. [*To Price*] Did you have a piece of bread?

PRICE [*with unction*]   Yes, miss; but Ive got the piece that I value more; and thats the peace that passeth hall hannerstennin.

RUMMY [*fervently*]   Glory Hallelujah!

Bill Walker, a rough customer of about 25, appears at the yard gate and looks malevolently at Jenny.

JENNY   That makes me so happy. When you say that, I feel wicked for loitering here. I must get to work again.

She is hurrying to the shelter, when the new-comer moves quickly up to the door and intercepts her. His manner is so threatening that she retreats as he comes at her truculently, driving her down the yard.

BILL   Aw knaow you. Youre the one that took awy maw girl. Youre the one that set er agen me. Well, I'm gowin to ev er aht. Not that Aw care a carse for er or you: see? Bat Aw'll let er knaow; and Aw'll let you knaow. Aw'm gowing to give her a doin thatll teach er to cat awy from me. Nah in wiv you and tell er to cam aht afore Aw cam in and kick er aht. Tell er Bill Walker wants er. She'll knaow wot thet means; and if she keeps me witin itll be worse. You stop to jawr beck at me; and Aw'll stawt on you: d'ye eah? Theres your wy. In you gow. [*He takes her by the arm and slings her towards the door of the shelter. She falls on her hand and knee. Rummy helps her up again*].

PRICE   [*rising, and venturing irresolutely towards Bill*]   Easy there, mate. She aint doin you no arm.

BILL   Oo are you callin mite? [*Standing over him threateningly*] Youre gowin to stend ap for er, aw yer? Put ap your ends.

RUMMY   [*running indignantly to scold him*]   Oh, you great brute—[*He instantly swings his left hand back against her face. She screams and reels back to the trough, where she sits down, covering her bruised face with her hands and rocking herself and moaning with pain*]

JENNY   [*going to her*]   Oh, God forgive you! How could you strike an old woman like that?

BILL   [*seizing her by the hair so violently that she also screams, and tearing her away from the old woman*]   You Gawd forgimme again an Aw'll Gawd forgive you one on the jawr thetll stop you pryin for a week. [*Holding her and turning fiercely on Price*] Ev you ennything to sy agen it?

PRICE   [*intimidated*]   No, matey: she aint anything to do with me.

BILL   Good job for you! Aw'd pat two meals into you and fawt you with one finger arter, you stawved cur. [*To Jenny*] Nah are you gowin to fetch aht Mog Ebbijem; or em Aw to knock your fice off you and fetch her meself?

JENNY   [*writhing in his grasp*]   Oh please someone go in and tell Major Barbara— [*she screams again as he wrenches her head down; and Price and Rummy flee into the shelter*].

BILL   You want to gow in and tell your Mijor of me, do you?

JENNY   Oh please dont drag my hair. Let me go.

BILL   Do you or downt you? [*She stifles a scream*]. Yus or nao?

JENNY   God give me strength—

BILL   [*striking her with his fist in the face*]   Gow an shaow her thet, and tell her if she wants one lawk it to cam and interfere with me. [*Jenny, crying with pain, goes into the shed. He goes to the form and addresses the old man*]. Eah: finish your mess; an git aht o maw wy.

SHIRLEY   [*springing up and facing him fiercely, with the mug in his hand*]   You take a liberty with me, and I'll smash you over the face with the mug and cut your eye out. Aint you satisfied—young whelps like you—with takin the bread out o the mouths of your elders that have brought you up and slaved for you, but you must come shovin and cheekin and bullyin in here, where the bread of charity is sickenin in our stummicks?

BILL [*contemptuously, but backing a little*]   Wot good are you, you aold palsy mag? Wot good are you?

SHIRLEY   As good as you and better. I'll do a day's work agen you or any fat young soaker of your age. Go and take my job at Horrockses, where I worked for ten year. They want young men there: they cant afford to keep men over forty-five. Theyre very sorry—give you a character and happy to help you to get anything suited to your years—sure a steady man wont be long out of a job. Well, let em try you . Theyll find the differ. What do you know? Not as much as how to beeyave yourself—layin your dirty fist across the mouth of a respectable woman!

BILL   Downt provowk me to ly it acrost yours: d'ye eah?

SHIRLEY [*with blighting contempt*]   Yes: you like an old man to hit, dont you, when youve finished with the women. I aint seen you hit a young one yet.

BILL [*stung*]   You loy, you aold soupkitchener, you. There was a yang menn eah. Did Aw offer to itt him or did Aw not?

SHIRLEY   Was he starvin or was he not? Was he a man or only a crosseyed thief an a loafer? Would you hit my son-in-law's brother?

BILL   Oo's ee?

SHIRLEY   Todger Fairmile o Balls Pond. Him that won £20 off the Japanese wrastler at the music hall by standin out 17 minutes 4 seconds agen him.

BILL [*sullenly*]   Aw'm nao music awl wrastler. Ken he box?

SHIRLEY   Yes: an you cant.

BILL   Wot! Aw cawnt, cawnt Aw? Wots thet you sy [*threatening him*]

SHIRLEY [*not budging an inch*]   Will you box Todger Fairmile if I put him on to you? Say the word.

BILL [*subsiding with a slouch*]   Aw'll stend ap to enny menn alawv, if he was ten Todger Fairmawls. But Aw dont set ap to be a perfeshnal.

SHIRLEY [*looking down on him with unfathomable disdain*]   You box! Slap an old woman with the back o your hand! You hadnt even the sense to hit her where a magistrate couldnt see the mark of it, you silly young lump of conceit and ignorance. Hit a girl in the jaw and ony make her cry! If Todger Fairmile'd done it, she wouldnt a got up inside o ten minutes, no more than you would if he got on to you. Yah! I'd set about you myself if I had a week's feedin in me instead o two months' starvation. [*He turns his back on him and sits down moodily at the table*].

BILL [*following him and stooping over him to drive the taunt in*]   You loy! youve the bread and treacle in you that you cam eah to beg.

SHIRLEY [*bursting into tears*]   Oh God! it's true: I'm only an old pauper on the scrap heap. [*Furiously*] But youll come to it yourself; and then youll know. Youll come to it sooner than a teetotaller like me, fillin yourself with gin at this hour o the mornin!

BILL   Aw'm nao gin drinker, you oald lawr; bat wen Aw want to give my girl a
        bloomin good awdin Aw lawk to ev a bit o devil in me: see? An eah Aw emm,
        talkin to a rotten aold blawter like you sted o givin her wot for. [*Working
        himself into a rage*] Aw'm gowin in there to fetch her aht. [*He makes vengefully
        for the shelter door*].

SHIRLEY Youre goin to the station on a stretcher, more likely; and they'll take the
        gin and the devil out of you there when they get you inside. You mind what
        youre about: the major here is the Earl o Stevenage's granddaughter.

BILL [*checked*]   Garn!

SHIRLEY Youll see.

BILL [*his resolution oozing*]   Well, Aw aint dan nathin to er.

SHIRLEY Spose she said you did! who'd believe you?

BILL [*very uneasy, skulking back to the corner of the penthouse*]   Gawd! theres no jastice
        in this cantry. To think wot them people can do! Aw'm as good as er.

SHIRLEY Tell her so. It's just what a fool like you would do.

*Barbara, brisk and businesslike, comes from the shelter with a note book, and addresses
herself to Shirley. Bill, cowed, sits down in the corner on a form, and turns his back on
them.*

BARBARA   Good morning.

SHIRLEY [*standing up and taking off his hat*]   Good morning, miss.

BARBARA   Sit down: make yourself at home. [*He hesitates; but she puts a friendly
        hand on his shoulder and makes him obey.*] Now then! since youve made friends
        with us, we want to know all about you. Names and addresses and trades.

SHIRLEY Peter Shirley. Fitter. Chucked out two months ago because I was too
        old.

BARBARA [*not at all surprised*]   Youd pass still. Why didnt you dye your hair?

SHIRLEY I did. Me age come out at a coroner's inquest on me daughter.

BARBARA   Steady?

SHIRLEY Teetotaller. Never out of a job before. Good worker. And sent to the
        knackers like an old horse!

BARBARA   No matter: if you did your part God will do his.

SHIRLEY [*suddenly stubborn*]   My religion's no concern of anybody but myself.

BARBARA [*guessing*]   I know. Secularist?

SHIRLEY [*hotly*]   Did I offer to deny it?

BARBARA   Why should you? My own father's a Secularist, I think. Our Father—
        yours and mine—fulfils himself in many ways; and I daresay he knew what
        he was about when he made a Secularist of you. So buck up, Peter! we can
        always find a job for a steady man like you. [*Shirley, disarmed and a little bewil-
        dered, touches his hat. She turns from him to Bill*]. Whats your name?

BILL [*insolently*]   Wots thet to you?

BARBARA [*calmly making a note*]   Afraid to give his name. Any trade?

BILL   Oo's afride to give is nime? [*Doggedly, with a sense of heroically defying the*

House of Lords in the person of Lord Stevenage] If you want to bring a chawge agen me, bring it. [*She waits, unruffled*]. Moy nime's Bill Walker.

BARBARA [*as if the name were familiar: trying to remember how*] Bill Walker? [*Recollecting*] Oh, I know: youre the man that Jenny Hill was praying for inside just now. [*She enters his name in her note book*].

BILL   Oo's Jenny Ill? And wot call as she to pry for me?

BARBARA   I dont know. Perhaps it was you that cut her lip.

BILL [*defiantly*]   Yus, it was me that cat her lip. Aw aint afride o you .

BARBARA   How could you be, since youre not afraid of God? Youre a brave man, Mr Walker. It takes some pluck to do our work here; but none of us dare lift our hand against a girl like that, for fear of her father in heaven.

BILL [*sullenly*]   I want nan o your kentin jawr. I spowse you think Aw cam eah to beg from you, like this demmiged lot eah. Not me. Aw downt want your bread and scripe and ketlep. Aw dont blieve in your Gawd, no more than you do yourself.

BARBARA [*sunnily apologetic and ladylike, as on a new footing with him*]   Oh, I beg your pardon for putting your name down, Mr Walker. I didnt understand. I'll strike it out.

BILL [*taking this as a slight, and deeply wounded by it*]   Eah! you let maw nime alown. Aint it good enaff to be in your book?

BARBARA [*considering*]   Well, you see, theres no use putting down your name unless I can do something for you, is there? Whats your trade?

BILL [*still smarting*]   Thets nao concern o yours.

BARBARA   Just so. [*Very businesslike*] I'll put you down as [*writing*] the man who— struck—poor little Jenny Hill—in the mouth.

BILL [*rising threateningly*]   See eah. Awve ed enaff o this.

BARBARA [*quite sunny and fearless*]   What did you come to us for?

BILL   Aw cam for maw gel, see? Aw cam to tike her aht o this and to brike er jawr for er.

BARBARA [*complacently*]   You see I was right about your trade. [*Bill, on the point of retorting furiously, finds himself, to his great shame and terror, in danger of crying instead. He sits down again suddenly*]. Whats her name?

BILL [*dogged*]   Er nime's Mog Ebbijem: thets wot her nime is.

BARBARA   Mog Habbijam! Oh, she's gone to Canning Town, to our barracks there.

BILL [*fortified by his resentment of Mog's perfidy*]   Is she? [*Vindictively*] Then Aw'm gowin to Kennintahn arter her. [*He crosses to the gate; hesitates; finally comes back at Barbara*]. Are you loyin to me to git shat o me?

BARBARA   I dont want to get shut of you. I want to keep you here and save your soul. Youd better stay: youre going to have a bad time today, Bill.

BILL   Oo's gowin to give it to me? You, preps?

BARBARA   Someone you dont believe in. But youll be glad afterwards.

BILL [*slinking off*]   Aw'll gow to Kennintahn to be aht o reach o your tangue. [*Suddenly turning on her with intense malice*] And if Aw downt fawnd Mog there, Aw'll cam beck and do two years for you, selp me Gawd if Aw downt!

BARBARA [*a shade kindlier, if possible*]   It's no use, Bill. She's got another bloke.

BILL   Wot!

BARBARA   One of her own converts. He fell in love with her when he saw her with her soul saved, and her face clean, and her hair washed.

BILL [*surprised*]   Wottud she wash it for, the carroty slat? It's red.

BARBARA   It's quite lovely now, because she wears a new look in her eyes with it. It's a pity youre too late. The new bloke has put your nose out of joint, Bill.

BILL   Aw'll put his nowse aht o joint for him. Not that Aw care a carse for er, mawnd thet. But Aw'll teach her to drop me as if Aw was dirt. And Aw'll teach him to meddle with maw judy. Wots iz bleedin nime?

BARBARA   Sergeant Todger Fairmile.

SHIRLEY [*rising with grim joy*]   I'll go with him, miss. I want to see them two meet. I'll take him to the infirmary when it's over.

BILL [*to Shirley, with undissembled misgiving*]   Is thet im you was speakin on?

SHIRLEY   Thats him.

BILL   Im that wrastled in the music awl?

SHIRLEY   The competitions at the National Sportin Club was worth nigh a hundred a year to him. He's gev em up now for religion; so he's a bit fresh for want of the exercise he was accustomed to. He'll be glad to see you. Come along.

BILL   Wots is wight?

SHIRLEY   Thirteen four. [*Bill's last hope expires*].

BARBARA   Go and talk to him, Bill. He'll convert you.

SHIRLEY   He'll convert your head into a mashed potato.

BILL [*sullenly*]   Aw aint afride of im. Aw aint afride of ennybody. Bat e can lick me. She's dan me. [*He sits down moodily on the edge of the horse trough*].

SHIRLEY   You aint goin. I thought not. [*He resumes his seat*].

BARBARA [*calling*]   Jenny!

JENNY [*appearing at the shelter door with a plaster on the corner of her mouth*]   Yes, Major.

BARBARA   Send Rummy Mitchens out to clear away here.

JENNY   I think she's afraid.

BARBARA [*her resemblance to her mother flashing out for a moment*]   Nonsense! she must do as she's told

JENNY [*calling into the shelter*]   Rummy: the Major says you must come.

Jenny comes to Barbara, purposely keeping on the side next Bill, lest he should suppose that she shrank from him or bore malice.

BARBARA   Poor little Jenny! Are you tired? [*Looking at the wounded cheek*] Does it hurt?

JENNY   No: it's all right now. It was nothing.

BARBARA [*critically*]   It was as hard as he could hit, I expect. Poor Bill! You dont feel angry with him, do you?

JENNY   Oh no, no, no: indeed I dont, Major, bless his poor heart! [*Barbara kisses her; and she runs away merrily into the shelter. Bill writhes with an agonizing return of his new and alarming symptoms, but says nothing. Rummy Mitchens comes from the shelter*].

BARBARA [*going to meet Rummy*]   Now Rummy, bustle. Take in those mugs and plates to be washed; and throw the crumbs about for the birds.

Rummy takes the three plates and mugs; but Shirley takes back his mug from her, as there is still some milk left in it.

RUMMY   There aint any crumbs. This aint a time to waste good bread on birds.

PRICE [*appearing at the shelter door*]   Gentleman come to see the shelter, Major. Says he's your father.

BARBARA   All right. Coming [*Snobby goes back into the shelter, followed by Barbara*].

RUMMY [*stealing across to Bill and addressing him in a subdued voice, but with intense conviction*]   I'd av the lor of you, you flat eared pignosed potwalloper, if she'd let me. Youre no gentleman, to hit a lady in the face. [*Bill, with greater things moving in him, takes no notice*].

SHIRLEY [*following her*]   Here! in with you and dont get yourself into more trouble by talking.

RUMMY [*with hauteur*]   I aint ad the pleasure o being hintroduced to you, as I can remember. [*She goes into the shelter with the plates*].

SHIRLEY   Thats the—

BILL [*savagely*]   Downt you talk to me, d'ye eah? You lea me alown, or Aw'll do you a mischief. Aw'm not dirt under your feet, ennywy.

SHIRLEY [*calmly*]   Dont you be afeerd. You aint such prime company that you need expect to be sought after. [*He is about to go into the shelter when Barbara comes out, with Undershaft on her right*].

BARBARA   Oh, there you are, Mr. Shirley! [*Between them*] This is my father: I told you he was a Secularist, didnt I? Perhaps youll be able to comfort one another

UNDERSHAFT [*startled*]   A Secularist! Not the least in the world: on the contrary, a confirmed mystic.

BARBARA   Sorry, I'm sure. By the way, papa, what is your religion? in case I have to introduce you again.

UNDERSHAFT   My religion? Well, my dear, I am a Millionaire. That is my religion.

BARBARA   Then I'm afraid you and Mr Shirley wont be able to comfort one another after all. Youre not a Millionaire, are you, Peter?

SHIRLEY   No; and proud of it.

UNDERSHAFT [*gravely*]   Poverty, my friend, is not a thing to be proud of.

SHIRLEY [*angrily*]   Who made your millions for you? Me and my like. Whats kep us poor? Keepin you rich. I wouldnt have your conscience, not for all your income.

UNDERSHAFT   I wouldnt have your income, not for all your conscience, Mr Shirley. [*He goes to the penthouse and sits down on a form*].

BARBARA [*stopping Shirley adroitly as he is about to retort*]   You wouldnt think he was my father, would you, Peter? Will you go into the shelter and lend the lasses a hand for a while: we're worked off our feet.

SHIRLEY [*bitterly*]   Yes: I'm in their debt for a meal, aint I?

BARBARA   Oh, not because youre in their debt, but for love of them, Peter, for love of them. [*He cannot understand, and is rather scandalized*] There! dont stare at me. In with you; and give that conscience of yours a holiday [*bustling him into the shelter*].

SHIRLEY [*as he goes in*]   Ah! it's a pity you never was trained to use your reason, miss. Youd have been a very taking lecturer on Secularism.

Barbara turns to her father.

UNDERSHAFT   Never mind me, my dear. Go about your work; and let me watch it for a while.

BARBARA   All right.

UNDERSHAFT   For instance, whats the matter with that outpatient over there?

BARBARA [*looking at Bill, whose attitude has never changed, and whose expression of brooding wrath has deepened*]   Oh, we shall cure him in no time. Just watch [*She goes over to Bill and waits. He glances up at her and casts his eyes down again, uneasy, but grimmer than ever*]. It would be nice to just stamp on Mog Habbijam's face, wouldnt it, Bill?

BILL [*starting up from the trough in consternation*]   It's a loy: Aw never said so. [*She shakes her head*]. Oo taold you wot was in moy mawnd?

BARBARA   Only your new friend.

BILL   Wot new friend?

BARBARA   The devil, Bill. When he gets round people they get miserable, just like you.

BILL [*with a heartbreaking attempt at devil-may-care cheerfulness*]   Aw aint miserable. [*He sits down again, and stretches his legs in an attempt to seem indifferent*].

BARBARA   Well, if youre happy, why dont you look happy, as we do?

BILL [*his legs curling back in spite of him*]   Aw'm eppy enaff, Aw tell you. Woy cawnt you lea me alown? Wot ev I dan to you ? Aw aint smashed your fice, ev Aw?

BARBARA [*softly: wooing his soul*]   It's not me thats getting at you, Bill.

BILL   Oo else is it?

BARBARA   Somebody that doesnt intend you to smash women's faces, I suppose. Somebody or something that wants to make a man of you.

BILL [*blustering*]   Mike a menn o me . Aint Aw a menn? eh? Oo sez Aw'm not a menn?

BARBARA   Theres a man in you somewhere, I suppose. But why did he let you hit poor little Jenny Hill? That wasnt very manly of him, was it?

BILL [*tormented*]   Ev dan wiv it, Aw tell you. Chack it. Aw'm sick o your Jenny Ill and er silly little fice.

BARBARA   Then why do you keep thinking about it? Why does it keep coming up against you in your mind? Youre not getting converted, are you?

BILL [*with conviction*]   Not ME. Not lawkly.

BARBARA   Thats right, Bill. Hold out against it. Put out your strength. Dont lets get you cheap. Todger Fairmile said he wrestled for three nights against his salvation harder than he ever wrestled with the Jap at the music hall. He gave in to the Jap when his arm was going to break. But he didnt give in to his salvation until his heart was going to break. Perhaps youll escape that. You havnt any heart, have you?

BILL   Wot d'ye mean? Woy aint Aw got a awt the sime as ennybody else?

BARBARA   A man with a heart wouldnt have bashed poor little Jenny's face, would he?

BILL [*almost crying*]   Ow, will you lea me alown? Ev Aw ever offered to meddle with you, that you cam neggin and provowkin me lawk this? [*He writhes convulsively from his eyes to his toes*].

BARBARA [*with a steady soothing hand on his arm and a gentle voice that never lets him go*]   It's your soul thats hurting you, Bill, and not me. Weve been through it all ourselves. Come with us, Bill. [*He looks wildly round*]. To brave manhood on earth and eternal glory in heaven. [*He is on the point of breaking down*]. Come. [*A drum is heard in the shelter; and Bill, with a gasp, escapes from the spell as Barbara turns quickly. Adolphus enters from the shelter with a big drum*]. Oh! there you are, Dolly. Let me introduce a new friend of mine, Mr Bill Walker. This is my bloke, Bill: Mr Cusins. [*Cusins salutes with his drumstick*].

BILL   Gowin to merry im?

BARBARA   Yes

BILL [*fervently*]   Gawd elp im! Gaw-aw-aw-awd elp im!

BARBARA   Why? Do you think he wont be happy with me?

BILL   Awve aony ed to stend it for a mawnin: e'll ev to stend it for a lawftawm.

CUSINS   That is a frightful reflection, Mr. Walker. But I cant tear myself away from her.

BILL   Well, Aw ken. [*To Barbara*] Eah! do you knaow where Aw'm gowin to, and wot Aw'm gowin to do?

BARBARA   Yes: youre going to heaven; and youre coming back here before the week's out to tell me so.

BILL   You loy. Aw'm gowin to Kennintahn, to spit in Todger Fairmawl's eye. Aw beshed Jenny Ill's fice; an nar Aw'll git me aown fice beshed and cam beck and shaow it to er. Ee'll itt me ardern Aw itt er. Thatll mike us square. [*To Adolphus*] Is thet fair or is it not? Youre a genlmn: you oughter knaow.

BARBARA   Two black eyes wont make one white one, Bill.

BILL   Aw didnt awst you. Cawnt you never keep your mahth shat? Oy awst the genlmn.

CUSINS [*reflectively*]   Yes: I think youre right, Mr Walker. Yes: I should do it. It's curious: it's exactly what an ancient Greek would have done.

BARBARA   But what good will it do?

CUSINS   Well, it will give Mr Fairmile some exercise; and it will satisfy Mr Walker's soul.

BILL   Rot! there aint nao sach a thing as a saoul. Ah kin you tell wevver Awve a saoul or not? You never seen it.

BARBARA   Ive seen it hurting you when you went against it.

BILL   [with compressed aggravation]   If you was maw gel and took the word aht o me mahth lawk thet, Aw'd give you sathink youd feel urtin, Aw would. [To Adolphus] You tike maw tip, mite. Stop er jawr; or youll doy afoah your tawm [With intense expression] Wore aht: thets wot youll be: wore aht. [He goes away through the gate].

CUSINS [looking after him]   I wonder!

BARBARA   Dolly! [indignant, in her mother's manner].

CUSINS   Yes, my dear, it's very wearing to be in love with you. If it lasts, I quite think I shall die young.

BARBARA   Should you mind?

CUSINS   Not at all. [He is suddenly softened, and kisses her over the drum, evidently not for the first time, as people cannot kiss over a big drum without practice. Undershaft coughs].

BARBARA   It's all right, papa, weve not forgotten you. Dolly: explain the place to papa: I havnt time. [She goes busily into the shelter].

Undershaft and Adolphus now have the yard to themselves. Undershaft, seated on a form, and still keenly attentive, looks hard at Adolphus. Adolphus looks hard at him.

UNDERSHAFT   I fancy you guess something of what is in my mind, Mr. Cusins. [Cusins flourishes his drumsticks as if in the act of beating a lively rataplan, but makes no sound.] Exactly so. But suppose Barbara finds you out!

CUSINS   You know, I do not admit that I am imposing on Barbara. I am quite genuinely interested in the views of the Salvation Army. The fact is, I am a sort of collector of religions; and the curious thing is that I find I can believe them all. By the way, have you any religion?

UNDERSHAFT   Yes.

CUSINS   Anything out of the common?

UNDERSHAFT   Only that there are two things necessary to Salvation.

CUSINS [disappointed, but polite]   Ah, the Church Catechism. Charles Lomax also belongs to the Established Church.

UNDERSHAFT   The two things are—

CUSINS   Baptism and—

UNDERSHAFT   No. Money and gunpowder.

CUSINS [surprised, but interested]   That is the general opinion of our governing classes. The novelty is in hearing any man confess it.

UNDERSHAFT   Just so.

CUSINS   Excuse me: is there any place in your religion for honor, justice, truth, love, mercy and so forth?

UNDERSHAFT   Yes: they are the graces and luxuries of a rich, strong, and safe life.

CUSINS   Suppose one is forced to choose between them and money or gunpowder?

UNDERSHAFT   Choose money and gunpowder; for without enough of both you cannot afford the others.

CUSINS   That is your religion?

UNDERSHAFT   Yes.

The cadence of this reply makes a full close in the conversation. Cusins twists his face dubiously and contemplates Undershaft. Undershaft contemplates him.

CUSINS   Barbara wont stand that. You will have to choose between your religion and Barbara.

UNDERSHAFT   So will you, my friend. She will find out that that drum of yours is hollow.

CUSINS   Father Undershaft: you are mistaken: I am a sincere Salvationist. You do not understand the Salvation Army. It is the army of joy, of love, of courage: it has banished the fear and remorse and despair of the old hell-ridden evangelical sects: it marches to fight the devil with trumpet and drum, with music and dancing, with banner and palm, as becomes a sally from heaven by its happy garrison. It picks the waster out of the public house and makes a man of him: it finds a worm wriggling in a back kitchen, and lo! a woman! Men and women of rank too, sons and daughters of the Highest. It takes the poor professor of Greek, the most artificial and self-suppressed of human creatures, from his meal of roots, and lets loose the rhapsodist in him; reveals the true worship of Dionysos to him; sends him down the public street drumming dithyrambs [*he plays a thundering flourish on the drum*].

UNDERSHAFT   You will alarm the shelter.

CUSINS   Oh, they are accustomed to these sudden ecstasies. However, if the drum worries you—[*he pockets the drumsticks; unhooks the drum; and stands it on the ground opposite the gateway*].

UNDERSHAFT   Thank you.

CUSINS   You remember what Euripides says about your money and gunpowder?

UNDERSHAFT   No.

CUSINS [*declaiming*]

One and another
In money and guns may outpass his brother;
And men in their millions float and flow
And seethe with a million hopes as leaven;
And they win their will; or they miss their will;
And their hopes are dead or are pined for still;

> But who'er can know
> As the long days go
> That to live is happy, has found his heaven.

My translation: what do you think of it?

UNDERSHAFT   I think, my friend, that if you wish to know, as the long days go, that to live is happy, you must first acquire money enough for a decent life, and power enough to be your own master.

CUSINS   You are damnably discouraging. [*He resumes his declamation*].

> Is it so hard a thing to see
> That the spirit of God—whate'er it be—
> The law that abides and changes not, ages long,
> The Eternal and Nature-born: these things be strong?
> What else is Wisdom? What of Man's endeavor,
> Or God's high grace so lovely and so great?
> To stand from fear set free? to breathe and wait?
> To hold a hand uplifted over Fate?
> And shall not Barbara be loved for ever?

UNDERSHAFT   Euripides mentions Barbara, does he?

CUSINS   It is a fair translation. The word means Loveliness.

UNDERSHAFT   May I ask—as Barbara's father—how much a year she is to be loved for ever on?

CUSINS   As Barbara's father, that is more your affair than mine. I can feed her by teaching Greek: that is about all.

UNDERSHAFT   Do you consider it a good match for her?

CUSINS [*with polite obstinacy*]   Mr Undershaft: I am in many ways a weak, timid, ineffectual person; and my health is far from satisfactory. But whenever I feel that I must have anything, I get it, sooner or later. I feel that way about Barbara. I dont like marriage: I feel intensely afraid of it; and I dont know what I shall do with Barbara or what she will do with me. But I feel that I and nobody else must marry her. Please regard that as settled.—Not that I wish to be arbitrary; but why should I waste your time in discussing what is inevitable?

UNDERSHAFT   You mean that you will stick at nothing: not even the conversion of the Salvation Army to the worship of Dionysos.

CUSINS   The business of the Salvation Army is to save, not to wrangle about the name of the pathfinder. Dionysos or another: what does it matter?

UNDERSHAFT [*rising and approaching him*]   Professor Cusins: you are a young man after my own heart.

CUSINS   Mr. Undershaft: you are, as far as I am able to gather, a most infernal old rascal; but you appeal very strongly to my sense of ironic humor.

Undershaft mutely offers his hand. They shake.

UNDERSHAFT [*suddenly concentrating himself*]   And now to business.

CUSINS   Pardon me. We are discussing religion. Why go back to such an uninteresting and unimportant subject as business?

UNDERSHAFT   Religion is our business at present, because it is through religion alone that we can win Barbara.

CUSINS   Have you, too, fallen in love with Barbara?

UNDERSHAFT   Yes, with a father's love.

CUSINS   A father's love for a grown-up daughter is the most dangerous of all infatuations. I apologize for mentioning my own pale, coy, mistrustful fancy in the same breath with it.

UNDERSHAFT   Keep to the point. We have to win her; and we are neither of us Methodists.

CUSINS   That doesnt matter. The power Barbara wields here—the power that wields Barbara herself—is not Calvinism, not Presbyterianism, not Methodism—

UNDERSHAFT   Not Greek Paganism either, eh?

CUSINS   I admit that. Barbara is quite original in her religion.

UNDERSHAFT [*triumphantly*]   Aha! Barbara Undershaft would be. Her inspiration comes from within herself.

CUSINS   How do you suppose it got there?

UNDERSHAFT [*in towering excitement*]   It is the Undershaft inheritance. I shall hand on my torch to my daughter. She shall make my converts and preach my gospel—

CUSINS   What! Money and gunpowder!

UNDERSHAFT   Yes, money and gunpowder. Freedom and power. Command of life and command of death.

CUSINS [*urbanely: trying to bring him down to earth*]   This is extremely interesting, Mr. Undershaft. Of course you know that you are mad.

UNDERSHAFT [*with redoubled force*]   And you?

CUSINS   Oh, mad as a hatter. You are welcome to my secret since I have discovered yours. But I am astonished. Can a madman make cannons?

UNDERSHAFT   Would anyone else than a madman make them? And now [*with surging energy*] question for question. Can a sane man translate Euripides?

CUSINS   No.

UNDERSHAFT [*seizing him by the shoulder*]   Can a sane woman make a man of a waster or a woman of a worm?

CUSINS [*reeling before the storm*]   Father Colossus—Mammoth Millionaire—

UNDERSHAFT [*pressing him*]   Are there two mad people or three in this Salvation shelter today?

CUSINS   You mean Barbara is as mad as we are?

UNDERSHAFT [*pushing him lightly off and resuming his equanimity suddenly and com-*

pletely] Pooh, Professor! let us call things by their proper names. I am a millionaire; you are a poet; Barbara is a savior of souls. What have we three to do with the common mob of slaves and idolaters? [*He sits down again with a shrug of contempt for the mob*].

CUSINS   Take care! Barbara is in love with the common people. So am I. Have you never felt the romance of that love?

UNDERSHAFT [*cold and sardonic*]   Have you ever been in love with Poverty, like St Francis? Have you ever been in love with Dirt, like St Simeon! Have you ever been in love with disease and suffering, like our nurses and philanthropists? Such passions are not virtues, but the most unnatural of all the vices. This love of the common people may please an earl's granddaughter and a university professor; but I have been a common man and a poor man; and it has no romance for me. Leave it to the poor to pretend that poverty is a blessing: leave it to the coward to make a religion of his cowardice by preaching humility: we know better than that. We three must stand together above the common people: how else can we help their children to climb up beside us? Barbara must belong to us, not to the Salvation Army.

CUSINS   Well, I can only say that if you think you will get her away from the Salvation Army by talking to her as you have been talking to me, you dont know Barbara.

UNDERSHAFT   My friend: I never ask for what I can buy.

CUSINS [*in a white fury*]   Do I understand you to imply that you can buy Barbara?

UNDERSHAFT   No; but I can buy the Salvation Army.

CUSINS   Quite impossible.

UNDERSHAFT   You shall see. All religious organizations exist by selling themselves to the rich.

CUSINS   Not the Army. That is the Church of the poor.

UNDERSHAFT   All the more reason for buying it.

CUSINS   I dont think you quite know what the Army does for the poor.

UNDERSHAFT   Oh yes I do. It draws their teeth: that is enough for me as a man of business.

CUSINS   Nonsense! It makes them sober—

UNDERSHAFT   I prefer sober workmen. The profits are larger.

CUSINS   —honest—

UNDERSHAFT   Honest workmen are the most economical.

CUSINS   —attached to their homes—

UNDERSHAFT   So much the better: they will put up with anything sooner than change their shop.

CUSINS   —happy—

UNDERSHAFT   An invaluable safeguard against revolution.

CUSINS   —unselfish—

UNDERSHAFT   Indifferent to their own interests, which suits me exactly.

CUSINS   —with their thoughts on heavenly things—

UNDERSHAFT [*rising*]   And not on Trade Unionism nor Socialism. Excellent.

CUSINS [*revolted*]   You really are an infernal old rascal.

UNDERSHAFT [*indicating Peter Shirley, who has just come from the shelter and strolled dejectedly down the yard between them*]   And this is an honest man!

SHIRLEY   Yes; and what av I got by it? [*he passes on bitterly and sits on the form, in the corner of the penthouse*].

Snobby Price, beaming sanctimoniously, and Jenny Hill, with a tambourine full of coppers, come from the shelter and go to the drum, on which Jenny begins to count the money.

UNDERSHAFT [*replying to Shirley*]   Oh, your employers must have got a good deal by it from first to last. [*He sits on the table, with the one foot on the side form. Cusins, overwhelmed, sits down on the same form nearer the shelter. Barbara comes from the shelter to the middle of the yard. She is excited and a little overwrought*].

BARBARA   Weve just had a splendid experience meeting at the other gate in Cripps's lane. Ive hardly ever seen them so much moved as they were by your confession, Mr Price.

PRICE   I could almost be glad of my past wickedness if I could believe that it would elp to keep hathers stright.

BARBARA   So it will, Snobby. How much, Jenny?

JENNY   Four and tenpence, Major.

BARBARA   Oh Snobby, if you had given your poor mother just one more kick, we should have got the whole five shillings!

PRICE   If she heard you say that, miss, she'd be sorry I didnt. But I'm glad. Oh what a joy it will be to her when she hears I'm saved!

UNDERSHAFT   Shall I contribute the odd twopence, Barbara? The millionaire's mite, eh? [*He takes a couple of pennies from his pocket*].

BARBARA   How did you make that twopence?

UNDERSHAFT   As usual. By selling cannons, torpedoes, submarines, and my new patent Grand Duke hand grenade.

BARBARA   Put it back in your pocket. You cant buy your salvation here for two-pence: you must work it out.

UNDERSHAFT   Is twopence not enough? I can afford little more, if you press me.

BARBARA   Two million millions would not be enough. There is bad blood on your hands; and nothing but good blood can cleanse them. Money is no use. Take it away. [*She turns to Cusins*]. Dolly: you must write another letter for me to the papers. [*He makes a wry face*]. Yes: I know you dont like it; but it must be done. The starvation this winter is beating us: everybody is unemployed. The General says we must close this shelter if we cant get more money. I force the collections at the meetings until I am ashamed: dont I, Snobby?

PRICE   It's a fair treat to see you work it, miss. The way you got them up from three-and-six to four-and-ten with that hymn, penny by penny and verse by verse, was a caution. Not a Cheap Jack on Mile End Waste could touch you at it.

BARBARA   Yes; but I wish we could do without it. I am getting at last to think more of the collection than of the people's souls. And what are those hatfuls of pence and halfpence? We want thousands! tens of thousands! hundreds of thousands! I want to convert people, not to be always begging for the Army in a way I'd die sooner than beg for myself.

UNDERSHAFT [*in profound irony*]   Genuine unselfishness is capable of anything, my dear.

BARBARA [*unsuspectingly, as she turns away to take the money from the drum and put it in a cashbag she carries*]   Yes, isnt it? [*Undershaft looks sardonically at Cusins*].

CUSINS [*aside to Undershaft*]   Mephistopheles! Machiavelli!

BARBARA [*tears coming into her eyes as she ties the bag and pockets it*]   How are we to feed them? I cant talk religion to a man with bodily hunger in his eyes. [*Almost breaking down*] It's frightful.

JENNY [*running to her*]   Major, dear—

BARBARA [*rebounding*]   No: dont comfort me. It will be all right. We shall get the money.

UNDERSHAFT   How?

JENNY   By praying for it, of course. Mrs Baines says she prayed for it last night; and she has never prayed for it in vain: never once. [*She goes to the gate and looks out into the street*].

BARBARA [*who has dried her eyes and regained her composure*]   By the way, dad, Mrs Baines has come to march with us to our big meeting this afternoon; and she is very anxious to meet you, for some reason or other. Perhaps she'll convert you.

UNDERSHAFT   I shall be delighted, my dear.

JENNY [*at the gate: excitedly*]   Major! Major! heres that man back again.

BARBARA   What man?

JENNY   The man that hit me. Oh, I hope he's coming back to join us.

Bill Walker, with frost on his jacket, comes through the gate, his hands deep in his pockets and his chin sunk between his shoulders, like a cleaned-out gambler. He halts between Barbara and the drum.

BARBARA   Hullo, Bill! Back already!

BILL [*nagging at her*]   Bin talkin ever sence, ev you?

BARBARA   Pretty nearly. Well, has Todger paid you out for poor Jenny's jaw?

BILL   Nao e aint.

BARBARA   I thought your jacket looked a bit snowy.

BILL   Sao it is snaowy. You want to knaow where the snaow cam from, downt you?

BARBARA   Yes.

BILL   Well, it cam from orf the grahnd in Pawkinses Corner in Kennintahn. It got rabbed orf be maw shaoulders: see?

BARBARA   Pity you didnt rub some off with your knees, Bill! That would have done you a lot of good.

BILL   [*with sour mirthless humor*]   Aw was sivin another menn's knees at the tawm. E was kneelin on moy ed, e was.

JENNY   Who was kneeling on your head?

BILL   Todger was. E was pryin for me: pryin camfortable wiv me as a cawpet. Sow was Mog. Sao was the aol bloomin meetin. Mog she sez "Ow Lawd brike is stabborn sperrit; bat downt urt is dear art." Thet was wot she said. "Downt urt is dear art"! An er blowk—thirteen stun four!—kneelin wiv all is wight on me. Fanny, aint it?

JENNY   Oh no. We're so sorry, Mr Walker.

BARBARA   [*enjoying it frankly*]   Nonsense! of course it's funny. Served you right, Bill! You must have done something to him first.

BILL   [*doggedly*]   Aw did wot Aw said Aw'd do. Aw spit in is eye. E looks ap at the skoy and sez, "Ow that Aw should be fahnd worthy to be spit upon for the gospel's sike!" e sez; an Mog sez "Glaory Allelloolier!"; and then e called me Braddher, and dahned me as if Aw was a kid and e was me mather worshin me a Setterda nawt. Aw ednt jast nao shaow wiv im at all. Arf the street pryed; an the tather arf larfed fit to split theirselves. [*To Barbara*] There! are you settisfawd nah?

BARBARA   [*her eyes dancing*]   Wish I'd been there, Bill.

BILL   Yus: youd a got in a hextra bit o talk on me, wouldnt you?

JENNY   I'm so sorry, Mr Walker.

BILL   [*fiercely*]   Downt you gow bein sorry for me: youve no call. Listen eah. Aw browk your jawr.

JENNY   No, it didnt hurt me: indeed it didnt, except for a moment. It was only that I was frightened.

BILL   Aw downt want to be forgive be you, or be ennybody. Wot Aw did Aw'll py for. Aw trawd to gat me aown jawr browk to settisfaw you—

JENNY   [*distressed*]   Oh no—

BILL   [*impatiently*]   Tell y' Aw did: cawnt you listen to wots bein taold you? All Aw got be it was bein mide a sawt of in the pablic street for me pines. Well, if Aw cawnt settisfaw you one wy, Aw ken another. Listen eah! Aw ed two quid sived agen the frost; an Awve a pahnd of it left. A mite o mawn last week ed words with the judy e's gowin to merry. E give er wot-for; an e's bin fawnd fifteen bob. E ed a rawt to itt er cause they was gowin to be married; but Aw ednt nao rawt to itt you; sao put another fawv bob on an call it a pahnd's worth. [*He produces a sovereign*]. Eahs the manney. Tike it; and lets ev no more o your forgivin an pryin and your Mijor jawrin me. Let wot Aw dan be dan an pide for; and let there be a end of it.

JENNY   Oh, I couldnt take it, Mr Walker. But if you would give a shilling or two to poor Rummy Mitchens! you really did hurt her; and she's old.

BILL   [*contemptuously*]   Not lawkly. Aw'd give her another as soon as look at er. Let her ev the lawr o me as she threatened! She aint forgiven me: not mach.

Wot Aw dan to er is not on me mawnd—wot she [*indicating Barbara*] mawt call on me conscience—no more than stickin a pig. It's this Christian gime o yours that Aw wownt ev plyed agen me: this bloomin forgivin an neggin an jawrin that mikes a menn thet sore that iz lawf's a burdn to im. Aw wownt ev it, Aw tell you; sao tike your manney and stop thraowin your silly beshed fice hap agen me.

JENNY Major: may I take a little of it for the Army?

BARBARA No: the Army is not to be bought. We want your soul, Bill; and we'll take nothing less.

BILL [*bitterly*] Aw knaow. Me an maw few shillins is not good enaff for you. Youre a earl's grendorter, you are. Nathink less than a anderd pahnd for you.

UNDERSHAFT Come, Barbara! you could do a great deal of good with a hundred pounds. If you will set this gentleman's mind at ease by taking his pound, I will give the other ninety-nine.

Bill, dazed by such opulence, instinctively touches his cap.

BARBARA Oh, youre too extravagant, papa. Bill offers twenty pieces of silver. All you need offer is the other ten. That will make the standard price to buy anybody who's for sale. I'm not; and the Army's not. [*To Bill*] Youll never have another quiet moment, Bill, until you come round to us. You cant stand out against your salvation.

BILL [*sullenly*] Aw cawnt stend aht agen music awl wrastlers and awtful tangued women. Awve offered to py. Aw can do no more. Tike it or leave it. There it is. [*He throws the sovereign on the drum, and sits down on the horse-trough. The coin fascinates Snobby Price, who takes an early opportunity of dropping his cap on it*].

Mrs Baines comes from the shelter. She is dressed as a Salvation Army Commissioner. She is an earnest looking woman of about 40, with a caressing, urgent voice, and an appealing manner.

BARBARA This is my father, Mrs Baines. [*Undershaft comes from the table, taking off his hat with marked civility*]. Try what you can do with him. He wont listen to me, because he remembers what a fool I was when I was a baby. [*She leaves them together and chats with Jenny*].

MRS BAINES Have you been shewn over the shelter, Mr Undershaft? You know the work we're doing, of course.

UNDERSHAFT [*very civilly*] The whole nation knows it, Mrs Baines.

MRS BAINES No, sir: the whole nation does not know it, or we should not be crippled as we are for want of money to carry our work through the length and breadth of the land. Let me tell you that there would have been rioting this winter in London but for us.

UNDERSHAFT You really think so?

MRS BAINES   I know it. I remember 1886, when you rich gentlemen hardened your hearts against the cry of the poor. They broke the windows of your clubs in Pall Mall.

UNDERSHAFT [*gleaming with approval of their method*]   And the Mansion House Fund went up next day from thirty thousand pounds to seventy-nine thousand! I remember quite well.

MRS BAINES   Well, wont you help me to get at the people? They wont break windows then. Come here, Price. Let me shew you to this gentleman [*Price comes to be inspected*]. Do you remember the window breaking?

PRICE   My ole father thought it was the revolution, maam.

MRS BAINES   Would you break windows now?

PRICE   Oh no, maam. The windows of eaven av bin opened to me. I know now that the rich man is a sinner like myself.

RUMMY [*appearing above at the loft door*]   Snobby Price!

SNOBBY   Wot is it?

RUMMY   Your mother's askin for you at the other gate in Cripps's Lane. She's heard about your confession [*Price turns pale*].

MRS BAINES   Go, Mr Price; and pray with her.

JENNY   You can go through the shelter, Snobby.

PRICE [*to Mrs Baines*]   I couldnt face her now, maam, with all the weight of my sins fresh on me. Tell her she'll find her son at ome, waitin for her in prayer. [*He skulks off through the gate, incidentally stealing the sovereign on his way out by picking up his cap from the drum*].

MRS BAINES [*with swimming eyes*]   You see how we take the anger and the bitterness against you out of their hearts, Mr Undershaft.

UNDERSHAFT   It is certainly most convenient and gratifying to all large employers of labor, Mrs Baines.

MRS BAINES   Barbara: Jenny: I have good news: most wonderful news. [*Jenny runs to her*]. My prayers have been answered. I told you they would, Jenny, didnt I?

JENNY   Yes, yes.

BARBARA [*moving nearer to the drum*]   Have we got money enough to keep the shelter open?

MRS BAINES   I hope we shall have enough to keep all the shelters open. Lord Saxmundham has promised us five thousand pound—

BARBARA   Hooray!

JENNY   Glory!

MRS BAINES   —if—

BARBARA   "If!" If what?

MRS BAINES   —if five other gentlemen will give a thousand each to make it up to ten thousand.

BARBARA   Who is Lord Saxmundham? I never heard of him.

UNDERSHAFT [*who has pricked up his ears at the peer's name, and is now watching Barbara curiously*]   A new creation, my dear. You have heard of Sir Horace Bodger?

BARBARA   Bodger! Do you mean the distiller? Bodger's whisky!

UNDERSHAFT   That is the man. He is one of the greatest of our public benefactors. He restored the cathedral at Hakington. They made him a baronet for that. He gave half a million to the funds of his party: they made him a baron for that.

SHIRLEY   What will they give him for the five thousand?

UNDERSHAFT   There is nothing left to give him. So the five thousand, I should think is to save his soul.

MRS BAINES   Heaven grant it may! Oh Mr Undershaft, you have some very rich friends. Cant you help us towards the other five thousand? We are going to hold a great meeting this afternoon at the Assembly Hall in the Mile End Road. If I could only announce that one gentleman had come forward to support Lord Saxmundham, others would follow. Dont you know some-body? couldnt you? wouldnt you? [*her eyes fill with tears*] oh, think of those poor people, Mr. Undershaft: think of how much it means to them, and how little to a great man like you.

UNDERSHAFT   [*sardonically gallant*]   Mrs Baines: you are irresistible. I cant disap-point you; and I cant deny myself the satisfaction of making Bodger pay up. You shall have your five thousand pounds.

MRS BAINES   Thank God!

UNDERSHAFT   You dont thank me?

MRS BAINES   Oh sir, dont try to be cynical: dont be ashamed of being a good man. The Lord will bless you abundantly; and our prayers will be like a strong fortification round you all the days of your life. [*With a touch of caution*] You will let me have the cheque to shew at the meeting, wont you? Jenny: go in and fetch a pen and ink. [*Jenny runs to the shelter door*].

UNDERSHAFT   Do not disturb Miss Hill: I have a fountain pen [*Jenny halts. He sits at the table and writes the cheque. Cusins rises to make room for him. They all watch him silently*].

BILL   [*cynically, aside to Barbara, his voice and accent horribly debased*]   Wot prawce selvytion nah?

BARBARA   Stop. [*Undershaft stops writing: they all turn to her in surprise*]. Mrs Baines: are you really going to take this money?

MRS BAINES   [*astonished*]   Why not, dear?

BARBARA   Why not! Do you know what my father is? Have you forgotten that Lord Saxmundham is Bodger the whisky man? Do you remember how we implored the County Council to stop him from writing Bodger's Whisky in letters of fire against the sky; so that the poor drink-ruined creatures on the Embankment could not wake up from their snatches of sleep without being reminded of their deadly thirst by that wicked sky sign? Do you know that the worst thing I have had to fight here is not the devil, but Bodger, Bodger, Bodger, with his whisky, his distilleries, and his tied houses? Are you going to make our shelter another tied house for him, and ask me to keep it?

BILL   Rotten dranken whisky it is too.

MRS BAINES   Dear Barbara: Lord Saxmundham has a soul to be saved like any of us. If heaven has found the way to make a good use of his money, are we to set ourselves up against the answer to our prayers?

BARBARA   I know he has a soul to be saved. Let him come down here; and I'll do my best to help him to his salvation. But he wants to send his cheque down to buy us, and go on being as wicked as ever.

UNDERSHAFT [*with a reasonableness which Cusins alone perceives to be ironical*]   My dear Barbara: alcohol is a very necessary article. It heals the sick—

BARBARA   It does nothing of the sort.

UNDERSHAFT   Well, it assists the doctor: that is perhaps a less questionable way of putting it. It makes life bearable to millions of people who could not endure their existence if they were quite sober. It enables Parliament to do things at eleven at night that no sane person would do at eleven in the morning. Is it Bodger's fault that this inestimable gift is deplorably abused by less than one per cent of the poor? [*He turns again to the table; signs the cheque; and crosses it*].

MRS BAINES   Barbara: will there be less drinking or more if all those poor souls we are saving come tomorrow and find the doors of our shelters shut in their faces? Lord Saxmundham gives us the money to stop drinking—to take his own business from him.

CUSINS [*impishly*]   Pure self-sacrifice on Bodger's part, clearly! Bless dear Bodger! [*Barbara almost breaks down as Adolphus, too, fails her*].

UNDERSHAFT [*tearing out the cheque and pocketing the book as he rises and goes past Cusins to Mrs Baines*]   I also, Mrs Baines, may claim a little disinterestedness. Think of my business! think of the widows and orphans! the men and lads torn to pieces with shrapnel and poisoned with lyddite! [*Mrs Baines shrinks; but he goes on remorselessly*] the oceans of blood, not one drop of which is shed in a really just cause! the ravaged crops! the peaceful peasants forced, women and men, to till their fields under the fire of opposing armies on pain of starvation! the bad blood of the fierce little cowards at home who egg on others to fight for the gratification of their national vanity! All this makes money for me: I am never richer, never busier than when the papers are full of it. Well, it is your work to preach peace on earth and goodwill to men. [*Mrs Baines's face lights up again*]. Every convert you make is a vote against war. [*Her lips move in prayer*]. Yet I give you this money to help you to hasten my own commerical ruin. [*He gives her the cheque*].

CUSINS [*mounting the form in an ecstasy of mischief*]   The millennium will be inaugurated by the unselfishness of Undershaft and Bodger. Oh be joyful! [*He takes the drum-sticks from his pocket and flourishes them*].

MRS BAINES [*taking the cheque*]   The longer I live the more proof I see that there is an Infinite Goodness that turns everything to the work of salvation sooner or later. Who would have thought that any good could have come out of war and drink? And yet their profits are brought today to the feet of salvation to do its blessed work. [*She is affected to tears*].

JENNY [*running to Mrs Baines and throwing her arms around her*]   Oh dear! how blessed, how glorious it all is!

CUSINS [*in a convulsion of irony*]   Let us seize this unspeakable moment. Let us march to the great meeting at once. Excuse me just an instant. [*He rushes into the shelter. Jenny takes her tambourine from the drum head*].

MRS BAINES   Mr. Undershaft: have you ever seen a thousand people fall on their knees with one impulse and pray? Come with us to the meeting. Barbara shall tell them that the Army is saved, and saved through you.

CUSINS [*returning impetuously from the shelter with a flag and a trombone, and coming between Mrs Baines and Undershaft*]   You shall carry the flag down the first street, Mrs Baines [*he gives her the flag*]. Mr Undershaft is a gifted trombonist: he shall intone an Olympian diapason to the West Ham Salvation March. [*Aside to Undershaft, as he forces the trombone on him*] Blow, Machiavelli, blow.

UNDERSHAFT [*aside to him, as he takes the trombone*]   The trumpet in Zion! [*Cusins rushes to the drum, which he takes up and puts on. Undershaft continues, aloud*] I will do my best. I could vamp a bass if I knew the tune.

CUSINS   It is a wedding chorus from one of Donizetti's operas; but we have converted it. We convert everything to good here, including Bodger. You remember the chorus. "For thee immense rejoicing—immenso giubilo—immenso giubilo." [*With drum obbligato*] Rum tum ti tum tum, tum tum ti ta—

BARBARA   Dolly: you are breaking my heart.

CUSINS   What is a broken heart more or less here? Dionysos Undershaft has descended. I am possessed.

MRS BAINES   Come, Barbara: I must have my dear Major to carry the flag with me.

JENNY   Yes, yes, Major darling.

CUSINS [*snatches the tambourine out of Jenny's hand and mutely offers it to Barbara*].

BARBARA [*coming forward a little as she puts the offer behind her with a shudder, whilst Cusins recklessly tosses the tambourine back to Jenny and goes to the gate*]   I cant come.

JENNY   Not come!

MRS BAINES [*with tears in her eyes*]   Barbara: do you think I am wrong to take the money?

BARBARA [*impulsively going to her and kissing her*]   No, no: God help you, dear, you must; you are saving the Army. Go; and may you have a great meeting!

JENNY   But arnt you coming?

BARBARA   No. [*She begins taking off the silver S brooch from her collar*].

MRS BAINES   Barbara: what are you doing?

JENNY   Why are you taking your badge off? You cant be going to leave us, Major.

BARBARA [*quietly*]   Father: come here.

UNDERSHAFT [*coming to her*]   My dear! [*Seeing that she is going to pin the badge on his collar he retreats to the penthouse in some alarm*].

BARBARA [*following him*]   Dont be frightened. [*She pins the badge on and steps back towards the table, shewing him to the others*] There! It's not much for £5000, is it?

MRS BAINES   Barbara: if you wont come and pray with us, promise me you will pray for us.

BARBARA   I cant pray now. Perhaps I shall never pray again.

MRS BAINES   Barbara!

JENNY   Major!

BARBARA [*almost delirious*]   I cant bear any more. Quick march!

CUSINS [*calling to the procession in the street outside*]   Off we go. Play up, there! Immenso giubilo. [*He gives the time with his drum; and the band strikes up the march, which rapidly becomes more distant as the procession moves briskly away*].

MRS BAINES   I must go, dear. Youre overworked: you will be all right tomorrow. We'll never lose you. Now Jenny: step out with the old flag. Blood and Fire! [*She marches out through the gate with her flag*].

JENNY   Glory Hallelujah! [*flourishing her tambourine and marching*].

UNDERSHAFT [*to Cusins, as he marches out past him easing the slide of his trombone*]   "My ducats and my daughter"!

CUSINS [*following him out*]   Money and gunpowder!

BARBARA   Drunkenness and Murder! My God: why hast thou forsaken me?

She sinks on the form with her face buried in her hands. The march passes away into silence. Bill Walker steals across to her.

BILL [*taunting*].   Wot prawce selvytion nah?

SHIRLEY   Dont you hit her when she's down.

BILL   She itt me wen aw wiz dahn. Waw shouldnt Aw git a bit o me aown beck?

BARBARA [*raising her head*]   I didnt take your money, Bill. [*She crosses the yard to the gate and turns her back on the two men to hide her face from them*].

BILL [*sneering after her*]   Naow, it warnt enaff for you. [*Turning to the drum, he misses the money*] Ellow! If you aint took it sammun else ez. Weres it gorn? Bly me if Jenny Ill didnt tike it arter all!

RUMMY [*screaming at him from the loft*]   You lie, you dirty blackguard! Snobby Price pinched it off the drum when he took up his cap. I was up here all the time an see im do it.

BILL   Wot! Stowl maw manney! Waw didnt you call thief on him, you silly aold macker you?

RUMMY   To serve you aht for ittin me acrost the fice. It's cost y'pahnd, that az. [*Raising a pæan of squalid triumph*] I done you. I'm even with you. Ive ad it aht o y —[*Bill snatches up Shirley's mug and hurls it at her. She slams the loft door and vanishes. The mug smashes against the door and falls in fragments*].

BILL [*beginning to chuckle*]   Tell us, aol menn, wot o'clock this mawnin was it wen im as they call Snobby Prawce was sived?

BARBARA [*turning to him more composedly, and with unspoiled sweetness*]   About half past twelve, Bill. And he pinched your pound at a quarter to two. *I* know. Well, you cant afford to lose it. I'll send it to you.

BILL [*his voice and accent suddenly improving*]   Not if Aw wiz to stawve for it. Aw
   aint to be bought.

SHIRLEY   Aint you? Youd sell yourself to the devil for a pint o beer; ony there aint
   no devil to make the offer.

BILL [*unshamed*]   Sao Aw would, mite, and often ev, cheerful. But she cawnt baw
   me. [*Approaching Barbara*] You wanted maw saoul, did you? Well, you aint
   got it.

BARBARA   I nearly got it, Bill. But weve sold it back to you for ten thousand
   pounds.

SHIRLEY   And dear at the money!

BARBARA   No, Peter: it was worth more than money.

BILL [*salvationproof*]   It's nao good: you cawnt get rahnd me nah. Aw downt blieve
   in it; and Awve seen tody that Aw was rawt. [*Going*] Sao long, aol soupkitchener! Ta, ta, Mijor Earl's Grendorter! [*Turning at the gate*] Wot prawce selvytion
   nah? Snobby Prawce! Ha! ha!

BARBARA [*offering her hand*]   Goodbye, Bill.

BILL [*taken aback, half plucks his cap off; then shoves it on again defiantly*]   Git aht.
   [*Barbara drops her hand, discouraged. He has a twinge of remorse*]. But thets aw
   rawt, you knaow. Nathink pasnl. Naow mellice. Sao long, Judy. [*He goes*].

BARBARA   No malice. So long, Bill.

SHIRLEY [*shaking his head*]   You make too much of him, miss, in your innocence.

BARBARA [*going to him*]   Peter: I'm like you now. Cleaned out, and lost my job.

SHIRLEY   Youve youth an hope. Thats two better than me.

BARBARA   I'll get you a job, Peter. Thats hope for you: the youth will have to be
   enough for me. [*She counts her money*]. I have just enough left for two teas at
   Lockharts, a Rowton doss for you, and my tram and bus home. [*He frowns
   and rises with offended pride. She takes his arm*]. Dont be proud, Peter: it's sharing between friends. And promise me youll talk to me and not let me cry.
   [*She draws him towards the gate*].

SHIRLEY   Well, I'm not accustomed to talk to the like of you—

BARBARA [*urgently*]   Yes, yes: you must talk to me. Tell me about Tom Paine's
   books and Bradlaugh's lectures. Come along.

SHIRLEY   Ah, if you would only read Tom Paine in the proper spirit, miss! [*They
   go out through the gate together*].

ACT III

*Next day after lunch Lady Britomart is writing in the library in Wilton Crescent. Sarah is
reading in the armchair near the window. Barbara, in ordinary fashionable dress, pale and
brooding, is on the settee. Charles Lomax enters. He starts on seeing Barbara fashionably
attired and in low spirits.*

LOMAX   Youve left off your uniform!

Barbara says nothing; but an expression of pain passes over her face.

LADY BRITOMART [*warning him in low tones to be careful*]   Charles!

LOMAX [*much concerned, coming behind the settee and bending sympathetically over Barbara*]   I'm awfully sorry, Barbara. You know I helped you all I could with the concertina and so forth. [*Momentously*] Still, I have never shut my eyes to the fact that there is a certain amount of tosh about the Salvation Army. Now the claims of the Church of England—

LADY BRITOMART   Thats enough, Charles. Speak of something suited to your mental capacity.

LOMAX   But surely the Church of England is suited to all our capacities.

BARBARA [*pressing his hand*]   Thank you for your sympathy, Cholly. Now go and spoon with Sarah.

LOMAX [*dragging a chair from the writing table and seating himself affectionately by Sarah's side*]   How is my ownest today?

SARAH   I wish you wouldnt tell Cholly to do things, Barbara. He always comes straight and does them. Cholly: we're going to the works this afternoon.

LOMAX   What works?

SARAH   The cannon works.

LOMAX   What? your governor's shop!

SARAH   Yes.

LOMAX   Oh I say!

Cusins enters in poor condition. He also starts visibly when he sees Barbara without her uniform.

BARBARA   I expected you this morning, Dolly. Didnt you guess that?

CUSINS [*sitting down beside her*]   I'm sorry. I have only just breakfasted.

SARAH   But weve just finished lunch.

BARBARA   Have you had one of your bad nights?

CUSINS   No: I had rather a good night: in fact, one of the most remarkable nights I have ever passed.

BARBARA   The meeting?

CUSINS   No: after the meeting.

LADY BRITOMART   You should have gone to bed after the meeting. What were you doing?

CUSINS   Drinking.

LADY BRITOMART	Adolphus!
SARAH	Dolly!
BARBARA	Dolly!
LOMAX	Oh I say!

LADY BRITOMART   What were you drinking, may I ask?

CUSINS   A most devilish kind of Spanish burgundy, warranted free from added alcohol: a Temperance burgundy in fact. Its richness in natural alcohol made any addition superfluous.

BARBARA Are you joking, Dolly?

CUSINS [*patiently*] No. I have been making a night of it with the nominal head of this household: that is all.

LADY BRITOMART Andrew made you drunk!

CUSINS No: he only provided the wine. I think it was Dionysos who made me drunk. [*To Barbara*] I told you I was possessed.

LADY BRITOMART Youre not sober yet. Go home to bed at once.

CUSINS I have never before ventured to reproach you, Lady Brit; but how could you marry the Prince of Darkness?

LADY BRITOMART It was much more excusable to marry him than to get drunk with him. That is a new accomplishment of Andrew's, by the way. He usent to drink.

CUSINS He doesnt now. He only sat there and completed the wreck of my moral basis, the rout of my convictions, the purchase of my soul. He cares for you, Barbara. That is what makes him so dangerous to me.

BARBARA That has nothing to do with it, Dolly. There are larger loves and diviner dreams than the fireside ones. You know that, dont you?

CUSINS Yes: that is our understanding. I know it. I hold to it. Unless he can win me on that holier ground he may amuse me for a while; but he can get no deeper hold, strong as he is.

BARBARA Keep to that; and the end will be right. Now tell me what happened at the meeting?

CUSINS It was an amazing meeting. Mrs Baines almost died of emotion. Jenny Hill simply gibbered with hysteria. The Prince of Darkness played his trombone like a madman: its brazen roarings were like the laughter of the damned. 117 conversions took place then and there. They prayed with the most touching sincerity and gratitude for Bodger, and for the anonymous donor of the £5000. Your father would not let his name be given.

LOMAX That was rather fine of the old man, you know. Most chaps would have wanted the advertisement.

CUSINS He said all the charitable institutions would be down on him like kites on a battle-field if he gave his name.

LADY BRITOMART Thats Andrew all over. He never does a proper thing without giving an improper reason for it.

CUSINS He convinced me that I have all my life been doing improper things for proper reasons.

LADY BRITOMART Adolphus: now that Barbara has left the Salvation Army, you had better leave it too. I will not have you playing that drum in the streets.

CUSINS Your orders are already obeyed, Lady Brit.

BARBARA Dolly: were you ever really in earnest about it? Would you have joined if you had never seen me?

CUSINS [*disingenuously*] Well—er—well, possibly, as a collector of religions—

LOMAX [*cunningly*] Not as a drummer, though, you know. You are a very clear-headed brainy chap, Dolly; and it must have been apparent to you that there is a certain amount of tosh about—

LADY BRITOMART   Charles: if you must drivel, drivel like a grown-up man and not like a schoolboy.

LOMAX [*out of countenance*]   Well, drivel is drivel, dont you know, whatever a man's age.

LADY BRITOMART   In good society in England, Charles, men drivel at all ages by repeating silly formulas with an air of wisdom. Schoolboys make their own formulas out of slang, like you. When they reach your age, and get political private secretaryships and things of that sort, they drop slang and get their formulas out of The Spectator or The Times. You had better confine yourself to The Times. You will find that there is a certain amount of tosh about The Times; but at least its language is reputable.

LOMAX [*overwhelmed*]   You are so awfully strongminded, Lady Brit—

LADY BRITOMART   Rubbish! [*Morrison comes in*]. What is it?

MORRISON   If you please, my lady, Mr Undershaft has just drove up to the door.

LADY BRITOMART   Well, let him in. [*Morrison hesitates*]. Whats the matter with you?

MORRISON   Shall I announce him, my lady; or is he at home here, so to speak, my lady?

LADY BRITOMART   Announce him.

MORRISON   Thank you, my lady. You wont mind my asking, I hope. The occasion is in a manner of speaking new to me.

LADY BRITOMART   Quite right. Go and let him in.

MORRISON   Thank you, my lady. [*He withdraws*].

LADY BRITOMART   Children: go and get ready. [*Sarah and Barbara go upstairs for their out-of-door wraps*]. Charles: go and tell Stephen to come down here in five minutes: you will find him in the drawing room. [*Charles goes*]. Adolphus: tell them to send round the carriage in about fifteen minutes. [*Adolphus goes*].

MORRISON [*at the door*]   Mr Undershaft.

Undershaft comes in. Morrison goes out.

UNDERSHAFT   Alone! How fortunate!

LADY BRITOMART [*rising*]   Dont be sentimental, Andrew. Sit down. [*She sits on the settee: he sits beside her, on her left. She comes to the point before he has time to breathe*]. Sarah must have £800 a year until Charles Lomax comes into his property. Barbara will need more, and need it permanently, because Adolphus hasnt any property.

UNDERSHAFT [*resignedly*]   Yes, my dear: I will see to it. Anything else? for yourself, for instance?

LADY BRITOMART   I want to talk to you about Stephen.

UNDERSHAFT [*rather wearily*]   Dont, my dear. Stephen doesnt interest me.

LADY BRITOMART   He does interest me. He is our son.

UNDERSHAFT   Do you really think so? He has induced us to bring him into the world; but he chose his parents very incongruously, I think. I see nothing of myself in him, and less of you.

LADY BRITOMART   Andrew: Stephen is an excellent son, and a most steady, capable, highminded young man. You are simply trying to find an excuse for disinheriting him.

UNDERSHAFT   My dear Biddy: the Undershaft tradition disinherits him. It would be dishonest of me to leave the cannon foundry to my son.

LADY BRITOMART   It would be most unnatural and improper of you to leave it to anyone else, Andrew. Do you suppose this wicked and immoral tradition can be kept up for ever? Do you pretend that Stephen could not carry on the foundry just as well as all the other sons of the big business houses?

UNDERSHAFT   Yes: he could learn the office routine without understanding the business, like all the other sons; and the firm would go on by its own momentum until the real Undershaft—probably an Italian or a German—would invent a new method and cut him out.

LADY BRITOMART   There is nothing that any Italian or German could do that Stephen could not do. And Stephen at least has breeding.

UNDERSHAFT   The son of a foundling! Nonsense!

LADY BRITOMART   My son, Andrew! And even you may have good blood in your veins for all you know.

UNDERSHAFT   True. Probably I have. That is another argument in favor of a foundling.

LADY BRITOMART   Andrew: dont be aggravating. And dont be wicked. At present you are both.

UNDERSHAFT   This conversation is part of the Undershaft tradition, Biddy. Every Undershaft's wife has treated him to it ever since the house was founded. It is mere waste of breath. If the tradition be ever broken it will be for an abler man than Stephen.

LADY BRITOMART [*pouting*]   Then go away.

UNDERSHAFT [*deprecatory*]   Go away!

LADY BRITOMART   Yes: go away. If you will do nothing for Stephen, you are not wanted here. Go to your foundling, whoever he is; and look after him.

UNDERSHAFT   That fact is, Biddy—

LADY BRITOMART   Dont call me Biddy. I dont call you Andy.

UNDERSHAFT   I will not call my wife Britomart: it is not good sense. Seriously, my love, the Undershaft tradition has landed me in a difficulty. I am getting on in years; and my partner Lazarus has at last made a stand and insisted that the succession must be settled one way or the other; and of course he is quite right. You see, I havnt found a fit successor yet.

LADY BRITOMART [*obstinately*]   There is Stephen.

UNDERSHAFT   Thats just it: all the foundlings I can find are exactly like Stephen.

LADY BRITOMART   Andrew!!

UNDERSHAFT   I want a man with no relations and no schooling: that is, a man who would be out of the running altogether if he were not a strong man. And I cant find him. Every blessed foundling nowadays is snapped up in his infancy by Barnardo homes, or School Board Officers, or Boards of Guardians; and if he shews the least ability he is fastened on by schoolmasters; trained to win scholarships like a racehorse; crammed with secondhand ideas; drilled and disciplined in docility and what they call good taste; and lamed for life so that he is fit for nothing but teaching. If you want to keep the foundry in the family, you had better find an eligible foundling and marry him to Barbara.

LADY BRITOMART   Ah! Barbara! Your pet! You would sacrifice Stephen to Barbara.

UNDERSHAFT   Cheerfully. And you, my dear, would boil Barbara to make soup for Stephen.

LADY BRITOMART   Andrew: this is not a question of our likings and dislikings: it is a question of duty. It is your duty to make Stephen your successor.

UNDERSHAFT   Just as much as it is your duty to submit to your husband. Come, Biddy! these tricks of the governing class are of no use with me. I am one of the governing class myself; and it is waste of time giving tracts to a missionary. I have the power in this matter; and I am not to be humbugged into using it for your purposes.

LADY BRITOMART   Andrew: you can talk my head off; but you cant change wrong into right. And your tie is all on one side. Put it straight.

UNDERSHAFT [disconcerted]   It wont stay unless it's pinned [he fumbles at it with childish grimaces]—

Stephen comes in.

STEPHEN [at the door]   I beg your pardon [about to retire].

LADY BRITOMART   No: come in, Stephen. [Stephen comes forward to his mother's writing table].

UNDERSHAFT [not very cordially]   Good afternoon.

STEPHEN [coldly]   Good afternoon.

UNDERSHAFT [to Lady Britomart]   He knows all about the tradition, I suppose?

LADY BRITOMART   Yes. [To Stephen] It is what I told you last night, Stephen.

UNDERSHAFT [sulkily]   I understand you want to come into the cannon business.

STEPHEN   I go into trade! Certainly not.

UNDERSHAFT [opening his eyes, greatly eased in mind and manner]   Oh! in that case—

LADY BRITOMART   Cannons are not trade, Stephen. They are enterprise.

STEPHEN   I have no intention of becoming a man of business in any sense. I have no capacity for business and no taste for it. I intend to devote myself to politics.

UNDERSHAFT [rising]   My dear boy: this is an immense relief to me. And I trust it may prove an equally good thing for the country. I was afraid you would consider yourself disparaged and slighted [He moves towards Stephen as if to shake hands with him].

LADY BRITOMART [rising and interposing]   Stephen: I cannot allow you to throw away an enormous property like this.

STEPHEN [*stiffly*]   Mother: there must be an end of treating me as a child, if you please. [*Lady Britomart recoils, deeply wounded by his tone*]. Until last night I did not take your attitude seriously, because I did not think you meant it seriously. But I find now that you left me in the dark as to matters which you should have explained to me years ago. I am extremely hurt and offended. Any further discussion of my intentions had better take place with my father, as between one man and another.

LADY BRITOMART   Stephen! [*She sits down again, her eyes filling with tears*].

UNDERSHAFT [*with grave compassion*]   You see, my dear, it is only the big men who can be treated as children.

STEPHEN   I am sorry, mother, that you have forced me—

UNDERSHAFT [*stopping him*]   Yes, yes, yes, yes: thats all right, Stephen. She wont interfere with you any more: your independence is achieved: you have won your latchkey. Dont rub it in; and above all, dont apologize. [*He resumes his seat*]. Now what about your future, as between one man and another—I beg your pardon, Biddy: as between two men and a woman.

LADY BRITOMART [*who has pulled herself together strongly*]   I quite understand, Stephen. By all means go your own way if you feel strong enough. [*Stephen sits down magisterially in the chair at the writing table with an air of affirming his majority*].

UNDERSHAFT   It is settled that you do not ask for the succession to the cannon business.

STEPHEN   I hope it is settled that I repudiate the cannon business.

UNDERSHAFT   Come, come! dont be so devilishly sulky: it's boyish. Freedom should be generous. Besides, I owe you a fair start in life in exchange for disinheriting you. You cant become prime minister all at once. Havnt you a turn for something? What about literature, art, and so forth?

STEPHEN   I have nothing of the artist about me, either in faculty or character, thank Heaven.

UNDERSHAFT   A philosopher, perhaps? Eh?

STEPHEN   I make no such ridiculous pretension.

UNDERSHAFT   Just so. Well, there is the army, the navy, the Church, the Bar. The Bar requires some ability. What about the Bar?

STEPHEN   I have not studied law. And I am afraid I have not the necessary push— I believe that is the name barristers give to their vulgarity—for success in pleading.

UNDERSHAFT   Rather a difficult case, Stephen. Hardly anything left but the stage, is there? [*Stephen makes an impatient movement*]. Well, come! is there anything you know or care for?

STEPHEN [*rising and looking at him steadily*]   I know the difference between right and wrong.

UNDERSHAFT [*hugely tickled*]   You dont say so! What! no capacity for business, no knowledge of law, no sympathy with art, no pretension to philosophy; only a simple knowledge of the secret that has puzzled all the philosophers, baffled all the lawyers, muddled all the men of business, and ruined most of the artists: the secret of right and wrong. Why, man, youre a genius, a master of masters, a god! At twentyfour, too!

STEPHEN [*keeping his temper with difficulty*]   You are pleased to be facetious. I pretend to nothing more than any honourable English gentleman claims as his birthright [*he sits down angrily*].

UNDERSHAFT   Oh, thats everybody's birthright. Look at poor little Jenny Hill, the Salvation lassie! she would think you were laughing at her if you asked her to stand up in the street and teach grammar or geography or mathematics or even drawing room dancing; but it never occurs to her to doubt that she can teach morals and religion. You are all alike, you respectable people. You cant tell me the bursting strain of a ten-inch gun, which is a very simple matter; but you all think you can tell me the bursting strain of a man under temptation. You darent handle high explosives; but youre all ready to handle honesty and truth and justice and the whole duty of man, and kill one another at that game. What a country! What a world!

LADY BRITOMART [*uneasily*]   What do you think he had better do, Andrew?

UNDERSHAFT   Oh, just what he wants to do. He knows nothing and he thinks he knows everything. That points clearly to a political career. Get him a private secretaryship to someone who can get him an Under Secretaryship; and then leave him alone. He will find his natural and proper place in the end on the Treasury Bench.

STEPHEN [*springing up again*]   I am sorry, sir, that you force me to forget the respect due to you as my father. I am an Englishman and I will not hear the Government of my country insulted. [*He thrusts his hands in his pockets, and walks angrily across to the window*].

UNDERSHAFT [*with a touch of brutality*]   The government of your country! *I* am the government of your country: I, and Lazarus. Do you suppose that you and half a dozen amateurs like you, sitting in a row in that foolish gabble shop, can govern Undershaft and Lazarus? No, my friend: you will do what pays us. You will make war when it suits us, and keep peace when it doesnt. You will find out that trade requires certain measures when we have decided on those measures. When I want anything to keep my dividends up, you will discover that my want is a national need. When other people want something to keep my dividends down, you will call out the police and military. And in return you shall have the support and applause of my newspapers, and the delight of imagining that you are a great statesman. Government of your country! Be off with you, my boy, and play with your caucuses and leading articles and historic parties and great leaders and burning questions and the rest of your toys. I am going back to my counting-house to pay the piper and call the tune.

STEPHEN [*actually smiling, and putting his hand on his father's shoulder with indulgent patronage*]   Really, my dear father, it is impossible to be angry with you. You dont know how absurd all this sounds to me. You are properly proud of having been industrious enough to make money; and it is greatly to your credit that you have made so much of it. But it has kept you in circles where you are valued for your money and deferred to for it, instead of in the doubtless very old-fashioned and behind-the-times public school and university where I formed my habits of mind. It is natural for you to think that money governs England; but you must allow me to think I know better.

UNDERSHAFT   And what does govern England, pray?

STEPHEN   Character, father, character.

UNDERSHAFT   Whose character? Yours or mine?

STEPHEN   Neither yours nor mine, father, but the best elements in the English national character.

UNDERSHAFT   Stephen: Ive found your profession for you. Youre a born journalist. I'll start you with a high-toned weekly review. There!

Before Stephen can reply Sarah, Barbara, Lomax, and Cusins come in ready for walking. Barbara crosses the room to the window and looks out. Cusins drifts amiably to the armchair. Lomax remains near the door, whilst Sarah comes to her mother.

Stephen goes to the smaller writing table and busies himself with his letters.

SARAH   Go and get ready, mamma: the carriage is waiting. [*Lady Britomart leaves the room*].

UNDERSHAFT [*to Sarah*]   Good day, my dear. Good afternoon, Mr Lomax.

LOMAX [*vaguely*]   Ahdedoo.

UNDERSHAFT [*to Cusins*]   Quite well after last night, Euripides, eh?

CUSINS   As well as can be expected.

UNDERSHAFT   Thats right [*To Barbara*] So you are coming to see my death and devastation factory, Barbara?

BARBARA [*at the window*]   You came yesterday to see my salvation factory. I promised you a return visit.

LOMAX [*coming forward between Sarah and Undershaft*]   Youll find it awfully interesting. Ive been through the Woolwich Arsenal; and it gives you a ripping feeling of security, you know, to think of the lot of beggars we could kill if it came to fighting. [*To Undershaft, with sudden solemnity*] Still, it must be rather an awful reflection for you, from the religious point of view as it were. Youre getting on, you know, and all that.

SARAH   You dont mind Cholly's imbecility, papa, do you?

LOMAX [*much taken aback*]   Oh I say!

UNDERSHAFT   Mr Lomax looks at the matter in a very proper spirit, my dear.

LOMAX   Just so. Thats all I meant, I assure you.

SARAH   Are you coming, Stephen?

STEPHEN   Well, I am rather busy—er—[*Magnanimously*] Oh well, yes: I'll come. That is, if there is room for me.

UNDERSHAFT   I can take two with me in a little motor I am experimenting with for field use. You wont mind its being rather unfashionable. It's not painted yet; but it's bullet proof.

LOMAX [*appalled at the prospect of confronting Wilton Crescent in an unpainted motor*] Oh I say!

SARAH   The carriage for me, thank you. Barbara doesnt mind what she's seen in.

LOMAX   I say, Dolly, old chap: do you really mind the car being a guy? Because of course if you do I'll go in it. Still—

CUSINS   I prefer it.

LOMAX   Thanks awfully, old man. Come, my ownest. [*He hurries out to secure his seat in the carriage. Sarah follows him*].

CUSINS [*moodily walking across to Lady Britomart's writing table*]   Why are we two coming to this Works Department of Hell? that is what I ask myself.

BARBARA   I have always thought of it as a sort of pit where lost creatures with blackened faces stirred up smoky fires and were driven and tormented by my father. Is it like that, dad?

UNDERSHAFT [*scandalized*]   My dear! It is a spotlessly clean and beautiful hillside town.

CUSINS   With a Methodist chapel? O do say theres a Methodist chapel.

UNDERSHAFT   There are two: a Primitive one and a sophisticated one. There is even an Ethical Society; but it is not much patronized, as my men are all strongly religious. In the High Explosives Sheds they object to the presence of Agnostics as unsafe.

CUSINS   And yet they dont object to you!

BARBARA   Do they obey all your orders?

UNDERSHAFT   I never give them any orders. When I speak to one of them it is "Well, Jones, is baby doing well? and has Mrs Jones made a good recovery?" "Nicely, thank you, sir." And thats all.

CUSINS   But Jones has to be kept in order. How do you maintain discipline among your men?

UNDERSHAFT   I dont. They do. You see, the one thing Jones wont stand is any rebellion from the man under him, or any assertion of social equality between the wife of the man with 4 shillings a week less than himself, and Mrs Jones! Of course they all rebel against me, theoretically. Practically, every man of them keeps the man just below him in his place. I never meddle with them. I never bully them. I dont even bully Lazarus. I say that certain things are to be done; but I dont order anybody to do them. I dont say, mind you, that there is no ordering about and snubbing and even bullying. The men snub the boys and order them about; the carmen snub the sweepers; the artisans snub the unskilled laborers; the foremen drive and bully both the laborers and artisans; the assistant engineers find fault with the foremen; the chief engineers drop on the assistants; the departmental managers worry the chiefs; and the clerks have tall hats and hymnbooks and keep up the social tone by refusing to associate on equal terms with anybody. The result is a colossal profit, which comes to me.

CUSINS [*revolted*]   You really are a—well, what I was saying yesterday.

BARBARA   What was he saying yesterday?

UNDERSHAFT   Never mind, my dear. He thinks I have made you unhappy. Have
I?

BARBARA   Do you think I can be happy in this vulgar silly dress? I! who have
worn the uniform. Do you understand what you have done to me? Yesterday
I had a man's soul in my hand. I set him in the way of life with his face to
salvation. But when we took your money he turned back to drunkenness and
derision. [*With intense conviction*] I will never forgive you that. If I had a child,
and you destroyed its body with your explosives—if you murdered Dolly
with your horrible guns—I could forgive you if my forgiveness would open
the gates of heaven to you. But to take a human soul from me, and turn it
into the soul of a wolf! that is worse than any murder.

UNDERSHAFT   Does my daughter despair so easily? Can you strike a man to the
heart and leave no mark on him?

BARBARA [*her face lighting up*]   Oh, you are right: he can never be lost now: where
was my faith?

CUSINS   Oh, clever clever devil!

BARBARA   You may be a devil; but God speaks through you sometimes. [*She takes
her father's hands and kisses them*]. You have given me back my happiness: I feel
it deep down now, though my spirit is troubled.

UNDERSHAFT   You have learnt something. That always feels at first as if you had
lost something.

BARBARA   Well, take me to the factory of death; and let me learn something more.
There must be some truth or other behind all this frightful irony. Come,
Dolly. [*She goes out*].

CUSINS   My guardian angel! [*To Undershaft*] Avaunt! [*He follows Barbara*].

STEPHEN [*quietly, at the writing table*]   You must not mind Cusins, father. He is a
very amiable good fellow; but he is a Greek scholar and naturally a little
eccentric.

UNDERSHAFT   Ah, quite so. Thank you, Stephen. Thank you. [*He goes out*].

*Stephen smiles patronizingly; buttons his coat responsibly; and crosses the room to the
door. Lady Britomart, dressed for out-of-doors, opens it before he reaches it. She looks round
for the others; looks at Stephen; and turns to go without a word.*

STEPHEN [*embarrassed*]   Mother—

LADY BRITOMART   Dont be apologetic, Stephen. And dont forget that you have
outgrown your mother. [*She goes out*].

*Perivale St Andrews lies between two Middlesex hills, half climbing the northern one. It is
an almost smokeless town of white walls, roofs of narrow green slates or red tiles, tall trees,
domes, campaniles, and slender chimney shafts, beautifully situated and beautiful in itself.
The best view of it is obtained from the crest of a slope about half a mile to the east, where*

the high explosives are dealt with. The foundry lies hidden in the depths between, the tops of its chimneys sprouting like huge skittles into the middle distance. Across the crest runs an emplacement of concrete, with a firestep, and a parapet which suggests a fortification, because there is a huge cannon of the obsolete Woolwich Infant pattern peering across it at the town. The cannon is mounted on an experimental gun carriage: possibly the original model of the Undershaft disappearing rampart gun alluded to by Stephen. The firestep, being a convenient place to sit, is furnished here and there with straw disc cushions; and at one place there is the additional luxury of a fur rug.

Barbara is standing on the firestep, looking over the parapet towards the town. On her right is the cannon; on her left the end of a shed raised on piles, with a ladder of three or four steps up to the door, which opens outwards and has a little wooden landing at the threshold, with a fire bucket in the corner of the landing. Several dummy soldiers more or less mutilated, with straw protruding from their gashes, have been shoved out of the way under the landing. A few others are nearly upright against the shed; and one has fallen forward and lies, like a grotesque corpse, on the emplacement. The parapet stops short of the shed, leaving a gap which is the beginning of the path down the hill through the foundry to the town. The rug is on the firestep near this gap. Down on the emplacement behind the cannon is a trolley carrying a huge conical bombshell with a red band painted on it. Further to the right is the door of an office, which, like the sheds, is of the lightest possible construction.

Cusins arrives by the path from the town.

BARBARA Well?

CUSINS Not a ray of hope. Everything perfect! wonderful! real! It only needs a cathedral to be a heavenly city instead of a hellish one.

BARBARA Have you found out whether they have done anything for old Peter Shirley?

CUSINS They have found him a job as gatekeeper and timekeeper. He's frightfully miserable. He calls the time-keeping brainwork, and says he isnt used to it; and his gate lodge is so splendid that he's ashamed to use the rooms, and skulks in the scullery.

BARBARA Poor Peter!

Stephen arrives from the town. He carries a fieldglass.

STEPHEN [*enthusiastically*] Have you two seen the place? Why did you leave us?

CUSINS I wanted to see everything I was not intended to see; and Barbara wanted to make the men talk.

STEPHEN Have you found anything discreditable?

CUSINS No. They call him Dandy Andy and are proud of his being a cunning old rascal; but it's all horribly, frightfully, immorally, unanswerably perfect.

Sarah arrives.

SARAH   Heavens! what a place! [*She crosses to the trolley*]. Did you see the nursing home!? [*She sits down on the shell*].

STEPHEN   Did you see the libraries and schools!?

SARAH   Did you see the ball room and the banqueting chamber in the Town Hall!?

STEPHEN   Have you gone into the insurance fund, the pension fund, the building society, the various applications of co-operation!?

Undershaft comes from the office, with a sheaf of telegrams in his hand.

UNDERSHAFT   Well, have you seen everything! I'm sorry I was called away. [*Indicating the telegrams*] Good news from Manchuria.

STEPHEN   Another Japanese victory?

UNDERSHAFT   Oh, I dont know. What side wins does not concern us here. No: the good news is that the aerial battleship is a tremendous success. At the first trial it has wiped out a fort with three hundred soldiers in it.

CUSINS [*from the platform*]   Dummy soldiers?

UNDERSHAFT [*striding across to Stephen and kicking the prostrate dummy brutally out of his way*]   No: the real thing.

Cusins and Barbara exchange glances. Then Cusins sits on the step and buries his face in his hands. Barbara gravely lays her hand on his shoulder. He looks up at her in whimsical desperation.

UNDERSHAFT   Well, Stephen, what do you think of the place?

STEPHEN   Oh, magnificent. A perfect triumph of modern industry, Frankly, my dear father, I have been a fool: I had no idea of what it all meant: of the wonderful forethought, the power of organization, the administrative capacity, the financial genius, the colossal capital it represents. I have been repeating to myself as I came through your streets "Peace hath her victories no less renowned than War." I have only one misgiving about it all.

UNDERSHAFT   Out with it.

STEPHEN   Well, I cannot help thinking that all this provision for every want of your workmen may sap their independence and weaken their sense of responsibility. And greatly as we enjoyed our tea at that splendid restaurant—how they gave us all that luxury and cake and jam and cream for threepence I really cannot imagine!—still you must remember that restaurants break up home life. Look at the continent, for instance! Are you sure so much pampering is really good for the men's characters?

UNDERSHAFT   Well you see, my dear boy, when you are organizing civilization you have to make up your mind whether trouble and anxiety are good things or not. If you decide that they are, then, I take it, you simply dont organize civilization; and there you are, with trouble and anxiety enough to make us all angels! But if you decide the other way, you may as well go through with it. However, Stephen, our characters are safe here. A sufficient dose of anxiety is always provided by the fact that we may be blown to smithereens at any moment.

SARAH   By the way, papa, where do you make the explosives?

UNDERSHAFT   In separate little sheds, like that one. When one of them blows up, it costs very little; and only the people quite close to it are killed.

Stephen, who is quite close to it, looks at it rather scaredly, and moves away quickly to the cannon. At the same moment the door of the shed is thrown abruptly open; and a foreman in overalls and list slippers comes out on the little landing and holds the door for Lomax, who appears in the doorway.

LOMAX [*with studied coolness*]   My good fellow: you neednt get into a state of nerves. Nothing's going to happen to you; and I suppose it wouldnt be the end of the world if anything did. A little bit of British pluck is what you want, old chap. [*He descends and strolls across to Sarah*].

UNDERSHAFT [*to the foreman*]   Anything wrong, Bilton?

BILTON [*with ironic calm*]   Gentleman walked into the high explosives shed and lit a cigaret, sir: thats all.

UNDERSHAFT   Ah, quite so. [*Going over to Lomax*] Do you happen to remember what you did with the match?

LOMAX   Oh come! I'm not a fool. I took jolly good care to blow it out before I chucked it away.

BILTON   The top of it was red hot inside, sir.

LOMAX   Well, suppose it was! I didn't chuck it into any of your messes.

UNDERSHAFT   Think no more of it, Mr. Lomax. By the way, would you mind lending me your matches.

LOMAX [*offering his box*].   Certainly.

UNDERSHAFT   Thanks. [*He pockets the matches*].

LOMAX [*lecturing to the company generally*]   You know, these high explosives dont go off like gunpowder, except when theyre in a gun. When theyre spread loose, you can put a match to them without the least risk; they just burn quietly like a bit of paper. [*Warming to the scientific interest of the subject*] Did you know that, Undershaft? Have you ever tried?

UNDERSHAFT   Not on a large scale, Mr. Lomax. Bilton will give you a sample of gun cotton when you are leaving if you ask him. You can experiment with it at home. [*Bilton looks puzzled*].

SARAH   Bilton will do nothing of the sort, papa. I suppose it's your business to blow up the Russians and Japs; but you might really stop short of blowing up poor Cholly. [*Bilton gives it up and retires into the shed*].

LOMAX   My ownest, there is no danger. [*He sits beside her on the shell*].

Lady Britomart arrives from the town with a bouquet.

LADY BRITOMART [*impetuously*]   Andrew: you shouldnt have let me see this place.

UNDERSHAFT   Why, my dear?

LADY BRITOMART   Never mind why: you shouldnt have: thats all. To think of all that [*indicating the town*] being yours! and that you have kept it to yourself all these years!

UNDERSHAFT   It does not belong to me. I belong to it. It is the Undershaft inheritance.

LADY BRITOMART   It is not. Your ridiculous cannons and that noisy banging foundry may be the Undershaft inheritance; but all that plate and linen, all that furniture and those houses and orchards and gardens belong to us. They belong to m e: they are not a man's business. I wont give them up. You must be out of your senses to throw them all away; and if you persist in such folly, I will call in a doctor.

UNDERSHAFT [*stooping to smell the bouquet*]   Where did you get the flowers, my dear?

LADY BRITOMART   Your men presented them to me in your William Morris Labor Church.

CUSINS   Oh! It needed only that. A Labor Church! [*he mounts the firestep distractedly, and leans with his elbows on the parapet, turning his back to them*].

LADY BRITOMART   Yes, with Morris's words in mosaic letters ten feet high round the dome. NO MAN IS GOOD ENOUGH TO BE ANOTHER MAN'S MASTER. The cynicism of it!

UNDERSHAFT   It shocked the men at first, I am afraid. But now they take no more notice of it than of the ten commandments in church.

LADY BRITOMART   Andrew: you are trying to put me off the subject of the inheritance by profane jokes. Well, you shant. I dont ask it any longer for Stephen: he has inherited far too much of your perversity to be fit for it. But Barbara has rights as well as Stephen. Why should not Adolphus succeed to the inheritance? I could manage the town for him; and he can look after the cannons, if they are really necessary.

UNDERSHAFT   I should ask nothing better if Adolphus were a foundling. He is exactly the sort of new blood that is wanted in English business. But he's not a foundling; and theres an end of it. [*He makes for the office door*].

CUSINS [*turning to them*]   Not quite. [*They all turn and stare at him*]. I think—Mind! I am not committing myself in any way as to my future course—but I think the foundling difficulty can be got over. [*He jumps down to the emplacement*].

UNDERSHAFT [*coming back to him*]   What do you mean?

CUSINS   Well, I have something to say which is in the nature of a confession.

SARAH
LADY BRITOMART
BARBARA   }   Confession!
STEPHEN

LOMAX   Oh I say!

CUSINS   Yes, a confession. Listen, all. Until I met Barbara I thought myself in the main an honorable, truthful man, because I wanted the approval of my conscience more than I wanted anything else. But the moment I saw Barbara, I wanted her far more than the approval of my conscience.

LADY BRITOMART Adolphus!

CUSINS It is true. You accused me yourself, Lady Brit, of joining the Army to worship Barbara; and so I did. She bought my soul like a flower at a street corner; but she bought it for herself.

UNDERSHAFT What! Not for Dionysos or another?

CUSINS Dionysos and all the others are in herself. I adored what was divine in her, and was therefore a true worshipper. But I was romantic about her too. I thought she was a woman of the people, and that a marriage with a professor of Greek would be far beyond the wildest social ambitions of her rank.

LADY BRITOMART Adolphus!!

LOMAX Oh I say!!!

CUSINS When I learnt the horrible truth—

LADY BRITOMART What do you mean by the horrible truth, pray?

CUSINS That she was enormously rich; that her grandfather was an earl; that her father was the Prince of Darkness—

UNDERSHAFT Chut!

CUSINS —and that I was only an adventurer trying to catch a rich wife, then I stooped to deceive her about my birth.

BARBARA [rising] Dolly!

LADY BRITOMART Your birth! Now Adolphus, dont dare to make up a wicked story for the sake of these wretched cannons. Remember: I have seen photographs of your parents; and the Agent General for South Western Australia knows them personally and has assured me that they are most respectable married people.

CUSINS So they are in Australia; but here they are outcasts. Their marriage is legal in Australia, but not in England. My mother is my father's deceased wife's sister; and in this island I am consequently a foundling. [Sensation].

BARBARA Silly! [She climbs to the cannon, and leans, listening, in the angle it makes with the parapet].

CUSINS Is the subterfuge good enough, Machiavelli?

UNDERSHAFT [thoughtfully] Biddy: this may be a way out of the difficulty.

LADY BRITOMART Stuff! A man cant make cannons any the better for being his own cousin instead of his proper self [she sits down on the rug with a bounce that expresses her downright contempt for their casuistry].

UNDERSHAFT [to Cusins] You are an educated man. That is against the tradition.

CUSINS Once in ten thousand times it happens that the schoolboy is a born master of what they try to teach him. Greek has not destroyed my mind: it has nourished it. Besides, I did not learn it at an English public school.

UNDERSHAFT Hm! Well, I cannot afford to be too particular: you have cornered the foundling market. Let it pass. You are eligible, Euripides: you are eligible.

BARBARA Dolly: yesterday morning, when Stephen told us all about the tradition, you became very silent; and you have been strange and excited ever since. Were you thinking of your birth then?

CUSINS When the finger of Destiny suddenly points at a man in the middle of his breakfast, it makes him thoughtful.

UNDERSHAFT   Aha! You have had your eye on the business, my young friend, have you?

CUSINS   Take care! There is an abyss of moral horror between me and your accursed aerial battleships.

UNDERSHAFT   Never mind the abyss for the present. Let us settle the practical details and leave your final decision open. You know that you will have to change your name. Do you object to that?

CUSINS   Would any man named Adolphus—any man called Dolly!—object to be called something else?

UNDERSHAFT   Good. Now, as to money! I propose to treat you handsomely from the beginning. You shall start at a thousand a year.

CUSINS [*with sudden heat, his spectacles twinkling with mischief*]   A thousand! You dare offer a miserable thousand to the son-in-law of a millionaire! No, by Heavens, Machiavelli! you shall not cheat me. You cannot do without me; and I can do without you. I must have two thousand five hundred a year for two years. At the end of that time, if I am a failure, I go. But if I am a success, and stay on, you must give me the other five thousand.

UNDERSHAFT   What other five thousand?

CUSINS   To make the two years up to five thousand a year. The two thousand five hundred is only half pay in case I should turn out a failure. The third year I must have ten per cent on the profits.

UNDERSHAFT [*taken aback*]   Ten per cent! Why, man, do you know what my profits are?

CUSINS   Enormous, I hope: otherwise I shall require twentyfive per cent.

UNDERSHAFT   But, Mr Cusins, this is a serious matter of business. You are not bringing any capital into the concern.

CUSINS   What! no capital! Is my mastery of Greek no capital? Is my access to the subtlest thought, the loftiest poetry yet attained by humanity, no capital? My character! my intellect! my life! my career! what Barbara calls my soul! are these no capital? Say another word; and I double my salary.

UNDERSHAFT   Be reasonable—

CUSINS [*peremptorily*]   Mr Undershaft: you have my terms. Take them or leave them.

UNDERSHAFT [*recovering himself*]   Very well. I note your terms; and I offer you half.

CUSINS [*disgusted*]   Half!

UNDERSHAFT [*firmly*]   Half.

CUSINS   You call yourself a gentleman; and you offer me half!!

UNDERSHAFT   I do not call myself a gentleman; but I offer you half.

CUSINS   This is your future partner! your successor! your son-in-law!

BARBARA   You are selling your own soul, Dolly, not mine. Leave me out of the bargain, please.

UNDERSHAFT   Come! I will go a step further for Barbara's sake. I will give you three fifths; but that is my last word.

CUSINS   Done!

LOMAX   Done in the eye! Why, *I* get only eight hundred, you know.

CUSINS By the way, Mac, I am a classical scholar, not an arithmetical one. Is three fifths more than half or less?

UNDERSHAFT More, of course.

CUSINS I would have taken two hundred and fifty. How you can succeed in business when you are willing to pay all that money to a University don who is obviously not worth a junior clerk's wages!—well! What will Lazarus say?

UNDERSHAFT Lazarus is a gentle romantic Jew who cares for nothing but string quartets and stalls at fashionable theatres. He will be blamed for your rapacity in money matters, poor fellow! as he has hitherto been blamed for mine. You are a shark of the first order, Euripides. So much the better for the firm!

BARBARA Is the bargain closed, Dolly? Does your soul belong to him now?

CUSINS No: the price is settled: that is all. The real tug of war is still to come. What about the moral question?

LADY BRITOMART There is no moral question in the matter at all, Adolphus. You must simply sell cannons and weapons to people whose cause is right and just, and refuse them to foreigners and criminals.

UNDERSHAFT [*determinedly*] No: none of that. You must keep the true faith of a Armorer, or you dont come in here.

CUSINS What on earth is the true faith of an Armorer?

UNDERSHAFT To give arms to all men who offer an honest price for them, without respect of persons or principles: to aristocrat and republican, to Nihilist and Tsar, to Capitalist and Socialist, to Protestant and Catholic, to burglar and policeman, to black man, white man and yellow man, to all sorts and conditions, all nationalities, all faiths, all follies, all causes and all crimes. The first Undershaft wrote up in his shop IF GOD GAVE THE HAND, LET NOT MAN WITHHOLD THE SWORD. The second wrote up ALL HAVE THE RIGHT TO FIGHT: NONE HAVE THE RIGHT TO JUDGE. The third wrote up TO MAN THE WEAPON: TO HEAVEN THE VICTORY. The fourth had no literary turn; so he did not write up anything; but he sold cannons to Napoleon under the nose of George the Third. The fifth wrote up PEACE SHALL NOT PREVAIL SAVE WITH A SWORD IN HER HAND. The sixth, my master, was the best of all. He wrote up NOTHING IS EVER DONE IN THIS WORLD UNTIL MEN ARE PREPARED TO KILL ONE ANOTHER IF IT IS NOT DONE. After that, there was nothing left for the seventh to say. So he wrote up, simply, UNASHAMED.

CUSINS My good Machiavelli, I shall certainly write something up on the wall; only, as I shall write it in Greek, you wont be able to read it. But as to your Armorer's faith, if I take my neck out of the noose of my own morality I am not going to put in into the noose of yours. I shall sell cannons to whom I please and refuse them to whom I please. So there!

UNDERSHAFT From the moment when you become Andrew Undershaft, you will never do as you please again. Dont come here lusting for power, young man.

CUSINS If power were my aim I should not come here for it. You have no power.

UNDERSHAFT None of my own, certainly.

CUSINS I have more power than you, more will. You do not drive this place: it drives you. And what drives the place?

UNDERSHAFT [*enigmatically*]   A will of which I am a part.

BARBARA [*startled*]   Father! Do you know what you are saying; or are you laying a snare for my soul?

CUSINS   Dont listen to his metaphysics, Barbara. The place is driven by the most rascally part of society, the money hunters, the pleasure hunters, the military promotion hunters; and he is their slave.

UNDERSHAFT   Not necessarily. Remember the Armorer's Faith. I will take an order from a good man as cheerfully as from a bad one. If you good people prefer preaching and shirking to buying my weapons and fighting the rascals, dont blame me. I can make cannons: I cannot make courage and conviction. Bah! you tire me, Euripides, with your morality mongering. Ask Barbara: she understands. [*He suddenly reaches up and takes Barbara's hands, looking powerfully into her eyes*] Tell him, my love, what power really means.

BARBARA [*hypnotized*]   Before I joined the Salvation Army, I was in my own power; and the consequence was that I never knew what to do with myself. When I joined it, I had not time enough for all the things I had to do.

UNDERSHAFT [*approvingly*]   Just so. And why was that, do you suppose?

BARBARA   Yesterday I should have said, because I was in the power of God. [*She resumes her self-possession, withdrawing her hands from his with a power equal to his own*]. But you came and shewed me that I was in the power of Bodger and Undershaft. Today I feel—oh! how can I put it into words? Sarah: do you remember the earthquake at Cannes, when we were little children?—how little the surprise of the first shock mattered compared to the dread and horror of waiting for the second? That is how I feel in this place today. I stood on the rock I thought eternal: and without a word of warning it reeled and crumbled under me. I was safe with an infinite wisdom watching me, an army marching to Salvation with me; and in a moment, at a stroke of your pen in a cheque book, I stood alone; and the heavens were empty. That was the first shock of the earthquake: I am waiting for the second.

UNDERSHAFT   Come, come, my daughter! dont make too much of your little tinpot tragedy. What do we do here when we spend years of work and thought and thousands of pounds of solid cash on a new gun or an aerial battleship that turns out just a hairsbreadth wrong after all? Scrap it. Scrap it without wasting another hour or another pound on it. Well, you have made for yourself something that you call a morality or a religion or what not. It doesnt fit the facts. Well, scrap it. Scrap it and get one that does fit. That is what is wrong with the world at present. It scraps its obsolete steam engines and dynamos; but it wont scrap its old prejudices and its old moralities and its old religions and its old political constitutions. Whats the result? In machinery it does very well; but in morals and religion and politics it is working at a loss that brings it nearer bankruptcy every year. Dont persist in that folly. If your old religion broke down yesterday, get a newer and a better one for tomorrow.

BARBARA   Oh how gladly I would take a better one to my soul! But you offer me a worse one. [*Turning on him with sudden vehemence*]. Justify yourself: shew me some light through the darkness of this dreadful place, with its beautifully clean workshops, and respectable workmen, and model homes.

UNDERSHAFT   Cleanliness and respectability do not need justification, Barbara: they justify themselves. I see no darkness here, no dreadfulness. In your Salvation shelter I saw poverty, misery, cold and hunger. You gave them bread and treacle and dreams of heaven. I give from thirty shillings a week to twelve thousand a year. They find their own dreams; but I look after the drainage.

BARBARA   And their souls?

UNDERSHAFT   I save their souls just as I saved yours.

BARBARA [*revolted*]   You saved my soul! What do you mean?

UNDERSHAFT   I fed you and clothed you and housed you. I took care that you should have money enough to live handsomely—more than enough; so that you could be wasteful, careless, generous. That saved your soul from the seven deadly sins.

BARBARA [*bewildered*]   The seven deadly sins!

UNDERSHAFT   Yes, the deadly seven. [*Counting on his fingers*] Food, clothing, firing, rent, taxes, respectability and children. Nothing can lift those seven millstones from Man's neck but money; and the spirit cannot soar until the millstones are lifted. I lifted them from your spirit. I enabled Barbara to become Major Barbara; and I saved her from the crime of poverty.

CUSINS   Do you call poverty a crime?

UNDERSHAFT   The worst of crimes. All the other crimes are virtues beside it: all the other dishonors are chivalry itself by comparison. Poverty blights whole cities; spreads horrible pestilences; strikes dead the very souls of all who come within sight, sound, or smell of it. What you call crime is nothing: a murder here and a theft there, a blow now and a curse then: what do they matter? they are only the accidents and illnesses of life: there are not fifty genuine professional criminals in London. But there are millions of poor people, abject people, dirty people, ill fed, ill clothed people. They poison us morally and physically: they kill the happiness of society: they force us to do away with our own liberties and to organize unnatural cruelties for fear they should rise against us and drag us down into their abyss. Only fools fear crime: we all fear poverty. Pah! [*turning on Barbara*] you talk of your half-saved ruffian in West Ham: you accuse me of dragging his soul back to perdition. Well, bring him to me here; and I will drag his soul back again to salvation for you. Not by words and dreams; but by thirtyeight shillings a week, a sound house in a handsome street, and a permanent job. In three weeks he will have a fancy waistcoat; in three months a tall hat and a chapel sitting; before the end of the year he will shake hands with a duchess at a Primrose League meeting, and join the Conservative Party.

BARBARA   And will he be the better for that?

UNDERSHAFT   You know he will. Dont be a hypocrite, Barbara. He will be better fed, better housed, better clothed, better behaved; and his children will be pounds heavier and bigger. That will be better than an American cloth mattress in a shelter, chopping firewood, eating bread and treacle, and being forced to kneel down from time to time to thank heaven for it: knee drill, I think you call it. It is cheap work converting starving men with a Bible in one hand and a slice of bread in the other. I will undertake to convert West Ham to Mahometanism on the same terms. Try your hand on my men: their souls are hungry because their bodies are full.

BARBARA   And leave the east end to starve?

UNDERSHAFT [*his energetic tone dropping into one of bitter and brooding remembrance*]   I was an east ender. I moralized and starved until one day I swore that I would be a full-fed free man at all costs; that nothing should stop me except a bullet, neither reason nor morals nor the lives of other men. I said "Thou shalt starve ere I starve"; and with that word I became free and great. I was a dangerous man until I had my will: now I am a useful, beneficent, kindly person. That is the history of most self-made millionaires, I fancy. When it is the history of every Englishman we shall have an England worth living in.

LADY BRITOMART   Stop making speeches, Andrew. This is not the place for them.

UNDERSHAFT [*punctured*]   My dear: I have no other means of conveying my ideas.

LADY BRITOMART   Your ideas are nonsense. You got on because you were selfish and unscrupulous.

UNDERSHAFT   Not at all. I had the strongest scruples about poverty and starvation. Your moralists are quite unscrupulous about both: they make virtues of them. I had rather be a thief than a pauper. I had rather be a murderer than a slave. I dont want to be either; but if you force the alternative on me, then, by Heaven, I'll choose the braver and more moral one. I hate poverty and slavery worse than any other crimes whatsoever. And let me tell you this. Poverty and slavery have stood up for centuries to your sermons and leading articles: they will not stand up to my machine guns. Dont preach at them: dont reason with them. Kill them.

BARBARA   Killing. Is that your remedy for everything?

UNDERSHAFT   It is the final test of conviction, the only lever strong enough to overturn a social system, the only way of saying Must. Let six hundred and seventy fools loose in the streets; and three policemen can scatter them. But huddle them together in a certain house in Westminster; and let them go through certain ceremonies and call themselves certain names until at last they get the courage to kill; and your six hundred and seventy fools become a government. Your pious mob fills up ballot papers and imagines it is governing its masters; but the ballot paper that really governs is the paper that has a bullet wrapped up in it.

CUSINS   That is perhaps why, like most intelligent people, I never vote.

UNDERSHAFT   Vote! Bah! When you vote, you only change the names of the cabinet. When you shoot, you pull down governments, inaugurate new epochs, abolish old orders and set up new. Is that historically true, Mr Learned Man, or is it not?

CUSINS   It is historically true. I loathe having to admit it. I repudiate your sentiments. I abhor your nature. I defy you in every possible way. Still, it is true.

But it ought not to be true.

UNDERSHAFT   Ought! ought! ought! ought! ought! Are you going to spend your life saying ought, like the rest of our moralists? Turn your oughts into shalls, man. Come and make explosives with me. Whatever can blow men up can blow society up. The history of the world is the history of those who had courage enough to embrace this truth. Have you the courage to embrace it, Barbara?

LADY BRITOMART   Barbara: I positively forbid you to listen to your father's abominable wickedness. And you, Adolphus, ought to know better than to go about saying that wrong things are true. What does it matter whether they are true if they are wrong?

UNDERSHAFT   What does it matter whether they are wrong if they are true?

LADY BRITOMART [rising]   Children: come home instantly. Andrew: I am exceedingly sorry I allowed you to call on us. You are wickeder than ever. Come at once.

BARBARA [shaking her head]   It's no use running away from wicked people, mamma.

LADY BRITOMART   It is every use. It shews your disapprobation of them.

BARBARA   It does not save them.

LADY BRITOMART   I can see that you are going to disobey me. Sarah: are you coming home or are you not?

SARAH   I daresay it's very wicked of papa to make cannons; but I dont think I shall cut him on that account.

LOMAX [pouring oil on the troubled waters]   The fact is, you know, there is a certain amount of tosh about this notion of wickedness. It doesnt work. You must look at facts. Not that I would say a word in favor of anything wrong; but then, you see, all sorts of chaps are always doing all sorts of things; and we have to fit them in somehow, dont you know. What I mean is that you cant go cutting everybody; and thats about what it comes to. [Their rapt attention to his eloquence makes him nervous]. Perhaps I dont make myself clear.

LADY BRITOMART   You are lucidity itself, Charles. Because Andrew is successful and has plenty of money to give to Sarah, you will flatter him and encourage him in his wickedness.

LOMAX [unruffled]   Well, where the carcase is, there will the eagles be gathered, dont you know. [To Undershaft] Eh? What?

UNDERSHAFT   Precisely. By the way, may I call you Charles?

LOMAX   Delighted. Cholly is the usual ticket.

UNDERSHAFT [to Lady Britomart]   Biddy—

LADY BRITOMART [violently]   Dont dare call me Biddy. Charles Lomax: you are a fool. Adolphus Cusins: you are a Jesuit. Stephen: you are a prig. Barbara: you are a lunatic. Andrew: you are a vulgar tradesman. Now you all know my opinion; and my conscience is clear, at all events [she sits down with a vehemence that the rug fortunately softens].

UNDERSHAFT   My dear: you are the incarnation of morality. [She snorts]. Your conscience is clear and your duty done when you have called everybody names.

Come, Euripides! it is getting late; and we all want to go home. Make up your mind.

CUSINS   Understand this, you old demon—

LADY BRITOMART   Adolphus!

UNDERSHAFT   Let him alone, Biddy. Proceed, Euripides.

CUSINS   You have me in a horrible dilemma. I want Barbara.

UNDERSHAFT   Like all young men, you greatly exaggerate the difference between one young woman and another.

BARBARA   Quite true, Dolly.

CUSINS   I also want to avoid being a rascal.

UNDERSHAFT [*with biting contempt*]   You lust for personal righteousness, for self-approval, for what you call a good conscience, for what Barbara calls salvation, for what I call patronizing people who are not so lucky as yourself.

CUSINS   I do not: all the poet in me recoils from being a good man. But there are things in me that I must reckon with. Pity—

UNDERSHAFT   Pity! The scavenger of misery.

CUSINS   Well, love.

UNDERSHAFT   I know. You love the needy and the outcast: you love the oppressed races, the negro, the Indian ryot, the underdog everywhere. Do you love the Japanese? Do you love the French? Do you love the English?

CUSINS   No. Every true Englishman detests the English. We are the wickedest nation on earth; and our success is a moral horror.

UNDERSHAFT   That is what comes of your gospel of love, is it?

CUSINS   May I not love even my father-in-law?

UNDERSHAFT   Who wants your love, man? By what right do you take the liberty of offering it to me? I will have your due heed and respect, or I will kill you. But your love! Damn your impertinence!

CUSINS [*grinning*]   I may not be able to control my affections, Mac.

UNDERSHAFT   You are fencing, Euripides. You are weakening: your grip is slipping. Come! try your last weapon. Pity and love have broken in your hand: forgiveness is still left.

CUSINS   No: forgiveness is a beggar's refuge. I am with you there: we must pay our debts.

UNDERSHAFT   Well said. Come! you will suit me. Remember the words of Plato.

CUSINS [*starting*]   Plato! You dare quote Plato to me!

UNDERSHAFT   Plato says, my friend, that society cannot be saved until either the Professors of Greek take to making gunpowder, or else the makers of gunpowder become Professors of Greek.

CUSINS   Oh, tempter, cunning tempter!

UNDERSHAFT   Come! choose, man, choose.

CUSINS   But perhaps Barbara will not marry me if I make the wrong choice.

BARBARA   Perhaps not.

CUSINS [*desperately perplexed*]   You hear!

BARBARA   Father: do you love nobody?

UNDERSHAFT   I love my best friend.

LADY BRITOMART   And who is that, pray?

UNDERSHAFT   My bravest enemy. That is the man who keeps me up to the mark.

CUSINS   You know, the creature is really a sort of poet in his way. Suppose he is a great man, after all!

UNDERSHAFT   Suppose you stop talking and make up your mind, my young friend.

CUSINS   But you are driving me against my nature. I hate war.

UNDERSHAFT   Hatred is the coward's revenge for being intimidated. Dare you make war on war? Here are the means: my friend Mr Lomax is sitting on them.

LOMAX [springing up]   Oh I say! You dont mean that this thing is loaded, do you? My ownest: come off it.

SARAH [sitting placidly on the shell]   If I am to be blown up, the more thoroughly it is done the better. Dont fuss, Cholly.

LOMAX [to Undershaft, strongly remonstrant]   Your own daughter, you know!

UNDERSHAFT   So I see. [To Cusins] Well, my friend, may we expect you here at six tomorrow morning?

CUSINS [firmly]   Not on any account. I will see the whole establishment blown up with its own dynamite before I will get up at five. My hours are healthy, rational hours: eleven to five.

UNDERSHAFT   Come when you please: before a week you will come at six and stay until I turn you out for the sake of your health. [Calling] Bilton! [He turns to Lady Britomart, who rises]. My dear: let us leave these two young people to themselves for a moment. [Bilton comes from the shed]. I am going to take you through the gun cotton shed.

BILTON [Barring the way]   You cant take anything explosive in here, sir.

LADY BRITOMART   What do you mean? Are you alluding to me?

BILTON [unmoved]   No, maam. Mr Undershaft has the other gentleman's matches in his pocket.

LADY BRITOMART [abruptly]   Oh! I beg your pardon. [She goes into the shed].

UNDERSHAFT   Quite right, Bilton, quite right: here you are. [He gives Bilton the box of matches]. Come, Stephen. Come, Charles, Bring Sarah. [He passes into the shed].

Bilton opens the box and deliberately drops the matches into the fire-bucket.

LOMAX   Oh! I say [Bilton hands him the empty box]. Infernal nonsense! Pure scientific ignorance! [He goes in].

SARAH   Am I all right, Bilton?

BILTON   Youll have to put on list slippers, miss: thats all. Weve got em inside. [She goes in].

STEPHEN [very seriously to Cusins]   Dolly, old fellow, think. Think before you decide. Do you feel that you are a sufficiently practical man? It is a huge undertaking, an enormous responsibility. All this mass of business will be Greek to you.

CUSINS   Oh, I think it will be much less difficult than Greek.

STEPHEN   Well, I just want to say this before I leave you to yourselves. Dont let anything I have said about right and wrong prejudice you against this great chance in life. I have satisfied myself that the business is one of the highest character and a credit to our country. [*Emotionally*] I am very proud of my father. I—[*Unable to proceed, he presses Cusins' hand and goes hastily into the shed, followed by Bilton*].

Barbara and Cusins, left alone together, look at one another silently.

CUSINS   Barbara: I am going to accept this offer.

BARBARA   I thought you would.

CUSINS   You understand, dont you, that I had to decide without consulting you. If I had thrown the burden of the choice on you, you would sooner or later have despised me for it.

BARBARA   Yes: I did not want you to sell your soul for me any more than for this inheritance.

CUSINS   It is not the sale of my soul that troubles me: I have sold it too often to care about that. I have sold it for a professorship, I have sold it for an income. I have sold it to escape being imprisoned for refusing to pay taxes for hangmen's ropes and unjust wars and things that I abhor. What is all human conduct but the daily and hourly sale of our souls for trifles? What I am now selling it for is neither money nor position nor comfort, but for reality and for power.

BARBARA   You know that you will have no power, and that he has none.

CUSINS   I know. It is not for myself alone. I want to make power for the world.

BARBARA   I want to make power for the world too; but it must be spiritual power.

CUSINS   I think all power is spiritual: these cannons will not go off by themselves. I have tried to make spiritual power by teaching Greek. But the world can never be really touched by a dead language and a dead civilization. The people must have power; and the people cannot have Greek. Now the power that is made here can be wielded by all men.

BARBARA   Power to burn women's houses down and kill their sons and tear their husbands to pieces.

CUSINS   You cannot have power for good without having power for evil too. Even mother's milk nourishes murderers as well as heroes. This power which only tears men's bodies to pieces has never been so horribly abused as the intellectual power, the imaginative power, the poetic, religious power that can enslave men's souls. As a teacher of Greek I gave the intellectual man weapons against the common man. I now want to give the common man weapons against the intellectual man. I love the common people. I want to arm them against the lawyers, the doctors, the priests, the literary men, the professors, the artists, and the politicians, who, once in authority, are more disastrous and tyrannical than all the fools, rascals, and imposters. I want a power simple enough for common men to use, yet strong enough to force the intellectual oligarchy to use its genius for the general good.

BARBARA   Is there no higher power than that [*pointing to the shell*]?

CUSINS Yes: but that power can destroy the higher powers just as a tiger can destroy a man: there Man must master that power first. I admitted this when the Turks and Greeks were last at war. My best pupil went out to fight for Hellas. My parting gift to him was not a copy of Plato's Republic, but a revolver and a hundred Undershaft cartridges. The blood of every Turk he shot—if he shot any—is on my head as well as on Undershaft's. That act committed me to this place for ever. Your father's challenge has beaten me. Dare I make war on war? I dare. I must. I will. And now, is it all over between us?

BARBARA [*touched by his evident dread of her answer*] Silly baby Dolly! How could it be!

CUSINS [*overjoyed*] Then you—you—you—Oh for my drum! [*He flourishes imaginary drumsticks*].

BARBARA [*angered by his levity*] Take care, Dolly, take care. Oh, if only I could get away from you and from father and from it all! if I could have the wings of a dove and fly away to heaven!

CUSINS And leave me!

BARBARA Yes, you, and all the other naughty mischievous children of men. But I cant. I was happy in the Salvation Army for a moment. I escaped from the world into a paradise of enthusiasm and prayer and soul saving; but the moment our money ran short, it all came back to Bodger: it was he who saved our people: he, and the Prince of Darkness, my papa. Undershaft and Bodger: their hands stretch everywhere: when we feed a starving fellow creature, it is with their bread, because there is no other bread; when we tend the sick, it is in the hospitals they endow; if we turn from the churches they build, we must kneel on the stones of the streets they pave. As long as that lasts, there is no getting away from them. Turning our backs on Bodger and Undershaft is turning our backs on life.

CUSINS I thought you were determined to turn your back on the wicked side of life.

BARBARA There is no wicked side: life is all one. And I never wanted to shirk my share in whatever evil must be endured, whether it be sin or suffering. I wish I could cure you of middle-class ideas, Dolly.

CUSINS [*gasping*] Middle cl—! A snub! A social snub to me! from the daughter of a foundling!

BARBARA That is why I have no class, Dolly: I come straight out of the heart of the whole people. If I were middle-class I should turn my back on my father's business; and we should both live in an artistic drawing room, with you reading the reviews in one corner, and I in the other at the piano, playing Schumann: both very superior persons, and neither of us a bit of use. Sooner than that, I would sweep out the guncotton shed, or be one of Bodger's barmaids. Do you know what would have happened if you had refused papa's offer?

CUSINS I wonder!

BARBARA I should have given you up and married the man who accepted it.

After all, my dear old mother has more sense than any of you. I felt like her when I saw this place—felt that I must have it—that never, never, never could I let it go; only she thought it was the houses and the kitchen ranges and the linen and china, when it was really all the human souls to be saved: not weak souls in starved bodies, sobbing with gratitude for a scrap of bread and treacle, but fulfilled, quarrelsome, snobbish, uppish creatures, all standing on their little rights and dignities, and thinking that my father ought to be greatly obliged to them for making so much money for him—and so he ought. That is where salvation is really wanted. My father shall never throw it in my teeth again that my converts were bribed with bread. [She is transfigured]. I have got rid of the bribe of bread. I have got rid of the bribe of heaven. Let God's work be done for its own sake: the work he had to create us to do because it cannot be done except by living men and women. When I die, let him be in my debt, not I in his; and let me forgive him as becomes a woman of my rank.

CUSINS   Then the way of life lies through the factory of death?

BARBARA   Yes, through the raising of hell to heaven and of man to God, through the unveiling of an eternal light in the Valley of The Shadow. [Seizing him with both hands] Oh, did you think my courage would never come back? did you believe that I was a deserter? that I, who have stood in the streets, and taken my people to my heart, and talked of the holiest and greatest things with them, could ever turn back and chatter foolishly to fashionable people about nothing in a drawing room? Never, never, never, never: Major Barbara will die with the colors. Oh! and I have my dear little Dolly boy still; and he has found me my place and my work. Glory Hallelujah! [She kisses him].

CUSINS   My dearest: consider my delicate health. I cannot stand as much happiness as you can.

BARBARA   Yes: it is not easy work being in love with me, is it? But it's good for you. [She runs to the shed, and calls, childlike] Mamma! Mamma! [Bilton comes out of the shed, followed by Undershaft]. I want Mamma.

UNDERSHAFT   She is taking off her list slippers, dear. [He passes on to Cusins]. Well? What does she say?

CUSINS   She has gone right up into the skies.

LADY BRITOMART [coming from the shed and stopping on the steps, obstructing Sarah, who follows with Lomax. Barbara clutches like a baby at her mother's skirt] Barbara: when will you learn to be independent and to act and think for yourself? I know as well as possible what that cry of "Mamma, Mamma," means. Always running to me!

SARAH [touching Lady Britomart's ribs with her finger tips and imitating a bicycle horn] Pip! pip!

LADY BRITOMART [highly indignant]   How dare you say Pip! pip! to me, Sarah? you are both very naughty children. What do you want, Barbara?

BARBARA   I want a house in the village to live in with Dolly. [Dragging at the skirt] Come and tell me which one to take.

UNDERSHAFT [to Cusins]   Six o'clock tomorrow morning, Euripides.

BERTOLT BRECHT

1898–1956

Born and raised in Augsburg, a Bavarian city in western Germany, where his father worked in the local paper factory, Brecht took up writing while still in high school and had his first play produced there when he was sixteen. After a year of medical study in Munich, he was inducted into the army, and following the first world war became involved in an unsuccessful revolution in Bavaria, a disenchanting political experience that provoked his first major theatrical success, *Drums in the Night* (1922). In 1924, after four years as resident playwright at a theater in Munich, Brecht moved to Berlin, where his contact with *avant garde* writers and producers led him to develop his radical and influential approach to drama, known as "epic theater," which he used through his subsequent career. His aim in "epic theater" was to shock spectators into a heightened political and social consciousness, rather than to involve them in a complex emotional or psychological situation. To achieve this goal, he deliberately used an episodic structure of scenes, shifting rapidly from one locale to another, moving back and forth quickly from prose dialogue, to verse, to song; he trained his actors to distance themselves from the characters they were performing and to deliver their lines in a theatrically self-conscious manner; and he used various nonrealistic staging devices, such as posters, slide projections, and garish lighting effects. His earliest and most successful piece of "epic theater" was *The Threepenny Opera* (1928). During the early thirties, he wrote a series of dogmatically Marxist plays. During the late thirties and early forties, when his communist sympathies had forced him to flee Nazi Germany and take up residence in the United States, he wrote his other well-known works, *Mother Courage and her Children* (1939), *Galileo* (1939), *The Good Woman of Setzuan* (1943), and *The Caucasian Chalk Circle* (1943).

The Threepenny Opera
After John Gay: The Beggar's Opera

Collaborators: E. Hauptmann, K. Weill
Translators: Ralph Manheim and John Willett

CHARACTERS

MACHEATH, called Mac the Knife
JONATHAN JEREMIAH PEACHUM, proprietor of "Beggar's Friend Ltd."
CELIA PEACHUM, his wife
POLLY PEACHUM, his daughter
BROWN, High Sheriff of London
LUCY, his daughter
LOW-DIVE JENNY

SMITH	THE GANG
THE REVEREND KIMBALL	BEGGARS
FILCH	WHORES
A BALLAD SINGER	CONSTABLES

PROLOGUE

The Ballad of Mac the Knife

Fair in Soho

The beggars are begging, the thieves are stealing, the whores are whoring. A ballad singer sings a ballad:

> See the shark with teeth like razors.
> All can read his open face.
> And Macheath has got a knife, but
> Not in such an obvious place.

> See the shark, how red his fins are
> As he slashes at his prey.
> Mac the Knife wears white kid gloves which
> Give the minimum away.

> By the Thames's turbid waters
> Men abruptly tumble down.
> Is it plague or is it cholera?
> Or a sign Macheath's in town?

> On a beautiful blue Sunday
> See a corpse stretched in the Strand.
> See a man dodge round the corner . . .
> Mackie's friends will understand.

> And Schmul Meir, reported missing
> Like so many wealthy men:
> Mack the Knife acquired his cash box.
> God alone knows how or when.

[*Peachum goes walking across the stage from left to right with his wife and daughter*]

> Jenny Towler turned up lately
> With a knife stuck through her breast
> While Macheath walks the Embankment
> Nonchalantly unimpressed.

Where is Alfred Gleet the cabman?
Who can get that story clear?
All the world may know the answer
Just Macheath has no idea.

And the ghastly fire in Soho—
Seven children at a go—
In the crowd stands Mac the Knife, but he
Isn't asked and doesn't know.

And the child-bride in her nightie
Whose assailant's still at large
Violated in her slumbers—
Mackie, how much did you charge?

[*Laughter among the whores. A man steps out from their midst and walks quickly away across the square*]

LOW-DIVE JENNY   That was Mac the Knife!

ACT I

SCENE 1

To combat the increasing callousness of mankind, J. Peachum, businessman, has opened a shop where the poorest of the poor can acquire an exterior that will touch the hardest of hearts.

Jonathan Jeremiah Peachum's outfitting shop for beggars

Peachum's Morning Hymn

You ramshackle Christian, awake!
Go on with your sinful employment
Show what an old crook you could make.
The Lord will soon cut your enjoyment.

Betray your own brother, you rogue
And sell your old woman, you rat.
You think the Lord God's just a joke?
He'll give you His Judgment on that.

PEACHUM [*to the audience*]   Something must be done. My business is too hard, for my business is arousing human sympathy. There are a few things that stir men's souls, just a few, but the trouble is that after repeated use they lose their effect. Because man has the abominable gift of being able to deaden his feelings at will, so to speak. Suppose, for instance, a man sees another man standing on the corner with a stump for an arm; the first time he may be shocked enough to give him tenpence, but the second time it will only be fivepence, and if he sees him a third time he'll hand him over to the police without batting an eyelash. It's the same with the spiritual approach. [*A large sign saying "It is more blessed to give than to receive" is lowered from the grid*] What good are the most beautiful, the most poignant sayings, painted on the most enticing little signs, when they get expended so quickly? The Bible has four or five sayings that stir the heart; once a man has expended them, there's nothing for it but starvation. Take this one, for instance—"Give and it shall be given unto you"—how threadbare it is after hanging here a mere three weeks. Yes, you have to keep on offering something new. So it's back to the good old Bible again, but how long can it go on providing?

[*Knocking. Peachum opens. Enter a young man by the name of Filch*]

FILCH   Messrs. Peachum & Co.?

PEACHUM   Peachum.

FILCH   Are you the proprietor of the "Beggar's Friend Ltd."? I've been sent to you. Fine slogans you've got there! Money in the bank, that is. Got a whole library full of them, I suppose? That's what I call really something. What chance has a bloke like me got to think up ideas; and how can business flourish without education?

PEACHUM   What's your name?

FILCH   It's like this, Mr. Peachum, I've been down on my luck since I was a boy. My mother drank, my father gambled. Left to my own resources at an early age, without a mother's tender hand, I sank deeper and deeper into the quicksands of the big city. I 've never known a father's care or the blessings of a happy home. So now you see me . . .

PEACHUM   So now I see you . . .

FILCH   [*confused*]   . . . bereft of all support, a prey to my base instincts.

PEACHUM   Like a derelict on the high seas and so on. Now tell me, derelict, which district have you been reciting that fairy story in?

FILCH   What do you mean, Mr. Peachum?

PEACHUM   You deliver that speech in public, I take it?

FILCH   Well, it's like this, Mr. Peachum, yesterday there was an unpleasant little incident in Highland Street. There I am, standing on the corner quiet and miserable, holding out my hat, no suspicion of anything nasty . . .

PEACHUM   [*leafs through a notebook*]   Highland Street. Yes, yes, right. You're the bastard that Honey and Sam caught yesterday. You had the impudence to be molesting passers-by in District 10. We let you off with a thrashing because we had reason to believe you didn't know what's what. But if you show your face again it'll be the ax for you. Got it?

FILCH   Please, Mr. Peachum, please. What can I do, Mr. Peachum? The gentlemen beat me black and blue and then they gave me your business card. If I
took off my coat, you'd think you were looking at a fish on a slab.

PEACHUM   My friend, if you don't look like a bloater, then my men haven't been
doing their job. Along come these young whippersnappers, imagining
they've only got to hold out their paws to land a steak. What would you say
if somebody started fishing the best trout out of your pond?

FILCH   It's like this, Mr. Peachum—I haven't got a pond.

PEACHUM   Licenses are issued to professionals only. [*Points in a businesslike way to
a map of the city*] London is divided into fourteen districts. Any man who
intends to practice the craft of begging in any of them needs a license from
Jonathan Jeremiah Peachum & Co. Why, anybody could come along—a prey
to his base instincts.

FILCH   Mr. Peachum, only a few shillings stand between me and utter ruin.
Something must be done. With two shillings in my pocket I . . .

PEACHUM   One pound.

FILCH   Mr. Peachum!

[*Points imploringly at a sign saying "Do not turn a deaf ear to misery!" Peachum points
to the curtain over a showcase, on which is written: "Give and it shall be given unto you!"*]

FILCH   Ten bob.

PEACHUM   Plus fifty percent of your take. Settle up once a week. With outfit seventy percent.

FILCH   What does the outfit consist of?

PEACHUM   That's for the firm to decide.

FILCH   Which district could I start in?

PEACHUM   Baker Street. Numbers 2 to 104. That comes even cheaper. Only fifty
percent, including the outfit.

FILCH   Very well. [*He pays*]

PEACHUM   Your name?

FILCH   Charles Filch.

PEACHUM   Right. [*Shouts*] Mrs. Peachum! [*Mrs. Peachum enters*] This is Filch.
Number three-fourteen. Baker Street district. I'll do his entry myself. Trust
you to pick this moment to apply, just before the Coronation, when for once
in a lifetime there's a chance of making a little something. Outfit C. [*He opens
a linen curtain before a showcase in which there are five wax dummies*]

FILCH   What's that?

PEACHUM   Those are the five basic types of misery, those most likely to touch the
human heart. The sight of such types puts a man into that unnatural state
where he is willing to part with money.
Outfit A: Victim of the traffic speed-up. The merry cripple, always cheerful
[*he acts it out*], always carefree, emphasized by arm-stump.
Outfit B: Victim of the Higher Strategy. The Tiresome Trembler, molests passers-by, operates by inspiring nausea [*he acts it out*], attenuated by medals.

Outfit C: Victim of modern Technology. The Pitiful Blind Man, the Cordon Bleu of Beggary. [*He acts out, staggering toward Filch. The moment he bumps into Filch, Filch cries out in horror. Peachum stops at once, looks at him with amazement and suddenly roars*] He's *sorry* for me! You'll never be a beggar as long as you live! You're only fit to be begged from! Very well, outfit D! Celia, you've been drinking again. And now you can't see straight. Number one-thirty-six has complained about his outfit. How often do I have to tell you that a gentleman doesn't put on filthy clothes? Number-one-thirty-six paid for a brand-new suit. The only thing about it that could inspire pity was the stains and they should have been added by just ironing in candle wax. Use your head! Have I got to do everything myself? [*To Filch*] Take off your clothes and put this on, but mind you, look after it!

FILCH   What about my things?

PEACHUM   Property of the firm. Outfit E: young man who has seen better days or, if you'd rather, never thought it would come to this.

FILCH   Oh, you use them again? Why can't *I* do the better days act?

PEACHUM   Because nobody can make his own suffering sound convincing, my boy. If you have a bellyache and say so, people will simply be disgusted. Anyway, you're not here to ask questions but to put these things on.

FILCH   Aren't they rather dirty? [*After Peachum has given him a penetrating look*] Excuse me, sir, please excuse me.

MRS. PEACHUM   Shake a leg, son, I'm not standing here holding your trousers till Christmas.

FILCH   [*suddenly emphatic*]   But I'm not taking my shoes off! Absolutely not. I'd sooner drop the whole business. They're the only present my poor mother ever gave me, I may have sunk pretty low, but never . . .

MRS. PEACHUM   Stop driveling. We all know your feet are dirty.

FILCH   Where am I supposed to wash my feet? In mid-winter?

[*Mrs. Peachum leads him behind a screen, then she sits down on the left and starts ironing candle wax into a suit*]

PEACHUM   Where's your daughter?

MRS. PEACHUM   Polly? Upstairs.

PEACHUM   Has that man been here again? The one who always comes round when I'm out?

MRS. PEACHUM   Don't be so suspicious, Jonathan, there's no finer gentleman. The Captain takes a real interest in our Polly.

PEACHUM   I see.

MRS. PEACHUM   And if I've got half an eye in my head, Polly thinks he's very nice too.

PEACHUM   Celia, the way you chuck your daughter around anyone would think I was a millionaire. Wanting to marry her off? The idea! Do you think this lousy business of ours would survive a week if those ragamuffins our customers had nothing better than *our* legs to look at? A husband! He'd have us in his clutches in three shakes! In his clutches like this! Do you think your daughter can hold her tongue in bed any better than you?

MRS. PEACHUM A fine opinion of your daughter you have.

PEACHUM The worst. The very worst. A lump of sensuality, that's what she is.

MRS. PEACHUM If so, she didn't get it from you.

PEACHUM Marriage! I expect my daughter to be to me as bread to the hungry [*he leafs in the Book*]; it even says so in the Bible somewhere. Anyway marriage is disgusting. I'll teach her to get married.

MRS. PEACHUM Jonathan, you're just a barbarian.

PEACHUM Barbarian! What's this gentleman's name?

MRS. PEACHUM They never call him anything but "the Captain."

PEACHUM So you haven't even asked him his name? Interesting.

MRS. PEACHUM We wouldn't be so rude as to ask him for his birth certificate when he's so distinguished and invited the two of us to the Cuttlefish Hotel for a little hop.

PEACHUM Where?

MRS. PEACHUM To the Cuttlefish for a little hop.

PEACHUM Captain? Cuttlefish Hotel? Hm, hm, hm . . .

MRS. PEACHUM A gentleman who has always handled my daughter and me with kid gloves.

PEACHUM Kid gloves!

MRS. PEACHUM It's quite true, he always does wear gloves, white ones: white kid gloves.

PEACHUM I see. White gloves and a cane with an ivory handle and spats and patent-leather shoes and an over-powering personality and a scar . . .

MRS. PEACHUM On his neck. What! Isn't there anybody you don't know? [*Filch crawls out from behind the screen*]

FILCH Mr. Peachum, couldn't you give me some tips, I've always believed in having a system and not just shooting off my mouth any old how.

MRS. PEACHUM A system!

PEACHUM Let him be a half-wit. Come back this evening at six, we'll teach you the rudiments. Now clear out!

FILCH Thank you very much indeed, Mr. Peachum. Many thanks. [*Goes out*]

PEACHUM Fifty percent!—And now I'll tell you who this gentleman with the gloves is—Mac the Knife! [*He runs up the stairs to Polly's bedroom*]

MRS. PEACHUM God in Heaven! Mac the Knife! Lord alive! For what we are about to receive, the Lord—Polly! What's become of Polly? [*Peachum comes down slowly*]

PEACHUM Polly? Polly's not come home. Her bed is untouched.

MRS. PEACHUM Then she's gone to supper with that wool merchant. That'll be it.

PEACHUM Let's hope to God it is the wool merchant!

[*Mr. and Mrs. Peachum step before the curtain and sing. Song lighting: golden glow. The organ is lit up. Three lamps are lowered from above on a pole, and the signs say:*]

The "No They Can't" Song

1

PEACHUM

No, they can't
Bear to be at home all tucked up tight in bed.
It's fun they want
You can bet they've got some fancy notions brewing up instead.

MRS. PEACHUM

So that's your Moon over Soho
That is your infernal "d'you feel my heart beating?" line.
That's the old "wherever you go I shall be with you, honey"
When you first fall in love and the moonbeams shine.

2

PEACHUM

No, they can't
See what's good for them and set their mind on it.
It's fun they want
So they end up on their arses in the shit.

BOTH

Then where's your Moon over Soho?
What's come of your infernal "d'you feel my heart beating?" bit?
Where's the old "wherever you go I shall be with you, honey"?
When you're no more in love and you're in the shit.

SCENE 2

Deep in the heart of Soho the bandit Mac the Knife is celebrating his marriage to Polly Peachum, the beggar king's daughter

Bare Stable

MATTHEW [*known as Matt of the Mint, holds out his revolver and examines the room with a lantern*]   Hey, hands up if anybody's here!

[*Macheath enters and makes a tour of inspection along the footlights*]

MACHEATH   Well, is anybody here?
MATTHEW   Not a soul. Just the place for our wedding.
POLLY [*enters in wedding dress*]   But it's a stable!
MAC   Sit on the feed-bin for the moment, Polly. [*To the audience*] Today this stable

will witness my marriage to Miss Polly Peachum, who has followed me for
love in order to share my life with me.

MATTHEW   All over London they'll be saying this is the most daring job you've
ever pulled, enticing Mr. Peachum's only child from his home.

MAC   Who's Mr. Peachum?

MATTHEW   He'll tell you he's the poorest man in London.

POLLY   But you surely don't intend to have our wedding here? Why, it is a common stable. You can't ask the vicar to a place like this. Besides, it isn't even
ours. We really oughtn't to start our new life with a burglary, Mac. Why, this
is the biggest day of our life.

MAC   Dear child, everything shall be done as you wish. We can't have you embarrassed in any way. The trimmings will be here in a moment.

MATTHEW   That'll be the furniture.

[*Large vans are heard driving up. Half a dozen men come in, carrying carpets, furniture,
dishes, etc., with which they transform the stable into an exaggeratedly luxurious room*]

MAC   Junk.

[*The gentlemen put the presents down left, congratulate the bride, and report to the bridegroom*]

JAKE [*known as Crook-fingered Jake*]   Congratulations! At 14 Ginger Street there
were some people on the second floor. We had to smoke them out.

BOB [*known as Bob the Saw*]   Congratulations! A copper got bumped in the Strand.

MAC   Amateurs.

NED   We did all we could, but three people in the West End were past saving.
Congratulations!

MAC   Amateurs and bunglers.

JIMMY   An old gent got hurt a bit, but I don't think it's anything serious. Congratulations.

MAC   My orders were: avoid bloodshed. It makes me sick to think of it. You'll
never make businessmen! Cannibals, yes, but not businessmen!

WALTER [*known as Dreary Walt*]   Congratulations. Only half an hour ago, madam,
that harpsichord belonged to the Duchess of Somerset.

POLLY   What is this furniture anyway?

MAC   How do you like the furniture, Polly?

POLLY [*in tears*]   Those poor people, all for a few sticks of furniture.

MAC   And what furniture! Junk! You have a perfect right to be angry. A rosewood
harpsichord with a Renaissance sofa. That's unforgivable. What about a
table?

WALTER   A table?

[*They lay some planks over the bins*]

POLLY   Oh, Mac, I'm so miserable! I only hope the vicar doesn't come.

MATTHEW   Of course he'll come. We gave him exact directions.

WALTER [*introduces the table*]   A table!

MAC [*seeing Polly in tears*]   My wife is very much upset. Where are the rest of the chairs? A harpsichord and no chairs! Use your heads! For once I'm having a wedding, and how often does that happen? Shut up, Dreary! How often does it happen that I leave you to do something on your own? And when I do you make my wife unhappy right at the start.

NED   Dear Polly . . .

MAC [*knocks his hat off his head*]   "Dear Polly"! I'll bash your head through your kidneys with your "dear Polly," you squirt. Have you ever heard the like? "Dear Polly"! I suppose you've been to bed with her?

POLLY   Mac!

NED   I swear . . .

WALTER   Dear madam, if any items of furniture should be lacking, we'll be only too glad to go back and . . .

MAC   A rosewood harpsichord and no chairs. [*Laughs*] Speaking as a bride, what do you say to that?

POLLY   It could be worse.

MAC   Two chairs and a sofa and the bridal couple has to sit on the floor.

POLLY   Something new, I'd say.

MAC [*sharply*]   Get the legs sawn off this harpsichord! Go on!

FOUR MEN [*saw the legs off the harpsichord and sing*]

> Bill Lawgen and Mary Syer
> Were made man and wife a week ago.
> When it was over and they exchanged a kiss
> He was thinking "Whose wedding dress was this?"
> While his name was a thing she would have liked to know.
> Hooray!

WALTER   The final result, madam: there's your bench.

MAC   May I now ask the gentlemen to take off those filthy rags and put on some decent clothes? After all this isn't just anybody's wedding. Polly, may I ask you to look after the grub?

POLLY   Is this our wedding feast? Was the whole lot stolen, Mac?

MAC   Of course. Of course.

POLLY   I wonder what you will do if there's a knock at the door and the sheriff steps in.

MAC   I'll show you what your husband will do in such a situation.

MATTHEW   It couldn't happen today. The mounted police are all sure to be in Daventry. They'll be escorting the Queen back to town for Friday's Coronation.

POLLY   Two knives and fourteen forks! One knife per chair.

MAC What incompetence! That's the work of apprentices, not experienced men! Haven't you any sense of style? Fancy not knowing the difference between Chippendale and Louis Quatorze.

[*The gang comes back. The gentlemen are now wearing fashionable evening dress, but unfortunately their movements are not in keeping with it*]

WALTER We only wanted to bring the most valuable stuff. Look at that wood! Really first class.

MATTHEW Ssst! Ssst! Permit us, Captain . . .

MAC Polly, come here a minute.

[*Mac and Polly assume the pose of a couple prepared to receive congratulations*]

MATTHEW Permit us, Captain, on the greatest day of your life, in the bloom of your career, or rather the turning point, to offer you our most indispensable and at the same time most sincere congratulations, and so forth. That posh talk don't half make me sick. So to cut a long story short [*shakes Mac's hand*]— keep a stiff upper lip, old mate.

MAC Thank you, that was kind of you, Matthew.

MATTHEW [*shaking Polly's hand after embracing Mac with emotion*] It was spoken from the heart, all right—Anyway, keep a stiff upper lip, old girl, I mean [*grinning*] he should keep it stiff.

[*Roars of laughter from the guests. Suddenly Mac with a deft movement sends Matthew to the floor*]

MAC Shut your trap. Keep that filth for your Kitty, she's the kind of slut that appreciates it.

POLLY Mac, don't be so vulgar.

MATTHEW Here, I don't like that. Calling Kitty a slut . . . [*stands up with difficulty*]

MAC Oh, so you don't like that?

MATTHEW And besides, I never use filthy language with her. I respect Kitty a lot too much for that. But maybe you wouldn't understand that, the way you are. You're a fine one to talk about filth. Do you think Lucy didn't tell me the things you've told her? Compared to that, I'm a kid glove.

[*Mac stares at him*]

JAKE Cut it out, this is a wedding. [*They pull him away*]

MAC Fine wedding, isn't it, Polly? Having to see trash like this around you on the day of your marriage. You wouldn't have thought your husband's friends would let him down so. Let it be a lesson to you.

POLLY I think it's nice.

ROBERT   Blarney. Nobody's letting you down. What's a difference of opinion between friends? Your Kitty's as good as the next girl. But now bring out your
wedding present, mate.

ALL   Yes, hand it over!

MATTHEW [offended]   Here.

POLLY   Oh, a wedding present. How kind of you, Mr. Matt of the Mint. Look,
Mac, what a lovely nightgown.

MATTHEW   Another bit of filth, eh, Captain?

MAC   Forget it. I didn't mean to hurt your feelings on this festive occasion.

WALTER   What do you say to this? Chippendale! [He unveils an enormous Chippendale grandfather clock]

MAC   Quatorze.

POLLY   It's wonderful. I'm so happy. Words fail me. You're so unbelievably kind.
Oh, Mac, isn't it a shame we haven't got a flat to put it in?

MAC   Hm, it's a start in the right direction. The great thing is to get started. Thank
you kindly, Walter. Go on, clear the stuff away now. Food!

JAKE [while the others start setting the table]   Trust me to come empty-handed again.
[Intensely to Polly] Believe me, young lady, I find it most distressing.

POLLY   It doesn't matter in the least, Mr. Crook-fingered Jake.

JAKE   Here are the boys flinging presents right and left, and me standing here
like a fool. What a situation to be in! It's always the way with me. Situations!
It's enough to make your hair stand on end. The other day I meet Low-Dive
Jenny; well, I say, you old cow . . . [Suddenly he sees Mac standing behind him
and goes off without a word]

MAC [leads Polly to her place]   This is the best food you'll taste today, Polly. Gentlemen! [All sit down to the wedding feast]

NED [indicating the china]   Beautiful dishes. Savoy Hotel.

JAKE   The plover's eggs are from Selfridge's. There was supposed to be a bucket
of foie gras. But Jimmy ate it on the way, he was mad because it had a hole
in it.

WALTER   We don't talk about holes in polite society.

JIMMY   Don't bolt the eggs like that, Ned, not on a day like this.

MAC   Couldn't somebody sing something? Something delectable?

MATTHEW [choking with laughter]   Something delectable? That's a first-class word.
[He sits down in embarrassment under Mac's withering glance]

MAC [knocks a bowl out of someone's hand]   I didn't intend us to start eating yet.
Instead of seeing you people wade straight into the trough, I would have
liked a little something for the heart. That's what other people do on an occasion like this.

JAKE   What, for instance?

MAC   Am I supposed to think of everything myself? I'm not asking you to put on
an opera. But you might have arranged for something else besides stuffing
your bellies and making filthy jokes. Oh well, it's a day like this that you find
out who your friends are.

POLLY   The salmon is marvelous, Mac.

NED   I bet you've never eaten anything like it. You get that every day at Mac the Knife's. You've landed in the honey pot all right. That's what I've always said: Mac is the right match for a girl with a feeling for higher things. As I was saying to Lucy only yesterday.

POLLY   Lucy? Mac, who is Lucy?

JAKE [*embarrassed*]   Lucy? Oh, nothing serious, you know.

[*Matthew has risen; standing behind Polly, he is waving his arms to shut Jake up*]

POLLY [*sees him*]   Do you want something? Salt perhaps . . . ? What were you saying, Mr. Jake?

JAKE   Oh, nothing, nothing at all. The main thing I wanted to say really was nothing at all. I'm always putting my foot in it.

MAC   What have you got your hand, Jake?

JAKE   A knife, Captain.

MAC   And what have you got on your plate?

JAKE   A trout, Captain.

MAC   I see. And with the knife you are eating the trout, are you not? It's incredible. Did you ever see the like of it, Polly? Eating his fish with a knife! Anybody who does that is just a plain swine, do you get me, Jake? Let that be a lesson to you. You'll have your hands full, Polly, trying to turn trash like them into human beings. Have you boys got the least idea what that means?

WALTER   A human being or a human pee-ing?

POLLY   Really, Mr. Walter!

MAC   So you won't sing a song, something to brighten up the day? Has it got to be a miserable gloomy day like any other? And come to think of it, is anybody guarding the door? I suppose you want me to attend to that myself too? Do you want me on this day of days to guard the door so you lot can stuff your bellies at my expense?

WALTER [*sullenly*]   What do you mean at your expense?

JIMMY   Stow it, Walter boy, I'm on my way. Who's going to come here anyway? [*Goes out*]

JAKE   A fine joke on a day like this if all the wedding guests were pulled in.

JIMMY [*rushes in*]   Hey, Captain. The cops!

WALTER   Tiger Brown!

MATTHEW   Nonsense, it's the Reverend Kimball. [*Kimball enters*]

ALL [*roar*]   Good evening, Reverend Kimball!

KIMBALL   So I've found you after all. I find you in a lowly hut, a humble place but your own.

MAC   Property of the Duke of Devonshire.

POLLY   Good evening, reverend. Oh, I'm so glad that on the happiest day of our life you . . .

MAC   And now I request a rousing song for the Reverend Kimball.

MATTHEW How about Bill Lawgen and Mary Syer?

JAKE Good. Bill Lawgen might be the right thing.

KIMBALL Be nice if you'd do a little number, boys.

MATTHEW Let's have it, gentlemen.

[*Three men rise and sing hesitantly, weakly and uncertainly:*]

Wedding Song for the Less Well-off

Bill Lawgen and Mary Syer
Were made man and wife a week ago.
(Three cheers for the happy couple: hip, hip, hooray!)
When it was over and they exchanged a kiss
He was thinking "Whose wedding dress was this?"
While his name was a thing she would have liked to know.
Hooray!

Do you know what your wife's up to? No!
Do you like her sleeping round like that? No!
(Three cheers for the happy couple: hip, hip, hooray!)
Billy Lawgen told me recently
Just one part of her will do for me.
The swine.
Hooray!

MAC Is that all? Paltry!

MATTHEW [*chokes again*] Paltry is the word, gentlemen. Paltry.

MAC Shut your trap!

MATTHEW Oh, I only meant no gusto, no fire, and so on.

POLLY Gentlemen, if none of you wishes to perform, I myself will sing a little
song; it's an imitation of a girl I saw once in some twopenny halfpenny dive
in Soho. She was washing the glasses, and everybody was laughing at her,
and then she turned to the guests and said things like the things I'm going to
sing to you. All right. This is a little bar, I want you to think of it as filthy.
She stood behind it morning and night. This is the bucket and this is the rag
she washed the glasses with. Where you were sitting, the customers were
sitting laughing at her. You can laugh too, to make it exactly the same; but if
you can't, you don't have to. [*She starts pretending to wash glasses, muttering to
herself*] Now, for instance, one of them—it might be you [*pointing at Walter*]—
says: Well, when's your ship coming in, Jenny?

WALTER Well, when's your ship coming in, Jenny?

POLLY And another says—you, for instance: Still washing up glasses, Jenny the
pirate's bride?

MATTHEW Still washing up glasses, Jenny the pirate's bride?

POLLY   Good. And now I'll begin.

[*Song lighting: golden glow. The organ is lit up. Three lamps are lowered from above on a pole, and the signs say:*]

Pirate Jenny

1

Now you gents all see I've the glasses to wash
If a bed's to be made I make it.
You may tip me with a penny, and I'll thank you very well
And you see me dressed in tatters, and this tatty old hotel
And you never ask how long I'll take it.
But one of these evenings there will be screams from the harbor
And they'll ask: what can all that screaming be?
And they'll see me smiling as I do the glasses
And they'll say: how she can smile beats me.
  And a ship with eight sails and
  All its fifty guns loaded
  Has tied up at the quay.

2

They say: get on, dry your glasses, my girl
And they tip me and don't give a damn.
And their penny is accepted, and their bed will be made
(Although nobody is going to sleep there, I'm afraid)
And they still have no idea who I am.
But one of these evenings there will be explosions from the harbor.
And they'll ask: what kind of a bang was that?
And they'll see me as I stand beside the window
And they'll say: what's she got to smile at:
  And that ship with eight sails and
  All its fifty guns loaded
  Will lay siege to the town.

3

Then, you gents, you aren't going to find it a joke
For the walls will be knocked down flat
And in no time the town will be razed to the ground.
Just one tatty old hotel will be left standing safe and sound
And they'll ask: did someone special live in that?
Then there'll be a lot of people milling round the hotel
And they'll ask: what made them let that place alone?
And they'll see me as I leave the door next morning
And they'll say: don't tell us she's the one.

And that ship with eight sails and
All its fifty guns loaded
Will run up its flag.

4

And a hundred men will land in the bright midday sun
Each stepping where the shadows fall.
They'll look inside each doorway and grab anyone they see
And put him in irons and then bring him to me
And they'll ask: which of these should we kill?
In that noonday heat there'll be a hush round the harbor
As they ask which has got to die.
And you'll hear me as I softly answer: the lot!
And as the first head rolls I'll say: hoppla!
    And that ship with eight sails and
    All its fifty guns loaded
    Will vanish with me.

MATTHEW   Very pretty. Cute, eh? And the way the missus puts it across!

MAC   What do you mean pretty? It's not pretty, you idiot! It's art, it's not pretty. You did that marvelously, Polly. But it's wasted on trash like this, if you'll excuse me, Your Reverence. [*In an undertone to Polly*] Anyway, I don't like you play-acting; let's not have any more of it. [*Laughter at the table. The gang is making fun of the parson*] What you got in your hand, Your Reverence?

JAKE   Two knives, Captain.

MAC   What you got on your plate, Your Reverence?

KIMBALL   Salmon, I think.

MAC   And with that knife you are eating the salmon, are you not?

JAKE   Did you ever see the like of it, eating fish with a knife? Anybody who does that is just a plain . . .

MAC   Swine. Do you understand me, Jake? Let that be a lesson to you.

JIMMY [*rushing in*]   Hey, Captain, cops. The sheriff in person.

WALTER   Brown. Tiger Brown!

MAC   Yes, Tiger Brown, exactly. It's Tiger Brown himself, the high sheriff of London, that pillar of the Old Bailey, who will now enter Captain Macheath's humble cabin. Let that be a lesson to you.

[*The bandits creep away*]

JAKE   It'll be the gallows for us!

[*Brown enters*]

MAC   Hullo, Jackie.

BROWN   Hullo, Mac! I haven't much time, got to be leaving in a minute. Does it
have to be somebody else's stable? Why, this is breaking and entering again!

MAC   But Jackie, it's so conveniently located. I'm glad you could come to old
Mac's wedding. Let me introduce my wife, née Peachum. Polly, this is Tiger
Brown, what do you say, old man? [*Slaps him on the back*] And these are my
friends, Jackie, I imagine you've seen them all before.

BROWN [*pained*]   I'm here unofficially, Mac.

MAC   So are they. [*He calls them. They come in with their hands up*] Hey, Jake.

BROWN   That's Crook-fingered Jake. He's a dirty dog.

MAC   Hey, Jimmy; hey Bob; hey, Walter!

BROWN   Well, just for today I'll turn a blind eye.

MAC   Hey, Ned; hey, Matthew.

BROWN   Be seated, gentlemen, be seated.

ALL   Thank you, sir.

BROWN   I'm delighted to meet my old friend Mac's charming wife.

POLLY   Don't mention it, sir.

MAC   Sit down, ya old blighter, and pitch into the whiskey!—Polly and gentlemen! You have today in your midst a man whom the king's inscrutable decree
has placed high above his fellow men and who has none the less remained
my friend throughout the storms and perils, and so on. You know whom I
mean, and you too know whom I mean, Brown. Ah, Jackie, do you remember how we served in India together, soldiers both of us? Ah, Jackie, let's sing
the Cannon Song right now.

[*They sit down on the table*]

[*Song lighting: golden glow. The organ is lit up. Three lamps are lowered from above on a
pole, and the signs say:*]

The Cannon Song

1

John was all present and Jim was all there
And Georgie was up for promotion.
Not that the army gave a bugger who they were
When confronting some heathen commotion.
The troops live under
The cannon's thunder
From Sind to Cooch Behar.
Moving from place to place
When they come face to face
With men of a different color
With darker skins or duller
They quick as winking chop them into beefsteak tartare.

2

Johnny found his whiskey too warm
And Jim found the weather too balmy
But Georgie took them both by the arm
And said: never let down the army.
The troops live under
The cannon's thunder
From Sind to Cooch Behar.
Moving from place to place
When they come face to face
With men of a different color
With darker skins or duller
They quick as winking chop them into beefsteak tartare.

3

John is a write-off and Jimmy is dead
And they shot poor old Georgie for looting
But young men's blood goes on being red
And the army goes on recruiting.
The troops live under
The cannon's thunder
From Sind to Cooch Behar.
Moving from place to place
When they come face to face
With men of a different color
With darker skins or duller
They quick as winking chop them into beefsteak tartare.

MAC Though life with its raging torrents has carried us boyhood friends far apart, although our professional interests are very different, some people would go so far as to say diametrically opposed, our friendship has come through unimpaired. Let that be a lesson to all of you. Castor and Pollux, Hector and Andromache and so on. Seldom have I, the humble bandit, well, you know what I mean, made even the smallest haul without giving him, my friend, a share, a sizable share, Brown, as a gift and token of my unswerving loyalty, and seldom has he, take that knife out of your mouth, Jake, the all-powerful police chief, staged a raid without sending me, his boyhood friend, a little tip-off. Well, and so on and so forth, it's all a matter of give and take. Let that be a lesson to you. [*He takes Brown by the arm*] Well, Jackie, old man, I'm glad you've come, I call it real friendship. [*Pause, because Brown has been looking sadly at a carpet*] Genuine Shiraz.

BROWN From the Oriental Carpet Company.

MAC Yes, we never go anywhere else. Do you know, Jackie, I had to have you here today, I hope it's not too unpleasant for you in your position.

BROWN You know, Mac, that I can't refuse you anything. I must be going, I've really got so much on my mind; if the slightest thing should go wrong at the Queen's Coronation . . .

MAC   See here, Jackie, my father-in-law is a rotten old stinker. If he tries to make trouble for me, is there anything on record against me at Scotland Yard?

BROWN   There's nothing whatsoever on record against you at Scotland Yard.

MAC   I knew it.

BROWN   I've taken care of all that. Good night.

MAC   Aren't you fellows going to stand up?

BROWN [to Polly]   Best of luck. [Goes out accompanied by Mac]

JAKE [who along with Matthew and Walter has meanwhile been conferring with Polly]   I must admit I couldn't repress a certain alarm a while ago when I heard Tiger Brown was coming.

MATTHEW   You see, dear lady, we have connections with the top authorities.

WALTER   Yes, Mac always has an iron in the fire that the rest of us don't even suspect. But we have our own little iron in the fire. Gentlemen, it's half-past nine.

MATTHEW   And now comes the high point.

[All go upstage behind the carpet that conceals something. Mac enters]

MAC   I say, what's going on?

MATTHEW   Hey, Captain, another little surprise.

[Behind the carpet they sing the Bill Lawgen song softly and with much feeling. But at "his name was a thing she would have liked to know" Matthew pulls down the carpet and all go on with the song, bellowing and pounding on the bed that has been disclosed]

MAC   Thank you, friends, thank you.

WALTER   And now we shall quietly take our leave. [The gang go out]

MAC   And now the time has come for softer sentiments. Without them man is a mere working animal. Sit down, Polly.

[Music]

MAC   Look at the moon over Soho.

POLLY   I see it, dearest. Feel my heart beating, my beloved.

MAC   I feel it, beloved.

POLLY   Where'er you go I shall be with you.

MAC   And where you stay, there too shall I be.

BOTH [sing]
    And though we've no paper to say we're wed
    And no altar covered with flowers
    And nobody knows for whom your dress was made
    And even the ring is not ours—
    That platter off which you are eating your bread

Give it one brief look; fling it far.
For love will endure or not endure
Regardless of where we are.

SCENE 3

To Peachum, aware of the hardness of the world, the loss of his daughter means
utter ruin

Peachum's Outfitting Shop for Beggars

To the right Peachum and Mrs. Peachum. In the doorway stands Polly in her coat and hat,
holding her traveling bag.

MRS. PEACHUM   Married? First you rig her fore and aft in dresses and hats and
gloves and parasols, and when she's cost as much as a sailing ship, she
throws herself in the garbage like a rotten pickle. Are you really married?

[*Song lighting: golden glow. The organ is lit up. Three lamps are lowered from above on a*
pole and the signs say:]

In a little song Polly gives her parents to understand that she has married the
bandit Macheath

Barbara Song

1
I once used to think, in my innocent youth
(And I once was as innocent as you)
That someone someday might come my way
And then how would I know what best to do?
And if he'd got money
And seemed a nice chap
And his workday shirts were white as snow
And if he knew how to treat a girl with due respect
I'd have to tell him: No.
That's where you must keep your head screwed on
And insist on going slow.
Sure, the moon will shine throughout the night
Sure, the boat is on the river, tied up tight.
That's as far as things can go.
Oh, you can't lie back, you must stay cold at heart
Oh, you must not let your feelings show.
Oh, whenever you feel it might start
Ah, then your only answer's: No.

2

The first one that came was a man of Kent
And all that a man ought to be.
The second one owned three ships down at Wapping
And the third was crazy about me.
And as they'd got money
And all seemed nice chaps
And their workday shirts were white as snow
And as they knew how to treat a girl with due respect
Each time I told them: No.
That's where I still kept my head screwed on
And I chose to take it slow.
Sure, the moon could shine throughout the night
Sure, the boat was on the river, tied up tight
That's as far as things could go.
Oh, you can't lie back, you must stay cold at heart
Oh, you must not let your feelings show.
Oh, whenever you feel it might start
Ah, then your only answer's: No.

3

But then one day, and that day was blue
Came someone who didn't ask at all
And he went and hung his hat on the nail in my little attic
And what happened I can't quite recall.
And as he'd got no money
And was not a nice chap
And his Sunday shirts, even, were not like snow
And as he'd no idea of treating a girl with due respect
I could not tell him: No
That's the time my head was not screwed on
And to hell with going slow.
Oh, the moon was shining clear and bright
Oh, the boat kept drifting downstream all that night
That was how it simply had to go.
Yes, you must lie back, you can't stay cold at heart
In the end you have to let your feelings show.
Oh, the moment you know it must start
Ah, then's no time for saying: No.

PEACHUM So now she's associating with criminals. That's lovely. That's delightful.

MRS. PEACHUM If you're immoral enough to get married, did it have to be a horse
thief and a highwayman? That'll cost you dear one of these days! I ought to

have seen it coming. Even as a child she had a swelled head like the Queen of England.

PEACHUM   So she's really got married!

MRS. PEACHUM   Yes, yesterday, at five in the afternoon.

PEACHUM   To a notorious criminal. Come to think of it, it shows that the fellow is really audacious. If I give away my daughter, the last prop of my old age, my house will cave in and my last dog will run off. I'd think twice about giving away the dirt under my fingernails, it would mean risking starvation. If the three of us can get through the winter on one log of wood, maybe we'll live to see the new year. Maybe.

MRS. PEACHUM   What got into you? This is our reward for all we've done, Jonathan. I'm going mad. My head is swimming. I'm going to faint. Oh! [*she faints*] A glass of Cordial Médoc.

PEACHUM   You see what you've done to your mother. Quick! Associating with criminals, that's lovely, that's delightful! Interesting how the poor woman takes it to heart. [*Polly brings in a bottle of Cordial Médoc*] That's the only consolation your poor mother has left.

POLLY   Go ahead, give her two glasses. *My* mother can take twice as much when she's not quite herself. That will put her back on her feet. [*During the whole scene she looks very happy*]

MRS. PEACHUM [*wakes up*]   Oh, there she goes again, pretending to be so loving and sympathetic!

[*Five men enter*]

BEGGAR   I'm making a complaint, see, this thing is a mess, it's not a proper stump, it's a botch-up, and I'm not wasting my money on it.

PEACHUM   What do you expect? It's as good a stump as any other; it's only that you don't keep it clean.

BEGGAR   Then why don't I take as much money as the others? Naw, you can't do that to me. [*Throws down the stump*] If I wanted crap like this, I could cut off my real leg.

PEACHUM   What do you fellows want anyway? Is it my fault if people have hearts of flint? I can't make you five stumps. In five minutes I can turn any man into such a pitiful wreck it would make a dog weep to see him. Can I help it if people don't weep? Here's another stump for you if one's not enough. But look after your equipment!

BEGGAR   This one will do.

PEACHUM [*tries a false limb on another*]   Leather is no good, Celia; rubber is more repulsive. [*To the third*] That swelling is going down and it's your last. Now we'll have to start all over again. [*Examining the fourth*] Obviously natural scabies is never as good as the artificial kind. [*To the fifth*] You're a sight! You've been eating again. I'll have to make an example of you.

BEGGAR   Mr. Peachum, I really haven't eaten anything much. I'm just abnormally fat, I can't help it.

PEACHUM   Nor can I. You're fired. [*Again to the second beggar*] My dear man, there's an obvious difference between "tugging at people's heart strings" and "getting on people's nerves." What I need is artists. Only an artist can tug at anybody's heart strings nowadays. If you fellows performed properly, your audience would be forced to applaud. You just haven't any ideas! So obviously I can't extend your engagement.

[*The beggars go out*]

POLLY   Look at him. Is he particularly handsome? No. But he makes a living. He can support me. He is not only a first-class burglar but a farsighted and experienced stick-up man as well. I've been into it, I can tell you the exact amount of his savings to date. A few successful ventures and we shall be able to retire to a little house in the country just like that Mr. Shakespeare father admires so much.

PEACHUM   It's all perfectly simple. You're married. What does a girl do when she's married? Use your head. Well, she gets divorced, see, is that so hard to figure out?

POLLY   I don't know what you're talking about.

MRS. PEACHUM   Divorce.

POLLY   But I love him. How can I think of divorce?

MRS. PEACHUM   Really, have you no shame?

POLLY   Mother, if you've ever been in love . . .

MRS. PEACHUM   In love! Those damn books you've been reading have turned your head. Why, Polly, everybody's doing it.

POLLY   Then I'm an exception.

MRS. PEACHUM   Then I'm going to tan your behind, you exception.

POLLY   Oh yes, all mothers do that, but it doesn't help because love goes deeper than a tanned behind.

MRS. PEACHUM   Don't strain my patience.

POLLY   I won't let my love be taken away from me.

MRS. PEACHUM   One more word out of you and you'll get a clip on the ear.

POLLY   But love is the finest thing in the world.

MRS. PEACHUM   Anyway, he's got several women, the blackguard. When he's hanged, like as not half a dozen widows will turn up, each of them like as not with a brat in her arms. Oh, Jonathan!

PEACHUM   Hanged, what made you think of that, that's good idea. Run along, Polly. [*Polly goes out*] Quite right. That'll earn us forty pounds.

MRS. PEACHUM   I see. Report him to the sheriff.

PEACHUM   Naturally. And besides, that way we get him hanged free of charge . . . Two birds with one stone. Only we've got to find out where he's holed up.

MRS. PEACHUM   I can tell you that, my dear, he's holed up with his tarts.

PEACHUM   But they won't turn him in.

MRS. PEACHUM   Just let me attend to that. Money rules the world. I'll go to Turnbridge right away and talk to the girls. Give us a couple of hours, and after
that if he meets a single one of them he's done for.

POLLY [*has been listening behind the door*]   Dear mama, you can spare yourself the
trip. Mac will go to the Old Bailey of his own accord sooner than meet any of
those ladies. And even if he did go to the Old Bailey, the sheriff would serve
him a cocktail; they'd smoke their cigars and have a little chat about a certain
shop in this street where a little more goes on than meets the eye. Because,
papa dear, the sheriff was very cheerful at my wedding.

PEACHUM   What's this sheriff called?

POLLY   He's called Brown. But you probably know him as Tiger Brown. Because
everyone who has reason to fear him calls him Tiger Brown. But my husband, you see, calls him Jackie. Because to him he's just dear old Jackie.
They're boyhood friends.

PEACHUM   Oh, so they're friends, are they? The sheriff and Public Enemy No. 1,
ha, they must be the only friends in this city.

POLLY [*poetically*]   Every time they drank a cocktail together, they stroked each
other's cheeks and said: "If you'll have the same again, I'll have the same
again." And every time one of them left the room, the other's eyes grew moist
and he said: "Where'er you go I shall be with you." There's nothing on record
against Mac at Scotland Yard.

PEACHUM   I see. Between Tuesday evening and Thursday morning Mr. Macheath, a gentleman who has assuredly been married many times, enticed my
daughter from her home on pretext of marriage. Before the week is out, he
will be taken on that account to the gallows, which he has deserved. "Mr.
Macheath, you once had white kid gloves, a cane with an ivory handle, and
a scar on your neck, and frequented the Cuttlefish Hotel. All that is left is
your scar, undoubtedly the least valuable of your distinguishing marks, and
today you frequent nothing but prison cells, and within the foreseeable future no place at all . . . "

MRS. PEACHUM   Oh, Jonathan, you'll never bring it off. Why, he's Mac the Knife,
whom they call the biggest criminal in London. He takes what he pleases.

PEACHUM   Who's Mac the Knife? Get ready, we're going to see the Sheriff of London. And you're going to Turnbridge.

MRS. PEACHUM   To see his whores.

PEACHUM   For the villainy of the world is great, and a man needs to run his legs
off to keep them from being stolen from under him.

POLLY   I, papa, shall be delighted to shake hands with Mr. Brown again.

[*All three step forward and sing the first finale. Song lighting. On the signs is written:*]

FIRST THREEPENNY FINALE

Concerning the Insecurity of the Human State

POLLY

Am I reaching for the sky?
All I'm asking from this place is
To enjoy a man's embraces.
Is that aiming much too high?

PEACHUM [*with a Bible in his hands*]

Man has a right, in this our brief existence
To call some fleeting happiness his own
Partake of worldly pleasures and subsistence
And have bread on his table rather than a stone.
Such are the basic rights of man's existence.
But do we know of anything suggesting
That when a thing's a right one gets it? No!
To get one's rights would be most interesting
But in our present state this can't be so.

MRS. PEACHUM

How I want what's best for you
How I'd deal you all the aces
Show you things and take you places
As a mother likes to do.

PEACHUM

Let's practice goodness: who would disagree?
Let's give our wealth away: is that not right?
Once all are good His Kingdom is at hand
Where blissfully we'll bask in His pure light.
Let's practice goodness: who would disagree?
But sadly on this planet while we're waiting
The means are meagre and the morals low.
To get one's record straight would be elating
But in our present state this can't be so.

POLLY AND MRS. PEACHUM

And that is all there is to it.
The world is poor, and man's a shit.

PEACHUM

Of course that's all there is to it.
The world is poor, and man's a shit.
Who wouldn't like an earthly paradise?
Yet our condition's such it can't arise.
Out of the question in our case.

Let's say you brother's close to you
But if there's not enough for two
He'll kick you smartly in the face.
You think that loyalty's no disgrace?
But say your wife is close to you
And finds she's barely make do
She'll kick you smartly in the face.
And gratitude: that's no disgrace
But say your son is close to you
And finds your pension's not come through
He'll kick you smartly in the face.
And so will all the human race.

POLLY AND MRS. PEACHUM

That's what you're all ignoring
That's what's so bloody boring.
The world is poor, and man's a shit
And that is all there is to it.

PEACHUM

Of course that's all there is to it
The world is poor, and man's a shit.
We should aim high instead of low
But in our present state this can't be so.

ALL THREE

Which means He has us in a trap:
The whole damn thing's a load of crap.

PEACHUM

The world is poor, and man's a shit
And that is all there is to it.

ALL THREE

That's what you're all ignoring
That's what's so bloody boring.
That's why He's got us in a trap
And why it's all a load of crap.

ACT II

SCENE 4

Thursday afternoon: Mac the Knife takes leave of his wife and flees from his
father-in-law to the heaths of Highgate.

The Stable

POLLY [*enters*]   Mac! Mac, don't be frightened.

MAC [*lying on the bed*]   Well, what's up? Polly, you look a wreck.

POLLY   I've been to see Brown, my father went too, they decided to pull you in; my father made some terrible threats and Brown stood up for you, but then he weakened, and now he thinks too that you'd better bestir yourself and make yourself scarce for a while, Mac. You must pack right away.

MAC   Pack? Nonsense. Come here, Polly. You and I have got better things to do than pack.

POLLY   No, we mustn't now. I'm so frightened. All they talked about was hanging.

MAC   I don't like it when you're moody, Polly. There's nothing on record against me at Scotland Yard.

POLLY   Perhaps there wasn't yesterday, but today there's suddenly a terrible lot. You—I've brought the charges with me, I don't even know if I can get them straight, the list goes on and on—you've killed two shopkeepers, more than thirty burglaries, twenty-three hold-ups, and God knows how many acts of arson, attempted murder, forgery and perjury, all within eighteen months. You're a dreadful man. And in Winchester you seduced two sisters under the age of consent.

MAC   They told me they were over twenty. What did Brown say? [*He stands up slowly and goes whistling to the right along the footlights*]

POLLY   He caught up with me in the corridor and said there was nothing he could do for you now. Oh, Mac! [*She throws herself on his neck*]

MAC   All right, if I've got to go away, you'll have to run the business.

POLLY   Don't talk about business now, Mac, I can't bear it. Kiss your poor Polly again and swear that you'll never never be . . .

[*Mac interrupts her brusquely and leads her to the table where he pushes her down in a chair.*]

MAC   Here are the ledgers. Listen carefully. This is a list of the personnel. [*Reads*] Right. First of all, Crook-fingered Jake, a year and a half in the business. Let's see what he's brought in. One, two, three, four, five gold watches, not much, but clean work. Don't sit on my lap, I'm not in the mood right now. Here's Dreary Walter, an unreliable dog. Sells stuff on the side. Give him three weeks grace, then get rid of him. Just turn him in to Brown.

POLLY [*sobbing*]   Just turn him in to Brown.

MAC   Jimmy II, an impertinent bastard; good worker but impertinent. Swipes bed sheets right out from under ladies of the best society. Give him a rise.

POLLY   Give him a rise.

MAC   Robert the Saw: small potatoes, not a glimmer of genius. Won't end on the gallows, but he won't leave any estate either.

POLLY   Won't leave any estate either.

MAC In all other respects you will carry on exactly the same as before. Get up at seven, wash, bathe once a week and so on.

POLLY You're perfectly right, I've got to grit my teeth and attend to the business. What's yours is mine now, isn't it, Mackie? What about your rooms, Mac? Should I let them go? I don't like having to pay the rent.

MAC No, I still need them.

POLLY What for, it's just a waste of our money!

MAC You seem to think I'm never coming back.

POLLY What do you mean? You can rent other rooms. Mac . . . Mac, I can't go on. I keep looking at your lips and then I don't hear what you say. Will you be faithful to me, Mac?

MAC Of course I'll be faithful, I'll do as I'm done by. Do you think I don't love you? It's only that I see farther ahead than you.

POLLY I'm so grateful to you, Mac. Worrying about me when they're after you like bloodhounds . . .

[*Hearing the word "bloodhounds" he goes stiff, stands up, goes to the right, throws off his coat and washes his hands*]

MAC [*hastily*] You will go on sending the profits to Jack Poole's banking house in Manchester. Between you and me it's only a matter of weeks before I go over to banking altogether. It's safer and it's more profitable. In two weeks at the most the money will have to be taken out of this business, then off you to go Brown and give the list to the police. Within four weeks all this scum of humanity will be safely in the cells at the Old Bailey.

POLLY Why, Mac! How can you look them in the eye when you've written them off and they're as good as hanged? How can you shake hands with them?

MAC With who? Robert the Saw, Matt of the Mint, Crook-fingered Jake? Those jailbirds?

[*Enter the gang*]

MAC Gentlemen, it's a pleasure to see you.

POLLY Good evening, gentlemen.

MATTHEW Captain, I've got hold of the Coronation program. It looks to me like we have some days of very hard work ahead of us. The Archbishop of Canterbury is arriving in half an hour.

MAC When?

MATTHEW Five thirty. We'd better be shoving off, Captain.

MAC Yes, you'd better be shoving off.

ROBERT What do you mean: you?

MAC For my part, I'm afraid I'm obliged to take a little trip.

ROBERT Good God, are they out to nab you?

MATTHEW It would be just now, with the Coronation coming up! A Coronation without you is soup without a spoon.

MAC   Shut your trap! In view of that, I am temporarily handing over the manage-
     ment of the business to my wife. [*He pushes her forward and goes to the rear
     where he observes her*]

POLLY   Well, boys, I think the Captain can go away with an easy mind. We'll
     swing this job, you bet. What do you say, boys?

MATTHEW   It's not for me to say. But at a time like this I'm not so sure that a
     woman . . . I'm not saying anything against you, Ma'am.

MAC [*from upstage*]   What do you say to that, Polly?

POLLY   You shit, that's a fine way to start in. [*Screaming*] Of course you're not
     saying anything against me! If you were, these gentlemen would have ripped
     your pants off long ago and tanned your arse for you. Wouldn't you,
     gentlemen?

[*Brief pause, then all clap like mad*]

JAKE   Yes, there's something in that, you can take her word for it.

WALTER   Hurrah, the missus knows how to lay it on! Hurrah for Polly!

ALL   Hurrah for Polly!

MAC   The rotten part of it is that I won't be here for the Coronation. There's a
     gilt-edged deal for you. In the daytime nobody's home and at night the toffs
     are all drunk. That reminds me, you drink too much, Matthew. Last week
     you were implying that it was you who set the Greenwich Children's Hos-
     pital on fire. If such a thing happens again, you're out. Who set the
     Children's Hospital on fire?

MATTHEW   I did.

MAC [*to the others*]   Who set it on fire?

THE OTHERS   You, Mr. Macheath.

MAC   So who did it?

MATTHEW [*sulkily*]   You, Mr. Macheath. At this rate our sort will never rise in the
     world.

MAC [*with a gesture of stringing up*]   You'll rise all right if you think you can com-
     pete with me. Who ever heard of one of those professors at Oxford College
     letting some assistant put his name to his errors? He puts his own.

ROBERT   Ma'am, while your husband is away, you're the boss. We settle up every
     Thursday, ma'am.

POLLY   Every Thursday, boys.

[*The gang goes out*]

MAC   And now farewell, my heart. Look after your complexion, and don't forget
     to make up every day, exactly as if I were here. That's very important, Polly.

POLLY   And you, Mac, promise me you won't look at another woman and that
     you'll leave town right away. Believe me, it's not jealousy that makes your
     little Polly say that; no, it's very important, Mac.

MAC   Oh, Polly, why should I go round drinking up the empties? I love only you.

As soon as the twilight is deep enough I'll take my black stallion from somebody's stable and before you can see the moon from your window, I'll be on
the other side of Highgate Heath.

POLLY   Oh, Mac, don't tear the heart out of my body. Stay with me and let us be
happy.

MAC   But I must tear my own heart out of my body, for I must go away and no
one knows when I shall return.

POLLY   It's been such a short time, Mac.

MAC   Does it have to be the end?

POLLY   Oh, last night I had a dream. I was looking out of the window and I heard
laughter in the street, and when I looked out I saw our moon and the moon
was all thin like a worn-down penny. Don't forget me, Mac, in strange cities.

MAC   Of course I won't forget you, Polly. Kiss me, Polly.

POLLY   Good-bye, Mac.

MAC   Good-bye, Polly. [On his way out]
    For love will endure or not endure
    Regardless of where we are.

POLLY [alone]   He never will come back. [She sings]
    Nice while it lasted, and now it is over
    Tear out your heart, and good-bye to your lover!
    What's the use of grieving, when the mother that bore you
    (Mary, pity women!) knew it all before you?

[The bells start ringing]

POLLY
    Into this London the Queen now makes her way.
    Where shall we be on Coronation Day?

INTERLUDE

[Mrs. Peachum and Low-Dive Jenny step out before the curtain]

MRS. PEACHUM   So if you see Mac the Knife in the next few days, run to the
nearest constable and turn him in; it'll get you ten shillings.

JENNY   Shall we see him, though, if the constables are after him? If the hunt is
on, he won't go spending his time with us.

MRS. PEACHUM   Take it from me, Jenny, even with all London at his heels, Macheath is not the man to give up his habits. [She sings]

The Ballad of Sexual Obsession

1
There goes a man who's won his spurs in battle
The butcher, he. And all the others, cattle.

The cocky sod! No decent place lets him in.
Who does him down, that's done the lot? The women.
Want it or not, he can't ignore that call.
Sexual obsession has him in its thrall.
    He doesn't read the Bible. He sniggers at the law.
    Sets out to be an utter egoist
    And knows a woman's skirts are what he must resist
    So when a woman calls he locks his door
    So far, so good, but what's the future brewing?
    As soon as night falls he'll be up and doing.

2

Thus many a man watched men die in confusion:
A mighty genius, stuck on prostitution!
The watchers claimed their urges were exhausted
But when they died who paid the funeral? Whores did.
Want it or not, they can't ignore that call.
Sexual obsession has them in its thrall.
    Some fall back on the Bible. Some set out to change the law.
    Some turn to Christ. Others turn anarchist.
    At lunch you pick the best wine on the list
    Then meditate till half past four.
    At tea: what high ideals you are pursuing!
    Then soon as night falls you'll be up and doing.

SCENE 5

Before the coronation bells had died away, Mac the Knife was sitting with the whores of Turnbridge. The whores betray him. It is Thursday evening.

Whorehouse in Turnbridge

An afternoon like any other; the whores, mostly in their shifts, are ironing clothes, playing draughts, or washing: a bourgeois idyll. Crook-fingered Jake is reading the newspaper. No one is paying attention to him. He is rather in the way.

JAKE   He won't come today.
WHORE   No?
JAKE   I don't think he'll ever come again.
WHORE   That would be too bad.
JAKE   Think so? If I know him, he's out of town by now. This time he's cleared out.

[*Enter Macheath, hangs his hat on a nail, sits down on the sofa behind the table*]

MAC   My coffee!

VIXEN [*repeats admiringly*]   "My coffee!"

JAKE [*horrified*]   How come you're not in Highgate?

MAC   It's my Thursday. Do you think I can let such trifles interfere with my habits? [*Throws the warrant on the floor*] Anyhow, it's raining.

JENNY [*reads the warrant*]   In the name of the Queen, Captain Macheath is charged with three . . .

JAKE [*takes it away from her*]   Am I in it too?

MAC   Naturally, the whole team.

JENNY [*to the other whore*]   Look, that's the warrant. [*Pause*] Mac, let's see your hand.

[*He gives her his hand*]

DOLLY   That's right, Jenny, read his palm, you're so good at it. [*Holds up an oil lamp*]

MAC   Coming into money?

JENNY   No, not coming into money.

BETTY   What's that look for, Jenny? It gives me the shivers.

MAC   A long journey?

JENNY   No, no long journey.

VIXEN   What do you see?

MAC   Only the good things, not the bad, please.

JENNY   Oh well, I see a narrow dark place and not much light. And then I see a big T, that means a woman's treachery. And then I see . . .

MAC   Stop. I'd like some details about that narrow dark place and the treachery. What's this treacherous woman's name?

JENNY   All I see is it begins with a J.

MAC   Then you've got it wrong. It begins with a P.

JENNY   Mac, when the Coronation bells start ringing at Westminster, you'll be in for a sticky time.

MAC   Go on! [*Jake laughs uproariously*] What's the matter? [*He runs over to Jake, and reads*] They've got it wrong, there were only three.

JAKE [*laughs*]   Exactly.

MAC   Nice underwear you've got there.

WHORE   From the cradle to the grave, underwear first, last and all the time.

OLD WHORE   I never wear silk. Makes gentlemen think you've got something wrong with you.

[*Jenny slips stealthily out by the door*]

SECOND WHORE [*to Jenny*]   Where are you off to, Jenny?

JENNY   You'll see. [*Goes out*]

MOLLY   But homespun underwear can put them off, too.

OLD WHORE I've had very good results with homespun underwear.

VIXEN It makes the gentlemen feel at home.

MAC [to Betty] Have you still got the black lace border?

BETTY Still the black lace border.

MAC What kind of underwear do you have?

SECOND WHORE Oh, I don't like to tell you. I can't take anybody to my room because my aunt is so crazy about men, and in doorways, you know, I just don't wear any.

[Jake laughs]

MAC Finished?

JAKE No, I've just got to the rapes.

MAC [back by the sofa] But where's Jenny? Ladies, long before my star rose over this city . . .

VIXEN "Long before my star rose over this city . . . "

MAC . . . I lived in the most impoverished circumstances with one of you, dear ladies. And though today I am Mac the Knife, my good fortune will never lead me to forget the companions of my dark days, especially Jenny, whom I loved the best of all. Now listen, please.

[While Mac sings, Jenny stands to the right outside the window and beckons to Constable Smith. Then Mrs. Peachum joins her. The three stand under the street lamp and watch the house]

Ballade of Immoral Earnings

1

MAC

There was a time, now very far away
When we set up together, I and she.
I'd got the brain, and she supplied the breast.
I saw her right, and she supported me—
A way of life then, if not quite the best.
And when a client came I'd slide out of our bed
And treat him nice, and go and have a drink instead
And when he paid up I'd address him: Sir
Come any time you feel you fancy her.
That time's long past, but what would I not give
To see that whorehouse where we used to live?

[Jenny appears in the door, Smith behind her]

2

JENNY

That was the time, now very far away
He was so sweet and bashed me where it hurt.
And when the cash ran out the feathers really flew
He'd up and say: I'm going to pawn your skirt.
A skirt is nicer, but no skirt will do.
Just like his cheek, he had me fairly stewing
I'd ask him straight to say what he thought he was doing
Then he'd lash out and would knock me headlong downstairs.
I had the bruises off and on for years.

BOTH

That time's long past, but what would I not give
To see that whorehouse where we used to live?

3

BOTH [*together and alternating*]

That was the time, now very far away

MAC

Not that the bloody times seem to have looked up.

JENNY

When afternoons were all I had for you

MAC

I told you she was generally booked up.
(The night's more normal, but daytime will do.)

JENNY

Once I was pregnant, so the doctor said.

MAC

So we reversed positions on the bed.

JENNY

He thought his weight would make it premature.

MAC

But in the end we flushed it down the sewer.
That could not last, but what would I not give
To see the whorehouse where we used to live?

[*Dance. Mac picks up his sword stick, she hands him his hat, he is still dancing when Smith lays a hand on his shoulder*]

SMITH   Coming quietly?
MAC   Is there still only one way out of this dump?

[*Smith tries to put the handcuffs on Macheath; Mac gives him a push in the chest and he reels back. Mac jumps out of the window. Outside stands Mrs. Peachum with constables*]

MAC [*with poise, very politely*]   Good afternoon, ma'am.

MRS. PEACHUM   My dear Mr. Macheath. My husband says the greatest heroes in history have tripped over this humble threshold.

MAC   May I ask how your husband is doing?

MRS. PEACHUM   Better, thank you. I'm so sorry, you'll have to be bidding the charming ladies good-bye now. Come, constable, escort the gentleman to his new home. [*He is led away. Mrs. Peachum through the window*] Ladies, if you wish to visit him, you'll invariably find him in. From now on the gentleman's address will be the Old Bailey. I knew he'd be in to see his whores. I'll settle the bill. Good-bye, ladies [*Goes out*]

JENNY   Wake up, Jake, something has happened.

JAKE [*who has been too immersed in his reading to notice anything*]   Where's Mac?

JENNY   The coppers were here.

JAKE   Good God! And me just reading, reading, reading . . . Boy, oh boy, oh boy!
    [*Goes out*]

SCENE 6

Betrayed by the whores, Mac is freed from prison by the love of yet another woman.

The Old Bailey, a cage

Enter Brown.

BROWN   If only my men don't catch him! Good God, I only hope he's riding out beyond Highgate Heath, thinking of his Jackie. But he's so frivolous, like all great men. If they bring him in now and he looks at me with his faithful friendly eyes, I won't be able to bear it. Thank God, at least the moon is shining; if he is riding across the heath, at least he won't stray from the path. [*Sounds backstage*] What's that? Oh, my God, they're bringing him in.

MAC [*tied with heavy ropes, accompanied by six constables, enters with head erect*]   Well, flatfeet, thank God we're home again. [*He notices Brown who has fled to the far corner of the cell*]

BROWN [*after a long pause, under the withering glance of his former friend*]   Oh, Mac, it wasn't me . . . I did everything in my . . . don't look at me like that, Mac . . . I can't stand it . . . Your silence is killing me. [*Shouts at one of the constables*] Stop tugging at that rope, you swine . . . Say something, Mac. Say something to your poor Jackie . . . A kind word in his tragic . . . [*Rests his head against the wall and weeps*] He doesn't deem me worthy even of a word. [*Goes out*]

MAC   That miserable Brown. The living picture of a bad conscience. And he calls himself a chief of police. It was a good idea not shouting at him. I was going to at first. But then it occurred to me in the nick of time that a deep withering stare would send much colder shivers down his spine. It worked. I looked at him and he wept bitterly. That's a trick I got from the Bible.

[*Enter Smith with handcuffs*]

MAC   Well, Mr. Warder, I suppose these are the heaviest you've got? With your kind permission I should like to apply for a more comfortable pair. [*He takes out his checkbook*]

SMITH   Of course, Captain, we've got them here at every price. It all depends how much you want to spend. From one guinea to ten.

MAC   How much would none at all cost?

SMITH   Fifty.

MAC   [*writes a check*]   But the worst of it is that now this business with Lucy is bound to come out. If Brown hears that I've been carrying on with his daughter behind his friendly back, he'll turn into a tiger.

SMITH   As you make your bed, so must you lie on it.

MAC   I'll bet you the tart is waiting outside right now. I can see happy days between now and the execution.

> Is this a life for one of my proud station?
> I take it, I must frankly own, amiss.
> From childhood up I heard with consternation:
> One must live well to know what living is!

[*Song lighting: golden glow. The organ is lit up. Three lamps are lowered on a pole, and the signs say:*]

Ballade of Good Living

1

> I've heard them praising single-minded spirits
> Whose empty stomachs show they live for knowledge
> In rat-infested shacks awash with ullage.
> I'm all for culture, but there are some limits.
> The simple life is fine for those it suits.
> I don't find, for my part, that it attracts.
> There's not a bird from here to Halifax
> Would peck at such unappetizing fruits.
> What use is freedom? None, to judge from this.
> One must live well to know what living is.

2

The dashing sort who cut precarious capers
And go and risk their necks just for the pleasure
Then swagger home and write it up at leisure
And flog the story to the Sunday papers—
If you could see how cold they get at night
Sullen, with chilly wife, climbing to bed
And how they dream they're going to get ahead
And how they see time stretching out of sight—
Now tell me, who would choose to live like this?
One must live well to know what living is.

3

There's plenty that they have. I know I lack it
And ought to join their splendid isolation
But when I gave them more consideration
I told myself: my friend, that's not your racket.
Suffering ennobles, but it can depress.
The paths of glory lead but to the grave.
You once were poor and lonely, wise and brave.
You ought to try to bite off rather less.
The search for happiness boils down to this:
One must live well to know what living is.

[*Enter Lucy*]

LUCY   You dirty dog, you—how can you look me in the face after all there's been
between us?
MAC   Have you no bowels, no tenderness, my dear Lucy, seeing a husband in
such circumstances?
LUCY   A husband! You monster! So you think I haven't heard about your goings-
on with Miss Peachum! I could scratch your eyes out!
MAC   Seriously, Lucy, you're not fool enough to be jealous of Polly?
LUCY   You're married to her, aren't you, you beast?
MAC   Married! It's true, I go to the house, I chat with the girl. I kiss her, and now
the silly jade goes about telling everyone that I'm married to her. I am ready,
my dear Lucy, to give you satisfaction—if you think there is any in marriage.
What can a man of honor say more? He can say nothing more.
LUCY   Oh, Mac, I only want to become an honest woman.
MAC   If you think marriage with me will . . . all right. What can a man of honor
say more? He can say nothing more.

[*Enter Polly*]

POLLY Where is my dear husband? Oh, Mac, there you are. Why do you turn away from me? It's your Polly. It's your wife.

LUCY Oh, you miserable villain!

POLLY Oh, Mackie in prison! Why didn't you ride across Highgate Heath? You told me you wouldn't see those women any more. I knew what they'd do to you; but I didn't say anything, because I believed you. Mac, I'll stay with you till death.—Not one kind word. Mac? Not one kind look? Oh, Mac, think what your Polly must be suffering to see you in this condition.

LUCY Oh, the slut.

POLLY What does this mean, Mac? Who on earth is that? You might at least tell her who I am. Tell her I'm your wife, will you? Aren't I your wife? Look at me. Tell me, aren't I your wife?

LUCY You low-down sneak! Have you got two wives, you monster?

POLLY Say something, Mac. Aren't I your wife? Haven't I done everything for you? I was innocent when I married, you know that. Why, you even put me in charge of the gang, and I've done everything the way we arranged, and Jake wants me to tell you that he . . .

MAC If you two could only shut your traps for two minutes I'll explain every-thing.

LUCY No, I won't shut my trap, I can't bear it. It's more than flesh and blood can bear.

POLLY Yes, my dear, naturally the wife has . . .

LUCY The wife!!

POLLY   . . . the wife deserves some preference. Or at least the appearance of it, my dear. All this fuss and bother will drive the poor man mad.

LUCY Fuss and bother, that's a good one. What have you gone and picked up now? This filthy little tart! So this is your great conquest! So this is your Rose of Old Soho!

[*Song lighting: golden glow. The organ is lit up. Three lamps are lowered on a pole and the signs say:*]

Jealousy Duet

1

LUCY

Come on out, you Rose of Old Soho!
Let us see your legs, my little sweetheart!
I hear you have a lovely ankle
And I'd love to see such a complete tart.
They tell me that Mac says your behind is so provoking.

POLLY

Did he now, did he now?

LUCY

If what I see is true he must be joking.

POLLY

Is he now, is he now?

LUCY

Ho, it makes me split my sides!

POLLY

Oh, that's how you split your side?

LUCY

Fancy you as Mackie's bride!

POLLY

Mackie fancies Mackie's bride.

LUCY

Ha ha ha! Catch him sporting
With something that the cat brought in.

POLLY

Just you watch your tongue, my dear.

LUCY

Must I watch my tongue, my dear?

BOTH

Mackie and I, see how we bill and coo, man
He's got no eyes for any other woman.
The whole thing's an invention
You mustn't pay attention
To such a bitch's slanders.
Poppycock!

2

POLLY

Oh, they call me Rose of Old Soho
And Macheath appears to find me pretty.

LUCY

Does he now?

POLLY

They say I have a lovely ankle
And the best proportions in the city.

LUCY

Little whippersnapper!

POLLY

Who's a little whippersnapper?
Mac tells me that he finds my behind is most provoking.

LUCY

Doesn't he? Doesn't he?

POLLY

I do not suppose that he is joking.

LUCY

Isn't he, isn't he?

POLLY

Ho, it makes me split my sides!

LUCY

Oh, that's how you split your side?

POLLY

Being Mackie's only bride!

LUCY

Are you Mackie's only bride?

POLLY [to the audience]

Can you really picture him sporting

With something that the cat brought in?

LUCY

Just you watch your tongue, my dear.

POLLY

Must I watch my tongue, my dear?

BOTH

Mackie and I, see how we bill and coo, man

He's got no eyes for any other woman.

The whole thing's an invention

You cannot pay attention

To such a bitch's slanders.

Poppycock!

MAC   All right, Lucy. Calm down. You see it's just a trick of Polly's. She wants to come between us. I'm going to be hanged and she wants to parade as my widow. Really, Polly, this isn't the moment.

POLLY   Have you the heart to disclaim me?

MAC   And have you the heart to go on about my being married? Oh, Polly, why must you add to my misery? [Shakes his head reproachfully] Polly! Polly!

LUCY   It's true, Miss Peachum, you're putting yourself in a bad light. Quite apart from the fact that it's barbarous of you to worry a gentleman in his situation!

POLLY   The most elementary rules of decency, my dear young lady, ought to teach you, it seems to me, to treat a man with a little more reserve when his wife is present.

MAC   Seriously, Polly, that's carrying a joke too far.

LUCY   And if, my dear lady, you start raising a row here in this prison, I shall be obliged to send for the warder to show you the door. I'm sorry, my dear Miss Peachum.

POLLY   Mrs., if you please! Mrs. Macheath. Just let me tell you this, young lady.

The airs you give yourself are most unbecoming. My duty obliges me to stay
with my husband.

LUCY   What's that? What's that? Oh, she won't leave! She stands there and we
throw her out and she won't leave! Must I speak more plainly?

POLLY   You—you just hold your filthy tongue, you slut, or I'll knock your block
off, my dear young lady.

LUCY   You've been thrown out, you interloper! I suppose that's not clear enough.
You don't understand nice manners.

POLLY   You and your nice manners! Oh, I'm forgetting my dignity! I shouldn't
stoop to . . . no, I shouldn't. [She starts to bawl]

LUCY   Just look at my belly, you slut! Did I get that from out of nowhere? Haven't
you eyes in your head?

POLLY   Oh! So you're in the family way! And you think that gives you rights? A
fine lady like you, you shouldn't have let him in!

MAC   Polly!

POLLY [in tears]   This is really too much. Mac, you shouldn't have done that. Now
I don't know what to do.

[Enter Mrs. Peachum]

MRS. PEACHUM   I knew it. She's with her man. You little trollop, come here immediately. When they hang your man, you can hang yourself too. A fine way
to treat your respectable mother, making her come and get you out of jail.
And he's got two of them, what's more—the Nero!

POLLY   Leave me here, mama; you don't know . . .

MRS. PEACHUM   You're coming home this minute.

LUCY   There you are, it takes your mama to tell you how to behave.

MRS. PEACHUM   Get going.

POLLY   Just a second. I only have to . . . I only have to tell him something . . .
Really . . . it's very important.

MRS. PEACHUM [giving her a box on the ear]   Well, this is important too. Get going!

POLLY   Oh, Mac! [She is dragged away]

MAC   Lucy, you were magnificent. Of course I felt sorry for her. That's why I
couldn't treat the slut as she deserved. Just for a moment you thought there
was some truth in what she said. Didn't you?

LUCY   Yes, my dear, so I did.

MAC   If there were any truth in it, her mother wouldn't have put me in this situation. Did you hear how she laid into me? A mother might treat a seducer like
that, not a son-in-law.

LUCY   It makes me so happy to hear you say that from the bottom of your heart.
I love you so much I'd almost rather see you on the gallows than in the arms
of another. Isn't that strange?

MAC   Lucy, I should like to owe you my life.

LUCY   It's wonderful the way you say that. Say it again.

MAC   Lucy, I should like to owe you my life.

LUCY   Shall I run away with you, dearest?

MAC   Well, but you see, if we run away together, it will be hard for us to hide. As soon as they stop looking, I'll send for you post haste, you know that!

LUCY   What can I do to help you?

MAC   Bring me my hat and cane.

[Lucy comes back with his hat and cane and throws them into his cage]

MAC   Lucy, the fruit of our love which you bear beneath your heart will hold us forever united.

[Lucy goes out]

SMITH [enters, goes into the cage, and says to Mac]   Let's have that cane.

[After a brief chase, in which Smith pursues Mac with a chair and a crowbar, Mac jumps over the bars. Constables run after him. Enter Brown]

BROWN [off]   Hey, Mac!—Mac, answer me please. It's Jackie. Mac, please be a good boy, answer me, I can't stand it any longer. [Goes in] Mackie! What's this? He's gone, thank God! [He sits down on the bed]

[Enter Peachum]

PEACHUM [to Smith]   My name is Peachum. I've come to collect the forty pounds reward for the capture of the bandit Macheath. [Appears in front of the cage] Excuse me! Is that Mr. Macheath? [Brown is silent] Oh. I suppose the other gentleman has gone for a stroll? I come here to visit a criminal, and who do I find sitting here but Mr. Brown! Tiger Brown is sitting here and his friend Macheath is not sitting here.

BROWN [groaning]   Oh, Mr. Peachum, it wasn't my fault.

PEACHUM   Of course not. How could it be? You yourself would never . . . when you think of the situation it'll land you in . . . it's out of the question, Brown.

BROWN   Mr. Peachum, I'm beside myself.

PEACHUM   I believe you. You must be feeling terrible.

BROWN   Yes, it's this feeling of helplessness that gets a man down. Those fellows do just as they please. It's dreadful, dreadful.

PEACHUM   Wouldn't you care to lie down awhile? Just close your eyes and pretend nothing has happened. Imagine you're on a lovely green meadow with little white clouds overhead. The main thing is to forget all about those terrible things, those that are past, and most of all, those that are still to come.

BROWN [alarmed]   What do you mean by that?

PEACHUM   I'm amazed at your fortitude. In your position I should simply collapse, crawl into bed and drink hot tea. And above all, I'd find someone to lay a soothing hand on my forehead.

BROWN   Damn it all, it's not my fault if the fellow escapes. There's not much the police can do about it.

PEACHUM   I see. There's not much the police can do about it. You don't believe we'll see Mr. Macheath back here again? [*Brown shrugs his shoulders*] In that case, your fate will be hideously unjust. People are sure to say—they always do—that the police shouldn't have let him escape. No, I can't see that glittering Coronation procession just yet.

BROWN   What do you mean?

PEACHUM   Let me remind you of a historical incident which, despite having caused a great stir at the time, in the year 1400 B.C., is unknown to the public of today. On the death of the Egyptian king Ramses II, the police captain of Nineveh, or it may have been Cairo, committed some minor offense against the lower classes of the population. Even at that time the consequences were terrible. As the history books tell us, the coronation procession of Semiramis, the new queen "developed into a series of catastrophes because of the unduly active participation of the lower orders." Historians still shudder at the cruel way Semiramis treated her police captain. I only remember dimly, but there was some talk of snakes that she fed on his bosom.

BROWN   Really?

PEACHUM   The Lord be with you, Brown. [*Goes out*]

BROWN   Now only the mailed fist can help. Sergeants! Report to me at the double!

[*Curtain. Macheath and Low-Dive Jenny step before the curtain and sing to song lighting*]

SECOND THREEPENNY FINALE

What Keeps Mankind Alive?

1

MAC

You gentlemen who think you have a mission
To purge us of the seven deadly sins
Should first sort out the basic food position
Then start your preaching: that's where it begins.
You lot, who preach restraint and watch your waist as well
Should learn for all time how the world is run:
However much you twist, whatever lies you tell
Food is the first thing. Morals follow on.
So first make sure that those who now are starving
Get proper helpings when we all start carving.

VOICE [*off*]

What keeps mankind alive?

MAC

    What keeps mankind alive? The fact that millions
    Are daily tortured, stifled, punished, silenced, oppressed.
    Mankind can keep alive thanks to its brilliance
    In keeping its humanity repressed.

CHORUS

    For once you must try not to shirk the facts:
    Mankind is kept alive by bestial acts.

    2

JENNY

    You say that girls may strip with your permission.
    You draw the lines dividing art from sin.
    So first sort out the basic food position
    Then start your preaching: that's where we begin.
    You lot, who bank on your desires and our disgust
    Should learn for all time how the world is run:
    Whatever lies you tell, however much you twist
    Food is the first thing. Morals follow on.
    So first make sure that those who now are starving
    Get proper helpings when we all start carving.

VOICE [*off*]

    What keeps mankind alive?

JENNY

    What keeps mankind alive? The fact that millions
    Are daily tortured, stifled, punished, silenced, oppressed.
    Mankind can keep alive thanks to its brilliance
    In keeping its humanity repressed.

CHORUS

    For once you must try not to shirk the facts:
    Mankind is kept alive by bestial acts.

ACT III

SCENE 7

That night Peachum prepares his campaign. He plans to disrupt the coronation procession by a demonstration of human misery.

Peachum's Outfitting Shop for Beggars

The beggars paint little signs with inscriptions such as "I gave my eye for my king," etc.

PEACHUM   Gentlemen, at this moment, in our eleven branches from Drury Lane to Turnbridge, one thousand four hundred and thirty-two gentlemen are working on signs like these with a view to attending the Coronation of our Queen.

MRS. PEACHUM   Get a move on! If you won't work, you can't beg. Call yourself a blind man and can't even make a proper K? That's supposed to be child's writing, anyone would take it for an old man's.

[*A drum roll*]

BEGGAR   That's the Coronation guard presenting arms. Little do they suspect that today, the biggest day in their military careers, they'll have us to deal with.

FILCH [*enters and reports*]   Mrs. Peachum, there's a dozen sleepy-looking hens traipsing in. They claim there's some money due them.

[*Enter the whores*]

JENNY   Madam . . .

MRS. PEACHUM   Hm, you look as if you'd fallen off your perches. I suppose you've come to collect the money for that Macheath of yours? Well, you'll get nothing, do you understand, nothing.

JENNY   How are we to understand that, ma'am?

MRS. PEACHUM   Bursting in here in the middle of the night! Coming to a respectable house at three in the morning! With the work you do, I should think you'd want some sleep. You look like sicked-up milk.

JENNY   Then you won't give us the stipulated fee for turning in Mr. Macheath, ma'am?

MRS. PEACHUM   Exactly. No thirty pieces of silver for you.

JENNY   Why not, ma'am?

MRS. PEACHUM   Because your fine Mr. Macheath has scattered himself to the four winds. And now, ladies, get out of my parlor.

JENNY   This is too much. Just don't you try that on us. That's all I've got to say to you. Not on us.

MRS. PEACHUM   Filch, the ladies wish to be shown the door.

[*Filch goes toward the ladies, Jenny pushes him away*]

JENNY   I'd advise you to hold your filthy tongue. If you don't, I'm likely to . . .

[*Enter Peachum*]

PEACHUM   What's going on, you haven't given them any money, I hope? Well, ladies, how about it? Is Mr. Macheath in jail, or isn't he?

JENNY   Don't talk to me about Mr. Macheath. You're not fit to black his boots. Last night I had to let a customer go because it made me cry into my pillow to think how I had sold that gentleman to you. Yes, ladies, and what do you think happened this morning? Less than an hour ago, just after I had cried myself to sleep, I heard somebody whistle, and out on the street stood the very gentleman I'd been crying about, asking me to throw down the key. He wanted to lie in my arms and make me forget the wrong I had done him. Ladies, he's the last gentleman left in London. And if our friend Suky Tawdry isn't here with us now, it's because he went on from me to her to comfort her too.

PEACHUM [*muttering to himself*] Suky Tawdry . . .

JENNY So now you know that you're not fit to black that gentleman's boots. You miserable stool pigeon.

PEACHUM Filch, run to the nearest police station, tell them Mr. Macheath is at Miss Suky Tawdry's place. [*Filch goes out*] But ladies, why are we arguing? The money will be paid out, that goes without saying. Celia dear, you'd do better to make the ladies some coffee instead of slanging them.

MRS. PEACHUM [*on her way out*] Suky Tawdry! [*She sings the third stanza of the Ballade of Sexual Obsession*]

There stands a man. The gallows loom above him.
They've got the quicklime mixed in which to shove him.
They've put his neck just under where the noose is
And what's he thinking of, the idiot? Floozies.
They've all but hanged him, yet he can't ignore that call.
Sexual obsession has him in its thrall.
  She's sold him down the river heart and soul
  He's seen the dirty money in her hand
  And bit by bit begins to understand:
  The pit that covers him is woman's hole.
  Then he may rant and roar and curse his ruin—
  But soon as night falls he'll be up and doing.

PEACHUM Get a move on, you'd all be rotting in the sewers of Turnbridge if in my sleepless nights I hadn't worked out how to squeeze a penny out of your poverty. I discovered that though the rich of this earth find no difficulty in creating misery, they can't bear to see it. Because they are weaklings and fools just like you. They may have enough to eat till the end of their days, they may be able to wax their floors with butter so that even the crumbs from their tables grow fat, but they can't look on unmoved while a man is collapsing from hunger, though of course that only applies so long as he collapses outside their own front door.

[*Enter Mrs. Peachum with a tray full of coffee cups*]

MRS. PEACHUM You can come by the shop tomorrow and pick up your money, but only when the Coronation's over.

JENNY Mrs. Peachum, you leave me speechless.

PEACHUM   Fall in. We assemble in one hour outside Buckingham Palace. Quick
    march.

[*The beggars fall in*]

FILCH [*dashes in*]   Cops! I didn't even get to the police station. The police are here
    already.
PEACHUM   Hide, gentlemen! [*To Mrs. Peachum*] Call the band together. Shake a
    leg. And if you hear me say "harmless," do you understand, *harmless* . . .
MRS. PEACHUM   Harmless? I don't understand a thing.
PEACHUM   Naturally you don't understand. Well, if I say *harmless* . . . [*knocking at
    the door*] Thank God, this is the answer, *harmless*, then you play some kind of
    music. Get a move on!

[*Mrs. Peachum goes out with some beggars. The others except for the girl with the sign "A
Victim of Military Tyranny," hide with their things upstage right behind the clothes rack.
Enter Brown and constables*]

BROWN   Here we are. And now Mr. Beggar's Friend, drastic action will be taken.
    Put him in chains, Smith. Oh, here are some of those delightful signs. [*To the
    girl*] "A Victim of Military Tyranny"—is that you?
PEACHUM   Good morning, Brown, good morning. Sleep well?
BROWN   Huh?
PEACHUM   Morning, Brown.
BROWN   Is he saying that to me? Does he know one of you? I don't believe I have
    the pleasure of your acquaintance.
PEACHUM   Really? Morning, Brown.
BROWN   Knock his hat off.

[*Smith does so*]

PEACHUM   Look here, Brown, as long as you're *passing by, passing*, I say, Brown,
    I may as well ask you to put a certain Macheath under lock and key, it's high
    time.
BROWN   The man's mad. Don't laugh, Smith. Tell me, Smith, how is it possible
    that such a notorious criminal should be running around loose in London?
PEACHUM   Because he's your friend, Brown.
BROWN   Who?
PEACHUM   Mac the Knife. Not me. I'm no criminal. I'm a poor man, Brown. You
    can't abuse me, Brown, you've got the worst hour in your life ahead of you.
    Care for some coffee? [*To the whores*] Girls, give the chief of police a sip, that's
    no way to behave. Let's all be friends. We are all law-abiding people! The law
    was made for one thing alone, for the exploitation of those who don't under-
    stand it, or are prevented by naked misery from obeying it. And anyone who
    wants a crumb of this exploitation for himself must obey the law strictly.

BROWN   I see, then you believe our judges are corruptible?

PEACHUM   Not at all, sir, not at all! Our judges are absolutely incorruptible: It's
more than money can do to make them give a fair verdict!

[*A second drum roll*]

PEACHUM   The troops are marching off to line the route. The poorest of the poor
will move off in half an hour.

BROWN   That's right, Mr. Peachum. In half an hour the poorest of the poor will
be marched off to winter quarters in the Old Bailey. [*To the constables*] All
right, boys, round them all up, all the patriots you find here. [*To the beggars*]
Have you fellows ever heard of Tiger Brown? Tonight, Peachum, I've hit on
the solution and, I believe I may say, saved a friend from mortal peril. I'll
simply smoke out your whole nest. And lock up the lot of you for—hm, for
what? For begging on the street. You seem to have intimated your intention
of embarrassing me and the Queen with these beggars. I'll just arrest the
beggars. Let that be a lesson to you.

PEACHUM   Excellent, but—what beggars?

BROWN   These cripples here. Smith, we'll take these patriots along with us.

PEACHUM   I can save you from a hasty step; you can thank the Lord, Brown, that
you came to me. You see, Brown, you can arrest these few, they're harmless,
harmless . . .

[*Music starts up, playing a few measures of the "Song of the Insufficiency of Human
Endeavor"*]

BROWN   What's that?

PEACHUM   Music. They play as well as they can. The Song of Insufficiency. You
don't know it? Let this be a lesson to you.

[*Song lighting: golden glow. The organ is lit up. Three lamps are lowered from above on a
pole and the signs say:*]

Song of the Insufficiency of Human Endeavor

1

Mankind lives by its head
Its head won't see it through
Inspect your own. What lives off that?
At most a louse or two.
    For this bleak existence
    Man is never sharp enough.
    Hence his weak resistance
    To its tricks and bluff.

2

Aye, make yourself a plan
They need you at the top!
Then make yourself a second plan
Then let the whole thing drop.
   For this bleak existence
   Man is never bad enough
   Though his sheer persistence
   Can be lovely stuff.

3

Aye, race for happiness
But don't you race too fast.
When all chase after happiness
Happiness comes in last.
   For this bleak existence
   Man is never undemanding enough.
   All his loud insistence
   Is a load of guff.

PEACHUM   Your plan, Brown, was brilliant, but hardly realistic. All you can arrest
in this place is a few young fellows celebrating their Queen's Coronation by
arranging a little fancy dress party. When the real paupers come along—there
aren't any here—there will be thousands of them. That's the point, you've
forgotten what an immense number of poor people there are. When you see
them standing outside the Abbey, it won't be a festive sight. You see, they
don't look good. Do you know what the rose is, Brown? Yes, but how about
a hundred thousand faces all flushed with the rose: Our young Queen's path
should be strewn with roses not with the rose. And all those cripples at the
church door. That's something one wishes to avoid, Brown. You'll probably
say the police can handle us poor folk. You don't believe that yourself. How
will it look if six hundred poor cripples have to be clubbed down at the Coronation? It will look bad. It will look disgusting. Nauseating. I feel faint at the
thought of it, Brown. A small chair, if you please.

BROWN [to Smith]   That's a threat. See here, you, that's blackmail. We can't touch
the man, in the interests of public order we simply can't touch him. I've
never seen the like of it.

PEACHUM   You're seeing it now. Let me tell you something: You can behave as
you please to the Queen of England. But you can't tread on the toes of the
poorest man in England, or you'll be brought down, Mr. Brown.

BROWN   So you're asking me to arrest Mac the Knife? Arrest him? That's easy to
say. You've got to find a man before you can arrest him.

PEACHUM   If you say that, I can't contradict you. So I'll find your man for you;
we'll see if there's any morality left. Jenny, where is Mr. Macheath at this
moment?

JENNY   21 Oxford Street, at Suky Tawdry's.

BROWN   Smith, go at once to Suky Tawdry's place at 21 Oxford Street, arrest Macheath and take him to the Old Bailey. In the meantime, I must put on my gala uniform. On this day of all days I must wear my gala uniform.

PEACHUM   Brown, if he's not on the gallows by six o'clock . . .

BROWN   Oh, Mac, it was not to be. [*Goes out with constables*]

PEACHUM [*calling after him*]   That was a lesson to you, eh, Brown?

[*Third drum roll*]

PEACHUM   Third drum roll. Change of direction. You will head for the dungeons of the Old Bailey. March!

[*The beggars go out*]

PEACHUM [*sings the fourth stanza of the "Song of the Insufficiency of Human Endeavor"*]:

Man could be good instead
So slug him on the head
If you can slug him good and hard
He may stay good and dead.
  For this bleak existence
  Man's not good enough just yet.
  Don't wait for assistance.
  Slug him on the head.

[*Curtain. Jenny steps before the curtain with a hurdy-gurdy and sings the*]

Solomon Song

1
You saw sagacious Solomon
You know what came of him.
To him complexities seemed plain.
He cursed the hour that gave birth to him
And saw that everything was vain.
How great and wise was Solomon!
But now that time is getting late
The world can see what followed on.
It's wisdom that had brought him to this state—
How fortunate the man with none!

2
You saw the lovely Cleopatra

You know what she became.
Two emperors slaved to serve her lust.
She whored herself to death and fame
Then rotted down and turned to dust.
How beautiful was Babylon!
But now that time is getting late
The world can see what followed on.
It's beauty that had brought her to this state—
How fortunate the girl with none!

3
You saw the gallant Caesar next
You know what he became.
They deified him in his life
Then had him murdered just the same.
And as they raised the fatal knife
How loud he cried "You too, my son!"
But now that time is getting late
The world can see what followed on.
It's courage that had brought him to this state—
How fortunate the man with none!

4
You know the ever-curious Brecht
Whose songs you liked to hum.
He asked, too often for your peace
Where rich men get their riches from.
So then you drove him overseas.
How curious was my mother's son!
But now that time is getting late
The world can see what followed on.
Inquisitiveness brought him to this state—
How fortunate the man with none!

5
And now look at this man Macheath
The sands are running out.
If only he'd known where to stop
And stuck to crimes he knew all about
He surely would have reached the top.
Then suddenly his heart was won.
But now the time is getting late
The world can see what followed on.
His sexual urges brought him to this state—
How fortunate the man with none!

SCENE 8

Property in Dispute

A young girl's room in the Old Bailey.

Lucy.

SMITH [*enters*]   Miss, Mrs. Polly Macheath wishes to speak with you.
LUCY   Mrs. Macheath? Show her in.

[*Enter Polly*]

POLLY   Good morning, madam. Madam, good morning!
LUCY   What is it, please?
POLLY   Do you recognize me?
LUCY   Of course I know you.
POLLY   I've come to beg your pardon for the way I behaved yesterday.
LUCY   Very interesting.
POLLY   I have no excuse to offer for my behavior, madam, but my misfortunes.
LUCY   I see.
POLLY   Madam, you must forgive me. I was stung by Mr. Macheath's behavior.
   He really ought not to have put us in such a situation, and you can tell him
   so when you see him.
LUCY   I . . . I . . . shan't be seeing him.
POLLY   Of course you will see him.
LUCY   I shall not see him.
POLLY   Forgive me.
LUCY   But he's very fond of you.
POLLY   Oh no, you're the only one he loves. I'm sure of that.
LUCY   Very kind of you.
POLLY   But, madam, a man is always afraid of a woman who loves him too much.
   And then he's bound to neglect and avoid her. I could see at a glance that he
   is more devoted to you than I could ever have guessed.
LUCY   Do you mean that sincerely?
POLLY   Of course, certainly, very sincerely, madam. Do believe me.
LUCY   Dear Miss Polly, both of us have loved him too much.
POLLY   Perhaps [*Pause*] And now, madam, I want to tell you how it all came
   about. Ten days ago I met Mr. Macheath for the first time at the Cuttlefish
   Hotel. My mother was there too. Five days later, about the day before yesterday, we were married. Yesterday I found out that he was wanted by the
   police for a variety of crimes. And today I don't know what's going to happen. So you see, madam, twelve days ago I couldn't have imagined ever
   losing my heart to a man.

[*Pause*]

LUCY   I understand, Miss Peachum.

POLLY   Mrs. Macheath.

LUCY   Mrs. Macheath.

POLLY   To tell the truth, I've been thinking about this man a good deal in the last few hours. It's not so simple. Because you see, miss, I really can't help envying you for the way he behaved to you the other day. When I left him, only because my mother made me, he didn't show the slightest sign of regret. Maybe he has no heart and nothing but a stone in his breast. What do you think, Lucy?

LUCY   Well, my dear miss—I really don't know if Mr. Macheath is entirely to blame. You should have stuck to your own class of people, dear miss.

POLLY   Mrs. Macheath.

LUCY   Mrs. Macheath.

POLLY   That's quite true—or at least, as my father always advised me, I should have kept everything on a strictly business footing.

LUCY   Definitely.

POLLY [*weeping*]   But he's my only possession in all the world.

LUCY   My dear, such a misfortune can befall the most intelligent woman. But after all, you are his wife on paper. That should be a comfort to you. Poor child, I can't bear to see you so depressed. Won't you have a little something?

POLLY   What?

LUCY   Something to eat.

POLLY   Oh yes, please, a little something to eat. [*Lucy goes out. Polly aside*] The hypocritical strumpet.

LUCY [*comes back with coffee and cake*]   Here. This ought to do it.

POLLY   You've really gone to too much trouble, madam. [*Pause. She eats*] That's a lovely picture of him you've got. When did he bring it?

LUCY   Bring it?

POLLY [*innocently*]   I mean when did he bring it up here to you?

LUCY   He didn't bring it.

POLLY   Did he give it to you right here in this room?

LUCY   He never was in this room.

POLLY   I see. But there wouldn't have been any harm in it. The paths of fate are so dreadfully crisscrossed.

LUCY   Must you keep talking such nonsense? You only came here to spy.

POLLY   Then you do know where he is?

LUCY   Me? Don't you know?

POLLY   Tell me this minute where he is.

LUCY   I have no idea.

POLLY   So you don't know where he is. Word of honor?

LUCY   No, I don't know. Hm, and you don't either?

POLLY   No. This is terrible. [*Polly laughs and Lucy weeps*] Now he has two commitments. And he's gone.

LUCY   I can't stand it any more. Oh, Polly, it's so dreadful.

POLLY [*gaily*]   I'm so happy to have found such a good friend at the end of this tragedy. That's something. Would you like a little more to eat? Some more cake?

LUCY   Just a bit! Oh, Polly, don't be so good to me. Really, I don't deserve it. Oh, Polly, men aren't worth it.

POLLY   Of course men aren't worth it, but what else can we do?

LUCY   No! Now I'm going to make a clean breast of it. Will you be very cross with me, Polly?

POLLY   About what?

LUCY   It's not real!

POLLY   What?

LUCY   This here! [*She indicates her belly*] And all for that criminal!

POLLY [*laughs*]   Oh, that's magnificent! Is it a cushion? Oh, you really are a hypocritical strumpet! Look—you want Mackie? I'll make you a present of him. If you find him you can keep him. [*Voices and steps are heard in the corridor*] What's that?

LUCY [*at the window*]   Mackie! They've caught him once more.

POLLY [*collapses*]   This is the end.

[*Enter Mrs. Peachum*]

MRS. PEACHUM   Ha, Polly, so this is where I find you. You must change your things, your husband is being hanged. I've brought your widow's weeds. [*Polly changes into the widow's dress*] You'll be a lovely widow. But you'll have to cheer up a little.

SCENE 9

Five o'clock, Friday morning: Mac the Knife, who has been with the whores again, has again been betrayed by whores. He is about to be hanged.

Death cell.

The bells of Westminster ring. Constables bring Macheath shackled into the cell.

SMITH   Bring him in here. There go the bells of Westminster. Stand up straight, I'm not asking you why you look so worn out. I'd say you were ashamed. [*To the constables*] When the bells of Westminster ring for the third time, that will be at six, he's got to have been hanged. Make everything ready.

A CONSTABLE   For the last quarter of an hour all the streets around Newgate have been so jammed with people of every class you can't get through.

SMITH   Strange! Then they already know?

CONSTABLE   If this goes on, all London will know in another quarter of an hour.

All the people who would otherwise have gone to the Coronation will come here. And the Queen will ride through empty streets.

SMITH   All the more reason for us to move fast. If we're through by six, that will give people time to get back to the Coronation by seven. So now, get going.

MAC   Hey, Smith, what time is it?

SMITH   Haven't you got eyes? Five-oh-four.

MAC   Five-oh-four.

[Just as Smith is locking the cell door from outside, Brown enters]

BROWN [his back to the cell, to Smith]   Is he in there?

SMITH   You want to see him?

BROWN   No, no, no, for God's sake. I'll leave it all to you.

[Goes out]

MAC [suddenly bursts into a soft unbroken flow of speech]   All right, Smith, I won't say a word, not a word about bribery, never fear. I know all about it. If you let yourself be bribed, you'd have to leave the country for a start. You certainly would. You'd need enough to live on for the rest of your life. A thousand pounds, eh? Don't say anything! In twenty minutes I'll tell you whether you can have your thousand pounds by noon. I'm not saying a word about feelings. Go outside and think it over carefully. Life is short and money is scarce. And I don't even know yet if I can raise any. But if anyone wants to see me, let them in.

SMITH [slowly]   That's a lot of nonsense, Mr. Macheath.

[Goes out]

MAC [sings softly and very fast the "Call of the Grave":]

Hark to the voice that's calling you to weep.
Macheath lies here, not under open sky
Not under treetops, no, but good and deep.
Fate struck him down in outraged majesty.
God grant his dying words may reach a friend.
The thickest walls encompass him about.
Is none of you concerned to know his fate?
Once he is gone the bottles can come out
But do stand by him while it's not too late.
D'you want his punishment to have no end?

[Matthew and Jake appear in the corridor. They are on their way to see Macheath. Smith stops them]

SMITH   Well, son. You look like a soused herring.

MATTHEW   Now the Captain's gone it's my job to get our girls in the family way, so when they're brought into court they can plead irresponsibility. It's a job for a horse. I've got to see the Captain.

[*Both continue toward Mac*]

MAC   Five twenty-five. You took your time.

JAKE   Yes, but, you see, we had to . . .

MAC   You see, you see, I'm being hanged, man! But I've not time to waste arguing with you. Five twenty-eight. All right: How much can you people draw from your savings account right away?

MATTHEW   From our . . . what, at five o'clock in the morning?

JAKE   Has it really come to this?

MAC   Can you manage four hundred pounds?·

JAKE   But what about us? That's all there is.

MAC   Who's being hanged, you or me?

MATTHEW [*excitedly*]   Who was lying around with Suky Tawdry instead of clearing out? Who was lying around with Suky Tawdry, us or you?

MAC   Shut your trap. I'll soon be lying somewhere other than with that slut. Five-thirty.

JAKE   Matt, if that's how it is, we'll just have to do it.

SMITH   Mr. Brown wishes to know what you'd like for your . . . meal.

MAC   Don't bother me. [*To Matthew*] Well, will you or won't you [*To Smith*] Asparagus.

MATTHEW   Don't you shout at me. I won't have it.

MAC   I'm not shouting at you. It's only that . . . Well Matthew, are you going to let me be hanged?

MATTHEW   Of course I'm not going to let you be hanged. Who said I was? But that's the lot. Four hundred pounds is all there is. No reason why I shouldn't say that, is there?

MAC   Five thirty-eight.

JAKE   We'll have to run, Matthew, or it'll be no good.

MATTHEW   If we can only get through. There's such a crowd. Scum of the earth! [*Both go out*]

MAC   If you're not here by five to six, you'll never see me again. [*Shouts*] You'll never see me again . . .

SMITH   They've gone. Well, what about it? [*Makes a gesture of counting money*]

MAC   Four hundred. [*Smith goes out shrugging his shoulders. Mac, calling after him*] I've got to speak to Brown.

SMITH [*comes back with constables*]: Got the soap?

CONSTABLE   Yes, but not the right kind.

SMITH   You can set the thing up in ten minutes.

CONSTABLE   But the trap doesn't work.

SMITH It's got to work. The bells have gone a second time.

CONSTABLE What a shambles!

MAC [*sings*]

> Come here and see the shitty state he's in.
> This really is what people mean by bust.
> You who set up the dirty cash you win
> As just about the only god you'll trust
> Don't stand and watch him slipping around the bend!
> Go to the Queen and say that her subjects need her
> Go in a group and tell her of his trouble
> Like pigs all following behind their leader.
> Say that his teeth are wearing down to rubble.
> D'you want his punishment to have no end?

SMITH I can't possibly let you in. You're only number sixteen. Wait your turn.

POLLY What do you mean, number sixteen? Don't be a bureaucrat. I'm his wife, I've got to see him.

SMITH Not more than five minutes, then.

POLLY Five minutes! That's perfectly ridiculous. Five minutes! How is one to say all one has to say? It's not so simple. This is good-bye forever. There's an exceptional amount of things for man and wife to talk about at such a moment . . . where is he?

SMITH What, can't you see him?

POLLY Yes, of course. Thank you.

MAC Polly!

POLLY Yes, Mackie, here I am.

MAC Yes, of course!

POLLY How are you? Are you quite worn out? It's hard!

MAC But what will you do now? What will become of you?

POLLY Don't worry, the business is doing very well. That's the least part of it. Are you very nervous, Mackie? . . . By the way, what was your father? There's so much you still haven't told me. I just don't understand. Your health has always been excellent.

MAC Polly, can't you help me to get out?

POLLY Oh yes, of course.

MAC With money, of course. I've arranged with the warder . . .

POLLY [*slowly*] The money has gone off to Manchester.

MAC And you've got none on you?

POLLY No, I've got nothing on me. But you know, Mackie, I could talk to somebody, for instance . . . I might even ask the Queen in person. [*She breaks down*] Oh, Mackie!

SMITH [*pulling Polly away*] Well, have you raised those thousand pounds?

POLLY All the best, Mackie, take care of yourself, and don't forget me! [*Goes out*]

[*Smith and a constable bring in a table with a dish of asparagus on it*]

SMITH   Is the asparagus tender?

CONSTABLE   Absolutely. [*Goes out*]

BROWN [*appears and goes up to Smith*]   Smith, what does he want me for? It's good you didn't take the table in earlier. We'll take it right in with us, to show him how we feel about him. [*They enter the cell with the table. Smith goes out. Pause*] Hello, Mac. Here's your asparagus. Won't you have some?

MAC   Don't you bother, Mr. Brown. There are others to show me the last honors.

BROWN   Oh, Mackie!

MAC   Would you be so good as to produce your accounts? You don't mind if I eat in the meantime, after all it is my last meal. [*He eats*]

BROWN   I hope you enjoy it. Oh, Mac, you're turning the knife in the wound.

MAC   The accounts, sir, if you please, the accounts. No sentimentality.

BROWN [*with a sigh takes a small notebook from his pocket*]   I've got them right here, Mac. The accounts for the past six months.

MAC [*bitingly*]   Oh, so all you came for was to get your money before it's too late.

BROWN   You know that isn't so.

MAC   Don't worry, sir, nobody's going to cheat you. What do I owe you? But I want an itemized bill, if you don't mind. Life has made me distrustful . . . In your position, sir, you should be able to understand that.

BROWN   Mac, when you talk like that, I just can't think.

[*A loud pounding is heard rear*]

SMITH [*off*]   All right, that'll hold.

MAC   The accounts, Brown.

BROWN   Very well—if you insist. Well, first of all the rewards for murderers arrested thanks to you or your men. The government paid you a total of . . .

MAC   Three instances at forty pounds apiece, that makes a hundred and twenty pounds. One quarter for you comes to thirty pounds, so that's what we owe you.

BROWN   Yes—yes—but really, Mac, I don't think we ought to spend our last . . .

MAC   Kindly stop sniveling. Thirty pounds. And for the job in Dover eight pounds.

BROWN   Why only eight pounds, there was . . .

MAC   Do you believe me or don't you believe me? Your share in the transactions of the last six months comes to thirty-eight pounds.

BROWN [*wailing*]   For a whole lifetime . . . I could read . . .

BOTH   Your every thought in your eyes.

MAC   Three years in India—John was all present and Jim was all there—, five years in London, and this is the thanks I get. [*Indicating how he will look when hanged*]

Here hangs Macheath who never wronged a flea
A faithless friend has brought him to this pass.
And as he dangles from the gallowstree
His neck finds out how heavy is his arse.

BROWN   If that's the way you feel about it, Mac . . . The man who impugns my
honor, impugns me. [*Runs furiously out of the cage*]

MAC   Your honor . . .

BROWN   Yes, my honor. Time to begin, Smith! Let them all in! [*To Mac*] Excuse
me, would you.

SMITH [*quickly to Macheath*]   I can still get you out of here, in another minute I
won't be able to. Have you got the money?

MAC   Yes, as soon as the boys get back.

SMITH   There's no sign of them. The deal is off.

[*People are admitted. Peachum, Mrs. Peachum, Polly, Lucy, the whores, the vicar, Matthew and Jake*]

JENNY   They didn't want to let us in. But I said to them: If you don't get those
pisspots you call heads out of my way, you'll hear from Low-Dive Jenny.

PEACHUM   I am his father-in-law. I beg your pardon, which of the present company is Mr. Macheath?

MAC [*introduces himself*]   I'm Macheath.

PEACHUM [*walks past the cage, and like all who follow him stations himself to the right of
it*]   Fate, Mr. Macheath, has decreed that though I don't know you, you
should be my son-in-law. The occasion of this first meeting between us is a
very sad one. Mr. Macheath. You once had white kid gloves, a cane and an
ivory handle, and a scar on your neck, and you frequented the Cuttlefish
Hotel. All that is left is your scar, no doubt the least valuable of your distinguishing marks. Today you frequent nothing but prison cells, and within the
foreseeable future no place at all . . .

[*Polly passes the cage in tears and stations herself to the right*]

MAC   What a pretty dress you're wearing.

[*Matthew and Jake pass the cage and take up positions on the right*]

MATTHEW   We couldn't get through because of the terrible crush. We ran so hard
I was afraid Jake was going to have a stroke. If you don't believe us . . .

MAC   What do my men say? Have they got good places?

MATTHEW   You see, Captain, we thought you'd understand. You see, a Coronation doesn't happen every day. They've got to make some money when
there's a chance. They send you their best wishes.

JAKE   Their very best wishes.

MRS. PEACHUM [*steps up to the cell, takes up a position on the right*]   Mr. Macheath, who would have expected this a week ago when we were dancing at a little hop at the Cuttlefish Hotel.

MAC   A little hop.

MRS. PEACHUM   But the ways of destiny are cruel here below.

BROWN [*at the rear to the vicar*]   And to think that I stood shoulder to shoulder with this man in Azerbaidjan under a hail of bullets.

JENNY [*approaches the cage*]   We Drury Lane girls are frantic. Nobody's gone to the Coronation. Everybody wants to see you. [*Stations herself on the right*]

MAC   To see me.

SMITH   All right. Let's go. Six o'clock. [*Lets him out of the cage*]

MAC   We mustn't keep them waiting. Ladies and gentlemen. You see before you a declining representative of a declining social group. We lower-middle-class artisans who work with humble jemmies on small shopkeepers' cash registers are being swallowed up by big corporations backed by the banks. What's a jemmy compared with a stock certificate? What's breaking into a bank compared with founding a bank? What's murdering a man compared with hiring a man? Fellow citizens, I hereby take my leave of you. I thank you for coming. Some of you were very close to me. That Jenny should have turned me in amazes me greatly. It is proof positive that the world never changes. A convergence of several unfortunate circumstances has brought about my fall. So be it—I fall.

[*Song lighting: golden glow. The organ is lit up. Three lamps are lowered on a pole, and the signs say:*]

Ballade in which Macheath begs all men for forgiveness

You fellow men who live on after us
Pray do not think you have to judge us harshly
And when you see us hoisted up and trussed
Don't laugh like fools behind your big mustaches
Or curse at us. It's true that we came crashing
But do no judge our downfall like the courts.
Not all of us can discipline our thoughts—
Dear fellows, your extravagance needs slashing
Dear fellows, we've shown how a crash begins.
Pray then to God that He forgive my sins.

The rain washes away and purifies.
Let it wash down the flesh we catered for
And we who saw so much, and wanted more—
The crows will come and peck away our eyes.
Perhaps ambition used too sharp a goad
It drove us to these heights from which we swing

> Hacked at by greedy starlings on the wing
> Like horses' droppings on a country road.
> O brothers, learn from us how it begins
> And pray to God that He forgive our sins.
>
> The girls who flaunt their breasts as bait there
> To catch some sucker who will love them
> The youths who slyly stand and wait there
> To grab their sinful earnings off them
> The crooks, the tarts, the tarts' protectors
> The models and the mannequins
> The psychopaths, the unfrocked rectors
> I pray that they forgive my sins.
>
> Not so those filthy police employees
> Who day by day would bait my anger
> Devise new troubles to annoy me
> And chuck me crusts to stop my hunger.
> I'd call on God to come and choke them
> And yet my need for respite wins:
> I realize that it might provoke them
> So pray that they forgive my sins.
>
> *Someone must take a hugh iron crowbar*
> *And stave their ugly faces in.*
> *All I ask is to know it's over*
> *Praying that they forgive my sins.*

SMITH   If you don't mind, Mr. Macheath.
MRS. PEACHUM   Polly and Lucy, stand by your husband in his last hour.
MAC   Ladies, whatever there may have been between us . . .
SMITH [*leads him away*]   Get a move on!

Procession to the Gallows.

[*All go out through doors left. These doors are on projection screens. Then all reenter from the other side of the stage with shaded lanterns. When Macheath is standing at the top of the gallows steps Peachum speaks*]

PEACHUM

> Dear audience, we now are coming to
> The point where we must hang him by the neck
> Because it is the Christian thing to do
> Proving that men must pay for what they take.

But as we want to keep our fingers clean
And you are people we can't risk offending
We thought we'd better do without this scene
And substitute instead a different ending.

Since this is opera, not life, you'll see
Justice give way before Humanity.
So now, to throw our story right off course
Enter the royal official on his horse.

[*The signs read:*]

THIRD THREEPENNY FINALE

Appearance of the messenger on horseback

CHORUS
Hark, who's here?
A royal official on horseback's here!

[*Enter Brown on horseback as the messenger*]

BROWN   I bring a special order from our beloved Queen to have Captain Macheath set at liberty forthwith [*all cheer*] since it's her Coronation, and raised
to the hereditary peerage. [*Cheers*] The castle of Marmarel, likewise a pension
of ten thousand pounds, to be his in usufruct until his death. To any bridal
couples present Her Majesty bids me to convey her gracious good wishes.

MAC   Reprievéd! Reprievéd! I was sure of it.
When you're most despairing
The clouds may be clearing.

POLLY   Reprievéd, my dearest Macheath is reprievéd. I am so happy.

MRS. PEACHUM   So it all turned out nicely in the end. How nice everything would
be if these saviors on horseback always appeared when they were needed.

PEACHUM   So please remain all standing in your places, and join in the hymn of
the poorest of the poor, whose most arduous life you have seen portrayed
here today, for in fact the fate they meet is bound to be grim. Saviors on
horseback are seldom met with in practice once the man who's kicked about
has kicked back. Which all means one shouldn't persecute wrongdoing too
much.

ALL [*come forward, singing to the organ*]
Don't punish our wrongdoing too much. Never
Will it withstand the frost, for it is cold.
Think of the darkness and the bitter weather
The cries of pain that echo through this world.

LANGSTON HUGHES
1902–1967

Born in Joplin, Missouri, Hughes grew up in Kansas, Illinois, and Ohio, where he lived at various times with his grandmother, his aunt, and his mother, whom he credited with giving him his sense of courage and racial pride. After a year at Columbia University, he took a job as a sailor and made his way to Europe and Africa, where he spent a few years as a vagabond, and then returned to complete his undergraduate education at Lincoln University. During the 1920s, he became a leading figure in the literary movement known as the Harlem Renaissance, which was marked by the appearance of an outstanding group of black writers who devoted themselves to celebrating the values of black culture rather than encouraging black aspirations to middle-class white society. Hughes was a prolific writer of journalistic essays, short stories, novels, poems, plays, musical librettos, and filmscripts. His best-known work for the theater is *Simply Heavenly* (1957), a musical comedy based on his popular stories about Simple, an amiable character who humorously echoed the thoughts and feelings of urban blacks about racial discrimination. Hughes' two autobiographies, *The Big Sea* (1940), and *I Wonder as I Wander* (1960), provide not only a revealing self-portrait, but also a clear and powerful statement of his anti-middle class values and of his abiding interest in depicting the painful experience of common black people with humor, irony, and understanding, rather than bitterness.

Mother and Child
A Theater Vignette

CHARACTERS

The characters are typical Negro women to be found in any farm community on the edge of the South. They are not well dressed, nor very well educated.

LOTTIE MUMFORD	MRS. SAM JONES
MATTIE CRANE	SISTER JENKINS
LUCY DOVES	MADAM PRESIDENT
SISTER WIGGINS	SISTER PRIME
CORA PERKINS	SISTER HOLT

The parlor of a small farmhouse in southern Ohio, overcrowded with old-time furniture. Springtime. Bright sunlight through the lace curtains at the windows.

The monthly meeting of the Salvation Rock Missionary Society, a religious organization of rural colored ladies, is being held. The members are beginning to gather. Sister Wiggins,

Mattie Crane, Cora Perkins, and Sister Holt are already present. They are gossiping as usual, but today the gossip centers persistently around a single tense and fearful topic—a certain newborn child that has come to Boyd's Center. As the curtain rises, the hostess, Lottie Mumford, her apron still on, is answering the door. Enter Lucy Doves and Mrs. Sam Jones.

LOTTIE MUMFORD [*at the door*]   Howdy, you-all! Howdy! 'Scuse my apron, Sister Jones. I'm makin' some rolls for the after-part. [*Laughs.*]

OTHER SISTERS   Howdy! Howdy-do!

LOTTIE MUMFORD   Lucy Doves, all I wants to know is what news you got? Is you seen that chile?

MATTIE CRANE   Yes, is you seen it? You lives right over there by 'em.

LUCY DOVES [*bursting to talk*]   Ain't nobody seen it. Ain't nobody seen it, but the midwife and the doctor. And her husband, I reckon. They say she won't let a soul come in the room.

LOTTIE MUMFORD   Ain't it awful?

LUCY DOVES   But it's still livin' cause Mollie Ranson heard it cryin'. And the woman from Downsville what attended the delivery says it's as healthy a child as she ever seed, indeed she did.

SISTER WIGGINS [*from a rocking chair*]   Well, it's a shame it's here.

MATTIE CRANE   Sho' is!

SISTER WIGGINS   I been livin' in Boyd's Center for twenty-two years, at peace with these white folks, ain't had no trouble yet, till this child was born—now look at 'em. Just look what's goin' on! People actin' like a pack o' wolves.

CORA PERKINS   It's ter'ble, ter'ble.

MRS. SAM JONES [*taking off her hat*]   Poor little brat! He ain't been in the world a week yet, and done caused more trouble than all the rest of us in a lifetime. I was born here, and I ain't never seen the white folks up in arms like they are today. But they don't need to think they can walk over Sam and me . . .

SISTER HOLT   Nor me!

MRS. SAM JONES [*continuing*]   For we owns our land, it's bought and paid for, and we sends our children to school. Thank God, this is Ohio. It ain't Mississippi.

CORA PERKINS   Thank God!

LUCY DOVES   White folks is white folks, honey, South or North, North or South. I's lived both places and I know.

SISTER WIGGINS   Yes, but in Mississippi they'd lynched Douglass by now.

MATTIE CRANE   Where is Douglass? You-all know I don't know much about this mess. Way back yonder on that farm where I lives now, you don't get nothin' straight. Where is Douglass?

LUCY DOVES   Douglass is here! Saw him just now out in de field doin' his spring sowin' when I drive down de road, as stubborn and bold-faced as he can be. We told him he ought to leave here.

SISTER HOLT   Huh! He's a *man*, ain't he?

SISTER WIGGINS   Well, I wish he'd go on and get out, if that would help any. His brother's got more sense than he has, even if he is a seventeen-year-old child. Clarence left here yesterday and went to Cincinnati. But their ma, poor Sister Carter, she's still tryin' to battle it out.

LOTTIE MUMFORD   She told me last night, though, she thinks she have to leave. They won't let her have no more provisions at de general store. And they ain't got their spring seed yet. And they can't pay cash for 'em.

CORA PERKINS   Po' souls.

MRS. SAM JONES   Don't need to tell me! Old man Hartman's got evil as de rest of de white folks. Didn't he tell ma husband Saturday night he'd have to pay up every cent of his back bill, or he couldn't take nothin' out of that store? And we been tradin' there for years!

LUCY DOVES   That's their way o' strikin' back at us colored folks.

MRS. SAM JONES   Yes, but Lord knows my husband ain't de father o' that child.

LUCY DOVES   Nor mine.

MRS. SAM JONES   Sam's got too much pride to go foolin' 'round any old loose white woman.

SISTER WIGGINS   Child, you can't tell about men.

MATTIE CRANE   I knowed a case once in Detroit where a colored man lived ten years with a white woman, and her husband didn't know it. He was their chauffeur.

SISTER WIGGINS   That's all right in the city, but please don't come bringing it out here to Boyd's Center where they ain't but a handful o' us colored—and we has a hard enough time as it is.

LOTTIE MUMFORD   You right! This sure has brought de hammer down on our heads. [*Jumps*] Oh, lemme go see about my rolls! [*Exits into kitchen.*]

SISTER WIGGINS   Lawd knows we's law-biding people, ain't harmed a soul, yet some o' these white folks talkin' 'bout trying to run all de colored folks out o' de county on account o' Douglass.

SISTER HOLT   They'll never run me out!

MRS. SAM JONES   Nor me!

LUCY DOVES   Don't say they *won't* do, 'cause they might. [*A knock and the door opens* Sister Jenkins *enters.*] Howdy, Sister Jenkins.

OTHERS   Howdy!

SISTER JENKINS   Good evenin'! Is you 'bout to start?

MRS. SAM JONES   Yes, de meetin' due to start directly.

MATTIE CRANE   Soon as Madam President arrives. Reckon she's havin' trouble gettin' over that road from High Creek.

SISTER WIGGINS   Sit down and tell us what you's heard, Sister Jenkins.

SISTER JENKINS   About Douglass?

SISTER HOLT   Course 'bout Douglass. What else is anybody talking 'bout?

SISTER JENKINS   Well, my daughter told me Douglass' sister say they was in love.

MATTIE CRANE   Him and that white woman?

SISTER JENKINS   Yes. Douglass' sister say it's been goin' on 'fore de woman got married.

MRS. SAM JONES   Uh-huh! Then why didn't he stop foolin' with her after she got married? Bad enough, colored boy foolin' 'round a unmarried white woman, let alone a married one.

SISTER JENKINS   Douglass' sister say they was in love.

SISTER WIGGINS   Well, why did she marry the *white* man, then?

MATTIE CRANE   She's white, ain't she? And who wouldn't marry a rich white man? Got his own farm, money and all, even if he were a widower with grown children gone to town. He give her everything she wanted, didn't he?

SISTER HOLT   Everything but the right thing.

MRS. SAM JONES   Well, she must not o' loved him, sneakin' 'round meetin' Douglass in de woods.

CORA PERKINS   True, true!

MATTIE CRANE   But what you reckon she went on and had that colored baby for?

SISTER WIGGINS   She must a thought it was the old man's baby.

LUCY DOVES   She don't think so now! Mattie say when the doctor left and they brought the child in to show her, she like to went blind. It were near black as me.

MATTIE CRANE   Do tell!

CORA PERKINS   And what did her husband say?

LUCY DOVES   Don't know, Don't know.

SISTER HOLT   He must a fainted.

[*Reenter* Lottie Mumford, *pulling off her apron.*]

LUCY DOVES   That old white woman lives across the crick from us said he's gonna put her out soon's she's able to walk.

MRS. SAM JONES   Ought to put her out!

SISTER JENKINS   Maybe that's what Douglass waitin' for.

MATTIE CRANE   I heard he wants to take her away.

SISTER WIGGINS   He better take his fool self away 'fore these white folks get madder. Ain't nobody heard it was a black baby till day before yesterday. Then it leaked out. And now de white folks are rarin' to kill Douglass!

CORA PERKINS   I sure am scared!

LOTTIE MUMFORD   And how come they all said right away it were Douglass?

LUCY DOVES   Honey, don't you know? Colored folks knowed Douglass been eyein' that woman since God know when, and she been eyein' back at him. You ought to seed 'em when they meet in de store. Course, they didn't speak no more 'n Howdy, but their eyes followed one another 'round just like dogs.

SISTER JENKINS   They was in love, I tell you. Been in love.

MRS. SAM JONES   Mighty funny kind o' love. Everybody knows can't no good come out o' white and colored love. Everybody knows that. And Douglass ain't no child. He's twenty-six years old, ain't he? And Sister Carter sure did try to raise her three children right. You can't blame her.

SISTER WIGGINS   Blame that fool boy, that's who, and that woman. Plenty colored girls in Camden he could of courted ten miles up de road. One or two right here in Boyd's Center. I got a daughter myself.

MRS. SAM JONES   No, he had to go foolin' 'round with a white woman.

LOTTIE MUMFORD   Yes, a white woman.

MATTIE CRANE   They say he loved her, though.

LOTTIE MUMFORD   What do Douglass say, since it happened?

LUCY DOVES   He don't say nothin'. Just goes on with his plowin'.

SISTER HOLT   He's a *man*, ain't he?

MRS. SAM JONES   What could he say?

SISTER WIGGINS   Well, he needn't think he's gonna keep his young mouth shut and let de white folks take it out on us. Down yonder at de school today, my Dorabelle says they talkin' 'bout separatin' de colored from de white and makin' all de colored children go in a nigger room next term.

MRS. SAM JONES   Ain't nothin' like that ever happened in Boyd's Center long as I been here—these twenty-two years.

LUCY DOVES   White folks is mad now, child, mad clean through.

LOTTIE MUMFORD   Wonder they ain't grabbin' Douglass and lynched him.

CORA PERKINS   It's a wonder!

LUCY DOVES   And him calmly out yonder plowin' de field this afternoon.

MATTIE CRANE   He sure is brave.

SISTER HOLT   Douglass is a *man*.

SISTER WIGGINS   Woman's husband's liable to kill us.

MRS. SAM JONES   Her brother's done said he's gunnin' for him.

CORA PERKINS   They liable to burn us Negroes' houses down.

SISTER WIGGINS   Anything's liable to happen. Lawd, I'm nervous as I can be.

LUCY DOVES   You can't tell about white folks.

LOTTIE MUMFORD   I ain't nervous. I'm *scared*.

SISTER HOLT   Huh! Ain't you-all got no weapons?

CORA PERKINS   Don't say a word! It's ter'ble!

MATTIE CRANE   Why don't Sister Carter make him leave here?

MRS. SAM JONES   I wish I knew.

LOTTIE MUMFORD   She told me she were nearly crazy.

SISTER WIGGINS   And she can't get Douglass to say nothin', one way or another— if he go, or if he stay. [*A knock and the door opens. Enter* Madam President *and* Sister Prime.] Howdy, Madam President.

OTHERS   Good evenin', Madam President.

[*The gossip does not halt.* Madam President *goes to a little table and takes a small bell from her purse.*]

SISTER JENKINS   I done told you Douglass loves her.

MATTIE CRANE   He wants to see that white woman once more again, that's what
    he wants.
MRS. SAM JONES   A white hussy!
SISTER WIGGINS   He's foolin' with fire.
LOTTIE MUMFORD   Poor Mis' Carter. I'm sorry for his mother.
CORA PERKINS   Poor Mis' Carter.
SISTER JENKINS   Why don't you all say poor Douglass? Poor white woman? Poor
    child?

[*The* President *taps importantly on her bell, but the women continue in an undertone.*]

MATTIE CRANE   Madam President's startin' de meetin'.
SISTER PRIME   Is it a boy or girl?
LUCY DOVES   Sh-s-s! There's de bell.
SISTER WIGGINS   I hear it's a boy.
SISTER PRIME   Thank God, ain't a girl then.
MATTIE CRANE   I hope it looks like Douglass, cause Douglass a fine-looking
    nigger.
SISTER HOLT   And he's a *man*!
SISTER WIGGINS   He's too bold, too bold.
MRS. SAM JONES   Shame he's got us all in this mess.
CORA PERKINS   SHAME, SHAME, SHAME.
SISTER PRIME   Sh-s-s!
LOTTIE MUMFORD   Yes, indeedy!
SISTER HOLT   Mess or no mess, I got ma Winchester.
MRS. SAM JONES   They'll never run Sam and me out, neither!
MATTIE CRANE   Amen!
MADAM PRESIDENT   Sisters, can't you hear this bell?
LUCY DOVES   Sh-s-s!
MADAM PRESIDENT   Madam Secretary, take your chair.

[Mrs. Sam Jones *comes forward.*]

CORA PERKINS   Ter'ble, ter'ble! [*Again the bell taps.*] Sh-s-s!
MADAM PRESIDENT   The March meetin' of the Salvation Rock Ladies' Missionary
    Society for the Rescue o' the African Heathen is hereby called to order. Sister
    Holt, raise a hymn. All stand! [*As the talking continues.*] Will you-all ladies
    please be quiet? What are you talkin' 'bout back there, anyhow?
LUCY DOVES   Heathens, daughter, heathens.
SISTER WIGGINS   They ain't in Africa neither!

SISTER HOLT [*singing from her chair in a deep alto voice as the others join in*].

> I shall not be,
> I shall not be moved.
> Oh, I shall not be,
> I shall not be moved,
> Like a tree that's
> Planted by the waters,
> I shall not be moved.

Curtain

TENNESSEE WILLIAMS
1911–

Thomas Lanier Williams, who adopted his college nickname, Tennessee. during the late 1930s, was born in Columbus, Mississippi, where he spent his early childhood, and in 1918 moved to St. Louis, Missouri, an experience that he later described as "tragic." His southern accent, his small town background, his physically weakened condition brought on by diptheria, and his parents' relative poverty altogether made him acutely conscious of being an outsider, a condition that Williams has variously portrayed in virtually all of his plays. Williams' years in St. Louis were also complicated by the emotional pressures of his family—by his overprotective mother, by his domineering father who called him "Miss Nancy" in mockery of his literary interests, and by his psychologically frail sister who gradually withdrew into a permanent state of mental illness. Echoes of Williams' family and of himself can be found in the long-suffering women, the tyrannical men, the artists, the dreamers, and the mentally disturbed persons who figure as characters in all of his major plays, *The Glass Menagerie* (1944), *Streetcar Named Desire* (1947), *Cat on a Hot Tin Roof* (1955), and *The Night of the Iguana* (1961). But Williams' plays are by no means restricted to characters echoing his past, nor are they merely autobiographical even with respect to characters who are based on his personal experience, for Williams has always shaped his characters and plots to reflect and explore the enduring problems of loneliness and illusion in human experience.

Cat on a Hot Tin Roof

CHARACTERS

MARGARET
BRICK
MAE, sometimes called Sister Woman
BIG MAMA
DIXIE, a little girl
BIG DADDY
REVEREND TOOKER
GOOPER, sometimes called Brother Man
DOCTOR BAUGH, pronounced "Baw"
LACEY, a Negro servant
SOOKEY, another
CHILDREN

NOTES FOR THE DESIGNER

The set is the bed-sitting-room of a plantation home in the Mississippi Delta. It is along an upstairs gallery which probably runs around the entire house; it has two pairs of very wide doors opening onto the gallery, showing white balustrades against a fair summer sky that fades into dusk and night during the course of the play, which occupies precisely the time of its performance, excepting, of course, the fifteen minutes of intermission.

Perhaps the style of the room is not what you would expect in the home of the Delta's biggest cotton-planter. It is Victorian with a touch of the Far East. It hasn't changed much since it was occupied by the original owners of the place, Jack Straw and Peter Ochello, a pair of old bachelors who shared this room all their lives together. In other words, the room must evoke some ghosts; it is gently and poetically haunted by a relationship that must have involved a tenderness which was uncommon. This may be irrelevant or unnecessary, but I once saw a reproduction of a faded photograph of the verandah of Robert Louis Stevenson's home on that Samoan Island where he spent his last years, and there was a quality of tender light on weathered wood, such as porch furniture made of bamboo and wicker, exposed to tropical suns and tropical rains, which came to mind when I thought about the set for this play, bringing also to mind the grace and comfort of light, the reassurance it gives, on a late and fair afternoon in summer, the way that no matter what, even dread of death, is gently touched and soothed by it. For the set is the background for a play that deals with human extremities of emotion, and it needs that softness behind it.

The bathroom door, showing only pale-blue tile and silver towel racks, is in one side wall; the hall door in the opposite wall. Two articles of furniture need mention: a big double bed which staging should make a functional part of the set as often as suitable, the surface of which should be slightly raked to make figures on it seen more easily; and against the wall space between the two huge double doors upstage: a monumental monstrosity peculiar to our times, a *huge* console combination of radio-phonograph (hi-fi with three speakers) TV set *and* liquor cabinet, bearing and containing many glasses and bottles, all in one piece, which is a compostition of muted silver tones, and the opalescent tones of reflecting glass, a chromatic link, this thing, between the sepia (tawny gold) tones of the interior and the cool (white and blue) tones of the gallery and sky. This piece of furniture (?!), this monument, is a very complete and compact little shrine to virtually all the comforts and illusions behind which we hide from such things as the characters in the play are faced with. . . .

The set should be far less realistic than I have so far implied in this description of it. I think the walls below the ceiling should dissolve mysteriously into air; the set should be roofed by the sky; stars and moon suggested by traces of milky pallor, as if they were observed through a telescope lens out of focus.

Anything else I can think of? Oh, yes, fanlights (transoms shaped like an open glass fan) above all the doors in the set, with panes of blue and amber, and above all, the designer should take as many pains to give the actors room to move about freely (to show their restlessness, their passion for breaking out) as if it were a set for a ballet.

An evening in summer. The action is continuous, with two intermissions.

ACT I

At the rise of the curtain someone is taking a shower in the bathroom, the door of which is half open. A pretty young woman, with anxious lines in her face, enters the bedroom and crosses to the bathroom door.

MARGARET [*shouting above roar of water*] One of those no-neck monsters hit me with a hot buttered biscuit so I have t' change!

Margaret's voice is both rapid and drawling. In her long speeches she has the vocal tricks of a priest delivering a liturgical chant, the lines are almost sung, always continuing a little beyond her breath so she has to gasp for another. Sometimes she intersperses the lines with a little wordless singing, such as "da-da-daaaa!"

Water turns off and Brick calls out to her, but is still unseen. A tone of politely feigned interest, masking indifference, or worse, is characteristic of his speech with Margaret.

BRICK   Wha'd you say, Maggie? Water was on s' loud I couldn't hearya. . . .

MARGARET   Well, I!—just remarked that!—one of th' no-neck monsters messed up m' lovely lace dress so I got t'—cha-a-ange. . . . [*She opens and kicks shut drawers of the dresser.*]

BRICK   Why d'ya call Gooper's kiddies no-neck monsters?

MARGARET   Because they've got no necks! Isn't that a good enough reason?

BRICK   Don't they have any necks?

MARGARET   None visible. Their fat little heads are set on their fat little bodies without a bit of connection.

BRICK   That's too bad.

MARGARET   Yes, it's too bad because you can't wring their necks if they've got no necks to wring! Isn't that right, honey? [*She steps out of her dress, stands in a slip of ivory satin and lace.*]   Yep, they're no-neck monsters, all no-neck people are monsters . . .

Children shriek downstairs.

Hear them? Hear them screaming? I don't know where their voice boxes are located since they don't have necks. I tell you I got so nervous at that table tonight I thought I would throw back my head and utter a scream you could hear across the Arkansas border an' parts of Louisiana an' Tennessee. I said to your charming sister-in-law, Mae, honey, couldn't you feed those precious little things at a separate table with an oilcloth cover? They make such a mess an' the lace cloth looks *so* pretty! She made enormous eyes at me and said, "Ohhh, noooooo! On Big Daddy's birthday? Why, he would never forgive me!" Well, I want you to know, Big Daddy hadn't been at the table two minutes with those five no-neck monsters slobbering and drooling over their food before he threw down his fork an' shouted, "Fo' God's sake, Gooper, why don't you put them pigs at a trough in th' kitchen?"—Well, I swear, I simply could have di-ieed!

Think of it, Brick, they've got five of them and number six is coming. They've brought the whole bunch down here like animals to display at a county fair. Why, they have those children doin' tricks all the time!

"Junior, show Big Daddy how you do this, show Big Daddy how you do
that, say your little piece fo' Big Daddy, Sister. Show your dimples,
Sugar. Brother, show Big Daddy how you stand on your head!"—It goes
on all the time, along with constant little remarks and innuendos about
the fact that you and I have not produced any children, are totally
childless and therefore totally useless!—Of course it's comical but it's
also disgusting since it's so obvious what they're up to!

BRICK [without interest]   What are they up to, Maggie?

MARGARET   Why, you know what they're up to!

BRICK [appearing]   No, I don't know what they're up to.

*He stands there in the bathroom doorway drying his hair with a towel and hanging
onto the towel rack because one ankle is broken, plastered and bound. He is still
slim and firm as a boy. His liquor hasn't started tearing him down outside. He has
the additional charm of that cool air of detachment that people have who have
given up the struggle. But now and then, when disturbed, something flashes
behind it, like lightning in a fair sky, which shows that at some deeper level he is
far from peaceful. Perhaps in a stronger light he would show some signs of
deliquescence, but the fading, still warm, light from the gallery treats him gently.*

MARGARET   I'll tell you what they're up to, boy of mine!—They're up to
cutting you out of your father's estate, and—

*She freezes momentarily before her next remark. Her voice drops as if it were
somehow a personally embarrassing admission.*

—Now we know that Big Daddy's dyin' of—*cancer.* . . .

*There are voices on the lawn below: long-drawn calls across distance. Margaret
raises her lovely bare arms and powders her armpits with a light sigh.*

*She adjusts the angle of a magnifying mirror to straighten an eyelash, then rises
fretfully saying:*

There's so much light in the room it—

BRICK [softly but sharply]   Do we?

MARGARET   Do we what?

BRICK   Know Big Daddy's dyin' of cancer?

MARGARET   Got the report today.

BRICK   Oh . . .

MARGARET [letting down bamboo blinds which cast long, gold-fretted shadows
over the room]   Yep, got th' report just now . . . it didn't surprise me,
Baby. . . .

Her voice has range, and music; sometimes it drops low as a boy's and you have a sudden image of her playing boy's games as a child.

I recognized the symptoms soon's we got here last spring and I'm willin' to bet you that Brother Man and his wife were pretty sure of it, too. That more than likely explains why their usual summer migration to the coolness of the Great Smokies was passed up this summer in favor of—hustlin' down here ev'ry whipstitch with their whole screamin' tribe! And why so many allusions have been made to Rainbow Hill lately. You know what Rainbow Hill is? Place that's famous for treatin' alcoholics an' dope fiends in the movies!

BRICK   I'm not in the movies.

MARGARET   No, and you don't take dope. Otherwise you're a perfect candidate for Rainbow Hill, Baby, and that's where they aim to ship you—over my dead body! Yep, over my dead body they'll ship you there, but nothing would please them better. Then Brother Man could get a-hold of the purse strings and dole out remittances to us, maybe get power of attorney and sign checks for us and cut off our credit wherever, whenever he wanted! Son-of-a-bitch!—How'd you like that, Baby?— Well, you've been doin' just about ev'rything in your power to bring it about, you've just been doin' ev'rything you can think of to aid and abet them in this scheme of theirs! Quittin' work, devoting yourself to the occupation of drinkin'!—Breakin' your ankle last night on the high school athletic field: doin' what? Jumpin' hurdles? At two or three in the morning? Just fantastic! Got in the paper. *Clarksdale Register* carried a nice little item about it, human interest story about a well-known former athlete stagin' a one-man track meet on the Glorious Hill High School athletic field last night, but was slightly out of condition and didn't clear the first hurdle! Brother Man Gooper claims he exercised his influence t' keep it from goin' out over AP or UP or every goddam "P."

But, Brick? You still have one big advantage!

During the above swift flood of words, Brick has reclined with contrapuntal leisure on the snowy surface of the bed and has rolled over carefully on his side or belly.

BRICK [*wryly*]   Did you *say* something, Maggie?

MARGARET   Big Daddy dotes on you, honey. And he can't stand Brother Man and Brother Man's wife, that monster of fertility, Mae. Know how I know? By little expressions that flicker over his face when that woman is holding fo'th on one of her choice topics such as—how she refused twilight sleep!—when the twins were delivered! Because she feels motherhood's an experience that a woman ought to experience fully!—

in order to fully appreciate the wonder and beauty of it! HAH!—and how she made Brother Man come in an' stand beside her in the delivery room so he would not miss out on the "wonder and beauty" of it either!—producin' those no-neck monsters. . . .

A speech of this kind would be antipathetic from almost anybody but Margaret; she makes it oddly funny, because her eyes constantly twinkle and her voice shakes with laughter which is basically indulgent.

—Big Daddy shares my attitude toward those two! As for me, well—I give him a laugh now and then and he tolerates me. In fact!—I sometimes suspect that Big Daddy harbors a little unconscious "lech" fo' me. . . .

BRICK   What makes you think that Big Daddy has a lech for you, Maggie?

MARGARET   Way he always drops his eyes down my body when I'm talkin' to him, drops his eyes to my boobs an' licks his old chops! Ha ha!

BRICK   That kind of talk is disgusting.

MARGARET   Did anyone ever tell you that you're an ass-aching Puritan, Brick?

I think it's mighty fine that that ole fellow, on the doorstep of death, still takes in my shape with what I think is deserved appreciation!

And you wanta know something else? Big Daddy didn't know how many little Maes and Goopers had been produced! "How many kids have you got?" he asked at the table, just like Brother Man and his wife were new acquaintances to him! Big Mama said he was jokin', but that ole boy wasn't jokin', Lord, no!

And when they infawmed him that they had five already and were turning out number six!—the news seemed to come as a sort of unpleasant surprise . . .

Children yell below.

Scream, monsters!

Turns to Brick with a sudden, gay, charming smile which fades as she notices that he is not looking at her but into fading gold space with a troubled expression.

It is constant rejection that makes her humor "bitchy."

Yes, you should of been at that supper-table, Baby.

Whenever she calls him "baby" the word is a soft caress.

Y'know, Big Daddy, bless his ole sweet soul, he's the dearest ole thing in the world, but he does hunch over his food as if he preferred not to notice anything else. Well, Mae an' Gooper were side by side at the table, direckly across from Big Daddy, watchin' his face like hawks while they jawed an' jabbered about the cuteness an' brillance of th' no-neck monsters!

She giggles with a hand fluttering at her throat and her breast and her long throat arched.

She comes downstage and recreates the scene with voice and gesture.

And the no-neck monsters were ranged around the table, some in high chairs and some on th' *Books of Knowledge*, all in fancy little paper caps in honor of Big Daddy's birthday, and all through dinner, well, I want you to know that Brother Man an' his partner never once, for one moment, stopped exchanging pokes an' pinches an' kicks an' signs an' signals!—Why, they were like a couple of cardsharps fleecing a sucker.—Even Big Mama, bless her ole sweet soul, she isn't th' quickest an' brightest thing in the world, she finally noticed, at last, an' said to Gooper, "Gooper, what are you an' Mae makin' all these signs at each other about?"—I swear t' goodness, I nearly choked on my chicken!

Margaret, back at the dressing table, still doesn't see Brick. He is watching her with a look that is not quite definable—Amused? shocked? contemptuous?—part of those and part of something else.

Y'know—your brother Gooper still cherishes the illusion he took a giant step up the social ladder when he married Miss Mae Flynn of the Memphis Flynns.

But I have a piece of Spanish news for Gooper. The Flynns never had a thing in this world but money and they lost that, they were nothing at all but fairly successful climbers. Of course, Mae Flynn came out in Memphis eight years before I made my debut in Nashville, but I had friends at Ward-Belmont who came from Memphis and they used to come to see me and I used to go to see them for Christmas and spring vacations, and so I know who rates an' who doesn't rate in Memphis society. Why, y'know ole Papa Flynn, he barely escaped doing time in the Federal pen for shady manipulations on th' stock market when his chain stores crashed, and as for Mae having been a cotton carnival queen, as they remind us so often, lest we forget, well, that's one honor that I don't envy her for!—Sit on a brass throne on a tacky float an' ride down Main Street, smilin', bowin', and blowin' kisses to all the trash on the street—

She picks out a pair of jeweled sandals and rushes to the dressing table.

Why, year before last, when Susan McPheeters was singled out fo' that honor, y' know what happened to her? Y'know what happened to poor little Susie McPheeters?

BRICK [*absently*]   No. What happened to little Susie McPheeters?

MARGARET   Somebody spit tobacco juice in her face.

BRICK [*dreamily*]   Somebody spit tobacco juice in her face?

MARGARET   That's right, some old drunk leaned out of a window in the Hotel Gayoso and yelled, "Hey, Queen, hey, hey, there, Queenie!" Poor Susie looked up and flashed him a radiant smile and he shot out a squirt of tobacco juice right in poor Susie's face.

BRICK   Well, what d'you know about that.

MARGARET [*gaily*]   What do I know about it? I was there, I saw it!

BRICK [*absently*]   Must have been kind of funny.

MARGARET   Susie didn't think so. Had hysterics. Screamed like a banshee. They had to stop th' parade an' remove her from her throne an' go on with—

She catches sight of him in the mirror, gasps slightly, wheels about to face him. Count ten.

—Why are you looking at me like that?

BRICK [*whistling softly, now*]   Like what, Maggie?

MARGARET [*intensely, fearfully*]   The way y' were lookin' at me just now, befo' I caught your eye in the mirror and you started t' whistle! I don't know how t' describe it but it froze my blood!—I've caught you lookin' at me like that so often lately. What are you thinkin' of when you look at me like that?

BRICK   I wasn't conscious of lookin' at you, Maggie.

MARGARET   Well, I was conscious of it! What were you thinkin'?

BRICK   I don't remember thinking of anything, Maggie.

MARGARET   Don't you think I know that—? Don't you—?—Think I know that—?

BRICK [*cooly*]   Know *what*, Maggie?

MARGARET [*struggling for expression*]   That I've gone through this—hideous!—transformation, become—hard! Frantic! [*Then she adds, almost tenderly:*]   —cruel!!

That's what you've been observing in me lately. How could y' help but observe it? That's all right. I'm not—thin-skinned any more, can't afford t' be thin-skinned any more. [*She is now recovering her power.*] —But Brick? Brick?

BRICK   Did you say something?

MARGARET   I was *goin'* t' say something: that I get—lonely. Very!

BRICK   Ev'rybody gets that . . .

MARGARET   Living with someone you love can be lonelier—than living entirely *alone!*—if the one that y' love doesn't love you. . . .

There is a pause. Brick hobbles downstage and asks, without looking at her:

BRICK   Would you like to live alone, Maggie?

Another pause: then—after she has caught a quick, hurt breath:

MARGARET   *No!—God!—I wouldn't!*

Another gasping breath. She forcibly controls what must have been an impulse to cry out. We see her deliberately, very forcibly, going all the way back to the world in which you can talk about ordinary matters.

Did you have a nice shower?

BRICK   Uh-huh.

MARGARET   Was the water cool?

BRICK   No.

MARGARET   But it made y' feel fresh, huh?

BRICK   Fresher. . . .

MARGARET   I know something would make y' feel *much* fresher!

BRICK   What?

MARGARET   An alcohol rub. Or cologne, a rub with cologne!

BRICK   That's good after a workout but I haven't been workin' out, Maggie.

MARGARET   You've kept in good shape, though.

BRICK   [*indifferently*]   You think so, Maggie?

MARGARET   I always thought drinkin' men lost their looks, but I was plainly mistaken.

BRICK   [*wryly*]   Why, thanks, Maggie.

MARGARET   You're the only drinkin' man I know that it never seems t' put fat on.

BRICK   I'm gettin' softer, Maggie.

MARGARET   Well, sooner or later it's bound to soften you up. It was just beginning to soften up Skipper when— [*She stops short.*] I'm sorry. I never could keep my fingers off a sore—I wish you *would* lose your looks.

If you did it would make the martyrdom of Saint Maggie a little more bearable. But no such goddam luck. I actually believe you've gotten better looking since you've gone on the bottle. Yeah, a person who didn't know you would think you'd never had a tense nerve in your body or a strained muscle.

There are sounds of croquet on the lawn below: the click of mallets, light voices, near and distant.

Of course, you always had that detached quality as if you were playing a game without much concern over whether you won or lost, and now that you've lost the game, not lost but just quit playing, you have that rare sort of charm that usually only happens in very old or hopelessly sick people, the charm of the defeated.—You look so cool, so cool, so enviably cool.

REVEREND TOOKER [*off stage right*]   Now looka here, boy, lemme show you how to get outa that!

MARGARET   They're playing croquet. The moon has appeared and it's white, just beginning to turn a little bit yellow. . . .

You were a wonderful lover. . . .

Such a wonderful person to go to bed with, and I think mostly because you were really indifferent to it. Isn't that right? Never had any anxiety about it, did it naturally, easily, slowly, with absolute confidence and perfect calm, more like opening a door for a lady or seating her at a table than giving expression to any longing for her. Your indifference made you wonderful at lovemaking—*strange?*—but true. . . .

REVEREND TOOKER   Oh! That's a beauty.

DOCTOR BAUGH   Yeah. I got you boxed.

MARGARET   You know, if I thought you would never, never, *never* make love to me again—I would go downstairs to the kitchen and pick out the longest and sharpest knife I could find and stick it straight into my heart, I swear that I would!

REVEREND TOOKER   Watch out, you're gonna miss it.

DOCTOR BAUGH   You just don't know me, boy!

MARGARET   But one thing I don't have is the charm of the defeated, my hat is still in the ring, and I am determined to win!

There is the sound of croquet mallets hitting croquet balls.

REVEREND TOOKER   Mmm—You're too slippery for me.

MARGARET   —What is the victory of a cat on a hot tin roof?—I wish I knew. . . .

Just staying on it, I guess, as long as she can. . . .
DOCTOR BAUGH   Jus' like an eel, boy, jus' like an eel!

More croquet sounds.

MARGARET   Later tonight I'm going to tell you I love you an' maybe by that
time you'll be drunk enough to believe me. Yes, they're playing croquet. . . .

Big Daddy is dying of cancer. . . .

What were you thinking of when I caught you looking at me like that?
Were you thinking of Skipper?

Brick takes up his crutch, rises.

Oh, excuse me, forgive me, but laws of silence don't work! No, laws of
silence don't work. . . .

Brick crosses to the bar, takes a quick drink, and rubs his head with a towel.

Laws of silence don't work. . . .

When something is festering in your memory or your imagination, laws
of silence don't work, it's just like shutting a door and locking it on a
house on fire in hope of forgetting that the house is burning. But not
facing a fire doesn't put it out. Silence about a thing just magnifies it. It
grows and festers in silence, becomes malignant. . . .

He drops his crutch.

BRICK   Give me my crutch.

*He has stopped rubbing his hair dry but still stands hanging onto the towel rack in
a white towel-cloth robe.*

MARGARET   Lean on me.
BRICK   No, just give me my crutch.
MARGARET   Lean on my shoulder.
BRICK   *I don't want to lean on your shoulder, I want my crutch!*

This is spoken like sudden lightning.

Are you going to give me my crutch or do I have to get down on my knees on the floor and—

MARGARET   *Here, here, take it, take it!*   [*She has thrust the crutch at him.*]

BRICK   [*hobbling out*]   Thanks . . .

MARGARET   We mustn't scream at each other, the walls in this house have ears. . . .

He hobbles directly to liquor cabinet to get a new drink.

—but that's the first time I've heard you raise your voice in a long time, Brick. A crack in the wall?—Of composure?

—I think that's a good sign. . . .

A sign of nerves in a player on the defensive!

Brick turns and smiles at her coolly over his fresh drink.

BRICK   It just hasn't happened yet, Maggie.

MARGARET   What?

BRICK   The click I get in my head when I've had enough of this stuff to make me peaceful. . . .

Will you do me a favor?

MARGARET   Maybe I will. What favor?

BRICK   Just, just keep your voice down!

MARGARET   [*in a hoarse whisper*]   I'll do you that favor, I'll speak in a whisper, if not shut up completely, if *you* will do *me* a favor and make that drink your last one till after the party.

BRICK   What party?

MARGARET   Big Daddy's birthday party.

BRICK   Is this Big Daddy's birthday?

MARGARET   You know this is Big Daddy's birthday!

BRICK   No, I don't, I forgot it.

MARGARET   Well, I remembered it for you. . . .

They are both speaking as breathlessly as a pair of kids after a fight, drawing deep exhausted breaths and looking at each other with faraway eyes, shaking and panting together as if they had broken apart from a violent struggle.

BRICK   Good for you, Maggie.

MARGARET   You just have to scribble a few lines on this card.

BRICK   You scribble something, Maggie.

MARGARET   It's got to be your handwriting; it's your present, I've given him
my present; it's got to be your handwriting!

The tension between them is building again, the voices becoming shrill once more.

BRICK   I didn't get him a present.

MARGARET   I got one for you.

BRICK   All right. You write the card, then.

MARGARET   And have him know you didn't remember his birthday?

BRICK   I didn't remember his birthday.

MARGARET   You don't have to prove you didn't!

BRICK   I don't want to fool him about it.

MARGARET   Just write "Love, Brick!" for God's—

BRICK   No.

MARGARET   You've *got* to!

BRICK   I don't have to do anything I don't want to do. You keep forgetting
the conditions on which I agreed to stay on living with you.

MARGARET   [*out before she knows it*]   I'm not living with you. We occupy the
same cage.

BRICK   You've got to remember the conditions agreed on.

SONNY   [*off stage*]   Mommy, give it to me. I had it first.

MAE   Hush.

MARGARET   They're impossible conditions!

BRICK   Then why don't you—?

SONNY   I want it, I want it!

MAE   Get away!

MARGARET   HUSH! Who is out there? Is somebody at the door?

There are footsteps in hall.

MAE   [*outside*]   May I enter a moment?

MARGARET   OH, *you!* Sure. Come in, Mae.

Mae enters bearing aloft the bow of a young lady's archery set.

MAE   Brick, is this thing yours?

MARGARET   Why, Sister Woman—that's my Diana Trophy. Won it at the
intercollegiate archery contest on the Ole Miss campus.

MAE   It's a mighty dangerous thing to leave exposed round a house full of
nawmal rid-blooded children attracted t'weapons.

MARGARET   "Nawmal rid-blooded children attracted t'weapons" ought t'be
taught to keep their hands off things that don't belong to them.

MAE   Maggie, honey, if you had children of your own you'd know how funny that is. Will you please lock this up and put the key out of reach?

MARGARET   Sister Woman, nobody is plotting the destruction of your kiddies. —Brick and I still have our special archers' license. We're goin' deer-huntin' on Moon Lake as soon as the season starts. I love to run with dogs through chilly woods, run, run leap over obstructions— [*She goes into the closet carrying the bow.*]

MAE   How's the injured ankle, Brick?

BRICK   Doesn't hurt. Just itches.

MAE   Oh, my! Brick—Brick, you should've been downstairs after supper! Kiddies put on a show. Polly played the piano, Buster an' Sonny drums, an' then they turned out the lights an' Dixie an' Trixie puhfawmed a toe dance in fairy costume with *spahkluhs!* Big Daddy just beamed! He just beamed!

MARGARET   [*from the closet with a sharp laugh*]   Oh, I bet. It breaks my heart that we missed it! [*She reenters.*] But Mae? Why did y'give dawgs' names to all your kiddies?

MAE   *Dogs'* names?

MARGARET   [*sweetly*]   Dixie, Trixie, Buster, Sonny, Polly!—Sounds like four dogs and a parrot . . .

MAE   Maggie?

Margaret turns with a smile.

Why are you so catty?

MARGARET   Cause I'm a cat! But why can't *you* take a joke, Sister Woman?

MAE   Nothin' pleases me more than a joke that's funny. You know the real names of our kiddies. Buster's real name is Robert. Sonny's real name is Saunders. Trixie's real name is Marlene and Dixie's—

Gooper downstairs calls for her. "Hey, Mae! Sister Woman, intermission is over!"—She rushes to door, saying:

Intermission is over! See ya later!

MARGARET   I wonder what Dixie's real name is?

BRICK   Maggie, being catty doesn't help things any . . .

MARGARET   I know! *WHY!*—Am I so catty?—Cause I'm consumed with envy an' eaten up with longing?—Brick, I'm going to lay out your beautiful Shantung silk suit from Rome and one of your monogrammed silk shirts. I'll put your cuff links in it, those lovely star sapphires I get you to wear so rarely. . . .

BRICK   I can't get trousers on over this plaster cast.

MARGARET   Yes, you can, I'll help you.

BRICK   I'm not going to get dressed, Maggie.

MARGARET   Will you just put on a pair of white silk pajamas?

BRICK   Yes, I'll do that, Maggie.

MARGARET   *Thank* you, thank you so *much!*

BRICK   Don't mention it.

MARGARET   *Oh, Brick!* How long does it have t' go on? This punishment? Haven't I done time enough, haven't I served my term, can't I apply for a—pardon?

BRICK   Maggie, you're spoiling my liquor. Lately your voice always sounds like you'd been running upstairs to warn somebody that the house was on fire!

MARGARET   Well, no wonder, no wonder. Y'know what I feel like, Brick?

I feel all the time like a cat on a hot tin roof!

BRICK   Then jump off the roof, jump off it, cats can jump off roofs and land on their four feet uninjured!

MARGARET   Oh, yes!

BRICK   Do it!—fo' God's sake, do it . . .

MARGARET   Do what?

BRICK   Take a lover!

MARGARET   I can't see a man but you! Even with my eyes closed, I just see you! Why don't you get ugly, Brick, why don't you please get fat or ugly or something so I could stand it? [*She rushes to hall door, opens it, listens.*]   The concert is still going on! Bravo, no-necks, bravo! [*She slams and locks door fiercely.*]

BRICK   What did you lock the door for?

MARGARET   To give us a little privacy for a while.

BRICK   You know better, Maggie.

MARGARET   No, I don't know better. . . .

She rushes to gallery doors, draws the rose-silk drapes across them.

BRICK   Don't make a fool of yourself.

MARGARET   I don't mind makin' a fool of myself over you!

BRICK   I mind, Maggie. I feel embarrassed for you.

MARGARET   Feel embarrassed! But don't continue my torture. I can't live on and on under these circumstances.

BRICK   You agreed to—

MARGARET   I know but—

BRICK   —Accept that condition!

MARGARET   *I CAN'T! I CAN'T! CAN'T!*   [*She seizes his shoulder.*]

BRICK   Let go!

He breaks away from her and seizes the small boudoir chair and raises it like a lion-tamer facing a big circus cat.

Count five. She stares at him with her fist pressed to her mouth, then bursts into shrill, almost hysterical laughter. He remains grave for a moment, then grins and puts the chair down.

Big Mama calls through closed door.

BIG MAMA   Son? Son? Son?

BRICK   What is it, Big Mama?

BIG MAMA [*outside*]   Oh, son! We got the most wonderful news about Big Daddy. I just had t' run up an' tell you right this—   [*She rattles the knob.*]   —What's this door doin', locked, faw? You all think there's robbers in the house?

MARGARET   Big Mama, Brick is dressin', he's not dressed yet.

BIG MAMA   That's all right, it won't be the first time I've seen Brick not dressed. Come on, open this door!

Margaret, with a grimace, goes to unlock and open the hall door, as Brick hobbles rapidly to the bathroom and kicks the door shut. Big Mama has disappeared from the hall.

MARGARET   Big Mama?

Big Mama appears through the opposite gallery doors behind Margaret, huffing and puffing like an old bulldog. She is a short, stout woman; her sixty years and 170 pounds have left her somewhat breathless most of the time; she's always tensed like a boxer, or rather, a Japanese wrestler. Her "family" was maybe a little superior to Big Daddy's, but not much. She wears a black or silver lace dress and at least half a million in flashy gems. She is very sincere.

BIG MAMA [*loudly, startling Margaret*]   Here—I come through Gooper's and Mae's gall'ry door. Where's Brick? *Brick*—Hurry on out of there, son, I just have a second and want to give you the news about Big Daddy.—I hate locked doors in a house. . . .

MARGARET [*with affected lightness*]   I've noticed you do, Big Mama, but people have got to have *some* moments of privacy, don't they?

BIG MAMA   No, ma'am, not in *my* house. [*without pause*] Whacha took off you' dress faw? I thought that little lace dress was so sweet on yuh, honey.

MARGARET   I thought it looked sweet on me, too, but one of m' cute little table-partners used it for a napkin so—!

BIG MAMA [*picking up stockings on floor*]   What?

MARGARET   You know, Big Mama, Mae and Gooper's so touchy about those
children—thanks, Big Mama . . .

Big Mama has thrust the picked-up stockings in Margaret's hand with a grunt.

—that you just don't dare to suggest there's any room for improvement
in their—
BIG MAMA   Brick, hurry out!—Shoot, Maggie, you just don't like children!
MARGARET   I do SO like children! Adore them!—well brought up!
BIG MAMA [*gentle—loving*]   Well, why don't you have some and bring them
up well, then, instead of all the time pickin' on Gooper's an' Mae's?
GOOPER [*shouting up the stairs*]   Hey, hey, Big Mama, Betsy an' Hugh got to
go, waitin' t' tell yuh g'by!
BIG MAMA   Tell 'em to hold their hawses, I'll be right down in a jiffy!
GOOPER   Yes ma'am!

She turns to the bathroom door and calls out.

BIG MAMA   Son? Can you hear me in there?

There is a muffled answer.

We just got the full report from the laboratory at the Ochsner Clinic,
completely negative, son, ev'rything negative, right on down the line!
Nothin' a-tall's wrong with him but some little functional thing called a
spastic colon. Can you hear me, son?
MARGARET   He can hear you, Big Mama.
BIG MAMA   Then why don't he say something? God Almighty, a piece of
news like that should make him shout. It made *me* shout, I can tell you. I
shouted and sobbed and fell right down on my knees!—Look! [*She
pulls up her skirt.*]   See the bruises where I hit my kneecaps? Took both
doctors to haul me back on my feet!

She laughs—she always laughs like hell at herself.

Big Daddy was furious with me! But ain't that wonderful news?

Facing bathroom again, she continues:

After all the anxiety we been through to git a report like that on Big
Daddy's birthday? Big Daddy tried to hide how much of a load that
news took off his mind, but didn't fool *me*. He was mighty close to
crying about it *himself!*

Goodbyes are shouted downstairs, and she rushes to door.

GOOPER   Big Mama!

BIG MAMA   *Hold those people down there, don't let them go!*—Now, git dressed, we're comin' up to this room fo' Big Daddy's birthday party because of your ankle.—How's his ankle, Maggie?

MARGARET   Well, he broke it, Big Mama.

BIG MAMA   I know he broke it.

A phone is ringing in hall. A Negro voice answers: "Mistuh Polly's res'dence."

I mean does it hurt him much still.

MARGARET   I'm afraid I can't give you that information, Big Mama. You'll have to ask Brick if it hurts much still or not.

SOOKEY [*in the hall*]   It's Memphis, Mizz Polly, it's Miss Sally in Memphis.

BIG MAMA   Awright, Sookey.

Big Mama rushes into the hall and is heard shouting on the phone:

Hello, Miss Sally. How are you, Miss Sally?—Yes, well, I was just gonna call you about it. *Shoot!*

MARGARET   Brick, don't!

Big Mama raises her voice to a bellow.

BIG MAMA   *Miss Sally? Don't ever call me from the Gayoso Lobby, too much talk goes on in that hotel lobby, no wonder you can't hear me!* Now listen, Miss Sally. They's nothin' serious wrong with Big Daddy. We got the report just now, they's nothin' wrong but a thing called a—spastic! SPASTIC!—colon . . . [*She appears at the hall door and calls to Margaret.*]   —Maggie, come out here and talk to that fool on the phone. I'm shouted breathless!

MARGARET [*goes out and is heard sweetly at phone*]   Miss Sally? This is Brick's wife, Maggie. So nice to hear your voice. Can you hear *mine?* Well, *good!*—Big Mama just wanted you to know that they've got the report from the Ochsner Clinic and what Big Daddy has is a spastic colon. Yes. Spastic colon, Miss Sally. That's right, spastic colon. *G'bye, Miss Sally, hope I'll see you real soon!*

Hangs up a little before Miss Sally was probably ready to terminate the talk. She returns through the hall door.

She heard me perfectly. I've discovered with deaf people the thing to do is not shout at them but just enunciate clearly. My rich old Aunt Cornelia was deaf as the dead but I could make her hear me just by sayin' each word slowly, distinctly, close to her ear. I read her the *Commercial Appeal* ev'ry night, read her the classified ads in it, even, she never missed a word of it. But was she a mean ole thing! Know what I got when she died? Her unexpired subscriptions to five magazines and the Book-of-the-Month Club and a LIBRARY full of ev'ry dull book ever written! All else went to her hellcat of a sister . . . meaner than she was, even!

Big Mama has been straightening things up in the room during this speech.

BIG MAMA [*closing closet door on discarded clothes*]   *Miss Sally sure is a case!* Big Daddy says she's always got her hand out fo' something. He's not mistaken. That poor ole thing always has her hand out fo' somethin'. I don't think Big Daddy gives her as much as he should.

GOOPER   Big Mama! Come on now! Betsy and Hugh can't wait no longer!

BIG MAMA [*shouting*]   I'm comin'!

She starts out. At the hall door, turns and jerks a forefinger, first toward the bathroom door, then toward the liquor cabinet, meaning: "Has Brick been drinking?" Margaret pretends not to understand, cocks her head and raises her brows as if the pantomimic performance was completely mystifying to her.

Big Mama rushes back to Margaret.

Shoot! Stop playin' so dumb!—I mean has he been drinkin' that stuff much yet?

MARGARET [*with a little laugh*]   Oh! I think he had a highball after supper.

BIG MAMA   Don't laugh about it!—Some single men stop drinkin' when they git married and others start! Brick never touched liquor before he—!

MARGARET [*crying out*]   *THAT'S NOT FAIR!*

BIG MAMA   Fair or not fair I want to ask you a question, one question: D'you make Brick happy in bed?

MARGARET   Why don't you ask if he makes *me* happy in bed?

BIG MAMA   Because I know that—

MARGARET   *It works both ways!*

BIG MAMA   Something's not right! You're childless and my son drinks!

GOOPER   Come on, Big Mama!

Gooper has called her downstairs and she has rushed to the door on the line above. She turns at the door and points at the bed.

—When a marriage goes on the rocks, the rocks are *there*, right *there!*

MARGARET   *That's*—

Big Mama has swept out of the room and slammed the door.

—not—*fair* . . .

Margaret is alone, completely alone, and she feels it. She draws in, hunches her shoulders, raises her arms with fists clenched, shuts her eyes tight as a child about to be stabbed with a vaccination needle. When she opens her eyes again, what she sees is the long oval mirror and she rushes straight to it, stares into it with a grimace and says: "Who are you?"—Then she crouches a little and answers herself in a different voice which is high, thin, mocking: "I am Maggie the Cat!"—Straightens quickly as bathroom door opens a little and Brick calls out to her.

BRICK   Has Big Mama gone?
MARGARET   She's gone.

He opens the bathroom door and hobbles out, with his liquor glass now empty, straight to the liquor cabinet. He is whistling softly. Margaret's head pivots on her long, slender throat to watch him.

She raises a hand uncertainly to the base of her throat, as if it was difficult for her to swallow, before she speaks:

You know, our sex life didn't just peter out in the usual way, it was cut off short, long before the natural time for it to, and it's going to revive again, just as sudden as that. I'm confident of it. That's what I'm keeping myself attractive for. For the time when you'll see me again like other men see me. Yes, like other men see me. They still see me, Brick, and they like what they see. Uh-huh. Some of them would give their—

Look, Brick!

She stands before the long oval mirror, touches her breast and then her hips with her two hands.

How high my body stays on me!—Nothing has fallen on me—not a fraction. . . .

Her voice is soft and trembling: a pleading child's. At this moment as he turns to glance at her—a look which is like a player passing a ball to another player, third down and goal to go—she has to capture the audience in a grip so tight that she can hold it till the first intermission without any lapse of attention.

Other men still want me. My face looks strained, sometimes, but I've kept my figure as well as you've kept yours, and men admire it. I still turn heads on the street. Why, last week in Memphis everywhere that I went men's eyes burned holes in my clothes, at the country club and in restaurants and department stores, there wasn't a man I met or walked by that didn't just eat me up with his eyes and turn around when I passed him and look back at me. Why, at Alice's party for her New York cousins, the best-lookin' man in the crowd—followed me upstairs and tried to force his way in the powder room with me, followed me to the door and tried to force his way in!

BRICK   Why didn't you let him, Maggie?

MARGARET   Because I'm not that common, for one thing. Not that I wasn't almost tempted to. You like to know who it was? It was Sonny Boy Maxwell, that's who!

BRICK   Oh, yeah, Sonny Boy Maxwell, he was a good end-runner but had a little injury to his back and had to quit.

MARGARET   He has no injury now and has no wife and still has a lech for me!

BRICK   I see no reason to lock him out of a powder room in that case.

MARGARET   And have someone catch me at it? I'm not that stupid. Oh, I might sometime cheat on you with someone, since you're so insultingly eager to have me do it!—But if I do, you can be damned sure it will be in a place and a time where no one but me and the man could possibly know. Because I'm not going to give you any excuse to divorce me for being unfaithful or anything else. . . .

BRICK   Maggie, I wouldn't divorce you for being unfaithful or anything else. Don't you know that? Hell. I'd be relieved to know that you'd found yourself a lover.

MARGARET   Well, I'm taking no chances. No, I'd rather stay on this hot tin roof.

BRICK   A hot tin roof's 'n uncomfo'table place t' stay on. . . .   [*He starts to whistle softly.*]

MARGARET   [*through his whistle*]   Yeah, but I can stay on it just as long as I have to.

BRICK   You could leave me, Maggie.

He resumes whistle. She wheels about to glare at him.

MARGARET   *Don't want to and will not!* Besides if I did, you don't have a cent to pay for it but what you get from Big Daddy and he's dying of cancer!

For the first time a realization of Big Daddy's doom seems to penetrate to Brick's consciousness, visibly, and he looks at Margaret.

BRICK   Big Mama just said he *wasn't*, that the report was okay.

MARGARET   That's what she thinks because she got the same story that they gave Big Daddy. And was just as taken in by it as he was, poor ole things. . . .

But tonight they're going to tell her the truth about it. When Big Daddy goes to bed, they're going to tell her that he is dying of cancer. [*She slams the dresser drawer.*]—It's malignant and it's terminal.

BRICK Does Big Daddy know it?

MARGARET Hell, do they *ever* know it? Nobody says, "You're dying." You have to fool them. They have to fool *themselves.*

BRICK Why?

MARGARET *Why?* Because human beings dream of life everlasting, that's the reason! But most of them want it on earth and not in heaven.

He gives a short, hard laugh at her touch of humor.

Well. . . . [*She touches up her mascara.*] That's how it is, anyhow. . . . [*She looks about.*] Where did I put down my cigarette? Don't want to burn up the home-place, at least not with Mae and Gooper and their five monsters in it!

She has found it and sucks at it greedily. Blows out smoke and continues:

So this is Big Daddy's last birthday. And Mae and Gooper, they know it, oh, *they* know it, all right. They got the first information from the Ochsner Clinic. That's why they rushed down here with their no-neck monsters. Because. Do you know something? Big Daddy's made no will? Big Daddy's never made out any will in his life, and so this campaign's afoot to impress him, forcibly as possible, with the fact that you drink and I've borne no children!

He continues to stare at her a moment, then mutters something sharp but not audible and hobbles rather rapidly out onto the long gallery in the fading, much faded, gold light.

MARGARET [*continuing her liturgical chant*] Y'know, I'm *fond* of Big Daddy, I am genuinely fond of that old man, I really *am*, you know. . . .

BRICK [*faintly, vaguely*] Yes, I know you are. . . .

MARGARET I've always sort of admired him in spite of his coarseness, his four-letter words and so forth. Because Big Daddy *is* what he *is*, and he makes no bones about it. He hasn't turned gentleman farmer, he's still a Mississippi redneck, as much of a redneck as he must have been when he was just overseer here on the old Jack Straw and Peter Ochello place. But he got hold of it an' built it into th' biggest an' finest plantation in the Delta.—I've always *liked* Big Daddy. . . .

She crosses to the proscenium.

> Well, this is Big Daddy's last birthday. I'm sorry about it. But I'm facing the facts. It takes money to take care of a drinker and that's the office that I've been elected to lately.

BRICK   You don't have to take care of me.

MARGARET   Yes, I do. Two people in the same boat have got to take care of each other. At least you want money to buy more Echo Spring when this supply is exhausted, or will you be satisfied with a ten-cent beer?

> Mae an' Gooper are plannin' to freeze us out of Big Daddy's estate because you drink and I'm childless. But we can defeat that plan. We're *going* to defeat that plan!

> *Brick, y'know, I've been so God damn disgustingly poor all my life!*—That's the *truth*, Brick!

BRICK   I'm not sayin' it isn't.

MARGARET   Always had to suck up to people I couldn't stand because they had money and I was poor as Job's turkey. You don't know what that's like. Well, I'll tell you, it's like you would feel a thousand miles away from Echo Spring!—And had to get back to it on that broken ankle . . . without a crutch!

> That's how it feels to be as poor as Job's turkey and have to suck up to relatives that you hated because they had money and all you had was a bunch of hand-me-down clothes and a few old moldly three-per-cent government bonds. My daddy loved his liquor, he fell in love with his liquor the way you've fallen in love with Echo Spring!—And my poor Mama, having to maintain some semblance of social position, to keep appearances up, on an income of one hundred and fifty dollars a month on those old government bonds!

> When I came out, the year that I made my debut, I had just two evening dresses! One Mother made me from a pattern in *Vogue,* the other a hand-me-down from a snotty rich cousin I hated!

> —The dress that I married you in was my grandmother's weddin' gown. . . .

> So that's why I'm like a cat on a hot tin roof!

Brick is still on the gallery. Someone below calls up to him in a warm Negro voice, "Hiya, Mistuh Brick, how yuh feelin'?" Brick raises his liquor glass as if that answered the question.

MARGARET   You can be young without money, but you can't be old without it. You've got to be old *with* money because to be old without it is just too awful, you've got to be one or the other, either *young* or *with money*, you can't be old and *without* it.—That's the *truth*, Brick. . . .

Brick whistles softly, vaguely.

Well, now I'm dressed, I'm all dressed, there's nothing else for me to do. [*Forlornly, almost fearfully.*]   I'm dressed, all dressed, nothing else for me to do. . . .

She moves about restlessly, aimlessly, and speaks, as if to herself.

What am I—? Oh!—my bracelets. . . .

She starts working a collection of bracelets over her hands onto her wrists, about six on each, as she talks.

I've thought a whole lot about it and now I know when I made my mistake. Yes, I made my mistake when I told you the truth about that thing with Skipper. Never should have confessed it, a fatal error, tellin' you about that thing with Skipper.

BRICK   Maggie, shut up about Skipper. I mean it, Maggie; you got to shut up about Skipper.

MARGARET   You ought to understand that Skipper and I—

BRICK   You don't think I'm serious, Maggie? You're fooled by the fact that I am saying this quiet? Look, Maggie. What you're doing is a dangerous thing to do. You're—you're—you're—foolin' with something that—nobody ought to fool with.

MARGARET   This time I'm going to finish what I have to say to you. Skipper and I made love, if love you could call it, because it made both of us feel a little bit closer to you. You see, you son of a bitch, you asked too much of people, of me, of him, of all the unlucky poor damned sons of bitches that happen to love you, and there was a whole pack of them, yes, there was a pack of them besides me and Skipper, you asked too goddam much of people that loved you, you—superior creature!—you godlike being!—And so we made love to each other to dream it was you, both of us! Yes, yes, yes! Truth, truth! What's so awful about it? I like it, I think the truth is—yeah! I shouldn't have told you. . . .

BRICK [*holding his head unnaturally still and uptilted a bit*]   It was Skipper that told me about it. Not you, Maggie.

MARGARET   I told you!

BRICK   After he told me!

MARGARET   What does it matter who—?

DIXIE   I got your mallet, I got your mallet.
TRIXIE   Give it to me, give it to me. IT's mine.

Brick turns suddenly out upon the gallery and calls:

BRICK   Little girl! Hey, little girl!
LITTLE GIRL [*at a distance*]   What, Uncle Brick?
BRICK   Tell the folks to come up!—Bring everybody upstairs!
TRIXIE   It's mine, it's mine.
MARGARET   I can't stop myself! I'd go on telling you this in front of them all,
    if I had to!
BRICK   Little girl! Go on, go on, will you? Do what I told you, call them!
DIXIE   Okay.
MARGARET   Because it's got to be told and you, you!—you never let me!

She sobs, then controls herself, and continues almost calmly.

It was one of those beautiful, ideal things they tell about in the Greek
legends, it couldn't be anything else, you being you, and that's what
made it so sad, that's what made it so awful, because it was love that
never could be carried through to anything satisfying or even talked
about plainly.
BRICK   Maggie, you gotta stop this.
MARGARET   Brick, I tell you, you got to believe me, Brick, I *do* understand all
    about it! I—I think it was—*noble!* Can't you tell I'm sincere when I say I
    respect it? My only point, the only point that I'm making, is life has got
    to be allowed to continue even after the *dream* of life is —all—over. . . .

*Brick is without his crutch. Leaning on furniture, he crosses to pick it up as she
continues as if possessed by a will outside herself:*

Why I remember when we double-dated at college, Gladys Fitzgerald
and I and you and Skipper, it was more like a date between you and
Skipper. Gladys and I were just sort of tagging along as if it was
necessary to chaperone you!—to make a good public impression—
BRICK [*turns to face her, half lifting his crutch*]   Maggie, you want me to hit
    you with this crutch? Don't you know I could kill you with this crutch?
MARGARET   Good, Lord, man, d' you think I'd care if you did?
BRICK   One man has one great good true thing in his life. One great good
    thing which is true!—I had friendship with Skipper.—You are naming it
    dirty!
MARGARET   I'm not naming it dirty! I am naming it clean.
BRICK   Not love with you, Maggie, but friendship with Skipper was that one
    great true thing, and you are naming it dirty!
MARGARET   Then you haven't been listenin', not understood what I'm

saying! I'm naming it so damn clean that it killed poor Skipper!—You two had something that had to be kept on ice, yes, incorruptible, yes!—and death was the only icebox where you could keep it. . . .

BRICK   I married you, Maggie. Why would I marry you, Maggie, if I was—?

MARGARET   Brick, let me finish!—I know, believe me I know, that it was only Skipper that harbored even any *unconscious* desire for anything not perfectly pure between you two!—Now let me skip a little. You married me early that summer we graduated out of Ole Miss, and we were happy, weren't we, we were blissful, yes, hit heaven together ev'ry time that we loved! But that fall you an' Skipper turned down wonderful offers of jobs in order to keep on bein' football heroes—pro-football heroes. You organized the Dixie Stars that fall, so you could keep on bein' teammates forever! But somethin' was not right with it!—*Me included!*—between you. Skipper began hittin' the bottle . . . you got a spinal injury—couldn't play the Thanksgivin' game in Chicago, watched it on TV from a traction bed in Toledo. I joined Skipper. The Dixie Stars lost because poor Skipper was drunk. We drank together that night all night in the bar of the Blackstone and when cold day was comin' up over the Lake an' we were comin' out drunk to take a dizzy look at it, I said, "SKIPPER! STOP LOVIN' MY HUSBAND OR TELL HIM HE'S GOT TO LET YOU ADMIT IT TO HIM!"—one way or another!

HE SLAPPED ME HARD ON THE MOUTH!—then turned and ran without stopping once, I am sure, all the way back into his room at the Blackstone. . . .

—When I came to his room that night, with a little scratch like a shy little mouse at his door, he made that pitiful, ineffectual little attempt to prove that what I had said wasn't true. . . .

Brick strikes at her with crutch, a blow that shatters the gemlike lamp on the table.

—In this way, I destroyed him, by telling him truth that he and his world which he was born and raised in, yours and his world, had told him could not be told?

—From then on Skipper was nothing at all but a receptacle for liquor and drugs. . . .

—Who shot cock robin? I with my—   [*She throws back her head with tight shut eyes.*]   —merciful arrow!

Brick strikes at her; misses.

Missed me!—Sorry,—I'm not tryin' to whitewash my behavior, Christ, no! Brick, I'm not good. I don't know why people have to pretend to be good, nobody's good. The rich or the well-to-do can afford to respect moral patterns, conventional moral patterns, but I could never afford to, yeah, but—I'm honest! Give me credit for just that, will you *please?*— Born poor, raised poor, expect to die poor unless I manage to get us something out of what Big Daddy leaves when he dies of cancer! But Brick?!—*Skipper is dead! I'm alive!* Maggie the cat is—

Brick hops awkwardly forward and strikes at her again with his crutch.

—alive! I am alive, alive! I am . . .

He hurls the crutch at her, across the bed she took refuge behind, and pitches forward on the floor as she completes her speech.

—alive!

A little girl, Dixie, bursts into the room, wearing an Indian war bonnet and firing a cap pistol at Margaret and shouting: "Bang, bang, bang!"

Laughter downstairs floats through the open hall door. Margaret had crouched gasping to bed at child's entrance. She now rises and says with cool fury:

Little girl, your mother or someone should teach you—[*gasping*]—to knock at a door before you come into a room. Otherwise people might think that you—lack—good breeding. . . .

DIXIE   Yanh, yanh, yanh, what is Uncle Brick doin' on th' floor?

BRICK   I tried to kill your Aunt Maggie, but I failed—and I fell. Little girl, give me my crutch so I can get up off th' floor.

MARGARET   Yes, give your uncle his crutch, he's a cripple, honey, he broke his ankle last night jumping hurdles on the high school athletic field!

DIXIE   What were you jumping hurdles for, Uncle Brick?

BRICK   Because I used to jump them, and people like to do what they used to do, even after they've stopped being able to do it. . . .

MARGARET   That's right, that's your answer, now go away, little girl.

Dixie fires cap pistol at Margaret three times.

Stop, you stop that, monster! You little no-neck monster! [*She seizes the cap pistol and hurls it through gallery doors.*]

DIXIE   [*with a precocious instinct for the cruelest thing*]   You're *jealous!*—You're just jealous because you can't have babies!

She sticks out her tongue at Margaret as she sashays past her with her stomach stuck out, to the gallery. Margaret slams the gallery doors and leans panting against them. There is a pause. Brick has replaced his spilt drink and sits, faraway, on the great four-poster bed.

MARGARET   You see?—they gloat over us being childless, even in front of their five little no-neck monsters!

Pause. Voices approach on the stairs.

Brick?—I've been to a doctor in Memphis, a—a gynecologist. . . .

I've been completely examined, and there is no reason why we can't have a child whenever we want one. And this is my time by the calendar to conceive. Are you listening to me? Are you? Are you LISTENING TO ME!

BRICK   Yes. I hear you, Maggie. [*His attention returns to her inflamed face.*]   —But how in hell on earth do you imagine—that you're going to have a child by a man that can't stand you?

MARGARET   That's a problem that I will have to work out. [*She wheels about to face the hall door.*]

MAE [*off stage left*]   Come on, Big Daddy. We're all goin' up to Brick's room.

From off stage left, voices: Reverend Tooker, Doctor Baugh, Mae.

MARGARET   *Here they come!*

The lights dim.

Curtain

ACT II

There is no lapse of time. Margaret and Brick are in the same positions they held at the end of Act I.

MARGARET [*at door*]   *Here they come!*

Big Daddy appears first, a tall man with a fierce, anxious look, moving carefully not to betray his weakness even, or especially, to himself.

GOOPER   I read in the *Register* that you're getting a new memorial window.

Some of the people are approaching through the hall, others along the gallery: voices from both directions. Gooper and Reverend Tooker become visible outside gallery doors, and their voices come in clearly.

They pause outside as Gooper lights a cigar.

REVEREND TOOKER [*vivaciously*]   Oh, but St. Paul's in Grenada has three memorial windows, and the latest one is a Tiffany stained-glass window that cost twenty-five hundred dollars, a picture of Christ the Good Shepherd with a Lamb in His arms.

MARGARET   Big Daddy.

BIG DADDY   Well, Brick.

BRICK   Hello Big Daddy.—Congratulations!

BIG DADDY   —Crap. . . .

GOOPER   Who give that window, Preach?

REVEREND TOOKER   Clyde Fletcher's widow. Also presented St. Paul's with a baptismal font.

GOOPER   Y'know what somebody ought t' give your church is a *coolin'* system, Preach.

MAE [*almost religiously*]   —Let's see now, they've had their *tyyy*-phoid shots, and their tetanus shots, their diptheria shots and their hepatitis shots and their polio shots, they got *those* shots every month from May through September, and—Gooper? Hey! Gooper!—What all have the kiddies been shot faw?

REVEREND TOOKER   Yes, siree, Bob! And y'know what Gus Hamma's family gave in his memory to the church at Two Rivers? A complete new stone parish-house with a basketball court in the basement and a—

BIG DADDY [*uttering a loud barking laugh which is far from truly mirthful*]   Hey, Preach! What's all this talk about memorials, Preach? Y' think somebody's about t' kick off around here? 'S that it?

Startled by this interjection, Reverend Tooker decides to laugh at the question almost as loud as he can.

How he would answer the question we'll never know, as he's spared that embarrassment by the voice of Gooper's wife, Mae, rising high and clear as she appears with "Doc" Baugh, the family doctor, through the hall door.

MARGARET [*overlapping a bit*]   Turn on the hi-fi, Brick! Let's have some music t' start off th' party with!

BRICK   You turn it on, Maggie.

The talk becomes so general that the room sounds like a great aviary of chattering birds. Only Brick remains unengaged, leaning upon the liquor cabinet with his faraway smile, an ice cube in a paper napkin with which he now and then rubs his forehead. He doesn't respond to Margaret's command. She bounds forward and stoops over the instrument panel of the console.

GOOPER   We gave 'em that thing for a third anniversary present, got three speakers in it.

The room is suddenly blasted by the climax of a Wagnerian opera or a Beethoven symphony.

BIG DADDY   *Turn that dam thing off!*

Almost instant silence, almost instantly broken by the shouting charge of Big Mama, entering through hall door like a charging rhino.

BIG MAMA   *Wha's my Brick, wha's mah precious baby!!*
BIG DADDY   *Sorry! Turn it back on!*

Everyone laughs very loud. Big Daddy is famous for his jokes at Big Mama's expense, and nobody laughs louder at these jokes than Big Mama herself, though sometimes they're pretty cruel and Big Mama has to pick up or fuss with something to cover the hurt that the loud laugh doesn't quite cover.

On this occasion, a happy occasion because the dread in her heart has also been lifted by the false report on Big Daddy's condition, she giggles, grotesquely, coyly, in Big Daddy's direction and bears down upon Brick, all very quick and alive.

BIG MAMA   Here he is, here's my precious baby! What's that you've got in your hand? You put that liquor down, son, your hand was made fo' holdin' somethin' better than that!
GOOPER   Look at Brick put it down!

Brick has obeyed Big Mama by draining the glass and handing it to her. Again everyone laughs, some high, some low.

BIG MAMA   Oh, you bad boy, you, you're my bad little boy. Give Big Mama a kiss, you bad boy, you!—Look at him shy away, will you? Brick never liked bein' kissed or made a fuss over, I guess because he's always had too much of it!

Son, you turn that thing off!

Brick has switched on the TV set.

I can't stand TV, radio was bad enough but TV has gone it one better, I mean—[*plops wheezing in chair*]—one worse, ha ha! Now what'm I sittin' down here faw? I want t' sit next to my sweetheart on the sofa, hold hands with him and love him up a little!

Big Mama has on a black and white figured chiffon. The large irregular patterns, like the markings of some massive animal, the luster of her great diamonds and many pearls, the brilliants set in the silver frames of her glasses, her riotous voice, booming laugh, have dominated the room since she entered. Big Daddy has been regarding her with a steady grimace of chronic annoyance.

BIG MAMA [*still louder*]   Preacher, Preacher, hey, Preach! Give me you' hand an' help me up from this chair!
REVEREND TOOKER   None of your tricks, Big Mama!
BIG MAMA   What tricks? You give me you' hand so I can get up an'—

Reverend Tooker extends her his hand. She grabs it and pulls him into her lap with a shrill laugh that spans an octave in two notes.

Ever seen a preacher in a fat lady's lap? Hey, hey, folks! Ever seen a preacher in a fat lady's lap?

Big Mama is notorious throughout the Delta for this sort of inelegant horseplay. Margaret looks on with indulgent humor, sipping Dubonnet "on the rocks" and watching Brick, but Mae and Gooper exchange signs of humorless anxiety over these antics, the sort of behavior which Mae thinks may account for their failure to quite get in with the smartest young married set in Memphis, despite all. One of the Negroes, Lacy or Sookey, peeks in, cackling. They are waiting for a sign to bring in the cake and champagne. But Big Daddy's not amused. He doesn't understand why, in spite of the infinite mental relief he's received from the doctor's report, he still has these same old fox teeth in his guts. "This spastic condition is something else," he says to himself, but aloud he roars at Big Mama:

BIG DADDY   *BIG MAMA, WILL YOU QUIT HORSIN'?*—You're too old an' too fat fo' that sort of crazy kid stuff an' besides a woman with your blood pressure—she had two hundred last spring!—is riskin' a stroke when you mess around like that. . . .

Mae blows on a pitch pipe.

BIG MAMA   *Here comes Big Daddy's birthday!*

Negroes in white jackets enter with an enormous birthday cake ablaze with candles and carrying buckets of champagne with satin ribbons about the bottle necks.

Mae and Gooper strike up song, and everybody, including the Negroes and Children, joins in. Only Brick remains aloof.

EVERYONE
    Happy birthday to you.
    Happy birthday to you.
    Happy birthday, Big Daddy—

Some sing: "Dear, Big Daddy!"

    Happy birthday to you.

Some sing: "How old are you?"

Mae has come down center and is organizing her children like a chorus. She gives them a barely audible: "One, two, three!" and they are off in the new tune.

CHILDREN
    Skinamarinka—dinka—dink
    Skinamarinka—do
    We love you.
    Skinamarinka—dinka—dink
    Skinamarinka—do.

All together, they turn to Big Daddy.

    Big Daddy, you!

They turn back front, like a musical comedy chorus.

    We love you in the morning;
    We love you in the night.
    We love you when we're with you,
    And we love you out of sight.
    Skinamarinka—dinka—dink
    Skinamarinka—do.

Mae turns to Big Mama.

    Big Mama, too!

Big Mama bursts into tears. The Negroes leave.

BIG DADDY   Now Ida, what the hell is the matter with you?

MAE   She's just so happy.

BIG MAMA   I'm just so happy, Big Daddy, I have to cry or something.

Sudden and loud in the hush:

>   Brick, do you know the wonderful news that Doc Baugh got from the clinic about Big Daddy? Big Daddy's one hundred per cent!

MARGARET   Isn't that wonderful?

BIG MAMA   He's just one hundred per cent. Passed the examination with flying colors. Now that we know there's nothing wrong with Big Daddy but a spastic colon, I can tell you something. I was worried sick, half out of my mind, for fear that Big Daddy might have a thing like—

Margaret cuts through this speech, jumping up and exclaiming shrilly:

MARGARET   Brick, honey, aren't you going to give Big Daddy his birthday present?

Passing by him, she snatches his liquor glass from him.

She picks up a fancily wrapped package.

>   *Here it is, Big Daddy, this is from Brick!*

BIG MAMA   This is the biggest birthday Big Daddy's ever had, a hundred presents and bushels of telegrams from—

MAE [*at same time*]   What is it, Brick?

GOOPER   I bet 500 to 50 that Brick don't *know* what it is.

BIG MAMA   The fun of presents is not knowing what they are till you open the package. Open your present, Big Daddy.

BIG DADDY   Open it you'self. I want to ask Brick somethin'! Come here, Brick.

MARGARET   Big Daddy's callin' you, Brick. [*She is opening the package.*]

BRICK   Tell Big Daddy I'm crippled.

BIG DADDY   I see you're crippled. I want to know how you got crippled.

MARGARET [*making diversionary tactics*]   Oh, look, oh, look, why, it's a cashmere robe! [*She holds the robe up for all to see.*]

MAE   You sound surprised, Maggie.

MARGARET   I never saw one before.

MAE   That's funny.—Hah!

MARGARET [*turning on her fiercely, with a brilliant smile*]   Why is it funny? All my family ever had was family—and luxuries such as cashmere robes still surprise me!

BIG DADDY [*ominously*]   Quiet!

MAE [*heedless in her fury*]   I don't see how you could be so surprised when you bought it yourself at Loewenstein's in Memphis last Saturday. You know how I know?

BIG DADDY   I said, Quiet!

MAE   —I know because the salesgirl that sold it to you waited on me and said, Oh, Mrs. Pollitt, your sister-in-law just bought a cashmere robe for your husband's father!

MARGARET   Sister Woman! Your talents are wasted as a housewife and mother, you really ought to be with the FBI or—

BIG DADDY   QUIET!

Reverend Tooker's reflexes are slower than the others'. He finishes a sentence after the bellow.

REVEREND TOOKER [*to Doc Baugh*]   —the Stork and the Reaper are running neck and neck!

He starts to laugh gaily when he notices the silence and Big Daddy's glare. His laugh dies falsely.

BIG DADDY   Preacher, I hope I'm not butting in on more talk about memorial stained-glass windows, am I, Preacher?

Reverend Tooker laughs feebly, then coughs dryly in the embarrassed silence.

    Preacher?

BIG MAMA   Now, Big Daddy, don't you pick on Preacher!

BIG DADDY [*raising his voice*]   You ever hear that expression all hawk and no spit? You bring that expression to mind with that little dry cough of yours, all hawk an' no spit. . . .

The pause is broken only by a short startled laugh from Margaret, the only one there who is conscious of and amused by the grotesque.

MAE [*raising her arms and jangling her bracelets*]   I wonder if the mosquitoes are active tonight?

BIG DADDY   What's that, Little Mama? Did you make some remark?

MAE   Yes, I said I wondered if the mosquitoes would eat us alive if we went out on the gallery for a while.

BIG DADDY   Well, if they do, I'll have your bones pulverized for fertilizer!

BIG MAMA [*quickly*]   Last week we had an airplane spraying the place and I think it done some good, at least I haven't had a—

BIG DADDY [*cutting her speech*]   Brick, they tell me, if what they tell me is

true, that you done some jumping last night on the high school athletic
field?

BIG MAMA   Brick, Big Daddy is talking to you, son.

BRICK [smiling vaguely over his drink]   What was that, Big Daddy?

BIG DADDY   They said you done some jumping on the high school track field
last night.

BRICK   That's what they told me, too.

BIG DADDY   Was it jumping or humping that you were doing out there?
What were you doing out there at three A.M., layin' a woman on that
cinder track?

BIG MAMA   Big Daddy, you are off the sick-list, now, and I'm not going to
excuse you for talkin' so—

BIG DADDY   Quiet!

BIG MAMA   —nasty in front of Preacher and—

BIG DADDY   QUIET!—I ast you, Brick, if you was cuttin' you'self a piece o'
poon-tang last night on that cinder track? I thought maybe you were
chasin' poon-tang on that track an' tripped over something in the heat of
the chase—'sthat it?

Gooper laughs, loud and false, others nervously following suit. Big Mama stamps
her foot, and purses her lips, crossing to Mae and whispering something to her as
Brick meets his father's hard, intent, grinning stare with a slow, vague smile that
he offers all situations from behind the screen of his liquor.

BRICK   No, sir, I don't think so. . . .

MAE [at the same time, sweetly]   Reverend Tooker, let's you and I take a stroll
on the widow's walk.

She and the preacher go out on the gallery as Big Daddy says:

BIG DADDY   Then what the hell were you doing out there at three o'clock in
the morning?

BRICK   Jumping the hurdles, Big Daddy, runnin' and jumpin' the hurdles,
but those high hurdles have gotten too high for me, now.

BIG DADDY   Cause you was drunk?

BRICK [his vague smile fading a little]   Sober I wouldn't have tried to jump the
low ones. . . .

BIG MAMA [quickly]   Big Daddy, blow out the candles on your birthday cake!

MARGARET [at the same time]   I want to propose a toast to Big Daddy Pollitt
on his sixty-fifth birthday, the biggest cotton planter in—

BIG DADDY [bellowing with fury and disgust]   I told you to stop it, now stop it,
quit this—!

BIG MAMA [*coming in front of Big Daddy with the cake*]   Big Daddy, I will not
allow you to talk that way, not even on your birthday, I—

BIG DADDY   I'll talk like I want to on my birthday, Ida, or any other goddam
day of the year and anybody here that don't like it knows what they can
do!

BIG MAMA   You don't mean that!

BIG DADDY   What makes you think I don't mean it?

*Meanwhile various discreet signals have been exchanged and Gooper has also gone
out on the gallery.*

BIG MAMA   I just know you don't mean it.

BIG DADDY   You don't know a goddam thing and you never did!

BIG MAMA   Big Daddy, you don't mean that.

BIG DADDY   Oh, yes, I do, oh, yes, I do, I mean it! I put up with a whole lot of
crap around here because I thought I was dying. And you thought I was
dying and you started taking over, well, you can stop taking over now,
Ida, because I'm not gonna die, you can just stop now this business of
taking over because you're not taking over because I'm not dying, I went
through the laboratory and the goddam exploratory operation and
there's nothing wrong with me but a spastic colon. And I'm not dying of
cancer which you thought I was dying of. Ain't that so? Didn't you think
that I was dying of cancer, Ida?

*Almost everybody is out on the gallery but the two old people glaring at each other
across the blazing cake.*

Big Mama's chest heaves and she presses a fat fist to her mouth.

Big Daddy continues, hoarsely:

Ain't that so, Ida? Didn't you have an idea I was dying of cancer and now
you could take control of this place and everything on it? I got that
impression, I seemed to get that impression. Your loud voice everywhere,
your fat old body butting in here and there!

BIG MAMA   Hush! The Preacher!

BIG DADDY   Fuck the goddam preacher!

Big Mama gasps loudly and sits down on the sofa which is almost too small for her.

Did you hear what I said? I said fuck the goddam preacher!

*Somebody closes the gallery doors from outside just as there is a burst of fireworks
and excited cries from the children.*

BIG MAMA   I never seen you act like this before and I can't think what's got in you!

BIG DADDY   I went through all that laboratory and operation and all just so I would know if you or me was boss here! Well, now it turns out that I am and you ain't—and that's my birthday present—and my cake and champagne!—because for three years now you been gradually taking over. Bossing. Talking. Sashaying your fat old body around the place I made! I made this place! I was overseer on it! I was the overseer on the old Straw and Ochello plantation. I quit school at ten! I quit school at ten years old and went to work like a nigger in the fields. And I rose to be overseer of the Straw and Ochello plantation. And old Straw died and I was Ochello's partner and the place got bigger and bigger and bigger and bigger and bigger! I did all that myself with no goddam help from you, and now you think you're just about to take over. Well, I am just about to tell you that you are not just about to take over, you are not just about to take over a God damn thing. Is that clear to you, Ida? Is that very plain to you, now? Is that understood completely? I been through the laboratory from A to Z. I've had the goddam exploratory operation, and nothing is wrong with me but a spastic colon—made spastic, I guess, by *disgust!* By all the goddam lies and liars that I have had to put up with, and all the goddam hypocrisy that I lived with all these forty years that we been livin' together!

Hey! Ida!! Blow out the candles on the birthday cake! Purse up your lips and draw a deep breath and blow out the goddam candles on the cake!

BIG MAMA   Oh, Big Daddy, oh, oh, oh, Big Daddy!

BIG DADDY   What's the matter with you?

BIG MAMA   *In all these years you never believed that I loved you??*

BIG DADDY   Huh?

BIG MAMA   *And I did, I did so much, I did love you!*—I even loved your hate and your hardness, Big Daddy!   [*She sobs and rushes awkwardly out onto the gallery.*]

BIG DADDY   [*to himself*]   *Wouldn't it be funny if that was true. . . .*

A pause is followed by a burst of light in the sky from the fireworks.

BRICK! HEY, BRICK!

He stands over his blazing birthday cake.

After some moments, Brick hobbles in on his crutch, holding his glass.

Margaret follows him with a bright, anxious smile.

I didn't call you, Maggie. I called Brick.
MARGARET   I'm just delivering him to you.

She kisses Brick on the mouth which he immediately wipes with the back of his hand. She flies girlishly back out. Brick and his father are alone.

BIG DADDY   Why did you do that?
BRICK   Do what, Big Daddy?
BIG DADDY   Wipe her kiss off your mouth like she'd spit on you.
BRICK   I don't know. I wasn't conscious of it.
BIG DADDY   That woman of yours has a better shape on her than Gooper's but somehow or other they got the same look about them.
BRICK   What sort of look is that, Big Daddy?
BIG DADDY   I don't know how to describe it but it's the same look.
BRICK   They don't look peaceful, do they?
BIG DADDY   No, they sure in hell don't.
BRICK   They look nervous as cats?
BIG DADDY   That's right, they look nervous as cats.
BRICK   Nervous as a couple of cats on a hot tin roof?
BIG DADDY   That's right, boy, they look like a couple of cats on a hot tin roof. It's funny that you and Gooper being so different would pick out the same type of woman.
BRICK   Both of us married into society, Big Daddy.
BIG DADDY   Crap . . . I wonder what gives them both that look?
BRICK   Well. They're sittin' in the middle of a big piece of land, Big Daddy, twenty-eight thousand acres is a pretty big piece of land and so they're squaring off on it, each determined to knock off a bigger piece of it than the other whenever you let it go.
BIG DADDY   I got a surprise for those women. I'm not gonna let it go for a long time yet if that's what they're waiting for.
BRICK   That's right, Big Daddy. You just sit tight and let them scratch each other's eyes out. . . .
BIG DADDY   You bet your life I'm going to sit tight on it and let those sons of bitches scratch their eyes out, ha ha ha. . . .

But Gooper's wife's a good breeder, you got to admit she's fertile. Hell, at supper tonight she had them all at the table and they had to put a couple of extra leafs in the table to make room for them, she's got five head of them, now, and another one's comin'.
BRICK   Yep, number six is comin'. . . .
BIG DADDY   Six hell, she'll probably drop a litter next time. Brick, you know, I swear to God, I don't know the way it happens?

BRICK   The way what happens, Big Daddy?

BIG DADDY   You git you a piece of land, by hook or crook, an' things start growin' on it, things accumulate on it, and the first thing you know it's completely out of hand, completely out of hand!

BRICK   Well, they say nature hates a vacuum, Big Daddy.

BIG DADDY   That's what they say, but sometimes I think that a vacuum is a hell of a lot better than some of the stuff that nature replaces it with.

Is someone out there by that door?

GOOPER   Hey Mae.

BRICK   Yep.

BIG DADDY   Who? [He has lowered his voice.]

BRICK   Someone int'rested in what we say to each other.

BIG DADDY   Gooper?——GOOPER!

After a discreet pause, Mae appears in the gallery door.

MAE   Did you call Gooper, Big Daddy?

BIG DADDY   Aw, it was you.

MAE   Do you want Gooper, Big Daddy?

BIG DADDY   No, and I don't want you. I want some privacy here, while I'm having a confidential talk with my son Brick. Now it's too hot in here to close them doors, but if I have to close those fuckin' doors in order to have a private talk with my son Brick, just let me know and I'll close 'em. Because I hate eavesdroppers, I don't like any kind of sneakin' an' spyin'.

MAE   Why, Big Daddy—

BIG DADDY   You stood on the wrong side of the moon, it threw your shadow!

MAE   I was just—

BIG DADDY   You was just nothing but *spyin'* an' you *know* it!

MAE   [begins to sniff and sob]   Oh, Big Daddy, you're so unkind for some reason to those that really love you!

BIG DADDY   Shut up, shut up, shut up! I'm going to move you and Gooper out of that room next to this! It's none of your goddam business what goes on in here at night between Brick an' Maggie. You listen at night like a couple of rutten peekhole spies and go and give a report on what you hear to Big Mama an' she comes to me and says they say such and such and so and so about what they heard goin' on between Brick an' Maggie, and Jesus, it makes me sick. I'm goin' to move you an' Gooper out of that room, I can't stand sneakin' an' spyin', it makes me puke. . . .

Mae throws back her head and rolls her eyes heavenward and extends her arms as if invoking God's pity for this unjust martyrdom; then she presses a handkerchief to her nose and flies from the room with a loud swish of skirts.

BRICK [*now at the liquor cabinet*]   They listen, do they?

BIG DADDY   Yeah. They listen and give reports to Big Mama on what goes on in here between you and Maggie. They say that— [*He stops as if embarrassed.*]   —You won't sleep with her, that you sleep on the sofa. Is that true or not true? If you don't like Maggie, get rid of Maggie!—What are you doin' there now?

BRICK   Fresh'nin' up my drink.

BIG DADDY   Son, you know you got a real liquor problem?

BRICK   Yes, sir, yes, I know.

BIG DADDY   Is that why you quit sports-announcing, because of this liquor problem?

BRICK   Yes, sir, yes, sir, I guess so.

He smiles vaguely and amiably at his father across his replenished drink.

BIG DADDY   Son, don't guess about it, it's too important.

BRICK [*vaguely*]   Yes, sir.

BIG DADDY   And listen to me, don't look at the damn chandelier. . . .

Pause. Big Daddy's voice is husky.

—Somethin' else we picked up at th' big fire sale in Europe.

Another pause.

Life is important. There's nothing else to hold onto. A man that drinks is throwing his life away. Don't do it, hold onto your life. There's nothing else to hold onto. . . .

Sit down over here so we don't have to raise our voices, the walls have ears in this place.

BRICK [*hobbling over to sit on the sofa beside him*]   All right, Big Daddy.

BIG DADDY   Quit!—how'd that come about? Some disappointment?

BRICK   I don't know. Do you?

BIG DADDY   I'm askin' you, God damn it! How in hell would I know if you don't?

BRICK   I just got out there and found that I had a mouth full of cotton. I was always two or three beats behind what was goin' on on the field and so I—

BIG DADDY   Quit!

BRICK [*amiably*]   Yes, quit.

BIG DADDY   Son?

BRICK   Huh?

BIG DADDY [*inhales loudly and deeply from his cigar; then bends suddenly a little*

forward, exhaling loudly and raising a hand to his forehead]   —Whew!—ha
ha!—I took in too much smoke, it made me a little lightheaded. . . .

The mantel clock chimes.

Why is it so damn hard for people to talk?
BRICK   Yeah. . . .

The clock goes on sweetly chiming till it has completed the stroke of ten.

—Nice peaceful-soundin' clock, I like to hear it all night. . . .

*He slides low and comfortable on the sofa; Big Daddy sits up straight and rigid
with some unspoken anxiety. All his gestures are tense and jerky as he talks. He
wheezes and pants and sniffs through his nervous speech, glancing quickly, shyly,
from time to time, at his son.*

BIG DADDY   We got that clock the summer we wint to Europe, me an' Big
    Mama on that damn Cook's Tour, never had such an awful time in my
    life, I'm tellin' you, son, those gooks over there, they gouge your
    eyeballs out in their grand hotels. And Big Mama bought more stuff than
    you could haul in a couple of boxcars, that's no crap. Everywhere she
    wint on this whirlwind tour, she bought, bought, bought. Why, half
    that stuff she bought is still crated up in the cellar, under water last
    spring!   [*He laughs.*]

    That Europe is nothin' on earth but a great big auction, that's all it is,
    that bunch of old worn-out places, it's just a big firesale, the whole
    fuckin' thing, an' Big Mama wint wild in it, why, you couldn't hold that
    woman with a mule's harness! Bought, bought, bought!—lucky I'm a
    rich man, yes siree, Bob, an' half that stuff is mildewin' in th' basement.
    It's lucky I'm a rich man, it sure is lucky, well, I'm a rich man, Brick, yep,
    I'm a mighty rich man.   [*His eyes light up for a moment.*]

    Y'know how much I'm worth? Guess, Brick! Guess how much I'm
    worth!

Brick smiles vaguely over his drink.

    Close on ten million in cash an' blue-chip stocks, outside, mind you, of
    twenty-eight thousand acres of the richest land this side of the valley
    Nile!

    But a man can't buy his life with it, he can't buy back his life with it when his life has been spent, that's one thing not offered in the Europe fire-sale or in the American markets or any markets on earth, a man can't buy his life with it, he can't buy back his life when his life is finished.

That's a sobering thought, a very sobering thought, and that's a thought that I was turning over in my head, over and over and over— until today. . . .

I'm wiser and sadder, Brick, for this experience which I just gone through. They's one thing else that I remember in Europe.

BRICK   What is that, Big Daddy?

BIG DADDY   The hills around Barcelona in the country of Spain and the children running over those bare hills in their bare skins beggin' like starvin' dogs with howls and screeches, and how fat the priests are on the streets of Barcelona, so many of them and so fat and so pleasant, ha ha!—Y'know I could feed that country? I got money enough to feed that goddam country, but the human animal is a selfish beast and I don't reckon the money I passed out there to those howling children in the hills around Barcelona would more than upholster the chairs in this room, I mean pay to put a new cover on this chair!

Hell, I threw them money like you'd scatter feed corn for chickens, I threw money at them just to get rid of them long enough to climb back into th' car and—drive away. . . .

And then in Morocco, them Arabs, why, I remember one day in Marrakech, that old walled Arab city, I set on a broken-down wall to have a cigar, it was fearful hot there and this Arab woman stood in the road and looked at me till I was embarrassed, she stood stock still in the dusty hot road and looked at me till I was embarrassed. But listen to this. She had a naked child with her, a little naked girl with her, barely able to toddle, and after a while she set this child on the ground and give her a push and whispered something to her.

This child come toward me, barely able t' walk, come toddling up to me and—

Jesus, it makes you sick to' remember a thing like this!
It stuck out its hand and tried to unbotton my trousers!

That child was not yet five! Can you believe me? Or do you think that I am making this up? I wint back to the hotel and said to Big Mama, Git packed! We're clearing out of this country. . . .

BRICK   Big Daddy, you're on a talkin' jag tonight.

BIG DADDY [*ignoring this remark*]   Yes, sir, that's how it is, the human animal is a beast that dies but the fact that he's dying don't give him pity for others, no, sir, it—

—Did you say something?

BRICK   Yes.

BIG DADDY   What?

BRICK   Hand me over that crutch so I can get up.

BIG DADDY   Where you goin'?

BRICK   I'm takin' a little short trip to Echo Spring.

BIG DADDY   To where?

BRICK   Liquor cabinet. . . .

BIG DADDY   Yes, sir, boy— [*he hands Brick the crutch.*] —the human animal is a beast that dies and if he's got money he buys and buys and buys and I think the reason he buys everything he can buy is that in the back of his mind he has the crazy hope that one of his purchases will be life everlasting!—Which it never can be. . . . The human animal is a beast that—

BRICK [*at the liquor cabinet*]   Big Daddy, you sure are shootin' th' breeze here tonight.

There is a pause and voices are heard outside.

BIG DADDY   I been quiet here lately, spoke not a word, just sat and stared into space. I had something heavy weighing on my mind but tonight that load was took off me. That's why I'm talking.—The sky looks diff'rent to me. . . .

BRICK   You know what I like to hear most?

BIG DADDY   What?

BRICK   Solid quiet. Perfect unbroken quiet.

BIG DADDY   Why?

BRICK   Because it's more peaceful.

BIG DADDY   Man, you'll hear a lot of that in the grave. [*He chuckles agreeably.*]

BRICK   Are you through talkin' to me?

BIG DADDY   Why are you so anxious to shut me up?

BRICK   Well, sir, ever so often you say to me, Brick, I want to have a talk with you, but when we talk, it never materializes. Nothing is said. You sit in a chair and gas about this and that and I look like I listen. I try to look like I listen, but I don't listen, not much. Communication is—awful hard between people an'—somehow between you and me, it just don't—happen.

BIG DADDY   Have you ever been scared? I mean have you ever felt downright terror of something? [*He gets up.*]   Just one moment.   [*He looks off as if he were going to tell an important secret.*]

BIG DADDY   Brick?

BRICK   What?

BIG DADDY   Son, I thought I had it!

BRICK   Had what? Had what, Big Daddy?

BIG DADDY   Cancer!

BRICK   Oh . . .

BIG DADDY   I thought the old man made out of bones had laid his cold and heavy hand on my shoulder!

BRICK   Well, Big Daddy, you kept a tight mouth about it.

BIG DADDY   A pig squeals. A man keeps a tight mouth about it, in spite of a man not having a pig's advantage.

BRICK   What advantage is that?

BIG DADDY   Ignorance—of mortality—is a comfort. A man don't have that comfort, he's the only living thing that conceives of death, that knows what it is. The others go without knowing which is the way that anything living should go, go without knowing, without any knowledge of it, and yet a pig squeals, but a man sometimes, he can keep a tight mouth about it. Sometimes he—

There is a deep, smoldering ferocity in the old man.

—can keep a tight mouth about it. I wonder if—

BRICK   What, Big Daddy?

BIG DADDY   A whiskey highball would injure this spastic condition?

BRICK   No, sir, it might do it good.

BIG DADDY   [*grins suddenly, wolfishly*]   Jesus, I can't tell you! The sky is open! Christ, it's open again! It's open, boy, it's open!

Brick looks down at his drink.

BRICK   You feel better, Big Daddy?

BIG DADDY   Better? Hell! I can breathe!—All of my life I been like a doubled up fist. . . .   [*He pours a drink.*]   —Poundin', smashin', drivin'!—now I'm going to loosen these doubled-up hands and touch things *easy* with them. . . .

He spreads his hands as if caressing the air.

You know what I'm contemplating?

BRICK   [*vaguely*]   No, sir. What are you contemplating?

BIG DADDY   Ha ha!—*Pleasure!*—pleasure with *women!*

Brick's smile fades a little but lingers.

—Yes, boy. I'll tell you something that you might not guess. I still have
desire for women and this is my sixty-fifth birthday.

BRICK   I think that's mighty remarkable, Big Daddy.

BIG DADDY   Remarkable?

BRICK   *Admirable,* Big Daddy.

BIG DADDY   You're damn right it is, remarkable and admirable both. I realize
now that I never had me enough. I let many chances slip by because of
scruples about it, scruples, convention—crap. . . . All that stuff is bull,
bull, bull!—It took the shadow of death to make me see it. Now that
shadow's lifted, I'm going to cut loose and have, what is it they call it,
have me a—ball!

BRICK   A ball, huh?

BIG DADDY   That's right, a ball, a ball! Hell!—I slept with Big Mama till, let's
see, five years ago, till I was sixty and she was fifty-eight, and never
even liked her, never did!

The phone has been ringing down the hall. Big Mama enters, exclaiming:

BIG MAMA   Don't you men hear that phone ring? I heard it way out on the
gall'ry.

BIG DADDY   There's five rooms off this front gall'ry that you could go
through. Why do you go through this one?

Big Mama makes a playful face as she bustles out the hall door.

Hunh!—Why, when Big Mama goes out of a room, I can't remember
what that woman looks like—

BIG MAMA   Hello.

BIG DADDY   —But when Big Mama comes back into the room, boy, then I see
what she looks like, and I wish I didn't.

*Bends over laughing at this joke till it hurts his guts and he straightens with a
grimace. The laugh subsides to a chuckle as he puts the liquor glass a little
distrustfully down the table.*

BIG MAMA   Hello, Miss Sally.

Brick has risen and hobbled to the gallery doors.

BIG DADDY   Hey! Where you goin'?

BRICK   Out for a breather.

BIG DADDY   Not yet you ain't. Stay here till this talk is finished, young fellow.

BRICK   I thought it was finished, Big Daddy.

BIG DADDY   It ain't even begun.

BRICK   My mistake. Excuse me. I just wanted to feel that river breeze.

BIG DADDY   Set back down in that chair.

Big Mama's voice rises, carrying down the hall.

BIG MAMA   Miss Sally, you're a case! You're a caution, Miss Sally.

BIG DADDY   Jesus, she's talking to my old maid sister again.

BIG MAMA   Why didn't you give me a chance to explain it to you?

BIG DADDY   Brick, this stuff burns me.

BIG MAMA   Well, goodbye, now, Miss Sally. You come down real soon. Big Daddy's dying to see you.

BIG DADDY   Crap!

BIG MAMA   Yaiss, goodbye, Miss Sally. . . .

She hangs up and bellows with mirth. Big Daddy groans and covers his ears as she approaches.

Bursting in:

Big Daddy, that was Miss Sally callin' from Memphis again! You know what she done, Big Daddy? She called her doctor in Memphis to git him to tell her what that spastic thing is! Ha-*HAAAA!*—And called back to tell me how relieved she was that—Hey! Let me in!

Big Daddy has been holding the door half closed against her.

BIG DADDY   Naw I ain't. I told you not to come and go through this room. You just back out and go through those five other rooms.

BIG MAMA   Big Daddy? Big Daddy? Oh, Big Daddy!—You didn't mean those things you said to me, did you?

He shuts door firmly against her but she still calls.

Sweetheart? Sweetheart? Big Daddy? You didn't mean those awful things you said to me?—I know you didn't. I know you didn't mean those things in your heart. . . .

The childlike voice fades with a sob and her heavy footsteps retreat down the hall. Brick has risen once more on his crutches and starts for the gallery again.

BIG DADDY   All I ask of that woman is that she leave me alone. But she can't admit to herself that she makes me sick. That comes of having slept with her too many years. Should of quit much sooner but that old woman she never got enough of it—and I was good in bed . . . I never should of wasted so much of it on her. . . . They say you got just so many and each one is numbered. Well, I got a few left in me, a few, and I'm going to pick me a good one to spend 'em on! I'm going to pick me a choice one, I don't care how much she costs, I'll smother her in—minks! Ha ha! I'll strip her naked and smother her in minks and choke her with diamonds! Ha ha! I'll strip her naked and choke her with diamonds and smother her with minks and hump her from hell to breakfast. *Ha aha ha ha ha!*

MAE [*gaily at door*]   Who's that laughin' in there?

GOOPER   Is Big Daddy laughin' in there?

BIG DADDY   Crap!—them two—*drips*. . . .

He goes over and touches Brick's shoulder.

Yes, son. Brick, boy.—I'm—*happy!* I'm happy, son, I'm happy!

He chokes a little and bites his under lip, pressing his head quickly, shyly against his son's head and then, coughing with embarrassment, goes uncertainly back to the table where he set down the glass. He drinks and makes a grimace as it burns his guts. Brick sighs and rises with effort.

What makes you so restless? Have you got ants in your britches?

BRICK   Yes, sir . . .

BIG DADDY   Why?

BRICK   —Something—hasn't—happened. . . .

BIG DADDY   Yeah? What is that!

BRICK [*sadly*]   —the click. . . .

BIG DADDY   Did you say click?

BRICK   Yes, click.

BIG DADDY   What click?

BRICK   A click that I get in my head that makes me peaceful.

BIG DADDY   I sure in hell don't know what you're talking about, but it disturbs me.

BRICK   It's just a mechanical thing.

BIG DADDY   What is a mechanical thing?

BRICK   This click that I get in my head that makes me peaceful. I got to drink till I get it. It's just a mechanical thing, something like a—like a—like a—

BIG DADDY   Like a—

BRICK   Switch clicking off in my head, turning the hot light off and the cool night on and— [*He looks up, smiling sadly.*]   —all of a sudden there's —peace!

BIG DADDY [*whistles long and soft with astonishment; he goes back to Brick and*

clasps his son's two shoulders]   Jesus! I didn't know it had gotten that bad
with you. Why, boy, you're—*alcoholic!*

BRICK   That's the truth, Big Daddy. I'm alcoholic.

BIG DADDY   This shows how I—let things go!

BRICK   I have to hear that little click in my head that makes me peaceful.
Usually I hear it sooner than this, sometimes as early as—noon, but—

—Today it's—dilatory. . . .

—I just haven't got the right level of alcohol in my bloodstream yet!

This last statement is made with energy as he freshens his drink.

BIG DADDY   Uh—huh. Expecting death made me blind. I didn't have no idea
that a son of mine was turning into a drunkard under my nose.

BRICK [*gently*]   Well, now you do, Big Daddy, the news has penetrated.

BIG DADDY   UH-huh, yes, now I do, the news has—penetrated. . . .

BRICK   And so if you'll excuse me—

BIG DADDY   No, I won't excuse you.

BRICK   —I'd better sit by myself till I hear that click in my head, it's just a
mechanical thing but it don't happen except when I'm alone or talking to
no one. . . .

BIG DADDY   You got a long, long time to sit still, boy, and talk to no one, but
now you're talkin' to me. At least I'm talking to you. And you set there
and listen until I tell you the conversation is over!

BRICK   But this talk is like all the others we've ever had together in our lives!
It's nowhere, nowhere!—it's—it's *painful*, Big Daddy. . . .

BIG DADDY   All right, then let it be painful, but don't you move from that
chair!—I'm going to remove that crutch. . . .   [*He seizes the crutch and
tosses it across room.*]

BRICK   I can hop on one foot, and if I fall, I can crawl!

BIG DADDY   If you ain't careful you're gonna crawl off this plantation and
then, by Jesus, you'll have to hustle your drinks along Skid Row!

BRICK   That'll come, Big Daddy.

BIG DADDY   Naw, it won't. You're my son and I'm going to straighten you
out; now that *I'm* straightened out, I'm going to straighten out you!

BRICK   Yeah?

BIG DADDY   Today the report come in from Ochsner Clinic. Y'know what
they told me?   [*His face glows with triumph.*]   The only thing that they
could detect with all the instruments of science in that great hospital is a
little spastic condition of the colon! And nerves torn to pieces by all that
worry about it.

A little girl bursts into room with a sparkler clutched in each fist, hops and shrieks like a monkey gone mad and rushes back out again as Big Daddy strikes at her.

Silence. The two men stare at each other. A woman laughs gaily outside.

I want you to know I breathed a sigh of relief almost as powerful as the Vicksburg tornado!

There is laughter outside, running footsteps, the soft, plushy sound and light of exploding rockets.

Brick stares at him soberly for a long moment; then makes a sort of startled sound in his nostrils and springs up on one foot and hops across the room to grab his crutch, swinging on the furniture for support. He gets the crutch and flees as if in horror for the gallery. His father seizes him by the sleeve of his white silk pajamas.

Stay here, you son of a bitch!—till I say go!
BRICK   I can't.
BIG DADDY   You sure in hell will, God damn it.
BRICK   No, I can't. We talk, you talk, in—circles! We get no where, no where! It's always the same, you say you want to talk to me and don't have a fuckin' thing to say to me!
BIG DADDY   Nothin' to say when I'm tellin' you I'm going to live when I thought I was dying?!
BRICK   Oh—*that!*—Is that what you have to say to me?
BIG DADDY   Why, you son of a bitch! Ain't that, ain't that—*important?!*
BRICK   Well, you said that, that's said, and now I—
BIG DADDY   Now you set back down.
BRICK   You're all balled up, you—
BIG DADDY   I ain't balled up!
BRICK   You are, you're all balled up!
BIG DADDY   Don't tell me what I am, you drunken whelp! I'm going to tear this coat sleeve off if you don't set down!
BRICK   Big Daddy—
BIG DADDY   Do what I tell you! I'm the boss here, now! I want you to know I'm back in the driver's seat now!

Big Mama rushes in, clutching her great heaving bosom.

BIG MAMA   Big Daddy!
BIG DADDY   What in hell do you want in here, Big Mama?
BIG MAMA   Oh, Big Daddy! Why are you shouting like that? I just cain't stainnnnnnnd—it. . . .

BIG DADDY [*raising the back of his hand above his head*]   GIT!—outa here.

She rushes back out, sobbing.

BRICK [*softly, sadly*]   Christ. . . .
BIG DADDY [*fiercely*]   Yeah! Christ!—is right . . .

Brick breaks loose and hobbles toward the gallery.

Big Daddy jerks his crutch from under Brick so he steps with the injured ankle. He utters a hissing cry of anguish, clutches a chair and pulls it over on top of him on the floor.

Son of a—tub of—hog fat. . . .
BRICK   Big Daddy! Give me my crutch.

Big Daddy throws the crutch out of reach.

Give me that crutch, Big Daddy.
BIG DADDY   Why do you drink?
BRICK   Don't know, give me my crutch!
BIG DADDY   You better think why you drink or give up drinking!
BRICK   Will you please give me my crutch so I can get up off this floor?
BIG DADDY   First you answer my question. Why do you drink? Why are you throwing your life away, boy, like somethin' disgusting you picked up on the street?
BRICK [*getting onto his knees*]   Big Daddy, I'm in pain, I stepped on that foot.
BIG DADDY   Good! I'm glad you're not too numb with the liquor in you to feel some pain!
BRICK   You—spilled my—drink . . .
BIG DADDY   I'll make a bargain with you. You tell me why you drink and I'll hand you one. I'll pour the liquor myself and hand it to you.
BRICK   Why do I drink?
BIG DADDY   Yea! Why?
BRICK   Give me a drink and I'll tell you.
BIG DADDY   Tell me first!
BRICK   I'll tell you in one word.
BIG DADDY   What word?
BRICK   DISGUST!

The clock chimes softly, sweetly. Big Daddy gives it a short, outraged glance.

Now how about that drink?

BIG DADDY   What are you disgusted with? You got to tell me that, first. Otherwise being disgusted don't make no sense!

BRICK   Give me my crutch.

BIG DADDY   You heard me, you got to tell me what I asked you first.

BRICK   I told you, I said to kill my disgust!

BIG DADDY   DISGUST WITH WHAT!

BRICK   You strike a hard bargain.

BIG DADDY   What are you disgusted with?—an' I'll pass you the liquor.

BRICK   I can hop on one foot, and if I fall, I can crawl.

BIG DADDY   You want liquor that bad?

BRICK   [dragging himself up, clinging to bedstead]   Yeah, I want it that bad.

BIG DADDY   If I give you a drink, will you tell me what it is you're disgusted with, Brick?

BRICK   Yes, sir, I will try to.

The old man pours him a drink and solemnly passes it to him.

There is silence as Brick drinks.

Have you ever heard the word "mendacity"?

BIG DADDY   Sure. Mendacity is one of them five dollar words that cheap politicians throw back and forth at each other.

BRICK   You know what it means?

BIG DADDY   Don't it mean lying and liars?

BRICK   Yes, sir, lying and liars.

BIG DADDY   Has someone been lying to you?

CHILDREN   [chanting in chorus offstage]
    We want Big Dad-dee!
    We want Big Dad-dee!

Gooper appears in the gallery door.

GOOPER   Big Daddy, the kiddies are shouting for you out there.

BIG DADDY   [fiercely]   Keep out, Gooper!

GOOPER   'Scuse me!

Big Daddy slams the doors after Gooper.

BIG DADDY   Who's been lying to you, has Margaret been lying to you, has your wife been lying to you about something, Brick?

BRICK   Not her. That wouldn't matter.

BIG DADDY   Then who's been lying to you, and what about?

BRICK   No one single person and no one lie. . . .

BIG DADDY   Then what, what then, for Christ's sake?

BRICK   —The whole, the whole—thing. . . .

BIG DADDY   Why are you rubbing your head? You got a headache?

BRICK   No, I'm tryin' to—

BIG DADDY   —Concentrate, but you can't because your brain's all soaked
with liquor, is that the trouble? Wet brain! [*He snatches the glass from
Brick's hand.*]   What do you know about this mendacity thing? Hell! I
could write a book on it! Don't you know that? I could write a book on it
and still not cover the subject? Well, I could, I could write a goddam
book on it and still not cover the subject anywhere near enough!!—
Think of all the lies I got to put up with!—Pretenses! Ain't that
mendacity? Having to pretend stuff you don't think or feel or have any
idea of? Having for instance to act like I care for Big Mama!—I haven't
been able to stand the sight, sound, or smell of that woman for forty years
now!—even when I *laid* her!—regular as a piston. . . .

Pretend to love that son of a bitch of a Gooper and his wife Mae and
those five same screechers out there like parrots in a jungle? Jesus! Can't
stand to look at 'em!

Church!—it bores the bejesus out of me but I go!—I go an' sit there and
listen to the fool preacher!

Clubs!—Elks! Masons! Rotary!—*crap!*

*A spasm of pain makes him clutch his belly. He sinks into a chair and his voice is
softer and hoarser.*

You I *do* like for some reason, did always have some kind of real feeling
for—affection—respect—yes, always. . . .

You and being a success as a planter is all I ever had any devotion to in
my whole life!—and that's the truth. . . .

I don't know why, but it is!

I've lived with mendacity!—Why can't *you* live with it? Hell, you *got* to
live with it, there's nothing *else* to *live* with except mendacity, is there?

BRICK   Yes, sir. Yes, sir there is something else that you can live with!

BIG DADDY   What?

BRICK   [*lifting his glass*]   This!—Liquor. . . .

BIG DADDY   That's not living, that's dodging away from life.

BRICK   I want to dodge away from it.

BIG DADDY   Then why don't you kill yourself, man?

BRICK   I like to drink. . . .

BIG DADDY   Oh, God, I can't talk to you. . . .

BRICK   I'm sorry, Big Daddy.

BIG DADDY   Not as sorry as I am. I'll tell you something. A little while back
when I thought my number was up—

This speech should have torrential pace and fury.

—before I found out it was just this—spastic—colon. I thought about
you. Should I or should I not, if the jig was up, give you this place when
I go—since I hate Gooper an' Mae an' know that they hate me, and since
all five same monkeys are little Maes an' Goopers.—And I thought,
No!—Then I thought, Yes!—I couldn't make up my mind. I hate Gooper
and his five same monkeys and that bitch Mae! Why should I turn over
twenty-eight thousand acres of the richest land this side of the valley
Nile to not my kind?—But why in hell, on the other hand, Brick—should
I subsidize a goddam fool on the bottle?—Liked or not liked, well,
maybe even—*loved!*—Why should I do that?—Subsidize worthless behavior? Rot? Corruption?

BRICK [*smiling*]   I understand.

BIG DADDY   Well, if you do, you're smarter than I am, God damn it, because
I don't understand. And this I will tell you frankly. I didn't make up my
mind at all on that question and still to this day I ain't made out no
will!—Well, now I don't *have* to. The pressure is gone. I can just wait and
see if you pull yourself together or if you don't

BRICK   That's right, Big Daddy.

BIG DADDY   You sound like you thought I was kidding.

BRICK [*rising*]   No, sir, I know you're not kidding.

BIG DADDY   But you don't care—?

BRICK [*hobbling toward the gallery door*]   No, sir, I don't care. . . .

*He stands in the gallery doorway as the night sky turns pink and green and gold
with successive flashes of light.*

BIG DADDY   *WAIT!*—Brick. . . .

*His voice drops. Suddenly there is something shy, almost tender, in his restraining
gesture.*

Don't let's—leave it like this, like them other talks we've had, we've
always—talked around things, we've—just talked around things for
some fuckin' reason, I don't know what, it's always like something was
left not spoken, something avoided because neither of us was honest
enough with the—other. . . .

BRICK I never lied to you, Big Daddy.

BIG DADDY Did I ever to *you*?

BRICK No, sir. . . .

BIG DADDY Then there is at least two people that never lied to each other.

BRICK But we've never *talked* to each other.

BIG DADDY We can *now*.

BRICK Big Daddy, there don't seem to be anything much to say.

BIG DADDY You say that you drink to kill your disgust with lying.

BRICK You said to give you a reason.

BIG DADDY Is liquor the only thing that'll kill this disgust?

BRICK Now. Yes.

BIG DADDY But not once, huh?

BRICK Not when I was still young an' believing. A drinking man's someone who wants to forget he isn't still young an' believing.

BIG DADDY Believing what?

BRICK Believing. . . .

BIG DADDY Believing *what*?

BRICK [*stubbornly evasive*] Believing. . . .

BIG DADDY I don't know what the hell you mean by believing and I don't think you know what you mean by believing, but if you still got sports in your blood, go back to sports announcing and—

BRICK Sit in a glass box watching games I can't play? Describing what I can't do while players do it? Sweating out their disgust and confusion in contests I'm not fit for? Drinkin' a coke, half bourbon, so I can stand it? That's no goddam good any more, no help—time just outran me, Big Daddy—got there first . . .

BIG DADDY I think you're passing the buck.

BRICK You know many drinkin' men?

BIG DADDY [*with a slight, charming smile*] I have known a fair number of that species.

BRICK Could any of them tell you why he drank?

BIG DADDY Yep, you're passin' the buck to things like time and disgust with "mendacity" and—crap!—if you got to use that kind of language about a thing, it's ninety-proof bull, and I'm not buying any.

BRICK I had to give you a reason to get a drink!

BIG DADDY You started drinkin' when your friend Skipper died.

Silence for five beats. Then Brick makes a startled movement, reaching for his crutch.

BRICK What are you suggesting?

BIG DADDY I'm suggesting nothing.

The shuffle and clop of Brick's rapid hobble away from his father's steady, grave attention.

—But Gooper an' Mae suggested that there was something not right exactly in your—
BRICK [*stopping short downstage as if backed to a wall*]   "Not right"?
BIG DADDY   Not, well, exactly *normal* in your friendship with—
BRICK   They suggested that, too? I thought that was Maggie's suggestion.

Brick's detachment is at last broken through. His heart is accelerated; his forehead sweat-beaded; his breath becomes more rapid and his voice hoarse. The thing they're discussing, timidly and painfully on the side of Big Daddy, fiercely, violently on Brick's side, is the inadmissible thing that Skipper died to disavow between them. The fact that if it existed it had to be disavowed to "keep face" in the world they lived in, may be at the heart of the "mendacity" that Brick drinks to kill his disgust with. It may be the root of his collapse. Or maybe it is only a single manifestation of it, not even the most important. The bird that I hope to catch in the net of this play is not the solution of one man's psychological problem. I'm trying to catch the true quality of experience in a group of people, that cloudy, flickering, evanescent—fiercely charged!—interplay of live human beings in the thundercloud of a common crisis. Some mystery should be left in the revelation of character in a play, just as a great deal of mystery is always left in the revelation of character in life, even in one's own character to himself. This does not absolve the playwright of his duty to observe and probe as clearly and deeply as he legitimately can: but it should steer him away from "pat" conclusions, facile definitions which make a play just a play, not a snare for the truth of human experience.

The following scene should be played with great concentration, with most of the power leashed but palpable in what is left unspoken.

Who else's suggestion is it, is it *yours?* How many others thought that Skipper and I were—
BIG DADDY [*gently*]   Now, hold on, hold on a minute, son.—I knocked around in my time.
BRICK   What's that got to do with—
BIG DADDY   I said "Hold on!"—I bummed, I bummed this country till I was—
BRICK   Whose suggestion, who else's suggestion is it?
BIG DADDY   Slept in hobo jungles and railroad Y's and flophouses in all cities before I—
BRICK   Oh, *you* think so, too, you call me your son and a queer. Oh! Maybe that's why you put Maggie and me in this room that was Jack Straw's

and Peter Ochello's, in which that pair of old sisters slept in a double
bed where both of 'em died!

BIG DADDY *Now just don't go throwing rocks at—*

Suddenly Reverend Tooker appears in the gallery doors, his head slightly, playfully, fatuously cocked, with a practised clergyman's smile, sincere as a bird call blown on a hunter's whistle, the living embodiment of the pious, conventional lie.

Big Daddy gasps a little at this perfectly timed, but incongruous, apparition.

—What're you lookin' for, Preacher?
REVEREND TOOKER The gentleman's lavatory, ha ha!—heh, heh . . .
BIG DADDY [*with strained courtesy*] —Go back out and walk down to the
    other end of the gallery, Reverend Tooker, and use the bathroom
    connected with my bedroom, and if you can't find it, ask them where it
    is!
REVEREND TOOKER Ah, thanks. [*He goes out with a deprecatory chuckle.*]
BIG DADDY It's hard to talk in this place . . .
BRICK Son of a—!
BIG DADDY [*leaving a lot unspoken*] —I seen all things and understood a lot of
    them, till 1910. Christ, the year that—I had worn my shoes through,
    hocked my—I hopped off a yellow dog freight car half a mile down the
    road, slept in a wagon of cotton outside the gin—Jack Straw an' Peter
    Ochello took me in. Hired me to manage this place which grew into this
    one.—When Jack Straw died—why, old Peter Ochello quit eatin' like a
    dog does when its master's dead, and died, too!
BRICK Christ!
BIG DADDY I'm just saying I understand such—
BRICK [*violently*] Skipper is dead. I have not quit eating!
BIG DADDY No, but you started drinking.

Brick wheels on his crutch and hurls his glass across the room shouting.

BRICK YOU THINK SO, TOO?

Footsteps run on the gallery. There are women's calls.

Big Daddy goes toward the door.

Brick is transformed, as if a quiet mountain blew suddenly up in volcanic flame.

BRICK You think so, too? You think so, too? You think me an' Skipper did,
    did, did!—*sodomy!*—together?

BIG DADDY   Hold—!

BRICK   That what you—

BIG DADDY   —ON—a minute!

BRICK   You think we did dirty things between us, Skipper an'—

BIG DADDY   Why are you shouting like that? Why are you—

BRICK   —Me, is that what you think of Skipper, is that—

BIG DADDY   —so excited? I don't think nothing. I don't know nothing. I'm simply telling you what—

BRICK   You think that Skipper and me were a pair of dirty old men?

BIG DADDY   Now that's—

BRICK   Straw? Ochello? A couple of—

BIG DADDY   Now just—

BRICK   —fucking sissies? Queers? Is that what you—

BIG DADDY   Shhh.

BRICK   —think?

He loses his balance and pitches to his knees without noticing the pain. He grabs the bed and drags himself up.

BIG DADDY   Jesus!—Whew. . . . Grab my hand!

BRICK   Naw, I don't want your hand. . . .

BIG DADDY   Well, I want yours. Git up!

He draws him up, keeps an arm about him with concern and affection.

You broken out in a sweat! You're panting like you'd run a race with—

BRICK [*freeing himself from his father's hold*] Big Daddy, you shock me, Big Daddy, you, you—*shock* me! Talkin' so— [*He turns away from his father.*]   —casually!—about a—thing like that . . .

—Don't you know how people *feel* about things like that? How, how *disgusted* they are by things like that? Why, at Ole Miss when it was discovered a pledge to our fraternity, Skipper's and mine, did a, *attempted* to do a, unnatural thing with—

We not only dropped him like a hot rock!—We told him to git off the campus, and he did, he got!—All the way to— [*He halts, breathless.*]

BIG DADDY   —Where?

BRICK   —North Africa, last I heard!

BIG DADDY   Well, I have come back from further away than that, I have just now returned from the other side of the moon, death's country, son, and I'm not easy to shock by anything here. [*He comes downstage and faces out.*]   Always. anyhow, lived with too much space around me to be infected by ideas of other people. One thing you can grow on a big place more important than cotton!—is *tolerance!*—I grown it. [*He returns toward Brick.*]

BRICK Why can't exceptional friendship, *real, real, deep, deep friendship!* between two men be respected as something clean and decent without being thought of as—

BIG DADDY It can, it is, for God's sake.

BRICK —*Fairies.* . . .

In his utterance of this word, we gauge the wide and profound reach of the conventional mores he got from the world that crowned him with early laurel.

BIG DADDY I told Mae an' Gooper—

BRICK Frig Mae and Gooper, frig all dirty lies and liars!—Skipper and me had a clean, true thing between us!—had a clean friendship, practically all our lives, till Maggie got the idea you're talking about. Normal? No!—It was too rare to be normal, any true thing between two people is too rare to be normal. Oh, once in a while he put his hand on my shoulder or I'd put mine on his, oh, maybe even, when we were touring the country in pro-football an' shared hotel-rooms we'd reach across the space between the two beds and shake hands to say goodnight, yeah, one or two times we—

BIG DADDY Brick, nobody thinks that that's not normal!

BRICK Well, they're mistaken, it was! It was a pure an' true thing an' that's not normal.

MAE [*off stage*] Big Daddy, they're startin' the fireworks.

They both stare straight at each other for a long moment. The tension breaks and both turn away as if tired.

BIG DADDY Yeah, it's—hard t'—talk. . . .

BRICK All right, then, let's—let it go. . . .

BIG DADDY Why did Skipper crack up? Why have you?

Brick looks back at his father again. He has already decided, without knowing that he has made this decision, that he is going to tell his father that he is dying of cancer. Only this could even the score between them: one inadmissible thing in return for another.

BRICK [*ominously*] All right. You're asking for it, Big Daddy. We're finally going to have that real true talk you wanted. It's too late to stop it, now, we got to carry it through and cover every subject.

He hobbles back to the liquor cabinet.

Uh-huh.

He opens the ice bucket and picks up the silver tongs with slow admiration of their frosty brightness.

Maggie declares that Skipper and I went into pro-football after we left "Ole Miss" because we were scared to grow up . . .

He moves downstage with the shuffle and clop of a cripple on a crutch. As Margaret did when her speech became "recitative," he looks out into the house, commanding its attention by his direct, concentrated gaze—a broken, "tragically elegant" figure telling simply as much as he knows of "the Truth":

—Wanted to—keep on tossing—those long, long!—high, high!—passes that—couldn't be intercepted except by time, the aerial attack that made us famous! And so we did, we did, we kept it up for one season, that aerial attack, we held it high!—Yeah, but—

—that summer, Maggie, she laid the law down to me, said, Now or never, and so I married Maggie. . . .
BIG DADDY   How was Maggie in bed?
BRICK [*wryly*]   Great! the greatest!

Big Daddy nods as if he thought so.

She went on the road that fall with the Dixie Stars. Oh, she made a great show of being the world's best sport. She wore a—wore a—tall bearskin cap! A shako, they call it, a dyed moleskin coat, a moleskin coat dyed red!—Cut up crazy! Rented hotel ballrooms for victory celebrations, wouldn't cancel them when it—turned out—defeat. . . .

MAGGIE THE CAT! Ha ha!

Big Daddy nods.

—But Skipper, he had some fever which came back on him which doctors couldn't explain and I got that injury—turned out to be just a shadow on the X-ray plate—and a touch of bursitis. . . .

I lay in a hospital bed, watched our games on TV, saw Maggie on the bench next to Skipper when he was hauled out of a game for stumbles, fumbles!—Burned me up the way she hung on his arm!—Y'know, I think that Maggie had always felt sort of left out because she and me never got any closer together than two people just get in bed, which is not much closer than two cats on a—fence humping. . . .

So! She took this time to work on poor dumb Skipper. He was a less than average student at Ole Miss, you know that, don't you?!—Poured in his mind the dirty, false idea that what we were, him and me, was a frustrated case of that ole pair of sisters that lived in this room, Jack Straw and Peter Ochello!—He, poor Skipper, went to bed with Maggie to prove it wasn't true, and when it didn't work out, he thought it *was* true!—Skipper broke in two like a rotten stick—nobody ever turned so fast to a lush—or died of it so quick. . . .

—Now are you satisfied?

Big Daddy has listened to this story, dividing the grain from the chaff. Now he looks at his son.

BIG DADDY   Are *you* satisfied?
BRICK   With what?
BIG DADDY   That half-ass story!
BRICK   What's half-ass about it?
BIG DADDY   Something's left out of that story. What did you leave out?

The phone has started ringing in the hall.

GOOPER [*off stage*]   Hello.

As if it reminded him of something, Brick glances suddenly toward the sound and says:

BRICK   Yes!—I left out a long-distance call which I had from Skipper—
GOOPER   Speaking, go ahead.
BRICK   —In which he made a drunken confession to me and on which I hung up!
GOOPER   No.
BRICK   —Last time we spoke to each other in our lives . . .
GOOPER   No, sir.
BIG DADDY   You musta said something to him before you hung up.
BRICK   What could I say to him?
BIG DADDY   Anything. Something.
BRICK   Nothing.
BIG DADDY   Just hung up?
BRICK   Just hung up.
BIG DADDY   Uh-huh. Anyhow now!—we have tracked down the lie with which you're disgusted and which you are drinking to kill your disgust with, Brick. You been passing the buck. This disgust with mendacity is disgust with yourself.

You!—dug the grave of your friend and kicked him in it!—before you'd
face truth with him!

BRICK   *His* truth, not *mine!*

BIG DADDY   His truth, okay! But you wouldn't face it with him!

BRICK   Who *can* face truth? Can *you?*

BIG DADDY   Now don't start passin' the rotten buck again, boy!

BRICK   *How about these birthday congratulations, these many, many happy
returns of the day, when ev'rybody knows there won't be any except you!*

*Gooper, who has answered the hall phone, lets out a high, shrill laugh; the voice
becomes audible saying: "No, no, you got it all wrong! Upside down! Are you
crazy?"*

*Brick suddenly catches his breath as he realizes that he has made a shocking
disclosure. He hobbles a few paces, then freezes, and without looking at his
father's shocked face, says:*

Let's, let's—go out, now, and—watch the fireworks. Come on, Big
Daddy.

*Big Daddy moves suddenly forward and grabs hold of the boy's crutch like it was a
weapon for which they were fighting for possession.*

BIG DADDY   Oh, no, no! No one's going out! What did you start to say?

BRICK   I don't remember.

BIG DADDY   "Many happy returns when they know there won't be any"?

BRICK   Aw, hell, Big Daddy, forget it. Come on out on the gallery and look at
the fireworks they're shooting off for your birthday. . . .

BIG DADDY   First you finish that remark you were makin' before you cut off.
"Many happy returns when they know there won't be any"?—Ain't that
what you just said?

BRICK   Look, now. I can get around without that crutch if I have to but it
would be a lot easier on the furniture an' glassware if I didn' have to
go swinging along like Tarzan of th'—

BIG DADDY   FINISH! WHAT YOU WAS SAYIN'!

An eerie green glow shows in sky behind him.

BRICK [*sucking the ice in his glass, speech becoming thick*]   Leave th' place to
Gooper and Mae an' their five little same little monkeys. All I want is—

BIG DADDY   "LEAVE TH' PLACE," did you say?

BRICK [*vaguely*]   All twenty-eight thousand acres of the richest land this side
of the valley Nile.

BIG DADDY   Who said I was "leaving the place" to Gooper or anybody? This

is my sixty-fifth birthday! I got fifteen years or twenty years left in me!
I'll outlive *you!* I'll bury you an' have to pay for your coffin!

BRICK   Sure. Many happy returns. Now let's go watch the fireworks, come
on, let's—

BIG DADDY   Lying, have they been lying? About the report from th'—clinic?
Did they, did they—find something——*Cancer.* Maybe?

BRICK   Mendacity is a system that we live in. Liquor is one way out an'
death's the other. . . .

*He takes the crutch from Big Daddy's loose grip and swings out on the gallery
leaving the doors open.*

A song, "Pick a Bale of Cotton," is heard.

MAE *[appearing in door]*   *Oh, Big Daddy, the field hands are singin' fo' you!*

BRICK   I'm sorry, Big Daddy. My head don't work any more and it's hard for
me to understand how anybody could care if he lived or died or was
dying or cared about anything but whether or not there was liquor left in
the bottle and so I said what I said without thinking. In some ways I'm
no better than the others, in some ways worse because I'm less alive.
Maybe it's being alive that makes them lie, and being almost *not* alive
makes me sort of accidentally truthful—I don't know but—anyway—
we've been friends . . .

—And being friends is telling each other the truth. . . .

There is a pause.

You told *me!* I told *you!*

BIG DADDY *[slowly and passionately]*   CHRIST—DAMN—

GOOPER *[off stage]*   Let her go!

Fireworks off stage right.

BIG DADDY   —ALL—LYING SONS OF—LYING BITCHES!

*He straightens at last and crosses to the inside door. At the door he turns and looks
back as if he had some desperate question he couldn't put into words. Then he nods
reflectively and says in a hoarse voice:*

Yes, all liars, all liars, all lying dying liars!

This is said slowly, slowly, with a fierce revulsion. He goes on out.

—Lying! Dying! Liars!

Brick remains motionless as the lights dim out and the curtain falls.

Curtain

ACT III

There is no lapse of time. Big Daddy is seen leaving as at the end of ACT II.

BIG DADDY   ALL LYIN'—DYIN'!—LIARS! LIARS!—LIARS!

Margaret enters.

MARGARET   Brick, what in the name of God was goin' on in this room?

Dixie and Trixie enter through the doors and circle around Margaret shouting. Mae enters from the lower gallery window.

MAE   Dixie, Trixie, you quit that!

Gooper enters through the doors.

Gooper, will y' please get these kiddies to bed right now!
GOOPER   Mae, you seen Big Mama?
MAE   Not yet.

Gooper and kids exit through the doors. Reverend Tooker enters through the windows.

REVEREND TOOKER   Those kiddies are so full of vitality. I think I'll have to be starting back to town.
MAE   Not yet, Preacher. You know we regard you as a member of this family, one of our closest an' dearest, so you just got t' be with us when Doc Baugh gives Big Mama th' actual truth about th' report from the clinic.
MARGARET   Where do you think you're going?
BRICK   Out for some air.
MARGARET   Why'd Big Daddy shout "Liars"?
MAE   Has Big Daddy gone to bed, Brick?

GOOPER [*entering*]   Now where is that old lady?

REVEREND TOOKER   I'll look for her.   [*He exits to the gallery.*]

MAE   Cain'tcha find her, Gooper?

GOOPER   She's avoidin' this talk.

MAE   I think she senses somethin'.

MARGARET [*going out on the gallery to Brick*]   Brick, they're goin' to tell Big
Mama the truth about Big Daddy and she's goin' to need you.

DOCTOR BAUGH   This is going to be painful.

MAE   Painful things caint always be avoided.

REVEREND TOOKER   I see Big Mama.

GOOPER   Hey, Big Mama, come here.

MAE   Hush, Gooper, don't holler.

BIG MAMA [*entering*]   Too much smell of burnt fireworks makes me feel a
little bit sick at my stomach.—Where is Big Daddy?

MAE   That's what I want to know, where has Big Daddy gone?

BIG MAMA   He must have turned in, I reckon he went to baid . . .

GOOPER   Well, then, now we can talk.

BIG MAMA   What *is* this talk, *what* talk?

Margaret appears on the gallery, talking to Doctor Baugh.

MARGARET [*musically*]   My family freed their slaves ten years before aboli-
tion. My great-great-grandfather gave his slaves their freedom five years
before the War between the States started!

MAE   Oh, for God's sake! Maggie's climbed back up in her family tree!

MARGARET [*sweetly*]   What, Mae?

The pace must be very quick: great Southern animation.

BIG MAMA [*addressing them all*]   I think Big Daddy was just worn out. He
loves his family, he loves to have them around him, but it's a strain on
his nerves. He wasn't himself tonight, Big Daddy wasn't himself, I could
tell he was all worked up.

REVEREND TOOKER   I think he's remarkable.

BIG MAMA   Yaisss! Just remarkable. Did you all notice the food he ate at that
table? Did you all notice the supper he put away? Why he ate like a
hawss!

GOOPER   I hope he doesn't regret it.

BIG MAMA   What? Why that man—ate a huge piece of cawn bread with
molasses on it! Helped himself twice to hoppin' John.

MARGARET   Big Daddy loves hoppin' John.—We had a real country dinner.

BIG MAMA [*overlapping Margaret*]   Yaiss, he simply adores it! an' candied
yams? Son? That man put away enough food at that table to stuff a *field*
hand!

GOOPER [*with grim relish*]   I hope he don't have to pay for it later on . . .

BIG MAMA [*fiercely*]   What's *that*, Gooper?

MAE   Gooper says he hopes Big Daddy doesn't suffer tonight.

BIG MAMA   Oh, shoot, Gooper says, Gooper says! Why should Big Daddy suffer for satisfying a normal appetite? There's nothin' wrong with that man but nerves, he's sound as a dollar! And now he knows he is an' that's why he ate such a supper. He had a big load off his mind, knowin' he wasn't doomed t'—what he thought he was doomed to . . .

MARGARET [*sadly and sweetly*]   Bless his old sweet soul . . .

BIG MAMA [*vaguely*]   Yais, bless his heart, where's Brick?

MAE   Outside.

GOOPER   —Drinkin' . . .

BIG MAMA   I know he's drinkin'. Cain't I see he's drinkin' without you continually tellin' me that boy's drinkin'?

MARGARET   Good for you, Big Mama! [*She applauds.*]

BIG MAMA   Other people *drink* and *have* drunk an' will *drink*, as long as they make that stuff an' put it in bottles.

MARGARET   That's the truth. I never trusted a man that didn't drink.

BIG MAMA   *Brick? Brick!*

MARGARET   He's still on the gall'ry. I'll go bring him in so we can talk.

BIG MAMA [*Worriedly*]   I don't know what this mysterious family conference is about.

Awkward silence. Big Mama looks from face to face, then belches slightly and mutters, "Excuse me . . ." She opens an ornamental fan suspended about her throat. A black lace fan to go with her black lace gown, and fans her wilting corsage, sniffing nervously and looking from face to face in the uncomfortable silence as Margaret calls "Brick?" and Brick sings to the moon on the gallery.

MARGARET   Brick, they're gonna tell Big Mama the truth an' she's gonna need you.

BIG MAMA   I don't know what's wrong here, you all have such long faces! Open that door on the hall and let some air circulate through here, will you please, Gooper?

MAE   I think we'd better leave that door closed, Big Mama, till after the talk.

MARGARET   Brick!

BIG MAMA   Reveren' Tooker, will *you* please open that door?

REVEREND TOOKER   I sure will, Big Mama.

MAE   I just didn't think we ought t' take any chance of Big Daddy hearin' a word of this discussion.

BIG MAMA   *I swan!* Nothing's going to be said in Big Daddy's house that he caint hear if he want to!

GOOPER   Well, Big Mama, it's—

Mae gives him a quick, hard poke to shut him up. He glares at her fiercely as she circles before him like a burlesque ballerina, raising her skinny bare arms over her head, jangling her bracelets, exclaiming:

MAE   *A breeze! A breeze!*

REVEREND TOOKER   I think this house is the coolest house in the Delta.—Did you all know that Halsey Banks's widow put air-conditioning units in the church and rectory at Friar's Point in memory of Halsey?

General conversation has resumed; everybody is chatting so that the stage sounds like a bird cage.

GOOPER   Too bad nobody cools your church off for you. I bet you sweat in that pulpit these hot Sundays, Reverend Tooker.

REVEREND TOOKER   Yes, my vestments are drenched. Last Sunday the gold in my chasuble faded into the purple.

GOOPER   Reveren', you musta been preachin' hell's fire last Sunday.

MAE   [*at the same time to Doctor Baugh*]   You reckon those vitamin B12 injections are what they're cracked up t' be, Doc Baugh?

DOCTOR BAUGH   Well, if you want to be stuck with something I guess they're as good to be stuck with as anything else.

BIG MAMA   [*at the gallery door*]   Maggie, Maggie, aren't you comin' with Brick?

MAE   [*suddenly and loudly, creating a silence*]   I have a strange feeling, I have a peculiar feeling!

BIG MAMA   [*turning from the gallery*]   What feeling?

MAE   That Brick said somethin' he shouldn't of said t' Big Daddy.

BIG MAMA   Now what on earth could Brick of said t' Big Daddy that he shouldn't say?

GOOPER   Big Mama, there's somethin'—

MAE   NOW, WAIT!

She rushes up to Big Mama and gives her a quick hug and kiss. Big Mama pushes her impatiently off.

DOCTOR BAUGH   In my day they had what they call the Keeley cure for heavy drinkers.

BIG MAMA   Shoot!

DOCTOR BAUGH   But now I understand they just take some kind of tablets.

GOOPER   They call them "Annie Bust" tablets.

BIG MAMA   *Brick* don't need to take *nothin'*.

Brick and Margaret appear in gallery doors, Big Mama unaware of his presence behind her.

That boy is just broken up over Skipper's death. You know how poor Skipper died. They gave him a big, big dose of that sodium amytal stuff at his home and then they called the ambulance and give him another big, big dose of it at the hospital and that and all of the alcohol in his system fo' months an' months just proved too much for his heart . . . I'm scared of needles! I'm more scared of a needle than the knife . . . I think more people have been needled out of this world than— [*She stops short and wheels about.*]
Oh—here's Brick! My precious baby—

She turns upon Brick with short, fat arms extended, at the same time uttering a loud, short sob, which is both comic and touching. Brick smiles and bows slightly, making a burlesque gesture of gallantry for Margaret to pass before him into the room. Then he hobbles on his crutch directly to the liquor cabinet and there is absolute silence, with everybody looking at Brick as everybody has always looked at Brick when he spoke or moved or appeared. One by one he drops ice cubes in his glass, then suddenly, but not quickly, looks back over his shoulder with a wry, charming smile, and says:

BRICK   I'm sorry! Anyone else?
BIG MAMA [*sadly*]   No, son. I *wish* you wouldn't!
BRICK   I wish I didn't have to, Big Mama, but I'm still waiting for that click in my head which makes it all smooth out!
BIG MAMA   Ow, Brick, you—BREAK MY HEART!
MARGARET [*at same time*]   Brick, go sit with Big Mama!
BIG MAMA   I just cain't staiiiiii-nnnnnnnd-it . . . [*She sobs.*]
MAE   Now that we're all assembled—
GOOPER   We kin talk . . .
BIG MAMA   Breaks my heart . . .
MARGARET   Sit with Big Mama, Brick, and hold her hand.

Big Mama sniffs very loudly three times, almost like three drumbeats in the pocket of silence.

BRICK   You do that, Maggie. I'm a restless cripple. I got to stay on my crutch.

Brick hobbles to the gallery door; leans there as if waiting.

Mae sits beside Big Mama, while Gooper moves in front and sits on the end of the couch, facing her. Reverend Tooker moves nervously into the space between them; on the other side, Doctor Baugh stands looking at nothing in particular and lights a cigar. Margaret turns away.

BIG MAMA   Why're you all *surroundin'* me—like this? Why're you all starin' at me like this an' makin' signs at each other?

Reverend Tooker steps back startled.

MAE   Calm yourself, Big Mama.

BIG MAMA   Calm you'self, *you'self*, Sister Woman. How could I calm myself with everyone starin' at me as if big drops of blood had broken out on m'face? What's this all about, annh! What?

Gooper coughs and takes a center position.

GOOPER   Now, Doc Baugh.

MAE   Doc Baugh?

GOOPER   Big Mama wants to know the complete truth about the report we got from the Ochsner Clinic.

MAE [*eagerly*]   —on Big Daddy's condition!

GOOPER   Yais, on Big Daddy's condition, we got to face it.

DOCTOR BAUGH   Well . . .

BIG MAMA [*terrified, rising*]   Is there? Something? Something that I? Don't—know?

In these few words, this startled, very soft, question, Big Mama reviews the history of her forty-five years with Big Daddy, her great almost embarrassingly true-hearted and simple-minded devotion to Big Daddy, who must have had something Brick has, who made himself loved so much by the "simple expedient" of not loving enough to disturb his charming detachment, also once coupled, like Brick, with virile beauty.

Big Mama has a dignity at this moment; she almost stops being fat.

DOCTOR BAUGH [*after a pause, uncomfortably*]   Yes?—Well—

BIG MAMA   I!!!—want to—*knowwwwww* . . .

Immediately she thrusts her fist to her mouth as if to deny that statement. Then for some curious reason, she snatches the withered corsage from her breast and hurls it on the floor and steps on it with her short, fat feet.

Somebody must be lyin'!—I want to know!

MAE   Sit down, Big Mama, sit down on this sofa.

MARGARET   Brick, go sit with Big Mama.

BIG MAMA   *What is it, what is it?*

DOCTOR BAUGH   I never have seen a more thorough examination than Big
    Daddy Pollitt was given in all my experience with the Ochsner Clinic.
GOOPER   It's one of the best in the country.
MAE   It's THE best in the country—bar *none*!

*For some reason she gives Gooper a violent poke as she goes past him. He slaps at
her hand without removing his eyes from his mother's face.*

DOCTOR BAUGH   Of course they were ninety-nine and nine-tenths per cent
    sure before they even started.
BIG MAMA   Sure of what, sure of what, sure of—*what?—what?*

*She catches her breath in a startled sob. Mae kisses her quickly. She thrusts Mae
fiercely away from her, staring at the Doctor.*

MAE   Mommy, be a brave girl!
BRICK   [*in the doorway, softly*]   "By the light, by the light, Of the sil-ve-ry
    mo-oo-n . . ."
GOOPER   Shut up!—Brick.
BRICK   Sorry . . .   [*He wanders out on the gallery.*]
DOCTOR BAUGH   But now, you see, Big Mama, they cut a piece off this
    growth, a specimen of the tissue and—
BIG MAMA   Growth? You told Big Daddy—
DOCTOR BAUGH   Now wait.
BIG MAMA   [*fiercely*]   You told me and Big Daddy there wasn't a thing wrong
    with him but—
MAE   Big Mama, they always—
GOOPER   Let Doc Baugh talk, will yuh?
BIG MAMA   —little spastic condition of—[*Her breath gives out in a sob.*]
DOCTOR BAUGH   Yes, that's what we told Big Daddy. But we had this bit of
    tissue run through the laboratory and I'm sorry to say the test was
    positive on it. It's—well—malignant . . .

Pause.

BIG MAMA   —Cancer?! Cancer?!

Doctor Baugh nods gravely. Big Mama gives a long gasping cry.

MAE AND GOOPER   Now, now, now, Big Mama, you had to know . . .
BIG MAMA   WHY DIDN'T THEY CUT IT OUT OF HIM? HANH? HANH?
DOCTOR BAUGH   Involved too much, Big Mama, too many organs affected.
MAE   Big Mama, the liver's affected and so's the kidneys, both! It's gone way
    past what they call a—

GOOPER A surgical risk.

MAE —Uh-huh . . .

Big Mama draws a breath like a dying gasp.

REVEREND TOOKER Tch, tch, tch, tch, tch!

DOCTOR BAUGH Yes it's gone past the knife.

MAE *That's why he's turned yellow, Mommy!*

BIG MAMA *Git away from me, git away from me, Mae!* [*She rises abruptly.*] I want Brick! Where's Brick? Where is my only son?

MAE Mama! Did she say "*only son*"?

GOOPER What does that make *me*?

MAE A sober responsible man with five precious children!—*Six!*

BIG MAMA I want Brick to tell me! Brick! Brick!

MARGARET [*rising from her reflections in a corner*] Brick was so upset he went back out.

BIG MAMA *Brick!*

MARGARET Mama, let *me* tell you!

BIG MAMA No, no, leave me alone, you're not my blood!

GOOPER *Mama, I'm your son!* Listen to *me!*

MAE Gooper's your son, he's your first-born!

BIG MAMA Gooper never liked Daddy.

MAE [*as if terribly shocked*] *That's not TRUE!*

There is a pause. The minister coughs and rises.

REVEREND TOOKER [*to Mae*] I think I'd better slip away at this point. [*Discreetly*] Good night, good night, everybody, and God bless you all . . . on this place . . .

He slips out.

Mae coughs and points at Big Mama.

DOCTOR BAUGH Well, Big Mama . . . [*He sighs.*]

BIG MAMA It's all a mistake, I know it's just a bad dream.

DOCTOR BAUGH We're gonna keep Big Daddy as comfortable as we can.

BIG MAMA Yes, it's just a bad dream, that's all it is, it's just an awful dream.

GOOPER In my opinion Big Daddy is having some pain but won't admit that he has it.

BIG MAMA Just a dream, a bad dream.

DOCTOR BAUGH That's what lots of them do, they think if they don't admit they're having the pain they can sort of escape the fact of it.

GOOPER [*with relish*] Yes, they get sly about it, they get real sly about it.

MAE   Gooper and I think—

GOOPER   Shut up, Mae! Big Mama, I think—Big Daddy ought to be started on morphine.

BIG MAMA   Nobody's going to give Big Daddy morphine.

DOCTOR BAUGH   Now, Big Mama, when that pain strikes it's going to strike mighty hard and Big Daddy's going to need the needle to bear it.

BIG MAMA   I tell you, nobody's going to give him morphine.

MAE   Big Mama, you don't want to see Big Daddy suffer, you know you—

Gooper, standing beside her, gives her a savage poke.

DOCTOR BAUGH [*placing a package on the table*]   I'm leaving this stuff here, so if there's a sudden attack you all won't have to send out for it.

MAE   I know how to give a hypo.

BIG MAMA   Nobody's gonna give Big Daddy morphine.

GOOPER   Mae took a course in nursing during the war.

MARGARET   Somehow I don't think Big Daddy would want Mae to give him a hypo.

MAE   You think he'd want *you* to do it?

DOCTOR BAUGH   Well . . .

Doctor Baugh rises.

GOOPER   Doctor Baugh is goin'.

DOCTOR BAUGH   Yes, I got to be goin'. Well, keep your chin up, Big Mama.

GOOPER [*with jocularity*]   She's gonna keep *both* chins up, aren't you, Big Mama?

Big Mama sobs.

Now stop that, Big Mama.

GOOPER [*at the door with Doctor Baugh*]   Well, Doc, we sure do appreciate all you done. I'm telling you, we're surely obligated to you for—

Doctor Baugh has gone out without a glance at him.

—I guess that doctor has got a lot on his mind but it wouldn't hurt him to act a little more human . . .

Big Mama sobs.

Now be a brave girl, Mommy.

BIG MAMA   It's not true, I know that it's just not true!

GOOPER   Mama, those tests are infallible!

BIG MAMA   Why are you so determined to see your father daid?

MAE   Big Mama!

MARGARET [*gently*]   I know what Big Mama means.

MAE [*fiercely*]   Oh, do you?

MARGARET [*quietly and very sadly*]   Yes, I think I do.

MAE   For a newcomer in the family you sure do show a lot of understanding.

MARGARET   Understanding is needed on this place.

MAE   I guess you must have needed a lot of it in your family, Maggie, with your father's liquor problem and now you've got Brick with his!

MARGARET   Brick does not have a liquor problem at all. Brick is devoted to Big Daddy. This thing is a terrible strain on him.

BIG MAMA   Brick is Big Daddy's boy, but he drinks too much and it worries me and Big Daddy, and, Margaret, you've got to cooperate with us, you've got to co-operate with Big Daddy and me in getting Brick straightened out. Because it will break Big Daddy's heart if Brick don't pull himself together and take hold of things.

MAE   Take hold of *what* things, Big Mama?

BIG MAMA   The place.

There is a quick violent look between Mae and Gooper.

GOOPER   Big Mama, you've had a shock.

MAE   Yais, we've all had a shock, but . . .

GOOPER   Let's be realistic—

MAE   —Big Daddy would never, would *never*, be foolish enough to—

GOOPER   —put this place in irresponsible hands!

BIG MAMA   Big Daddy ain't going to leave the place in anybody's hands; Big Daddy is *not* going to die. I want you to get that in your heads, all of you!

MAE   Mommy, Mommy, Big Mama, we're just as hopeful an' optimistic as you are about Big Daddy's prospects, we have faith in *prayer*—but nevertheless there are certain matters that have to be discussed an' dealt with, because otherwise—

GOOPER   Eventualities have to be considered and now's the time . . . Mae, will you please get my brief case out of our room?

MAE   Yes, honey.   [*She rises and goes out through the hall door.*]

GOOPER [*standing over Big Mama*]   Now, Big Mom. What you said just now was not at all true and you know it. I've always loved Big Daddy in my own quiet way. I never made a show of it, and I know that Big Daddy has always been fond of me in a quiet way, too, and he never made a show of it neither.

Mae returns with Gooper's brief case.

MAE   Here's your brief case, Gooper, honey.

GOOPER [*handing the brief case back to her*] Thank you . . . Of cou'se, my relationship with Big Daddy is different from Brick's.

MAE You're eight years older'n Brick an' always had t' carry a bigger load of th' responsibilities than Brick ever had t' carry. He never carried a thing in his life but a football or a highball.

GOOPER Mae, will y' let me talk, please?

MAE Yes, honey.

GOOPER Now, a twenty-eight-thousand-acre plantation's a mighty big thing t' run.

MAE Almost singlehanded.

Margaret has gone out onto the gallery and can be heard calling softly to Brick.

BIG MAMA You never had to run this place! What are you talking about? As if Big Daddy was dead and in his grave, you had to run it? Why, you just helped him out with a few business details and had your law practice at the same time in Memphis!

MAE Oh, Mommy, Mommy, Big Mommy! Let's be fair!

MARGARET Brick!

MAE Why, Gooper has given himself body and soul to keeping this place up for the past five years since Big Daddy's health started failing.

MARGARET Brick!

MAE Gooper won't say it, Gooper never thought of it as a duty, he just did it. And what did Brick do? Brick kept living in his past glory at college! Still a football player at twenty-seven!

MARGARET [*returning alone*] Who are you talking about now? Brick? A football player? He isn't a football player and you know it. Brick is a sports announcer on T.V. and one of the best-known ones in the country!

MAE I'm talking about what he was.

MARGARET Well, I wish you would just stop talking about my husband.

GOOPER I've got a right to discuss my brother with other members of MY OWN family, which don't include *you*. Why don't you go out there and drink with Brick?

MARGARET I've never seen such malice toward a brother.

GOOPER How about his for me? Why, he can't stand to be in the same room with me!

MARGARET This is a deliberate campaign of vilification for the most disgusting and sordid reason on earth, and I know what it is! It's *avarice, greed, greed!*

BIG MAMA Oh, I'll scream! I will scream in a moment unless this stops!

Gooper has stalked up to Margaret with clenched fists at his sides as if he would strike her. Mae distorts her face again into a hideous grimace behind Margaret's back.

BIG MAMA [*sobs*]   Margaret. Child. Come here. Sit next to Big Mama.
MARGARET   Precious Mommy. I'm sorry, I'm, sorry, I—!

She bends her long graceful neck to press her forehead to Big Mama's bulging shoulder under its black chiffon.

MAE   How beautiful, how touching, this display of devotion! Do you know why she's childless? She's childless because that big beautiful athlete husband of hers won't go to bed with her!
GOOPER   You jest won't let me do this in a nice way, will yah? Aw right—I don't give a goddam if Big Daddy likes me or don't like me or did or never did or will or will never! I'm just appealing to a sense of common decency and fair play. I'll tell you the truth. I've resented Big Daddy's partiality to Brick ever since Brick was born, and the way I've been treated like I was just barely good enough to spit on and sometimes not even good enough for that. Big Daddy is dying of cancer, and it's spread all through him and it's attacked all his vital organs including the kidneys and right now he is sinking into uremia, and you all know what uremia is, it's poisoning of the whole system due to the failure of the body to eliminate its poisons.
MARGARET   [*to herself, downstage, hissingly*] *Poisons, poisons! Venomous thoughts and words! In hearts and minds!—That's poisons!*
GOOPER   [*overlapping her*] I am asking for a square deal, and, by God, I expect to get one. But if I don't get one, if there's any peculiar shenanigans going on around here behind my back, well, I'm not a corporation lawyer for nothing, I know how to protect my own interests.

Brick enters from the gallery with a tranquil, blurred smile, carrying an empty glass with him.

BRICK   Storm coming up.
GOOPER   Oh! A late arrival!
MAE   Behold the conquering hero comes!
GOOPER   The fabulous Brick Pollitt! Remember him?—Who could forget him!
MAE   He looks like he's been injured in a game!
GOOPER   Yep, I'm afraid you'll have to warm the bench at the Sugar Bowl this year, Brick!

Mae laughs shrilly.

Or was it the Rose Bowl that he made that famous run in?—

Thunder.

MAE   The punch bowl, honey. It was in the punch bowl, the cut-glass punch
   bowl!

GOOPER   Oh, that's right, I'm getting the bowls mixed up!

MARGARET   Why don't you stop venting your malice and envy on a sick boy?

BIG MAMA   *Now you two hush, I mean it, hush, all of you, hush!*

DAISY, SOOKEY   Storm! Storm comin'! Storm! Storm!

LACEY   Brightie, close them shutters.

GOOPER   Lacey, put the top up on my Cadillac, will yuh?

LACEY   Yes, suh, Mistah Pollitt!

GOOPER   [*at the same time*].   Big Mama, you know it's necessary for me t' go
   back to Memphis in th' mornin' t' represent the Parker estate in a
   lawsuit.

Mae sits on the bed and arranges papers she has taken from the brief case.

BIG MAMA   Is it, Gooper?

MAE   Yaiss.

GOOPER   That's why I'm forced to—to bring up a problem that—

MAE   Somethin' that's too important t' be put off!

GOOPER   If Brick was sober, he ought to be in on this.

MARGARET   Brick is present; we're present.

GOOPER   Well, good. I will now give you this outline my partner, Tom
   Bullitt, an' me have drawn up—a sort of dummy—trusteeship.

MARGARET   Oh, that's it! You'll be in charge an' dole out remittances, will
   you?

GOOPER   This we did as soon as we got the report on Big Daddy from th'
   Ochsner Laboratories. We did this thing, I mean we drew up this
   dummy outline with the advice and assistance of the Chairman of the
   Boa'd of Directors of th' Southern Plantahs Bank and Trust Company in
   Memphis, C. C. Bellowes, a man who handles estates for all th'
   prominent fam'lies in West Tennessee and th' Delta.

BIG MAMA   Gooper?

GOOPER   [*crouching in front of Big Mama*]   Now this is not—not final, or
   anything like it. This is just a preliminary outline. But it does provide a
   basis—a design—a—possible, feasible—*plan!*

MARGARET   Yes, I'll bet it's a plan.

Thunder.

MAE   It's a plan to protect the biggest estate in the Delta from irresponsibility an'—

BIG MAMA   Now you listen to me, all of you, you listen here! They's not
   goin' to be any more catty talk in my house! And Gooper, you put that
   away before I grab it out of your hand and tear it right up! I don't know

what the hell's in it, and I don't want to know what the hell's in it. I'm
talkin' in Big Daddy's language now; I'm his *wife* not his *widow*, I'm still
his *wife!* And I'm talkin' to you in his language an'—

GOOPER   Big Mama, what I have here is—

MAE [*at the same time*]   Gooper explained that it's just a plan . . .

BIG MAMA   I don't care what you got there. Just put it back where it came
from, an' don't let me see it again, not even the outside of the envelope
of it! Is that understood? Basis! Plan! Preliminary! Design! I say—what is
it Big Daddy always says when he's disgusted?

BRICK [*from the bar*]   Big Daddy says "crap" when he's disgusted.

BIG MAMA [*rising*]   That's right—CRAP! I say CRAP too, like Big Daddy!

Thunder.

MAE   Coarse language doesn't seem called for in this—

GOOPER   Somethin' in me is *deeply outraged* by hearin' you talk like this.

BIG MAMA   *Nobody's goin' to take nothin'!*—till Big Daddy lets go of it—
maybe, just possibly, not—not even then! No, not even then!

Thunder.

MAE   Sookey, hurry up an' git that po'ch furniture covahed; want th' paint
to come off?

GOOPER   Lacey, put mah car away!

LACEY   Caint, Mistah Pollitt, you got the keys!

GOOPER   Naw, you got 'em, man. Where th' keys to th' car, honey?

MAE   You got 'em in your pocket!

BRICK   "You can always hear me singin' this song, Show me the way to go
home."

Thunder distantly.

BIG MAMA   Brick! Come here, Brick, I need you. Tonight Brick looks like he
used to look when he was a little boy, just like he did when he played
wild games and used to come home when I hollered myself hoarse for
him, all sweaty and pink cheeked and sleepy, with his—red curls
shining . . .

*Brick draws aside as he does from all physical contact and continues the song in a
whisper, opening the ice bucket and dropping in the ice cubes one by one as if he
were mixing some important chemical formula.*

Distant thunder.

Time goes by so fast. Nothin' can outrun it. Death commences too early—almost before you're half acquainted with life—you meet the other . . . Oh, you know we just got to love each other an' stay together, all of us, just as close as we can, especially now that such a *black* thing has come and moved into this place without invitation.

Awkwardly embracing Brick, she presses her head to his shoulder.

A dog howls off stage.

Oh, Brick, son of Big Daddy, Big Daddy does so love you. Y'know what would be his fondest dream come true? If before he passed on, if Big Daddy has to pass on . . .

A dog howls.

. . . you give him a child of yours, a grandson as much like his son as his son is like Big Daddy . . .

MARGARET   I know that's Big Daddy's dream.

BIG MAMA   That's his dream.

MAE   Such a pity that Maggie and Brick can't oblige.

BIG DADDY [*off down stage right on the gallery*]   Looks like the wind was takin' liberties with this place.

SERVANT [*off stage*]   Yes, sir, Mr. Pollitt.

MARGARET [*crossing to the right door*]   Big Daddy's on the gall'ry.

Big Mama has turned toward the hall door at the sound of Big Daddy's voice on the gallery.

BIG MAMA   I can't stay here. He'll see somethin' in my eyes.

Big Daddy enters the room from up stage right.

BIG DADDY   Can I come in?

He puts his cigar in an ash tray.

MARGARET   Did the storm wake you up, Big Daddy?

BIG DADDY   Which stawm are you talkin' about—th' one outside or th' hullballoo in here?

Gooper squeezes past Big Daddy.

GOOPER   'Scuse me.

Mae tries to squeeze past Big Daddy to join Gooper, but Big Daddy puts his arm firmly around her.

BIG DADDY   I heard some mighty loud talk. Sounded like somethin' impor-
tant was bein' discussed. What was the powwow about?
MAE [*flustered*]   Why—nothin', Big Daddy . . .
BIG DADDY [*crossing to extreme left center, taking Mae with him*]   What is that
pregnant-lookin' envelope you're puttin' back in your brief case,
Gooper?
GOOPER [*at the foot of the bed, caught, as he stuffs papers into envelope*]   That?
Nothin', suh—nothin' much of anythin' at all . . .
BIG DADDY   Nothin'? It looks like a whole lot of nothin'!

He turns up stage to the group.

You all know th' story about th' young married couple—
GOOPER   Yes, sir!
BIG DADDY   Hello, Brick—
BRICK   Hello, Big Daddy.

The group is arranged in a semicircle above Big Daddy, Margaret at the extreme right, then Mae and Gooper, then Big Mama, with Brick at the left.

BIG DADDY   Young married couple took Junior out to th' zoo one Sunday,
inspected all of God's creatures in their cages, with satisfaction.
GOOPER   Satisfaction.
BIG DADDY [*crossing to up stage center, facing front*]   This afternoon was a
warm afternoon in spring an' that ole elephant had somethin' else on his
mind which was bigger'n peanuts. You know this story, Brick?

Gooper nods.

BRICK   No, sir, I don't know it.
BIG DADDY   Y'see, in th' cage adjoinin' they was a young female elephant in
heat!
BIG MAMA [*at Big Daddy's shoulder*]   Oh, Big Daddy!
BIG DADDY   What's the matter, preacher's gone, ain't he? All right. That
female elephant in the next cage was permeatin' the atmosphere about
her with a powerful and excitin' odor of female fertility! Huh! Ain't that
a nice way to put it, Brick?
BRICK   Yes, sir, nothin' wrong with it.
BIG DADDY   Brick says th's nothin' wrong with it!
BIG MAMA   Oh, Big Daddy!
BIG DADDY [*crossing to down stage center*]   So this ole bull elephant still had a

couple of fornications left in him. He reared back his trunk an' got a whiff of that elephant lady next door!—began to paw at the dirt in his cage an' butt his head against the separatin' partition and, first thing y'know, there was a conspicuous change in his *profile*—very *conspicuous!* Ain't I tellin' this story in decent language, Brick?

BRICK Yes, sir, too fuckin' decent!

BIG DADDY So, the little boy pointed at it and said, "What's that?" His mama said, "Oh, that's—nothin'!"—His papa said, "She's spoiled!"

Big Daddy crosses to Brick at left.

You didn't laugh at that story, Brick.

Big Mama crosses to down stage right crying. Margaret goes to her. Mae and Gooper hold up stage right center.

BRICK No, sir, I didn't laugh at that story.

BIG DADDY What is the smell in this room? Don't you notice it, Brick? Don't you notice a powerful and obnoxious odor of mendacity in this room?

BRICK Yes, sir, I think I do, sir.

GOOPER Mae, Mae . . .

BIG DADDY There is nothing more powerful. Is there, Brick?

BRICK No, sir. No, sir, there isn't, an' nothin' more obnoxious.

BIG DADDY Brick agrees with me. The odor of mendacity is a powerful and obnoxious odor an' the stawm hasn't blown it away from this room yet. You notice it, Gooper?

GOOPER What, sir?

BIG DADDY How about you, Sister Woman? You notice the unpleasant odor of mendacity in this room?

MAE Why, Big Daddy, I don't even know what that is.

BIG DADDY You can smell it. Hell it smells like death!

Big Mama sobs. Big Daddy looks toward her.

What's wrong with that fat woman over there, loaded with diamonds? Hey, what's-you-name, what's the matter with you?

MARGARET [*crossing toward Big Daddy*] She had a slight dizzy spell, Big Daddy.

BIG DADDY You better watch that, Big Mama. A stroke is a bad way to go.

MARGARET [*crossing to Big Daddy at center*] Oh, Brick, Big Daddy has on your birthday present to him, Brick, he has on your cashmere robe, the softest material I have ever felt.

BIG DADDY Yeah, this is my soft birthday, Maggie . . . Not my gold or my silver birthday, but my soft birthday, everything's got to be soft for Big Daddy on this soft birthday.

Maggie kneels before Big Daddy at center.

MARGARET   Big Daddy's got on his Chinese slippers that I gave him, Brick. Big Daddy, I haven't given you my big present yet, but now I will, now's the time for me to present it to you! I have an announcement to make!
MAE   What? What kind of announcement?
GOOPER   A sports announcement, Maggie?
MARGARET   Announcement of life beginning! A child is coming, sired by Brick, and out of Maggie the Cat! I have Brick's child in my body, an' that's my birthday present to Big Daddy on this birthday!

Big Daddy looks at Brick who crosses behind Big Daddy to down stage portal, left.

BIG DADDY   Get up, girl, get up off your knees, girl.

Big Daddy helps Margaret to rise. He crosses above her, to her right, bites off the end of a fresh cigar, taken from his bathrobe pocket, as he studies Margaret.

Uh-huh, this girl has life in her body, that's no lie!

BIG MAMA   BIG DADDY'S DREAM COME TRUE!
BRICK   JESUS!
BIG DADDY   [*crossing right below wicker stand*]   Gooper, I want my lawyer in the mornin'.
BRICK   Where are you goin', Big Daddy?
BIG DADDY   Son, I'm goin' up on the roof, to the belvedere on th' roof to look over my kingdom before I give up my kingdom—twenty-eight thousand acres of th' richest land this side of the valley Nile!

He exits through right doors, and down right on the gallery.

BIG MAMA   [*following*]   Sweetheart, sweetheart, sweetheart—can I come with you?

She exits down stage right.

Margaret is down stage center in the mirror area. Mae has joined Gooper and she gives him a fierce poke, making a low hissing sound and a grimace of fury.

GOOPER   [*pushing her aside*]   Brick, could you possibly spare me one small shot of that liquor?

BRICK   Why, help yourself, Gooper boy.

GOOPER   I will.

MAE [shrilly]   Of course we know that this is—a lie.

GOOPER   Be still, Mae.

MAE   I won't be still! I know she's made this up!

GOOPER   Goddam it, I said shut up!

MARGARET   Gracious! I didn't know that my little announcement was going to provoke such a storm!

MAE   That woman isn't pregnant!

GOOPER   Who said she was?

MAE   She did.

GOOPER   The doctor didn't. Doc Baugh didn't.

MARGARET   I haven't gone to Doc Baugh.

GOOPER   Then who'd you go to, Maggie?

MARGARET   One of the best gynecologists in the South.

GOOPER   Uh huh, uh huh!—I see . . . [He takes out a pencil and notebook.] —May we have his name, please?

MARGARET   No, you may not, Mister Prosecuting Attorney!

MAE   He doesn't have any name, he doesn't exist!

MARGARET   Oh, he exists all right, and so does my child, Brick's baby!

MAE   You can't conceive a child by a man that won't sleep with you unless you think you're—

Brick has turned on the phonograph. A scat song cuts Mae's speech.

GOOPER   Turn that off!

MAE   We know it's a lie because we hear you in here; he won't sleep with you, we hear you! So don't imagine you're going to put a trick over on us, to fool a dying man with a—

A long drawn cry of agony and rage fills the house. Margaret turns the phonograph down to a whisper. The cry is repeated.

MAE   Did you hear that, Gooper, did you hear that?

GOOPER   Sounds like the pain has struck.

MAE   Go see, Gooper!

GOOPER   Come along and leave these lovebirds together in their nest!

He goes out first. Mae follows but turns at the door, contorting her face and hissing at Margaret.

MAE   Liar!

She slams the door.

Margaret exhales with relief and moves a little unsteadily to catch hold of Brick's arm.

MARGARET   Thank you for—keeping still . . .
BRICK   O.K., Maggie.
MARGARET   It was gallant of you to save my face!

He now pours down three shots in quick succession and stands waiting, silent. All at once he turns with a smile and says:

BRICK   *There!*
MARGARET   What?
BRICK   The *click* . . .

His gratitude seems almost infinite as he hobbles out on the gallery with a drink. We hear his crutch as he swings out of sight. Then, at some distance, he begins singing to himself a peaceful song. Margaret holds the big pillow forlornly as if it were her only companion, for a few moments, then throws it on the bed. She rushes to the liquor cabinet, gathers all the bottles in her arms, turns about undecidedly, then runs out of the room with them, leaving the door ajar on the dim yellow hall. Brick is heard hobbling back along the gallery, singing his peaceful song. He comes back in, sees the pillow on the bed, laughs lightly, sadly, picks it up. He has it under his arm as Margaret returns to the room. Margaret softly shuts the door and leans against it, smiling softly at Brick.

MARGARET   Brick, I used to think that you were stronger than me and I didn't want to be overpowered by you. But now, since you've taken to liquor—you know what?—I guess it's bad, but now I'm stronger than you and I can love you more truly! Don't move that pillow. I'll move it right back if you do!—Brick?

She turns out all the lamps but a single rose-silk-shaded one by the bed.

I really have been to a doctor and I know what to do and—Brick?—this is my time by the calendar to conceive?
BRICK   Yes, I understand, Maggie. But how are you going to conceive a child by a man in love with his liquor?
MARGARET   By locking his liquor up and making him satisfy my desire before I unlock it!
BRICK   Is that what you've done, Maggie?

MARGARET   Look and see. That cabinet's mighty empty compared to before!
BRICK   Well, I'll be a son of a—

He reaches for his crutch but she beats him to it and rushes out on the gallery, hurls the crutch over the rail and comes back in, panting.

MARGARET   And so tonight we're going to make the lie true, and when that's done, I'll bring the liquor back here and we'll get drunk together, here, tonight, in this place that death has come into . . . —What do you say?
BRICK   I don't say anything. I guess there's nothing to say.
MARGARET   Oh, you weak people, you weak, beautiful people!—who give up with such grace. What you want is someone to—

She turns out the rose-silk lamp.

—take hold of you.—Gently, gently with love hand your life back to you, like somethin' gold you let go of. I *do* love you, Brick, I *do!*
BRICK [*smiling with charming sadness*]   Wouldn't it be funny if that was true?

The End

SAMUEL BECKETT

1906–

Born and raised near Dublin, where his father was a well-to-do purveyor, Beckett was sent to a boarding school at the age of fourteen, and then went on to receive a B.A. at Trinity College, Dublin, where he distinguished himself as a scholar of French and Italian. His academic distinction won him a lectureship in Paris, where he met James Joyce, became his literary disciple, and began writing experimental poetry and fiction. After receiving his M.A. from Trinity College in 1931, he gave up the academic life, returned to the continent and continued to write fiction, while he travelled around France and Germany, leading a vagabond existence. He settled in Paris in 1937, subsequently became a member of the French resistance movement, and at the end of the second world war began writing the plays that were to make him internationally famous as the first and leading practitioner of absurdist drama. His best-known plays, *Waiting for Godot* (1953), *Endgame* (1957), and *Krapp's Last Tape* (1958) repeatedly challenge conventional dramatic expectations through their depiction of bizarre vaudeville-like characters, in outlandish settings, engaged in purposeless activities, exchanging frequently illogical and comically nonsensical dialogue with each other or with themselves. And in challenging traditional forms of theater, they ultimately challenge traditional views of human existence, suggesting that it may be as illogical, as absurd, as the dramatic spectacles they portray.

Krapp's Last Tape
A Play in One Act

A late evening in the future.

Krapp's den.

Front centre a small table, the two drawers of which open towards audience. Sitting at the table, facing front, i.e. across from the drawers, a wearish old man: Krapp.

Rusty black narrow trousers too short for him. Rusty black sleeveless waistcoat, four capacious pockets. Heavy silver watch and chain. Grimy white shirt open at neck, no collar. Surprising pair of dirty white boots, size ten at least, very narrow and pointed.

White face. Purple nose. Disordered grey hair. Unshaven.

Very near-sighted (but unspectacled). Hard of hearing.

Cracked voice. Distinctive intonation.

Laborious walk.

On the table a tape-recorder with microphone and a number of cardboard boxes containing reels of recorded tapes.

Table and immediately adjacent area in strong white light. Rest of stage in darkness.

Krapp remains a moment motionless, heaves a great sigh, looks at his watch, fumbles in his pockets, takes out an envelope, puts it back, fumbles, takes out a small bunch of keys, raises it to his eyes, chooses a key, gets up and moves to front of table. He stoops, unlocks first drawer, peers into it, feels about inside it, takes out a reel of tape, peers at it, puts it back, locks drawer, unlocks second drawer, peers into it, feels about inside it, takes out a large banana, peers at it, locks drawer, puts keys back in his pocket. He turns, advances to edge of stage, halts, strokes banana, peels it, drops skin at his feet, puts end of banana in his mouth and remains motionless, staring vacuously before him. Finally he bites off the end, turns aside and begins pacing to and fro at edge of stage, in the light, i.e. not more than four or five paces either way, meditatively eating banana. He treads on skin, slips, nearly falls, recovers himself, stoops and peers at skin and finally pushes it, still stooping, with his foot over the edge of stage into pit. He resumes his pacing, finishes banana, returns to table, sits down, remains a moment motionless, heaves a great sigh, takes keys from his pockets, raises them to his eyes, chooses key, gets up and moves to front of table, unlocks second drawer, takes out a second large banana, peers at it, locks drawer, puts back keys in his pocket, turns, advances to edge of stage, halts, strokes banana, peels it, tosses skin into pit, puts end of banana in his mouth and remains motionless, staring vacuously before him. Finally he has an idea, puts banana in his waistcoat pocket, the end emerging, and goes with all the speed he can muster backstage into darkness. Ten seconds. Loud pop of cork. Fifteen seconds. He comes back into light carrying an old ledger and sits down at table. He lays ledger on table, wipes his mouth, wipes his hands on the front of his waistcoat, brings them smartly together and rubs them.

KRAPP [*briskly*]   Ah! [*He bends over ledger, turns the pages, finds the entry he wants, reads.*] Box . . . thrree . . . spool . . . five. [*He raises his head and stares front. With relish.*] Spool! [*Pause.*] Spooool! [*Happy smile. Pause. He bends over table, starts peering and poking at the boxes.*] Box . . . thrree . . . thrree . . . four . . . two . . . [*with surprise*] nine! good God! . . . seven . . . ah!

the little rascal!   [*He takes up box, peers at it.*] Box thrree. [*He lays it on table, opens it and peers at spools inside.*] Spool . . . [*he peers at ledger*] . . . five [*he peers at spools*] . . . five . . . five! . . . ah! the little scoundrel! [*He takes out a spool, peers at it.*] Spool five. [*He lays it on table, closes box three, puts it back with the others, takes up the spool.*] Box thrree, spool five. [*He bends over the machine, looks up. With relish.*] Spooool! [*Happy smile. He bends, loads spool on machine,* rubs his hands.] Ah! [*He peers at ledger, reads entry at foot of page.*] Mother at rest at last . . . Hm . . . The black ball . . . [*He raises his head, stares blankly front. Puzzled.*] Black ball? . . . [*He peers again at ledger, reads.*] The dark nurse . . . [*He raises his head, broods, peers again at ledger, reads.*] Slight improvement in bowel condition . . . Hm . . . Memorable . . . what? [*He peers closer.*] Equinox, memorable equinox. [*He raises his head, stares blankly front. Puzzled.*] Memorable equinox? . . . [*Pause. He shrugs his shoulders, peers again at ledger, reads.*] Farewell to—[*he turns the page*]—love.

He raises his head, broods, bends over machine, switches on and assumes listening posture, i.e. leaning forward, elbows on table, hand cupping ear towards machine, face front.

TAPE [*strong voice, rather pompous, clearly Krapp's at a much earlier time.*]   Thirty-nine today, sound as a—[*Settling himself more comfortably he knocks one of the boxes off the table, curses, switches off, sweeps boxes and ledger violently to the ground, winds tape back to beginning, switches on, resumes posture.*] Thirty-nine today, sound as a bell, apart from my old weakness, and intellectually I have now every reason to suspect at the . . . [*hesitates*] . . . crest of the wave—or thereabouts. Celebrated the awful occasion, as in recent years, quietly at the Winehouse. Not a soul. Sat before the fire with closed eyes, separating the grain from the husks. Jotted down a few notes, on the back of an envelope. Good to be back in my den, in my old rags. Have just eaten I regret to say three bananas and only with difficulty refrained from a fourth. Fatal things for a man with my condition. [*Vehemently.*] Cut 'em out! [*Pause.*] The new light above my table is a great improvement. With all this darkness round me I feel less alone. [*Pause.*] In a way. [*Pause.*] I love to get up and move about in it, then back here to . . . [*hesitates*] . . . me. [*Pause.*] Krapp.

Pause.

The grain, now what I wonder do I mean by that, I mean . . . [*hesitates*] . . . I suppose I mean those things worth having when all the dust has—when all *my* dust has settled. I close my eyes and try and imagine them.

Pause. Krapp closes his eyes briefly.

Extraordinary silence this evening, I strain my ears and do not hear a sound. Old Miss McGlome always sings at this hour. But not tonight. Songs of her girlhood, she says. Hard to think of her as a girl. Wonderful woman though. Connaught, I fancy. [*Pause.*] Shall I sing when I am her age, if I ever am? No. [*Pause.*] Did I sing as a boy? No. [*Pause.*] Did I ever sing? No.

Pause.

Just been listening to an old year, passages at random. I did not check in the book, but it must be at least ten or twelve years ago. At that time I think I was still living on and off with Bianca in Kedar Street. Well out of that, Jesus yes! Hopeless business. [*Pause.*] Not much about her, apart from a tribute to her eyes. Very warm. I suddenly saw them again. [*Pause.*] Incomparable! [*Pause.*] Ah well . . . [*Pause.*] These old P.M.s are gruesome, but I often find them—[*Krapp switches off, broods, switches on*]—a help before embarking on a new . . . [*hesitates*] . . . retrospect. Hard to believe I was ever that young whelp. The voice! Jesus! And the aspirations! [*Brief laugh in which Krapp joins.*] And the resolutions! [*Brief laugh in which Krapp joins.*] To drink less, in particular. [*Brief laugh of Krapp alone.*] Statistics. Seventeen hundred hours, out of the preceding eight thousand odd, consumed on licensed premises alone. More than 20%, say 40% of his waking life. [*Pause.*] Plans for a less . . . [*hesitates*] . . . engrossing sexual life. Last illness of his father. Flagging pursuit of happiness. Unattainable laxation. Sneers at what he calls his youth and thanks to God that it's over. [*Pause.*] False ring there. [*Pause.*] Shadows of the opus . . . magnum. Closing with a—[*brief laugh*]—yelp to Providence. [*Prolonged laugh in which Krapp joins.*] What remains of all that misery? A girl in a shabby green coat, on a railway-station platform? No?

Pause.

When I look—

Krapp switches off, broods, looks at his watch, gets up, goes backstage into darkness. Ten seconds. Pop of cork. Ten seconds. Second cork. Ten seconds. Third cork. Ten seconds. Brief burst of quavering song.

KRAPP [*sings*]   Now the day is over,
                 Night is drawing nigh-igh,
                 Shadows—

Fit of coughing. He comes back into light, sits down, wipes his mouth, switches on, resumes his listening posture.

TAPE   —back on the year that is gone, with what I hope is perhaps a glint of the old eye to come, there is of course the house on the canal where mother lay a-dying, in the late autumn, after her long viduity [*Krapp gives a start*], and the—[*Krapp switches off, winds back tape a little, bends his ear closer to machine, switches on*]—a-dying, after her long viduity, and the—

Krapp switches off, raises his head, stares blankly before him. His lips move in the syllables of "viduity." No sound. He gets up, goes backstage into darkness, comes back with an enormous dictionary, lays it on table, sits down and looks up the word.

KRAPP [*reading from dictionary*] State—or condition of being—or remaining—a widow—or widower. [*Looks up. Puzzled.*] Being—or remaining? . . . [*Pause. He peers again at dictionary. Reading.*] "Deep weeds of viduity" . . . Also of an animal, especially a bird . . . the vidua or weaver-bird . . . Black plumage of male . . . [*He looks up. With relish.*] The vidua-bird!

Pause. He closes dictionary, switches on, resumes listening posture.

TAPE   —bench by the weir from where I could see her window. There I sat, in the biting wind, wishing she were gone. [*Pause.*] Hardly a soul, just a few regulars, nursemaids, infants, old men, dogs. I got to know them quite well—oh by appearance of course I mean! One dark young beauty I recollect particularly, all white and starch, incomparable bosom, with a big black hooded perambulator, most funereal thing. Whenever I looked in her direction she had her eyes on me. And yet when I was bold enough to speak to her—not having been introduced—she threatened to call a policeman. As if I had designs on her virtue! [*Laugh. Pause.*] The face she had! The eyes! Like . . . [*hesitates*] . . . chrysolite! [*Pause.*] Ah well . . . [*Pause.*] I was there when— [*Krapp switches off, broods, switches on again*]—the blind went down, one of those dirty brown roller affairs, throwing a ball for a little white dog, as chance would have it. I happened to look up and there it was. All over and done with, at last. I sat on for a few moments with the ball in my hand and the dog yelping and pawing at me. [*Pause.*] Moments. Her moments, my moments. [*Pause.*] The dog's moments. [*Pause.*] In the end I held it out to him and he took it in his mouth, gently, gently. A small, old, black, hard, solid rubber ball. [*Pause.*] I shall feel it, in my hand, until my dying day. [*Pause.*] I might have kept it. [*Pause.*] But I gave it to the dog.

Pause.

Ah well . . .

Pause.

Spiritually a year of profound gloom and indigence until that memorable night in March, at the end of the jetty, in the howling wind, never to be forgotten, when suddenly I saw the whole thing. The vision, at last. This I fancy is what I have chiefly to record this evening, against the day when my work will be done and perhaps no place left in my memory, warm or cold, for the miracle that . . . [*hesitates*] . . . for the fire that set it alight. What I suddenly saw then was this, that the belief I had been going on all my life, namely—[*Krapp switches off impatiently, winds tape forward, switches on again*]— great granite rocks the foam flying up in the light of the lighthouse and the wind-gauge spinning like a propellor, clear to me at last that the dark I have always struggled to keep under is in reality my most—[*Krapp curses, switches off, winds tape forward, switches on again*]—unshatterable association until my dissolution of storm and night with the light of the understanding and the fire—[*Krapp curses louder, switches off, winds tape forward, switches on again*]— my face in her breasts and my hand on her. We lay there without moving. But under us all moved, and moved us, gently, up and down, and from side to side.

Pause.

Past midnight. Never knew such silence. The earth might be uninhabited.

Pause.

Here I end—

Krapp switches off, winds tape back, switches on again.

—upper lake, with the punt, bathed off the bank, then pushed out into the stream and drifted. She lay stretched out on the floorboards with her hands under her head and her eyes closed. Sun blazing down, bit of a breeze, water nice and lively. I noticed a scratch on her thigh and asked her how she came by it. Picking gooseberries, she said. I said again I thought it was hopeless and no good going on, and she agreed, without opening her eyes. [*Pause.*] I asked her to look at me and after a few moments—[*pause*]—after a few moments she did, but the eyes just slits, because of the glare. I bent over her to get them in the shadow and they opened. [*Pause. Low.*] Let me in. [*Pause.*] We drifted in among the flags and stuck. The way they went down, sighing, before the stem! [*Pause.*] I lay down across her with my face in her breasts and my hand on her. We lay there without moving. But under us all moved, and moved us, gently, up and down, and from side to side.

Pause.

Past midnight. Never knew—

Krapp switches off, broods. Finally he fumbles in his pockets, encounters the banana, takes it out, peers at it, puts it back, fumbles, brings out the envelope, fumbles, puts back envelope, looks at his watch, gets up and goes backstage into darkness. Ten seconds. Sound of bottle against glass, then brief siphon. Ten seconds. Bottle against glass alone. Ten seconds. He comes back a little unsteadily into light, goes to front of table, takes out keys, raises them to his eyes, chooses key, unlocks first drawer, peers into it, feels about inside, takes out reel, peers at it, locks drawer, puts keys back in his pocket, goes and sits down, takes reel off machine, lays it on dictionary, loads virgin reel on machine, takes envelope from his pocket, consults back of it, lays it on table, switches on, clears his throat and begins to record.

KRAPP   Just been listening to that stupid bastard I took myself for thirty years ago, hard to believe I was ever as bad as that. Thank God that's all done with anyway. [*Pause.*] The eyes she had! [*Broods, realizes he is recording silence, switches off, broods. Finally.*] Everything there, everything, all the—[*Realizes this is not being recorded, switches on.*] Everything there, everything on this old muckball, all the light and dark and famine and feasting of . . . [*hesitates*] . . . the ages! [*In a shout.*] Yes! [*Pause.*] Let that go! Jesus! Take his mind off his homework! Jesus! [*Pause. Weary.*] Ah well, maybe he was right. [*Pause.*] Maybe he was right. [*Broods. Realizes. Switches off. Consults envelope.*] Pah! [*Crumples it and throws it away. Broods. Switches on.*] Nothing to say, not a squeak. What's a year now? The sour cud and the iron stool. [*Pause.*] Revelled in the word spool. [*With relish.*] Spooool! Happiest moment of the past half million. [*Pause.*]. Seventeen copies sold, of which eleven at trade price to free circulating libraries beyond the seas. Getting known. [*Pause.*] One pound six and something, eight I have little doubt. [*Pause.*] Crawled out once or twice, before the summer was cold. Sat shivering in the park, drowned in dreams and burning to be gone. Not a soul. [*Pause.*] Last fancies. [*Vehemently.*] Keep 'em under! [*Pause.*] Scalded the eyes out of me reading *Effie* again, a page a day, with tears again. Effie . . . [*Pause.*] Could have been happy with her, up there on the Baltic, and the pines, and the dunes. [*Pause.*] Could I? [*Pause.*] And she? [*Pause.*] Pah! [*Pause.*] Fanny came in a couple of times. Bony old ghost of a whore. Couldn't do much, but I suppose better than a kick in the crutch. The last time wasn't so bad. How do you manage it, she said, at your age? I told her I'd been saving up for her all my life. [*Pause.*] Went to Vespers once, like when I was in short trousers. [*Pause. Sings*]

Now the day is over.
Night is drawing nigh-igh,
Shadows—[*coughing, then almost inaudible*]—of the evening
Steal across the sky.

[*Gasping.*] Went to sleep and fell off the pew. [*Pause.*] Sometimes wondered in the night if a last effort mightn't—[*Pause.*] Ah finish your booze now and get to your bed. Go on with this drivel in the morning. Or leave it at that. [*Pause.*] Leave it at that. [*Pause.*] Lie propped up in the dark—and wander. Be again in the dingle on a Christmas Eve, gathering holly, the red-berried. [*Pause.*] Be again on Croghan on a Sunday morning, in the haze, with the bitch, stop and listen to the bells. [*Pause.*] And so on. [*Pause.*] Be again, be again. [*Pause.*] All that old misery. [*Pause.*] Once wasn't enough for you. [*Pause.*] Lie down across her.

Long pause. He suddenly bends over machine, switches off, wrenches off tape, throws it away, puts on the other, winds it forward to the passage he wants, switches on, listens staring front.

TAPE   —gooseberries, she said. I said again I thought it was hopeless and no good going on, and she agreed, without opening her eyes. [*Pause.*] I asked her to look at me and after a few moments—[*pause*]—after a few moments she did, but the eyes just slits, because of the glare. I bent over her to get them in the shadow and they opened. [*Pause. Low.*] Let me in. [*Pause.*] We drifted in among the flags and stuck. The way they went down, sighing, before the stem! [*Pause.*] I lay down across her with my face in her breasts and my hand on her. We lay there without moving. But under us all moved, and moved us, gently, up and down, and from side to side.

Pause. Krapp's lips move. No sound.

Past midnight. Never knew such silence. The earth might be uninhabited.

Pause.

Here I end this reel. Box—[*pause*]—three, spool—[*pause*]—five. [*Pause.*] Perhaps my best years are gone. When there was a chance of happiness. But I wouldn't want them back. Not with the fire in me now. No, I wouldn't want them back.

Krapp motionless staring before him. The tape runs on in silence.

Curtain

Glossary and Index
of Critical Terms

FICTION

ALLEGORY   A story in which the events and characters are symbolic of another
order of meaning, in a frame of reference outside that of the fictional
world, the way killing a dragon may symbolize defeating the devil. See
pp. 13–14.

CHARACTER   A name or title and a set of qualities that make a fictional person.
See pp. 11–12, 38, 44, 48.

COMEDY   The story of a person's rise to a higher station in life through education or improvement of personality. See pp. 8–9.

DESIGN   The shape of a story when it is considered as a completed object
rather than an ongoing process. See pp. 19–21.

DIALOGUE   The parts of a story in which the words of characters are directly
reported. See p. 15.

FABLE   A story that makes a moral point through the actions of characters,
often using animals to represent human behavior. See pages 25–26.

FABULATION   Fiction that violates normal probabilities to make some point
about the nature of existence. See p. 79.

FACT   A thing that has been done, or a true statement. See pp. 3–4.

FANTASY   A story of events that violate our sense of natural possibilities in this
world; the more extreme the violation, the more fantastic the story.
See pp. 5–7.

FICTION   Something made up, usually a made-up story. See pp. 3–4.

HISTORY   The events of the past, or a re-telling of those events in the form of a
story; the most factual kind of fiction. See pp. 5–7, 39.

IRONY   The result of some difference in point of view or values between a
character in fiction and the narrator or reader. See pp. 15–16.

JUXTAPOSITION   The way episodes or elements of a plot are located next to one another to contribute to the design of a story. See pp. 19–21.

METAFICTION   A special kind of fabulation that calls into question the nature of fiction itself. See p. 79.

METAPHOR   The way rich and complex thoughts can be conveyed by the linking of different images and ideas. See pp. 15–19, 62, 71.

MYTH   A story that expresses a deep human concern, often involving the actions of gods or other superhuman figures. See pp. 22–23.

NARRATION   The parts of a story that summarize events and conversations. See p. 15.

NARRATOR   The person who tells a story. See p. 15.

PARABLE   A story that takes the form of a simple allegory, using humble characters and situations as a way of suggesting more important moral or religious concerns. See pp. 25–26.

PATHOS   The emotion generated by the story of a character's fall or persecution through no fault of his own. See p. 8–9.

PICARESQUE   A kind of story that blends comedy and satire to narrate the adventures of a rogue passing through a low or debased version of contemporary reality. See p. 9.

PLOT   The order of events in a story as an ongoing process. See p. 10–11.

POINT OF VIEW   The voice and vision through which the events of a story reach the reader. See pp. 15–19.

REALISM   A mode of fiction that is not specifically factual but presents a world recognizably bound by the same laws as the world of the author. See pp. 7, 60.

REPETITION   The way certain features or elements of a story may be presented more than once to make a thematic point. See pp. 19–21.

ROMANCE   A story that is neither wildly fantastic nor bound by the conventions of realism, but offers a heightened version of reality. See pp. 7, 60.

SATIRE   A story that offers a world that is debased in relation to the world of the author. See pp. 8–9.

STORY   A complete sequence of events, as told about a single character or group of characters. See p. 4.

STREAM OF CONSCIOUSNESS   A fictional technique in which the thoughts of a character are entirely opened to the reader, usually being presented as a flow of ideas and feelings, apparently without logical organization. See p. 11.

SYMBOL   A particular object or event in a story which acquires thematic value through its function or the way it is presented. See pp. 21, 71.

TALE   A story that is told for its own sake, because it has a satisfying shape. See pp. 30–31.

THEME   The ideas, values, or feelings that are developed or questioned by a work of fiction. See pp. 12–14.

TONE   The way in which attitudes are conveyed through language without being presented directly as statements, as in sarcasm. See pp. 15–17.

TRAGEDY   The story of a character's fall from a high position through some flaw of personality. See pp. 8–9.

POETRY

ACCENT   The rhythmical alternation of light and heavy (soft and loud) sounds in verse. See pp. 451–58; see also STRESS.

ALLITERATION   The use of the same sound at the beginning of two or more words in the same line (or two adjacent lines) of verse. See pp. 460–61.

ANIMATION   The endowment of inanimate objects with some of the qualities of living creatures. See p. 443.

BALLAD   A poem that tells a story, usually meant to be sung. See p. 430.

BLANK VERSE   Unrhymed iambic pentameter lines. See pp. 478–79; see also FOOT and LINE.

CAESURA   The point or points within a line of verse where a pause is noticeable. See pp. 478–79.

CONCEIT   An elaborately developed and sometimes farfetched metaphor. See pp. 440–41.

DESCRIPTION   The use of visual images and appeals to other senses in poetry. See pp. 433–35.

DRAMA   The quality of poetry that is like theatrical drama, requiring the reader to grasp the nature of speaker, listener, and situation. See pp. 427–31; see also Drama Glossary.

DRAMATIC MONOLOGUE   A poem in which a single speaker addresses remarks to one or more listeners at some significant moment in the speaker's life. See pp. 428–29.

END-STOPPED   A line of verse that ends where one would normally pause in speech or punctuate in writing. See p. 450.

ENJAMBMENT   The use of run-on lines in verse. See p. 450.

FEMININE RHYME   When rhyme words end in an unaccented syllable, two rhyming sounds are required, as in *yellow* and *fellow*. See pp. 455, 461.

FOOT   A unit of meter or rhythm, of which five kinds are normally recognized: the iamb (da-dum), the anapest (da-da-dum), the trochee (dum-da), the dactyl (dum-da-da), and the spondee (dum-dum). See pp. 452–58.

FREE VERSE   Unrhymed lines in which no particular meter is maintained. See p. 450.

HEROIC COUPLET   A rhymed, iambic pentameter pair of lines, usually both end-stopped, with a period or other full stop at the end of the second line. See pp. 459–60; see also FOOT and LINE.

IMAGERY   The use of sensory details (images) in poetry: sounds, scents, tastes, textures, and especially sights. See p. 439.

IRONY   A deliberate gap or disparity between the language in which a thing is discussed and language usually considered appropriate for that particular subject. See pp. 444–47.

LINE   The line of verse as normally printed on a page. Lines may be divided into feet and labeled according to the number of feet per line. In English the most common lines are pentameter (five feet) and tetrameter (four feet). See p. 450; see also FOOT.

MEDITATION   The movement from images to ideas in poetry. See pp. 434–35.

METAPHOR   The discovery of likeness or similarity in different things—a major resource of poetical expression. See pp. 436–40.

METRICS   The part of poetry that has to do with sound rather than sense. See pp. 449–61.

NARRATION   The quality of poetry that is like fiction, requiring the reader to follow shifts in time and space, and to observe significant details, so as to understand a poem as a kind of story. See pp. 430–32.

NARRATOR   One who tells a story. See pp. 430–31.

PERSONIFICATION   The endowment of non-human things or creatures with distinctly human qualities. See pp. 443–44.

PUN   A word used in a context that obliges it to carry two conflicting meanings. See pp. 442–43.

RHYME   A sound pattern in which both vowel and consonant sounds at the end of words match (as in *rhyme* and *chime*), especially when these words come at the ends of nearby lines. See pp. 460–61.

RUN-ON   A line of verse that ends where one would not normally pause in speech or punctuate in writing. See p. 450.

SCANSION   To "scan" a poem is to determine its metrical structure and rhyme scheme. See pp. 451–61.

SIMILE   A kind of metaphor in which the likeness of two things is made explicit by such words as *like, as, so.* See pp. 436–37.

SITUATION   In a narrative or dramatic poem, the circumstances of the characters or speaker. See pp. 427–29.

SONNET   A verse form featuring intricate rhyming, usually employing fourteen iambic pentameter lines. See pp. 477–80.

STANZA   A regularly repeated metrical pattern of the same number of lines in groups throughout a poem, sometimes including repeated patterns of rhyme as well. See pp. 455–56.

STRESS   The ways in which verse sounds are accented, of which three types may be recognized in poetry: *grammatical stress,* the normal pronunciation of a word or phrase; *rhetorical stress,* change in pronunciation to emphasize some part of the meaning of an utterance; *poetical stress,* the regular rhythm established in metrical verse. See pp. 451–52.

SYMBOL   An extension of metaphor in which one thing is implicitly discussed by means of the explicit discussion of something else. See pp. 441–42.

TACT   A reader's ability to observe the conventions operating in any particular poem and to pay attention to the idiom of every poet. See pp. 426–27.

DRAMA

ABSURDIST DRAMA   A mode of drama which does not provide any rational source of explanation for the behavior and fate of its characters and thus expresses the possibility that human existence may be meaningless. See pp. 692–94.

BLOCKING   Arrangement of characters on stage during any particular moment in the production of a play. See pp. 674–77.

CHARACTER   A dramatic being, known by name, word, and deed. See pp. 699–700.

CHORIC CHARACTER   A character who takes part in the action of a play but is not directly involved in the outcome of the action, and thus can provide a source of commentary upon it. See pp. 681–88.

CHORIC COMMENTARY   Commentary upon characters and events provided either by a chorus or by choric characters. See p. 681.

CHORUS   A group of characters who comment upon the action of a play but do not take part in it. See pp. 681, 702–3.

CLOSET DRAMA   Drama written only to be read, rather than to be produced in a theater. See pp. 673–74.

COMEDY   Dramatization of a hero's and heroine's change in fortune (from frustration to satisfaction) brought about not only by the effort of the hero and heroine themselves but also by some element of chance, coincidence, or luck. See pp. 686–90, 748–49.

COSTUME   A piece of physical apparel worn by actors to create a visual illusion appropriate to the characters they are pretending to be. See pp. 674, 701, 748, 787, 815.

CUE   A word, phrase, or statement in the text of a play which provides explicit or implicit information relevant to theatrical production of the play. See pp. 674–77.

DIALOGUE   Specialized form of conversation peculiar to drama, in that it is designed to convey everything about the imaginative world of a play, as well as to provide all of the cues necessary for production of a play. See pp. 674–77, 680–81, 695–96.

DISCOVERY   A change from ignorance to knowledge on the part of a dramatic hero and/or heroine which brings about a significant change in the fortune of the hero and/or heroine. See pp. 689, 691, 692; see also REVERSAL.

DRAMA   Imitative action created through the words of imaginary beings talking to one another rather than to a reader or spectator. See pp. 673–74, 679–80, 685–87, 695.

DRAMATIC UNIT   A segment of the scenario that is determined by the entrance or exit of a character or group of characters. See pp. 698–99; see also SCENARIO.

EXPOSITION   Dialogue at the beginning of a play that includes background information about characters and events in the imaginative world of a play. See pp. 680, 698.

GESTURE   A physical movement made by actors appropriate to the attitudes and intentions of the characters they are pretending to be. See pp. 674, 676–77, 701, 748, 815, 913.

INTERACTION   Verbal and physical deeds performed by dramatic characters in relation to one another. See pp. 676–77, 679–82.

INTONATION   Particular manner (including pronunciation, rhythm, and volume) in which actors deliver the lines of the characters they are pretending to be. See pp. 674, 701.

MEDITATIVE DRAMA   A form of drama that is primarily concerned with representing the internalized thoughts and feelings of its characters. See pp. 682–83.

NARRATION   An element in drama that is like the act of storytelling, in that it tells about characters and events, or comments upon characters and events, rather than showing them directly. See pp. 679–82; see also CHORIC CHARACTER, CHORIC COMMENTARY, CHORUS, EXPOSITION, REPORTED ACTION, and RETROSPECTION.

NATURALISTIC DRAMA   A mode of drama which embodies a view of men and women as being influenced by psychological, social, and economic forces beyond their control and comprehension. See pp. 692–94, 965–67.

PACING   Tempo of activity on stage during any particular moment in the production of a play. See pp. 674, 676–77.

PERSUASIVE DRAMA   A form of drama that uses dialogue, plot, and character primarily as a means of testing ideas, expounding ideas, or demonstrating the superiority of one set of ideas over another. See p. 684.

PLOT   Specialized form of experience peculiar to drama, in that it consists of a wholly interconnected system of events, deliberately selected and arranged to fulfill both the imaginative and theatrical purposes of a play. See pp. 687–90, 695, 697–99; see also SCENARIO.

PROP   Any physical item (other than costume and set) which is used by actors on stage during the production of a play. See pp. 674, 702, 815, 966.

REPORTED ACTION   Action taking place during the time of the play which is reported by one or more of the characters rather than being directly presented. See pp. 680–81, 697–99.

REPRESENTED ACTION   Action taking place during the time of the play which is directly presented rather than reported by one or more of the characters. See pp. 673–75, 680–81, 697–99.

RETROSPECTION   Post-expository dialogue in which characters survey, explore, and seek to understand action which took place well before the time of the play. See p. 680.

REVERSAL   An incident or sequence of incidents that go contrary to the expectations of a hero and/or heroine. See p. 689.

ROMANCE   A mode of drama that uses characters and events to present an intensified but not completely idealized view of human excellence. See pp. 685, 690–92.

SATIRE   A mode of drama that uses characters and events to present an intensified but not completely negative view of human imperfection. See pp. 685, 690–92, 912–13.

SCENARIO   Action that is directly presented (i.e., on stage), and thus embodies everything that takes place in the imaginative world of a play (i.e., the plot). See pp. 697–99.

SCRIPT   Text of a play interpreted as a set of cues for theatrical production. See pp. 674–77.

SET   Physical construction placed on stage to represent an interior or exterior location in the imaginative world of a play. See pp. 674, 678–79, 702, 787, 815–16, 913, 965–68.

SOLILOQUY   Lines spoken by a character that are meant to represent the unspoken thoughts and feelings of the character. See pp. 682–83.

SPECTACLE   Sights and sounds of performance by means of which the imaginative world of a play is brought to life in the theater. See pp. 674–79, 701–3, 748–49, 787, 815–16, 913, 965–68. See also BLOCKING, COSTUME, GESTURE, INTONATION, PACING, PROP, SET.

TRAGEDY   Dramatization of a hero's or heroine's change in fortune (from prosperity to catastrophe) brought about by some great error in judgment on the part of the hero or heroine. See pp. 686–89, 702–3.

TRAGICOMEDY   A mode of drama that does not embody a clear-cut pattern of catastrophe or rebirth (as in tragedy or comedy), or present clear-cut images of good or evil (as in romance or satire), and thus presents an ambiguous and problematic view of human experience. See pp. 692–94; see also ABSURDIST DRAMA; NATURALISTIC DRAMA.

Index

Names of authors and film directors appear in SMALL CAPITALS, titles of readings and films in *italics*, and first lines of poems in roman type. If title and first line coincide, the title alone is entered; if title begins the first line, it appears in *italics*, the rest of the line in [roman bracketed]. Titles supplied for untitled works appear in [*italic bracketed*].

1273